This Book
Donated by Henry Worthy
Please pray for him
Rest in Peace

GW00657408

Plate 1: The Inscription of Adam Sedbar, Abbot of Jervaulx, whilst a prisoner in the Beauchamp Tower, Tower of London.
© Historic Royal Palaces.

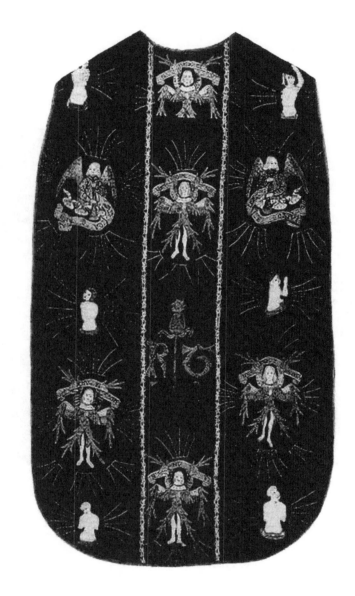

Plate 2: The Mourning Chasuble of Robert Thornton, Abbot of Jervaulx (1511-1532).
© *The Victoria and Albert Museum.*

Plate 3: A Corrodian's Chamber: The Home from 1535 of Edward Walker at Cleeve Abbey.
© English Heritage.

*Plate 4: The Initial Letter of the Esholt Priory Charter of 1484.
(West Yorkshire Archive Service, Leeds., WYL 1530).*

THE TUDOR CISTERCIANS

By the same Author and published by Gracewing

The Cistercians in the Early Middle Ages (1998)

The Welsh Cistercians (2001)

The Five Wounds of Jesus (2004)

THE TUDOR CISTERCIANS

DAVID H. WILLIAMS

GRACEWING

First published in England in 2014
by
Gracewing
2 Southern Avenue
Leominster
Herefordshire HR6 0QF
United Kingdom
www.gracewing.co.uk

No part of this publication may be reproduced, stored in a
retrieval system, or transmitted in any form or by any means,
electronic, mechanical, photocopying, recording or otherwise,
without the written permission of the publisher.

The right of David H. Williams to be identified
as the author of this work has been asserted in accordance
with the Copyright, Designs and Patents Act 1988.

© 2014 David H. Williams

ISBN 978 085244 826 7

Typeset by Gracewing

Cover design by Bernardita Peña Hurtado

Cover picture: Fountains Abbey and Abbot Huby's Tower.
(*Collectanea Archaeologica* 2, 1871).
By permission of the Society of Antiquaries of London.

Dedicated to

All my Friends in the Cistercian Order

Past and Present

CONTENTS

FIGURES

FOREWORD

IN WRITING THIS volume I have been much assisted by the staff of several libraries, and of a number of county and other record offices in England and Wales. They will I hope recognise themselves when they read these words of thanks. This book owes much to the professionalism of Mr Tom Longford, the Revd. Dr Paul Haffner and Gracewing, and once again I am grateful for their kind co-operation. I am indebted also to those corporate bodies who have given permission for the reproduction of plates and figures; due acknowledgement is made in the text. I have also been assisted by several scholars who have responded to my enquiries.

It is fifty years since in 1964 my first article relating to Cistercian history was published in *The Monmouthshire Antiquary*, concerning the small abbey of Grace Dieu near Monmouth. I remember with gratitude Mr Cefni Barnett who as editor put that journal on a sure foundation, and Col Llewellyn Hughes of the Griffin Press, Pontypool, who published not only the early numbers of that journal, but also my first books. I also recall with affection Fr Edmund Mikkers, OCSO, who as editor accepted several earlier articles of mine for publication in *Cîteaux, commentarii cistercienses*.

The research undertaken for this volume could not have been accomplished without the grants kindly made to me, in aid of subsistence and travel to several archival repositories, by the Ethel and Gwynne Morgan Charitable Trust and the Cambrian Archaeological Association.

David H. Williams
College of St Barnabas,
Lingfield, Surrey

ABBREVIATIONS

f(f):	folio(s).
m(m):	membrane(s).
p(p):	page(s).
Appx:	Appendix.
r:	recto
v:	verso.

BAR:	British Archaeological Reports.
N.S.:	New Series.
R.O.:	Record Office/County Archives.
S.P.C.K.:	The Society for Promoting Christian Knowledge.
U.P.:	University Press.
VCH:	The Victoria County History of England (published by the Institute for Historical Research; in London until the 1970s, thereafter in Oxford.

Repositories

BL:	The British Library, London.
CCA:	Canterbury Cathedral Archives, Kent.
CIY:	The Cistercians in Yorkshire Project, Sheffield University.
CUL:	Cambridge University Library microfilm collection.
LMA:	London, The Metropolitan Archives.
LPL:	Lambeth Palace Library, London.
NLW:	The National Library of Wales, Aberystwyth.
SAL:	Library of the Society of Antiquaries of London.
SSC:	Stratford-on-Avon, Shakespeare Centre.
TNA:	The National Archives, Kew, Surrey.

Periodicals

AC:	Archaeologia Cambrensis.
BHRS:	Bedfordshire Historical Record Series.
CY:	The Canterbury and York Society.
Cîteaux:	Cîteaux, commentarii cistercienses.
EHR:	English Historical Review.
JBAA:	Journal of the British Archaeological Association.
LCRS:	Lancashire and Cheshire Record Society.
MA:	The Monmouthshire Antiquary.
MC:	The Montgomeryshire Collections.
MS:	Monastic Studies, Headstart History (Bangor, Wales).
NH:	Northern History.
ODNB:	Oxford Dictionary of National Biography (online edn.)
OHS:	Oxford Historical Society.
PTS:	Publications of the Thoresby Society.
RTDA:	Report and Transactions, The Devonshire Association.
SAC:	Surrey Archaeological Collections.
SRS:	Somerset Record Society.
SxAC:	Sussex Archaeological Collections.
SxRS:	Sussex Record Society.
TBGAS:	Transactions of the Bristol and Gloucestershire Archaeological Society.
TCWAA:	Transactions of the Cumberland and Westmorland Antiquarian and Archaeological Society.
TEAS:	Transactions of the Essex Archaeological Society.
THSC:	Transactions of the Honourable Society of the Cymmrodorion.
THSLC:	Transactions of the Historical Society of Lancashire and Cheshire.
TLAS:	Transactions of the Leicestershire Architectural and Archaeological Society.
YAJ:	Yorkshire Archaeological Journal.
YASRS:	Yorkshire Archaeological Society Record Series.

Primary Sources

AF:	*Annales Furnesienses*, ed. T. A. Beck, London: Payne & Foss, 1844.
Augm.:	*Records of the Court of Augmentations relating to Wales*, ed. E. A. Lewis and J. Conway Davies, Cardiff: University of Wales Press, 1954.
BAC:	*The Book of the Abbot of Combermere*, ed. J. Hall, Lancashire and Cheshire Record Soc., 1896.
BRUO (1):	*A Biographical Register of the University of Oxford to 1500*, ed. A. B. Emden, Oxford: Clarendon Press, 1957–59.
BRUO (2):	*A Biographical Register of the University of Oxford, 1501 to 1540*, ed. A. B. Emden, Oxford: Clarendon Press,
BW:	*Bedfordshire Wills, 1480–1519*, ed. P. L. Bell, BHRS **45**, 1966.
Cartae Glam.:	*Cartae et alia Munimenta quae ad Dominium de Glamorgan pertinent*, ed. G. T. Clark; Cardiff: William Lewis, 1910.
Charter:	*Calendar of the Charter Rolls*, London: Public Record Office, 1903–.
CHA:	'The Cartulary of Hailes Abbey, 1469–1539', ed. D. N. Bell. In: *Cîteaux* **60**, 2009, pp. 79–138.
CL:	*Clergy in London in the Late Middle Ages*, V. Davis, London: Institute of Historical Research, 2000.
Close:	*Calendar of the Close Rolls*, London: Public Record Office, 1902–.
CPA:	*Calendar of Probate and Administrative Acts, 1447–1550, in the Consistory Court of the Bishops of Hereford*, ed. M. A. Faraday, Logaston: Logaston Press, 2008.
CPL:	*Calendar of Entries in the Papal Registers relating to Great Britain and Ireland*, Letters; London: Public Record Office,1893–, Vols. 1–14; from Vol. 15: Dublin: Irish MSS Commission.
DCL:	*Pleadings and Depositions in the Duchy Court of Lancaster*, ed. H. Fishwick, LCRS **32**, 1896.
DCP:	Lincolnshire R.O., Dioc/Court Papers/Box 92/Religious Houses/5.
DKR:	Appendix 1 to the *Eighth Report of the Deputy Keeper of the Public Records*, London: Public Record Office, 1847.
ECW:	*Act Book of the Ecclesiastical Court of Whalley, 1510–1538*, ed. A. M. Cooke, Chetham Soc., 1901.

EPD:	*The Episcopal Registers of the Diocese of St David's, 1397 to 1518*, ed. R. F. Isaacson, London: Cymmrodorion Record Series **6**, 1917.
Fine:	*Calendar of the Fine Rolls*, London: Public Record Office, 1911–.
FLB:	*The Fountains Abbey Lease Book*, ed. D. J. H. Michelmore, Leeds: YAS **140**, 1981.
FOR:	*Faculty Office Registers, 1534–1549*, ed. D. S. Chambers, Oxford: Clarendon Press, 1966.
Itin:	*The Itinerary of John Leland*, ed. L. T. Smith, London: Centaur Press, 1964.
Itin. Wm. Worcestre:	*William Worcester, Itineraries*, ed. J. H. Harvey, Oxford: Clarendon Press, 1969.
LB:	*The Ledger Book of Vale Royal Abbey*, ed. J. Brownbill, LCRS **68**, 1914.
LC:	*Letters to Cromwell*, ed. G. H. Cook, London: J. Baker, 1965.
LCCS:	*Lancashire and Cheshire Cases in the Court of Star Chamber*, Part 1, ed. R. Stewart–Brown, Lancashire and Cheshire Record Society, **71**, 1916.
Letters:	*Letters from English Abbots to Cîteaux*, ed. C. H. Talbot, Camden Soc., 4th Ser. No. 4; London: Royal Hist. Soc. 1967.
LP:	*Letters and Papers, Foreign and Domestic, of the Reign of Henry VIII*, London: Public Record Office, 2nd edn. 1920–.
LW:	*Lincoln Wills, 1532–34*, ed. D. Hickman, Lincoln Record Society, **89**, 2001.
MCP:	*Monastic Chancery Proceedings*, ed. J. S. Purvis, YAS **88**, 1934,
MF:	*Memorials of the Abbey of St Mary of Fountains*, ed. J. R. Walbran, Durham: Andrews, **1**. 1863, **2**. 1878.
Monasticon:	*Monasticon Anglicanum*, ed. W. Dugdale, London: Brown & Smith, 1718.
MSS in BM:	*A catalogue of the manuscripts relating to Wales in the British Museum*, ed. E. Owen, London: Honourable Society of the Cymmrodorion, 1900–1922.
MW:	*Monmouthshire Wills Proved in the Prerogative Court of Canterbury, 1560–1601*, ed. J. Jones, Cardiff: South Wales Record Soc., 1997.
Patent:	*Calendar of the Patent Rolls*, London: Public Record Office, 1903–.
PCSC:	*Proceedings in the Court of Star Chamber*, ed. G. Bradford, SRS **27**, 1911.

RC:	*The Rufford Charters*, ed. C.J. Holdsworth, Nottingham: Thoroton Soc., 1972–1981.
SAE:	*The Sibton Abbey Estates, Select Documents, 1325–1509*, ed. A. H. Denney, Suffolk Record Soc., **2**, 1960.
SAP:	*Supplications from England and Wales in the Registers of the Apostolic Penitentiary* **1**, 1410– 1464, ed. P. D. Clarke and P. N. R. Zutshi, Woodbridge: Boydell & Brewer, CY **103**.
SAP(2):	*Supplications from England and Wales in the Registers of the Apostolic Penitentiary* **2**, 1464–1492, Woodbridge: Boydell Press, 2014.
SBC:	*Sibton Abbey Cartularies and Charters*, ed. P. Brown, Woodbridge: Boydell Press, 1980–1988.
SCR:	*Sussex Chantry Records*, ed. J. E. Ray, SxRS **36**, 1931.
SCSC:	*Select Cases before the Court of Star Chamber* I, ed. J.S. Leadam, London: Bernard Quaritch for the Selden Soc. **16**, 1903.
Statuta:	*Statuta Capitulorum Generalium Ordinis Cisterciensis ab anno 1116 ad annum 1786*, ed. J-M. Canivez, Bibliothèque de la Revue d'histoire ecclésiastique, vols. 9–14, Louvain, 1933–1941.
SW:	*Sussex Wills*, **4**, ed. W. H. Godfrey, SxRS XLV, 1940.
VDL:	*Visitations of the Diocese of Lincoln*, ed. A. H. Thompson, **1**, 1940; **2**. 1944; **3**. 1947, Lincoln Record Society, **33**, **35**, **37**.
VDY:	*Visitation in the Diocese of York holden by Archbishop Edward Lee (A.D. 1534–5)*, YAJ **16**, 1901, pp. 424–58; no author cited.
VE:	*Valor Ecclesiasticus, temp. Henry VIII*, ed. J. Caley *et al.*, London: Record Commission, 1810–1834.
WIB:	*Wills and Inventories from Bury St Edmunds*, ed. S. Tymms, Camden Soc., **49**, 1850.
WIR:	*Wills and Inventories of the Archdeaconry of Richmond*, ed. J. Raine, Surtees Soc., **26**, 1853.

Episcopal Registers

Reg. J. Alcock:	*Register of John Alcock, Bishop of Worcester, 1476–1486*, Worcestershire R. O.
Reg. J. Arundel:	*Register of John Arundel, Bishop of Coventry and Lichfield, 1476–1502*, Lichfield R.O., CUL.
Reg. W. Atwater:	*Register of William Atwater, Bishop of Lincoln, 1514–1521*, CUL.

Reg. E. Audley:	_Register of Edmund Audley, Bishop of Salisbury, 1502–1524,_ Wiltshire R.O.
Reg. C. Bainbridge:	_Register of Christopher Bainbridge, Archbishop of York, 1508–1514,_ Borthwick Institute, York.
Reg. W. Barons:	_Register of William Barons, Bishop of London, 1504–1505,_ LMA.
Reg. T. Bekynton:	_The Register of Thomas Bekynton, Bishop of Bath and Wells, 1443–1465,_ Pt. 2, ed. H. C. Maxwell–Lyte and M. C. B. Dawes, SRS **50**, 1934.
Reg. G. Blyth:	_Register of Geoffrey Blyth, Bishop of Coventry and Lichfield, 1503–1531,_ Lichfield R.O.
Reg. J. Blyth:	_Register of John Blyth, Bishop of Salisbury, 1493–1499_ , Wiltshire R.O.
Reg. C. Bothe:	_The Register of Charles Bothe, Bishop of Hereford, 1516–1535,_ ed. A. T. Bannister, Hereford: Cantilupe Soc., 1921.
Reg. L. Booth:	_Register of Lawrence Booth, Archbishop of York, 1476–1480,_ Borthwick Institute, York.
Reg. W. Booth:	_Register of William Booth, Archbishop of York, 1452–1464,_ Borthwick Institute, York.
Reg. L. Campeggio:	_Register of Lorenzo Campeggio, Bishop of Salisbury, 1524–1534,_ Wiltshire R.O.
Reg. J. Carpenter:	_Register of John Carpenter, Bishop of Worcester, 1443–1476,_ Worcestershire R.O.
Reg. H. de Castello:	_Register of Hadrian de Castello, Bishop of Bath and Wells, 1504–1518,_ Somerset R.O.
Reg. J. Clerk:	_Register of John Clerk, Bishop of Bath and Wells, 1523–1541,_ Somerset R.O.
Reg. P. Courtenay:	_Register of Peter Courtenay, Bishop of Winchester, 1482–1492,_ Hampshire R.O.
Reg. R. Fitzjames:	_Register of Richard FitzJames, Bishop of London, 1506–1522,_ LMA.
Reg. J. Fisher:	_Register of St John Fisher, Bishop of Rochester, 1504–1535,_ Kent R.O.
Reg. R. Fox (1):	_The Register of Richard Fox, Bishop of Bath and Wells, 1492–1494,_ ed. F. C. Batten, London: privately printed, 1889: this published register is now online.
Reg. R. Fox:	_The Register of Richard Fox, Lord Bishop of Durham, 1494–1501,_ ed. M. P. Howden, (Surtees Soc., Durham: Andrews & Co., 1932.

Reg. R, Fox (2) and (3): *Register of Richard Fox, Bishop of Winchester, 1501–1528, Hampshire R.O., Winchester.*

Reg. G. Ghinucci: *Register of Geronimo Ghinucci, Bishop of Worcester, 1522–1535, Worcestershire R.O.*

Reg. G. Gigli: *Register of Giovanni de Gigli, Bishop of Worcester, 1497–1498, Worcestershire R.O.*

Reg. S. Gigli: *Register of Silvestro de Gigli, Bishop[of Worcester, 1498–1521, Worcestershire R.O.*

Reg. J. Goldwell: *Register of James Goldwell, Bishop of Norwich, 1472–1499, Norfolk R.O.*

Reg. J. Hales: *Register of John Hales, Bishop of Coventry and Lichfield, 1459–1490, Lichfield R.O.,*

Reg. R. Hill: *Register of Richard Hill, Bishop of London, 1489–1496, LMA.*

Reg. O. King: *Register of Oliver King, Bishop of Bath and Wells, 1495–1503, Somerset R.O.*

Reg. T. Langton: *The Register of Thomas Langton, Bishop of Salisbury, 1485–93,* ed. D. P. Wright, CY 1985.

Reg. E. Lee: *Register of Edward Lee, Archbishop of York, 1531–1544, Borthwick Institute, York.*

Reg. J. Longland: *Register of John Longland, Bishop of Lincoln, 1521–1547, CUL microfilm.*

Reg. R. Mayew: *The Register of Richard Mayew, Bishop of Hereford, 1504–1516,* ed. A. T. Bannister, Hereford: Cantilupe Soc., 1919.

Reg. J. Morton: *The Register of John Morton, Archbishop of Canterbury, 1486–1500,* II, ed. C. Harper–Bill, CY, 1991.

Reg. J. Morton: *The Register of John Morton, Archbishop of Canterbury, 1486–1500;* Norwich sede vacante, III, ed. C. Harper–Bill, CY, 2000.

Reg. R. Morton: *Register of Robert Morton, Bishop of Worcester, 1486–1497, Worcestershire R.O.*

Reg. T. Myllyng: *Register of Thomas Myllyng, Bishop of Hereford, 1474–1492,* ed. A. T. Bannister, Hereford: Cantilupe Soc., 1919.

Reg. G. Neville: *Register of George Neville, Archbishop of York, 1465–1476, Borthwick Institute, York.*

Reg. H. Oldham: *Register of Hugh Oldham, Bishop of Exeter, 1505–1519, Devon R.O.*

Reg. R. Redmayne: *Register of Richard Redmayne, Bishop of Exeter, 1496–1502, Devon R.O.*

Reg. T. Rotherham:	*Register of Thomas Rotherham, Archbishop of York, 1480–1500*, ed. E. E. Barker, CY, **69**; Torquay, 1976.
Reg. J. Russell:	*Register of John Russell, Bishop of Lincoln, 1480–1494* (CUL).
Reg. T. Savage:	*Register of Thomas Savage, Bishop of London, 1496–1501*, LMA.
Reg. T. Savage:	*Register of Thomas Savage, Archbishop of York, 1501–1507*, Borthwick Institute, York.
Reg. R. Sherburne:	*A Calendar of the Register of Richard Fitzjames, 1504–1516 and Part of the Register of Robert Sherburne, 1508–1536, Bishops of Chichester*, ed. W. D. Peckham, typescript of 1927, a copy is in BL.
Reg. W. Smyth:	*Register of William Smyth (Smyth), Bishop of Coventry and Lichfield,1493–1494*, Lichfield R.O., CUL.
Reg. W. Smyth:	*Register of William Smyth, Bishop of Lincoln, 1495–1514* (CUL microfilm).
Reg. J. Stafford:	*Register of John Stafford, Bishop of Bath and Wells, 1424–1443*, Somerset R.O.
Reg. J. Stanbury:	*Register of John Stanbury, Bishop of Hereford, 1453–1474*, ed. J. H. Parry, Hereford: Cantilupe Soc., 1918.
Reg. R. Stillington:	*Register of Robert Stillington, Bishop of Bath and Wells, 1465–1491*, Somerset R.O.
Reg. J. Stokesley:	*Register of John Stokesley, Bishop of London, 1530–1539*, LMA.
Reg. E. Story:	*Register of Edward Story, Bishop of Chichester, 1478–1503*, West Sussex R.O.
Reg. C. Tunstall:	*Register of Cuthbert Tunstall, Bishop of London, 1522–1530*, LMA.
Reg. C. Tunstall:	*Register of Cuthbert Tunstall, Bishop of Durham, 1530–39*, ed. G. Hinde, Surtees Soc. **161**, 1952.
Reg. J. Vesey:	*Register of John Vesey, Bishop of Exeter, 1519–1551*, Devon R.O.
Reg. W. Warham:	*Register of William Warham, Archbishop of Canterbury, 1503–1532*, LPL.
Reg. W. Whittlesey:	*Register of William Whittlesey, Bishop of Worcester, 1363–1368*, Worcestershire R.O.
Reg. T. Wolsey:	*Register of Thomas Wolsey, Bishop of Lincoln, 1514–1515*, Lincolnshire R.O.
Reg. T. Wolsey:	*Register of Thomas Wolsey, Bishop of Bath and Wells, 1518–1523*, Somerset R.O.
Reg. T. Wolsey:	*Register of Thomas Wolsey, Archbishop of York, 1514–1530*, Borthwick Institute, York.

Note: The Purchasing Power of the Pound Sterling

Estimates of the modern equivalent of one pound sterling as between the Middle Ages and the present day vary widely. A conservative estimate would put the value of one pound, in say 1535, to correspond with £400 if not £500 today. An annuity granted by a monastery in 1535 of say £2, would if awarded today bring the recipient close on £1,000.

1 THE MONASTERIES: BACKGROUND, FABRIC AND WORSHIP

Introduction

THE TUDOR YEARS were a difficult time both for the Cistercian Order in general as well as in England and Wales. In 1487 Pope Innocent VIII called on the energetic abbot of Cîteaux, Jean de Cirey (1476–1501), to instigate a thorough reform of the Order. Unfortunately Cirey's authoritarian nature provoked for a time a schism between himself and the abbot of Clairvaux and his affiliated houses.[1] Sharp and relentless polemic was prolonged between the two houses—especially from 1484 to 1486, and there was a real fear of the abbeys of the filiation of Clairvaux seceding from the Order, but Innocent gave his backing to Cîteaux.[2] The tension reached Wales where the family of Clairvaux predominated; the abbot of Stratford Langthorne writing to the abbot of Cîteaux (12 March 1487) told him that 'some Welsh fathers are leaning away from your rule'.[3]

The difficulties may also have been reflected in the advice given at Henry VII's court by the abbot of Aberconwy (of the generation of Clairvaux) which thwarted a proposed visit to England in 1491 by the abbot of Cîteaux.[4] To the contrary, John Darnton, abbot of Fountains, also of Clairvaux's family, was said to be 'a faithful man of integrity towards the abbot of Cîteaux.'[5] When harmony had been restored between the two proto-abbots, in March 1491, Abbot Darnton expressed his 'joy and rejoicing' at the termination of the split.[6]

Jean de Cirey had been able to adopt a semi-monarchical style because of the weakness and unrepresentative nature of the Order's annual General Chapter, its supreme legislature. Instead of the hundreds of abbots who centuries before had attended the annual General Chapter held in mid-September each year at the 'first house' of Cîteaux in Burgundy, now only a small minority did so. Fifty abbots were present in 1515 and 1520, but only thirty-three had attended in 1510. This undermined the authority of the central government of the Order.

Nevertheless, Cirey was determined on returning the Order to its core values, and early in 1494 held a meeting of forty-five French abbots at the College of St Bernard in Paris.[7] This resulted in the *Confirmation of a Charter for the Reform of the Order*, promulgated at that autumn's General Chapter held at Cîteaux.[8] Its provisions showed the need for renewal within the Order, and were stipulated to be equally binding on monks and nuns. The charter called for the reverent and proper keeping of the divine office 'whether by day or by night,' and insisted that in choir and chapter-house the cowl must be worn. The daily chapter was to be held to amend faults and to promote regular observance. Fasting from meat was compulsory on all but Sundays, Tuesdays and Thursdays, and even then meat was forbidden in Advent, Lent, Rogation-tide, on Days of Sermon and other accustomed fast days. When meat was eaten it was to be in a place specially assigned.

Unless an abbot had made proper exceptions, all monks were to sleep in the dorter. The doors of the cloister, dorter, refectory and other places, were to be locked after Compline, so that none might enter nor leave. Silence was to be maintained in the regular places, and everywhere after Compline. The presence of women was forbidden, save for the visits of noble patrons and those women hired to milk the animals. If working on a Sunday ladies could hear Mass in the gate-house chapel, along with other members of the house-hold. Young monks were to be educated and sent to the *studia* of the Order; sick monks were to be cared for. A father-abbot, or his delegate, should inspect his daughter-houses each year, but not take a sizeable entourage which might cause grave expense. Abbots were instructed to avoid pomp and superfluity. Lastly, rules were laid down for the work of monastic bursars, and for monks going on a journey. The need for these prescriptions shows that in some monasteries there had been a departure from the Order's norms of simplicity and uniformity. There were no abbots present at the 1494 Chapter from England and Wales; indeed, Henry VIII's conflict with France meant that in most years no British abbot was present at all. In 1489 the abbot of Stratford sent two monks to represent him at the Chapter, and in 1497 he promised to attend every two or three years.[9] The records are incomplete, but it is known that Abbot Wynchcombe of Strata Marcella was present in 1496 and 1510, and was appointed as one of the definitors—the steering committee of the Chapter, on both occasions. Abbot Chard of Ford attended in 1515 and 1518; Abbot Lleision of Neath was also there in 1518, and when Abbot Lewis

Thomas of Margam was present in 1530, he was made one of the three confessors to the Chapter.

Surprisingly, considering the difficulties of his monastery at the time, an abbot of Furness accompanied the abbot of Ford in 1515.[10] Central authority, and the General Chapter, may have been seen by Tudor times as remote concepts in some of the Cistercian houses of England and Wales, and this in turn accounted for deviations from the Cistercian spirit, which Abbot Huby of Fountains was quick to lament. Huby was concerned with bishops wishing to undo the exemptions of the Order, and said that a number of members of the Order, especially university graduates, favoured jurisdiction passing from the General Chapter to the Pope and the bishops. He told of Cistercians having recourse to secular courts when dissatisfied with abbatial elections and depositions, and how some called in nobles and patrons to settle their difficulties. He also lamented a sprinkling of Cistercian monks seeking, and obtaining from Rome, 'capacities' permitting them to live and work as secular priests.[11] Huby and his fellow Reformator, Abbot William Hickman of Stratford—with whom he did not always agree, had the 'Paris Articles' and the 1494 Charter as up-to-date supports in endeavouring to maintain the Cistercian way of life in England and Wales.

Geographical Distribution

Of the seventy-five monasteries of white monks in England and Wales at the accession of Henry VII (1485), the great majority, forty-nine, traced their ancestry back either to St Bernard's abbey of Clairvaux, or to the monastery of Savigny whose congregation was absorbed into the Cistercian Order in 1147. These abbeys dominated the monastic landscape in north and eastern England, as well as in Wales. A substantial minority of the monasteries, nineteen, derived ultimately from the mother-house of Cîteaux itself; they prevailed in southern England and in what might be called a 'midland triangle'. It was a separation which reflected itself in the late-fifteenth century, during the breakdown of relations between the abbeys of Cîteaux and Clairvaux. In 1487 a monk named William Marlow, and accounted by Henry VII as the 'rightful abbot' of Strata Florida, was said to have evaded capture by monks loyal to Cîteaux as he guided a monk sent from Clairvaux to the king's court at Winchester.[12] There were no representative abbeys of the filiation of La

Ferté or Pontigny, but three abbeys of the generation of Morimond (Dore, Grace Dieu and Vale Royal) lay close to the Welsh border.

Fig. 1: The Cistercian Abbeys of England and Wales in Tudor Times

Occasionally, even as late as Tudor times, a monastery might be referred to by an alternative colloquial name; as Llantarnam, cited as Dewma abbey in the verse of Huw Cae Llwyd (*d.*1504),[13] and as Caerleon abbey in a bishop's register of 1521.[14] Earlier, in 1485, one episcopal register gave the alternatives of Caerleon and Llantarnam within the record of one ordination.[15] St Mary Graces in London was occasionally referred to as Eastminster (as distinct from Westminster) or as Tower Hill abbey (from its location).[16] The abbey was also referred to as 'the monastery of graces, otherwise called New Abbey, besides the Tower of London.'[17]

Reflective of its foundation by the 'grey monks' of Savigny in 1135, a deed of 1512 referred to Stratford as 'Grey Abbey beside Stratford Langthorne, Essex,'[18] and similarly a will of 1515 mentioned 'the monastery of grey abbey otherwise Stratford Langthorne.'[19] On the Welsh border, deriving its *alias* from nearby Welshpool, Strata Marcella was still given its alternative name of 'Pola' as late as 1496.[20] More colloquial names of those days included 'Crokesden' for Croxden, 'Meryvall' for Merevale, and 'Rivers' for Rievaulx.

The Evidence of John Leland

Occasional glimpses of certain abbeys can be obtained from documentation and eye-witness accounts of those days. In 1491 the abbot of Loos, northern France, had commented upon the site of Medmenham, 'close to the bank of the river Thames.'[21] Thomas, Lord Howard, drew attention to the coastal site of an Isle of Wight monastery when he scribbled in 1513 a letter 'in the Mary Rose before Quarr abbey.'[22] A lease of 1568 referred at Tintern, sited by the tidal river Wye, to an orchard 'towards low water mark.'[23]

Other deeds referred to the stone crosses which stood close by several abbeys, as at Dore[24] and Merevale.[25] A stone cross at Calder stood 'beside a void place nigh unto the gate of the monastery,'[26] and one at Stanley outside the outer gate.[27] That at Tintern lay by the road from the abbey to the village.[28] Excavation has shown that a large stone cross lay west of the main buildings of Cleeve.[29] The base of a stone cross remains in the forecourt of Fountains.[30] William Worcester (1478) described the east window of Tintern as containing eight lights, and as being glazed with the arms (a red lion rampant on a background of gold and green) of Earl Roger Bigod, its late thirteenth-century benefactor.[31] The Glamorgan poet, Lewis Morgannwg (*c.*1520) told of the coats of arms on the glass of Neath.[32]

Robert Aske, prominent in the Pilgrimage of Grace (1536), described Salley abbey as 'being the charitable relief of those parts and standing in a mountain country and amongst three forests.'[33] Sir Arthur Darcy, present at the closure of Jervaulx in May 1537, wrote to Cromwell to tell him that the church there was wholly roofed in lead. He reported that it was 'one of the fairest churches I have seen, fair meadows and the river running by it, and a great demesne.[34] The visitation commissioners of 1537 commented upon the site of Furness: 'It standeth in a valley, and hath a great course of water running through, and is inclosed with a great stone wall in circuit about a mile.'[35]

The most comprehensive review of the sites of monasteries come from the travels in the late 1530s of the antiquary, John Leland, a bibliophile much favoured over the years by Henry VIII, Wolsey and Cromwell. He was fortunate in that his years of travel led him to monasteries still in existence as well as to those recently closed. In his English peregrination Leland made much mention of the riverine sites of the Cistercian abbeys he visited. He saw Ford abbey by the Axe, 'standing on the farther ripe [bank] of it'; Bindon, by the Frome, was he observed 'a little lower than Wool Bridge, and standeth on the right hand and ripe as the river descendeth'; Llanllŷr nunnery in Wales stood 'upon the brook of Aeron', and in Shropshire, Buildwas was 'upon the right bank of the Severn and hard by it.'[36]

Leland commented on the woodland sites of Jervaulx, Newminster, Bordesley (in Feckenham Forest), and Pipewell—which he wrote 'standeth in Rockingham Forest.'[37] He also mentioned two of the Gwent monasteries, Grace Dieu and Llantarnam, as 'standing in woods.'[38] He noted in the wood next to Vaudey a 'great quarry of a coarse marble,' which he said had been much used in the abbey buildings.[39] He noticed the salt pits of Combermere and the stone bridge at Buildwas, as well as the 'good pasture, corn and wood' at Bruern.[40]

Leland told also of the later history of Rufford, as granted by Henry VIII to the earl of Shrewsbury in exchange for his lands in Ireland.[41] Visiting Ripon he saw a chapel of Our Lady close to the new minster there, and records how Abbot Huby of Fountains, having obtained the chapel from Archbishop Savage of York in 1501, pulled down its ancient east end and built a 'new work with squared stone,' but left the old west end standing.[42] Nearly four hundred years after it happened, he tells how 'the houses of the Order called Savigniac, otherwise Grey Friars, were reduced on to the Order called Cistercian.' Elsewhere he more correctly terms them 'the grey brothers,' and he lists five of the abbeys concerned: Basingwerk, Bordesley, Buckfast, Buildwas and Neath. It was a significant comment, as it shows that their ancestry was still important in the eyes of the monks themselves.[43] As for humble Medmenham which in its last years never had more than two monks, Leland dismisses it curtly as 'a cell to Woburn.'[44]

Following his journey in Wales, Leland was able to describe Llantarnam as 'lately suppressed', but also to note that 'Ty Gwyn ar Tav (*Whitland*), Barnardines, still stondeth.'[45] These comments place his journey in Wales firmly to the years 1537 or 1538. He conversed with surviving monks. The abbot of Whitland spoke to him in Welsh, and told him 'a meri tale'. A seemingly bilingual monk of Strata Florida told him 'for a certainty that Newport in Kemeysland is called Tredraith in Welsh.'[46] Neath, it seemed to Leland, was 'the fairest abbey of all Wales', but he saw: 'no church of such length' as that at Cwmhir.[47] He noted the wastage of woodland around Strata Florida, and told of the partial state of ruin of that abbey; but also mentioned its 'meanly walled cemetery', the extent of its estates, its lead mine and its inland fishing potential.[48] Another visitor to Strata Florida in its last days was Edward Waters, one of the Particular Receiver for the monasteries already dissolved, who thanked its abbot for the 'good cheer' afforded him there.[49]

Physical State of the Monasteries

By the time they closed, the fabric of several monasteries was in a poor condition; a consequence in part of major donations being a thing of the past, and of few monks now inhabiting abbeys which once had housed many. On the other hand, there were some monasteries which for much of Tudor times were engaged in considerable renovations and even in the erection of new buildings.

By 1490 even the grand abbey of Tintern was said to be 'threatened in ruin in its walls, roofs, houses and granges, by passage of years, and by negligence and incompetence.'[50] This assessment may have been exaggerated as it was justification used by Abbot William Kere for his request to the Holy See for leave to hold a secular benefice, and thereby obtain extra income. The abbot of Melrose, visiting his daughter-house of Holm Cultram in 1472, ordered that the infirmary there be rebuilt as soon as possible.[51] At a visitation of Warden in

1492 one monk alleged that the church and various claustral buildings were 'in great ruin', and that little remedial work was being undertaken.[52]

In 1512 the bishop of Hereford granted an indulgence to those who contributed to the 'repair of the ruinous refectory and buildings' of Flaxley.[53] Later, in 1525, the church at Flaxley was said to have been destroyed by fire, and to gain funds for its repair its bells were melted down and the metal sold.[54] There appears to have been 'a fraternity or chapel of St Whyte' in the monastery at Flaxley, as about 1530/31 one Thomas Medley found himself in Ilchester gaol, Somerset, on a charge of counterfeiting the king's seal in his efforts to collect money for the chapel. The bishop of Hereford in June 1530, authorising him to collect alms as 'proctor' of the abbey, referred rather to its chapel of SS Candida and Radegund.[55]

Fig. 2: The Strata Marcella Indulgence (1528).
(By permission of Llyfrgell Genedlaethol Cymru / National Library of Wales).

By about 1528 the 'greater part' of Strata Marcella was 'broken down.' To obtain funds for its renovation, Abbot John ap Rhys issued an indulgence reciting privileges granted by Pope Clement VII and Cardinal Wolsey to those who visited the monastery on certain named feasts, and/or 'extended helping hands towards it'. One of the feasts was Holy Cross Day (14 September), perhaps because the abbey possessed a relic of the True Cross. The indulgence was the earliest known printed document relating to Wales, and was the work of Richard Pynson, partner of the celebrated printer, Wynkyn de Worde.[56] Two copies survive.[57]

Other abbeys which in their closing years were in need or renovation included Revesby—the duke of Norfolk telling Cromwell of its buildings being 'in great ruin and decay;'[58] Garendon—which the suppression commissioners found 'great, old and partly ruinous',[59] Stoneleigh which they reported as being 'ruinous and in decay,'[60] and Medmenham, 'wholly in ruin.'[61] John Leland had told how the refectory and infirmary of Strata Florida were 'mere ruins,' and in 1535 it was reported that both the church and monastery of Valle Crucis were 'in great decay,'[62]—little wonder considering the problems of that abbey in its final years. This sad story was not true everywhere. The suppression commissioners found the buildings of Stanley as being 'in a very good state, part rebuilt,'[63] and the fabric of Buildwas as being 'in convenient repair,'[64] This conflicts with the reason given for the grant of a corrody to Edward Lakyn at Buildwas in April 1535; it was 'for forty marks [given] to us in our necessity to build and repair the church.'[65]

Those monasteries which could carried out running repairs. This was facilitated for Vale Royal by regular Crown grants between 1486 and 1534 of timber from Delamere Forest to assist maintenance.[66] Coggeshall re-roofed part of its church in the early 1530s.[67] Warden appointed John Clerke (1531), a local freemason (in the true original meaning of that word) as 'mason of its church and cloister and all its houses.' It was a life appointment, unless 'apparent sickness or evident age do not let him.' He was to be in residence at the monastery with the usual entitlements of chamber, clothing, food and drink. He was also given a building 'with lock and key' in which to securely keep his 'scaffold timber, barrows, ladders' and other tools of his trade. Having completed necessary work for the monastery, he could work for one month on his own account.[68]

At least six monasteries placed an emphasis in this period on the renewal of their cloister ranges. Abbot Walton at the close of the fifteenth century re-roofed the claustral buildings at Croxden.[69] In 1534 Hugh Roper, the vicar of Stogumber, bequeathed the sizeable sum of £60 to Cleeve for 'the new building of its cloister.'[70] Abbot Dovell did, at some stage, renew a section of its cloister.[71] Sir Edward Raleigh of Farnborough, by his will bearing date 20 June, 1509, bequeathed £30 to build the south side of the cloister at Combe and to glaze the windows.[72] In the later fifteenth century at Kirkstall not only was the cloister remodelled, but a gothic window replaced the rose window in the presbytery, and the roofs of the church and east range were covered with lead sheet.[73] The suppression accounts refer to the glass windows of the chapter-houses of Dieulacres, Dore and Merevale, and of the cloisters at Merevale and Pipewell. The chapter-house and cloister at Merevale accounted for 'xxviii panys of payntyd glasses.'[74] Much earlier it is thought that many Cistercian cloisters were open to the elements.

The prosperity brought to Hailes by pilgrims visiting the shrine of the Precious Blood led to the rebuilding of its cloister from the later fifteenth-century. Heraldic bosses in the west cloister, and encaustic tiles bearing the initials and arms of Abbots Thomas Stafford (1483–1504) and Anthony Melton (1509–1527), suggest that this work was prolonged. Renovation was not confined to its cloister, as in her will of 1519/1520 Lady Huddleston instructed that, 'if I die before all the aisles of the abbey church at Hailes are fully finished, leaded and embattled, it should be finished by my executors at my cost without delay.'[75] Clearly much work was in progress. In the account of the spoliation of Hailes on its closure mention is made of the 'bachelors haile chamber', this was probably its novitiate rather than a room reserved for its Oxford graduates.[76]

At Merevale in the 1490s stone from its own local quarry was employed for 'the foundation and undersetting' of the south side of its cloister. In the year of 1499 alone, Merevale's kiln on its Pinley grange fired 20,000 tiles and the same number of bricks. Apart from renovation work on its cloister, and the replacement of tiles and guttering, work at Merevale was carried out on a range of ancillary buildings, including 'the white chamber' and the 'new chamber' in the monastery, the guest stable and the abbot's stable, as well as repairs being made to four barns and two dovecots on its properties. Even new estate houses were built.[77]

It may be that renovation works were referred to when Thomas Nichol lent £44 to Abbot Richard Pyttemister for 'new work and building of the church' at Dunkeswell. Abbot Richard being sick and aged resigned in 1498, and his successor, John Whitmore, had to be sued for repayment of the loan.[78] At Whalley Abbot Paslew (1507–1537) built a fine Lady Chapel with a buttressed roof, but its location is now unknown. It was the work of two named masons, Nicholas Craven and Thomas Sellars.[79] When Burnley church was restored the same masons were employed, and instructed to give to each of the buttresses a funnel on top 'according to the fashion of the funnels upon the new chapel of Our Lady at Whalley.'[80] At Llantarnam as late as 1532 it was hoped to build 'an arch in the body of the church', as well as a new processional entrance off the cloister.[81] At Vaudey, when Abbot Henry Saxton was forced to resign in 1533, he told how he had spent £100 on rebuilding when 'the body of my church fell down.'[82]

When John Darnton became abbot of Fountains (1478–1490) parts of its abbey church were in a poor condition, and extensive repair work was necessary, including the replacement of the stone vault of the church with a timber roof. Darnton installed in the west wall of the nave and the east end of the Nine Altars Chapel great new windows in Perpendicular style. To support the east wall of the chapel buttresses were constructed, while by the sixteenth century the aisles of the infirmary were made into separate rooms, perhaps for elderly monks. Marmaduke Huby continued Darnton's work inserting a massively moulded arch below another giving entrance to the south aisle of the presbytery but which was badly cracked.[83] In 1501, at Fountains, came mention of 'the chapel near the new chamber near the church.'[84]

A fine relic of Cistercian adornment of their churches of these times was the porch added to Holm Cultram abbey church by Abbot Robert Chambers in 1507. It gives his name and the year of erection, and bears in Latin texts from the liturgy for the consecration of a church, including 'Let us rejoice in the Lord, who has blessed this house' (*Cf.* 1 K 9, v. 3), and 'This is none other than the house of God, the gate of heaven' (Gn 28, v. 17). The heraldry displayed include the arms of the abbey: a cross moline and a lion rampant, as well as Chambers' initials to either side of a bear chained to a crosier.[85]

A porch of a different kind was embellished at Cleeve early in the sixteenth century when Abbot Dovell found it necessary to add buttresses to its gate-house, and to rebuild its upper storey completely. In so doing, a fine crucifixion scene as well as the abbot's name, was added and in addition the motto: *Porta Patens Esto / Nulli Claudaris Honesto.*[86] This has been translated as 'Gate be open, Be shut to no honest person.' Tree-ring analysis of timbers in the modern conference centre at Whalley date them to the years between 1478 and 1508, and they may relate to the building of its north-west gateway in 1480.[87]

Abbots' Houses

Some abbots' lodgings were also renovated or built anew in the Tudor period. At Thame Abbot Robert King (*c.*1530) added a battlemented tower to the abbot's hall. A chamber in the hall on the first floor has a frieze carved with his name, while his parlour on the first floor of the tower is inscribed with his initials. That parlour was 'sumptuously decorated in Italian Renaissance style' between 1520 and 1530, but probably by English artists. The whole is now incorporated into Thame Park House.[88] At Rievaulx Abbot William Burton (1489–1510) converted the twelfth-century infirmary into a new and grand first floor abbot's dwelling. The abbot's chamber at first floor level was approached by a stone staircase, and over the entry was a sculpture of the Annunciation to Our Lady—akin to a relief found at Fountains.[89]

One of the remaining, though much altered, edifices at Combermere is a hall, formerly thought of as being the monastic refectory, but now postulated as the abbot's house. It possesses a false hammer-beam roof, the timbers of which are dated by tree-ring evidence to have been felled in the year 1502. Whatever its original function, it shows very active building improvements at the abbey. The arched braces of the roof bear heraldry, including a shield portraying a crozier and the arms of the abbey.[90]

At Valle Crucis part of the dormitory was converted into its abbot's house with a private adjacent chamber built over the sacristy. The spiral staircase leading to the dorter was narrow and restricted, so a new entrance was made into the abbot's lodgings reached by an external wooden staircase.[91] This conversion may have been the work of Abbot Dafydd ap Ieuan who ruled at Valle Crucis, from about 1480 to 1503. The additional building may have been that referred to by Gutun Owain, a Welsh poet of the period who was a frequent guest at the abbey, when he wrote of the abbot's house 'with its skilfully wrought roof, which he has walled about.'[92]

At Whalley the last abbot, John Paslew, built himself a fine new house with a hall measuring sixteen by eight metres. Only low foundations of it now survive, but the abbey accounts tell of the furniture it contained, and record that there was a 'hanging candlestick,' probably a chandelier, in the middle of the hall to give light on a dark evening.[93] At Fountains improvements to the abbatial quarters were reflected when in 1517 Thomas Twisilton did homage to Abbot Marmaduke Huby 'in his new lower chamber.'[94] At Bruern one William Thorpe towards the Suppression loaned £10 to the monastery for the building of a prior's chamber; not repaid when the abbey closed, the Court of Augmentations awarded him only £4 in recompense. [95]

The abbot's chamber at Bordesley contained three beds: a feather bed and two woollen beds.[96] On 26 July 1499 new bedsheets were provided for the abbot's chamber at Merevale.[97] When Llantarnam and its home demesne was demised in 1539 to John Parker, esq., of the king's stable, mention was made that the grant included 'Skylbor courte' [Ysgubor-cŵrt], 'in the personal occupation of the late abbot,' suggesting a home a little way removed from the monastery, perhaps at the modern Court Farm.[98] The enhanced status of the abbot was reflected at Whitland in stones 'set up for the picture of the abbot.'[99]

One preoccupation of a few Tudor abbots lay in the improvement of belfries and in the erection of impressive towers. Abbot William Marshall of Kirkstall (1509–1527) took down his church spire, and raised the tower to twice its former height above the roof, giving it shields bearing his initials. The weight of the new tower eventually proved too much, and it collapsed in 1779.[100] Money was bequeathed so that at Robertsbridge (1502) 'the belfry over the bell on Our Lady's Chapel, be new made and covered with lead.'[101] A benefactor of Sibton bequeathed that abbey no less than £20 in 1469/70 'for the fabric of the bell tower.'[102]

Abbot Chard (1505–1539) of Ford built a new entrance tower inscribed with his name, the ground floor of which formed the entrance porch to his brand new hall or refectory, as well as renewing the cloister; all these still stand. Shields bearing his initials adorn the tower, and above a series of new chambers he erected appear his name and the date of construction: 1528. On his visit to Ford John Leland was able to comment that 'the abbot at considerable expense is now restoring the monastery most gloriously.'[103] Chard also renovated the Abbot's house in Charmouth (later the Queen's Arms), again gracing the building with his initials engraved. To Abbot John King of Buckfast (1466-?1497) may be ascribed the renovation of its fourteenth-century Abbot's Tower.[104]

Fig. 3: A Panel over the cloister at Ford displaying the initials and armorial bearings of Abbot Chard (1505–1539). (Sidney Heath, 1911)

Huby's Tower

Perhaps the most impressive Cistercian monument from Tudor times was the great tower, forty-eight metres tall, built by Abbot Marmaduke Huby (1495–1526) at Fountains, adjoining the north transept of the church.[105] The tower still has three statues remaining: of St Catherine, St James the Great and (probably) St Bernard. It bears Huby's arms: a mitre impaled by a crosier with his initials, and his motto: *Soli Deo Honor et Gloria*: 'To the only God, be honour and glory' (1 Tm 1, v. 17). The texts of three bands of inscriptions around the tower's upper storeys come from the Cistercian office for Sundays, and suggest a devotion to the Holy Name, though this did not become a Cistercian feast until 1644. The texts (given in Latin) include 'Blessed be the

Name of the Lord Jesus Christ from this time forth and for evermore' (*Cf.* Ps 113, v. 2), and 'At the Name of Jesus, every knee shall bow' (Ph 2, v. 10). The bell tower has often been regarded as self-aggrandizement by Huby,[106] but one author points out that the inscriptions, and the identity and location of the three saints' images on the tower, mean that 'the structure can be interpreted as an expression of Huby's personal devotions and of his dedication to monastic reform.'[107] One fact remains to this day—the statement regarding Huby in the *Memorials of Fountains*: 'While the tower of Fountains raises its head above the vale, he will not be deprived of a memorial.'[108]

Church and Other Furnishings

Something of the dignity of the worship afforded by the Cistercians, and of the wealth of a few monasteries, comes in the itemised lists of furnishings made for a special reason: as at a time of visitation, or in the survey of a house prior to its suppression, or at the sales of goods made at its dissolution. The monastery church of Merevale was noted (in 1538) as having a partition of old timber in the body of the church—the *pulpitum* separating the quire of the monks from the former quire of the *conversi*. There was a high altar—'a table of alabaster', and six 'old altars with images'.[109] The monks' seats were of timber, there were six gravestones inlaid with brass, and a brass holy water stoup.

One Richard Merywether desired in 1518 to be buried at Warden 'before the rood.'[110] There was a similar wooden partition at Dieulacres, which monastery had an high altar bearing four latten candlesticks, as well as four side altars in the aisles and a further four 'in the body of the church'. In its quire stood a great lectern of latten.[111] In a style foreshadowing that accustomed to be seen in later Anglican churches, Sawtry had 'a lectern with an eagle of latten.'[112] Dore possessed a gospel book plated with silver, as well as a silver-plated cross containing the relic of a saint.[113]

A benefactor providing for Stratford abbey in his will of 1522 desired to be buried there 'before the image of St John the Baptist over against Our Lady of Pity.'[114] Hailes (1511) and Rievaulx (1521)[115] had like images of Our Lady caressing the body of her dead Son. At Jervaulx 'a great image of Saint Anne' stood in the cloister.[116] When Cwmhir in mid-Wales closed early in March 1537, its 'picture of Jesus' was bought by abbot Talley of Strata Florida at its sale of goods. Within six weeks its return was sought by the people of Cwmhir as it was planned to build a parish chapel to replace the ministrations they had formerly received from the monks.[117] The chapel was built, but the division of Abbey Cwmhir remained extra-parochial.

An examination of the state of Vale Royal in 1509 credited it with thirty copes and more than ten sets of vestments (meaning chasuble, dalmatic and tunicle).[118] Tilty's twenty-nine pieces of vestments in 1536 included those of white damask, green velvet and green baudekyn; its thirteen copes comprehended one of blue damask, and three of silk, 'branched and wrought with beasts of gold.'[119] Dore abbey owned 'a cope of blue silk with angels.' At Thame, where amongst the lesser altars was one 'of the dead,' there were eight copes and nineteen sets of vestments.[120] A black chasuble survives decorated with last judgement imagery, and the initials and the rebus of Abbot Robert Thornton of Rievaulx who died in 1533.[121] Fountains, in the early 1530s, surpassed all others with eighty copes and twenty-two silver chalices, as well as much else.[122] It had a monstrance for Corpus Christi weighing 506 ounces.[123]

Whalley had twenty-one copes, one of them having 'a portrait of Christ upon a cloth of gold;' that and another bore the arms of Lord Monteagle (*d.*1523), and were probably the gift of that peer. Another cope bore the image of St John, yet another that of St Martin. Whalley's twenty-five chasubles included one of green velvet with an image of St Michael enbroidered on the back, and another of white satin bearing an image of the Trinity. Apart from these splendid vestments, there were fifteen others 'that are daily occupied in the church.' Some of the vestments were kept in a 'standard' or large chest in the church, others in 'little revestries' adjacent to the gallery and the library.[124]

Altar cloths also gave colour—like those at Tilty made from white Bruges satin and sprinkled with spots 'like drops of blood,' and lectern falls, of which Sawtry had four—three of white and green, and the other of tawny baudekyn. It also possessed 'a cloth to be placed before the abbot of fustian mapys with arms.'[125] Vale Royal ornamented its statue of the Blessed Virgin with a collar of gold, and a choice of two velvet vestments and four silk and velvet tunics.[126]

The plate of Stoneleigh included eight chalices, three silver thuribles, a pyx for containing the Body of Christ, a silver 'ampulla'—perhaps the vessel in which to keep the holy oil, and other items of plate.[127] Sawtry had four silver-gilt chalices, one of them being 'a great chalice.' Tilty had a silver and gilt censer, as also the boat for containing the incense—'a ship with a spoon.'[128] So did Whalley, which also possessed a large cross of silver and gilt bearing the images of Our Lady and St John, the beloved disciple, and another cross displaying the four evangelists. Ancient statues of Our Lady have been found close to the sites of Hailes (hidden in the floorboards of a house), and Whalley (discovered in a river bank).[129]

Claustral Chambers

The several surveys afford interesting insights into the domestic quarters of the monasteries. By Tudor times a number of chambers came to have specific individual names, as at Merevale where were to be found 'the chief parlour, the inner chamber, the great old chamber, the chamber called "ye Bredames," the white chamber, and the porter's chamber.'[130] Amongst the accommodation provided at Dieulacres were the 'ryders' chamber, the butler chamber, the labourer's chamber, and the corner chamber.[131] The latter, with its feather-bed and mattress and a tester of dornyx, might well have been the residence of a retired abbot or a corrodian. Dore had its "St Thomas of Lancaster's Chamber"—Earl Thomas who after his execution in 1322 achieved a considerable measure of public acclaim, but was never officially canonised. At Dore also was its 'New Chamber,' the home in its closing years of retired Abbot Thomas Cleubery.[132]

At Sawtry, in 'the lord's chamber' was a feather bed with a baster with white curtains, and feather beds were also found in its chapel chamber and its kitchen chamber—perhaps for sacristan and domestic staff respectively.[133] The abbot's dining chamber at Tilty had hangings of red say, 'a carpet of gaunt work' for the table, and sundries including a pair of tongs and 'a fire fork.' In its guest chamber were hangings of painted cloth and a trussing bed, and in the servant's chamber a feather bed with bolster and an old coverlet.[134] Contrary to earlier Cistercian custom, each monk of Hailes (enquiry testimony of 1542),[135] Jervaulx (archaeological evidence),[136] and of Pipewell (noted at the dissolution, 1538),[137] had their own individual chamber in the dorter. When Pipewell closed each monk was allowed to take away the contents of his chamber. In 1481 abbots on visitation at Rufford directed that a chamber, well appointed, be assigned in the infirmary for the care of the sick and aged religious.[138]

The washing trough before the refectory ('a laver of ley metall and lead') is mentioned at Merevale,[139] whilst the combined brew-house and bakehouse of Sawtry, had 'a pipe of lead to convey water in,' and a bag of hops was noted in its store-house. Its buttery's utensils included ten candlesticks, eight hogsheads for ale, and 'an old bin for bread.'[140] The brew-house at Dieulacres had a mashing fat and twelve 'kelers' of lead;[141] the brew-house of Tilty contained 'three brass pots hanging in a furnace and three brewing vats,' whilst in its cellar were 'two joists covered with lead to lay on barrels of beer.'[142] In 1547 a 'Brewhouse Croft' was noted on the site of the now closed Kirkstall.[143] In the kitchen of Sawtry were found fifteen pewter platters and twelve saucers; sixteen platters of 'old fashioned pewter' were noted in Tilty's kitchen, and the goods sold at Dieulacres included no less than thirty-eight platters, dishes and saucers.

The Liturgy

An indication of how Cistercian worship was offered comes in the visitation charters of Tudor times. By their nature these do not give an overall description, but simply address points for improvement. At Rufford, visited in 1481,[144] the charter directed that the monks were to worship with 'their eyes directed to the ground, their hearts lifted to the Holy Trinity and the Mother of God.' They were to make a decent pause in the middle of every verse when chanting the psalms, and 'always and everywhere, according to the definitions,[145] they were to incline the head at the names of Jesus and Mary.' With the exception of those in the dormitory at the sound of the sacring bell, indicating the elevation of 'the Most Holy', all everywhere were to genuflect and not rise from the ground until the act of consecration was complete.

After the *Salve Regina* had been sung at the close of Compline, all were to be sprinkled with holy water and then with covered heads to ascend to the dormitory. Rising at the third hour for vigils, the sacristan was to give the signal by ringing the small dormitory bell, and none were to absent themselves from choir. On Sundays and feasts of Twelve Lessons two Masses were sung in choir at the second hour after cock-crow. The prescriptions given to the community of Thame, when visited by the father-abbot of Waverley in 1526, also made mention of the *Salve Regina* being sung, the bell rung and holy water sprinkled after Compline. It was also enjoined that three lamps were to be always burnt in the church during Vigils, 'as expressly laid down in the Book of Usages.'[146]

When Warden was inspected in 1492[147] the monks were instructed to chant the offices devoutly and soberly and keeping in time, in neither too high nor too low a voice, but in a middling tone and dove-like voice, and none were to leave the choir except for grave infirmity or necessity or on important business of the monastery. Priests not assigned for the conventual Masses were to celebrate their own Masses at least three times in the week. Monks who were not priests were to receive Holy Communion on Sundays and Feasts of Sermon. Further insight into the liturgy at Warden came in 1507 when the Crown permitted it to alienate from Sir John Fisher, a justice of the bench, a gift of over 250 acres of land.[148] In return the community promised that a monk would celebrate Mass daily at the altar of St Nicholas and St John Baptist in the north part of the monastery, for the good estate of the king and of the grantor and his family, and by way of obit after their deaths.

Other favours granted by a monarch resulted in monks offering spiritual services in gratitude. Flaxley (1502) granted Henry VII in consideration of a heavy debt he forgave it, a daily Mass of the Blessed Virgin at her altar in the south side of the church, as well as a solemn obit to be celebrated for ever.[149] Beaulieu (1508) in acknowledgement of a pardon given by Henry VIII, promised that 'for the king's prosperous estate' one Mass of the Holy Spirit would be said by a monk on one day of each week, and on one Sunday each quarter a solemn Mass of the Holy Trinity would be celebrated. After the king's death, these provisions were to be replaced each quarter by a solemn Mass of requiem with a special collect, together with *placebo* and *dirige*. On these occasions, the bells were to be solemnly rung and 'knolled'.[150] At Holm Cultram (1535) a Mass had long been said annually in its St Saviour Chapel for the soul of Richard II, but now the intention also included the good estate of Henry VIII.[151]

In November 1504, in common with eighteen other religious and collegiate foundations in the London area, St Mary Graces entered into a tripartite agreement with the abbey of St Peter, Westminster and the mayor and commonalty of the City.[152] In return for an annuity of £3-6-8 paid to St Mary Graces by Westminster abbey, the monastery by Tower Hill bound itself to the mayor and commonalty, to observe, 'while the world shall endure,' a solemn commemoration on 11 November each year, being the anniversary of the death of Queen Elizabeth on that day in 1503. After Henry VII's own death, the commemoration was to be transferred to the anniversary of the day of his sepulture, which in the event was 11 May 1509.[153] In addition each monk that day was to say a Requiem Mass for the same intentions 'unless let by sickness or bound by other duty.'

The community of St Mary Graces were to 'sing solemnly with note *placebo* and *dirige* with nine lessons, as well as Lauds.' The prayers to be used were inserted into the agreement, as well as the collect, secret prayer and post-communion prayers for the Requiem Mass. If the anniversary fell on a Sunday it was to be kept the preceding day. If it fell during the sacred triduum, then it was to be observed on the Saturday of Easter week. During the entire obsequies the abbey bells were to be rung, and a hearse was to be set up in the midst of the quire surrounded by four candles each of eight pounds weight. If the abbot celebrated the Mass he was to receive, out of the annuity, 6s. 8d; the costs of the hearse, bells and candles were also to be met from the annuity. Any surplus money was to be divided between the members of the community; they cannot each have received very much.

Service to another queen consort was afforded when the body of Queen Katherine lay overnight at Sawtry in January 1536, en route for burial at Peterborough Abbey, and the bishop of Ely celebrated there a requiem Mass. Sawtry abbey church was illuminated for the night vigil, and at the requiem 'in the middle of the church, forty-eight torches of rosin were carried by as many poor men, with mourning hoods and garments.'[154]

By these years the Cistercian kalendar was firmly established, but in 1496 Abbot Huby of Fountains (early in his days as a Reformator of the Order), gained the upgrading of the commemoration of St Oswald (5 August), in the Cistercian monasteries of the province of York, as a feast of Twelve Lessons with two Masses and a proper collect. This was in part, he said, because some of the abbeys contained relics of the saint.[155] Other notes of liturgy come in mention of the daily Mass of Our Lady (as celebrated at Buckland, Newenham, and Cleeve); Cleeve also having a votive of the Holy Name of Jesus on Fridays.[156] A daily 'Mass of Jesus' was assumed by a benefactor in 1533 of Swineshead.[157]

An undated manuscript records the names of thirteen monks of Tilty as being paid 7d. each for Masses offered, but how many and for what purpose is not stated.[158] As for private daily Masses these were assisted by secondary chapels and altars. The dissolution accounts list these at Pipewell, which had chapels dedicated in honour of Saints Benet [Benedict], Michael, Nicholas and Stephen, as well as altars named the Trinity Altar and St Katherine's

Altar.[159] In the heralds' visitations of Wales in 1531 note was made at Tintern of an altar dedicated to St John Baptist 'on the north side of the church', and another of St Mary Magdalene 'on the south side of the monastery.'[160]

At Vaudey (1531/32) the church expenses included the purchase of bread and wine for Mass, twelve gallons of oil to burn in the lamps of the church, eight 'tartari' also to burn in the church, three dozen tallow candles, and payments for the mending of vestments and tuning of the bells.[161] Stratford (1488) supplemented the income of its sacristy by levying three shillings yearly from the lessee of its manor of Bumpstead, in addition to his nine marks annual rent.[162] In demising two mills within the precincts for £10 annually, a further 2s. were payable each year to the sacristan.[163] Individuals continued to make small grants to facilitate specific items of worship, as in 1497/98 when Edward Hubande gave a rent of 4s. arising from land at Astwode, Buckinghamshire, for 'lighting' the daily Mass of the Blessed Virgin Mary at Bordesley.[164]

The sacrist of Sibton (1483/84) received rents and oblations totalling over £5 annually for the purchases made by the sub-sacrist of bread, wine and wax, and for mending the bells and the candlelabra. His purchases also included 'oil for the chrism'—used in confirmations and the like.[165] The annual expenditure of the sacristan of Furness (1538) amounted to £12, and covered the purchase of wine, oil, wax and 'syngengebrede.'[166] In 1493 the Chamberlain of Chester accounted for two casks of wine, a royal gift by ancient charters to Vale Royal.[167]

When in 1526 the abbot of Waverley made a visitation of Thame, the lengthy charter stipulated that 'the liturgy was to be celebrated according to the form of blessed father Benedict and as in the mother-house of Cîteaux.'[168] Lay cantors, whether men or boys, were to be excluded from the choir in time of divine service; broken chant, called in English 'prick song,' was not to be used but the organ might be played by a secular if no monk had the necessary skill. It was a reminder that lay involvement and organ music had an increasing role in Cistercian worship.

Fig. 4: An anthem, Felix namque es sacra virgo Maria', written into a composite volume assembled by Abbot Thomas Cleubery of Dore (1516–1523) (Exeter College, Oxford, MS1, f.75v).
(Published with permission of the Rector and Fellows of Exeter College, Oxford)

At Buckland in 1522 Abbot Whyte agreed with one Robert Derkham, that he was to assist daily in the choir, and encourage 'better and smoother singing' by four boys of the monastery 'that they may serve adequately in the choir.' He was to train one boy, and any of the monks who might wish, 'in the musical skill, art and expertise of playing the organs.' He was to be paid an annuity of £2-13-4, to be provided with a decent table, to have a furnished room over the west gate of the monastery, and a gown yearly of the value of 12s. In addition, he was to have the reversion of a tenement at Milton—this perhaps was meant to afford him a retirement abode. His room was cold and dreary in winter, but he was also granted daily five ounces of bread and a quart of beer, and a wax candle every night, together with thirty horse-loads of faggots annually for fuel. Derkham must have stayed in the service of the abbey until its closure, for on 18 December 1540 the Court of Augmentations allowed him a yearly pension of £4-13-4 as 'full satisfaction' for his loss of position and lodging.[169]

Boxley in 1532 was fortunate in gaining the services of John Trapham as organist and Master of its Song School; previously he had been a gentleman of the chapel of Archbishop Warham. He was to 'teach, instruct and inform, four children within the monastery in singing, as plainsong, priksong and descant, and to play at the organs at all times necessary and requisite, and all other instruments which he hath any sight and knowledge in.'[170] It was a departure from Cistercian simplicity. John was granted a substantial residential corrody, and his services seems to have been appreciated, as eighteen months after his appointment he received for his 'good and faithful service' an annuity of 30s.[171] Still in office when the abbey closed, the Court of Augmentations awarded him £4 annually for loss of home and perquisities.

Hailes was another abbey with an organist-cum-chorister having a residential corrody. He was Robert Blokeley, appointed in September 1533 and responsible 'for keeping and playing of our organs and singing within our choir.'[172] Kingswood's organ player, at its suppression in 1538, was John Pulfford. He received only a £1 stipend, but undoubtedly had full residential rights.[173] When Newminster closed in 1537 it had four choir boys on the establishment—this seems to have been the average number. The commissioners awarded Edward Wilborne, its 'singing-man,' an annuity of 13s 4d.[174] The abbey school at Furness comprised both a grammar school and a song school.[175] Byland (1529) awarded an annuity of £2 to John Yonger, 'our singing man, for good services before this time;' perhaps he was retiring.[176]

At Cleeve, where John Mitchell (1518) was engaged as a chorister, the musical standard will have come under the critical ear of Richard Smyth, vicar-choral of Wells Cathedral (1528), during his periods of residence there.[177] On three days of each week, Mitchell was, 'while he is strong in health of body and voice until he comes to the age of fifty years,' to assist at the sung mass of Our Lady, on Fridays at the sung mass of the Name of Jesus, on Saturdays at the mass of Our Lady in her chapel in Cleeve, as well as at mass and vespers every Sunday. Receiving an annual stipend of £2-13-4, he was to be given 'an honest chamber' and adequate rights of food and fuel. Moreover, he could take ten days leave each year.[178]

At Newenham (1519) John fitzWilliam, one of the abbot's servants, had to double up as a chorister. As well as ministering at the abbot's table and riding out on business with him, John was to 'sing every day at the mass of the Blessed Virgin Mary, and on all feast-days to be present in the choir with the convent (community) chanting at the Mass and at the hour of Vespers.' There is no mention of residential entitlement (perhaps he lived nearby), but he was to receive a stipend of 33s 4d. for life, as well as a horse and its harness. The Court of Augmentations (23 January 1541) awarded him the continuance of his stipend.[179] At Stanley (1513)[180] and Coggeshall (1512, 1529, 1532) where the Crown awarded corrodies to former members of the Chapel Royal, the musical standards may have found critical ears. In those years, three choristers of the Chapel Royal succeeded one another in residence at Coggeshall.[181] There are frequent references to the use of organs in Cistercian houses, and there were certainly other lay organists as at Merevale in 1496. That abbey had the services of one Robert Organplayer granting him a stipend of £1-6-8. The monastery had acquired its organ that year from Northampton via Coventry.[182] Coggeshall abbey had a 'pair of organs' on order in 1475,[183] while in remote mid-Wales, Cwmhir was left a bequest in 1524 in order 'to buy a pair of organs to honour God within the abbey.'[184] A 'pair of organs' were also among the effects at the closure of Merevale,[185] Tilty[186] and Sawtry (two in its case).[187] The term may refer to the 'regal organ', a small portable instrument with reed pipes and two bellows.[188] At Croxden (1538) comes reference to its organ loft.[189] When Pipewell closed in November 1538 it was owing £6-16-8 to one Richard Baynton, clerk, 'for making new organs' in the monastery church.[190]

At the dissolution of Vale Royal the last abbot, John Harwood, requested to be able to possess the abbey's organ, but there is no certainty that he did.[191] The organ of Merevale sold for but £1,[192] whilst 'the organs in the quire' at Dore were bought as part of a package for only £2 by the Particular Receiver of the Herefordshire monasteries, John Scudamore.[193] When, however, the organ of Strata Marcella abbey on the Welsh border was sold to St Mary's Church, Shrewsbury, it realised the handsome sum of £13-6-8.[194]

The employment of organs in Tudor time must have greatly enhanced the worship in an abbey church. At Valle Crucis in north Wales, where the steps ascending the *pulpitum* may have led to an organ loft, the Celtic poets of Tudor times noted that in the abbot's hall 'during dinner will arise the strains of organs, vocal and instrumental music.' The blind and deaf resident poet there, Guto'r Glyn, regretted that he could no longer 'hear an organ and bells!'[195]

Refectories, and Food Supply

As part of his reconstruction work Abbot Chard of Ford built there in the 1520s a new refectory measuring 115 x 28 feet, and with a painted panelled roof. A first-floor dining hall, it may have been intended as the place where meat could lawfully be eaten.[196] At Cleeve Abbot David Juyner in the mid-fifteenth century had built a first floor refectory on an east-west axis, and tree-ring analysis of its roof timbers confirms this date. While Cleeve's refectory may later have been additionally used as the abbot's hall the pulpitum shows its primary purpose. Behind the position of the high table was formerly a wall painting depicting the Crucfixion. All but adjoining is a chamber with a late-fifteenth century wall painting depicting St Catherine with her wheel and St Margaret standing on a dragon.[197] Less happily, by 1512 the refectory of Flaxley was in a state of ruin. The same was true of the refectory of Strata Florida in 1538; on its foundations were later built a substantial dwelling house which still exists. Restoration work at Vale Royal House in the 1990s uncovered the original fifteenth-century timber framing with wattle and daub of its former refectory.[198]

At Pipewell's suppression (1538) note was made of its 'salt chamber, fish chamber and cheese chamber', all presumably ancillary to its refectory and kitchen.[199] When Tilty was 'surveyed' on 3 March 1536, the third day of Lent that year, there were noted in its larder forty-six couple of salt fishes, twelve couple of lings, and thirty-one couple of stock fishes.[200] In 1519/20 fish were a major element in the diet of the monks of Sibton, costing in total over £22 and mostly bought via the ports of Dunwich and Great Yarmouth. The stock purchased included over two hundred salt fish in addition to ling and stockfish, as well as twelve 'cades' of white and six 'cades' of red herrings, and sprats. Two salmon were received: the one cost two shillings, the other was a gift for the acting abbot—Abbot Clifton having just died or resigned. Whelks and eels were also bought at Yarmouth; two of the eels were a gift for the new abbot, John Goodwyn.[201]

In 1531/32, fish accounted for £27 of the £52 spent on food at Vaudey. The fish bought included 'goodes saltfish' and 'lobbe' saltfish, five barrels of white herrings and seven 'cades' of red herrings, as also ling, stockfish, eels and pike. Other purchases for its monks' food supply included salt and meat, capons, pullets and piglets.[202] When Merevale closed (13 October 1538) it was still owing five shillings to one Thomas Wilcocke for 'salt fish called ling' bought from him eighteen months beforehand.[203] Salt and fresh salmon and other fish were prominent in the diet of the monks of Whalley in its last months; they also consumed eggs, butter and cheese, but little meat as it was Lent. Fasting was maintained to the last! Mustard was also available to them, while no less than nine gallons and eight pots of honey were bought for monastic use between 31 December 1536 and 24 March 1537![204]

The diet of the monasteries, apart from the produce realised by direct cultivation and from tithes, might also be supplemented by rents paid in kind. This was especially true in Wales, where the tenants of Strata Florida in Ceredigion rendered yearly 90 teils of oats (about 500 bushels), over 1500 bushels of oatmeal, several hundred 'truggs' of corn, 450 capons and pullets, about 120 topstans of wool and, every second year, 120 sheep. In the instance of Margam, by 1532 commutation was permitted of kind rents into cash payments where fish were concerned. This was fufilled at the rate of 8d per salmon due, 4d per gilling and ½d per sewin. Partial rents in kind continued to be paid until the Suppression by certain tenants of Basingwerk ('clean and winnowed wheat' from its Caldy Grange), and of Tintern (110 quarters of wheat being outstanding from its Merthyr Gerain Grange tenants when the Dissolution came).[205]

In the Isle of Wight only three of Quarr's granges still paid rents in kind, but the tenant of Combley was expected to cart to the abbey fixed quantities of wheat, barley and oats, and also to render eight pigs, twenty geese, sixteen capons, thirty pullets, eight brace of rabbits, and 100lb. of cheese.[206] In Sussex, Robertsbridge demising Woodrove Manor (1534) required an annual rent of £35-13-4, but also in kind ten quarters of corn and ten of barley, two bushels of mustard and 1200 reeds. On Humberside, the following year, Meaux granted for twenty-one years the lease of the rectory of Affreton (Arreton), with the mansion house and all lands pertaining; no monetary payment was expected of the tenant, Dame Isabel Tunstall, but rather yearly sixty-eight quarters of wheat, 126 of barley, 120 of peas, and twenty-one of oats, as well as ten swine, twelve capons, twelve goats, twelve hens and 100 eggs.[207] Fowls and eggs were also received by Stratford from a property in Woolwich.[208]

In the Midlands the tenants of Rufford's Babworth and Kyrketon Granges (1535) proferred rents in money and kind: oats (valued at 20d a quarter), rye (3s 8d. per qtr.), barley (at 3s. per qtr.), and wheat (5s per qtr.).[209] In the north-west kind rents formed part of tenants' remit on at least eighteen properties of Furness, while the tenant of its Southend holding (valued in total at an annual rent of over £10), paid a small part of that in silver, but also rendered oats and barley, young pigs and fixed quantities of butter (16 lb.) and cheese (40 lb).[210]

Provisions such as these made for a varied and constant supplement to an abbey's food supply, but when the penultimate abbot of Coggeshall, William Love, made several late leases, and granted one solely in return for a rent in cheese, his action one of his monks thought would deprive the Crown of income after the Suppression.[211] At St Mary Graces, one boar was consumed annually on the feast of St Catherine.[212] When Abbot Henry More of St Mary Graces around 1530 received from a 'Mr Spyncke,' a London grocer, spices and other groceries for use in the monastery, he declined to pay the £6 bill, and refused to have further dealings with Spyncke. He said this was because he had been charged for more items than were delivered, and since Spyncke's prices were much greater than those of other London grocers.[213]

Small quantities of food or drink might be promised in wills. Bryan Cryar of Swineshead (1532) left the abbey there 'till a pot with ale, xxd', and—perhaps to assist its brewing—John Pape bequeathed a quarter of barley to Kirkstead.[214] Local produce was supplemented at Furness by the import yearly of 100 quarters of wheat from its lands in Ireland,[215] whilst (for church purposes as well as drink) one tun of wine each came in 1526 through the port of Southampton for Beaulieu, Netley and Waverley.[216]

By Tudor times meat might be eaten on non-abstinence days (like Sundays, Tuesdays and Thursdays), but never in Lent and never in the refectory. Meat could only be consumed in a room specially set aside or in the infirmary. The meat consumed at Sibton (in 1519–1520) came mainly from the demesne stock, and whilst accounted for in-house it was valued in total as worth over £74. Sheep were prominent, but there were also hens and eggs, geese, doves and rabbits received by the kitchener. Spices bought in included pepper and ginger, sugar and cinnamon, dates and prunes, raisins and nutmegs. Almost 5,000 eggs were consumed, two hundred of these were gifts from neighbours and 124 came from dues payable by tenants. The bake-house account of Sibton in the same years tells of wheat and rye being used for the baking of bread, of barley being employed in making malt for the brewing of ale, of oats for horse fodder, and peas for pottage.[217]

By Tudor times it was common for monks to take breakfast and to have mid-afternoon refreshments. The community of Vaudey in 1533 were 'wont daily to command bread, meat and drink in the buttery and in the kitchen at breakfast time and at afternoon;' 'meat' in this instance is to be equated with 'food'.[218] The day of the lay brethren was long past, and in its last days

Fountains granted an annuity of £2 to Christopher Hebden, its 'principal cook.'[219]

Repositories and Safe Keeping

Many a monastery was seen as a place of relative security where layfolk might deposit for safe keeping, deeds, money and jewels. In especial abbeys might keep safely the inheritance of a gentleman's offspring. Robert Aske, noted for his leadership in the Pilgrimage of Grace, told how gentlemen entrusted the monasteries of the North with 'their evidences and money left to the uses of infants, always sure there.'[220] Added to that, a number of abbots were from time to time appointed sub-collectors of a subsidy or tenth granted to the Crown or the papacy. That involved the handling of large sums of cash, and the need to protect it. It has been suggested that abbey treasuries were commonly at dorter level above the book-room and the sacristy, though Abbot Thomas of Garendon kept muniments relating to a loan to one William Acton 'in a locked coffer in his chamber.'[221] The charters and other 'evidences' of Pipewell (1538) were kept in a strong press in the dorter. This was forced open at its dissolution, 'but what was wanting not known.'[222]

Even monasteries were not immune from assaults, invasions and internal discord, so the abbot of Margam by the south Wales coast had to admit in 1533 that 'the place of his abbey was too perilous to receive treasure.'[223] Holm Cultram, close to the shores of the Solway Firth, had nearby its own safe place for storage of plate and deeds, the crenellated Wolsty Castle. Incursions by the Scots 'and other perverse men' caused the monks to withdraw there for a time in 1507/08.[224] The keeper of Wolsty Castle in 1537 was Robert Chamber, undoubtedly a relative of Abbot Robert Chamber (1502–1527).

At Furness after the death of Abbot Bank (1533) Hugh Brown, a monk who was entrusted with the key of the abbot's chamber, employed a smith to break open the chest in that chamber in which the abbey's common seal was kept. Allegedly Brown then used the seal to authenticate several blank parchments, which were the means of granting four manors to the earl of Cumberland. In proceedings before the Duchy of Lancaster Court in 1543, Brown—now forty-seven years old and living at Ayrton, Cumbria, admitted breaking into the safe, saying that for this he had been 'committed to ward' by the commissioners Doctors Layton and Legh, but he denied issuing any such leases. He also said that three fellow monks agreed to the breaking open of the chest, but they were not named in the proceedings.[225] In 1524 Abbot Bank, during a dispute regarding the manor of Kirkby, Lancashire, said that he had relevant deeds in a casket 'closed and locked.'[226]

The amounts of money that might need protection could be huge. When Henry VIII in 1531 was in need of immediate funds he demanded of the abbots of Beaulieu and of St Mary Graces no less than 1,000 marks, supposed to be in their hands after being levied from the Cistercian houses of England and Wales by the late Cardinal Wolsey.[227] In 1537 the abbot of Buckland had gathered in no less than £402 for the monarch's use.[228] Earlier, after Lord Monteagle's death in 1523, £360 of his money held in safe keeping at Whalley was appropriated by the monarch. In modern equivalent that amounted perhaps to nearly £150,000.[229] After the death around 1523 of Abbot Elys of Newenham, three of his 'familiar servants' allegedly removed from the monastery its charters and deeds and also some £600 in money, spent the money and refused to return the muniments.[230]

Other dignitaries who deposited money in a Cistercian house included Bishop Standish of St Asaph at Whalley—a locked casket containing cash, jewels and plate;[231] and Dr John Rayne, chancellor of the bishop of Lincoln, at Pipewell—£106 worth of gold, £20 in groats, and other money.[232] Whalley was again seen as a trustworthy repository when in 1524 Thomas Hesketh deposited there for safe keeping £1,400 worth of plate as heirlooms for his son, Robert. In all these instances security precautions must have been tight.

Banking services were afforded when in 1508 George Lewis of Netherwent arranged for Tintern to hold £9 yearly for ten years to provide for the marriage of his children,[233] and when in 1534 £240 was deposited at Valle Crucis to yield £20 p.a. for the children of Robert ap Rhys, the abbot's father.[234] When Margaret Bulkely died (1528), her will provided that the deeds proving her possessions were to be put in a coffer in the custody of the abbot of Whalley, he to have one of the three keys.[235] This meant that an unscrupulous superior could not open the chest, unless the other key holders were in agreement and present.

Between 1485 and 1538 there were more than fifty instances involving over thirty Cistercian monasteries where, it was alleged, deeds and documents had been deposited in safe-keeping at an abbey, but that in later years its abbot refused to deliver them up when requested. The known allegations resulted in lawsuits mostly before the Court of Chancery, though it is possible that there were others of which the records have not survived, or which were dealt with more locally. Whilst most abbeys had only one or at most two cases brought against them in this respect, Roche was involved in five such lawsuits and Stanley in no less than six. Only in a few instances is an abbot's rejoinder or explanation of the circumstances on record.

A typical example came in the mid-1530s when Robert Eysterby of Brandsby, North Yorkshire, complained in the Court of Chancery that his father, Thomas, had possessed six ox-gangs of land, twenty acres of pasture and ten acres of meadow in the town fields of Brandsby, as well as common rights. He had entered into the property after his father died, but the deeds proving his title had come into the possession of the abbot of Jervaulx—undoubtedly because his father had deposited them at the monastery. The abbot not only refused to give him the title deeds, but rather one of the monks and the abbot's servant had used them to cause him 'vexation and trouble.' Moreover he did not know whether 'the said evidences be in bags, boxes or chests, sealed or unsealed, nor yet the number of them.' The abbot responded that the abbey had never held any such evidences 'from the beginning of the world unto this day.'[236]

A like case arose when around 1516 Thomas and Elizabeth Brasbridge 'having special trust and confidence' in the abbot of Garendon, Thomas Syston, placed before their marriage monies, plate and deeds into his custody. Later they were to allege that the abbot after their wedding refused to return them. The matter they said was especially worrying as they did not know the exact number of deeds nor the weight of the plate.[237] After John Shipton became abbot of Hulton in 1517 he allegedly refused to deliver up the obligations of both parties to a dispute of which his predecessor had been an arbitrator.[238]

In the mid-1520s, Katherine Brynston asserted that in November 1478 Abbot John Wormesley of Boxley demised to her husband and herself a mease in Aylesford, Kent, known as the Sign of the Bull. After she was widowed her husband's executor asked the new abbot, John Adcock, and one Robert Fisher, to draw up the inventory of his goods. They took away the title deed for the Sign of the Bull and evicted her. The abbot responded that he had not removed any deeds, but that Katherine was behind in the payment of rent.[239]

In a similar case, perhaps around 1520, one Henry Carver alleged in the Court of Chancery that a previous abbot of Combermere had demised to his father a certain waste ground called Wychwood Green in Cheshire on which to build a house. In his lifetime his father made his wife, Elyn, his executrix, but after his death the new abbot persuaded Elyn to come and live at the monastery. She did so, bringing with her all her deeds, goods and chattels. In time she also died, and so all her papers came into the hands of the new abbot who refused to deliver them up. The abbot responding said that he had no such deeds.[240]

In many instances there is no extant explanation by an abbot as to the truth or otherwise of such accusations. There may have been a few unscrupulous abbots who saw in this way a means of increasing their abbeys' estates, but there is also the real probability (as with the case of a prioress of Wykeham related later) that false claimants or pretended heirs came forward, and an abbot was only doing his duty in refusing them the evidences they sought. Noteworthy also is the close similarity of phraseology employed in several of these cases: 'whether they be closed in bags, boxes or chest' (Roche, 1486/1515);[241] 'be they contained in box or chest locked' (Cleeve, 1518/29),[242] or 'in bags or chests or boxes or locked' (Kirkstall, 1518/20).[243] It may well be that there were specialist lawyers dealing with such cases in chancery, or a model formula to be alluded to.

In an interesting Herefordshire episode of about 1520/25, Philip Scudamore of Kentchurch alleged to the Court of Chancery that Miles ap Harry, son of Abbey Dore's former steward, had conveyed out of that abbey deeds relating to his lands. Miles ap Harry countered that Philip's father, James, in his lifetime had allowed the use of the lands to Miles' wife, Eleanor. He did not doubt Philip's ownership of the lands, but as he felt the documents concerned him more than Philip he had removed the coffer containing the 'charters, writings and muniments' from the monastery to his house a mile away. He did so also because he was 'perceiving that the monastery of Dore standeth in a wild quarter where there resided many persons of light demeanour, and some of the monks being of that condition, for fear lest the coffer and evidence should be embezzled or misordered by such persons.'[244] The troubles of Dore in those years give some veracity to his explanation.[245]

Over the centuries there have been occasional finds of buried treasure at a Cistercian site, usually money secreted away for whatever reason. It was in different circumstances that one James Huddleston, clearly a relative of the then Abbot William Huddleston, dwelling and having a barn within the precincts of Stratford abbey, hid for safety in a post in that barn 'a great quantity of gold being in angel nobles.' In late August 1532 he rode to Cumberland with his son, Miles, to visit a relative, but died there intestate.

His son returned and took the hidden money. This meant, his stepmother, Ellen, alleged to the Court of Chancery, that she could not administer James' estate of which the abbot had appointed her executrix. Clearly there was no love lost between stepmother and stepson.[246] A find in 1534 of gold and silver close to Furness turned out to be coins from the Roman period.[247]

Notes

1   L. J. Lekai, *The Cistercians, Ideals and Reality*, Kent State U.P., 1977, pp. 110–11.

2   Ibid. p. 111.

3   C. H. Talbot (ed.), *Letters from English Abbots to Cîteaux*, London, Royal Historical Soc., 1967, pp. 97–98 [40].

4   Ibid. pp. 123–26 [61–62], 128–30 [64].127 [63].

5   *Statuta* 5, p. 387.

6   Talbot, *Letters*, 1967, p. 126 [No. 62].

7   Lekai, *Cistercians*, 1977, pp. 111–12.

8   *Statuta* 6, pp. 87–90 [90–96].

9   Talbot, *Letters*, 1967, pp. 193–96 [96]. He sent the abbot of Cîteaux 'a young horse, firm on its feet, and of a gentle pace.' The horse, and a packet of letters, were transmitted by the abbot of Vauluisant, Dépt. Aube, France, but was the term 'horse' a cover for monies sent?

10   *Statuta* 6, pp. 123, 377–78, 468, 525, 531, 546–47, 674–75.

11   Talbot, *Letters*, 1967, pp. 186–89 [92–93].

12   Ibid. 97–98 [40]; D. H. Williams, *The Welsh Cistercians*, Leominster, Gracewing, 2001, p. 64.

13   L. Harries, *Gwaith Huw Cae Llwyd ac Eraill*, Cardiff, Gwasg Prifysgol Cymru, 1953, p. 112.

14   Somerset R.O., *Reg. T. Wolsey*, f. 28.

15   Worcestershire R.O., *Reg. J. Carpenter*, f. 546.

16   BL, Harley MS 544, f. 111.

17   TNA, C1/426/49.

18   *LP* 1, p. 1166 [No. 2672].

19   E. A. B. Barber, *Cistercian Abbey of St Mary, Stratford Langthorne, Museum of London*, 2004, p. 57; TNA, PROB11/18, f.83v.

20   *Letters*, p. 191.

21   *Letters*, pp. 112–13 [No. 52].

22   *LP* 1, Part 1, p. 900 [No. 1992].

23   NLW, Badminton Manorial 1524, m. 44.

24   Kentchurch Court, Herefordshire: *Herald's MS*, pp. 21–22 (consulted by permission of the late Mr J. Lucas Scudamore).

25   J. Youings, *Dissolution of the Monasteries*, London, Allen and Unwin, 1971, p. 211.

26   A. G. Loftie, *Calder Abbey*, London, Bemrose and Sons, 1892, p. 3; Cumbria R.O. Cu/4/99; TNA, E315/405, f.1r.

27   TNA, E32/225.

28   NLW, Badminton Manorial 2445, p. 9.

29   *Cleeve Abbey, Washford,* Somerset Historic Environment Record, Somerset County Council.

30   G. M. Hills, 'Fountains Abbey.' In : *Collectanea Archaeologica* **2**, 1871, p. 276.

31   J. H. Harvey, *Itin. Wm. Worcestre*, Oxford, Clarendon Press, 1969, p. 61, D. M. Robinson, *Tintern Abbey*, Cardiff: CADW, 1990, p. 37.

32   W. de Gray Birch, *A History of Neath Abbey*, London, Richards, 1902, p. 139, T. Dineley, *Official Progress of the First Duke of Beaufort through Wales, 1684*; London, Hambledon, 1888, p. 309.

33   *LP* **12**, Part 1, p. 6 [No. 6].

34   *LP* **12**, Part 2, p. 21 [No. 59].

35   *AF* p. lxii.

36   L. T. Smith (ed.), *Itinerary of John Leland*, London, Centaur Press, 1964, **1**, pp. 243, 249; **3**, p. 51; **5**, p. 159, respectively.

37   Ibid. **5**, pp. 139, 63, 160; **4**, p. 21, respectively.

38   Ibid. **3**, p. 50.

39   Ibid. **1**, p. 23.

40   Ibid. **1**, p. 6; **4**, p. 4; **2**, 84; **5**, p. 74, respectively.

41   Ibid. **4**, p. 17; *Cf. LP* **12**, Part 2, pp. 350–51 [No. 1008/9].

42   Smith, *Itinerary of John Leland.* **1**, p. 80.

43   Ibid. **5**, pp. 159–60.

44   Ibid. **1**, p. 111.

45   Ibid. **3**, pp. 45, 58.

46   Ibid. **3**, p. 23.

47   Ibid. **3**, pp. 51–52.

48   Ibid. **3**, pp. 118–23; S. W. Williams, *Cistercian Abbey of Strata Florida*, London, Whiting, 1889, Appendix pp. iii-vii.

49   *LP* **12**, Part 1, p. 424 [No. 932].

50   *CPL* **16**, pp. 3–4 [No. 5].

51   VCH, *Cumberland* **2**, 1905, pp. 170–71

52   Talbot, *Letters*, 1967, pp. 156–58 [No. 79].

53   A. T. Bannister (ed.), *Reg. R. Mayew*, Hereford, Cantilupe Soc., 1919, p. 286.

54   VCH, *County of Gloucester* **2**, London, 1907, p. 95.

55   TNA, C1/658/26; A. T. Bannister (ed.), *Reg. C. Bothe*, Hereford, Cantilupe Soc., 1921, p. 359.

56   *Y Cymmrodor* **29**, 1919, pp. 4–13.

57   BL, Egerton MS 2410, f.4; NLW (Dept. of Printed Books) Ws 1528.

58 VCH, *County of Lincoln* **2**, London, 1906, p. 142.

59 TNA, E36/154, ff.110v-111r; M. E. C. Walcott, 'Chantries of Leicestershire,' in *TLAS* **4**, (1874—attached sheet).

60 TNA, E36/154, ff.146v–147r; R. Bearman, *Stoneleigh Abbey*, Stoneleigh Abbey Ltd., 2004, p. 213.

61 A. H. Plaisted, *Manor of Medmenham*, London: Longmans, Green & Co., 1925, p. 188.

62 *LP* 9, p. 83 [No. 244].

63 TNA, SC12/33/27; G. Brown, *Stanley Abbey and its Estates*, BAR British Series **566**, 2012, p. 101.

64 VCH, *Shropshire* 2, London, 1973, p. 58.

65 TNA, E315/92, ff. 2v–3r.

66 VCH, *Cheshire* 3, London, 1980, p. 162.

67 *LP* 10, pp. 59–60 [164].

68 TNA, E315/100/195v–196.

69 J. Hall, *Croxden Abbey: buildings and community*, York University, Ph. D. thesis, 2003, p. 23.

70 VCH, *Somerset* 2, London, 1911, p. 117.

71 N. Pevsner, *South and West Somerset*, Harmondsworth, Penguin, 1958, p. 128.

72 G. Baskerville, 'Dispossessed Religious of Gloucestershire,' in *TBGAS* **49**, 1927, p. 20; VCH, *County of Warwick* **2**, 1908, p. 74.

73 B. Sitch, *Kirkstall Abbey*, Leeds City Council, 2000p. 23.

74 VCH, *Warwickshire* **2**, London, 1908, p. 78.

75 D. Winkless, *Hailes Abbey*, Stocksfield, Spredden, 1990, pp. 49–51.

76 E. A. B. Barnard, *The Last Days of Hailes Abbey*, Evesham: Evesham Journal, 1928, p. 6; TNA, SP5/5/10–18.

77 M. H. Bloxam, 'Merevale Abbey,' in *TLAS* **2**, 1870, pp. 324–34; *Warwickshire History* **9**, No. 3, Summer, 1994, pp. 93–94.

78 TNA, C1/1216/36.

79 C. Hartwell and N. Pevsner, *Lancashire North*, Yale U.P. and London, Penguin, 2009, pp. 691, 694; G. Moorhouse, *The Pilgrimage of Grace*, London: Weidenfeld & Nicolson, 2002, pp. 317–18.

80 G. Moorhouse, *The Pilgrimage of Grace*, London: Weidenfeld & Nicolson, 2002, p. 280.

81 TNA, PROB11/14, f.21.

82 *LP* 5, p. 621 [No. 1477].

83 G. Coppack and R. Gilyard-Beer, *Fountains Abbey*, London, English Heritage, 1993, pp. 8, 21; B. Jennings, *Yorkshire Monasteries*, Otley, Settle Smith, 1999, pp. 105–06.

84 *FLB*, p. 78 [No. 89].

85 G. E. Gilbanks, *Some Records of a Cistercian Abbey*, Holm Cultram, Cumberland, no publisher noted, 1899, pp. 120–21, and *illus.*; M. Carter, 'The Tower of Marmaduke Huby,' *YAJ* **82**, 2010, p. 274.

86 R. Gilyard-Beer, *Cleeve Abbey, Somerset*, London, Historic Buildings and Monuments

Commission, 1960, p. 13; N. Pevsner, *South Somerset*, 1958, p. 128; J. H. Bettey, *Suppression of Monasteries in the West Country*, Gloucester: Alan Sutton, 1989, p. 59.

87   Bridge, M., *Tree-ring Analysis of Timbers, The Conference Centre, Whalley Abbey*, London: English Heritage, Research Dept. Report Series **66**, 2007, non-paginated.

88   J. Sherwood and N. Pevsner, *Oxfordshire*, Harmondsworth, Penguin, 1974, pp. 809–11.

89   P. Fergusson and S. Harrison, *Rievaulx Abbey*, Yale U.P., 1999, pp. 67, 118–19, 128–35; A. Squire, *Aelred of Rievaulx*, London, S.P.C.K., 1969, pp. 129–30; M. Carter, 'Late Medieval Relief Sculptures from Rievaulx and Fountains,' in *Cîteaux* **60**, 2009, pp. 140–41.

90   P. de Figueiredo and J. Treuberz, *Cheshire Country Houses*, Chichester, Phillimore, 1981, p. 60; C. Hartwell *et al,. Cheshire*, Yale U.P. and Penguin, p. 294; R.E. Howard, *et al., Tree-Ring Analysis of Oak Timbers from Combermere Abbey*, English Heritage: Centre for Archaeology Report **83**, 2003, p. 2.

91   D. H. Evans, *Valle Crucis Abbey*, Cardiff: CADW, 1995, pp. 60–62.

92   G. V. Price, *Valle Crucis Abbey*, Liverpool, Hugh Evans & Son, 1952, p. 278.

93   G. Ashmore, *Whalley Abbey*, Blackburn Diocesan Board of Finance, 6th edn., 2003, pp. 21–22.

94   *FLB*, p. 69 [No. 77].

95   TNA, E315/91, f.26.

96   TNA, SC12/16/75.

97   TNA, E315/283.

98   *LP* **14**, Part 2, p. 101 [No. 264/21].

99   G. D. Owen, *Agricultural Conditions in West Wales*, Ph. D. thesis, University of Wales, 1935, p. 363.

100   W. H. St John Hope and J. Bilson, *Architectural Description of Kirkstall Abbey*, Leeds, *PTS* **16**, 1907, p. 16; Sitch, *Kirkstall Abbey*, 2000, p. 23.

101   *SW*, p. 90.

102   *CPL* **12**, p. 753.

103   S. Heath, *The Story of Ford Abbey*, London, Francis Griffiths, 1911, pp. 49–51; D. M. Smith, *The Heads of Religious Houses, England and Wales*, **3**, *1377–1540*, Cambridge U.P., 2008, p. 291.

104   B. Cherry and N. Pevsner, *Devon*, London, Penguin, 2nd. edn., 1989, p. 222; J. Stéphan, *A History of Buckfast Abbey*, Bristol, Burleigh Press, 1970, p. 172.

105   Carter, *Tower of Marmaduke Huby*, 2010, pp. 270–78. ? 888

106   As by Jennings, *Yorkshire Monasteries*, 1999, p. 106.

107   Carter, *Tower of Marmaduke Huby*, 2010, p. 285.

108   C. H. Talbot, 'Marmaduke Huby, Abbot of Fountains,' in *Analecta Sacri Ordinis Cisterciensis* **20**, 1964, p. 184.

109   VCH, *County of Warwick* **2**, London, 1908, p. 78.

110   A. F. Cirket, 'English Wills, 1498–1526, in *BHRS* **37**, 1957, p. 74.

111   F. A. Hibbert, *The Dissolution of the Monasteries*, London, Pitman, 1910, p. 237.

[112] TNA, E315/405, f.42.

[113] D. H. Williams, *White Monks in Gwent and the Border*, Pontypool, Griffin Press, 1976, pp. 29–30.

[114] Barber, *Stratford Langthorne*, 2004, p. 57; TNA, PROB11/21, f. 37v.

[115] Winkless, *Hailes Abbey*, 1990, pp. 49–51; M. Aveling, 'The Monks of Byland after the Dissolution,' in *YAJ* **60**, Part 1, 1955, p. 3, respectively.

[116] *LP* **8**, p. 421 [No. 1069].

[117] *LP* **12**, Part 1, p. 397 [No. 890], p. 428 [No. 932].

[118] *LB*, p. 191.

[119] *LP* **10**, p. 164 [No. 408/2]; R. C. Fowler, 'Essex Monastic Inventories,' in *TEAS*, N.S. **10**, 1908, pp. 14–15.

[120] Lincoln R.O., *Reg. J. Longland*, f. 109r–v.

[121] M. Carter, 'The mourning vestment of Robert Thornton, abbot of Jervaulx,' in *Textile History* **41**, 2010, pp. 145–60; also *ODNB* (online, 2013).

[122] G. Coppack, *Fountains Abbey*, Stroud, Tempus, 2003, p. 129.

[123] G. M. Hills, 'Fountains Abbey.' In: *Collectanea Archaeologica* **2**, 1871, p. 272.

[124] Moorhouse, *Pilgrimage of Grace*, 2002, p. 318; M. E. C. Walcott, 'Inventory of Whalley Abbey,' in *THSLC*, N.S. **7**, 1867, pp. 6–7; TNA, E36/154, ff. 183r–193r.

[125] TNA, E315/40, f. 42v.

[126] TNA, E315/3/16.

[127] SSC, DR18/1/723.

[128] *LP* **10**, p. 164 [No. 408/2].

[129] C. Nash, 'The Fate of the English Cistercian Abbots,' in *Cîteaux* **2**, 1965, 104 (Hailes); information of the parish priest (Whalley).

[130] VCH, *County of Warwick* **2**, London, 1908, p. 78.

[131] Staffordshire Archives, 2/32/00, pp. 238–39.

[132] Williams, *White Monks in Gwent and the Border*, 1976, pp. 192–95.

[133] TNA, 315/40, f. 42v.

[134] *LP* **10**, p. 164 [No. 408/2].

[135] TNA, SP5/5/10–18; Barnard, *Last Days of Hailes Abbey*, 1928, p. 3.

[136] G. Coppack, *Abbeys and Priories*, Stroud, Tempus, 2006, p. 96.

[137] VCH, *County of Northampton* **2**, London, 1906, p. 120: 'in the dormitory every monk had his chamber given him by the king's commissioners at the suppression which the same monks took away.'

[138] *RC* **3**, pp. 560–61 [No. 1004].

[139] VCH, *County of Warwick* **2**, London, 1908, p. 78.

[140] TNA, E315/40, f. 42v.

[141] Staffordshire R.O., 2/32/00, pp. 238–39.

[142] Fowler, 'Essex Monastic Inventories,' 1908, p. 15.

[143] Yorkshire, East Riding Archives, DD/CC/131/34.

[144] *RC* **3**, pp. 555–61 (No. 1004).

[145] The codifications of Cistercian statutes compiled in the thirteenth century.

[146] G. G. Perry, 'The Visitation of the Monastery of Thame,' in *EHR* **3**, 1888, pp. 713–14. [The Book of Usages was the Cistercian customary compiled in the twelfth century but much modified in later years.]

[147] Talbot, *Letters*, 1967, pp. 159–62 (No. 80).

[148] *Patent* 1507, p. 556.

[149] *Close* 1502, pp. 70–71 [No. 197/xiii.]

[150] *Close* 1508, pp. 332–33 [No. 891]. *Placebo*—Vespers of the Dead, from the words of its opening antiphon, 'I will walk/please the Lord in the land of the living' (Ps. 116, v. 9); *Dirige* or 'dirge'—Matins of the Dead, from the words of the first antiphon, 'Lead me O Lord in thy righteousness' (Ps. 5, v. 9).

[151] *VE* **5**, 282.

[152] TNA, E33/18/1–3. (Interestingly, Maundy Thursday is referred to as Shere Thursday.)

[153] I am grateful to Mr Matthew Payne, Westminster Abbey Archives, for supplying me with the date of his burial.

[154] *LP* **10**, p. 105 [No. 284].

[155] Talbot, *Letters*, 1967, p. 190 [No. 94]; *Statuta VI*, p. 108 [No. 1495/30], 143 [No. 1496/36].

[156] D. H. Williams, 'Corrodians and Residential Servants in Tudor Cistercian Monasteries,' in *Cîteaux* **34**, 1983, p. 299.

[157] *LW*, **89**, pp. 153–54 [No. 224].

[158] TNA, E314/101.

[159] VCH, *County of Northampton* **2**, London, 1906, p. 120.

[160] M. P. Siddons, ed. *Visitations by the Heralds in Wales*, London, Harleian Soc., 1966, p. 38.

[161] TNA, SC6/HENVIII/2003, f. 10.

[162] Essex R.O., D/DL/T1/518. [3s then is worth about £50 today].

[163] *LP* **14**, p. 162 [No. 103/47/9].

[164] TNA, E326/164.

[165] *SAE*, pp. 139–40.

[166] *AF*, p. 333.

[167] *LB*, p. 16–61; *Cf.* pp. 55, 128, 157, 170–71, 176.

[168] Perry, 'Visitation of Thame,' 1888, pp. 705–07.

[169] TNA, 315/96, f. 68r–v.

[170] TNA, E315/92, ff. 27r–28v.

[171] TNA, E315/100, f. 2.

[172] TNA, E315/101, f. 88r–v.

[173] TNA, E36/152, f. 224. [When Kingswood was suppressed on 6 March 1538, he was paid his wages until Lady Day, 25 March: *LP* **13**, Part 1, p. 160 [No. 433/iii].

[174] F. M. Gasquet, *Henry VIII and the English Monasteries*, London, J.C. Nimmo, 2nd. edn. 1899, p. 268; TNA, SC12/30, f. 4

[175] VCH, *County of Lancaster* **2**, London, 1908, p. 122.

[176] TNA, LR1/176, f. 41r–v.

[177] TNA, E315/91, ff. 32v–33; *Cf.* f. 27r.

[178] TNA, E315/91, ff. 54v–55v; *Proc. Somerset Arch. and Nat. Hist. Soc*, **52**, 1906, pp. 26–27.

[179] TNA, 315/97, f. 16r–v.

[180] *LP* **1**, Part 1, p. 705 [No. 11].

[181] *LP* **1**, Part 1, 549 [13]; 4, Part 3, p. 2437 [No. 28]; 5, p. 633 [No. 1499/15].]

[182] A. Watkins, 'Merevale Abbey in the Late 1490s', in *Warwickshire History* **9**, No. 3, Summer, 1994, p. 91.

[183] Barber, *Stratford Langthorne*, 2004, p. 85.

[184] TNA, PROB11/21, f. 35.

[185] Watkins, *Merevale*, 1994, pp. 89–90.

[186] Fowler, 'Essex Monastic Inventories,' 1908, p. 15.

[187] TNA, E315/405, f. 42.

[188] *Wikipedia* online.

[189] Hibbert, *Dissolution*, 1910, p. 255; BL. Add MS 11041.

[190] TNA, SC6/HENVIII/7339.

[191] *LP* **13**, Part 2, p. 123 [No. 315].

[192] VCH, *County of Warwick* **2**, London, 1908, p. 78.

[193] TNA, C115/D.21/1937.

[194] D. H. Williams, 'White Monks in Powys,' in *Cistercian Studies* XI, 1976., pp. 176–77; Owen, 1919, 'Strata Marcella', pp. 27–28; TNA, E315/516/25–27.

[195] T. Parry, *Oxford Book of Welsh Verse*, Oxford, 1962, p. 553. I am grateful to Dr Paul Bryant-Quinn of Exeter University, and Mr David Greaney of the National Library of Wales, with assistance in translation.

[196] Heath, *Ford Abbey*, 1911, pp. 49–51; R. Tyler, *Forde Abbey*, St Ives: Beric Tempest Co., 1995, p. 10.

[197] R. Gilyard-Beer, *Cleeve Abbey*, 1960, p. 29–32; I. Tyers, *Tree-Ring Analysis of Oak Timbers from the Frater Roof of Cleeve Abbey*, London: English Heritage, Centre for Archaeology, 2003, non-paginated.

[198] Bostock, T. and Hogg, S., *Vale Royal Abbey, 1277–1538*, Vale Royal Borough Council, 1999, p. 4.

[199] VCH, *Northamptonshire* 2, London, 1970, p. 120.

[200] Fowler, 'Monastic Inventories,' 1908, p. 15.

[201] J. Ridgard and R. Norton, *Food and Ale, Farming and Worship: Daily Life at Sibton Abbey*, Leiston, Suffolk; Leiston Press, 2011, pp. 39–40.

[202] TNA, SC6/HENVIII/2005B. [A 'barrel' contained 1000 herrings, a 'cade' was a cask holding 500 herrings].

[203] Watkins, *Merevale*, 1994, p. 98.

[204] TNA, E315/427/3, f. 39.

[205] Williams, *Welsh Cistercians*, 2001, p. 281.

206 S.F. Hockey, *Quarr Abbey and its Lands*, Leicester U.P., 1970, p. 177.

207 TNA, E315/95, f. 8r–v. (She had previously received from Meaux the rectory of Skipsea in return for five marks a year and smaller kind rents: E315/95, ff. 44r–45r).

208 TNA, C1/568/95.

209 *VE* **5**, p. 172.

210 Ibid. **5**, pp. 269–70.

211 *LP* **10**, pp. 59–60 [No. 164].

212 I. Grainger and C. Phillpotts, *The Cistercian Abbey of St Mary Graces, East Smithfield*, London: Museum of London, 2011, p. 90.

213 TNA, C1/990/41.

214 *LW*, pp. 29 (No. 37), 247 (No. 361), respectively.

215 *Patent* 1486, p. 178; 1487, p. 197.

216 VCH, *Hampshire* 2, London, 1973, p. 144.

217 Ridgard and Norton, *Sibton*, 2011, pp. 40–43, 47–48.

218 TNA, E315/92, ff. 43v–44v.

219 R. Hoyle, 'Monastic Leasing Before the Dissolution', in *YAJ* **61**, 1989, p. 137.

220 *LP* **12**, Part 1, p. 406 [No. 901].

221 TNA, C4/7/9.

222 VCH, *Northamptonshire* **2**, London, 1970, pp. 120–21.

223 *Calendar of Chancery Warrants*, London, Public Record Office, I, p. 517.

224 *CPL* **19**, p. 57 (No. 98).

225 *AF*, pp. 315, 317, xc.

226 *DCL*, pp. 116–18.

227 *LP* **5**, p. 196 [No. 394].

228 *LP* **13**, Part 1, p. 127 [No. 370].

229 *LP* **3**, Part 2, p. 1256 [No. 2968]; **4**, Part 1, p. 6 [No. 13/1].

230 TNA, C1/548/16.

231 *LP* **9**, p. 9 [Nos. 32, 34], p. 16 [No. 57].

232 *LP* **11**, p. 559 [No. 1407/2].

233 TNA, PROB11/16/266.

234 TNA, E315/131, f. 45r.

235 Lancashire R.O., DDM 17/67.

236 TNA, C1/785/21–22; *MCP*, pp. 68–69 [No. 58].

237 TNA, C1/390/26.

238 TNA, C1/344/67.

239 TNA, C4/8/41.

240 TNA, C1/483/2.

241 TNA, C1/119/26.

242 TNA, C1/557/18.

243 TNA, C1/516/2.

244 TNA, C1/899/14–15; Williams, *White Monks in Gwent and the Border*, 1976, p. 25.

245 Williams, *White Monks in Gwent and the Border*, 1976, pp. 24–27.
246 TNA, C1/813/1–2.
247 *LP 7*, 1534, p. 181 [No. 432].

2 THE COMMUNITIES: COMPOSITION AND CHARACTER

Numerical Strength

SOME OF THE suppression returns are incomplete, but within the monasteries of the Order in England and Wales there were certainly close upon nine hundred monks when their houses were dissolved. Before this time, in the survey of 1535/36, monks under the age of twenty-four were supposed to be dismissed from their houses by the various sets of commissioners. It is not known how far this policy was enforced but, taking it into account, it could well be that in the early 1530s there were well in excess of nine hundred Cistercian monks in England and Wales; perhaps a figure even approaching one thousand.

The age of the once numerous lay-brethren, the *conversi*, had long since passed by, and there is only one certain note of a Tudor-age *conversuus*, Thomas Seymour of Kingswood. When his house was suppressed (1538), not probably being able to write his name, he made his mark on its surrender deed.[1] He appears to have had the alternative surname of Lawrence, and under that name received no pension when Kingswood was closed, but was to be 'sent to remain in another religious house according to his desire and request.'[2] To which monastery he went is not known. Another monk who made his mark was John Wright of Stratford (1538); of him it was said 'which can not wrytte'; but he may have been a monk debilitated by a stroke, and as his name does not appear in the dispensation list perhaps soon after died.[3]

The average number of monks in any one monastery on closure was almost twelve, but numbers varied greatly. A few monasteries had next to no known monks apart from their abbot. This was true of Medmenham whose community in 1491 consisted of the abbot and one other monk, and the same appears to have been true in 1536.[4] A similar situation appear to have existed in Wales by 1536 at Cymer, Grace Dieu and Strata Marcella. The largest monastic community was that at Fountains with thirty-seven religious This reflects the influence of Abbot Marmaduke Huby who told in 1520 that the numbers at

Fountains had increased more than double since his abbacy commenced. He claimed that he had fifty-two monks in his community, of whom forty-one were priests, as opposed to the twenty-two religious there when he had become abbot in 1495.[5]

Generally speaking the monasteries with the most sizeable communities were in the somewhat far flung areas of England, like Kirkstall in Yorkshire (thirty-one monks), Furness (thirty-four, including those non-resident) and Whalley (twenty-eight religious) in Lancashire. Rievaulx, also in Yorkshire, and Holm Cultram (despite their problems) had twenty-five monks, though Calder, also in Cumbria, had but eight monks. There were usually modest numbers in the houses of central England, like Biddlesden and Rufford (eleven each), Croxden and Dieulacres (thirteen apiece), Warden (twelve) and Hulton (nine). There were exceptions, such as the pilgrimage abbey of Hailes with twenty-four religious. Overall, recruitment seems to have been most successful in the north of England. A balance also had to be struck between the resources of an abbey and the number of religious it could support.

Another pointer to the numerical strength of individual monasteries should be the ordination lists in the episcopal registers of the times. Unfortunately these are wanting in this period for the dioceses of Carlisle and of Durham, while the rebound registers of Bishops Sherburne (1518–1536) and Sampson (1536–1543) of Chichester contain no ordination lists. No ordinations are recorded in the registers of Bishop John Hilsey of Rochester (1535–1540), and of Bishop Hugh Latimer of Worcester (1536–1539), nor in the register of Archbishop Cranmer (1533–1555) held at Lambeth Palace Library. The register of Bishop Peter Courtenay of Exeter (1478–1487) lists no ordinations after 1480. Apart from a few exceptions, the Welsh episcopal registers are mostly lacking. Very occasionally, the monastery or a monk or his grade of ordination may be erroneously recorded, or wrongly copied from earlier documentation. Richard Burford and John Burton, monks of Dore, were recorded in the register of Bishop Charles Bothe of Hereford, as being made acolyte on 15 March 1522 (the Lenten Ember Saturday) and again on the 5th of April that year, 'Sitientes' Saturday, when in fact on that day they must have proceeded to the subdiaconate.[6] There were other such misleading entries.

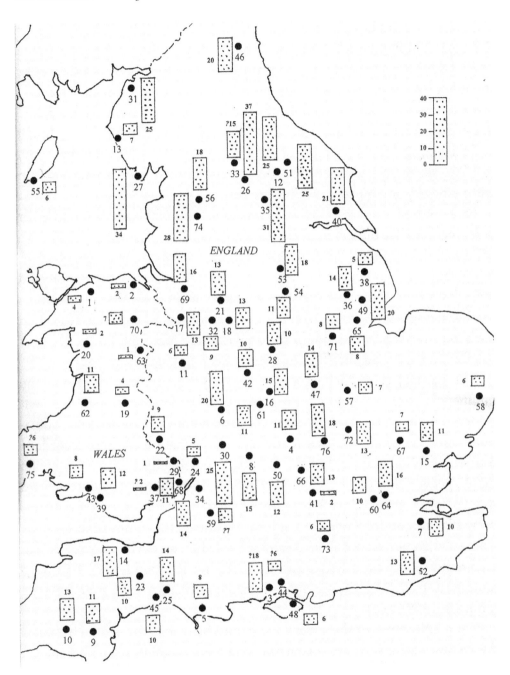

Fig. 5: The Numbers of Monks in Cistercian Abbeys at their Dissolution
(The larger print number refers to the house concerned, the smaller number denotes the
number of its monks)

A further complication comes in the fact that in 1510 Bishop Thomas Skevington of Bangor who was also abbot of Beaulieu where he resided, the year after becoming abbot received permission from the bishop of Winchester to ordain his own monks.[7] This permission, granted originally for two ordinations that year, seems thereafter to have been taken for granted, and Skevington appears to have ordained all his own monks in his abbey church at Beaulieu, and probably most of those of Netley abbey, down to his death in 1533. Skevington also received a dated and limited permission to ordain within the city and diocese of Winchester.[8]

No known register exists of those ordinations, nor of the admission to lesser orders permitted to the abbots of Furness. In 1484 Sixtus IV gave Abbot Laurence of Furness the authority to ordain his monks, and indeed canons of other Orders, to the four minor orders and to the subdiaconate, because of the remote and difficult situation of the monastery 'on the island of Furness'. After Pope Sixtus's death that August, Innocent VIII confirmed this privilege.[9] Leo X in 1516 granted the abbots of Whalley like power to administer the four minor orders both at Whalley and in its daughter-houses, given the consent of the local ordinary.[10]

This partial lack of documentation makes it impossible to determine the number of Cistercian monks in any particular year. There is though sufficient evidence to determine trends. Based on sixteen hundred known first ordinations, and averaging from five yearly figures, ordinations (where recorded) were static in the years from 1495 to 1504, averaging thirty-three Cistercian monks per year. For the short period of 1505 to 1509 there is a definite upward trend of forty-seven ordinations yearly which thereafter decreases. Could this be a reflection of the Jubilee of 1500 having stirred the minds of the young? Thereafter some, but not all houses, may have shown a decline. Merevale had a community of ten at its closure in 1538, but its complement had been fourteen in 1497.[11] Vale Royal showed a much smaller decrease, from eighteen monks in 1509 to sixteen in 1539.[12]

The graphs can only show trends, and must be seen in the light of technical difficulties. The 'first' known ordination on record might be of an aspirant as a lowly acolyte or a fully-pledged priest—a limited correction has been made for this in the table. The other problem for accuracy is that some monasteries held back monks due for ordination, until there were several ready to travel to their cathedral church to receive holy orders. This meant that the 'first' ordination of some monks took place two or three years later than would normally have been the case. In 1502 for instance no less than ten monks of Furness were ordained to the priesthood at York.[13] In 1507 Revesby had nine of its monks made deacon in the diocese of Lincoln.[14] In 1509 six monks of Roche were made deacon together in the York diocese,[15] whilst a batch of five monks of Buckfast received the different grades of holy orders together between 1517 and 1521.[16] This holding back for a couple of years of those ready for ordination hinders our knowledge of the dates of their first entry into the Order, and of the actual numbers of professed monks in any particular year.

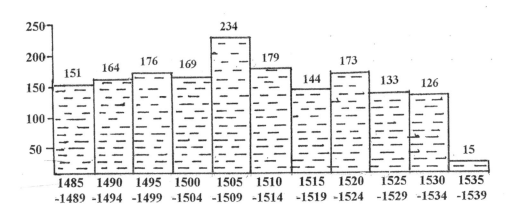

Fig. 6: Known ordinations of Cistercian monks in five-yearly periods
(Based upon the actual and estimated dates of admission to the rank of acolyte of
1,664 monks)

There is only an occasional record of an ordination being held in a Cistercian monastery church. The bishop of Worcester did so in Kingswood abbey on 21 March 1516—surprisingly Good Friday that year. The entry of the day as 'xxi' of the month may probably be an error for 'xxii', in which case the ordination took place as is far more likely on Holy Saturday. No monks were ordained; it was for the bishop a conveniently placed church.[17] Six monks of Stratford's community were ordained at a general ordination held on 21 March 1535 in their abbey by Thomas Swillington, titular bishop of Philadelphia.[18] That ordination was held on one of the four quarterly Saturdays favoured for the conferring of ministerial authority, in this case, the eve of

Passion Sunday commonly called 'Sitientes', from the opening words of the Introit at the Eucharist that day: 'All you who are thirsty, come to the waters' (Ps. 55, v. 1).

Cistercian ordinands were usually ordained in the cathedral church of their diocese or some other church appointed for that purpose, either by the diocesan bishop or a suffragan or titular bishop acting on his behalf. To that church the monk concerned would come carrying letters dimissory from his abbot. A model letter for this purpose, for a later abbot's clerk to copy when occasion arose, is to be found both in the Cartulary of Hailes (dating from the time of Abbot Anthony Melton, 1504–1527),[19] and in Exeter College, Oxford, MS 1 (emanating from Dore and drafted around 1420, probably in the time of Abbot Richard Moyne).[20]

A monastic official would often also attend to present his abbey's candidates. This might be an abbot himself (as from Robertsbridge in 1495); a prior (Tilty, 1529), a sub-prior (Coggeshall, 1509), a cellarer (Waverley, 1510), a kitchener (Stratford, 1514), a sacristan (Coggeshall, 1522), or a simple monk (Coggeshall, 1510). When Thomas Walker of Flaxley was made deacon in the chapel of Ludlow Castle by the visiting bishop of Rochester in 1476 he simply presented a letter of commendation from his abbot.[21] As the Reformation took hold and there was an anti-papalist agenda, and given the recent history of their house, a group of six monks of Woburn were examined prior to their ordination in September 1537 by the prior of St Andrew's, Northampton—Francis Apree, soon to be appointed dean of Peterborough.[22]

A further difficulty in assessing precisely the numbers of Cistercian personnel derives from many of the monks having dual nomenclature where their surname was concerned. Of the twenty-two monks of Rievaux who signed its surrender in 1538, no less than fifteen did so giving both a family name and a place-name indicting their locality of origin. John Pynder, for example, had the *alias* of Malton, and Richard Jenkinson of Ripon. The suppression papers for Biddlesden, of 1536, show that each of its twelve monks, save the abbot, bore a patronymic and a place-name. John Dawkins, for instance, was also known as John Northampton, and Robert Taylor as Robert Northampton.

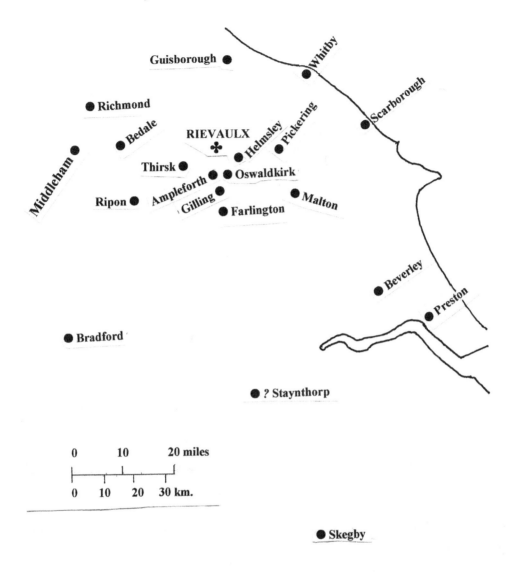

Fig. 7: Localities from which some of the monks of Rievaulx came.

This leads to confusion of identification, but also shows that many monks came from within a reasonable vicinity of their monastery. The 'place surnames' of Kirkstall's monks show that the majority came from within about a twenty mile radius. Four monks of Warden bore the surname of nearby Biggleswade. Three monks of Merevale had the *alias* of adjacent Atherstone, the surname also of its sub-steward.[23] Other 'place surnames' were more widely dispersed:

seventeen monks in various parts of England and Wales bore the name of London, while in central England fourteen were named Chester.

Other examples of local recruitment were to be found at Ford, where mention is made of monks bearing the alternative surnames of Bridgwater, Exmestre, and Ylmyster; at Rievaulx of monks hailing from Ampleforth, Bedale, Guisburn, Helmsley, and Whitby. Numerous other examples indicate a local origin: as at Garendon, James and Robert Loughborough; at Newminster, Roger and Thomas Morpeth; at Stanley, William Chippenham and John Devizes, whilst Maurice Dovery of Strata Florida probably sprang from not far distant Llandovery.

The family surnames of the monks, where known, also seem to indicate, though it cannot be always proven, that a monk professed in his monastery and perhaps by now an abbot, might attract a brother or nephew to enter the same abbey. This may have been the case at Cleeve where two monks bearing the surname of Dovell were ordained in 1504 and 1505, one becoming its abbot; another Dovell followed there in 1525. At Hailes whilst Anthony Melton was abbot, a John Melton was made deacon there in 1512. A John Orpe was abbot of Croxden until 1490; a monk of the same name was professed there about 1509. At Furness the rebellious Richard Bank of the 1530s, may well have been a nephew of the controversial abbot Alexander Banks who died in 1533.

A Richard Pyerson was made subdeacon whilst a monk of Byland in 1499, there followed in that abbey Henry Pyerson, made subdeacon in 1537. At Revesby a monk named Richard Layton, in its community in 1507, was followed by a Henry Layton in 1528. A Thomas Okeley, monk of Pipewell was made subdeacon in 1488, and another monk of the same name in 1528. The community of Calder contained a Richard Ponsonby in 1507, and a Matthew Ponsonby in 1535. Might John Whitingdon of Bordesley, made acolyte in 1499, and Richard Whitingdon of the same abbey advanced to the same order in 1504, have been brothers? Three monks bearing the surname of Squire inhabited Robertsbridge between.1501 and 1523. Some of these instances may be coincidences, but there are sufficient to suggest a trend.

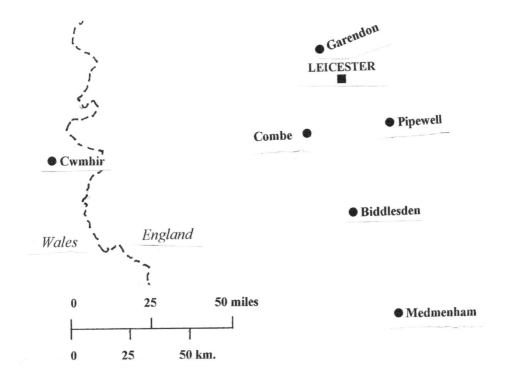

Fig. 8: Some of the abbeys which gained vocations from Leicester.

Strictly speaking, Cistercian monks owned all they possessed in common, but all the evidence points to them receiving by the Tudor period pocket-money known as 'wages'. When Abbot Robert Salusbury took over at Valle Crucis (1528), he was forced he said to pay wages to monks he had to hire, as others left at his coming. When in 1532 Richard Piggott became a corrodian at Coggeshall, part of his settlement was an annual payment of 20s, 'as one of our brethren is paid.'[24] Much earlier, in 1490, Abbot Clerkenwell of Stoneleigh had requested each priest-monk to say at the Requiem altar a collect daily for his welfare and that of a benefactor, and after their deaths to keep their obit fully. In return, the monks were each to receive an additional 6s 8d to their rate of 20s.[25] Taken together, these evidences suggest that Cistercian monks may have received 'wages' or pocket-money of £1 yearly; in modern terms a sum well in excess of £300.

Occasional payments to individual monks were noted in various wills. In 1479 John Pilkington left £10 to the abbot of Fountains, and half-a-mark to each of its monks.[26] In 1534 Robert Barnyt of Keddington, Lincolnshire, bequeathed 4d. to each monk of Louth Park, without specifying any obit obligations.[27] Frequently each monk participating in funeral rites was left a few pence. When Roger Robynson died in 1533, he desired burial in the abbey church of Swines-head—he had been dwelling within the precincts, and desiring vespers and lauds of, and Mass for the dead, on the day of burial and on the week's and month's mind; he left 4d. to each monk taking part for each of those three days.[28] The previous year one benefactor willed 6d. to a monk from Swineshead going to the parish church there to see that his obit 'be surely kept.'[29]

William Chamfer (1521), desiring to be buried in the monastery church at Byland, bequeathed ten shillings to its abbot, and four pence to each monk present at his funeral, and in addition each monk was to receive a share of ten shillings for the saying of two trentals of Masses for his soul.[30] A benefactor of Stratford and trusting for of burial there left in 1522, 3s 4d. to every monk of the monastery.[31] Another will in favour of the same house in 1512 provided £1 for its abbot, 3s 4d. for every priest monk, and 20d. to each novice.[32] A testator also in 1512 left 3s 4d. for the abbot of Sibton, 4d for each priest-monk and 2d. for each novice there..[33] William Joye of Bedford (1503) bequeathed 'to every monk of Warden being a priest, 3s 4d., and every novice, 12d.'[34] Sir Edward Raleigh of Farnborough (1509) bequeathed, expecting his obit to be kept there, 6s 8d. to each of the monks of Combe save for those not yet ordained priest who were each to receive 3s 4d.[35] In these ways, individual monks might well have accrued a small nest-egg.

Age Structure

The average age of the monks in any particular community can often be derived from the lists drawn up at the Suppression, but as by this time a number of young monks under the age of twenty-four may have been expelled, a false picture could be given of a community which ten years previously might well have had a lower average age. The dissolution records indicate an average age for the monks of Kirkstall of forty-three, of Rievaulx forty-one, and of Byland forty.

The age of the monks of Buckfast when it closed varied from sixty-one to twenty-five. It seems that there, as at Newminster, the clearance of young monks was carried out. At the latter monastery in 1536 the twenty remaining monks ranged in age from twenty-five to eighty-five, but half of its monks were still only in their thirties.[36] It was a relatively young community with every prospect for a future which was not to be. The commissioners visiting Buildwas in 1536 reported only nine monks, 'and the more part of them ancient men,' yet when the monastery closed the following year it had three novices on its books.[37]

That there were young monks, some perhaps very young, was illustrated by the case of Edward Paynter. Interrogated in 1532 for possessing a copy of the New Testament in English, he told how when younger he had been a monk of Jervaulx, but was press-ganged into its novitiate. Now about nineteen years old, he said: 'I was bound apprentice at the age of thirteen, and sold by my master to the abbot in the first year, who shaved my head and put on me a white coat.' He ran away but a trap was set, and he was returned to his abbey and punished. Later he left again, and after visiting other religious houses, married and settled down in Colchester. Imprisoned by the bishop of London for some six months on account of possession of vernacular scriptures, Jervaulx told Cromwell that the abbey did not want him back. His real name was 'Freez', but he was called Paynter on account of having been apprenticed to a painter in York.[38] In January 1537 a monk of Coggeshall alleged that Abbot Love had 'unlawfully used' Robert Goswill ten years before; he was then young but now a monk there.'[39]

A quarter of a century before the Tudor period, but worthy of note, two professed Cistercian monks had by Decmber 1450, petitioned the papal penitentiary to affirm that they were 'not bound to the Order.' The first was William London, monk of Dore, who alleged that he had been persuaded to enter the monastery at the age of eleven, and forced to make profession whilst under age. Later, he said, he escaped. The second monk was Ieuan ap Dafydd of Aberconwy who wrote that he had been persuaded to enter at the age of twelve, and made profession, but after three months left his abbey. Both former monks were clearly anxious to regularise their position.[40] In the same year, the penitentiary noted the appeal of Thomas Domet, a priest of the London diocese, who told how his parents had forced him to enter Coggeshall abbey as a boy but he 'wished to remain in the world.' The papal registers further tell that he was only thirteen at the time, that he was 'moved by reasonable fear,' and that after profession he left the monastery as soon as he could.[41] George Sanderson, a professed monk of Louth Park by the 1520s, was said to have entered the abbey at the age of fourteen.[42]

The minimum age for reception of a Cistercian novice was meant to be eighteen years, though these cases demonstrate that this rule was by no means scrupulously observed. If professed at eighteen years, there would be a delay of several years before ordination. Given the right atmosphere and order in a community, this could be a positive time for education and spiritual formation. Three monks of Robertsbridge, who were members of its community by 1491/92 [Henry Fanne/Vane, Stephen Warre and Robert Bekeryng] did not proceed to the first stage of ordination, the lowly position of acolyte, until 1496.[43]

Two monks of Merevale (John Lenton and John Tamworth,) monks there in 1497, did not achieve ordination as priests until seven years later.[44] Their youth was probably a factor, but there may also have been an insistence on proper preparation. It was a time when educationally-minded Reformators like Marmaduke Huby were making their mark. Seven monks of Hailes who had been advanced to the priesthood from 1478 onwards, all petitioned the Holy See in 1487 for absolution as they had been ordained under age.[45] It was hardly their fault!

At least a dozen monks, if not fifteen, are known to have been *jubilarians* by the time of the dissolution of their monastery, and others fell not far short of that mark. They included Richard Albrighton of Dore, Griffith Hampton at Beaulieu, and Thomas Rolleston of Croxden, whilst Richard Cowper of Netley, professed by 1489, would have reached that status had not his monastery been closed in 1536. Runners-up included John Paslew of Whalley, and John Browne at Kirkstall, both of whom were professed for at least forty-eight years. Occasionally allowance would be made for a monk's age as for John Stickford of Revesby who in 1450, on account of old age, sought and received 'dispensation to read by candlelight and wear linen clothes; also that he may use a light when saying the night office.'[46] When Garendon was suppressed, one of its community was 'blind, impotent and in extreme age.'[47]

At least fifteen former Cistercian monks lived on into the 1580s. Some of these died in harness, so to speak; as John Rooper (formerly of Newenham) still in office as rector of West Stafford, Dorset, in 1582; William Forrest (Thame) who resigned as vicar of Adwell, Oxon, only in 1585; Richard

Woodward (Hailes) who died in 1580 whilst vicar of Chedworth, Gloucs., and Robert Slingsby (Woburn) dying in 1585 when rector of Aston-in-the-Walls, Northamptonshire. Thomas Moke, formerly of Rufford, making his will in 1586 expressed his wish to be buried at Farndon, Nottinghamshire.[48] All these, and others, would have been jubilarians had their monasteries survived.

So too would have been three former Cistercians who died in custody: Thomas Reade of Hailes may be the cleric of that name who died in the Marshalsea in 1579;[49] Thomas Mudde, formerly of Jervaulx, who had been fervently opposed to the new ways, died in 1583, after several years custody in the North Block House at Hull;[50] while John Alman of Croxden ended his earthly life in prison in Hull castle in 1585, where he had been incarcerated since 1579.[51] .

The distinction of being the Cistercian who survived longest *may* rest with Richard ap Robert ap Rhys, appointed in 1536 to the abbacy of Aberconwy when only 24 years old, as a result of family influence and intrigue, and a recommendation from the bishop of Coventry and Lichfield to Cromwell, who wrote that he was 'a man of good qualities and loved by his brethren'. He survived until 1588/89 as rector of Eglwys-bach and Llanbadrig in Gwynedd.[52] Next in terms of survivorship may have been Thomas Dickinson, formerly of Fountains, if he was the cleric of that name who died at the close of 1587 whilst vicar of Hampthwaite, Yorkshire.[53] .

Character of the Monks

Given that there were probably over one thousand Cistercian monks in the opening decades of the fifteenth century, there are remarkably and relatively few religious against whom complaints might be lodged—and these often came in the closing days from the prejudged minds of royal commissioners like Doctors Layton and Legh. There is, however, also evidence of the bad character of a few monks from visitation charters and other records. Happily, there were those houses, like Garendon, where the commissioners gave a very favourable report. They told of their being there 'fourteen monks with the abbot and the prior of Bindon; one of them blind, impotent and of extreme age; all of good conversation and good service, and desire to continue.'[54] A similar picture was painted of Stanley; all there were 'by report, of honest conversation and desiring continuance in religion.'[55]

It is important to remember that only when there was bad news, were the activities of medieval monks reported upon. Many, if not most of the Cistercians of Tudor times, very probably lived exemplary lives devoted to their vocation. Unfortunately, the extant documentation is mostly silent in their praise. Only occasionally does good news come to the fore, as in the instance of William Leicester, a monk of Cwmhir for over thirty years when passed over for its abbacy in 1535, only to be supplanted with Cromwell's help by John Glyn, a monk with powerful friends who had already been deposed from the abbacy of Dore. The earl of Shrewsbury pointed out that Leicester was 'a good religious man, and hath the love of all his neighbours.'[56]

In north Wales in 1528 the prior of Valle Crucis, Richard Bromley, a monk there for at least a quarter of a century, was passed over for the abbacy giving way to Robert Salusbury, a youthful ne'er-do-good. In compensation perhaps, Cardinal Wolsey granted Bromley a series of privileges on account of infirmity: he might wear linen next his skin, he could use long leggings of a decent colour, and a 'head warmer' under his hood. He could talk quietly in the dorter, and eat and drink in his own prior's chamber. He could also be promoted to an abbacy, despite being the bastard son of a monk, but when the opportunity for this arose a few years later, he declined it. The commissioners surveying the abbey in August 1535 saw him as 'a virtuous and well-disposed man,' and of the six monks there the only one fit to be abbot. A monk from St Mary Graces was imported to fulfil the position.[57]

It is regrettable that little written evidence is extant to tell of the lives of the many more monks there must have been like Humphrey Chester (*al.* Lightfoot) of Combermere, patient, devout and versed in the Scriptures. In the early 1530s Chester corresponded with Robert Joseph, a monk of Evesham, his letters being carried by an itinerant fishmonger. The exchange of letters reveals that Chester was an avid reader of the Bible, 'going hither and thither among the flowers of scripture like a bee;' but that his knowledge of Latin was poor. He was ashamed that he could only write to Joseph in the vernacular. Some references might suggest Chester's concern at the state of his monastery. Certainly he had problems there, but more happily about February 1532 Joseph was able to write to him saying, 'I am glad that you now lead a quiet life and have only one adversary; he is sent to exercise your virtue.'[58] It was a reminder that there had to be give-and-take, and tolerance of others, in a monastic community.

Unfortunately extent documentation ignores most of what was good in Cistercian life, but highlights the moral and other failings. One of the most common accusations against monks were of having improper relations with members of the opposite sex. Again, one must be wary of allegations stemming from the pens of the suppression commissioners. Even abbots were not counted blameless. Thomas Doncaster, the last abbot of Rufford and about sixty years old in 1536, allegedly had immoral relations with two married women and four others.[59] A disaffected monk alleged that Thomas Carter, only abbot of Holm Cultram for a year before his death in 1537, 'brought divers women into the inward parts of the monastery to dine and sup.' The informant had been passed over for the abbacy and spied on Abbot Carter for the civil authorities.[60]

In south Wales a Celtic poet praised Abbot David ap Thomas of Margam (1500–1517) with the words, 'Never did a white habit adorn a fairer owner,' but he openly kept concubines by whom he had at least one son and four daughters. The Reformator for Wales, Abbot Lleision of Neath, insisted upon his resignation, though Abbot Huby implied that this was because of his loyalty to Clairvaux—Neath was of Savigniac descent. Huby, who was not too well disposed towards the abbot of Neath who had taken over his own jurisdiction in Wales, said that the effective deposition with only one investigating abbot had been irregular, and that Abbot David resigned 'in fear of death and terror of armed force.'[61] In north Wales Thomas Pennant (abbot of Basingwerk, perhaps c.1481–1523) bore three sons, the youngest of whom succeeded him in the abbacy, and none seem to have thought the worse of Abbot Thomas. Rather, he was praised for his stature and accomplishments.[62]

Monks who were adjudged by the Crown visitors to have played loose with women included Richard Scarborough of Rievaulx, and John Melsonby (once his abbot's chaplain) and Lawrence Smyth of Fountains. At the time of the accusations, in 1536, Scarborough and Melsonby were perhaps about fifty years old, but Smyth must have been in his late 60s.[63] Unless offences of earlier years were referred to, these ages suggest that perhaps nothing too improper occurred. It is important also to remember that whereas five monks of Fountains were rightly or wrongly adjudged of immorality, thirty-two were not. More independent and trustworthy evidence comes in the case of a monk of Warden, Thomas Luton, who at his abbey's visitation in 1492 by the abbots of Stratford and St Mary Graces, was accused of bringing 'suspect women' into the monastery, and of joining with his concubine in the feasting after her purification rite following childbirth.[64]

A few monks were accused by the Suppression commissioners of unspecified 'incontinence' or 'uncleanness', and a very few of 'self-abuse'—but how could that be even known to the commissioners, let alone proved? Given the numbers of boys and young men in some monasteries—as servants, choristers or pupils, it is no wonder that some monks were accused of sodomy, but the figure of six religious of Calder and five of Garendon alleged to be guilty of this crime when suppressed is hard to accept, particularly when a few months earlier the initial commissioners had found the religious of Garendon free of any blame.[65] Moreover the crime is only noted at a few other houses.

Other shortcomings recorded of a few monks included a tendency to over indulge in alcoholic drink. This was a particular problem at Warden, where three of its monks were described by their abbot in 1535 as 'common drunkards'. Abbot Emery, who had previously been abbot of Sibton and was not happy in his new post, also accused one monk, Thomas Warden, a ring-leader in the opposition to him, of spending all night in an ale-house in Shesford and refusing correction.[66] Fortunately, there were at least eight other monks at Warden of a sober character.

An occasional offence was the uttering of false coinage, the forging of money. Richard Woodward of Flaxley, after committing this and other crimes, was rehabilitated by the General Chapter in 1486;[67] in 1521 a monk of Kirkstall accused of coining was held in Pontefract Castle.[68] Richard Smith of Strata Florida (1534) was for the same misdemeanour committed for several months to prison, first at Carmarthen and then in Aberystwyth Castle, before being brought before the Commissioners in the Marches at Shrewsbury. He seems to have been a rebellious monk and the Commissioners ordered him to be obedient to Abbot Talley.[69]

More serious were those isolated monks who minds were set on murder. John Yvynge, a monk of Warden, was in 1492 convicted of trying to poison his abbot, John Bright. There had long been differences between them. He was sentenced to perpetual imprisonment and to be confined, firstly at Sibton Abbey (daughter-house of Warden) and then at Stratford (the monastery of an abbot-reformator).[70] One of the early acts, as a Reformator, of Abbot

Marmaduke Huby (1496), and whilst visiting Wales, was to imprison John ap Hywel ap Morgan, a monk of Neath, for the premeditated murder of a secular priest in the cloister of Whitland. John's presence at Whitland suggests that he was already an evildoer who had been banished there.[71]

Stability and Apostasy

Misdoing apart and not counting those elected to an abbacy elsewhere, monks might occasionally but rarely move to another abbey of the Order. In 1516, for instance, and with the agreement of both abbots, Henry Tutbury, a monk of Hailes, transferred to Dore 'for good and reasonable grounds,' which appear to have been his age and peace of mind.[72] The abbots of Stratford and St Mary Graces, on visitation at Warden in 1493, were critical of the 'insolence and presumption' of monks coming across the seas to English houses, mentioning a German ('Teuton') who had recently been newly professed at Warden. This monk was a weak if not lewd character, and he did not speak the English language.[73] From Fürstenfeld abbey in Bavaria where he was originally professed, John Ffranck came to be 'canonically translated' to Medmenham. In 1502 he gained the advantage of being dispensed to receive a secular benefice.[74]

The shortage of monks in some of the monasteries of Wales may have accounted for the presence at Cwmhir in 1537 of William Laken, perhaps the monk of that name at St Mary Graces in 1506; at Llantarnam in 1537 of Prior Henry Wydon, probably a monk of Cleeve in 1508; at Strata Florida in 1539 of Richard Mayott, possibly at Dieulacres in 1495, and at Strata Marcella in 1515 of Benjamin Godson, seemingly a monk of Fountains in 1510.[75] Contrariwise, Rewley (possibly because of the Oxford connection) numbered in its ranks two monks of Welsh origin: William Vaghan (Vaughan) in 1507,[76] and Henry Aphoel (Ap Hywel) in 1510.[77]

At Valle Crucis in north Wales, the violent reputation of a youthful new abbot, Robert Salusbury in 1528, preceded him. Owing his appointment to family pressure and being perhaps under-age, necessitating a dispensation from Cardinal Wolsey, his 'coming thither' was not to the liking of the seven professed monks then at Valle Crucis. Five promptly left for other monasteries, and in evidence he later gave Salusbury acknowledged that 'he was forced to get seven other strange monks, and give them wages to serve with him'.[78] This statement reveals that nine monks were felt necessary to maintain divine service there, and points to the now prevalent custom of giving even Cistercian monks pocket-money ('wages').

Early Cistercian writers, including St Bernard, discouraged monks from going on pilgrimages, for a monk's earthly and lifelong pilgrimage was his progression in sanctity within his own monastery.[79] Yet when the great jubilee occurred in 1500, the Reformators of the Order in England complained of junior monks going to Rome for the jubilee, 'not on account of devotion, but led by levity and curiosity.'[80] Their names are not on record, nor whether they had their abbots' permission. Known Cistercian pilgrims to Rome at a later date, staying at the English Hospital (later the English College) of the Most Holy Trinity and St Thomas of Canterbury, included in 1505, Richard Bromley, monk and later prior of Valle Crucis; in 1506, William Wright, a scholar of Byland, and in 1507, William Wode, from Thame.[81]

Abbots might have occasion to visit Rome, such as Thomas Oliver whose hold on the abbacy of Buckland was challenged. Unfortunately whilst in Rome somewhere between 1475 and 1485 he ran short of money, and borrowed the equivalent of £4 from one John Burton, clerk. On his return the abbot broke his promise of hasty repayment, and Burton had to appeal to the bishop of Lincoln, as Chancellor of England, for its return.[82] In 1496, John Longdon, a monk of Hailes and later abbot of Dore, visited the Holy See on the business of his monastery.[83]

There were those monks, not many, who abandoned their vocation and their white habit; technically termed apostates. Recourse to the civil power for their return was seemingly not always sought. Were they so returned, by that or other means—like the young Edward Paynter to Jervaulx, they would have been very probably flogged and for a time imprisoned. All the abbot of Boxley could do in 1521 was to bemoan the fact that his four missing monks were 'a scandal to the Christian faithful,'[84] while the abbot of Hulton told in 1518 how his monk, John Micklewright, had absconded twenty years before.[85] Even Beaulieu, Hailes and Rievaulx, had the occasional absentee monk.[86]

Earlier (on 17 May 1499) when the archbishop of Canterbury's commissary held a visitation at Bungay in Suffolk, John Hengham, a professed Cistercian—perhaps of Sibton—but now a parochial chaplain, was cited for wearing secular dress without apostolic dispensation, and thus incurring apostasy. He admitted the charge, and the commissary imposed penance and ordered him to wear the habit of his profession. When the court met at Beccles on 14 June, he appeared again, but now 'reformed and clad in the habit of his profession.'[87] The papacy, Alexander VI in this instance, could be very forgiving. In 1500 Thomas Rydforth (*alias* Hethe), a monk of Bruern, was absolved by the pontiff from apostasy, allowed to hold a secular benefice, and to wear his habit under the dress of a secular priest. He was to perform 'a suitable penance,' but permitted to choose his own confessor to impose it.[88]

In 1518 it was said of Richard Rotter, a monk of Grace Dieu, that he was apostate but had a chantry at St Briavel's church in the Forest of Dean.[89] This was very close to property the abbey held there, yet there seems to have been no effort to recall him. In 1491 the papal register noted that about 1460 Robert Cornwall (*alias* Burton]), a monk of Kirkstead, 'had laid aside the habit of his Order, assumed that of a secular priest, and had remained as such for the past thirty years, thereby incurring apostasy and excommunication.' In 1487/88, he had become vicar of Broughton-by-Kettering. Innocent VIII absolved him but ordered him to resume his Cistercian habit, so 'then he might receive and retain the said church, or exchange it for another.' It is noteworthy that the pontiff did not require him to return to conventual life.[90]

The prior of Hailes in 1480 was Thomas Bristow but he had all but abandoned monastic life. He had become vicar of Rodbourne Cheney, Wiltshire, was at variance with his abbot, and said to be 'going about dressed in fine linen with a belt ornamented with gold, pearls, and with gold and silver clasps.' Although he had effectively left the Order, in 1494 he returned to Hailes and purchased a corrody there for £20 which gave him comfort in his old age.[91] In 1485 John Easingwold, *alias* Smythson, a monk of Rievaulx, sought a dispensation from the Holy See on account of his apostasy and requested permission to transfer to another monastery. He had been disobedient to his abbot and imprisoned, but had broken out of prison and fled.[92]

A case which drew the attention both of the General Chapter and of the Holy See was that of Thurstin Watson (*alias* Trustin Lofthouse). A Cistercian of Kirkstall by 1467 (when he was made sub-deacon), after eleven years he was professed as a Carthusian monk at Mount Grace Priory, also in Yorkshire, but without permission of his abbot. The case came before the General Chapter in 1485, which appointed the abbots of Stratford, Woburn and Fountains to investigate, and to cause Thurstin either to return to his monastery of Kirkstall or to remain in the Carthusian Order, as might best serve peace and concord between the two Orders.[93]

After being told to return by the abbot of Kirkstall, having failed for seven years to do so, the abbot cautioned him under penalty of excommunication, and so Thurstin returned to the Cistercian fold. He then travelled to Rome, where in February 1489 both he and the abbot of Cîteaux were present in the Roman Curia. Innocent VIII ordered the abbot of Cîteaux to absolve him from his apostasy and appoint a penance. The abbot was also told to grant Thurstin permission to remain in the Cistercian Order 'and to preach the Word of God to the people.' The abbot did this, but sixteen months later, Thurstin was said to be still in the Carthusian Order and wishing to remain there; the pontiff now allowed him so to do 'for ever.'[94] The bull he brought back from Rome in favour of the Order was felt to be not all that had been hoped.[95]

Secular Benefices received before the Dissolution

The papal registers reveal the names of a sprinkling of Cistercian monks who, well before the Suppression, were allowed to retain benefices usually held by secular clerics. It was not a new phenomenon: from the early fifteenth century monks of Hailes had been appointed as vicars of several churches of their appropriation, including Didbrook and Pinnock almost adjacent to the abbey, and personally served those parishes.[96] During the pontificate of Innocent VIII (1484–1492) twenty-one English Cistercians from seventeen of the abbeys received papal dispensation to receive a secular benefice,[97] This growing trend of Cistercian monks seeking capacities from the Holy See troubled the Reformators of the Order in England, the abbots of Fountains, Stratford and St Mary Graces, who in 1496 asked the procurator-general of the Order in Rome to curb the practice.[98] This petition may have had its effect, no such dispensations are recorded after 1497 in the registers of Alexander VI (1492–1503)—though there were eleven by that year, but twelve more Cistercian monks did receive such leave during the pontificate of Julius II (1503–1513).

One unusual case was that of a monk of Jervaulx, Thomas Huschwayte, who in 1482 received the necessary permission from the Holy See, as a result of which he came to possess the church of St Medard at Oye near Calais. Not content with this, the pontiff surprisingly gave him in 1491 leave to hold two more benefices. This cannot have been for the good of the monastery or his own spiritual life. His surname, and the location of his first church, suggest that he was perhaps a Frenchman.[99]

Being granted leave to hold secular benefices did not always mean (if at all) that the monks concerned were abandoning their parent monastery. Certainly in two cases it was made clear that they continued 'to enjoy the privileges of the Cistercian Order'. This was true in 1487 for Edmund Hepham, a monk of Vaudey, and in 1491 for John Longdon, mentioned above, a monk of Hailes and later abbot of Dore.[100] Robert Irby, a monk of Revesby who, by papal dispensation was vicar of the parish church of St Mary's, Wymondham, Norfolk, from 1479 to 1499, pleaded in 1490 that he could not 'with peace of mind and in tranquillity serve the church, nor remain therein, while publicly wearing the habit of monks of his Order;' so the pope allowed him 'to wear a decent gown of a fitting colour over the said habit.'[101]

In a later instance, Richard Pyrly, a monk of Quarr, was granted release by Cardinal Wolsey from all monastic obligations,[102] and became in 1527 curate of St Helen's, Isle of Wight, and then in 1528, priest-in-charge of the chapel of the Holy Ghost, Limerston, Brightstone; all this despite being suspended by the bishop of Winchester from officiating in the diocese. He, too, remained a member of his community, being eventually dispensed from monastic vows in 1538.[103] A non-resident monk of Boxley (1512) was William Roger, who was a chantry priest in Ash church, Kent, and was that year allowed to cover his habit with the garb of a secular priest.[104]

When in 1494 Thomas Stickney of Swineshead, received papal leave to secure a secular benefice, the pontiff ordered that he was to 'receive the customary portion of wine from the monastery', and to have 'a stall in the choir, and a place and a voice in the chapter.' In other words, he remained very much a member of the community.[105] Likewise William Harbotell (1516), a monk of Coggeshall, was to be afforded 'for life, a stall in the choir, a place and an active and passive voice in the chapter, and the usual monachal portion'.[106] So too in 1536, did Richard Estgate, a monk of Sawley, who was permitted to hold a benefice but also to retain 'a stall in choir, a seat in the chapter and a portion in any monastery' to which the king might assign him. Later he was executed for his involvement in the Pilgrimage of Grace.[107]

Thomas Ireby, abbot of Holm Cultram, complained to Cromwell in July 1533 that 'for the great favour we bore him' the monastery had granted one of its monks, Thomas Graham, the proctorship of its church of Wigton, Cumbria, 'expecting it would be to the advantage of our house, which has proved otherwise.'[108] Graham, the abbot wrote, refused to withdraw from the proctorship and had obtained a dispensation from Rome allowing him to hold a secular benefice. 'By this dispensation', the abbot said, 'he has become the earl of Northumberland's chaplain, which is contrary to the rules of our religion.' Holm Cultram bribed Cromwell with an annual grant of ten marks, and asked for Graham to 'be reformed.' In 1537, back in his monastery, Graham sought the abbacy but had to be content with the position of being its last cellarer.[109]

Several dispensations to hold a benefice were granted to Cistercian monks in the years immediately preceding the dissolution of their houses; some but two or three months before their closure. Such licences came now not from Rome but from the faculty office of the archbishop of Canterbury. Unlike the permissions granted when a house was finally dissolved, some of these faculties saw a fee of £4 being charged (in to-day's terms well over £1,000). Monks subject to such a charge included Wybert Gilboye of St Mary Graces, Edmund Staynforth of Furness, and Ralph Castleton of Vale Royal. More fortunate were William Ottrey of Ford and Henry Huskyn of Neath in whose cases the fee was waived. In some instances it was specified that the grantee must obtain his superior's permission, as specified for William Watson of Byland, and for William Parson of Newenham.[110] Robert Eltryngham of Stratford, dispensed a year before his abbey's closure, had to pay £8 for the privilege.[111]

Most dispensations permitted the recipient to wear his Cistercian habit beneath that of a secular priest, uncomfortable though that must surely have been. John Goday of Coggeshall (1496) was permitted to 'wear the habit and sign usually borne by monks of his Order under a robe or garment of a secular priest.'[112] Robert Wilkinson of Revesby (1508) received papal dispensation not only to receive a secular benefice, but also to 'wear the habit under the honest dress of a secular cleric, being dark and of a decent colour.' Moreover, 'he may not be compelled to wear the habit otherwise.'[113] Thomas Garforth of Kirkstead (1500), already dispensed to hold a benefice, received like permission so that he might 'live among secular clerics more honestly, and without scandal to the people.'[114]

Another sign that a number of these monks did not altogether abandon the Order comes in the evidence that many remained on the books of their monasteries. These included Thomas Farre, a monk of Hailes, who received the parish of Pinnock, close to the monastery, in 1530 but was also the last cellarer of his abbey. John Holme, of the same monastery, was also given a living that same year of nearby Didbrook, which may account for the relatively small pension of £2-13-4 awarded him on the closure of Hailes in 1539. Richard Deane, also of Hailes, became vicar of Longborough in 1527, and he had eventually a pension of only £1-6-8.

Thomas Spratt, of Robertsbridge, became vicar of Bodiam, Suusex, in 1536, with dispensation to give up his habit, but seemingly taken ill returned to his monastery. Edward Lune, of Woburn, became vicar of Fortho, Northants, in 1533, but also remained Cistercian.[115] Byland, in November 1536 and three years before its closure, gave to Robert Webster, 'sometime our fellow brother and monk,' the rents and profits of its rectory of Bubwith, Yorkshire. Webster was also still on the books of his abbey at its suppression.[116]

There were monks permitted by the Holy See to acquire more than one benefice. In 1494 William Mallyng of Boxley, previously dispensed and now holding the church of Leybourne, Kent, was allowed to hold a second church.[117] Henry Radelyf of Rushen was in 1495 also granted the right to hold two churches.[118] All these foregoing instances were at variance with the early customs and spirit of the Order, but papal authority over-rode any potential criticism on that account, and was given as in the case of John Hengham of Sibton (1494), 'not withstanding the statutes and customs of the monastery.'[119]

Educational Achievements

Little is on record of the education Cistercian novices had received before they entered the Order. That in some instances it was minimal was indicated at a visitation of Rufford in 1481, when the abbot was bidden to appoint a master, regular or secular, to teach his young monks the basis of grammar, 'so that they would be useful monks they were to learn to speak and write Latin correctly.' Further, no novice was to be professed unless he knew the psalter by heart, and all young monks—until they had been in the Order for fifteen years, were to learn to sing the antiphons and hymns correctly by heart. The abbot was encouraged to send suitable monks to study the major sciences at Oxford, 'to add wisdom and knowledge to the splendour of the house of God.'[120]

In 1526 Stanley appointed Thomas Counser as its school-master with a residential corrody. He was to 'diligently instruct and teach the monks in all the skills he comprehends and understands, in the appropriate time and accustomed hours', with fifteen days annual leave 'to delight himself as he pleases, mixing or dividing.'[121] He could also absent himself for the duration of any 'common plague or pestilence' affecting the monastery. His residential corrody included an annuity of £4, and a healthy chamber with rights of food and fuel, of service and of privacy. In January 1537 the Court of Augmentations awarded Counser an annuity of only £2-6-8 in recompense of his loss of office and perquisites.[122]

There was a degree of concern regarding the abilities of some young monks, but the real effort to improve matters came only close to the Dissolution when for pragmatic reasons—the countering of the position of the papacy, Cromwell and his visitors in 1535/1536 insisted that a lecturer should be appointed in each house to interpret the Scriptures to the community.[123] Seemingly this, if fulfilled, was performed by selecting a suitable monk, as there are but few notes of outside lecturers being employed. At Furness it was noted in 1536 that 'the abbot and brethren have not kept the injunction of the Visitors to hear a lecture of scripture and keep a schoolmaster.'[124] Very much earlier, in 1472, the visiting abbot of Melrose had ordered that 'a man learned in grammar' be employed at Holm Cultram to instruct its younger monks in Holy Scripture.[125]

Ford, however, at the late date of 3 September 1537, engaged a faithful servant, William Tyler, A.M., of Axminster, not only to teach the boys of the monastery, but also 'whenever asked, at appropriate times, to interpret and explain any of the Scriptures in the refectory.' He received a residential corrody and a fee of £3 annually.[126] The abbot of Hailes informed Cromwell that, unless he brought his scholars home from Oxford, he had no monk sufficiently learned to read the scriptures to the brethren, so he secured for this purpose a divinity scholar, by the name of George Cotes, a divinity graduate from Magdalene College, Oxford, and, later in life, Master of Balliol College.[127]

It is perhaps surprising that Hailes had no senior monk able to fulfil the role. Might it not be that there were such qualified monks, but that being of traditional views they did not wish to assume such a duty?[128] One Anthony Sawnder, another Oxford graduate but with an arts degree, had been appointed by Cromwell to be the lecturer for Winchcombe abbey, was not pleased with Cotes; whom he saw as 'trying to catch me in my sermons.'[129] Cotes was inherently Catholic in his views, Sawnder indubitably of Lutheran leanings. Sawnder sent copies of Cotes's sermons to Cromwell and Bishop Latimer. The upshot was that Cromwell that around December 1535 summoned Cotes to London to explain himself. He did not return to Hailes but, after Mary's accession to the throne twenty years later, and after being Master of Balliol, he was rewarded with the bishopric of Chester.

After the visitation of Warden by Dr Legh and John Ap Rhys, Henry Emery, only lately appointed as abbot, tried to resign his position for his community were in rebellious mood. He did request a monk, Thomas London, to give the daily divinity lecture, but when this was done few, if any of the community would attend. Worse still, Thomas did not fulfil his duty but read instead from the homilies of John Eck, the German theologian and champion of the papacy, which the abbot said did 'entreat of many things clean against the determination of the Church of England.' Abbot Emery also commented that 'perceiving ignorance was a great cause of his monks continual unquietness, he bought grammar books for each of them, and assigned his brother [the retired Abbot Edmund Emery of Tilty, now living at Warden] to instruct them.' It was a fruitless exercise, because only two of the monks would attend his classes. Further, the abbot pointed out, only three of his fifteen monks had any real knowledge of the rule and statutes of their Order. It was a sad situation, with the monks of Warden seemingly almost out of control.[130]

St Bernard's College, Oxford

During the course of the thirteenth century, Cistercian *studia*, basically perhaps halls of residence for young monks attending the local university, emerged in several countries of Europe; the leading house being St Bernard's College, Paris.[131] Rewley abbey, close to Oxford, was designated as the English *studium*, but in 1437 Archbishop Chicheley gave a site at Oxford for the erection of a Cistercian college. It was here that in Tudor times several leading English and Welsh abbots obtained divinity or canon law degrees, for there seems to have been a conscious feeling that abbots should be well qualified. Amongst them were personalities like Thomas Chard of Ford, Gabriel Dunne of Buckfast, Lleision ap Thomas of Neath, and Richard Wyche of Tintern.

The General Chapter in 1482 decreed that in every monastery with at least twelve monks, one was to be sent to their Oxford college; if an abbey had twenty-six or more religious, then two monks were to be sent to Oxford. Smaller monasteries were to join their resources together to make it possible to send one monk.[132] In 1490 the abbot of Cîteaux ordered the abbots of Fountains and Stratford, as his commissaries in England, to enforce this statute. He also enjoined that students must remain at the college until they had graduated.[133] At any one time only one or two monks from an individual abbey would be resident, and consequently they were often referred to by their monastery's name. Thomas Grey recalled in later years how in 1517 he became 'the bible clerk and butler' at St Bernard's College, sharing chambers with 'Mr Byland, Mr Rivers [Rievaulx] and Mr Buckfast.'[134] The surnames of Thomas Robertsbridge and Thomas Kingswood, both gaining their B.D. in 1532, denote their home monastery.[135]

There was not always much enthusiasm for this foundation in the later fifteenth century. The abbot of Fountains in 1489 referred to the 'vacation of the college as many and great'—probably referring to a paucity of students or a frequency of closures.[136] The abbey which, in its latter years, did treasure the college was Hailes. At least four of its monks, still alive in December 1539, had obtained their bachelor of divinity degrees there.[137] The penultimate provisor or superior, William Alynger (perhaps William Alyng, the last abbot of now dissolved Waverley), died at the turn of the year 1539/1540. In his will (made on 26 September 1539) he left to the three student monks from Hailes various items of clothing.[138]

The office of superior or 'provisor' was sometimes a stepping-stone to an abbacy. This was true for Oliver Adams of Combe (gaining his B. D. in 1507; abbot from 1513); John Cabull/Ilmyster of Newenham (provisor, 1517–18; abbot from 1525); and Thomas Scott of Revesby (provisor in 1502; abbot from 1504). By the mid-1490s, the provisor received a £5 annual stipend.[139] In 1460, John King, then prior of Buckfast was appointed the second provisor to hold that position, but allowed to retain his office as prior. Unfortunately he preferred to live mostly at the monastery, so the students did much as they pleased. In 1464 the General Chapter ordered him to reside in Oxford, but this rebuke did not hinder him from becoming a long-serving abbot of Buckfast two years later.[140]

The obtaining of their Oxford degree made *some* of the St Bernard's ex-students think highly of themselves. The General Chapter of 1500 noted that back in their monasteries they expected to sit next to the abbot in choir; they were not humble but proud and indeed haughty; they abandoned the simplicity of the Order; they went bare headed in public, looked down on the cowl and scapular, and disregarded divine service, 'whether by day or by night.'[141] It is hard to believe that these faults were to be found in more than a handful of the

St Bernard's graduates. The Vice-Chancellor in 1515 instructed John Ford, a senior Cistercian, perhaps provisor at the time, to see that 'the student brethren of his Order and other scholars of St Bernard's should behave themselves honestly both within the college and without'.[142] This might imply that non-Cistercian undergraduates found lodgings in the college.

In 1518 the provisor reported to the General Chapter that two rebellious ring-leaders were leading some of the other young monks astray. The culprits were the principal offender—William, a monk from Holm Cultram—several there bore that Christian name, and Edward from Rievaulx,—who must have been Edward Kirkby, later abbot of his house from 1530 to 1533, and then deposed. The provisor said of William and Edward that they frequently went out without permission, disturbed the common peace, and had even broken the doors of the college and of his own chamber. The General Chapter ordered an investigation and punishment.[143]

A few years later in 1521 further abuses were noted including women going into the college, and it was reported that 'the students are fewer and returning home.' The then Reformators appointed by the Order for southern England, the abbots of Stratford and St Mary Graces, sought power to make an official visitation of the college.[144] It does seem that in the years leading up to the Suppression, matters may have greatly improved. The consecration of the new college chapel, and the popularity of the college with the monks of Hailes bear witness to that. The Crown in 1532, also required the abbots of Fountains and others to visit and reform the college 'from time to time, for the increase of virtue and learning,' and to punish transgressors 'by expulsion or otherwise.'[145] The provisor of 1534, probably Robert a monk of Combe, appears to have been conservative in his theological views, and not given to the 'New Learning.' Michael Drome, a student at Oxford, wrote in a letter (9 March 1534) that the abbot of Rewley had asked a Mr Elyott to teach his monks, 'but by reason of another "pekyshe pyed monk" who is provisor of Barnard College, he is not only warned from his living, but accused of teaching heresy.'[146]

The chief and prolonged problem that the college had to face was the slowness of completing proper facilities, and in this respect Abbot Marmaduke Huby of Fountains proved to be a pillar of strength. Indeed whilst he was still bursar of Fountains, the then provisor of the College recommended his election as its abbot (which took place by 17 August 1495), saying that Huby was 'a lover and defender of the college.'[147] Huby not only became abbot of

Fountains but, in harness with the abbot of Stratford—with whom his relations were difficult at first, a Reformator of the Order in England and Wales. Huby was not the only person to strive hard for the success of St Bernard's College; he had already worked hard in this respect with Robert Greyne, a highly praised monk of Stratford.[148]

By the 1480s little appears to have been done to provide adequate and sufficient buildings at the college. In 1482 letters were read from the child king, Edward V, and the archbishop of Canterbury to the General Chapter, and in 1483 to the abbots of the southern province, concerning the extension of the buildings of the college, as nothing had been done for nearly ten years.[149] In 1488 the abbot of Fountains claimed that the college was only one-third finished, and sought authority of the Chapter for himself and the abbot of Stratford to make a collection for seven years for this purpose.[150]

A problem was that the Order expected annual contributions towards its general funds, and for the maintenance of St Bernard's College in Paris. There were conflicting loyalties, and in some years like 1480 payments overseas from England were deferred to divert money for the good of the college.[151] It is noticeable that in the *Valor Ecclesasticus* of 1535, few abbeys are on record as paying annual subscriptions to the college; exceptions included Furness (£4), Whalley (£2-13-4) and Vaudey (13s 4d).[152] Furness also spent annually £10 on its scholars residing at the college; this figure suggests that it maintained at least two students there. It has been suggested that £5 was the annual cost of maintaining a student in the college.[153]

In 1495, soon after he became abbot and a Reformator, Marmaduke Huby gave a set of golden silk vestments with a similar cope to the college, as well as a chalice and twenty books of sacred scripture for its library. He also sought authority to make a collection of between eight and twelve books from all the English monasteries for the college's library. Moreover, he urged his fellow Reformator, the abbot of Stratford, himself a former pupil of the college, to be more supportive of its needs [154]Throughout the 1490s monies were spent on the building works, £20 for instance, in 1493,[155] while in 1501 Huby arranged for a supply for stone from a Headington quarry.[156]

In 1503 the General Chapter noted that the commissioners (the abbots of Fountains, Stratford and St Mary Graces) were active in reparations to the college, but ordered these to cease until 'the state of the temporalities of the Order were ascertained.'[157]The work that year may have been in the hands of a master mason, William Orchard, who had been responsible for the great quadrangle at Magdalene College; he died in 1540. It was he with whom Huby contracted two and a half year's supply of stone.[158] It was a slow project, but in 1517 when a new chapel and hall were being built, Huby hoped that the work would be finished within two years.[159] It was not until May 1530, four years after Huby's death, that the new college chapel was consecrated by the Cistercian Robert King, abbot of Thame, and titular bishop of Rion (Transcaucasus), on behalf of the diocesan bishop of Lincoln.[160]

A survey of perhaps the 1540s of 'Barnard college,' tells of it being without the north gate of Oxford and in the parish of St Mary Magdalene.[161] A two storeyed gateway gave entrance from West Street into a quadrangle measuring 112 by 100 feet, around the walls of which various buildings were ranged. In the north-west of the quadrangle was a 'fair hall,' thirty feet by twenty-seven feet, with a buttery at its east end and a cellar underneath, and over it was a large chamber—perhaps the provisor's abode. East of the kitchen, which measured forty-two by twenty-seven feet, stood 'a fair chapel' measuring eighty by twenty-seven feet. It had three altars, and a great window at the east end of fourteen lights. The kitchen was orientated from north to south, and by it on the north side an opening gave access into the fields. Land, including a garden ,was held in 'the fields of St Giles.'

The library stood on the eastern side of the quadrangle, and measured 112 feet by nineteen.[162] Apart from the great chamber, twenty other chambers find mention, half of them having a 'study' attached. There was a large garden and, for water supply, a well on the south side of the quadrangle. Mostly the buildings ranged roughly north-south and east-west and measured twenty-seven feet in breadth, giving a total area of the property as 17,563 square feet. From the various parts, twenty-five windows looked out through the walls; those on the east side (perhaps open to the street) were secured by iron bars.

The long struggle had been worthwhile for the college had facilitated the higher education of several abbots, and it survived for a few years the closure of the monasteries. It was still an entity in 1542 when note was made of a rent due to it.[163] In 1544 or slightly later Edward Glynton, the 'manciple' or 'steward' of the college appealed to the new Chancellor of England, Lord Wriothesley, regarding a former monk of Buckfast, Arnold Gye, who had for four years been resident there but had now left without paying for his board and lodging, his 'weekly commons.'[164] This appeal must post-date 3 May 1544, when Wriothesley was appointed Lord Chancellor.

Gye had gained his B.D. at Oxford in 1518, when he was noted as owing £9 for books to the university stationer.[165] He was provisor of the college from 1528 to 1531, and was to become the last prior of Buckfast.[166] After the Suppression, it seems he returned to live at St Bernard's College. The 'commons book' showed he owed £16, so the cost for one year of board and lodging at the college must have been £4. In Glynton's appeal, Gye was described as 'late provisor,' which seems that after Alynger (who died at the close of 1539) and Philip Brode, formerly of Kingswood noted as provisor in 1541, Gye must have reoccupied that position. Glynton asserted that Gye had now 'privily conveyed himself forth of the premises.' Made deacon in 1500, he must have been in his mid-sixties by 1544. It is the last that is heard of the college before the Crown survey, and the subsuming of its buildings into the new St John's College.

A monk might perhaps seek or be sent to study at St Bernard's College in Paris. When William Mayun, a monk of Bindon, sought leave in 1492 to study and lecture for seven years in a *studium generale*, the educational establishment he had in mind was not named.[167]

Libraries, and Books

The Cistercians of the Tudor period were able to enhance their libraries with a novel acquisition: the printed book, and the evidence is that they were good Europeans in this respect. In all some thirty-five printed books survive from Cistercian libraries: Woburn had a volume of Cicero printed in Mainz in 1466; Fountains a Bible published in Basle in 1498, and Holm Cultram a copy of the writings of St John of Damascus printed in Paris in 1519.[168]

Nine printed books are known to have been acquired by Hailes, ranging in date between 1521 (Bede's commentaries on the New Testament, published by the noted printer Ascensius in Paris, and intended for use in the chapter-house), and 1532 (a Bible printed by Estienne, also in Paris). The volumes included the *Letters* of St Jerome (printed in Lyon in 1518), and the *Sentences* of Peter Lombard (also published in Lyon in 1527). Other works derived from Cologne and Hagenau. Some of Hailes books were bought for the abbey by Philip Acton, one of its Oxford scholars, who also gave his monastery ten volumes of the collected works of St Augustine of Hippo, which had been printed in Paris in 1531.[169]

In the west country the retired abbot of Dore, Thomas Cleubery, was very much a bibliophile. He arranged a composite volume including three printed sections, including Lichtenberger's *Prognosticatio* (Strasbourg, c.1500). The first folio bears evidence of his authorship: 'This little new work is compiled and put together by Cleubery, this long time of Dore.' On folio 47 of the *Prognosticatio* the prophecy of 1512 relating to the extinction of the monasteries has 'A.D. 1539' added in manuscript in the margin, and a mention of two years of tribulation has '1522' appended, for that is when Cleubery was gravely harassed and forced out of office.[170] Cleubery also appears to have been responsible for assembling a composite manuscript volume including large sections of the *Ecclesiastica Officia* and a valuable Cistercian kalendar.[171] After its closure, a chamber at Furness (1542) was described as having been its 'Screpter', meaning the scriptorium, where books and manuscripts may well have been compiled.[172] Manuscript books made in the fine and active scriptorium at Buildwas were traded in Oxford by the early-fifteenth century.[173]

When Sir John Huddleston and his wife passed away (1512, 1519, respectively), Hailes inherited two books elaborately decorated and made for the Huddlestons as a gift by Sir Christopher Urswyck, formerly great almoner to Henry VII: they were a Psalter and a Commentary by St John Chrysostom on St Matthew's gospel. The former has the *ex libris* inscription: 'Liber monasterii de Hayles.' Both were copied by the one-eyed Louvain graduate, Pieter Meghen, and both are now in Wells Cathedral Library.[174] Another monk and scholar of Hailes was Roger Coscomb who provided for the abbey a copy of the *Letters of St Jerome*, printed in Oxford in 1518, and who had in his possession a composite text, *Libellus sophistarum ad usum Oxonien'*, also printed perhaps that year, but in London by Wynkyn de Worde..[175]

Individual monks occasionally might receive a gift of books. Guy Oswaldkirk, a monk of Rievaulx, was left in the will of the vicar of Oswaldkirk drawn up in 1524, 'some of my books, such as he most desireth and is most expedient for him.'[176] John Winchcombe, a monk of Hailes, in the early 1530s lent books carried by itinerant traders to Robert Joseph, a monk of Evesham. They included volumes of Erasmus, Homer and Ulysses. Humphrey Chester of Combermere was also able to send books to Joseph; these Joseph wrote to

Chester in 1531 he had 'distributed as you wished'—for Chester had several friends in the Evesham community.[177]

When John Palmer, last abbot of Tilty, made his will (proved February 1539), he bequeathed to William Wyke, the parson of Great Easton, 'all his Latin books.' Palmer was also able to bequeath 'a book called polychronicon and a pair of tables.'[178] Such monastic wills show former Cistercian monks as retaining books or purchasing them in later life. The will of Richard Hall (*al.* Gilling), a monk of Rievaulx, proved in 1566, shows that he possessed a number of books, including Erasmus's New Testament in Latin but also a New Testament in English.[179]

The Work of the Reformators

The usual means of ensuring uniformity and high standards in a Cistercian monastery were achieved by a father abbot inspecting each of his daughter houses annually, and compiling a charter recording his stipulations for improvement. Whilst this visitatorial system continued to an extent, by the late fifteenth century the General Chapter appointed commissaries known as 'reformators' for England and Wales, who had over-all visitatorial duties and also responsibility for ensuring the collection of the annual subsidy for the Order. Their appointment was made more urgent since it was feared in 1488 that Pope Innocent VIII was to issue a bull transferring the visitation and reformation of the Order in England and Wales to the archbishops of Canterbury and York; in other words, the Cistercians would lose their long and cherished independence from episcopal control.[180] The need for local reformators was also emphasised in 1491 when Henry VII refused to permit the abbot of Cîteaux to make a personal visitation.[181] The General Chapter had in 1489 requested the abbot to reform 'the many monasteries in the British Isles that were transgressing by poor adherence to the rule and way of life.'[182]

The abbots chosen as reformators varied from time to time, but successive abbots of Stratford served by 1486 down to 1533, while abbots of Fountains occupied the position from 1489 down also to 1533. In 1486 the General Chapter appointed the abbots of Combe (William Whityngton), Cleeve (Humphrey Quicke) and of Stratford (Hugh Watford) as its commissaries in England, Wales and Ireland.[183] Theirs was a huge task, which could only have allowed visitations of monasteries of which there had been a bad report. Two years later, at the request of the abbots of Combe and Stratford, Quicke was appointed again as a Reformator for England and Wales. This choice was not altogether welcome in the Order, and Quicke, now abbot of Beaulieu, faded from the scene.[184]

Abbot Darnton of Fountains said in a letter sent in 1488 to Cîteaux that it was rumoured that Humphrey Quicke, now abbot of Beaulieu, had pocketed much money he had collected for the Order, but Quicke rejoined that he had been badly treated by the abbot of Stratford, and recommended that the abbot of Fountains took over Stratford's position as a Reformator. Stratford remained but in harness with Darnton.[185] This difference between the reformators may reflect the then schism between the abbeys of Cîteaux (of whose family Beaulieu formed part) and of Clairvaux (Fountains and Stratford being of its generation). Abbot Darnton of Fountains in 1491 expressed his pleasure at the healing of that rupture between two of the first monasteries of the Order.[186]

In 1489 the abbots of Stratford and Fountains were appointed to visit all the monasteries of the Order, of both sexes, in the provinces of Canterbury and York for a five-year period.[187] This authority was repeated in 1491 with the additional responsibility of the houses in Ireland and Scotland.[188] An impossible task! By 1493 there were three reformators—the abbot of St Mary Graces now also a commissary. On a further commission that year, Abbot Darnton of Fountains was empowered both to inspect English monasteries, but also those 'of adjacent parts'—principally Wales. His wide-ranging powers included the suspension and deposition of abbots. He died two years later, when Huby his bursar and successor, praised his work highly and sought a continuation of Darnton's commission.[189]

About 1514 the abbot of Ford became a fourth reformator, and in 1517 appeared before Cardinal Wolsey on behalf of the Order,[190] In 1514 also Leo X appointed the abbots of Waverley, St Mary Graces, Thame, Ford and Combe, as 'defendants of appellants to Rome.'[191] In 1517 Abbot Huby of Fountains lamented that whereas there had once been two commissaries in each province sharing the work, now there were five instead of four, and some English abbots were trying to avoid their authority by appealing to the Holy See. Nevertheless, he asked for the abbot of Rievaulx to share his burden in his old age. The fifth was Abbot Lleision ap Thomas of Neath, now reformator for Wales where previously, and as he said for twenty years, Huby had laboured; Lleision's decisions were not always to Huby's liking.[192]

From about 1517 the abbeys under the abbot of Ford were in the south and south-west of England, those of northern England were placed under Huby of Fountains and the abbot of Rievaulx—now included on account of Huby's age and at his request.[193] the houses of Stratford and St Mary Graces were to be divided between them as they pleased, whilst Wales now passed to the abbot of Neath. Their commission was extended for a five-year period. Around 1520 the abbot of Vale Royal sought eighteen abbeys and three nunneries to be placed under his jurisdiction, but Abbot Huby wished to expel him as a commissary, and a list attributed to September of that year detailing monasteries to be inspected by the abbots of St Mary Graces and Stratford, includes six of those he sought as well as the three convents.[194] The position of the Abbot of Ford, as a reformator was strengthened in 1521 when he was one of several abbots given by General Chapter the power to absolve their monks in all cases, where hitherto an appeal might have had to be made to Cîteaux.[195]

Huby of Fountains recalled in 1517 that his job had not been easy with some abbots straying from the spirit and privileges of the Order, and his expenses had cost the treasury of Fountains no less over the years than 1,000 marks.[196] The reformators could themselves find criticism as when in 1521 the abbot of Combe (no longer himself a commissary) wrote to Cîteaux implying that the commissaries had done little to stop many breaches of the rules in certain houses, including whole families entering monasteries and drinking at all hours of the day.[197]

Because of the perceived problems in England and Wales, the General Chapter in 1531 delegated the abbot of Chaâlis to make a visitation there. Henry VIII objected, saying that he would not allow anybody to meddle in the affairs of his kingdom, and that 'it was not convenient to admit him, being a stranger and inhabitant of France.'[198] The consequence was that in 1532 the Crown appointed as Visitors the abbots of Woburn and St Mary Graces to cover the south of England, and those of Byland and Fountains the north, and Neath for Wales. These appointments were confirmed for a five year period by the General Chapter in 1533.[199] This did not run its course since in 1535 Henry VIII took it upon himself to appoint the abbots of Ford (Thomas Chard) and Stanley (Thomas Calne) as Visitors of more than thirty Cistercian abbeys in the south of England and the Midlands. Stratford which had previously occupied a pre-eminent position, was now made subject to the Crown Visitors.[200]

The reformators did not work in isolation but held regular joint meetings. These sometimes included the presence of many more superiors, and were essentially provincial chapters. In 1486 a meeting of abbots was held at Northampton 'for the reform of the Order', and its decisions were approved by the General Chapter.[201] Abbot Huby told of regular meetings of the commissaries either in London or in the centrally placed town of Leicester, as in 1495, 1497 and 1498. [202]At such a meeting in Leicester in 1498 the differences between Huby and Abbot Hickman of Stratford which had marred relations since Huby became abbot Fountains were resolved.[203]

In 1500 the reformators met in London but, because of an infestation in the city, removed to Barnet in Hertfordshire.[204] The year 1517 saw two meetings: one in York, where a number of abbots 'zealous for the Order' convened', but the abbot of Rievaulx bewailed of others that they acted secretly and unjustly, hypocritically and pitiably.[205] The second meeting that year, of the abbots of Stratford, St Mary Graces and nearby Waverley, was held at Guildford, when the abbot of Ford queried why certain abbeys had been removed from his jurisdiction.[206] Other known meetings took place in London: a Cistercian chapter in 1519,[207] and a meeting at St Mary Graces in 1520, apparently summoned by the Abbot Lleision of Neath.[208]

The reformators could be jealous of their rights, as when Huby of Fountains, not long a reformator, took it upon himself to install in 1497 a new abbot at Furness. This offended the abbot of Stratford, who said that Huby was acting outside his commission. Huby pointed out that he had been summoned by the monks of Furness because of the urgent situation there—a divided community, and he went as his monastery was very much closer to Furness than London.[209] In 1518 Abbot Gill of Buckfast was rebuked by the General Chapter for allowing a delegate sent by the abbot of Savigny (of whose family Buckfast was a member) to make the official visitation of his monastery, as this was now within the jurisdiction of the abbot of Ford.[210]

In 1533, as reformators for the north of England, the abbots of Byland and Fountains warned Abbot Banks of Furness not to intervene in the case of Gawain Borrowdale, a monk of Holm Cultram alleged to have poisoned his abbot.[211] When the General Chapter heard in 1500 of conspiracies at Newminster, and of many novelties being introduced there which departed 'from the way of the holy fathers', it delegated the abbots of Fountains and St Mary Graces to investigate. The matter was to come back at the next year's Chapter when the abbot of Newminster was to be present. If the reformators found the allegations to be true then, until that Chapter, they were to suspend the abbot from holding visitations at his daughter houses of Pipewell and Roche.[212] The abbot was probably Robert de Charlton, and he was perhaps deposed.

When the abbot of Woburn, perhaps Robert Chorley, was a reformator in the late 1470s/early 1480s a considerable amount of the Order's business was carried out by one of his monks, John Cok(e). Described later as 'a zealot of the Order', he reportedly 'sold' the abbacy of Aberconwy in 1479, presumably using delegated visitatorial powers. The next year he carried monies from the Order in England to Loos abbey in France for onward transmission to the General Chapter. Not universally liked, a gathering of twenty Cistercian abbots meeting in Shrewsbury in 1482, addressed a letter to the abbot of Cîteaux expressing their concern at the defamation of Abbot Cromboke of Hailes, himself newly appointed as a reformator, by John Coke and his abbot. Coke continued his activities, conveying a letter from the abbot of Woburn to Cîteaux in April 1484.[213]

Abbot Chorley having resigned, Coke was sent with a letter to Cîteaux by the abbots of Vaudey and Warden in July 1491. He seems to have visited Loos abbey en route, taking opportunity to let its abbot know that his former abbot was retired without pension. The abbot of Loos, writing to Cîteaux told how Coke had disparaged the new abbot of Woburn, and hinted at an irregular and simonical appointment to the abbacy of Medmenham in which Coke was involved. No more is heard of Coke after that year.[214]

Another significant personality in the affairs of the Order in England and Wales was John Haryngton, B.C.L. (Cantab), Yorkshire-born, clerk to Richard III and serving under Henry VII. He was also the registrar of the consistory court of York, and later a counsellor in the court of Henry VII.[215] He showed a keen interest in the well-being of the Cistercians, addressing a letter to the abbot of Cîteaux in 1489, when he compared unfavourably the flourishing facilities of the mendicant orders in Oxford, compared to the 'poverty' of provision for the Cistercians there. He did, however, commend highly Robert Greyne of Stratford and Marmaduke Huby of Fountains for their work in connection with St Bernard's College.[216]

In 1490 Harington was involved in the case of the deposed prioress of Cook Hill (*Chapter 8*), and he reported to Cîteaux the deposition of Abbot Maurice of Whitland. In 1491, in London and together with Marmaduke Huby, then bursar of Fountains, he arranged the transmission of the Order's dues to France by the hands of Florentine merchants. In July 1493 he was in Rome endeavouring to obtain a bull in favour of the English Cistercians. His last letter is dated 1499 when he lay ill in Orleans.[217]

A major responsibility of the Reformators was the collection from individual monasteries of their annual contribution payable to the General Chapter of the Order, and the transmission of the monies to Cîteaux. In some years sending money abroad was impossible on account of a sovereign's conflict with France. In 1487 England was mentioned as one of six countries sending little or nothing, and the Chapter noted that if this continued 'the final ruin of the Order would be imminent.'[218] There were other years when the transmission of the subsidy was impracticable, and when it was feasible the nature of the cargo was masked in the correspondence by referring to the names of the flowers stamped on coinage rather than the money itself, or to use misleading phraseology such as 'one thousand weights of tin.'[219]

The annual tax on individual monasteries was not over-large. In 1491 the total collected by one Reformator (the abbot of Stratford) amounted to £26 from twenty-seven monasteries, and ranged from the £1-10-0 paid by St Mary Graces, and £1-5-0 paid by each of Beaulieu, Buxckfast, Combermere, Ford, Hailes and Tintern, down to the 13s 4d. levied on nine of the abbeys in his commission, including Flaxley, Sawtry and, surprisingly, Waverley. In 1513/14 the total collected by the four Reformators (Fountains, Stratford, St Mary Graces and Ford), and receipted by Cîteaux, amounted to £73-10-0.[220] Collection within the country would be by trusted monks, like William Waldegrave of Pipewell who operated in 1505/06 from St Mary Graces in London.[221] Transmission abroad likewise—as by John of Hailes who paid over his monies during the General Chapter of 1486; or as a brother John Budelar who transmitted the monies to Cîteaux in 1510, or by lay agents such as the 'bank of Capone' at Lyons (1491).[222]

The work of the Reformators necessitated expense, and this was either met by lessening the amounts of money sent to Cîteaux or, as Abbot Huby once implied, by their own monasteries. In 1493 and 1498 the Reformators paid the £5 stipend of the provisor of St Bernard's College, Oxford; in 1497 they made good a debt of £4 owing to the manciple of the college by a former provisor who had become abbot of Strata Florida, and they also placed money towards new building at the college. In 1495 the abbot of Stratford claimed

£6 expenses in attending a meeting of abbots in Leicester, and in 1497 £3-6-8 met the needs of the messenger sent by the Reformators to Cîteaux.[223]

The Evidence of Visitations

The visitation 'charters' drawn up by a reformator or a father-abbot at the conclusion of his visitation of a monastery rarely mentioned the positive aspects of the common life and worship there. All too often the charters list only those points where improvement was necessary, and thus give a misleading picture of that abbey at the time, making it appear as if everything was disordered, whereas the conventual life there may well have been for the most part holy and praiseworthy. It is very important to read the visitation charters in that light. Nevertheless, the charters do give insights into many aspects of a community's life, and therefore the few charters which are extant are worthy of closer study. A manuscript volume of the late fifteenth century, perhaps to be ascribed to Robertsbridge,[224] and a register emanating from Hailes abbey, both outline the lines of enquiry to be made at a visitation.[225]

A very lengthy visitation charter was compiled on the occasion of the inspection of *Rufford* in 1481 by the abbots of Loos (north-eastern France) and of Woburn, as commissaries of the abbot of Cîteaux and the General Chapter.[226] Its liturgical requirements have been noted (*Chapter 1*), while the other stipulations included the dismantling of private chambers in the dorter—save those of the prior and sub-prior; the locking at night of all doors of the cloister and dorter, and the keeping of the 'holy silence' in the dorter, as also in the church, cloister and refectory. Those breaking the rules were to be flogged and/or imprisoned on a diet of bread and water.

Juniors, not yet priests, were after confession to receive Holy Communion on all Sundays and feasts of Sermon. Meat was not to be eaten in the cloister refectory, and no meat at all was to be consumed in Advent and Lent, on Mondays, Wednesdays, Fridays and Saturdays, nor on the vigils of major feasts. In the refectory the monks were to listen in silence to the reading from the Bible or the lives of the Saints; they wearing their scapular, the reader his cowl. After lunch in the summer months, the monks could for a time rest on their beds. On Sundays, Tuesdays and Thursdays, when meat was served to the community in the infirmary hall, a period of 'recreation' could follow, when in a low voice conversation of an edifying character was permitted. Reference was also made to the Saturday foot washing; in cold weather the washing of hands might be substituted.

Private property was not to be held, and women were not to enter the precincts—except for an annual visit by ladies of noble birth; this to favour the descendants of patrons and important benefactors. All monastic officials were to render monthly accounts to the abbot and senior monks. Lastly the monks were bidden to be obedient to the abbot, and the junior monks respectful to their seniors. Given that the charter lacks any specific references to Rufford itself, it is possible that it was in part compiled before the Visitors arrived at the monastery. Be that so or not, there are several reminders within the charter that the community should observe the prescriptions of the *Benedictina*, the constitution for the Cistercian Order promulgated in 1335 by Pope Benedict XII.

A visitation which was clearly necessary was that carried out by two reformators, the abbots of Stratford and St Mary Graces at *Warden* (a daughter-house of Rievaulx) on 26 September 1492, when eight monks alleged various short-comings.[227] The abbot, John Bright, came in for severe criticism, even from John Stanford, his aged prior, who blamed the abbot for 'great destruction of the wealth of the monastery.' This had been done by selling three corrodies, and pawning much of the abbey's plate, including four silver gilt chalices, seven silver dishes and two silver basins, as well as twelve large volumes, including St Augustine's, *The City of God*. In this way the abbot had realised in excess of twenty pounds. The prior said that brother Thomas Luton ('Lucy'), who had brought women into the monastery was now apostate; that the brethren did not rise for vigils at the appointed hour; that some wore linen garments; that some did not 'keep' the refectory, nor process after lunch chanting the *Miserere* to the church in order to say grace; that the psalms were chanted with maximum speed; that the Saturday foot-washing was not observed; that there was no uniformity in the tonsure of the monks, they did not bow in the church, and stood in choir with their hands crossed. These were serious allegations.

Others of the community added their voice: that the evening cloister reading was not given; that the distinctions and statutes were not read in chapter; that monks going on or returning from a journey were not given a blessing; that the daily Mass for the dead was not celebrated; that two of their number frequented taverns, both by day and by night, and that 'suspect women' even stayed in the abbot's chamber. One of the monks, who also told of Luton's shortcomings, was himself accused of illicitly leaving the dorter during the night.

In their charter the visitors responded to these quite serious shortcomings.[228] Amongst their stipulations was insistence that all the ceremonies of the Order 'as left us by our holy fathers' be observed, with silence in the appointed places and at the appointed times; and uniformity in chant, behaviour, habit and tonsure, in reading and in prayer. Each year, between All Saints Day (1 November) and Easter, the prior or his deputy were to read to the community, and explain if necessary, the 'ancient and new distinctions, together with the *Benedictina* and the other statutes of the Order.' All monks were to spend the reading time in the cloister, and to perform manual labour outside the cloister; those who without leave left the precincts or gave way to sins of the flesh were to be imprisoned.

The monks were reminded to make the procession on fish-days to the church after dinner to say grace, chanting the *Miserere* as they walked; to perform the Saturday feet or hand washing, and not to wear linen under garments. A lengthy paragraph exhorted mutual love and respect between the abbot and the monks. All were forbidden to reveal what had been said during the visitation to any outsider. The precentor was to have custody of the charter of visitation, and four times a year to read it to the assembled community, word by word. Finally, the precepts of the charter were to be fully observed. But were they?; of that there is no knowledge.

Another visitation that gave cause for concern was that of *Thame* in 1526 by its father abbot of Waverley, acting on twenty-two allegations levelled against its abbot [John Warren] and the community by the bishop of Lincoln.[229] Amongst the bishop's accusations were that the abbot had in his company several young men and boys, sleeping in bed with one of them; that he kept no proper accounts; that he had demised lands unfairly to a particular friend, John Cowper; that he was given to providing feasts for his friends; that women were frequently in the monastery leading to 'bad feelings between the brothers'; that the monks were ignorant of the Rule of St Benedict, and of the way of life and ceremonies of their Order; and that monks freely left the abbey, even to engage in archery, and were sometimes improperly dressed. The abbot made a detailed rebuttal of these claims, but the bishop did not accept his protestations, nor the abbot of Waverley's prescriptions for reform.

The abbot of Waverley did issue a detailed visitation charter the prescriptions of which regarding the liturgy have already been alluded to. Other stipulations made insisted that all were to sleep during the great silence in single beds, and that no lay person was to rest in the dorter; a light was to burn in the dorter so that the 'president' could ensure that no one was absent, and so that any who needed to go to the necessarium [the reredorter or toilet block] could do so safely; the doors of the dorter and proptuarium [the store room] were to be locked at night, whilst 'singing and clamour' by the door of the dorter was prohibited; the Rule of St Benedict, the Book of Usages and the Old and New Definitions were to be read and explained to the monks over the course of a year; study and reading was to be encouraged, with manual labour on ferial days; monks were not to go out without proper cause, nor to take part in archery with seculars. They could, however, amongst themselves only, have 'honest and religious recreation within the bounds of the monastery on two or three days of the week.' Finally, and as was normal, the charter concludes with the stipulation, by way of reminder, that it was to be read to the assembled community in chapter by the precentor four times a year. In connection with the visitation, Abbot Warren—who appears to have resigned or been deposed, compiled on 4 February 1526 an inventory of the monastery's possessions and debts.[230]

At a visitation at Holm Cultram held in 1472 by the father-abbot of Melrose, Scotland, the priests were ordered to receive the Eucharist four times a week, and those monks not priests at least twice a fortnight. Unless accompanied by 'a companion of honest conversation' a monk was not to visit anyone outside the precincts, and no woman was to enter. The inner doors of the monastery were to be supplied with locks to keep out unwanted visitors. It is clear that not all was as it ought to have been in the monastery.[231] The abbot of Dore visited his daughter-house of Vale Royal on 16 March 1509, but the only record that survives is a statement of the goods and wealth of the house at that time.[232]

Notes

[1]   *DKR*, p. 25.
[2]   TNA, E36/152, f. 22.
[3]   *DKR*, p. 52.
[4]   *Letters*, pp. 112–13 [No. 82].
[5]   Ibid. p. 259 [No. 131].
[6]   *Reg. C. Bothe*, pp. 311–12.
[7]   *Reg. R. Fox* (2), f. 146.
[8]   *Reg. R. Fox* (3), f. 51r–v.
[9]   *CPL* **15**, p. 23 [No. 43].
[10] *CPL* **20**, pp. 492–93 [No. 696].
[11] TNA, E315/283, f. 1.
[12] TNA, E135/3/16; *FOR*, pp. 125, 162.
[13] *Reg. T. Savage*, f. 113.
[14] *Reg. W. Smyth*, n.f.
[15] C. Cross, and N. Vickers, *Monks, friars and nuns in sixteenth century Yorkshire*, YAS 1995, p. 187.
[16] J. Stéphan, *A History of Buckfast Abbey*, Bristol, Burleigh Press, 1970, p. 177.
[17] *Reg.S. Gigli*, f. 330 [170v in later pagination].
[18] *Reg. J. Stokesley*, ff. 129v–130r.
[19] *CHA*, pp. 207–08.
[20] D. H. Williams, 'Exeter College, Oxford, MS1,' in *Cîteaux* **62**, 2011, p. 120.
[21] *Reg. T. Myllyng*, p. 157.
[22] *Reg. J. Longland*, f. 55v.
[23] TNA, E315/283, f. 1.
[24] TNA, E315/105, f. 84r.
[25] SSC, DR 10/996.
[26] D. B. Foss, 'Marmaduke Bradley, Last Abbot of Fountains,' in *YAJ* **61**, 1989, p. 105.
[27] *LW*, p. 255 [No. 373].
[28] Ibid. pp. 153 [No. 224]; the abbot if taking part was to receive 3s 4d.
[29] Ibid. p. 81 [No. 122].
[30] M. Aveling, 'The Monks of Byland after the Dissolution,' in *YAJ* **60**, Part 1, 1955, p. 3.
[31] TNA, PROB11/21, f. 37v; B. Barber *et al.*, *The Cistercian Abbey of St Mary, Stratford Langthorne, Essex*, Museum of London, 2004, p. 57.
[32] TNA, PROB11/22, f. 62.
[33] J. L. M. Moore, 'Sibton Church'. In: *Proc. Suffolk Institute of Archaeology and History*, **8**, Part 1, p. 64.
[34] A. F. Cirket, 'English Wills, 1498–1526.' In *BHRS* **37**, 1957, p. 13.
[35] VCH, *County of Warwick 2*, London, 1908, p. 74.

36   TNA, SC12/13/65.

37   W. G. Clark-Maxwell, 'Buildwas Abbey—The survey of 1536', in *Trans. Shropshire Archaeological Soc.*, **44**, 1931, 68; *FOR*, **p.** 92.

38   *LP* **5**, pp. 527 [No. 1203], 773–74 [Appx. 34]; G. Baskerville, *English Monks and the Suppression of the Monasteries*, London, Jonathan, Cape, 1937, p. 137; M. Carter, *ODNB* online.

39   *LP* **10**, p. 60 [No. 164/5].

40   *SAP* pp. 15556 [Nos. 703–04], and *footnote*. London may have been the William London ordained priest in 1424, and who in 1451 vacated the Childeshall portion in the church of Pontesbury, Herefs.

41   *SAP*, p. 147 [No. 664]; *CPL* **12**, 66–67.

42   TNA, C1/475/16.

43   SAL, MS 14, and see the Appendix.

44   TNA, E315/283, f. 1r, and see the Appendix.

45   *SAP*(2), pp. 388–89 [No. 3143].

46   *SAP*, pp. 143 [No. 637], 156 [No. 709].

47   *LP* **10**, p. 496 [No. 1191].

48   Cross, *Monks, friars and nuns*, 1995, p. 149.

49   Baskerville, *English Monks*, 1937, p. 90; F.A. Gasquet, *Henry VIII and the English Monasteries*, London, J.C. Nimmo, 2nd edn., 1899, p. 458.

50   Cross, *Monks, friars and nuns*, 1995, pp. 135–36.

51   Gasquet, *Henry VIII and the English Monasteries*, p. 458.

52   R.W. Hays, *History of the Abbey of Aberconway*, Cardiff: University of Wales Press, 1963, pp. 140, 160–61, 178–79; Williams, *Cistercians*, 2001, p. 77.

53   Cross, *Monks, friars and nuns*, 1995, pp. 113, 115, 120.

54   Walcott, *Leicester chantries*, 1874, attached sheet.

55   TNA, SC12/33/27.

56   D. H. Williams, 'The White Monks in Powys.' In: *Cistercian Studies* **11**, 1976, pp. 83–84.

57   D. H. Williams, *The Welsh Cistercians*, Leominster: Gracewing, 2001, p. 68.

58   H. Aveling and W.A. Pantin, ed. *The Letter Book of Robert Joseph*, OHS, N.S. **19**, 1967, pp. 84, 146, 187–88 [No. 121]; VCH, *County of* Chester **3**, London, 1980, p. 154.

59   *LP* **10**, p. 138 [No. 364].

60   VCH, *Cumberland*, **2**, London, 1968, p. 171.

61   *Letters*, p. 251 [No. 129]; L. Thomas, *The Reformation in the Old Diocese of Llandaff*, Cardiff: William Lewis, 1930, 31; G. Williams, *Welsh Church from Conquest to Reformation*, Cardiff: University of Wales Press, 1962, pp. 398–99; Williams, *Welsh Cistercians*, 2001, pp. 63, 70.

62   Williams, *Welsh Cistercians*, 2001, p. 69; D. H. Williams, 'The Monks of Basingwerk.' In: *Flintshire Historical Soc. Jnl.* **39**, 2012, pp. 47–49.

63   See the Appendix for relevant references.

64   *Letters*, p. 158 [No. 79].

[65] W. Humphrey, *Garendon Abbey*, Loughborough University: East Midlands Study Unit, 1982, p. 64.

[66] *LC*, p. 59 [No. XXIX].

[67] *Statuta* **5**, pp. 562–63 [No. 1486/120].

[68] *LP* **12**, Part 2, p. 66 [No. 186/23].

[69] S. W. Williams, *The Cistercian Abbey of Strata Florida*, London: Whiting & Co., 1889, Appendix. pp. lxxvii–lxxx; *LP* **7**, p. 477 [No. 1264].

[70] *Letters*, pp. 154–57 [No. 78], 163–64 [No. 81].

[71] Ibid. p. 191 [No. 94].

[72] *CHA*, p. 104 [36]; SSC, DR18/31/5, f. 17.

[73] *Letters*, p. 65 [No. 81].

[74] *CPL* 1, p. 597 [No. 973].

[75] See the Appendix for relevant references.

[76] Reg. G. Audley, ff. 7r–9r, Wiltshire R.O

[77] *CPL* **19**, p. 207 [No. 345].

[78] TNA, E315/117, f. 42; E. Owen, 'Vale Crucis Abbey.' In: *Wrexham Guardian*, 4 November 1931, p. 1.

[79] D. H. Williams, *The Cistercians in the Early Middle Ages*, Leominster: Gracewing, 1998, p. 63.

[80] *Letters*, p. 223 [No. 109].

[81] H. Foley, 'The Pilgrim Book of the Ancient English Hospice, Rome. In: *Records of the English Province of the Society of Jesus*, London: Burns and Oates, **6**, 1880, pp. 545–47.

[82] TNA, C1/59/38.

[83] TNA, E315/33/31; Williams, *White Monks in Gwent*, 1976, pp. 23–24.

[84] TNA, C81/1788/7.

[85] TNA, REQ2/11/40.

[86] TNA, C81/1788/2; C1/1788/30; C1/1788/42, respectively.

[87] C. Harper–Bill, ed. *Register of John Morton, Archbishop of Canterbury*, **3**: *Norwich sede vacante*, CY, 2000, p. 172 [No. 351].

[88] *CPL* **17**, Part 2, p. 176 [No. 177].

[89] Williams, *The Welsh Cistercians*, 2001, p. 73.

[90] *CPL* **15**, pp. 358–59 [No. 682]. His possession of the church was challenged in 1492: *CPL* **16**, pp. 5–6 [No. 6].

[91] *CHA*, pp. 337–38.

[92] *SAP*(2), pp. 328–29 [No. 2988].

[93] *Statuta* **5**, p. 501 (No. 1485/26).

[94] *CPL* **15**, p. 158 [No. 320], pp. 296–97 [No. 577].

[95] *Letters*, p. 135.

[96] D. N. Bell, 'A Tudor Chameleon: the Life and Times of Stephen Sagar, Last Abbot of Hailes.' In: *Cîteaux* **62**, 2011, p. 298

[97] *CPL* **15**, *passim*. and **16**, p. cxix

98 *Letters*, pp. 186–89 [Nos. 92–93].

99 *CPL* **13**, Part 1, p. 744; **15**, p. 385 [No. 728].

100 *CPL* **15**, pp. 41 [No. 73], 430 [No. 823], respectively

101 *CPL* **15**, pp. 270–71 [No. 537]. I am grateful to Richard Barton-Wood for his dates as vicar there. [In 1499, with a personal bequest of 20s., Irby was asked to be one of the 'supervisors' of the will of William Lombe of Wymondham (*Reg. J. Morton* **3**, p. 87 [No. 128]).

102 TNA, E326/8894.

103 S. F. Hockey, *Quarr Abbey and its Lands*, Leicester U.P., 1970, pp. 201, 231.

104 *CPL* **19**, p. 357 [No. 634].

105 *CPL* **16**, p. 224 [No. 314]; *Cf. CPL* **19**, p. 503 [No. 868] John Carvegh, Rewley, 1512.

106 *CPL* **20**, p. 457 [No. 643].

107 F.O.R., p. 58.

108 LP **6**, pp. 348–49 [No. 781].

109 Gasquet, *Henry VIII and the English Monasteries*, 1899, pp. 279–81; S. M. Harrison, *The Pilgrimage of Grace in the Lake Countiest*, Royal Historical Soc., 1981, p. 129; *DKR*, p. 24.

110 See the Appendix for the authorities for these named monks.

111 J. E. Oxley, *The Reformation in Essex*, Manchester U.P., 1965, p. 118.

112 *CPL* **16**, p. 416 [No. 626]; *Cf.* p. 524 [No. 762]; **18**, p. 332 [No. 424]; **20**, p. 577 [note 55]..

113 *CPL* **18**, p. 548 [No. 803], pp. 582–83 [No. 869]).

114 *CPL* **17**, Part 1, p. 294 [No. 447]).

115 See the Appendix for the references for these monks.

116 TNA, LR1/175, f. 314r.

117 *CPL* **16**, pp. 199–200 [No. 281].

118 Ibid. p. 281 [No. 392].

119 Ibid. p. 278 [No. 382].

120 *RC* **3**, pp. 555–61 [No. 1004].

121 i.e: 'with others or by himself'.

122 TNA, E315/91, ff. 16v–17v.

123 Gasquet, *English Monasteries*, 1899, p. 93.

124 *LP* **12**, Part 1, p. 370 [No. 841/5].

125 VCH, *Cumberland* **2**, London, 1968, pp. 170–71.

126 TNA, E315/100, ff. 217v–218v.

127 D. Winkless, *Hailes Abbey, Gloucestershire*, Stocksfield: Spredden, 1990, p. 54; *LP* **7**, p. 640 [No. 35].

128 Bell, *A Tudor Chameleon*, 2011, pp. 290–96, where a full analysis of the situation

129 Ibid. p. 293; Gasquet, *English Monasteries*, 1899, p. 93.

130 *LP* **9**, pp. 383–84 [No. 1118], 397–98 [No. 1167].

131 Williams, *Cistercians in the Early Middle Ages*, 1998, pp. 98–99.

[132] *Statuta* **5**, p. 441 (No. 41).

[133] Stevenson and Salter, *St John's College*, 1939, p. 26.

[134] M. Aveling, 'The Rievaulx Community after the Dissolution.' In: *Ampleforth Journal*, LVII, 1952, pp. 101–02. A student monk in Oxford in 1533 was a Mr Boxley: Canterbury Cathedral Archives, CC/JQ/333/vii. Another student at Oxford *c*.1515 was a Thomas Buckland, but he was a scholar of London College: TNA, STAC2/26/371

[135] W. H.Stevenson and H. E. Salter, *The Early History of St John's College, Oxford*, Oxford: Oxford Historical Soc., 1939, p. 32.

[136] *Letters*, p. 93 [No. 37].

[137] *LP* **14**, Part 2, p. 291 [[No. 771]. They were Philip Brode, John Dawson, Richard Eddon and Roger Rede, all bachelors of divinity.

[138] Stevenson and Salter, *The Early History of St John's College*, p. 37: To Philip Acton 'a riding cloak and my studying frock,' to Roger Whalley 'a riding cloak, short frock and feather bed,' and to Richard Hailes, 'a worsted frock.'

[139] *Letters*, p. 198

[140] Stéphan, *Buckfast Abbey*, 1970, pp.163–65.

[141] *Statuta* **5**, pp. 237–38 [No. 1500/24].

[142] Stevenson and Salter, *St John's College*, 1939, p. 29.

[143] Aveling, 'The Rievaulx Community,' 1952, pp. 101–02; *Statuta* **6**, p. 540 [No. 1518/69].

[144] *Letters*, pp. 265–66 [No. 137].

[145] *LP* **5**, p. 456 [No. 978/6].

[146] *LP* **7**, p. 133 [No. 308].

[147] *Letters*, p. 173 [No. 86].

[148] Ibid. pp. 121 [No. 59], 132 [No. 66], 196 [No. 97].

[149] Stevenson and Salter, *St John's College*, 1939, p. 40.

[150] *Letters*, p. 115 [No. 54].

[151] Ibid. p. 115 [54].

[152] *VE* **5**, p. 270; VCH, *County of Lancaster* **2**, London, 1908, p. 138; *VE* **4**, p. 99, respectively

[153] Stevenson and Salter, *St John's College*, 1939, pp. 26–27.

[154] *Letters*, pp. 182 [No. 89], 190–92 [Nos. 94–95], 195–96 [No. 97], 207, 210–11.

[155] Ibid. pp. 195–96 [No. 97].

[156] H. E. Salter, ed. *Snappe's Formulary*, Oxford U.P., 1924, p. 217.

[157] *Letters*, p. 230 [No. 114].

[158] Stevenson and Salter, *St John's College*, 1939, pp.28–29; C. Wilson, 'Orchard, William', *ODNB* online; VCH, *County of Oxford* **3**, 1965, p. 204n.

[159] Ibid. pp. 240–41 No. 125], 244–45 [No. 126].

[160] VCH, *County of Oxford* **2**, 1907, p. 86.

[161] TNA, SC11/548; Stevenson and Salter, *St John's College*, 1939, pp. 90–91.

[162] *Letters*, p. 198: In 1498 the Reformators contributed £15 for work on the college, including the building of 'a large chamber at the end of the eastern part'—was this the library?

163 VCH, *County of Oxford* **2**, 1907, p. 86.

164 TNA, C1/1125/15.

165 Stevenson and Salter, *St John's College*, 1939, p. 29.

166 Stéphan, *Buckfast*, 1970, pp. 177, 212; Stevenson, *St John's College*, 1939, p. 43; D. M. Smith, ed. *The Heads of Religious Houses, England and Wales* **3**, *1377–1540*, Cambridge U.P., 2008, p. 319.

167 *SAP* (2), p. 373 [No. 3102].

168 D.N. Bell, *An Index of Authors and Works in Cistercian Libraries in Great Britain*, Kalamazoo: Cistercian Publications, 1992, pp. 291–94.

169 D.N. Bell, 'Hailes Abbey and its Books.' In: *Cîteaux* **61**, 2010, pp. 335–53.

170 A.G. Watson, 'A book belonging to Thomas Cleubery.' In: *Transactions of the Woolhope Naturalists Field Club*, **40**, Part 1, 1970, pp. 133–36; D.H. Williams, *White Monks in Gwent*, 1976, p. 26. The original is BL, Harley MS 218

171 D.H. Williams, 'Exeter College, Oxford, MS 1.' In: *Cîteaux* **62**, 2011, pp. 119–139.

172 *AF*, p. lxxxviii.

173 J.M. Sheppard, *The Buildwas Books*, Oxford: Oxford: Bibliographical Soc., 1997, p. lviii.

174 Winkless, *Hailes Abbey*, 1990, 51.

175 D.N. Bell, 'Hailes Abbey and its Books.' In: *Cîteaux* **61**, 2010, pp. 346–47.

176 Cross, *Monks and friars*, 1995, p. 179

177 Aveling and Pantin, *Letter Book of Robert Joseph*, 1967, pp. 106 [No. 74], 163–64 [No. 110], 215–16 [No. 143]; Bell, *Hailes and its Books*, 2010, pp. 350–53.

178 Essex R.O. D/ABW 28/46.

179 Cross, *Monks and friars*, 1995, p. 176.

180 *Letters*, p. 108 [No. 50]; *Statuta* **5**, pp. 643–44 [No. 1488/34].

181 *Letters*, pp. 123–26, 128–30 [Nos. 61–62, 64]. The then bursar of Fountains, Marmaduke Huby, blamed the abbot of Aberconwy for this royal refusal. The abbot of Chaâlis had been permitted in October 1531 to pass through England to make a visitation of the Scottish Cistercian houses: *LP* **5**, p. 233 [No. 494/2].

182 *Statuta* **5**, p. 687 [No. 1489/43].

183 Ibid. V, p. 543 [No. 1486/42].

184 *Letters*, pp. 103–05 [Nos. 45–47]; S.F. Hockey, *Beaulieu, King John's Abbey*, Beaulieu: Pioneer Publns., 1976, pp. 140–41.

185 *Letters*, pp.109–10 [No. 50], 113–14 [No. 53]; Hockey, *Beaulieu*, 1976, p. 141.

186 *Letters*, pp. 124–26 [No. 62].

187 Ibid. pp. 116–17 [No. 55]; *Statuta* **5**, p. 692 [No. 1489/54]

188 *Statuta* **6**, pp. 411–12 [No. 1491/22].

189 *Letters*, pp. 166–69 [No. 83], 174–81 [Nos. 87–88], 183 [No. 89].

190 Ibid. pp. 233 [No. 119], 250–51 [No. 129].

191 *LP* **2**, Part 1, p. 1529 [No. 3617].

192 Ibid. pp. 242–45 [No. 126]; 251–52 [No. 129].

193 Ibid. p. 242 [No. 126]. As reformators, the abbots of Ford and Stratford were not well

pleased in 1515 when Bishop Thomas Skevington, Abbot of Beaulieu, instituted a new abbot at St Mary Graces, although he was its father abbot: *Statuta* **6**, p. 475 [No. 1515/22).

194   *Letters*, pp. 257–58 [No. 130], 260 [No. 132].

195   *Statuta* **6**, p. 589 [No. 1521/86].

196   *Letters*, p. 242 [No. 126].

197   Ibid. p. 263 [No. 135]; Cf. *Statuta* **5**, pp. 692 [No. 1489/54], 695 [No. 1489/63].

198   *Statuta* **6**, p. 702–03 [No. 50]; *LP* **5**, pp. 168 [No. 361]; 456 [No. 978/6].

199   Ibid. **6**, pp. 718–19 [No. 45]: the abbots of *Woburn and St Mary Graces* were to have oversight of: Stratford, Boxley, Coggeshall, Robertsbridge, Tilty, Warden, Sawtry, Sibton, Pipewell, Garendon, Merevale, Bordesley, Stanley, Hailes, Biddlesden, Flaxley, Bruern, Stoneleigh, Thame, Rewley, Medmenham, Waverley, Beaulieu, Netley, Quarr, Bindon, Newenham, Dukeswell, 'Lynterna' [Tintern], Cleeve, Buckland, St Mary Graces, Buckfast, Kingswood, and the nunneries of Pinley, Cook Hill, Tarrant and Marham; [46]. the abbots of *Fountains and Byland* were to supervise Furness, Rievaulx, Calder, Ford [surely misplaced], Newminster, Sawley, Whalley, Kirkstead, Vaudey, Louth Park, Combermere, Vale Royal, Buildwas, Swineshead, Hulton, Croxden, Woburn and Combe, and the nunneries of Nun Appleton, Sinningthwaite, Esholt, Hampole, Wallingwells, Ardington, Ellerton, Swine, Greenfield, Kirklees, Gokewell, Nun Cotham and Newcastle.

200   *LP* **8**, pp. 23–24 [No. 74].

201   *Statuta* **5**, p. 536 [No. 1486/18].

202   *Letters*, pp. 192 [No. 95]; 198–99 [No. 97]), 210–11 [No. 103]), (213–16 [Nos. 104. 105].

203   Ibid. pp 185–86 [No. 91], 217–18 [No. 105]; Cf. *Statuta* **5**, p. 181 [No. 1497/37].

204   *Letters*, p. 220 [No. 109].

205   Ibid. pp. 239–41 [No. 125].

206   Ibid. p. 235 [No. 121].

207   TNA, E135/21/14: citation by the abbot of St Mary Graces to the abbot of Stoneleigh to attend.

208   TNA, E326/12613.

209   *Letters*, pp. 200–04 [Nos. 99–101].

210   Stéphan, *Buckfast*, 1970, pp. 181–82.

211   C. Haigh, *Last Days of the Lancashire Monasteries and the Pilgrimage of Grace*, Manchester U.P. for the Chetham Society, 1969, p. 19.

212   *Statuta* **6**, pp. 235–37 [No. 1500/22].

213   *Letters*, pp. 64 [No. 15], 73 [No. 22], 86 [No. 32].

214   Ibid. pp. 94 [No. 38], 112–13 [No. 52].

215   Elizabeth Ashworth, online entry.

216   *Letters*, pp. 120–22 [No. 59].

217   Ibid. pp. 138–39 [No. 67], 152 [No. 76], 170–72 [No. 85], 218 [No. 107].

218   *Statuta* **5**, p. 577 [No. 1487/23].

219   *Letters*, pp. 185–86 [No. 91].

220   Ibid. pp. 195–96, 232–333.

221   TNA, E328/26/vi, xvii.

222   *Letters*, pp. 96–97 [No. 39], 232 [No. 117], 151–52 [Nos. 75–76], respectively.

223   Ibid. pp. 196–98.

224   Society of Antiquaries of London MS 14, a Cistercian manual written perhaps before 1492, gives on folios 15–23 the form and order for a Cistercian visitation by a father abbot; folios 23–35 ff. 23–35: detail the proceedings for cession, resignation and election of abbots. The two lists of monks entered on the final folios suggest that this manual was once in the possession of Robertsbridge abbey, or possibly of one of the Reformators, the abbot of St Mary Graces.

225   SSC, DR18/31/5, ff. 104–105.

226   *RC*, **3**, pp. 555–61 [No. 1004], where a full transcription.

227   *Letters*, pp. 156–58 [No. 79].

228   Ibid. pp. 159–62 [No. 80].

229   G. G. Perry, 'The Visitation of the Monastery of Thame.' In: *EHR* **3**, 1888, pp. 705–22. For a summary: VCH, *County of Oxford* **2**, 1907, pp. 84–85; Baskerville, *English Monks*, 1937, p. 91.

230   *Reg. J. Longland*, Lincoln R.O., ff. 109r–110r.

231   VCH, *Cumberland* **2**, London, 1968, pp. 170–71.

232   TNA, E135/3/16.

3 THE CLAUSTRAL OFFICERS AND THE ABBOTS

THE SMOOTH LIFE of a religious community meant that talented monks would be given specific posts within their monastery, which in some cases led to higher promotion as the years passed by. Thomas Marston of Fountains progressed from being his abbot's chaplain to the office of bursar by 1507, and then served as cellarer there from 1509 to 1517. William Kere, cellarer of Tintern from 1476 became its abbot in 1488. William Huddleston, kitchener of Stratford in 1514, was later to be sub-prior (1521) and then abbot (from 1524).

Other posts which needed to be filled included those of: sub-cellarer [this may have been equivalent to 'kitchener' and 'provisioner']—as Anthony Symondson, Holm Cultram, 1538)]; pitancier (as John Foster at Whalley, 1536); porter (now the days of the *conversi* were past) as Richard Marston (Whalley, 1536); precentor (as Richard Eddon, Hailes, 1537); sacrist (like William Robinson at Merevale, 1538), granger/granary keeper (as William Wotton, Kingswood, 1538); monk of the bakehouse (Stephen Burghe, Rievaulx, 1533) and monk of the brew-house (like Stephen Staynthorpe, Rievaulx, 1533). By the Suppression some of these latter positions were fulfilled by laity. At the apex of community life stood the sub-prior (such as Thomas Lilborne, the last sub-prior of Louth Park), prior (like Brian Gardner, the last prior of Furness), and then the abbot, in ascending order.

Bursars

The position of bursar, a monastery's chief financial and accounting officer, was an important and influential one, and could be a prelude to greater things, and the names of seven who served in this position are known. It was in this office that Marmaduke Huby of Fountains first made his mark on the English Cistercian scene; a later abbot there, Marmaduke Bradley, also briefly served in this role (1515–1517). Yet another Fountains bursar, Thomas Merston, went on to become that abbey's cellarer for some years (1509–1517). For Robert Langton, the last bursar of Holm Cultram, the position meant a slightly enhanced pension, £6 rather than the average there of £4 or £4-13-4. For the bursar of Whalley, it gave a special office—"the bursar's house", the chattels of which in 1537 included two 'playent bowlls,' a minstrel's scutcheon, a little scutcheon bearing a black lion and a large standing parcel gilt pounced bowl.[1] The penultimate bursar of Meaux, George Throstill, was bequeathed 7s 6d in 1539 for acting as executor of a will.[2]

A few bursars played a not unimportant part in the tense time of the Reformation. It was in the chamber of Richard Newport, bursar of Woburn in 1538, that a conversation took place that was reported to the authorities concerning the dangerous book *De Potestate Petri* by Sir John Milward of Toddington.[3] Henry Jenkinson, a monk of Kirkstead, claimed that during the Lincolnshire Rising (Chapter 4) all except his abbot joined a rebel host at Horncastle with 'the cellarer and bursar horsed and with battle axes, the rest unhorsed'.[4] It was the bursar who brought the rebels money and provisions.[5] When it was alleged by the curate of Woburn (William Shirborne) that some of the papal bulls favouring that abbey had been hidden in his chapel, its abbot testified that his bursar had collected all papal bulls and handed them over to the Visitor, Dr Petre.[6]

Cellarers

If the position of bursar was significant, even much more so was that of the monastic cellarer. Having a general oversight of an abbey's estate and of its trade, the Cistercian cellarer was often well travelled and possessive of a wide range of contacts. No wonder that a number of cellarers proceeded to abbatial status directly from running the business affairs of his monastery. The names of over thirty cellarers of the Tudor period are on record, no less than twelve of these served Tintern abbey between 1476 and 1536. Those cellarers' names are on record in a series of extant court rolls, as they sat taking second place to the presiding lay steward or his deputy at the abbey courts.[7] Unless Tintern had two successive monks bearing the same name, then one of its cellarers was John Earl who performed the duties of cellarer there for much of the years stretching from 1448 to 1493.[8] When Tintern was suppressed in 1536, one of its monks, Nicholas Acton, performed the duties of cellarer at its daughter-house of Kingswood until that abbey closed two years later.[9]

Generally speaking cellarers, because of their previous responsibilities, were awarded slightly higher pensions at the Suppression than most of their confrères. It was usually a marginal difference: the monks of Combe mostly received an annual pension of £5-6-8; their last cellarer £6. Other cellarers so to do included those of Combe, Dunkeswell and Vale Royal.[10] A £6 pension was also recommended for that officer at Biddlesden.[11] Thomas Graham at Holm Cultram gained the sum of £6-13-4—possibly in compensation for having been passed over for the abbacy there. When in 1538 Beaulieu was dissolved, its cellarer, Richard Frye, was awarded but a £5 pension, which prompted his former abbot to seek for him an increase to £6-13-4, but in 1539 he became rector of Farley, Hampshire.[12]

The offices of the Cistercian cellarer were generally housed in the lower part of the west range, and part of the cellarer's store survives at Dunkeswell;[13] more completely elsewhere as at Furness. His 'little chamber' found mention when Hailes was suppressed.[14] Occasionally cellarers' accounts are extant showing the breadth of their activity. In 1536 the cellarer of Whalley balanced his books chiefly because of rents from tenants in the villages of Whalley and of Staining in the Fylde. His expenditure included payments for hay-making, the grinding and winnowing of barley and oats, and wages to servants, including the abbey's merchants. One of his purchases was 'sea-coal'.[15] The two extant cellarers' rolls from Tintern are early and mid-fifteenth century in date.[16]

The cellarer would be a constant visitor to all his monastery's properties; the cellarer of Fountains being harassed in 1526 at its Lune fishery.[17] He could need to travel further afield on business, as when John Ledys, the cellarer of Byland, journeyed to York in 1522 to hand over a £50 loan from his monastery.[18] In Tudor times with the growing importance of lay stewards, and in the closing years the emergence of lay receivers-general for monastic lands, the significance of the cellarer's office waned. Thus Fountains in 1538 appointed Sir Henry Norton as its receiver-general 'in the same way that Thomas Ripon, cellarer, had hitherto done.'[19]

The position of cellarer as a stepping-stone towards the holding of an abbacy was quite common within the Cistercian Order. Indeed, in 1238, its General Chapter had insisted that no monk was to be appointed prior or cellarer unless he was of such quality that he might be considered fit to be promoted abbot.[20] The records are sketchy, and the number of cellarers promoted to an abbacy must be far higher than the eight on record, while of those eight four were cellarers of Tintern. One cellarer, William Stile, cellarer of Woburn and cousin of its abbot, became in 1533 abbot of Vaudey; both were 'sister-abbeys', having been directly colonised from Fountains. William Fladbury, cellarer of Warden, became in late 1534 abbot of its daughter house of Sibton.[21]

Not all cellarers who aspired to become abbot were fortunate: John Dalton, cellarer of Furness by 1515/16 did become its abbot briefly in an undignified and divisive dispute, whilst Thomas Graham was passed over at Holm Cultram losing out to Gawin Borowdale, a much favoured monk, despite offering Cromwell a bribe of 400 marks.[22] In the last months of its existence, in May 1538, the last cellarer of Bordesley, Richard Whittington, tried to engineer the resignation of its abbot, John Day (abbot 1519–1538), whom he said had been abbot for twenty years and was 'aged, impotent, sick, and also not of perfect remembrance.' He sought the assistance of an influential layman, Thomas Evans, asking him to assure Cromwell that if he became abbot he would surrender the monastery, He failed in his bid, but Evans got what he wanted—a lease of the abbey site and home farm.[23]

Sub-cellarers

There is little note of the work of the cellarer's deputy in documentation of the Tudor period, and only a few monks who held that office are known by name. It is very probable that the terms 'sub-cellarer', 'kitchener' and 'provisioner' were interchangeable.[24] This was certainly the case at Whalley where James More was described both as kitchener and sub-cellarer.[25] His accounts for 1536 show that he obtained two-thirds of his income from the sale of animal skins. It exceeded his expenditure, which included the buying in of honey, capons and pullets, geese and goslings. He had care of the fish-pond—a traditional duty of sub-cellarers, but no expenditure was necessary with regard to it.[26] The food purchases of the 'kitchener' of Vaudey suggests that he was also the sub-cellarer.[27] The last sub-cellarer of Furness was Richard Skales who, on his monastery's closure in 1537, transferred to Rushen abbey (Isle of Man).

Closely associated with the work of the sub-cellarer was that of the *pitancier* whose job it was to provide for special supplementary dishes from funds bequeathed, and on days allotted by a benefactor of former years. The *pitancier* at Whalley (John Foster in 1536) gained his income mostly by a grant from the bursars and by the sale of animal skins; his income that year was £47 but his expenditure £93. Half of his expenditure was on meat [beef, mutton, lamb, chiefly, but also pork, chicken and goose]; fish accounted for half as much, and was mostly 'fresh fish', but with lesser quantities of dried and salted fish, red and white herrings, salmon and eels. The pitancier also paid for almonds, olive oil, honey, butter and cheese, pepper and saffron, as well as for timber (for fuel) and the wages of the kitchen servants.[28]

The Priors

An abbot's second-in-command, and stand-in when he was absent was the prior (the 'first' of the brethren), sitting opposite him in quire. His regular duties included presiding in the refectory, arranging the daily labour, and making the periodic arrangements for blood-letting; they came to the fore when taking charge during a vacancy in an abbacy. The thirteenth-century regulations provided that they be chosen by the abbot after consulting with 'God-fearing brethren,' and they were to be monks of such calibre that they could be promoted to an abbacy themselves.[29] In Tudor times, such elevations include those of Oliver Adams at Combe, John Corne [Cory] at Netley, John King at Buckfast and John Palmer at Tilty. Some priors remained in their position until middle-aged or elderly. Such included John Stanford of Warden—who was not fearful of severely criticising his abbot during a visitation; Christopher Smyth of Whalley, eighty years old when the house closed in 1537, and Richard Bromley of Valle Crucis—passed over for the abbacy in 1528, then declining it in 1534.

There were priors who had known difficulties in their earlier monastic life. Michael Hamerton, the last prior of Furness, had been imprisoned in The Fleet in 1515/1516 during the schism in his community between Abbots Banks and Dalton. Richard Norton, the last prior of Bruern, rose to the office of prior despite being for two lengthy periods detained in The Fleet prison; firstly, from 7 April 1526 until 22 June 1527 'for various crimes and offences,' and then again from about the spring of 1529 until early 1530. On the former occasion, his abbot refused to pay the £14 account for Richard's board and lodging in The Fleet, saying that whilst there he had been saying Masses and acting as chaplain of The Fleet.[30] Writing a letter 'in the Fleet, Monday after Twelfth Day' [10 January 1530] Richard told that he had been detained there for three-quarters of a year on the order of Cardinal Wolsey, on charges of stealing his abbey's common seal—which he denied, and of bringing his abbey's plate to the abbot of Garendon in London. He explained that the plate was pledged to a Mr Horne of Oxford, now deceased, and redeemed by the abbot of Garendon who delivered it back to Bruern.[31] Bruern and Garendon were sister abbeys, both founded by Waverley. Richard's eventual appointment as prior cannot have been much consolation for his sufferings.

In charge at Aberconwy around 1481/1482, following the death of its Abbot Reginald, was its prior, Gruffydd Goch. Despite 'the poverty of the abbey', Gruffydd awarded two sizeable annual pensions to two of the monks—one the son of the late abbot, and also granted that monk's mother a house. The General Chapter in 1482 ordered an investigation into these arrangements.[32] The son was probably Ieuan ap Reginald, a scholar in 1468 when said to have been born of an unmarried woman and a Cistercian abbot.[33] Gruffydd again took control at Aberconwy when a Welsh element in the community challenged the appointment of David Wynchcombe, a monk of Hailes, as its abbot. The Crown therefore in 1484 ordered the abbey's tenants to render their rents to Prior Gruffydd.[34] By 1494 he appears to have become a short-lived abbot of Cymer.

A prior whose name became known for the wrong reasons was Thomas Hamond of Combermere. On 11 February 1520 John Jenyns, a tanner and servant of the abbey, slew one of the monks (surnamed Ottewell) with a dagger thrust to the heart. The dead man's brother alleged later to the Court of Star Chamber that the prior tried to cover up the event, saying that 'this abbey is already in an evil name for using of misrule.' He refused to make the murder public and swore all to secrecy, allowing Jenyns to stay on as a barker. Eventually, however, Jenyns was arrested on a charge of felony and placed in Chester prison. The prior seems to have taken the initiative in this evasion of the facts; the abbot's view is not known.[35]

Another prior who took the lead, perhaps because his abbot, William Bewdley, was absent, was Thomas Reding, the prior of Kingswood. Early in 1535 he had tried to ingratiate himself with Thomas Cromwell with a thesis in support of the king's supremacy. On 19 September 1536 or 1537, together with Nicholas Acton, the cellarer, Reding wrote again to Cromwell pleading for forgiveness for any shortcomings. Acton wrote: 'You have tempered mercy with justice. In discharging our consciences we did acknowledge our offences through the scrutiny made by your commissary, submitting ourselves to you. Begging that you will regard us with an eye of pity.' It was an appeal for the continuance of their monastery, but it was suppressed on 1 February 1538.[36] Not unknown for monks in those days, Reding found relaxation in hunting. Alas for him, while taking part in illegal hunting in Crown forest land in Gloucestershire in June/July 1535, he was severely beaten by the keepers.[37]

Something of the duties of a prior, as they were seen in Tudor times, comes in the prescriptions of the visitations alluded to. At Warden in 1492, where the aged prior seemed unable to control his monks, he was reminded to ensure that they heard and understood the statutes and customs of the Order. Similar instructions were given to the prior of Thame (1526). At Rufford (1481) there was mention of the prior and sub-prior making an inspection of the dorter both at night and at mid-day, to ensure that no monks were absent from the house.

The position of the prior meant that certainly in this period he had sleeping accommodation of his own. When the visitors at Rufford (1481) insisted that the private chambers that had been made in the dorter be dismantled, the chambers of the prior and sub-prior were excepted. In its last years, a prior's chamber was built at Bruern at a cost of £10.[38] When Hailes closed, not only were all the glass and iron of its prior's chamber sold, but also its ceiling—perhaps this was of carved oak or even painted.[39] The remains of the supposed prior's chamber of Tintern are yet to be seen.

The former responsibilities of a prior also meant that his pension in later life was generally raised two or three pounds above the level received by the ordinary monks of his old house. It was still very lowly compared to that of the abbot whom he had served. For some reason, Alexander Sedon of Vale Royal, was awarded the princely sum of £12 annually. The best most priors could hope for was £8—as granted to the former priors of Combermere, Fountains, Ford, Hailes, and Stratford. Richard Green of Thame received £7; the priors of Byland, Kingswood and Newenham, £6-13-4—about the average; the prior of Dieulacres but £6, and of Holm Cultram but £5-6-8.

A special case was the last prior of Bindon, John Andrews, who received an annuity of £8 'in consideration of a corrody of £10 which he had under convent seal and which he hath surrendered to the king.'[40] For some reason, when Garendon was 'surveyed' on 24 June 1536, Andrews was staying there.[41] Another prior who received a corrody in his house was John Webb when in 1528 he retired as prior of Cleeve. On account of his 'good and diligent service' in that office he was given the use of the 'firmary chamber in the posterior part of the monastery', a stipend of £3 annually, and the usual rights of firewood, bread and ale. He had the right to a place in choir and chapter, but if he wished he could live elsewhere and still draw his pension. Presenting the evidence of his corrody at the Court of Augmentations on 14 May 1539, he was awarded an annual compensatory pension of £8, together with £16 arrears.[42]

Sub-Priors

The sub-prior was the monk who generally assisted the prior, and took his place if he were absent or ill. In particular he had an especial concern for the discipline of his community, while the Order's statutes prescribed that he should 'animate' the monks in quire, and make good any short-comings on the part of the precentor or sacristan.[43] A sub-prior might well play an occasional role outside the precincts of his abbey, whilst at Hailes[44] and Rufford,[45] and very probably at other monasteries, he came to have a chamber of his own. The expertise he acquired from his duties might give him a stepping-stone to an abbacy, as for William Huddleston at Stratford and Christopher Massey of Combermere. After the Suppression a sub-prior's pension might be greater than that afforded his confrères: as at Roche £6-13-4 as opposed to £5, at Tilty, £6-13-4 against £5-6-8, and at Biddlesden £6 as opposed to £5-6-8, but at Kingswood and Holm Cultram only £4. The best rewarded sub-prior was John Lawrence of Bindon with £7 yearly.[46]

It was the sub-prior of Furness who, when its abbot died in 1497, sought on behalf of the monks the presence of Abbey Huby of Fountains to conduct the election for a new abbot.[47] Similarly, when Abbot Ireby of Holm Cultram died in 1534, the list of signatures appealing to Cromwell for leave to elect a new abbot was headed by that of Christopher Nevinson, its sub-prior.[48] The need in both instances was urgent: at Furness because of a divided community, at Holm Cultram because the monks were 'continually exposed to danger from raids of the Scots.' At both Boxley (1516) and Rufford (1523) the sub-prior played a major part in the election of a new abbot. In August 1500 the sub-prior of Stratford accompanied the abbot of Strata Marcella to the following month's General Chapter, as the representatives of all the abbots. His character was highly praised.[49] John Wakerley, the sub-prior of Stoneleigh, arbitrated in 1510 in a local dispute.[50]

Alas! Not all sub-priors were plaster saints: the sub-prior of Warden was said in 1492 to frequent taverns; a successor there in 1535 was allegedly caught with a woman in the monastery vineyard.[51] When his abbot, Richard Prehest, died in 1516, John Palmer, the sub-prior of St Mary Graces who was present at his death, took his keys and opened a chest in the abbot's chamber containing £500 of which he took £200. He then absconded, using the money 'to buy a capacity,' and was 'walking abroad and living unreligiously.' The new abbot, Henry More, sought his summons to appear before the Court of Chancery.[52] Palmer, however, on 31 July 1516 obtained his 'capacity'—permission from the papacy to hold a secular benefice. He was also allowed by the Holy See to have for life not only 'a stall in the choir, and an active and passive voice in the chapter,' but also 'a room in the dormitory'.[53] Could he be the John Palmer who was the last abbot of Tilty?

When in 1535 Abbot Emery of Warden sought to resign, one of his laments was that he had 'often commanded the sub-prior and the *custos ordinis* that no secular boys should be conversant with any of the monks or lie in the dorter.'[54] This statement draws attention to another monastic official but rarely mentioned: the 'keeper of order' or 'the keeper of the Order'. This, presumably senior monk, clearly had a role to play in upholding high standards in his monastery. He was a feature of at least some Cistercian monasteries from the mid-thirteenth century, but his duties were seemingly never clearly defined.[55] Presumably the 'keeper' was appointed rather than elected by his fellows, and might have had an equivalent role to that of foreman in a factory.

The 'keeper' is perhaps to be equated with the 'president' named in certain Cistercian abbeys. The visitors at Warden in 1492 enjoined that 'no-one was to absent themselves from reading time, divine office or the refectory without permission from the president,' who was also to ensure that none were missing from the dorter.[56] The visitors at Thame in 1526 required its 'president' to ensure that no one was absent from the daily chapter meeting.[57] On first reading it might be assumed that 'president' meant who-ever was in charge at a particular time. That he was an assigned monk bearing this title was shown, however, when Thomas More as 'president' of St Mary Graces presented a candidate for ordination in 1521/22,[58] and in the listing of Thomas Longbothom in 1538 as the last 'president' at Revesby.[59] It has been suggested that within the Order the term 'president' initially referred to the 'abbot'.[60]

The Abbots: Election and Benediction

When a vacancy occurred in an abbacy, its community proceeded to the election of a new superior.[61] The abbot of its mother-house would normally preside with another abbot assisting him. The early customs of the Order provided that the election should be conducted 'according to the will and counsel of the father-abbot,'—he could very much influence the outcome of the proceedings. A papal bull granted in 1265 in favour of the Cistercians provided that henceforth the prior, sub-prior and cellarer, of a vacant monastery were to play a prime role in deciding upon nominations.[62] This could limit the free choice of the community as a whole, and it explains why at abbatial elections at Rufford in 1516[63] and at Robertsbridge in 1523[64] the sub-prior had a prominent part.

At Rufford the sub-prior and two of the senior monks denoted the names of the candidates chosen; at Boxley election was by the sub-prior and 'the electors' in the chapter-house. Did all the monks have a vote, or only the seniors? When Abbot Huby conducted an election at Furness in 1497 the total number of votes cast was twenty-six; in that instance all the community appear to have voted, though perhaps there were a couple of abstentions.[65] When in 1514 Abbot Skevington presided at the election of Richard Prehest at St Mary Graces, 'the convent met in one body for the election.' Although the monks are said to have 'harmoniously elected' Richard, the need to obtain papal confirmation suggests that there were some not content.[66]

The centuries-old procedures were followed at both elections. At Rufford after the death of Abbot Roger Balke on 25 June 1516, Abbot William of Rievaulx, assisted by the abbot of Newminster, held the election on 4 July in its chapter-house; fulfilling the statutory requirement of an election within fifteen days.[67] After the invocation of the Holy Spirit and the casting of votes, the votes were received before the high altar by the scrutineers and notaries. One of the monks, Roland Blyton, was chosen unanimously, and by the Visitors 'confirmed and admitted.' The Te Deum was sung, the church bells were rung, and the new abbot placed in his stall in the quire. Installed again in his seat in the chapter-house, he swore on the gospels to observe the customs of the Order, the keys and abbey seal were delivered to him, and the monks singly made their profession of obedience before him.

The same sequence of events took place at Robertsbridge, following the death of Abbot William Brekyn.[68] Its father-abbot of Boxley, accompanied by the abbot of St Mary Graces, presided there at the election not of one of its community, but of Thomas Taylor, a monk of Boxley. After his installation in quire and chapter-house, all the 'obstinate' monks pledged their obedience to him, whilst the Visitors exhorted peace and tranquillity in the community. Does the term 'obstinate' mean here 'difficult' or 'rebellious', or does it rather mean 'unwavering' in their monastic vocation? Writing in 1479 to the archbishop of York, the abbot of Newminster told how, as father-abbot of Roche and with the abbot of Rufford assisting him, he had presided at the election of William Tickhill as abbot of Roche. He told how 'we confirmed him and led him into the church and installed him, and brought him back into the chapter-house, and bound him by an oath and did all other things requisite.'[69]

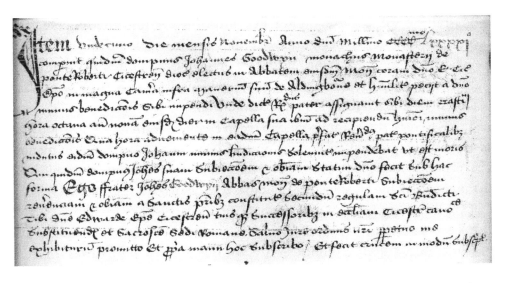

Fig. 9: The Record of the Blessing and Profession of Obedience of Abbot John Goodwin of Robertsbridge (1491)
By kind permission of West Sussex Record Office: EPI/1/3, folios 91/92

Certainly the appointment of a new abbot was not always appreciated, as Abbot Henry Emery of Sibton found when he was translated to Warden (1534), where some monks 'vexed him with many uncharitable surmises and opprobious words.'[70] At Furness Abbot Roger Pyle, who took over in 1531, found it necessary to imprison within two years a group of rebellious monks led by Richard Banks, perhaps a relative of his predecessor. Eventually Banks was exiled to the Isle of Man to take charge of one of the abbey's churches there.[71] Even the caring Thomas Stevens, who transferred in 1536 from the abbacy of Netley to that of Beaulieu, found some of his new monks uncooperative. When Beaulieu had closed, Stevens wrote: 'Thank God, I am rid of my lewd monks.'[72] These cases were sad, and should not be taken as typical.

Shortly after being elected and installed, a new Cistercian abbot would travel to where-ever the local diocesan bishop happened to be, or a suffragan acting on his behalf, in order to promise him 'canonical subjection and obedience,' and to receive his blessing. As Cistercians were exempt from direct episcopal jurisdiction, this obedience would related to the possession by a monastery of spiritualities—churches and tithes, within the diocese. To respect Cistercian privilege a new abbot's promise was qualified by the insertion of the phrase 'saving my Order,' or 'saving our Order,' or 'saving the right of my Order.' In other words, he pledged his obedience to the diocesan bishop so far as Cistercian law and custom would allow.

It was to make this promise and to receive a blessing, that Abbot Goodwin of Robertsbridge went to the bishop of Chichester's Aldingbourne manor chapel on 12 November 1491;[73] that Abbot London of Tilty presented himself in the church of the Hospital of St Thomas Martyr of Acon, London on 7 April 1515 to be blessed by John de Riperia, O. Pr. titular bishop of Gallipoli;[74] and that Thomas Chalner, abbot of Croxden went to the bishop of Lichfield at his palace at Beaudesert, Cannock Chase, for this purpose on 21 May 1531.[75] Abbot Thomas Oliver of Buckland in 1463 and John Toker of the same house in 1528, both received their benediction in Exeter Cathedral.[76]

It may have been doubts as to his suitability which caused a two year delay before Abbot Glyn of Dore was blessed by the bishop of Hereford on 22 March 1526 at the chapel of his Whitbourne manor.[77] In 1509 two Cistercian abbots were blessed by the bishop of Winchester in his Esher manor chapel—Richard Totnam of Quarr [3 March] and John Cory of Netley [22 December].[78] Exceptionally, Abbot Henry More of St Mary Graces made his obedience in his own monastery church before Bishop John de Riperia on 7 May 1516.[79] Either urgency or difficult circumstances in Wales meant that Abbot Wynch-combe of Aberconwy, a monk of Hailes, was blessed on 31 January 1482, by leave of the bishop of Bangor, by the bishop of Worcester in the chapel of his country residence, Hartlebury Castle.[80]

Newly elected abbots generally had held positions of responsibility in their monastery,[81] like John Palmer who had been sub-prior (1521) and prior (1528) of Tilty before becoming its abbot. Oliver Adams of Combe had previously been its prior; John Alanbridge of Byland was formerly its cellarer, and Thomas Stevens of Netley was once its 'receiver'. Monks of a mother-house might be elected superior of a daughter abbey—Warden provided John Clifton to the abbacy of Sibton, and Henry Clopton and William Angell to the abbacy of Sawtry. William Bewdley, a monk of Bordesley, became abbot of its daughter-house of Flaxley, and then of Kingswood (a foundation from Tintern). Lawrence Marre (1514) and John Clapham (1522) moved from Furness to assume the abbacy of Calder, its daughter-house.

Other monks promoted from a mother house to a daughter abbey included Edward Tyrry going from Fountains to Newminster and Thomas Taylor from Boxley to Robertsbridge. Some moves paid no respect to the particular 'family' or 'generation' of a monastery. Abbot Quicke moved from his abbacy at Cleeve (of the family of Clairvaux) to Beaulieu (of the generation of Cîteaux); William Ripon, a monk of Beaulieu, moved to be abbot of Quarr, once of the congregation of Savigny, whilst Richard Wyche transferred from Whalley (of the Clairvaux family) to Tintern (of the generation of Cîteaux). The hand of two successive abbots of St Mary Graces, as Reformators of the Order in England, may be seen in two of its monks going to abbacies elsewhere: John London to Tilty in 1515 and John Redborne to Dore in 1529.

A striking feature of Tudor Cistercian life was the number of abbots who received a university education; frequently completing their studies after their installation. This seems to have been a deliberate policy for the good of the Order, and the monasteries with graduate-abbots were often the most stable as the dissolution approached. Some fifteen Cistercian abbots of England in Tudor times were Oxford graduates, and there may be others whose education has not been traced. They included well known personalities like Chard of Ford, Dunne of Buckfast, King of Bruern and Skevington of Beaulieu, but also lesser known abbots such as Adams of Combe, Deveys of Holm Cultram and Scrope of Meaux.

In the period of 1501–40 at least seven Welsh abbots studied at Oxford.[82] They included: (presumably) Abbot John Lloyd of Valle Crucis ('doctor of both laws' by 1518);[83] David ab Owain, abbot of Strata Marcella and Aberconwy (D.C.L.); Lleision ap Thomas of Neath (abbot by 1510, B.Can.L. in 1511, B.D. in 1512); and Richard Talley of Strata Florida (abbot perhaps by 1516, B.D. in 1526).). It did not bode well for the Order in north Wales that two monks became abbots whilst still quite young; and both undoubtedly owing their promotion to being members of locally important and influential families.

One was the youthful Hugh ap Rhys of Aberconwy who died in 1528 whilst a Cambridge undergraduate, and was buried at Saffron Walden. The other was Robert Salusbury, created abbot of Valle Crucis by March, 1528, with a dispensation from Cardinal Wolsey—perhaps because he was under-age. After life at the monastery deteriorated under his rule, the Reformator for Wales (Lleision ap Thomas of Neath) and other Visitors sent him to Oxford 'there to continue at his school and learning.' Alas! once there he became the leader of a robber band, and was committed for at least three months to the Tower of London.[84] He was replaced by a monk of St Mary Graces, John Heron (*al.* Durham), who borrowed £200 from Sir William Penyson to meet the expenses of 'his induction and installation.' The terms of the agreement were such that in December 1536 the Court of Augmentations awarded Sir William £110 in satisfaction of the debt.[85]

It is not certain how many British Cistercian abbots received papal authority to wear pontifical insignia: mitre and gloves. The first appears to have been Abbot Richard Gower of Jervaulx, who distinguished himself by representing at their behest the clergy of the province of York at the General Council called to meet at Pisa in 1409, to endeavour to mend the schism in the papacy. Shortly afterwards he and his successors were empowered by Pope Alexander V to wear the mitre, ring, and other pontifical insignia, and in the monastery and its subject priories and the churches belonging to it to give solemn benediction after mass, vespers and matins, provided that no bishop or papal legate were present. [86] The continuance of these rights meant that the mitre was included in the rebus on a surviving chasuble bearing the initials of Abbot Robert Thornton (1511–1533).[87]

Abbot John Ripon of Fountains around 1412 received the like privilege, but it was annulled in 1420 as his entitlement had been granted by the deposed anti-pope John XXIII.[88] It was renewed when in 1459 Abbot John Grenewell of Fountains gained papal leave to wear 'the mitre, ring, gloves and other pontifical insignia.' Again, he was not to give a solemn blessing at a service when a bishop was present. In the request for the re-granting of this entitlement it was pointed out that Abbot Greenwell was 'held in great honour and reverence', that he was 'the visitor and reformator of all monasteries of the Cistercian Order in England and adjacent parts,' and that his monastery was 'reputed very important, notable and very opulent.'[89] The like privilege was granted to the abbots Beaulieu and of St Mary Graces in 1415, Coggeshall in 1427, Warden in 1429 and Stratford in 1448.[90] Again, apart from pontificating in their own abbeys, they could also do so in their daughter-houses and appropriated churches.

That other abbots possessed the privilege of pontificals comes from knowledge of their accoutrements. At a survey of the effects of Fountains made by Abbot Kirkby of Rievaulx and the dean of Ripon in around 1530 two mitres encrusted with silver gilt were recorded as well as two crosiers with silver heads.[91] The abbot of Ford included a mitre in his heraldic bearings.[92] Hailes had mitres also furnished with silver gilt, and its last abbot, Stephen Sagar, faced with the costs of a journey to London in August 1538, feared that the sale of the best mitre might be necessary to recoup costs.[93] Abbot Huby of Fountains had a mitre as part of his coat of arms.

The abbot of Thame was present, mitred, at the funeral in Peterborough Cathedral in January 1536 of Queen Katherine,[94] whilst on 10 April 1524 Richard Bank wrote from Hornby Castle to Lord Darcy, that the abbot of Furness had been at Lord Monteagle's funeral 'with all his pontifical stuff.'[95]. The abbot of Thame was mitred because he was now a suffragan bishop. When in 1526 an inventory of the goods of Thame was made, shortly before his predecessor resigned or was deposed, three pastoral staffs for the abbot's use were noted in the abbey's sacristy, but there was no mention of a mitre.[96] No record tells when abbots of Rievaulx became mitred, but the inventory made there at its closure mentions a 'mitour of paest set with perles.'[97]

Leo X in 1516 granted Abbot John Paslew of Whalley and his successors the right to use pontificals, namely 'an embroidered mitre adorned with gems, dalmatic, episcopal gloves adorned with gems, grey almuce, ring, pastoral staff and other episcopal insignia.' The inventory of the goods of Whalley made at the Suppression bears this out, referring to a mitre of silver and gold set with sapphires, emeralds and other jewels, as well as a pair of gloves adorned with pearls and sapphires, a mitre of needlework and two silver pastoral staffs.[98] It is difficult to believe the abbots of Whalley had not previously been granted the right to the mitre. It is possible that the deed of 1517 was a confirmatory grant, as it includes powers permitting the conferring of the minor orders, and the blessing of sacred vessels, 'even tabernacles in which the sacrament of the Eucharist is kept.'

Julius II, in 1508, gave the same pontifical privileges, and of conferring admission to the four minor orders, to Robert Chambers, abbot of Holm Cultram, but with the *caveat* that he did not impart a solemn blessing if a bishop were present.[99] Amongst the effects recorded at Tintern on its closure was a crosier but no mitre.[100]

Controversial Appointments and Elections

The ability of a Cistercian community to freely elect whom they chose to be their new abbot faded somewhat in Tudor times; firstly, because of the over-riding authority of the Reformators; secondly, because of the influence of Cardinal Wolsey, thirdly, on account of the wide-ranging rights Thomas Cromwell came to enjoy as vicar-general, and fourthly, where powerful secular neighbours pressurised monks into choosing an abbot of their liking. Election of an abbot could now be a costly business, and it was not unknown for Cromwell to be offered large sums of money in an attempt to secure an abbacy. As the Suppression approached there may also have been a determined effort on the part of some monks to gain an abbacy in the hope of a large pension when their monastery closed.

One of the longest serving abbots was Thomas Oliver of Buckland who, after it seems an Oxford education,[101] was blessed as abbot in Exeter Cathedral on 20 March 1463. A few years later he was deprived of his abbacy by his father-abbot from Quarr, who by 1469 had installed the prior, William Breton, in his place. Oliver did not accept his demotion, but imprisoned Breton and held the abbey by force. He was certainly *de facto* abbot by 1476 and was such until the early years of the sixteenth century. A Lancastrian by sympathy and proscribed by Richard III, when Henry VII became monarch in 1485, Oliver's position was assured.[102]

One of the first acts of Marmaduke Huby of Fountains as a Reformator was to travel to Furness abbey in July 1497 at the request of its community to preside at the election of a new abbot. Both candidates Huby saw as 'ambitious monks'; the one was the cellarer who gained fifteen votes, the other a monk with a B. Th. degree who received eleven votes. Huby felt that this result might lead to further division in its community so, after consulting with his assessors and the 'wiser and senior' monks, he laid the election aside and appointed a thirty-year old monk, Alexander Banks, said to be 'learned in science and literature and who led a virtuous life.'[103] It was an appointment which in retrospect proved to be regrettable, as was shown in 1500 when the General Chapter gave Banks a dispensation on account of various irregularities, simony and other crimes. His rehabilitation was the work of Huby and his fellow reformators, the abbots of Stratford and St Mary Graces. By this time, too, it was noted that John Dalton, the former cellarer, had with others been allegedly conspiring against Banks.[104]

Banks' abbacy continued to give grave concern, and eventually Henry VIII ordered a visitation of the monastery. It was carried out by the abbots of Stratford (a Reformator), Whalley, Sawley and Calder (adjacent abbeys), who came to Furness on 27 February 1514 only to find that Banks had gathered a protective force of three hundred mercenaries. It was ten days before he could be deposed, and in his place the cellarer, John Dalton, unanimously elected, seemingly with the support of the abbey Steward, the earl of Derby.

Banks was furious, appealed to the court of the archbishop of York, and for the space of six months frequented the king's court. Bank also appealed to Rome and on 16 May 1514 Leo X requested the abbots of Fountains, Byland and Meaux, to investigate the matter. The pontiff understood that the abbot of Stratford, Reformator of the Order, at the instigation of Thomas Stanley, earl of Derby, and Alexander's 'capital enemy,' had summoned Alexander to appear before him, not at Furness but in the chapter-house of the Dominican friary in Lancaster. Alexander had told Rome that Lancaster 'was a place well known to be unsafe for him to appear in person,' and that in his absence William Hickman of Stratford had deprived him of his abbacy, appointed Dalton and intruded him into the abbey. Leo X told the three investigating abbots to lift the sentence of excommunication of Alexander, and to remedy the principal matter if they found Alexander was in the right, and to invoke the aid of the secular arm if necessary.[105]

With the help of influential people Alexander had Abbot Dalton and four of his monks thrown into the Fleet Prison on 9 September 1514, and there they languished for sixty-seven weeks.[106] That done, Banks returned to Furness with an armed force, and cast a further four of its monks into Lancaster prison. He then remained as abbot until his death in 1531. On 2 February 1516 Nicholas de Aretis, auditor in Rome of the Apostolic Chamber, issued a decree in favour of Dalton and the eight confined monks.[107] This may have been the cause of their release by the king and his council, but Dalton was still in The Fleet when he wrote a letter of appeal to Cîteaux on 29 April 1517.[108] Their board and lodging together with fuel at the Fleet amounted to a total of £146-11-4. They left without paying this, and Abbot Banks refused to reimburse this sum to the Fleet authorities.[109] Dalton himself told how he had survived in The Fleet 'on the charity of the faithful.'[110]

As for Dalton, once back at Furness life must have been very difficult; he was described as 'pretended abbot' in 1528, and was still alive in 1532 when no more than a simple monk.[111] As for Banks his troubles were not over. In his efforts to regain the abbacy he had promised its steward, Sir William Compton, a close friend of Henry VIII, £200 for his assistance. He laid down £50, and then as he had not helped Banks, Sir William remitted the remainder to him, but did not return the bond. Compton died in 1528 and, having the bond, his executors commenced an action of debt against the abbot.[112] The whole episode is an indication that the Order's machinery could be weak and unable to enforce rightful decisions.

Another instance where influential laity played a role came when a new abbot of Hulton had to be found. The earl of Shrewsbury gave his backing to a monk of the abbey, William Chalner, whose brother was abbot of Croxden. Shrewsbury wrote from his seat at Sheffield Castle on 28 August 1535 to Cromwell, saying that Chalner was supported by most of his brethren and was a person of 'good learning, living and wisdom.' The very next day Sir Philip Draycot, the monastery's steward, also wrote to Cromwell giving a very different report, telling him, 'I am bold to tell the truth,' and asserted that Chalner 'instead of being a good man, as he will be reported, is very vicious and exceeding drunken.' He advised that there was no monk at Hulton of suitable age fit for the office of abbot, that there was division in the community, and that 'it would be better to put over them some good monk of another house.' Chalner was passed over; by 1536 Edward Wilkins was abbot. It it is not known from which abbey he came.[113]

The vacancy at Hulton had arisen because of the promotion of its abbot, John Harwood (Hareware) to the like position at Vale Royal, another controversial appointment. In 1535 after the death of Abbot John Butler, no less than three notable persons sought the election of their favoured candidate for Vale Royal: Queen Anne Boleyn pressed for an unnamed monk to be chosen,[114] Sir Piers Dutton, lord of the local manor of Dutton, suggested Ralph Winslow,[115] while William Brereton, then a king's favourite and Escheator of Cheshire, put forward the name of Ralph Goldsmith (*al.* Golson).[116] Both Goldsmith and Wilmslow were monks of Vale Royal, and both had entered holy orders when made acolyte in 1521. In the event a 'free election' was allowed, and the community chose John Harwood, abbot of Hulton.[117]

This enraged Brereton who said that he would do unto the new abbot 'such a displeasure that it would be very hard for him to abide in Cheshire.' Abbot Harwood, in order to pacify him, promised Brereton £100, to be paid over a period. Brereton was caught up in the accusations against Anne Boleyn, and executed with her on 17 May 1536. His widow sought payment from the Crown of the remaining debt.[118] As for Harwood, he was accused but cleared in court of complicity in the murder one of his monks, Hugh Chalner; it being found that Chalner had stabbed himself in the refectory. On 31 March 1539 Cromwell laid charges against Harwood in person at Vale Royal. These included dissuading a tenant from fighting against the rebels in the Northern Rising, and that one of his vicars had refused to marry a couple upon a license obtained from the king as Supreme Head. The trial was a ruse to get him to surrender the abbey, for he was pensioned off with an annuity of £60 and possession of the abbey plate.[119] As for Goldsmith, he was dispensed before the closure of the abbey to wear his Cistercian abbot beneath that of a secular priest. Wilmslow may have been the Ralph Bent who signed the deed of suppression in December 1538.

When the abbacy of Bindon fell vacant in 1534, Henry, duke of Richmond, wrote to Cromwell asking that the monks might have 'liberty to elect their own abbot, as the king has licensed you to take order in such cases.' Richmond, a bastard son of Henry VIII had a vested interest, for he added: 'Bindon adjoins lands of mine in Purbeck, and the convent will look after my deer.'[120] All abbatial elections were subject now to Cromwell's whim, who also expected payment for services rendered. William Arnold, abbot of Merevale told Cromwell in 1529 that he was 'very short of money, but at Christmas he will pay most of his duty.' He sent a token with the letter of 53s 4d. as a reward for Cromwell's trouble at his election. He had the previous year been noted as a debtor of Cromwell.[121].

On the death of Abbot Ireby of Holm Cultram in 1536, Sir Thomas Wharton wrote to Cromwell that a monk there, Thomas Graham, would if appointed abbot give Cromwell 400 marks.[122] He was unsuccessful in his bid, but it was later alleged that the new abbot, Thomas Carter, gave the abbot of Byland [a Crown visitor of the abbeys in the north] 'for helping him to his promotion, a salt of gold and silver worth twenty shillings.'[123] When a Richard Andrews was advocating the cause of a monk of Rewley to become abbot of Biddlesden, his letter to Cromwell said that 'I gave here £60 in angels, part of your 100.'[124] In another instance one John Mille wrote to Cromwell, on 25 April 1533, that 'the bearer shall be abbot of Quarr,' and would give Cromwell an annuity of £2 yearly, but there was no vacancy at Quarr at that date, so perhaps the letter has been misplaced or mistranscribed.[125] In July 1535 Nicholas Austen, the abbot of Rewley, had hoped to bribe Cromwell in order to become abbot of Merevale, offering to give him an annuity of £2.[126]

Cardinal Wolsey, before his downfall, had also played a role in the appointment of abbots. In 1526 the abbots of Rievaulx and Roche wrote to Wolsey praising William Thirsk, the abbot-elect of Fountains. Wolsey had wished to be so informed before he confirmed Thirsk's election.[127] For what was to be a short and troubled abbacy, John Chaffcombe (*al.* Macy) bought his abbacy at Bruern from Cardinal Wolsey for 250 marks of money, and 280 oaks of the greatest and best from the woods of the monastery—these were to aid the construction of Cardinal's college at Oxford. He recouped himself from the abbey's coffers.[128] Chaffcombe also granted an annuity of 4 marks to Edward Fetiplace, a member of an old Oxfordshire family, for good offices in helping him regain the abbacy after he was ousted in 1529 by rioters.[129] The officers of Wolsey also demanded £100 of of a new abbot, John Butler of Vale Royal (1517–1530). When there was a delay in payment of a £20 instalment, the abbot was fearful that he might be deprived of the abbacy.[130]

In north Wales, there was favouritism and nepotism indeed! This resulted from the friendship with Wolsey of Robert ap Rhys, the vicar-general of the diocese of St Asaph. Of his twelve illegitimate sons, Hugh ap Rhys (1528) who died young and then Richard ap Rhys, became abbots of Aberconwy (1535–1537), while John ap Rhys took over the abbacy of Strata Marcella in 1527. He may have been a worthy choice, coming to the abbey towards the close of ten years study in philosophy, civil law and theology, for the Oxford B.Th.[131] By 1535 his father had died, but Richard owed his abbacy to another of his father's friends, Bishop Lee , President of the Council of the Marches. The bishop saw Richard as 'much loved by his brethren,' but Abbot Geoffrey Johns who had to stand down in his favour, thought that he was 'a wilful and misruled person who would utterly destroy the abbey.'[132] From all the foregoing examples, it is clear that the Cistercian ideal of a 'free' election was now often held more in the breach than in the observance.

Lastly, the hunger for an abbatial pension—honoured by the Court of Augmentations after the dissolution—was blatantly shown at Grace Dieu where there were no less than four abbots between 1530 and 1536, three of them being awarded pensions. The monastery by this time was little more than a cell of Abbey Dore, and these four abbots may all have been temporary imports from other houses: John Rothwell from Buildwas (1530–1533), William Ipsley from Flaxley (1533), Thomas Perpin, perhaps from Flaxley (1534), and John Gruffydd, possibly a deposed abbot of Margam (1534/36). It was a deliberate device to secure additional income for favoured monks.[133]

Resigned and Deposed Abbots

Most Cistercian abbots died in office, but there were in Tudor times some thirty superiors who are recorderd as having resigned or having been deposed. The circumstances of others is not known, nor of all those said to have 'resigned'. The greater majority, at least twenty of the thirty were either deposed during an official visitation, or were effectively deposed by being pressured to resign, and perhaps offered inducements to do so. In some instances the pressure came not from within a monastery or the Order, but from local laity of influence; persons who may have had a genuine concern for the well-being of a monastery, or else had their own favourite candidate in mind.

At Tilty three abbots were removed or resigned within a few years because they fell into disfavour with the formidable marchioness of Dorset who lived at the abbey. One went to Warden where his brother was abbot, another to Dublin![134] The latter, Roger Beverley, who was effectively deposed in 1530 by being forced to resign, five years later wrote from Dublin to Cromwell with the words: 'The late marquess of Dorset sent to the fathers of the region to cause him to resign, and assured him of £20 under the convent seal, which had not been truly paid. He was content to take £10, but had nothing since Michaelmas.'[135] It was an example of how local dignitaries could engineer the resignation of an abbot they disliked.

A letter to Cîteaux in 1491 told how the abbots of Combe and of Waverley had retired due to age and infirmity.[136] In the instance of Gerard Duxfeld of Newminster, in his mid-eighties when he retired in 1527, age also probably played a part in his stepping down.[137] The same was true of Philip Morgan, abbot of Dore from 1478 to 1495 and a monk there by 1455. Deposed 'for certain great causes,' he was released from obedience to his successor, given an annuity of £12, and technically professed as a monk of Whitland. In fact, 'for his comfort in his age,' he was given leave to live at the house of Friars Preachers in Hereford, and there a few years later he died. When he left Dore he allegedly took with him 'divers books, writings, charters and muniments concerning the monastery, and also money, jewels and goods to the value of £200.' After his death in Hereford these items came into the hands of David Lewis and Hugh Vaughan, who 'utterly refused' to return anything. The case came to the Court of Chancery. [138]

Of similar age when they resigned were Thomas Kilburn, abbot of Byland from 1479 to 1497, and a monk there by 1452, and perhaps Robert Sutton, abbot of Stoneleigh for twenty-eight years from 1504 to 1532. Richard Benet, abbot of Biddlesden from 1512 to 1534, also perhaps stepped down on account of age, and enjoyed a corrody in and a pension of £13-6-6 from his house. He was described as 'a very honest man.'[139] Other elderly abbots, like Marmaduke Huby—despite being in his eighties and afflicted by 'paralysis and the stone', laboured to the end of their lives.[140]

Thomas White, having been abbot of Buckland for twenty years, was pressurised by the marquis of Exeter in 1527 to resign. Abbot White rejoined that 'his age has not caused debility of reason, but given him better experience how to govern.' He could do everything, he said, 'except ride about the country.' He begged the marquis to allow him to remain in office, but he died not long after.[141] It was one example of monastic constitutional procedures being set aside at the whim of a powerful 'patron'. What was worse, Thomas White felt he had to advise the marquis that when he died he should 'not give the office to

Sir Toker,' on account of his 'untoward conversation and the intolerable charges he has caused to the monastery.' Not only did the marquis appear to have the effective power to depose, but also to appoint. The advice was disregarded, and John Toker was blessed as abbot in Exeter Cathedral on 7 June 1528.[142]

There were abbots who wished to resign but could or did not do so. When Henry Emery of Warden, formerly abbot from 1522 to 1534 of its daughter-house at Sibton, was translated to Warden he found some of the monks there disobedient and rebellious, very lax in their morals, sobriety and keeping of the Rule [as described in earlier chapters], and given to do as they wanted. This was especially true after Dr Legh and John Ap Rice visited the house on 16 October 1535 and bade the monks maintain strict enclosure. Emery described how 'they have since vexed him with many uncharitable surmises and opprobrious words,' how one had said the abbot had no authority to correct him, and how another threatened the abbot and his servants. He was 'in such fear that he commanded his servants to watch his chamber three nights after till their fury was somewhat assuaged.' Emery made an agreement to step down in favour of Thomas London, a monk of the house favoured by the earl of Rutland, and resigned on 5 August 1537. London reneged on the terms of the agreement between them and, with the support of Cromwell and the duke of Norfolk, Emery was reinstated and was still in office when Warden closed on 4 December 1537.[143]

Amongst those abbots whose resignation was forced was the scholarly Thomas Cleubery, from 1516 abbot of Dore. His abbacy came to an end in the autumn of 1523 or thereabouts, after months of harassment of himself and his family by a number of local armed men. Matters came to a head on Sunday 20 September when fifteen or more persons bearing 'bows and arrows, swords, bucklers, bills and spears' invaded the quire and chancel during high mass, seeking the abbot who fled from the church for fear of his life.[144]

On the other hand, when in 1517 Abbot Chard of Ford as a Reformator deposed Robert Woolaston, the abbot of Kingswood, local people came to Robert's support.[145] On Saturday 25 April thirty-nine persons 'riotously assembled' at Kingswood, some of them entering the monastery 'through a garden by the infirmary,' and shouting at the abbot of Ford. On Sunday some twenty entered the cloister through the abbey church 'which is the common way to the monastery,' and spoke 'many high and cruel words' at the chapter-house door. On the Monday rioters assembled again, including a man wearing 'a green coat and black bonnet with sword and buckler.'

Their efforts were unsuccessful; Abbot Robert was deposed leaving the chapter-house 'sore weeping and lamenting,' and complaining of maltreatment both at Kingswood and at Tintern, the mother-house. The rioters were quelled by men sent by the duke of Buckingham, resident at nearby Thornbury. The deposition seems to have been at the duke's behest; the three abbots [Ford, Tintern and Kingswood] having visited him on the Friday. The local vicar of nearby Wootton said the abbot would not have ben deposed 'if it had not been for the duke's displeasure.' Abbot Huby, who was not entirely happy with the new Reformators, reported the deposition to Cîteaux.[146]

A questionable forced resignation was that of Abbot Henry Saxton, abbot of Vaudey from 1510 to 1533. In late October 1532 the abbots of Fountains, William Thirsk—who was himself forced to resign four years on, and of Woburn, Crown Visitors, as well as the abbot of Pipewell, carried out a visitation of Vaudey, and charged Abbot Henry with mismanagement and neglect of divine service, despite his assertion that he had brought the abbey out of very significant debt and restored a collapsed nave. The visitors were determined to depose him, but after Cromwell intervened he was allowed to resign with a yearly pension of £20 and a residential corrody. His resignation was effective from 2 August 1533, but the real motive for his dismissal was the abbot of Woburn's determination to see his cousin, William Stile who was cellarer of Woburn, installed as abbot at Vaudey. Abbot Hobbes further said that to get his cousin the position 'he would spend large sums of money.'[147] Stile did succeed, but it is further proof that financial inducements were offered to Cromwell for such promotions.

Marmaduke Bradley, a monk of Fountains rehabilitated after part of a scheme to remove Abbot Marmaduke Huby from office, continued to endeavour to obtain an abbacy. Unsuccessful in attempts in 1529 and 1533 to become abbot of Rievaulx, he schemed to have Abbot Thirsk of Fountains removed from office, with a bribe to Cromwell of 600 marks if he replaced Thirsk, which he did. Doctors Layton and Legh forced Thirsk to resign on 19 January 1536, several allegations of mishandling of the monastery's goods and economy having been made against him. In part these were trumped up charges, and whilst they called Thirsk an 'idiot', this was not the case; for only a few years previously he was identified by the abbots of Rievaulx and Roche when he became abbot of Fountains as being of 'good and virtuous living, of good experience and gravity, the best man for the place.'[148] After refusing to hand over monies Bradley asserted were the monastery's due, Thirsk retired to Jervaulx and eventually suffered death.

Bradley succeeded Thirsk, although one author has described him as 'a troublemaker, simoniac, liar and trickster'. He already held the prebend of Thorpe in Ripon collegiate church which led Layton and Legh to describe him as 'a wealthy fellow,' but also as 'the wisest monk within England' of his Order. Once in office as abbot of Fountains, Bradley tried to avoid paying to the Crown the first-fruits of £1,000 which the Visitors had asserted he could. He issued eighteen leases in the half-year from June to December 1538, whereas there had been no more than nine in any full year since 1495. On Fountain's closure he received an annual pension of £100 and retired to his prebend and to life as a canon residentiary, being president of the chapter at Ripon despite long periods of non-residence. He did though contribute substantially towards very necessary renovations of the collegiate church. Bradley died and was buried at Ripon in 1553.[149] On 31 August 1536 William Love, abbot of Coggeshall from 1527, was said to have 'freely resigned,' and was permitted to hold a secular benefice. In January 1536 he had been accused by some of his community of serious shortcomings: undervaluing to the commissioners the worth of the abbey plate; leasing at less than true value certain lands, aware that one day they would be the property of the monarch; omitting the collect for the king and queen at high mass; declaring that Cromwell was an arch-heretic, and various other charges. The earls of Oxford and Essex held an enquiry and cleared Love, finding him to be 'a true subject', but later Dr Legh, Cromwell's agent, secured his resignation. It appears the charges were brought at the instigation of John Sampford, Love's predecessor as abbot, who had been deprived nine years before.

Some doubt remains: did Henry More, abbot of St Mary Graces and one of those charged by Henry VIII with inspecting the English Cistercian monasteries, have anything to do with the affair? Love's removal meant that More, on payment of a fee of £125, obtained the abbacy of Coggeshall for himself, in addition to holding on to his own monastery.[150] The amount of Love's compensatory pension is uncertain, but he had in the years following the abbey's closure a house known as "Sympson's Lodging" in which to dwell, with an annual allowance of twelve bales of wood for fuel.[151]

In Wales the character of three or four abbots was less than might be expected. Richard Dorston had been effectively deposed at Dore in 1500 on account of 'inordinate rule and governance,' yet managed by 1509 to become for a few years abbot of Strata Florida. John Glyn became the last abbot of Cwmhir about 1534/35, despite having been 'the cause of decay at two other houses for which he was expelled.' Dore was one of those abbeys, Cymer may have been the second.[152] The trouble caused to Valle Crucis by its extremely youthful abbot, Robert Salusbury, finds mention before. Sent back to study at Oxford in 1534, he became the leader of a band of robbers, and found himself incarcerated first in Holt and Chester castles, and then in the Tower of London. His disliked abbacy had ended in ignominy.[153]

Three other abbatial depositions are worthy of especial note. The abbot of Dieulacres, William Alben, with some of his monks, servants and tenants, was party in 1516 to a riot in Leek aimed at obstructing the king's commissioner appointed to investigate a murder.[154] The result was that Abbot Alben was confined for a long time in The Fleet Prison in London. When he returned to the abbey, only in 1519, certain of his monks did not want him, he was in fear of his life, and he was deposed by his father-abbot of Combermere.[155]

A hostile community faced John Chaffcombe (*alias* Macy) when he bought his abbacy at Bruern in 1527 by paying 250 marks to Cardinal Wolsey and giving him 280 of the monastery's best oaks. At the instigation of some of the monks, he alleged, he was expelled 'and kept out of the monastery for a great season,' taking refuge at Rewley abbey The cardinal restored him, but in Easter Week 1529 fifteen armed local rioters threatened him so that he was 'forced to keep to his chamber.'[156]. Chaffcombe said that his opponents boasted that they would spent £100 to keep him out of the abbacy, and that the local justice of the peace who had been commanded to guard against the riot 'little regards it.'[157]

Chaffcombe was a monk of Ford when he became abbot of Bruern, aided by his bribery of Wolsey and because Abbot Chard of Ford was then a Reformator of the Order. His coming to Bruern was, it was alleged, to the grave undoing of that abbey, and his father-abbot of Garendon, as well as the now Reformators, the abbots of St Mary Graces and of Woburn, more than once attempted to visit the monastery but the gates were closed against them and a hired band of local men, 'gadzed out of Burford and other places' was there to make sure they did not enter. Henry VIII, learning of the problems commanded 'under his great seal of flame coloured wax' a local squire, Sir Simon Harcourt, to assist the reformators, and ordered an investigation at Bruern. This took place in the chapter-house of the abbey on 26 April 1532.[158]

Evidence was heard firstly from the prior, and then from ten other monks (including the bursar) who agreed with all the prior said and added some detail of their own. The first complaint related to the 200 marks of money and the 280 of the greatest and best oaks of the monastery which on taking up office he gave to Cardinal Wolsey for the building of his Cardinal's College at Oxford. The second charge was that Chaffcombe had bound his monastery in an obligation of £280 to the abbot of Ford; a sum which exceeded the total income of the house. Several of his brethren resisted this move, but Chaffcome either imprisoned them or persuaded Abbot Chard of Ford, in his capacity as a reformator, to move them to other abbeys.

Other charges related to the selling off of church plate, including a gold chalice, and the granting of annuities which the monastery could not afford, including one of £2 with rights of food and drink to a John Macy, clearly a relative. Another annuity, of four marks, was awarded to Edmund Fetiplace in November 1530, for his services in assisting Chaffcombe secure the abbacy. The abbot had demised from the monastery demesne a pasture never let out before and capable of sustaining four hundred sheep. In his five years of abbot the stock, it was said, depreciated by half: He also sold six hundred elms, but one of of the monks emphasised that not a penny from the sale of the timber was bestowed to the profit of the house. The prior affirmed that Chaffcombe had let the abbey's farms and pastures unprofitably so that 'he might be better supported to his pleasure.'

Worse still were the allegations made against him of sexual misconduct. The prior asserted that Chaffcombe kept for six weeks a harlot in his chamber, and that 'divers other suspect women resorted there.' The bursar alleged that the abbot had 'fourteen concubines which oft-times resorted to him and he to them.' He had seen the abbot in bed with women. Other articles drawn up against Chaffcombe asserted that he had a child by a woman he kept at Tingley Grange, and that he maintained another woman at Sandbrouck Grange. He also kept a woman in nearby Sydenham, but shortly before he was deposed she was driven out of the village.

This situation could not continue; Chaffcombe was deposed, but surprisingly was granted a pension of £13-6-8 and appears to have still been on the books of the monastery, under his *alias* of John Macy when Bruern was suppressed. In 1536/37 Fetiplace complained to the Court of Chancery that he was owed £40 on account of non-receipt of his annuity. The abbot of Ford, one of its guarantors, responded that Fetiplace had been for seven years 'well and truly paid.'[159]

The amount claimed by Fetiplace was far in excess of seven years non-payment and suggests that he was not a truthful witness.

The most serious abbatial deposition, because of the stature of the monastery concerned, was that of Abbot Kirkby of Rievaulx in 1533. An Oxford graduate, he had only been abbot since 1530 but by May 1533 had offended Henry VIII, and it was alleged against him that he had imprisoned and otherwise punished some of his brethren who criticised him and his dissolute living and, further, that he took from an aged monk all his money with which 'he should have made his jubilee.' After some of the monks wrote to their patron, the earl of Rutland, he in turn complained to Cromwell who ordered an enquiry by the abbot of Fountains, Dr Legh—Rutland's cousin, and others.[160]

Kirkby was formally deposed on Cromwell's instructions and, as the abbot of Fountains could not or did not wish to attend, the abbot of Byland visited Rievaulx at the close of September 1533, and took depositions from each monk 'so that none of them knew what was the answer of the others.'[161] The community was deeply divided. Nine monks voted for a fresh abbatial election, but thirteen did not agree saying that Abbot Kirkby had been wrongly deposed. Even one of the monks who voted in favour of a fresh election asserted that the deposition had been engineered by the earl of Rutland.[162]

The upshot was that Abbot Blyton of Rufford was imposed upon the community, after a delay which irked the king.[163] His installation took place on 6 December 1533 (St Nicholas's Day) and former Abbot Kirkby attended.[164] In May 1534 at a meeting in Ripon the abbots of Fountains, Kirkstall and Rievaulx, agreed that Kirkby should received a yearly pension of £44, though Abbot Blyton was slow to agree. At some point in 1535 Kirkby had to complain to Cromwell that the pension was not being paid, whereupon Cromwell ordered his reinstatement as abbot if it was not forthcoming. The duke of Norfolk wrote to Cromwell to say that it had been by his command that the pension be stopped when Kirkby was suspected of treason.[165]

As for Kirkby, he was in some way involved in the Pilgrimage of Grace and tried but reprieved. His six week sojourn in the Tower of London cost 6s 8d.[166] In later life Blyton referred to himself as 'abbot of Rufford;' it may be that his translation to Rievaulx was not entirely to his liking. Around 1536 the duke of Norfolk described him as 'an old man, ill able to ride and of as honest a sort as any religious in these parts.'[167] Praise indeed!

Whether abbots resigned freely or under pressure, they were generally accorded a fair pension and corrodial rights in their or another monastery. This not only made their loss of status easier to accept, but also made them more amenable to accepting demands that they resign voluntarily. The relevant indentures were usually made out to two laymen on their behalf, as being religious they could not in theory hold individual property. This also acted as a guarantee that the monastery concerned would fulfil its part of the bargain. In the instance of Abbot Cleubery of Dore (1526), the bargain was struck with the mayor of Hereford, Thomas Warncombe, and Richard Gittins, who succeeded Warncombe as mayor.[168] When Richard Emery was deposed from the abbacy of Buildwas (1520), a pension of £12-6-8 was awarded on his behalf to the earl of Shrewsbury and four others.[169] Alas for John Cresshale, once abbot of Tilty who resigned around 1420, he had to complain that whilst his successor had granted a pension on his behalf to John Wolff, parson of Hildersham, Cambs., William Skrene and John Basset, they were refusing to pay him.[170]

Richard Benet at Biddlesden on his retirement (1535) was granted the 'Ffowkes Chamber' in the monastery with its garden;[171] Edmund Emery who moved from Tilty to Warden (1533) was given there the chamber called 'Angels'—'next to the kitchen of the west part.'[172] At Dore (1526) Thomas Cleubery was allotted the New Chamber, on the north side of the monastery, with the chapel adjacent;[173] and at Newminster, the aged Gerard Duxfeld had the Castle Chamber 'situated above the cloister'.[174] These were not insubstantial dwelllings, nor was the chamber granted to Henry Saxton at Vaudey (1533); it lay at 'the eastern end of the dormitory' and with it went adjoining 'buildings, sub-cellars, gardens and closes adjacent.'[175]

In all cases rights of food and drink were normally awarded together with fuel, candles, and the like, together frequently with provision for a servant or servants. When Abbot William Huby of Woburn retired in 1477 his residential corrody included weekly twenty-four loaves of white bread and fifteen gallons of ale, and daily two dishes of meat or fish.[176] In addition an annuity would be paid, as the £20 for Abbot Saxton and the £10 granted Abbot Benet. If the retired superiors were still alive, then they were recompensed in part by the Court of Augmentations: Abbot Benet was awarded in 1539 £13-6-8 p.a., Henry Saxton in 1537 was granted £16 p.a. Technically when an abbot retired he became a monk subject to the authority of the new abbot and to enclosure; so important clauses were added to allow him 'free egress and regress' (Abbot

Benet); or to 'walk or ride where-ever he wished and be free from monastic observances' (Abbot Duxfeld).

Not all resigned or deposed abbots were so fortunate. When William Johns retired in 1516 as abbot of Cwmhir, a relatively poor monastery, the details of any corrody granted are not known, but his monetary pension was only £2. Acting as the recipients on his behalf were George Traherne and Roger ap Johns; both probably minor gentry.[177] In a sad case, it was left to the abbot of Loos in France to tell in 1488 how Robert Chorley, the former abbot of Woburn, was 'in a state of destitution.' He had to wait until 1491, but then the General Chapter and the abbot of Cîteaux ordered that his pension was to be paid without delay. His free movement in and out of the chamber assigned to him was also confirmed.[178]

Abbots receiving Secular Benefices

At least thirteen Cistercian abbots held parish churches not of their abbey's appropriation, which would normally have had a secular rector or vicar. In most instances this will have been a means of supplementing their personal income, or that of their monastery. Two abbots, William Breken of Roberts-bridge (1516) and John Birde of Boxley (1523) held in succession the living of Salehurst, Kent. When John Burton became abbot of Rievaulx (1499) he was instituted to the vicarage of Normanton, Yorkshire, and the same year, Robert Reyfeld, newly abbot of Boxley, received the parishes of Headcorn and Huntingdon in Kent.[179]

During his time as abbot of Bruern (1515–1527), the later bishop Robert King held the living of Charlbury in Oxfordshire, whilst the Cistercian bishop of Bangor, Thomas Skevington, favoured his confrère, Abbot John Baddesley of Merevale, with the parish of Llangynhafal in Gwynedd (1515–1525). By way of partial compensation Abbot John Bryan of Bindon received the rectory of Tarrant Keynstone, Dorset, after his deposition in 1504, whilst after his resignation in 1509 Abbot William Henley of Netley was collated to the living of Hound, Hampshire.[180]

Because of the supposedly ruinous state of his monastery, William Kere, abbot of Tintern (1487–1493), in order 'to enable him to sustain his position in accordance with abbatial dignity more suitably,' could receive a secular benefice and hold it *in commendam* for life, and if he resigned the abbacy to still hold it, and to have a place in choir and chapter and a monk's portion.[181] In other words, he very probably would not have resided on his benefice, and as the grant was made the year before he resigned he thus secured some comfort in old age. John Addingham, abbot of Swineshead, was in 1516 given leave to acquire two secular benefices, once again 'to keep up his position in accordance with abbatial dignity more fittingly.'[182]. When the abbots of Rewley (1513) and Bindon (1514) were given leave to acquires benefices, no causatory factor was referred to.[183]

Abbatial Duties

A respected abbot's community might suffer by reason of the amount of time their superior might have to spend away from the monastery. From time to time both the papacy and the Crown might require of abbots to undertake commissions of various kinds. They would also be involved in attendance at the Convocation of Canterbury when it took place, and a minority of abbots would also have parliamentary duties; while most would have one or more daughter-houses which they should inspect annually. When Convocation was held in 1529 all Cistercian abbots appear to have been summoned, but eleven of their number were represented by the abbot of St Mary Graces, the abbot of Biddlesden stood in for the abbot of Garendon, and the abbot of Stratford for the abbot of Hailes.[184] There is occasional note of abbots like those of Stratford[185] and Waverley[186] undertaking parliamentary duties.

A tiresome burden for many abbots was the supervision of collection of tenths levied for the Crown or subsidies for the Holy See, whilst the Reformators had the additional responsibilty of taking in the annual contributions expected by the Order's General Chapter. Of more local concern, might be the administration of wills and grants of probate, and defending the rights of their abbey. Abbots might be called upon to settle local disputes. The Welsh poet, Iorwerth Fynglwys (*fl. c.*1480–1527), anxious for his patrons, Sir Thomas Gamage and Sir Edward Stradlyng, to settle their differences, wrote: 'Let four men go to arbitrate, and let one be the abbot of Neath.'[187]

That abbots took their duties seriously, and attended to them in person when necessary, is seen in remarks made to Cromwell by the mayor and citizens of Winchester in January 1536, in a case involving the statute of sewers: 'My lord of Bangor and the other Commissioners have been at Wood Mills, which you saw, and had a great part of it pulled down. On Monday next, the Commissioners are appointed to be there for further execution of the same.'[188] In other words, Abbot Skevington of Beaulieu and his colleagues fulfilled in person what was expected of them, time consuming as it must have been.

The abbots in several coastal and flood plain regions were placed repeatedly on commissions 'of sewers' or of 'banks and ditches', the prime object being to deal with drainage problems. Such commissions being mostly headed by a bishop (as of London) or a magnate (like the earl of Northumberland). In this way abbots of Meaux served in Holderness;[189] abbots of Kirkstead and Revesby, and occasionally of Louth Park and Swineshead, in Holland and neighbouring districts;[190] an abbot of Sibton in Suffolk,[191] an abbot of Stratford in south-east Essex,[192] of St Mary Graces there and in the Lea valley area,[193] and an abbot of Robertsbridge in Sussex.[194]

In 1532 commissioners were appointed for Yorkshire 'for the reformation of weirs and fish-garths and other nuisances in the great rivers;' those nominated included the abbots of Byland, Kirkstall and Meaux.[195] As late as 1538 the abbot of Beaulieu served on a commission of sewers 'for the sea coast and marsh ground extending from the river running from Blackridge to Southampton.'[196] The commissioners could produce results. After Abbot Skevington's visits to Wood Mills it was reported that 'the streams are already greatly improved, the lands of the abbot of Netley which were drowned are now perfectly dried, and the rivers are full of salmon kyppers.'[197]

Many other duties were entrusted to religious superiors. In 1505 the abbot of Bordesley headed a commission taking evidence regarding the city of Worcester's wish 'to take toll on vessels laden with merchandise passing under the bridge or putting in there;'[198] in 1513 the abbot of Stratford was one of a commission of eight for Essex, whose duty it became 'to seize property of all born subjects of the king of Scotland in the county;'[199] in 1528 the abbot of Jervaulx was listed in a commission whose duty it was, that year being one of dearth, 'to search all barns for wheat or grain kept there.'[200]

Abbots might be placed on commissions of the peace, with a responsibility for good order in their area. Such abbots included Marmaduke Huby of Fountains [from 1502 to 1508, and again in 1525];[201] the abbot of Swineshead, the long serving John Addingham, for the Holland district of Lincolnshire (1532),[202] and William Huddleston, abbot of Stratford (for the county of Essex; 1536).[203] Such duties given to an abbot made them formidable opponents when lowlier parties sought to sue them for perceived wrongdoing. A few abbots had the potential duty of raising soldiery from their tenantry to support the Crown: in this regard, Furness was assessed as being able to provide no less than four hundred horsemen and 858 foot soldiers![204] It was said that in 1513 Abbot Stratford of Vale Royal, with the assistance of Sir George Holford and John Bostock, personally led about three hundred of his tenants to the Battle of Flodden.[205]

In the twenty-first year of the reign of Henry VII (1505–06), Abbot Roger Balke of Rufford chaired no less than seven commissions of enquiry, several of them sitting in Nottingham. Mostly they were concerned with the theft of trees from Crown lands: oak trees from Sherwood Forest and ash trees from royal land at Wheatley; both oak and ash trees from the king's park at Gringley.[206] In 1506 Abbot Roger was also a member of an enquiry into £200 found in gold royals in the font of Newark church, years before in 1490.[207] It is clear that Abbot Roger was a person trusted, and he was rewarded by the monarch in 1505 with the office for life of master or provost of Stainthorpe College, Yorkshire, in the hands of the the the king due to the minority of the earl of Westmorland.[208] The abbot of Robertsbridge in 1536/37 chaired a commission taking depositions in a dispute regarding the manor of Iklysham, Sussex.[209]

The ability of a bishop to delegate to an abbot the collection of a tenth due to the Crown was on the basis of that monastery possessing appropriated churches and their tithes within his diocese. The abbots were essentially sub-collectors for the bishop, and they in turn would appoint vice-collectors to do the work. In Devon the abbot of Buckland's vice-collector in 1537 was one John Croft, and he expected a payment of 8d for every pound he raised.[210] The many instances include the abbot of Bordesley frequently appointed a collector in the archdeaconry of Worcester; an entire manuscript volume records the work of the abbots of that house in this respect.[211]

There could be difficulties in raising the monies assessed on the clergy. To counter this, the abbot of Boxley (1490) as a collector in the Canterbury diocese had 'the power of canonical coercion against defaulters.'[212] The abbot of Furness, made a collector for the archdeaconry of Richmond in 1532, found that one of his adversaries, Master Seyton, would not pay up.[213] The abbot of Neath encountered difficulties when expecting All Souls College, Oxford, to pay in respect of its church at Llangennydd in Glamorgan.[214] When in November 1536 the abbot of Whalley, a collector in Cheshire, demanded several times payment of £50 due from St Werburgh's Abbey, Chester, its abbot wrote to Cromwell saying that of the £50 due, 'I have paid him £30, and as soon as I can after Christmas will pay him the residue.'[215]

It was the difficulties experienced by sub-collectors, in this case the abbots of Buckland, Ford and Dunkeswell, that found note in a letter of February 1537 from the bishop of Exeter and the archdeacon of Barnstaple to the king, noting arrears from the collection of a subsidy of £171 in the case of the abbot of Ford and £1,453 in the instance of the abbot of Buckland—though the latter had so far paid in £402. As for the abbot of Dunkeswell 'for whom we have often sent, he comes not.'[216] In December 1538 the abbots of Ford and Buckland were noted as being over a year behind in their payment to the Crown.[217] Monies collected by the last abbot of Dore were, allegedly, only partly raised and paid in by the time the house was suppressed.[218] It is clear that the collection of tenths due to the Crown was time-consuming and a problem for all concerned.

There could be errors and misunderstandings. About 1516 John Baptist, the parson of Alwoldeby, Lincolnshire, took to the Court of Chancery, George Walker, the abbot of Louth Park. His cause for complaint was that he had paid the abbot who was collector of a tenth in Lincolnshire, his due of twelve shillings and had his receipt, but the abbot had failed to discharge him at the Exchequer, and he had therefore been fined for non-payment.[219]

A special subsidy, which saw all monasteries being assessed in 1522, was an 'annual grant for the recovery of France by the king.' The sums expected must have been an extremely heavy drain on the resources of most abbeys: £100 each was levied on Dunkeswell, Ford, Hailes and Woburn; the lowest figure quoted was £20 payable by Dore, Medmenham, Rewley and Waverley. Forty-four Cistercian abbeys are named in what appears to be an incomplete list. The majority paid either £44 or £66-13-4; the basis of the valuations is difficult to understand.[220] It may have been this 'loan' was that referred to when in 1525 the Marquis of Dorset wrote to Cardinal Wolsey to inform him that Abbot Chard of Ford refused to comply.[221]

Commissions delegated by the papacy involved usually purely ecclesiastical affairs, and a Cistercian abbot might be appointed a judge delegate in company with a bishop or other religious superior. In 1493 the abbots of St Mary Graces and Stratford were appointed to assist the bishop of Rochester to enquire into the presentation of a canon of St Stephen's, Westminster, to the living of Cheshunt. Hertfordshire.[222] That same year the abbot of Bordesley was to join with the superior of Evesham to enquire into the presentation of David Hugh to the church of Newbold-on-Avon, Worcestershire.[223] Abbots might be appointed to commissions involving tithe disputes (Boxley, 1515), marriage cases (Swineshead, 1513), and parish affairs (Dunkeswell, 1514).[224]

Another time consuming duty which might fall to an abbot, but which also sometimes led to acrimony and dispute, was the executor-ship of the will of a local lay person. In 1500 the abbot of Combermere was an executor of the will of Richard Chomundeley;[225] in around 1505 the abbot of Meaux acted for Robert Ingram of Ottringham,[226] and in 1511/12 the abbot of Hailes was the sole executor of Sir John Huddleston.[227] Richard Kyrke (1533) of Horncastle, Lincolnshire, appointed three lay executors, but above them placed the abbot of Kirkstead as 'the supervisor, to see it [the will] be performed, fulfilled and kept.'[228] He was to receive ten shillings for his pains. Richard Lambeson (1534) willed that one of his properties be sold on the advice of the abbot of Swineshead, and the money received to benefit the abbey and its community in return for a 'solemn dirge and mass with ringing.'[229] Abbot Richard Stopes of Meaux (1525) was the 'supervisor' of the will of Thomas Baker of Holderness.[230] Abbot Thomas Hogeson of Woburn (1500) performed the same duty, together with Sir Hugh Kingsley, in the case of the will of John Shyngleshurt who appointed his widow as executrix.[231]

An abbot might occasionally find himself entrusted with the guardianship of a minor, in those times a person aged under twenty-one.[232] Around 1508 a hundred-strong group of armed people made an assault on Dunkeswell abbey during divine service, but fortunately the abbot of Ford was present and was able to pacify them. The rioters were protesting on the seizure of a ward by the abbot of Dunkeswell on the death of the ward's father, by virtue the abbot said of the terms of his will.[233] In 1533 the abbot of Furness ceded to Dame Frances Pennington, widow of Sir William Pennington, the custody of her son, William, still 'within the age of twenty-one years,' as well as the keeping of Pennington manor for twenty-five marks to be paid upon the altar of St John in the abbey church of Furness.[234]

For some abbots their manifold duties might be made easier by the position they came to hold in local society, and the influence that allowed them to bring to bear. Local and national events could give them an enhanced status. Abbot Hickman of Stratford was amongst those bidden in 1515 to receive Katherine of Aragon when she came to England for her marriage to Prince Arthur.[235] In

1533 Abbot Huddleston, also of Stratford, was one of the supporting prelates at the baptism of Princess Elizabeth in the Church of the Friars Minor at Greenwich; he also assisted at the funeral of Queen Jane Seymour at Windsor in 1537.[236] That same October he with the abbot of St Mary Graces, were present at the baptism of Prince Edward at Hampton Court.[237] In 1515 Abbot Duxfeld of Newminster accompanied Lord Dacre to meet in Morpeth the widowed Margaret Tudor, Queen of the Scots, on her journey to stay at Morperth Castle.[238] In May 1509 Abbot Langton of St Mary Graces had been the celebrant at one of three Masses sung in the royal chapel on the Saturday of the funeral obsequies of Henry VII.[239]

Abbatial Jurisdiction

Monastic courts dealt with petty offences as well as ingress to tenements on an abbey estate (Chapter 6). There is evidence also of some abbots asserting their jurisdiction over the probate of wills of their tenants of lands which they considered to be exempt from normal ecclesiastical jurisdiction. They might do this in person, or else appoint a legally qualified delegate. Kingswood abbey had at the time of its closure a 'Mr Browne, priest, commissary of the peculiar jurisdiction of the monastery.'[240] For his services, he received an annuity of £1-6-8, so it was not seemingly a full-time appointment—unless it was coupled with a residential corrody.

The claim of such 'ordinary' jurisdiction, could lead to hard feelings. In the 1520s Richard Yonge of Magdalen-by-Wiggenhall, Lincolnshire, chaplain, complained to Cardinal Wolsey, both chancellor and papal legate, that when his brother-in-law, John Haryson of Revesby, whose executor he was, died, Abbot Thomas of Revesby, having 'ordinary jurisdiction' within the town of Revesby had detained John's goods and cattle, claiming that Haryson had died intestate. The cattle concerned comprised twenty 'oike,' eight bullocks, two oxen, forty sheep, and eight mares and colts; a small but valuable flock.[241]

Such a right of jurisdiction might be challenged. After William Dene of Chaldon, Dorset, died, his wife, Alice, married one John Brody who proved Dene's will before Abbot Thomas of Bindon, as the abbot was 'possessed of the peculiar jurisdiction in the town of Chaldon, out of remembrance of man, and ought to have the probate of the testament and last wills of all such persons dying in Chaldon.' Brody had later to appeal to Thomas Audley, the chancellor, saying that before Cardinal Wolsey died, Nicholas Chaunterell his commissary detained the will claiming the cardinal's jurisdiction, and made Alice prove the will again; this time before himself on 22 September 1527 in Dorchester, charging her a fee of £1-13-4.[242]

Whalley had the exempt ecclesiastical jurisdiction of the royal forests of Pendle, Trawden, Rosendale, Bowland and Blackburnshire, and its ecclesiastical court was again presided over by a commissary appointed by the abbot. The court was usually held in Whalley parish church, but on at least one occasion met in Clitheroe parish church. It had jurisdiction of all ecclesiastical offences and causes in the region: such as probate of wills, non-payment of tithes; marriage cases—including divorce and legal separation and adjudication and forced marriages; libel, breach of faith, talking in church, work on Sundays and holydays, washing clothes on Saturday evenings, as well as grave immorality and adultery. Penances might be imposed as (at an unknown date in the 1530s) on Margaret Hutchin, who had borne a child out of wedlock. She was, clad in white and with bare head and feet, made to walk around the church of Burnley, and to receive discipline at the hands of the curate. No mention though of any penance for Nicholas Heype, by whom she bore the child; he lay outside the jurisdiction of the court.[243]

Notable Abbots

Marmaduke Huby, abbot of Fountains from August 1495 until his death in the summer of 1526, was undoubtedly the most influential and noteworthy Cistercian abbot of these times.[244] Of an old Yorkshire family with long links to Fountains abbey, he was made subdeacon on 19 September 1467 in the church of the Friars Minor, York; deacon on 17 March 1469 in the church of the Austin Friars, York, and was ordained priest on 19 September 1472 in the Benedictine church of the Holy Trinity at Micklegate, York. His obvious scholarship and biblical knowledge shows that at some stage he had received a thorough education.[245] It might well be that he attended St Bernard's College, Paris.[246] By 1482 he was undertaking tasks on behalf of his abbot, John Darnton, in the latter's capacity as a Reformator of the Order; on one occasion even suffering imprisonment at the hands of two men. By 1489 he held the important post of bursar of his monastery. Darnton described Huby as 'a faithful and prudent man.' John Harington, the lawyer much engaged in Cistercian affairs, referred to him as Darnton's right-hand man, "Darnton's Marmaduke."[247] A fervent zealot for the well-being of the Order, Huby was the natural choice to be elected abbot of Fountains when Darnton died early in 1495.[248]

Huby's labours as abbot in building works and increasing the numerical strength of his community, his massive support of St Bernard's College, and his work as a Reformator have been noted. In the latter capacity he showed a lifelong concern for the Cistercian monasteries of Wales,[249] despite in his travels there enduring 'many dangers to his body.'[250] In 1497 he had to tell how many Welsh monks had 'digressed from the path of holy religion, as well in habit and tonsure as in other uses.'[251] Nothing much is known of Huby's activities between 1500 and 1517, but then he showed sympathy for the 'very poor' monasteries of the Principality; it was, he said, 'as if the skins have been stripped off their backs,' and he sought to give them new hope and strength.[252] Another endeavour was to try to ensure that the annual subsidy expected of the English and Welsh monasteries safely reached Cîteaux. This was difficult as the export of money to the Continent was prohibited, and one of his ploys to circumvent the ban was to describe the cash being transmitted by the names of flowers: angels, roses and lilies; these being also the images stamped on the coins of the time: the angel, the rose noble and the florin.[253]

By 1519 Huby was feeling the effects of his age, and on 16 October that year excused himself from a meeting called by Cardinal Wolsey, writing that he was 'eighty, and subject to paralyis and the stone.'[254] Thoughts at Fountains turned to who might one day succeed him, and in 1520 one monk, Edward Tyrry, led a disaffected group of some seven monks whose aim was for Tyrry to succeed should Huby resign or die.[255] They seem to have met and eaten and drunk secretly in hidden corners of the abbey. This displeased Huby who sent the seven conspiring monks to other monasteries, with a demand that they by imprisoned. Against Huby's wishes they appear to have been eventually rehabilitated, but despite that Tyrry seems to have moved permanently to Newminster where in 1523 Lord Dacre described him as 'my monk,'[256] and where by 1527 he was abbot.

When Huby died in 1526 he had been a monk of Fountains for over sixty years, and abbot for thirty. He had left his mark on his beloved Order in no small measure, and had worn himself out in its service, but even he could not escape involvement in local politics and troubles. He defended the rights of his abbey, which meant an agreement in 1499 between Huby and John Norton of Norton Conyers regarding conflicting pasture rights, but only after 'divers controversies, troubles, debates and variances.'[257] The only other note of discord during his administration came in 1521/22, when Huby allegedly supported Sir William Gascoigne and his servants in riotous trespass on the lands of Miles Wilsthorpe of Wilsthorpe, East Yorkshire.[258] Given his age and infirmity, Huby can hardly have been actively involved.

Stephen Sagar (*alias* Whalley), abbot of Hailes from 1527 until its closure, was of a family whose ancestral home was at Catlow in the parish of Whalley, Lancashire. Stephen received his early education at that abbey under the tutelage or oversight of the later Abbot John Paslew who came to regard him as a son. Stephen, however, entered the monastery of Hailes, being made deacon as a monk of that house in 1512, and ordained priest in 1513. By 1527 he became known to Cromwell who probably recommended his appointment as abbot to Cardinal Wolsey. Stephen retained a friendship with Cromwell until after the Suppression, but at the same time managed to remain attached quietly and unobtrusively to the old faith. He broke with his Catholic-minded lecturer, George Cotes, when it suited him and, in royal and Cromwell's favour, was in 1537 appointed king's chaplain. In the spring and autumn seasons, he suffered from ague [malaria], and spent much time them in 'the clear air' of his nearby upland country lodging at Coscombe.

In the years leading up to the Suppression, Stephen ensured that members of his family were provided for by monastic grants, and he himself was granted a large pension of £100 at the dissolution of his abbey, with continuance of life at Coscombe for a few more years. He had managed the affairs of his monastery well, built up its library, and ensured it remained debt free. Later Stephen became a 'mature student' at Oxford, and then a pluralist and a wealthy man, able to lend £66-13-4 to Henry VIII in 1544 towards the defence of British interests in France. The money was repaid a little over two years later.[259] Stephen died in 1551 and was buried besides his brother, Otho, at Warmfield, Yorkshire. One scholar sums up his life with the words: 'He had an eye to himself as well as to his friends and family, (and) he was certainly no saint, but (there is) no evidence in his character of evil or malice.'[260]

Gabriel Dunne (*Donne*), the last abbot of Buckfast, found his vocation as a Cistercian monk seemingly by 1505 when his wealthy father, Angel Dunne, a London alderman and merchant, describing Gabriel as a monk, bequeathed him £10 to assist him to receive a university education.[261] At that date he may have been still in his upper teens for five years were to elapse before, as a monk of Stratford in Essex, he was ordained sub-deacon (1510), then deacon (1511) and finally priest (1516) in the diocese of London.[262] Gabriel appears to have been a monk of no small ability, and in the early 1530s acted as proctor for his abbot in law-suits concerning the vicar of its appropriated church at West Ham.[263]

Gabriel was also an academic; he supplicated for the degree of Bachelor of Theology at Oxford in October 1521, after a period of study which lasted twelve years, and which was partly spent at St Bernard's College. A promising monk, he then matriculated in 1530 at the University of Louvain hoping to obtain a doctorate, and it is possible that this was accomplished.[264] At least in the latter part of his studies in Louvain, he lived in the same house as Henry Phillips who was instrumental in the capture of William Tyndale. Phillips asserted that 'there was no one of his counsel' except Gabriel Dunne.[265] There is no evidence to suggest that Gabriel was, as formerly thought, an active participant in Tyndale's arrest. Foxe's *Book of Martyrs* makes no mention of Dunne in this connexion, and it is likely he had left Louvain before Tyndale's capture.[266]

Gabriel finally returned to England in July 1535, having already been assured of the abbacy of Buckfast even though Abbot John Rede had not then retired or died.[267] It seems that he stood high in Cromwell's favour who facilitated his promotion, but his appointment did not come cheaply, he—or a wealthy patron on his behalf, paid over to Cromwell's use £100 in late August 1535,[268] and in the following years sent him from Buckfast gifts of fish. He may have recouped his payment from monies received as the monastery from January 1536 onwards made numerous grants and leases of its properties.[269] His standing with Cromwell may have owed something to the fact that his niece, Frances Mirfin, was to marry Cromwell's nephew, Richard Williams.[270]

When Buckfast was suppressed in 1539 Gabriel was awarded the highest pension that any Cistercian abbot received, £120 each year.[271] In addition he became in 1541 a canon of St Paul's cathedral, as well as being from 1544 rector of Stepney without cure in 1544, and from 1549 absentee rector of Langtree, Devon.[272] After Bishop Bonner of London's deprivation Gabriel was constituted in September 1549 by Archbishop Cranmer as 'the official keeper of the spirituality, and to exercise all manner of episcopal jurisdiction within the city and diocese.'[273] He was clearly an influential priest who managed to survive unscathed the religious changes of his times, and he died on 5 December 1558 as a wealthy man.

His generous will allowed a scholarship worth £120 at Trinity Hall, Cambridge, where his arms and initials are amongst the shields in the roof of the chapel, and a bequest of forty-five books to St John's College, Oxford, which had grown out of St Bernard's College. He also made provision in his will for silver plate for St Paul's high altar; for an iron railing there to fence off the sanctuary, and for an altar or monument commemorating the Annunciation.[274] These provisions suggest continuing Catholic sympathies. He was buried in the cathedral on 9 December 1558, and his tomb before the high altar bore an inscription which concluded, *Corpus in Elyzii pace quiescat. Amen.*[275]

Another abbot whose tenure was short-lived and clearly had the backing of Thomas Cromwell was *Gawain Borrowdale* of Holm Cultram (1537–1538), who was a 'notable abbot' for all the wrong reasons. His background is not known, save that he was described by Dr Thomas Legh as one who 'has done the King good service.' If the accusations levelled against him were correct then, seething with indignation at the election of a monk of the house and Oxford graduate, Matthew Deveys, as abbot of Holm Cultram in 1531, he caused him and others to be poisoned, thus causing the abbot's death. Witnesses alleged that Gawain had threatened to kill the abbot, uttering such words before 'brethren of the London house,'—so Gawain had previously stayed for a time at either St Mary Graces or Stratford. It was also suggested that he tried to cover his tracks by riding to Penrith after the abbot was taken ill, and that 'so soon after his death' he took the late abbot's mother's goods.[276]

In September 1532 (if the letter is correctly dated), Sir John Lamplugh informed Cromwell of Gawain as being suspected of being implicated in Abbot Deveys' death.[277] At some stage the new abbot, Thomas Ireby, examined witnesses as to the affair when several of the community testified against Gawain.[278] For at least five months, in perhaps the autumn of 1533 and the spring of 1534, Gawain was held in custody at Furness abbey—'in prison at night, and during the day he goes to the church, and "melleth" with no one except the prior.'[279] This displeased the abbots of Byland and Fountains who as Reformators saw it as their business to investigate the affair, so Gawain was transferred on Cromwell's orders to the custody of the abbot of Byland.[280] In August 1533 Dr Thomas Legh had reported that both these abbots testified to Gawain's innocence, and that Gawain should be allowed to return to Holm Cultram. Abbot Pyle of Furness was not so sure, describing

Gawain as 'a masterful man (who) hath secret bearers.' Meanwhile Gawain appealed directly to Cromwell himself.[281]

Abbot Ireby died in 1536 and his successor, Thomas Carter, on 10 August 1537. Possibly because Cromwell felt that Gawain would surrender the house without difficulty, he did at last become abbot of Holm Cultram[282]—but only for a few months because his monastery closed on 6 March 1538. Gawain must have had friends in high places for although he had been abbot for only half-a-year, he was rewarded on 1 June, *in lieu* of a potential pension of £100 p.a., with the rectory of Holm Cultram and its tithes, two chambers in the now closed monastery and a stable. In November that year Henry VIII additionally demised to him for an annual payment of 26s 8d. the abbey site and adjacent lands, together with rights of firebote, ploughbote and cartbote.[283] For one against whom the evidence for deliberate murder seemed overwhelming, Gawain retired very comfortably indeed.

In Wales two abbots played a significant role in endeavouring to maintain the good state of the Order. The first (in time) was *David Wynchcombe*, an Englishman whose surname denotes his Gloucestershire origins. He first finds mention when in 1461 and then a monk of Hailes in adjoining Worcestershire, he was permitted by the abbot of Cîteaux to wear linen clothing 'out of consideration for his ailments.'[284] What-ever his ill-health at that time it did not prevent him from his appointment as abbot of Aberconwy in Gwynedd in 1482 being approved by the General Chapter, in time to attend a meeting of Cistercian abbots in Shrewsbury.[285] The circumstances were unusual, and it is doubtful how much he saw of his abbey for his abbatial blessing took place not in Wales but, on commission from the bishop of Bangor, on 13 January 1482 by the bishop of Worcester at his residence of Hartlebury Castle.[286]

Hailes was of the 'generation' of Cîteaux, but Aberconwy of the 'family' of Clairvaux, and in the growing tension of those years between Cîteaux and Clairvaux, Wynchcombe's appointment must have been a deliberate effort to extent the influence of Cîteaux in Wales. He does not appear to have been freely elected by the Aberconwy community, and his abbacy was soon challenged by another contender, a Welshman, David Lloyd. The Crown at the end of May 1484 had therefore to order the abbey's tenants to pay their rents not to the abbot but to the prior, Gruffydd Goch, 'during the variance and controversy between Dom David Wynchcombe and Dom David Lloyd.'[287] David Lloyd eventually ousted Wynchcombe and was certainly abbot in November 1489.[288] It may well be he who, the next autumn, resisted a visitation of the English and Welsh houses by the abbot of Cîteaux himself.[289]

Wynchcombe appears to have returned to Hailes, but was obviously of high standing in the Order and appears to have briefly held office as abbot of Cymer in 1495/96.[290] If so it was he whom Marmaduke Huby, still bursar of Fountains, entrusted in April 1495 with letters to the abbot of Cîteaux who was on visitation in Flanders. In August that year, Huby now abbot of Fountains, also sent the abbot of Cymer bearing letters to Cîteaux 'under a simple covering of cloth.'[291] Visiting Wales in 1496 Huby deposed the abbot of Strata Marcella on the Welsh border and personally installed Wynchcombe, for whom he had a high regard, as abbot there in his place. Huby described Wynchcombe as a man 'well proven in religion,' and 'a faithful lover and observer of the Order.' Huby also inhibited the father-abbot of Whitland from interfering in the affairs of his daughter-house at Strata Marcella, thus giving Wynchcombe a free hand.[292]

Wynchcombe attend the General Chapter at Cîteaux in September 1496, at which he was named as a definitor for the abbeys of the generation of Pontigny.[293] Huby drew attention to the divergences in Welsh monasteries at this time from the true Cistercian way of life. One reason for this, Wynchcombe claimed, was that 'by the reception of secular priests and noble sons from the Welsh nation, the sacred Order of Cîteaux is very much denigrated.'[294] The influx of vocations cannot have been a bad thing, but perhaps a lack of formation was.

Wynchcombe travelled again to Cîteaux in late August 1500 to represent the English Reformators, the abbots of Fountains, St Mary Graces and Stratford, regarding an internal Cistercian matter. Note was then made of his faithfulness over the years.[295] Attending General Chapter again in 1510, Wynchcombe acted as definitor for the line of La Ferté.[296] He was perhaps the abbot David of Strata Marcella who, whilst staying at Llantarnam abbey, wrote to the abbot of Dore requesting payment of a subsidy due to the General Chapter.[297] For such purposes, Dore was seen by this time as within 'the province of Wales.'[298] No more is heard of Wynchombe after 1513 when he presumably died. An abbot who showed concern for the well-being of his Order, he must have been in his early seventies when in 1510 he travelled to Cîteaux for the last time.

Huby did not show the same appreciation for Abbot *Lleision ap Thomas* of Neath (1510–1539) as he had for David Wynchcombe, whose death left a void Lleision undoubtedly filled. A monk of Neath when made deacon in 1509,[299] Llesion had spent several years of study at Oxford; indeed, a pardon roll of 1510 refers to him as 'late of Oxford.'[300] Although scarcely ordained, the emphasis of the time for learned abbots saw Lleision's education achievements secure him the abbacy of his house in 1510, even before he was awarded the degree of bachelor of canon law in 1511 and of divinity in 1512.[301] He remained abbot until the closure of his abbey in 1539.

Appointed a Reformator for Wales by perhaps 1514, Lleision's actions were not always to Abbot Huby's liking; after all Huby had for years laboured for the good of the Order in Wales. In 1517 Huby criticised Lleision for effectively deposing David ap Thomas ap Hywel, who had been abbot of Margam since 1500. Huby pointed out that his action had been irregular, as only one assisting abbot had been present when there should have been two. Further, he said, Abbot David had been forced to resign 'in fear of death and terror of armed force,' and that an unlearned monk, John Gruffydd, had been substituted in his place.[302] Lleision though was undoubtedly aware that Abbot David supposedly openly kept concubines and had sired a son and four daughters.[303]

Huby was also critical when about 1514 Lleison had allegedly effected 'a triple translation within two years' of David Floyd, abbot of Aberconwy, first to Cymer and then to Strata Marcella.[304] Had Huby been still alive, he could have found no cause for complaint when in June 1534, Lleision—who was staying at the White Hind-without-Cripplegate in London, was sent for to travel north and effect the very necessary deposition of the youthful Abbot Salusbury of Valle Crucis.[305]

Abbot Lleision was to be well travelled, attending the General Chapter at Cîteaux in 1517 and 1518; it was a mark of his ability, that he was appointed definitor for the family of Clairvaux in the former year, and for the lineage of Cîteaux in the latter.[306] In 1520 he summoned the abbot of Dore to a meeting held for the reform of the Order at St Mary Graces in London.[307] The next year he travelled to France, staying at Chaâlis abbey, with such monies as he had been able to raise in Wales for its abbeys' subsidy to the General Chapter. He explained that the inability of some houses to pay was a result of 'famine and the high price of corn, such as has not been known for fifty years.' He had hoped to meet the abbot of Cîteaux in Paris but did not find him there, and had the money forwarded on to Dijon.[308] When the Crown in 1532 found it 'not convenient' to allow the abbot of Chaâlis to enter England to conduct a visitation of Cistercian houses, Lleision was one of the five abbots appointed to take his place.[309]

At home in Glamorgan Lleision was named in commissions of the peace in 1513 and 1536.[310] In 1532 he played an important part in dealing with affrays between the western and eastern parts of Gower,[311] and it was to his monastery that the evidences in the Turberville-Loughor land dispute were committed for safe keeping in 1535.[312] His last years as abbot were spent in raising money for the survival of his house, and when it was suppressed in 1539 Lleision received both an annual pension of £40 and the rectory of Cadoxton-iuxta-Neath (Llangatwg-iuxta-Nedd), a living he held until at least 1547.[313] At the closure of his abbey one of the suppression commissioners said of Lleision that 'he had ever lived worshipfully and well.'[314] In the verses addressed to Lleision by Lewis Morgannwg, the Glamorgan bard *par excellence* of the period, the poet admired 'the peaceful songs of praise' chanted at Neath but, after the Suppression, Lewis changed his views and sang instead of 'the false religious of the choir.'[315]

Few Cistercian abbots have received a full biographical study, and details of their lives are mostly scanty. What is known is summarised in the *Appendix* which follows, or recounted in greater detail elsewhere in this book. Certain other abbots are worthy of special mention. *Oliver Adams* (Combe, 1513–1518) who was troubled by the undue presence of women in monasteries of the Order; *John Alanbridge* (Byland, 1525–1538), a Crown Visitor for the Order who presided at the deposition of Abbot Kirkby of Rievaulx; *John Baddesley* (Merevale, 1488-1525), the length of whose service probably gave stability to his house; *Roland Blyton* (Rufford, 1516–1533; Rievaulx, 1533–1538), who retained his affection for Rufford, and appears to have lived into his eighties; and *John Harwood* (Hulton, 1528–1535; Vale Royal, 1535–1539), falsely accused of murdering a monk who had taken his own life.

William Hickman (Stratford, 1490–1516), a Reformator of the Order was much involved in supervising the monasteries in his charge; *Henry More* (St Mary Graces, 1516–1539) gained the abbey of Coggeshall *in commendam*; *Thomas Stevens* (Netley, 1529–1536; Beaulieu, 1536–1538), showed concern for the welfare of the debtors in sanctuary there; *Richard Stopes* (Meaux, 1523–1539), politically astute, kept his abbey away from serious involvement in the Pilgrimage of Grace; *Robert Thornton* (Jervaulx, 1511–1533), in whose time young Edward Paynter was forcibly made a novice; and *Richard Wyche* (Tintern, 1521–1536), who delayed answering a summons to attend upon Cromwell until his abbey had kept the feast of the Nativity of Our Lady. These are a few of the abbots whose fuller biographies have yet to be compiled.

Cistercian Bishops

In the decades preceding the Dissolution six Cistercian abbots are known to have been consecrated to the episcopate, three as diocesans (Dafydd ap Ieuan and Dafydd ap Owain, both of St Asaph, and Thomas Skevington of Bangor) and three as suffragans (Abbots Church of Thame, Rawlinson of Kirkstead and King of Bruern and Thame.) After the Suppression King was promoted to his own diocese of Oxford, while John Hooper (from Cleeve) eventually became bishop of Worcester. Thomas Calne, abbot of Stanley, became suffragan bishop of Marlborough, and Lewis ap Thomas, formerly abbot of Cymer, was appointed suffragan bishop of Shrewsbury.

The best known of these bishops prior to the Reformation was *Thomas Skevington*, a member of the Pace family of Leicestershire, and taking his surname from the village so called.[316] A monk of Merevale, to which his will shows he remained strongly attached, he was ordained sub-deacon, deacon and priest, in Lichfield Cathedral (1482/83).[317] Nothing is on record regarding his Oxford education. A monk who stood out, he was abbot of Waverley from about 1492 until translated to Beaulieu in 1508. This happened despite his being pardoned that year for offences against the statute of liveries.[318] His reputation by this time must have been considerable since on 17 June 1509 he was consecrated at Lambeth to be bishop of Bangor, continuing to hold the abbacy of Beaulieu *in commendam*.[319] He was empowered to continue all jurisdiction over Beaulieu, 'and the other monasteries subject to it'—Netley, Hailes, Newenham and St Mary Graces.[320] As has been noted he appears to have occasionally been at variance with others in his Order. This was so when in 1514/15 he installed an abbot at his daughter-house of St Mary Graces whom the General Chapter saw as a 'rebellious' monk and 'pretended abbot'. He was Richard Prehest who died two years into his abbacy.[321]

Little is recorded regarding his quarter-of-a-century as abbot and bishop. His ordinations of his own monks were held at Beaulieu, and it was said in 1533 that he had not visited his diocese of Bangor for fourteen years, but he did not forget it.[322] In 1515 he gave Abbot John Baddesley of Merevale, the house of his own profession, the parish of Llangynhafal in Gwynedd.[323] Skevington vigorously defend the rights of his monastery when officers of Cardinal Wolsey wished to assume ownership of Beaulieu's valuable holdings at St Keverne in Cornwall.[324] His relations with Wolsey were extremely poor, partly because of his non-residence at Bangor and partly because in 1524 Wolsey's candidate for the archdeaconry of Anglesey was passed over in favour of Skevington's nominee.[325] He was nominated in 1526 for a period of nine years, together with Abbot Henry More of St Mary Graces, to collect from the Cistercian monasteries of England and Wales no less than 3,150 marks, 'proxies legatine' payable to Cardinal Wolsey.[326] In 1531, after Wolsey's downfall and death, Henry VIII called upon the two abbots to render the 1,000 marks supposed so far to have been collected.[327]

In a separate issue, in May 1532 the King acknowledged the receipt of 100 marks from Cromwell, in full payment of 500 marks due for a fine 'made and concluded with the bishop of Bangor.' This fine had been imposed on Skevington 'for offences against the statutes of provisions [1393] and praemunire [1351].' Both these limited the scope of papal authority in Britain, and the huge fine was imposed seemingly for offences as bishop rather than as abbot..[328] In his last years Skevington was also in the king's disfavour on account of 'offences [in Hampshire] against the King's game.'[329] Despite this the abbot's name was placed in 1533 on the commission of the peace for Hampshire.[330]

In that year of his death, which took place on 17 August 1533, Skevington was then said to be 'the richest monk in England.'[331] A letter, perhaps wrongly ascribed to 1538 and sent to an unknown correspondent, says that about 1530 the bishop had 10,000 marks in the keeping of John Milles, a prominent Southampton citizen and merchant, and that he visited Southampton once a year to check his money, 'wher any lackyd or noo.'[332] Perhaps with the wide variety of refugees from justice finding sanctuary at Beaulieu, Skevington thought that to safeguard his assets at Southampton was a safer bet!

The same letter tells that Skevington after rising on the morning of 17 August 'called for water to wash his hands, and then washing his hands and face, the palsy took him so that he never spoke after.' John Mills and one Pace (indubitably a family member)[333] and others placed a pen in his hands, and Skevington 'wrote a will after their pleasure, and he was verily dead before they finished, and other will he made none.' This was not true for on 21 August 1533 probate was granted for his will seemingly dated 10 May 1528. There is a discrepancy in the National Archives copy of the will; it purports to have been made on 10 May 1528, but also says in the 25th year of Henry VIII, which would give a date of 10 May 1533. In the will he made provision for his burial and obits, both at Beaulieu and Bangor. He requested no less than 2,000 Masses to be 'sung and said' for his soul; he wished his body to be buried at Beaulieu, but his heart at Bangor cathedral, 'before the picture of St Deiniol,' its patron saint.[334]

Skevington left two pounds towards the reparations of St Bernard's College, Oxford, and to Merevale abbey, where he had been professed, a suit of vestments or £22 and silver-gilt plate. To Waverley, where he had previously been abbot, he willed a suit of vestments valued at £20 and two parcel gilt cups, and he also bequeathed £2 to one Dan Thomas Johnson. He showed concern for his faithful lay servants—desiring that they should be paid for half-a-year (in some instances for a whole year) after his demise. In his life-time Skevington completed work on the bishop's palace at Bangor, commenced by Bishop Henry Deane (1496–1500), and in his latter years he restored the nave of Bangor Cathedral, and initiated work on its tower. Now, in his will, he directed that the steeple be finished and a fourth bell hung there. Of his work for the cathedral fabric, the priest-poet, Dafydd Trefor, said the bishop had spent 'a chestful of gold.'[335] Inscriptions at the cathedral and palace record his work, whilst the gatehouse chapel of Merevale had a window inscribed with the date of his death and the arms of the see of Bangor, placed there at his wish. There was formerly also a window in his memory at Skeffington church.[336]

In north Wales two Cistercian abbots in succession occupied the relatively poor see of St Asaph.[337] The first was *Dafydd ap Ieuan ap Iorwerth* of a local Denbighshire family, who was professed before 1480 as a monk of Aberconwy. Dispensed for illegitimacy in 1480 (as he was the son of a Cistercian monk and an unmarried woman),[338] he was elected that year abbot of Valle Crucis; an election confirmed by the abbot of Cîteaux at the request of the abbot of Woburn who was currently making a visitation of the Welsh monasteries.[339] In 1485 Dafydd himself was appointed as a deputy to the abbots of Fountains and Woburn as reformators.[340] Dafydd was much praised in the verse of two Welsh bards, Guto'r Glyn and Gutun Owain, who told of his hospitality, his learning and his building works.[341] It may well be he who converted and extended part of the dorter of Valle Crucis to make new abbatial quarters.

By 1496 Dafydd held in plurality the wardenship of the collegiate establishment of St Peter, Ruthin, bringing him an additional income of £200 yearly. He was permitted to retain this when, on 8 January 1500, he was named as bishop of St Asaph by Pope Alexander VI. Henry VII must have played a major role in his appointment, but the pontiff made it very clear that St Asaph was a see whose provision he reserved to himself.[342] The episcopal palace lay in ruins, so undoubtedly Dafydd continued to reside at Valle Crucis. His was to be a short-lived episcopate for no later than mid-December 1503, Dafydd was dead. His place of burial is not on record, nor his will extant. At Valle Crucis he was succeeded as abbot, but not as bishop, by *John Lloyd* noted as being 'the king's chaplain and doctor of both laws', and who was one of those entrusted with compiling the Welsh pedigree of King Henry VII.[343]

Another abbot who gained the favour of Henry VII was *Dafydd ab Owain,* a native of Meifod, Powys, and later a monk of Strata Marcella who was made deacon and ordained priest in Lichfield cathedral in 1466.[344] Said to have studied at Oxford gaining a degree in canon law, he may have served for a time John Tiptoft, earl of Worcester and chief justice of north Wales, a Yorkist, but who by 1485 had aligned himself with the Tudor cause. A Denbighshire poet praised Dafydd in verse: 'When Harry had need you gave silver and gold ... Harry was glad to repay you what was owed, he has given you an abbacy.'[345] Dafydd was successively abbot of Strata Marcella (1485–), Strata Florida (*c.*1496–1500), and then Aberconwy (1501–1513)—where he restored the monastic buildings. He was named as bishop of St Asaph on 18 December 1503, being permitted to hold the abbacy of Aberconwy *in commendam.*[346]

Dafydd is credited with continuing the restoration work of Abbot Morgan ap Rhys at Strata Florida, repairing the episcopal palace at St Asaph, with building a wooden bridge [Pont Dafydd Esgob] over the River Clwyd nearby, and with the raising in 1507 of the landmark tower of Wrexham parish church—a possession of Valle Crucis.[347] Death, on 11 or 12 February 1513, seems to have taken the bishop unawares. In his will, seemingly dictated and written in the third person, he asked to be buried on the south side of the high altar in his cathedral; he made the usual gifts of vestments and provision for his obit.[348] With one possible exception, no Cistercian monk appears to have been present at his unexpected passing. After Dafydd's death, Henry VIII suggested to Cardinal Wolsey that the now abbot of Valle Crucis, John Lloyd, should succeed him. In the event, a Franciscan, Henry Standish, obtained the see.[349]

The first Cistercian monk of Tudor times to be consecrated as a suffragan bishop was Abbot *Augustine Church* of Thame. Appointed early in 1488 as bishop of Lydda [Lod in Israel today], he was required to live there in person although also permitted to hold Thame abbey *in commendam*. In May 1488, this requirement was varied as Lydda was *in partibus infidelium* and he therefore could not go nor remain there safely. He acted as a suffragan in the diocese of Lincoln (1488–1512), and of Salisbury (1488–1499); also assisting in the diocese of Exeter.[350]

In July 1488 at the petition of Henry VII, because he could derive no income from Lydda, he received papal dispensation to hold two benefices. He was instituted to the churches of Boscombe, Wiltshire (1497) and Washingborough, Lincolnshire (1509).[351] His appointment saw a visit to him paid by the abbot of Stratford, a Reformator of the Order, noting that the new bishop wished to hold the abbey *in commendam*; the expenses of this journey were noted as being £1-5-0 under the year 1492, so this claim must have been for a back-payment. Did Abbot William Hickman, the Reformator, wish to dissuade Abbot Augustine from undertaking this dual role?[352]

Less is known of Abbot *John Rawlinson* of Kirkstead from 1509 to 1521. Made deacon as a monk of that house in 1500, and ordained priest in 1502,[353] on 10 September 1512 he was appointed a suffragan within the diocese of York, and titular bishop of 'Ariensis', holding his abbacy *in commendam*.[354] He also acted in the Lincoln diocese between 1519 and 1522. Like most suffragans, and many abbots, it was necessary for him to hold secular benefices, in order to maintain the dignity of his office. By 1509 Rawlinson was rector of Newton Kyme, North Yorkshire, and from 1511 rector of Kirkby-on-Bain, Lincolnshire.[355] He retained these parishes once a bishop.

Another abbot of Thames to be elevated to the episcopate was *Robert King*, abbot there from 1527, having been transferred from the abbacy of Bruern.[356] His father was a Thame yeoman, but Robert became a monk of Rewley and also attending St Bernard's College, Oxford (whose chapel he later consecrated), obtained his B. Th. degree in 1507.[357] In January 1527 King was nominated as titular bishop of Rheon (in the Transcaucasus) as a suffragan to the bishop of Lincoln.[358] On 5 May that year, in the bishop's chapel at Lincoln, he made his profession of obedience as abbot of Thame, and the next day was consecrated as bishop.[359] He was as a bishop both to consecrate the chapel at St Bernard's College, and to bless Richard Grene as new abbot of Biddlesden in 1535.[360] His financial position was eased by receiving in 1535 a prebend in Lincoln cathedral which he exchanged in 1536 for the church of Biggleswade. From 1530 he was also vicar of Charlbury, Oxfordshire. His building work at Thame has been noted (Chapter 1).

A letter written, perhaps to Cromwell, by a 'eucharistic minister' from Stamford, Lincolnshire, on 14 October 1535, described a sermon Bishop King allegedly gave on 19 September in Stamford church. If the report was true, then the bishop was not in accord with the 'New Learning' which became fashionable in those years. In his address he apparently rebuked those 'young men who carried the New Testament in their hands or at their girdles,' especially those who explained it in taverns. Further, King was reported as maintaining the efficacy of mediation by the Blessed Virgin and the saints, and deploring the destruction of their statues. He also said that 'the Lord's Prayer should not be said by heretics, infidels or imperfect men.' The correspondent said that he would not have dared to report the matter, 'on account of the power of the bishop,' but for the fact of there being reliable witnesses present.[361]

The sermon did Robert King no harm. In December 1537 he was elected abbot of Augustinian Oseney, an appointment organised by Cromwell to facilitate that abbey's surrender. Thame was dissolved on 17 November 1539, Oseney the next day. King was appointed to the new bishopric of Oseney and Thame, eventually to become the first bishop of the new diocese of Oxford in 1546. It does not seem to have been difficult for him to adjust his theological positions with the succession of Edward VI and then Mary. Indeed in 1555 he was one of the prosecuting (or as some would have it 'persecuting') bishops presiding at the trial of Archbishop Thomas Cranmer. Dying in 1557 he was interred in his Oxford cathedral at Christ Church, where his canopied tomb now stands in the south transept.[362]

Alleged at his trial in 1554 to have been formerly a monk of Cleeve, though his ordination has not been traced, *John Hooper* was destined to become a man of protestant sympathies and bishop of Gloucester and Worcester.[363] Gaining his first degree at Oxford in 1519, in 1538 (the year after Cleeve was suppressed) he appears as rector of Liddington, Wiltshire, a living in the gift of Sir Thomas Arundell, one of Cromwell's commissioners for the suppression of the monasteries. His protestant sympathies saw Hooper—for safety's sake—spend much of the 1540s in Paris, Strasbourg and then Zürich, where he developed lasting friendship with the theologian of like views, Bullinger. After Edward VI's accession Hooper returned to Britain in 1549, and was consecrated bishop of the new see in 1551. Despite having supported Mary's accession to the throne, Hooper was tried for heresy and, on 4 February 1555, burnt at the stake in Gloucester.

Two former Cistercian abbots were appointed as suffragan bishops almost immediately following the suppression of their houses: Thomas Morley as bishop of Marlborough, and Lewis ap Thomas as bishop of Shrewsbury. Morley (*alias* Calne), a monk of Stanley, was made subdeacon and deacon and ordained priest in 1506,[364] and from 1527 to 1536 was the last abbot of his monastery, gaining an annual pension of £24 on its closure.[365] As then had become the rule, Bishop Shaxton of Salisbury submitted two names to Henry VIII for the appointment to the new suffragan bishopric of Marlborough. The monarch's choice fell on Morley,[366] he was consecrated on 4 November 1537 and died perhaps not until 1561.[367]

Lewis ap Thomas, was a monk of Valle Crucis when made deacon in 1514.[368] Abbot of Cymer from 1517 to 1537, he was described as 'a good husband,' that is, a wise guardian of the monastery and its assets.[369] When a new abbot had to be appointed at Valle Crucis in 1534, Lewis hoped to be preferred to that house of his profession himself, but it was not to be. Consecrated bishop of Shrewsbury at Lambeth on 24 June 1537,[370] it must have been with a heavy heart that on Ember Saturday, 17 December 1541, he ordained to the priesthood John Lloyd ap Rhys, in Llandegla church, not far from the now closed Valle Crucis.[371] Lewis was a co-consecrator on 3 May 1545 in Westminster Abbey of Bishop Anthony Kitchin of Llandaff,[372] and his income was supplemented from 1545 by the vicarage of Bloxham, Oxfordshire. His monastic pension was but £6-13-4, and he also died in 1561.[373]

Notes

[1] M. E. C. Walcott, ed. 'Inventory of Whalley Abbey.' In: *THSLC*, N.S. 7, 1867, pp. 103–04.

[2] C. Cross and N. Vickers, *Monks, friars and nuns in sixteenth century Yorkshire*, Leeds: Yorkshire Archaeological Soc., 1995, p. 165.

[3] G. S. Thomson, 'Woburn Abbey and the Dissolution of the Monasteries.' In: *Trans. Royal Historical Soc.*, 4th Series, **16**, 1933, pp. 132–33.

[4] A. N. Shaw, 'The Involvement of the Religious Orders in the Northern Risings.' In:

Downside Review **117**, No. 407, April, 1999, p. 102.

5   M. H. Dodds, *The Pilgrimage of Grace and the Exeter Conspiracy*, I, Cambridge U.P., 1915, p. 106.

6   Thomson, *Woburn Abbey*, 1933, p. 157.

7   NLW, Badminton Manorial Deeds.

8   NLW, Badminton Deeds, Group 1, No. 1657; Group 2, Nos. 14471, 14481–82.

9   D. H. Williams, *White Monks in Gwent and the Border*, Pontypool: Griffin Press, 1976, p.111.

10   For these individual cellarers, see the references given in the Appendix.

11   C. W. Green, *Biddlesden and its Abbey*, Buckingham: E.N. Hillier and Sons, 1974, pp. 25, 63–64.

12   S. F. Hockey, *Beaulieu, King John's Abbey*, Beaulieu: Pioneer Publns., 1976, pp. 182, 186–87.

13   J. A. Sparks, *In the Shadow of the Blackdowns*, Bradford-on-Avon: Moonraker Press, 1978, p. 114.

14   E. A. B. Barnard, *The Last Days of Hailes Abbey*, Evesham: Evesham Journal, 1928, p. 7.

15   TNA, SC6/HENVIII/1796.

16   NLW, Badminton Manorial 1575–1576; Williams, *White Monks in Gwent*, 1976, pp. 118–19.

17   TNA, STAC2/15, f. 281.

18   *LP* **3**, Part:2, p. 1976 [No. 2535/2].

19   TNA, LR 1/174, f. 35 [11-11-1538].

20   *Statuta* **2**, p. 200 [No. 1238/76].

21   See the Appendix for relevant references.

22   S. M. Harrison, *The Pilgrimage of Grace in the Lake Counties*, Royal Historical Society, 1981, p. 129.

23   J. Youings, *The Dissolution of the Monasteries*, London: Blandford Press, 1972, p. 69; VCH, *County of Worcester* **2**, London, 1906, p. 153.

24   C. Haigh, *The Last Days of the Lancashire Monasteries and the Pilgrimage of Grace*, Manchester U.P., 1969, pp. 147, 245

25   TNA, E315/427/3, ff. 39r, 40r.

26   TNA, SC6/HENVIII/1796.

27   TNA, SC6/HENVIII/2005B.

28   TNA, SC6/HENVIII/1796.

29   D. H. Williams, *Cistercians in the Early Middle Ages*, Leominster: Gracewing, 1998, p. 77.

30   TNA, C1/828/23–26.

31   *LP* **4**, Part 3, p. 2741 [No. 6141].

32   *Statuta* **5**, pp. 438–39 [No. 1482/37]; Williams, *The Welsh Cistercians*, Leominster: Gracewing, 2001, pp. 65–66.

33   *SAP* **2**, p. 63 [1518].

34 *AC,.* 1882, p. 71.

35 *LCCS*, p. 129; *VCH, Cheshire* **3**, Oxford U.P., 1980, p. 154.

36 *LP* **9**, p. 131 [No. 394].

37 *LP* **8**, p. 413 [No. 1048/vii]

38 TNA, E315/91, f. 26.

39 Barnard, *The Last Days of Hailes Abbey*, p. 7.

40 TNA, E245, f. 145; E314/77.

41 'The prior of Bondon'—presumably Bindon: TNA, E36/154, ff. 110v–111r; *LP* **10**, p. 496 [No. 1191].

42 TNA, E315/100, ff. 249v–250v

43 Williams, *Cistercians in the Early Middle Ages*, 1998, p. 77.

44 Barnard, *Last Days of Hailes*, 1928, p. 7.

45 *RC*, **3**, pp. 555–61 [1004].

46 For these pensions, see the individuals listed in the Appendix.

47 *Letters*, pp. 200–02 [No. 99].

48 *LP* **11**, p. 115 [No. 276].

49 *Letters*, p. 222 [No. 109].

50 SSC, SR18/1/957.

51 *Letters*, pp. 156–58 [No. 79]; *LC*, pp. 59–60 [No. 29].

52 I. Grainger and C. Phillpotts, *The Cistercian Abbey of St Mary Graces*, London: Museum of London, 2011, p. 92; *Cf.* TNA, C1/426/49; *LP* **2**, Part 1, p. 533 [No. 1861].

53 *CPL* **20**, p. 497 [No. 709].

54 *LP* **9**, pp. 397–98 [No. 1167].

55 Williams, *Cistercians in the Early Middle Ages*, 1998, p. 77.

56 *Letters*, p. 160 [No. 80].

57 G. G. Perry, 'The Visitation of the Monastery of Thame.' In: *EHR* **3**, 1888, pp. 705–07.

58 *Reg. R. FitzJames*, f. 183v [194v].

59 Essex R.O., D/DRg 1/104.

60 Grainger and Phillpotts, *St Mary Graces*, 2011, p. 90.

61 SAL MS 14, ff. 23–35, is a fifteenth-century manuscript giving detailed proceedings for the cession, resignation and election of abbots.

62 Williams, *Cistercians in the Early Middle Ages*, 1998, p. 72.

63 *RC* **2**, pp. 388–89 [No. 732].

64 SAL, MS 14, ff. 58v–59r.

65 *Letters*, p. 206 [No. 99].

66 *CPL* **20**, pp. 108–09 [No. 165]

67 At Furness in 1497 Abbot Huby also acted promptly; Abbot Chamber died on 12 July; the election was fixed for a week later, 20 July [*Letters*, p. 173].

68 West Sussex R.O., EPI/1/3.

69 J. H. Aveling, *The History of Roche Abbey*, London: John Russell Smith, 1870, pp. 62–63.

70 Cook, *Letters to Cromwell*, 1965, pp. 59–60 [No. 29].

71 Haigh, *Lancashire Monasteries*, 1969, p. 18; *LP* **6**, p. 350 [No. 787].

72 *LP* **13**, Part 1, p. 314 [No. 848].

73 West Sussex R.O., EP1/1/3.

74 LMA, *Reg. R. Fitzjames*, f.59 [61]. See: Reg. C. Tunstall, f. 147r, for blessing of Abbot Love of Coggeshall [1527], and ff. 64v [67r], for the blessing of Abbot Etherway of Stratford [1516].

75 Lichfield R.O., *Reg. G. Blyth*, f. 31.

76 C. Gill, *Buckland Abbey*, Plymouth: s.n., 3rd edn. 1968, pp. 36, 40.

77 Bannister, *Reg. C. Bothe*, 1921, p. 177.

78 Winchester R.O., *Reg. R. Fox*, vol. 2, ff. 24r, 25v–26r, respectively.

79 LMA, *Reg. R. Fitzjames*, f. 64v [67r].

80 Worcester R.O., *Reg. J. Alcock*, f. 93.

81 For references to thse individual abbots, please refer to the Appendix.

82 For this section, see: Williams, *Welsh Cistercians*, 2001, p. 71.

83 *LP* **2**, Part 2, p. 1262 (No. 4070).

84 Williams, *Welsh Cistercians*, 2001, pp. 66–68; *LP* **12**, Part 2, pp. 59–60 [No. 181]: the cost of his board was 10s

85 TNA, E315/91, f. 24; C1/870, m.4; Williams, *Welsh Cistercians*, 2001, pp. 76–77.

86 *CPL* **6**, p. 159.

87 M. Carter, 'Robert Thornton', *ODNB* on-line.

88 *CPL* **7**, p. 144; *VCH, Yorkshire* **3**, 1913, p. 130.

89 *CPL* **12**, p. 34.

90 *CPL* **6**, pp. 159 465 (St Mary Graces), 467 (Beaulieu); **7**, pp. 514 (Coggeshall); **8**, p.142 (Warden), **10**, p. 413 (Stratford).

91 G. Coppack, *Fountains Abbey*, Stroud: Tempus, 2003, p. 129

92 C. Sherwin, 'The History of Ford Abbey,' *RTDA* **59**, 1927, p. 259

93 D. Winkless, *Hailes Abbey*, Stocksfield: Spredden, 1990, p. 76; D.N. Bell, 'The Life and Times of Stephen Sagar, Last Abbot of Hailes.' In: *Cîteaux* **62**, 2011, p. 305.

94 *LP* **10**, pp. 105–06 [No. 284].

95 *LP* **4**, Part 1, p. 94 [No. 235].

96 Lincoln R.O., *Reg. J. Longland*, f. 109v. A similar inventory was made at Stoneleigh on the resignation of Abbot Robert Sutton in 1532 [SSC, DR18/1/723].

97 *VCH, County of York*, **3** (London, 1974) p. 152.

98 G. Moorhouse, *The Pilgrimage of Grace*, London: Weidenfeld & Nicolson, 2002, pp. 317–18, M. E. C. Walcott, 'Inventory of Whalley Abbey.' In: *THSLC*, N.S. **7**, 1867, p. 107.

99 *CPL* **19**, p. 57 [No. 98].

100 TNA, LR6/152/1.

101 This is inferred from his obtaining in Oxford in 1462 a sum of money owing to Buckland by an Oxford surgeon: *BRUO* 1974, **2**, 1397–98.

102 C. Gill, *Buckland Abbey*, Plymouth: s.n. 1951, pp. 33–34; D. M. Smith, *Heads of Religious*

Houses, England and Wales **3**, Cambridge U.P., 2008, pp. 75–76; West Devon R.O., 70/135, gives him as abbot in 1466; 70/249 in 1476, 70/252 in 1486. He was succeeded by Thomas Whyte by 1508.

[103] *Letters*, pp. 200–09 [Nos. 99–101].

[104] *Statuta* **5**, pp. 237–38 [Nos. 1500/23, 25].

[105] *CPL* **20**, pp. 309–10 [No. 434]

[106] *Letters*, pp. 247–49 [No. 128]. Dalton had the B. Th. degree and was now cellarer; it is clear that as the latter he was one of the monks passed over by Huby in 1497. Dalton had earlier on behalf of the monastery been to the custom house at Richmond to receive payment of money owed to the abbey by William Spence, parson of Croft: he later deposed that 'how much money he knew not was laid out on a table there, but he did not take the money nor any part of it': TNA, E111/79). The other imprisoned monks were William Ambrose, John Grene, Hugh Egglestone, and Michael Hamerton.

[107] TNA, E135/2/30. The decree mentions the four monks cited above, and also John Harington, Hugh Morton, William Bulvist and John Fery—the later may have been the sub-prior, who died in prison.

[108] *Letters*, pp. 148–49 [No. 128].

[109] TNA, C1/586/63.

[110] *Letters*, pp. 247–49 [No. 128].

[111] Smith, *Heads of Houses* **3**, 2008, p. 295.

[112] TNA, C1/509/67.

[113] *LP* **7**, Part 2, pp. 423–24 [Nos. 1094: Shrewsbury, 1096: Draycot]; VCH, *County of Stafford* **2**, Oxford, 1967, p. 236. [*LP* assign these letters to 1534, but there was no vacancy until 1535 at Hulton]. Cf. Baskerville, *English Monks*, 1937, pp. 59–60; J.L. Tomkinson, *A History of Hulton Abbey, Staffordshire Archaeological Studies*, N.S. **10**, 1997, pp. 59–60.

[114] *LP* **8**, p. 417 [No. 1056].

[115] *LP* **7**, Part 1, p. 405 [No. 1037].

[116] VCH, *County of Chester* **3**, Oxford U.P., 1980, p. 162

[117] TNA, C1/902/16–18; Cf. TNA, E179/15/8b; E322/106; Lichfield R.O. B/A/1/1/14.

[118] TNA, C1/902/16–18.

[119] *LC*, pp. 196–97 [No. CXXIII]; Tomkinson, *Hulton Abbey*, 1985, p. 66; Wikipedia website; Cf. *LP* **13**, Part 2, p. 123 [No. 315]; *LB*, p. 23.

[120] *LP* **7**, Part 1, p. 311 [No. 821]. Baskerville, *English Monks*, 1937, p. 69.

[121] *LP* **4**, Part 3, pp, 2344 [No. 5330], 2653 [No. 5944].

[122] Harrison, *Pilgrimage of Grace*, 1981, p. 129; *LP* **11**, p. 132 [No. 319].

[123] F. A. Gasquet, *Henry VIII and the English Monasteries*, London: J.C. Nimmo, 2nd edn. 1899, p. 280; G.E. Gilbanks, *Some Records of a Cistercian Abbey, Holm Cultram, Cumberland*: s.n. 1899, pp. 92–98.

[124] *LP* **7**, Part 2, p. 471 [No. 1214], *LP* **8**, p. 259 [No. 689, where repeated]; Cf. *LP* **7**, Part 1, p. 360 [No. 943], *LP* **8**, p. 387 [No. 980] –a further repeat, the first may have been

misplaced. Andrews was probably the gentleman of Oxfordshire/Berkshire noted in TNA, E136/181/2 of 1536/38, and possibly a London wool merchant of *c.*1530 [TNA, C241/282/150].

125 *LP* **6**, Part 1, p. 177 [No. 386],

126 J. D. Austin, *Merevale Church and Abbey*, Studley: Brewin, 1998, p. 7.

127 *LP* **4**, p. 3103 [Appendix No. 85].

128 Baskerville, *English Monks*, 1937, pp. 63, 106.

129 TNA, C1/1501/56.

130 TNA, C1/685/10.

131 Williams, *Welsh Cistercians*, 2001, p. 68. After Wolsey's death several abbots wee in arrears for monies owed him for faculties granted, like dispensations on account of illegitimacy, including the abbots of Strata Marcella, Valle Crucis and Whitland (*LP* **4**, Part 3, p. 3048 [No. 6748/14]).

132 Williams, *Welsh Cistercians*, 2001, p. 77.

133 Ibid. p. 77.

134 Baskerville, *English Monks*, 1937, p. 54.

135 VCH, *Essex* **2**, London, 1907, pp. 134–36.

136 *Letters*, p. 144 [No. 71].

137 See the sources cited in the Appendix.

138 TNA, C1/304/36–38. [The response of David Lewis is mostly illegible, but it seems that the annuity was unpaid, and that as Philip Morgan's representatives they retained the monies in lieu].

139 Green, *Biddlesden*, 1974, pp. 24–5.

140 More fully described later in this chapter.

141 *LP* **6**, p. 547 [No. 1376]: the letter is misplaced here under the year of 1533; *Cf.* Baskerville, *English Monks*, 1937, p. 54.

142 Gill, *Buckland*, 1968, pp. 36, 40.

143 *LP* **9**, pp. 210, 398 [Nos. 621, 1167]; *LC*, 59–60 [No. 29].

144 TNA, STAC2/26/163; Williams, *White Monks in Gwent*, 1976, pp. 25–26.

145 TNA, STAC2/15, ff. 159–62; 2/17/259; *LP* **2**, Part 2, pp. 1021–22 [No. 3137]; **3**, Part 1, pp. 511–12 [No. 1288]; Williams, *White Monks in Gwent*, 1976, pp. 109–10; *TBGAS* **73**, 1954, p. 123; *Gloucestershire Notes and Queries* **4**, 1890, pp. 436–39.

146 *Letters*, pp. 249, 252.

147 *LP* **5**, pp. 621, [No. 1477]; **6**, p. 348 [Nos. 778–79]; **7**, p. 206 [No. 516].

148 *LP* **4**, p. 3103 [Appx. 85].

149 D. B. Foss, 'Marmaduke Bradley, Last Abbot of Fountains.' In: *YAJ* **61**, 1989, pp. 103–09; *Cf. LC*, pp. 77–78 [No. 41]; Cross anjd Vickers, *Monks, friars and nuns*, 1995, pp. 113, 115–16; J. S. Fletcher, *The Cistercians in Yorkshire*, London: S.P.C.K., 1919, pp. 254–55; *LP* **4**, Part 3, p. 2395 [No. 5445].

150 *LP* **10**, p. 32 [No. 94], pp. 59–60 [No. 164], 325 [No. 774]; *FOR*, p. 75; Baskerville, *English Monks*, 1937, p. 181.

151   TNA, SC12/7/34.

152   Williams, *Welsh Cistercians*, 2001, pp. 66, 69–70, 77.

153   Ibid. pp. 67–68.

154   VCH, *County of Stafford* II, London, 1908, p. 233; M .J. C. Fisher, *Dieulacres Abbey*, Leek: Hill Bros., 1969, pp. 45–47.

155   TNA, E135/22/21.

156   TNA, STAC2/27/15.

157   *LP* **4**, Part 3, p. 2363 [No. 5373].

158   *DCP*, pp.1–6.

159   TNA, C1/501/56.

160   *LP* **6**, pp. 237 [No. 546]; 391 [No. 913]; W. Brown, 'Edward Kirkby, Abbot of Rievaulx.' In: *YAJ* **21**, 1911, p. 45.

161   C. Nash, 'The Fate of the English Cistercian Abbots.' In: *Cîteaux* **2**, 1965, pp. 101–02; G. W. O. Woodward, *Dissolution of the Monasteries*, London: Blandford Press, 1966, pp. 55–56.

162   TNA, STAC2/7/217; Cf. M. Aveling, 'The Rievaulx Community after the Dissolution.' In: *Ampleforth Journal*, LVII, 1952, p. 111.

163   *LP* **6**, p. 561 [No. 1408].

164   *LP* **6**, [No. 513]

165   *LP* **7**, p. 280 [No. 724]; *LP* **9**, 171 [No. 1152]; *LP* **12**, Part 2, p. 289 [No. 822].

166   *LP* **12**, Part 2, pp. 59–60 [No. 181].

167   *LP* **12**, Part 2, p. 289 [No. 822].

168   TNA, SC6/HENVIII/7319, f.17v; Williams, *White Monks in Gwent*, 1976, p. 26, and note 135..

169   *LP* **12**, Part 2, p. 166 [No. 411/13].

170   TNA, C1/69/345.

171   TNA, E315/86, ff.38v–40r.

172   TNA, E315/92, ff.43v–44v.

173   Williams, *White Monks in Gwent*, 1976, p. 26.

174   TNA, LR1/173, f. 62; SC12/30/4, f. 3r.

175   TNA, E315/91, f. 19.

176   R. Bearman, *Stoneleigh Abbey*, Stoneleigh: Stoneleigh Abbey Ltd., 2004, p. 212.

177   TNA, C24/29 (part 2); E315/91, f. 56v; Williams, *Welsh Cistercians*, 2001, pp. 86, 88

178   *Letters*, pp. 113–14 [No. 52], 145–46 [No. 72]; *Statuta* **5**, pp. 22–23 [No. 1491/53].

179   For the relevant references, see the Appendix.

180   For the relevant references, see the Appendix.

181   *CPL* **16**, pp. 3–4 [No. 5]: 26–08–1492.

182   *CPL* **16**, pp. 494–95 [No. 700].

183   *CPL* **20**, pp. 20, 85 [No. 139], 197 [No. 280], respectively.

184   *LP* **4**, Part 3, pp. 2697–2701 [No. 6047].

185   TNA, E314/76, f. 464.

186 W. C. Smith, *The History of Farnham and the Ancient Cistercian Abbey of Waverley*, Farnham: s..n., 1829, p. 190.

187 L. Beverley Smith, ''Disputes and Settlements in Medieval Wales.' In: *EHR* **106**, 1990, p. 854.

188 *LP* **10**, p. 24 [No. 67].

189 *LP* **1**, Part 1, p. 82 [158/91]; *Patent*, 1486, p. 103; 1503, p. 328; 1507, p. 579.

190 *LP* **1**, Part 1, pp. 432 [No. 804/13], 490 [No. 969/52], 123–24 [No. 257/48]; *LP* **3**, Part 1, pp. 552–53 [No. 1379/16]; *LP* **4**, Part 1, p. 81 [No. 213/2]; *Patent*, 1497, p. 90; 1507, p. 547.

191 *LP* **7**, p. 596 [No. 1601/5].

192 *Patent*, 1499, pp. 180–81.

193 *LP* **1**, Part 2, pp. 489–90 [No. 969/45].

194 *LP* **7**, p. 559 [No. 1498/22].

195 *LP* **5**, p. 347 [No. 725].

196 *LP* **13**, Part 1, p. 563 [1519/18]; *Cf. LP* **13**, Part 1, p. 241 [March 1938; Grant 4].

197 *LP* **10**, p. 24 [No. 67].

198 *SCSC*, pp. 221–25.

199 *LP* **1**, Part 1, p. 996 [No. 2222/16].

200 *LP* **4**, p. 1701 [No. 3822].

201 *LP* **4**, Part 1, p. 721 [No. 1610/11].

202 *LP* **5**, p. 399 [No. 838/19].

203 *LP* **11**, p. 358 [No. 901/9].

204 *AF*, p. lxix.

205 T. Bostock and S. Hogg, *Vale Royal Abbey, 1277–1538*, Cheshire: Vale Royal Borough Council, 1999, p. 8.

206 TNA, C142/19/109–112, 115, 118–119; *Cf. Patent* 1504, p. 407; 1505, pp. 422, 457; 1506, pp. 457, 507–08

207 TNA, C142/19/110.

208 *Patent* 1505, p. 396

209 P. D. Mundy, 'Star Chamber Proceedings.' In: *Sussex Record Society* **16**, 1913, p. 38.

210 *LP* **13**, Part 1, p. 127 [No. 370].

211 TNA, E328/26; *Cf.* Worcester R.O., *Reg. G. Ghinucci*, f. 143.

212 *Reg. J. Morton*, Canterbury, I, p. 34 [No. 123].

213 Haigh, *Lancashire Monasteries*, 1969, pp. 18–19.

214 TNA, C1/205/24.

215 *LP* **5**, p. 638 [No. 1506].

216 *LP* **13**, Part 1, p. 127 [No. 370]; Sparks, *In the Shadow of the Blackdowns*, 1978, p. 107.

217 *LP* **13**, Part 2, p. 510 [No. 1217].

218 Williams, *White Monks in Gwent*, 1976, p. 30.

219 TNA, C1/388/44: ['Alwoldeby' might perhaps be correlated with 'Autby'].

220 *LP* **3**, Part 2, pp. 1047–48 [No. 2483]; *Cf.* pp. 1083 [No. 2552], 1976 [No.2535/2].

[221] Sherwin, 'Ford Abbey,' 1927, p. 255.

[222] *CPL* **16**, pp. 185–87 [No. 257].

[223] *CPL* **16**, pp. 214–15 [No. 209].

[224] *CPL* **20**, pp. 141–42 [No. 218], 325–25 [No. 462].

[225] Cheshire Archives, DCH/A/151.

[226] TNA, C1/327/31, 33.

[227] Winkless, *Hailes Abbey*, 1990, pp. 49–50.

[228] *LW*, p. 107 [No. 156].

[229] Ibid. p. 312 [No. 463].

[230] Cross, *Monks, friars and nuns*, 1995, p. 156

[231] *BW*, p. 3 [No. 6].

[232] See also Chapter 4.

[233] *Short History of Dunkeswell*, Honiton: Abbey Preservation Fund, 1974, pp. 5–6.

[234] TNA, DL25/3267.

[235] VCH, *Essex* **2**, 1907, p. 131.

[236] *LP* **6**, p. 465 [No. 111/4].

[237] *LP* **12**, Part 2, p. 320 [No. 911/ii].

[238] *LP* **2**, Part 1, p. 365 [No. 1350].

[239] *LP* **1**, Part 1, p. 20 [No. 20].

[240] TNA, E36/152, f. 7; possibly 'Bronne

[241] TNA, C1/599/21.

[242] TNA, C1/697/45.

[243] *ECW*, pp. vi–viii, 180; 'curate' here means the incumbent, not an assistant priest.

[244] Much of what follows is derived from C.H. Talbot, 'Marmaduke Huby, Abbot of Fountains.' In: *Analecta Sacri Ordinis Cisterciensis*, **20**, 1964, pp. 165–84.

[245] *Letters*, p. 173 [No. 86]. ??? 80?

[246] *CPL* **11**, p. 557 note.

[247] D. Knowles, *The Religious Orders in England* **3**: *The Tudor Age*, Cambridge U.P., 1971, p. 35.

[248] Ibid. p. 107 [No. 48].

[249] Williams, *Welsh Cistercians*, 2001, pp. 63–64.

[250] *Letters*, p. 132 [No. 66].

[251] Ibid. pp. 188 [No. 93], 208 [No. 101].

[252] Ibid. p. 247 [No. 127].

[253] Ibid. p. 213 [No. 104], Cf. Talbot, *Marmaduke Huby*, 1964, passim.

[254] *LP* **3**, Part 1, p. 166 [No. 475].

[255] *Letters*, p. 252 [No. 131].

[256] *LP* **3**, Part 2, p. 1324 [No. 3171].

[257] *FLB*, pp. 64–66 [No. 75].

[258] TNA, STAC1/2/58; 2/17/8.

[259] J. H. Bettey, *Suppression of Monasteries in the West Country*, Gloucester: Alan Sutton,

1989, p. 108.

260 This section is entirely based on Bell,
Life and Times of Stephen Sagar, 2011, pp. 283–318.

261 N. Orme, 'Dunne, Gabriel,' *ODNB*, 2008.

262 LMA, *Register Richard FitzJames*, ff. 158r [169v], 161v [172r], 182r.

263 J. Stéphan, *A History of Buckfast Abbey*, Bristol: Burleigh Press, 1970, p. 203.

264 N. Orme, 'Dunne, Gabriel,' *ODNB*, 2008.

265 *LP* **9**, p. 57, note 182.

266 Christopher Andersson in his *Annals of the English Bible* (1845) called Dunne 'the basest betrayer,' but Professor Orme vigorously refutes that: N. Orme, 'The Last Medieval Abbot of Buckfast.' In: *RTDA*, **133**, 2001, pp. 101–02.

267 *LP* **8**, p. 449 [No. 1151].

268 LP **9**, p. 171 [No. 522]: The entry has been construed as Gabriel receiving a gift from Cromwell; it reads 'for Sir Gabriel Donne, late abbot elect,' but it is in notes of receipts *by* Cromwell, and should undoubtedly read 'for the promotion of Sir Gabriel Dunne.'

269 Stéphan, *Buckfast*, 1970, p. 207.

270 Orme, 'Last Medieval Abbot,' 2001, p. 103.

271 TNA, E164/31, f. 34r.

272 Orme, 'Last Medieval Abbot,' 2001, p. 104.

273 Stéphan, *Buckfast*, 1970, pp. 209–10.

274 Orme, 'Last Medieval Abbot,' 2001, p. 104; W. H. Stevenson and H. E. Salter, *Early History of St John's College, Oxford*, Oxford: Oxford Historical Soc., 1939, p. 44.

275 Stéphan, *Buckfast*, 1970, p. 210.

276 *LP* **6**, pp. 425–26 [No. 988].

277 *LP* **5**, pp. 571–72 [No. 1317].

278 *LP* **6**, pp. 425–26 [No. 988].

279 Gilbanks, *Records of a Cistercian Abbey*, 1899, pp. 91–97.

280 Haigh, *Last Days of the Lancashire Monasteries*, 1969, p. 19; *LP* 6, p. 425 [No. 987].

281 *LP* **6**, pp. 425 [Nos. 985–86), 627 [No. 1557]. Only one of the several deeds is exactly dated, so it is not possibble to give a certain sequence of events.

282 TNA, LR1/173, f. 132r–v; E314/20/11, f. 3r.

283 TNA, LR1/173, ff. 141–143; *LP* **13**, Part 1, p. 161 [No. 436].

284 C. Harper-Bill, C., 'Cistercian Visitation.' In: *Bulletin of the Institute of Historical Research*, **53**, 1980, p. 112.

285 *Statuta* **5**, pp. 438–39 (No. 1482/37); D.H. Williams, 'White Monks in Powys.' In: *Cistercian Studies* **11**, 1976, pp. 172–73; R. Hays, *History of the Abbey of Aberconway*, Cardiff: University of Wales Press, 1963, p. 135.

286 Worcestershire R.O., *Reg. J. Alcock*, f. 93.

287 *AC*, 1882, p. 71.

288 Hays, *Aberconway*, 1963, p. 136.

289 *Letters*, pp. 127–30 [No. 64].

290 *Statuta* **5**, p. 536 [No. 1486/18].

291 *Letters*, pp. 176–77 {No. 88], 181 [No. 89], *Cf.* pp. 191–92 [No. 95].

292 Ibid. pp. 191 [No. 94], 221 [No. 109], 251 [No. 129].

293 *Statuta* **6**, p. 123.

294 *Letters*, p. 191 [No. 94].

295 Williams, *White Monks in Powys*, 1976, p. 173.

296 *Statuta* **6**, p. 377.

297 TNA, E315/48, m. 3.

298 *Letters*, p. 262.

299 *Reg. R. Mayew* (Hereford) p. 250. ?? 251

300 LP **1**, Part 1, p. 230 [No. 438/2, m. 27].

301 L. Thomas, *Reformation in the Old Diocese of Llandaff*, Cardiff: William Lewis, 1930, p. 30.

302 Ibid. p. 30.

303 G. Williams, *Welsh Church from Conquest to Reformation*, Cardiff: University of Wales Press, 1962, p. 399.

304 *Letters*, pp. 251–52 [No. 129].

305 D.H. Williams, *Welsh Cistercians*, 2001, p. 67.

306 *Statuta* **6**, pp. 509 [No. 1517/A], 525–26 [No. 1518/A.

307 TNA, E326/12613.

308 *Letters*, pp. 260–63.

309 LP **5**, p. 456 [No. 978/6].

310 LP **2**, p. 1836 [No. 18], 10, p, 159 [No. 392/48].

311 E.J. Saunders, 'Lleision ap Thomas.' In: *Dictionary of Welsh Biography*, London: Honourable Society of the Cymmrodorion, 1959, pp. 567–68.

312 *AC*, 1853, p. 243.

313 Thomas, *Reformation in the Old diocese of Llandaff*, 1930, p. 42; G. Williams, 'Neath Abbey.' In: E. Jenkins, ed. *Neath and District: A Symposium*, Neath: Elis Jenkins, 1974, p. 150.

314 G. Williams, *Welsh Reformation Essays*, Cardiff: University of Wales Press, 1967, p. 96.

315 T.B. Pugh (ed.), *Glamorgan County History*, **3**, Cardiff: University of Wales Press, 1971, pp. 510, 512.

316 For much of what follows, see: Glanmor Williams, 'Skevington, Thomas' (*ODNB* online). In about 1528 Skevington assumed temporary care of a kinsman and royal courtier, Richard Pace, who had suffered a nervous breakdown: C. Curtis, 'Richard Pace', *ODNB* on line.

317 *Reg. J. Hales*, ff.279r, 280r, 281v.

318 *Patent* 1508, 569. [This statute of 1506 restricted the issuing of livery badges by others than the king; it was a means of asserting royal authority. In what way Skevington had offended is not known.]

319 CPL **19**, p. 612 [No. 2246].

320 *CPL* **20**, p. 531 [No. 805].

321 *Statuta* 6, pp. 474–75 [No. 22–23].

322 *LP* **4**, , Part 3, p. 2449 [No. 5533].

323 A. I. Pryce, *Diocese of Bangor in the Sixteenth Century*, Bangor: Jarvis and Foster, 1923, p. 2.

324 Gasquet, *Henry VIII and the English Monasteries*, 1899, p. 27.

325 Williams, *Welsh Church*, 1962, pp. 304, 309–10.

326 TNA, E210/11308.

327 *LP* **5**, p. 196 [No. 394].

328 *LP* **5**, Part 1, pp. 295 [No. 657], 477 [No. 1052].

329 *LP* **6**, p. 431 [No. 1006].

330 VCH, *Hampshire* II, 1973, p. 144.

331 *LP* **4**, Part 3, p. 2449 [No. 5533].

332 *LP* **13**, Part 2, p. 544 [Appendix 12].

333 A Thomas Pace of Southampton made his will in 1560.

334 TNA, PROB 11/25/59; Hockey, *Beaulieu: King John's Abbey*, 1976, pp. 144–54, 225–28.

335 G. Williams, 'Skevington, Thomas', *ODNB* online.

336 Austin, *Merevale*, 1998, pp. 51–52, 89–90.

337 The paragraphs on these two abbots are mostly based on the present author's entries regarding them in *ODNB* online, where a full bibliography.

338 *CPL* **13**, Part 2, p. 728.

339 *Letters*, pp. 81–83 [Nos. 29–30].

340 Williams, *Welsh Church*, 1962, p. 397; BL, Harley MS 433, f. 209.

341 H.I. Bell, 'Translations from the Cywyddwyr.' In: *THSC*, 1940, p. 251; 1942, p. 146; Clancy, *Medieval Welsh Lyrics*, London: Macmillan, 1965, pp. 221, 224; G.V. Price, *Valle Crucis Abbey*, Liverpool: Hugh Evans & Son., 1952, pp. 270–76.

342 *CPL* **17**, pp. 380–81 [Nos. 594–596].

343 *LP* **2**, Part 2, p. 1262 [No. 4070]; J.Y.W. Lloyd, *The history of the princes, the lords marcher, and the ancient nobility of Powys Fadog* V, London: T. Richards Whiting, 1885, p. 250.

344 R. O. Lichfield, *Reg. J. Hales*, ff. 184, 185v.

345 M. P. Bryant-Quinn, *Gwaith Ieuan ap Llywelyn Fychan*, Aberystwyth University: Centre for Advanced Welsh and Celtic Studies, 2003, p. 88.

346 *CPL* **18**, pp. 200–05.

347 Williams, *Welsh Church*, 1962, pp. 384–85.

348 TNA, PROB 11/17, ff. 169–70.

349 *LP* **2**, Part 2, p. 1262 [No. 4070].

350 *CPL* **15**, pp. 117 [No. 247]:118 [No. 248], 118–19 [No. 250], 130 [No. 279]. *Cf. Letters*, 197 [97], 273. [[*Letters* 197].

351 D.M. Smith, 'Suffragan Bishops in the Medieval Diocese of Lincoln.' In: *Lincolnshire History and Archaeology* 17, 1982, p. 26; *Heads of Religious Houses* 3, 2008, p. 339.

352 *Letters*, pp. 197, 273.

353 Lincolnshire R.O., *Reg. W. Smith*, ff. 22v, 35v.

354 *CPL* **19**, pp. 247 [No. 420], 484–86 [Nos. 836–37].

355 L.A.S. Butler, 'Suffragan Bishops in the Medieval Diocese of York.' In: *NH* **37**, 2000, p. 59 [No. 52].

356 Much of this section is derived from: N. Doggett, 'King, Robert,' *ODNB* online.

357 *BRUO*, Part 2, p. 172.

358 Smith, *Heads of Religious Houses* **2**, 1982. 27.

359 Lincoln R.O., *Reg. J. Longland*, f. 135v.

360 Lincoln R.O., *Reg. J. Longland*, f. 259v.

361 *LP* **9**, p. 207 [No. 611].

362 N. Doggett, 'King,, Robert', *ODNB* on-line.

363 This paragraph is based on the entry by D.G. Newcombe in *ODNB* online.

364 Wiltshire R.O., *Reg. E. Audley*, non-foliated).

365 TNA, E315/255, no. 144; *Cf.* Somerset Archives, DD/WHb/988.

366 *LP* **12**, Part 2, p. 354 [No. 1008/34].

367 Smith, *Heads of Religious Houses* **3**, 2008, p. 336; VCH, *Wiltshire* **3**, London, 1956, p. 274.

368 Lichfield R.O., *Reg. G. Blyth*, non-foliated. For Lewis, see especially Williams, *Welsh Cistercians*, 2001, 65–68, 72, 76, 87–88. His abbacy at Cymer may have followed a brief spell as abbot of Strata Marcella, while he himself may have been displaced at Cymer in the years 1521–25 by an Abbot John.

369 *Letters*, p. 252.

370 Smith, *Heads of Religious Houses* **3**, 2008, p. 287

371 NLW, SA/MB/14, f. 13r.

372 W. de Gray Birch, *Memorials of the See and Cathedral of Llandaff*, Neath: J. E. Richards, 1912, p. 360.

373 Smith, *Heads of Religious Houses* **3**, 2008, p. 287.

4 THE SECULAR COMMUNITY

ITHIN OR ADJACENT to the precincts of all Cistercian monasteries were by Tudor times residents other than the monks. These included temporary and permanent lay staff: servants and officers assisting in the economy and daily life of the abbey; a wide variety of guests: travellers and family members, mostly accommodated in the guest hall; as well as visiting religious, and sick and infirm persons housed in the external infirmary; and corrodians who enjoyed (usually) residential rights on account of long service or a cash down-payment. The typical abbey as the Suppression approached had a diverse group of inhabitants who, when their monastery closed, were faced with homelessness, which was only partly alleviated by such compensation that the Court of Augmentations might decide to award them.[1] The accommodation afforded these lay residents give an insight into the domestic quarters of the abbeys.

Corrodians

The term 'corrody' derives from the medieval Latin, 'conredium', later 'corrodium'. The relevant grants of corrody in Tudor times themselves define the intrinsic meaning of the term. Corrodies were seen as synonymous with 'perpetual living and finding' (Bordesley, 1528), 'daily sustentation' (Buckfast, 1522), 'continual sustenance or provision of food, drink and fuel' (Robertsbridge, 1531), 'meat, drink, clothes and chamber' (Margam, 1531), an 'exhibition' (Neath, 1532), and other like phraseology. A more concise synonym was 'livery', employed for example at Garendon (1523) and Rufford (1525). The reasons for grants of corrody included reward for faithful service or indebtedness to the recipient, but in most cases they were bought by substantial financial down-payments. These both assisted a monastic community, but also offered security for the purchasers in their old age. Few monasteries would have much more than a couple of corrodians at any given time.

In its broadest sense, 'livery' was equivalent to the whole 'provision', hence its adjectival use in 'livery-bread (Margam, 1534).[2] 'Livery' had also on occasion a narrower connotation, referring to the provision of clothing particular for the residential servants. There was mention at Coggeshall of 'our gentlemen's livery' (1532), while Vaudey (1532) made a grant to one servant of 3½ yards of woollen cloth 'for his livery'. These phrases may refer sometimes to the quality of cloth provided, rather than a recognisable uniform. In a great house distinctive livery was certainly to be found; so it was noted of Robinson, a horse marshal during the Pilgrimage of Grace, that he 'weareth the abbot of Furness livery.'[3] The officers of Fountains received grants of clothing according to status: the more important 'of the suit of the gentlemen of the monastery;' the humbler yeoman servants a jacket such as "the yeoman's suit". One officer had as part of his perquisites from Fountains, 'one jacket of the abbot after the form of his livery.[4]'

Accommodation

A corrody mostly, though there were exceptions, implied residence within monastic precincts, whether by single persons or married couples.[5] It was, as implied in a grant made by Garendon (1523), a 'livery' to be taken 'of and in the monastery.'[6] Frequently little more is remarked of accommodation provided other than it being 'an honest chamber' (Calder, 1527) or a 'decent chamber' (Valle Crucis, 1530). Sometimes the nature of the chamber is spelt out: as 'a chamber having chimney and draught in it' (Buckfast, 1520);[7] 'a chamber with a chimney and a house of easement' (Combermere, 1532);[8] and 'a chamber with a chimney which he now lieth in' (Stoneleigh, 1533).[9] In the case of John Bristow, perpetual vicar of Rodbourne Cheney, who purchased for £20 a corrody at Hailes (1494), he was given a chamber in the infirmary showing that it was at least partly divided up.[10]

The location of the accommodation provided is frequently referred to, especially where there had been a substantial down payment and a suitably substantial home was offered. At Cleeve (1528) Stephen and Margaret Jopson who done the monastery 'a large pecuniary service', received 'the great chamber beyond the gate, with other chambers adjacent.'[11] Also at Cleeve (1535) Edward Walker who promised a loan of £100 and had paid £27 in hand, was rewarded with 'a chamber situate under the east part of the fratry house [the first floor refectory], with a door coming and going into the cloister, and another inner chamber for his servant.'[12] (Both Edward's chamber and that of his servant are still to be seen today). Stephen Jopson died, and Margaret perhaps married his brother, for in 1534 Rufford granted a corrody to Christopher [a merchant of 'Berweke'—perhaps one of the Wiltshire Berwicks] and Margaret Jopson which included inhabiting there 'all the new building at the west church door called the New Chambers.'[13]

For forty marks paid beforehand, Richard and Elizabeth Moteram gained at Rufford (1527) 'a lease or corrody,' including for their dwelling house 'the kitchen of the New Chambers, with two parlours and the entry betwixt the kitchen and the two parlours, with the well-house and the yard, and also a chamber over the well-house.'[14] For twenty pounds given the abbey 'at the making of these presents,' Thomas Milner (*al.* Rougedragon) also received from Rufford (1534), 'their house and chamber called the abbot's chamber lying within the monastery between the Chapel of St Bernard of the north side, and a chamber of the abbot and convent, of the south side, with the appurtenances, namely the nether chamber with the buttery, kitchen and wood-house and three other chambers.'[15] A substantial return for his down-payment, but perhaps he could afford it. He was from 1530 to 1536 a junior officer of the College of Arms as Rouge Dragon Pursuivant in Arms in Ordinary; the name being taken from the red dragon of Wales, and this purchase made for a comfortable retirement.[16]

At Ford (1533) Ralph and Agnes Bogshawe 'for £20 paid at ensealing hereof' received one house with a garden called the Lodge.[17] At Garendon (1523), for a downpayment of £40 John Crosby, a mercer late of Loughborough, and his wife Elizabeth were granted 'the house, chambers and kitchen, that Master Ralph Kenington had.'[18] At Grace Dieu (1534), Hywel ap John ap Jevan and his wife, Margaret, received the west end of its gate-house as their dwelling.[19] At Beaulieu (1535) John Mewe and his wife were given a 'hospice' within the walls near the bridge and called 'the Lodging', whilst Thomas Page (1537) was allowed residence in the 'lyme house' with the 'new garden' specially prepared for him.[20]

At Hailes (1518) Christopher and Elizabeth Layghlyn were provided with a substantial residence in a deed which tells that it lay close to the residence of one William Russell. Their corrody came at the request of Sir John Huddleston, described as 'a generous and extremely liberal benefactor' to the monastery.[21] At Hailes also, Lady Jane Huddleston made a generous grant to the abbey in 1513 for Elizabeth Parke, her maid-servant, wishing her to have a decent house and food after her own death.[22] After her husband's death in 1511/12 Lady Jane Huddleston resided in a chamber of the monastery at

Hailes, which boasted a portable altar, complete with linen, crucifix, cross, chalice and paten.[23]

The grant of accommodation was generally accompanied by relevant perquisites, such as candles and fuel, stabling and horse fodder. Lawrence Stanley at Calder (1527) was entitled to not only 'one honest chamber,' but also 'fire thereto with candlelight' and, further, one horse with fodder and 'to have his launderer, barber and tailor at the cost of the house.'[24] At Valle Crucis (1530) John Howe, who had placed '£20 at the use of the monastery,' was entitled to 'any week, adequate barbering and laundering, both of his shirts and personal linen and of his sheets.'[25] John and Alice Davy, given at Bindon (1534) 'our house at the gate called Newborough Place' in return for £20 and 'other benefits' afforded the abbey, also received the orchard adjacent, and ten cartloads of wood annually.[26]

Thomas and Eleanor Martin at Bordesley (1528) were to have yearly twelve loads of wood, felled and carried at the abbey's costs, and twenty pounds of tallow candles, as well as two kine with the keeping of an horse. They had made a down payment of £40.[27] The monks of Buckfast (1520) were indebted to John Knottesford in the sum of £100, and his generous corrody included 'a feather bed, bolster with blanket, sheets and coverlets,' and if sick he was to have 'an honest keeper.'[28] Formerly a servant of the royal household, and given a corrody at the monastery in 1517 on the king's nomination,[29] this new livery seems to have been a move by James to improve his conditions. John Howe at Valle Crucis (1530) was to be provided with 'an adequate bed with sheets and other necessaries for spending the night relaxing.'

Provision was sometimes made for the servant of a corrodian, or else a helper was provided. At Rufford (1534) Thomas Milner's servant was to have 'meat and drink, like as the abbot and convent doth give their yeomen.' At Cleeve (1535) meat and drink for Edward Walker's servant was to be received 'daily at the table with the servants of the abbot.' [His chamber has been noted]. Lawrence Stanley at Calder (1527) might have 'a child always to be at his commandment, of his own provision, and the said child to sit at the latter dinner,' [i.e: the second sitting]. At Combermere (1532) if Thomas Whittingham was sick, then 'a child was to fetch his livery for him.'[30]

Such references show the presence of children in some of the monasteries, as does the provision made for Thomas Hoggis at Stoneleigh (1519) to have 'a child to wait upon him, and he to have meat and drink as the children that wait upon the convent.'[31] Likewise, when a priest, Thomas Wells, was awarded a corrody at Fountains (1535) he could have 'one child or boy to serve him in his chamber and lie with him, and the child to be allowed meat and drink in the hall as other children hath.'[32] The corrodies afforded married couples demonstrate the presence of women within monastic precincts.

Food and Drink

All resident corrodians received supplies of meals from the kitchens, bread from the bakehouse and beer from the monastic brewhouse. Alternatively, or additionally, male single corrodians might be permitted to dine within an abbey refectory or infirmary or abbot's hall. The Martins at Bordesley (1528) were entitled daily to 'at every meal, a mess of meat' and weekly: six casts of convent bread and three loaves of yeoman's bread, with six gallons of convent ale and four of yeoman'a ale. Ralph and Agnes Bogshawe at Ford (1533) were to be supplied daily at the abbey kitchen with 'potage, fish and flesh, as much as for two monks,' and weekly to receive four casts of convent bread and three of yeoman bread at the bakehouse, as well as five gallons of ale at the brewhouse.[33]

At Rufford (1534) the Jopsons had a similar entitlement 'except that in the Advent of Our Lord when the convent be served with fish, that then they be served with flesh, and a mess of 'brewis'[34] (in other words, a dish of broth) and a piece of beef every flesh day.' A reminder that total abstinence was no longer a feature of Cistercian life. Thomas Hoggis at Stoneleigh (1519) had like rights with a variety of diet including butter, eggs and milk, a herring every day for his breakfast in Lent, and eight cheeses both at Lammas (1 August) and Martinmas (11 November).He too could receive 'upon every fasting day a competent mess of meat for the day.' (It is probable that 'meat' here refers to 'food', and 'competent' to 'appropriate/sufficient').

Unmarried beneficiaries, like Lawrence Stanley at Calder (1527), might eat 'at the table next the convent". James Knottesford at Buckfast (1520) might 'sit at the convent board at dinner and supper or else with the cellarer, steward or kitchener at the same mess.' In addition he was entitled to bread and ale at 8.am. for his breakfast, and again at 3.pm. and 8.pm. daily (a night-cap!). Edward Walker at Cleeve (1535) might have his food at the abbot's table, unless the abbot was absent and then to eat in his own chamber.

Thomas Milner at Rufford (1534) could eat with the abbot and convent, 'or else be served honestly like such a man as he is.' At Stoneleigh Anthony Walker (1533) might eat at the convent or the abbot's yeomen table, 'so long as God shall able him to come to their refection.'[35] If sick food was to be delivered to his room: this was a common provision. The same consideration was promised John Howe at Valle Crucis (1530), otherwise he could eat daily 'at the trestle table in the common hall of the abbot.'

Conditional Clauses

Where a married couple were the recipient of a corrody, it remained in force 'during the life of the longest liver,' but there was the fair provision that, if one partner died, then the food and drink entitlement was normally reduced by one-half for the survivor. On the death of the remaining partner, a few grants detail what should happen to their possessions. When the Crosbys residing at Garendon (1523) were deceased any 'household stuff and chattels' they had brought with them were to become abbey property, save for some carefully listed items—a safeguard for their child's future. At Rufford (1525) Elizabeth Paramour was to leave all her goods to the abbey, but it undertook to give her proper burial and an annual obit thereafter. Happily she outlived the life of the monastery itself. A corrody granted by Rufford (1489) to Edward and Margaret Bierley, required that when they died they left five marks to the monastery or goods to that value.[36]

A common restriction was the forbidding of a recipient to sell his corrody, but the prohibition was not always absolute. It could be that a community might wish to guard against unsuitable persons dwelling in their midst. Edward Lakyn at Buildwas (1535) was not 'to sell or assign his corrody,'[37] but at Stoneleigh (1519) Thomas Hoggis was 'not to sell nor make alienation of his corrody without the consent of the abbot and convent.' At Buckfast (1520) James Knottesford was 'not to give or sell his right or sustentation to any other person that is affected with the pox or other like unreasonable sickness.' Even that understandable clause could be waived by the abbot and community.

Nor did a community wish to have litigious people within the precincts. James Kottesford (Buckfast, 1520) was required not to 'support or aid any person' against the abbey. The Jopsons at Cleeve (1528) were to limit any litigation against the abbey to 'the court of Old Cleeve and in the Chapter

Court there.' Lawrence Stanley at Calder (1527) was not to be an intermediary for people wanting to borrow money. He was 'never to ask any "penny" through the supplication or desire of any great man unto us.'

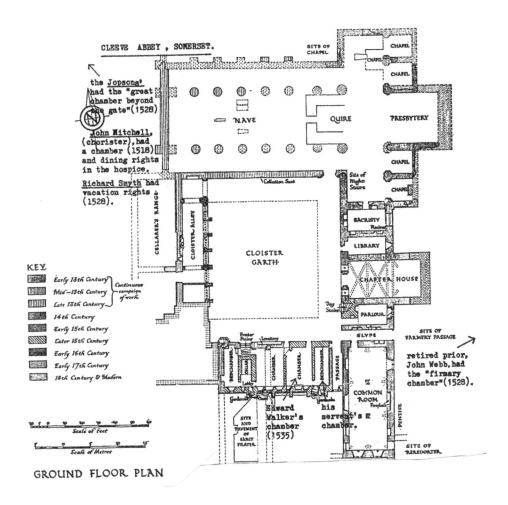

Fig. 10: Plan of Cleeve Abbey with the homes of lay residents
(By permission of English Heritage)

Corrody Values

On the rare occasions when a corrody was commuted for an annuity, some idea might be gleaned as to its relative worth. John Goodriche, a London grocer, and his wife Elizabeth were given a full residential corrody at Vale

Royal (1520), but if they chose not to reside then they could receive £4 yearly instead.[38] At Bindon, instead of the daily dish afforded of 'meat or fish as for one monk,' the Davys could receive 10 pence weekly.[39] The daily and weekly provisions for the Layghlyns at Hailes (1518) were reckoned to be worth 3s 4d. In Lent they could either receive 10 shillings in money or 'sixty white herrings, the same number of red, one ling, one salmon, and two hakes.'

When their abbeys were closed the corrodians were compensated, if they could prove their title, by the Court of Augmentations. Rarely did the annual payment awarded fully compensate for (in many cases) loss of home, and (in all cases) removal of associated perquisites. A few corrodians were more fortunate. The Davys at Bindon were awarded in 1541 an annuity of £4 by the court—they had laid down only in 1534 twenty pounds, but they were permitted to continue to occupy their house at the monastery gate. At Bordesley the Martins were allowed to continue to live in their messuage. At Grace Dieu Hywel ap John ap Ieuan and Margaret his wife were given an annuity of only 30 shillings, but were able to continue to live for term of their lives in the west end of its gate-house.

There was no such favourable decree for James Knottesford who had loaned £100 by 1520 to Buckfast. His recompense was an annuity of £5-6-8. Other post-Suppression annuities which can by no means have fully compensated the former residents, ranged from £11 in the case of the Layghlyns at Hailes, down to only £1 for Elizabeth Paramour at Rufford. The factors determining these individual payments are not known, but the court was fair in one respect: in all cases, it ordered arrears to be paid.

The value of a corrody granted at Margam (1535) to John and Margaret Dorman 'for praiseworthy helpfulness and service,' detailed the value of its several components.[40] Their food was valued at 3d. per day (equivalent to £4-11-3 each year); John received yearly a robe valued at 16s 8d., and they were entitled to 13s 4d. for fuel each year. All this amounted to £6-1-3 per annum, and in addition they received a chamber and daily allowances of bread and beer. Clearly their £4 compensation awarded by the Court of Augmenations was a poor return.

Rarely do disputes concern corrodies awarded or promised, but John Gardiner (*alias* Harry) complained to the Court of Chancery that in 1508-/09, one Walter Gardiner and his wife, Margaret, had bought a corrody or pension at Netley worth twenty marks yearly, After Walter died, having enjoyed the corrody for twenty-four years, Margaret remarried to a John Sampson. Sampson and the new abbot had 'compassed between them' to defraud John (presumably's Walter's son) of the pension. As corrodies were generally only valid for 'the life of the longest liver,' and Margaret although aged was still alive, it is difficult to see his grounds for complaint.[41] Nor are the circumstances known of the complaint to the court by a yeoman, Robert Wyndar, alleging that he had paid 'a sufficient sum of money' to Rievaulx for a corrody of 'meat and drink, and other things,' but after half-a-year of enjoying it, it was removed from him.[42]

Crown Corrodians

Both Henry VII, and more especially Henry VIII, might send a retiring royal servant to an eventide home in a monastery, often on the mythical basis that the monarch was founder or patron of that house. Some twenty-five such persons are on record as having received such a corrody at a total of fourteen Cistercian houses during the reign of Henry VIII, and at his direction.[43] They included Robert Riston, a yeoman of the chamber (Bordesley, 1509); Henry Stephenson, gentleman of the chapel (Coggeshall, 1512); William Dalbourne, groom of the bows (Waverley, 1517); Walron de Choen and Roger More (sewer of the chamber and clerk of the king's bakehouse respectively (Warden, 1521); John Robards, yeoman of the Guard (Vale Royal, 1532) and William Blyke, page of the pitcher house (Kirkstead, 1535).[44] In its closing days Fountains granted annuities of £4 and £6 respectively to Richard and John Smith, valets of the king's wardrobe. With some abbeys already suppressed, it dared not do otherwise.

When at those monasteries deemed to owe the king a service a royal corrodian resigned his livery or died, another person would be nominated in his stead. At Coggeshall, for example, Richard Pygot succeeded William Colman on the latter's resignation. Colman had similarly followed Henry Stephenson, who, in turn, had entered upon the vacancy created by the death of Edward Johns.[45] When it was decided in 1528 that the Princess Mary should live near the king, her household was dissolved, and ten Cistercian abbeys were amongst the houses directed to receive one of her poorest servants.[46]

Occasionally a monastery might attempt to resist a royal request. When in 1532 John Penne, a groom of the king's privy chamber, was directed to Thame on the basis that the house had been 'founded by the king's ancestors,' its community pointed out that 'the house was not so founded, but by the bishop of Lincoln.'[47] It did however not risk the monarch's wrath, but granted the provision demanded. Some Crown corrodies might be commuted in return for an annual financial payment. John Fisher, a retiring gentleman of the Chapel Royal (1513), was nominated for a 'royal' corrody at Stanley, 'or for the corrody seven marks.'[48] George Breggus (1518), a valet of the royal wardrobe, was pensioned with 'a corrody or sustenance of seven marks annually' at the same abbey. Payment in instalments is set down in detail, implying perhaps his corrody too was commuted.[49]

Where a royal corrodian actually resided, and mostly they perhaps did so, they enjoyed like perquisites to those who had purchased their livery. Robert Little, groom of the wardrobe of beds, receiving a corrody at Bordesley (1519) 'at the king's request and command,' was to be given there a chamber 'fit for his status' with sufficient fuel. Weekly he was to receive seven white loaves and seven gallons of connvent ale, and seven black loaves—as the abbot's servants. Daily he was to be given one kitchen dish of meat or fish as for one monk, and also one mark a year—perhaps to cover clothing.[50]

At Coggeshall (1532) Richard Piggott, a gentleman of the Chapel Royal, was to be given daily one convent loaf called 'miche' and another loaf called 'medling',[51] with one gallon of beer and food as for one of the monks. He was to receive sufficient barbering and laundering, and be provided with 'an adequate chamber' with bedding, fuel and candles. He was also to receive 'one *toga* of our gentlemen's livery.' In addition he was to be paid one pound a year, 'as one of our brethren is paid.' He could, if he so wished, commute his entitlement for an annual payment of £3.[52]

When the monasteries closed, and the Crown corrodians presented their clams for compensation to the Court of Augmentations, the annuity they were awarded cannot often have made up for their loss of home. John Bromfeld at Vale Royal, a former valet of the wardrobe, did reasonably well with an annuity of £6-6-8; seven marks were granted to John Fisher and George Bregus at Stanley, whilst Robert Little at Bordesley received but £3.[53]

Residential Servants

The day of the lay-brother (the *conversus*) long gone, every monastery relied on a number of lay officers and servants to maintain its daily life and economy.

Some of these lived within the precincts or close by and received corrodial rights; others may have come into work from their homes and been purely stipendiary. The wages bill must have been considerable at abbeys like Biddlesden with fifty-one servants on its books,[54] Stoneleigh with forty-five,[55] and Dieulacres with thirty.[56] Garendon had fifty-six male servants, as well as eleven women 'for the dairy and other necessities.[57] Tintern's thirty-five officers and servants included cooks, fishermen, an auditor, a coroner (part-time), a ferry man (for crossing the river Wye to Brockweir), and a keeper of horses.[58] Even the abbot of Aberconwy could write to Cromwell in 1536 saying, 'I keep forty persons besides poor people and strangers, at no small cost this year, when corn is so scant in these parts.'[59]

The ordinary or 'waiting servants', did not merit the care and expense of negotiated agreements, which seem to have been confined to the 'officers of the abbot' (as at Warden, 1533), the 'gentleman' of the abbey (Bruern, 1517), and the 'top servants.' (Robertsbridge, 1530). In their many contracts of employment and related perquisites, we find provision both for part-time officers—like receivers, surveyors, and auditors and clerks of court, but also a wide range of full-time officials—as porters, kitcheners, organists and choirmasters (detailed in Chapter 1), schoolmasters, brewers, blacksmiths, launderers, tailors, and the like.[60] Their entitlements were not dissimilar to those enjoyed by corrodians who had purchased their exhibitions, save that frequently provision is made for annual grants of livery cloth or cash *in lieu*. A few examples must suffice.

In February 1512 Abbot Huby and his monks at Fountains granted a corrody to Robert and Ellen Dawson, for which surprisingly they were expected to pay £2-13-4 each year.[61] Their duties were manifold: Robert was to serve the abbot within the abbey, especially on solemnities and festivals, and also in external affairs. He was further to be porter of the West Gates (a subsidiary entrance to the precincts), with the duty of closing them at night and in market time (as a right of way was then claimed through them). The abbot agreed to build a stable near their hospice for the abbot's guests whose duty it was for Robert to receive. Ellen, his wife, was to be the laundress and to wash, or cause to be washed, all the linen of the hall, store room, common hospice and the abbot's chamber, 'returning it to the servants clean and fair;' she was to mend any rents found.

For these considerable responsibilities, the Dawsons were given for life, 'a house or hospice newly built without the West Gates,' with various lands, including a water meadow by the river Skell. Weekly they were to receive seven loaves of the better and seven loaves of the secondary bread from the bake-house, and six flagons of the better beer and six of the secondary sort. Daily they were entitled to a dish of flesh or fish as for two monks. Further, they were have at the larder 'all intestines called the 'ashewes' of all animals and sheep killed there, excepting animals killed before Christmas and assigned for the larderers.' At least in 1512 and 1513 the Dawsons were given an ox by the monastery. By 1526 Ellen was widowed but continued to occupy the hospice and act as laundress.

At Bruern in July 1533 the Hill family, Robert Hill, his son and first grandson, were appointed to the office of blacksmith of the monastery.[62] As well as his smithy duties, Robert had the further role of 'riding with the abbot in time of his business and urgent causes.' For his accommodation he had on a three lives' lease 'the house in the monastery called the Porter's Gate, with sufficient meat and drink daily as the convent doth fare, and he to sit at the convent table.' There were also weekly allowances of bread and ale, housebote and firebote, a livery coat, and the finding of a horse. His entitlement was short-lived, for in April 1537 the Court of Augmentations granted a compensatory annuity of only twenty shillings.

Stephen Pele, appointed brewer at Buildwas in February 1533, also had to be 'ready at all times to ride and go in the business of the abbot and convent, so long as he shall be able.' His usual food entitlement makes no mention of residence, but that is implied, and he did additionally receive a stipend of £1-6-8. His decree from the Court in April 1543 allowed him just that sum. His main duty was 'to brew, bake and make malt at all times, and to teach and instruct a prentice in the same faculty.'[63] As a valued servant, but without specific duties noted, Thomas Okynthorp was granted by Combermere in January 1518 a stipend of 16s. yearly, with food and drink and 'a chamber with bed and bedding, shared or separately.' He promised to give 'good and faithful service,' and he was obliged not to 'recede' without leave. His decree in October 1539 awarding him 26s 8d. yearly, showed that he had remained a servant of the monastery until its closure in 1538, making twenty years' service.[64]

It was at Combermere that the potential of conflicts and disagreement between servants and members of the monastic community was illustrated when in 1520 John Jenyns, its tanner, slew one of the monks, Dom Ottewell, with a dagger stoke to the heart. The prior, Thomas Hamond, refused to let the matter become public saying that 'this abbey is already in an evil name for using of misrule,' and all were sworn to secrecy. Jenyns was kept on for six months as a barker, but then arrested on a charge of felony and placed in Chester prison.[65]

Gate-keepers-cum-gaolers were on record at Merevale and Tintern. At Merevale John Gresbrooke was in November 1535 appointed to 'the officer of Janitor or Keeper of the exterior "Janne"', with the usual food entitlements, and 'the chamber pertaining to the office from of old'[66] At Tintern in February 1536 John Edmund was granted the reversion of the office of 'our porter and keeper of our gaol and the garret,' on the death of the incumbent, Edward Tiler. It does not appear that he succeeded for the monastery closed that September. Had he done, then he would have been responsible for the opening and closing of the Great Gate at night, and for the custody of 'transgressors' in the 'gaol.' He was subject to a £40 penalty if a prisoner escaped.[67]

Receivers-General and/or Surveyors ('supervisors') to receive residential corrodies included Henry Norton at Fountains (1538), John Higgs at Kingswood (1527), Richard Leftwiche at Vale Royal (1533), and Edward Gostwyke at Warden (1536).[68] The post was of relatively late institution, at Fountains made almost on the eve of its closure with Norton taking over the work of the cellarer. At Kingswood, Higgs had to wait until the death of the current holder of the office, Patrick Thomas, before he could succeed, which he did. The stipend varied from £10 at Fountains to £2 at Vale Royal and Warden.

The position did not require full time residence. At Fountains Norton could appoint a deputy; at Kingswood, Higgs could sit at the abbot's or the convent's table 'whenever resident at the abbey;' whilst Gostwyke's entitlement at Warden took effect 'when he went to the abbey.' These were all 'top servants', generally accompanied by their own servants, and provided when in residence with suitable accommodation: set on the south part of the brew-house at Kingswood; and known as the Green Chamber at Warden. The recompense made at the Suppression was very generous for Norton at Fountains; no less than £15 annually for some-one who held the office for only a matter of months. £4 yearly was awarded by the Court for the Vale Royal receiver, £3 for Warden, and only £2-13-4 for Kingswood's officer.

Other servants enjoying part-time residence and/or work and entitlements at a Cistercian monastery included: *bailiffs*—as John ap Watkin (1533) of Dore, a full-time official with food and drink at the servant's table when he came to the abbey; *clerks of court:* as John Vaughan (1531) of Margam, food and drink whilst at the abbey on court-days; and *tailors:* as Harry ap Glyn at Dore (1527): food and drink whilst working at the abbey. He was responsible for 'making all manner of garments' and 'amending the vestments in the church,' he to provide 'all manner thread, silk excepted.'[69] Merevale in 1535 appointed Thomas Fowler, gent., as 'auditor and supervisor' of all its lands, with an annual stipend of £4. Later the Court of Augmentations was to reject his claim for compensation, saying that it had 'no vigour in law.'[70]

Stewards rarely lived in; but they too were well provided for when at a monastery on business. Rhesus ap Ieuan, steward of the local lands of Neath (1532), and Rhesus ap Rhys, a kinsman presumably, received a stipend of £2 as well as 'a corrody or exhibition' of food, hospice and stabling, when coming to the abbey for court-days, together with hay in the one acre Cadoc's Mead. Thomas Dalston, steward of Holm Cultram (1534), was dismissed at Christmas that year, evicted forcibly from his chamber, and 'all his stuff' was cast out. Given a chamber in the monastery at Bruern (1517) was Thomas King, brother of the then abbot. He occupied the position of *Sheep Reeve,* and was required to be there 'at washing, shearing and branding' of the sheep, so he may not have been always resident.[71]

Most grants to residential servants made provision either of a coat or gown, or the cloth for its manufacture, or else money *in lieu.* At Bruern it was 'a robe', at Buildwas 'a toga', at Kingswood 'a gown', and at Stoneleigh, 'a livery coat and apparel'. Cloth provided varied in length from three to four yards. It was always broad-cloth, but differed in quality. Mention was made at Bruern of 'the best cloth, as for their gentlemen,' but at Warden a servant received cloth as for 'the yeomen.' At Boxley 'broadcloth coloured' was prescribed, 'fustian' cloth at Valle Crucis, and 'woollen cloth' at Robertsbridge and Vaudey.

The livery of each house may have been distinctive. Strata Florida's bailiff at Nant Bau was granted in 1528 'one tunic, like the other servants.' John Edmund, porter-designate of Tintern, was to receive a 'toga' of our livery.'[72] The value of cloth varied usually from 3s. 4d. to 4s. per yard, and in most cases a whole outfit was worth between 12s. and 16s. A servant of Stoneleigh had an additional allowance of 2s. for a pair of boots.[73]

Rarely is anything known of individual servants, but George Carter, a thresher employed by Sawtry was interrogated by the chancellor of the diocese of Lincoln in 1525, because he asserted that he had a vision during Mass at 'Blakeburne'. He saw he maintained in the host over the priest's head the image of 'a child naked in flesh and blood and his arms abrode.'[74]

Other Monastic Residents of Interest

In the last days of certain monasteries, *family members* of the abbot appear to have been resident for a shorter or a greater period. When in August 1523 rioters attacked Dore in Herefordshire, they assaulted Alice Walker, Abbot Thomas Cleubery's sister, and 'beat, wounded and evil entreated' John Uncles, his brother and servant, so that he was 'in jeopardy of his life.'[75] When in October 1536 Abbot Adam Sedbar of Jervaulx fled to Witton Fell, his father was on hand to accompany him.[76] In 1518 Katherine, the mother of Abbot John, lived in a house close to Boxley abbey, and arrangements were made for her fuel supply.[77]

At Tilty Abbot John Palmer was permitted to retain there his impotent mother, Alice Mills, during the interval between 'survey' and 'suppression'.[78] At Kingswood, on the suppression of the house in 1538, the commissioners made a grant of £2 to Alice Padland, the last abbot's mother, as 'it was thought needful.'[79] In all these cases the surnames of the mothers do not correspond to those of their sons; not unusual in those days when a number of ladies appear to have outlived first and even second husbands.

The decrease in vocations in some houses, as well as the need for additional income, meant that more and more lay people might reside close to or within an abbey's precincts, as superfluous buildings were sold or demised. In 1530 Beaulieu leased out for life to Thomas Pace, a kinsman of Abbot Skevington, 'a hospice called Gaynesffordd lying within the gates of the monastery, with free ingress and egress between the hours of five in the dawn and nine at night.'[80] In 1533 Beaulieu further rented out to John Warde of Coventry and his wife, a tenement 'next to the tan-house'. They received various perquisites including 'the fruit of apples set lying and growing around the tan-house.'[81] Stratford abbey included a small parish with its church of All Hallows within the precincts, and its residents included George Boys (1461), Lettice Lee (1484) and John Williams (1522). Mostly on death they looked to the church of West Ham for burial. An exception was a cooper, William Bryggis, who in 1480 expressed his wish to be interred 'in the belfry of St Mary of Stratford.'[82]

In February 1536 Bordesley demised even its gate-house to Arthur Buknall for 18s. yearly. It was a lease not accepted by the Court of Augmentations.[83] Geoffrey Poole, making his will in 1478, bequeathed to his widow 'his mansion situated within the abbey of Medmenham,' though he himself had another address in that parish. Surprisingly he chose to be buried at Bisham priory.[84] At Coggeshall a priest, John Sharpe, occupied 'a mansion and lodging with a garden, next to the infirmary.' He had the right of the exclusive use of St Catherine's chapel in the monastery church. When he died in 1518 he bequeathed all this to his faithful friend, Isabel Damme, but in 1528 the abbey re-demised the property to one Clement Harleston.[85]

One such demise was to create problems for the abbots of Tilty. The abbey in 1529 and in return for the surrender of Tilty Grange, demised to its Steward, Thomas, Marquess of Dorset, a kinsman of the royal family and an influential dignitary, 'the pleasure of the new house over against the church.' Thomas, and Margaret, his wife, on giving eight weeks' notice, also had the right of entry into the Guest Hall, with the new lodging made by the marquess.[86]

Thomas died in October 1530, but the marchioness continued to reside at the monastery, and proved to be a very difficult neighbour. Before Thomas died, he forced the resignation of Abbot Roger Beverley, his widow ensuring the deposition in 1533 of Abbot Edmund Emery whom she said was 'unthrifty.'[87] She then thanked Cromwell for 'quieting the poor house of Tilty.' but in 1535 she wrote to Cromwell that 'it does not trouble me a little to hear that you think the abbey of Tilty is impaired by me.' She sent Cromwell a gift of ten pounds and a cup.[88] She received further residential rights in 1535, admitted by the Court of Augmentations,[89] and still dwelt there when Tilty was suppressed, but after she died in 1541 the site was granted to the Chancellor, Sir Thomas Audley. Clearly the marchioness was an imperious individual who endeavoured to rule the abbey.

Travellers and Guests

The reception of guests from all ranks in life was an integral part of Cistercian life. The various sixteenth-century accounts make mention of the guest stable at Merevale[90]—at which abbey £50 was set aside annually for the reception of wayfarers and other guests;[91] the guest hall of Stratford—demised in 1537 to the dean of Salisbury,[92] and the 'ostrey garth' of Calder.[93] The hostry at Whalley, to which there is note of oats being supplied,[94] had nine chambers, the chief having three feather beds, and there were three 'bishop's chambers—upper, lower and middle.'[95] Ordinary travellers perhaps had to suffice with simple accommodation; better class visitors would be housed in chambers like that at Tilty with 'hangings of painted cloth.'[96]

Twelve rooms were listed in the 'great hospice' or 'principal inn' at Hailes which was situated between its inner and outer gateways. Within the inn and adjoining buildings were no less than twenty-three bedsteads. The individual chambers bore names such as 'the crowne chamber', 'the good man's chamber' and 'the madyns chamber'—this being located above the buttery.[97] Buildwas also had in addition to hospitality in the guest-house an inn or hospice with a smithy by Buildwas bridge. The names of the tenants, who in 1536 were William Whitefolks and his wife Benet, perhaps suggest a close association with the abbey household.[98]

Monasteries close to well-travelled route-ways obviously attracted more persons wishing for at least an over-night stay. The Suppression commissioners commented on the usefulness of Quarr (on the Isle of Wight) and Netley (by the Solent channel) for travellers at sea.[99] Basingwerk, by the Dee estuary, was on a major route-way through north Wales to Ireland. It was said of its abbot Thomas Pennant (1480-1522) that he built new houses for guests, who were so numerous that they had to take their meals in two sittings.[100]

The first monastic official a traveller would normally encounter on arriving at a monastery would be its porter. Even at their closure Stratford[101] and Whalley still had monk-porters, but at many abbeys this function was now committed to stipendiary laymen with residential corrodies: as Edward Tiler at Tintern (noted above), and John Brown, 'the keeper of the hosterys' at Holm Cultram.[102] John Coo was the lay porter of St Mary Graces in 1536 when its abbot reported him to Cromwell 'for words spoken;' namely heretical views.[103] In the early thirteenth century, Abbot Stephen Lexington had bade the Cistercian porters of Ireland to show themselves 'more merciful and humane towards the poor.'[104]. It was in like manner that when Robert Dawson was entrusted with receiving the abbot's guests at the West Gates of Fountains, he was admonished to do so 'diligently and courteously in word and deed', and in settlement of their expenses to treat them as 'gently and mildly as he could.'[105]

Hailes had a lay porter by 1501, Ralph Wheler who doubled up as carpenter. For his duties as carpenter he was given a stipend of £2-6-8, with a further £6-13-4 in his capacity of porter. As carpenter his responsibilities included the maintenance and repair of the abbey's wagons, carts and ploughs; as porter his duties meant the taking care as to whom was admitted at the postern gate of the monastery, 'whether by day or by night.' He, and his wife Margaret, were given a house and garden to inhabit with the usual perquisites of food, fuel and candles. Each Lent their food entitlement included sixty white herrings. Ralph was not to alienate or sell his corrody, and provision was made for a reduction in stipend when he could no longer work as porter, and for Margaret should she be widowed.[106]

During their travels both Henry VII in 1490[107] and Henry VIII in 1511 stayed overnight at Pipewell; the latter occasion was a weekend visit during which state papers were issued, and on the Sunday (3 August) Henry VIII made an offering of 13s. 4d.[108] He then went on to Merevale where again he made an offering of one mark.[109] Henry VIII also dated letters and transacted business at Beaulieu in 1510, calling it 'our monastery,' and he was to stay at Woburn in 1524.[110]

Other notables who found hospitality in a Cistercian houses included a papal legate, Lawrence de Campeggio, spending the night of 25 July 1518 at Boxley, whilst en route from Canterbury to London,[111] In May 1538 Bishop Rowland Lee, President of the Council of the Welsh Marches, wrote of the 'gentle entertainment' given him at Combermere.[112] In 1536 the earl of Rutland stayed at Pipewell whilst journeying to see the king, and in 1537 the earl of Norfolk addressed a letter from Fountains.[113] Bishop John Longland of Lincoln was a frequent visitor at Woburn, suitably located to be a staging-post in his large diocese.

In Wales Celtic bards continued to be permanent or semi-permanent guests in several Cistercian monasteries, praising their abbots in their verse.[114] The abbot who attracted most attention was David ap Owain, superior of Strata Marcella, Strata Florida and then Aberconwy, successively, between 1485 and 513. No less than thirteen poets addressed him in their verse. Tudur Aled (1480-1526) praised an abbot of Aberconwy (David Lloyd) for his greatness and generosity,[115] and an abbot of Basingwerk (Thomas Pennant) as being 'a generous patron of bards.'[116] .At Valle Crucis, where the poet Lewis Môn

(1480-1527) lay 'sick to death', one of the monks was a witness to his will. He left the abbey one pound.[117]

The praise of the Celtic poets reflected the hospitality they received, and perhaps trusted to continue to receive. That conditions the validity of their poetic evidence, and gives a note of caution. Lewis Morgannwg (1520-1565) once wrote of Neath that 'the peaceful songs of praise proclaim the frequent thanksgivings of the white monks,' but after the abbey was closed—and he was no longer obligated to them—he wrote instead of 'the false religious of the choir.[118]

Short-stay guests might include family members. Robert Joseph, a monk of Evesham, wrote in January 1530, to Philip Acton at Hailes saying that 'our Acton, your uncle' and himself had decided to visit Hailes shortly. They may not have done so, because not much later Robert was confined to the cloister for disparaging remarks about the result of an abbatial election at Evesham.[119] In the northern counties a transient guest in 1530 was Thomas Tonge, Norroy King of Arms, in the course of his heraldic visitation, noting—as at Furness, the arms of several monasteries.[120]

The evidence for the presence of boys in certain monasteries has been noted, but their background is largely unknown. A specific instance occurred in the 1520s when John Rede of Oxford had brought up for twelve years the nephew of a priest, Thomas Phillip. When 'there was great plague of sickness' at Oxford, he took the boy to stay at Tilty 'to be kept out of danger of the plague.'[121] In 1508 when a freeholder died on one of Dunkeswell's manors, Abbot John Whitmore took in his orphan child, and laid claim to his land during the child's minority. This was contrary to the terms of the deceased's will; and led to court action and the abbot being menaced and threatened.[122] The wardship of an orphan child who had inherited land was the prerogative of the king, who in 1509 gave Abbot Whitmore a general pardon.

At the start of the sixteenth century, the abbot of Rewley was entrusted with the upbringing of a boy called William Noble by his father. The lad was at Rewley for three years, was sent to school, and was 'right well sped in learning,' when Abbot Alexander of Abingdon conveyed the boy away. Abbot Henry of Rewley was awarded by arbitrators five pounds for his unpaid costs regarding young William, but then Abbot Thomas of Abingdon died and his successor, Abbot John Coventry, refused to pay the money owing.[123]

There might be 'guests' sent to a monastery on account of doubts concerning them. When at the close of May 1536 the crown visitors enumerated the residents of Netley they found there two friars, committed to the monastery by the king. It could well be they were suspected of doubting the royal supremacy.[124] In a letter written to the abbot of Furness in March 1533, John Dakyn, a curial officer of the diocese of York and later to be its vicar-general, said he was surety for the good behaviour of the bearer, Henshawe, who 'is commanded not to teach without my licence, but as he says he has not sufficient living meanwhile, I ask you to keep him in meat and drink till he shall be ordained priest, unless he resort to suspect persons or evil opinions.'[125]

In a manner reminiscent of occasional practice in the early thirteenth century, an unwilling guest may have been a dying vicar of Dean, Devon, John Cleugger (Clengger). After the vicar had fallen ill, and having been shriven on Whitsun Eve 1527, Abbot Rede of Buckfast nearby caused him to be bound to a bier with ropes, and carried to the abbey where he died three days later. At the same time the abbot and his monks took away from the vicarage a coffer containing the deceased's last will and testament, and with-held his goods from Richard Cleugger, his brother and heir, pretending the abbey had them by a deed of gift. The vicar's brother-in-law and executor, Philip Brayen of Exeter, pursued the matter in the Court of Star Chamber.[126]

Next to nothing is on record in Tudor days of travellers and guests from the lower social spectrum of society, but it can be assumed that there was provision 'for all sorts and conditions of men.' A monastic guest-house was, as always, a melting-pot of people of varied skills, talents and trades, and of diverse temperaments and achievements, and a meeting-place for persons of differing dialects, some from far off localities. The conversations they held could not fail to broaden their minds and outlooks on life.

There are also but few mentions of the work of guest-masters in Tudor times. John Faucon, a monk, was in 1484 both sacrist and guest-master of Sibton. In this latter capacity that year he purchased a mattress for half-a-mark, and no less than a total of forty-six yards of linen cloth from three different suppliers for eighteen shillings. He also bought materials for washing the 'stuff' of his office.[127]

Refugees, and Sanctuary

When Abbot Skevington of Beaulieu died in August 1533 it was said of his abbey that 'the place standeth so wildly, and is a great sanctuary, and boundeth upon a great forest and upon the sea coast, where sanctuary men may do much displeasure if they be not very well and substantially looked upon.'[128] The Great Close of Beaulieu was an acknowledged place of refuge for debtors, thieves and murderers. By the suppression of the monastery in April 1538 they formed quite a settled community, with no less than thirty-two transgressors having there their houses, wives and children, but many of them were aged and sick.[129] When the abbey closed they wished to remain and the last abbot, Thomas Stevens, took pity on them. So, too, did one of the commissioners, Thomas Crayford, and they both wrote to Thomas Wriothesley (who had been granted the site) suggesting that if the felons and murderers were evicted, the debtors be allowed to remain. Seemingly, this happened.[130]

Such a sanctuary could be a cause for concern and irritation. After the death from 'sweating sickness' of his close friend, Sir William Compton in 1528, Henry VIII was concerned lest that some of Compton's goods which had been stolen might have found their way if not to the sanctuary of Beaulieu then to Bewdley. Apparently, Compton held jewels and plate which were rightly the property of the king.[131]

It was at Beaulieu's sanctuary that a man called Arnold, who had escaped from prison in Ilchester in September 1533, took refuge.[132] At an uncertain date the Court of Star Chamber demanded that the abbey hand over 'certain chests and coffers' left at Beaulieu by two men, Messaunger and Robyns, who had taken sanctuary there.[133] In 1537 when Cromwell demanded that a Florentine in sanctuary, James Manzi, be handed over, he escaped but was found hiding in a barn.[134] The most notable refugee at Beaulieu was Perkin Warbeck, the impostor who styled himself Duke of York and entertained ideas of supplanting Henry VII. In September 1497 when he realised his cause was lost, he fled to Beaulieu but then submitted to the monarch at Taunton. Eventually in 1499 he was hanged.[135]

Sanctuary rights also applied at Beaulieu's St Keverne property in Cornwall. When John Leland visited the area in 1535, he noted that at Churchtown there was 'a sanctuary with ten or twelve dwelling houses.'[136] There is record of some local men 'after riotous behaviour' taking sanctuary at St Keverne.[137]

Visiting Wales Leland wrote of Margam that 'it has the privilege of sanctuary, which the Welsh rarely or never made use of,' and of Tintern that 'there was a sanctuary granted, but it hath not been used many a day.'[138] Edward Lhuyd (about 1700) told how at Neath were remnants of 'ye Sanctuary wall,'[139] and proof positive comes in the post-Suppression Ministers' Accounts.[140]

Shrines, and Pilgrims

Those monasteries which could claim the possession of a miraculous image, or relics of the Holy Cross and/or of the saints, might well attract pilgrims whose offerings would help the finances of the abbey. Relics of the Holy Cross did attract pilgrims at Stratford,[141] and Strata Marcella.[142] The latter monastery issued an indulgence about 1528 which encouraged visitors there on various feasts including Holy Cross Day (14 September). Garendon had an image of the Holy Cross in its Rood Chapel. The offerings there amounted to £10 yearly, but half that was lost in payment of the chaplain's stipend.[143] At Sibton (1484) small offerings were received 'at the Cross' on Good Friday and Easter Day.[144]

Archbishop Warham wrote in May 1524 that the image of the Holy Cross of Grace at Boxley was much sought after by pilgrims from all over the realm, and that it was 'so holy a place where so many miracles be showed.'[145] After the closure of the abbey it was found that hidden wires and sticks, not miraculous powers, caused the eyes of the image to wink and its body to move. The image was burnt at Paul's Cross in London.[146] Boxley also had a stone image of St Romuald which only the pure in heart could lift. All this undoubtedly helped the finances of the monastery.[147]

Images venerated included a crucifix at Roche, said to have been discovered in the rocks there,[148] and of Our Lady at Penrhys, in the hills of Glamorgan, on lands belonging to Llantarnam. The Celtic poet, Rhisiart ap Rhys (1480-1520), addressing Our Lady of Penrhys wrote: 'The diseases of the multitude who wait upon thee, after their weeping are healed the second night.'[149] The very popularity of this statue led to its speedy removal, on Cromwell's orders (14 September 1538), when it was taken to Chelsea for public burning.[150] Despite this, offerings of wax continued to be made at Penrhys as late as 1550.[151]

Llantarnam had a secondary pilgrimage centre at Llanderfel on Mynydd Maen, Monmouthshire, where earthworks yet remain.[152] When the Crown demised this site on 2 December 1538 to Henry Kemeys (of a Gwent family, but resident in Portishead), the property conveyed was 'the chapel and oblation or relic of St Dervall, Llantarnam;'[153] so, it appears, offerings here also had not yet ceased. Derfel was a Celtic saint with a more celebrated shrine in Merionethshire (Meirionydd).

The principal Cistercian shrine in north Wales was that of St Winefride at Holywell, Flintshire, where the present Perpendicular-style buildings were erected during the abbacy of Thomas Pennant of Basingwerk (1481-1522), aided by the munificence of Margaret, countess of Richmond and mother of Henry VII.[154] In an enquiry after the Suppression deponents told how there was 'an image of St Winefride with a box before it, in which people have long put their oblations, and where they offered their oxen, kine and other things.'[155] Noted for its holy well—where modern pilgrims bathe, the shrine was visited by James II in 1680.[156]

Pilgrims were attracted to Rievaulx as it possessed an image of Our Lady of Pity, where Mary cradled the body of her Son taken down from the Cross.[157] Visitors to Vale Royal who heard Mass and prayed in the chapel of SS Clement and Mary Magdalene there were in 1489 granted forty days indulgence.[158] In Somerset pilgrims came to the coastal chapel of Our Lady belonging to Cleeve as when the old chapel there collapsed, due to a land-slip, the altar and the image of the Blessed Virgin had been seemingly miraculously preserved.[159] Other monasteries benefiting from lesser oblations included Swineshead (in its chapel of the Holy Trinity; 12s 1½d. p.a.); Pipewell (at its 'chapel in Holland'; 10s. p.a.), Warden (in its chapel of Our Lady, £4 p.a.), and Woburn (at its image of the Blessed Virgin, 6s 8d. p.a.).[160]

As Doctors Layton and Legh made their visitation of the province of York and the diocese of Coventry and Lichfield, they noted relics in the form of girdles adduced as being helpful to pregnant women to whom they might (as at Meaux) be lent. They included girdles of Our Lady at Calder, Fountains and Jervaulx, a girdle of St Aelred at Rievaulx, one of St Bernard at Kirkstall and at Meaux, and one of St Robert at Newminster. Also 'helpful to lying-in women' was a necklace called an 'Agnus Dei' at Holm Cultram, and the 'Virgin's Milk' at Rufford.[161]

The most surprising alleged relic was the head of St Anne, mother of Our Lady, at St Mary Graces. As that abbey was only founded in 1350 it is difficult to see how the monks could possibly have acquired it. Nevertheless in 1514 Leo X granted pilgrims there an indulgence as if they had been to Rome itself, on condition for prayers for the departed. The Holy See did strike a cautionary note in saying the head was 'piously believed' to be that of St Anne.[162] That was as well as Fountains claimed a piece of St Anne's scalp in addition to a rib of St Lawrence, and a relic of the Holy Cross which was enshrined in a pure gold cross.[163]

The most illustrious Cistercian shrine was that of the Precious Blood at Hailes,[164] which was 'enclosed within a round berall garnished and bound on every side with silver.'[165] Hugh Latimer, rector of West Kington, Wiltshire, wrote in 1533: 'I live within half a mile of the Fosseway, and you would wonder to see how they come by flocks out of the west country to many images, but chiefly to the blood of Hayles.'[166] Both monastery and shrine may have seen a resurgence in Tudor years,[167] helped by Innocent VIII (1484-1492) who gave its monks leave to minister the Eucharist to all pilgrims, even at Easter, and 'to bless the beads of such pilgrims who touch them against the place where the Blood is preserved.'[168]

Hailes held by the late fifteenth-century a copy of *De sanguine Christi et de potentia Dei*, composed by Pope Sixtus IV shortly before his elevation to the papacy in 1471.[169] It may have been a monk of Hailes who had printed in 1519 a book entitled *A Little Treatise of Divers Miracles*. The faithful could also become members of the Confraternity of Hailes.[170] Unfortunately when Latimer, now a prejudiced bishop of Coventry, examined the Blood in October 1538, he found it to be more of a honey and gum-like substance.[171] It has been formerly supposed that the relic was publicly destroyed at Paul's Cross in London by Bishop Hilsey of Rochester in November 1539, but this is far from certain.[172] Abbot Sagar of Hailes appears to have maintained a belief in the authenticity of the relic almost to the last, but finally changed his mind and on 23 September 1538, when it was wise to do so, asked Cromwell for permission to 'put it down, every stick and stone, so that no manner or token or remembrance of that forged relic shall remain.'[173] In 1535 the relic was bringing in £10 worth of oblations to Hailes; in modern equivalent close upon £4,000. Not as much as might have been expected.[174]

Schools, and Education

The presence of boys in a monastery, not condoned in the earlier centuries by the Order, rendered necessary a degree of formal education. Despite the evidence of the Crown visitors in 1536 that a schoolmaster had not been kept at Furness,[175] at a later enquiry (in about 1580) one deponent affirmed that he had been taught in the abbey school there; that the school comprehended both a grammar and a song school; that the pupils included the children of tenants, and that children and labourers were fed in the monastery.[176] The witness also implied that 'apt boys' might well become monks of the house. How the educational facilities fared at Furness during the times the community was divided must be a matter of conjecture; the criticism of the Crown visitors may have related to a lack of provision of scriptural exegesis for the younger monks. Of these monasteries in the North Robert Aske, a chief leader in the Pilgrimage of Grace, told that there the younger sons of gentlemen 'were succoured and in nunneries their daughters brought up in virtues.'[177]

At Woburn abbey (1538) where there is note in of an usher, a 'Mr James' was schoolmaster 'to the young gentlemen, Mr Norice, Mr Carye and Mr Hervye, when they were commensals in the house,'[178] There is an idea of 'higher boarding education' here. At Ford (1537) in addition to his duties of biblical interpretation to the community, William Tyler, A.M., was to 'teach and dogmatise in letters and grammar the boys of our monastery.' He was rewarded with a residential corrody and an annual stipend of £3-6-8.[179] Richard Mulhouse was the salaried schoolmaster at Merevale in 1496,[180] whilst Stanley had an unnamed schoolmaster at the time of its suppression.[181] Pipewell (1538) had a 'scole house',[182] while the Whalley Grammar School founded in 1549 must have been essentially a continuance of a school run by the monks there since the fourteenth century.[183]

Whalley had a say in the management of the college of Our Lady, Manchester. In 1519/20, its new Master, George West, told in the Duchy of Lancaster court, how in an agreement made by a predecessor and a former abbot of Whalley, as well as one Edmund Trayford, esq., provision was to be made for the support of four extra priests in the college, and for this the warden and fellows bound themselves in the sum of £500 to the abbot of Whalley. No lands or money came to the college, and the abbot started an action intending to regain the £500.[184] Whilst primarily the responsibility of Winchcombe abbey, Hailes had some connection with the establishment of a grammar school and song schoool in Winchcombe under the terms of the will of Lady Jane Huddleston (1518/19).[185]

In Lincolnshire Abbot Kirton of Peterborough (1496-1528) founded a grammar school in his native village of Kirton in Holland, but paid the abbot of Swineshead £10 yearly for undertaking the management of the school and the appointment of its master.[186] Suppression accounts reveal that Jervaulx was responsible for paying the salaries of two schoolmasters at Durham,[187] perhaps a condition laid down years before when granted some lands.

In north-east Wales a grammar school appears to have been associated with Basingwerk abbey, at which Abbot Thomas Pennant (1480-1522), or his son Thomas, may have been a pupil and/or a master at some stage. A book of Latin grammatical texts bears evidence of his ownership, mentions a Thomas Pennant as 'a good boy,' and gives a list of pupils and the fees they paid. Thomas Pennant, before he became abbot, is credited with making a copy of the fifteenth-century popular Latin-English glossary, *Medulla Grammatice*.[188]

In south Wales, Morgan Jones of Roxford, Hertfordshire, but probably of Monmouthshire origin, making his will in 1532, entrusted his son John to Llantarnam abbey, there to be 'intreated as well in his learning and bringing up in virtue.'[189] In like vein Thomas Leryffax, a draper of Beverley, left Abbot Stopes of Meaux (1530) a kirtle of tawny satin, and asked him to be 'a good lord' to his son.[190] Another testator entrusting his offspring to monastic guardianship was John Symson of Helmsley, Yorkshire, who in 1520 entrusted Rievaulx with his son Robert, and his portion of his estate, and his other son, Richard, with his portion to Byland.[191]

The Sick, and the Poor

There is plenty of evidence of accustomed Cistercian charity being performed to the very end. As for the north of England, Robert Aske, who led the Pilgrimage of Grace, asserted that 'in the north parts much of the relief of the commons was by succour of the abbeys.'[192] In north Wales the bard Guto'r Glyn said of Abbot David of Valle Crucis (1480–1503) that 'his strong hand maintains the poor, a whole township at the door of his hall.'[193] In a letter to Cromwell (1535) Sir William Parre praised the monks of Pipewell for 'keeping continual hospitality and relieving the poor.'[194] Provision varied: it has been calculated that the proportion of total gross income expended on alms and charity by Fountains was only 1.7%, by Meaux 3.7%, but 4.9% at Combermere, and at Whalley as much as 22.1%. These figures could perhaps reflect incomplete returns made for the compilation in 1535 of the *Valor Ecclesiasticus*.[195]

The larger abbeys maintained permanently a limited number of alms-people. At Whalley, by a provision of John de Lacy, the house was bound to keep twenty-four poor and feeble folk. This cost nearly £49 annually, but a further £62 was spent on the relief of the casual poor coming to the monastery.[196] It was the monastery with most thus spent charitably; in total nearly one-fifth of its gross income.[197] At Furness thirteen such poor people were kept out of its catering budget of nearly £22 annually,[198] though one record suggests that they had 'bought their living of the house.'[199] A further £12 was spent on providing eight widows with weekly allowances of bread and beer.

Furness was criticised by the vicar of Dalton in April 1537 to the commissioners enquiring into the conduct of its monks. He alleged that they did not 'distribute the reversion of their broken meat at dinner and supper to the poor, but hath taken in young men for their tenement, which they call their bedemen, and bestow all the broken meat on young men and lusty.' This suggests that these young heirs had surrendered small inheritances for a place in the monastery.[200] When Furness was suppressed in 1537 the twelve paupers received but one mark each on being turned out to beg for their living; in to-day's values each received perhaps nearly £300.[201] They were fortunate; eight poor bede-men at Dieulacres received but 26s 8d. between them,[202] whilst an unknown number of paupers at Kingswood had to share only 6s 8.d.[203]

The normal residence for the poor was probably either the secular infirmary or designated almshouses. At Warden (1535) seven poor people of both sexes were maintained in the abbey's 'house of charity or secular infirmary,' at an annual cost of £13-13-4.[204] There is mention at the closure of Stratford of its 'poor firmary' with its garden.[205] Tintern, whose lay infirmary may have lain a mile or two from the abbey' had in 1476 a holding nearby called 'the almshouse.'[206] Its Abbot Henry Newland of Tintern in 1501 built a church house (possibly as an almshouse, but more likely as a village hall) at the east end of its Woolaston churchyard.[207] Other monasteries which supported poor residents included: Buildwas ('three persons living of alms', 1536);[208] Garendon (five children and five impotent persons; 1536);[209] Holm Cultram (five poor people who had a duty to pray for the king);[210] Calder (four poor people, 1535),[211] and Stanley (seven almsmen, 1536, and three poor women).[212]

Maundy Thursday was always a day of accustomed charity, when alms would be distributed at a monastery gate. At Furness that day, in addition to dole at the gate, one shilling was given to each of one hundred poor boys in the cloister;

at Holm Cultram alms were given at the gate each Maundy Thursday, but also to 'the boys brought up in the cloister.'[213] Margam had been endowed with a gift of half-a-mark about 1200 for a 'maundy' for the poor on that day; and extra alms were also distributed by Tintern.[214] The value of the Maundy Thursday dole at Whalley amounted to £18; in to-days terms perhaps well in excess of £6,000.[215] At Merevale (1535) Maundy Thursday alms totalled of £6-3-0 in value, consisting of 5s. in money, twelve quarters of barley made into bread, three quarters of barley made into beer, and three thousand herrings.[216]

Combe distributed in alms on Maundy Thursday 4s. 8d. in money; but also each quarter to poor people at the gate: 10 quarters of rye made into bread, 3 quarters of malt made into beer, and three hundred herrings.[217] Hailes also distributed alms of money, bread and herrings, to the value of £2-16-8 on that day. In modern terms, its charity was in the order of £1,000.[218] Annual expenditure on almsgiving amounted to £21-13-4 at Furness, and included the distribution of bread, white herrings and money to the poor at the gates on Maundy Thursday.[219] Sometimes the dole afforded on Maundy Thursday was stated to be in memory of founders and benefactors, or of being a custom since the foundation. Such abbeys included Garendon, Vaudey and Warden.[220] Bindon spent one mark each Maundy Thurday on charity for the poor in memory of Roger Newborough and Matilda his wife, 'founders' of the house.[221]

Such almsgiving was not restricted to Maundy Thurday. Merevale each week gave a dole at its gate of oaten bread and of beer valued at £5-13-8 p.a. Cleeve, out of its endowments, was obliged to expend give yearly £25 to the poor.[222] Jervaulx spent around £23 annually on charity to the poor each Sunday and three days every week, including beer and fish distributed at the gate. It also spent £18-8-0 on bread and white and red herrings each year for 'the poor hermits and the boys.' All this came to nearly one-tenth of its gross income.[223]

Tintern gave regular alms of corn, perhaps at harvest-time, both at the monastery and on its properties at Woolaston (Gloucestershire), Acle (Norfolk) and Lydd (Kent).[224] Special factors and other feasts might provide the reason for charity. When in 1485 Buckland on account of its alleged impoverished state was permitted to appropriate Bampton church, Devon, one of the conditions was that 'a competent sum be distribute yearly among the poor.'[225] Two of the poor people supported by Revesby benefited from a provision in the will of a former archdeacon of Lincoln, and it also distributed 23s. worth of alms each year for the repose of the soul of one Edward Heven.[226]

Neath proffered charity in memory of its founder, Richard de Granville, as well as "Our Lady's loaf" of half a bushel weekly to the needy.[227] Tintern gave out alms on six feast-days to honour its thirteenth-century benefactor and restorer of its church, Earl Roger Bigod; one of those feasts being his anniversary of death, St Nicholas's Day (6 December).[228] At St Mary Graces one pound in money was given to the needy, and seven tunics, were distributed to seven poor people on the anniversary of Sir Nicholas Lovayne, of Burstow, Surrey.[229]

For Furness each feast of SS Crispin and Crispian (25 October) was a special day of charity, when five oxen were given to the poor.[230] Pipewell gave money to the poor at the feast of the Exaltation of the Holy Cross, stating this to be 'by the constitution of the religion of St Bernard.' At Fountains charity was afforded in especial on the five vigils of feasts of Our Lady 'by the institution and confirmation by the General Chapter.'[231] Other feasts which saw charity afforded included St Luke (Calder, 1535), and St Thomas the Apostle (Fountains, 1535).[232]

Little is known as to what, if any, medical provision was afforded to monastic residents and visitors. It may be hinted at by the presence in 1478 in Tintern's community of an alchemist-monk, Walter Brockweir. It is specifically adduced at Dore when, in the early sixteenth century, Thomas Cokeshutt was indebted to that abbey for 'a bleeding in his pins [legs] with cloves, spices and other things.'[233] Bleeding was then a normal way of regularly maintaining good health, and Cokeshutt must have regarded Dore abbey as his local surgery! Flaxley and Meaux held earlier medical works in their libraries, whilst the composite volume assembled by Abbot Cleubery at Dore included a printed thesis entitled 'Medicine for the Pestilence.'[234]

The Departed

John Leland, the travelling antiquary, visited Strata Florida abbey around 1538 and shortly before its closure, and noted there that 'the cemetery wherein the country about doth bury is very large, and meanly walled with stone.' Within it stood thirty-nine 'great yew trees.'[235] Earlier the poet Dafydd Nanmor (*d.*1490) had said of the monastery that 'between her walls are acres for burying lords.'[236] It was a reminder that medieval people would seek if they could to be buried close to a prestigious holy place and, if of sufficient status, actually seek interment within it. Earlier restrictions were forgotten by Tudor times when a monastery might welcome the funeral offerings, and obit monies that might attend a secular burial. Most that is on record relates to burials within an abbey church, as desired in the wills of the dying.

Drawings exist of the striking tomb monuments formerly at Tintern of the first and second earls of Pembroke of the eighth creation, both named William Herbert, who died in 1469 and 1491 respectively. The first monument supposedly lay 'in the quire before the high altar.'[237] Another significant funeral must have been that in January 1535 at Croxden of Joan de Verdun, the last representative of that abbey's founding family. She was buried before its high altar, the abbot of Croxden being assisted by five other abbots—three of them being Cistercian (Combermere, Dieulacres and Hulton).[238]

Amongst those who gave instructions for their burial at Hailes were Sir John and Lady Huddleston. He, dying in 1511/12, sought burial in the abbey 'before Our Lady of Pity' and, as well as leaving the monastery money for Masses, also bequeathed £20 for the improvement of local highways. When his widow died in 1518/19 she also desired interment before that image 'and in the chapel of St Nicholas, where my tomb is ready made.'[239] In 1514 Sir Rauf Shirley, of Staunton Harold, Leicestershire, directed that he be buried in Garendon abbey,[240] and William Chamfer indicated in 1521 his wish to be interred at Byland, bequeathing monetary gifts to its abbot and monks.[241] At Swineshead (1533) one of its resident servants, Roger Robynson 'otherwise called Maltmaker,' desired to be buried in the abbey church 'nigh to the grave of Agnes my wife.'[242]

In Wales Cymer profited in 1495 with an offering of one mark, and a further ten shillings gift for the abbey fabric, as well as a mark for tithes forgotten, when David ap Meurig Vychan willed to be buried there.[243] Gruffydd David Ddu, who died in 1538, sought annual obits from Whitland in return for financial assistance to the abbey which closed the following year.[244] A benefactor of Llantarnam, Morgan Jones, making his will in 1532, desired there over his grave 'a stone of marble with scripture in letters purporting my name with these words: *IH'V XTE FILI DEI MISERE MEI*: 'Jesus Christ, Son of God, have mercy on me.'[245]

The fullest extant list of burials in a Cistercian church is that made on 27 March 1533 at St Mary Graces by Thomas Benolte, Clarenceux King of Arms.[246] Before its high altar lay Dame Elizabeth (née Stafford), wife of the first earl of Sussex and dead by 1532, and her third son, George Radcliffe. Also in the quire lay her aunt, Dame Joan/Jane Stafford, who passed away in 1484.

Other burials at St Mary Graces included that of Thomas Charles, sometime Lieutenant of the adjacent Tower of London—in a chapel outside the quire; members of the Montgomery family—in the Lady Chapel, and at the quire door was the tomb of Walter Hayward, secretary to the lord treasurer, probably Thomas Howard, third duke of Norfolk. In his will of 1529 one John Moore also requested interment in the same church 'before the rood on the south side'[247] Such surveys and wills tell much of the component parts of that abbey church, and also indicate the social status of those admitted to burial.

Spiritual Fraternity

A further way into which Cistercian monks came in contact with the outside world was by means of promising other bodies and individuals spiritual fraternity; a share in their way of life without their actually being present in the monastery. It was a means of showing gratitude for favours granted, and/or a device to gain favour and support from those highly placed. Seven Cistercian abbeys between 1503 and 1506 accorded Henry VII a grant of fraternity, with the promise of the keeping of the anniversary of his death, and the addition of a specified prayer to be said for the Sovereign at every principal Mass at an abbey's high altar.[248] In 1509 Hailes favoured Charles Herbert, chamberlain of Henry VIII and later first earl of Worcester; with the privilege of spiritual fraternity,[249] and in 1526 Bordesley accorded St Thomas More a like grant.[250] In 1529 Hailes further received into fraternity the influential Charles Brandon, first duke of Suffolk and a brother-in-law of Henry VIII.[251] Meanwhile Abbot Huby of Fountains in 1517 requested Cîteaux to send a letter of confraternity to Cardinal Wolsey in order to gain his support for the Order.[252]

Roche in 1531 made such a grant to the Carthusian monks of Axholme (*al.* Epworth), Lincolnshire, for an unspecified 'kindness shown to us by your house.' The Carthusians there were assured of a participation 'in all Masses, vigils, prayers, fastings, disciplines, privileges and other indulgences,' practised not just by the monks of Roche but of the entire Cistercian Order. Further three requiem Masses were to be offered for each monk of Axholme known to have died, and those monks, professed but not priests, were to recite the psalter fifteen times a year with the same intention. It was a typical grant of fraternity, sealed in the chapter-house at Roche and bearing the individual signatures of the entire community.[253]

On occasion grants of fraternity were awarded by the General Chapter on behalf of the whole Order. This was done in 1517, at the request of the abbot of Ford who was present at the Chapter that September, firstly in favour of the widowed, Katherine of York, countess of Devon and an aunt of Henry VIII, and secondly in respect of Philip Underwood, 'a Carthusian of the diocese of London.'[254] Underwood had been a very energetic procurator of the London Charterhouse, and had wealthy relatives in the city of London. In 1514 by special dispensation he transferred to the Knights of St John at nearby Clerkenwell Priory, and this grant of fraternity was perhaps associated with that event.[255]

It is rare to find money being proffered for a grant of fraternity, but in a dispute regarding land in Baxterley with John Glover, junior, the abbot of Merevale insisted, rightly or wrongly, that the £1-6-8 paid by John's father on 14 March 1523 was not for making a lease, but in return for being made 'a brother of the monastery, and partaker of all suffrages and prayers done.'[256] In other words, John the elder became a 'brother' not by taking the habit, but yet in a real sense of spiritual fellowship. In like manner, Alan Story, a butcher of Coxwold, Yorkshire, gave Byland one pound for the prayers of its community, and to be made 'a brother, and his wife a sister' of the chapter.[257]

External Relations

Certain Cistercian communities did not always enjoy harmonious relations with their neighbours and their tenants. One frequent cause for complaint (described in Chapter 1) was that deeds held for safe-keeping in a monastery were not given up when an alleged heir wished to lay claim to his inheritance. Another was that monies lent to an abbey were not repaid, and some might still be outstanding at the time of an abbey's closure.

When Dieulacres was suppressed in 1538 it had forty-five creditors to whom the sum of £171 was due in total. Monies were owed to individuals as far distant as in London and Islington, as well as more local clergy and the parishioners of Sandbach. Nothing is recorded of the monastery's debtors.[258]. One creditor was Laurence Hergrever who had lent Dieulacres £29. The Court of Augmentations awarded him £20 in recompense. Either part of the debt had been repaid or else, more likely, two-thirds compensation was the going rate.[259] After the closure of Cleeve the executors of Robert Shirton who had loaned the abbey £13-6-8 were compensated with only £6-13-4; while John Shorte and John Wolfe who had lent £40 had a settlement from the court of but £26-13-4.[260] As late as 12 October 1538 Hugh Losse lent £20 to St Mary Graces; on 18 November 1540 the Court of Augmentations allowed him £13-6-8 'in full satisfaction.'[261]

In the late-fifteenth century Joan Adeane had to sue the abbot of Thame in the Court of Chancery; her late husband had sold the monastery oxen valued at £14-6-8, but so far only £4 had been paid.[262] In the early sixteenth century Abbot John Bryan of Bindon owed £4 for three hogsheads of wine. He was deposed before making payment and his successor, John Walshe, refused to cover the debt.[263] In much the same period another widow, Joan Palle, sought at chancery the payment of seven years wages and other entitlements, totalling nearly £10, due to her husband from Newenham at the time of his death.[264]

A new abbot of Buildwas, Stephen Green, in about 1520 declined to pay a bill a predecessor had run up for seven kine and forty cheeses, saying that the vendor had no sealed deed testifying to the amount owed.[265] At the Duchy of Lancaster court in 1530/31 it was alleged that Abbot Paslew of Whalley stood bound to one Robert Crombelholme, clerk, in the sum of £500. Robert died intestate, and the abbot 'intending to deceive' the plaintiffs who sought redress, sent for them and asked them to bring the bond with them. This they did that Good Friday. The abbot, they said, took the bond, conveyed it to his chamber, and refused to return it. In response, the abbot claimed that he had only owed Robert £40 and no more.[266]

There are a scattering of such cases. They must not be taken as typical, and they could arise from false claims (unlikely, if only because of the expense of going to court), or because of urgent demands on the funds of an abbey (as for a royal subsidy). Nevertheless there were sufficient such instances as to give cause for concern. Further, more than one complainant said that they could get no satisfaction locally against perceived wrongdoing by a monastery, as an abbot's word was more likely to be heeded than theirs. John Halwell, a tanner of Pensford, Somerset, and Elizabeth, his wife, executrix of Robert Roper, in a case at chancery pleaded that they were 'very poor people of small ability,' whilst Abbot William Dovell of Cleeve was 'a man of great substance and hath many friends in the county.'[267]

One abbot whose alleged behaviour in this respect fell short of high standards was William Huddleston of Stratford. His predecessor, William Tetter, borrowed in 1521 no less than £40 from John a Parys, stepfather of one of his monks, Robert Parker, in order to pay a loan demanded by the king—probably the levy on account of war with France. When Tetter was dying in 1523 Parys visited the abbey, only to be assured by William Huddleston, who succeeded Tetter, that his money was safe. Huddlestone desired Parys to ask his stepson to support his election as abbot, promising to repay the debt, but he never did.[268] Young Robert Parker was 'set in the cloister'—perhaps meaning confined to the house, by the abbot and made to keep silent about the matter.[269] Parys died, and when Robert Parker fell ill his mother, Elizabeth, lent the abbey for his comfort 'a royned bed and the bedding thereunto.' The son died, but Huddlestone refused to let her have the bed back.[270] Incidents such as these, isolated as they may have been, cast a blemish on the Order.

There were also occasions when a monastery itself was hard done by, if it lent money to individuals who failed to repay it. John Rede, the penultimate abbot of Buckfast, lent the considerable sum of £126-13-8 to Thomas Cole of 'Blade' in two instalments of £46-13-8 and £80. When his successor from 1535, Gabriel Dunne, tried to reclaim it Cole disputed the amount and refused to pay; the now abbot saying that this meant 'the utter undoing and impoverishment of his poor house.'[271] In modern values, this was a great sum indeed, some £45,000 perhaps. Dore was troubled by three tenants who for years on end failed to pay their rents until in 1477 they owed in total over £160.[272] Given the troubled nature of the area at the time, eviction was not an easy option. Abbot Helmsley of Rievaulx (1513-1528) bargained to sell eight loads of wood to John Garth for £5, but was never paid.[273] A careful abbot might require security when making a loan. At Fountains in 1518 two silver flagons of considerable value were deposited on behalf of Lord Darcy when Abbot Huby made him a short-term loan of £40.[274]

Where an abbey had far-flung properties the chances of trespass by strangers were increased. This was especially true for Furness, which suffered repeated attacks on its holdings, note of a few of which must suffice here. In June 1518, within the then extensive archdeaconry of Richmond, notice of excommunication was given of all persons who had interfered with the fisheries and other possessions of Furness at Beaumont on the river Lune in

Lancashire.[275] It was ineffective. In June 1526 riotous persons menaced the cellarer and the abbey fishermen there, and twice took the net, rent it in pieces and stole fish caught. The following April two hundred stakes of the weir at Beaumont were destroyed, and malefactors 'with arrows in their bows' threatened to shoot the abbey servants.[276] Furness also held the manor of Borrowdale in the far east of the Lake District, with its 300 acres of arable, 3000 acres of pasture and 3000 of woodland. The abbot complained to the Court of Star Chamber that on 11 May 1533 some twelve rioters 'arrayed with swords, bucklers, bills, daggers and staffs,' assembled there, broke up the sitting of the manorial court, and cut down three score of oak trees.[277]

Around 1507 Byland was troubled in its possessions at Blea Tarn and Warcop in Cumbria, both by John Jackson, the Crown steward in Westmorland and 'a man of great might in those parts,'[278] and by Robert Warcop, who pretended to be the monastery's steward for its holdings in Westmorland.[279] The activities of the former meant that the abbey's rent collectors did not dare to go to those localities; while the latter had taken over its properties, evicted its tenants and even maimed one, cutting off his thumb. Warcop denied the charges, and said that he had been given the stewardship by the king and his son, the duke of York. In Staffordshire, and close to the monastery, Hulton abbey had cause for complaint in 1527/28 when a gang of men made repeated attacks on a smithy in Horton it had leased from Sir William Brereton; the wheel was broken, wainloads of charcoal burnt, tools destroyed, and the great bellows cast into a nearby ditch.[280]

There were a number of accusations against the monasteries themselves, and especially Dieulacres in which members of the Brereton family were sometimes involved. In 1516 at the instigation of John Brereton, the abbot, William Alben, eight of his monks and some of his tenants were in a riotous group that tried to prevent the a Crown officer, William Egerton, from arresting a murderer who had taken refuge in Leek church. One of the monks, Thomas Whitney, carried the abbot's bow. For his part in the proceedings Alben found himself lodged for a long time in The Fleet prison.[281] Thomas Whitney, now himself abbot, in August 1529 and supported by Harry Brereton of Leek, yeoman, John Brereton of Leek, labourer, some of his monks and others in a twenty-strong band, 'riotously arrayed with bills, staves, knives and other weapons,' assaulted one of the abbey tenants, John Legh, 'put him in great jeopardy of his life,' and destroyed his fence and six acres of pasture land at Leek.[282] It was one of several incidents in which Abbot Whitney was involved.[283]

There were a number of incidents involving force where abbeys allegedly tried to dispossess tenants or others of lands or property or rights which they enjoyed. Rarely are the responses justifying such actions preserved, so it is difficult to know whether an abbot was in the right or in the wrong. Generally speaking only a small minority of abbots were involved in such alleged assaults over the fifty years of Tudor times. The potential difficulties of a lowly tenant obtaining justice against an abbot were again illustrated when Thomas Kenyon (1525) was in dispute regarding land in Accrington, Lancashire with Abbot Paslew of Whalley and Sir John Towneley. At the Duchy of Lancaster court it was said that they had 'such might of power that the plaintiff could not possibly stand against them.'[284]

The cases of alleged misconduct by monasteries which came before the courts included: the theft of cloth meant for the use of the king, taken with force by the abbot of Dieulacres 'with many malefactors' (1487);[285] the destruction of a pin-fold in Cumbria 'by the procuring, comfort and mainte-nance' of the abbot of Calder (1496);[286] the taking of two horses and their baggage in Lichfield by an abbot of Combe with 'persons unknown' (c.1500);[287] the stopping up of the Sidway at Luxborough, Somerset, to the hindrance of a local resident with 'the maintenance and great support' of the abbot of Cleeve (1506);[288] the taking away by the bursar of Rievaulx 'with riot, force and arms,' of seven wain-loads of turfs cut by a tenant on Mares Moor (1519);[289] eviction from the tenancy of Harnage Grange by an abbot Buildwas with 'other evil disposed and riotous persons' (1518/19);[290] and the plucking down of the hedges of Cressage Wood by a later abbot of Buildwas with a company of monks and servants, so that the corn of John Lyttelton growing there was 'utterly destroyed' (1530).[291]

If all the allegations made were justified, then clearly there were a very small number of abbots whose conduct fell far short of the high standard that might have been expected. One such was Abbot Robert Lylly of Sawtry who about 1533 was faced with a series of questions to which the Court of Star Chamber required answer.[292] They were a response to information laid by William Lokwode of Welborne, Bedfordshire, who—without saying how he fared personally, or where the family lived at the time, or giving any reason for the abbot's discontent—told how the abbot had arrested Agnes, his wife, and held her for three hours in the stocks at the monastery.

Lokwode further asserted that she, and her parents, Thomas and Joan Johnson, were held for nine weeks in "the sheriff's ward" at Huntingdon. Meanwhile the abbot had her coffers opened and money and jewels taken. At some stage Agnes and Joan Johnson's servant were allegedly stripped and paraded naked in the chapter-house, and William's five-year old son, Harry, was beaten to force him to disclose what goods his father and grandmother had. The abbot, personally, seeing Thomas Johnson in the cloister, struck him with his fist so forcibly in the stomach that within a few months he was dead. If true, it was a sad and distressing case, and the outcome is not on record, but by the next year Lylly was no longer abbot of Sawtry.

Fortunately the incidents recorded above were few and far between, when the number of Cistercian abbeys and the fifty years of the Tudor period are taken into account. More happily, abbeys like Sibton appear to have enjoyed very good relations with their neighbours. Its accounts for 1519/20 show numerous gifts made to its monks by local people of hens and eggs, as well as six swans and six peacocks.[293] Doubtless other abbeys were similarly favoured.

Church Houses

There are several references in Tudor times to the building of 'church houses', though only one in any particular locality. That at Heavitree, Devon, was also referred to as a 'poor house'; others may have been residences, but the likelihood is that they were essentially village halls. The erection of them on lands belonging to churches appropriated to the Cistercians can be traced in a few instances. In 1484 Quarr leased land at Arreton on which the church wardens of that parish were to erect a 'oompetent' house within three years. This must be the 'new Church House' referred to in 1514, a focus of parish social life and for church ales and meetings of guilds.[294] In 1526 a Church House is noted in a rent roll of Medmenham, but its location is uncertain.[295]

Abbot Henry Newland of Tintern in 1501 built a church house [possibly as an almshouse, but more likely as a village hall] at the east end of its Woolaston churchyard.[296] In 1517 Buckfast gave land for the building of a Church House in South Brent, the rents and profits from the house were to be used to maintain the parish church.[297] Again the house or hall seems to have been for social activities and meetings. When in 1531 Dunkeswell granted to the wardens of Broadhembury Church half-an-acre of newly enclosed land on the west side of the churchyard to make a Church House, Abbot Ley was fulfilling a promise made by his predecessor, Abbot Whitmore. The one condition was that the abbot's manorial court might be held there.[298]

Notes

[1] The following section is dealt with in greater detail in D. H. Williams, 'Corrodians and Residential Servants in Tudor Cistercian Monasteries.' In: *Cîteaux* **34**, 1983, pp. 77–91, 284–310.

[2] *Cartae Glam.***3**, pp. 1131–32.

[3] *LP* **12**, Part 1, p. 283 [No. 632].

[4] *FLB*, p. lxxxi; p. 97 [No. 111, of 1521].

[5] The reference for any particular corrody will only be given once in these end-notes.

[6] TNA, E315/92, f. 52v.

[7] TNA, E315/100, f. 292r–v.

[8] TNA, E315/100, f. 126r–v.

[9] TNA, E315/92, ff. 5r–6r.

[10] *CHA*, p. 94 [No. 4].

[11] TNA, E315/95, f. 22r–v.

[12] TNA, E315/91, f. 35r–v.

[13] TNA, E315/92, f. 4r–v.

[14] TNA, E315/92, ff. 33v–34r.

[15] TNA, E315/91, ff. 86v–87r.

[16] *Wikipedia* online.

[17] TNA, E315/94, ff. 39–40.

[18] TNA, E315/92, f.52v.

[19] TNA, 315/91, ff. 33v–34r; LR6/152/1.

[20] S. F. Hockey, *Beaulieu, King John's Abbey*, Beaulieu: Pioneer Publications, 1976, p. 167.

[21] TNA, E315/93, f. 101v.

[22] *CHA*, p. 104 [No. 38].

[23] D. Winkless, *Hailes Abbey*, Stocksfield: Spredden, 1990, p. 50.

[24] TNA, E315/92, ff. 24v–25r.

[25] TNA, E315/91, f. 61r–v.

[26] TNA, E315/93, f. 31r–v.

[27] TNA, E315/100, ff. 123v–124r.

[28] TNA, E315/100, f. 292r–v.

[29] *LP* **2**, Part 1, 1199 [3822].

[30] TNA, E315/100, f. 126r–v.

31   TNA, E315/91, ff. 77r–78r.

32   TNA, LR1/174, f. 43v; *FLB* pp. 254–55 [No. 240]: 'lie with him', be in his chamber or nearby so as to be on call.

33   TNA, E315/94, ff. 39–40

34   'mess' = 'a dish'; 'brewis' = 'broth'

35   TNA, E315/92, ff. 5r–6r.

36   *RC* 3, pp. 552–53 [No. 1002]; Nottinghamshire Archives, DDSR 102/200.

37   TNA, E315/92, ff. 2v–3r.

38   TNA, E315/100, f. 46r–v.

39   TNA, E315/91, ff. 33v–34r; LR6/152/1.

40   TNA, E315/101, f. 58r–v.

41   TNA, C1/702/48.

42   *MCP* 124 [122], TNA, C1/596/14.

43   Williams, 'Corrodians and Residential Servants,' 1983, pp. 301–02, 306.

44   *LP* **1**, Part 1, pp. 33 [No. 83; Riston]; 549 [No. 13; Stephenson]; *LP* **2**, Part 1, p. 556 [No. 1917; Dalbourne]; *LP* **3**, Part 2, p. 593 [No. 1451/9; Choen and More]; also TNA, E315/100, f.100v; *LP* **5**, p. 398 [No. 838/5; Robards); *LP* **8**, p. 305 [No. 28; Blyke].

45   Williams, 'Corrodians and Residential Servants,' 1983, 79.

46   *LP* **4**, Part 2, 1811 [4096/iii].

47   *LP* **5**, 150 [318/30]; TNA, E315/103, f. 83v.

48   TNA, E315/91, ff. 55v–56r.

49   TNA, E315/91, f. 8r.

50   TNA, E315/100, ff. 82v–83r.

51   'miche' = a small loaf; 'medling' = a medium sized loaf.

52   TNA, E315/105, f. 84r.

53   TNA, E315/100, f. 95v [Bromfeld]; E315/91, ff. 8r [Bregus], 55v–56r [Fisher], E315/100, ff. 82v–83r [Little].

54   VCH, *County of Buckingham* **1**, 1969, p. 366.

55   *LP* **10**, p. 498 [No. 1191/2]; TNA, E36/154, ff.146v–147r.

56   F. A. Hibbert, *The Dissolution of the Monasteries*, London: Pitman, 1910, p. 240; Staffordshire Archives, 2/32/00.

57   M. E. C. Walcott, 'Chantries of Leicestershire.' In: *TLAS* **4** , 1874, on attached sheet

58   D. H. Williams, *The Welsh Cistercians*, Leominster: Gracewing, 2001, p. 139.

59   *LP* **10**, p. 434 [No. 1046].

60   Williams, 'Corrodians and Residential Servants,' 1983, pp. 284–85.

61   G. M. Hills, 'Fountains Abbey.' In: *Collectanea Archaeologica* **2**, 1871, pp. 268–70.

62   TNA, E315/91, f. 47r–48r.

63   TNA, E315/103, f. 88r.

64   TNA, E315/96, ff. 93v–94r.

65   VCH, *Cheshire* **3**, 1980, p. 154; TNA, STAC2/19/158, 2/26/18.

66   TNA, E315/101, f. 171r–v.

67   TNA, LR1/228, f. 698v.

68   , E315/95, ff. 178v–179r; E315/100, ff. 156v–157r TNA; E315/100, ff. 18v–19r; E315/102, f. 183r–v, respectively.

69   TNA, E315/92, f. 88r–v; E315/91, f. 72v; E303/5, m.112, respectively.

70   TNA, E315/98, f. 57r–v.

71   TNA, LR1/228, ff. 82v–83r; *LP* **8**, p. 126 [No. 310]; TNA, E315/91, f. 8r–v, respectively.

72   TNA, LR1/228, ff. 98v, 698v, respectively.

73   Williams, 'Corrodians and Residential Servants,' 1983, pp. 293–94.

74   E. Peacock, 'Extracts from Lincoln Episcopal Visitations.' In: *Archaeologia* **48**, 1885, pp. 251–53.

75   TNA, STAC 2/26/163. [John Uncles' normal place of residence may have been Hereford: TNA, C1/1080/8–10].

76   M. H. Dodds, *The Pilgrimage of Grace*, Cambridge U.P., 1915, I. pp. 202–03.

77   TNA, E315/92, ff. 31v–32r [8 loads of fuel yearly].

78   *LP* **10**, p. 164 [No. 408].

79   TNA, E36/152, f. 25.

80   Hampshire (Winchester) R.O., 5M53/67.

81   Hampshire (Winchester R.O.), 5M53/68.

82   B. Barber *et al.*, *The Cistercian Abbey of Stratford Langthorne*, Museum of London, 2004, pp. 57, 94.

83   TNA, E315/100, ff. 17v–18r.

84   TNA, PROB11/6/457.

85   J. E. Oxley, *The Reformation in Essex*, Manchester U.P., 1965, pp. 52–53.

86   W. C. Waller, 'An Account of Some Records of Tilty Abbey.' In: *TEAS*, N.S. **8**, 1903, pp. 119–20.

87   *LP* **5**, p. 654 [No. 1557]; **6**, p. 527 [No. 1304]; .**8**, p. 273 [Nos. 728–29]; VCH, *County of Essex* **2**, 1907, pp. 134–36.

88   *LP* **8**, p. 66 [No. 188].

89   TNA, E315/100, ff. 12v–14r.

90   A. Watkins, 'Merevale Abbey in the Late 1490s.' In: *Warwickshire History* **9**: No. 3, Summer, 1994, pp. 93–94.

91   J. D. Austin, *Merevale Abbey and Church*, Studley: Brewin, 1998, p. 7.

92   *LP* **14**, Part 1, p. 162 [No. 403/47/1].

93   TNA, E315/405, f. 2; Cumbria (Whitehaven) Archives, DCU/4/99.

94   TNA, SC6/HENVIII/1796.

95   M. E .C. Walcott, 'Inventory of Whalley Abbey.' In: *THSLC*, N.S. **7**, 1867, pp. 105–06.

96   *LP* **10**, p. 164 [No. 408/12].

97   *CHA* pp. 99 [No. 18], 129–31; *Cf.* pp. 105 [No. 39], 114–15 [No. 59].

98   TNA, SC6/HENVIII//3006, m.9.

99   G. Baskerville, *English Monks and the Suppression of the Monasteries*. London: Jonathan Cape, 1937, p. 29.

100 A. Jones, 'Basingwerk Abbey.' In: J. G. Edwards *et al.* (ed.), *Historical Essays in honour of James Tait*, Manchester, privately printed, 1933, p. 176.

101 *LP* **14**, p. 162 [No. 403/47]: a curtilage and garden were attached to his office.

102 TNA, SC6/HENVIII/481, 931, ff. 2v–3r.

103 *LP* **11**, p. 161 [No. 393].

104 D. H. Williams, *Cistercians in the Early Middle Ages*, Leominster: Gracewing, 1998, p. 116.

105 Hills, 'Fountains Abbey,' 1871, pp. 268–70.

106 *CHA* 100 [22]; SSC, DR 18/31/5, ff. 9r–10r.

107 *Patent* 1490, p. 490 [No. 969/56].

108 *LP* **2**, pp. 454, 490 [Nos. 857/14; 969/56].

109 *LP* **2**, Part 2, p. 1452.

110 *LP* **1**, Part 1, pp. 325 [No. 555]; 475 [No. 924/28]; **4**, Part 1, p. 352 [No. 787], respectively.

111 *LP* **2**, p. 1336 [No. 4333].

112 VCH, *County of Chester* **3**, 1980, p. 155.

113 *LP* **11**, p. 417 [No. 1037]; **12**, Part 1, p.. XXXX [No. 419].

114 D. Pratt, 'The Impact of the Cistercians on Welsh Life and Culture in North and Mid-Wales.' In: *Denbighshire Historical Society Transactions* **50**, 2001, pp. 13–23; Williams, *Welsh Cistercians*, 2001, pp. 145–46.

115 R. W. Hays, *History of the Abbey of Aberconwy*, Cardiff: University of Wales Press, 1963), pp. 155–56.

116 Jones, 'Basingwerk Abbey,' 1933, pp. 169, 176

117 *AC* 1880, p. 218.

118 Ibid. pp. 537–38.

119 H. Aveling and W. A. Pantin (ed.), *The Letter Book of Robert Joseph*, OHS, N.S. **19**, 1967, p. 14 [No. 12].

120 *AF*, p. 313.

121 TNA, C1/560/18. [*Wikipedia* tells of recurring infectious diseases at Oxford].

122 J. A. Sparks, *In the Shadow of the Blackdowns*, Bradford-on-Avon: Moonraker Press, 1978, pp. 103–04.

123 TNA, C1/353/63.

124 VCH, *Hampshire* **2**, 1973, p. 148

125 *LP* **6**, p. 126 [No. 287].

126 *LP* **4**, Part 2, pp. 1667–68 [No. 3733], where 'Cleugger'; TNA, STAC2/6, f. 281 (where 'Clengger').

127 *SAE*, p. 141.

128 *LP* **6**, p. 432 [No. 1007].

129 *LC*, pp. 167–68 [No. CIV], Hockey, *Beaulieu, King John's Abbey*, 1976, pp. 161–62, 180; *LP* **13**, Part 1, p. 254 [No. 668].

130 *LP* **13**, Part 1, pp. 295–96 [Nos. 792, 796].

131 *LP* **4**, Part 2, p. 1989 [No. 4562].

132 *LP* **6**, Part 2, p. 391 [No. 914/iii]; *LP* **4**, Part 2, p. 1989 [No. 4562]; **6**, pp. 391–92 [No. 914].

133 TNA, STAC2/24/299.

134 Hockey, *Beaulieu, King John's Abbey*, 1976, pp. 158–61.

135 *Ibid.* pp. 128–29; Lambeth Palace Library MS 632, f. 251b.

136 Hockey, *Beaulieu, King John's Abbey*, 1976, p. 176.

137 TNA, STAC2/20/130.

138 *Monasticon* **5**, pp. 265 (Tintern), 740 (Margam).

139 E. Lhuyd, *Parochialia* 3, p. 69 [in supplement to *AC*, 1911).

140 TNA, SC6/HENVIII/5156, m. 3v.

141 It was adorned with silver: Oxley, *Reformation in Essex*, 1965, p. 118.

142 Williams, *Welsh Cistercians*, 2001, pp. 68–69.

143 TNA, E315/278, f. 49; SC12/30/4, f. 23r; W. Humphreys, *Garendon Abbey*, Loughborough University, 1982, p. 64; *VE* **4**, p. 173

144 *SAE*, pp. 139–40.

145 *LP* **4**, Part 1, p. 127 [No. 299].

146 *LP* **13**, Part 1, pp. 79 [No. 231], 117 [No. 339], 120 No. [348], 284 [No. 754].

147 D. Hook and A. Ambrose, *Boxley: The story of an English parish*, Maidstone: the authors, 1999, p. 8.

148 *LP* **10**, p. 138 [No. 364].

149 J. Ward, 'Our Lady of Penrhys.' In: *AC*, 1914, pp. 395–405.

150 Williams, *Welsh Cistercians*, 2001, pp. 148–50.

151 Sr. T. Alphonse, *Llantarnam Abbey*, Llantarnam: cyclostyled, 1979, p. 147.

152 B. J. Wood, 'Llanderfil.' In: *Pontypool and District Review* **5**, 1970; Williams, *White Monks in Gwent*, 1976, p. 81, *Welsh Cistercians*, 2001, p. 151.

153 *LP* **13**, Part 1, p. 579 [No. 1520].

154 Williams, *Welsh Cistercians*, 2001, pp. 147–48.

155 *Augm.* p. 96.

156 T. Charles Edwards, *Saint Winifred and her Well*, London: Catholic Truth Society, 1971, p. 7.

157 M. Aveling, 'The Monks of Byland after the Dissolution.' In: *YAJ* **60**, 1955, p. 3.

158 *Reg. T. Rotherham*, p. 227 [No. 1799].

159 VCH, *Somerset* **2**, London, 1911, p. 116.

160 *VE* **4**, pp. 96, 294, 193, 212, respectively.

161 *LP* **10**, pp. 138–40 [No. 364, *passim*].

162 *CPL* **20**, pp. 207–08 [No. 292].

163 G. M. Hills, 'Fountains Abbey.' In: *Collectanea Archaeologica* **2**, 1871, p. 272.

164 St Clair Baddeley, 'The Holy Blood of Hailes.' In: *TBGA* **23**, 1900, pp. 276–84.

165 *LP.***13**, Part 2, pp. 272–73 [Nos. 709–10].

166 Baskerville, *English Monks and the Suppression*, 1937, p. 22.

167 Winkless, *Hailes,* (1990, p. 49.

168 *CPL* **15**, p. 37 [No. 66].

169 D. N. Bell, 'Hailes and its Books,' *Cîteaux* **61**, 2010, pp. 335–36.

170 Winkless, *Hailes,* 1990, p. 49.

171 D. N. Bell, 'A Tudor Chameleon.' In: *Cîteaux* **62**, 2011, pp. 307, 318; pp. 300–08 give a fine account of the Blood of Hailes.

172 St Clair Baddeley, 'The Holy Blood of Hailes.'s.' In: *TBGA* **23**, 1900, pp 283; Bell, 'Tudor Chameleon,' 2011, p. 308.

173 Bodleian Library, Oxford, Tanner MS f. 23v.

174 *VE* **2**, 456.

175 *LP* **12**, Part 1, p. 370 [No. 841/3].

176 VCH, *County of Lancaster* **2**, 1908, p. 22; TNA, DL4/25/13.

177 *LP* **12**, Part 1, p. 406 [No. 901].

178 *LP* **13**, Part 1, p. 361 [No. 981].

179 TNA, E315/100, ff. 217v–218v. [The Court of Augmentations granted him an annuity of £3].

180 Watkins, 'Merevale,' 1994', p. 91; TNA, E315/283. His stipend was £1-6-8.

181 TNA, SC12/33/27.

182 VCH, *County of Northampton* **2**, p. 120.

183 Greater Manchester R.O., 2/M37/40.

184 *DCL*, pp. 81–83.

185 *CHA*, p. 93.

186 *VDL* **1**, pp. lx–lxi.

187 *LP* **14**, Part 2, p. 77 [No. 239].

188 D. Huws, *Medieval Welsh Manuscripts*, Cardiff: University of Wales Press, 2000, pp. 23, 33, 62; D. Thompson, 'Cistercians and Schools in Late Medieval Wales.' In: *Cambridge Medieval Celtic Studies* **3**, 1982, pp. 76–77; D. H. Williams, 'The Monks of Basingwerk.' In: *Flintshire Historical Society Journal,* **39**, 2012, p. 47.

189 Williams, *White Monks*, 1976, pp. 85–86; TNA, PROB. 11/24/73.

190 C. Cross and N. Vickers, *Monks, friars and nuns in sixteenth century Yorkshire*, YAS 1995, p. 156.

191 C. Cross, 'The End of Medieval Monasticism.' In: *YAJ* **78**, 2006, p. 149.

192 G. W. O. Woodward, *The Dissolution of the Monasteries*, London: Blandford Press, 1972, p. 23.

193 D. Pratt, *The Dissolution of Valle Crucis Abbey*, Wrexham: Bridge Books, 1997, p. 14.

194 *LP* **9**, p. 275 [No. 822].

195 Woodward, *Dissolution*, 1966, p. 22.

196 VCH, *County of Lancaster* **2**, 1908, p. 139.

197 *VE* **5**, pp. 229–30.

198 *VE* **5**, p. 270; *AF*, p. 333.

199 *LP* **12**, Part 2, p. 89 [No. 205].

[200] *LP* **12**, Part 1, p. 370 [No. 841/3].

[201] F. A. Gasquet, *Henry VIII and the English Monasteries*, London: J.C. Nimmo, 2nd edn., 1899, p. 278.

[202] *LP* **13**, Part 2, p. 348 [No. 839/5].

[203] TNA, E36/152, f. 25.

[204] *Monasticon* **5**, p. 374; *VE* **4**, p. 194.

[205] *LP* **14**, Part 1, p. 161 [No. 403/47 (I)].

[206] NLW, Badminton Manorial 1657, m. 17.

[207] S. Rudder, *A New History of Gloucestershire*, Cirencester, 1779, p. 845.

[208] W. G. Clark-Maxwell, 'Buildwas Abbey.' In: *Trans. Shropshire Archaeological Soc.* **46**, 1931, p. 68.

[209] Woodward, *Dissolution*, 1966, p. 23.

[210] F. Grainger, 'The Chambers Family.' In: *TCWAA*, N.S. **1**, 1901, p. 161.

[211] *VE* **5**, p. 264.

[212] Woodward, *Dissolution*, 1966, p. 23.

[213] Gasquet, *Henry VIII and the English Monasteries*, 1899, pp. 278–79.

[214] NLW, Penrice and Margam Charter 87; Williams, *Welsh Cistercians*, 2001, pp. 151–52, respectively.

[215] Woodward, *Dissolution*, 1966, p. 22.

[216] Austin, *Merevale*, 1998, p. 7.

[217] VCH, *County of Warwick* **2**, 1908, p. 74.

[218] *VE* **2**, p. 456.

[219] *AF*, p. 333.

[220] *VE* **4**, pp. 174, 99, 194, respectively.

[221] *VE* **1**, p. 241.

[222] VCH, *Somerset* **2**, London, 1911, p. 118.

[223] *VE* **5**, p. 242; J.S. Purvis, 'A Selection of Monastic Rentals.' In: *YASRS* **80**, 1931, pp. 41–42.

[224] Williams, *White Monks in Gwent*, 1976, p. 99.

[225] *Patent* 1485, p. 117.

[226] VCH, *County of Lincoln* **2**, 1906, p. 142.

[227] W. de Gray Birch, *A History of Neath Abbey*, Neath: Richards, 1902, p. 153.

[228] Williams, *White Monks in Gwent*, 1976, p. 95.

[229] *VE* **1**, p. 399.

[230] Gasquet, *Henry VIII and the English Monasteries*, 1899, p. 278.

[231] *VE* **4**, p. 296; **5**, p. 254, respectively.

[232] *VE* **5**, p. 264; **5**, p. 254, respectively. [St Thomas 'Apostol cuilibet Hermite'].

[233] TNA, E315/405[2]/22.

[234] BL, Harley MS 218; *Cf.* D.N. Bell, 'The English Cistercians and the Practice of Medicine.' In: *Cîteaux* **40**, 1989, pp. 157–60.

[235] *Itinerary* **3**, p. 118.

236 T. Roberts, *The Poetical Works of Dafydd Nanmor*, Cardiff: University of Wales Press, 1923, p. 74.
237 M. P. Siddons, M.P (ed.), *Visitations by the Heralds in Wales*, London: Harleian Soc., 1966, p. 38; Cardiff Central Library, Phillips MS 12134 [info. Dr David Robinson]; Williams, *Welsh Cistercians*, 2001, p. 154 (illus.).
238 J. Hall, 'Croxden Abbey Church.' In: *JBAA* **160**, 2007, p. 83.
239 Winkless, *Hailes Abbey*, 1990, pp. 49–51.
240 Leicester R.O., 26D53/1948.
241 Aveling, 'Monks of Byland,' 1955, p. 3.
242 *LW*, pp. 153–54 [No. 224].
243 NLW, Dol'rhyd Deed 2; W.W.E.W., 'The Will of David ap Meuric" In: *AC*, Supplement I, 1877, p. cxliii.
244 F. Green, 'Early Wills in West Wales.' In: *West Wales Historical Records* **7**, 1917–18, 155–56
245 Alphonse, *Llantarnam Abbey*, 1979, p. 129.
246 *LP* **14**, Part 2, p. 124 [No. 279]; BL, Harley MS 544, f. 111; I. Grainger and C. Phillpotts, *The Cistercian Abbey of St Mary Graces*, Museum of London, 2011, p. 107.
247 Grainger, *St Mary Graces*, 2011, p. 110.
248 *Close* 1506, pp. 246–48 [No. 647/vii (Sibton), xviii (Stoneleigh), xix (Vale Royal), xxviii (Woburn), xxvix (Combe), xxxiii (Dunkeswell), xxxv (Ford).
249 Gloucestershire R.O., D6799/3.
250 TNA, E328/26/5.
251 *CHA*, p. 110 [No. 52].
252 *Letters*, pp. 253–54.
253 TNA, E135/3/6; *Cf.* Baskerville, *English Monks*, 1937, p. 20.
254 *Statuta* **6**, p. 490 (Nos. 1515/63, 74, respectively).
255 VCH, *Middlesex* **1**, 1969, p. 161.
256 TNA, C1/802/30; *Cf.* C1/802/27–29, 40.
257 Cross, 'The End of Medieval Monasticism,' 2006, p. 148.
258 Hibbert, *Dissolution*, 1910, pp. 243–44; Staffordshire R.O. 2/32/00, pp. 46–48.
259 TNA, E315/98, f. 54r.
260 TNA, E315/92, ff. 38, 66, respectively.
261 TNA, E315/98, f. 13v.
262 TNA, C1/716/65.
263 TNA, C1/198/48; C1/115/60; C1/282/25.
264 TNA, C1/346/21.
265 TNA, C1/645/31 [Each cow was valued at 6s 8d; the cheeses totalled 13s 4d.].
266 *DCL*, pp. 201–05.
267 TNA, C1/1001/24.
268 TNA, STAC2/35/5; VCH, *Essex* **2**, 1907, p. 132.
269 Barber, *Stratford Langthorne*, 2004, pp. 57–58.

270 TNA, C1/874/21.

271 TNA, C1/745/401.

272 Williams, *White Monks in Gwent*, 1976, p. 45

273 *MCP*, p. 123–24 [No. 121].

274 TNA, SP46/187/47.

275 TNA, DL25/3317.

276 TNA, STAC2/15, f. 281; *LCCS*, p. 98.

277 TNA, STAC2/15, ff. 278–280.

278 TNA, C1/285/4.

279 *SCSC*, pp. 253–61.

280 TNA, STAC2/21/236; J. L. Tomkinson, 'The History of Hulton Abbey,' In: *Staffordshire Archaeological Studies* N.S. **2**, 1985, p. 64.

281 M. J. C. Fisher, *Dieulacres Abbey*, Leek: Hill Bros. 1969, pp. 45–47; VCH, *County of Stafford* **2**, 1967, p. 233.

282 TNA, STAC2/21/245.

283 Fisher, *Dieulacres*, 1969, pp. 48–50.

284 *DCL*, p. 128.

285 TNA, C1/142/23/218.

286 TNA, STAC1/1/11.

287 TNA, C1/160/21; C1/167/61.

288 *PCSC*, pp. 65–68.

289 Woodward, *Dissolution*, 1966, pp. 14–15.

290 TNA, REQ2/11/40.

291 TNA, STAC2/27/182.

292 TNA, STAC2/19/191.

293 J. Ridgard and R. Norton, *Food and Ale, Farming and Worship*, Leiston, Suffolk: Leiston Press, 2011, pp. 41–43.

294 S. F. Hockey, *Quarr Abbey and its Lands*, Leicester U.P., 1970, pp. 167–68.

295 TNA, SC12/21/17.

296 Rudder, *Gloucestershire*, 1779, p. 845. For later deeds, see: Gloucestershire R.O. P376 CW 3/1. I am grateful to Mr Andrew Parry for this information.

297 Devon R.O., 123M/Z1.

298 No author noted, *A Short History of Dunkeswell Abbey*, Honiton: Abbey Preservation Fund, 2nd edn. 1974, p. 15.

5 UPRISINGS AND MARTYRS

I N NOVEMBER 1534 Parliament passed the Act of Supremacy which acknowledged Henry VIII as 'the only supreme head on earth of the Church in England,' and there followed shortly after the Treason Act, which made it a capital offence to disavow the Act of Supremacy and thus to deprive the King of his 'dignity, title, or name.' This placed many spiritually minded persons in great difficulty of conscience, wishing to do their duty both to God and Man. The consequence was that a number of those who could not subscribe to the royal supremacy were put to death, including two who had been faithful servants of the monarch: Bishop John Fisher of Rochester, and Sir Thomas More, chancellor of the realm. Religious were not to be exempted from the death penalty, as was shown when, in May and June 1535, seven members of the Carthusian Order were executed at Tyburn, including one who had been a personal friend of the king.

Blessed George Lazenby

The first Cistercian martyr appears to have been George Lazenby, a monk of Jervaulx who had been ordained priest in 1526. He was perhaps in his mid-thirties when on 11 July 1535 he interrupted a sermon being given in his abbey church, which declared that every bishop and priest had the authority to remit sin.[1] The preacher was Thomas Garrard, who had recanted former strongly-held Lutheran beliefs, and was now chaplain to Sir Francis Bigod, a Yorkshire squire who had been in the service of both Cardinal Wolsey and now of Thomas Cromwell. It was Bigod who on 6 June 1535 obtained for Garrard an archiepiscopal licence permitting him to preach anywhere within the realm. Five weeks later at Jervaulx, and in the company of Sir Francis, Garrard was proclaiming the 'pure Word of God,' when Lazenby called out that the bishop of Rome had the authority over all other bishops.[2]

The sermon ended, Bigod examined Lazenby as to his beliefs in the presence of the abbot and all those present, and finding him to give 'heretical and highly traitorous' answers committed him to custody at Middleham Castle, until the king's pleasure was known. Bigod reported to Cromwell that he felt Lazenby had come under the influence of the Carthusians at not far distant Mount Grace priory—and there is some evidence for that.[3] He tried to denigrate Lazenby by saying that 'of learning he has none,' an undoubtedly disputable statement which was repeated by one of the justices at his trial. Lazenby may well have been a visionary, for Bigod also related to Cromwell two apparitions of which Lazenby told him. One was at Jervaulx as he was sleeping in bed—when he thought that Our Lady and her mother, St Anne, appeared to him; and the other in the chapel at Mount Grace—when Our Lady appeared and said to him, 'George, George, be of good cheer, for I may yet not spare thee.'[4]

On 6 August 1535 Lazenby was tried at York Assizes, adjudged guilty and 'speedily executed.'[5] Noteworthy, it was the feast of the Transfiguration. Seemingly he was beheaded for when after the Suppression another Jervaulx monk and confessor, Thomas Mudde, fled to Scotland he took the head of Blessed George Lazenby with him. On that day in July when Bigod had examined Lazenby, he also interrogated the rest of the Jervaulx community, and said that they 'made answer like true subjects.' It is clear that Mudde (and also Robert Hartlepool) felt otherwise for both monks in the aftermath of the Pilgrimage of Grace, if not before, took refuge north of the Border. As for Bigod and Garrard, both fell foul of the authorities not long after: Bigod was hanged at Tyburn in 1537, and Garrard in 1540.

The Lincolnshire Rising

Dissatisfaction with the closure of the monasteries, and more generally with the Reformation, led to a series of popular revolts in seven counties commencing in Lincolnshire in October 1536, and ending with the Cumberland Rising of February 1537.[6]

Feelings ran especially high in Lincolnshire where already thirty-seven religious houses had been suppressed. Rumour had it that the Crown was about to confiscate all church plate. When therefore the registrar of the bishop of Lincoln visited Louth on Monday 2 October 1536, an alarm bell was rung and the rising began. The following days there were musters of rebels, the 'commons' as they were called, in Caistor (Tuesday 3 October), and at Horncastle (Wednesday 4 October)—where the estimates of the number of riders present varied from three to ten thousand. Later even the bishop's palace in Lincoln was to be ransacked. The rising was short-lived; it was crushed by Crown forces led by the earl of Shrewsbury by Friday 13 October, but there was Cistercian involvement throughout, albeit mostly forced.[7]

On Wednesday 4 October the 'commons' sent notice to the monks of Kirkstead that if they did not join the rebellion the abbey would burnt. They had no option, neither did their servants, who had already been compelled to join he rebels. On Thursday 5 October, save the abbot who was ill, seventeen monks of Kirkstead joined the 'host' at Horncastle. The cellarer and the bursar were mounted and carried battle axes; the rest were on foot. The abbot contributed by giving the bursar twenty shillings and a horse laden with food.[8] Little by little the monks of Kirkstead were allowed to return home; their abbot, Richard Harrison, 'thanking God for their safe return, and that there was no business.'[9]

Three Kirkstead monks had played a prominent role in the rising: Reynold Kirby, William Ripon and Hugh Ledger. All three had transferred to Kirkstead from Vaudey abbey after its earlier closure, and were brought to Lincoln to give evidence in the inquiry held there that November. All three were sentenced to death.[10] So too was Abbot Richard Harrison, despite his peripheral involvement, his complicity being limited to the sending of money and food. He was condemned on 6 March 1537 and hanged at Lincoln on Wednesday 7 March 1537, along with three of his monks: Reynold Wade, William Swale and Henry Jenkynson.[11] As a result of the abbot's perceived 'treason', Kirkstead was 'attainted' and fell to the Crown; a survey of its possessions being made on 6 August 1537.[12]

Monks of Revesby were also said to have been involved in the rising, but if so none appear to have been brought to trial.[13] Two monks of the not long suppressed Louth Park did take part: William Moreland *alias* Borrowby, and another by the surname of Skerne. Little is known of the latter's implication, save that he was one of the ring-leaders during the array of rebels at Caistor.[14]

William Moreland was swept into the disturbances at Louth on Monday 2 October. He had been having breakfast in a butcher's house with another former monk of Louth Park, Robert Hert, when those in the church rang the 'common bell'. He did try to moderate the anger of the crowd against John Franks, the bishop's registrar. He failed to save his books being burnt, but he did see him safely out of town, though he himself was at some risk. The next day, at Caistor, Moreland shrieved a dying servant of Lord Brough.[15] Initially under some compulsion from the 'commons', by now Moreland seems to have been a willing participant in the revolt, and went briefly to Ovingham to force his former abbot to give him a gelding.[16] Moreland was one of eight 'outriders' who led the rebels from Louth to Caistor, wearing for a while sword and buckler, and at another times 'a breastplate and sleeves of mail with a gorget.' It was said that for a time he carried the banner of Sir Robert Constable, and that he had been encouraging the 'commons' to draw up a list of demands.[17]

When the rebellion began to dismantle at Lincoln Heath on Tuesday 10 October, Moreland returned to his home at Kedington. Passing through Louth on the way, he persuaded the 'commons' to release from custody three of Cromwell's officers: Bellowe, Milsent and Parker, who had been taken by a group of rebels whilst surveying the now closed Cistercian nunnery of Legbourne.[18] Neither this act, nor his later frank testimony, saved Moreland from a traitor's death. He was one of perhaps an hundred rebels held in the Tower of London or at Newgate prison. They were tried on 26 March 1537 and, Moreland included, were executed with the usual barbarities at Tyburn on 29 March. Their bodies were buried in the Pardon churchyard close to the London Charterhouse.[19]

Much of what is known of the rising comes from the testimony given by Moreland himself. Fearing for his life, on the advice of friends, on 19 October he went to Yorkshire and visited the abbeys of Meaux, Byland and Rievaulx, and then stayed with Richard Lascelles.[20] At some stage he was taken in for questioning, and was subject to a lengthy examination at York on 9 February 1537.[21] A further interrogation, when Moreland was 'more exactly examined', took place on 22 February before Doctors Layton, Legh and Petre, commissioners involved in the suppression of the monasteries.[22]

The Lincolnshire Rising had been short-lived and seemingly ineffective. So, too, was the wish of the 'commons' to restore religious to their former monasteries. This is suggested by a letter sent to Thomas Cromwell on 6 October by Christopher Ascough, saying that the rioters 'have made a nun in Legbourne and an abbot in Louth Park.'[23] If they did, it was but for a matter of a few days. As for Meaux, despite Moreland's visit, Abbot Stopes 'kept the abbey clear of any serious involvement.'[24]

The Pilgrimage of Grace

Sawley (Salley) Abbey

Hardly had the Lincolnshire rising been suppressed when a new series of rebellions broke out in the north of England, popularly called the Pilgrimage of Grace. They were fuelled not only by religious motives, but also by economic and political grievances. Once again the Cistercian monks of Lancashire and Yorkshire could not avoid involvement. The principal leader of the rebels was a member of the Yorkshire gentry, Robert Aske, who entered York on 15 October 1536 at the head of a band of nine thousand rebels.[25] One of his aims was the restoration of those monasteries already suppressed, with the effect that Sawley abbey in Yorkshire, closed on 14 May, had re-opened by 12 October, and was re-occupied by its abbot and twenty-one monks.[26]

On 19 October Henry VIII ordered the earl of Derby to take the restored abbot and his monks 'with violence' and to hang them in their monks' apparel.[27] This did not prove feasible as the earl of Derby was delayed by a muster in Kendal,[28] and Sawley remained a living entity until sometime after the Pilgrimage had faded away. That Christmas a neighbour, Sir Nicholas Tempest, bow-bearer of Bowland Forest, sent the community for its Christmas dinner a fat ox, a mutton and some geese,[29] while the rebels granted them the church of Gisburn, formerly a property of the closed Stainfield nunnery.[30] The abbot or one of his monks, preached a sermon justifying the use of force to defend the church.[31] They also sought the return of Tadcaster church, now in Sir Arthur Darcy's hands.[32]

The abbey was retaken by Sir Richard Tempest [brother of Nicholas, but not a rebel] on 13 February 1537, the monks now meekly complying on the advice of Sir Thomas Percy, and the 'commons' being nowhere at hand.[33] A few days later, Sir Arthur Darcy then arrived to take possession of the abbey which had been granted to him, and wrote to Cromwell: 'No man knew where the abbot was, but I got secret information and twelve of my servants took him. He makes as though he could neither ride nor go, and lays all the blame on the commons that put him in against his will.'[34]

In about January the abbot, Thomas Bolton,[35] had sent, by means of his chaplain, Richard Estgate, and a servant, George Shuttleworth, a letter to Sir Thomas Percy (himself implicated in the rising) seeking counsel and advice,[36] and apparently offering support if another rising was attempted, and enclosing a 'royal of gold'.[37] It was a time when 'all the North is ready to rise if any one put out the monks of Salley.'[38] After Percy had been arrested and sent to the Tower (he was hanged on 2 June 1537 at Tyburn),[39] the duke of Norfolk took an inventory of his possessions, and Lady Percy gave him the abbot's letter. The duke, writing to Cromwell said that the letter 'will touch the abbot very sore.'[40] Unfortunately for Sir Nicholas Tempest and Sir Stephen Hamerton, the abbot in his letter asked Sir Thomas to thank them for being his chief maintainers. Both were hung at Tyburn.

On 17 April 1537 Cromwell wrote to the duke of Norfolk instructing him 'to proceed against the abbot of Salley if you can find matter worth of it, as we doubt not you shall. You may remember the letter sent by him to Sir Thomas Percy.'[41] When Stephen Hamerton was examined (25 April 1537) he said that 'the abbot, when condemned to die, sent to ask his forgivenesss for having named him in the letter.'[42] The letter was obviously incriminating and the abbot sentenced to death, but it is unclear as to when and where. One source suggests that he was hung, drawn and quartered at Carlisle;[43] another implies that he may have died naturally after being sent to the Tower of London.[44]

Little is known of the fate of the monks of Sawley. On the closure of their house in early June 1536 they had been granted faculties enabling them to seek opportunities in the Church but outside the cloister.[45] Some of the monks moved to other houses, perhaps Kirkstall and Whalley, but four went to Furness. When Sawley was temporarily restored to the monks, three of the four went back to Sawley voluntarily, the other at the insistence of Abbot Pyle of Furness.[46]

The abbot's chaplain, Richard Estgate, fled to Whalley, where his brother, John, was a monk, and where its monks were said to have hidden him unknown to their abbot.[47] This is difficult to believe, as whilst at Whalley he is credited—together with another Sawley monk, Henry Banaster, of composing and distributing seditious bills throughout Blackburnshire.[48] On 21 March 1537 Cromwell sought a copy of the 'sayings' of Estgate, and on 24 March 1537 (if the letter is correctly dated), Henry VIII ordered that Estgate be 'sent up in safety,'[49] but he had already been tried at Lancaster Assizes, and executed there or at Whalley on 10 March, along with the abbot of Whalley and one of his monks.[50] When a pardon was granted in the summer of 1537, the duke of Norfolk asked for the names of two monks of Sawley, Henry Bradford and Christopher Parish, to be excepted, for they were associated with the abbot's letter. They may have escaped, and never brought to justice.[51]

Jervaulx Abbey

In a simultaneous rising in 'Richmond-shire' around 11 October 1536, a crowd of two or three hundred rebels occupied Jervaulx abbey, presumably to requisition its horses, but also to gain the co-operation of Adam Sedbar the abbot. Together with his father and a boy, Sedbar fled through a back door and took refuge on Witton Fell a mile or so east of the abbey, but coming home secretly at nights. He returned some four days later, one of his monks, William Nelson, having found him, as the rebels were threatening to burn the monastery down unless he came. In the meanwhile the rebels had unsuccessfully tried to get the monks to elect a new abbot. On his return, as Sedbar entered the abbey hall, one of the ring-leaders, twenty-seven year old Leonard Burgh, had to be restrained from stabbing Sedbar with a dagger. Another leader called him a 'whoreson traitor,' and called for his immediate execution. He had no choice but to provision the rebels, and allow two of his monks to join their number.[52]

Sedbar himself was forced to ride bareback with the 'commons' through Richmond-shire and into the Palatinate of Durham.[53] There, at Bishop Auckland, his chaplain was said to have carried a bow and a sheaf of arrows, whilst Sedbar—perhaps feeling under threat, gave a speech encouraging enlistment in the 'commons'. In so doing he is reported as saying: 'The king doth cry eighteen pence a day, and I trust that we shall have as many men for eight pence a day.'[54] On Wednesday 18 October Sedbar was allowed to return home. During his absence Jervaulx was used as a post office 'to despatch the posts with letters from host to host.'[55]

Kirkstall Abbey

Abbot John Ripley attended a meeting of rebels at Pontefract in December 1536 to discuss the Pilgrimage of Grace, but there after is supposed to have taken no further part in their cause. He has been described as 'a sober man and spoke little'. In fact, on 29 January 1537 Sir Henry Savile, an influential Yorkshireman, wrote to Cromwell to report that the abbot of Kirkstall, since the pardon granted rebels at the close of the previous year, had 'made a fray' on servants of Sir Nicholas Danby, a Yorkshire squire who had only initially associated himself with the 'commons.' During the affray several were hurt on either side, including 'a monk or two.'[56] Danby rose to prominence in the service of the Crown, and the abbot remained superior until Kirkstall's closure.

The Northern Rising

Unfortunately for Sedbar, two of his monks at Jervaulx, Roger Hartlepool and John Staynton, were instrumental in attempting another uprising early the following February. This they did by inciting 'men of bad character',[57] led by Ninian Stavely and Edward Middleton, to take part, and by posting bills on all the church doors in Richmondshire urging all those aged between sixteen and sixty to assemble on Middleham Moor.[58] It was said that the abbot sent a servant into Lincolnshire, outwardly to collect rents,[59] but really to gain information on the movements of the duke of Norfolk.[60] When it was heard on Sunday 4 February 1537 that the duke had reached Doncaster, the bills were posted.[61]

Hartlepool and Staynton urged on the band of rebels, so that 'their abbey might stand, and Holy Church be as it was in Henry VII's day, for if Norfolk came into the country their abbey would be put down and they would go a-begging.'[62] The abbot gave them food and drink, and the deposed abbot of Fountains, William Thirsk, resident at Jervaulx, gave two nobles to the cause, and offered twenty more if they restored him to the abbacy of Fountains.[63] The inicipient revolt was poorly attended and all went home. Staynton had been executed before mid-April, whilst Hartlepool fled into Scotland.[64] Abbot Sedbar fled for protection to Lord Scrope at Bolton Castle in Wensleydale, a move which cost Lord Scrope dear, for the king's forces fired the castle.

Abbots Sedbar and Thirsk were arrested and taken to the Tower of London. There Sedbar was examined on 24 April,[65] and is reputed to have said to Cromwell: 'Ye be greatly deceived thinking that monks and canons were the chief doers of this insurrection, for there were others of more reputation.'[66] Sedbar was held in the Tower for several weeks, and engraved his name on the inside wall of the Beauchamp tower. He had been forced by the weight of the 'commons' to take part in the October foray into Durham county. His involvement again the following February might have been out of fear. Nevertheless, after being examined in the Tower on 25 April before Master Tregonwell and Dr Legh, both abbots were tried on 17 May and condemned to death. They were hung, drawn and quartered at Tyburn: Thirsk on 25 May 1537 and Sedbar on 2 June; his head and those of other rebels being displayed on Tower Bridge.[67] Because of his perceived treason the monastery of Jervaulx fell by attainder to the Crown, and before the end of May its monks had been dispersed.[68]

Whalley Abbey[69]

Very little documentation survives to explain why John Paslew, the last abbot of Whalley, was executed in March 1537, as the charges against him are not extant. The only deed outlining an examination of some of the monks refers solely to allegations that Paslew, after becoming a mitred abbot in 1516 and to sustain his expenses, 'continually diminished the plate of the house.'[70] The abbot had also 'lent' to the rebel leader, Sir Nicholas Tempest, a chalice belonging to 'the chapel of Our Lady without the monastery of Whalley.'[71]

It was Tempest who on Monday 23 October 1536, arrived at Whalley with four hundred men. For two hour the abbey doors were closed to them, but in fear of the monastery being burnt the 'commons' were then allowed in. The abbot and eight of his monks had no option but to take the oath demanded, and to lend Tempest a horse but not money.[72] When it became apparent that the earl of Derby—who had intended to be at Whalley that night, had withdrawn, the rebels left.[73] Two months later, as if to mollify Cromwell, the abbey granted him an annuity of £6-13-4.[74]

The rebels were granted a pardon that autumn, yet Abbot Paslew remained suspect and his monks were viewed as 'traitors.'[75] One reason was that Whalley, unknown to him, had sheltered Richard Estgate of Sawley; indeed this may have been the chiefest reason.[76] Another factor may have lain in a letter Paslew sent by an Oxford baker, William Rede, who had been at Whalley, to take to Oxford for onward despatch to Abbot Sagar of Hailes, with a verbal message that Paslew felt 'sore stopped and acrased.' Rede, examined on 10 February 1537, carried other letters, including one from the monk who was proctor of Whalley's Blackburn church. Perhaps because he felt the 5d. he had been given to carry the letters was insufficient, Rede showed them to the constable at Wootton, who read them and took them to an official at Kenilworth castle. That officer arrested Rede. It is probable that the abbot's letters contained incriminatory material.[77]

What-ever the reason, Abbot Paslew, along with his penultimate prior, William Haydock—himself 'attainted of high treason,'[78] and Richard Estgate of Sawley, were tried at Lancaster, when Paslew pleaded guilty to five charges, and the three were executed on 10 March 1537.[79] Some traditions suggest that the executions took place at Whalley, or else the bodies were taken there and hung from its gate-house.[80] The monastery fell by attainder to the Crown, and an inventory was made of its possessions.[81] The earls of Sussex and Derby (the latter being the abbey's steward) felt that 'the accomplishment of the matter of Whalley was God's ordinance,' given the local support for the monks.[82]

The king was anxious that rather than take their 'capacities', the monks of Whalley could be persuaded to transfer to other monasteries, as 'it cannot be wholesome to permit them to wander abroad.'[83] In the event seventeen monks took their capacities—granted on 1 and 10 May 1537, with a further four doing so on 10 October that year—they could be monks who had transferred to another abbey.[84] One monk, John Estgate, seems to have moved to Furness, although he expressed a desire to transfer to Neath, which raised Henry VIII's suspicions.[85] The aged prior, Christopher Smyth, was permitted to remain at Whalley as one of the two chaplains serving the parish church.[86] Each monk was given "the king's reward" of forty shillings to help them buy secular clothing and immediate necessities.[87] They did not receive annual pensions.

Furness Abbey

In the spring of 1537 the earl of Sussex said in a letter to Cromwell that 'the monks of Furness have been as bad as any other.'[88] It is indeed surprising that of their number only one or two were eventually imprisoned, and this may have been due to the negotiating skills of Abbot Roger Pyle, forbearance on the part of the investigating earl of Sussex, and the patronage of the earl of Derby. Certain monks of the community did make assertions against the royal supremacy, even after a pardon had been granted at the close of 1536 to all but selected individuals. Some writers have belittled Abbot Pyle, but anxious and frightening as the autumn of 1536 and the spring of 1537 must have been to him, he did do what he considered best for his monastery.

There is no doubt but that several of his monks supported the 'commons' in their revolt, and when pressure was placed upon the abbey he encouraged his community to do what they could with the commons, but he himself left the monastery towards the end of October 1536, travelled by boat and reached Lathom further south in Lancashire, to stay with the abbey's steward, the young earl of Derby, who happened to have been brought up by Henry VIII after his own father died when he was thirteen. From Lathom Pyle sent his monks the message that he had 'taken a way to be sure both from king and commons.'[89]

Meanwhile, back at Furness on 30 October, four monks headed by Michael Hamerton, the cellarer, met the rebels at Swartmore and gave them £23-6-8 for their cause. The monks then marched with the rebels to Dalton where, on the 31st, the prior, John Garner, and another monk, John Green, called on the monastery's tenants on pain of destruction of their houses to arm and join the uprising. They gave the tenants the advice, 'Agree with them, as we have done.' On 9 November John Green went further and said that the monarch would never give them another abbot, 'but they would choose their own.'[90] This went directly contrary to the supremacy in church affairs which Henry VIII claimed.

When Abbot Pyle returned to his monastery he had little control over his monks, who required him to sign certain articles, presumably in favour of the rebels.[91] He was so afraid that he dared not enter the church alone after dark. When some of the monks circulated a prophecy that 'in England shall be slain the decorate rose in his mother's belly,' implying that the king would be murdered by a priest, and when one monk, Henry Salley, perhaps early in 1537, opined that 'there should be no lay knave head of the Church.' Pyle, although he knew these were treasonable statements, failed to report them to the authorities. Such gossip continued with another monk, John Broughton, saying that Henry VIII was not the rightful monarch, since his father only became king by the sword.

On the first Sunday of Lent (February 18) realising that royal commissioners would shortly be sitting at Lancaster, and fearful of his monks behaviour, Abbot Pyle in the chapter-house bade the community to observe the injunctions laid down during their visitation of the house in 1535 by Doctors Layton and Legh. The earls of Derby and Sussex, as royal commissaries, were hearing complaints regarding the state of affairs at Furness, and visited the monastery in mid-March; the abbot the previous Sunday strictly enjoining his monks not to disclose anything to them, on pain of imprisonment. Unfortunately from the abbey's point of view, there was an independent resident witness to the events at Furness, a conservative and traditionalist friar, Robert Legate, who had been, the earl of Derby noted, 'put into that monastery to read and preach to the brethren.'[92]

Legate's account to the commissioners detailing many of the above-mentioned accusations, was divided by the earl of Derby into offences committed before and after 'the indulgence'—the general pardon granted on 31 December 1536. The vicar of Dalton also proved to be an unhelpful witness so far as the abbey was concerned. He told of what the prior had said, and also deposed that the monks refused to allow Legate expound Scriptures to them, and that they did not give to the poor the left-overs from their dinner and supper. The vicar, who was an abbey appointee himself, was clearly sworn to give true evidence; he said he disclosed all he knew 'because of my book oath.' Yet another independent and unhelpful witness who gave corroborative detail was the abbey's own bailiff in Dalton.[93]

Abbot Pyle in his evidence disclosed that only a small minority of monks took the king's part; that Broughton had showed him certain prophecies, that he had been forced to sign the articles, and that as his monks mostly showed so much affection for the commons that he 'durst not go alone to the church this winter before day.'[94] Clearly he had been under considerable pressure for months. It was greatly held against him that he had not reported the perceived traitorous sayings of his monks to the king's commissioners when they had been at Furness, but rather had threatened the community with imprisonment for those individuals who gave away anything to the commissioners.

The earl of Sussex reported to Henry VIII on 6 April that, after 'closely examining them,' they could only find two monks guilty of offences committed since the pardon granted on 31 December 1536. They had been committed to prison in Lancaster Castle.[95] The earl also said that at his coming again to Furness he would investigate further.[96] It is generally assumed that the two monks incarcerated were Henry Salley and John Broughton, as their signatures do not appear on the surrender deed[97] At least three of the Furness monks, James Forster, Thomas Settle and John Thornton, were opposed to the rebels' cause.[98]

Abbot Pyle was summoned to Whalley abbey, where the earl of Sussex had his temporary headquarters, and was given an option, a way out of his difficulties; namely to agree to the immediate surrender of Furness. This he did speedily and willingly at Whalley on 5 April 1537, 'knowing the mis-order and evil life of his brethren,' and yielding to the king 'all his interest in the house and lands of Furness.'[99] The earl of Sussex immediately sent three officers, Sirs Thomas Butler, John Byron and Richard Houghton to Furness, 'to take the rule of the house into their hands, and prevent anything being embezzled.'[100] A few days later, on 9 April 1537, at Furness the formal deed of surrender was signed by Abbot Roger, Prior Brian Garner, and twenty-eight other monks.[101] Two or three others were not present, being resident upon their parishes.

The dispensations ('capacities') allowing the monks of Furness to seek and hold secular benefices, for most their only source of income when thrown out into the world, were dated the 14th of May, but what became of most of the Furness community is not known. Surprisingly, the monks were still in residence on 23 June when Sir Robert Southwell, an officer of the Court of Augmentations, arrived there 'expecting to find the monks ready to disperse on receiving their capacities and 20s. reward as the earl of Sussex at his last being there was thought to have concluded with them.' The monks clamoured that they had no such agreement with the earl of Sussex, and that they had not surrendered willingly. In the presence of several hundred lay people there that day, Sir Robert gave each instead 40s. to cover arrears, writing to Cromwell that 'the traitors of Whalley had no less.' He pointed out that much of this pocket money would in any case be spent on lay attire; 'their secular weed, without which he would not suffer them to pass out.'[102]

On 15 December 1537 Cromwell sent instructions to Sir John Lamplugh, to 'keep his household on the site of the late monastery,' thus securing the former monastery against spoliation. Mindful of local feeling, he was also charged with keeping a watchful eye for any signs of dissent in the area: curates (parish priests, in this context) were to do their duty 'in setting forth the king's supremacy', and any seditious person 'provoking diversity of opinion' was to be imprisoned.[103]

Holm Cultram Abbey

As rebellion spread in October 1536 into Cumberland, the new abbot of Holm Cultram, Thomas Carter was allegedly involved. It was later said that he ordered his tenants under pain of hanging to join a muster being held Kilwatling How on 25 October, that he himself personally joined the rebels near Cockermouth on Saturday 28 October, and that he gave 40s. to representatives from Penrith attending the pilgrims council at York on Tuesday 21 November.[104] At the assembly on the 28th at Mewtey Hill near Cockermouth, was the abbot was 'brought in' in by the vicar of Burgh and sworn by the 'commons.' The assembly appointed him and four others to go to Carlisle and desire the mayor and his brethren to also take the oath. At first the abbot feared to go, and there was ill-feeling towards him. On the 31st he did with others venture to Carlisle, but 'they were not suffered to enter the city.'[105] This information came from depositions made on 20 March 1537 by witnesses held in the Tower of London, and in later investigations at the monastery. Meanwhile, despite the granting of the king's pardon, an attack was planned by the 'commons' in mid-February 1537 on Carlisle, and the abbot commanded his tenants to take part. This, it is said, they refused to do, and the siege of Carlisle failed. Abbot Carter also, allegedly, instructed his community "to go daily with procession to speed the commons' journey;" possibly a reference to chanting the litany in procession. Thomas Graham, a fellow monk, asserted that 'all the insurrection there' was owing to the abbot.[106] On 11 April 1537, Dr Legh, one of Cromwell's commissioners, was at the abbey, but why is uncertain.[107]

Much information was gained by Sir Thomas Curwen, the sheriff that year of Cumberland, who heard on 21 May 1537 that 'there had been words between the abbot and Thomas Graham, monk there, which touched treason.' So Curwen and others went to the abbey and 'secretly examined' Graham and other monks and lay witnesses, without giving too much away. Graham also accused the abbot of having brought women into the monastery 'to dine and sup,' of selling £100 worth of monastery plate, and the 'jewels of our kirk.'[108] Later a commission of enquiry was held in the abbey church, but it dragged on and Abbot Carter appears to have died before its conclusion.[109] As for Graham, he very much wished to succeed to the abbacy, and that alone may have coloured his evidence.

Newminster Abbey

By all accounts, Newminster abbey had closed by 12 October 1536, on which day its monks were granted their 'capacities'.[110] Already the earl of Northumberland had asked Cromwell (13 September and 3 October 1536) for the preferment of Newminster for William Grene, an officer of the Court of Augmentations, which abbey he said was then held by Sir Oswald Wilthrop (Welstropp/Wolstrope).[111] If the dating of these letters is correct, then—as Cardinal Gasquet thought[112]—the community of Newminster, like that of its daughter-house at Sawley must, during the northern troubles, have regained their monastery. This is also suggested by the fact that on 22 February 1537 Henry VIII, hearing that its monks were offering resistance, ordered the duke of Norfolk that they—as well as the monks of Sawley and elsewhere, 'be tied up without further delay or ceremony.'[113] If, however, the letters of the earl of Northumberland have been misplaced a year early, and the faculty office register wrongly dated, the re-entry of the community at Newminster did not take place, but the monks simply tried to delay their eviction.

The New Learning

The 1530s were a time of considerable change. In June 1530 proclamation was made that all heretical books and all translations of the Scriptures into English were to be delivered up.[114] Unfortunately for the young, former press-ganged monk of Jervaulx, Edward Paynter now living in Colchester, he was found in 1532 to be in possession of a copy of the New Testament in English, and spent several months incarcerated and held in irons in the bishop of London's prison.[115] Yet when, but a few years later, Henry VIII in order to spite Rome authorised such a translation of the Scriptures, Abbot Sagar of Hailes was able to write to Cromwell saying: 'I thank God that I live in this time of light and knowledge, which I had never come to if I had not liberty to read Scripture in English.'[116]

This shows that, in their very last years, some of the monasteries did have access to the Word of God in the vernacular tongue. More than that, the prior of Kingswood (Thomas Redinge on 21 January 1535/36) after Cromwell had visited that abbey, wrote to him an ingratiating letter, saying that as 'you spoke unto me that the word of God, the gospel of Christ, is not only favoured but also set forth by you, it has emboldened me to make a little book concerning the supremacy of the King, which I have dedicated unto you.'[117] In September 1535 a friar who preached in Kingswood abbey spoke, according to the abbot, 'contrary to God's word,' saying that Peter was head of the Church. The abbot sent him up to Cromwell.[118] A monk of Kingswood, Thomas Lacock, was absent when his house was suppressed in 1538 as he was 'about the ministration of the Gospel.'[119] It does seem that an element of Kingswood's community favoured 'the new learning.' Abbot Austen of Rewley, after the suppression of his house, removed to study at Trinity Hall, Cambridge, from where he wrote that he was 'studying the Word of God sincerely.'[120]

Having to acknowledge the royal supremacy in matters ecclesiastical could not but offend the consciences of many religious, divide communities, and leave individual monks open to suspicion. Abbot Love of Coggeshall was in 1536 cleared of several charges (although his resignation soon followed), which included omitting the collect for the King and Queen at High Mass.[121] The last abbot of Garendon, Thomas Syston, was reported to Cromwell in 1536 as saying words to the effect that 'the king should be expelled from the realm and slain on his return.' His informant was John Beaumont, recorder of Leicester and a commissioner for the suppression of the monasteries. Writing to Cromwell (1 October 1537) he pointed out that he had informed Cromwell of the matter over a year before, and added that 'the publication of these things has encouraged divers persons to rebellion.'[122] No action then or later seems to have been taken against Syston who was involved, perhaps between 1537 and 1540 in a dispute regarding property in Loughborough, Leicestershire, where he, or a namesake or both, rented a house and shop called the Sign of the George.[123]

Surprisingly monks of Stratford (1535/36) reported their autocratic abbot, William Huddleston, to the Recorder of London, for causing their excommunication because they assented to the royal supremacy.[124] Huddlestone survived to retire on a handsome pension. Thomas Norton, the youngest monk of Rewley (1533), made subdeacon in 1525, was reported to Cromwell for quoting from Agrippa's book, *De Vanitate Scientiarum*, with treasonable application on the king's divorce.[125] Richard Yaxley, a monk of Thame since at least 1497, preached in 1538 the doctrines of purgatory and of veneration of the saints in St Mary Magdalene's, Oxford, but was quick to recant when arrested.[126] These are isolated examples, but they illustrate the difficulties in those times for monks of conscience. Much earlier in 1521 a priest named Adam Bradshaw was in prison at Maidstone for pulling down writings and seals 'set up at the abbey of Boxley against the ill opinions of Martin Luther.'[127]

One monk who adhered to traditional beliefs after the Dissolution was Robert Robinson, formerly of Meaux. Holding the chantry of St William in Beverley collegiate church until the chantries were suppressed in 1548, he then became a schoolmaster. In that reign of Edward VI, some of the local Beverley boys were warned against attending his school as he was reputed to be a papist. In Mary's reign he attested the orthodoxy of two Beverley men who wished to be ordained, and he was appointed in 1556 to oversee the penance of one John Pesegrave, accused of possessing protestant books.[128] In 1560 Anthony Clarke, formerly a monk of Stratford, was deprived of his livings—including his prebend in Chichester, for refusing to take the oath of supremacy. Instead he became chaplain to Lord Montague at Cowdray, who 'preferred the old ways.'[129] A former abbot of Rievaulx, Edward Kirkby deposed in 1533, also clung to his catholic belief, referring in his will of 1551 to 'our blessed lady virgin, Mary the mother immaculate of Jesus Christ our Lord.'[130]

Very much later, in 1571, Parliament passed a Subscription Act, which required all clerics to declare their assent to the Thirty-Nine Articles, the doctrinal formulary of the Church of England. A few elderly, surviving Cistercians are known to have declined, and spent at least part of their last years in prison, as John Alman (Almond) of Croxden who ended his earthly life in Hull Castle in 1585. Thomas Mudde (Madde), formerly of Jervaulx, who had carried Blessed George Lazenby's head to St Andrew's in Scotland, returned south of the Border in Queen Mary's reign. Living in Knaresborough he taught children there, dying in 1583 after six years custody in the North Block House at Hull. Thomas Reade of Hailes may be the cleric of that name who died in the Marshalsea in 1579.[131]

Christopher Symondson of Rievaulx was accused of recusancy in 1570;[132] William Walton, formerly of Byland, was deprived of his two Yorkshire livings in 1572 for declining to subscribe;[133] while John Barrowe, formerly of Meaux, did subscribe in 1571 to the articles, despite perhaps being the former monk of whom it was said in 1567, that he 'useth the communion for the dead.'[134] The same was said that year of Richard Sympson, who may well have been Richard Skerne, also a monk of Meaux.[135] All these may not have suffered a martyrs' crown, but they were 'confessors,' faithful witnesses to their life-long held beliefs.

An abbey where opinion was sharply divided between a few monks on either side, although blows were not struck, was Woburn in Bedfordshire.[136] One of its monks, Robert Salford, in favour of the 'new learning', addressed a letter to Thomas Cromwell which was carried to London by the curate of the local parish chapel; William Sherburn, an ex-friar who had already been rebuked by the abbot, Robert Hobbes, for making anti-papal utterances.[137] Salford and Sherburn effectively betrayed the abbot and others of conservative views within the monastery. Abbot Hobbes did not help himself when, in January 1538, he declared that "the bishop of Rome's authority is good and lawful within this realm."[138] The community was therefore examined on 11 and 12 May 1538, not in the Tower of London—as Gasquet supposed, but at Woburn itself.[139] The upshot was that the abbot, the sub-prior and the sexton were committed for trial, which took place at Abbot's Woburn on Friday 14 June.[140]

Against the abbot it was deposed that after the execution of the Carthusian martyrs he had ordered his monks to add Psalm 68 ('Let God arise, and let his enemies be scattered') every Friday to the Litany, and that daily after Lauds the antiphon, 'O Saviour of the word, save us all',[141] be sung. The abbot allegedly also, instead of having the pope's name deleted from the service-books, had caused it only to be crossed out in ink—against the day that papal power would be regained. Knowing that papal bulls in favour of the house were to be taken away, he made copies of them, and he instructed a monk, William Hampton, to make a copy of a book locally written and entitled 'Of the Power of Peter.'[142] In his own evidence the abbot agreed with several of the allegations laid against him—for there were more, but set them in a different and favourable context. He also asserted that he had seen a copy of the new English translation of the Bible, and thought it 'not well interpreted in many places.'[143]

The sub-prior of Woburn, Ralph Woburn, acknowledged that he had entertained doubts about the royal supremacy, and had preached many times without mentioning it, and also admitted that he thought the deaths of St John Fisher and St Thomas More meritorious, and wished that he had died with them. He had, however, seen the error of his ways, by reading Tyndale's, *The Obedience of a Christian Man*, and Henry VIII's prose dialogue, *A Glass of the Truth*.[144] The sexton, Laurence Blonham, agreed that he did 'not kiss the book'—put his hand out to touch it, the first time he was sworn, but because of others crowding around he could not reach it. He had a 'foolish scrupulous mind,' so that sometimes he was with the pope and sometimes against him, but now was 'put out of doubt of the truth' by Cromwell's instruction.[145]

There were others in the community at Woburn suspected of having reservations about the royal supremacy and with papalist leanings, but it was the abbot, the sub-prior and the sexton, who were condemned to be drawn through the town of Woburn and there be hung, drawn and quartered. It is probable that this took place on 20 June 1538. Tradition has it that abbot was hung from an oak tree within sight of his monastery.[146] The remaining eighteen monks of the abbey were granted their 'capacities' on 20 July, but as the monastery was 'attainted' there is no record of any pensions being awarded them. Those receiving their dispensations included others that their fellow monk, Robert Salford, thought to be 'papists': William Hampton, Richard Hopworth, Robert Nede and Thomas Toller.[147]

A week later, the earl of Oxford had occasion to write to Cromwell protesting his innocence regarding 'an accusation made against me in the deposition of that arrant traitor, the abbot of Woburn.' The earl said that he had not seen the abbot since the prorogation of the last parliament, and that he could not remember having any 'papistical cope or book.'[148]

Conclusion

Between 1535 and 1538, five Cistercian abbots, one former abbot, and eleven Cistercian monks, were executed, but can all of them be considered as having been 'martyrs' in the usual sense of that word? In all but the instance of Woburn, those who died had no choice but to support the 'commons' in their revolts. Had they not done so, monasteries might well have been burnt, individuals maltreated. The uprisings in Lincolnshire and the north each had a religious element, outwardly at least. Those affected will have been aware of the barbaric death meted out to the Carthusian martyrs a little while before. Compared to the total numbers taking part in the risings, monastic participants were to an extent singled out when retribution came. There was seemingly no consideration given by the judicial authorities, and certainly not by Henry VIII, as to why abbots and monks had become involved. At Woburn those charged admitted but in part tried to explain away their actions. There was a need for reformation in monastic life, but in the sense of renewal and redeployment. Religion and politics were interwoven; abbots and monks could not avoid being caught up in situations not of their own making. In the eyes of the Crown, recalcitrant religious could be seen as traitors; in retrospect, they suffered both needlessly and unjustly.

Notes

[1] C. H(ugh) Talbot, 'The English Cistercian Martyrs, I: George Lazenby, Monk of Jervaulx.' In: *Collectanea Cisterciensia* 2, 1935, pp. 70–75.

[2] *LP* 8, p. 4405 [No. 1025].

[3] *LP* 8, p. 408 [No. 1033]; Knowles, *Bare Ruined Choirs*, 1976, pp. 262–63.

[4] *LP* 8, p. 420 [No. 1069].

[5] *LP* 9, pp. 10 [No. 37], 184 [No. 557].

[6] A. N. Shaw, 'The Involvement of the Religious Orders in the Northern Risings.' In: *Downside Review* 117 (No. 407), 1999, pp. 89–90.

[7] F. A. Gasquet, *Henry VIII and the English Monasteries*, London: J.C. Nimmo, 2nd. edn. 1899, pp. 201, 207–10, 213; M. H. Dodds, *The Pilgrimage of Grace*, Manchester U.P., I, 1915, p. 106; *LP* 11, p. 217 [No. 536]; *LP* 12, Part 1, p. 227–28 [No. 481].

[8] *LP* 11, p. 325 [No. 828/2/viii]; Dodds, *Pilgrimage of Grace* I, 1915, pp. 104–06; Gasquet, *English Monasteries*, 1899, p. 219; Shaw, 'Northern Risings', 1999, p. 102.

[9] *LP* 11, p. 325 [No. 828/2/viii].

[10] *LP* 12, Part 1, pp. 268, 271 [Nos. 581, 590]; Cf. *LP* 11, pp. 320, 325 [Nos. 827/ii, 2viii; 828, ix, x]; Shaw, 'Northern Risings,' 1999, p. 94. [Two confusing earlier lists exist of

offenders admitted to bail: the one [*LP* **12**, Part 1, p. 268 [No. 581 fn.] would suggest
that Wade had the *alias* of 'Kirby,' and 'Swale' that of 'Ripon'; the other [*LP* .**11**, pp.
320–21 [No. 827] gives as put to bail, Henry Jenkinson, monk of Bardney (this must
be an error), and Reynold Kirby, William Ripon and Hugh Ledney, of Kirkstead.]

11   *LP* **12**, Part 2, p. 268 [No. 581/ii]; **13**, Part 1, p. 564 [No. 1519/21].
12   *LP* **12**, Part 2, p. 182 [No. 462].
13   *LP* **11**, p. 322 [No. 828/i(2)].
14   *LP* **11**, p. 225 [No. 568].
15   *LP* **12**, Part 1, pp. 175–76 [No. 380].
16   *LP* **11**, p. 399 [No. 974].
17   *LP* **12**, Part 1, pp. 177–78 [No. 380]; Shaw, 'Northern Risings,' 1999, p. 102.
18   *LP* **12**. Part 1, p. 175 [No. 380]; Dodds, *Pilgrimage of Grace* I, 1915, p. 102; *Cf. LP* **11**,
       pp. 343–44 [No. 854]. It had been reported to Cromwell that Mellesent had been
       hanged by the rebels and Bellew baited to death with dogs [*LP* **11**, p. 225 [No. 567].
19   Dodds, *Pilgrimage of Grace* II, 1915, pp. 153–54.
20   *LP* **12**, Part 1, pp. 179 [No. 380], 229 [No. 481].
21   *LP* **12**, Part 1, pp. 173–79 [No. 380].
22   *LP* **12**, Part 1, pp. 227–29 [No. 481].
23   *LP* **11**, p. 225 [No. 567].
24   C. Cross and N. Vickers, *Monks, friars and nuns in sixteenth century Yorkshire*, YAS, 1995,
       p. 156..
25   Gasquet, *English Monasteries*, 1899, pp. 232–33.
26   Shaw, 'Northern Risings,' 1999, pp. 95–96.
27   *LP* **11**, p. 304 [No. 783]; *Cf.* C. Nash, 'The Fate of the English Cistercian Abbots.' In:
       Cîteaux **2**, 1965, p. 98.
28   Dodds, *Pilgrimage of Grace* II, 1915, p. 217.
29   J. S. Fletcher, *The Cistercians in Yorkshire*, London: S.P.C.K., 1919, pp. 28–9; Dodds,
       Pilgrimage of Grace II, 1915, p. 39.
30   *LP* **11**, p. 305 [No. 786].
31   Cross and Vickers, *Monks, friars and nuns*, 1995, p. 202.
32   *LP* **11**, p. 304 [No. 784].
33   Dodds, *Pilgrimage of Grace* II, 1915, p. 128; G. Moorhouse, *The Pilgrimage of Grace*,
       London: Weidenfeld and Nicolson, 2002, pp. 278–79.
34   *LP* **12**, Part 1, p. 237 [No. 506].
35   Gasquet, *English Monasteries*, 1899, p. 270, perhaps following J. Harland, *A History of
       Sawley*, London, 1853, p. 47, gives William Trafford as the last abbot of Sawley, asserting
       he was hanged at Lancaster on 10 March 1537, but this cannot be correct.
36   *LP* **12**, Part 1, pp. 472–73 [No. 1034] for Hamerton's examination; *Cf. LP* **11**, p. 340
       [No. 785].
37   *LP* **12**, Part 1, p. 493 [No. 1086]; Moorhouse, *Pilgrimage of Grace*, 2002, pp. 316–17.
38   *LP* **12**, Part 1, pp. 375 [No. 847/13]; 378 [No. 848/13].

39 See *LP* **12**, Part 1, p. 496 [No. 1087]: Percy's examination.

40 *LP* **12**, Part 1, p. 266 [No. 577].

41 *LP* **12**, Part 1, p. 293 [No. 666].

42 *LP* **12**, Part 1, p. 472–73 [No. 1034].

43 Fletcher, *Cistercians in Yorkshire*, 1919, pp. 297–8 (but this may be a mistaken identity).

44 D. M. Smith, *Heads of Religious Houses* **3**, Cambridge U.P., 2008, p. 329.

45 *FOR*, p. 58.

46 Cross and Vickers, *Monks, friars and nuns*, 1995, p. 202.

47 Dodds, *Pilgrimage of Grace* II, 1915, p. 142.

48 Moorhouse, *Pilgrimage of Grace*. 2002, p. 281.

49 *LP* **12**, Part 1, pp. 306 [No. 695]; 315 [No. 706].

50 *LP* **12**, Part 1, p. 283 [No. 632].

51 Dodds, *Pilgrimage of Grace* II, 1915, pp. 83–85; Moorhouse, *Pilgrimage of Grace*, 2002, p. 279.

52 *LP* **12**, Part 1, pp. 473–74 [No. 1035]; M. L. Bush, 'The Richmondshire Uprising.' In: *NH* **29**, 1993, pp. 64–68, 83–84.

53 *LP* **12**, Part 1, p. 342 [No. 786/11]; John Dakyn, a prisoner, testified to force being used; p. 345 [No. 789].

54 Dodds, *Pilgrimage of Grace* I, 1915, pp. 202–03.

55 *LP* **12**, Part 1, pp. 345 [No. 789], 473–74 [No. 1035].

56 *LP* **12**, Part 1, p. 130 [No. 281].

57 Dodds, *Pilgrimage of Grace* II, 1915, p. 214.

58 *LP* **12**, Part 1, pp. 455–56 [No. 1012].

59 *LP* **12**, Part 1, pp. 473–74 [No. 1035].

60 *LP* **12**, Part 1, pp. 455–56 [No. 1012], 468 [No. 1023/ii].

61 Dodds, *Pilgrimage of Grace* II, 1915, p. 108.

62 Ibid. II, p. 107; *LP* **12**, Part 1, p. 455 [No. 1012].

63 *LP* **12**, Part 1, pp. 455–56 [No. 1012], 468 [No. 1023/ii].

64 Dodds, *Pilgrimage of Grace* II, 1915, p. 108. [His name was excepted from a proposed list of pardons.].

65 *LP* **12**, Part 1, pp. 473–74 [No. 1035].

66 Dodds, *Pilgrimage of Grace* I, p. 208.

67 Ibid. II, pp. 214–16.

68 Ibid. II, p. 139.

69 Much of this section is based upon: C. Haigh, *The Last Days of the Lancashire Monasteries*, Manchester U.P., 1969, pp. 94–99.

70 *LP* **12**, Part 1, p. 280 [No. 621].

71 *LP* **12**, Part 1, p. 395 [No. 879].

72 Dodds, *Pilgrimage of Grace* I, 1915, p. 219; *Cf. LP* **12**, Part 1, p. 461 [No. 1020].

73 *LP* **11**, pp. 379–80 [No. 947].

74 *LP* **12**, Part 2, p. 88 No. 205].

[75] VCH, *County of Lancaster* **2**, 1908, p. 125.

[76] Dodds, *Pilgrimage of Grace* II, 1915, p. 142.

[77] *LP* **12**, Part 1, p. 181 [No. 389].

[78] *LP* **12**, Part 1, pp. 378, 500 [Nos. 848/12, 1087]; Moorhouse, *Pilgrimage of Grace*, 2002, p. 282 (who tells that the abbot pleaded guilty to all his five charges, but Haydock only to one).

[79] *LP* **12**, Part 1, p. 283 [No. 632]; C. Haigh, 'John Paslew', *ODNB* on–line.

[80] Haigh, *Lancashire Monasteries*, 1969, p. 84; Nash, 'English Cistercian Abbots,' 1965, p. 103; Dodds, *Pilgrimage of Grace* II, 1915, p. 143, suggests the execution took place 'in a field opposite his birth–place.'

[81] *LP* **12**, Part 1, pp. 294, 399 [Nos. 668, 896]. For the inventory, see: M. E. C. Walcott (ed.), 'Inventory of Whalley Abbey.' In: *THSLC*, N.S. 7, 1867, pp. 103–110.

[82] *LP* **12**, Part 1, p. 282 [No. 630].

[83] *LP* **12**, Part 1, p. 294 [No. 668]. *Cf.* pp. 306 [No. 695], 368–69 [No. 840].

[84] *FOR*, pp. 91, 96, 110.

[85] *LP* **12**, Part 1, p. 315 [No. 706].

[86] *LP* **12**, Part 1, pp. 306, 399 [Nos. 840, 896].

[87] *LP* **12**, Part 2, p. 88 [No. 205].

[88] *LP* **12**, Part 1, p. 306 [No. 695].

[89] *LP* **12**, Part 1, p. 289 [No. 652]; VCH, *County of Lancaster* **2**, 1908, pp. 124–25..

[90] *LP* **12**, Part 1, p. 370 [No. 841/3].

[91] VCH, *County of Lancaster* **2**, 1908, p. 124.

[92] *LP* **12**, Part 1, pp. 369–72 [No. 841/1–3].

[93] *LP* **12**, Part 1, p. 289 [No. 652].

[94] *LP* **12**, Part 1, pp. 371–72 [No. 841/3ii].

[95] *LP* **12**, Part 1, pp. 368–69 [No. 840].

[96] *LP* **12**, Part 1, p. 369 [No. 841/1]—gives the fragmentary testimony of certain monks recorded at Furness.

[97] If, however, John Broughton can be equated with John Troughton, he did receive the usual dispensation to wear secular habit [Haigh, *Last Days*, 1969, p. 145; *FOR*, p. 97].

[98] Haigh, *Last Days*, 1969, p. 145.

[99] *LP* **12**, Part 1, p. 366 [No. 832].

[100] *LP* **12**, Part 1, pp. 369–69 [No. 840].

[101] *LP* **12**, Part 1, p. 395 [No. 880].

[102] *LP* **12**, Part 2, p. 88 [No. 205].

[103] *LP* **12**, Part 2, p. 429 [No. 1216].

[104] Dodds, *Pilgrimage of Grace* I, 1915, p. 312.

[105] *LP* **12**, Part 1, pp. 303–04 [No. 687].

[106] *LP* **12**, Part 1, pp. 575–76 [No. 1259].

[107] *LP* **12**, Part 1, p. 413 [No. 904].

[108] *LP* **12**, Part 1, pp. 575–76 [No. 1259].

109   *LC*, pp. 279–80.

110   *FOR*, p. 77.

111   *LP* **11**, pp. 181 [No. 449], 216 [No. 529].

112   Gasquet, *English Monasteries*, 1899, pp. 268–69, where he suggests that Newminster finally closed as late as 20 August 1537.

113   *LP* **12**, Part 1, p. 227 [No. 479].

114   *LP* **4**, Part 3, p. 2915 [No. 6487].

115   *LP* **5**, pp. 773–74 [Misc. 34]; *Cf. LP* **5**, p. 527 [No. 1203].

116   *LP* **13**, Part 1, p. 119 [No. 347].

117   *LP* **8**, p. 27 [No. 79]. In another letter, of September 1535, the prior asked Cromwell to cast an 'eye of pity' on his community: *LP* **9**, pp. 131 [394].

118   *LP* **9**, p. 106 [No. 315].

119   *LP* **13**, Part 1, p. 387 [No. 1051].

120   G. Baskerville, *English Monks and the Suppression of the Monasteries*, London: Jonathan Cape, 1937, pp. 147–48.

121   *LP* **10**, pp. 59–60 [No. 164].

122   *LP* **12**, Part 2, p. 283 [No. 800].

123   TNA, REQ2/10/57. [He pension was certainly paid up to the close of 1536: *LP* **13**, Part 2, p. 178 [No. 457], and he may have had the lease of the abbey's Staunton Grange: *LP* **13**, Part 2, p. 350 [No. 840/2].

124   *LP* **8**, p. 123 [No. 297].

125   *LP* **6**, p. 674 [No. 1677]..

126   *LP* **13**, Part 1, p. 391 [No. 1066]; W.H. Stevenson ahnd H.E. Salter, *Early History of St John's College, Oxford*, Oxford Historical Soc., 1939, p. 49.

127   *LP* **3**, Part1, pp. 541–42 [No. 1353].

128   Cross and Vickers, *Monks, friars and nuns*, 1995, p. 162.

129   Baskerville, *English Monks*, 1937, pp. 268–69.

130   M. Aveling, 'The Rievaulx Community after the Dissolution.' In: *Ampleforth Journal* **57**, 1952, pp. 102–03.

131   G. Baskerville, 'The Dispossessed Religious of Gloucestershire.' In: *TBGAS* **49**, 1927, p. 90; Cross and Vickers, *Monks, friars and nuns*, 1995, pp. 135–36.

132   Cross and Vickers, *Monks, friars and nuns*, 1995, p. 182.

133   Ibid. p. 109.

134   Ibid. p. 157.

135   Ibid. p. 163.

136   For this section see especially, VCH, *County of Bedford* **1**, 1904, pp. 368–70.

137   D. Knowles, *Saints and Scholars*, Cambridge U.P., 1963, p. 189.

138   N. Doggett, 'Hobbes, Robert', *ODNB* on–line.

139   *LP* **10**, p. 517 [No. 1239], **13**, Part 1, pp. 356 [No. 981]; 397 [No. 1086]

140   G.S. Thomson, 'Woburn Abbey.' In: *Trans. Royal Historical Soc.*, 4th Series, **16**, 1933, pp. 136–40.

[141] Gasquet, *English Monasteries*, 1899, pp. 284–87.

[142] *LP* **13**, Part 1, pp. 356, 360 [Nos. 981/6, 11).

[143] Gasquet, *English Monasteries*, 1899, pp. 286–88.

[144] *LP* **10**, p. 517 [No. 1239].

[145] *LP* **13**, Part 1, p. 397 [No. 1086].

[146] Baskerville, *English Monks*, 1937, p. 178; Knowles, *saints and Scholars*, 1963, pp. 190–91.

[147] *FOR*, p. 145.

[148] *LP* **13**, Part 1, p. 547 [No. 1477].

6 THE MONASTIC ECONOMY

T HE EARLY IDEAL of the Cistercian Order had been that monastic lands would be farmed by the labours of the monks themselves and their attendant lay-brothers, the *conversi*, whilst the oversight of the economy of individual houses would be the responsibility of the monk business-manager appointed as cellarer. By Tudor times this ideal situation had become a past memory. Since the Black Death there had been little recruitment of lay-brothers and, so far as is known, only one *conversus* was a member of an English Cistercian community by the Suppression. The lack of this labour force meant that monastic lands had been increasingly demised to tenants or even sold, so that little of their farming was overseen by the monks themselves.

The immediate monastic demesne usually remained in abbatial hands, as that of Biddlesden, valued at £19 in 1535.[1] Tintern by 1536 had taken back two of its granges into its own hands,[2] whilst activities like fishing and mining might be more directly controlled. The upshot of all this was for some abbeys a large wages bill, with laity appointed to a variety of supervisory tasks. One factor remained static: the desire of the monasteries to see that their economy was well managed, and to gain the greatest possible return from their assets. Contemporaneous surveys of an abbey's lands and rents due exist for Combermere. That record is prefaced with the words: 'This manuscript was begun by me John Massy, sub-prior, in the year of Our Lord, 1523, at the instance and bidding of Christopher Whalley, Bachelor of Divinity, Abbot.'[3] Such written evidence of a monastery's economy also exists for abbeys such as Sibton, Tintern and Whalley.

To safeguard and underpin their economy, as Henry VII's reign drew to its close, at least eight Cistercian abbeys gained confirmation from the Crown of earlier charters from a variety of benefactors including confirmations by previous sovereigns, granting them possessions and liberties. On the accession of Henry VIII some thirteen monasteries of the Order did the same between the years 1509 and 1511; they were clearly anxious that a new monarch should respect their rights.[4]

One of these abbeys was St Mary Graces; it obtained royal confirmation of charters ranging in date from the reign of Richard II to Henry VI in 1508, but in 1511, after the accession of Henry VIII, it requested and gained approval of twenty charters and letters patent from the reign of Edward III down to that of Henry VII.[5] Hailes in 1510 received confirmation of twenty-six previous charters and letters patent, including those of Edmund and Richard, earls of Cornwall, its founding family,[6] whilst Holm Cultram, the same year, gained recognisance of twenty-eight earlier charters, letters patent and exemplifications.[7] Newenham had fewer charters of which to seek approval, but one was dated 'at the siege of Bordeaux' during the reign of Henry III.[8] The printed records do not indicate the fees charged for these many deeds of authenticity. By the period under study the Cistercian estates were well settled and defined, but certain abbeys sought to increase the acreage of their estates. Because of the Statutes of Mortmain of 1279 and 1290, the passing of any land into the 'dead hand' (*mortmain*) of a religious corporation had to receive Crown approval. In each case the sheriff of the county concerned was directed to hold an inquiry as to what hurt or damage (*ad quod damnum*: alternatively, *ad quod dampnum*) there might be to the Crown or individuals by the loss of inheritance and other taxes by the lands concerned being now held in perpetuity. Such inquisitions were held at Northampton (1494/95) regarding a propose alienation in mortmain of lands in Thornby and elsewhere to Pipewell;[9] at Horncastle (1506/07) concerning a similar transfer of lands in Sibsey and other localities to Revesby, [10]and at Warwick (1515) relating to land in Ashow given to Stoneleigh.[11]

Several applications were approved: Pipewell (1495) might receive lands up to the yearly value of £4,[12] Stoneleigh (1505) of £7;[13] Boxley (1510) of £10,[14] and Stoneleigh again (1515) up to a value of £26-13-4.[15] One of the largest acquisitions was made by Warden (1507) when it alienated 254 acres, the gift of Sir John Fisher, a justice of the bench, in return for daily masses for the good estate of the king, the donor and his family, and for obits after their deaths, at 'the altar of St Nicholas and St John Baptist in the north part of the monastery.'[16] In the formative earlier centuries, the Cistercians employed a policy of land exchanges to consolidate their estates. A different transaction, but effectively an exchange, occurred in 1497 when Robertsbridge was permitted to acquire lands up to the annual value of £40, whilst granting to Sir Richard Guildford, controller of the royal household, 3,000 acres of its saltmarsh in Sussex and

Kent.[17] Conversely, when by 1492 Woburn had acquired lands in Eversold, Bedfordshire, without the requisite permission, they were forfeited and given to one of the king's servants.[18]

The Lay Officers and Monastic Courts

The several monastic officers and servants maintaining a monastic establishment, and perhaps mostly resident, have been described (Chapter 4). At the apex of their ranks was the lay official designated as the *Steward*, who was practically always a person living relatively locally, and usually an individual of influence and importance. His was an office which came to the fore in Tudor times, and in some abbeys relatively late. One of the chiefest duties of a Cistercian steward was to preside—usually by means of a deputy, at the abbey's manorial courts. He could be a person to whom a monastery might look for protection of its interests, but occasionally he might be interfering and overbearing. It is clear that some stewards actively involved themselves in the affairs of their abbey, with provision being made for their board if visiting an abbey grange.

It was to its steward, the earl of Derby, that Abbot Pyle of Furness went for advice during the Northern Rebellion); it was Sir Francis Bryan, steward of Woburn, who pleaded with Cromwell (1536) for the retention of a certain warren by that monastery;[19] and it was Sir Thomas Denys, 'chief steward' of Newenham who gave its abbot a supporting and laudatory letter when he was summoned to visit Cromwell.[20] It was to its steward, Sir Roger Cholmeley, the Recorder of London, that monks of Stratford reported in 1535 the scruples of their abbot regarding the royal supremacy.[21] It was a concerned steward of Hulton, Sir Philip Draycott (1534), who advised against the appointment of William Chalner as abbot there.[22]

It was to its new steward, William Brereton, that in 1534 Lewis ap Thomas, abbot of Cymer, unsuccessfully offered £40 in a bid to gain the abbacy of Valle Crucis for himself, after Brereton had imprisoned its young miscreant superior. Brereton had only just been appointed abbot of the house, but he immediately became its master.[23] Stewards could be of independent mind. The steward of Byland, Roger Lascelles (1534), went 'against the mind of the abbot,' when he indicted a malefactor for killing a stag 'within the close of the abbot.'[24] Thomas Cromwell, no less, imposed himself as steward upon Vale Royal, and held a court there in person.

A notable steward might hold several stewardships, as Sir Rhys ap Thomas in Wales (*d.*1532) who held no less than five,[25] and the earls of Derby, father and son, who were the principal stewards of Dieulacres, Furness and Whalley. The earl was also Steward of Chester Abbey.[26] The appointment in 1518 of Thomas, marquess of Dorset, and of his son, Henry Grey, in survivorship, as steward of Stanley, made for another family concern. Dorset became also steward of Merevale in 1520 and of Tilty in 1529, and also held two other but non-Cistercian stewardships.[27] Some monasteries had appointed lay stewards for decades, the earl of Shrewsbury claiming in 1536 that he had been steward of Combermere for forty years.[28]

Other houses may have managed to conduct their own affairs: to improve its situation, the appointment of a lay steward was envisaged at Warden only in 1537.[29] At Buckfast in 1537 and 1538 respectively, John Southcote, a local lawyer, was named as steward and his son, Thomas, as under-steward.[30] They were related to John Tregonwell, one of the suppression commissioners. In October 1538 St Mary Graces appointed Sir Richard Pollard, king's remembrancer of the exchequer, as 'general supervisor' of all its possessions, with an annuity of 5 marks.[31] These, and other very late grants of stewardship, suggest that the monasteries may have received hidden financial favours in return.

For many stewards, given their other commitments, the assistance of under-stewards might be necessary. In 1533 Newenham, at the request of its steward, Sir Thomas Denys, gave John Drake of Musbury, the post of stewardship of its lands in Newenham and Axminster.[32] Under-stewards or sub-stewards are also noted at Buckfast,[33] Merevale,[34] Dieulacres (for Poulton manor),[35] Ford[36] and Swineshead (Cottgrave manor).[37] When sometime around 1520 a manorial court was held at Dore, its steward, Henry Miles, was 'so diseased, that he could not well labour at that time.' He sent his son-in-law, John Vaughan, to keep the court, at which various disturbances occurred.[38]

In a very late appointment Fountains (1538) appointed Christopher Lyneley, steward of its lands in Yorkshire but excepting Craven.[39] Stewards were usually non-resident, but Beaulieu's two principal joint stewards had as part of their emoluments the "Old Abbot's Lodging" near Our Lady Gate. They were assisted by a sub-steward, Thomas Goddard, later mayor of Southampton, while there were also joint stewards for its Faringdon manor in Oxfordshire.[40]

The stipend of many stewards was not much more than £2 yearly—but at least perhaps £700 in modern terms; such was paid to Sir John Bridges (later

Baron Chandos), steward of Hailes from 1528,[41] to Robert Meynell, steward of Byland (a late appointment) from 1538,[42] and to William FitzWilliam (later earl of Southampton) at Kirkstall.[43] His appointment may well have been an effort to gain his favour, for he was chancellor of the Duchy of Lancaster and actively involved in the suppression of monasteries. The earl of Derby's Cistercian stewardships brought him yearly £17-6-8, equivalent in modern values to perhaps £7,000. The steward of Newenham for that manor and Axminster received but £1-6-8 yearly but it was, like most, a life appointment. Christopher Lyneley, working for Fountains, gained £1-6-8 each year, but with an extra 10s. for his additional work as the abbey's auditor.[44]

Valle Crucis in its closing years had William Brereton as its Steward with a stipend of £8, and Edward ap Rees as under-steward with a wage of £2. These two officials received between them one-sixth of the monastery's income from temporalities, which was extravagant but Brereton was a powerful personage and chamberlain of Chester who could exact what he wanted.[45] Most fortunate were the Southcotes at Buckfast: the father awarded a stipend of £6-13-4, the son of £2-13-6. At Kirkstead the steward, George Taylboys, was given an annuity of £2-13-4, but John Hussey gained £1-6-8 for his keeping of the court at Hamtree, whist its several *bailiffs* received between £3 and 3s 4d. depending on the size of the property they administered.[46]

Other non-resident lay officers of a Cistercian abbey may have included *receivers-general*, charged with the receipts and expenses of all the properties of an abbey. When Sir Henry Norton was given this post for Fountains in 1538, it was made clear that he was taking over these duties directly from its cellarer, Thomas Ripon.[47] In 1535 Rewley sought Cromwell's assent to the appointment of William Austen, its abbot's natural brother, as its 'surveyor and receiver' on account of the services he had rendered the community.[48] Assisting the earl of Derby at Whalley were no less than five receivers and eleven bailiffs on its wide-flung properties.[49] A receiver's work was aided by the engagement of *rent gatherers* like Robert Snowe (1533) acting for Stratford abbey.[50]

At both Strata Florida, Richard Devereux (appointed receiver-general in May 1538) and at Whitland, David Nash (receiver-general from October that year), must have played a major role in the numerous late demises those abbeys made.[51] Such officers would have received their meals when at their monastery on business; when in 1530 John Howe was granted a corrody at

Valle Crucis, he was to take his food: 'At the trestle table in the common hall of the abbot within the monastery, just as the Receiver and other officers did'.[52]

Other officials will have included, certainly in the larger monasteries, the *auditors* who presumably partly took over the work of the monastic bursars. Roger Kynsey occupied this office ta Ford in its closing years,[53] and Edmund Turner at Tintern (with an annuity of £2).[54] Richard Cromwell, Thomas's nephew, gained himself £2 yearly as auditor for Biddlesden (by 1535).[55] At Merevale, Thomas Fowler was its 'auditor and supervisor,' though the Court of Augmentations declined to award him any compensation for loss of office; perhaps because of the late date of his appointment.[56] Likewise disallowed, by the suppression commissioners, was Thomas Herbert's post as *coroner* of Tintern, since 'no cause could be shown.'[57] The Herberts were an influential local family, and Charles Herbert, was Tintern's steward for its Gwent lands.

The supervision of monastic *manorial courts* or *courts-leet* generally fell to an abbey's steward, but other provision might be made. At Tintern's Porthcaseg manor court by the sixteenth century the steward or his deputy always presided, with the cellarer present and presumably sitting by his side. At Fountains the receiver-general appointed in 1536 was also steward of its court. Furness, whose steward was the earl of Derby, gave in 1526 to Laurence Starkey, an under-sheriff of Lancashire and for a time member of parliament for Lancaster, the duty of holding 'all courts and sessions of the peace held at Dalton or elsewhere within the liberties of the abbey.'[58] Ford on 31 October 1538 made one Mark Hayes its 'sub-steward or clerk of courts,' with an annual fee of £2-13-4. The Court of Augmentations, probably because the appointment was made so close to the closure of the abbey, refused him compensation. His claim, it said, 'had no strength in law.'[59]

Monastic tenants were usually obliged to pay suit of court (be present and available for serving on a jury) twice a year. The courts of Tintern's Porthcaseg manor were held quarterly, as in 1514 when William Betson, deputy to the steward William Herbert, presided together with John Tintern, the cellarer.[60] At Kirkstead, two 'great courts' were held annually, where certain tenants had, in 1536, to 'make two appearances and be of the panel.'[61] At Fountains there was perhaps greater regularity: one of its tenants in Craven in 1505 was committed to suit of court in the abbot's manor of Melkham, 'one week in three.'[62] At Buckfast a tenant of the abbey in South Brent, had to pay suit of court twice a year at Easter and Michalemas, on being given eight days notice.[63]

At Rufford the monastic court was held twice a year at the abbey gates.[64] A tenant of Fountains in Craven (1525) who had care of a flock of the abbey's sheep was expected 'to come to the monastery every year to make account for the flock at the audit held by the steward or official at the gates.'[65] The monastery gate-way was, as of old, a favourite meeting place with the outside world. Courts might also be held in more distance locations; as at Borrowdale chapel in the case of Furness.

At all monastic courts a written record was kept, noting entry fees, rents and heriot paid; adjudication of disputes, and other matters. From Vaudey a series of such *court rolls* exist for the abbacy of Henry Saxton (1510-33) relating to certain of its properties.[66] They are preserved in Lincolnshire Record Office, but a number are now unfit for production. Those which can be seen regrettably do not give the name of the presiding cellarer or steward, but each court roll commences by naming the twelve or more jurors appointed to hear pleas—their names giving an indication of the local population at the time.

Apart from the usual court notes, there is mention in theVaudey rolls of 'the grange gate' at Burton (a little north of Lincoln), and of a payment due of 4 pence—sometimes in arrears—from the nuns of Stixwould for suit of court. The rolls yield the name of Ralph Syre, as chantry priest at Burton in 1525,[67] and they relate the entry of tenants into holdings—like Thomas Nyx who succeeded his father in having a lease of four or five agricultural properties in Burton and elsewhere in return for an annual rent of 42s.[68] The rolls also reflect the open field system, and the demand of the abbey for properties to be kept in good maintenance. They also tell of 'delinquents,' like Lawrence Seele who had stolen ash trees from the abbey woods.[69]

An intermittent series of court rolls, stretching from the thirteenth down to the sixteenth century, for Tintern's home manor of Porthcaseg, are held in the National Library of Wales.[70] As well as normal manorial court business, from time to time the courts laid down injunctions for the general and social well-being of the district; 'bye-laws' in modern parlance. The courts in 1528 forbade: the playing of dice and cards in the manor; the playing of hand ball within the abbey gates; the recourse to external courts until an issue had been 'tempted and committed' at the abbey court; the theft of other people's timber; and the washing of 'any dirty thing, neither clothes nor other corrupt matter, in the stream which runs through the middle of the abbey,'—its principal drainage channel.[71]

Tintern jealously guarded its sole rights of buying and selling on its lands, but by the fifteenth century there were several tenant traders within the manor. John Whitmyll, of the nearby Angidy valley, paid sixpence in 1506 for leave to sell bread and wine.[72] In 1524 and 1525, respectively, John Potley and the lessee of the Angidy Mill received from the abbey permission to sell 'bread, ale and other merchandise.' In these years it seems some traders, perhaps to increase their takings, wished to move their stalls or shops. In October 1528 Porthcaseg court therefore ordered that 'every butcher who sells meat, and anyone who sells victuals, shall remain in the definite place granted to them beforehand by deed.'[73]

The extant court rolls make no explicit mention of recourse to capital punishment, but field names of the time included Hangman's Field on Tintern's Woolaston Grange,[74] and Hangynghouse pasture on Stoneleigh's Milborne Grange,[75] while Coggeshall village had its Gallow Street.[76] On Sibton's property in Peasenhall (1491) was a 'gallow-close'.[77] A description was given in 1517 of the rolls of Jervaulx's court at Cuerdley; they were 'bound together and rolled together in divers paper rolls, and they were to the "mountenance" of a handful.'[78]

Land Utilisation

While much monastic land had been demised, monasteries normally continued to directly cultivate the home demesne and, by the conditions written into leases, to ensure that their tenants engaged in good agricultural practice. Merevale practised very careful and organised farming on its demesne. This meant that in the late spring of 1498 two men were employed for twenty-six days simply in 'spreading muk'—fertilising the soil. Later that year women were paid for weeding and hoeing. The monastery thus produced considerable quantities of wheat, barley and rye, and also of peas—which were sold locally.[79] Hailes abbey used grazing sheep to 'muk and composter' its demesne ground.[80] The need for fertile soil was clearly recognised. The presence of a 'lime-house' at Merevale might indicate the liming of heavy clay soils, in addition to the use of lime in building repairs. Fountains had access to marl-pits in Ripley (1517) to ameliorate the limestone soils of the Pennines.[81] The continuing importance of arable farming was also demonstrated in stock numbers—as the thirty 'plough oxen' at Vale Royal,[82] in farming equipment—like the five harrows and the three shares and coulters of Sawtry,[83] and in labour services required of tenants—as by Buckfast.[84]

The monastery of Dore in Herefordshire in 1533 entered into a shared-farming agreement with two local men, Philip Tew and Robert Balcott (Bulcote). They were for nine years to have the three fields called the 'odde marks,' comprising 126 acres of arable and forty-seven of pasture. In a complex deed Tew and Balcott were to sow the fields, or cause them to be sowed, and for their labour were to have the fourth part of the one half of the field and the third part of the other half. The abbey was to pay for the reaping and mowing of three parts of all corn growing on the land. The lessees were to pay for the fourth part, and to carry all manner of corn and ten loads of hay to the abbot's barn. The agreement also provided for housing for the men, shared labour costs, fodder for the oxen and the necessary ploughs and harrows 'with harrowing horses.' Tew and Balcott were to provide the seed required. The upshot was the production of not only wheat, but also of oats, rye, barley and pulse.[85]

Despite the significance of arable farming to a monastery's food supply, certain abbeys apparently engaged in two general trends of Tudor times: the enclosing of land and the conversion of arable into pasture. Both these phenomena led to the loss of jobs in the countryside and also to its depopulation, and were a matter of State concern; the first also might mean the loss of rights of common of pasture. Anti-enclosure Acts were passed in 1489 and 1516, and from 1515 the conversion from arable to pasture also became an offence. In both cases, and especially if houses were destroyed, half the profits resulting from these actions were payable to the Crown.[86]

The Cistercians were not entirely faultless in these regards. Intent on enclosing abbey land Abbot Alexander Bank of Furness in 1516, along with two of his monks and servants, forcibly evicted William Carre, his wife and family, from their holding on abbey territory.[87] After arbitration Whalley reached an agreement in 1512 with local squires that it might that enclose some land in Much Harewood 'lying by the Hole House field under the Fallyngstone,' but that the abbey's tenants could have common of pasture on Harewood Moor.[88] A jury of fifteen was empanelled in 1517 to enquire into the enclosing of a park by Whalley nine years previously: the property comprised twelve acres of arable land, forty acres of wood and ten acres of moor and meadow.[89]

Around 1530 Garendon enclosed local 'waste ground' at nearby Dishley, some one thousand acres in extent. The local farmers took the monastery to court, as they alleged they had thus lost the common of pasture they had always enjoyed there between Michaelmas (29 September) and the Annunciation (25 March) each year.[90] One tenant, Eustace Brane, said that it was to his 'dyfeert and hurt.'[91] The abbey of Meaux (*c.*1535) was accused not only of with-holding deeds to a lease of twenty acres of pasture in Potterflett, Yorkshire, made to the monastery over thirty years previously, but of 'subverting and pulling up its boundaries', and then ditching and bounding the twenty acres so that they formed one unit with monastic land. Consequently Miles Stavely, the aggrieved owner, said that he had 'no perfect knowledge where he may distrain for the same.'[92]

Both the abbeys of Stanley (in 1510) and of Bruern (in 1515) were reported to the relevant authorities for having converted three hundred and thirty acres of arable respectively into pastureland.[93] Around 1516 Thomas Broke complained that whereas Dunkeswell had demised Sheldon Grange to him for life, the abbot (John Whitmore) later enclosed and converted into pasture the common land adjacent to the grange. The abbot countered by saying that the common land was not included in the property leased out to Broke.[94] Towards the close of the abbey's life, twenty tenants of Hailes complained to the Court of Chancery that that they used to grow crops and pasture sheep on their holdings on Longbarrow Hill, but that now the abbot was converting the tillage there into pasture for his profit. They alleged that whereas the monastery used to keep 240 sheep on the hill, it now pastured nine hundred, and they, the complainants, were 'utterly undone.'[95]

Other monasteries took a different approach. In 1494 Rewley had demised the manor of Wilanston to one William Arden. Nearly thirty years later, his heir, John, converted some of its lands from arable into pasture, but the Court of Chancery was told that he had done so 'against the mind and will of the abbot.'.[96] When in 1523 Robertsbridge demised for twenty-one years its manor of Werd to one William Borther, it demanded that he 'brusche and rede two pieces of land, one called Bechefeld and the other Assherode, and leave them arable ground in his later years.' He was to 'suffer no land to wild within the manor which is now arable.'[97]

In 1510 it was reported that Furness felt 'grieved for so much as the tenants [in Furness Fells] hath inclosed common of pasture more largely than they ought to.' A new agreement was reached between the abbey and twenty-two of the tenants in the Fells, which permitted certain improvements but they were to be 'hedged with dyke or wall.' In 1532 the monastery placed similar restrictions upon its tenants at Hawkshead.[98]

Boundaries could be marked out legitimately. When in 1498 Combe abbey demised lands in Rodburn, Warwickshire, the tenant, William Catesby, had the duty to 'maintain and make dykes to distinguish the lands, and make other durable metes and meres of wood and stone.'[99] A schedule of 1517 detailing the lands of Fountains in Threshfield, mentions enclosing stone walls and mear [boundary] stones there. When in 1518 lands at Taitfield, Rigton, were partitioned between Fountains and a lay owner, 'metes and bounds' were placed there.[100] In 1536 Warden demised Drewswood in Northill, Bedfordshire, to Northill College, on condition that the college enclosed and hedged it.[101]

In Tudor times there was still unused or under-used wasteland to be found on monastic properties. When arbitration settled the dispute between Hailes and its complainants on Longbarrow Hill, one hundred of acres of wasteland there was to be equally divided between twenty-four tenants.[102] In 1486 a tenant of Buckland was given waste at Sticklepath, Devon, on which to build a fulling mill,[103] and at an uncertain date Combermere allowed a tenant to build a house in Cheshire on 'a certain waste ground called Wychwood Green.'[104] Two pieces of waste, 'Gregepole waste' and "Welshman's waste," formed part of Stoneleigh's Melborne manor, Warwickshire, in 1537.[105]

In the earlier Middle Ages a relatively dry climate allowed for a degree of *wine production* in the south of England but, by Tudor times, damper weather meant that little viticulture remained. It is not therefore known whether the vineyards noted at Quarr (1495),[106] Warden (1533)[107] and Tilty (1535)[108] actually produced wine at those dates. Beaulieu had its 'Viniary Croft'.[109] The purchase of wine can be demonstrated even for the three southern abbeys of Beaulieu, Netley and Waverley, who in 1526 each imported a tun of wine at Southampton.[110] Climate change possibly accounted for the coastal erosion which affected lands of Merevale and Whalley on the Lancashire coast. Seventy-five year old Hugh Tokwold of Halsall said in 1504 that he had heard that 'great lands' of those abbeys, lying within four miles of Halsall, were 'worn into the see.'[111]

The Milling Industry

Even though the great majority of them were leased out to tenants, all monasteries jealously guarded the well-being of their corn mills and the attendant profits from them. The revenue from its five mills in Rotherham brought Rufford an income yearly of £31.[112] There is plenty of evidence to demonstrate that tenants of monastic properties had to pay 'suit of mill'; that is, have their corn ground at an abbey-owned mill, as by the lessees of Buckland at Bickleigh and Cullompton, Devon.[113] In evidence given just after the Suppression, it was said of Llantarnam's home mill that there 'all tenants of the abbey, and all other resiants adjoining the abbey, time out of mind, have used to grind all their corn.'[114] Where a mill was not demised,—as at Vaudey, a stipendiary miller ('mylner') was employed.[115] A monastery might decide to keep a particular mill in its own hands, as did Stoneleigh in 1535 when demising Milburne Grange it retained 'the Wode Mylne' there.[116]

In demising a mill, the tenant-miller would normally pay an annual monetary rent to the monastery, which might vary from only 6s 8d. (expected for a mill of Buckland in Bickleigh)[117] to £4 (for each of two mills of Woburn in Crawley).[118] The rent paid frequently covered the tenancy holdings of land pertaining to a mill, as also the fishing of the mill-pond. The miller had the duty of grinding the abbey corn; Woburn's miller at Crawley had to do this 'truly and diligently.' Margam's tenant of its Garw Mill was expected to be 'able to grind and shell all manner of corn.'[119]

There might be a degree of nepotism in the granting of a mill. Abbot Dovell of Cleeve in 1522 demised two corn mills 'without the abbey gate' to one Barnard Dovell, surely a relative?[120] Abbot Stevens of Beaulieu immediately before surrendering the monastery let out its home mill and parsonage to his sister.[121] With a grant would inevitably be accommodation, like the Mill House at Stoneleigh's Rabcroft mill. Strata Florida (1533), in demising its Fulbrook mill, envisaged 'a place for erecting a small chamber in the confines of the mill.'[122]

The miller charged each tenant who brought his corn for grinding. At two mills of Whitland in Carmarthenshire this payment was rendered in kind. At Crugerydd mill each tenant had to pay a toll to the lessee of one bushel out of every twelve ground.[123] At its Llanwinio mill three 'dishes' of corn had to be rendered for every two bushels ground.[124] So that he had no competition, Byland (1538)—when demising for forty years its mill in Sutton, promised the tenant that the abbey 'shall permit and suffer no other corn mill to be built within the lordship all the foresaid years.'[125]

In 1615, and quite probably in monastic days, 'suit of mill' at Vale Royal's former mill at Llanbadarn Fawr close to Aberystwyth, meant not only grinding one's corn at the mill, but also a duty to assist in carrying timber to repair the mill, and cutting and carrying turfs and the like 'for making of the mill pond.'[126] Buckfast (1521) promised the new lessee of its mill in Kingsbridge, Devon, that tenants of its Churchstowe manor would once a year cleanse the mill-stream, 'as of ancient custom, from the white oak of Nordyn to the mill.'[127] At the Crawley mills the duty of keeping the bank of the watercourse in good condition lay with Woburn's tenant.

The tenant was expected to keep his mill in good repair, but usually the monastery provided much of the wherewithal. When Newminster demised its water-mills at Stannington, the abbey was to 'lay sufficient gross timber upon the ground' for this purpose.[128] When Fountains leased out a mill in Rigton in 1514 the tenant promised to maintain the mill at his cost 'in yeren gere, timber-work and thekynge,' but the abbey was to provide millstones and large timber.[129] The tenant of Buckfast's Kingsbridge mill could have his timber at Buckfast without payment, but had to cut and carry it at his own expense. Holm Cultram, demising its Dub Mill, promised to provide 'all manner of timber,' except for 'rongs, koggs and cryndalls'.[130]

Milling was a concomitant to arable farming and the production of cereals. Some monasteries therefore encouraged in Tudor times the erection of new mills. The poet Gutun Owain lauded Abbot Thomas Pennant of Basingwerk (1481–1521), saying that 'with mills he has filled every available glen and hill.'[131] Land might be rented out for layfolk to build mills upon: Cymer did this at Maes-y-poeth, Dore at Gwenddwr in Breconshire and Strata Florida at Blaenaeron in Ceredigion.[132] The two water-mills of Woburn demised in Crawley were described in 1535 as 'new-made.' Byland, in a late lease of 1538, granted Richard Lascelles 'one place or mylnestede to build a mill upon within the manor of Wyldon.' It necessitated a millstream (the 'mylne race') being cut through the lordship of Kilburn.[133]

The mills described above were all water-powered. Cistercian monasteries did have *wind-mills* sited in localities exposed to reasonably strong wind strength, like hill-tops and coastal borders. Wind-mills on the former lands of Robertsbridge were noted in the later sixteenth century, as was the locality there named Windmill Hill.[134] Two monasteries encouraged the building of windmills. Swineshead in 1506 granted land in Kynnalon, Lincolnshire, so that the tenant 'shall make or cause to be made a windmill, so that there be a wind mill upon the said ground.'[135] Pipewell in 1514 leased out the 'mill-hill' lying between Ashby and Thornby with view to the tenant 'building a wind-mill there.'[136] Its windmill at Dunchurch, Warwickshire, was restored just before the monastery was suppressed,[137] and in 1535 it had another wind-mill at its East Grange.[138] Wind-mills also found note (in 1535) at Sawtry Juet,[139] and at Holm Cultram exposed to winds off the Solway Firth.[140] An old fashioned *horse mill*, utilised more often where a water supply was wanting, was sited within the precincts of Holm Cultram (1535),[141] whilst another found note in 1540 on lands formerly of Woburn abbey at Carswell.[142] A horse mill was noted within the precincts at Furness in 1538, in addition to two water-mills.[143]

Sometimes deriving water from the same stream and therefore in close proximity to a water-mill, might be a *fulling-mill*, otherwise known as a 'walk mill' or 'tucking mill,' or in Wales as a 'pandy,' and used in the process of making cloth. At Newminster it was noted that there were 'two fulling mills nigh the monastery upon the stream that serveth the corn mill,' one, however, was in a ruinous state.[144] There was a combined fulling and corn mill within the precincts of Stanley abbey,[145] while Stratford had two mills under one roof, but their usage is unknown. Dunkeswell's corn mill at Hackpen had in 1536 a fulling-mill adjoining. Two monasteries permitted their tenants to erect new fulling-mills: Margam at Hafod-heulog, Glamorgan, in 1484,[146] and Aberconwy at Voelas, Denbighshire, in 1502.[147] Boxley's fulling mill (1535) was known as the Poll Mill.[148] Robertsbridge owned at Salehurst a close called 'Fullingmillfield.'[149] At Hulton the proximate field-names of 'Walk Mill Hill' and 'Little Walk Mill Hill' testify to a former fulling-mill there.[150]

When fulling mills were demised the owner abbey laid down the usual conditions of good maintenance. Combe in 1537 rented out for £3-6-8 per annum its 'walkynmylne' in Brawnedon called the 'New Mill.' The tenant, Richard Wilcocks, received also the meadows and pastures pertaining to the mill, and the fishing of the mill pond. He was to keep the mill in good repair, but the abbey was to provide the requisite tile and timber.[151] Buckland in 1486 granted William Fote, junior, leave to build a fulling-mill in the waste at Sticklepath, Devon.[152]

In Wales, fulling mills often appear to have been the poor relations of the nearby corn mills. Whitland's fulling-mill at Hen Dy Gwyn was demised for only one-third the rent paid for the corn mill there.[153] In England, in certain instances, the opposite was true. By 1535 Stoneleigh received £15-10-0 from its six mills, most of which had been converted for fulling. Its earlier court rolls make mention of cloth workers there.[154] By 1490 John Sparry, the parson of 'Asshgo', had newly built a 'Walkemyll' at Rabcroft, 'from which the abbey [Stoneleigh] was to receive the rents and profits for ever.' In return the community granted him daily prayers during his life and a full obit thereafter.[155]

Other mills which are occasionally noted on Cisterican lands in Tudor times included *bark mills*—employed in the tanning of leather. In 1532 Fountains demised its 'barkhouse nyghte to the monastery, with also one barke mylne kylne and all vessels to the barkhouse belongyng for tannyng.'[156] The lessee, Richard Paver, had a thirty year lease, together with food and drink for his workmen. His annual rent was six guineas, with an additional payment of twenty shillings yearly for 'all the slaughter hides as shall be slain to the use of the monastery,' and further small payments for 'all the bark that shall be felled within two or three miles of the monastery.' Additionally, he was to render to abbey free of charge 'one half dacre of whit ledder for all mortes under the age of two yeres.' This lease has been said to be 'a belated response to the Act of 1529 forbidding spiritual persons to keep tanneries or breweries except for their own use in their own houses.'[157]

Kingswood in 1516 had on it home demesne 'a water mill called le Berkemyll.'[158] The bark kiln of Newminster listed amongst its tools, 'doobs, prongs and knives.'[159] Tintern's 'tanhouse', mentioned in 1535, stood probably by the Angidy brook there.[160] Sir Arthur Darcy visiting Sawley abbey in June 1537 noted there 'a bark-house stored with leather.'[161] The income from Jervaulx's 'tan-house' (1535) was valued at £7.[162] Buckland, demising an estate at Leather Tor, Devon, included in the lease a *stamping mill* used in the winning of tin.[163]

Disputes regarding monastic mills occasionally reached the courts. Louth Park in 1516 demised its corn mill in Beddington, Lincolnshire, to one John Dyfflesey for thirty years at a rent of £4 p.a. After eleven years he sub-let the mill to Margaret Jackson of Louth, but she became in arrears with the rent and allegedly had neither ground the abbey corn nor repaired the mill. Her response, in the Court of Chancery, was vague, saying that she had given 26s 8d. in part payment. The abbot was demanding the full rent from Dyfflesey.[164]

Two tenants of mills pertaining to Buckfast found themselves dispossessed, and their cases came before the Court of Star Chamber. John and Joan Macy complained that they had been granted that abbey's Staverton Mill in 1516, but after being in possession for some time, at the 'excitation and stirring' of John Read 'a besyd monk, son of the monastery'—he became abbot in 1525, and at the commandment of Abbot Avery Gill, two monks, John Pope and William Sole, 'with many riotous and ill disposed persons, with force of arms, bows, staves and other weapons,' had evicted them and still kept them them out of possession of the mill. The rioters had removed iron work and taken away quantities of wheat, barley and malt. The monastery's defence is not on record.[165]

John Austen of Kilbury, Devon, told how Buckfast had in 1514 demised to him its 'chief mansion house' there, and asserted that he had built a second corn mill there at his own cost, as well as 'a great stone bridge over the river nigh by called Dart.' After Gabriel Dunne assumed the abbacy in 1535, the new abbot 'by plain force cruelly put out and expelled him' from the property. Dunne responded that Austen had allowed 'great destruction and waste' upon the premises, had sub-let land without permission, and that the bridge had been built at the cost of all the inhabitants. Dunne's friendship with Cromwell probably meant that his voice prevailed, but the late Dom John Stéphan felt that in some of these cases there was a degree of blackmail on the part of the complainant.[166]

Pastoral Farming

A traditional and valuable facet of Cistercian economy was the rearing of animals, and especially of *sheep* which yielded food but primarily wool for the production of cloth. Long gone were the days of the *conversus* shepherd, lay servants now fulfilled his role. Careful accounting continued as displayed in the 'Fountains Abbey Stock Book.'[167] This comprises twelve annual stock accounts covering the period from 1480 to 1495. Each account gives details of the animals of some twenty-five major properties of Fountains, as well as the summary accounts of the 'master of the sheep' and the 'master of the beasts'. Shorter sections yield details regarding the abbey's horses and pigs.

The total number of Fountains' sheep in a good year might well exceed ten thousand. On Coniston Moor around 1480 the keeper, John Leyland, was able to account for 411 'gimmers' and 420 fleeces; as well as eight skins; eleven of his sheep died from disease ('murrain'). At Fountains property at Brimham (Brimbem), there grazed ten rams, 325 ewes, and 199 lambs, whilst 360 fleeces and twenty-two skins were produced. Only four animals died from disease. As for *cattle* of various kinds, the accounts suggest that Fountains pastured approaching four thousand beasts. At Brimbem in 1482 the lady keeper, Eleanor Jenkynson, recorded a bull, eight oxen, forty cows and eight heifers, as well as the production of fifty-three stones of cheese and twenty-six of butter. Two-thirds of the butter and cheese were delivered to 'the warming house'. Another property producing butter and cheese for Fountains (1524) was Heyshaw in Dacre at its 'derehouse' there. The lessees were expected yearly to deliver at its 'cheese-house' forty stones of cheese and twenty of butter.[168] When Furness was dissolved 'people came from all parts of the south to buy cattle, but for the milch neat, in number six score, the inhabitants had the preference.'[169] When Holm Cultram closed 287 cattle were sold.[170]

What-ever the specialisation, every grange economy was of necessity a mixed one. When Thomas Atkinson was made keeper of Fountains' Haddock-stones Grange in 1533, he was yearly to make 'true reckoning and account of all manner grains that shall be gotten of the grange,' and wheat, barley and rye are mentioned. He was also to keep 'as many swine of the community as from year to year hath been accustomed,' and to carry out many other labours including 'shearing, mowing and hay-making.' He was also to deliver yearly his butter and cheese to the cheese-house at Fountains. The amounts due were not stated, but if he fell short he was to pay one shilling for every stone of butter wanting and eight-pence for every stone of cheese. Horses and oxen were also pastured at this truly mixed economy grange and, in addition, Atkinson had to 'bring up and keep certain chickens, capons and geese' for the community, but for these he was paid.[171]

At its closure, over two hundred hens were noted on various properties of Furness.[172] They were valued at one penny apiece. In addition Furness (1537) had 'a little isle called the Isle of Fowley, which at every full see is compassed about in salt water, and standeth a mile and more from the demesne lands, where bred innumerable fowl of divers kinds upon the earth among the grass and stones.' Usage of the island where eggs were abundant was reserved to the monastery.[173]

A mixed economy was probably also characteristic of Sibton's North (or Home) Grange whose dairy by 1511 was managed by a lady officer, Katherine Dowe. She received a stipend of £1 for doubling up as a cow-herd, and she and the six maid servants each received a clothing allowance. That year her dairy produced ninety-one weys of cheese, 17½ barrels of butter, twenty-eight gallons of quarter (a soft wey cheese) and forty-two gallons of milk. Boars, bacon hogs, piglets, geese, hens and ducks, were amongst the animals on the farm, whilst of the 102 calves, forty-eight were killed for the abbot's kitchen and twenty-six went to the grange hospice.[174] As well as its hens, the other fowl here included six swans and six peacocks, the gifts of neighbours.

Lowland monasteries, especially in more settled areas, did not have the space of overtly large flocks, but reasonably large numbers were frequently accommodated making use of an abbey's lands but also of areas where it enjoyed with others common of pasture. After enclosure Hailes' Longbarrow Hill could accommodate nine hundred sheep.[175] At Merevale's Pinwall grange in 1499 there were 320 sheep and that number was added to by the 140 lambs born there that year.[176] On Sewell, one of Bruern's pastures, four hundred sheep could graze, whilst until decay set in the flocks of Bruern totalled 3,200 sheep and 300 head of cattle.[177] In a time of financial stringency, and in return for a payment of £200, Cleeve in 1531 let out to Richard Smith, a vicar-choral of Wells, 1200 sheep: '1000 wethers and 200 ewes, good, whole and able.'[178] At the end of five years Smith was to be paid £108 or else the monastery forfeited the animals. All this attests to the continuing significance of sheep in the monastic economy.

Large flocks required plenty of space, and this was achieved by abbeys enjoying rights of common of pasture outside their own demesne lands: such rights accrued amongst others to Calder in the Copeland Hills and Forest,[179] and to Garendon in Charnwood Forest.[180] Some monasteries might require tenants to maintain a flock of abbey sheep in addition to their own, and be accountable for them: this was true of Fountains (1507–1525) for several of its tenants in Craven.[181] With a tenant's lease might come common of pasture on monastic land: Buckland so demised properties with rights of pasture on Bickleigh, Roborough and Shaugh Downs.[182] A tenant of Dunkeswell (1532) was permitted the right of pannage and mastage (feeding his swine on acorns, chestnuts and beech mast) on the wooded slopes of Riggewood.[183]

Pastoralism, and in particular sheep grazing, were not without their problems. Bad weather might necessitate a shelter, which could also be used as a
place for shearing: hence the 'sheep-house newly builded' noted of Hailes in
1538.[184] There might be disputes with neighbours: a complainant in 1509
alleged that Abbot Thomas of Bindon had forcibly taken 320 of his sheep,
chosen and kept 120 of the best, and sent the rest back twenty days later 'almost
destroyed and famished.'[185] There could be a fateful epidemic of disease: Abbot
Emery of Warden told Cromwell in 1532 that he had lost 1100 sheep in one
year 'by the rot.'[186] Sheep might wander away: one tenant of Fountains in
Thresfield (1517) had to promise not to impound any of the abbey's animals
which strayed, but rather 'return them to their customary pastures.'[187]

As a source of winter food supply and of dung for manure, *doves* were
important in medieval times. In the year of 1519/20 the dovecot of Sibton raised
169 doves, a valuable adjunct to its food supply.[188] Dovecots operating in Tudor
times were noted in the accounts and leases made by many monasteries: as on
Connersley Grange (of Vale Royal, 1543),[189] and at Sowthskyrland (on land of
Swine, 1535),[190] while two dovecots on lands of Merevale were renovated in
the 1490s.[191] The first post-suppression ministers' accounts (of 1539) noted
the 'colver-houses' at Neath's Gelli-garn and Monknash granges –the remains
of both are still to be seen.[192] The rearing of doves at Calder (1537) is surmised
by the field-name of Dovehouse Close.[193] St Mary Graces had two dovecots
within the precincts, one being in its 'pineapple garden', and another on its
Poplar manor.[194] A dovecot also stood by the abbot's house at Tintern.

As a source of meat supply and of skin, the rearing of *rabbits* might be
significant in a monastery's economy. Rabbit warrens or 'cony-garths' featured
at Cleybrooke, Whippingham (on lands of Quarr, 1487);[195] Wolvey (a
property of Combe in 1539);[196] and at The Warren at Woburn (valued at £7
p.a. in 1536).[197] Woburn also had a warren called Hare Warren on its Harne
Grange,[198] whilst a close of Ford in Monsbery was named Haregrove.[199]
Warren Park was sited at the angle of the Beaulieu river and the Solent.[200]
Merevale demised two of its warrens in 1499: that on Brookhull at Orton-on-
the–Hill measured forty by forty-six feet.[201] The term 'conygarth' occurred in
1506 (on lands by Tintern abbey), in 1536 (on lands of Basingwerk in the
Wirral),[202] and at its dissolution on property of Kingswood at Cherington.[203]

The home warren of Sibton, sited close to the monastery,[204] was a helpful
perquisite, for in the year of 1519/20 it produced 143 rabbits for the monas-

tery kitchen.[205] Another of Woburn's several warrens was that at its Crawley Grange. In 1536 Thomas Cromwell sought a lease of the grange for one of his officers or friends, a Richard Day. Sir Francis Bryan, the abbey's Steward, interceded with Cromwell saying that whilst the abbot had already promised to let another man have the grange, he would commit it to Day, but wished to exclude from the grant the 'warren of coneys' there, for that would be a loss to the abbey of £40 per year.[206] The outcome is not known.

Horses were a mainstay of any economy. Tintern (1535) had its 'keeper of the horses,'[207] whilst stable 'lads' perhaps occupied Whitland's 'room in the stable' (1539)[208]. A corrody granted by Byland (1526) gave the recipients "custody of the common stable."[209] Sir Arthur Darcy paid a compliment to Cistercian horse breeding, when he wrote to Cromwell (June 1537) that Jervaulx abbey would make a good place for the royal stud of mares, 'for surely the breed of Jervaulx for horses was the tried breed in the north.'[210] Amongst the Tudor servants of Merevale were numbered its horse-breaker, stable-man and cartwright.[211]

Marshland and Causeways

Pasture land might also be provided by the extensive areas of marsh which certain monasteries possessed—like Kirkstead and Swineshead in the Fens, Boxley in the Thames estuary, and Robertsbridge on the Sussex coast. Swineshead made grants of pasture rights in Bykar and Wigtoft, Lincolnshire (1501) and in Gostkirk (1528).[212] Robertsbridge (1525, 1528) rented out marshland in Playden;[213] Boxley (1533) demised two pieces of marsh called Boxley Lease and the Harp.[214] St Mary Graces' marshland holdings included 600 acres at Stayhill Marsh near Sittingbourne and Elemely Marsh near Tunbridge Wells.[215] In 1529 the abbey demised its marshland called the Wet Marsh in Stepney for ninety years, the tenant (Robert Amadas, master of the Jewel House) was to drain it within four years.[216] Its Wet Marsh in Poplar had flooded in 1448, but the abbey seems to have done little to reclaim it.[217]

Abbot John Browning of Beaulieu (1533–1536) was intent on enclosing a salt marsh it owned which was 'of little value and greatly decayed' because 'the sea at any tide did ebb and flow.'[218] He engaged one Richard Ricarde of Walberton, Sussex, to make a protecting sea wall. Ricarde later claimed to the Court of Chancery that the abbot did not give him sufficient men for the job, and therefore before the wall was finished 'the rages of the sea cast down the wall.' He re-built it, but was never paid and, having had to borrow money was left heavily in debt. Abbot Browning had died, and Abbot Stevens now refused his payment on the grounds that the wall had not been built on time.

Robert Aske, the leader of the Pilgrimage of Grace, once asserted of the monasteries that they were 'great maintainers of sea walls and dykes, maintainers and builders of bridges and highways.'[219] Their abbots did this in part when serving on commissions of sewers (*Chapter 3*), but they could be found wanting. The abbey of Roche was said by the justices of the sewers for Lindsey, Lincolnshire, in 1533 to have failed to scour eleven score roods of drainage ditches on its lands there, and was fined 110 marks.[220] Kirkstead was accused of neglecting its banks within the king's manor of Bolingbroke, Lincolnshire. Agreement between the duchy of Lancaster and the monastery was reached in 1533 stipulating that when a court leet was held in the manor, six persons should be deputed to examine the banks and, if found ruinous and in decay, the monastery was to be warned to repair its part of the bank.[221] Bolingbroke stood within the Fens, and the reference may be either to the local drainage ditches, or the river Steeping or the river Witham also nearby. That same year it was alleged that there were twelve great gaps in Witham Bank, which Kirkstead was bound to uphold and maintain, and that water remained on the banks.[222]

From the early thirteenth century Revesby abbey had been given property in return for which the abbey was to maintain the 'common highway, cawsey and bridge' called North Dyke. An enquiry held in 1527 heard that it was 'much decayed and greatly damaged,' that the inhabitants of Sibsey going to Boston went 'in peril and danger of their lives' unless they made a very long detour, and that the causeway was used by 'their horses, carts and all manner of carriage.' A twenty-three strong jury sworn in at Spilsby found the the dyke was indeed defective, and that its repair was the responsibility of Revesby from 'time out of mind.' The monastery asserted that forty years previously the monastery had employed one hundred men on the repair of the North Dyke, its cook preparing meat and drink for their sustenance.[223]

Fisheries

The traditional siting of Cistercian monasteries by rivers, seas and lakes, assured them of a constant and necessary supply of fish given their originally meat-less diet. Further, all monasteries could obtain a limited amount of fish by stocking their mill-ponds. When abbey mills were demised, the fishing rights might also be let out, but with conditions. In demising its Rabcroft fulling mill in 1522, Stoneleigh charged the tenant an extra 3s 4d. for 'the fishing in the Poole,' and reserved the right for the abbey to keep one eyrie of swans on the water there.[224] Basingwerk (1536) on a grange at West Kirby, Cheshire, had 'a pond with fishery and swans.'[225] When in 1521 Stanley demised its home fulling mill,[226] and when in 1537 Combe let its fulling mill in Brawnedon,[227] the tenants had the fishing rights included in their leases, but when Stoneleigh, in 1534, demised its Milburne grange it retained the 'Wode Mylne' there, together with the mill pool and its fishing.[228]

It is evident from several inventories that all Cistercian houses consumed a very great deal of fish, including salt-fish which, as at Sibton (*Chapter 1*) and Merevale,[229] had often had to be bought in. Monasteries with coastal outlets were more fortunate: as Calder (1538)[230] and Holm Cultram (1538)[231] with salmon fisheries on the shores of the Solway Firth, and Furness at its Lune fishery on the Lancashire coast.[232] Beaulieu (on the Solent)[233] and Buckfast (near the Dart estuary)—were both able to send gifts of salmon to Cromwell. Buckland and Ford were also able to send salmon as gifts; in their case to Katherine, countess of Devon (1524), while Newenham gave her congers[234]

Salmon fishing was important to Tintern both in the adjacent river Wye, and also offshore of its Woolaston Grange by the Severn estuary. John and William Gough, becoming tenants of the grange in 1530, received the liberty there 'to fish and make puttes and engens in the river of Severn.'[235] Strata Florida obtained herrings from its coastal fisheries in Cardigan Bay, and at least one of its tenants had the duty of conveying the fish to the monastery.[236] It was recorded in 1537 that a poor man taking fish from Beaulieu to Cromwell had his boat captured by the French. This was at a loss to him of £50. Worse still, one of his crew was killed.[237] In the Tudor-period even fishing was not without its occasional hazards.

Monasteries might own or have fishing rights for fresh-water fish in inland lakes, as Strata Florida—which could access eels and red and white trout in the Teifi Pools of Ceredigion, as vividly described by John Leland (1538).[238] Fountains (1525) demised fishing rights to a tenant in its Malewater Lake in Craven, but reserved the right to take fish there for the abbey 'of the due proportion allowed at that time of the year,' a clear policy of conservation of fish stocks.[239] Warden (1535) had its Fishers Grange.[240]

There is note in Tudor times of active fishing in the stretches of local rivers pertaining to certain abbeys: as by Bordesley in the Avon: at its Binto Grange 'from the pond above the bridge to the ford below it,'[241] Medmenham in the Thames: 'from Westmead to Medmenham Mead,'[242] Newenham 'on the banks of the Axe and the waters of the Yerty,'[243] and Stratford in the Thames: 'from the mouth of the river Lee to Stratford-at-Bow bridge.'[244] St Mary Graces, next the Tower of London, had a property called 'the Stewe' in the parish of St Michael, Queenshithe, where was 'a great cistern of lead' [presumably a fish tank] connected to the Thames by 'a gutter of lead.'[245] In Lincolnshire, both Kirkstead[246] and Revesby[247] fished in the river Witham and set up booths for their fishermen.

There are many mentions of the active use of fish-ponds, as at Whalley (where as was customary it was administered by the sub-cellarer), and at Cleeve (where in 1522 it was leased to Barnard Dovell, patently a relative of the abbot);[248] whilst Hailes (1519) had at Haughley in far distant Suffolk 'a grange called Fishpond.'[249] James More, the subcellarer of Whalley, supplemented the monastery's local supply of fish by buying in fish during the first quarter of 1537, including twenty-five salt salmon for the abbot's kitchen and eleven fresh salmon for the use of the house.[250] Beaulieu's fourteenth-century Sowley Pond found a different use in the seventeenth and eighteenth centuries, providing power for an ironworks which supplied guns to the East India Company![251]

During repeated assaults in 1526/27 riotous persons assembled at Furness's fishery in the Lune estuary on the Lancashire coast, menaced and threatened the cellarer and abbey fishermen; tore a fishing net and destroyed a weir, and stole fish caught.[252] The Lune was the chiefest of the monastery's eight fisheries.[253] On the other hand, the tenants of Skerton had cause to complain of Abbot Banks of Furness that he had 'edified' a fish-yard of 'such great height and strength, with great piles, stakes, stones and gravel,' that the water overflowed upon to the town and highway, making movement along the latter 'a perilous passage.' The abbot responded that the monastery had always owned the fish-garth, and that it repaired it as often as was needful.[254]

Woodland Resources

Monastic timber might be used for a variety of purposes: as a building and fencing material, in the manufacture of boats; for fuel, and for the perquisites of timber frequently granted in leases to tenants. It was a valuable and prized commodity. When the abbey closed it was said that if sold the woodland of Stanley could fetch £164.[255] In its last days Rufford made a sale of timber which fetched £25—around £10,000 in modern values;[256] The acreage of available woodland on Cistercian estates differed widely. Furness (1533) could claim 3,000 acres on its Borrowdale manor alone. Its immediate precincts (1537) contained 'many trees of oak, ash, and other wood'. Its twelve woods in Low Furness, comprising 2099 acres, included 'many fair oaks' as well as under-growth supplying fuel for the abbey; its woods in Furness Fells provided fuel for the abbey's smithies there.[257]

The abbeys of lowland England and Wales fared less well, but were not impoverished. Garendon (at the time of the Crown commissioners survey) possessed 998 acres of woodland (valued at £650), and Stoneleigh, 548; the latter had been 'sold before last Christmas',[258] In the fenland Sawtry had but 422 acres[259] and Kirkstead only 412 acres, but sufficient to make a yearly £20 profit.[260] Pipewell (1535) had 84 acres of woodland between four localities. Valued at 1s 8d. per acre, its total worth was but £7.[261] In his itinerary, John Leland (in the late 1530s) noted the wooded sites of several abbeys (Chapter 1). Coming to west Wales, he remarked that Whitland abbey stood 'in a vast wood as in a wilderness.'[262]

Such facts and statistics as are available suggest a policy of careful conservation and maintenance on the part of most monasteries. 'Foresters' and 'woodwards' might be appointed, though the former term usually denoted an official with other duties and not merely 'the keeping of woods.' In 1537 Beaulieu appointed Richard Benger as woodward for its Great Close,[263] whilst in 1538 Robert Everingham was made woodward of all the woodlands of Woburn.[264] The year before the abbey closed, Pipewell (1537) appointed William Goodyse as 'woodward ad keeper of all woods in the forest of Rockingham.'[265]

When Fountains in 1493 appointed William Haxby as keeper or forester of Wheldrake, Yorkshire, as well as safe keeping its woods and preventing animals from pasturing there, he had also to assist the reeves in the collection of rents. He had the further duty 'to go or ride on the business of the abbot as often as he is commanded.'[266] Indeed a number of the abbey's bailiffs acted also as foresters,[267] whilst in its last years Neath appointed William Hopkins, already its receiver-general, as also its 'forester-general.'[268] Amongst Tintern's (1535) stipendiary servants were listed its wood-cutters.[269]

Another evidence of woodland conservation comes in the known ages of groups of trees, suggesting that they were often allowed to grow to full maturity. At its closure the woodland of Buildwas woodland included 180 acres of trees of 100 years growth or more;[270] whilst in its Belsholme Wood, Kirkstead had seventy acres of forty-year old trees.[271] At Dore's Morehampton Grange (1540) its fifty acre wood was 'set with oaks of eighty and one hundred years growth'. Its Gilbert's Hill wood was 'closed with a hedge containing 150 acres, whereof thirteen acres be of fifty years growing, and the residue of an hundred years growing and above.' Even its daughter-house, the small abbey of Grace Dieu, had by the Suppression two hundred oaks of eighty and one hundred years growth.[272]

Conservation was also afforded by replacing timber which had been cut down: Stoneleigh had, of its 548 acres of woodland, forty-two acres of trees eight years old or younger, suggesting new planting in the last years of that abbey's life.[273] The making of enclosed coppices also promoted new growth: Fountains (1520) expected in one of several such leases a tenant to maintain the fences it erected around any coppices the abbey made. The customary length of time for the fencing of its coppices was seven years, during which stock were not permitted to be pastured within them.[274] Tintern's manorial Porthcaseg court (1528) assisted the preservation of its woodland by forbidding the keeping of goats within the lordship.[275] Robertsbridge (1531) in demising certain lands in Sussex reserved the oak and beech trees.[276]

Cistercian-grown timber was appreciated in its day by Cardinal Wolsey who robbed Bruern of so many oaks to build his Cardinal's college at Oxford (*Chapter 3*). The duke of Suffolk bought wood from Coggeshall to be employed in buildings in Southwark; it was to be delivered by a middle-man at St Olave's water-gate.[277] In January 1538, anticipating the Suppression, Cromwell restrained the last abbot of Meaux from cutting down woodland because the timber would be needed for 'the haven of Bridlington.'[278]

Merevale, perhaps exceptionally, in 1526 sold to the local parson 'all its woods now growing and standing in ye wood in Over Sherle called Shortwood,' with leave to 'cut down and carry away all the said wood.'[279] The agreement was to end after thirty-six years, but brought the monastery an immediate payment of £14 [around £5,000 or more in modern equivalent);

possibly this unusual grant was necessitated by a need for cash. Shortly after the closure of Llantarnam , 'twenty great oaks' were felled at Llantarnam's Gelli-lâs grange to build a ship for the navy, whilst no less than 116 oaks (sixteen of them 'great oaks') were cut down at Aberconwy's first site of Maenan to repair the Shire Hall in Caernarfon.[280] In 1537 William Cowper was appointed general surveyor of the woods of the suppressed monasteries of Wales, and a few years later David Clayton was enlisted to work with him.[281]

Malefactors might make forays into Cistercian woods to abstract timber. One John Warcop (1535) felled and took away sixty loads of timber from Boxley's Franklin Wood near Aylesford.[282] At about the same time, Lord Mordaunt and others cut down timber to the value of £60 in the woods of Coggeshall at Childerditch, Essex. The abbot could do little about it, for he said Lord Mordaunt was 'a man of great power, authority and substance.'[283] On 4 May 1506 John Snelling, in one of two known forays into Buckland's woodland, led a band of sixteen armed persons who 'in manner of war arrayed, that is to say, swords, bills and other weapons,' cut down and carried away a large quantity of timber (possibly one thousand 'seams') from the monastery's Shaugh Wood, Devon,[284] One might surmise that the idea of the closure of the monasteries was current, and that the communities had lost much of their inherent authority.

Trade, Mining and Industry

Isolated references suggest that in Tudor times some monasteries actively extracted the mineral wealth available beneath the surface of their lands. This was especially true of Fountains able to obtain ores contained in the Carboniferous Limestone on the eastern flanks of the Pennines in the region sometimes known as Knaresborough Forest and within the broad area termed Craven. Indeed in 1524 the Crown required an explanation of the aged Abbot Marmaduke Huby of Fountains, as it had been reported that 'ye cause our grounds within our forest of Knaresborough, part of our duchy of Lancaster, to be broken and digged, and cause mines to be made without our licence or authority.' The abbey was ordered to desist until an enquiry had been held; at this the monastery produced ancient charters commencing with the grant to mine given in 1317 by Baron John de Mowbray and confirmed by succeeding sovereigns.[285]

Fountains had *lead* mines in Nidderdale, and also further south-west at Netherbordeley east of Malham, with forges at Dacre. On demising land at

Netherbordeley in 1525 to one Geoffrey Procter the abbey reserved the 'mines of *iron*, lead or other minerals found there' to the use of the abbey.[286] This was a clause written into several of its demises of lands.[287] Its active participation in lead mining was again demonstrated in 1527 when it entered into an arrangement with Marmaduke Bayn, John Parkinson and William Lupton, of Brighouse in Nidderdale, whereby on Greenhow Hill, Bewerley, they would smelt the lead ore delivered to them by Fountains, in return for retaining a small fraction of the ore. They promised to 'truly burn and make in(to) cleyn and sufficient lead all such lead ore.'[288] When in June 1530 Merevale demised in several portions its Pilsbury Grange in Ashbourne, Derbyshire, the monastery reserved to itself the 'lead ore of and in the premises, and the profits of the same.'[289]

How far the monasteries of south Wales continued extracting *coal* as in former centuries is not on record, nor whether Merevale made use of that fuel at its nearby 'le Colput.'[290] Garendon had a coal mine at Worthington,[291] and Hulton by the sixteenth century owned coal mines at Hulton and Hanley.[292] Newminster leased a coal mine from the bishopric of Durham for fuel to serve its salt evaporation.[293] After the surrender of Robertsbridge in 1538 its lands were granted to Sir William Sidney; the monks had seemingly taken no advantage of their potential mineral wealth, but Sidney immediately set about establishing an iron works there.[294] Did the 'Glasewrighte bridge' at Sibton (1535) indicate glass-making there?[295] It has been pointed out that by using their own coal for fuel, the monks of Furness, Newminster and Flaxley had an invisible source of income which was not reflected in the *Valor Ecclesiasticus*.[296]

Salt was commonly used in medieval times not only to flavour food, but more especially to preserve meat in winter storage. Several nearby Cistercian houses had interests in the Cheshire salt-field, though many of their pits there were demised. Basingwerk,[297] Combermere,[298] Hulton[299] and Vale Royal[300] all owned 'wych-houses' or 'salt-cotes' in places such as Northwich, Middlewich and Wych Malbank. John Leland (*c*.1536/38) told that 'there be tokens in Cheshire of diverse salt pits beside them that be commonly now used, as by Combermere in a wood.' He went on to describe how 'in time of mind,' a mile from Combermere a new spring of salt water appeared and the monastery employed it to manufacture salt. The men of the 'wiches', fearful of competition, compounded with the abbot for this to cease.[301] In or close to Wych Malbank, Combermere had (in 1524) six wych-houses all demised. The total rental they produced of five pounds was not great. Whether there were others worked directly is not on record. In 1487 five of its wych-houses there had been demised: three of 'twelve leads' and two of five.[302]

Newminster (1536) had salt-pans at Blythe, Northumberland.[303] In demising seven of these in 1534 to Sir Philip Dacre and a yeoman, Roger Pye, it did so for an annual rent of £24, but in addition the lessees had to provide free of charge 'as much salt for the kitchen and other places of the monastery as may be needed.'[304] With the lease went a house called the 'garner', and the mine of coals.[305] The name 'Salterns Hill' indicates that Beaulieu used flats on the adjacent river bank for the evaporation of sea water for the production of salt. [306] After the closure of Bordesley, Roger Bedull, apparently a salt manufacturer, told how salt was always made for that abbey 'between Easter and Pentecost,' and of his costs in doing so. These included 6s 8d. for gathering of the rent and making of the salt; 5d. for 'drawing of the brine;' 16d for 'beryng of the brine', and 2s. for cutting wood for fuel.[307]

Salt was exploited from brine wells close to the Wyre estuary by the tenants of Furness's Stalmine grange there. In 1536 Abbot Roger of Furness complained to the Duchy of Lancaster court that Nicholas Butler and his servants had interfered with his tenants at Stalmine, as they were digging turfs for fuel to evaporate the salt and took away their digging spades, so that the tenants 'left all their labour and turfs, and the making of salt, to their great impoverishment.' Another affray had followed when the tenants were so threatened that 'for fear of their lives they dared not dig any more.'[308]

The manufacture of ploughs and cart wheels, and the shoeing of horses, was facilitated where an abbey had its own *forge*. Smithies are on record at Croxden (1538: 'the little smith's forge'), which also owned a smithy at Dog Cheadle;[309] Hailes (1483: 'the smith's house'),[310] and Merevale (1538).[311] Furness had sometimes up to three smithies for producing the iron it needed at the monastery.[312] At its closure the home grange forge of Sawtry numbered amongst its tools a pair of bellows, a vice, three hammers and a grindstone.[313] In 1538 Kirkstall demised its smithies in Hesywell and Weetwood to Sir Robert Neville; later they were operated by Thomas Pepper, a former monk of the house.[314]

Bruern (1533) granted to Robert Hill of Faringdon, smith, his son and first grandson [another family association], the office of blacksmith, which they were to hold 'every one of them successively'.[315] Provided with a house and food, but with no mention of a stipend, their job was 'to well and workmanly surely and substantially make all manner of iron and steel necessary to the husbandry and necessaries of the monastery.' The abbey was to provide the iron and steel, but the smiths the necessary coal, though that would be transported at the abbey's cost. Unfortunately for the family the dissolution soon terminated this arrangement.

Hulton appears to have had an active interest in iron working as in 1527 the abbot (perhaps John Harwood), complained to the Court of Star Chamber of attacks on his smithy in Horton Hey, which had been sub-let to his abbey by Sir William Brereton.[316] A gang of up to sixteen men were accused of assaulting the premises on six different occasions that summer, during which they broke the smithy wheel, pulled down the walls, burnt three wain-loads of charcoal, cast a pair of great bellows into a nearby ditch, and destroyed 'all the residue of tools and implements necessary for making of iron.' The rioters asserted that the monks of Hulton had previously evicted them by force from the premises.[317] It seems likely that in the background was the local unpopularity of the abbot.[318]

The available information tells little of the income gained by monasteries in, for example, selling wool and excess grain. Household accounts, where extant as for Merevale, show the purchase in Coventry and Tamworth of a range of items including various foodstuffs, wax and parchment skins, and cloth for the abbey tailor.[319] It also bought in much wine, as did Beaulieu, Furness[320] and Netley.[321] The domestic accounts of Sibton indicate the purchase of much fish,[322] but there is relatively little indication of what goods a monastery might have for sale. That Cistercian abbeys will have been essentially trading communities was exemplified by the fact that successive abbots of Buckland were members of the merchants' guild of Totnes, Devon.[323]

Furness about 1530, in the time of Abbot Banks, about 1530, was accused in the Duchy of Lancaster court of diminishing Crown revenues by having 'a free port in Furness', taking there anchorage and other tolls, to the loss to the king of £110 over thirty-three years. Abbot Banks responded that 'without remembrance of man' whenever a ship came into the local creek, anchoring there and putting up goods for sale, the abbey made a small charge. The revenue from such tolls amounted to only about one pound per year.[324]

The income of an abbey was also enhanced from the rents paid by stall-holders and from its own trade, when it was given by the Crown (in addition to privileges which several abbeys already had) *market* and *fair* rights. Waverley was given permission in 1512 to hold an annual three-day fair over St Bartholomew's-tide (23–25 August) on its Wanborough Grange in Surrey.[325] Buckfast was licensed in 1520 to hold a weekly market each Friday in the village of Buckfastleigh, and to have two three-day fairs annually—one at Buckfastleigh over the feast of St John before the Latin Gate (6 May), the other at South Brent, ending on the feast of St Gabriel (?24 March).[326] Woburn could from 1529 hold two fairs annually in Woburn town: one on the eve and morrow of the feast of Pope St Gregory (12 March or 3 September), the other on the morrow and eve of the visitation of Our Lady (2 July).[327]

There are very few mentions in the sixteenth century of those monasteries which possessed the privilege, of exercising their right to wreck of sea. It endured in the case of Margam until the closure of that abbey, and then passed to the Mansel family.[328] The deed is torn, but when in 1525 Quarr demised its Chewte Grange it appears to have reserved the right there of wreck of sea to itself.[329] When a ship named the New Anne 'perished and went to wreck on the rase of Portland' about 15th March 1533 'by chance and misfortune of the sea,' pipes of oil and wine were cast on to the shore. William Fforman, an alderman of London, and several other merchants, complained to the Court of Chancery, that the abbots of Bindon (Cistercian) and Abbotsbury (Benedictine), who had lands adjoining the sea coast there, took and conveyed away pipes of oil and wine and 'bestowed them in secret places where they knew not.'[330] The abbots were perhaps justifiably claiming their right to wreck of sea.

Urban Property

From their early years monasteries acquired warehouses in market towns and ports, where they could trade their goods. In later centuries, as more and more holdings were obtained in urban areas, many of them were no more than an additional source of income from the rents received. London, the capital city, attracted interest from several Cistercian houses. By the sixteenth century, Rufford owned a brew-house called The Bell at St Bartholomew's Gate close to Smithfield;[331] Woburn possessed the farm of Goldsmiths' Hall with an inn;[332] Combe had a house in Fleet Street;[333] Tilty property in Milk Street and Wood Street.[334] Coggeshall possessed properties in the parishes of All Hallows ad Fenum in Dowgate and St Botolph-withourt-Aldgate;[335] in the latter parish, Kirkstead owned no less than twenty-nine holdings.[336] Coggeshall's rents from property at Tower Hill amounted to over £10, and included the 'Spyghts house.'[337] Thame had the property called 'the Ledyn Porches' in St Sepulchre-without-Newgate.[338] Warden had shops in the city.[339]

While most of these holdings were demised, there was perhaps provision for a visiting abbot to have a base to stay. This was true of Beaulieu's Abbot's Lodging next to St Mary's Church, Southwark, but even this was demised in 1530.[340] One of the most valuable Cistercian London possessions would appear to have been Coggeshall's messuage and garden called Redegate, in East Smithfield next the Tower of London. With its houses, gardens and cellars, it was a valuable property which, when sold by Sir Thomas Seymour in 1544, realised £55.[341] Tilty in 1530 demised to Clement Edward, a London baker, all its property in the parishes of St Michael in Wood Street and St Mary Magdalene in Milk Street. The annual rent was £7, and in 1537 the Court of Augmentations accepted the validity of his lease.[342]

Not unnaturally the abbey of Tower Hill (St Mary Graces) had the greatest investment in London. As well as owning the manor of Poplar,[343] it received rents from properties in twenty city parishes; the highest income coming from St Botolph without Billingsgate; St Margaret Moses, and St Sepulchre without Newgate. In Wapping the abbey owned six breweries; one, the Swan's Nest, having its own wharf by the Thames. [344] In St Botulph it had a wharf, messuage and cellars, called the Fresh Wharf.[345] These wharves might help its trade and the import of food from its rural properties in Kent, where it had a wharf at Gravesend.[346] Its shops in St Nicholas Shambles included ones occupied by a grocer and a skinner.[347]

One of the more interesting Cistercian properties in the capital was that of Garendon in Cripplegate (now the site of the Barbican), once termed 'St James-in-the-Wall'.[348] Surrounded by a twenty-six foot wide and eight foot deep moat, until the Suppression it had a resident monk and was essentially a cell of the monastery in Leicestershire. In its royal chapel here of St James, the monk's daily duty was to pray for Garendon's mid-fourteenth century benefactor, the countess of Pembroke and her husband. Along with the chapel went other property including a house with shop and cellar. The annual value of the complex was in excess of £11, and formed almost three-quarters of Garendon's income from urban holdings. The abbey also had properties in Derby, Leicester, Norwich and Nottingham.

In Wales one of several houses with urban interests, was Neath, which owned hundreds of burgages in Cardiff; thirty-six of them in St Mary Street. It demised the whole of its Cardiff holdings in 1485 to Sir John Tyrrell for £15 p.a., and then in 1529 for only 10 guineas yearly to one Laurence Buller. The abbey also held 220 or so burgages in Cowbridge, Vale of Glamorgan, leasing them in 1504 to James Turberville.[349] In the Border, Dore owned from the thirteenth century several properties in Hereford. Unfortunately for one tenant, John Williams, in a dispute regarding his lease and unpaid rent, Abbot John Longdon came one day in 1508/09 and evicted him. Not content with that Longdon 'gathered the flowers of the saffron there growing.' John's widow, understandably aggrieved, took the case to court.[350]

Amongst the urban property of Fountains demised in the sixteenth century were houses in Scarborough,[351] Ripon[352] and York. In North Street, York, was 'the hospice of the monastery,' where local tenants paid their rents.[353] In 1529 Furness demised to Raynold Beysley, an officer of the ecclesiastical court of York, its tenement there without Micklegate called Furness House, on condition that he was not a counsel for any adversary in actions against the monastery.[354] Property in such a see city permitted of a base when negotiations were needed with the diocesan bishop. Buckfast had a town house within the cathedral close at Exeter; in 1545 it passed to one Richard Rolle.[355] Dunkeswell had its 'Abbot's House' also in that see city. [356] Holm Cultram had property in the cathedral city of Carlisle.[357]

Other Cistercian monasteries with urban possessions in Tudor times, to name but a few, included: Merevale (in Leicester at Apple Gate) and at Tamworth;[358] Kirkstall (two shops at the top of the Flesh Shambles in Leeds),[359] Quarr (in High Street, Newport, Isle of Wight: it measured forty by thirty-two paces),[360] and Rufford in Stonysgate, Nottingham,[361] as well as property in Newark[362] and Rotherham.[363] Combermere owned (1487) thirty-six tenements in Wych Malbank, Cheshire, including the Swan Inn and properties in the High Street, Hospel Stret, as well as a house in Pillory Street.[364] Newminster's urban holdings in eleven parts of Morpeth fetched an annual return of almost £30, and included tenements in Aldgate, Newgate, Sidegate, Brigstrete, Market Street and Bullers Green.[365]

A tenant might be expected to improve a property leased to him. A great deal was expected by Swineshead when it demised in 1506 a holding in Grantham, Lincolnshire, to William Lees, a dyer, for forty-one years. He was 'to make or cause to be made there a gate house with one pair of broad gates and one chamber above, thereupon one shop and one hall, with other houses of offices and all to be chambers above with one bay window and one chimney in the hall, one bay window and one chimney above in the chamber, one long house, one "thrust" (outhouse?) and one workhouse in the garth.'[366] Clearly it was to be a warm and well-appointed residence and place of work.

Beaulieu noted in 1537, of one of its tenants in Southampton, John Mille, that he had spent over one hundred marks in erecting new buildings on his holding. Clearly impressed, the monastery gave him a new ninety-nine year lease.[367] Fountains had a holding, including a mill, in far distant Boston, Lincolnshire, which once would have been for it a trading centre. When it was demised in 1531 the tenant inherited the duty of maintaining the tenement and its defences, 'making about the sea ditch for as much belongs to the abbot and his monastery.'[368]

Tithes, and Appropriated Churches

The acquisition of parish churches brought to some abbeys no inconsiderable income from the tithes levied and other offerings made, collectively referred to as the 'spiritualities' of a monastery. In all such cases, the income was diminished by the duty to present to a parish a vicar, and provide for his lodging and stipend; further, as rector the monastery had the obligation to keep the chancel of the church in good repair; there was also the expense of collecting and storing the greater tithes. In the late-fifteenth century, Abbot William Stratford of Vale Royal, restored Llanbadarn's chancel, and left his name inscribed there in stone.[369] Abbot Shipton of Croxden rebuilt the chancel of Alton church, Staffordshire, in the 1520s.[370]

Despite the outgoings, for many abbeys the possession of a church or churches formed a very significant element in their economy. In the valuations recorded in the *Valor Ecclesiasticus* of 1535 spiritualities accounted for over half, £301, of Vale Royal's gross value of £518. Of this no less than £133 was derived from one church alone, Llanbadarn Fawr in Ceredigion.[371] Hatfield, Hertfordshire, was Roche's only church, but it provided an income of £42 out of a gross valuation of £260.[372] Rotherham, Yorkshire, was Rufford's sole parish, but it supplied well over one-third of the abbey's income: £67 out of £254 gross. Its vicar there received the princely stipend of £16-13-4. The abbey also held the manor of Rotherham, valued at £86, so the importance of manor and church to the monastery was very considerable.[373] The spiritualities of Holm Cultram (£164) accounted for thirty per cent of its gross income (£535).[374]

At around £277 the spiritualities of Whalley equalled its temporalities (income from its estates), and were gained from four Lancashire churches: Blackburn, Eccles, Rochdale and Whalley itself.[375] At Blackburn, with papal leave from 1459 on the monastery had a resident monk as procurator.[376] There could be difficulties. Around 1500 Whalley appointed one Edmond Sudeyll to serve Low Chapel in Blackburn parish, but in July 1525 Thomas Langton of Walton, Lancs., 'bearing great malice and ill will' towards Edmond, would not allow him nor any other priest appointed by the abbot to serve the chapel. The matter surfaced in the Duchy of Lancaster court.[377]

Not all monasteries were so fortunate, but it is clear that without the possession of churches and tithes many a Cistercian houses would have been much the poorer. Mostly churches had been appropriated in preceding centuries, but there were a few abbeys which in the late fifteenth/sixteenth century obtained further parishes, and supplemented their income in this way. Buckland was permitted in 1485, in consideration of its alleged 'impoverished state,' to appropriate the church of Bampton, Devon, providing that a vicarage was endowed and 'a competent sum distributed yearly among the poor.'[378] The potential value of the parish was emphasised by the fee of £50 the monastery had to pay the Crown for this appropriation; it was not a free gift. In 1500 Buckland was also allowed to appropriate the distant church of Sulbury, Buckinghamshire.[379]

The next year Bindon was given licence to appropriate Chaldon church, Dorset, but without having to endow the vicarage; this unusual permission was granted 'at the contemplation of the queen consort, Elizabeth.'[380] Buckfast in 1534 was granted by the Crown the rectory of Churstowe, Devon, with the usual conditions of maintaining a vicar there, and contributing 'the usual sum to the poor of the parish.'[381] The two parish churches of Revesby, together with the detached chapels of St Lawrence and St Sithe, accounted for over one-tenth of its gross income (£37/£349), but resulting from earlier benefactions it had not only to make provision for their vicars but had outgoings of over £9 in paying the stipends of chantry priests at Horncastle and Bolingbroke, Lincolnshire.[382] Biddlesden paid the yearly £4 stipend of a chantry chaplain in St Giles Chapel, Littlecote, Buckinghamshire.[383]

Abbeys as 'rectors' of their parishes received the 'greater' tithes; the vicars the 'small' or 'lesser' tithes. Typically the greater tithes would consist of one-tenth of all cereal crops harvested in a parish, as well perhaps of wool produced; the lesser tithes might include wool, young animals (like lambs and piglets) and dairy produce. There was wide variation from parish to parish, and in the agreements drawn up when a vicar was instituted. Evidence of 1542 shows that in Gwent the abbey of Grace Dieu received yearly from one of its parishes, Skenfrith, around two horse-loads of wheat, twelve horse- and two wagon loads of barley, two loads of beans, and seven loads of oats.[384] These were typical 'greater tithes.'

In Cumbria the small house of Calder located in difficult climate and terrain had three churches, which yielded for the monastery tithes of barley, rye and oats, wool and lambs, geese and hens, as well as 'offerings on the three chief days.'[385]. Amongst the tithes Cleeve abbey (1533) could expect from its church of SS Michael and Helen on Lundy Island in the Bristol Channel were one tenth of the hens and eggs produced there, together with one-tenth of the birds and fishes caught there.[386] In Wales where tithes formed an important component in the economy of abbeys like Cymer and Margam,[387] Strata Florida and Whitland abbeys still enjoyed at the Suppression the privilege granted in the mid-fourteenth century of the 'tryanes': one-third of the tithes arising from lands they owned in parishes not of their own appropriation.[388]

William Stagger, vicar of West Ham of which Stratford abbey was rector, complained in the 1530s that for twelve years the abbot had taken away his vicarial tithes of hay, corn and calves, and that this had meant an effective loss to him of £100.[389] His difficulties and litigation with the monastery only ended after its closure, when in 1539 the Court of Augmentations awarded him a very generous annual stipend of £39-13-8.[390] More fairly, the vicar of Gwenddwr, Breconshire, who was entitled to the lesser tithes there, had a provision written into his deed of appointment by Dore abbey (1529) that if 'the abbot be willing to have the tithing lambs, the vicar shall see them to him for his money before any other man.'[391] In other words, the vicar would be reimbursed.

The portion of tithes to be assigned by Fountains to its vicar of Crosthwaite led for a long time to 'causes, actions and dissensions.' Eventually in 1488 mediation spear-headed by the dean of York, resulted in an agreement whereby the monastery would receive all tithes of grain, and an annual payment of £20, and would upkeep the chancel; the vicar was to have the accustomed house and ground, and the lesser tithes of hay, lambs and dairy produce, as well as Lenten offerings and surplice fees (for churchings, weddings, funerals).[392] The importance of the concord was such that a copy was kept in the custody of the prior of Carlisle. William Brit, vicar of Westleton, Suffolk, one of Sibton's churches, initiated proceedings in the Court of Star Chamber against Abbot Emery, whom he said on 17 May 1525 forcibly took two of his kine, and later brought him before the sessions at Bury St Edmunds on a false charge of felony. He had been kept in prison and in the stocks for twelve days. The abbot's response is not on record.[393]

In the last quarter of the fifteenth century, the vicar of Slaidburn disputed Whalley's rights to the tithes of detached portions there of its parish of Clitheroe. Matters came to a head when, on 22 November 1480, the monastery bursar driving away tithe calves from the disputed lands was set upon and severely beaten by a mob intent on killing him. Edward IV (1482), Richard III (1484) and Henry VII (1492) all confirmed that the abbey was in the right. The vicar, Christopher Parsons, continued to make trouble, and a further royal order was made in 1503 commanding the men of the forests to pay their tithes to Whalley.[394] A like situation regarding detached portions of Quarr's parish of Arreton, Isle of Wight, was settled amicably in 1488 'by the friendly coming together of gentlemen.'[395]

That the possession of tithes was a valuable asset, was demonstrated when lay people sought to obtain a lease of them from a religious house. As early as 1494 Hailes demised its rectory of St Breage in Cornwall to John Godolham of Helston. The high rent of £42 p.a. shows how valuable its tithes must have been. Since it was so far from Hailes, the abbey had problems with the collection of rents.[396] Thomas Ireby, abbot of Holm Cultram (1532–1536), demised its Camerton church to Sir Christopher Dacre and Richard Chyrden, chaplain, for five years at an annul rent of £8-13-4; provision being made for the vicar who was to receive an annual stipend of £5-13-4. Dacre had effectively to outlay over £14 each year, but must have thought it worthwhile.[397] There are many such instances.

The continuing value to a monastery even of distant chapelries was shown when Henry VIII in 1534 desired Furness to give him the right of presenting the next vicar to the benefice of Hawkshead in Lancashire. The abbot replied saying that it was not a benefice but only a chapel of ease to Dalton in Furness, and begged that the monastery might continue to receive its profits and tithes.[398] Abbot Roger also wrote to Cromwell, sending him ten 'royals' as a token, and saying that 'if any such presentation be made to Hawkeshead, the monastery is undone, and will be compelled to give up hospitality.'[399] More distant churches of Furness included St Mahold and St Michael on the Isle of Man.[400]

A priest, John Ayrsome, was aggrieved when after receiving in 1530 a lease of the vicarage of Meopham, Kent, from the abbot of Boxley for a term of five years, before that term was ended the abbot deprived him of the vicarage. It seems the abbot used as an excuse 'the statute lately made against spiritual persons for taking of benefices to farm,' which had been promulgated in 1529. The possibility is that the abbot's new tenant (John Hasteling) was willing to pay more. Ayrsome requested reinstatement at the Court of Chancery.[401] No such difficulty was felt when the Crown (1538) granted the church of Old Byland for life to one of Byland's monks,[402] Three years after his abbey closed, John Heron, the last abbot of Valle Crucis, was 'sworn and examined' in a case concerning the lease of Llansanffraid Chapel which one John Vaughan, clerk, 'pretendeth to have under the convent seal.'[403]

When a rectory was demised, the lessees had the same duties to fulfil as a monastery previously had accomplished. Vale Royal's last tenant of Llanbadarn Fawr (1536) was required to maintain the chancel of the church, pay the accustomed synodals to the bishop and archdeacon of St David's, and provide hospitality for the abbot (and a party of up to fourteen persons) on his visits to the parish. Such a number of travelling companions was undoubtedly necessary to give mutual strength and comfort in traversing restless areas of mid-Wales![404] There was a duty also on monasteries as rectors to maintain the rectory or vicarage buildings. When Pipewell was dissolved (1538) it was owing ten shillings for repairs done to the walls and windows of Cold Ashby rectory, Northants.[405]

The Tenantry

The economy of the Cistercians by the late-fifteenth century was one in large measure based upon a rent- and service-paying body of tenants. Holders of small properties, perhaps only a few strips of land, might be tenants-at-will—having perhaps only a verbal agreement by which their contracts could easily be terminated by either party; or they might hold 'by copy of court roll'—their agreement being entered into the written record of the abbey's manorial court, and the copy given to them being proof of their entitlement. Within the Great Close of Beaulieu some thirty-five copyholders and seventeen tenants-at-will held land of the abbey.[406] In Wales copyholding tenants were numerous on the lands of Llantarnam (186) and of Margam (115), whilst of fourteen holdings of Neath in Gelligarn (1540) it was said that they were 'never letted, but only by copy of court roll.'[407]

Tenants to whom a fairly substantial property was granted would receive an indenture detailing the length of the lease in time, the rent and other services expected, and provision made for distress if the contractual obligations were not fulfilled. The completed agreement would have the common seal of the monastery appended, usually in the chapter-house. The term of such leases varied widely, but forty years was frequent for lands of Fountains,[408] forty-one years in some of the leases granted by Swineshead.[409] One demise granted by Buildwas (1534) was for ninety-five years.[410] When Abbot Whitmore of Dunkeswell in 1521 demised a holding in nearby Ashill, with common of pasture on Hackpen Hill, to Robert Whitmore and his son, John, the lease was valid 'to the life of the longest liver.' The annual rent was, unusually, 9s. 6½d., and at 'the view of the bailiff' father and son could take 'firebote, haybote, ploughbote and foldbote' in the abbey's woods for the maintenance of the property. Robert and John were almost certainly close relations of the abbot.[411]

There are several other instances where an abbot in demising property favoured members of his family, and where those leases were granted in an abbey's closing years it seems probable that they were made with an eye to the future prosperity of the abbot himself. Around 1494 the abbot of Buildwas demised his monastery's estate at Harnage, Salop., to his brother for a period of fifty-one years.[412] Other brothers to benefit included William Jackson (brother of Abbot John Urton of Calder) who about 1495 received a grange in Urton by Egremont,[413] and Richard Cryar, brother to John Addyngham, abbot of Swineshead, who in 1506 was demised that abbey's East Harvnyg Grange.[414] It is noteworthy that these 'brothers' occasionally bear a different surname from that of the abbot involved.

It seems likely that there was a family connection when in 1522 Abbot Dovell of Cleeve demised to one Barnard Dovell two mills without the abbey gate, as well as the fish pond and various closes of land.[415] By 1535 a Henry Dovell was bailiff of Cleeve's lands in Dunster, Timberscombe, and elsewhere.[416] In 1535 and 1536, in the ten months preceding his abbey's dissolution, Abbot Toker of Buckland, leased for sixty years to his brother, Robert, and his nephew, William, the rectorial tithes of five parishes.[417] Amongst late leases made by abbot Nicholas Pennant of Basingwerk, were the tithes of Brynford granted to his brother, John. He bequeathed the tithes back to (the now former) abbot Nicholas, who in turn re-demised them to a younger generation of Pennants, ensuring that they stayed in the occupation of his family for generations.[418] Abbot Stevens of Beaulieu gave the abbey mill and Beaulieu parsonage to his sister at the close of his monastery's life.[419]

The worst degree of nepotism came at Dieulacres during the last abbacy of Thomas Whitney (1524–1538).[420] A Humphrey Whitney was bailiff of all the abbey's Cheshire lands, and he personally had a lease from the monastery of a salt-pit in Middlewich. The abbot's brother, John, in 1534 received a seventy-year lease of Swythamnley Grange, while Nicholas Whitney, the abbot's nephew, was given an annuity in 1536 of 5 marks,[421] as well as a partial sixty-year lease of Rossall Grange. A Geoffrey Whitney received a substantial annuity of £12-13-4 out of the revenues of the abbey's manor at Leek. The family fortunes were tempered when in 1540 Henry VIII granted Swythhamnley Grange to William Trafford of Wilmslow, and when in 1553 Edward VI gave Rossall Grange to Thomas Fleetwood and the Middlewich salt-pit to a Thomas Venables.

A frequent condition enjoined on a lease being granted was that the tenant should maintain the property well and perhaps improve it. For general maintenance a tenant would be supplied with 'all manner of timber necessary for reparations' (Fountains, 1530), or receive 'large timber and slate-stones' to assist repairs (Fountains; 1531).[422] Kirkstead's tenant of its Benniworth Grange (1529/30), John Marling, had to sue the abbey in the Court of Chancery because the monastery had failed to provide him with timber, tiles and lime, for the repair of the grange, although this had been agreed 'in the lease about nine years past.'[423] Not only farm buildings, but also (as noted above) the lands had to be kept in good order. A tenant of Fountains in Craven (1514) had to 'repair and scour all hedges and ditches;'[424] a lessee of Margam at its Cibwr Grange (1525) was expected to 'uproot and destroy all briars and thorns in the meadows;'[425] a copyholder in the Great Close of Beaulieu (1525) had the duty of keeping down the thistles on her holding.[426]

When Stoneleigh demised Stoneleigh Grange in 1528 for thirty years at a rental of £7 p.a., the tenant promised 'to build or make a new bay of housing containing eighteen foot square with a chimney.'[427] Basingwerk's tenant of forty acres at Overleigh Grange in Cheshire (1482) was to build upon it 'a house of two bays and two cross-chambers,' the abbey providing the timber required.[428] One of Beaulieu's tenants at its Upton manor (1523) was required to 're-erect the old hall there at its former size with hall, chamber and kitchen.'[429] When Dore demised Morehampton Grange (1527) for ninety-nine years to its Steward, Thomas Baskerville, he was expected to build or caused to be builded anew 'a barn, an ox house, a kitchen and a day house.'[430] With such conditions attached to a lease, monasteries could maintain the worth of their real estate.

In addition to the cash and rents in kind *(Chapter 1)* and customary dues like heriot expected of tenants, a variety of labour services might be required of them. John Wolnesley renting two farms from Dunkeswell and enjoying common of pasture had to spend ten days reaping the monastery corn each autumn.[431] Thomas Forde leasing property in Bickleigh from Buckland (1497) was more fortunate with only two days work at harvest time expected.[432] A tenant of Buckfast (1523) had to perform two days of carriage with a horse, or else pay 4d for each day.[433] A tenant of Furness had the annual duty of carriage of twenty loads of turfs.[434] In Carmarthenshire labour in times of seasonal agrarian need accounted for 150 man-days of work on three granges of Whitland (1539).[435] Such labour services could also be commuted, as the monetary payments permitted from tenants of Valle Crucis in Halghton. These lived 'up to five miles from the grange' where their labour lay, and they had to be rebuked 'for coming so late to work.' Individual payments of 10½d. were expected of them.[436]

Where an ancient or major possession was demised, the tenants might have to provide for monastic officials coming on business. The tenant of Louth Park's Colon Grange (1535) had to give 'honest food' to those coming to oversee the manorial court there twice a year.[437] The lessee of Buckfast's property at Norton in Churchstowe, Devon (1534) was also obliged to provide 'food, bedding and drink' for the cellarer, steward or understeward coming to hold court there or in Kingsbridge as well as 'hay, fodder and litter,' for their horses. [438] Beaulieu's tenant of its Upton manor in north-west Hampshire (1523) had to provide food, bedding and horse fodder, for the abbot and six attendants on four nights each year. The manor appears to have been a staging-post en route to the monastery's Faringdon manor in Berkshire.[439] Abbots and other monks might well stay on an abbey grange for reasons of pleasure more than of business. A deposition of 1607 told how Abbot Blyton of Rufford (1516–1533) would come with six or eight of his monks, at least once a year in summer time, to Skiplam Hall to hunt and hawk in the grounds of Skiplam and Welberne.[440] (One of his monks, Thomas Arthur, was bequeathed in 1523 a bow and shaft.)[441] Another abbot keen on the chase was Baddesley of Merevale, a frequent hunting companion of Sir Henry Willoughby, who often gave him gifts of game.[442] The abbot and convent of Fountains (1529) and their officers, hunted, hawked and fished, on their grange called the Chapelhouse in Kilnsey lordship in Craven.[443] Abbot John Longdon of Dore (1500–1516) once sought the help of the sub-dean of Hereford in borrowing a ferret for three days.[444] On his abbey's Maenor Forion Grange, the abbot of Whitland had 'a place of diversion for summer.'[445]Perhaps for like reasons when Bordesley (1535) demised its Bidford Grange, Warwickshire, the abbot reserved to his use certain chambers there, including the parlour, buttery and chapel.[446]

Pleasure, rather than business, was perhaps also implied when in 1509 Dieulaces demised for the first time its Poulton chapel and grange in Cheshire, the original site of that monastery. The lessees was required for two weeks in every year to entertain the abbot with twelve mounted companions, but on those occasions the tenants did not have to provide 'wine, fresh salmon and oysters.'[447] Basingwerk's lessees at Overeleigh Grange (1482) had to provide overnight sustenance for the abbot and eight persons, and the holder of its Caldy Grange (Wirral; 1535) an 'abbot's feast'—its 'stewards, tenants and servants dinner.'[448]

There were a number of instances where the granting of a monastic lease, or its with-holding, led to litigation. The Court of Chancery heard that in 1526 Swineshead promised a lease of a grange in North Rauceby, Lincolnshire, to one Thomas Quadryng who paid £6 for the completion of the lease. He then died, and the abbot refused to complete the deal, leaving his daughter, Joan Sapcote, and her husband Edward, to appeal for redress.[449] After the suppression, in 1539 four former monks of Dore gave evidence into who was the rightful tenant of that abbey's Hollings Grange. They alleged that Abbot Redborne had granted the demise of the property in 1530 to David ap Thomas ap Rhys but that, two years later, pressurised by people of influence, he granted the tenancy to one Watkin Seysil instead.[450]

Fault could though lie on the part of a tenant. A normal lease would make provision that if the rent fell behind for more than a month or two an abbey could enter the grange and distrain goods from the tenant to compensate, and 'the distress so taken to drive, carry away and with-hold.'[451] James Witton, occupying lands of Sawley (*c.*1510) in Gisburn Forest, Yorkshire, not only refused to pay his rent, but rather threatened that if abbey servants came to take distress 'he would shoot arrows at them.'[452]

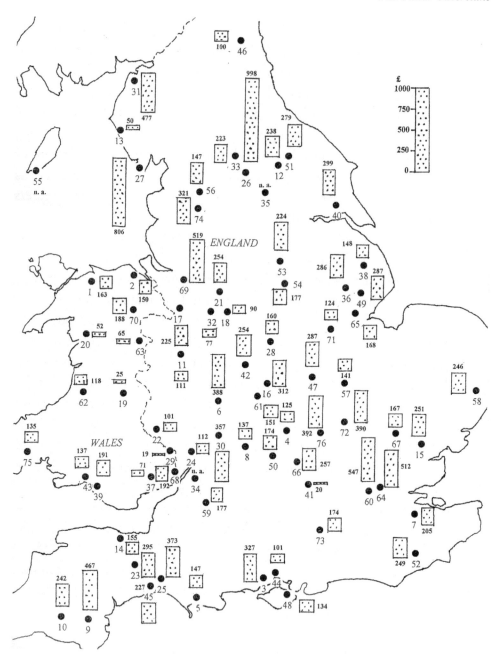

Fig. 11: Net Values of the Abbeys, 1535
(The larger figure indicates the number of an abbey given in the key on the next page;
the smaller figure its net value)

Number key to abbeys on previous page

1: Aberconwy; 2: Basingwerk; 3: Beaulieu; 4: Biddlesden; 5. Bindon; 6: Bordesley; 7. Boxley; 8: Bruern; 9. Buckfast; 10: Buckland; 11: Buildwas; 12: Byland; 13: Calder; 14: Cleeve; 15: Coggeshall; 16: Combe; 17: Combermere; 18: Croxden; 19: Cwmhir; 20: Cymer; 21: Dieulacres; 22: Dore; 23: Dunkeswell; 24: Flaxley; 25: Ford; 26: Fountains; 27: Furness; 28: Garendon; 29: Grace Dieu; 30: Hailes; 31: Holm Cultram; 32: Hulton; 33: Jervaulx; 34: Kingswood; 35: Kirkstall; 36: Kirkstead; 37: Llantarnam; 38: Louth Park; 39: Margam; 40: Meaux; 41: Medmenham; 42: Merevale; 43: Neath; 44: Netley; 45: Newenham; 46:Newminster; 47: Pipewell; 48: Quarr; 49: Revesby; 50: Rewley; 51: Rievaulx; 52: Robertsbridge; 53: Roche; 54: Rufford; 55: Rushen; 56: Sawley; 57: Sawtry; 58: Sibton; 59: Stanley; 60: St Mary Graces; 61: Stoneleigh; 62: Strata Florida; 63: Strata Marcella; 64: Stratford; 65: Swineshead; 66: Thame; 67: Tilty; 68: Tintern; 69: Vale Royal; 70: Valle Crucis; 71: Vaudey; 72: Warden; 73: Waverley; 74: Whalley; 75: Whitland; 76: Woburn.

The Valor Ecclesiasticus: Gross and Net Values

The great valuation of ecclesiastical property prepared for the compilation of the *Valor Ecclesiasticus* in 1535 gives a broad survey of the gross income of practically all the Cistercian monasteries of England and Wales. It was to be followed a very few years later by the Ministers' Accounts of receivers-general giving the gross and net values of monastic property in the year following the closure of an individual house, with further such accounts in the subsequent years. Mostly, but not always, the gross values accorded a monastery in the *Valor* are somewhat less than those itemised in the post-dissolution accounts. The reason for this is primarily that more time and care could be taken over the later accounts than in the rush to complete the 1535 survey; further, there was a degree of monetary inflation in those years.

A few examples illustrate the often slight but definite upgrading of values in the later accounts: A considerable increase in value was recorded for the properties of Stratford abbey in 1537/38 of no less than £69 above the figures stated in the *Valor*. The surveyor and receiver-general for the Crown in that case was one Geoffrey Chamber. Reference was made that his work saw the 'yearly increase gotten and improved.'[453] Likewise Woburn saw a greater estimated value, from £431 (1535) up to £529 (1538/39). Other increases were more moderate as in the instances of: Bindon's gross value estimated at £125 in 1535 was assessed at £164 in 1538; Swineshead's gross income given as £175 in the *Valor* but marked up to £185 two years later; Combermere's gross value rose from £258 in 1535 to £268 in 1538/39; Neath saw its estimated gross income rise from £150 in 1535 to £165 in 1539/40; An exception was Basingwerk where the value of £158 accorded in 1535 was levelled down to £153 in 1536/37.

The gross value accorded a monastery could be misleading on account of the outgoings that abbey might have had. The net value (as recorded in the *Valor*) was for practical purposes much more significant to the life of a monastery than the gross value, and was also the amount upon which tenths payable to the Crown were calculated. No figures are extant for a few abbeys, including Kirkstall and Kingswood –which was unintentionally bypassed,[454] but net values in 1535 ranged from £998 at Fountains down to but £20 at Medmenham. Yet that monastery, in effect no more now than a cell of Woburn, had a few years earlier been expected to pay £200 towards the costs of the war with France. Monasteries with a net value of over £500 also included Furness (£806), St Mary Graces (£547) and Vale Royal (£519).

After outgoings some abbeys were still reasonably healthy financially: Combermere had in the *Valor* outgoings of £33 reducing its gross value from £258 to a net value of £225; Vale Royal saw a like moderate reduction from £540 to £519. Jervaulx, on the other hand, burdened with annuities and stipends of various kinds amounting to £197, saw a gross value of £456 worth only £233 net. Whalley, notable for its charity costing £104, had its gross income lessened from £551 to £321. Vaudey's gross assessed value of £177-15-7¾ likewise reduced considerably to £124-5-11¼, on which basis its tenth was assessed at £12-8-7¼; the annuities and fees it paid amounted to £51.[455] Warden's net income of £390 saw its tenth assessed at £38-19-8. Jervaulx's net income being £234-18-5 had levied a tenth of £23-9-10¼. Louth Park's gross income was £169-5-6½, its net annual income £147-13-6¼, and its tenth £14-15-5½.

Compilation of the *Valor* was usually based upon reports received from local commissioners appointed for that purpose, and to a large extent depended on statements already prepared by a monastery and its officers. The entry for Kirkstead notes that the account of its possessions was 'presented by the abbot, Richard Haryson, and the convent as is declared below.'[456] The accounts for Ford and Dunkeswell were both presented to the Bishop of Exeter and his fellow commissioners by their respective abbots,[457] whilst the abbot of Thame signed the spiritualities income recorded in his return.[458] The return for Boxley was prefaced with the words: 'the Certificate of John, abbot of Boxley, made unto the commissioners of our Sovereign Lord the King, of the true yearly value' of all its possessions.[459]The declaration of the possessions of Cleeve was made in the presence of two local gentry, who also acted in the same capacity at Dunster Priory. They were Sir Andrew Luttrell of Dunster Castle (*d.*1538), and a former Sheriff of Somerset, and Hugh Malet, esq., of Corypole in the same county, with Hugh Trotter and John Plompton, themselves tenants of the abbey, acting as auditors.[460] The accounts for Waverley were signed off by Sir William fitzWilliam (who obtained the site) and four other local gentry.[461] In distant Monmouthshire the accounts of Llantarnam appear to have been presented by Abbot Jasper to the commissioners on 20 June 1535,[462] and those of Tintern by Abbot Wyche on 1 September that year.[463] The delay at Tintern may have been the reason Thomas Cromwell summoned Abbot Wyche that week to wait upon him.

Whatever the gross or net values of a monastery may have been, the profit to the crown by that abbey's closure was always considerably lessened by the pensions granted to former abbots and (in some cases) monks which might have to be paid for years to come. The gross income of Bindon was £241, but its annual pension bill amounted to £83; that of Biddlesden, £162, its pension bill came to £81, and of St Mary Grace's £603 gross income £115 would be swallowed up in pension payments.

Notes

1   *VE* **4**, 237.
2   D. H. Williams, *White Monks in Gwent*, Pontypool: Griffin Press, 1976, p. 116, *The Welsh Cistercians*, Leominster: Gracewing, 2001, p. 280.
3   *BAC*, 13.
4   *LP* **1**, passim.
5   *Patent* 1508, p. 590; *LP* **1**, Part 1, p. 375 [No. 682/32].
6   *LP* **1**, Part 1, p. 353 [No. 632/14].
7   Ibid. pp. 291–92 [No. 485/25].
8   Ibid. p. 291 [No. 485/21].
9   TNA, C142/11/28.
10   TNA, C142/21/78.
11   SSC, DR18/1/61.
12   *Patent* 1495, p. 58.
13   *Patent* 1505, p. 419.
14   *LP* **1**, Part 1, p. 344 [No. 604/20].].

15   *LP* **2**, Part 1, p. 302 [No. 1142].

16   *Patent 1507*, p. 556.

17   *Patent 1497*, p. 110.

18   *Patent 1492*, p. 390.

19   *LP* **11**, pp. 146–47 [No. 362].

20   *LP* **12**, Part 1, p. 420 [No. 920].

21   G. Baskerville, *English Monks and the Suppression of the Monasteries*, London: Jonathan Cape, 1937, p. 60.

22   *LP* **7**, Part 2, p. 425 [No. 1096].

23   Williams, *Welsh Cistercians*, 2001, pp. 67–68.

24   *LP* **7**, Part 1, p. 294 [No. 762].

25   G. Williams, *Welsh Church from Conquest to Reformation*, Cardiff: University of Wales Press, 1962, p. 367.

26   *LP* **4**, Part 2, p. 1975 [No. 4522]; *LP* **13**, Part 1, p. 152 [No. 406], Part 2, p. 348 [No. 839/5]; F.A. Hibbert, *Dissolution of the Monasteries*, London: Pitman, 1910, p. 240.

27   *LP* **XX**, Part 2, 1549 [59]; W. C. Waller, 'Some Records of Tilty Abbey.' In: *TEAS*, N.S. **8**, 1903, pp. 119–20.

28   *LP* **11**, p. 77 [No. 177].

29   VCH, *County of Bedford* **1**, 1904, p. 364.

30   J. Youings, *Dissolution of the Monasteries*, London: Allen and Unwin, 1971, p. 218.

31   TNA, E315/94, f. 93r–v.

32   TNA, E210/10787.

33   Devon R. O. 123M/TB86.

34   TNA, E315/238, f. 63.

35   Hibbert, *Dissolution*, 1910, p. 240.

36   TNA, E315/95, ff. 231v–232r.

37   TNA, E118/1/31, p.51.

38   TNA, E111/24.

39   TNA, LR1/174, f. 45.

40   S .F. Hockey, *Beaulieu, King John's Abbey*, Beaulieu: Pioneer Publns. 1976, p. 166.

41   *CHA*, p. 109 [No. 49].

42   TNA, LR1/175, f. 319r–v. Meynell was of an ancient Yorkshire family, based at North Kilvington.

43   TNA, E315/94, ff. 169v–170r.

44   TNA, LR1/174, f. 45.

45   D. Pratt, 'Valle Crucis abbey: lands and charters.' In: *Denbighshire Historical Transaction* **59**, 2011, p. 18.

46   *VE* **4**, p. 36.

47   TNA, E315/95, ff. 178v–179r; LR1/174, f. 35. [In early 1536 William Thirsk, who had to resign as abbot of Fountains, did labour for Sir William Mallory of Studley, to be appointed as 'receiver–general and steward of our Court,' but his successor appealed

to Cromwell not to confirm that deed: *LP* **10**, p. 170 [No. 424].

48   *LP* **9**, p. 263 [No. 782], of 6–11–1535.

49   VCH, *County of Lancaster* **2** (1908) 139.

50   Surrey History Centre, LM/1659/24: receipt issued by Snowe for 3s 10d. from a tenant in Stratford, ~Robert Swerder.

51   Williams, *Welsh Cistercians*, 2001, 79.

52   TNA, E315/91, f. 61.

53   TNA, E315/94, f. 59r–v.

54   *VE* **4**, p. 371.

55   Ibid. p. 238.

56   TNA, E315/98, f. 57r–v.

57   *VE* **4**, p. 371.

58   TNA, DL25/3316.

59   TNA, E315/95, ff. 231v–232r.

60   NLW, Badminton Manorial 1659.

61   Lincolnshire Archives, BNLW/1/1/62/7.

62   *FLB*, pp. 42–43 [No. 52].

63   Devon R.O., 123M/TB35 [1523].

64   *RC* **3**, pp. 552–53 [No. 1002]; Nottinghamshire Archives DDSR 102/200)].

65   *FLB*, pp. 51–53 [No. 62].

66   Lincolnshire Archives, 1ANC3/2/4–17, 3/8/13–21. A series of rolls for in the 1490s are also unfit for production [1ANC/2/9/1–8].

67   Lincolnshire Archives, 1ANC3/2/6r.

68   *Ibid.* 1ANC3/2/6v.

69   *Ibid.* 1ANC3/2/8.

70   In the Badminton Manorial collection.

71   NLW, Badminton Manorial 1663, mm. 3r–4d, 1654, m. 3r.

72   *Ibid.* 1658.

73   Williams, *White Monks in Gwent*, 1976, p. 101.

74   Gloucester City R.O., Badminton Plan 19: Photocopy 840.

75   *LP* **13**, Part 1, p. 326 [No. 887/12].

76   TNA, DL 28/33/3.

77   *SBC*, **4**, p. 63 [No. 1116].

78   *DCL*, p. 73.

79   A. Watkins, 'Merevale Abbey.' In: *Warwickshire History* **9**: No. 3, Summer, 1994, p. 94.

80   SSC, DR 18/31/5, f. 36.

81   *FLB*, pp. 225–26 [No. 226].

82   *LB*, p. 191.

83   TNA, E315/405, f. 45v.

84   Devon R.O., 123M/TB86.

85   Williams, *White Monks in Gwent*, 1976, pp. 47–48; TNA, E303/5/101.

[86]   Wikipedia entries.
[87]   Haigh (1969) 15.
[88]   Lancashire R.O., DDHE 57/12.
[89]   Lancashire R.O., DDTO 1/65; *Cf.* DDHE 57/12.
[90]   Humphrey (1982) 42.
[91]   TNA, STAC2/35/77
[92]   TNA, C1/895/58.
[93]   TNA, C43/2/19–20 respectively.
[94]   TNA, C1/382/1, C1/386/36.
[95]   TNA, C1/739/17; SSC, DR 18/31/5, ff. 77–78.
[96]   TNA, C1/563/5.
[97]   East Sussex R.O., SAS—RF/13/15.
[98]   *AF*, pp. 303–04, 313–14.
[99]   *Patent* 1498, pp. 141–42.
[100] *FLB*, pp. 62–64 [No. 71], 75–76 [No. 85].
[101] *LP* **10**, p. 432 [No. 1040].
[102] SSC, DR18/31/5, ff. 77–78; *CHA*, pp. 121–22 [Nos. 76–77].
[103] Plymouth and West Devon R.O., 70/182.
[104] TNA, C1/483/2.
[105] *LP* **13**, Part 1, p. 326 [No. 887/12]; *Cf.* SSC, DR18/3/59/2.
[106] TNA, SC7/64/58.
[107] *LP* **9**, p. 398 [No. 1167].
[108] Waller, 'Records of Tilty,' 1903, p. 121; TNA, E315/100, ff. 12v–14r. .
[109] *LP* **13**, Part 1, p. 569 [No. 1519/67].
[110] VCH, *Hampshire* **2**, 1973, p. 144.
[111] *DCL*, p. 24.
[112] TNA, SC11/542.
[113] West Devon R.O., 70/139 [Bickleigh, 1479]; Somerset R.O., DD/WY/Box 18/W6/2P
       [Cullompton, 1523].
[114] *Augm.* p. 132; Williams, *White Monks in Gwent*, 1976, p. 91.
[115] TNA, SC6/HENVIII/2005B, f. 10.
[116] SSC, DR10/1304.
[117] West Devon R.O., 70/150.
[118] TNA, E312/12/29.
[119] TNA, LR1/228, f. 158.
[120] *PCSC*, p. 175*n*.
[121] *LP* **13**, Part 1, p. 283 [No. 750].
[122] NLW, Cwrtmawr MS 973D, p. 33.
[123] G. D. Owen, *Agricultural Conditions in West Wales*, University of Wales: Ph. D,. thesis,
       1935, p. 225.
[124] TNA, C1/1397, m. 13.

[125] TNA, LR1/176, f. 66r–v.

[126] T. I. Jeffreys Jones, *Exchequer Proceedings Concerning Wales In Tempore James I*, Cardiff: University of Wales Press, 1955, p. 102.

[127] Devon R.O., 123M/TB83.

[128] TNA, LR1/173, f. 66r–v.

[129] *FLB*, pp. 74–75 [No. 84].

[130] TNA, LR1/173, f. 137.

[131] *AC* **1**, 1846, p. 111.

[132] TNA, LR1/213, f. 271; E315/50, f. 176; SC6/HENVIII/4868, m. 5d, respectively.

[133] TNA, C146/344.

[134] East Sussex R.O., RYE/25; RYE 123/4.

[135] TNA, E118/1/31, p. 22v [No. 34].

[136] TNA, E118/1/47.

[137] TNA, SC6/HENVIII/7339.

[138] *VE* **4**, p. 294.

[139] Ibid. p. 265.

[140] *VE* **5**, p. 282.

[141] Ibid. p. 283.

[142] *LP* **15**, p. 113 [No. 282/91].

[143] *AF*, p. lxii.

[144] TNA, SC12/30/4, f. 8v.

[145] G. Brown, *Stanley Abbey and its Estates*, BAR, British Series **566**, 2012, p. 100.

[146] W. de Gray Birch, *Margam Abbey*, London: 1907, p. 349.

[147] NLW, Cernioge Deed 48.

[148] *VE* **I**, p. 79.]

[149] R. H. D'Elboux, *Surveys of the Manors of Robertsbridge*, Sussex Record Society **47**, 1944, p. 181.

[150] J. L. Tomkinson, *A History of Hulton Abbey*, Staffordshire Archaeological Studies, N.S. **10**, 1997, p. 37.

[151] TNA, E118/1/121.

[152] Plymouth and West Devon R.O., 70/182.

[153] TNA, LR1/228, ff. 182–83.

[154] R. Bearman, *Stoneleigh Abbey*, Stoneleigh Abbey Ltd., 2004, p. 211

[155] SSC, DR 10/996–97.

[156] *FLB*, pp. 241–43.

[157] Ibid. p. 243*n*.

[158] Somerset R.O., DD/SE/15/1.

[159] TNA, SC12/30/4, f. 7v.

[160] Williams, *White Monks in Gwent*, 1976, p. 120.

[161] *LP* **12**, Part 2, p. 21 [No. 59].

[162] *VE* **5**, p. 241.

163 C. Gill, *Buckland Abbey*, Plymouth, 1968, p. 37.

164 TNA, C146/344.

165 TNA, STAC2/29/169; Stéphan, *Buckfast Abbey*, Bristol: Burleigh Press, 1970, pp. 183–84.

166 TNA, STAC2/2, f.237; Stéphan, *Buckfast*, 1970, pp. 189–94.

167 Yorkshire Archaeological Society, MD 335/4/2.

168 *FLB*, p. 208 [No. 212].

169 *LP* 12, Part 2, p. 89 [No. 205].

170 TNA, SC6/HENVIII/481.

171 *MF*, pp. 232–35 [No. LXII].

172 *AF*, pp. 325–28.

173 Ibid. p. lxv. This must be the modern Foulney Island.

174 J. Ridgard and R. Norton, *Food and Ale, Farming and Worship*, Leiston, Suffolk: Leiston Press, 2011, pp. 36–37, 41–42.

175 TNA, LR1/174, f. 45; C1/73917.

176 Watkins, 'Merevale Abbey,' 1994, pp. 95–96.

177 *DCP*, p. 4.

178 TNA, E315/91, ff. 26r–27r.

179 TNA, E315/405, f. 2; Cumbria R.O. D/Cu/4/99; *LP* 13, Part 1, p. 572 [No. 1519/71].

180 TNA, E315/278, f. 53.

181 *FLB*, pp. 45 [No. 55], 47–48 [No. 57], 53.

182 West Devon (Plymouth) R.O., 70/139, 141, 143, 148–49, of 1503–1517.

183 J. A. Sparks, *In the Shadow of the Blackdowns*, Bradford-on-Avon: Moonraker Press, 1978, p. 124.

184 *CHA*, pp. 126–27 [No. 90].

185 TNA, STAC2/1, ff. 28–30.

186 *LP* 5, p. 621 [No. 1477].

187 *FLB*, pp. 60–61 [70], of 1517.

188 Ridgard, *Food and Ale*, 2011, p. 42.

189 Lancashire R.O., DDX3.

190 TNA, LR 1/169, f. 389r–v.

191 Watkins, 'Merevale Abbey,' 1994, p. 94.

192 TNA, SC6/HENVIII/5156, m.11r; Royal Commission on Ancient and Historical Monuments in Wales, *Glamorgan 3*, Part 2 (1982), p. 260 (MG 16; Fig. 143, Pl. 42); 263 (MG 17), 265 (Fig. 145).

193 Whitehaven (Cumbria) Archives, DCU/4/99.

194 Grainger and Phillpotts, *Abbey of St Mary Graces*, 2011, pp. 88, 90.

195 TNA, E315/33/134.

196 SSC, DR10/1332.

197 *LP* 13, Part 1, pp. 469–70 [No. 1280].

198 *LP* 14, Part 1, p. 532 [No. 1192/5].

199 Somerset R.O., D/B/bw/181.

200 S. F. Hockey, *Quarr Abbey and its Lands*, Leicester U.P., 1970, pp. 169–70.

201 Watkins, 'Merevale Abbey,' 1994, p. 99.

202 Williams, *Welsh Cistercians*, 2001, p. 251.

203 *LP* **13**, Part 1, p. 160 [No. 433].

204 *VE* **3**, p. 432.

205 Ridgard, *Food and Ale*, 2011, pp. 40–41.

206 *LP* **11**, pp. 146–47 [No. 362].

207 *VE* **4**, p. 371.

208 Owen, *Agricultural Conditions*, 1935, p. 362.

209 TNA, LR1/176, f. 9r–v.

210 *LC*, pp. 131–32 [No. LXXX].

211 TNA, E315/283.

212 TNA, E118/1/31, pp. 24v, 49.

213 TNA, E315/92, f. 96; *LP* **14**, Part 1, p. 422, [No. 906/7/(2)].

214 TNA, E315/92, f. 50v.

215 Grainger, *Abbey of St Mary Graces*, 2011, p. 89.

216 *LP* **4**, Part 3, p. 2366 [No. 5378].

217 Grainger, *Abbey of St Mary Graces*, 2011, p. 89.

218 TNA, C1/877/71.

219 *LP* **12**, Part 1, p. 406 [No. 901].

220 *LP* **6**, p. 315 [No. 710].

221 TNA, DL41/326; *Cf. LP* **6**, pp. 620 [No. 1538], 630 [No. 1561].

222 TNA, DL 41/327–28.

223 TNA, STAC2/31/151. For earlier incidents at North Dyke, see TNA, E111/94; D. H. Williams, 'Cistercian Bridges.' In: *Tarmac Papers* **3**, 1999, pp. 150–51.

224 SSC, DR 10/997.

225 *LP* **15**, p. 561 [No. 1032].

226 Somerset R.O., DD/WHb/2086.

227 TNA, E118/1/121.

228 SSC, DR 10/1304.

229 Watkins, 'Merevale Abbey,' 1994, p. 98.

230 *LP* **13**, Part 1, p. 572 [No. 1519/71].

231 TNA, E315/405, f. 11.

232 *LP* **12**, Part 1, p. 509 [No. 1093].

233 Ibid. p. 211 [No. 438].

234 *LP* **4**. Part 1, p. 339 [No. 771].

235 Williams, *White Monks in Gwent*, 1976, p. 139.

236 Williams, *Welsh Cistercians*, 2001, pp. 267, 282.

237 *LP* **12**, Part 1, p. 211 [No. 438].

238 S. W. Williams, *Cistercian Abbey of Strata Florida*, London: Whiting & Co., 1889, Appx.

pp. v–vi; Williams, *Welsh Cistercians*, 2001, 267.

239 *FLB*, pp. 51–53 [No. 62].

240 *VE* **4**, p. 193.

241 Warwickshire R.O., Child-Villiers papers.

242 A. H. Plaisted, *Manor and Parish Records of Medmenham*, London: Longmans, Green and Co., 1925, p. 195.

243 Devon R.O., 49/26/6/1.

244 *LP* **14**, Part 1, pp. 162–63 [No. 403/47 (10)].

245 TNA, E315/212/ f. 31r–v.

246 BL, Harley MS 144, f. 1.

247 Lincolnshire R.O., RA/1/REVESBY/6/150.

248 *PCSC*, p. 175*n*.

249 *CHA*, pp. 93–94 [No. 5], 105 [No. 4].

250 TNA, E315/427/3: f. 39r.

251 Hockey, *Beaulieu*, 1976, p. 207.

252 *LCCS*, p. 98; TNA, STAC2/15, f.281. [Considerable damage had also been done in 1518 to the abbey's Beaumont fishery: TNA, DL25/3317].

253 *AF*, pp. 325, lxv.

254 *DCL* **2**, pp. 241–42.

255 TNA, SC12/3/27.

256 *LP* **13**, Part 2, p. 177 [No. 457/6].

257 *AF*, pp. lxii, lxvi.

258 TNA, E36/154,, ff. 110v–111r (Garendon); ff. 146v–147r (Stoneleigh); *LP* **10**, pp. 496, 498 [No. 1191/1].

259 *LP* **10**, p. 499 [1191/1–2]. It was valued at 12d. per acre.

260 BL, Harley MS 144, f. 47v.

261 *VE* **4**, p. 294.

262 *Itin.* **3**, p. 115.

263 Hockey, *Beaulieu*, 1976, p. 166.

264 G. S. Thomson, 'Woburn Abbey and the Dissolution.' In: *Trans. Royal Historical Soc.*, 4th Series, **16**, 1933, p. 145.

265 TNA, SC6/HENVIII/7339.

266 *FLB*, pp. 92–94 [No. 103]. The post seems to have run in the Haxby family, for a later William Haxby was bailiff there in 1535 [*FLB*, p. 94*n*.]

267 *FLB*, pp. lxvii–lxviii; pp. 13 [No. 9].

268 TNA, E315/103, f. 2v; SC6/HENVIII/5156, mm. 3v–4r.

269 *VE* **4**, p. 371.

270 VCH, *Shropshire* **2**, 1973, p. 58.

271 BL, Harley MS 144, f. 47v.

272 Williams, *White Monks in Gwent*, 1976, pp. 46–47, *Welsh Cistercians*, 2001, p. 230.

273 *TNA*, E36/154, ff. 146v–147r; *LP* 10, p. 499 [No. 1191/2].

274 *FLB*, p. lxiii.
275 NLW, Badminton Manorial 1663, m. 3v.
276 *LP* **14**, Part 1, p. 422 [No. 906, ii/5].
277 TNA, C1/626/17.
278 *LP* **13**, Part 1, p. 54 [No. 162].
279 TNA, E303/17, m. 335.
280 Williams, *Welsh Cistercians*, 2001, p. 230.
281 *LP* **13**, Part 1, p. 582 [No. 1520].
282 TNA, C1/738/19.
283 TNA, C1/755/26.
284 TNA, STAC1/2/96; *Cf.* STAC2/5, ff. 67–68.
285 TNA, DL41/302.
286 *FLB*, pp. 51–53 [No. 62].
287 *Cf. FLB*, pp. 52 [Nos. 61–62], 204 [No. 209].
288 *FLB*, pp. 194–95 [No. 203].
289 TNA, E303/17, f. 351,
290 Watkins, 'Merevale Abbey,' 1994, p. 98.
291 W. Humphrey, *Garendon Abbey*,Loughborough University: East Midlands Study Unit, 1982, p. 71.
292 VCH, *County of Stafford* **3**, 1970, p. 236.
293 TNA, SC12/30/4.
294 E. Straker, 'Westall's Book of Panningridge.' In: *SxAC* **72**, 1931, p. 253.
295 *SBC* **4**, pp. 64–65 [No. 1117], 85.
296 D. Knowles, *Bare Ruined Choirs*, Cambridge U.P., 1976 edn., p. 132.
297 E. Owen, 'Monastery of Basingwerk.' In: *Jnl. Flintshire Historical Soc.*, **7**, 1920, p. 57; G. Wrottesley, Notes in: *Collections for a History of Staffordshire*, William Salt Archaeological Soc., N.S. **9**, 1906, pp. 336, 339.
298 Cheshire Archives, DCH/Z/3 (of 1536).
299 VCH, *County of Stafford* **3**, 1970, p. 236.
300 TNA, C1/1499/48–51; E135/3/16.
301 *Itinerary.* **1**, p. 6; **4**, p. 4.
302 *BAC*, pp. 24, 31, 34, 37–8, 66–67.
303 Northumberland R.O., 324/M.1/7.
304 TNA, LR1/173, ff. 63v–64r.
305 TNA, SC12/30/4.
306 Hockey, *Beaulieu*, 1976, p. 169.
307 BL, Additional MS 11041, f. 48.
308 *LCCS* **2**, 1916, pp. 74–75.
309 Hibbert, *Dissolution*, 1910, p. 255.
310 SSC, DR18/31/5, f. 1.
311 Watkins, 'Merevale Abbey,' 1994, p. 90.

312 *AF*, p. lxvi.

313 TNA, E315/405, f. 45v.

314 G. D.Barnes, 'Kirkstall Abbey.' In: *PTS* **58**, No. 128, p. 83.

315 TNA, E315/91, f. 47r–v.

316 TNA, STAC2/21/230.

317 VCH, *County of Stafford* 3, 1970, p. 237.

318 Tomkinson, *Hulton Abbey*, 1997, p. 40.

319 Watkins, 'Merevale Abbey,' 1994, pp. 98–100; TNA, E315/283 *passim*.

320 *LP* **8**, p. 444 [No. 1132], **10**, p. 18 [No. 51].

321 *LP* **4**, Part 2, p. 1126 [No. 2528].

322 Ridgard and Norton, *Food and Ale*, 2011, pp. 39–40; *SAE*, pp. 77–109 (for Sibton's rent roll of February 1484).

323 C. Gill, *Buckland Abbey*, Plymouth: Plymouth Corporation, 1ˢᵗ edn., 1951, p. 19.

324 *DCL*, pp. 195–96.

325 *LP* **1**, Part 1, p. 508 [No. 1044/2].

326 *LP* **3**, Part 1, p. 267 [No. 754]; Stéphan, *Buckfast*, 1970, p. 185.

327 *LP* **4**, Part 3, p. 2772 [No. 6187/29].

328 Williams, *Welsh Cistercians*, 2001, p. 270.

329 TNA, E326/669.

330 TNA, C1/787/30–36:

331 TNA, SP5/4, ff. 26–27.

332 Thomson, 'Woburn Abbey,' 1933, p. 132; *VE* **4**, p. 213.

333 Warwickshire R.O., CR/1886/BL/234.

334 Gibson, 'Tilty Abbey.' In: *Essex Review* **5**, 1896, p. 97.

335 *LP* **13**, Part 1,pp. 246–47 [March, 1538, Grant 61].

336 *LP* **12**, Part 2, p. 358 [No. 1008/42].

337 *VE* **6**, p. xi.

338 TNA, C1/57/363.

339 *VE* **4**, p. 193.

340 Hockey, *Beaulieu*, 1976, p. 175.

341 TNA, E328/255.

342 TNA, E315/91, ff. 22v–23v.

343 LMA, ACC/0079/001.

344 Grainger, *St Mary Graces*, 2011, p. 89.

345 TNA, E315/97, f. 14.

346 Grainger, *St Mary Graces*, 2011, p. 89.

347 Corporation of London, R.O. CLA/007/EM/02/1/069, and 1/055.

348 Humphrey, *Garendon*, 1982, pp. 53–54; TNA, SC6/HENVIII/1825, SC12/30/4, f. 26r; *Patent*, 1504, p. 344.

349 Williams, *Welsh Cistercians*, 2001, p. 260.

350 Williams, *White Monks in Gwent*, 1976, p. 24; TNA, E111/28.

351 *FLB*, pp. 86–87 [No. 97].

352 TNA, LR1/174, f. 34.

353 *FLB*, p. 88 [No. 99].

354 *AF*, pp. 309–10.

355 L. S. Snell, *The Suppression of the Religious Foundations of Devon and Cornwall*, Marazion: Wordens Ltd., 1967, p. 118.

356 Sparks, *In the Shadow of the Blackdowns*, 1978, p. 128.

357 TNA, LR1/173, ff. 135, 149.

358 TNA, E315/283, f. 9; E303/17, f. 364, respectively.

359 Yorkshire Archaeol. Soc. DD12/1/31.

360 TNA, E326/4426; *Cf.* E326/2840, 2841, 2843.

361 Nottinghamshire R.O., DDD/ST/208/29; *RC* **1**, p. 23 [No. 35].

362 Nottinghamshire Archives, DD/SR/12/2.

363 Sheffield Archives, BGM/28.

364 *BAC*, p. 63.

365 TNA, SC12/30/4; E315/281, f. 1v; Northumberland R.O., 324/M.1/7; BMO/01/HENVII/2 and 9.

366 TNA, E118/1/31, pp. 43v–44r. It also in 1535 demised holdings in the port of Boston: E118/1/31, p. 23 [35].

367 Hockey, *Beaulieu*, 1976, pp. 173–74.

368 *FLB* pp. 88–89 [No. 100].

369 W. G. Thomas, 'The Chancel of Llanbadarn Fawr Church.' In: *AC* **127**, 1978, pp. 127–29.

370 Hall, J., *Croxden Abbey: buildings and community*, York University, Ph. D. thesis, 2003, p. 23.

371 *VE* **5**, p. 209.

372 VCH, *County of York* **3**, 1913, p. 154.

373 *VE* **5**, p. 173; TNA, SC11/542.

374 *VE* **5**, p. 282.

375 TNA, DL29/158/36; *VE* **5**, pp. 229–30.

376 *CPL* **11**, pp. 563–64.

377 *DCL*, pp. 153–55.

378 *Patent 1485*, p. 117.

379 *Patent 1500*, pp. 196; 1505, 399.

380 *Patent 1501*, p. 244.

381 *LP* 7, p. 293 [No. 761/25].

382 *VE* **4**, pp. 44–45.

383 *VE* **4**, p. 238.

384 *Augm.* pp. 141, 177; Williams, *White Monks in Gwent*, 1976, p. 71.

385 J. Thorley, 'Estates of Calder Abbey.' In: *TCWAA*, 3rd Series **4**, 2004, p. 153.

386 TNA, E315/91, f. 80; in 1535 the lease of Lundy rectory was worth 10s. p.a., A. E.

Blackwell, 'Lundy's Ecclesiastical History.' In: *RTDA* **92**, 1960, p. 92.

387 Williams, *Welsh Cistercians*, 2001, pp. 274–75.

388 Ibid. p. 274.

389 TNA, C1/361/66; C4/23/152.

390 TNA, E315/100, f. 194r–v.

391 Williams, *White Monks in Gwent*, 1976, p. 45; TNA, E303/5/96; *Cf.* E326/4660.

392 *FLB*, pp. 1–7 [1–2].

393 TNA, STAC2/6, f. 164.

394 VCH, *County of Lancaster* **2**, 1908, ff. 131–39.

395 TNA, E326/108; Hockey, *Quarr Abbey*, 1970, p. 161.

396 *CHA*, p. 95 [No. 6]; *Cf.* pp. 100 [No. 23]; 101 [No. 27].

397 TNA, LR1/173, f. 131r–v.

398 *LP* 7, p. 207 [No. 520].

399 Ibid. p. 215 [No. 531].

400 *AF*, p. lxix.

401 TNA, C1/602/40.

402 *FOR*, p. 153.

403 TNA, E315/118, f. 226.

404 Williams, 'The Cistercians in West Wales, II: Ceredigion.' In: *AC* **159**, 2010, pp. 269–70.

405 TNA, SC6/HENVIII/7339.

406 Hockey, *Beaulieu*, 1976, p. 169.

407 Williams, *Welsh Church*, 1962, pp. 361–82; *Welsh Cistercians*, 2001, p. 280.

408 TNA, LR1/174, ff. 27–28, 40–41.

409 TNA, E118/1/31, pp. 20 [No. 30], 21 [No. 32], 25v [No. 39].

410 Shropshire Archives, Lease 513/2/9/2/2.

411 TNA, E326/8507.

412 Robinson (2002) 31.

413 TNA, C1/832/17.

414 TNA, E118/1/31, p.44.

415 *PCSC*, p. 175*n.*

416 *VE* **1**, p. 217.

417 Brooking Rowe, J., 'Buckland Abbey.' In: *RTDA* 7, 1875, p. 341.

418 Williams, *Welsh Cistercians*, 2001, p. 78.

419 *LP* **13**, Part 1, p. 283 [No. 750].

420 Staffordshire R.O., 2/32/00, p.46; M.J.C. Fisher, *Dieulacres Abbey*, Leek: Hill Bros. 1969, pp. 56–57.

421 TNA, E315/96, ff. 101v–102r.

422 TNA, LR1/174, ff. 27–28, 41; *FLB*, pp. 46 [No. 37], 49 [No. 51]

423 TNA, C1/656/35.

424 *FLB*, pp. 19–20 [No. 21].

425 J. H. Matthews (ed.), *Records of the County Borough of Cardiff* **1**, 1898, pp. 204–05.

426 Hockey, *Beaulieu*, 1976, p. 169.

427 SSC, DR 18/1/722.

428 Owen, 'Basingwerk,' 1920, p. 58.

429 Hockey, *Beaulieu*, 1976, p. 172.

430 TNA, SC6/HENVIII/7319, f. 8r.

431 Sparks, *In the Shadow of the Blackdowns*, 1978, p. 122.

432 West Devon R.O., 70/139.

433 Devon R.O., 123M/TB35.

434 *VE* **4**, p. 269.

435 TNA, SC6/HENVIII/4903 *passim*.

436 NLW, Chirk Castle Deed, Group F, 12897.

437 TNA, E42/455.

438 Devon R.O., 123M/TB86.

439 Hockey, *Beaulieu*, 1976, p. 172.

440 M. Aveling, 'The Rievaulx Community.' In: *Ampleforth Jnl.*, **57**, 1952, p. 104.

441 C. Cross, 'The Reconstitution of Northern Religious Communities.' In: *NH* **29**, 1993, pp. 200, 203.

442 Watkins, 1994, p. 91.

443 *FLB*, pp. 59–60 [No. 69]:

444 Williams, *White Monks in Gwent*, 1976, p. 23; TNA, SP1/231/24.

445 E. Lhuyd, *Parochialia* (Supplement to *AC*) **3**, 1707, p. 77.

446 TNA, E118/1/132.

447 Fisher, *Dieulacres*, 1969, p. 45.

448 Williams, *Welsh Cistercians*, 2001, p. 282; Owen, 'Basingwerk,' 1920, pp. 54–55, 57–58.

449 TNA, C1/709/20.

450 Williams, *White Monks in Gwent*, 1976, pp. 28–29.

451 TNA, SC6/HENVIII/7319, f. 8r.

452 *MCP*, p. 130 [No. 131].

453 VCH, *County of Essex* **2**, 1907, p. 132.

454 J. H. Bettey, *Suppression of Monasteries in the West Country*, Gloucester: Alan Sutton, 1989, p. 24.

455 *VE* **4**, pp. 98–99.

456 Ibid. p. 34.

457 *VE* **2**, pp. 299, 304, respectively.

458 Ibid. p. 213.

459 *VE* **1**, p. 79.

460 Ibid. p. 217.

461 *VE* **2**, p. 35.

462 *VE* **4**, p. 365.

463 Ibid. p. 370.

7 THE SUPPRESSION AND THEREAFTER

K ING HENRY VIII and his chief minister and vicar-general, Thomas Cromwell, cannot be held entirely blameworthy in the matter of the suppression of all the monasteries and nunneries of England and Wales between 1535 and 1540. There were precedents, both abroad and in this country, made with papal approval, which perhaps suggested to them that they too could do the same. Bishop John Alcock of Ely (1486–1500), an influential prelate who served also as President of the Council of the Marches in Wales, in 1496 dissolved the ancient mid-twelfth century Benedictine St Radegund's nunnery in Cambridge, to convert it into what is now Jesus College. Even the saintly Bishop John Fisher of Rochester (1504–1535) in 1511 closed the Hospital of St John in Cambridge to found the new St John's College there. He did this as her executor to fulfil the wishes of the late Margaret, countess of Richmond. He also closed the Benedictine nunneries of Broomhall in Berkshire and Higham in Kent, so that their income could assist the new college's well-being.[1]

Far more impressive in the eyes of the king must have been the activity of Cardinal Wolsey. Not only archbishop of York and papal legate, but also from 1515 Chancellor of the realm, he closed no less than twenty-nine of the smaller monasteries between 1524 and 1529 in order to realise his two pet projects: the King's School, Ipswich, and Cardinal's College, Oxford (later to become Christchurch).[2] Indeed twenty of the monasteries were closed within a few months, between February and April 1524.[3] None of the houses suppressed were Cistercian, though one, Medmenham, had been included in the original plans.[4] All this was done with the with the support of Clement VII (1524), who permitted Wolsey to close St Frideswide's monastery of Augustinian canons in Oxford to give a site for his college there.[5]

Further papal bulls addressed to Wolsey on November 1528, permitted the closure of monasteries of lesser value and with less than seven religious, and the amalgamation of houses with under twelve religious.[6] None of this excuses the total extinction of monastic life from 1535 onwards, but they were precedents both King and Cromwell felt they could follow. Another scheme, mooted immediately after the Dissolution, was the establishment of a college at Westminster. The resources of the now-closed Swineshead abbey were amongst those ear-marked to provide an endowment for the college. The reference may be to Henry VIII's refoundation of Westminster School in 1540 after the closure of that abbey.[7]

(Sir) Thomas Cromwell, later Earl of Essex

Closely allied with Cardinal Wolsey in his suppression of religious houses was Thomas Cromwell who, after Wolsey fell from grace (1529) and then died from natural causes (1530), helped to fill the void left. An influential figure behind the scenes in Henry VIII's court, in April 1534 he was formally appointed the king's chief minister, and in January 1535 made vicar-general with sweeping powers. Of relatively lowly origins he became a very wealthy man, and a person not so much to be respected as to be feared. Cardinal Gasquet rightly described Cromwell's rule as 'a reign of terror.'[8]

Cromwell in the 1530s amassed a personal fortune by receiving annuities from thirty monasteries, from fees on the election of abbots, and bribes to try to persuade him to give an abbacy to a particular monk or to spare a house from closure. Between 1533 and 1537 Cromwell gained £4,000 in fees of one kind and another.[9] Amongst the sums Cistercian houses paid out in annuities to Cromwell by 1536, undoubtedly in order to keep in his favour, were Furness, Kingswood and Whalley (£6-13-4 apiece), Ford (£5), Merevale and Pipewell (£4 each), Holm Cultram (£3-6-8) and Robertsbridge (£2-13-4).[10] Neath granted an annual sum of £12 as late as 1536, perhaps hoping to escape closure.[11]

Some of these figures represented an increase on an earlier initial grant. Furness (1532) had only awarded an annuity of £4.[12] Pipewell (1531) had promised Cromwell an annuity of only £1-6-8 for 'his good and gratuitous counsel and aid, and for his good-will already shown to us, and to be shown.'[13] The thirty annuities Cromwell gained from Cistercian and other monasteries were, not surprisingly, all confirmed by the Court of Augmentations on 31 October 1539.[14] For Cromwell it was short-lived gain; eight months later he was dead.

The new abbot of Merevale, William Arnold, realised he owed Cromwell money 'for his trouble at the election,' but being hard-pressed only sent

(September 1529) a 'token' of £2-13-4 with the promise of more to come.[15] He was still in debt to Cromwell in the sum of £50, half of which he paid off in January 1532.[16] The abbot of Waverley was recorded in February 1535 as also owing Cromwell £50.[17] Marmaduke Bradley (1536) offered to give Cromwell the huge sum of six hundred marks (£400) immediately after his installation if he gained the abbacy of Fountains.[18] He did become abbot, and presumably paid up to the potential detriment of his monastery's finances. Other would-be abbots offered Cromwell unspecified goodwill if they obtained their desired post.Such offers of bribes were not always successful; Ralph Wilmslow of Vale Royal (1534) was willing to give Cromwell £100 'in hand', if given the abbacy of Vale Royal,[19] whilst Lewis ap Thomas, already abbot of Cwmhir (1535), offered Cromwell £20 if he might have the abbacy of Valle Crucis, his house of profession.[20] When a vacancy occurred at Holm Cultram (1536), Thomas Graham, a leading contender for its abbacy, was willing if chosen to give Cromwell 400 marks.[21] All three offers remained that, for they did not result in the hoped for promotions. The same was true when Abbot Richard ap Rhys of Aberconwy in January 1537 sent Cromwell a gift of £40 in the hope his abbey might continue.[22] His plea fell on deaf ears; two months later it was suppressed.

Cromwell also tried (as had Cardinal Wolsey),[23] and on at least twenty occasions, to advance the fortunes of his friends and acquaintances at monastic expense, by urging superiors and communities to demise to them quite substantial properties. The usual response of an abbot was that the income from a grange desired was necessary for the maintenance of hospitality. This was the case when Cromwell sought a farm of Quarr (December, 1535) for his servant, Mark Lee;[24] Dyxley grange of Garendon (November 1534) for his servant, John Sharpe;[25] and Sutton Grange of Fountains (February 1538) for his servant, William Dale.[26] In a typical reply the abbot of Croxden (January 1533) begged to be excused from Cromwell's request to demise Musden Grange to Francis Meverell, 'as without the grange neither God's service nor hospitality can be maintained. It has not been set to farm for forty years.'[27]

Cromwell did not always listen to such excuses proffered; he was a man to be reckoned with. In August 1538 he wrote a second time to the abbot of Fountains regarding Sutton Grange; the abbot replied that the reasons he had given were 'not an excuse, but unfeigned.'[28] When Cromwell sought Newhouse Grange of Merevale (July 1537) for his nephew, Richard Cromwell, its abbot realised that the community had no option but to submit.[29] Richard

Cromwell also benefited from a Crown lease of Sawtry abbey on its closure.[30] When Cromwell wrote to the abbot of Netley (December 1533) asking for a continuation of the tenancy of Roydon farm for John Cooke, his friend and a servant of the king in the Admiralty, a reply by return was expected.[31]

Seeking Darnhall (the prestigious first site of Vale Royal) for himself, Cromwell ignored letters of excuse sent to him by Abbot Harwood who, feeling pressurised, on 21 March 1538 granted Cromwell the manor, reserving the wood and waters and tithe barn to the monastery.[32] It is as well he did, for four months later Cromwell had himself appointed as Steward of Vale Royal. His appointment was not to take effect until after the death of the then long-term steward, the earl of Shrewsbury, but the fee of £20 was to be paid to Cromwell immediately![33] When Cromwell sought the parsonage of Child's Ercall, Shropshire, from Combermere for his servant, Roger Paddye, the abbot had already demised it to Robert Blount, a nominee of the earl of Shrewsbury who wrote to Cromwell to explain and intercede on the abbot's behalf.[34]

Late Leases and Grants of Annuity

Reluctant as some monasteries were to grant leases to Cromwell's nominees, in the years immediately preceding their closure most monasteries appear to have demised properties to lay-folk on a greater scale than in preceding decades. This it has been suggested allowed abbots 'to provide generously for friends and family,'[35] while the initial down payments provided ready cash to sustain an abbey's economy. There is no direct evidence, but it is quite possible that some monies benefited also the purses of members of the communities. The process was most marked in the case of those abbeys granted in 1536 a stay from closure, as then they had to find heavy payments to the Crown for the privilege of remaining open.

One abbey, which in the space of the ten years between 1527 and its closure in 1536, demised eight of its granges and manors was Swineshead.[36] In rapid succession it gave control to lay tenants of Casthropp manor, Cottgrave grange, North Rauceby Grange, Little Hale Grange, Kymalton Grange, Bolnes Grange and Burton Grange. The periods of demise granted, between forty-one and sixty years, meant that when the Suppression came those lands, but not their income, were lost to the Crown. The income from such rents which the Crown might later receive may not always have reflected the true value of the properties concerned. A monk of Coggeshall, at an enquiry held there in 1536 alleged that Abbot Love, expecting the abbey's properties to pass to the king, had let many lands at less than their true value.[37]

Merevale made a number of leases within the last year of its existence, including one but a month before its closure.[38] One typical lease was that of its Altker grange, made on 19 September 1537 with the tenant amongst other obligations having to pay a £5 annual stipend for the monk serving the grange chapel. The lessee had further to provide a week's hospitality each year to the abbot or his commissary and ten companions coming on visitation. As in like cases (Chapter 6) hunting and pleasure was probably intended, but thirteen months later the monastery closed, and the abbot and his friends no longer had that entitlement![39]

The authorities were not unaware of what was happening. The First Act of Suppression, which came into force with effect from 4 February 1536, provided that all such leases granted within the twelve months prior to the promulgation of the Act were 'utterly void and of none effect.'[40] It was stated in 1547, regarding Strata Marcella, that several tenants possessed 'parcels of the demesne lands of the late abbey', by virtue of leases granted then 'within one year before the Dissolution, contrary to the Statute.'[41] That such demises were made was exemplified when Dore also leased a property 'within the period disallowed by statute'.[42]

Of thirty-nine dated leases granted by Strata Marcella, twenty-nine were from the last abbacy of John ap Rhys (1527–1536). One was of Berriw church (1531) to Nicholas Purcell, burgess and draper of Shrewsbury, in return for a £300 loan.[43] The abbot completed the formalities of another later lease whilst in Ludlow, en route to London to surrender his monastery.[44] Cwmhir mortgaged Gwernygo Grange (1534) to the constable of Clun in recompense of a loan of £112, 'in ready money and other necessaries.'.[45] The need for ready cash was further assisted by writing substantial entry fines into relevant agreements. Whitland's new tenant of Ystlwyf Grange (1538) had to make a down-payment of £40. In each instance of four major late leases made by Strata Florida (1538) the grant was in return for a substantial sum 'beforehand paid.'[46]

Those monasteries which survived the 1536 round of closures found it necessary to further accelerate the rate at which they split up their estates. Byland between 20 August 1538 and 22 November 1538 made thirteen substantial grants or leases, four of them between 20 and 22 November. The monastery was dissolved a week later on 30 November. Oldstead Grange and lands at its first site, Old Byland, were amongst the properties demised.[47] From 1481 to 1535, Buckfast made only twenty-five major transactions regarding land, but there were fifty-three cases of alienations, leases and grants, between January and February 1539, its very last year.[48]

Of twenty-three individual leases recorded by Robertsbridge between March 1529 and December 1538, ten were made between January 1537 and December 1539.[49] Other abbeys where the same process can be exemplified included Biddlesden,[50] Dunkeswell[51] and Kirkstall.[52] In Wales, where Neath, Strata Florida and Whitland all participated in the same process,[53] the reason was spelt out in a grant by Whitland: the money was needed 'towards the 1,000 marks sterling [due] to the king for the redemption of the house.'[54] The earl of Essex (1576) who eventually gained the lands of Whitland found that he could make no profit out of them, because the abbot before the dissolution had demised them out for ninety-nine years'. The abbot had used to confirm certain leases the seal of the friars of Carmarthen, probably because his own monastery's common seal had been confiscated by the earlier visitation commissioners.[55]

At Fountains twenty-seven leases were made during the course of 1538, compared to only twenty-six in the ten-year abbacy of William Thirsk (1525–1536).[56] Abbot Bradley of Fountains, examined in London in January 1541, asserted that its late leases were made without thought of fraud, 'without covyn', but did admit that the imminence of dissolution had played a part. He said that at Christmas 1538 he and his monks 'were in fear of dissolution of the monastery, by cause thereof they made divers leases.'[57] Abbot Wilkins of Hulton, which closed on 23 September 1538, was summoned that November to the Court of Augmentations to explain some of the leases made during his short term of office which only commenced in 1536. He admitted that a grant of a two hundred acre pasture (that of Mixon Hay) had been made to the abbey's steward, Sir Philip Draycot, in anticipation of imminent dissolution of the monastery. It was granted he said 'at such time as the voice went in the country in the 27th year of our sovereign lord that divers religious houses could be suppressed.' The pasture had been demised for sixty years at a rental of £4; the Court gave Draycot a new lease, but only for twenty-one years and at an increased rental.[58]

Various alleged irregularities were reported in the making of some last-minute demises of land. Abbot Whitney of Dieulacres towards the end of 1537 allegedly sealed several blank deeds with the abbey's common seal. A few days *after* its dissolution, when he had no right to do so, he ante-dated these thus granting lands to various friends and former servants of the monastery.[59] At an enquiry held in 1582 a former monk of Newenham, John Roper, told how after its suppression Abbot Gill 'used often to come and bother me to agree to the making and sealing of lands of the monastery.' He refused, and said that the abbot and his servants patched up and glued together an old latten seal—for the abbey 's new silver seal had been confiscated, 'after which they proceeded to work.'[60]

Mis-use of seals was also alleged at Strata Florida. At an investigation held at Rhayader in 1542, Matthew Lewis of London, claiming the abbey's Aberdihonw Grange, complained that *after* the abbey closed Abbot Talley used a counterfeit seal, 'like the convent seal,' to demise the property to one Hugh Lewis. Hugh rejoined that the lease was made 'long before the dissolution' in return for a payment of £100.[61] A lease, allegedly made by Strata Florida in 1509 was queried around 1580 because the seal was the new seal made after the restoration of the abbey in 1537.[62] It is clear that, even after their houses had closed, a few superiors used unorthodox means to benefit their friends.

In addition to demising lands, monasteries commonly also made more grants of non-residential *annuities* than in previous years. The recipients might be family members of an abbot—as in the instance of Nicholas (1536) and Geoffrey Whitney (1537) at Dieulacres,[63] or personal friends—like Nicholas Fersay (1538) whom the abbot of Byland had baptised.[64] There may have been a genuine effort to ensure that loyal servants had some income to fall back upon when a monastery closed. This may have been the case for Thomas Dyke and Thomas Taston (1538) at Beaulieu, who at its suppression could have lost their livelihood.[65] It has been suggested that at Pipewell the community was cajoled into granting annuities at the last minute to Cromwell's officers, as well as to their servants and friends: that abbey gave no less than seventeen late annuities, including that to Edward Montagu, an influential lawyer and later to be knighted and become chief justice of the King's Bench.[66]

Many annuities may well have been granted, like that by Byland (1528) to Thomas Smythe, priest, in return for 'a certain sum of money aforepaid.'[67] John Dorman (1537) received annuities from Strata Florida for 'great liberalities' shown it,[68] and from Whitland 'for a certain pecuniary service.'[69] Such financial favours may well been masked in the reasons generally given for an award of annuity. One most common alleged causes of an annuity were 'in consideration of good and faithful service before this time.' Such terminology applied to annuities made to twelve persons by Byland in 1538.[70] Another vague reason proffered for grant of annuity was for 'good advice' or 'good counsel' rendered to a monastery, as when Swineshead (1532) allowed Anthony Irby a mark yearly.[71]

Where legal officers were concerned, there may have been justification for an award. Strata Florida awarded Maurice ap David its attorney, £1 (from 1533), and Gruffydd Leyson, 'doctor of laws', £1-6-8 (from 1538).[72] Pipewell allowed £2 p.a. to David Clapham, LL.B. (also from 1538).[73] The annuities several houses paid to Thomas Cromwell have been noted, and paid out of fear rather than real respect. The same was perhaps true of the considerable annual sum of £40 promised by Fountains (1537) to Dr William Petre, one of Cromwell's visitors,[74] and of the £16-13-4 p.a. guaranteed by Holm Cultram (1536) to Thomas Legh, one of the suppression commissioners.[75] From Kingswood, Richard Cromwell (Cromwell's nephew) and John Gostwicke (one of the judges who later sentenced the abbot of Woburn to death), each received a £2 annuity.[76] Richard Cromwell also claimed £4-8-4 for his expenses when involved in the surrender of Tilty.[77]

Most annuities were much more modest. Fountains (1538) granted Henry Audley, gent., £5 p.a. for 'good counsel before this time';[78] £4 annually was allowed by Basingwerk (1534) to Sir John Donne 'for favours and friendship shown,'[79] and by Whitland (1537) to John Prescott for 'various causes and considerations.'[80] John Aylworth received an annuity of £2-13-4 from Buckfast (1537) for 'good and laudable counsel;'[81] Nicholas Fersay received the same sum from Byland (1538) 'for good offices shown to the abbey by his father and progenitors'.[82] Tintern (1535) awarded Edmund Turner £2 for certain good turns in time of need.'[83] The value of an annuity might have been lessened by any expense in collecting it. Richard Hall, an annuitant of Netley in Hampshire, acknowledged his payment of £4 in 1508, 'between the hours of seven and eleven in the morning, in the church of St. Paul's, London, before the image of Holy Cross, at the north door.'[84]

Some of the individual annuities granted may not appear great, but a sum of £5 awarded in 1538 would be equivalent nowadays to at least £1500. Some abbeys granted a number of annuities, which, added up, formed a burden on their finances. Kirkstall awarded fifty-one annuities, in total they amounted to £58, which was over one-sixth of the abbey's net value.[85] Those granted by Kingswood totalled £33, about one-tenth of its gross income.[86] Abbot Dunne of Buckfast in the two years preceding its closure in 1539 granted new fees and annuities totalling £70.[87] Between May 1537 and August 1539, Fountains made thirty such grants, one of them at the behest of the earl of Northumberland.[88] The last abbot, Roger Pyle, of Furness, found it difficult to pay all the annuities promised by predecessor, Alexander Bank, but he had pragmatically no choice but to make further grants, including £10 to the duke of Suffolk, and £6-13-4 to the earl of Wiltshire (Anne Boleyn's father) by royal command.[89]

The lateness of many of these awards of annuity was looked upon with disfavour by the Court of Augmentations when, after the closure of the monasteries, the recipients sought their continuance. They formed, after all, a drain on the revenues which the Crown might otherwise have expected. The annuities given by Fountains (1537; £1-6-8) to John Brodbeld 'for good favour and service,'[90] by Kirkstall (1538; £1-13-4) to John Cootes 'for good service';[91] by Strata Florida (1537, £2) to John Gwyn and John Lloyd, and (in 1538, £1-6-8) to Richard Greneway and John Dorman;[92] by Vale Royal (1536; £2) to Dr Adam Beckensall for 'good counsel, help and usefulness',[93] and by Warden (1536; £6-13-4) to Anthony Rous 'for good counsel',[94] were amongst a number disallowed by the Court saying that their claims were 'void and of none effect' and had 'no vigour in law.' Where a recipient had made a cash down-payment for his annuity, he stood at a perhaps substantial loss. The only softening of such a blow was that arrears were paid up.

Mechanics of the Dissolution

In September 1534 Parliament passed the First Fruits and Tenths Act, which provided for the Crown to receive one-tenth of the net income of all ecclesiastical bodies. The result was a survey of the assets and outgoings of all dioceses, monasteries and parishes, mostly completed by May 1535. It also enabled the Crown to distinguish between monasteries with greater or lesser income. The survey, known as the *Valor Ecclesiasticus*, was largely carried out on the basis of returns submitted by the ecclesiastical bodies themselves (Chapter 6).

In January 1535 Thomas Cromwell was appointed vicar-general with sweeping powers. Following the publication of the *Valor* he appointed commissaries to visit and inspect the monasteries of England and Wales, and to report back as to their economic and spiritual state.[95] By and large the visitors gave a very poor impression of current monastic life. In part, this may have been justified, but as some of the commissioners were autocratic and self-seeking, relied in part on hearsay evidence and completed their task in rapid time, there must be grave doubt as to the validity of some of the conclusions they reached.

Chiefest amongst the Crown visitors of the monasteries in 1535/1536 and thereafter numbered amongst the suppression commissioners were Doctors Layton and Legh. Richard Layton, born about 1498, a cleric of northern extraction and holding an Oxford doctorate in civil law, was very much a pluralist, being by 1534 archdeacon of Buckingham and a clerk of the privy council. A servant of Wolsey and later a trusted emissary of Cromwell, he willingly fulfilled his role especially in the visitation of the northern monasteries. In his mid-thirties he can best be described as a young bully with little regard for the truth. Later becoming dean of York, he died of natural causes in 1544.[96]

It was Layton who, visiting Waverley on 25 September 1536, wrote to Cromwell to complain of the lack of respect there for the abbot by the servants. He emphasised how 'in the morning, sitting in my chamber in examination, I could get neither bread, drink nor fire, of these knaves until I was fretished.' The abbot was an honest man but 'durst not speak to them', Layton wrote, and he said that among the monks was to be found 'corruption of the worst sort, because they dwell in the forest [away] from all company.[97]

Thomas Legh, of similar age and with a Cambridge degree, was both an ecclesiastical lawyer and diplomat. Working at first in the Midlands, he was attended by John ap Rice, registrar-general in ecclesiastical causes and later a visitor in his own right, who bravely reported Legh to Cromwell as 'insolent and pompous', telling how he 'handleth the fathers where he cometh very roughly,' and criticising the excessive fees Legh charged. He saw Legh as 'young and of intolerable elation.' He told that after the election at Vale Royal he expected not only a £15 fee from the abbey, but also £6 costs and a 'reward.' He also told how Legh would have a retinue of twelve liveried attendants, and how he had abused an abbot for not being prepared to receive him although he had not received warning of his visit.[98] Cromwell remonstrated with Legh, who replied with an aggrieved letter saying that 'as touching my triumphant and sumptuous usage and gay apparel, I used myself no otherwise than I did before.'[99] Together with Layton, Legh visited over 120 monasteries and collegiate establishments in the province of York between December 1535 and the end of February 1536. This speed cannot have permitted a true assessment of current religious life.[100] It was one of the demands made by the leaders of the Pilgrimage of Grace in December 1536 that Layton and Legh be punished for the financial extortions of sums like £20 and more taken from the monasteries during the course of their visitations.[101] The same haste was exercised by Layton when, after accepting the surrender of Kirkstall on 22 November 1539, he dissolved St Mary's Abbey, York, and the nunneries of Arthington and Kirklees within seven days. Legh within a week dissolved not only Fountains and Hampole nunnery, but also Nostell and Pontefract priories.[102]

Other visitors involved in Cromwell's survey included Thomas Bedyll, B. Cn. L, a pluralist with many rectories who continued to harry the Carthusians and inspected houses in East Anglia.[103] The young William Petre, 'a doctor in both laws' was efficient and fair, 'avoiding the unsavoury reputation' of his fellow commissioners, but 'used his position to amass a substantial landholding,' mainly in his native Devon and in Essex.[104] John Tregonwell, D.C.L., a Cornish-man and much in the king's service visited monasteries in Somerset and Devon and south Lincolnshire.[105] He sought an abbey for himself, and had his eyes set on Bindon, Bruern or Cleeve,[106] but gained instead Milton Abbey. Tregonwell had an eye to his own needs and, amongst others, extracted a pension of £2 from Ford in its very last days.[107] In his suppression duties he became very wealthy and was able to pay the £1,000 required for Milton Abbey and its estates.[108] The surrenders of Ford and Newenham were taken on the same day, 8 March 1539: Ford by Wiliam Petre, Newenham by John Tregonwell.[109]

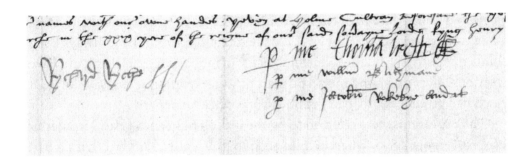

Fig. 12: Signatures of Officers of the Court of Augmentations,
appended to a pension warrant for John Jackson, monk of Holm Cultram, 16 March
1538.
(The National Archives, TNA: PRO. E314/77)
(The signatories are Sir Richard Riche, Chancellor; Dr Thomas Legh, a Suppression
Visitor; William Blithman, Particular Receiver for Yorkshire and Cumbria; James
Rokeby, Auditor.)

When Tregonwell closed Dunkeswell he came with a large retinue of horsemen to make sure the monks made no resistance. In south Wales, Dr John Vaughan, a Visitor in south Wales, wrote to Cromwell saying, 'help me to get one of the abbies.' He was granted the small house of Grace Dieu, but later the more prestigious monastery at Whitland. Vaughan also indicated the hurried nature of this visitation, and the tendency to listen to hearsay evidence. He added in his letter, 'I hear by the common people that the houses of Wales, also Tintern, are greatly abused, and have transgressed the king's injunctions.'[110] Certainly he, as well as Layton and Legh, had their minds made up even before they reached the monasteries. In Glamorgan and western Monmouthshire several commissioners were appointed, but most of the work was done by Sir William Morgan of Tredegar.[111] The commissioners in north Wales were led by William Stumpe, a justice of the peace and clothier from Malmesbury, Wiltshire. He received a lease of Aberconwy's Quirt (Court) Grange, but also Malmesbury Abbey itself, part of which he converted into a textile mill.[112]

The Crown visitors of 1535/1536 were furnished with a set of eighty-six articles of enquiry and twenty-five injunctions.. The commissioners paid particular attention in their reports to the morality or otherwise of some of the monks (Chapter 2, and also drew attention to the presence of relics of one kind or another in numerous monasteries (Chapter 4). Two prescriptions were not welcome to many, as all monks under the age of twenty-five or professed under the age of twenty, as well as all novices and postulants, were to be told to leave their abbey.[113] This regulation may not have always been fulfilled too strictly, but the Newminster list of monks suggests that it did have a serious effect on young monastic man-power. So does the mention that Dr Legh had given leave to 'half the house of Sawtry' to depart.[114]

The expulsions were referred to by the bishop of Faenza (Italy) in a letter of 3 November 1535, when he told seemingly a Vatican official that he had heard from England that Cromwell was 'visiting all the monasteries and driving out those under twenty-four years of age.'[115] The fate of the young men (and women) concerned is not on record. This age limit was a source of disagreement and of different practice amongst the Visitors. This is evident from the letter sent by John ap Rice to Cromwell in October 1535 saying that Legh 'does not follow your instructions, for whereas you ordered that all of both sexes between twenty-two and twenty-four might go abroad, he only allows that liberty to religious men. He has inserted a clause in his injunctions that all of any age may go abroad.' Eventually Cromwell decided that no one over the age of twenty should be compelled to go.[116]

The second unwelcome injunction was that from henceforth all monks were to be strictly enclosed; this was in tune with the early spirit of the Order, but not with the times, and it proved to be a hindrance. The monks of Warden chafed at this restriction, and blamed Abbot Emery as much as they did Dr Legh.[117] Abbot Chard of Ford begged Cromwell (in October 1535) for exemption for his monks from this rule. He himself could not travel far, and needed the facility to send monks out on business, for 'this is indispensable to the weal of our monastery.'[118] The following month Abbot Dovell of Cleeve wrote in like terms. Dr Tregonwell, he said, 'had commanded me and all my convent to keep within the precincts of our monastery.' This rule meant he wrote that the abbey could not be properly provisioned nor hospitality maintained. Further, he himself would be unable to preach within the diocese of Bath and Wells, as he was licensed to do.[119] Sir William Parre (11 November 1535) told Cromwell that the monks of Pipewell 'cannot now have access to make necessary provision for their house,' and sought a dispensation for the abbey.[120]

Parliament decreed in the spring of 1536 that those monasteries with a net income of under £200, were to be dissolved [£200 then was equivalent to perhaps £70,000 or more to day].[121] Thirty-five Cistercian monasteries were thus valued.[122] Even before the Parliament closed, on or about 1 April 1536, a new body was established to handle all matters relating to the forthcoming suppression of the lesser monasteries. That body was termed the Court of Augmentations of the Revenue of the Crown; its Chancellor was Sir Richard Riche, on a salary of £300 per year; and it had officers appointed for each region of the realm, headed by a Receiver and an Auditor, with warrants of appointment issued on the very day the Parliament closed. Their duties were manifold because whilst by the Act of Suppression the Crown took over the assets of each monastery, it also became responsible for the satisfaction of its debts.

The decision of Parliament meant a further visitation of all those abbeys meant for immediate closure. The responsibility for this new assessment lay with the Receiver and Auditor for each region appointed by the Court, with members of the local gentry co-opted on to the teams of investigators.[123] The commissioners now were required to 'survey' the state of each monastery—its income and debts, the number of religious—and whether any wish to leave the monastic life, the number of servants and corrodians, the value of the house and its possessions—the extent of woodland being particularly noted, and the value of other assets such as the bells and lead on the buildings.[124]

In the interval between the time of 'survey' and the actual date of closure the monasteries could no longer conduct any business as a corporate body and had to keep a careful note of all expenditure. The seals of each monastery were to be broken or kept safely to the King's use, so that no abbot could conduct any business.[125] Few Cistercians indicated any desire to leave the monastic life; at Stoneleigh, for instance, all wished 'to continue or be transferred' to other houses.[126] Likewise at Garendon all the monks were 'of good conversation, and God's service well maintained, all desire to continue or be assigned to some other house.'[127]

On the day of 'survey' the abbeys were effectively taken into the king's hands, and then left in a state of suspended animation for weeks or even months. The monks of Margam kept a book of accounts for this period which told of payments to twenty-seven people, totalling £33, including a launderer and the keeper of Briton Ferry. A further twenty-seven pounds was expended on essentials such as food, beer and the hospice.[128] The like accounts for Cwmhir noted precisely the 'twenty-four weeks and five days' of its suspension.[129] The detailed accounts of James More, the sub-cellarer and kitchener of Whalley, relate to this period suggesting its 'survey' was on 30/31 December 1536, and its dissolution on or close to 24 March 1537.[130] When the abbey closed a number of suppliers of foodstuffs remained unpaid.

In the accounts of Buildwas the initial date of 'survey' was referred to as the day of 'dissolution;' as opposed to the date of its actual closure, seen as the date of 'suppression.'[131] At Garendon the expenses of the house during this period amounted to £7-12-0, and the loss or decline in value of its goods came to £7-17-0, including £2-8-3 being the price set upon those animals which died from murrain.[132] At Stoneleigh the maintenance of its nine monks in this interval came only to £3-13-4, but the wages and upkeep of forty-five servants totalled £27-0-6. £8-6-8 was to be written off from the loss and spoliation of goods and the loss of animals from disease.[133]

At this stage a few abbeys tried to obtain the continuance of their house. In February 1536 Abbot Austen of Rewley wrote to Cromwell offering him £100 if his monastery could be spared even though converted into a college. His appeal was unavailing; his abbey closed later that year.[134] Later, an undated letter from Abbot Sagar of Hailes (perhaps in 1539) expressed a like desire for his monastery to continue as a college, but his hopes also fell on deaf ears.[135] Indeed, the Commissioner for the West, headed by Richard Southwell, found when he closed Hailes that it was out of debt and so well attended to as though the abbot 'looked for [expected] no alteration of his house.'[136] There were plans for Fountains to become a fully fledged cathedral establishment, but these were never consummated.[137] When Whalley fell in 1537 by attainder, Henry VIII thought of a new establishment there 'as shall be meet for the honour of God, our surety and the benefit of the county', but nothing happened.[138]

On 9 June 1536 the abbot of Waverley pleaded with Cromwell 'to help the preservation of this poor monastery, in the service of God, and to pray for the estate of our prince and your mastership.' Again it was not to be; six weeks later Waverley had closed.[139] In January 1537 Sir Thomas Arundell, the king's receiver, riding to Cornwall passed by Cleeve abbey in Somerset. He heard 'such lamentation for the dissolution thereof, and a bruit in the country', and passed on the wishes to Cromwell of 'the honest gentlemen of that quarter that the house may stand'. He referred to its 'seventeen priests of honest life who keep hospitality', to an earlier underestimate of its value, and to the the willingness of the house to give the King 1,000 marks for exemption from closure, but the abbey was suppressed that spring.[140]

Abbot Richard of Aberconwy in 1536 offered Cromwell an annuity if his house was spared, 'by a provision of this Parliament or a special licence from the king.' In January 1537 he sent Cromwell a gift, effectively a bribe, of £40, and promised him daily prayers 'as for a founder of this house.' His impassioned pleas fell on deaf ears; within two months Aberconwy was no more.[141] Another abbot reluctant to admit defeat was Abbot Harwood of Vale Royal. In an undated letter he protested to Cromwell that 'we never consented to surrender, and never will unless the King commands it. We trust your Lordship will be a means to His Grace that we may continue.' It did not.[142] It has been suggested that Harwood's signature on Vale Royal's surrender deed of 7 September 1538 was a forgery.[143]

On 6 July 1538 Sir William Parre transmitted to Cromwell the offer from the abbot of Pipewell of £200 that his abbey might stand. Parre pointed out that the monastery relieved 'the poor people for a great compass about by their hospitality and charitable deeds'. Parre wrote again, in September, to say that the monastery was now ready to surrender, requested pensions for the abbot and community for 'they used themselves like honest men', and successfully sought the site for himself. It closed that November.[144] Earlier on

7 April 1538 the duke of Norfolk sought the continuance of Byland, saying that 'no house in these parts is more charged with hospitality'; it did endure, but only for a further eight months.[145]

Especially in the second wave of closures, abbots reluctant to surrender their houses were summoned to London to appear before Cromwell or one of his officials. This must have been a frightening experience, and it was designed to bring pressure to bear upon them.[146] The abbot of Byland was 'repairing to Cromwell' in April 1538,[147] the abbot of Hulton somewhat later.[148] In May that year, the abbot of Combermere was summoned to London to surrender his monastery, he hoped that it might continue, and took with him to this effect a commendatory letter from Bishop Rowland Lee, President of the Council of the Welsh Marches, but to no effect: Combermere was dissolved on 27 July 1538.[149] It could be that Abbot Massey hoped that, despite dissolution, his community might survive for on 10 May he had written to Cromwell hoping that 'I and my poor brethren may continue in the monastery as his grace's true bedesmen and daily orators.'[150] It was not to be.

This hope of continuance, even when all must have seemed lost, was expressed before his martyrdom by Abbot Hobbes of Woburn when he said: 'surely brethren, there will come over us a good man that will re-edify those monasteries that are now suppressed'.[151] Some of the late leases issued by monasteries had a clause stating that they would be invalid should the monastery in fact survive. This was true at its mother-house of Dore which leased a property 'within the period disallowed by statute', on condition that should the monastery 'stand still' (*i.e:* not be closed), then the lease was to be surrendered.[152]

Abbot Harwood of Vale Royal rode to London personally to see Cromwell, following attempts by Thomas Holcroft, one of the king's commissioners and from 1538 crown receiver for Lancashire and Cheshire, to assert that he had dissolved the abbey on 7 September 1538. Holcroft prepared a list of eight questions to be put to the abbot, including charges of demising most of his demesne and felling over 5,000 oaks, and of asking for the sealing of an *ante*-dated lease to Sir William Brereton. On 31 March 1539, Cromwell (its Steward-in-waiting) personally held a court at Vale Royal at which the abbot was charged of complicity in the death of a monk, of dissuading a tenant from fighting against the rebels in the Northern Rising, and on account of one of his vicars refusing to marry a couple upon a licence obtained from the King as supreme head of the Church. Harwood was adjudged guilty, but received an annual pension of £60. It was a ruse to declare the abbey forfeit.[153]

Abbot Sagar of Hailes (1539) was another summoned to London, where he made a 'privy surrender' of his abbey; the monks signing the suppression deed on his return. The commissioners praised him for surrendering his house 'with such discreet and frank manner', but Dr Layton [in London] bound him over in a recognizance of £500 not to alienate any monastic property.[154] An abbot who declined to surrender his house was Oliver Adams, abbot of Combe from 1513. The consequence was that he was made to resign, and his place was taken by Robert Kynvar, B.D., who did yield up the house in January 1539. Dr London, the commissioner, noted that 'he surrendered the house the same day twelve month [that] he was made master and left it in a competent state.'[155]

That there was an element of coercion is apparent from a letter (3 June 1538) written by Sir John Neville, a member of the Council of the North, saying 'the abbot of Roche is come up, so Lee [Dr Legh] can use him as he thinks best.' The abbey closed three weeks later[156] There was a degree of fear: Abbot Pyle of Furness had been summoned to Whalley abbey by the commissioners, where on 5 April 1537, he consented to his monastery's closure. He had no room for manoeuvre, the body of its abbot was still perhaps hanging at Whalley's gate, and he would not have wished to suffer the same fate. He returned to Furness with Richard Southwell and two other commissioners, and there on Monday 9 April 1537, thirty-three monks signed the deed of surrender.[157]

There were inducements too: Abbot John Dey of Bordesley (20 May 1538), aged and infirm, wrote to Cromwell telling him that 'Master Evance came to day and persuaded me to surrender the monastery, assuring me a competent portion for life, with the grange of Bydford to dwell in.'[158] Dey had later to be told by Evance that he was 'not to meddle', for after his submission abbey crops had been sold, woodland felled and household implements purloined—all this to the loss of profit for the Crown.[159] About ten Cistercian monasteries valued at under £200 did survive, on payment of heavy fines. They included Bindon, which by Michaelmas 1538 had paid the Crown £300, Croxden (£100), Hulton (£66-13-4),[160] Neath (£150), Strata Florida (£66-13-4) and Whitland (£400). These sums beggared the abbeys concerned as they had to split up their estates and make late leases in return for substantial financial return.[161] Indeed the commissary John ap Rice said of Abbot Lleision of Neath, that he had 'dangered himself and his friends very far with the redemption of his house.'[162]

In all these instances the abbey concerned was technically dissolved and then refounded, with the outgoing abbot re-appointed by the Crown, not elected by his community. Letters patent were issued to this effect, like those reinstating John Norman as abbot of Bindon.[163] Thomas Chalner at Croxden,[164] and Edward Wilkins at Hulton.[165] Neath was to remain 'in pristino statu' (30 January 1537); in the case of Strata Florida, Henry VIII consented to 'erect and renew the abbey for ever' (25 April 1537), Whitland was formally re-founded 'by the king's restitution' (25 April 1537).[166] The large sums of money had been levied from them under false pretences, for two years on all these four monasteries, as others, had closed.

At Sibton it has been suggested that Abbot Flatbury was installed through the influence of the duke of Norfolk in order to bring about a quick submission of the house, even though its net income was £246. On 31 July 1536 Sibton sold out to the duke of Norfolk, who henceforth paid the abbot and monks an annual pension, and this arrangement was confirmed by Act of Parliament in 1539. The sale comprised 'all the site, ambit and precinct' of the monastery, with all its buildings and all its manors and churches[167] The sale was not to the liking of Sir Arthur Hopton of Yoxford, Suffolk, frequently in royal service, because as he later asserted to the Court of Chancery he had on 20 April 1536 been promised the sale at the forthcoming Michaelmas. Flatbury, he said, was no longer abbot and had taken from him a great deal of money.[168] The outcome is unknown, but in 1539 Hopton was granted the suppressed priory of Blytheburgh.

In a similar arrangement Revesby agreed in January 1538 to hand over all its properties, evidences and charters, to its Steward, Charles Brandon, duke of Suffolk, in return for his paying off a debt due of £369 to the king, as well as 'great sums of money' owed to other people. He also consented to give the abbot and monks generous annual pensions. Two months later the community was still in residence when Crown commissioners came, around 24 March, to accept its surrender. Whether the monks still received the promised pensions is unknown, but the duke, a favourite brother-in-law, of Henry VIII, was granted the monastery.[169] In the Welsh border Strata Marcella was later said to have been sold to Lord Powis by its community 'before the making of the Act.' The abbot's reward was presentation by the peer (as early as 13

March 1536) to a portion in Pontesbury church, Salop. He had left the monastery before its dissolution..[170]

Thirty-seven Cistercian abbeys, almost exactly half, were closed in the first wave of suppressions, commencing perhaps with Calder in February 1536. The precise dates of dissolution are not all on record, but some abbeys, like Cleeve, Newminster and Whalley, survived into the spring of 1537. A few, like Jervaulx in June 1537, fell by attainder. Despite monies paid and leave of continuance granted, the remaining thirty-seven monasteries closed mostly during the course of 1538 and 1539. George Rolle, Steward of Dunkeswell abbey and an officer of the Court of Common Pleas, was able to write to Lord Lisle that 'the abbeys go down as fast as they may.'[171] Boxley was the first abbey to fall—on 29 January 1538, Hailes the last, on Christmas Eve, 1539. A seventy-fifth monastery, Rushen on the Isle of Man, survived until 24 June 1540. Speed was again of the essence; in mid-September 1538 Thomas Legh closed down four monasteries in five days, including Croxden and Hulton.[172]

On 24 June 1536, Henry VIII issued a set of instructions concerning the closure of the monasteries.[173] In preparation for the day of dissolution, the commissioners were to appoint pensions for the abbots, and give to them and each monk a 'convenient reward' to help them on their way. The individual religious in the first wave of closure were not granted annual pensions but, if they did not wish to transfer to another monastery, the commissioners were to arrange for them to be issued free of charge with a 'capacity' allowing them to adopt secular clergy habit and seek a clerical living.

A careful inventory was to be made, not only of landed possessions and stock, but also of all household effects and any stores of corn and grain: such was the 'book of survey' drawn up at Boxley [1 February 1538] by Walter Hendle and his fellow commissioners.[174] A sale of these goods was to be held, but the lead, bells and plate were reserved to the Crown. All servants' wages and outstanding debts were to be paid by the commissioners, and they were to deliver each site to those whom the King wished.[175]

The detailed inventory made at Tilty on the effective day of suppression (3 March 1536) by Richard Cromwell and John Milsent, and counter-signed by Abbot John Palmer, told not only of the vestments in the church, but also of the furniture in the 'convent parlour', the utensils in the kitchen, the hangings of red say in the abbot's dining chamber and of painted cloth in the guest chamber, and the contents of the larder and the brew-house (*Chapter 1*). Two copies of the inventory were made, the names of Richard Cromwell and John Milsent, the commissioners, being subscribed to the one part, that of the outgoing abbot, John Palmer, to the other.[176]

A whole series of deeds of surrender exist for the Cistercian abbeys of England, generally bearing the signatures of their abbots and monks, and attested by the relevant commissioners. Dr William Petre signed in the case of Roche (23 June 1538), describing himself as 'one of the clerks of chancery of the King', as did John Tregonwell at the suppression of Dunkeswell (14 February 1538).[177] The formula is constant, and the deeds were clearly prepared in advance and brought with the officials. It would have been for the communities the last time they met in their chapter-house before being dispersed into the world. Stratford was closed, sadly, on St Benedict's Day (21 March) in 1539.[178]

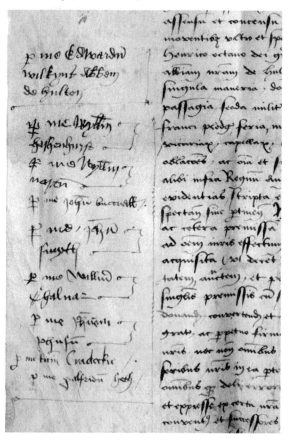

Fig. 13: Signatures of the Monks of Hulton on their Suppression Deed,
18 September 1538
(The National Archives, TNA: PRO. E322/106)

The monks of Biddlesden must have hidden their true feelings when in their deed of closure, of 25 September 1538 and couched unusually in English rather than Latin, they said that they surrendered their abbey 'profoundly considering the manner and trade of living which we have practised and used many days, [that] doth most primarily consist in dumb ceremonies.' Clearly prepared for their signatures in advance, the deed also had the monks acknowledging 'such discord of living and abuses as now have been found to have reigned amongst us,' and that they had now 'happily discovered by the study of the gospel that it was most expedient for them to be ruled by their Supreme Head the king.' Had any of the monks of Biddlesden been minded not to sign that deed, they would have been well aware of the fate which would await them![179]

The suppression deed of Coggeshall, dated 5 February 1538, now held *in commendam* by Abbot More of St Mary Graces, bears no signatures whatsoever, simply a notary's mark and a fine seal. It perhaps never even arrived at Coggeshall.[180] Sir Thomas Seymour was instructed to pay Abbot More the great sum of £340, 'in compensation of charges sustained by him for the house of Coggeshall before and since the suppression, and for debts for which the monastery of Tower Hill stands bound.'[181]

When Dr London came to suppress Combe (21 January 1539) he was informed by John Harford, sheriff of Coventry that year, that Abbot Kynvar of Combe had hidden £500 in a feather bed in his brother's house. London searched the bed but found only £25, and accepted the abbot's explanation that the money was placed there against certain debts due at Candlemas, and because he did not trust his servants. Dr London was concerned for the security of the abbey in the days immediately following its closure, and so wrote to Cromwell asking him 'to stay spoil, and for the safeguard of evidences, let the surveyors come as speedily after me as may be.'[182]

The surrender of Holm Cultram on 6 March 1538 was received by three commissioners: Thomas Legh, LL.D., described by the monarch as 'our trusty servant', William Blitheman, Receiver of the lands of suppressed houses in the county of York, and James Rokeby as auditor. They were 'with all convenient speed repairing to the monastery to take and receive of the abbot such sufficient writing under their convent seal as shall be expedient for the surrender.' Before the dissolution, with the abbot and brethren, they were to make 'a substantial and perfect inventory of all the lands, rents and farms belonging to the monastery, and take into their hands all jewels, plates, goods and cattle with the lead and all other things … and the same to utter and sell either for ready money or money to be paid at days as ye shall think best … with the money to satisfy and content all debts and other things which ye shall find.' The sale made here amounted to £941, half of this was accounted for by the value of the lead, and the outgoings of the house in annuities, debts, pensions and various costs– amounting to £594, greatly reduced this impressive figure.[183]

On 23 August 1538, John Scudamore, Auditor and Receiver of suppressed monasteries in four counties: Herefordshire, Shropshire, Staffordshire and Worcestershire, received like instructions as to his duties.[184] Doubtless the Particular Receivers of other counties were issued with a document couched in like terms. Scudamore was to examine the clear yearly value of each monastery, by deducting from the gross income all fees and other outgoings payable, but 'leaving the final determination to the king's court of Augmentations.' He was also to receive the accounts of all bailiffs of the lands of suppressed monasteries and others when suppressed. He was by his 'discreet wisdom' to sell all the bells of the closed abbeys as well as superfluous houses and buildings. Finally, he was given instructions as to the disposal of lead.

The Fate of the Monks

Generally speaking immediately a house was dissolved the monks were sent on their way. In later years, one who was a local boy at the time, told how the commissioners came to Roche abbey [23 June 1538] without notice, so that the monks could not convey away goods to help them when they were expelled. The former eye-witness wrote that 'the visitors took their dinner with them, and then turned them forth.'[185] Rather sad!

Sometimes there was a short period of grace. When Boxley was 'surveyed' and its goods valued in early February 1537, the commissioners wrote to Cromwell asking how long the monks should remain there.[186] Holm Cultram surrendered formally on 6 March 1538, but it was not until 18 March that Dr Legh could write to Cromwell saying, 'the monastery of Holm is quietly dissolved, and the monks, in secular apparel, having honest rewards in their purses are dispersed.'[187] Tilty was formally closed on 3 March 1536, but 'the late abbot and his five brethren were to remain in the abbey till the King's further pleasure.'[188] It was in the very early stages of monastic closures; could

Henry VIII have been considering putting the abbey to another use? For the time being Abbot Palmer's five servants, as well as his mother and two 'impotent persons' were to continue to find their home there.

Especially in the earlier wave of suppressions, monks of a house being dissolved were given the option of transferring to other as yet undissolved monasteries. Most of the monks of Cleeve, for example, found new homes in abbeys not too far distant: John Benet, John Gaye and John Webbe—by now elderly, moved to Dunkeswell; John Baker went to Newenham, whilst Thomas Orchard moved to either Kingswood or Stanley. Two of Cleeve's monks may have moved well before the suppression: Richard London might possibly be the monk of that name at Strata Marcella in 1525, whilst Henry Wydon was in position as prior of Llantarnam when that monastery was dissolved in 1536.

Cardinal Gasquet suggested that at its closure in 1536 all the monks of Netley went to live at Beaulieu where their former abbot, Thomas Stevens, was now superior, but this is not entirely borne out by the facts. Six monks of Netley were given 'capacities' to seek secular livings. Only two appear to have certainly moved to Beaulieu, John Bere and Thomas Evaw. Other monks to move to Beaulieu were John Kery from Waverley and Richard Curlew from Quarr and, possibly, William Austen from Tilty and William Baxterley from Merevale. Simon Rugewike of Quarr moved to Buckland.[189]

Altogether some three dozen monks can be traced as moving to another abbey when theirs was closed.[190] Amongst them were monks of Flaxley (Edward Fryer transferred to Kingswood and Thomas Were to Thame). Monks might move to a mother house (as Henry Norton moving from Strata Marcella to Whitland), or to a daughter-abbey (as Nicholas Acton and John Gethin of Tintern transferring to Kingswood—the former became its cellarer, the latter its parish priest). The last Cistercian monastery to be suppressed was that at Rushen in the Isle of Man in 1540, by which year its small community had been reinforced by Richard Skales, the sub-cellarer of Furness, and James More from Whalley

When Vaudey was dissolved (1536) three of its monks went to Kirkstead and there were so active in helping the rebels that they were executed. Four monks of Sawley played a like role. Refused admission at Furness when Sawley was closed (20 May 1536), they returned to the vicinity of Sawley, encouraged the commons to rebel, and found themselves briefly housed in their abbey once again *(Chapter 5)*.[191] When Whalley fell by attainder (17 March 1537)

Henry VIII preferred its monks to transfer to other houses rather than be given 'capacities', 'for it cannot be wholesome for them to wander abroad.'[192]. The king (24 March 1537), displeased with the perceived disloyalty of certain of the monks of Furness, realised the difficulty some abbeys might have in housing them. He therefore sent to the earl of Sussex and others, 'letters for bestowing the monks to other monasteries, with three or four blanks to be directed to other houses, as those in the list cannot well receive the numbers set upon them.'[193]

Monastic Pensions

In the first wave of monastic closures (1536/37) dispossessed abbots were awarded a modest pension, but the ordinary monks seemingly got nothing save a 'reward',—nothing more than pocket money to help them on their way, as well as any arrears of 'wages'. This was because they were given a choice between continuing their vocation in another monastic house, or of taking a 'capacity' allowing them to obtain other clerical employment. The monks of Whalley received no pension as it fell by attainder; this was also the fate of the monks of of Furness and seemingly of Jervaulx and of Kirkstead.[194].

The monks who did not wish to transfer to other abbeys, and most Cistercians in the second period of dissolution, were granted 'capacities', that is to say: dispensation from their monastic vows, and permission to wear the clothing of a secular cleric rather than monastic habit. These dispensations were a prerequisite before dispossessed monks might find other suitable employment. Unfortunately clerical positions were not always easy to find, and the weeks immediately following their eviction from their monasteries must have been a period for many religious of deep unhappiness and anxiety. William Moreland, the monk of Louth Park, who participated in the Pilgrimage of Grace, told how he and his brethren received their 'capacities', but with scant hope of finding opportunity to use them.[195]

By 8 July 1536 Eustache Chapuys, the influential ambassador to Britain of Emperor Charles V, had been able to write: 'It is a lamentable thing to see a legion of monks and nuns who have been chased from their monasteries wandering miserably hither and thither seeking means to live, and several honest men have told me that what with monks, nuns and persons dependent on the monasteries suppressed, there were over twenty thousand who knew not how to live.'[196] Amongst these will indubitably have been many Cistercians.

At Cleeve the 'pocket money' received was amounted to 26s 8d. per monk.[197] This was equivalent in modern terms to at most about £500. At Tintern its twelve monks had to share eight guineas between them; at nearby Llantarnam the four religious received a total payment of but 35s.[198] The nine religious of Stoneleigh received between them a total of but £14-13-4 to help them on their way, and the five monks remaining at Dore only a total of £6-13-4.[199] For many this was a cruel blow, and the outlook for those who could not speedily find alternative priestly employment must have been grim indeed, More than that, these figures sometimes included the 'wages' or personal income lost between the date of survey and the final days of closure.

At Louth Park, the ten monks had £4-6-8 divided amongst them as 'wages' due, with twenty shillings apiece to buy secular apparel.[200] At Kingswood, as at Holm Cultram, the 'reward and finding' was were given to the monks 'on the day of their departing out of the monastery'.[201] All these small grants were paid by the Receiver appointed for a particular monastery, but with the assent of the local commissioners. Their value was lessened by their need to buy clothing befitting a secular priest; at Holm Cultram, and probably generally, this was achieved before the monks left their house for good. At least one monk of Louth Park continued on at least one occasion to wear his monastic habit; he was William Moreland.

The religious evicted in the second round of suppressions of 1538/1539 were more fortunate. An analysis of 430 known Cistercian pensions from those years, leaving aside those higher awards known to have been made to abbots, priors, sub-priors and cellarers, suggest that the average Cistercian monk's pension amounted to almost precisely £5. One hundred and nine of those monks received exactly that amount, whilst a further one hundred were awarded £5-6-8. Fifty-seven monks (some possibly holding unknown offices in their monastery) received £6; a further sixty-two monks received £4 or more.

Fig. 14: Page 2 of the Pensions awarded to the monks of Bordesley, and the amount of subsidy payable thereupon, 1540
(By kind permission of the Bodleian Libraries, The University of Oxford, MS. Tanner 343, folio 2)

The warrants granting such pensions were signed by local commissioners or by two or more officials of the Court of Augmentations working in the field: Richard Riche, its chancellor and later Lord Chancellor, was to the fore –as at Bindon,[202] and other signatories included John Onley, its first solicitor; Thomas Pope, its treasurer, and later sworn of the privy council; and Robert Southwell, a career civil servant who did well financially out of the dissolution. The grants recommended by the local commissioners appear to have been approved from a central office: those, for instance, for Llantarnam and Margam in Wales, and for Cleeve and Stanley in England, were signed on the same day: 2 July 1536.[203]

At Biddlesden Dr John London assigned 'a convenient pension unto the abbot and monks there.'[204] He also determined the pensions to be paid to the monks of Combe. At Kingswood John Tregonwell and his fellow commisisoners awarded 'such stipends as is thought necessary and expedient by us.'[205]

His signature, and that of Walter Hendle, appear on the warrant for the monks of Robertsbridge. The list of pensions for the monks of Stratford was signed by Thomas Cromwell himself.[206] At Holm Cultram the pension warrants signed by Dr Legh survive for the entire community, he issuing them he said 'by virtue of our commission.'[207]

There were variations between the pensions granted to the monks of one monastery as opposed to another. The five Yorkshire abbeys exemplified this. Kirkstall led the way with an average pension of £6 for the ordinary monk, followed in descending order by Fountains (£5-65), Meaux (£5-60), Rievaulx (£5-20), Byland (£5—not counting unexplained above average pensions), and, least of all, Roche (£4-70). Whereas thirteen monks of Kirkstall received a pension of £6 or more, only two of Roche's monks did so. The monks of Combe, eight of whom received £5-6-8 and five £6, were more fortunate.[208] Their pensions were assigned by Dr London, the commissioner, who wrote to Cromwell (21 January 1539) asking for them to be ratified 'to encourage others.' His idea was that speedy and substantial pensions would weaken any resistance to suppression.[209]

In the west country the monks of Kingswood were mostly awarded but £4 apiece, whilst this was also the average figure gained by the monks of Holm Cultram—where the gross return to the Crown was lessened by the considerable provision made for its last abbot. In Wales, where perhaps the return expected of the monasteries was not great, the monks of Neath and Whitland had to be satisfied with an average pension of under £4, whilst the religious of the once noble Strata Florida were fortunate if they received much more than £3. In Kent the nine dispossessed monks of Boxley fared little better: with either £4 or £2-13-4 piece.[210] The situation was even worse for the six monks evicted from their abbey of Rushen on the Isle of Man in June 1540: they each received an annual pension pittance of £2-13-4.[211]

Various reasons might be adduced for the variation in individual pensions—willingness or reluctance to surrender, length of service, the policy of individual commissioners, or an appreciation of how much the pension bill would amount to in later years against the income to be expected from the monastery's lessees and estates. On dissolving Biddlesden, Dr John London, the commissioner, took into account in awarding pensions there the fact that the monks 'have already paid money to have their house continue, although under £200 value.' Each received £5-6-8.[212]

Within a community, there were variations in the amount of pension awarded to individual members. Length of service may have played a part in determining this. Some monks long professed do appear to have benefited slightly. Amongst their number may have been John Stone of Ford (made subdeacon in 1504; £8), James Austen of Meaux (ordained priest in 1509; £6), and a jubilarian, Griffin Hampton of Beaulieu (£6). On the other hand at Holm Cultram Richard Adamson and William Marten, neither priested by its dissolution, received but £2 annual pension each. Likewise Richard Baxbie of Byland, still a deacon at its closure, gained but £4 yearly. At Roche four of its eighteen monks received but £3-6-8 in pension; they were three novices and one a deacon.[213] At Kingswood most monks received a £4 pension but one, John Stonley, gained only £2 he 'being no priest.'[214]

Short service was not always a barrier to a fuller pension: Robert Kynvar, abbot of Combe for only and exactly one year, received £80 per year, perhaps because he had, unlike his predecessor, willingly surrendered his monastery.[215] William Wetherall of Byland, made an acolyte only in 1533, still managed to gain a £5 pension, whilst William Cromboke of Whalley and later of Byland, made deacon in 1535, yet obtained yearly £5-6-8. At Ford newly ordained Richard Kingsbury and William Deryngton both received a pension of £5.[216] At Warden two deacons received the same pension of £5-6-8 as did most of the other monks there, but two deacons of Stratford received £3-6-8 instead of the £5 awarded their confrères.[217] It is difficult therefore to determine that length of service played a major part in the amount of pension awarded.

It has been suggested that monks with an Oxford degree achieved an average pension of £8 each.[218] This may have been true of Robert Baynton of Byland (£10), Anthony Clerk of Stratford (£8), Roger/Robert Moreton of Combe (£8). and Richard Eddon of Hailes (£7)—though he was also the abbey's precentor. On the other hand, another monk of Hailes with an Oxford education and its custodian of the Holy Blood, Roger Rede, received but £5. Eight other monks elsewhere with no known degree or monastic office also gained an £8 pension.

What is of note, is that those monks accused in the 1535/36 visitation of sexual shortcomings and illcit relations with the opposite sex, did not see their pensions in any way affected. . Such monks included Gawin Berwik of Fountains and Paul Mason of Kirkstall. Occasionally a former monk is on record of selling his pension—perhaps to avoid pecuniary embarrassment.

William Hellay, of Roche, had sold his £3-6-8 pension by 1551 but was still assessed on it 1573.[219] Martin Wren of Meaux in about 1545 and then about forty-six, sold his pension of £6 to Henry Smith of York for £24. As Wren was still alive in 1556, Smith made a handsome profit on the transaction.[220]

In addition to their pensions the monks evicted in 1538/39 were, like those earlier dispossessed, given a 'regard' or 'reward' to help them on their way. These small payments were meant to cover the period from the date of dissolution until the first pension due was paid, as also 'for apparel' (Robertsbridge, 1538),[221] Most of the monks of Dieluacres received pocket-money of £2,[222] but the £1 of such pocket-money awarded the monks of Rushen (closed in 1540) was scant recompense for their meagre pensions.[223] At Kingswood the monks were fortunate their 'reward and finding' given 'at their departing out of the monastery' being mostly £2-13-4, their pension ranging from £4 to £4-13-4.[224] For their 'rewards' the twelve monks of Garendon shared £25-3-4 between them.[225] Dr Legh wrote of the dispossessed monks of Holm Cultram as dispersing 'having honest rewards in their purses.'[226] The monks of Roche (1538) were each to have at their departure 'their half-year's pension by way of reward, and 20s. beside towards their apparel'.[227] The abbot of Dieulacres received a 'reward' of £6, his prior of £2-10-0, and most of his community £2.[228]

Even when in receipt of their pensions problems remained for the ex-religious. Firstly, the pension awarded was a gross amount: they were subject to a 2s in the pound clerical subsidy—when one was levied, with a 4d. in the pound fee to the Receiver who paid them out, and the expense of collecting them. This could greatly lower their net value.[229] Richard West, for instance, formerly of Bordesley, was assessed in the first subsidy expected of ex-religious in 1540 to pay a subsidy of 12s. on his pension of £6; from the same abbey, John Johnson had to surrender in this way 10s out of £5; and William Austen 8s. on his pension of £4. These were no small sums to subtract from a small pension. Abbot Dey of Bordesley had to yield £5 from his pension of £50, and so the total subsidy expected that year from himself and his former community amounted to £14-7-3 being clawed back from the £143-13-4 paid out in pensions to the former Bordesley community.[230]

Secondly the pensions did not rise in pace with increases in the cost of living.[231] The value of the pound lowered considerably in the years following the suppression, so that by 1580—and a several monks survived beyond that year, its value was half that in the 1540s. Thus the pension of £5 granted

William Carter, formerly of Roche, in 1538 had by 1573 been subject to a depreciation in the value of the pound of at least 40%.

Thirdly, the pensions were paid out either by district Receivers of the Court of Augmentations or in London, twice-yearly. This might mean that pensioners had to make use of agents, who might be robbed en route.[232] When Biddlesden was suppressed in 1538, one of the commissioners, Dr London, wrote a kindly and thoughtful letter to Richard Rich, comptroller of the Court of Augmentations, asking for the assurance of the pensions of its monks, saying that 'divers of them be very aged, and pity it were to cause them to travel far in fetching of their pensions.'[233]

Six former monks of Croxden, initially at least, entrusted one Geoffrey Lee of 'Munkenschull' (? Moddershall, Staffs.) to obtain their pensions and relay the money to them. Their receipts for a half-year's payment received from Lee in May 1541 are extant, and make no mention of any deduction payable for his services.[234] The authority given to Lee to collect his money was dated by one of the five, John Orpe, on 29 April 1539.[235] Might Lee be the Geoffrey Lee who in 1532 was treasurer to the archbishop of York?

Fourthly, payments were frequently in arrears. No less than four former monks of Rievaulx, as well as their former abbot, complained in 1552/53 that their pension was a year or more in arrears.[236] When Robert Hemsworth of Kirkstall died in 1553 he left his sister 'my half-year's pension,' which indicates both that it was in arrears at the time of his passing, and that it was due to be paid half-yearly.[237] In response to the complaint of Thomas Jackson, formerly of Vaudey, and other appellants, the receiver for Lincolnshire by way of excuse reported in 1552 to a commission of enquiry, that 'at Mayday last he had a letter from the King's majesty's counsel, that he should not pay them that half year'. This commission set up that year to examine the problem, found that 148 of 315 Lincolnshire monastic pensions were in arrears.[238]

The pension problem was not entirely one-sided. The cost of monastic pensions (let alone the continuance of annuities and the like recognised by the Court of Augmentations) took away from the Crown a considerable portion of its profits from gaining and/or selling off monastic sites and lands.[239] The gross value of Combermere, for instance, after its suppression was £258, but of that £106 was taken up in pensions paid to the abbot and community.[240] The pensions awarded at Dieulacres amounted to £115, compared to its gross value of £243; the pension bill of Beaulieu was £152 out of its gross value of £428.

The profits gained by the Crown from the suppression of any abbey were also lessened by the necessity to pay the immediate expenses of the commissioners, and for years to come those of the Particular Receivers for each region. In 1536 the commissioners involved in the closure of Dore charged £9-17-2½ 'in riding and staying in various places.'[241] In February 1537 Walter Hendle leading the commissioners suppressing Boxley, wrote to Cromwell saying, surprisingly, that 'it is costly to lie here.'[242] John Scudamore, Receiver for four counties, was assured of being reimbursed for his work in melting down lead and transferring it to a royal castle.[243]

Later Employment, and Chantry Priests[244]

The majority of dispossessed monks were able to supplement their pensions by seeking clerical employment as chantry chaplains, parish curates and parish priests. This was not usually possible when a monk was presented to a benefice by the Crown, when a pension was foregone or reduced;[245] as for John Harrison, a monk of Byland, granted at the time of suppression the church of Old Byland for life. Usually, however, pension and the fruits of a benefice or chaplaincy went hand in hand.

Before endeavouring to find clerical employment, each monk required the 'dispensation' or 'capacity' granted by the faculty office of the Archbishop of Canterbury and often given to them as they left their monastery. For those seeking positions in the diocese of York there was for a time a problem, in as much as that Archbishop Lee of York also insisted on seeing their letters of orders. This meant Richard Ingworth, bishop of Dover, pointed out to Cromwell that 'some must go a hundred miles to seek them, and when come there the charges for giving the registrar is so great that they cannot pay it, so they come home again confounded.'[246] Happily for the monks of Biddlesden (suppressed in 1538), Thomas Wriothesley, active in the closure of some monasteries from which he personally benefited, did write to a local commissioner, 'Mr Townsend', requiring him 'to make out dispensations for these persons as shortly as you may conveniently.'[247] These faculties were granted free of payment, unlike those given to monks who opted out before the Suppression, when a fee of £4 was not an uncommon sum expected.[248]

There are numerous instances of some monks gaining worthwhile clerical office (*detailed in the Appendix*): as Walter Bartholomew of Beaulieu, Richard Bateson of Kirkstall, and Thomas Chester of Pipewell, to name but a few. Such additional income clearly made the lot of many former monks more bearable. A few monks did well, like Anthony Clerk of Stratford with a headmastership and an incumbency; Richard Eddon of Hailes with both a Somerset rectory and a prebendary-ship of Winchester cathedral, and Thomas Cordell of Warden, holding two livings in plurality. In the instance of Robert Webster of Byland, and more than one Hailes monk, they had been presented to abbey livings before their suppression.

Life cannot have been easy perhaps for a number of monks of whom, later in life, it was noted that—apart from their pension—they had no other ecclesiastical preferment. These may have included the majority of the monks of Furness.[249] Such was also the lot of William Robinson of Merevale, Thomas House of Warden, Thomas Best of Neath and William Ashenhurst of Hulton, amongst others. With the inflation of the 1540s they must have lived in straitened circumstances. The question remains: how did a monk of Holm Cultram with his £4 pension feel when realising that his last abbot—in office but for a short while and controversial—was in receipt of residence, living and emoluments valued at least £100 per annum? There was always a large gap between an abbot's pension and that of his former subordinates.

At least thirty Cistercian monks may have become chantry priests after the closure of their abbeys. As all chantries were suppressed in 1548, this was frequently a stepping-stone to better things, and it assured them of a further pension in addition to their monastic annuity. Several former monks of Rievaulx served as chantry priests including Richard Allerton, once its infirmarian who, fifty-six years old in 1548, had a pension of £5-3-10 from his position as priest of the Guild of St Katherine in Rotherham, in addition to his £5-6-8 monastic pension. This must have given him added security and comfort in old age. Similarly favoured were Henry Wilson, formerly of Roche: a monastic pension of £5 and an annual sum of £3-12-0 from his former chantry at Heckington, Lincolnshire; and Thomas Twellis, once of Rufford: enjoying in 1554 his monastic pension of £5 and in receipt of £3-11-8 for his former services as Stretton Wolfe chaplain in Lincoln Cathedral.

Amongst chantry priests who proceeded to better livings were Robert Gylling, formerly of Rievaulx, who after being a chantry priest in Holy Trinity,

Hull, later received the cure of Laytham, Yorkshire, and Matthew Tort, once of Rievaulx, who from being a chantry priest in Southwell Minster, became a prebendary there and rector of Hockerton, Nottinghamshire. Thomas Perpin, once monk of Flaxley and for a short while abbot of Grace Dieu, was a chantry priest at Holy Trinity, Bristol, before becoming perpetual curate of Cirencester. The chantry certificates of 1548 pass comment upon the priests concerned. Christopher Dixson, formerly of Jervaulx, if he was the priest of that name who held a chantry at Dale Grange, Aysgarth, was said to be 'forty six, and well-learned,' Thomas Swaledale of the same monastery, if the priest of that name in Bedale, was 'seventy-four but indifferently learned.' Richard Gill, last abbot of Newenham, was for a time one of two chaplains at the altar of the Rood in Exeter Cathedral.[250]

One abbot and one monk are worthy of especial note in that they later became members of the Benedictine community of Westminster abbey restored in Queen Mary's reign. John Redborne, the last abbot of Dore and now an elderly man, formed a part of the community. He was accompanied by a Welsh servant named Ap Thomas but died in September 1557, aged about seventy-seven years old.[251] Richard Eddon, formerly a monk of Hailes and Oxford graduate, gave up a Somerset living and Winchester prebend in order to be at Westminster, where he acted as cellarer. When he resigned, it was noted that he had done so 'to enter religion.'[252] Later he is believed to have been principal of Gloucester Hall, Oxford (1563), then returning as a pensioner, or a fellow, to the former St Bernard's, now St John's, College there (1564).[253]

Thomas Whitney, the last abbot of Dieulacres, normally resided at his own house in Mill Street, Leek, Staffordshire, but although not seemingly joining the new community he certainly gravitated towards Westminster. Dying in August 1558, probably in London, his will was proved there and it mentions Oliver Lingard, a curate at St Margaret's Westminster, as his 'good and special friend;' Lingard was the first witness attesting the will. The 'overseers' of his will were to be a cousin, Peter Whitney, and Richard Eddon (Eden), now a monk of Westminster.[254] Whitney desired to be buried in Westminster abbey, and he bequeathed to Nicholas Whitney, his nephew and executor of his will, both the house in Leek and also a silver and gilt chalice. This he was to surrender should Dieulacres be re-established. No Cistercian abbey was re-founded in the Marian reign, but Edward Heptonstall, a monk of Kirkstall also dying in 1558, made like provision. He bequeathed to his nephew the books he had years before brought away from that monastery, on the condition that should Kirkstall be re-established the books were to return there.[255]

Not unnaturally monks who had lived in their abbey for years will have formed an attachment to that place. Bewildered at their eviction as they may well have been, William Moreland of Louth Park told how for a while its dispossessed monks lived as near as they might to their old monastery, only going out to hear Mass in the parish church, and once or twice to meet and speak with one another.[256] For those who had true vocations it must have been a distressing and fearful time. A few Cistercians were fortunate in being appointed to serve the parishioners of their former abbey parish: Edward Pedley (*al.* Manchester) thus became vicar of Whalley in 1538, John Harrison was already incumbent of Old Byland, and Stephen Farsy served the cure of Bindon. In 1554 one of its former monks, Robert Taylor (*al.* Northampton) was vicar of Biddlesden, enjoying a stipend of £8-17-1 in addition to his monastic pension of £5-6-8.

John York, a monk of the house, was nominated to look after the former parishioners of Strata Florida, whilst former religious Walter Bartholomew of Beaulieu, John Watts at Buckfast, and William Merbury of Dore did the same for a while in their respective monastic parishes. Former monks who ministered at grange chapels once belonging to their monastery included William ap Thomas of Cwmhir at Gwernygo Grange in Powys, and John Dydebroke of Dore at Llanfair Cilgoed Grange in Gwent. John Genynge of Dunkeswell lived in the 1540s on former monastic land in the vicinity of his abbey, whilst Thomas Bertlot of Kirkstall resided at that monastery's Allerton Grange.

Keeping in Contact

It was said of the dispossessed monks of Llantarnam that they continued their community life at their pilgrimage centre of Pen-rhys in the Rhondda, that there they were protected by the 'sixteen Stradling bastards', and where (as late as 1550) there was 'a full choir of monks.'[257] If this account, written in 1550 were true then it is the reason that only two monks of Llantarnam were granted faculties after the abbey was closed. Local tradition, but not backed by any documentary evidence—for all the monks received faculties, has it that the seven aged monks remaining at Strata Florida moved to the house of

Nanteos near Aberystwyth, taking with them a mazer cup, later seen as the Cup of the Last Supper.[258]

In England there is no certain evidence of former Cistercians attempting to live in community, though several monks of Kirkstall did congregate in the nearby Leeds area.[259] It was said that Abbot Huddleston and his monks of Stratford retired to a small mansion at Plaistow, and there lived out their lives as a community.[260] At least two former monks of Byland lived at Kilburn close to their old monastery, and must have been in frequent contact, if not dwelling together: John Moyser who in 1552 was bequeathed £4 in return for singing Mass daily for the testator in Kilburn church for a year; and Thomas Metcalf, who making his will in 1558 desired to be buried in Kilburn church.[261] That monks continued to keep in contact so far as they could was shown in 1555 when a former novice of Roche, Richard Moysley, now a deacon and living in Kellington, North Yorkshire, was ordained priest. No less than eleven former Cistercians (five from Roche and six from Rufford) signed his letters testimonial.[262] Nicholas Colles (Toller), formerly a monk of Roche, was until 1548 a chantry priest in Tickhill church, Yorkshire, during the incumbency there of his abbot, Henry Cundall.

Several former Cistercian monks remembered their fellows when making their wills.[263] Robert Smith (1549), formerly of Rievaulx, left 12d. 'to every one of my brethren being of life,' whilst Roger Watson (1555), also formerly of Rievaulx, bequeathed 2d. and requested the prayers of 'every of my brethren that was in Ryval the day of our suppression and that be on live.'[264] Yet another monk of Rievaulx, John Pynder (1539), left 12d. to each of his former brethren so long as they said three Masses for his soul.[265] Thomas Spratt, formerly of Robertsbridge, made one of his former fellow monks, Geoffrey Iden, his executor, and left him a gown, a book case and a 'stool of ease'. He also did not forget another former monk of the house, William Senden.[266]

A generous benefactor was Richard Ellis (1550) formerly of Kirkstall, who in his will bequeathed to Anthony Jackson, a confrère, his best gown, vestments and an altar cloth. Jackson's godson, Thomas Pepper, also a monk of Kirkstall and now an industrialist, left him land in Cookridge; he also made bequests to other Cistercians of Kirkstall: Richard Wood (a lease at Cookridge), Leonard Wyndresse (a camlet jacket), and William Lupton (including a feather-bed.).[267] Other monks had less to bequeath: Gabriel Lofthouse seems to have died in poor circumstances, leaving to his brother only bedding, a shirt, a long gown, a spoon and just over a pound in cash.[268]

Pepper had eventually inherited the Weetwood iron works from his father, he had acquired much property, and his cash bequests totalled £86, a not inconsiderable sum.[269]

The Marital State

Wills and later surveys tell us that many former Cistercians remained unmarried. In some instances this was helpful for they had no income apart from their monastic pension with which to support a family. Such monks included Thomas Best of Neath, William Robinson of Merevale and Thomas House of Warden. It seems that Matthew Tort of Rievaulx (1576) also remained celibate for in his will he made bequests only to cousins, nephews and nieces.[270] Those, perhaps a relatively small minority of former Cistercians, who did marry faced possible deprivation from their livings when Mary acceded to the throne. Such a lot befell John Cartwright of Robertsbridge, Thomas Longbottom of Revesby and William Stapleton of Rievaulx; though in some instances the deprived monks found other cures quite speedily. Stapleton had married one Joan Raby, whom he was forced to divorce in 1554, and on which account he was enjoined to do public penance in Eastrington church from which vicarage he had just been deprived.[271] Another monk of Kirkstall, Paul Mason, who may have become vicar of Bishopthorpe (1563), is shown by his later will to have born a son, two daughters and a 'baseborn' daughter.[272]

Fate of the Abbots

The 1536 Act of Suppression ordered that religious superiors were to be provided with 'such yearly pensions and benefices as for their degrees and qualities shall be reasonable and convenient,' whilst John Oxley, clerk of the Court of Augmentations, suggested that the abbots of the Duchy of Lancaster should receive a pension of 'the tenth part of the clear yearly value of every house' as they were reassessed when surveyed in 1535/1536.[273] The suggestion does not appear to have been put into practice so far the Cistercian houses were concerned, as the abbot of Furness received a parish *in lieu* of a pension, whilst the abbot of Whalley was hanged.

The average pension awarded the abbots of those monasteries closed in 1536/37 was around £20, but ranged from the £30 p.a. granted to Abbot Tyrry of Newminster and Abbot Syston of Garendon, to but £5-6-8 in the instance of the last abbot of Cwmhir and only £4 in the case of the last abbot of Grace Dieu. These were not large sums, but put them in better stead than their former subordinates who received no pension at all.

The abbatial pensions awarded in the 1538/39 wave of suppressions were far more generous, averaging around £55—nearly three times as much as those previously granted. They ranged from the £120 awarded Abbot Dunne of Buckfast down to the £20 received by the abbot of Hulton and £10 granted the abbot of Rushen. In lieu of pension Abbot Pyle of Furness received the rectory of Dalton (valued at £66-13-4), Abbot Borrowdale of Holm Cultram the vicarage and monastery site and lands there (estimated to be worth £100 yearly), whilst Abbot Doncaster of Rufford was granted the living of Rotherham instead of a £25 pension.[274] Abbot Richard ap Rhys of Aberconwy was granted the rectories of Eglwys-bach and Llanbadrig in Caernarfonshire instead of a £20 annuity.[275]

Dispossessed abbots might be granted additional perquisites, or find for themselves other residences. William Alynger of Waverley, who Dr Layton described as 'honest but none of the children of Solomon', became provisor of St Bernard's College, Oxford, until his death in 1539. He requested burial in St Mary Magdalene's Church, Oxford.[276] When Hailes was dissolved in 1539 Abbot Sagar was permitted to live in his former summer house at Coscombe, on the hill above the monastery, with forty loads of timber yearly for firebote and housebote.[277] He moved to be rector of Adel, Yorkshire, in 1541, and the house was granted to Robert Acton. Sagar also held the prebend of Givendale in York Minster and became a chaplain to the King. With his pension of £100 p.a., he was comfortably off. As abbot he had he made long stays at Coscombe on account, he said, of his health.[278] Abbot Chard of Ford became vicar of Thorncombe, Dorset, having in addition to his abbatial pension of £80 p.a. the entitlement to forty wain loads of fire wood yearly.[279]

Abbot Borrowdale of Holm Cultram, although only abbot for little more than a year and of dubious reputation, received on 16 November 1538 a lease for only 26s 8d. p.a. of the abbey site and buildings, with the demesne lands and rights of firebote, ploughbote and cartbote. Earlier, on 1 June, he had been given accommodation and the tithes of the parish in lieu of a pension, in a package which was estimated as worth at least £100 pa.[280] Abbot John Alanbridge of Byland found an eventide home with the Calverley family at Calverley Hall, not far north-west of his native Leeds. The house had a late-medieval chapel, and Alanbridge died there in the porch chamber of the Hall in 1563, making provision in his will for the local poor.[281] The penultimate abbot of Rievaulx, Edward Kirkby, making his will in 1551 referred to his ability to have purchased 'both chantry and lamp lands.'[282]

The last abbot of Beaulieu, Thomas Stevens, previously abbot of Netley, in his short abbacy at Beaulieu suffered from uncooperative monks who spoke against him to the surrender commissioners. After Beaulieu's closure he exclaimed, 'Thank God, I am rid of my lewd monks.' Immediately after retirement he took up the problems of the debtors in sanctuary at Beaulieu, and asked that his cellarer's pension be increased. Settling first at St Leonard's, probably on monastic property he had demised to his sister immediately before the suppression but which he acknowledged as coming into the hands of the Crown, he became rector of Bentworth, Hants (1539), and later treasurer of Salisbury Catheral (1548), dying in 1550. His induction at Bentworth had to be accompanied by force, as the previous rector, John Palmys, married and unordained, wished to keep it for himself.[283]

The abbot of Roche, Henry Cundall (1538), received a generous settlement. When his house closed he received an annual pension of £33-6-8, but he was also allowed to take away with him his books, a fourth part of the abbey plate, a chalice and a vestment, and cattle and household effects.[284] Becoming vicar of Tickhill, Yorks., he bequeathed in 1555 forty shillings to the poor of Tickhill and twenty shillings to the poor of Crowle.[285] Abbot Chard of Ford, in addition to his large £80 pension, was entitled to receive forty wain-loads of timber yearly.[286] Abbot Ripley of Kirkstall is said to have been able to reside in its inner gate-house until his death.[287] Abbot Gyllam of Pipewell was granted 'the panelling and "delling" of the walls of the refectory,' and took this away.[288] Abbot Syston of Garendon also was permitted to take some of his monastery's plate.[289] Not all abbots received such generous settlements. Abbot Richard Wyche of Tintern, closed in September 1536, had to be content with a pension of £23 and became more or less a curate in his former parish of Woolaston, Gloucestershire. Probably previously a monk of Whalley, with an Oxford degree, he had been abbot since 1521. In retirement his curate's stipend of £4-13-4 supplemented his monastic pension, and he was able to have the services of two faithful retainers as well as female servants. It must have been hard to be a mere curate in a parish of which he had once been the rector. His early years of retirement were not unclouded, for he was sued at the Court of

Chancery by one of his former monks, John Gethin, regarding an annuity previously granted Gethin out of the income of the abbey's Trelech Grange.[290]

Abbot John Palmer of Tilty appears to have lived in retirement with his mother and a servant in Great Easton, Essex. Making his will in January 1539, he died the following month, expressing catholicity of faith, bequeathing his soul 'to almighty God and lady saynt mary with all the holy company of heaven.' Desiring to be buried in the church of St Giles, Great Easton, he left all his Latin books to the parson there as well as well as his bonnet, best doublet and tippet of sarsenet. Might the latter have been his degree hood? The bonnet he wore on 'holidays' he left to a friend; perhaps 'holy days' is meant here rather than times away of pleasure. Four children were to receive one penny each for bearing four pound tapers at his funeral.[291]

In December 1540 Thomas Whitney, formerly abbot of Dieulacres and once a powerful personality in Staffordshire, had to write a touching letter from his house in Mill Street, Leek, to John Scudamore, the Particular Receiver for that county and others, saying that he had to borrow £8 from his brother, and asking not only for his pension unpaid since the previous Michaelmas, but also for 'the pensions of my poor brethren that are not able to labour for them.'[292] This shows his concern for his former monks, five of whom were still drawing their pensions in 1557. Whitney had already suffered loss when in 1539 £4 of his pension had been kept back because of a debt incurred by his predecessor as abbot. Whitney then wrote to Scudamore pointing out that debts unpaid had on the closure of a monastery become the responsibility of the Crown.[293] Whitney died in 1558. Another former abbot who had cause to complain of arrears of payment was (in Edward VI's reign) Abbot Alanbridge of Byland.[294]

Fate of Sites and Buildings

On the day of suppression or very shortly thereafter the Particular Receiver for each monastery oversaw a sale of its goods and effects, reserving plate, lead and (often) bells to the Crown. The details afforded by these sales give us an insight into the furnishings of the Cistercian houses. On 20 October 1538 Dr Legh took the surrender of Dieulacres; the very next day the sale of goods and chattels, corn and cattle, raised £63-14-10. The purchaser was the abbey steward, the earl of Derby, who also took possession of the abbey

site and demesne on behalf of the Crown.[295] The itemised inventory of the
sale tells of the contents of all the principal buildings (described in Chapter
1), and also notes the animal stock (which fetched £9-10-0), and that oats,
hay and rye, remained in the granary.[296] Even gravestones were included in
the sale, as well as the cloister laver.

In his work Dr Legh, together with William Cavendish, who acted as
auditor, kept a book of accounts, and appointed for each monastery a jury of
twelve men whose duty it was to 'appraise the goods' of the several houses.
Their accounts itemised the goods sold under various heads, as in the case of
Merevale (15 November 1538): items from the church, vestry, cloister and
chapter-house; the buttery, parlour, kitchen , brew-house, smithy, barn, and
the like. The book of accounts also listed the 'rewards' given to monks and
servants, the expenses of the commissioners, goods unsold (plate, lead and
bells), rents received and unpaid, fees and annuities due, as well as debts due
to and owing by a particular monastery in their commission.[297] The jurors at
Dieulacres were led by one William Butler. Its thirty servants received
'rewards' ranging from 3s 4d. to 20s, and totalling £14-5-10. Small alms were
also given to the eight poor bead women there, three of whom were married.[298] Between them, the fifty-five junior officers and servants of Holm
Cultram shared £18-8-0 by way of reward'. Three 'bede-men' were given just
one shilling each to help them on their way.[299]

The sale of goods at Abbey Dore on 1 March 1537 'at the dissolution of
the house there,' was conducted by John Scudamore (*supra*), whose family
still live at nearby Kentchurch Court; and who the previous day presided at
the sale of goods of Monmouth Priory. The sale at Dore netted £51, of which
goods to the value of over £41 was purchased by Scudamore himself; who
bought *inter alia* all the equipment in the kitchen parlour, buttery, brew-house,
all the cattle of the demesne, the corn in the barn and the corn sown in the
ground, as well as the plough-gear, the organs in the quire, and the roof of the
refectory. Scudamore, with other local gentry, also bought up the glass and
iron of the windows of the dorter, frater, and the now vanished polygonal
chapter-house.[300]

The last abbot of Dore, John Redborn, spent 24s 8d on church vestments,
including a cope of blue silk with angels. Not on sale were goods which the
last abbot admitted in 1541 taking away from the monastery before its closure,
including a set of vestments which he gave to the parish church, but also a

gospel book plated with silver and a silver-plated cross including a small bone, the relic of a saint.[301] Was this the 'portion of wood of the holy cross adorned with gold and precious stones' presented to Dore in 1321 by Sir William de Grandison?[302]

The sale of effects at Croxden took place on 15 October 1538, a month after the closure of the abbey, and included a little gate-house on 'the north side of the common way', the organ loft, the little smith's forge, all the old timber in the cloister, and the roof of the church—the latter to Sir Thomas Gilbert and Edmund Wetheyn of Chekley parish.[303] The sale however only raised nine guineas, which suggests that the delay may have allowed time for looting of the buildings.[304] The last sale of goods at a Cistercian monastery was at Rushen, Isle of Man, in June 1540, which showed its barn to be well stocked and bore witness to a flourishing pastoral economy.[305]

Details of the sale of goods at Hailes emerged in a commission of enquriy held at Winchcombe, Gloucestershire, three years later, on 4 January 1542.[306] The sale had been overseen by officers of Robert Acton to whom custody of the site had been committed. Evidence was given that among the purchasers were a parson, Nicholas Wike, who bought substantial quantities of stained glass and this was carried away by cart, packed between two boards. John Isodde of Toddington bought 'a blue marble stone to grind colours on,' as well as a plummet of lead of a clock which weighed about 1 cwt. Christopher Wenar, a smith of Stow, received about 7 cwt. of iron and lead. The ceilings, probably painted, of the chambers of the prior, sub-prior and cellarer were locked up in the monastic inn at Hailes as items reserved for Robert Acton.

The inquiry was held because not all the sales were authorised, indeed there was plunder and theft. It was alleged that to obtain pickings many 'flocked to Hailes from all over the countryside, priests and people.' One of the monks, Thomas Hopkins (later chaplain to the Acton family), actively involved himself in the demolition of the monastery, causing two loads of squared timber to be cast out of the steeple, and selling off the washing lavers and six hundredweight of lead out of the bake-house. It was alleged of Christopher Wenar and others that they moved various items by night, presumably to avoid detection. Three years after the abbey closed, the commission of enquiry concluded that 'there still be many divers spoils daily done within the late monastery.'

Roche was also ransacked. In an account given in 1591 by one whose uncle was present and 'well acquainted with certain of the monks.' Once doors and locks had been removed different people 'went in and took what they found, filched it away.' This included 'the service books that lied in the church', while some hid their ill-begotten gains in the hay they had bought. Others took pewter vessels and hid them in the rocks surrounding the abbey.[307] Richard Riche, chancellor of the Court of Augmentations, learning in September 1538 that 'the late monastery of Bordesley has been defaced and plucked down and the substance thereof sold', wrote to John Scudamore, the Receiver for Worcestershire, asking him 'by whose authority those who have so defaced the house have acted, who were the purchasers and what has been paid.'[308]

Sir William Parre, to whom the site of Pipewell had been granted, complained as to the misuse of the former abbey. Consequently a commission of enquiry took place in 1540, one of the commissioners being the last abbot. This found that several parts of the monastery including the hall with the chambers over it and the chapter-house were still in good repair. The abbot legitimately had taken away 'the panelling and delling of the refectory,' each monk the contents of his chamber in the dorter, and Sir William Parre the paving of the dorter. Much had been stolen, including doors and window glass from the cellarer's chamber, and items from the salt, fish and cheese chambers. A tinker who had stolen iron and lead had been hanged at Northampton.[309]

In Wales Nicholas Purcell, Crown tenant of Strata Marcella and later sheriff of Montgomeryshire (1553), was accused of destroying the monastery by selling large amounts of stone to local inhabitants, and allowing the removal of the church windows and the disappearance of church plate and vestments. Whitland was ravaged by Sir John Vaughan—the former commissioner to whom the site had been leased, together with Sir John Perrot and Richard Vaughan, elder and younger. Perrot took much freestone to Laugharne to erect a house for himself, whilst Richard Vaughan exchanged cart-loads of freestone in return for livestock. As late as 1584 several local inhabitants were accused of making severe depredations to the 'mansion house' of Valle Crucis, and pulling down its 'great and high stone walls.'[310]

The suppression commissioners themselves had to a degree despoiled monastery buildings and effects, perhaps to keep them from thieving hands. In the autumn of 1538 this came to Cromwell's notice, and he ordered them to desist. Thomas Legh and William Cavendish, writing to Cromwell on 25 October, said that 'we received your letter admonishing us in no wise to deface the monastery of Pipewell, and will observe the same.'[311] A few days later John

London wrote to Cromwell in similar terms: 'I will henceforth deface no house without special command'.He said that he thought he had acted for the best, and that the accounts Cromwell had received were exaggerated. He pointed out that 'if there be no surveyor to do it at once or sure man to inhabit them, the houses will be spoiled.'[312] For this reason Sir John Lamplieu was ordered 'to keep household' at the site of Furness.[313] Sir Thomas Holcroft of Holcroft, Lancashire, an officer of both Henry VIII and Cromwell who took the surrender of Vale Royal on about 9 September 1538, within a few weeks wrote to the king saying that he had 'plucked down' the abbey church there.[314]

Where a powerful personage was granted the site of an abbey, his protection meant that the abbey buildings were saved from immediate plunder, though still subject to the ravages of the weather once the lead had been removed from the roofs. Tintern had been granted to the earl of Worcester in 1537, and he resided there for a time. His care of the site meant that when in 1568 he let out some of the buildings, they must have been fairly intact, and included a laundry-house, two stables, a bark-loft, a kiln-house and a graveyard. By 1579 'le library and le cloyster' were also demised. Sir Rice Mansel turned part of Margam into his principal residence, whilst Neath similarly converted formed a mansion for the Herbert family.[315] Grants of site were not made free of charge; Sir Thomas Denys in 1540 paid £315 for the privilege of obtaining Buckfast and many of its lands.[316]

Legitimate removal on behalf of the Crown of portions of monastic fabric included twenty-five foot of glass taken from Valle Crucis to ornament Holt Castle; stone from Aberconwy as well as over a hundred oaks from abbey land were removed by water to repair the Shire Hall and town walls of Caernarfon.[317] Stone from Beaulieu was used to build block-houses at East and West Cowes and its lead was intended for the Barbican at the Tower.[318] Stone from Roche was used in building the Earl of Shrewsbury's chapel in Sheffield parish church, Yorkshire.[319] Doubtless much monastic stone was also used when the gentry who inherited sites such as Beaulieu, Buildwas, Cwmhir and Neath converted parts of the remains into palatial dwellings. Much of Stanley was robbed of stone by Sir Edward Baynton, soon after its closure, in order to build his new mansion at Bromham.[320] In Elizabethan times, Cymer was said to be 'a quarry for stones.'[321] Sir Stephen Proctor around 1600 built himself at Fountains 'a very beautiful house, with stone got at hand out of the abbey walls.'[322]

Plate, Lead and Bells

The suppression commissioners noted carefully by weight and value the plate a house possessed, including items such as chalices. Plate, ornaments and jewels, were reserved to the Crown,[323] and when Sawtry was dissolved (4 June 1536) it was noted that its 'seal, evidences and plate,' which included four silver-gilt chalices, were 'in safe custody'.[324] The amount of plate an abbey possessed varied considerably with its fortunes. Fountains possessed 2,480 oz. of plate, including twenty-two silver chalices,[325] though Abbot Bradley had allegedly disposed of some plates and jewels,[326] while poor Cwmhir in Wales recorded only 9½ oz. of silver plate.[327] Stratford owned 279 oz. of gilt plate and 966 oz. of parcel gilt and white plate.[328] Merevale had 132 oz. of gilt plate and 26 oz. of white plate, totalling in value £32; a further 47 oz. of silver plate worth over £8 had, exceptionally, been sold.[329] The quantity of plate recorded at Roche was small, and a tabernacle was in pledge for £40. Might this suggest some plate was secreted away from the eyes of the commissioners?[330]

The site of Dunkeswell was granted to Lord John Russell, president of the King's Council in the West, in July 1539. He in November that year sold it on to John Heydon of Ottery St Mary. An unusual feature of the agreement was that, whilst lead was excepted from the sale, any treasure found in or around the church during the next ten years was to be shared between Russell and Heydon. This included treasure discovered 'within any tomb or monument under the ground.'[331]

Some perceived valuables were hidden away, like the statue of Our Lady—found in 1890 in the flooring of a house near Hailes,[332] and a further statue of the Blessed Virgin, discovered in a stream bank close to Whalley and now preserved in the local Roman Catholic church.[333]

The lead of monastic roofs was a valuable commodity reserved to the use of the Crown, though some was sold off, presumably when there was no potential royal demand for it. The lead of Hulton in Staffordshire was carried away to Tutbury castle.[334] Lead from Hailes went by water to Bristol.[335] Lead from Basingwerk (in 1546) was used to cover Dublin castle and other royal buildings in Ireland.[336] The stripping of a lead covering was a major factor in allowing natural weathering to assist the process of destruction of the abbey buildings. The several suppression surveys attempted to estimate its worth. In October 1538 the lead of Dieulacres was valued at £720; after its sale of goods lead to the value of £340 remained.[337] The lead of Beaulieu, destined for the Barbican at the Tower and estimated to be 180 'fothers' in weight was also valued at £720.[338]

In several surveys it is clear that much lead, although melted down, remained on site, sometimes for years either because of lack of an immediate need for it, or because of the problem of transporting it. When in November 1537 Jervaulx had been stripped of its lead, Richard Bellais who did the demolition wrote to Cromwell telling him that the metal could not be immediately carried away because 'the ways in that country are so foul and deep that no carriage can pass in winter.'[339] The lead of Strata Florida was eventually removed to storage at Aberystwyth Castle, where as late as 1555 much remained unused.[340] At Holm Cultram the lead roofing the now parish church, sixty fothers in all, was spared. The total value of its lead amounted to £466, being 140 fothers 'by the weight of the city of York,' and some was sold to George Pulleyn, a York merchant. [341] Some of the Fountains lead was pilfered, but the bulk was not transported from the site until 1544, when it was removed to Hull by way of Boroughbridge and York.[342] Robert Southwell, the responsible commissioner, wrote to Cromwell telling him that all the lead of Furness had been melted down, and thanking him for teaching him 'how to melt the ashes.'[343]

The lead, once taken down, was always melted on site into block described as 'pigs' or 'sows'; this perhaps explains two possible furnace sites excavated in front of the high altar of Hailes.[344] This liquefaction was a further cause of abbey despoliation, for it demanded a source of considerable heat. At some monasteries, and certainly at Fountains where huge fires were made—including one in the crossing, using the wood of the roofs, choir stalls and rood screen as fuel, the timber nearest to hand was employed.[345] This dismayed an eye witness of the destruction of Roche, who later recalled that 'the persons that cast the lead into fodders, plucked up all the seats in the choir, and burned them and melted the lead therewith all, although there was wood plenty within a flight shot of them.'[346]

John Scudamore, the particular receiver for four counties, had the duty of causing the lead of each suppressed house in his charge 'to be molten into 'plocks' and 'sows', to weight them, mark them with the king's mark, and then cause them to be conveyed to the nearest royal castle. There he was to surrender them to the constable or keeper of the castle; his costs being reimbursed.[347] The lead of Tintern (dissolved in 1536) remained on site until 1541, when "the king's plumbers," William Wilson and Christopher Dray, were paid £8 to melt it down. At Llantarnam, where the work was completed within a year, the 'plumbers, carpenters, tilers and labourers,' involved in cutting down the bells and melting the lead received the sum of £15 in payment, whilst a further 18s, was paid for the carriage of wood for charcoal.[348]

It is difficult to estimate the precise amounts of lead removed and melted down, as the terminology varies. Sometimes there is reference to lead being melted down into blocks called 'pigs', on other occasions the term used is 'sows', believed to be larger blocks. The late medieval weight represented by the term 'fother' (originating from 'cart-load') varied between 2184 and 2520 lb., and thus one fother was very roughly equivalent to one ton. Eight pigs, by one source, made a 'fother'. The lead of Strata Florida, stored at Aberystwyth, was described as consisting of 'eleven score sows', with each sow weighing 100 lb.[349] Another estimate makes a 'sow' equivalent to half-a-ton.[350]

At Merevale the lead amounted to 11 fothers, 421 lb., suggesting that each of the twenty-five sows there was weighed some 96 pounds.[351] The ninety tons of lead at Margam were melted down into 415 sows, valued at £372. To complicate matters further the lead of Sawtry was described as consisting of 272 'webbes', nineteen pipes and a gutter.[352] There was also a considerable disparity between the value placed upon a fother of lead by different officials and receivers. A fother of lead was estimated at Beaulieu as being worth £4, at Buildwas, Garendon and Stoneleigh valued at around £3-13-4, but at Dieula-cres and Newminster at well under £2.[353]

Monastic bells were mostly sold, but not always immediately. In some instances the bells were bought by the local parishioners so that they contin-ued to call them to worship. This was the case at Buckfast,[354] Medmenham,[355] Strata Florida and Whitland. Some bells went to serve reasonably local churches: the bells of Strata Marcella passed to the parish of Chirk, those of Valle Crucis to the churches of Baschurch and Great Ness in Shropshire.[356] The alleged twelve bells of Bindon were dispersed: four to Wool parish church, three to Combe Keynes nearby and five to Fordington. Two of those at Fordington bear the stamp of John Walgrave, a fifteenth-century London founder. Their presence led to a local rhyme: 'Wool streams and Combe Keynes wells, Fordington cuckolds stole Bindon bells!'[357]

Some bells went much further afield. In 1538 the abbot of St Peter's, Gloucester, acknowledged receipt of four bells and a clock 'lately called the bells and clock of Stanley.'[358] John White, a London grocer, bought for £40 the five bells of Beaulieu, but had not paid for them by 1539.[359] The bells of Grace Dieu remained on site until 1545 when bought by John Coore, another London grocer, who had them transported, presumably by water, to Bristol. He had already bought the bells of Margam and Neath.[360] When Richard Bellais dismantled the bells of Jervaulx in 1537, he had to write to Cromwell saying that 'I can only get fifteen shillings a hundredweight for them', and wanted to know whether to accept that price or send them up to London.[361]

As late as 1555 five bells of the former abbey remained standing upon the green outside the monastery of Hailes; the great bell—weighing 2016 lb.- was damaged. Leave was given for the bells to serve the church of Stratford-on-Avon, but there is no evidence that they arrived; local tradition has it that they went to Sutton-under-Brailes church.[362] The number of bells varied, according to the prosperity of a house: Fountains had ten bells weighing in all 10,000 lb.[363] Newminster had but five, and of little value (£15): three were 'great bells' and two were small bells 'for ferial days.'[364] Sawtry's fourth bell was one yard in both depth and head.[365] Where bells were not sold immediately their safe custody was the responsibility of those to whom the abbey site had been granted, as Sir Walter Devereux at Merevale and William Wigston at Combe.[366]

Provision for Parishioners

After the closure of Bordesley in July 1538 the local inhabitants petitioned the Court of Augmentations, saying that before the dissolution the abbot provided a curate to officiate in the parish church of Bordesley, but now they were 'without spiritual comfort'. They could not travel to any other church, they wrote, because the area was surrounded by rivers which flooded, and they therefore petitioned for a minister to be appointed to serve their needs.[367] The villagers of Holm Cultram wrote to Cromwell begging the preservation of the abbey church, as it was also their parish church.[368] Their request was granted, the nave survives, and Gavin Borrowdale, the last abbot, became their vicar. At Dore, the presbytery and crossing survived to serve the same purpose; at Margam, the nave.

The parishioners of Strata Florida, some dwelling up to seven or more miles from a parish church, had a chapel within the monastery to serve them. Local pressure ensured that this continued after the Suppression, and a former monk of the house, John York was appointed to serve them 'in the chapel of Stratflur' with a stipend of £5-6-8 p.a. When Cwmhir closed Edward Beawpe and others immediately set about building 'a chapel in Maelienydd in the honour of Jesus to have the sacraments and sacramentals administered,' and sought the return from Strata Florida of 'a famed picture of Jesus,' formerly owned by Cwmhir.[369] By 1540 the refectory at Beaulieu had been converted into the parish church; the steps leading up to the reader's pulpitum yet exist.[370]

At a few English abbeys the former gate-house chapels survive and serve as places of worship.[371] St Mary's, Whitegate, once the outer gate chapel of Vale Royal has been a parish church practically since the Dissolution,[372] as has the gate-house chapel of Our Lady at Merevale. It possesses a fourteenth-century Tree of Jesse widow, which probably came from the abbey. Other former gate-house chapels still in use for divine service are those at Coggeshall (St Nicholas; with a brick-lined sedilia, double piscina and mural consecration cross); Hailes (with fine medieval decorative painting); Kirkstead (bearing remnants of a grey masonry pattern), and Tilty (where the stepped sedilia bears carvings in stone of the heads of a monk and a layman). St Margaret's chapel at Tintern's former Trelech Grange, recently restored, also survives as a parish church. Dore's medieval grange and chantry chapel at Llanfair Cilgoed in northern Monmouthshire continued in use for recusant worship through-out the seventeenth century; until his death in 1570, John Didbroke, a former monk of the abbey, was the resident priest.[373] The church of Sawtry Judith, outside the monastery gates but served by a Cistercian monk in 1470, has long been demolished.[374]

Apart from the numerous jobs which may have been lost when the monas-teries closed, Vale Royal's tenants of Overham and Weaverham had another regret. They missed the 'bountiful dinners' and at divers times of the year 'comfort of meat and drink' they had enjoyed in return for their seed-time and harvest duties. Now all this was gone, as were grants of timber for their fuel.[375] For their part, the leaders of the Pilgrimage of Grace had emphasised that the abbeys of the North had been a source of sustenance to many, whilst the commissioners in the south had singled out the usefulness of Quarr and Netley to travellers at sea.[376] When the abbeys closed, all this was lost. Robert Aske, before his execution, told how many of the servants of the monasteries 'were their fee'd servants, who now want refreshing by meat, clothes and wages, and know not where to have any living.'[377] Robert Southwell, responsible for the closure arrangements at Furness took pity on those who had served that abbey. Writing to Cromwell he suggested that 'divers parcels of the demesne should be distributed to four or five poor men who were headmen, and had wages of the house, and are now destitute.'[378]

In the post-Suppression years new owners incorporated parts of the monastic buildings into the new comfortable homes they built on their site, but not all former abbeys were so fortunate; Jervaulx was blown up,[379] and the church of Ford was razed to the ground,[380] whilst the duke of Suffolk is said to have pulled down Vaudey in order to enlarge his residence at Grimsthorpe in time for a visit there by Henry VIII.[381] The rood screen and abbot's stall of Jervaulx were saved, and found their way to nearby Aysgarth church. The stall bears the hazel bush and barrel (tun) device of Abbot Heslington (abbot, 1475-?1487).[382] At Combermere the late medieval abbot's house was incorporated into a new mansion, and much the same happened at Buildwas and Hailes. Beaulieu Abbey House is today one of the foremost dwellings on a former Cistercian site, and incorporates its great gate-house.

Epilogue

Any account of monastic history is bound to be somewhat lop-sided, and a false impression perhaps given of Cistercian life in the sixteenth century. This is inevitable since—as with modern newspapers, very often only bad news surfaces in the deeds of the times. The holy lives led by many, perhaps the majority of the monks, rarely hit the headlines. Theirs was indeed a 'hidden life', of which we have little cognisance. The lack of our knowledge of all that was good in the lives of the Tudor religious is reminiscent of the words of Scripture: 'Behold, the half was not told me!' (1 K 10, v. 7).

This is not to say that there was no room for improvement in the Cistercian abbeys of the period, there was. There were a few abbots who acted dishonestly, and may be a sprinkling of monks whose lives were not as pure as could have been—though the evidence of the suppression commissioners in this respect is hardly to be trusted. The desire of many monks not to leave their calling when offered the opportunity to do so, the self-sacrifice made by the martyrs, and the adherence of a number in later life to catholicity, points to a high degree of spirituality on their part.

There was a need for reform—but in the sense of renewal, and there was a need to embrace the early principles of the Order—including austerity and simplicity in all aspects of life and worship. Several of the abbeys with but few remaining inhabitants could well have been closed, but not allowed to fall into rack and ruin. They might well have become places of caring, healing and education. The nine hundred Cistercian monks still following their vocation in 1536 could have been redistributed between say forty houses, allowing a reasonably sized community of over twenty monks in each.

There was a need for reform, of return to first principles, indeed of a new beginning, but given the avaricious nature of Henry VIII and his ministers, this was not possible, and the fault lay not with the Order.

Notes

[1]   G. Baskerville, *English Monks and Suppression of the Monasteries*, London: Jonathan Cape, 1937, pp. 100–01; J. Youings, *Dissolution of the Monasteries*, London: Allen and Unwin, 1971, p. 45.

[2]   *LC*, p. 262, F. A. Gasquet, *Henry VIII and the English Monasteries*, London: J.C. Nimmo, 2nd. edn. 1899, pp. 17–22.

[3]   *LP* 4, Part 1, pp. 501–02 [No. 1137].

[4]   TNA, E24/23/1; *LP* 4, Part 1, pp. 432 [No. 989]; 985–89 [No. 2217]. Certain properties of Beaulieu, Biddlesden, Pipewell and Woburn, were considered for appropriation to raise funds: *LP* 4, Part 1, p. 987 [No. 2217].

[5]   J. S. Fletcher, *Cistercians in Yorkshire*, London: S.P.C.K., 1919, pp. 200–01.

[6]   *LP* 4, pp. 272–73 [No. 610]; TNA, SC7/63/22, 24.

[7]   TNA, SC11/429.

[8]   Gasquet, *English Monasteries*, 1899, pp. 142–43.

[9]   *LP* 9, pp. 156–57 [No. 478].

[10] *LP* 11, p. 597 [Appx. 16].

[11] *LP* 14, Part 2, p. 321 [No. 782].

[12] *LP* 5, Part 2, p. 557 [No. 1285/vi].

[13] Youings, *Dissolution*, 1971, pp. 143–44.

[14] Ibid. p. 143.

[15] *LP* 4, Part 3, p. 2653 [No. 5944]; Cf. J. D. Austin, *Merevale Abbey*, Studley: Brewin, 1998, p. 7.

[16] *LP* 5, Part 1, p. 353 [No. 740].

[17] *LP* 8, p. 56 [No. 169].

18 *LP* **10**, pp. 45–46 [No. 137].
19 *LP* **7**, Part 1, p. 322 [No. 868].
20 *LP* **9**, p. 83 [No. 244].
21 Gasquet, *English Monasteries*, 1899, pp. 280–81.
22 *LP* **10**, p. 434 [No. 1046]; **12**, Part 1, p. 108 [No. 215]; **13**, Part 1, p. 577 [No. 1520].
23 G.W.O. Woodward, *Dissolution of the Monasteries*, London: Blandford Press, 1966, pp. 57–58.
24 *LP* **9**, p. 313 [No. 925].
25 *LP* **7**, p. 542 [No. 1447].
26 *LP* **13**, Part 1, p. 102 [No. 299].
27 *LP* **6**, p. 16 [No. 35].
28 *LP* **11**, p. 138 [No. 342; misplaced in date].
29 VCH, *County of Warwick* **2**, 1908, p. 77.
30 *LP* **13**, Part 1, p. 578 [No. 1520].
31 *LP* **6**, p. 608 [No. 1502].
32 *LP* **13**, Part 1, pp. 208–09 [No. 567].
33 VCH, *County of Chester* **3**, 1980, p. 162, n.89.
34 *LP* **11**, pp. 77 [No. 177], 106 [No. 247], 183 [No. 459].
35 A. Jones, 'The Estates of the Welsh Abbeys at the Dissolution.' In: *AC* **92**, 1937, p. 177; *Cf.* pp. 272–73.
36 TNA, E118/1/31, pp. 20–26v.
37 J. E. Oxley, , *The Reformation in Essex*, Manchester U.P., 1965, p. 102–03; *LP* **10**, p. 60 [164/5].
38 TNA, E303/17, m.370. [In E303/17 are several batches of Merevale demises forming together a veritable 'Merevale Lease Book.']
39 Lancashire R.O. DDM 19/24.
40 *LC*, p. 238, Woodward, *Dissolution*, 1966, p. 79; Youings, *Dissolution*, 1971, p. 157.
41 E. Owen, 'Strata Marcella immediately before and after its Dissolution.' *Y Cymmrodor* **29**, 1919, p. 27.
42 TNA, E321/32, m.84.
43 Glamorgan Archives, CL/Deeds II/Montgomery Box 3.
44 Owen, 'Strata Marcella,' 1919, p. 30.
45 D. H. Williams, 'White Monks in Powys.' In: *Cistercian Studies* **11**, 1976, p. 91.
46 Ibid., *The Welsh Cistercians*, Leominster: Gracewing, 2001, p. 79.
47 TNA, LR1/175, ff. 293r–307r.
48 J. Stéphan, *History of Buckfast Abbey*, Bristol: Burleigh Press, 1970, p. 207.
49 *LP* **14**, Part 1, pp. 421–23 [No. 906/7].
50 C.W. Green, *Biddlesden and its Abbey*, Buckingham: E.N. Hiller and Sons., 1974, pp. 25–26.
51 J. A. Sparks, *In the Shadow of the Blackdowns*, Bradford-on-Avon: Moonraker Press, 1978, pp. 121–28.

[52] G. D. Barnes, *Kirkstall Abbey*, PTS **58**: No. 128, 1982, p. 81.

[53] Williams, *Welsh Cistercians*, 2001, pp. 78–79.

[54] TNA, SC6/HENVIII/4903, f. 27.

[55] M. S. Giuseppi and G. D. Owen (ed.), Calendar of the Manuscripts of the Marquis of Salisbury, London: Historical Manuscripts Commission **9**, 1883; II, pp. 134–35.

[56] R. Hoyle, 'Monastic Leasing Before the Dissolution.' In: *YAJ* **61**, 1989, p. 117.

[57] TNA, E321/39/3.

[58] J. L. Tomkinson, *A History of Hulton Abbey*, Staffordshire Archaeological Studies, N.S. **10**, 1997, pp. 68–69; TNA, E315/118, ff. 224–25.

[59] M. J. C. Fisher, *Dieulacres Abbey*, Leek: Hill Bros., 1969, p. 56.

[60] Baskerville, *English Monks*, 1937, pp. 200–01.

[61] TNA, SP1 (HEN.VIII) XVII/380, f.197; E318/186, f.22; E321/10, m.45.

[62] *Augm.* Pp. 29–31; this seal was engraved with the royal arms, but no impressions from it are known [NLW, Cwrtmawr MS 873D, p. 25].

[63] Staffordshire R.O. 2/32/00, p. 46; Fisher, *Dieulacres*, 1969, pp. 56–57; TNA, E315/96, ff. 101r–102r.

[64] TNA, LR1/176, f. 3r–v.

[65] S. F. Hockey, *Beaulieu, King John's Abbey*, Beaulieu: Pioneer Publns., 1976, p. 167.

[66] VCH, *County of Northampton* **3**, 1970, p. 120.

[67] TNA, LR1/175, f. 312r–v.

[68] TNA, E315/94, f. 247; Tomkinson, *Hulton Abbey*, 1997, pp. 68–69.

[69] TNA, E315/99, f. 31v.

[70] TNA, LR1/175, ff. 293–326, LR1/176, ff. 1–101.

[71] TNA, E118/1/31, p. 46.

[72] TNA, LR1/228, f. 59v; E315/102, f. 19v, respectively.

[73] TNA, E315/94, ff. 136v–137r.

[74] Hoyle, 'Monastic Leasing,' 1989, p. 137.

[75] TNA,LR1/173, f. 150r–v.

[76] TNA, E36/152.

[77] *LP* **11**, p. 152 [No. 381b].

[78] TNA, LR1/174, f. 18.

[79] TNA, E315/91,f. 88; 315/100, f. 19v.

[80] TNA, E315/104, f. 126v.

[81] TNA, E315/94, f. 131r.

[82] TNA, LR1/176, f. 3r–v.

[83] D. H.Williams, *White Monks in Gwent and the Border*, Pontypool: Griffin Press, 1976, pp. 112–13.

[84] TNA, E210/815.

[85] Woodward, *Dissolution*, 1966, p. 26.

[86] TNA, E36/152.

[87] Youings, *Dissolution*, 1971, p. 59.

88 Hoyle, 'Monastic Leasing,' 1989, p. 137.

89 C. Haigh, *The Last Days of the Lancashire Monasteries*, Manchester U.P., 1969, p. 18.

90 TNA, E315/98, f. 82r–v.

91 TNA, E315/95, ff. 245v–246r.

92 TNA, E315/94, f. 247r

93 TNA, E315/98, f. 97r–v.

94 TNA, E315/95, f. 236.

95 A very good account of their journeyings is given in: D. Knowles, *Bare Ruined Choirs*, Cambridge U.P., 1976 edn., pp. 166–73.

96 P. Cunich, 'Layton, Richard,' *ODNB* online.

97 *LP* **9**, p. 147 [No. 452].

98 Ibid. pp. 210–11 [No. 622].

99 Ibid. p. 210 [No. 621].

100 A.N. Shaw, 'Legh, Thomas,' *ODNB* online.

101 A.N. Shaw, 'The Northern Visitation of 1535/6.' In: *Downside Review* **116**, 1998, p. 287; Gasquet, *English Monasteries*, 1899, p. 166.

102 M. Collinson, 'Monastic Cash at the Dissolution.' In: *YAJ* **80**, 2008, pp. 132–33.

103 P. R. N. Carter, 'Bedyll, Thomas,' *ODNB* online.

104 C. S. Knighton, 'Petre, William,' *ODNB* online.

105 A. N. Shaw, 'Tregonwell, John,' *ODNB* online.

106 *LP* **10**, p. 155 [No. 388].

107 TNA, E315/96, ff. 199v–200r. [Indeed, Tregonwell's deed appear to be dated one month after the closure of the abbey].

108 J. H. Bettey, *Suppression of Monasteries in the West Country*, Gloucester: Alan Sutton, 1989, p. 138.

109 L. S. Snell, *The Suppression of the Religious Foundations of Devon and Cornwall*, Marazion: Wordens Ltd, 1967, p. 85.

110 *LP* **10**, p. 160 [No. 393].

111 G. Williams, *Welsh Reformation Essays*, Cardiff: University of Wales Press, 1967, p. 93.

112 *LP* **13**, Part 1, p. 584 [No. 1520]; D. Pratt, *Dissolution of Valle Crucis Abbey*, Wrexham: Bridge Books, 1997, pp. 34–35.

113 Gasquet, *English Monasteries*, 1899, pp. 82–84.

114 VCH, *County of Huntingdon* **1**, 1974, p. 391.

115 *LP* **9**, pp. 258 [No. 758] 621 [No. 622].

116 Knowles, *Bare Ruined Choirs*, 1976, p. 170.

117 *LC*, pp. 59–60 [No. XXIX].

118 *LP* **9**, p. 195 [No. 590].

119 Ibid. p. 266 [No. 790].

120 Ibid. p. 275 [No. 822].

121 Woodward, *Dissolution*, 1966, p. 59.

122 *LP* **10**, pp. 515–17 [No. 1238].

[123] Woodward, *Dissolution*, 1966, p. 79.

[124] *LP* **10**, pp. 496, 498–99 [No. 1191].

[125] *LP* **11**, p. 596 [Appx. 15]; *Cf. LP* **11**, p. 37 [No. 75].

[126] *LP* **10**, p. 498 [No. 1191].

[127] Ibid. p. 496 [No. 1191].

[128] TNA, LR6/152/1, m. 8v.

[129] TNA, LR6/152/1, m. 3v.

[130] TNA, E315/427/3, f. 39r; ff. 1–5 [debts].

[131] TNA, E315/278, f. 26.

[132] *Ibid.* f. 56.

[133] *Ibid.* ff. 85–86.

[134] *LP* **10**, p. 155 [No. 387].

[135] *LP* **13**, Part 2, p. 190 [No. 488].

[136] *LC*, pp. 228–29 [No. CXLVIII].

[137] VCH, *County of York* **3**, 1974, p. 137.

[138] VCH, County of Lancaster **2**, 1908, p. 138.

[139] F. G. Baigent, 'In the Abbey of the Blessed Mary of Waverley.' In: *SAC* **8**, p. 202; *LP* **10**, p. 462 [No. 1097].

[140] *LP* **12**, Part 1, p. 2 [No. 4].

[141] *LP* **10**, p. 434 [No. 1046]; **12**, Part 1, p. 108 [No. 215].

[142] *LP* **13**, Part 2, p. 122 [No. 314].

[143] *LB*, p. 23.

[144] *LP* **13**, Part 1, p. 495 [No. 1330].

[145] Ibid. Part 2, p. 267 [No. 702].

[146] Ibid. Part 2, p. 71 [No. 180].

[147] Ibid. Part 1, p. 267 [No. 702], *Cf.* Part 1, p. 153 [No. 409].

[148] Tomkinson, 'Hulton Abbey,' 1985, p. 67.

[149] *LP* **13**, Part 1, p. 397 [No. 1087]; VCH, *County of Chester* **3**, 1980, p. 155.

[150] Youings, *Dissolution*, 1971, pp. 173–74.

[151] Gasquet, *English Monasteries*, 1899, pp. 285, 287.

[152] Williams, *White Monks in Gwent*, 1976, p. 30; TNA, E321/32/84.

[153] *LP* **11**, p. 173 [No. 433]; **14**, Part 1, p. 248 [No. 639]; **13**, Part 2, pp. 118 [No. 297], 123 [No. 315]; Wikipedia online; Youings, *Dissolution*, 1971, p. 228, n.3.

[154] Gasquet, *English Monasteries*, 1899, p. 349, *LC*, pp. 205–06; *Cf. LP* **13**, Part 2, p. 71 [No. 180].

[155] *LP* **14**, Part 1, p. 44 [No. 113]; *LC*, pp. 225–26.

[156] *LP* **13**, Part 1, p. 420 [No. 1130], *Cf.* p. 460 [No. 1248].

[157] Baskerville, *English Monks*, 1937, pp. 185–86; Youings, *Dissolution*, 1971, pp. 63–64..

[158] *LP* **13**, Part 1, p. 393 [No. 1073], *Cf.* p. 459 [No. 1243].

[159] Ibid. pp. 500–01 [No. 1343], of 8 July 1538.

[160] Ibid. Part 2, p. 177 [No. 457]; Youings, *Dissolution*, 1971, pp. 28, 221.

161 Williams, *Welsh Cistercians*, 2001, pp. 79–80.

162 *LP* **14**, Part 1, p. 150 [No. 395].

163 Dorset History Centre, D/WLC/T3 [original deed]; *LP* **11**, p. 490 [No. 1217/13, of 2-10-1536].

164 *LP* **12**, Part 2, p. 165 [No. 411/2].

165 Staffordshire Archives, D1798/H.M.ASTON/6/2, of 1-10-1537; the great seal remains attached; *Cf. LP* **12**, Part 2p. 349 [No. 1008/1].

166 Williams, *Welsh Cistercians*, 2001, pp. 79–80.

167 *SBC* **4**, pp. 110–11 [No. 1187].

168 TNA, C1/815/40; *SBC* **4**, pp. 109–10 [1187].

169 Essex Archives, D/DRg1/103–05; D.M. Smith, *The Heads of Religious Houses* **3**, Cambridge U.P., 2008, p. 322.

170 Williams, *Welsh Cistercians*, 2001, p. 79.

171 *LP* **13**, Part 1, p. 81 [No. 235].

172 Woodward, *Dissolution*, 1966, p. 111.

173 *LP* **10**, pp. 495–96 [No. 1191].

174 *LP* **13**, Part 1, p. 67 [No. 195].

175 *LP* **11**, p. 596 [Appx. 15].

176 *LP* **10**, p. 164 [No. 408/2]; R. C. Fowler., 'Essex Monastic Inventories,' *TEAS*, N.S. 10. 1908, p. 15.

177 TNA, E322/204, 76, respectively.

178 *LP* **13**, Part 1, p. 208 [No. 564].

179 *LP* **13**, Part 2, 161–62 [421]; Woodward, *Dissolution*, 1966, pp. 118–19

180 TNA, E322/57.

181 *LP* **10**, pp. 59–60 [No. 164]; *LP* **13**, Part 1, p. 75 [No. 221].

182 *LP* **14**, Part 1, p. 44 [No. 113].

183 TNA, SC6/HENVIII/481.

184 BL, Additional MS 11041, f. 12.

185 Gasquet, *English Monasteries*, 1899, p. 356.

186 *LP* **13**, Part 1, p. 67 [No. 195].

187 Ibid. pp. 160–61 [No. 434], 203 [No. 547].

188 *LP* **10**, p. 164 [No. 408].

189 LP **15**, p. 544 [No. 1032].

190 See the Appendix for sources regarding these monks.

191 Woodward, *Dissolution*, 1966, pp. 86–87.

192 *LP* **12**, Part 1, p. 294 [No. 668].

193 Ibid. p. 315 [No. 706].

194 Haigh, *Lancashire Monasteries*, 1969, p. 112.

195 VCH, *County of Lincoln* **2**, 1906, p. 139.

196 *LP* **11**, p. 26 [No. 42].

197 Gasquet, *English Monasteries*, 1899, p. 436.

[198] Williams, *White Monks in Gwent*, 1976, pp. 87, 111.

[199] TNA, E315/278, ff. 87, 146.

[200] VCH, *County of Lincoln* **2**, 1906, p. 139.

[201] TNA, E36/152, ff. 19–22.

[202] TNA, E314/77.

[203] TNA, E315/244.

[204] TNA, E315/245, f. 14.

[205] *LP* **13**, Part 1, p. 68 [No. 199/iii].

[206] TNA, E314/77.

[207] TNA, E314/77; LP **13**, Part 1, p. 160 [No. 433/iii].

[208] TNA, E314/77.

[209] *LP* **14**, Part 1, p. 44 [No. 113].

[210] TNA, E314/77.

[211] J. P. Davey and J. R. Roscow., *Rushen Abbey and the Dissolution of the Monasteries*, Isle of Man Natural History and Antiquarian Society, Monograph **1**, 2010, pp. 174–75.

[212] *LP* **13**, Part 2, p. 162 [No. 422].

[213] C. Cross and N. Vickers, *Monks, friars and nuns in sixteenth century Yorkshire*, Yorkshire Archaeological Soc., 1995, p. 188; TNA, E134/77.

[214] *LP* **13**, Part 1, p. 68 [No. 199/iii].

[215] *LP* **14**, Part 1, p. 44 [No. 113].

[216] Youings, *Dissolution*, 1971, p.186.

[217] TNA, E314/77.

[218] W. H. Stevenson and H. E. Salter, *Early History of St John's College, Oxford*, Oxford Historical Soc., 1939, p. 47.

[219] Cross and Vickers, *Monks, friars and nuns*, 1995, p. 193.

[220] Ibid. 166.

[221] *LP* **13**, Part 1, p. 292 [No. 776].

[222] Staffordshire Archives 2/32/00.

[223] Davey and Roscow, *Rushen Abbey*, 2010, p. 174.

[224] *LP* **13**, Part 1, p. 160 [No. 433/iii]; TNA, E36/152.

[225] *LP* **13**, Part 1, p. 68 [No. 199/iii].

[226] Ibid. p. 160 [No, 433/iii].

[227] Ibid. Part 2, p. 550 [Appx. 25].

[228] M. E. C. Walcott, 'Inventories and Valuations of Religious Houses.' In: *Archaeologia* **43**, 1871, p. 216.

[229] A. G. Dickens, *Reformation Studies*, 1982, p. 384; Woodward, *Dissolution*, 1966, pp. 145–46.

[230] Bodleian Library, Oxford; Tanner MS 343.

[231] Woodward, *Dissolution*, 1966, p. 23.

[232] Stéphan, *Buckfast Abbey*, 1970, p. 212, Sparks, *In the Shadow of the Blackdowns*, 1978, pp. 110–11.

[233] Green, *Biddlesden*, 1974, p. 27.

[234] BL, Additional MS 11041, ff. 5, 9.

[235] Ibid. f. 4; *LP* **14**, Part 1, p. 412 [No. 886].

[236] Cross and Vickers, *Monks, friars and nuns*, 1995, pp. 176, 184–85.

[237] A. Lonsdale, 'The Last Monks of Kirkstall Abbey.' In: *PTS* **53**: No. 118, Part 3, 1972, p. 209.

[238] Dickens, *Reformation Studies*, 1982, pp. 383, 400.

[239] Cheshire Archives, ZCR 72A/S/112.

[240] VCH *County of Chester* **3**1980, p. 155.

[241] TNA, E315/278, f. 143.

[242] *LP* **13**, Part 1, p. 67 [No. 195].

[243] BL, Additional MS 11041, f. 12.

[244] Where individual monks are cited, see the Appendix for bibliographical references.

[245] Lonsdale, 'Last Monks,' 1972, p. 210.

[246] Youings, *Dissolution*, 1971, p. 249.

[247] *LP* **10**, p. 521 [No. 1248].

[248] *Cf. LP* **13**, Part 2, p. 550 [Appx. 25]; *FOR.*, passim., Stéphan, *Buckfast Abbey*, 1970, p. 215.

[249] Haigh, *Lancashire Monasteries*, 1969, p. 121.

[250] Orme, N., 'The Dissolution of the Chantries in Devon,' *RTDA* **42**, 1960, p. 94.

[251] Williams, *White Monks in Gwent*, 1976, p. 28.

[252] W. H. Pearce, *The Monks of Westminster*, Cambridge U.P., 1916, pp. 214–16. I am grateful to Miss Christine Reynolds, Lambeth Palace Muniments, for yielding this reference. Could a 'Mr Strotford', also a monk of Westminster, have been previously a religious of Stratford?; Baskerville, 1927, p. 89.

[253] D. N. Bell, 'Hailes Abbey and its Books.' In: *Cîteaux* **61**, 2010, p. 349; D. Knowles, *The Religious Orders in England* **3**: *The Tuor Age*, Cambridge U.P., 1971, p. 442.

[254] TNA, PROB11/40/398.

[255] CIY; B. Sitch, *Kirkstall Abbey*, Leeds: Leeds City Council, 2000, p. 25.

[256] VCH, *County of Lincoln* **2**, 1906, pp. 139–40.

[257] L. Thomas, *Reformation in the Old Diocese of Llandaff*, Cardiff: William Lewis, 1930, pp. 146–47; D. and A. Mathew, 'The Survival of the Dissolved Monasteries in Wales.' In: *Dublin Review* **184**, 1929, p. 75.

[258] D. H. Williams, 'The Cistercians in West Wales, II: Ceredigion.' In: *AC* **159**, 2010, p. 280, *n.*197.

[259] C. Cross, 'Community Solidarity among Yorkshire Religious.' In: *MS* **1**, 1990, p. 247.

[260] J. A. Sparvel-Bayly, 'The Cistercian Abbey of Stratford Langthorne.' In: *Essex Review* **4**, 1895, p. 258.

[261] M. Aveling, 'The Monks of Byland after the Dissolution.' In: *Ampleforth Jnl.*, **60**, 1955, pp. 8–9.

[262] Cross and Vickers, *Monks, friars and nuns* Cross, 1995, p. 195.

263   Cross, 'Community Solidarity,' 1990, pp. 249–52.

264   Cross and Vickers, *Monks, friars and nuns*, 1995, p. 557; C. Cross, 'The End of Medieval Monasticism in the North Riding.' In: *YAJ* **78**, 2006, p. 155.

265   Cross and Vickers, *Monks, friars and* nuns, 1995, p. 180.

266   L. F. Salzman, 'Sussex Religious at the Dissolution.'In: *SxAC* **92**, 1954, p. 34.

267   Woodward, *Dissolution*, 1966, pp. 157–61 (transcription).

268   Cross and Vickers, *Monks, friars and nuns*, 1995, pp. 147–48.

269   Woodward, *Dissolution*, 1966, pp. 150–52.

270   M. Aveling, 'The Rievaulx Community after the Dissolution.' In: *Ampleforth Jnl.*, **57**, 1952, pp. 112–13.

271   Cross and Vickers, *Monks, friars and nuns*, 1995, p. 181.

272   Ibid., pp. 142, 148–49.

273   Youings, *Dissolution*, 1971, pp. 44, 52.

274   *LP* **13**, Part 1, pp. 574 [No. 520: Rufford], 583 [No. 1520: Furness].

275   Ibid. p. 577 [No. 1520].

276   Smith, *Heads of Religious Houses* **3**, 2008, p. 348, *BRUO*, p. 7.

277   TNA, SC6/HENVIII/4523, f. 73r–v.

278   G. Baskerville, 'The Dispossessed Religious of Gloucestershire.' In: *TBGAS* **49**, 1927, p. 89; Gasquet, *English Monasteries*, 1899, pp. 259, 349.

279   C. Sherwin, 'The History of Ford Abbey.' In: *RTDA* **59**, 1927, p. 257.

280   TNA, LR1/173, ff. 141–43.

281   Aveling, 'Monks of Byland,' 1955, pp. 4–7.

282   Aveling, 'Rievaulx Community,' 1952, pp. 102–03.

283   *LP* **13**, Part 1, p. 314 [No. 847]; Hockey, *Beaulieu*, 1976, pp. 183–86, 189

284   VCH, *County of York* **3**, 1974, p. 154; *LP* **13**, Part 2, p. 550 [Appx. 25].

285   CIY project; probate granted, 4-05-1555: Smith, *Heads of Religious Houses* **3**, 2008, p. 327).

286   Youings, *Dissolution*, 1971, p. 186.

287   Lonsdale, 'Last Monks of Kirkstall,' 1972, p. 204.

288   VCH, *County of Northampton* **2**, 1906, p. 121.

289   *LP* **13**, Part 2, pp. 349–50 [No. 840].

290   D. H. Williams, 'The Last Abbot of Tintern.' In: *MA* **23**, pp. 67–74.

291   Essex R.O. D/ABW 28/46.

292   BL, Add. MS 11041, ff. 68r–71v; VCH, *County of Stafford* **2**, 1970, p. 234.

293   *LP* **14**, Part 1, p. 385 [No. 814].

294   TNA, E164/31, f. 55r; Cross and Vickers, *Monks, friars and nuns*, 1995, pp. 9–101.

295   VCH, *County of Stafford* **3**, 1970, p. 234., *LP* **13**, Part 2, p. 251 [No. 656].

296   F. A. Hibbert, *Dissolution of the Monasteries*, London: Pitman, 1910, pp. 237–39, being a transcription of Staffordshire Archives, 2/32/00.

297   *LP* **13**, Part 2, p. 348 [No. 839]; VCH, *County of Warwick* **2**, London, 1908, p. 78. For a full record, see: Walcott, 'Inventories and Valuations,' 1871, pp. 214–15.

[298] Walcott, 'Inventories and Valuations,' 1871, pp. 214, 216.

[299] TNA, SC6/HENVIII/481.

[300] TNA, C115/D.21/1937; D.H. Williams, 'Sale of Goods at Abbey Dore.' In: *MA* **3**: Parts 3–4, 1975, pp. 192–97; *White Monks in Gwent*, 1976, pp. (1976) 31–32.

[301] TNA, E321/32/84; Williams (1976) 29–30.

[302] Williams (1976) 15.

[303] Hibbert, *Dissolution*, 1910, p. 255.

[304] J. Hall, *Croxden Abbey: buildings and community*, York University, Ph. D. thesis, 2003, p. 9.

[305] Davey, *Rushen Abbey*, 2010, p. 155.

[306] TNA, SP5/5, ff. 10–18; E.A.B. Barnard, *Last Days of Hailes Abbey*, Evesham: Evesham Journal, 1928, pp. 3–13.

[307] VCH, *County of York* **3**, 1974, pp. 154–55.

[308] *LP* **13**, Part 1, p. 556 [No. 1505]; BL, Add MS 11,041, f. 26.

[309] VCH, *County of Northampton* **2**, London, 1906, pp. 120–21.

[310] Williams, *Welsh Cistercians*, 2001, p. 90.

[311] *LP* **13**, Part 2, p. 261 [No. 689].

[312] Ibid. pp. 275–76 [No. 719].

[313] *LP* **12**, Part 2, p. 429 [No. 1216].

[314] T. Bostock, and S. Hogg., *Vale Royal Abbey, 1277–1538*, Vale Royal Borough Council, 1999, p. 7.

[315] .Williams, *Welsh Cistercians*, 2001, p. 92.

[316] Snell, *Suppression*, 1967, p. 161.

[317] Williams, *Welsh Cistercians*, 2001, p 89.

[318] Hockey, *Beaulieu*, 1976, p. 180; *LP* **14**, Part 1, pp. 415–16 [No. 899].

[319] Lambeth Palace Library, Talbot MS 3206.

[320] Bettey, *Suppression of Monasteries*, 1989, p. 35.

[321] T. P. Ellis, *Welsh Benedictines of the Terror*, Newtown: Welsh Outlook Press, 1936, p. 46.

[322] G. M. Hills, 'Fountains Abbey.' In: *Collectanea Archaeologica* **2**, 1871, p. 301.

[323] Youings, *Dissolution*, 1971, 157.

[324] TNA, E31/405, f. 42.

[325] D. B. Foss, 'Marmaduke Bradley, Last Abbot of Fountains.' In: *YAJ* **61**, 1989, p. 108.

[326] C. Nash, 'The Fate of the English Cistercian Abbots.' In: *Cîteaux* **2**, 1965, p.100.

[327] TNA, LR6/152/2.

[328] VCH, *Essex* **2**, 1907, p. 132.

[329] *LP* **13**. Part 2, pp. 347–48 [No. 839].

[330] J. H.Aveling, *The History of Roche* Abbe, London: John Russell Smith, 1870, p. 88

[331] Sparks, *In the Shadow of the Blackdowns*, 1978, p. 111.

[332] Nash, 'Fate of English Cistercian Abbots,' 1965, p. 104.

[333] pers. comm. The parish priest.

334   Tomkinson, 'Hulton Abbey,' 1985, p. 67.

335   Winkless, *Hailes Abbey*, 1990, pp. 59–60.

336   Williams, *Welsh Cistercians*, 2001, p. 89.

337   VCH, *County of Stafford* **2**, 1967, p. 233; *Staffordshire Record Office*, 2/32/00.

338   Hockey, *Beaulieu*, 1976, p. 180; *LP* **13**, Part 2, p. 348 [No. 839/5].

339   Gasquet, *English Monasteries*, 1899, p. 273; *LC*, 136–37 [No. LXXXV].

340   Williams, *Welsh Cistercians*, 2001, p. 89.

341   TNA, SC6/HENVIII/481.

342   G. Coppack, *Fountains Abbey*, Stroud, Tempus, 2003, p. 130.

343   *LP* **12**, Part 2, p. 88 [No. 205].

344   Winkless, *Hailes Abbey*,' 1990, pp. 59–60.

345   Coppack, 'Fountains Abbey,' 2003, p. 130; F.A. Gasquet, *The Greater Abbeys of England*, London: Chatto and Windus, 1908, p. 97.

346   VCH, *County of York* **3**, 1974, pp. 154–55.

347   BL, Additional MS 11041, f. 12.

348   Williams, *Welsh Cistercians*, 2001, pp. 89–90.

349   Ibid. p. 89.

350   Coppack, *Fountains Abbey*, 2003, p. 130.

351   TNA, SC6/HENVIII/7339.

352   *LP* **10**, p. 499 [No. 1191/4].

353   TNA, E315/278, ff. 18–19, 40–41; 71; SC12/30/4.

354   Gasquet, *Greater Abbeys*, 1908, p. 41; Stéphan, *Buckfast Abbey*, 1970, pp. 222.

355   TNA, E117/14/185.

356   Williams, *Welsh Cistercians*, 2001, p. 89.

357   L. B. Clarence, 'Church Bells of Dorset.' In: *Proc. Dorset Natural History and Antiquarian Field Club* **19**, 1898, p. 30.

358   Gloucestershire Archives, P201/CW 3/1.

359   Hockey, *Beaulieu*, 1976, pp. 191–92.

360   Williams, *White Monks in Gwent*, 1976, p. 66; *Welsh Cistercians*, 2001, p. 89.

361   Gasquet, *English Monasteries*, 1899, p. 173.

362   Winkless, *Hailes Abbey*, 1990, p. 76, n. 101.

363   Gasquet, *Greater Abbeys*, 1908, p. 97.

364   TNA, SC12/30/4, f. 4.

365   Walcott, 'Inventories and Valuations,' 1871, p. 240.

366   TNA, SC6/HENVIII/7339.

367   SSC, DR37/2/Box 125/7.

368   Nash, *Fate oif English Cistercian Abbots*, 1965, p. 103.

369   Williams, *Welsh* Cistercians, 2001, p. 88.

370   Hockey, *Beaulieu*, 1976, p. 207.

371   Williams, *The Cistercians in the Early Middle Ages*, Leominster: Gracewing, 1998, pp. 203–04.

372 BL, Harley MS 2060.

373 Williams, *Welsh Cistercians*, 2001, p. 199; *MW*, p. 89 [No. 28].

374 *SAP* (2), p. 286 [No. 2762].

375 Youings, *Dissolution*, 1971, pp. 227–28.

376 Baskerville, *English Monks*, 1937, p. 29.

377 *LP* **12**, Part 1, p. 405 [No. 901].

378 *LP* **12**, Part 2, pp. 88–89 [No. 205].

379 Nash, 'Fate of English Cistercian Abbots,' 1965, p. 101.

380 J. H. Pring, 'Memoir of Thomas Chard, D.D.' In: *JBAA* **18**, 1862, p. 202,

381 J. Wild, *The history of Castle Bytham*, Stamford: Johnson, Houlson, 1871, p. 114.

382 'Touring Monastic Yorkshire in Britannia', website.

8 THE NUNNERIES

Introduction

T HERE WERE IN medieval England and Wales thirty nunneries which are generally accepted as having been within the Cistercian fold. They were not evenly distributed geographically, rather they were mostly concentrated in Yorkshire and Lincolnshire. The former county possessed no less than twelve female monasteries accounted as Cistercian: Basedale (Baysdale), Ellerton, Esholt, Hampole, Handale, Keldholme, Kirklees, Nun Appleton, Rosedale, Sinningthwaite, Swine and Wykeham. In the latter shire stood six Cistercian nunneries: Gokewell (Goykewell), Greenfield, Heynings, Legbourne, Nun Cotham (Nun Coton) and Stixwould. Northamptonshire and Worcestershire each had two Cistercian convents: Catesby and Sewardsley; Cook Hill (Cokehill) and Whistones, respectively. The remaining houses were to be found in Dorset (Tarrant), Norfolk (Marham), Warwickshire (Pinley), and on the Isle of Man (Douglas). Two Cistercian nunneries lay in Wales: Llanllugan in Powys, and Llanllŷr in Ceredigion.

Occasionally some of these convents were referred to by other names. Handale was also known as Grendale or Gryndale.[1] Basedale had the *alias* of Nunthorp, from the locality of 'Torp' to which the nuns moved from their first site at Hutton near Guisborough.[2] The nuns of Cook Hill (Cokehill in some records) were also referred to as 'The White Ladies outside Worcester'.[3] Catesby nunnery had a rarely used alternative name of 'Shopys'.[4] Marham was once called 'Marham Barbara', undoubtedly an allusion to its last abbess. Barbara Mason.[5] The title given to Heynings on its deed of surrender described it as being 'of the Order of St Bernard and of the Rule of St Benedict.' The National Archives listing gives Heynings an *alias* of Knaith, from the lordship in which the nunnery was situated. Tarrant was commonly called Tarrant Kaines, on the basis that its founder was a member of the Kaines family.[6]

The considerable influx, earlier in the medieval period, into the Order of female monasteries calling themselves Cistercian, sometimes led to uncertainty as to how many were really of the family; that is, founded by a male abbey, and/or incorporated formally into the Order and subject to its rule.[7] Another pointer to the uncertain origin of some of the accepted Cistercian nunneries comes in the fact that not all were dedicated to the Blessed Virgin Mary: Cook Hill had a dual dedication to St John and St Mary; Whistones's patron was St Mary Magdalene.[8] Esholt had for its patron, St Leonard.[9]

The evidence of Abbot Marmaduke Huby suggests that some nunneries originally proclaiming to be Cistercian to avoid the strictness of that rule sought episcopal oversight when it pleased them. There may in fact only have been four nunneries actually incorporated formally by the General Chapter, and/or founded by Cistercian abbots. They were it seems Marham and Tarrant in England, and Llanllugan and Llanllŷr in Wales. Those four always ranked as 'abbeys'; the remaining Cistercian nunneries were invariably termed 'priories', though Stixwould styled itself as an abbey at the head of its accounts for 1528/29.[10] The topic is a complex one, but has recently been exhaustively analysed in a very fine scholarly article.[11]

It is this uncertainty which may explain, together with clerical error, why of the nunneries listed above, episcopal registers occasionally refer to Basedale and Rosedale as having been Benedictine;[12] and why Hampole in the suppression papers was listed as 'priory or house of nuns of the Order of Saint Augustine and of the Cistercian rule of Saint Benedict.'[13] Confusing indeed, but may it be that Hampole had swung from one allegiance to another?

The same doubts apply to two listings made by the General Chapter in 1533 of Cistercian nunneries subject to oversight for visitatorial purposes, in a move perhaps designed to bring these houses more firmly into the Order and away from episcopal authority, but also necessary as visitation from the Continent was politically no longer possible. In one of those listings, the abbots of St Mary Graces and Woburn were appointed for a period of five years as reformators or visitors for the well-being not only of a number of male abbeys, but also of the nunneries at Cook Hill, Tarrant and Marham.[14]

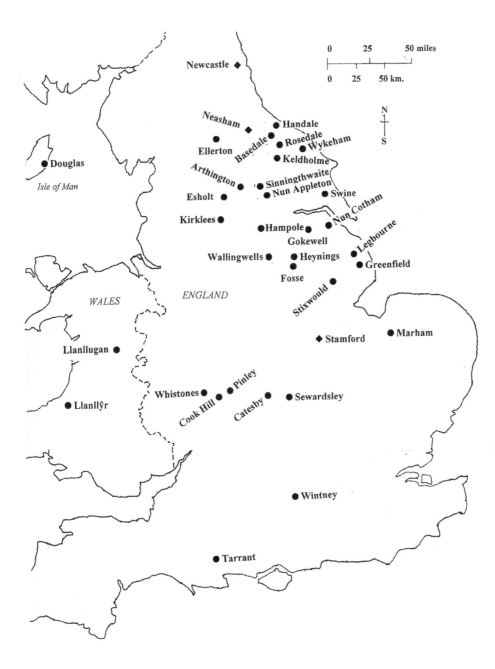

Fig. 15: The Cistercian Nunneries of England and Wales

The second listing commits to the care of the abbots of Byland and Fountains as official visitors several male abbeys and in addition no less than fifteen of the nunneries named above, clearly acknowledging them as being Cistercian.[15] The statute also includes the names of three nunneries commonly regarding as belonging to other Orders, and referred to as 'Ardythone, Newcastell and Walyngierett.' Arthington (Ardington) nunnery in Yorkshire was a Cluniac house, and noted as being 'of the Order of St Benedict' when a new prioress was installed in 1492,[16] though accounted Cistercian not only by this statute, but also by one suppression document.[17] Yet another deed of 1466 does indeed refer to it as a Cluniac monastery.[18] 'Walyngierett' must refer to the Nottinghamshire nunnery of Wallingwells, generally regarded as being Benedictine—as in a papal register for 1504,[19] but thrice referred to in the registers of the archbishops of York as being Cistercian. This happened when in 1505 Elizabeth Kirkby was chosen as its prioress, again in 1508 when Isabel Croft was elected to that position, and yet again in 1522 when Margaret Goldsmith became prioress.[20] Yet other convents which fifteenth-century records record as being Cistercian were Benedictine Neasham and St Michael's, Stamford. About 1270 the nuns of Stamford claimed that they had come from Nun Appleton, where they had been instructed in the ways of the Cistercians.[21]

In 1523 Abbot Huby of Fountains claimed that for the sixty years he had been a monk the convent of St Bartholomew's, Newcastle, had been under the jurisdiction of the Cistercian abbot of Newminster, but he was over-stating his case.[22] It had happened that in 1484 the diocesan bishop of Durham being absent in Rome, the then abbot of Newminster did supervise the election of a new prioress at Newcastle. When Huby did the same in July 1523 the vicar-general of the diocese annulled the election, saying that it was a matter not for Huby but for the bishop of Durham and the cardinal archbishop of York.[23]

Part of this confusion may relate to nunneries, for whatever reason, being at one time wanting to be free of the strict austerity and simplicity of Cistercian life, or at other times wishing to be independent of episcopal control and heavy fees. Abbot Huby told of this, and also wrote that he would not challenge the cardinal, but would let the nuns of Newcastle 'trip and dance in the same trace that all other their sisters have done.'[24]

Huby was also able to write that same year to Cîteaux that he had brought 'three southern nunneries' away from the oversight of their local bishop, and back under the authority of their father-abbots.[25] Unfortunately he does not specify which the houses were, but might one of them have been Wallingwells, and might they have included Cook Hill and Pinley, mentioned in the only other reference to a visitation ordered by the General Chapter—this time in 1520, when Huby was still alive.[26] . Another undated listing of Cistercian houses, seemingly on the command of Henry VIII, notes the names of almost all the Cistercian abbeys of England (but duplicates seven) and only two of the Welsh abbeys. It does proclaim as Cistercian the abbey of Marham and the priories of Legbourne, Nun Appleton, Nun Cotham and Swine.[27]

Save for the abbeys of Marham and Tarrant in England and of Llanllugan and Llanllŷr in Wales, the Cistercian nunneries ranked as priories with a prioress, rather than an abbess, as their superior. The origins of this distinction may lie in the early history of those priories *vis-à-vis* the Cistercian Order as a whole. It is reflected in the fact that whereas Marham appears to have come under the aegis of the abbot of Waverley,[28] and later was subject to visitation by the abbots of Warden and Sawtry,[29] and Llanllugan and Llanllŷr under the oversight of the abbots of Strata Marcella and Strata Florida respectively,[30] the priories were (so far as can be established) subject to visitation by their diocesan bishop or an official on his behalf. Male Cistercian abbeys were exempt from such episcopal control. Tarrant may have owed its abbatial status to its practical re-foundation by Bishop Richard le Poor of Salisbury.[31]

When a Cistercian abbot on assuming his abbacy was blessed by, and professed obedience to, his diocesan bishop, he always included the phrase 'saving my Order', in that promise. In other words, he professed obedience except where Cistercian privilege provided otherwise. When the prioresses of Kirklees (in 1492 and 1499),[32] of Swine (in 1521),[33] of Basedale (in 1524 and 1527), and of Sinningthwaite (in 1529 and 1535)[34] made their profession of obedience there was no such saving clause. The new superiors, like Katherine Forster at Sinningthwaite in 1535, limited themselves to promising obedience 'in all things lawful and honest'. It is apparent that the English Cistercian nunneries (as distinct from the four abbeys) did not enjoy the considerable degree of exemption from episcopal authority that their male counterparts did. The General Chapter's statutes in 1533 may well have been an endeavour to rectify this.

In a letter to Lord Dacre, Warden of the Marches, of July 1523,[35] written just after he had returned from Newcastle, Abbot Huby commenced by stating that within a century of the white monks first coming to England, there were no less than eighty-two monasteries and sixty-four nunneries of the Order in

England and Wales. This appears to be a very exaggerated claim, but Huby might have been including all the earlier sites of those abbeys which transferred to a new location.

The nuns he wrote were 'clearly and strongly exempt from all manner of jurisdiction of the ordinaries [bishops], and under the yoke of obedience and jurisdiction of the Visitors and father abbots of our religion'. This continued, Huby asserted, until about two hundred years previously when they 'began to wax wanton and remissly kept the vow of chastity.' This Huby said was 'sharply looked upon in those days and straitly punished, for the which correction the nuns groaned and murmured and one by one and little by little slipped away from the obedience of our religion unto the jurisdiction of the ordinaries.'

Abbot Huby wrote that in doing so the nuns hoped 'to find more favour and tolerance,' but as a consequence 'they clearly lost the exemption the which full fore now they repent.' He pointed out that when visited by the father abbots, as at elections and institutions of superiors, the sisters had to pay but twenty shillings or four nobles, but that the bishops charged at least £5 with a further £2 or 4 marks for the costs of their officials. Huby went on to assert that in France, Flanders, Picardy, Germany and 'all other regions christian,' all Cistercian nunneries were under the subjection of the father abbots. He wrote that this was not the case in England, but that there were 'three places in the south parts the which in my days reduced to the subjection of the Order again.' This lengthy epistle of Abbot Huby tells us perhaps why the sisters had lost their immunity from episcopal visitation, but it does not explain why—save four—their houses ranked only as priories and not as abbeys.

This concern by Abbot Huby, and indeed the General Chapter, for the well-being of the Cistercian nunneries, has recently been the focus of scholarly attention. The conclusion has been that 'towards the end of the Middle Ages Cistercian commissioners and the General Chapter understood Cistercian reform to be something involving both monks and nuns, and something involving the English Cistercian nuns who for centuries had otherwise been left to gain their monastic guidance from local sources rather than national or international sources.'[36]

The Communities

Within these thirty female monasteries lived in the mid-1530s at least two hundred and fifty nuns. The largest communities were those of Tarrant (twenty nuns at the dissolution),[37] Nun Appleton (nineteen sisters),[38] Hampole (nineteen nuns).[39] Stixwould (twelve perhaps—before its premature closure).[40] There were much smaller numbers, only four or five sisters at Douglas,[41] Gokewell[42] and Marham.[43] These figures cannot take into account very young nuns who may have been discharged prior to their house's suppression. If they are included then perhaps close to three hundred sisters occupied the Cistercian nunneries at say around 1530. A fine contemporaneous illustration of the Cistercian nuns of Tudor times has recently been published.[44]

Profession as a Cistercian nun was for life, normally within the monastery of one's novitiate. Stability was enforced when the General Chapter in 1213 forbade the nuns of the Order to leave their monastic precincts.[45] There were exceptions—as when a superior or her cellarer needed to travel on the business of their house, but the statute meant strict enclosure for the sisters, and therefore an inability to work in their own fields at any distance away.[46] This enclosure, together with the relatively small size of the nunneries, makes it difficult to compare them like-by-like with the male abbeys of the Order. This insistence on stability did not preclude the election of a nun of one convent to be prioress of another house, nor did it prevent sad cases of apostasy. At the dissolution several sisters of necessity moved from their convent to a priory not yet suppressed.

Such statistics as are available suggest that in 1536 the average age of a Cistercian nun was forty years old. The eldest was ninety-year old Joan Scott, a long time prioress of Handale (1504–1532), but now blind and aged. An octogenarian was Alice Stable of Basedale who on her house's closure gained a pension of £1-6-8, slightly more than the £1 awarded the other members of that convent. There were four known septuagenarians: Joan Hollynraws of Esholt, said to be 'lame and not able to ride'; Catherine Nendyk, the last prioress of Wykeham; Agnes Pighan of Handale, and Elizabeth Pudsey, the penultimate prioress of Esholt, also said to be 'decrepit and unable to ride'.[47]

It is quite evident that girls in their teens were professed as Cistercian sisters. Dr John London, writing to Cromwell on 27 July 1539 after taking he surrenders of Fosse, Heynings and Nun Cotham and two non-Cistercian houses, asserted that 'many of these nuns were professed at ten and twelve years.'[48] The youngest nuns on record were Isabel Cockeson and Joan Pulleyn, both of Hampole, only nineteen when their priory was suppressed in 1539, while Joan Gore of Nun Appleton can only have been seventeen when first listed as a nun in 1520. Margaret Sturmy, sub-prioress of Whistones in 1485, may well be the nun of that name who in 1427 had been one of the electors of a new prioress.[49] Agnes Nellys, who was twenty-nine in 1539 was a member of Basedale's community in 1524, when she can only have been about fourteen years old![50]

There were at the time of the Suppression a number of nuns in their twenties, but not as might have been expected a bevy of young nuns in their teens. This resulted from the deliberate policy of expelling religious under the age of twenty-four from their monasteries at the time they were 'surveyed' by the commissioners prior to their dissolution. A letter of November 1535 refers to Cromwell as 'driving out those nuns who are under the age of twenty-four'.[51] This policy was also referred to in the somewhat enigmatic letter written from Wintney nunnery to Cromwell on 24 September 1535 by John ap Rice, the notary of the Court of Augmentations. He said: 'You have the injunctions concerning nuns, without that temperance concerning young women under twenty-four, which Mr Doctor would not suffer me to alter, as I had in the other touching monks. I think there is much greater reason in the former case as women come to maturity two years before men, and more slander is caused by the misconduct of one of them going out than that by twenty men.'[52]

Officially everything the sisters possessed was owned in common, but the 'wages' given at the closure of a house, and the evidence of wills, is that by Tudor times each nun was allowed a limited mount of pocket-money. In 1487 John Wolewrowe, desiring burial there, left the prioress of Kirklees 10s and each nun 3s 4d, as well as 20d. for the fabric of its campanile.[53] In 1534 John Cocke, parson of Ketsby in Little Grimsby, bequeathed not only 6s 8d. to Anne Goderick, the prioress of Greenfield, but also 12d to each nun there, and 8d to 'the sister'—perhaps an extern religious able to do business outside the house. He also left the prioress of Legbourne, 6s. 8d., each nun there, 12d. and the novice 8d. In the same year, Legbourne nunnery received 12d. in the will of William Thore of Ingoldmells, with a further 4d. to each nun of the house. In all these cases, no obit services were specified.[54] One of the nuns of Legbourne, Elizabeth Martyn, perhaps a family member, was bequeathed in

1534 two shillings yearly by Lawrence Mylforde of Bardney 'of my stock, so long as it will endure.'[55]

Cistercian nunneries might attract more than one member of the same family. At Esholt in 1536 were two nuns who may have been natural sisters: Agnes Dogeson aged forty, and Barbara Dogeson, thirty-seven years old. At Catesby in 1530 the prioress and another nun, perhaps a niece, were both named Joyce Bikerley. At Basedale Elizabeth Cowper, aged fifty-seven in 1536, might well have been the aunt of thirty-one year old Margaret Cowper. When Wykeham closed in 1539 the last prioress, Catherine Nendyk was perhaps a relative of the nun named Isabel Nendyk, whilst the community also included the prioress's god-child, Catherine Gayle. At Hampole the last prioress named Isabel Arthington and a nun there called Elizabeth Arthington may have been blood relations, but their surnames also suggest that they may have originally been nuns of Arthington priory.[56]

Some nuns, if not most, were from reasonably well-to-do families. Catherine Nendyk, the prioress of Wykeham (1539) had as one of her nuns, Elizabeth Percy, a relation of Catherine, countess of Northumberland. The prioress making her will left to the countess a silver cross, a standing mazer and a corporax 'for such costs and charges as I put her unto.'[57] Perhaps the countess had given a financial helping hand to the nunnery. Two of the Handale nuns, Anne Benson and Isabel Norman, were daughters of prosperous local families.

The Prioresses

None of the Cistercian prioresses of the times appear to have been famed beyond the doors of their convent, but several served in their office for many years which may well have given their nunneries a long period of stability, and of spiritual and economic well-being. Amongst them was Joyce Bikerley, last prioress of Catesby, who held office from 1508 to 1536, and whom the king's commissioners described as 'a pure, wise, discreet and very religious woman.'[58]

Other long-serving superiors included Elizabeth Pudsey of Esholt (1513–1535), and Jane Skipwith of Greenfield (1490–1518). Ann Castelforth was only twenty-six when she became prioress of Gokewell (1534), but she had to pay a fee of £5 for the privilege.[59] The best known Cistercian nun may have been Alice Cranmer, sister of the archbishop and of the archdeacon of Canterbury.

Sacrist of Stixwould in 1525, she was elected in 1534 on the nomination of her episcopal brother as abbess of Benedictine Minster Abbey in Kent.[60]

The canonical procedures for the election of a prioress were well exemplified in the case of Joan Fletcher of Basedale.[61] On 5 August 1524, as Margaret Bucton the prioress there had died, the vicar-general of York commissioned the official of the archdeacon of Clevedon and the rural dean of Clevedon to supervise the election of a new prioress. Accordingly, on 12 August, after a Mass of the Holy Spirit in the priory church, the six nuns chose three of their number [the hosteler, the chantress and the sacristan] to determine the outcome. They left the chapter-house, and on their return announced their unanimous election of Joan Fletcher, a nun of Rosedale, to the community in choir and then to the people in the nave. The *Te Deum* was then sung. The next day, Joan made her profession of obedience before the archbishop's two commissaries, after which she received their promise of obedience from her six new sisters.

The choice of Joan had seemingly been predetermined, as the prioress of Rosedale had already given her consent to Joan leaving Rosedale if elected a prioress elsewhere. Joan was thirty-five years old and of legitimate birth. She had been professed at Rosedale in 1503, so she cannot have been more than fifteen years old when she became a nun.[62] Alas, her election to Basedale was to end after three years in ruin and acrimony.

When a sister of the house, Joan Morton, was elected as prioress of Whistones on 15 December 1485, subsequent to the death of Margery Swinson, the bishop of Worcester was described as 'the founder and patron' of the convent. His delegate for the proceedings was Dr John Moore, and the nuns named as making the choice were Margaret Sturmy (probably sub-prioress), Agnes Osborne ('president') and Katherine Goldsmith. The election completed, Dr Moore committed to the new prioress the cure and administration of the spiritual and temporal possessions of the nunnery,[63] and placed her in her stall in the choir and on her seat in the chapter-house. Her sisters then professed to her their vow of obedience. The election was not a 'closed shop': those present included the registrar—Robert Enkbarow, the notaries—Richard Grynne and Robert Charlemont, as well as Thomas Swinnerton, Joan Goldsmith, Joan Grene and 'many others'.[64]

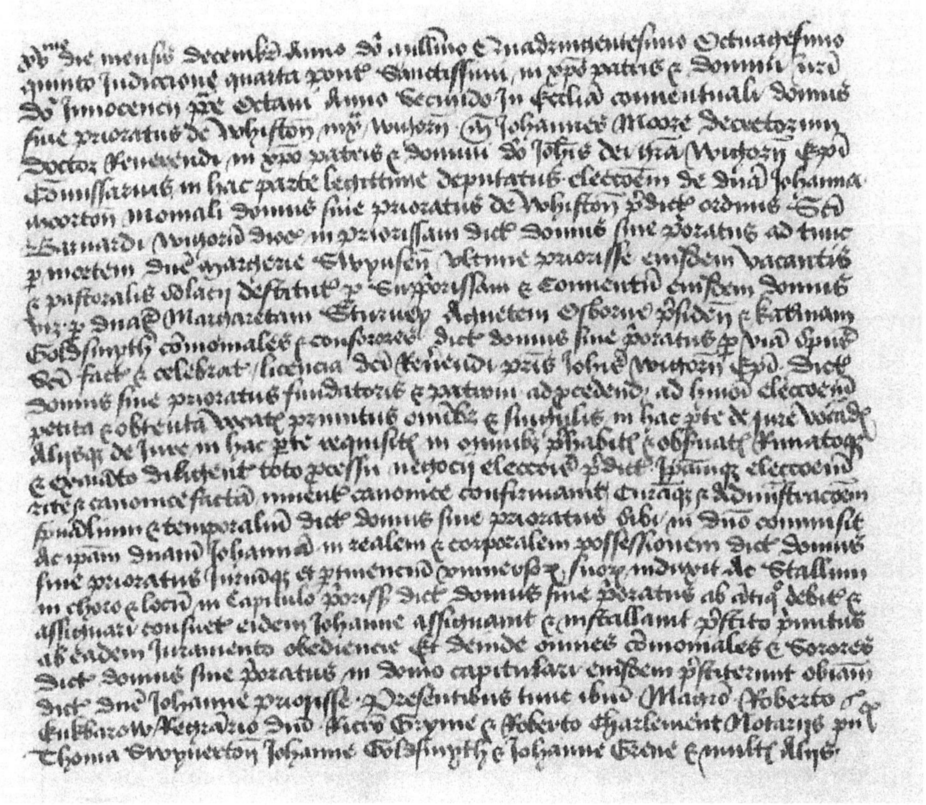

Fig. 16: The Election of Joan Morton, Prioress of Whistones (1483)
By kind permission from the Diocese of Worcester.
(Worcestershire Archive and Archaeology Service: b716.093 BA2648/7)

In the instance of Greenfield, when a vacancy arose in 1518, it was the patron, William, Lord Willoughby, who gave leave for the nuns to elect a new superior, Elizabeth Billesby.[65] It was not to be long before all such elections had to be referred to Thomas Cromwell as vicar-general. So it was that in 1534 Henry, Marquis of Exeter, pressed Cromwell that the office of prioress at Wintney should pass to a kinswoman of his wife.[66] The nun appointed was Elizabeth Martyn. When Katherine Fforster was made prioress of Sinningthwaite in 1534, she had been nominated by the archbishop, seemingly at the community's request.[67] When Abbess Edith died at Tarrant in 1535, it was the Crown which issued its *congé d'élire* allowing the community to elect her sucessor. Dr Legh who seemingly presided charged the nuns a substantial fee of £20 and also claimed £4 in costs.[68]

There were several instances of nuns of one convent being promoted to become prioress of another house. They included Mary Marshall, a nun of Nun Appleton, who became prioress of Rosedale (1527); Elizabeth Roughton, nun of Keldholme who was transferred to be prioress of Basedale (1527), and Margery Wigston, nun of Catesby, who became prioress of Pinley (1534).[69] Much earlier, in 1497, Elizabeth Davell, already prioress of Basedale, moved to the like position at Keldholme. Her young age when she was elected at Basedale in 1482 necessitated a dispensation, and continuing as superior of Keldholme until her death in 1534 she was one of the longest serving of Cistercian prioresses—for fifty-two years. Her experience and wisdom hopefully gave Keldholme a long period of stability.[70] Her predecessor at Keldholme who had resigned, Katharine Anlaby, rightly or wrongly took part in Elizabeth's election. It may well be that she had suggested her, and felt happy to continue living there under her successor's rule.

The election of a prioress was (in the diocese of York) presided over by a commissary of the archbishop, and that cleric confirmed the outcome. John Reynolds, LL.B., vicar-general, performed this duty in 1488 when Katherine Ward was elected as prioress of Wykeham, and he did the same for Elizabeth Lasyngby's accession to Esholt in 1497.[71] In the first instance, the office was vacant because of the death of Elizabeth Edmundson, in the second case on account of the 'free resignation' of Joan Warde. At both confirmations the profession of obedience omitted any reference to limitations on account of their being Cistercian superiors, but the oath was taken 'on the holy evangelists', and Elizabeth Lasyngby concluded 'so God me help'. When in 1492 Joan Stansfeld made her profession of obedience as prioress of Kirklees, the proceedings were overseen by a commissary of the archbishop of York; when in 1499 Margaret Tarlton succeeded her she made her profession before the rural dean of Pontefract.[72]

In at least two professions of obedience, as the Suppression approached and perhaps because of knowledge of a convent's problems, an addition was made to the oath the superiors swore. It was to ensure the economic stability of the priory concerned, and the new prioresses of Keldholme and Sinningthwaite—elected on 14 January and 9 May 1534 respectively, had to agree 'not to alienate the goods, jewels and possessions of the house, nor to farm, let the lands, granges or tenements, the same above three years without the consent of the archbishop.'[73]

The prioresses had their own separate accommodation off the cloister. At Kirklees her twenty-four feet long chamber was sited at the north side of the nether end of the church. At Baysdale it lay over the west part of the cloister, and had a fireplace with chimney and 'a fair round bay glazed window.'. It had timber walls and a roof of thak board. At Wykeham her two-storied chamber stood hard by the church, was twelve feet square and had the very necessary chimney.[74]

Depositions

There were at least three instances where an unsatisfactory prioress was deposed or forced to resign. One such superior was Ann Goldesburg of Sinningthwaite who stood down at the close of 1533 after a critical visitation report. She was treated honourably, being given after her 'free resignation' a pension of £10, as well as a chamber with a parlour within the precincts of the nunnery, lying on the 'south side of the cloister and the church'. Nothing was specified as to her food entitlements.[75] There were two other instances which attracted much more attention from the authorities either of the Order or the diocese. They were, indeed, sad cases.

The second case occurred in 1490 when the abbot of Hailes removed the prioress of Cook Hill, Joan Franklin, from office; weakness of the flesh is hinted at as being the reason. The abbot replaced her with Elizabeth Webbe, who had already been prioress there, certainly in 1485.[76] Joan Franklin did not take her deposition lightly, and perhaps had influential friends, as she was able to cause the dean of the Arches (the principal court of the archbishops of Canterbury) to summon both the abbot and the new prioress to explain why she, Joan, had been dismissed.[77] Such summons were, it was argued, contrary to the privileges of the Cistercian Order, and involved John Haryngton, LL.D., an advocate of the Court of Arches who partly specialised in Cistercian affairs.[78] He requested that the original papal bull of exemption be sent to England, and the case was adjourned until Lent 1491 to give time for the bull to arrive.[79]

Meanwhile an appeal had been made to Rome, and the Holy See in February 1491) commissioned the bishops of London and of Rochester to enquire into the affair.[80] The General Chapter, meeting in September 1491, approved Joan's deposition and Elizabeth's accession.[81] The Court of Arches repeated its citation in December 1491, but the outcome is unknown. The affair involved the abbot of Stratford, a Reformator of the Order in England, in considerable labour and expense; he termed the deposed prioress 'that evil one.'[82] The case must have been a minor cause celèbre within the Order. Elizabeth appears to have still been in office in 1493. It would be coincidental to identify her with the Elizabeth Webbe installed as prioress of Benedictine Sopwell in 1481, but later deposed.[83]

The third sad case involved Joan Fletcher, the nun of Rosedale described above as being singled out to become prioress of Basedale, making her profession of obedience on 13 August 1524. Unfortunately, her record in office was a bad one, and from fear of deposition after three years she resigned, cast aside her habit and left the house. Seven years later, on 1 September 1534, Archbishop Lee of York wrote two letters: one to the nunnery of Rosedale, to which after her apostasy she had been sent, and the other to Basedale. In the latter the archbishop said that Joan had set a bad example at Rosedale and that her penitence was false, and so he was transferring her back to Basedale. He exhorted its nuns to receive her with affection, but not to permit her to go outside the precincts of the convent.[84] By the next year, if not earlier, she had borne a child.[85] After the suppression she received, and probably until her death before 1564, a £1 pension given her on the closure of Basedale, and an annuity of £3-6-8 awarded her on her resignation as prioress.[86]

Initially after her resignation Joan was awarded by her successor a generous retirement package, if the deed she or her attorney presented to the Court of Augmentations (10 February 1541) was genuine.[87] The provision made for her was in response to the archbishop's ruling that Joan should have 'a sufficient and competent finding for her and her maiden yearly going out of the house of Basedale.' In the grant made on 11 March 1528 by her successor as prioress, Joan was to receive an annuity of £3-6-8, and to have the farm at Nunthorp that Dame Agnes Thomlynson (prioress, 1497–1524) had formerly as part of her retirement entitlement.

Even the farm animals to be given her were spelt out in precise detail, and indeed how they were to be spayed. They included eighty wethers, forty hogs and forty ewes and their lambs, as well as twelve hens and capons and three geese. At her departing out of this life, she was to leave the same numbers of stock 'to the behoof of Basedale.' When she returned to the nunnery she was to be free from any duties or making obeisance. She could have the same stall in choir that Dame Agnes had occupied, and she was to have 'her own chamber with the high parlour with all the hangings and beddings that she left when she went forth.' If she came to dinner and supper, she was to pay one penny for each companion.

In return for her resignation, Joan seems to have a struck a hard bargain, for the agreement also provided that the nuns who had given evidence on oath against her [Joan Absie, Barbara Brymley, Agnes Nellis and Agnes Addison] should go without their veils a twelve-month, and rank below the lowest sister, until she [Joan] should forgive them. It is hard to believe that such conditions could be imposed by a disgraced superior, and it is also difficult to understand how this grant fits into the accepted account of her life. The Court of Augmentations did not question the authenticity of the deed, but said it had 'no vigour in law'. She was to receive arrears of the pension, but no more. It could be that after occupying Nunthorp for a time, she had pangs of conscience and was then sent to Rosedale.

Other Breaches of Stability

It is clear that in Tudor times a certain degree of prudence was lacking in a few nunneries. Several of the convents received high praise from the suppression commissioners, and for a number documentation of any kind is scanty, but there was here and there a neglect of strict enclosure with consequent problems, not least the procreation of children. At least nine Cistercian nuns are recorded has having given birth to offspring, but that must be seen in perspective: it amounts to only one nun in twenty-five (and that over fifty years) failing to live up to her chosen life of chastity. Even Barbara Mason, the abbess of Marham, had improper relations with the prior of nearby Augustinian Pentney; something the prior admitted, but no child of their liaison is on record.[88] A scholar of the St David's diocese, Richard ap Lewis, was mentioned in 1475 as being the son of a priest and an abbess, though the Order is not given.[89]

Those nuns who did bear children included Margaret Newcombe of Greenfield who, by 1525, had been imprisoned on this account by her prioress. Her excuse was that whilst staying in the diocese of London, she had been raped by one William Wharton.[90] On 21 March 1530 the bishop of Lincoln quashed the election of Agnes Carter as prioress of Sewardsley, on the grounds that she was 'a corrupt and apostate woman, and mother of a child.'[91] He then changed his mind, and did appoint her one month later.[92] Others who became mothers were Alice Brampton of Handale, Isabel Rhodes of Kirklees and Joan Fletcher of Basedale (recounted above). The instance of Elizabeth Copley of Swine, twenty-nine years old in 1536, was more serious as the father was a priest.[93]

The problem of child-bearing appears to have been worst at Ellerton Priory where two sisters were found in the Crown visitation in February 1536 to have born children: Agnes Bayne and Cecilia Swale. Bayne was now fifty-two years old, so presumably she had given birth some years before. In September 1534 the archbishop of York ordered a nun of Esholt to be severely punished. She was Joan Hutton, not yet thirty years old, who was sentenced for bearing a child to spend two years in solitary confinement, 'in prison or some secret chamber in the dorter.' She was to receive only bread and ale on Wednesday and Fridays, and each Friday was to be disciplined in chapter. Fortunately for her, the archbishop reserved the right to shorten her penance. He called her offence a 'horrible crime' done 'contrary to the great danger of her soul.' She survived her penance, and was pensioned off when Esholt closed in August 1539.[94]

Visitation Charters

The regulations, the charter, issued by a bishop or his delegate at the conclusion of their visitation of a Cistercian nunnery, are almost always couched in negative terms. Their purpose was to end any shortcomings found in the life and worship of the sisters, and therefore they do not of necessity suggest that a house was in a particularly bad state. The prescriptions made ignore completely all that was good in a nunnery, and being one-sided can appear to suggest that it was completely lacking. This was often far from the truth, and in reading the visitation reports it is well to remember in the words of the queen of Sheba: 'Behold, the half was not told me' (1 K 10, 7). It is important to take note of other evidences as to the lives of the sisters. As their dissolution approached their vocation still meant something. This was shown in 1530 when Katharine Dodd, a nun of Augustinian Limebrook sought to transfer to Cistercian Llanllugan where, as the bishop of Hereford noted, 'the rule is stricter' and the way 'greater and straiter.'[95]

Another source of information comes in the reports of the commissioners sent out in 1535/36 to investigate the nuns' way of life. Some convents (like Heynings, Fosse and Marham) received bad reports, but mostly this was due to national commissioners, such as Layton, Legh and London, whose minds were made up before they accomplished their task, and whose prejudiced information was sometimes second-hand. Their investigation was often a hurried one—five commissioners, headed by Dr Layton, were sent in February 1539 to peruse no less than ten monasteries in Lincolnshire, though some survived until that summer.[96] When Doctors Layton and Legh dissolved Esholt (in August 1539) they did not even visit the nunnery, but sent for the community to attend upon them at Nostell Priory. On that occasion, Legh claimed that three nuns of Esholt were guilty of child-bearing, whereas the archiepiscopal visitation only four months before had mentioned only one sister. This discrepancy between the two sets of visitations does suggest that sometimes Legh looked for fault.[97]

Where more local and fair-minded commissioners were involved there is a different picture: the sisters of Pinley[98] and Wintney[99] were said to be 'by report of good conversation,' the nuns of Wykeham were noted as 'all of good living,'[100] while Hampole nunnery was said to be 'of good name, fame and rule'—there no fault could be found.[101] Catesby was reported as being 'in very perfect order, as good as we have ever seen.' The king was displeased with this report, and thought the commissioners there must have been bribed.[102] This despite the Visitors assertion that its nuns 'do much to the relief of the king's people and his grace's poor subjects there likewise much relieved.'[103] Another example of the need to take the findings of certain investigators with caution comes in the instance of Handale. There the initial royal visitors 'surveying' the monastery recorded Alice Brampton as having become a mother. Four months later, the suppression commissioners declared that all the nuns of the house were 'of good living', and noted Alice's age as being seventy![104]

The fourteen extant visitation charters must be read with such favourable comments in mind and, despite their inherent negativity, it is important to present them in detail, for while they certainly suggest a slackening of some aspects of religious life in certain houses, the records also give insights into the daily lives of the sisters.

Catesby, Northamptonshire

A visitation was held at Catesby on 19 June 1520 by Richard Roston, chancellor of the bishop of Lincoln, assisted by John Burges, B.Th.[105] The prioress (Joyce Bykerley) and seven nuns were present, the subprioress (Joan Stichenayll) being sick. The visitation commenced with the reading of the Visitors' mandate from the bishop, and a sermon in English preached by John Burges on the text: 'We have this treasure in earthen vessels' (2 Cor. 4, v. 7). The prioress exhibited the deed of the founder, Robert fitz Philip, as well as the deed of Henry III in 1272 and the bull of Innocent IV (1243–54) confirming the privileges of the house, its ownership of churches, and its freedom from paying tithe newly brought under cultivation. Exhibited also were the annual receipts of the revenues from its three appropriated churches. The senior nuns said that the house was free of debt. The sisters were separately examined by the vicar-general. The prioress was urged to each year to make an account of her administration before her sisters and she said she would do this. Otherwise nothing untoward found mention.

A later visitation on 10 September 1530 was not as positive.[106] The same prioress and ten nuns were present. Since the 1520 visitation three nuns appear to have died, but five new names appear: two of them perhaps relatives of the prioress: Agnes and Joyce Bykerley. The prioress reported that the dormitory, cloister and chapter-house were in disrepair. The former subprioress (Joan Stichenayll) alleged that the prioress did not render an annual account of her administration and that she had to stay numerous relatives, who were a burden on the convent. She also said that the dorter, cloister, bakehouse, chapter-house, mill and barn were in disrepair; that it was not agreeable that children played in the cloister and sat in the choir, and that there were many boys and girls in the monastery.

Much concern centred on Margaret Kelk, a nun of Nun Cotham, who was staying at Catesby—perhaps sent there on account of bad behaviour. She was not diligent in attending divine service; she was disobedient and a cause of discord in the community. She had at night left the dorter to go to the cloister to meet in the hall Thomas Catesby, a servant of the founding family of the house. Six of the nuns mentioned the shortcomings of Kelk and two her nocturnal wanderings. Only two nuns said that all was well without making any further comment.

The prioress was instructed by the Visitors to repair as soon as possible the buildings mentioned; to render an annual account of her administration to the sisters in writing; not to allow children to play in the cloister nor in the church nor to sit in the choir amongst the nuns; she was not to burden the convent with an excessive number of relatives; and while the house was defective in repair she was not to receive a new nun without the bishop's consent. The question has been asked of the children of this nunnery: 'Were they choristers, young scholars or just the local children at their play?'[107]

Esholt, Yorkshire

A visitation was held in August 1534 by the vicar-general of the diocese of York.[108] The consequent injunctions demanded that sufficient locks be placed on the cloister doors and the door of the dorter, and stipulated (as noted later for Sinningthwaite) the holders of keys and the opening and closing times. Part of St Benedict's rule was to be read in the chapter-house daily,—seemingly this custom had fallen into abeyance. No ale house was to be kept within the precincts,—presumably drink had been a problem. No person, secular or religious other than the sisters, was to be lodged or allowed to lie within the cloister or any chamber opening on to it. With the case of Joan Hutton in mind, it was prescribed that no sister might have leave to go out without a just reasonable cause, and then to be accompanied by 'a discrete and wise sister,' with the time of return fixed by the prioress. A strong and high wall was to be built to close off the open way from the back side of certain chambers on the south side of the church—where the sisters worked, going to the waterside and the bridge.

Greenfield, Lincolnshire

At a visitation held on 18 July 1519 by the bishop of Lincoln personally, it was alleged that Margaret Newcombe was disobedient to her superiors; and that the prioress (Elizabeth Billesby) constantly had at her table Margaret Billesby and Agnes Stanley, rather than invite the sisters in turn.[109]

At a further visitation held on 3 July 1525 by John Rayne, the vicar-general, the prioress and seven sisters were present, and three of the sisters came in for particular criticism[110]. *Agnes Graunde (Growance)* was accused of being a scold; her penance—to lie prostrate in the chapter house on Wednesdays and Fridays for the next two months, so that the sisters entering had to walk over her. Agnes was also said to be of a weak disposition and friendly with one James Smyth. *Margaret Newcombe*—noted above as having borne a child, was once again accused of disobedience and of absenting herself from matins. She was enjoined to be obedient, not to absent herself from divine office, and not to talk to strangers. For her penance she was to lie prostrate in the chapter house on Wednesdays and Fridays for the next month so that the sisters entering had to walk over her.

Isabella Smyth, the prioress, rejected on oath the rumour of her enemies that a year before she had born a child. It was also laid against her that she burdened the house by admitting relatives and neighbours; and that she intended to receive as a nun one Agnes Kettyll who was a source of discord. Two witnesses said of Kettyll that she was not fit to be a nun.[111] Seven witnesses came to the defence of the prioress, including Graunde and Newcombe. Three of the lay witnesses for her defence said that when the prioress had been ill, and the rumour of her being pregnant was spread, they had examined her body. The charge of giving birth was dismissed by the Visitor, who reminded Graunde and Newcombe that they must accept the penances imposed, and not to be absent from divine service.

Legbourne, Lincolnshire

At a visitation held at Legbourne on 19 July 1519 by the bishop of Lincoln personally, the bishop noted that a Gilbertine canon, also vicar of Little Cawthorp, was the nuns' confessor; that the infirmary was not in a good state of repair, nor were there adequate arrangements for sick nuns; and that some nuns had on occasion been labouring in making hay, albeit in the presence of the prioress.[112]

At a further visitation of Legbourne 1 July 1525 by John Rayne, the vicar-general, the prioress (Agnes Otteley) and ten nuns were present, of whom nine asserted that all was well in the nunnery.[113] The prioress and one sister (Elizabeth Pinchebek) criticised one nun, Ursula Tathewell (Taylwode), for disobedience to the prioress, for over-familiarity with local priests, especially John, the chantry priest of Legbourne—though it was thought nothing evil had taken place. It was alleged that she had passed on to friends two silver spoons and four yards of woollen cloth which the prioress had given her. It was enjoined that Ursula was not to talk to outsiders save by permission of the prioress, and then only in the presence of two or three sisters. She was to return the spoons and cloth, and before Michaelmas to fast on bread and water on six Fridays; John, the priest, was not to be admitted into the community nor to spend the night.

The Visitor reminded the nuns to accept penances imposed, and enjoined that they should not talk to any outsider save in the presence of two sisters, and that they should not take any relative to their chamber unless by express permission of the prioress or subprioress, and then only in the presence of two or three of their fellow nuns. It was alleged that one sister, Alice Fillvaron, was 'fickle in her speech.'

Nun Appleton

A visitation held in 1489 gives detailed stipulations making for greater stability of the sisters.[114] They are worth reproducing in full:

> First and principally we command and enjoin that divine service and the rules of your religion be observed and kept according to your order that ye be professed to. Item, that the cloister doors be shut and 'sparn' in winter at 7. and in summer at 8. of the clock at night, and the keys nightly be delivered to your Prioress, and ye after the said hours suffer no person come in or forth without a cause reasonable. Item, that the Prioress suffer no man lodge under the dorter nor on the 'Bakside', but if it be such sad persons by whom your house may be holpen and secured without slander or suspicion. Item, that the Prioress and all your sisters lodge nightly in the dorter, saving if ye or your sisters be sick or diseased, then ye or they so sick or diseased to keep a chamber. Item, that none of your sisters use the alehouse nor the waterside where concourse of strangers daily resort. Item, that none of your sisters have their service of meat and drink to the chamber but keep the frater and the hall according to your religion, except any of them be sick. Item, that none of your sisters bring in, receive, or take any lay man religious or secular into their chamber or any secret place day or night, nor with them in such private place to commune, etc. or drink without licence of you Prioress. Item, that ye Prioress licence none of your sisters to go pilgrimage or visit their friends without a great cause, and then such a sister so licensed to have with her one of the most sad and well disposed

sisters [to accompany her] to she come home again. Item, that ye grant
or sell no corrodies nor liveries of bread nor ale or other victual to any
person or persons from henceforward without authority and special
license of us or our vicar general. Item, that ye see (that) such servants
as (be)longeth to your place come in to meat and drink, and not have
their liveries of bread and ale outward but if ye think it necessary and
for the wealth of your house. Item, that ye take no boarders or sojourners into your place from henceforward, but they be children or else old
persons by which a 'vaile biliklyhod' may grow to your place.

A much later visitation of the nunnery in 1534[115] stipulated that wholesome
bread and ale were to be provided for the nuns—the same as for the prioress;
as some sisters had sent out of the nunnery for ale.[116] No secular persons were
to be in the hall when the sisters were at meals—save for serving women; at
both dinner and supper enough spoons were to be laid on the table as there
were sisters. Sick sisters were to be looked after, and given 'lighter' rather than
'grosse meats'. A laundress was to be appointed to wash her sisters' clothes
'according to the old laudable custom of that house.' A fire was to be provided
in the hall 'from the feast of All Saints unto Good Friday, according to the old
laudable custom of that house.'

Nun Cotham, Lincolnshire

The scanty records of an episcopal visitation conducted in July 1519 merely
forbid the nuns from talking or drinking with relatives, unless in a public place
assigned by the prioress, and with other nuns present. A further inspection in
June 1525 enjoined that no lay person was to speak with any nun except in
the presence of two or three other sisters, and that no secular person was to
enter the chamber of a nun, unless authorised by the prioress. Delinquent
nuns in these respects were to be imprisoned.[117]

A visitation conducted by Bishop Longland in 1531 does not give a very
satisfactory account of the nunnery.[118] He stipulated that it must not be
compulsory for money to be given on the admission of a novice—this was
important because in nunneries seen as havens for those of gentle birth, young
ladies of lower class whom the Holy Spirit might be calling to the religious life
could not possibly fulfil that vocation if a dowry was expected. In response to
what had clearly been the practice, it was enjoined that boys were not to be

brought up nor taught in the convent, and none but the sisters were to sleep in the dorter.

The bishop noted 'the miserable poverty and the ruin and extreme decay' of the convent. To counter this the prioress should reduce the excessive numbers of both men and women servants, and refrain from burdening the house with large numbers of her kinsfolk. It was meet to have her mother about her for their mutual comfort, but the liberality shown to her brother, George Thomson and his children, was to cease. This had involved 'grazing of [his] cattle, occupying your lands, making of ironworks to plough, and cart, and other like of your stuff in your forge.' Furthermore, the church, infirmary and other buildings which were in ruin were to be if possible repaired within a twelve-month.

The visitation charter forbade the hasty recitation of the hours, and in a reference perhaps to the Feast of Fools the prioress was instructed 'no more to suffer any lord of misrule to be within your house, neither to suffer hereafter any such disguisings as in times past have been used in your monastery in nuns apparel nor otherwise.'

The problems of breaches of enclosure were once again to the fore. Sisters had apparently been causing scandal and inconvenience by leaving the monastery at will to visit friends or to go out under the pretext of pilgrimage. Sometimes there had only been six nuns in choir, as the others had wandered to other religious houses—Augustinian Thornton and Premonstratensian Newsham were both but a few miles distant. It was not unknown for sisters even to go to Hull—across the Humber estuary from the nunnery, 'which is abominable, shameful and displeasing to God.' These wanderings had to cease: no nun was to leave the convent without permission, and then only in the company of 'a wise, sober and discrete sister.'

Lastly, under pain of excommunication, the prioress was ordered no longer to permit Sir John Warde and others (four named clerics it seems) to come within the precincts, and if they do by chance come unawares 'that ye straight banish them and none of your sisters commune with them.' Further, the prioress was enjoined 'to avoid out of your house Robert Lawrence, and [that] he no more resort to the same.'

Sinningthwaite, Yorkshire

At a visitation held on 14 October 1534 by the archbishop of York, several of the articles of the charter bear a close similarity to those issued in the case of

Esholt by the vicar-general two months previously.[119] Again the sisters were exhorted to obey the prioress 'without grudge or murmur,' but she was not to 'rebuke or worse intreat' any sister for anything said during the visitation; and the sisters were likewise not to murmur at the prioress. These regulations allowed the nuns to speak freely when interviewed individually by the archbishop. More than that, the proceedings of the daily chapter meeting were to be kept a secret.

The need for stability was again a major element in the injunctions: the cloister doors were to be surely locked every night after Compline, and not unlocked until 7 am. in winter and 6.am. in summer. The prioress or a 'discreet and religious sister' was to have custody of the keys; likewise the door of the dorter was to be 'surely and fast locked' every night, so that none of the sisters could get out until service time and that no person might get in to them. All nuns, but no secular women whomsoever they might be, were to lie in the dorter; nor were the sisters to be allowed to see any visitors but close family members. Sisters were only to be given leave to go out of the nunnery for short periods, on the convent's business or to visit near kinsfolk, and were to be accompanied by a 'sad and discrete' sister.

The refectory and diet also found mention. All the sisters 'to have dinner and supper in one house [sitting] and one table, and not severally in their chambers.' They were to have sufficient meat and drink, their dinner was to be at 11. of the clock or thereafter; their supper at 5 of the clock or thereafter. Other prescriptions included the requirement for the nuns to keep silence in quire, cloister, refectory and dorter, regular attendance in quire, and the need for an infirmary sister to be designated.

No new nun was to be admitted without the archbishop's permission, and no money was to be taken on such an admission—'for that is simony,'—unless 'it be given freely without any formal pact.' The common seal was to be kept under three keys—held by the prioress and two of the wisest sisters, and no deeds were to be executed without the agreement of a majority of the nuns and, in the case of corrodies and annuities, without the archbishop's licence. Accounts were to be rendered twice a year.

Lastly, but importantly, these injunctions were to be strictly observed, and read out in chapter once a month.

Stixwould, Lincolnshire

The bishop of Lincoln held a visitation personally on 8 July 1519, and the following day sitting in the chapter house issued his injunctions.[120] Sisterly relations were recommended by the enjoinder that the sub-prioress assign at least three nuns to eat with the prioress, and better care was to be taken of the infirm; they were to be ministered to 'by diligent and trustworthy servants with all humility and diligence.' It was not satisfactory for fourteen of the sisters to be living in the 'house' of the prioress, one in the house of the sub-prioress, and one living alone; this was to be amended as previously suggested. The prioress did not spend the night in the cloister range, but outside with secular ladies. This was not good enough; she was to provide herself with a proper residence within the cloister, and spend the night there. Her present quarters could be used for recreational purposes and to receive visitors. Dr Sheffield, rector of nearby Bucknall, was not to be permitted frequent recourse to the convent and was to return to his normal place of residence. He was, however, together with the vicar of Stixwould, named as one of the community's confessors.

A further visitation was held on 15 May 1525 by John Rayne, the vicar-general.[121] The prioress (Helen Key) and sixteen were present. Nine of the community asserted that all was well in the house, but one said that 'the nuns come never with the prioress nor the prioress come never among them unless it be in the church and chapter house some time.' Four of the nuns (including Alice Cranmer, the archbishop's sister) alleged that the prioress was too close to the Steward—he having the upper chamber of the prioress's house, she sleeping in her lower chamber. Moreover he grazed horses and cows on the convent's pastures.

The prioress was enjoined to have two or three of her sisters at her table at every meal. Under pain of excommunication she was not to permit the Steward to stay overnight within the gates of the nunnery, and at least one other sister should be present when she talked to him, nor was he to pasture his animals on the convent's land. Another nun (Dorothy Waltham) said that at the time of the prioress's election there had been £100 in the treasury, but in the three years that had elapsed £40 had been spent on 'grains' for the monastery. The prioress responded that £60 had been spent on necessary business, but that £40 remain for the use of the monastery.

Another visitation was held, by the bishop of Lincoln personally, on 21 October 1528; no record remains of his injunctions, but the expenses of the nunnery on that occasion amounted to £6-13-10.[122]

Wintney, Hampshire

A brief visitation of this nunnery took place in its chapter-house on 3 April 1501 by Thomas Hede, LL. D. Two nuns asserted that all was well, and the prioress, Anna Thomas reported the annual value to be of the order of £50;—this compares to the £52 observed at its dissolution in 1536. She also placed on record that the house had been twenty marks in debt when she became prioress in 1498, but that so far fifteen marks had been repaid. The only discordant note was struck by the sacrist, Joan Swayne, who alleged that the previous prioress, Petronilla Pigeon, had given a sealed but blank charter to the vicar of Herriard. The visitation appears to have been cut short—for only four nuns gave evidence, yet there were ten sisters here in 1536; it was adjourned to 3 July.[123]

The Secular Community

The nunneries were not entirely feminine establishments. In earlier centuries the typical Cistercian convent had one or more lay-brethren *(conversi)* to look after the house's commercial interests and to supervise work in the fields. The nuns could not themselves do that because of their strict enclosure. By Tudor times such help was a thing of the past, but every house had one or more residential chaplains and a number of servants, some of them at least living in.

Chaplains

Each convent requiring clergy as chaplains, or to serve churches of their appropriation, would present such clerics for ordination: the priory was their 'title'—an assurance that when ordained the clerics had the wherewithal to live by. Amongst such 'titles' granted were those by Swine to Richard Huetsam (diocese of York, 1491),[124] and by Basedale to John Gran (Winchester, 1499).[125] To name but two of the resident chaplains: Thomas Henryson (Handale, 1539) and Nicholas Williamson (Basedale, 1536–1539).[126] The annual stipends of the resident chaplains were low, varying from £1 at Esholt[127] to £2-13-4 at Marham,[128] but they also had food and accommodation provided. The chaplains of Nun Appleton (Robert Raynald and Robert Turner) each had a stipend of £2-10-0.[129]

John Jenkinson, chaplain of the Plumpton chantry in Esholt priory, was more fortunate with a stipend of £4, though this was seemingly halved by the Court of Augmentations.[130] The vicars and curates of a nunnery's appropriated churches had just salaries. Hampole gave a stipend of £6-13-4 to Robert Skott, curate of Marre, and also to William Watson, curate of Melton.[131] There are plenty of notes of the appointment of vicars to a nunnery's churches: Catesby, for instance, in 1497 named Richard Woddus as the new vicar of the village there, Hugh Deye having died; but two years later Woddus resigned, and John Clerke was appointed in his stead.[132] Hampole gave Robert Parkyn, priest, the reversion of the church of Ankerwyke after the decease of Peter Scott, then incumbent there. He was to receive only a £1 annual stipend, but he did gain a house and lands, the accustomed offerings, and the lesser tithes—including those of wool, pigs, fowls, pears, wardens and walnuts![133]

Stixwould's church at Wainfleet St Mary had by 1528 been placed in the hands of a priest-procurator, Edward Clarke, the vicar there receiving a stipend of £10 annually. The oblations and tithes amounted in value to over £22, and included oblations at weddings and funerals, and the tithe of fish, lambs ad sheaves. When it demised the parsonage of Lavington (1535) for £6-16-8 yearly, it reserved the advowson to the sisters.[134] At the priory the nuns had (1528/29) two chaplains: Simon Brinkhille and Andrew Speight, both receiving a £2-6-8 stipend, and undoubtedly their meals as well.[135]

At Kirklees were two chambers for the chaplains at the northern part of the inner court,' at Wykeham was 'a house where the priest lieth,'[136] and at Wintney also two chaplains lived in.[137] At Keldholme the "chaplain's chamber" was demised to John Potter in 1533. His entitlement included 'sufficient hay and provender or an horse for him to ride on in winter in the needful business of the house.'[138] He appears to have been both chaplain and intermediary.

At Swine the "vicar's mansion and four priests' chambers" were all under one roof measuring 100 x 16 ft.[139] The vicar (of Swine parish) received a stipend of £5-6-8; his curate ('the parish priest') £2-13-4, and the other clerics, £2 apiece. Their food and drink was valued at £2 each per year. The vicar had other perquisites, including provender and stable room for his horse. Apart from the vicar and curate, the other clerics were 'the lady priest' within the parish church, the 'Durham priest' and the "nuns' priest" within the abbey. There was also a deacon, whose lowly stipend was 15s p.a.[140]

Servants

Live-in servants are listed in the dissolution papers, and 'chambers for servants' are noted at Swine and Esholt,—in the latter case, on the home farm.[141] Wintney had a total of twenty-three servants, perhaps not all resident, including 'a waiting servant,' three male servants ('hinds') and nine women servants.[142] Wykeham had nineteen servants, including 'three little maids of the house,'[143] whilst boys were among the twelve servants of Keldholme.[144] The bishop of Lincoln, in his visitation charter for Nun Cotham (1531) urged its sisters 'to straight upon sight hereof diminish the number of your servants, as well men as women, which excessive number is one of the great causes of your miserable poverty and the ruin and extreme decay of your house.'[145]

At Basedale, with only five servants, the two female helpers had to double up: one as butler and cook, the other as baker and brewer.[146] At Esholt Jane Brerey was butler with an annual wage of 13s 4d, and Margaret Parkinson was cook and paid 10s, but Richard Jenkinson, 'a serving man', received £1 p.a.[147] Nun Appleton's male servants were headed by Christopher Smyth, its 'sergeant of husbandry,' and included a slaughter-man and a swineherd, as well as a man whose duty it was 'to keep the fires'—which probably included gathering the necessary fuel. Its lady servants comprehended a butler, a cook, two brewers and the prioress's maid.[148]

Amongst the eleven servants of Handale were two boys, and a lady butler—Mary Lutton, who was very probably a relative of the last prioress, Anne Lutton.[149] Christopher Nendyk, the collector of rents for Wykeham and also its Clerk of the Court, was clearly a relative of the last prioress, Catherine Nendyk. She seems to have made the nunnery something of a family concern.[150] Including its officers and farm servants, Hampole had twenty-seven men and women on its pay-roll. Eighteen of them were entitled to allowances of bread and ale. One of the perquisites of the under-brewer was to receive at every baking eight loaves of bread, and at every brewing ten gallons of ale. Additionally each servant had yearly 4 quarters and a windle of wheat, and the same of barley. The convent had its laundry woman.[151]

When the convents were closed the servants, who might not be able to find other jobs, were granted any arrears of wages, and also a 'reward'—pocket money to help them adjust to their new life. At Handale John Sawyer, the 'chief husband servant', received for his quarter wages due at Lammas, 4s. 3d, and 'in reward' 2s 5d. John Coverdale, the miller, received 2s 9d. and 2s 3d., and Margaret Hodson, the cook, 2s 3d. and 2s 9d, respectively. Thomas Henryson, the chaplain, too, had to look for a new posting. He was awarded his quarter wages of 10s. and 3s. 4d. to soften the blow of leaving.[152]

Corrodians

A faithful servant might be granted a permanent place in the monastery, a corrody (like those in the male houses) with usually entitlements of board and lodging. So it was that on 2 December 1538 Nun Appleton granted to George Godson 'our servant, for good service,' an annual payment of 10s., together with weekly three convent loaves and one of rye bread, and three gallons of ale, and also once a year three yards of coloured cloth for his clothing. In this instance, residence is not mentioned, so possibly the recipient lived close by. After the Suppression the Court of Augmentations awarded him an annual payment of £1-11-0 in *lieu* of his former corrody.[153] A corrody at Wykeham was held by one Thomas Nendyk, surely a relation of the last prioress, Katherine Nendyk. The circumstances are unknown.[154]

Other corrodians might purchase a corrody as an insurance against old age. Esholt, in 1518, granted a livery to John and Agnes Hudson, in return for a payment of £1 and a gift to the nunnery of thirteen cattle, three calves, forty sheep, two wethers and twenty-four lambs. They were also to find forty ewes yearly to be pastured by the convent with half the profits going to the Hudsons, but after their death the ewes were to become the property of the priory. In return the Hudsons received the house called 'hole hall', with each week 6lb of white bread and 'such a rye loaf as is baked,' and six gallons of the best convent ale. If one of the Hudsons died, the food entitlement was halved. They were also granted pasture and fuel rights. The corrody was valued at £2-19-10. By the time of the Suppression, John had died and Agnes was over eighty years old.[155]

Handale, at an unknown date, granted a corrody to Richard and Agnes Loghan, he perhaps being a relation of one of the nuns. They were given a house to live in, daily amounts of bread and ale, half a cow yearly and a pig yearly; 1½ bushels of salt yearly, 6 salt fishes and 100 white and red herrings yearly; a portion of every mutton killed, fire wood, milk of a cow winter and summer, each week from Easter to Martinmas a quart of milk, 1lb. of candles yearly, and the right to dine with the prioress and community every principal feast. No indication was given as to why the corrody was awarded. Agnes continued to enjoy this livery in her widowhood, and when the convent closed was given a 5 shillings 'reward' to help her on he way.[156]

Other Guests and Visitors

There is a little evidence of care for the elderly at this time. At the visitation of Nun Appleton in 1489 the nuns were ordered to receive no more boarders or sojourners, children and old persons excepted—which 'a vaile liliklyhod' may grow towards the nunnery.[157] At Kirklees there were two almshouses, 'one by the backside, and another within the gate where a poor man dwelleth.'[158] The income of Marham was enhanced by its giving a home to six boarders. Marham would also have received funeral offerings, as it had the right to bury lay people in the abbey cemetery. The abbey might also have received possibly unwanted seculars, as it had the legal privilege of affording sanctuary to accused wrong-doers.[159]

Charity was extended in the customary distribution of 'dole' on Maundy Thursday. That day, at Marham, one penny was given to each of thirteen poor people, together with a distribution of bread,[160] whilst at Tarrant bread to the value of £3 was given away principally in memory of the foundress, 'Eleanor, sometime queen of England'.[161] At Handale alms were distributed for the soul of Robert Percy valued at £4-9-2 p.a. They consisted of weekly handouts of two measures of corn and 3d. in cash.[162] At its suppression Catesby was described as having been 'a great relief to the poor.'[163] In 1535 5.6% of Swine's gross income was expended in such charity.[164] A helping hand might be extended to an outsider, as when around 1525 the sub-prioress of Catesby loaned ten marks to William Botry on the occasion of his marriage to her kinswoman, Joan Gibbons. The money was not repaid.[165]

Certain nunneries may have gained a small income from pilgrims. Recorded during the Suppression were relics in various houses, mostly adduced as being helpful to lying-in women, including: the Virgin's milk at Basedale nunnery; girdles of the Blessed Virgin at Arthington and Nun Appleton; a relic of the Holy Cross and a finger of St Stephen at Keldholme, a comb of St Edmund at Wallingwells; and an arm of St Margaret and a tunic of St Bernard at Sinningthwaite.[166] There was particular devotion, attracting pilgrims, at Hampole to St Richard, 'a saint not canonised', and at Wykeham to St Scytha. At Hampole the reference is to the hermit Richard Rolle. There was a church dedicated to Scytha the Virgin in London, and an altar in St Alban's abbey. For more local devotion, Swine had its 'Rood of the Pity.'[167]

There is plenty of evidence of boys and girls in certain of the nunneries, but how far did they receive any formal education? Certainly, there had been provision for this at Nun Appleton, where the survey of 1535/36 noted in the inner yard, adjacent to the church and cloister, 'an old school house, with ill daubed walls.'[168] Richard Dickson of Helmsley, Yorkshire, making his will in 1520 gave his daughter, Joan, to Keldholme, with her inheritance of £10, but perhaps this was as a religious rather than as a pupil.[169]

Sinningthwaite played a further role in education when 'at the special request and desire of one John Exilbe, gent., it did content and pay to Master James Scheffyld of York, then being schoolmaster of the high school there, 40s. for the board and learning of the son of the same John Exilbe.' Unfortunately John Exilbe, having twice married, died, and the second husband of his wife, John Baylton, 'often and many times' refused to reimburse the forty shillings loan, forcing the prioress, Elizabeth Swer (1489–1529), to take the case to the Court of Chancery.[170]

Guests who might have proved an embarrassment at Hampole were leaders of the Pilgrimage of Grace, Lord Darcy and Sir Robert Constable who, with Robert Bowes, lodged there one night in September 1536 whilst en route to an engagement in Doncaster. The chief rebel, Robert Aske, one night that same month 'lodged under Hampall the nunnery', whilst a number of rebels also stopped off there.[171] A more welcome guest visiting the nunnery of Llanllŷr might have been the Celtic poet, Huw Cae Llwyd (fl. 1431–1504) He appears to have been staying at the convent when he addressed verse to Sir William Herbert of Coldrook, Monmouthshire, praising the abbess. He wrote: 'Holy Llanllŷr, where there's a full moon. It is Dame Annes who, if she were at your court, would wish to have an ape from you.'[172]

Repositories

Another contact with the outside world came when nunneries, like male abbeys, were seen as places of security and stability, and so layfolk deposited deeds, money and jewels in them for safety. There were instances when a prioress would refuse to deliver up such items to those who alleged that they had the right to them. The responses of the superiors are either vague or unknown, but at least one prioress (*infra*) asserted that a claimant was not the rightful heir of a deceased depositor. The truth of the matters may never be known.

One Richard Ripley complained in 1530 to the Court of Chancery that although he was cousin and heir to Thomas Boston who had died, the prioress of Wykeham, Catherine Nendyk, refused to hand over deeds relating to a messuage called Roston. The prioress rejoined that it was not true that Richard was cousin to Thomas, and that she had no deeds showing that Thomas had been in possession of Roston. Rather she had various documents relating to Roston, 'which evidences, charters and muniments, she and all her predecessors in all time of two hundred years and more keepeth and hath kept for preservation of her and their good title.'[173]

Similar problems arose at Hampole where Dame Lucy Fitzwilliam, executrix of one John Fitzwilliam, complained at the close of the fifteenth century that the prioress refused to deliver up 'jewels, plate, household stuff and deeds' which John had deposited at the nunnery. Moreover, Lucy said, she 'knoweth not the certainty nor what manner of jewels and what was every piece of plate delivered, nor the content of the evidences.' The prioress's response is not on record.[174]

Like complaints were made regarding the 'evidences and charters' relating to a holding in Wombwell, Yorkshire (the property of Sinningthwaite),[175] and the manor of Ganstead (owned by Swine).[176] The first complainant—around 1500, had no idea how many evidences there were, nor how they were housed, whether 'in bag, box or chest.' The second plaintiff—about 1531, said that because the priory refused to deliver up the deeds he was 'disturbed and letted [*hindered*] to take possession of the premises.'

The Conventual Buildings

Relatively scant remains now exist of the nunneries.[177] Churches are found at Douglas (now part of an educational centre), Llanllugan (with medieval stained glass portraying a nun)[178] and Swine (where medieval misericords survive).[179] The latter two are still in use for public worship. Cook Hill is now in private hands, while remnants at Pinley now form a barn. At Marham and Wykeham portions of the church walls still stand, while the church tower survives at Ellerton,[180] as does a late Norman arch at Sinningthwaire,[181] and a thirteenth-century stair turret at Rosedale.[182] At Esholt, Keldholme, and Stixwould all that remains are coffin slabs. Excavation has shown the chancel

of the church at Cook Hill to have measured 42' x 23'6" and have demonstrated that the church of Kirkless was 80 feet long with a cloister 40ft square.
These figures are supported by the documentary evidence given below. At
least twelve of the nunneries have now no physical visible remains, though
they are evidenced by the remnants of a moated site at Greenfield, and
earthworks at Heynings.[183]

Churches

A detailed survey of six of the Yorkshire nunneries compiled probably in 1536
in the period between the 'survey' of a house and its actual closure—though
amended where the ages of the nuns was concerned in 1539, has recently been
painstakingly transcribed and interpreted.[184] It gives a considerable amount
of information regarding the conventual churches. The surveys tell us that the
churches of Esholt, Kirklees and Wykeham, were eighty feet in length with a
breadth of a little over twenty feet. Kirklees had a slate roof, but those of Swine
and Wykeham were covered with lead. Apart from their high altar, Both
Basedale and Handale had two altars in the quire and two in the body of the
church. In the 'upper chancel' of Catesby stood 'an altar stone of marble, a
yard broad and eight feet long.' It sold at the Suppression for 6s 8d.[185]

At Handale were noted thirty-six 'good seats' for the nuns, at Kirklees were
twenty-two stalls and at Esholt, eighteen. At the latter nunnery a rood loft
separated the quire from the nave, where there were fourteen stools for layfolk
to sit upon. The little steeple of Handale was roofed by thak board.[186] The
church roof of Legbourne was 108 feet in length; it and the steeple were
lead-covered.[187] Nun Appleton had a church 150 feet long with fifteen glazed
windows. It's high altar had a fine gilt front valued at £27. In the choir were
two altars and twenty-six stalls for the sisters, as opposed to thirty-six at Swine.
There was a north aisle, and a chapel of Our Lady on the north side of the high
altar.[188] A fifteenth-century alabaster statue of the Virgin and Child reputed
to have belonged to Whistones still survives.[189]

The valuations made around the time of closure of a nunnery show that,
so far as material goods were concerned, the convents were the poor relations
of their male counterparts. Often most valuable were the roof lead and the
bells, these being usually reserved to the Crown when a sale of goods was
made. Taken together, the lead and bells of Legbourne were valued at £84,
but at Wintney only £28; at Marham—despite its abbatial status, far less:

£4-4-0.[190] At Catesby, 'lead torn from the roofs' was worth £110, but the seven fothers of lead surveyed at Sewardsley only £26.[191] The 24½ fothers of lead "from pulling down of the priory" at Ellerton, together with a further fother 'in the ashes at the burning and milling of the lead' was valued at the fair sum of £81.[192] No lead was noted at Llanllŷr or Pinley.

Whistones had three bells weighing 100 lbs. in total, but valued at only £4-13-4.[193] The two bells of Keldholme were estimated as worth 10s; at Legbourne the steeple contained a 'great bell' and a 'small bell', and at Pinley there were two bells (weighing 122 lbs. together).[194] What happened to the bells of Pinley was the subject of an enquiry as late as 1556.[195] The four 'small bells' of Ellerton were valued together at only £2.[196] The two bells of Llanllŷr were sold to William Thomas of Carmarthen.[197]

So far as plate and ornaments were concerned, Douglas, Keldholme, Llanllŷr and Sinningthwaite, boasted little more than a single chalice and paten, usually of parcel gilt.[198] Sinningthwaite had been permitted in 1535 to pawn its silver vessels up to the value of £15 to assist in the necessary repair of its buildings.[199] Wintney and Catesby were more fortunate—the former having plate and jewels worth £35, and ornaments valued at £50;[200] the latter possessed plate assessed at £29, but its ornaments, vestments and house furnishings together were estimated at no less than £400.[201]

Legbourne had two chalices and patens of parcel gilt, an ivory pyx, thirteen copes, two suits of vestments—one being of green and blue silk, the other of back worsted. Amongst its other furnishings were a hearse cloth of baudekyn, Lenten altar cloths, and a 'painted cloth for the sepulchre' on Maundy Thursday.[202] A survey of Marham (in 1535) notes *inter alia* a latten censer, a sacring bell, a cross plated with silver gilt, and a cope of green Bruges satin.[203] Some church goods there had found their way to the dorter, which suggests a degree of disorder. As winter approached, in the week of St Catherine [25 November], Marham purchased oil for the lamps in its church.[204] Stixwould spent £4-5-8 in 1528/29 on bread and wine for the Eucharist and oil for lighting its church; another 4s. was expended on extra lighting at certain stated feasts.[205]

Apart from the visitation injunctions for Nun Cotham (1531) which urged less speed and more devotion in the chanting of the offices, and the need for much better and regular attendance in the quire, there is nothing to suggest (at least in those houses for which visitation charters are extant), but that the Eucharist was celebrated and the hours sung regularly and properly.

A note of interest concerning the liturgy comes, a little earlier (1476), in the statement by Margery Swinson, prioress of Whistones, that Edward I had in 1461 (the first year of his reign) granted £10 yearly to the convent on condition that the sisters kept the annual obit of his father (Prince Richard, Duke of York), 'with placebo, dirige and mass.' Prioress Swinson also promised prayers for the Royal Family after the gospel at the conventual mass on Sundays, Wednesdays and Fridays. In addition every Friday the nuns would say devoutly in procession 'the seven [penitential] psalms and the litany, for the tranquillity and peace of the realm of England.'[206] This annuity was confirmed by successive sovereigns in 1487 and in 1515.[207]

The Claustral Buildings

The most impressive nunnery *cloister* may have been that at Swine: seventy-six feet long and nine feet broad; it was lead covered and had glazed windows. The cloisters of Wykeham (sixty feet square), Baysdale (fifty feet), Handale (forty-eight feet) and Kirklees (forty feet) were smaller and unglazed. At Esholt the square cloister in circuit by estimation 120ft and six feet broad, was slate covered. Above the bolting house (where flour was sifted) at the west end of the cloister at Kirklees were five little chambers 'for the ladies to work in.'[208] The cloister of Nun Appleton lay on the south side of its church, was eighty feet square but unglazed.[209] The cloister of Legbourne was fifty-feet square and with a lead-covered roof.[210] A new cloister was being built at Nun Cotham in 1525, and it appears that some at least of its nuns had their own individual chambers.[211]

Off the cloisters were the usual ancillary buildings. The *chapter-house* of Kirklees, at the east end of the cloister, was relatively small being but sixteen feet square. The chapter-house at Wykeham stood at the south part of the church, was twenty feet long and eight feet broad, and had a glass window and a lead roof.[212] The stone-built chapter-house at Nun Appleton measured thirty-eight by eighteen feet and had seven glazed windows.[213]

The *refectory* of Kirklees was stone walled, thirty-four feet long and eighteen feet broad. At its west end was 'a little house to keep bread in,' and beneath the refectory was a larder. The refectory of Wykeham was sited over the south part of the cloister, measured thirty-six feet by twelve feet, and was lead covered. At Swine the refectory, off the south part of the cloister, measured sixty-eight by twenty-four feet. Lead covered, it had no less than twelve glazed windows.[214]

The Nun Appleton refectory, thirty-six by twenty feet, was on the upper floor of a two-storey building on the south side of its cloister; beneath it was a "nun's chamber" which might have been used for the elderly or infirm.[215]

The *kitchen* of Kirklees was twenty-four feet in length, and other ancillary buildings noted there included the bake-house, brew-house and 'cole house.' At Wykeham the kitchen was at the 'nether end' of the refectory, measuring fourteen by eight feet. There was a bed-chamber over the 'milk house' there. At Esholt was 'a kitchen of the old fashion' with a range of twelve feet in length and 'fair ovens.' The brew house adjoined the kitchen under the same roof. At Swine the kitchen measured thirty by sixteen feet, and had 'a fair chimney of brikkes.'[216] Nun Appleton's kitchen, thirty by twenty-four feet, was timber built with a slate roof.[217]

The descriptions of the *dorters* suggest that these were now partitioned. This was certainly the case at Esholt where the forty by fifteen foot dorter had in it 'seven cells for the ladies,' and at its south end were 'three little parlours each with a stone chimney, called the ladies parlours.' One had a small kitchen attached. The nuns of Catesby also had cells in their dorter, at the Suppression they sold for 6s 8d. each.[218] The longest dorter may have been that of Swine measuring one hundred feet. The forty-eight by sixteen feet dorter of Handale, at the east end of its church, had 'timber walls within and stone walls without.'. The fifty-six by eighteen foot dorter of Wykeham had a lead roof; that at Basedale, fifty by sixteen feet, was covered by thak board.[219] The dorter of Nun Appleton was seventy feet long and was sited at the east end of the cloister. Four 'nun's chambers' by its chapter-house suggest that some nuns slept out of the dorter.[220]

Amongst other buildings noted in the 1535/36 survey were the timber framed *porter's lodge* with a chamber over the gates at Wykeham, and the two chambers over the gates leading into the inner court at Handale. There was 'a pretty lodging' over the gate-house of Esholt. Mention is also made of the thirty-six by eighteen foot infirmary chamber of Swine, with its tiled roof.[221] At Nun Appleton the guest-house had several chambers over a parlour.[222] At Pinley the house was said in 1536 to be 'in meatly good repair, and most of it old.'[223] The 'Guest Hall' at Swine became the mansion house of the rectory of Swine, and was granted as his residence to the vicar of Swine, Richard Wright, by Dorothy Knight, the last prioress.[224]

Much of what is known of the books in the *libraries* of the Cistercian nuns comes from the evidence afforded by fifteenth-century wills. In 1448, for instance, Lady Agnes Stapilton bequeathed to Esholt a copy of the late-fourteenth century spiritual work, *The Chastising of God's Children*, while in 1486 a York priest, Thomas Hornby, left to Agnes Vavasour, a nun of Swine, a book written in English of the *Life of St Katherine*. It is known that Hampole possessed a copy of the 'Vernon Psalter', which included the Hours of the Passion and the Hours of Our Lady, while Matilda Wade, who resigned as prioress of Swine in 1482, gave a copy of *The Contemplation of the Dread and Love of God* to Joan Hyltoft, a sister of Nun Cotham.[225]

The Economy

Stewards

By Tudor times the lay-brethren *(conversi)* who would earlier have assisted in the management of the economy of a Cistercian nunnery were no more, and so each convent had to engage a completely lay agricultural staff. A lay officer, usually a gentleman of influence, was—even if only in the latter days—appointed as Steward of each convent, as a general superintendent and as convenor of any manorial courts held by a nunnery. He performed this duty for a relatively small fee, and often 'by means of a sufficient deputy.'.

Stewards could sometimes be overbearing and more of a hindrance than a help to a religious house—like the resident Steward noted in the visitation of Stixwould (1525). The power a Steward might assert was hinted at when in 1534 Ellerton appointed John, Lord le Scrope, as its Steward, giving him 'sway over the tenants and inhabitants.'[226] Few court rolls exist from nunnery properties, but a court held in 1526 at Catesby's 'Stareton' property with six jurors saw a tenant, John Moll', presented for allowing his property to fall into decay.[227]

In Ceredigion Sir Rhys ap Thomas held the stewardship of Llanllŷr nunnery until his death in 1525; later Lord Ferrers, Chief Justice of South Wales, occupied the position as one of six monastic stewardships he held.[228] Sir William Percy (1535) held the stewardships of both Hampole and Handale, but between them received only an annuity of £1-13-4.[229] Certain nunneries appointed stewards within months of their forthcoming suppression, as if they had no such officer before. This may have been a permanent reward for a financial favour shown them, or a means of gaining a powerful friend in the run-up to their eventual closure.

It seems likely that until the 1530s some convents at least tried to maintain control and management of their own affairs. As late as 1528 Alice Cranmer, the archbishop's sister, took over the office of 'receiver' at Stixwould from another nun, Margaret Stainburn. Alice appears to have been a very efficient business manager. She was assisted in some affairs by one John Huses, and an auditor, John Hill.[230]

A year before its suppression Swine appointed Sir Francis Bryan (who was also Steward of Woburn abbey, and 'a gentleman of the privy chamber') as its Steward on 20 August 1538.[231] Hampole gave the office to Leonard Beckwith on 8 January 1539, ten months before its closure.[232] Beckwith (in 1550–1551 to be Sheriff of Yorkshire) also received the stewardship of Nun Appleton (on 1 November 1538) a little over a year before its suppression. He was further in possession of a small annuity from Swine.[233] As the Particular Receiver in Yorkshire (save for the archdeaconry of Richmond) Beckwith oversaw the estates after their closure of Arthington, Keldholme, Hampole, Handale, Kirklees, Nun Appleton, Sinningthwaite and Wykeham. A favourite of Henry VIII, Beckwith had a legal background and he amassed no less than £54 p.a., in fees and annuities from monastic houses.[234] It was perhaps a relative, Ambrose Beckwith, who was already collector of rents at Handale,

Such late appointments were frequently not honoured by the Court of Augmentations, as being 'void and having no force in law.' Hampole on 16 February 1537 appointed Avary Hustrofte as 'bailiwick of the receipts and gathering of the rents' of its properties. The court later allowed him any arrears of payment at the time of the house's suppression over two years later, but not a continuance of the promised annuity of £2.[235]

Farm Servants

Among the farming staff noted in Tudor times were 'mylners'—water-mills are on record at most houses; windmills were listed at Gokewell[236] and Nun Cotham[237]—both open to winds from the North Sea, and horse mills at Legbourne and Swine.[238] Other servants included the plough-wright of Hampole whose job it was to make 'ploughs, axles, wains,' as well as 'hewing felewes and old timber.' His fellow labourers included threshers, dykers, hedgers and mowers, some of these were perhaps part-timers.[239] The miller of Marham received £1 p.a., its thresher and winnower, £1-4-0.[240] Esholt had eight farm servants, including two boys.[241]

Farm Buildings

The monastic survey of 1535/36 itemises the farm buildings of the nunneries it comprehends, and by this time not all were in good repair. At Kirklees, as well as corn barn, ox-house, stable, dove-cot and swine-cot, there was a kiln house measuring forty-four by eighteen feet. One half of it was old, but the other half 'late burned and new builded.' There was also an orchard 'enclosed by an old stone wall.' At Basedale the thirty-foot long barn and the twenty-seven foot long 'house where they lay turfs' were seemingly in good condition. Not so the cow house and the bakehouse, nor the overshot water wheel hard by the gate—'the whole is in decay, the mill goeth not.'[242]

At Wykeham, the house for turfs, the barn, swine-cot, cow house and lime house were in poor condition, but not so the kiln house in the outer yard. There was a bed-chamber over the milk house. Esholt had two 'fair barns'— their lower walls being of stone, the upper of timber. Both were orientated from west to east, and measured 100 by 32 feet and 60 by 35 feet, respectively. Its ox-house had a little chamber attached; there was also a servant's chamber, a wood house and a 'cole house'. Handale's buildings included a stable at the end of the brew house, and a little overshot wheel 'going with a little water.' It, too, had 'an old house where they lay turf or fuel with old mud walls.'[243]

Several of Swine's buildings were 'decayed', as the bakehouse and bulting house under one roof and fifty feet long. The forty foot long brew-house was also 'decayed', as were one of the barns, and the 'ox house and two stables for husbandry, all under one roof'. Its dove-house was 'well down.' Swine also had 'the mill house in the outer yard with a horse mill,' and 'a malting house to lay malt upon the floor.'[244] At Legbourne the granary was empty 'until new corn comes in'. Its brewhouse had two 'ledes', its bake-house, bulting and kneading tubs.[245]

Nun Appleton had two barns: one for hay measuring fifty by twenty-four feet, the other for corn and nearly twice as large. Its other farm buildings included: a timber walled sixteen-foot square dovecot; a swine cote and a horse mill. There were also the very necessary bake-house and brew-house.[246]

Stock and Food Supply

The animal numbers of most nunneries did not compare with those possessed by the male monasteries, but they were not always inconsiderable. At its closure Legbourne had (at 'Fenne House, Somesotes') thirty-one milk cows, 283 sheep and lambs, thirteen oxen, one bull, and forty-two hogs and pigs, as well as horses of various kinds.[247] Even the small nunnery of Douglas, Isle of Man, had in 1540 twenty-five cattle, eight pigs, twenty horses and foals, twenty-five lambs, 166 sheep, fifty-four goats, and eighteen kids: these were sold in total for £18.[248] Llanllŷr's animals in 1537 were smaller in number: on its home grange were only eight oxen, eighteen cows, and a further fifteen dairy cows called 'heyfords'—perhaps a specialised breed.[249]

Out of Marham's small gross income of £47 in 1492/93, one-quarter came from the sale of corn and stock. In true Cistercian style it also sold sixteen stone of wool (at 20d. per stone).[250] Despite its resources, in its closing months Marham bought in food, including beef, lamb and mutton, fish—including herrings, bread, butter, salt and hops.[251] Stixwould (1529) purchased for its nuns' Lenten diet sixty-four ling and 'lobbe,'[252] as well as two barrels of white herrings and four 'weights' of red herrings. In total that year its Lenten fish supply cost the sisters £4-12-8. There is an implication that at other seasons meat may have formed part of the sisters' meals.[253]

Part of Esholt's food supply came from the adjacent river Aire where it could fish at its pleasure 'from the lordship of West Esholt unto Apperley bridge, which is by the space of half a myle or more,' but the nuns were responsible for maintaining the nearby river bridge.[254] Swine had an orchard of fruit trees, close to which were 'divers ponds and stews [fishponds].' Other orchards there were 'about the houses'.[255] Remnants of the fish ponds at Cook Hill still survive.[256] As for arable Swine was well endowed with 802 acres, as well as 144 acres of meadow and 127 acres of pasture.[257]

Woodland Utiliation

Timber remained in the sixteenth century a very important commodity. Wykeham convent had eleven pieces of woodland, including 'the brew-house garth' and 'the garth before the house.'[258] Its most common trees were ash and elder. Pinley was less fortunate, and was said to have 'no woods except upon the demesne and copyholds; no forests.'[259] Five woods were noted at Esholt, including the ten acre 'Nonnewoode', which had three hundred great oaks of two hundred years growth and was valued at £10. Its 'keeper of the wood' had an annual wage of one mark [13s 4d].[260] Esholt had a 'wood house', and also 'a house to set carts or wains in, and to lay in timber'.[261] Its very name means stems from 'ash wood,' suggesting it was sited formerly in the heart of woodland.[262] Hampole's 'High Wood' covered 120 acres, and its timber—if all were to be sold—was valued at £100. It also had £10 worth of timber in 'the oaks and ashes growing in the hedgerows upon the east part of the house.'[263]

The value of timber was shown when Stixwould in 1514 demised its Basingthorpe Grange. The lessee could take timber from the nuns' wood there for reparation and new buildings, but he had to render in writing an account of the timber taken, and he was also to enclose or cause the wood to be enclosed. A later lease in 1535 of the priory's Honington Grange, allowed the tenant to have great timber from Basingthorpe Wood, but he was to bear the cost of its carriage.[264]

An abbess of Tarrant, Edith Goold, at the close of the fifteenth century, had to complain to the Court of Chancery when her coppice wood in Hurstbourne was lost to her, allegedly fraudulently. She asserted that the nunnery had sold to one John Douse twenty-three acres of coppice for £10, but that Douse had prevailed upon the vicar of Hurstbourne to draw up a forged deed suggesting that the priory had sold him the entire forty-five acre coppice. 'By colour and force of the same,' Douse had 'cut down all the underwood in the coppice,' and sold every acre thereof for 13s 4d an acre, 'to the great deceit and hurt of her poor abbey.'[265]

The loss of timber was also to the fore when one William Slocome complained in chancery that Joan Watson, prioress of Fosse, had demised a grange in Harwyke on 20 August 1507 to James Barnes for 41 years at £2-6-8 p.a.; he died, and his wife, Agnes, entered upon the holding. Later she married William and in her right he became the tenant. He should have paid the rent by the fifteenth day after Easter 1520, but was one day late in paying, so the prioress re-entered on the grange, where James in his time had built a barn and other edifices. William said he paid the prioress twenty shillings as she agreed to make a new lease of Harwyke to him for twenty-eight years. Instead, she let the grange to one William Remington. The prioress replied that not only was the rent unpaid, but that the tenant had 'done great waste in the felling and carrying away of timber and had broken all other covenants which should have been performed.' The twenty shillings, she argued, was meant to cover the damages for loss of the timber, and for her agreement to cease a suit against him, which she had commenced at the common law.[266]

Demising

In common with their male counterparts, by the sixteenth century much nunnery land was leased out, and this process accelerated as the Suppression approached. The usual conditions were written into the relevant deeds, frequently with a view to improving a property. When Stixwould for example on 31 May 1528 demised its Hundilbe Grange to John Bryan for twenty-one years at an annual rental of £5, he was obliged within three months to 'stake or bound all such lands, meadows, closes, that belong to the grange, that they may be well known from other mens' lands.' The convent was to provide timber for the work, but John to find or cause to be found the meat and drink of the workmen.[267] When Greenfield (1535) demised a close in Halton, it required the tenant at his own expense 'to dyke, plache, sette and hedge' it.[268]

The major return expected in the demise of monastic property was an annual cash rent, but sometimes there was a partial element of the rent being paid in kind. For Stixwould's Basingthorp Grange (1514), Thomas Elys had to render yearly not only £14 but also twelve stones of cheese.[269] Such a requirement was clearly advantageous for the food supply of the sisters. In Wales Llanllŷr (1537) received an annual cash income from its demised lands of about £25, but was also paid rents of oatmeal, and other oats called 'horsechettes'—presumably animal fodder. Taken together these payments were worth around £11.[270] As for cash payments, one tenant of Hampole paid yearly 'pence called Mawndy Silver on the Saturday before the day called Palm Sunday;' it amounted to 7s 6d.[271]

Occasionally a certain degree of nepotism can be detected in the leases: Indeed the bishop of Lincoln in 1530 instructed the prioress of Nun Cotham to stop granting leases and corrodies to members of her family; more than that, she was not to make any more demises at all for five years.[272] Swine (1535) leased out land and a dovecot at 'Southskyrland' to one Anthony Deyn, surely a relative of the last prioress, Eleanor Dean?[273] For the historical geographer the detail spelt out in some nunnery leases gives place-names which may, or may not, still exist. When Marham demised land in Marham itself (1530) mention was made of 'the street called Estgate.'[274] Nun Appleton's three holdings in York were at yet recognisable locations: Copgate, Skeldergate and Walmgate.[275]

An unnamed prioress of Catesby appears to have shown some solicitude for her tenants. An undated memorandum tells how for part of each year she allowed certain of them to pasture their flocks on nunnery land. Four of them had let to them 'a yard of land apiece, and also three horse pastures apiece, and four kine pastures apiece, and twenty sheep pastures and three loads of hay apiece, and also a certain plot of furze.' The terms of these grants are not recorded. Further, 'she hath granted to two other of her tenants to keep their lambs unto Martinmas (11 November), and calves unto they be a year old, and then to avoid [remove] them.'[276]

Disputes with External Parties

Demises of property granted by the nunneries could lead to later litigation, especially in the Court of Chancery. Richard Marks, yeoman, around 1530 complained that for three years he had been a sub-tenant of land in Colby granted by Prioress Agnes of Basedale to William and Alice Chamber, and which had passed to the two sons of Richard Croft of Myton, who had married Alice when widowed. After the accession of a new prioress—Elizabeth Roughton in 1527, and by her command, certain men had taken the sealed indentures, broken and defaced the seal, and to his loss made a new grant of the property. The prioress rejoined that this was wishful thinking, she doubted that any such lease had been made. Further she said he paid yearly and his rent was in arrears, and she rejected Marks claim that his cattle had been driven away.[277]

No response is extant of Anne Thomas, prioress of Wintney, to the allegations made against her, and her brother, Thomas, by one Robert Bayly, a husbandman who was a tenant in Hartley Wintney of a mease and one hundred acres of land demised to him by one Thomas Pykiner—it would seem that Robert was a sub-tenant of the nunnery. He alleged that on four occasions between the 7 November 1527 and 27 July the next year, Anne and Thomas sent a band of six or seven men 'in manner of war arrayed, with staffs, swords, bucklers and short daggers,' and forcibly abducted twenty-six beasts and cattle, two hogs, and ten loads of hay.' This was, Robert complained to the Court of Star Chamber, to the 'utter impoverishment' of himself, his wife and his children. On one occasion three of his beasts died 'in a strange pound unknown to him' by lack of nourishment. It is one of many cases where no rejoinder exists, and therefore it is difficult to pass judgement.[278] There is no suggestion that the prioress herself was part of the raiding party!

The plaintiff might be not a lessee but a lessor. Joyce Bykerley, prioress of Catesby (1508–1536), in her submission to the archbishop of York as chancellor of England, said that a predecessor—Aleine Steynton, prioress until 1484, had demised two yardlands in Daventry, Northamptonshire, for 20s p.a. The tenancy had passed into the hands of the priory of St Austin in Daventry, which since 1485, despite repeated requests, had paid no rent.[279]

Late Leases and Annuities

When it had become obvious that Esholt nunnery would be suppressed, Sir William Musgrave who hoped to receive the priory wrote (on 17 March 1537) to the Lord Privy Seal (Thomas Cromwell) asking him to send a letter quickly forbidding the prioress and nuns from making any further demises of property. He hoped that the letter would be despatched 'in brief time to stay further sales and grants.'[280] It was a clear sign that, like the male abbeys, some nunneries were as their end approached issuing hurried leases and grants of annuity.

Nun Appleton, in the five months between 1 November 1538 and 4 April 1539,—it closed on 5 December 1539, made no less than nine leases—including the tithes of Erlyngham, and granted three annuities.[281] A more extreme case was that of Swine. It did not surrender until 9 September 1539, but perhaps fearing the worst made no less than eight demises and four grants of annuity on one day alone, 20 August 1538.[282] The leases included that of Skyrleyght Mill on a twelve-year lease for £2-4-0 annually. One wonders whether all these grants were in fact made that day? Were some of them issued much nearer to its day of closure, but backdated so that they appeared to have been granted just over a year before its suppression, and therefore more likely to have been countenanced by the Court of Augmentations?

The annuities granted at the close of monastic life—six at least by Tarrant in the autumn of 1538,[283] were frequently, the relevant deeds report, for 'good and gratuitous service to us before this time' (Swine, 1538);[284] 'for good service, counsel and help' (Heynings, 1533);[285] 'for good help, aid and counsel given [and to be] given hereafter unto us' (Stixwould, 1524),[286] and for 'good counsel and favour' (Tarrant, 1538).[287] What was the 'aid', 'favour', 'help', 'counsel' or 'service' given? Perhaps legal advice, perhaps acting as an intermediary, or perhaps a monetary gift or loan—and the annuity a means of repaying it.

Where chaplains are mentioned as recipients like Robert Kirk at Nun Appleton, 'for true and diligent service,'[288] and William Estuke at Swine for 'good and gratuitous service before this time,'[289] it may well be that their annuities were a genuine reward for services rendered over a period of years. Occasionally late annuities were granted to persons who appear to have been a close relative of the prioress or abbess: this was true at Heynings (John Sandford, £2, 1538);[290] Llanllugan (David ap Llywelyn ap John, £1-6-8 and 24 bushels of oatmeal, 1534),[291] and at Tarrant (Sir John Russell, £6-13-4, 1538).[292] Could such payments to kinsfolk have been a means of ensuring an income for the superior herself when, thrown out of her convent, she might have to find refuge with her kinsfolk? Margaret Russell, the last abbess of Tarrant, was a cousin of the Duke of Bedford and after the Suppression lived very comfortably at Bere Regis. Dying in 1568, she left a great quantity of silver plate, as well as 'a collection of elegant, fashionable clothes, far removed from a nun's sombre habit.'[293]

The Suppression

The Cistercian nunneries endured the same fate of closure as did the male abbeys. Over one-third were closed in the first wave of suppression between the early summer of 1536 and the spring of 1537. The first convent to be closed was perhaps Gokewell (as early as 4 February 1536),[294] Ellerton may also have been taken into Crown hands at this time.[295] the last (in early 1537) may have been Sewardsley and the Welsh abbeys of Llanllugan and Llanllŷr.

There was usually an interval between a nunnery being 'surveyed' and later closed. There were limitations on the activities of a convent during this period, but the last prioress of Sinningthwaite managed to sell a portion of woodland, and to buy in hides and pelts of beasts.[296] Keldholme, for example, was 'surveyed' by the commissioners on 8 June 1535, but not suppressed until 5 or 7 August.[297] Careful note was made of the expenses during this waiting period; £4-18-2 in the case of Pinley.[298] The nuns remained in residence, but when the day of dissolution came they were generally expected to leave without delay. When Nun Appleton was 'surveyed' the commissioners gave a bad report, despite the lack of any mention of bad behaviour in Archbishop Lee's visitation a few months earlier. Worse still, Dr Layton did not even visit the house on that occasion; rather the sisters had to go to present themselves before him in Selby.[299]

When the commissioners returned to dissolve each house, the sisters were all expected to sign their deed of surrender. In the case of the nunneries this did not always happen, and the result was anyway a foregone conclusion. The surrender deed of Tarrant, and probably others, was clearly prepared before-hand in London, with simply a space being left for the insertion of the rank of the local superior; in this case 'abbess.' The Tarrant deed does bear the names of twenty nuns, but they are not individual signatures—for all are written in the same hand.[300] The like deed for Heynings has its community as stating that 'our names [are] underwritten,' when in fact they are not.[301] The surrender document of Swine also bears no signatures, nor does it say they were meant to be added.[302] All this points to the cursory and insensitive way in which the convents were often suppressed. It might also be that in some cases the sisters resisted giving their signatures.

On the day of dissolution of a particular house, apart from the lead and bells reserved to the Crown, a sale of other goods and chattels commonly took place. This brought to the benefit of the Crown often relatively small amounts. The sale of goods at Marham totalled £26 in value, leaving aside £3 worth of plate;[303] various chattels and the corn and animals of Pinley came to £21,[304] while the flocks of Douglas were sold for £18.[305]

Over half the nunneries surveyed in 1536 were eventually given formal exemption from immediate closure, and their superiors were usually reap-pointed by the Crown. Cook Hill received such exemption on 5 March 1537 and survived until 26 January 1540; Elizabeth Hewes, perhaps formerly a nun of the closed Gokewell was named as prioress.[306] Later in 1537 Cook Hill made a lease to Thomas Brough, a London merchant, 'in consideration that by his labour the nunnery was saved from suppression.' He had influence as he was one of the king's creditors.[307]

Kirklees was spared closure on 13 May 1538, and Cecilia Topcliff continued as prioress, though she retired shortly afterwards. There were two stipulations: the sisters who were resident on 4 February 1536, the day Parliament met to commence the Dissolution procedures, were to form the community, and all tithes and first fruits were to be paid to the Crown. After eighteen months, and then in its chapter-house in the presence of Dr Layton, 'one of the clerks in chancery,' on 24 November 1539 the community surrendered.[308]

It has been argued that small nunneries were spared immediate dissolution because of the difficulty of housing elsewhere those sisters who wished to continue in the religious life. Only one Yorkshire nunnery, Swine, was worth very much (£82), and the others would have struggled to take in an influx of sisters from other houses.[309] In the case of Hampole, a local squire, Sir Brian

Hastings of Fenwick Court, Campsall, pleaded on 13 April 1537 for its continuance, saying that the nuns were 'near neighbours of mine, and of good fame.'[310]
The convent survived until 19 November 1539; the next year Hastings died.

The last patent for exemption was granted for Nun Appleton on 12 July
1538, but it finally surrendered on 5 December 1539.[311] The first house to be
closed in the second wave may have been Tarrant [13 March 1539], and the
last was Douglas (Isle of Man, 24 June 1540). In the summer of 1539, three
Yorkshire nunneries closed within a few days of each other: Wykeham [21
August], Handale [23 August] and Basedale [24 August].[312]

A nunnery might become the base for sisters of another Order (as Stixwould), if closed it might be briefly resurrected (Legbourne), it might
endeavour to avoid closure (as Catesby), or it might be uncooperative (as
Llanllŷr). Henry VIII ordered the closure of Stixwould as a Cistercian house
on 12 August 1536, all the religious there (perhaps twelve in number) were
to be evicted, and the Benedictine sisters of nearby Stainfield were transferred
there. One of the Cistercian nuns, Jane Amcettes, transferred to Heynings,[313]
but the fate of the others is unknown. The Benedictine foundation at Stixwould ran into difficulties and was short-lived. It was re-founded by the king
as a Premonstratensian nunnery on 9 July 1537.[314]

The last prioress of Legbourne, Joan Missenden, in an undated letter
perhaps of the early summer of 1536, sought to avoid the closure of her house,
of which for some reason Cromwell was seen as 'founder'. She wrote to
Cromwell to say that 'as God has endued you with the just title of founder of
the priory of Legbourne, we trust you will hear no complaints against us, and
be a suitor for your own poor priory that it may be preserved, and you shall
be a higher founder to us than he who first founded our house.'[315]

Her appeal was unsuccessful for Cromwell himself was granted a lease of
the priory on 7 August 1536,[316] and later had two of his servants, John Milsent
and John Bellow on site surveying the property. Early that October, during
the course of the Lincolnshire Rising, a party of rebels went to Legbourne and
forcibly removed both of Cromwell's servants. The rumour went round that
the rebels had hanged Milsent and baited Bellow to death with dogs.[317] They
were, however, still alive and back at work according to a letter from Richard
Cromwell to his uncle on 2 November that autumn.[318] The rebels were also
credited with 'having made a nun at Legbourne.'[319] This suggests that they
tried for a very brief period to restore religious life there.

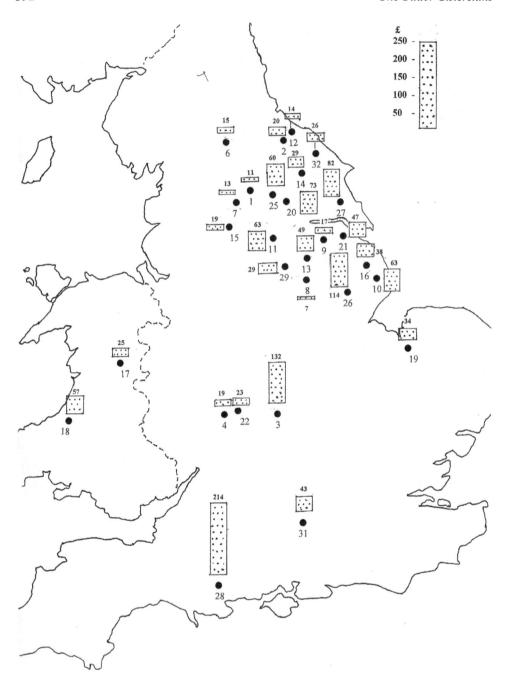

Fig. 17: Net Values of the Cistercian Nunneries, 1535

Number key to nunneries on previous page

1: Arthington; 2: Basedale; 3: Catesby: 4: Cook Hill; 5: Douglas; 6: Ellerton; 7: Esholt; 8: Fosse; 9: Gokewell; 10: Greenfield; 11: Hampole; 12: Handale; 13: Heynings; 14: Keldholme; 15: Kirklees; 16: Legbourne; 17: Llanllugan; 18: Llanllŷr; 19: Marham; 20: Nun Appleton; 21: Nun Cotham; 22: Pinley; 23: Rosedale; 24: Sewardsley; 25: Sinningthwaite; 26: Stixwould; 27: Swine; 28: Tarrant; 29: Wallingwells; 30: Whistones; 31: Wintney; 32: Wykeham.

Another prioress who tried to secure the continuance of her house was Joyce Bikerley of Catesby. She gained the support of the queen (presumably Anne Boleyn) who offered the monarch 2,000 marks to allow the nunnery to avoid closure. The prioress, asking Cromwell to intercede with the king, offered Cromwell 100 marks so he might buy a gelding, in addition to the prayers of the community; and reminded him that nominally he was their Steward and talked of 'her great sorrow.'[320] Catesby found high praise from the commissioners for Northamptonshire (led by Edmund Knightley) inspecting it on 12 May 1536, a week before the queen's execution. They wrote to Cromwell that if any monastery ought not to be suppressed, 'none is more meet for the King's charity and pity than Catesby. We have not found any such elsewhere.'[321] The king was not well pleased.[322] It was all in vain, Catesby was taken into the king's hands on 27 June,[323] and the nuns eventually left on 27 September that autumn.[324] In the prelude to its dissolution, the last abbess of Llanllŷr, Elizabeth Baynham, proved to be singularly unhelpful. When Henry VIII's survey of church income and property, the *Valor Ecclesiasticus*, was drawn up in 1535, she refused at first to declare her convent's income, and as a consequence it was arbitrarily assessed at £40 per annum [at least £14,000 in modern terms]. The nuns afterwards sent in 'a certain schedule', estimating their lands and spiritualities at around £18. The compilers then seem to have added both figures together, giving Llanllŷr the surprisingly high assessment of £57, as compared to an average of £25 in the Ministers' Accounts of the immediate post-Suppression years.[325] The survey of the abbey prior to its suppression came on 29 September 1536, and its actual dissolution on 26 February 1537. In the intervening 21 weeks and 2 days, £6 0s 5d. was allowed by the Receiver for the household expenses of the abbess, the sisters (alas, no number is cited), and the servants.[326]

Generally speaking, the value of the nunneries when closed was far less than that of their male counterparts. The wealthiest nunnery was Tarrant with a net income as given in the *Valor Ecclesiasticus* in 1535 of £214, followed by Catesby (£132), whilst not far behind was Stixwould with a net figure of £114. Thirteen convents had a net income of less than £40, and seven of those of under £20. There was very little spare cash available at Esholt (£13 net) and Handale (£14 net); one hopes that wealthier relatives helped to supply their needs. In the middle ground stood Swine (£82 net), Greenfield and Hampole (£63 net each), and Welsh Llanllŷr (£57).

The Fate of the Nuns

Several sisters (and there may well be others not yet traced) moved when their convent was dissolved to a nunnery which remained standing. Nun Appleton received four, if not six, such sisters: Agnes Aslaby and Elizabeth Parker of Ellerton, and Joan Fairfax and Alice Sheffelde from Sinningthwaite. It is possible that Joan Gascoyne (its last sub-prioress) and Agnes Snaynton of Hampole also transferred to Nun Appleton, only to find that nunnery was closed a fortnight later. Sinningthwaite was not many miles from Nun Appleton, but Ellerton was much further distant. Other nuns who moved included: Margaret Dyson from Ellerton to Cook Hill, and Katherine Stockes from Sinningthwaite to Hampole. Margaret Dyson had a considerable distance to travel from Yorkshire to Worcestershire.[327]

One testator, George Norman of Thirkleby, Yorkshire, aware of what was happening and making his will on 2 January 1539, took the precaution of providing that Isabel, his daughter and a nun of Handale, should have her due portion of his estate if her nunnery was closed.[328]

Pensions

For most sisters evicted from their convents in 1536/37 the outlook must have been very bleak, unless they had a family home—like the abbess of Marham, to which they could return. Only their superiors received a lasting pension, this was moderate and official confirmation of it could be months in coming. Only one prioress, Joyce Bykerley of Catesby, received a generous pension (£20), perhaps because of her long service in that position, and since the commissioners praised that nunnery highly, and indeed had suggested its continuance. The prioress of Hampole received £10, and of Legbourne £7.

At least six prioresses were granted £6-13-4, but the superiors of two early closed houses (Gokewell and Pinley) received only £4, and the abbess of Llanllugan but £3-6-8.[329]

The ordinary nuns of the houses closed in 1539 were more fortunate in that they were awarded pensions, albeit on a moderate scale. The amounts were fixed by the suppression commissioners, and reported back to Thomas Cromwell as vicar-general and Lord Privy Seal. The most a sister received was £2-13-4 p.a. (as at Cook Hill and Hampole), at worst but 16s 8d. (at Fosse).[330] A common sum to be granted was £1-6-8 or £1-13-4. There was a distinction in at least two instances based on age, and presumably therefore length of service. At Handale nuns over the age of forty years received a pension of £1-13-4 p.a., those younger but £1-6-8. At Heynings, the 'aged women' gained a pension of £1-13-4, but the 'young women' somewhat less, £1-10-0.[331]

In the years which followed dissolution, pensions were not always paid on time. Two former sisters of Basedale (Elizabeth Cowper and Agnes Nellys) were told in 1553 by the Yorkshire commissioners that their pensions had been in arrears from the previous Michaelmas because they, the commissioners, had no money. That year, another sister of Basedale, Barbara Bromley, reported that her pension was two years behind in payment. Other sisters at that time who were unpaid for a year or so included Felicity Chapman of Wykeham and Joan Messodyn, the past prioress of Legbourne.[332] Elizabeth Clifton of Swine, twenty-seven years old in 1539, sold her pension sometime before 1552. She was still alive in 1573, so the purchaser will have enjoyed at least twenty years return on his outlay, but how did Elizabeth survive meanwhile?[333]

The nuns, like the monks, were subject to taxation when a clerical subsidy was granted to the Crown. The former prioress of Whistones, Jane Burghill, saw in 1540 the deduction of 11s from her pension of £5-5-0, and her predecessor, Margaret Welsh, 4 shillings from her tiny pension of £2.[334] When in 1534 Anne Goldesburgh resigned as prioress of Sinningthwaite she was assigned a yearly pension of £10, but on account of a subsidy around 1536, she received in one half of that year—for the pensions were paid half-yearly, only £4-10-0.[335] The pensions of the sisters were small, but there was no exception from taxation.

Fig. 18: The pensions awarded to the nuns of Cook Hill,
with the subsidies payable thereupon (1540).
(By kind permission of the Bodleian Libraries, The University of
Oxford, MS. Tanner 343, folio 3)

Dr London, writing to Sir Richard Rich in July 1539, said that 'all these pensions were to be paid at Michaelmas [29 September] and Lady Day [25 March] by equal portions.' He wrote further a passage of uncertain meaning, that 'since the parties be at the cost of coming to London to sue for their pensions, I assigned the first payment to be at Michaelmas.'[336] This letter was in respect of Nun Cotham, which had been closed on 18 July; for its sisters there was to be a three month interval before any pension would be paid, but perhaps the need to make a claim in London had been averted.

It was partly to cover this gap, as also to give the nuns pocket money with which to buy lay clothes, that in addition to the promised pension they were also given an immediate 'regard' or 'reward'. The nuns of Esholt were awarded an eventual pension of £1-6-8, but also a 'reward' of one mark (13s 4d.). The nuns of Basedale and of Douglas each received 10s. in this respect.[337] The nuns of houses closed in 1536/1537 were given no pension, but they did receive this small sum of money to help them into civilian life. The sisters of Gokewell, perhaps the first convent to close, were each given £1 'for apparel.'[338]

It was this limited bounty to which Dr London (writing to Cromwell in 1539 regarding the nunneries he had closed in Lincolnshire, including Fosse and Nun Cotham, was able to say: 'In every house, they be in all manner gone that [very] night [that] I have taken their surrender, and straightway in new apparel'.[339] Instructions had been given to Dr Layton and the other commissioners closing religious houses in Lincolnshire in February 1539, including Heynings and Nun Cotham, to afford part of their assets to the departing religious.[340] It seems likely that at least some nuns had some personal pocket-money for in 1527 Thomas Ryther left 26s 8d. to be divided amongst the nuns of Nun Appleton, with an additional 26s 8d to Dame Joan Gower

Departing servants were also given this small 'reward' or gratuity on the closure of a priory. The sum total of such small grants amounted at Marham (25 January 1537) to £12-13-6.[341] Elizabeth Plummer seems to have been paid most (£2-15-0), and Mary Coo came next with £1-6-8. The chaplain received but one mark (13s 4d), while other beneficiaries included John Lawson (11s 8d) and Edward Williams (7s 6d).

Later Years

After the Suppression, the nuns dispersed to a variety of locations. Joan Hollynraws of Esholt, seventy-four years old and decrepit, may have left her house a little before its closure; she went to live with friends, but continued to wear her habit.[342] Abbess Barbara Mason of Marham appears to have moved to dwell with her brother at 'Hayle' in Suffolk, but died within a couple of years.[343] Leaving this world within a few days of 4 September 1538, she made no mention in her will of her former sisters, but made bequests, mostly of chattels, to some ten relatives and godchildren. She presented 'Hayle' church, where she desired to be buried, with a 'vestment of green silk betyn with gold'. She asked to have 'a marble stone to lie on my grave, and scripture [writing] on it'. She was not wealthy, but not impecunious either.[344]

Amongst other locations where sisters found an abode were Riccall, Yorkshire (Elizabeth Arte of Swine); Northallerton (Elizabeth Elsley, also from Swine), and Halifax (Isabel Saltynstall, formerly of Kirklees). In 1577, when she was about sixty-two years old and known locally as 'the nun', Isabel was cleared of a charge of calling one Marjory Hall a whore.[345] Agnes Broke of Kirklees may be the Dame Agnes Broke who, making her will in 1558, desired to be buried in Huddersfield parish church. Agnes Cutler, late of Hampole, may be the Anne Dodgeson *alias* Cutler who requested in 1557 interment in St Cuthbert's church, York.[346] Agnes Aunger of Nun Appleton found a home with her brother-in-law, Henry Burton of Bardsey, until his death in 1558. His will provided that after his death his executors were to provide her with 'sufficient meat and drink and cloth during her life, if she do so suffer them to receive and have her pension,' which was but £2.[347]

The marital status of the sisters in these years is not always evident, but at least six sisters of Heynings were still single in 1553, including Jane Amcettes, formerly of Stixwould and then of Heynings.[348] Other known to have remained unmarried included Alice Fyddell of Nun Cotham—she lived at Barton-on-Humber, and Cecilia Steward, formerly of Fosse and resident now at nearby Torksey.[349] It is probable that quite a number of former sisters remained single, but there were those who embraced married life, not always with happy consequences. The Six Articles Act of 1539 had forbidden ex-religious to marry, but it was repealed in Edward VI's reign.[350]

Tradition has it that Ellen Calcot, the last prioress of Douglas, Isle of Man, wed (under the name of Margaret Goodman) Robert Calcot, who was comptroller of the island, bit it is perhaps more likely that she was his sister.[351] Agnes Aslaby, of Ellerton, married Brian Spofforth, rector of Burton in Ryedale, but in 1554 he was deprived of his living and made to divorce from Agnes. Another casualty of the Marian revival, was Joan Fairxfax once of Sinningthwaite. In the world she was close to one Guy Fairxfax of Laysthorpe, and had a child by him around 1552. The Court of Chancery in 1555 ordered her to perform public penance in Stonegrave church, and to end the liaison.[352] Another to marry was Joan Messodyn, the last prioress of Legbourne; her husband was one William Ottbie/Otley and they resided at Corby, Lincs.[353]

There are signs that some nuns kept in contact with each other, and even possibly lived together. Tradition has it that Joan Kyppes/Kyppax, the last prioress of Kirklees, retired with four of her sisters to dwell at a house called Paper or Papist Hall in the parish of Mirfield. This is a feasible tradition since Mirfield church was of Kirklees's appropriation, and the nuns may have carefully arranged that a property was available to them when their convent was closed.

Joan died, aged 75 or 76 in 1562, and that may have meant the end of the community.[354] Between them the sisters had a consolidated income of £20.[355]

Elizabeth Thorne, formerly a nun of Swine and aged 60 in 1552, was domiciled in Hull and seemingly had in her household Elizabeth Patricke from her old community. When Thorne made her will in September 1557 she showed a concern for the welfare of that city and especially for its poor, as well as the mending of the highways. Her bequests show her to have been a lady of not inconsiderable means with a silver and gilt mazer, a gold ring with a turquoise, much household furniture and utensils and over £10 in cash. She left Patricke her house for life, and made her sole executrix, referring to her as her 'well beloved in Christ'[356]

Another former nun to be appointed an executrix was Alice Sheffield by her former superior, Katherine Forster, last prioress of Sinningthwaite, and now living in Tadcaster. Alice, on that nunnery's closure had moved on to Nun Appleton, despite allegedly having borne a child. She was pensioned off there in 1539, but was clearly still in contact with Katherine, and presumably living near her if not with her.[357]

The provisions made in the wills of other former nuns also show ties with those once their sisters in religion. Catherine Nendyk, the last prioress of Wykeham, in her will dated 7 May 1541 requested burial in the chancel of Kirby Moorside church where her parents were buried. Clearly she had returned to the family home. Among her bequests was 6s 8d. to be given to each of 'eight of my sisters that was professed in Wikham Abbey.' Her other provisions, including the stipend of a chantry priest for a year, and a silver cross to the countess of Northumberland 'for such costs and charges as I put her unto,' show that Catherine was not of inconsiderable means.[358] For a time after the dissolution she may have remained at her nunnery, as her relation Christopher Nendyk was not only the collector of rents there for the Crown, but had also been granted a lease of the site.[359]

In similar vein the last prioress of Ellerton, Joan Harkey, making her will in 1550 gave small bequests to four former nuns of the house: Alice Thomson, Cecilia Swale, Agnes Aslaby, and Elizabeth Parker, though she only had the means to leave them 12d. each.[360] She appointed another of her former nuns, Margaret Dowsone, to be her executrix 'if the law would allow.' Her belongings in her retirement in Richmond were modest: a cushioned chair and a feather bed, kitchen utensils, a coat and linen gear, two little chests and a coffer.

Despite being made during the reign of Edward VI, her will entrusted her soul to God and the prayers of blessed Mary and the saints, and she desired to be buried 'in the church of Richmond of Our Lady side.'[361] Her ready money amounted to only £3-12-4, and perhaps all her bequests could not be fulfilled. Amongst her beneficiaries, receiving one shilling, was Gabriel Lofthouse, formerly a monk of Kirkstall.

A last point: thirteen Cistercian nuns are known to have survived into the 1580s, and quite possibly so did others. They included no less than five former nuns of Swine, and at least one former sister of each of six other nunneries. It is worth noting the observation that 'the number of ex-religious upon whose post-dissolution lives we can throw any really positive light is relatively very small.'[362] Probably the last Cistercian religious in England and Wales was Isabel (Elizabeth) Coxson (Cockeson) of Hampole who still drew her pension in 1602, when she must have been about eighty-five years old.[363]

Fate of Nunnery Sites

In the months that followed the closure of a nunnery it and its lands were leased out by the Crown, and frequently among the recipients of former convents were those who served the monarch at close quarters. The first demise of Wintney was to Sir William Poulet, 'comptroller of the king's household', and brother of two of the suppression commissioners (August 1536);[364] the first lease of Rosedale was granted to John Berwyk 'of the Household' (20 June 1537);[365] that of Catesby to John Onley, "the king's attorney in the Court of Augmentations" (5 March 1537),[366] that of Marham to Thomas Bukworth, 'sergeant-at-arms' (16 June 1537), and again 'of the Household',[367] Llanllugan was demised to Maurice ap Knyvet, a yeoman of the Household (10 March 1538).[368]

Some of the nunnery sites leased or sold by the Crown remained in a family's hands for generations. This was true of Pinley, demised by the Crown in March 1537 to John Wigston, son of Sir Roger Wigston of Wolston, Warwickshire, a surveyor of the monasteries and also the Recorder of Coventry; Pinley was still in the family's hands in 1556. John was clearly a relative of the last prioress, Margery Wigston, and the demise of Pinley in this way may have assured her of an eventide home.[369]

Other nunneries which stayed in family hands for at least for a period included Greenfield. It was granted on 16 August 1536 to Mary Willoughby, the widow of the nunnery's patron, Lord Willoughby of Eresby, the largest land-owner in Lincolnshire, who bequeathed a set of vestments to the convent. She herself was a forceful personality, and it was in her arms that Catherine of Aragon died.[370] Another like grant was perhaps that of Gokewell to its former Steward, Sir William Tyrwhytt, of Kettelby and in 1535 Sheriff of Lincolnshire. Leased to him on 16 July 1538, it was regranted on 22 November the same year.[371] His brother, Robert Tyrwhytt, who had played an active part on behalf of the Crown during the Lincolnshire Rising, had received the nunnery of Stainfield when it closed in 1536.[372] Whistones was demised to a Walter Welshe, perhaps a relative of the penultimate prioress, Margery Welshe, perhaps allowing her to remain in residence.[373]

In other instances, an initial lease of a former convent may have been made and a few years later the site sold, with seemingly a sitting tenant. Basedale (closed 24 August 1539) was initially demised on 26 November 1539 to William Snowball 'of the Household' for 21 years, together with its grange at Nunthorpe, though the prioress retained some priory lands in her own hands at the dissolution. In 1544 it was effectively sold for £539 to Sir Ralph Bulmer, junior, of Willton, Yorkshire—a loyal soldier of the Crown, and John Thynne—Steward to Edward Seymour, Viscount Beauchamp,[374] who were granted the reversion of the site and its lands, and the rent reserved on the lease. In like manner, the reversion of the lease of Handale, originally given in December 1539 to Robert Kirk, 'clerk of the market of the King's household', passed in 1543 to Ambrose Beckwith, brother of Sir Leonard Beckwith, and both of Stillingfleet.[375] Handale became the family seat of Ambrose's branch of the Beckwiths.[376]

The evidence for the fate of Rosedale appears to be contradictory. Initially the site and lands were leased on 20 July 1536 to one William Smythwyke 'of the Household'. The lease was transferred to Sir William Bowner 'and by him forfeited.' A new Crown lease was therefore granted to one Thomas Greenhalgh on 20 June 1537. A year later on 6 July 1538, when the reversion of the lease and the rent received was granted to Ralph, earl of Westmorland, it was a John Berwyk 'of the Household', who is named as being the lessor of 20 June 1537.[377]

The grant of Legbourne priory in August 1536 to Thomas Cromwell came to an untimely end with his execution in August 1540. That December it was re-granted to Sir Thomas Heneage, a gentleman of the privy chamber and a friend of the king.[378] The Welsh convent at Llanllŷr was demised in 1537 to John Henry ap Rhydderch of Cedweli, but was sold in 1553 William Sackville and John Dudley.[379] Sewardsley priory, leased in 1537 to Thomas Broke, a man with many monastic interests and later to be Speaker of the House of Commons, passed in 1550 into the possession of Sir Richard Fermor, long rehabilitated after a sentence of life imprisonment, and who was to die naturally the following year.[380]

The scant remains of the fabric of the Cistercian nunneries reminds us that whilst the lead and bells were reserved to the Crown on a house's closure, the removal of the lead from a roof left it open to weathering and to speedy deterioration. As early as 27 March 1536, five months before its official surrender, Richard Southwell (sheriff of Norfolk in 1534/35 and a friend of Cromwell) wrote, with one Robert Hogen, to the vicar-general, to tell him that John Deriche, of Bircham Well, Norfolk, acting in the name of a king's sergeant, had 'spoiled the house of Marham of all the lead, and left it uncovered and bare.' They wrote that this was 'a very lewd and evil example [which] may encourage others to the like without the king's licence.'[381] This spoliation presumably took place soon after the preliminary 'survey' of the convent. By the time of its closure, on 8 August, it was said to be 'ruinous.'[382]

At Catesby nunnery, dissolved on 27 September 1536, by the end of that year the lead was said to have been torn from its roofs.[383] In at least one instance preventive steps were taken to avoid too hasty demolition of a priory's buildings. In an undated letter (which must precede June 1538), Richard Poulet, the receiver-general for the Court of Augmentations in Hampshire, Wiltshire and Gloucestershire, wrote to a Mr Hill, 'sergeant of the king's cellar,' ordering him, unless he could show sufficient authority to the contrary, not to deface any of the buildings of Wintney, other than that he had been to do—namely the cloister and the dorter.[384] Nun Appleton church was not immediately demolished, for the chantry of St John the Baptist within it survived until 1548, and on the grant of the site to William Fairfax in 1553, 'the steeple and churchyard' were included.[385]

Conclusion

In this sad way, the Cistercian way of life in some thirty nunneries with close on three hundred sisters came to its close. There were but few nuns in some of the houses, and in several convents there was a need for reform, but could not small communities have been amalgamated to form living entities, and could not superfluous nunnery buildings have been put to other good purposes? It was not to be, for greed and profit ruled the day, and saw the nunnery sites very often leased or granted to favourite royal servants. As for the history of the Cistercian nuns in Tudor times, the knowledge of it is fragmentary to say the least. Some convents have left little record behind them, almost as if they had never been; for most few documents are now extant. For the scholar today, the Cistercian nunneries of those days had indeed a 'hidden life'.

Notes

[1] *LP* **10**, p. 515 [No. 1238]; TNA, SP5/2, f.9; *VE* **5**, p. 87.
[2] VCH, *County of York* **3**, 1974, p. 158.
[3] *LP* **2**, p. 166 [No. 607]; Worcestershire R.O., *Reg. J. Alcock*, f. 241.
[4] *LP* **12**: Part 1, p. 350 [No. 795/10].
[5] *LP* **10**, p. 516 [No. 1238].
[6] VCH, *Dorset* **2**, 1908, p. 87.
[7] D. H. Williams, *Cistercians in the Early Middle Ages*, Leominster: Gracewing, 1998, pp. 401–02.
[8] M. Goodrich, *Worcester Nunneries*, Chichester: Phillimore, 2008, p. 17.
[9] No cited author, 'The Cistercian Abbey of S. Leonard at Esholt*, London: J.C. Hotten, 1866.
[10] BL, Add. Ch. 67119.
[11] E. Freeman, 'Houses of a Peculiar Order: Cistercian Nunneries in Medieval England.' In: *Cîteaux* **55**, Parts 3–4, 2004, pp. 245–87.
[12] Rosedale was termed Benedictine in a papal document of 1448 and in a dissolution paper: K. Seekings and D. Herd, *Rosedale Abbey*, Lastingham: United Benefice of Lastingham, 2005, p. 7.
[13] VCH, *County of York* **3**, 1974, pp. 174–76.
[14] *Statuta* **6**, p. 719 [No. 1533/45].
[15] Ibid. p. 719 [No. 1533/46].
[16] York; *Reg. T. Rotherham*, f. 78v.
[17] *LP* **13**, Part 1, p. 242 [No. 646/17].
[18] *SAP* (2), p. 57 [No. 1470]).
[19] *CPL* **18**, p. 355 [No. 471].
[20] York, *Reg. T. Savage* f. 76; *Reg. Sede vacante*, ff. 558v–559r; *Reg. T. Wolsey*, ff. 43v–44r.
[21] Freeman, 'Houses of a Peculiar Order,' 2004, pp. 264–65, 267, 279–80; M. J. Harrison, *The Nunnery of Nun Appleton*, University of York, Borthwick Paper **98**, 2001, p. 9.

22   D. M. Smith, *The Heads of Religious Houses* **3**, Cambridge U.P., 2008, pp. 673–74.

23   Freeman, 'Houses of a Peculiar Order,' 2004, pp. 273–74 give a full account of this episode;.Cf. *LP* **3**, Part 2, p. 1324 [No. 3171].

24   *LP* **3**, Part 2, p. 1329 [No. 3189].

25   Freeman, 'Houses of a Peculiar Order,' 2004, p. 272.

26   *Statuta* **6**, p. 557 [No. 1520/29].

27   Essex R.O., D/DP Q4.

28   F. G. Baigent, 'On the Abbey of Blessed Mary of Waverley.' In: *SAC* **8**, 1883, p. 172.

29   Freeman, 'Houses of a Peculiar Order,' 2004, p. 256*fn*.

30   D. H. Williams, *The Welsh Cistercians*, Leominster: Gracewing, 2001, p. 8. In 1534, for example, an annuity was granted by Llanllugan 'with the assent of the reverend father lord David, abbot of Strata Marcella' :TNA, E315/104, f. 177v (2ⁿᵈ nos); SC6/HENVIII/5257, m. 1r–2v.

31   VCH, *County of Dorset* **2**, 1975, p. 87.

32   S. J. Chadwick, 'Kirklees Priory.' In: *YAJ* **16**, 1902, pp. 364–65.

33   York, *Reg. T. Wolsey*, f. 53r.

34   *VDY*, p. 439.

35   BL, Add. MS 67119.

36   By Elizabeth Freeman in a paper given at the International Medieval Congress, Leeds, 2013.

37   TNA, E322/233.

38   *LP* **14**, Part 2, p. 232 [No. 636].

39   Ibid. p. 193 [No. 551].

40   VCH, *County of Lincoln* **2**, 1906, p. 148.

41   P. J. Davey and J. R. Roscow, *Rushen Abbey and the Dissolution of the Monasteries in the Isle of Man*, Isle of Man Natural History and Antiquarian Soc., Monograph I, 2010, p. 157.

42   *FOR*, p. 80.

43   TNA, E117/14/22.

44   W. Connor, 'The Esholt Priory Charter of 1485.' In: *YAJ* **80**, p. 123

45   *Statuta* **1**, p. 405 (No. 1213/3).

46   When synods were held in the Norwich diocese, as in 1499, the abbess of Marham was expected to be present on account of her convent possessing parish churches, but it may well be she sent a proctor: *Reg. J. Morton* **3**, 2000, pp. 30–31 [No. 45].

47   See the Appendix for relevant references.

48   *LP* **14**, Part 1, p. 576 [No. 1321].

49   Goodrich, *Worcester Nunneries*, 2008, p. 43

50   C. Cross and N. Vickers, *Monks, friars and nuns in sixteenth century Yorkshire*, Yorkshire Archaeological Soc., 1995, p. 558.

51   *LP* **9**, pp. 257–58 [No. 758].

52   Ibid. p. 137 [No. 423]. The 'doctor' was perhaps Dr Legh.

53 Chadwick, 'Kirklees Priory,' 1902, pp. 366–67.

54 *LW*, pp. 340–41 [No. 510; Greenfield, Legbourne], 310 [No. 461; Legbourne]

55 Ibid. p. 375 [No. 560].

56 For references to all these individual nuns, see the sources quoted for them in the Appendix

57 Cross and Vickers, *Monks, friars and nuns*, 1995, pp. 594–95; C. Cross, 'End of Medieval Monasticism in the North Riding.' In: *YAJ* **78**, 2006, p. 147.

58 *LP* **10**, p. 354 [No. 858].

59 *FOR*, p. 1.

60 G. Baskerville, 'A Sister of Archbishop Cranmer.' In: *EHR* **51**, 1936, pp. 287–89.

61 J. E. Burton, 'The election of Joan Fletcher as prioress of Basedale.' In: *Borthwick Institute Bulletin* **1**, 1975 78), pp. 146–150; York: *Reg. T. Wolsey*, f. 77r.

62 Burton, 'Joan Fletcher,' pp. 149–50.

63 All the sixteenth-century prioresses of York diocese were placed 'in the real and corporal possession' of their house.

64 Worcester R.O., *Reg. J. Alcock*, f. 214 (pencil nos.)

65 Lincolnshire Archives, 2ANC1/18/13.

66 *LP* **7**, p. 185 [No. 446].

67 York, *Reg. E. Lee*, f. 10.

68 *LP* **9**, pp. 79 [No. 236/6], 211 [No. 622].

69 See the Appendix for the relevant references.

70 York, *Reg. T. Rotherham* (partly on-foliated).

71 Ibid.

72 Chadwick, *Kirklees Priory*, 1902, pp. 364–65.

73 York; *Reg. E. Lee*, ff. 11, 42.

74 G. Coppack, 'Cistercian Nunneries in Early Sixteenth-Century Yorkshire.' In: *Cîteaux* **59**: Parts 3–4, 2008, pp. 258, 262, 264, 267.

75 York, *Reg. E. Lee*, f. 11v.

76 Smith, *Heads of Religious Houses* **3**, 2008, p. 639.

77 *Letters*, pp. 130–39 [Nos. 65–67], 146–48 [No. 73], 152–53 [No. 77], 199 [No. 97].

78 TNA, C1/205/42.

79 *Letters*, pp. 130–39 [Nos. 65–67]. Freeman, 'Houses of a Peculiar Order,' 2004, p. 271, explains that this was a 'tutorial' or double appeal: for substance to the Holy See; for leave for a year's protection while that case was being heard in the Court of Arches.

80 *CPL* **15**, pp. 231–32 [No. 464].

81 *Statuta* **6**, p. 22 [No. 1491/49].

82 *Letters*, pp. 131 [No. 65], 146–48, 153 [No. 77], 199 [No. 97]..

83 E. Power, *Medieval English Nunneries*, Cambridge U.P., 1922, pp. 479–80; *CPL* **15**, pp. 231–32 [No. 464]..

84 VCH, *County of York* **3**, 1974, pp. 159–60; Chadwick, 'Kirklees Priory,' 1902, pp. 431–32.

85 Cross and Vickers, *Monks, friars and nuns*, 1995, p. 557.

[86]   J. S. Purvis, 'Monastic Rentals and Dissolution Papers.' In: *YASRS* **80**, 1931, pp. 79–80.

[87]   TNA, LR1/169, ff. 444–446; E315/98, ff. 69v–70r.

[88]   *LP* **10**, p. 143 [No. 364].

[89]   *SAP* (2), p. 222 [No. 2332].

[90]   *VDL* **2**, pp. 160–63.

[91]   Smith, *Heads of Religious Houses* **3**, 2008, p. 689; VCH, *County of Northampton* **2**, 1906, p. 126.

[92]   Lincoln, *Reg. J. Longland*, f. 121v.

[93]   For references to these nuns, see the sources quoted in the Appendix.

[94]   VCH, *County of York* **3**, 1974, p. 162; *VDY*, pp. 451–53.

[95]   A. T. Bannister (ed.), *The Register of Charles Bothe*, Hereford, 1917, pp. 241–43. Dodd's name appears on the pension list of Limebrook at its suppression: *LP* **14**, Part 2, p. 283 [No. 752]); did she go to Llanllugan and then return to Limebrook when the Welsh house was dissolved?

[96]   *LP* **14**, Part 2, pp. 636 [No. 176]; *LC*, pp. 178–79 [No. CXI].

[97]   H. E. Bell, 'Esholt Priory.' In: *YAJ* **33**, 1938, pp. 23–24; G.W.O. Woodward, *Dissolution of the Monasteries*, London: Blandford Press, 1966, pp. 36–37).

[98]   *LP* **10**, p. 498 [No. 1191/2]; TNA, E36/154, ff. 142v–143r. Only one nun of Pinley was noted as wishing to depart.

[99]   VCH, *Hampshire* **2**, 1973, p. 151

[100] VCH, *County of York* **3**, 1974, pp. 165, 183.

[101] *LP* **12**, Part 1, p. 422 [Nos. 929–30].

[102] *LP* **10**, p. 354 [No. 858]; Cf. *LC*, pp. 107–110 [Nos. LXI–LXIII].

[103] D. Knowles, *Bare Ruined Choirs*, Cambridge U.P., 1976 edn., p. 194.

[104] Woodward, *Dissolution*, 1966, p. 40.

[105] *VDL*, **3**, pp. 101–02.

[106] Ibid. pp. 103–04

[107] Woodward, *Dissolution*, 1966, p. 19.

[108] *VDY*, pp. 451–53.

[109] *VDL*, pp. 160–61.

[110] Ibid. pp. 161–63.

[111] In the 1530s a John Kettill was the steward of the Worcestershire nunnery at Whistones: Goodrich, *Worcester Nunneries*, 2008, p. 25.

[112] *VDL*, p. 181.

[113] Ibid. pp. 182–83.

[114] York, *Reg. T. Rotherham*, pp. 229–30 [No. 1816].

[115] *VDY*, pp. 443–44.

[116] V. G. Spear, *Leadership in Medieval English Nunneries*, Woodbridge: Boydell Press, 2005, p. 146.

[117] *VDL* **3**, pp. 36–37.

[118] E. Peacock, 'Injunctions of John Longland, Bishop of Lincoln.' In: *Archaeologia* **47**, pp.

55–60.

119 *VDY*, pp. 439–43.

120 *VDL* **3**, pp. 101–03.

121 Ibid. pp. 103–04.

122 BL. Add. Ch. 67119.

123 Canterbury Cathedral Archives, DCc/Register R, f.139r. [I am grateful to Mrs Cressida Williams and Mr Daniel Korachi-Alaoui of the Archives, for locating this entry for me]. Unfortunately, the register gives no trace as to whether and when the visitation was resumed.

124 York, *Reg. P. Courtenay*, f. 17 v.

125 Winchester, *Reg. T. Langton*, f.34 r.

126 Purvis, 'Monastic Rentals,' 1931, pp. 79–83.

127 Ibid. pp. 82–83

128 Norwich Record Office, Hare 2211.

129 Purvis, 'Monastic Rentals,' 1931, p. 148.

130 Unknown author, *The Cistercian Priory of S. Leonard at Esholt in Airedale*, London: J. C. Hotten, 1866, pp. 24, 29. The chantry obligation derived from lands given in the early fourteenth century by Robert de Plumpton.

131 J. W. Clay, 'Yorkshire Monasteries Suppression Papers.' In: *YASRS* **48**, 1912, p. 117.

132 Lincoln; *Reg. W. Smith*, ff. 188 (160 pencil nos.), 193.

133 TNA, LR1/169, f. 462.

134 TNA, E118/1/37, No. 57.

135 BL, Add. Ch. 67119.

136 Coppack, 'Cistercian Nunneries,' 2008, pp. 258, 268.

137 VCH, *Hampshire* **2**, 1973, p. 151.

138 VCH, *County of York* **3**, 1974, 169 [*fn.* 35].

139 Coppack, 'Cistercian Nunneries,' 2008, p. 284.

140 Purvis, 'Monastic Rentals,' 1931, pp. 100–01.

141 Coppack, 'Cistercian Nunneries,' 2008, pp. 283, 271 respectively.

142 VCH, *Hampshire* **2**, 1903, p. 151.

143 Purvis, 'Monastic Rentals,' 1931, p. 95.

144 VCH, *Yorkshire* **3**, 1974, p. 169.

145 *Archaeologia* **48**, pp. 56–58; Power, *Medieval English Nunneries*, 1922, p. 153.

146 Purvis, 'Monastic Rentals,' 1931, pp. 79–80.

147 Ibid. pp. 82–83; Bell, 'Esholt Priory,' 1938, p. 30.

148 Purvis, 'Monastic Rentals,' 1931, p. 148; Harrison, *Nun Appleton*, 2001, p. 8.

149 Purvis, 'Monastic Rentals,' 1931, p. 78.

150 Clay, 'Suppression Papers,' 1912, p. 169.

151 Ibid. pp. 124–25.

152 Woodward, *Dissolution*, 1966, pp. 89–90.

153 LR1/169, ff. 477–78.

154 TNA, E315/443.

[155] Purvis, 'Monastic Rentals,' 1931, pp. 85–87; TNA, SP5/2, f. 37.

[156] Purvis, 'Monastic Rentals,' 1931, pp. 75, 79; TNA, SP5/2, f.8; Woodward, *Dissolution*, 1966, p. 90...

[157] York, *Reg. T. Rotherham*, pp. 229–30 [No. 1816]

[158] Coppack, 'Cistercian Nunneries,' 2008, p. 258.

[159] M. Oliva, *The Convent and Community in Late Medieval England*, Woodbridge: Boydell Press, 1998, pp.27, 136.

[160] Norwich R.O. Hare 2211.

[161] *VE* **1**, p. 267.

[162] VCH, *County of York* **3**, 1974, p. 166.

[163] *LP* **10**, p. 354 [No. 858].

[164] *VE* **5**, p. 114

[165] TNA, C1/187/15.

[166] *LP* **10**, pp. 138–41 [No. 364–364ii].

[167] Named in a will of 1504: [*VDL*, pp. 48, where 'a cross at the foot of which Mary sat with the dead body of Christ in her lap'].

[168] Harrison, *Nun Appleton*, 2001, pp. 16–17.

[169] Cross, 'End of Medieval Monasticism,' 2006, p. 149.

[170] TNA, C1/356/27; *MCP*, p. 135 [No. 138]:

[171] *LP* **12**, Part 1, pp. 191 [No. 392], 194 [No. 393], 431 [No. 946/118].

[172] J. Cartwright, 'Abbes Annes and the Ape.' In: J. Burton and K. Stöber, ed., *Monastic Wales*, Cardiff: University of Wales Press, 2013, pp. 192–94.

[173] *MCP*, pp. 145–47 [No. 149].

[174] Ibid. p. 54 [No. 47]; TNA, C1/202/6.

[175] TNA, C1/227/68.

[176] TNA, C1/896/12.

[177] J.A. Nichols, 'Medieval English Cistercian Nunneries', In: B. Chauvin (ed.), *Mélanges à la Mémoire du Père Anselme Dimier*, Arbois, France: Benoît Chauvin Pupillin, **5**/III, 1982, pp. 151–75.

[178] M. Lewis, *Stained Glass in North Wales*, Altrincham: Sherratt, 1970, pp. 7, 11, 39, 68–69.

[179] N. Pevsner and D. Neave, *Yorkshire: York and the East Riding*, London: Penguin, 2nd. edn., 1995, p. 719.

[180] N. Pevsner, *Yorkshire: The North Riding*, Harmondsworth: Penguin, 1966, p. 159.

[181] N. Pevsner, *Yorkshire: The West Riding*, Harmondsworth, Penguin, 1974, p. 506.

[182] Seekings and Herd, *Rosedale Abbey*, 2005, p. 18; called 'the priory tower' by E.H. Mowforth, *Rosedale Priory*, s.n., 1972, p. 5.

[183] N. Pevsner and J. Harris, *Lincolnshire*, London: Penguin, 1989, pp. 91, 429.

[184] Coppack, 'Cistercian Nunneries,' 2008, pp. 253–98.

[185] M. E. C. Walcott, 'Inventories and Valuations of Religious Houses.' In: *Archaeologia* **43**, 1871, p. 241.

[186] Coppack, 'Cistercian Nunneries,' 2008, pp. 257, 262, 267, 277, 281. 'Thak' could refer

to 'thatch,' but also to other coverings.

[187] M. Whitworth, 'Original Document.' In: *Lincolnshire Historian* **2**, No. 5, 1958, p. 32.

[188] Harrison, *Nun Appleton*, 2001, pp. 14–17.

[189] Goodrich, *Worcester Nunneries*, 2008, pp. 80–81.

[190] Whitworth, 'Original Document,' 1958, p. 32 [Legbourne]; VCH, *Hampshire* **2**,1973, p. 151 [Wintney]; F.A. Gasquet, *Henry VIII and the English Monasteries*, London: J.C. Nimmo, 2nd edn., 1899, p. 191 [Marham].

[191] VCH, *County of Northampton* **2**, 1970, p. 125 (Catesby); TNA, E315/278, f.101 (Sewardsley).

[192] Clay, 'Suppression Papers,' 1912, pp. 108–09.

[193] TNA, E315/278, f. 11.

[194] VCH, *County of York* **3** (1974) 169; [Keldholme]; Whitworth, 'Original Document,' 1958, p. 32 [Legbourne]; TNA, E315/290/1, f. 28 [Pinley].

[195] TNA, E117/14/99.

[196] Clay, 'Suppression Papers,' pp. 108–09.

[197] TNA, LR6/152/2.

[198] Davey and Roscow, Rushen Abbey, 2010, p. 161 [Douglas], VCH, *County of York* **3**, 1974, p. 178; TNA, LR6/152/2 [Llanllŷr], VCH, *County of York* **3**, 1974, p. 178 [Sinningthwaite].

[199] VCH, *County of York* **3**, 1974, p. 177.

[200] VCH, *Hampshire* **2**, 1973, p. 151

[201] VCH, *County of Northampton* **2**, 1970, p. 125.

[202] Whitworth, 'Original Document,' 1958, pp. 32–33.

[203] VCH, *Notfolk* **2**, 1906, p. 370.

[204] TNA, SC6/HENVIII/2612.

[205] BL. Add. Ch. 67119.

[206] Worcester R.O., *Reg. J. Alcock*, f. 241.

[207] *LP* **2**, Part 1, p. 166 [No. 607].

[208] Coppack, 'Cistercian Nunneries,' 2008, pp. 257, 262, 267, 272, 277, 281.

[209] Harrison, *Nun Appleton*, 2001, p. 15.

[210] Whitworth, 'Original Document, 1958, p. 32.

[211] *VDL* **3**, p. 37.

[212] Coppack, 'Cistercian Nunneries,' 2008, pp. 257, 267.

[213] Harrison, *Nun Appleton*, 2001, p. 15.

[214] Coppack, 'Cistercian Nunneries,' pp. 257, 267, 281.

[215] Harrison, *Nun Appleton*, 2001, p. 15.

[216] Coppack, 'Cistercian Nunneries,' 2008, pp. 258, 267, 272, 282.

[217] Harrison, *Nun Appleton*, 2001, p. 16.

[218] Walcott, 'Inventories and Valuations,' 1871, p. 241.

[219] Coppack, 'Cistercian Nunneries,' 2008, pp. 257, 267, 273, 277, 281.

[220] Harrison, *Nun Appleton*, 2001, p. 15.

[221] Coppach, 'Cistercian Nunneries,' 2008, pp. 268, 270, 278, 283.

[222] Harrison, *Nun Appleton*, 2001, p. 16.

[223] TNA, E36/154, ff. 142v–143r.

[224] T. Thompson, *History of the Priory and Church of Swine*, Hull: T. Topping, 1824, pp. 45–46.

[225] D. N. Bell, *What Nuns Read*, Kalamazoo: Cistercian Publications, 1995, pp. 138, 140, 170–71.

[226] TNA, Warwickshire R.O., CR26/1/12/L/69.

[227] TNA, SC2/195/80.

[228] G. Williams, *Welsh Church from Conquest to Reformation*, Cardiff: University of Wales Press, 1962, p. 367; TNA, LR 6/152/2, SC 6/HEN.VIII/4861; E 315/210/54; *VE* **4**, p. 397

[229] *VE* **5**, pp. 44, 87, respectively.

[230] BL. Add. Charter 67119.

[231] TNA, E315/94, ff. 101v–102r.

[232] TNA, LR1/169, f. 455.

[233] TNA, LR1/169. ff. 481, 382r–v, respectively.

[234] Clay, 'Suppression Papers,' 1912, passim; Woodward, *Dissolution*, 1972, p. 110; TNA, SC6/HENVIII) 4523, ff. 6–7.

[235] TNA, E315/98, ff. 107v–108r.

[236] *LP* **13**, Part 1, p. 568 [No. 1519/59].

[237] *LP* **15**, p. 342 [No. 733/19].

[238] Whitworth, 'Original Document,' 1958, p. 32, Coppack, 'Cistercian Nunneries,' 2008, p. 283, respectively.

[239] Purvis, 'Monastic Rentals,' 1931, pp. 124–25.

[240] Norwich R.O., Hare 2211.

[241] Bell, 'Esholt Priory,' 1938, p. 22.

[242] Coppack, 'Cistercian Nunneries,' 2008, pp. 258, 264, respectively. Another source tells of two dove-cots at Hampole.

[243] Ibid. pp. 268, 271–73, 278.

[244] Ibid. pp. 283–84.

[245] Whitworth, 'Original Document,' 1958, pp. 36–37.

[246] Harrison, 'Nun Appleton,' 2001, p. 17.

[247] Whitworth, 'Original Document,' 1958, p. 37.

[248] Davey and Roscow, *Rushen Abbey*, 2010, p. 157.

[249] TNA, LR6/152/2.

[250] Norwich R.O., Hare 2211.

[251] TNA, E117/14/22.

[252] ? the 'lobe' or 'lung-fish.'

[253] BL. Add. Ch. 67119.

[254] Coppack, 'Cistercian Monasteries,' 2008, p. 272.

[255] Ibid. p. 284.

[256] Goodrich, *Worcester Nunneries*, 2008, pp. 47, 83.

[257] Thompson, *Priory of Swine*, 1824, p. 41.

[258] Purvis, 'Monastic Rentals, 1931, pp. 96–97.

[259] *LP* **10**, p. 498 [No. 1191/2].

[260] TNA, E315/443, f. 1.

[261] Coppack, 'Cistercian Nunneries,' 2008, p. 271.

[262] No cited author, 'The Cistercian Abbey of S. Leonard at Esholt*, London: J. C. Hotten, 1866, p. 6.

[263] Chadwick, 'Kirklees,' 1902, pp. 122–23.

[264] TNA, E118/1/31, ff. 55–56, 52r, respectively.

[265] TNA, C1/137/40.

[266] TNA, C1/572/30–31.

[267] TNA, E118/1/31, f. 56.

[268] Lincolnshire Archives, 2ANC/1/18/5.

[269] TNA, E118/1/31, ff.55–56.

[270] TNA, E315/104, f. 177v (2nd nos); SC6/HENVIII/5257, m.1r–2v.

[271] Purvis, 'Monastic Rentals,' 1931, p. 119.

[272] G. Baskerville, *English Monks and the Suppression of the Monasteries*, London: Jonathan Cape, 1937, p. 210.

[273] TNA, LR1/169, f. 389r–v.

[274] Norwich R.O., Hare 2315, 2317.

[275] TNA, SC6/HENVIII/4523.

[276] TNA, E118/1/32.

[277] *MCP*, p. 3 [No. 2]; TNA, C1/658/32.

[278] TNA, STAC2/3, f. 314; STAC10/1/7.

[279] TNA, E135/2/52.

[280] *LP* **12**, Part 1, p. 295 [No. 670].

[281] TNA, LR1/169, ff. 466r–493r.

[282] TNA, LR1/169, ff. 368r–400r.

[283] TNA, E315/94, ff. 41v–42r, 101r–v, 170v–171r, 183v–184r, 192r; E315/96, f. 18v.

[284] TNA, LR1/169, ff. 370r–v, 372r–v.

[285] TNA, E315/95, f. 97r–v.

[286] TNA, E118/1/31, f. 57.

[287] TNA, E315/94, f. 170v–171r.

[288] TNA, LR1/169, ff. 468v–469r.

[289] TNA, LR1/169, f. 372r–v.

[290] TNA, TNA, E315/95, f. 97r–v.

[291] TNA, LR 6/152/2, SC 6/HEN.VIII/4861; E 315/210/54.

[292] TNA, E315/94, ff. 41v–42r.

[293] J. H. Bettey, *Suppression of Monasteries in the West Country*, Gloucester: Alan Sutton,

　　1989, p. 110.

[294]　*LP* **13**, Part 1, p. 568 [No. 1519/59].

[295]　Clay , 'Suppression Papers,' 1912, pp. 108–09.

[296]　Ibid. p. 159.

[297]　VCH, *County of York* **3**, 1974, p. 169.

[298]　TNA, E315/278, f. 89.

[299]　Harrison, 'Nun Appleton,' 2001, p. 19.

[300]　TNA, E322/233; Gasquet, *English Monasteries*, 1899, p. 303.

[301]　TNA, E322/98.

[302]　TNA, E322/231.

[303]　VCH, *Norfolk* **2**, 1906, p. 370.

[304]　TNA, E315/278, f. 71.

[305]　Davey and Roscow, *Rushen Abbey*, 2010, p. 157.

[306]　*LP* **12**, Part 1, p. 350 [No. 795/9]; **15**, p. 35 [No. 110].

[307]　Goodrich, *Worcester Nunneries*, 2008, p. 67.

[308]　Chadwick, 'Kirklees Priory,' 1902, pp. 322, 329–34; *LP* **13**, Part 1, p. 410 [No. 1115/19]; **14**, Part 2, p. 204 [No. 577].

[309]　Woodward, *Dissolution*, 1972, pp. 74–75.

[310]　*LP* **12**, Part 1, pp. 422–23 [No. 929].

[311]　Youings, *Dissolution*, 1971, pp. 49–50.

[312]　Cross, 'End of Medieval Monasticism,' 2006, p. 153.

[313]　*LP* **14**, Part 1, p. 563 [No. 1280].

[314]　Gasquet, *English Monasteries*, 1899, pp. 187, 192–93; VCH, *County of Lincoln* **2**, 1906, pp. 147–48; *LP* **11**, p. 593 (Appendix 4).

[315]　*LP* **10**, p. 154 [No. 384]; *LC*, pp. 88–89.

[316]　TNA, E315/209, f. 7.

[317]　*LP* **11**, pp. 225 [No. 567], 238 [No. 585], 323 [No. 828], 343 [No. 854].

[318]　*LP* **11**, p. 385 [No. 959].

[319]　*LP* **11**, p. 225 [No. 567].

[320]　*LP* **10**, p. 154 [No. 383]. This letter is not dated, but presumably was written in the spring of 1536.

[321]　*LP* **10**, p. 354 [No. 858].

[322]　*LP* **10**, p. 487 [No. 1166].

[323]　*LP* **10**, p. 508 [No. 1215].

[324]　*LC*, pp. 107–10 [Nos. LXI–LXIII]; Gasquet, *English Monasteries*, 1899, pp. 295–97.

[325]　*VE* **4**, p. 397; TNA, E 315/201/54; SC 6/HENVIII/4861.

[326]　TNA, LR 6/152/1–2.

[327]　It is of course possible that there was a nun of this name in each house.

[328]　Cross, 'End of Medieval Monasticism,' 2006, p. 153.

[329]　*LP* **13**, Part 1, pp. 575–77 [No. 1520].

[330]　Bodleian Library, Oxford, Tanner MS 343, f. 3 [Cook Hill], *LP* **14**, Part 2, p. 193 [No.

551; Hampole]; **14**, Part 1, p. 563 [No. 1256; Fosse].

331 *LP* **14**, Part 1, p. 563 [No. 1280].

332 Cross and Vickers, *Monks, friars and nuns*, 1995, pp. 557–59.

333 Woodward, *Dissolution*, 1966, p. 147.

334 Bodleian Library, Tanner MS 343.

335 VCH, *Yorkshire* **3**, 1913, p. 178.

336 *LP* **14**, Part 1, p. 563 [No. 1280].

337 Bell, *Esholt Priory*, 1938, pp. 31–32 (Esholt); Cross and Vickers, *Monks, friars and nuns*, 1995, pp. 558–59; Purvis, 'Monastic Rentals,' 1931, pp. 79–80 (Basedale), Davey and Roscow, *Rushen Abbey*, 2010, p. 157 (Douglas).

338 VCH, *County of Lincoln* **2**, 1906, pp. 156–57.

339 *LP* **14**. Part 1, p. 575 [No. 1321].

340 Youings, *Dissolution*, 1971, pp. 176–77.

341 TNA, E101/631/26.

342 Bell, 'Esholt Priory,' 1938, p. 31, Purvis, 'Monastic Rentals,' 1931, pp. 81–82.

343 Another author suggests she retired to Bury St Edmund's: M. Oliva, *Convent and Community in Late Medieval England*, Woodbridge: Boydell Press, 1998, p. 202.

344 *WIB*, pp. 133–35.

345 Cross and Vickers, *Monks, friars and nuns*, 1995, p. 577; Woodward, *Dissolution*, 1972, p. 154..

346 Cross and Vickers, *Monks, friars and nuns*, 1995, pp. 577–78, 569, respectively.

347 Woodward, *Dissolution*, 1972, p. 155.

348 C. A. J. Hodgett, *The state of the ex-Religious in the Diocese of Lincoln*, Lincoln Record Society **53**, 1959, p. 81.

349 Hodgett, *The state of the ex-Religious*, 1959, pp. 42, 109; 81, respectively.

350 Goodrich, *Worcester Nunneries*, 2008, p. 68.

351 Davey and Roscow, *Rushen Abbey*, 2010, make no mention of this. It seems more likely that she as the comptroller's brother. Calcott was the official receiver of the earl of Derby.

352 Cross and Vickers, *Monks, friars and nuns*, 1995, pp. 582, 587.

353 Goodrich, *Worcester Nunneries*, 2008, p. 68; Hodgett, *State of the ex–Religious*, 1959, pp. 57, 112.

354 Chadwick, 'Kirklees Priory,' 1902, pp. 322, 335; *LP* **15**, p. 296 [No. 613/19]; Woodward, *Dissolution*, 1972, p. 154.

355 Knowles, *Bare Ruined Choirs*, 1976, p. 299.

356 Cross and Vickers, *Monks, friars and nuns*, 1995, p. 593.

357 C. Cross, 'Community Solidarity among Yorkshire Religious after the Dissolution.' In: *MS* **1**, 1990, p. 252.

358 Cross and Vickers, *Monks, friars and nuns*, 1995, pp. 295–96.

359 TNA, SC6/HENVIII/4523, f. 6.

360 Cross, 'Community Solidarity,' 1990, p. 273; Woodward, *Dissolution*, 1966, pp. 161–62 (transcription).

361 Cross and Vickers 561; Smith (2008) 642; Woodward (1966) 156. For the complete will, see Woodward (2006) 161–62.

362 Woodward (2006) 156–57.

363 Cross and Vickers, *Monks, friars and nuns*, 1995, p. 568.

364 *LP* 11, p. 155 [No. 385/3]; It was part of a package which also included Netley Abbey.

365 TNA, E315/209, f. 9.

366 *LP* 12, Part 1, p. 350 [No. 795/10].

367 *LP* 13, Part 1, p. 585 [No. 1520/95]

368 D. H. Williams, 'Cistercian Nunneries in Medieval Wales.'. In: *Cîteaux* 26, 1975, p. 163.

369 *LP* 13, Part 1, p. 581 [No. 1520/64]; TNA, E117/14/99.

370 *LP* 13, Part 1, p. 578 [No. 1520/80]; Lincolnshire Archives, 2ANC/3/A/41.

371 *LP* 13, Part 1, pp. 568 [No. 1519/59]; 13, Part 2, p. 407 [Nos. 967/29, 30].

372 *LP* 11, Part 2, p. 593 [No. 4]. A Richard Tyrwhyt was vicar of Stixwould's appropriated church at Wainfleet in 1528/29: BL, Add. Ch. 67119..

373 Goodrich, *Worcester Nunneries*, 2008, p. 69.

374 *LP* 15, pp. 559–60 [No. 1032]; *LP* 19, Part 2, p. 413 [No. 690/33]; TNA, E315/212/f. 15 [Sir Ralph Bulmer had been temporarily detained in the Tower in 1538 on suspicion of complicity in the Pilgrimage of Grace, but was later restored to favour].

375 *LP* 15, p. 561 [No. 1032/36b]; 18, Part 1, p. 533 [No. 981/43].

376 BL, Lansdowne MS 903/3.

377 *LP* 13, Part 1, pp. 564, [No. 1519/29], 578 [No. 1520], 583 [No. 1520].

378 *LP* 13, Part 1, p. 578 [No. 1520/7]; 16, p. 177 [No. 379/59].

379 *LP* 13, Part 1, pp. 224 [No. 605], 295 [No. 790], 347 [No. 944], 564 [No. 1519/29], 585 [No. 11520/101b–103]; 19, Part 2, p. 413 [No. 690/33]. William Sackville was a yeoman of the chamber by 1530, and later briefly a Member of Parliament.

380 *LP* 13, Part 1, p. 579 [No. 1520/30].

381 *LP* 10, pp. 220–21 [No. 563].

382 TNA, E117/14/22.

383 VCH, *County of Northampton* 2, 1970, p. 125.

384 *LP* 13, Part 1, p. 475 [No. 1292]. His brother, Sir William Poulet, had been granted the site, perhaps in a caretaker capacity, in August 1536. It passed to Richard and Elizabeth Hill on very favourable terms on 4 June 1538. After Richard died, his widow was assured, in 1540, of the priory for her life: *LP* 15, p. 218 [No. 498/iii.c.68].

385 Harrison, *Nun Appleton*, 2001, pp. 21–22.

APPENDIX
KNOWN CISTERCIAN MONKS: 1485–1540

A few names are included of pre-Tudor times where noted in passing during research and of interest, and being of monks likely to have lived on into that age. Where manuscript episcopal registers are cited, they are generally to be found in the appropriate county archives, though the University Library at Cambridge holds microfilm sets for those of the dioceses of Carlisle, Chester, Durham, Coventry and Lichfield, Lincoln, London, Salisbury, and York. Lambeth Palace Library holds microfilms of the Canterbury registers, though original *sede vacante* registers are held at Canterbury, whilst the new London Metropolitan Archives possess the original registers for that diocese. A valuable resource is the compact disk enclosed with Virginia Davis, *Clergy in London in the Late Middle Ages* (Centre for Metropolitan History, Institute of Historical Research, 2000), which records all ordinations of regular and secular clergy in the diocese of London between 1361 and 1539.

ac: date of elevation to the ministry of acolyte.
d: date of ordination as a deacon.
ex: date of admission to the grade of exorcist.
p: date of ordination as a priest/presbyter.
sd: date of entry to the subdiaconate.
t: date of tonsure being imposed.
disp.: papal dispensation to hold a benefice normally possessed by a secular clerk, and (in the case of dispensations granted at the Suppression) licence to wear the habit of a secular priest and not that of a monk.

f(f): folio(s).
n–f.: no apparent foliation.
p(p).: page(s).
r: recto.
v: verso.

In references to episcopal registers, where a page number is given, it indicates the printed version as given in the Abbreviations, where folio numeration is used it relates to the original manuscript. Where two folio numbers are given, one being bracketed, these relate to the original folio number and a later number added by an archivist and often in pencil.

The following listing cannot be exhaustive.

(1) For the greater part the ordination lists in the episcopal registers of the period have been employed, but a number of registers are no longer extant – especially from the Welsh dioceses.

(2) Occasional sections in a register may have completely faded or else greatly darkened.

(3) Several monks may have received orders whilst studying abroad.

(4) Others may have been legitimately ordained by a visiting bishop but without a register entry.

(5) From 1509 to 1533 the monks of Beaulieu and Netley were ordained by Beaulieu's abbot, Bishop Thomas Skevington.

Some duplication is inevitable, as many monks bore a place–name as an *alias* surname, and it is not always possible to determine this.

Reference will need to be made to the List of Abbreviations **(pp. xv-xxiii)** and the Bibliography **(pp. 563-72).**

Abe, John: Combermere; *sd.* 1500, *d.* 1501 (Lichfield; *Reg. J. Arundel*, ff. 288, 293v).

Abraham, Thomas: Margam, *d.* and *p.* 1487 (St David's; *EPD* **2**, pp. 491, 509).

Abingdon, Adam: Rewley; *p.* 1514 (Lincoln; *Reg. W. Atwater*, f. 111r).

Abyngdon, William: Bruern; *sd.* 1510, *d.* and *p.* 1511 (Lincoln; *Reg. W. Smith*, n–f.); in house at suppression, 1536 (Baskerville, 1930, p. 334).

Acastre/Alaster, Robert: Vaudey; *sd.* and *d.* 1500, *p.* 1502 (Lincoln, *Reg. W. Smith*, ff.20r, 21v, 33r.).

Acclam, William: Meaux; *sd.* 1489, *d.* 1491 *p.* 1495 (York; Cross and Vickers, 1995, p. 153).

Acon, Nicholas: *see* Woldham.

Acton, Nicholas: Tintern, 1525–37, *sd.* 1525 (Hereford); monk, Kingswood, 1537–38 – where cellarer; *disp.* 1538, 'reward and finding', £2–13–4, pension, £4–13–4 (TNA, E36/152, f.21); stipendiary priest, Wickwar, Gloucs. 1540, and later (with the *alias* of Page) may have been vicar of Hewelsfield, Gloucestershire, until 1576 (*DKR*, p. 25, *FOR*, p. 131; Hereford, *Reg. C. Bothe*, p. 318; *TBGAS* **49**, 1927, p. 88; **73**, 1954, p. 185); in receipt of his pension of £4–13–4 as late as 1555 (TNA, E164/31, f. 29r).

Acton, Philip/*al.* Brode: Hailes; *sd.* 1527, *p.* 1533 (Worcester; *Reg. R. Morton addenda*, ff. 165, 174); scholar, St Bernard's College, Oxford, 1538; last provisor, St Bernard's College, 1540–1541/42; pension, £8, 31–12–1539; B.D. 1538, D.D. 1543; vicar, Huddersfield, 1541–51; rector, Adel, Yorks., 1545–51; prebendary of Givendale in York Minster and prebendary of Lichfield, 1547–51, when dies (Smith, 2008, p. 319; Stevenson, 1939, pp. 41, 43; *CHA*, pp. 85–86).

Acton, Thomas: Kingswood: *sd.* 1511 (Worcester; *Reg. S. Gigli*, f. 307).

Acworth/Arworth, Thomas: Roche, in community, 1531, and at suppression, 1538. Not noted in the Faculty Office Register, but possibly prebendary of Ryton in Lichfield cathedral, 1560, and rector of Wrestlingworth, Bedfordshire, 1561 (Cross and Vickers, 1995, p. 189; TNA, E135/3/6; E322//204)..

Adams/*al.* Bradake/Braddock, Richard: Combe, *sd.* 1531, *d.* 1532 (Lichfield; *Reg. G. Blyth* n–f.); *disp.* 1538 (*DKR*, pp. 16–17, *FOR*, p. 176); pension, £5–6–8 (TNA, E314/77).

Adams/*al.* Symmynge, Oliver: Combe; Sir William Ralegh, kt., left 1 mark for him to be a Doctor of Divinity at St Bernard's College, Oxford, 1509; provisor St Bernard's College, Oxford; B.D., 1507; B. Th. 1507, after nine years study; abbot, Combe, 1513–1538; in 1521 asks the abbot of Cîteaux for legislation forbidding women to enter monasteries; retired a twelve–month before Combe's suppression; *disp.* 1539, and still in residence though now no longer abbot (*BRUO*, **1**, p. 13; *LP* **2**, Part 1, p. 800 [No. 2575], **14**, Part 1, p. 44 [No. 111]); *Letters*, p. 263 [No. 135]; Stevenson, 1939, p. 41).

Adamson, Richard: Holm Cultram; in house, 11–08–1536 (*LP* **11**, p. 115 [No. 276]); not yet ordained priest when signed deed of surrender and *disp.* 1538 (*DKR*, p. 23, *FOR*, p. 123–24). His short service accounted for a pension of but £2, of which he was still in receipt in 1555 (TNA, E164/31, f. 73v).

Adcok, John: abbot, Boxley, before 1533 (Smith, 2008, p. 271); in arrears to the late Cardinal Wolsey for a faculty granted prior to 23 October 1530 (*LP* **4**, Part 3, p. 3048 (No. 6748/14).

Adderley, William: St Mary Graces; *p.* 1522 (Canterbury; LPL: *Reg. W. Warham* **2**, f. 296v).

Addisun (Addison), Christopher: Roche, *sd.* and *d.* 1525 (Cross and Vickers, 1995, p. 187); in house, 1531 (TNA, E135/3/6).

Addyngham, John: last abbot, Swineshead, ? 1497–1536 (TNA, E118/1/31/34–35, 41; Smith, 2008, p. 338); general pardon, 1509 (*LP* **1**, Part.1, p. 213 [No. 438/1, m.20]; after he once paid a visit to Spalding Priory, £500 was missing there, and its monks implied he might have taken it (*LP* **8**, p. 789 [No. 1001]; *disp.* 1516 (*CPL* **20**, pp. 494–95 [No. 700); pension £24, 1536 (TNA, E118/1/31, p. 50).

Adell, Anthony: *see* Jackson.

?Agraham, John: Rewley; *sd.* 1506 (Lincoln; *Reg. W. Smith*, n–f.).

Aiskarth, Brian: Jervaulx; *sd.* 1484, *d.* and *p.* 1486 (York; Cross and Vickers, 1995, p. 129).

Alanbridge, *al.* Leeds, John: Byland; *ac.* and *sd.* 1503, *d.* 1504, *p.* 1506 (York); cellarer, 1522; last abbot, 1525–1538; a Crown Visitor of the Order in England, 1532; deposed Abbot Kirkby of Rievaulx, 1534; involved in a dispute regarding money held in his custody (TNA, C1/1182/11–12); *disp.* 1539 (*FOR*, p. 181); complained regarding late payment of his £50 pension, 1555 (TNA, E164/31, f. 55r); died 1563, at Calverley Hall in the porch chamber (Aveling, 1955, pp. 4–7; Cross and Vickers, 1995, pp. 99–101.

Aland, Edmund: *see* Kirkham.

Alane/Alawe, John: Rushen; in receipt of his pension of £2–13–4 in 1555 (TNA, E164/31; Davey and Roscow, 2010, p. 174).

Alben/Albion/Allen, William: Dieulacres; *sd.* 1495 (Lichfield; *Reg. W. Smith*, f. 188); *d.* 1496 (Canterbury, for Coventry and Lichfield; *Reg. J. Morton* **2**, p. 118 [No. 428]; *p.* 1496 (Lichfield; *Reg. J. Arundell*, f. 259v); abbot by 1516, deposed 1519/20 (VCH, *Staffordshire* **2**, 1967, p. 235).

Alberton/Albrighton, Richard: Dore, *ac., sd.* and *d.* 1482; *p.* 1484 (Hereford; *Reg. T. Myllyng*, pp. 165–67, 170), *disp.* 1537, when nearly eighty years old (*FOR*, p. 98). A jubilarian.

Alborn/Alburn, Richard: Biddlesden; *ac.* 1515, *sd.* 1518, *d.* and *p.* 1520 (Lincoln; *Reg. W. Atwater*, ff. 117r, 127r, 132r, 133v).

Albrighton al. Blymmyl, Thomas: Bordesley; *ac.* and *sd.* 1478, *d.* 1480, (Worcester; *Reg. J. Alcock*, ff. 251, 261); *p.* 1483 (Lichfield; *Reg. J. Hales*, f. 284v); *disp.* 1487 (*CPL* **15**, p. 103 [No. 221]). If *Thomas Lylly/Bylly*, q.v. then just a jubilarian.

Alcester, Henry: Hailes; said on 16 November 1483 to be apostate (TNA, C81/1788/30).

Alcetur/Alcester, Thomas: Hailes; *sd.* and *d.* 1512 (Worcester; *Reg. S. Gigli*, ff. 312, 315).

Alcetur/Alcester, William: Bordesley; *ac.* 1507, *d.* 1510, *p.* 1515 (Worcester; *Reg. S. Gigli*, ff. 296, 305, 325).

Alchmer(s)he, Richard: Bordesley; *ac.* 1533 (Worcester; *Reg. R. Morton addenda*, f. 173).

Alderley, Richard: Kingswood; *ac.* and *sd.* 1481, *d.* 1482 (Worcester; *Reg. J. Alcock*, ff. 263–64, 268).

Alderton, William: Thame; *ac.* 1494 (Lincoln; *Reg. J. Russell*, f. 54r).

Aldham, John: Coggeshall; *sd.* 1496, *d.* snd *p.* 1501 (London; *Reg. R. Hill,* f. 34r; *Reg. T. Savage,* f. 66v; *Reg. W. Warham,* f. 2r).

Alen, Thomas: *see* Arlen.

Al(e)yn/Alen, Alexander: Beaulieu, *disp.* 1538 (TNA, E314/20/11, ff. 1d–2r; *FOR,* p. 131); curate, Otterbourne, Hants. 1551 (Hockey, 1976, p. 187); pension of £5 received in 1555 (TNA, E164/31, f. 13r).

Aleyng, Richard: Stratford; *sd.* 1507 (London; *Reg. R. Fitzjames, f. 95v*).

Alford, Richard: Coggeshall; *disp.* 1512 (*CPL* **19**, p. 486 [No. 838]).

Alford, Richard: Newenham; *sd.* 1530, *d.* 1532 (Exeter; *Reg. J. Vesey, ff. 171v, 179r*); *disp.* 1540 (*FOR,* p. 216); pension of £4–13–4 received as late as 1555 (TNA, E164/31, f. 34v).

Alford, Thomas: *see* Alresford.

Alford, William: Buckland; *sd.* and *d.* 1514, *p.* 1518 (Exeter; *Reg. H. Oldham, ff. 115r, 117v, 129r*). *disp.* 1539 (DKR, p. 12, FOR, p. 178); pension, £5, received as late as 1555 (TNA, E164/31, f.34r). Alkelond: *see* Todd.

Allanbridge: *see* Alanbridge.

Allerton/Alverston/*al.* Lyng/*al.* Malton, Richard: Rievaulx; *sd.* 1517, *d.* 1519, *p.* 1520 (York); infirmarian, 1533 (TNA, STAC2/7/217); signed deed of surrender, 1538 (*DKR,* p. 38); *disp.* 1538, pension. £5–6–8 (*FOR,* p. 156); in receipt of this pension until at least 1556; by 1548 – when said to be fifty–six years old, he received a stipend of £5–3–10 as chantry priest of the guild of St Katherine in Rotherham parish church (Cross and Vickers, 1995, pp. 169–70, 178; Aveling, 1952, p. 107); his father in 1531 bequeathed 4d. to each of the monks of Rievaulx (Aveling, 1955, p. 15).

Allerton, William: Cistercian monk, diocese Lincoln; *sd.* 1495 (Salisbury; *Reg. J. Blyth,* f. 103v).

Allyford, John: Netley; in community, 1518, by which time priested (TNA, E314/101).

Alman/Almon(d), John: Croxden, signed deed of surrender and *disp.* 1538 (Hibbert, 1910, p. 222; TNA, E314/20/11, ff. 7d–8r; *FOR,* p. 151); in receipt of pension of £4 as late as 1555 (TNA, E164/31, f. 46v); in prison in Hull Castle, 1579 to 1585, when died aged about 76 (Gasquet, 1899, p. 458).

Alresford/Alford/Abesforde, Thomas: Beaulieu; *ac.* and *sd.* 1488, *p.* 1490 (Winchester; *Reg. P. Courtenay,* ff. 13r, 13v, 17r.)

Alriche, Richard: at Stoneleigh before 1536, later vicar of Cubbington, Warwickshire (TNA, REQ2/4/58; 2/6/77).

Altam *al.* ?Preston, John: Rievaulx; *sd.* 1531; signed deed of surrender, 1538; pension, £5 (*DKR,* p.38); still alive and in receipt of his pension in 1582 (Cross and Vickers, 1995, pp. 170, 173).

Alton, Francis: Dieulacres; *sd.* 1509, *p.* 1510 (Lichfield; *Reg. G. Blyth,* n–f.).

Alton, John: Croxden: *p.* 1504 (Lichfield, *Reg. G. Blyth,* n–f). Might he be the *John Almon* given above?

Alton/Awton, John: Croxden; *d.* 1513, *p.* 1514 (Lichfield; *Reg. G. Blyth,* n–f).

Alton/Alneton/Halton, Thomas: Croxden; *ac.* 1507, *sd.* and *d.* 1508, *p.* 1510 (Lichfield; *Reg. G. Blyth,* n–f).

Alveston, William: Tintern; *p.* 1458 (Worcester; *Reg. J. Carpenter* **1**, p. 552).

Alyng/Alynger, William: last abbot, Waverley, 1533–36; described by Dr Layton in Sept. 1535 as 'honest, but none of the children of Solomon' (Smith, 2008, p. 348); pension, £70 (Ware, 1976, p. 36); provisor of St Bernard's College, Oxford; 1536–39, briefly rector of Yoxall, Staffs; died at very close of 1539; bequeathed all his books to three monk–scholars of Hailes (Stevenson, 1939, pp. 37–38); requested burial in St Mary Magdalene's church, Oxford (*BRUO* **2**, p. 7).

Alynson, John: Quarr; *d.* and *p.* 1509 (Winchester; *Reg. R. Fox* **2**, ff. 24r, 25r).

Alysson/Alison, William: Combe; *sd.* 1520, *d.* and *p.* 1522 (Lichfield; *Reg. G. Blyth* n–f).

Amberley, Richard: Dore, 1486; *p*. 1488 (Hereford, *Reg. T. Myllyng*, p. 173).

Ambrose, William: Furness; detained in the Fleet Prison, 1516/17 (TNA, C1/586/63; E135/2/30).

Amersler, John: house unknown; provisor, St Bernard's College, Oxford, 1518 (*Statuta* **6**, pp. VI, 538 [No. 1518/65]).

Ampilford/*al.* Christalowe, Marmaduke: Byland; *ac.* and *sd.* 1485, *d.* 1487, *p.* 1489 (York); *disp.* 1538; in 1522, an executor of his brother's will, receiving his best horse; pension, £5–6–8; died in 1540; a jubilarian (Aveling, 1955, p. 8; Cross and Vickers, 1995, pp. 98, 100, 103; *DKR*, p. 13, *FOR*, p. 181).

Ampleforth/*al.* Tort, Matthew: Rievaulx; *ac.* and *sd.* 1531, *d.* 1532, *p.* 1535 (York); *disp.* 1538 (*FOR*, p. 156), pension, £5; became a chantry priest at Southwell and later prebendary there; rector, Kettlethorpe, Nottinghamshire, 1554; rector, Hockerton, 1561, where he died in 1576. His will made provision for the poor of Southwell, Hockerton and Kettlethorpe parishes; remained unmarried (TNA, STAC2/7/217; Aveling, 1952, pp. 112–13, Cross and Vickers, 1995, pp. 169–70; 182–83).

Ampilford/Ampleforth, Thomas: Rievaulx; *sd.* and *d.* 1485, *p.* 1486 (York; Cross and Vickers, 1995, p. 167).

Ancell/Auncell, Richard: Quarr; *ac.* 1509, *sd.* 1510 (Winchester; *Reg. R. Fox* **2**, ff. 24r, 26v).

Andrew(s), John: last prior, Bindon, 1539 (TNA, E322/21; *DKR*, p. 10); awarded a pension of £8 'in consideration that he had a corrody of £10 under convent seal which he hath restored unto the king' (TNA, E245, f. 145, E314/77).

Angell, William: Warden; *d.* 1501 (Lincoln; *Reg. W. Smith*, f. 26v); abbot, Sawtry, a daughter–house, by 1534–1536 (*LP* **7**, p. 568 [No. 1518]; Smith, 2008, p. 330).

Anlaby/ Alenbye, John: Holm Cultram, by 1533 *LP* **6**, p. 426 [No. 988]);.sacristan, 1538 (TNA, E314/20/11, f. 3r–d), *disp.* 1538 (*FOR*, pp. 123–24). In receipt of his pension of £5 in 1555 (TNA, E164/31, f. 73v).

Antilbye, John: Sibton; *disp.* 28-04-1535, fee of £4, if given leave by his prior (*FOR*, p. 23).

Aphoel [Ap Hywel], Henry: Rewley; *disp.* 1510 (*CPL* **19**, p. 207 [No. 345]).

Apiggam (?Ap Reginald), David: Aberconwy, brother of former abbot Reginald (*Statuta* **5**, p. 439; and see Chapter 3).

Apleby/Appilby, Richard: Pipewell; *sd.* 1507, *d.* and *p.* 1508 (Lincoln; *Reg. W. Smith*, n–f.).

Ap(p)ley/Applebi, Robert: Kirkstead; *ac.* 1528, *sd.* 1529, *d.*1531, *p.* 1532 (Lincoln; *Reg. J. Longland*, ff. 21r, 24r, 28r, 30v); *disp.* 1537 (*FOR*, p. 96).

Archarde: *see* /Orchard, Thomas :

Arlen/Alen/Alyn, Thomas: Pipewell; signed deed of surrender and *disp.* 1538 (*DKR*, p. 37; *FOR*, p. 160); in receipt of pension of £6 as late as 1555 (TNA, E164/31, f. 43r).

Arlyngham: *see* Erlyngham.

Arncliff, Edward: Jervaulx; *p.* 1490 (York; Cross and Vickers, 1995, p. 129).

Arncliff: *see als* Touclif.

Arnold, Richard: monk, Kirkstead; *sd.* 1528, *p.* 1532 (Lincoln; *Reg. J. Longland*, ff. 21r, 30v); *disp.* 1537 (*FOR*, p. 96).

Arnold, *al.* Atherston, William: Merevale; *sd.* 1494, *d.* and *p.* 1497 (Lichfield; *Reg. W. Smith*, f. 176v, *Reg. J. Arundel*, ff. 263v, 268); last abbot, Merevale, 1525–1538 (*LP* **4**, Part 3, p. 2653 [No. 5944]; (LPL, Talbot Papers, MS 3192, p. 54 [No. 4]; Smith, 2008, p. 314); signed deed of surrender, 1538 (TNA, E322/151); 'reward,' £2–13–4, pension, £40 (*LP* **13**, Part 2, pp. 347–48 [No. 839]).

Artor/Arthur, Thomas: Rufford, was bequeathed a bow and shafts in 1523; signed letters testimonial in 1555; *disp.* 1536; vicar, Walesby, Nottinghamshire. 1549– (Cross and Vickers, 1995, p. 171; *FOR*, p. 74)..

Arwcombe, Thomas: Furness; *p.* 1502 (York; *Reg. T. Savage*, f. 113r).

Asheby/Ayshby, Henry: St Mary Graces; *sd.*and *d.* 1510 (London; *Reg. R. Fitzjames*, ff. 158r [169r], 159r [170v]).

Asheby: *see also* Ayshby.

Askington, William: Jervaulx; *sd.* 1515 (York; Cross and Vickers, 1995, p. 131).

Asshenhurst/Hashenhurst, William: Hulton, signed deed of surrender and *disp.* 1538 (TNA, E322/106; *FOR*, p. 154); died in 1544, wishing to be buried in the parish church of St Peter Ad Vincula, Stoke-on-Trent (Lichfield R.O., MB/C/11, Asshenhurst, Wm. – 1544); only income was his pension of £4–13–4 (Tomkinson, 985, pp. 66, 68; TNA, E315/233, f. 22r). His will describes him as 'late of the monastery of Hylton,' but makes no further allusion to this.

Assteley/Ashley, Edmund: Thame; *sd.* and *d.* 1505 (Lincoln; *Reg. W. Smith*, n.f.).

Astbury, William: Hulton; *sd.* and *d.* 1487; *p.* 1488 (Lichfield; *Reg. J. Hales*, ff. 222, 223v, 236v, 240v).

Astheley, John: Hailes; *d.* 1515 (Worcester; *Reg. S. Gigli*, f. 327).

AstonAscheton, John: Stoneleigh; *d.* 1514, *p.* 1518 (Lichfield; *Reg. G. Blyth*, n-f.).

Aston, Thomas: Biddlesden, 1538; pension, £5–6–8 (*DKR*, p. 10; TNA, E322/22).

Atherley, William: Stratford; *ac.* 1510 (London, *Reg. R. Fitzjames*, f. 158r [169v]).

Atherston, John: Combe; *sd.* 1524, *d.* 1525, *p.* 1526 (Lichfield; *Reg. G. Blyth*, n-f.).

Atherston: *see also* Arnold, Gilbert, Talley.

Atkinson, William: Louth Park; *ac.* 1498, *sd.* 1499, *d.* 1501, *p.* 1504 (Lincoln; *Reg. W. Smith*, ff. 28v, 46v).

Atkinson: *see* Ripon.

Auckeland, Richard: : Jervaulx; *sd.* and *d.* 1519, *p.* 1521 (York; Cross and Vickers, 1995, p. 131).

Aukland/Robinson, John: Biddlesden; *sd.* 1531, *d.* 1532, *p.* 1535 (Lincoln; *Reg. J. Longland*, ff. 28v, 31r, 45r); *disp.* 1538 (*FOR*, p. 179; TNA, E322/22); pension, £5–6–8 (TNA, E314/77), still received in 1555 (TNA, E164, f. 24r).

Austen/Harpeham, James: Meaux; *p.* 1509 (York); pension, £6 p.a., 1539; he was sixty–six in 1552 and died in 1555; Harpham was his family home (Cross and Vickers, 1995, pp. 154,156–57).

Austen, Nicholas: last abbot, Rewley, 1533–1536; member of Coventry Trinity Guild, *disp.* 1536; offered Cromwell £100 to save the monastery but to no avail, then studied 'the Word of God sincerely' at Trinity Hall, Cambridge, A.M. by 1540, an executor of *William Alynger*, q.v; incumbent of Whatcote, Warwickshire, from 1542 until his death in 1571, his income there being £12 p.a., in receipt of his abbatial pension of £22; will proved, 1571 (TNA, E164/31, f. 42r; *FOR*, p. 78; *BRUO* **2**, p. 18; Smith, 2008, pp. 323–24).

Auston, Thomas: Roche; *sd.* and *d.* 1490, *p.* 1491 (Cross and Vickers, 1995, p. 186).

Austen/Awstey, Thomas: sub–prior, St Mary Graces, 1520–21 (London; *Reg. R. Fitzjames*, ff. 180v–181r [191v–192r], 181v [192v]).

Austen, William: Tilty; *d.* 1520 (London; *Reg. R. Fitzjames*, f. 181r [192r]); may have transferred to Beaulieu in 1536 and be the under–mentioned monk.

Austen, William: Beaulieu, 1538 (*DKR*, p. 9). Pension not stated (*LP* **14**, Part 1, p. 596 [No. 1355/iii]).

Austen/Augustyne, William: Bordesley; *ac.* and *sd.* 1532 (Worcester; *Reg. R. Morton addenda*, f. 171); *disp.* 1538 (*FOR*, p. 149; TNA, E322/26); pension, £4 (TNA, E314/77); assessed for subsidy in 1540 (Bodleian Library, Oxford, Tanner MS 343).

Augustine/Austyn, William: Robertsbridge, probably by 1490 – 1523 (SAL, MS 14, f. 59v); *disp.* 1503 (*CPL* **17**, p. 589 [No. 962]).

Avenell, Richard: Bindon; *ac.* and *sd.* 1491, *d.* 1493 (Salisbury; *Reg. T. Langton*, pp. 109 [No. 575], 111 [No. 578], 117 [No. 585]); *p.* 1496 (Salisbury; *Reg. J. Blyth*, f. 108r).

Avery/Alvery, William: Buckfast, *sd.* 1535, *p.* 1538 (Exeter; *Reg. J. Vesey*, ff. 187r, 189r); in house at suppression, 1539 (*DKR*, p. 12); in receipt of pension of £5–6–8 in 1555 (TNA, E164/31, f. 34r).

Awdefeld, Marmaduke: Fountains; *sd.* and *d.* 1521, *p.* 1524 (York; Cross and Vickers, 1995, p. 114); *and see:* **Jenkinson.**

Awkland/Aukeland, John: *see* **Aukland.**

Awkeland, Thomas: Biddlesden; *ac.* 1529, *sd.* and *d.* 1530, *p.* 1532. (Lincoln; *Reg. J. Longland*, ff. 24v, 26v, 27r, 31v).

Awse, John: Buckfast, *disp.* to change habit, 1538; fee, £4 (*FOR*, p. 141).

Awstey: *see* **Austen.**

Awter(y), William: Ford; *sd.* 1511, *d.* 1512 (Exeter; *Reg. H. Oldham*, ff. 106v, 109r).

Axmi(n)ster, Richard: Newenham; *sd.* and *d.* 1508, *p.* 1509 (Exeter; *Reg. H. Oldham*, ff. 92v, 97r, 100v).

Ayleston/Elston, William: Garendon; *sd.* and *d.* 1514, *p.* 1517 (Lincoln; *Reg. T. Wolsey*, ff. 14r, 15r; *Reg. W. Atwater*, f. 123v); *disp.* 1536 (*FOR*, p. 76).

Ayreton, Robert: Fountains, *sd.* and *d.* 1497 (York; Cross and Vickers, 1995, p.112).

Ayshby/Asheby/Asche, John: Garendon; *d.* 1513 (Lincoln; *Reg. W. Smith*, n–f.); *p.* 1516 (*Reg. W. Atwater*, f. 119r); in house 15–03–1536 (*LP* **10**, p. 194 [No. 475]);.disp. 1536 (*FOR*, p. 76).

Ayshby: *see also* **Ascheby.**

Ayton, Ralph: Vale Royal; *p.* 1493 (York; *Reg. T. Rotherham*, n–f.).

Baddesley, John: Merevale; *sd.* 1464, *d.* 1465, *p.* 1466 (Lichfield; *Reg. J. Hales*, ff. 193v, 196r, 198v); abbot, Merevale, by 1488–1525; dispensed to hold a secular benefice *in commendam*, 1502 (*CPL* **17**, p. 458 [No. 754]); held rectory of Llangynhafal, Denbighshire, 1515–25; dies 1525 (Pryce, 1923, p. 2; Smith, 2008, p. 314); member of the fraternal guilds at Coventry and Knowle, and by the 1520s a frequent hunting companion of Sir Henry Willoughby (Watkins, 1994, p. 91).

Badger/Baker, Richard: Bordesley, signed deed of surrender and *disp.* 1538 (TNA, E322/6; *FOR*, p. 149); in receipt of pension of £6 as late as 1555 (TNA, E164/31, f. 44r).

Bafford: *see* **Darfford.**

Bagby/Bageley, Richard: Kirkstead; *ac.* and *sd.* 1485, *d.* 1486, *p.* 1487 (Lincoln; *Reg. J. Russell*, ff. 17r, 18r, 21v, 25r).

Bageley/Baguley, Robert: Dieulacres; *sd.* and *d.* 1514; *p.* 1516 (Lichfield; *Reg. G. Blyth*, n–f.); last prior, Dieulacres, *disp.* 1538; 'reward' £2–10–0; pension, £6 (Walcott, 1871, p. 216; Staffordshire Archives 2/32/00, p. 45).

Baker, Henry: Rufford, *disp.* 1536 (*FOR*, p. 74).

Baker, John: Cleeve; *sd.* 1518 (Exeter; *Reg. H. Oldham*, f. 130r); *p.* 1519 (Wells; *Reg. T. Wolsey*, f. 26). May be the next mentioned monk, having moved to Newenham on the earlier suppression of Cleeve.

Baker, John: Newenham, *disp.* 1540 (*FOR*, p. 216); pension, £5 (*LP* **14**, Part 1, p. 184 [No. 469]).

Baker, Robert: Cleeve; *p.* 1481 (Wells; *Reg. R. Stillington*, f.210v).

Baker/Badg', Richard: *see* **Badger.**

Baldock, Richard: one of the more compliant monks of Warden in Abbot's Emery's time, 1535 (*LC*, p. 59 [No. XXIX]; there at its suppression, when still a deacon, 1538 (*DKR*, p. 47; TNA, E314/77); in receipt of his pension of £5–6–8 as late as 1555 (TNA, E164/31, f. 25v).

Baljon, John: Rewley; *p.* 1501 (Lincoln; *Reg. W. Smith*, f.30v).

Balke, Roger: abbot, Rufford, by 1501 to 1516 (Derbyshire R.O., D239M/T1847); in 1505 granted the office for life of master of Stainthorpe Collge, Yorks, by Henry VIII (*Patent* 1505, p. 396);

resigning it in 1510 (Smith, 2008, p. 328) dies 25 June 1516 (Nottinghamshire R.O. DD/SR/208/64; *RC* 2, pp. 388–89 [No. 732]).

Ball, Robert: abbot, Pipewell, by 1518–1520 (Smith, 2008, p. 320).

Balle, Thomas: Pipewell; signed deed of surrender and *disp.* 1538 (TNA, E314/20/11, f. 9r; *FOR*, p. 160); in receipt of pension of £5–6–8 as late as 1555 (TNA, E164/31, f. 43r).

Banaster: *see* Sawley.

Banbury: *see* Pere.

Banion/Benyon, John: Vale Royal, signed deed of surrender and *disp.* 1538 (*DKR*, p. 46; *FOR*, p. 162). In receipt of his £5 pension in 1555 (TNA, E164/31, f. 69r).

Bank(s), Alexander: abbot of Furness, 1497–1514; his election was controversial and he was deposed by 1514 by the abbot of Stratford at the instigation of the earl of Derby, though papal judges ruled in his favour, and he regained the abbacy (See Chapter 3). Died in 1533 (Smith, 2008, pp. 295–96).

Banke, Richard: Furness; *sd.* and *d.* 1520, *p.* 1521 (York; *Reg. T. Wolsey*, ff. 188v, 189r, 193r); imprisoned by his abbot for disobedience by 8–07–1533 (*LP* 6, p. 350 [No. 787]); released, he served a cure in the Isle of Man (TNA, SC12/9/73; Haigh, 1969, p. 120).

Banks, Richard: Louth Park; *disp.* 6–08–1536 (*FOR*, p. 69).

Bank(es)/Baucke, Robert: Holm Cultram; gave evidence in an enquiry, 1533 (*LP* 6, p. 426 [No. 988]); signed deed of surrender and *disp.* 1538 (TNA, E314/20/11, f. 3r–d; *FOR*, pp. 123–24). In receipt of his pension of £3–6–8 in 1555 (LR1/173, ff. 145r, 147).

Barbor, Henry: Rufford; *d.* 1531, *p.* 1533 (York; *Reg. E. Lee*, ff. 184r, 186r).

Barber, John: monk, Margam; *p.* 1471 (Wells; *Reg. R. Stillington*, f. 185v.)

Barbor, Richard: Kirkstall, *sd.*1484, *d.* 1485, *p.*1489 (York; Cross and Vickers, 1995, p. 139); could he be the same monk as *Richard Bateson*, q.v. (Lonsdale, 1972, pp. 205–06]).

Barbor, William: Rufford; *sd.* and *d*, 1489, *p.* 1492 (York; *Reg. T. Rotherham*, n.f.).

Barbur, Richard: abbot, Bordesley, 1501–1526 (Smith, 2008, pp. 270–71).

Bardesey/Barsey, Richard: Tilty, 1491–92 (*Letters*, pp. 152 [No. 77], 155 [No. 78]).

Bardfeld/Bardfield, John: monk, Tilty; *ex.* 1498, *sd.*, *d.* and *p.* 1500 (London; *Reg. T. Savage*, ff. 59r, 60v, 61r, 64v).

Bardisley, Thomas: Flaxley; *p.* 1506 (Hereford, *Reg. R. Mayew*, p. 247).

Barker, Henry: Kirkstead; *d.* and *p.* 1490: entry of ordination as priest repeated in 1492, unless another monk of the same name (London; *Reg. J. Russell*, ff. 37r, 40r, 45/46v).

Barker, John: St Mary Graces; *sd.* and *d.* 1504 (London; *Reg. W. Barons*, ff. 88d, 89r).

Barker, Robert: Revesby; *ac.* 1502, *d.* 1503 (Lincoln; *Reg. W. Smith*, ff. 37v, 42r).

Barker, Robert: Stratford; *ac.* 1511 (London; *Reg. R. Fitzjames*, f. 160v [171v]).

Barkar/Barker, *al.* Yarm, Robert: Byland; *sd.* 1499, *d.* 1500, *p.* 1502 (York; Cross and Vickers, 1995, pp. 99, 103); sacristan, 1525; last prior, *disp.* 1538, pension, £6–13–4 (TNA, E315/244; *DKR*, p. 13); retired to live with Thomas Butler at Nunnington, with provision for him to continue there after Butler's death in 1539 (Aveling, 1955, p. 7); perhaps vicar of Driffield, Yorkshire, 1541–1548 (Cross and Vickers, 1995, pp. 100–01).

Barkeley/Berkeley, Robert: Llantarnam; *p.* 1521 (Wells; *Reg. T. Wolsey*, f. 28); monk, Quarr, *disp.* 1537 (*FOR*, 87). Did he move to Quarr on Llantarnam's closure?

Barking/Berking, John: Coggeshall; *d.* 1527 (London; *Reg. C. Tunstall*, f.159r). Perhaps the same monk as *John Leswell*, q.v.

Barming, Thomas: Boxley; *ac.*and *sd.* 1508 (Rochester; *Reg. J. Fisher*, f. 33r).

?Barnewell, William: Rewley; *p.* 1514 (Lincoln; *Reg. W. Atwater*, f. 111r).

Barneys/Barnes, Ralph/Randall: Dieulacres; 'reward', £2, 1538 (Walcott, 1871, p. 216) , *disp.* 1538; pension, £5–6–8 (Hibbert, 1910, pp. 239, 242; *FOR*, p. 160).

Bardon, Thomas: *see* Bawdon.

Barking/Berkyng, William: monk, Stratford; *sd.* 1533, *d.* 1534 (London; *Reg. R. Stokesley*, ff. 129r, 130r).

Barnard, Henry: Boxley; *t.* and *a.* 1522, *sd.* 1523 (Rochester; *Reg. J. Fisher*, f. 92v).

Barnard, Nicholas: Waverley; *ac.* and *sd.* 1514 (Winchester; *Reg. R. Fox* [3] ff. 55v, 56r); *d..* 1516 (London; *Reg. R. Fitzjames*, f. 182r); vicar, Boldre, Hants. 1540; incumbent, Free Chapel, South Baddesley, 1543–48; died 1553 (Baskerville, 1941, p. 19; Baigent, 1883, p. 210).

Barnes: *see* Woburn.

Barnewell, Thomas: Combe; *d.* 1485 (Lichfield; *Reg. J. Hales*, f. 211).

Baron, George: Combermere, 1538 (*DKR*, p. 17); pension, £3–6–8 (TNA, E315/233, f. 78r–v).

Barsey, … : Tilty; 1492, when allegedly detained vestments and other goods of Warden of a value in excess of £100 (*Letters*, p. 155 [No. 78])

Barrat, John: Warden, *disp.* 1538 (TNA, E314/20/11, f. 1r–d); pension, £5–6–8 (TNA, E314/77).

Barrington: *see* Baryngton.

Barrowe/Mapleton/Wythornwike, John: Meaux; *ac.* 1536, *sd.* 1537 (York); pension, 1539, £5; said to be forty–four years old in 1552, he was still alive in 1582. He was possibly the curate of Beeford in 1567 when it was said 'he useth the communion for the dead', and at Nunkeeling by 1571 until 1575; in the former year he subscribed to the articles of religion, in the latter he was teaching catechism to the boys of the parish. He may also be identified with *John Hawnsley* (Cross and Vickers, 1995, pp. 155–56, 157, 159).

Bartholomew, Walter: Beaulieu; *ac.* 1507 (London; *Reg. R. Fitzjames*, f. 9r); *disp.* 1538, pension at first was £6–13–4 as he ministered after the suppression for a year or so as parish priest of Beaulieu, by 1545 he was curate at Littleton, Hampshire, and by 1555 his pension was the standard £5 (TNA, E314/20/11, f. 1d–2r; *FOR*, p. 131; Hockey, 1976, pp. 187–88).

Bartlot/Bertlett, Thomas: Kirkstall, *sd.* and *d.* 1490, *p.* 1491 (York); pension, 1539, £6–13–4. Hailed from Leeds, after the dissolution lived at Allerton Grange, and died in 1542, leaving his vestments to the chapel at Chapeltown (Cross and Vickers, 1995, p. 142; Lonsdale, 1972, p. 206).

Barton/Burton, John: Rievaulx: *sd.* 1495, *d.* 1497 (York; Cross and Vickers, 1995, p. 168).

Barton/Burton, John: Dore; *p.* 1523 (Hereford; *Reg. C. Bothe*, p. 314).

Barton, Robert: Byland; *sd.* and *d.* 1485, *p.* 1487 (York; Cross and Vickers, 1995, p. 98).

Barton/Burton, Thomas: Newminster, *disp.* 1536, when thirty–five years old (TNA, SC12/13/65; *FOR*, p. 77).

Barwik, Edward: monk, Swineshead; *ac.* 1511, *d.* 1513 (Lincoln; *Reg. W. Smith*, n–f.); *p.* 1515 (*Reg. W. Atwater*, f. 112v).

Barwyke/Barwisse, William: Furness; *p.* 1502 (York; *Reg. T. Savage*, f.113r); signed deed of surrender and *disp.* 1537 (TNA, E322/91; *FOR*, p. 97). Was he the William Bulvist detained in The Fleet Prison, 1516/17? (TNA, C1/586/63; E135/2/30).

Baryngton/Caryngton, William: Bruern; *d.* 1525 (Lincoln; *Reg. J. Longland*, f. 18r); *p.* 1525; still in house at the suppression, 1536 (Baskerville, 1930, p. 334).

?Basham, John: Warden; *sd.* 1527 (Lincoln; *Reg. J. Longland*, f. 19v).

Baskerley/Baskerville/Baxterley, William: Beaulieu, *disp.* 1538 (*FOR*, p. 131); vicar of Hound, Hampshire, from 1548, pension of £5 received in 1555 (TNA, E164/31, f. 13r, Hockey, 1976, pp. 186–87). Could he be the William Baxterley (*infra*), formerly a monk of Merevale, moving to Beaulieu before the suppression of Merevale in October 1538; not named in the Merevale suppression list (TNA, E322/151).

Bate/Bait, Robert: *see* Kynvar.

Bate, Thomas: *see* Stafford.

Bateson/Batson, Richard: Kirkstall; pension, 1539, £7 (Cross and Vickers, 1995, pp. 142, 144); in receipt of pension in 1555 (TNA, E164/31, f.53v); in 1545 was curate of Spofforth and rector of Birkin, Yorkshire., Was he the monk, *Richard Barber*, q.v. (Lonsdale, 1972, p. 205).

Bathe, Richard: Quarr; *ac.* 1527 (Winchester; *Reg. R. Fox* 5, f. 37v); *disp.* 1537 (*FOR*, p. 87).

Battell, William: Waverley; *sd.* and *d.* 1524 (Winchester; *Reg. R. Fox* 5, ff. 35v, 37v).

?Baughill, Richard: Louth Park; *sd.* 1533 (Lincoln; *Reg. J. Longland*, f. 33r).

Bawden/Bawdewyn, Edward: Robertsbridge, 1523 (SAL, MS 14, f. 59v); *disp.* 1536, before the monastery's closure (*FOR*, p. 44).

Bawdon/Bardon, Thomas: Vale Royal, *d.* 1506 (Lichfield; *Reg. G. Blyth*, n.f.); kitchener, signed deed of surrender and *disp.* 1538 (*DKR*, p. 46; *FOR*, p. 162); pension, £5 (TNA, E315/233, f. 68r).

Bawe, John: Rewley; *sd.* 1497 (Lincoln; *Reg. W. Smith*).

Baxbie/Baxby, *al.* Judson, Richard: Byland; *sd.* 1537 (York); *disp.* 1538 (*DKR*, p. 13; *FOR*, p. 181); *d.* 1539, *p.* 1540 (on title of his monastic pension of £4); he *may* have been chantry priest and schoolmaster at Pickering, Yorkshire, in 1548, and then vicar of Kirby Moorside in 1548, resigning his living in 1592 (Aveling, 1955, p. 14; Cross, 1995, pp. 99–100, 105–06).

Baxter, Richard: Warden; *p.* 1530 (Lincoln: *Reg. J. Longland*, f. 27v).

Baxter, Robert: Jervaulx; *ac.* 1466 (York; *Reg. G. Neville*, f.193); that year he sought a papal dispensation on account of defect of birth allowing him to proceed to holy orders (*SAP* 2, p. 55 [No. 1455]).

Baxter, Thomas: Bordesley, signed deed of surrender and *disp.* 1538 (E322/6; *FOR*, p. 149); pension, £6 (*TNA, E314/77*); assessed for subsidy in 1540 (Bodleian Library, Oxford, Tanner MS 343).

Baxter, William: Byland, *disp.* 1538, pension, £5–6–8 (*DKR*, p. 13; *FOR*, p. 181); perhaps the same monk as William Kilburn, q.v. (Aveling, 1955, p. 9).

Baxterley, William: Merevale; *ac.* and *sd.* 1519, *d.* 1520, *p.* 1521 (Lichfield; *Reg. G. Blyth*, n-f.); **and .see Baskerley.**

Baynbridge/Baynbrok, Arthur: Vaudey; *sd.* 1524, *d.* and *p.*1525 (Lincoln; *Reg. J. Longland*, ff. 10v, 11r, 12r); *disp.* 1536 (*FOR, p. 67*).

Baynton, John: Meaux; *d.* 1482, *p.* 1485 (York; Cross and Vickers, 1995, p. 153).

Baynton/Bainton, Robert: Byland, *d.* 1512, *p.* 1518 (York); *disp.* 1538 (*FOR*, p. 181); may have studied at St Bernard's College, Oxford, in the 1520s; pension, £10, receiving this as late as 1573. Perhaps chantry priest, St Katherine's chapel, Towthorpe in parish of Wharram Percy, Yorkshire, in 1545, when defamed by one John Reeves, clearing his good name in the archbishop's court. Vicar of Hinderskelfe, 1571, and then of Hutton–on–the–Hill, where he died in 1578, leaving practically his whole estate to his servant, Jane Warde (Aveling, 1955, pp. 10–11; Cross and Vickers, 1995, pp. 99–100, 102).

Beare, John: Buckfast, *ac.* and *sd.* 1517, *d.* 1518, *p.* 1521 (Exeter; *Reg. H. Oldham*, ff. 127v, 128r, 130r, *Reg. J. Vesey*, f. 144v); present at the dissolution, 1539 (TNA, C1/950/23), but not in pension list (TNA, E315/233, f. 305).

Becwithe, John: Strata Florida, 1539; *disp.* 1540 (*FOR*, p. 206).

Bedale, *al.* Stapylton, William: Rievaulx; *p.* 1531 (York); signed deed of surrender and *disp.* 1538; pension, £5–6–8 (*DKR*, p. 38; *FOR*, p. 156); vicar, Eastrington, Yorkshire, from 1549, but deprived in June 1554, divorced from his 'pretended wife', Joan Raby, and ordered to do penance in Eastrington church; still in receipt of pension in 1556 (Cross and Vickers, 1995, pp. 169–70, 181).

Bedford, John: Warden; *sd.* and *d.* 1518, *p.* 1520 (Lincoln; *Reg. W. Atwater*, ff. 125r, 127r, 134r).

Bedford, Thomas: Warden; *d.* and *p.* 1530 (Lincoln; *Reg. J. Longland*, ff. 26v, 27v); in the monastery at its suppression, 1538 (TNA, E314/20/11, f. 1r–d); pension, £5–6–8 (TNA, E314/77).

Bedyng: *see* Redyng, Thomas.

Bekeryng, *al.* Sandherst, Robert: Robertsbridge; *ac.* and *sd.* 1496, *d.* 1497, *p.* 1498 (Chichester; *Reg. E. Story*, ff. 190r, 190v, 192r, 193r); noted when not ordained priest (SAL, MS 14, f. 59v); *disp.* 1502 (*CPL* **17**, p. 557 [No. 926].

Belamy, Thomas: Rufford; *p.* 1533 (York; *Reg. E. Lee*, f. 186r).

Belch(e)ford, Gilbert: Kirkstead; *sd.* 1499, *d.* 1500 (Lincoln; *Reg. W. Smith*, f. 22v).

Bellam, Thomas: Rufford, *disp.* 1536 (*FOR*, p. 74).

Belworthy, John: abbot, Buckfast, general pardon, 1509 (*LP* **1**, Part 1, p. 240 [No. 438/3, m.9]); *c.*1510 (Devon R.O., 123M/TB37); dies 1511/12 (Stéphan, 1970, pp. 174–77).). Could his surname be an *alias* of *John Rede* I? q.v.

Bemysley, William: Meaux; *d.* 1482, *p.* 1485 (York; Cross and Vickers, 1995, p. 153).

Benion: *see* **Banion.**

Benne, Laurence: Fountains, 1539; pension, £6–13–4 (Cross and Vickers, 1995, p. 115).

Bennett, Alan: Stratford; *d.* 1493, *p.* 1496 (London; *Reg. R. Hill*, ff. 27v, 34v).

Bennet, Henry: Dieulacres; *sd.* and *d.* 1514; *p.* 1515 (Lichfield; *Reg. G. Blyth* n–f.); *disp.* 1538; 'reward' £2–10–0 (Walcott, 1871, p. 216); pension, £6 (Hibbert, 1910, pp. 239, 242; TNA, E314/20/11, f. 9d); continued to live in the neighbourhood (Fisher 1969, p. 58).

Benett, John: Pipewell; signed deed of surrender and *disp.* 1538 (*DKR*, p. 37; *FOR*, p. 160); in receipt of pension of £5–6–8 as late as 1555 (TNA, E164/31, f. 43r).

Benet, John: Cleeve; *sd.* 1509 (Wells), *d.* 1510 (Exeter); *p.* 1510 (Wells; *Reg. H. de Castello*, ff. 150–51; *Reg. H. Oldham*, f. 103r); perhaps moved to Dunkeswell when Cleeve was suppressed in 1537.

Benet, John: Dunkeswell, at its suppression, 1539; pension, £4–13–4 (*DKR*, p. 19; Sparks, 1978, pp. 109–110); perhaps formerly at Cleeve.

Benet, Richard: Garendon; *sd.* 1503, *d.* 1504, *p.* 1505 (Lincoln; *Reg. W. Smith*, ff. 42v, 46v, n–f.).

Benett, Richard: monk, and later abbot, Biddlesden, 1512–1534; *disp.* 1536 (*LP* **10**, p. 521 [No. 1248]; allowed his annuity of £13–6–4, 1538, when described by Dr John London writing to Cromwell, as 'a very honest man' (TNA, E315/245, f. 14); dead by 1552 (Green, 1974, pp. 24–25, 63–64; Smith, 2008, p. 268).

Benson, Thomas: Merevale; signed surrender deed, 1538 (TNA, E322/151); pension, £5 (TNA, E315/233, f. 63r).

Benstede, John: Quarr; *sd., d.* and *p.* 1509 (Winchester; *Reg. R. Fox* **2**, ff. 24r, 25r).

Bent, Henry: Bruern; *sd.* 1517 (Lincoln; *Reg. W. Atwater*, f.122r); still in house at its suppression, 1536 (Baskerville, 1930, p. 334).

Bent(t)e/Bennett, Ralph: Vale Royal, signed deed of surrender and *disp.* 1538 (*DKR*, p. 46; *FOR*, p. 162); in receipt of his £5 pension in 1555 (TNA, E164/31, f. 69r.)

Bentley, Richard: Pipewell; *sd.* and *d.* 1492, *p.* 1496 (Lincoln; *Reg. J. Russell*, f.44/45r, 46/47r; *Reg. W. Smith*, n.f.).

Benvell, John: Rewley, *disp.* 1536 (*FOR*, p. 78).

Berdmore: *see* Kingsley.

Bere, John: monk, perhaps of Netley but transferring to Beaulieu, *disp.* 1538 (*FOR*, p. 131; Hockey, 1976, p. 183); pension, £5 (TNA, E314/77). Could he be the monk, *John Kerry*, q.v?

Berking: *see* Barking.

Berkley, Walter: Stratford: *p.* 1505 (London; *Reg. W. Barons*, f. 90r).

Berkley, John: Kingwood; *d.* 1442 (Wells; *Reg. J. Stafford*, f. 242v).

Berkeley, William: Flaxley, 1476 (*Gloucestershire Notes and Queries* **4**, 1890, p. 597 [No. 1915]).
Berkeley: *see also* Barkley.

Bernard, Thomas: Coggeshall; *d.* 1491 (where named as 'John'), *p.* 1493 (London; *Reg. R. Hill*, ff. 23v, 28r).

Bernys, Ralph: Woburn, 1496 (SSC, BRT 1/3/105]).
Bertelet: *see* Weston.

Berwell, Thomas: abbot, Biddlesden; general pardon, 1509 (*LP* **1**, Part 1, p. 247 [No. 438/3, m.20]).

Berwik/Byrtleson, Gawin: Fountains, *d.* and *p.* 1509 (York; in February 1536 charged, perhaps spuriously, with having committing sodomy with five boys; pension, 1539, £6 (Cross and Vickers, 1995, pp. 113, 115, 119).
Berwike, Thomas: *see* Ellis.

Bery, Gregory: Rievaulx; *sd.* 1504, *p.* 1509 (York; Cross and Vickers, 1995, p. 168).

Beryll/Burrill/Byrall/Birell, Robert: Revesby, *sd.* 1528, *d.* 1529, *p.* 1531 (Lincoln; *Reg. J. Longland*, ff. 21r, 24r, 28r); *disp.* 1538 (*FOR*, p. 128); described as 'chaplain' when signing surrender deed, March 1538 (Essex R.O., D/DRg 1/104).

Best, Richard: Vaudey; *sd.* 1517, *d.* 1518, *p.* 1519 (Lincoln; *Reg. W. Atwater*, ff. 120r, 125v, 129r).

Best, Roger: Furness; *sd.* 1516, *d.* 1517 (York; *Reg. T. Wolsey*, ff. 174v, 175v).

Best(e), Thomas: Neath, *disp.* 1539, when sub–prior (TNA, E314/77); pension, £4 p.a., (Birch, 1902, pp. 150, 154; *FOR*, p. 170); in 1554, unmarried and living at Southhill, Bedfordshire; still in receipt of his £4 pension in 1555, he had no other ecclesiastical preferments (Hodgett, 1959, p. 91; TNA, E164/31, f. 77v).

Bethom/Bothome, John: abbot, Calder, 1501–03 (Loftie, 1888, pp. 235–36; 1892, p. 78.

Bets, Robert: Sibton, *disp.* 1536 (*FOR*, p. 70). Could be an *alias* for Robert Bungey or Robert Elmam, q.v.

?Betanns, Oliver: Rufford; *p.* 1517 (York; *Reg. T. Wolsey*, f. 179r).

Beverley, Edward: Jervaulx; *ac.* 1524 (York; Cross and Vickers, 1995, p. 131).

Beverley, John: Jervaulx; *sd.* 1452 (York; *Reg. W. Booth*, f. 413r).

Beverley, John: Rievaulx; *sd.* and *d.* 1495 (York), *p.* 1498 (Cross and Vickers, 1995, p. 168).

Beverley, Richard: Meaux; *p.* 1466 (York; *Reg. G. Neville*, f. 193).

Beverley, Robert: Rievaulx; *sd.* and *d.* 1509, *p.* 1514 (York; Cross and Vickers, 1995, p. 168).

Beverley/Elys, Roger: abbot, Tilty, 1517–1530 (TNA, E40/5429; E41/306/(a); profession of obedience, 30 November, 1517, when blessed by John, titular bishop of Gallipoli in the church of St Thomas Martyr of Acon, London; received rectory of Staines, 1520 (BL, *Harley MS 6955*, ff. 76 [39v]; 77 [40r]; deposed and moved to Ireland, 1530 (VCH, *Essex* **2**, 1907, pp. 135); in dispute regarding his pension a little thereafter (TNA, C1/607/18; E40/5429).

Beverley/?Robinson, William: Meaux; *ac.* and *sd.* 1523, *d.* 1524, *p.* 1526; pension, £6 (York; Cross and Vickers, 1995, pp. 155, 162).

Beverley/Beverlay, William: Kirkstead: *sd.* 1523, *d.* 1524, *p.* 1527 (Lincoln; *Reg. J. Longland*, ff. 8r, 9r, 19v).

Bewdley, *al.* French, William: Bordesley; *ac.* and *sd.* 1507, *d.* 1508, *p.* 1510 (Worcester; *Reg. S. Gigli*, ff.. 296–98, 305); abbot, Flaxley; 1526–1533; B. Th. Oxon, 1528 (*BRUO* **2**, p. 48; Stevenson, 1939, p. 42); licence to hear confessions and preach in the diocese of Hereford, with forty days indulgence for his hearers, 1529 (Hereford; *Reg. C. Bothe*, pp. 208–09); last abbot, Kingswood, 1533, *disp.* 1538 (*DKR*, p. 25; *FOR*, p. 131); 'reward and finding', 1538, £6–13–4; pension, £50 (TNA, E36/152, f. 19); vicar of Hawkesbury, Gloucs., by 1540 to 1548 when dies; married and had a daughter (Baskerville, 1927, p. 88).

Biddlesden, Richard: Biddlesden; *ac.* 1523, *sd.* and *d.* 1525, *p.* 1527 (Lincoln; *Reg. J. Longland*, ff. 5v, 10v, 12r, 19v).

Bikleswade/?Biggleswade, Edmund: Warden; *ac.* 1508, *sd.* 1509, *d.* 1510 (Lincoln; *Reg. W. Smith*, n–f.); *p.* 1514 (*Reg. T. Wolsey*, f. 14v).

Bikleswade/?Biggleswade, Henry: Warden; *sd.* 1508, *d.* 1509 (Lincoln; *Reg. W. Smith*, n–f.).

Bykeleswade, Thomas: Warden: *d.* and *p.* 1530 (Lincoln; *Reg. J. Longland*, ff. 26v, 27v); said by Abbot Emery, 1535, to be 'a common drunkard' (*LC*, p. 59 [No. XXIX]); pension, £5–6–8 (TNA, E314/77).

Bikleswade/?Biggleswade, William: Warden; *sd.* 1508 (Lincoln; *Reg. W. Smith*, n–f.).

Biland: *see* Byland.

Billington, James: Combermere; *sd.* 1525, *d.* and *p.* 1526 (Lichfield; *Reg. G. Blyth*, n–f.).

Billington, William: Hailes; *p.* 1489 (Worcester; *Reg. R. Morton*, f. 144).

Bilton: *see also* Bolton.

Byrd/Bird, John: abbot, Kirkstead, 1491–1497 (Lincolnshire Archives, 2ANC2/9/1, 4, 5; Smith, 2008, p. 306).

Bird (Byrde), John: abbot, Boxley, 1523, when instituted to the vicarage of Salehurst, Kent; instituted to vicarage of Boxley, 1528, and later made rector, Cooling, 1535, when disp. to change habit (*FOR*, p. 11). He may well be the last abbot, *John Dobbes*, q.v. (Smith, 2008, pp. 271–72).

Birell: *see* **Beryll.**

Birkenham, Robert: Sawtry; *sd.* 1512 (Lincoln; *Reg. W. Smith*, n–f.).

Birmingham: *see* Byrmencham.

Birnley, Nicholas: Vale Royal; *p.* 1493 (York; *Reg. T. Rotherham*, n.f.)

Birstall, Richard: Kirkstall, *sd.* and *d.* 1522, *p.* 1525 (York); pension, 1539, £5–6–8. He may have been the priest of Leeds, *Richard Elles*,who in 1550 bequeathed his best gown, his horse and a vestment to another Kirkstall former monk, Anthony Jackson (Cross and Vickers, 1995, pp. 141–42, 145).

Birtlesone, Gawin: Fountains; pension, 1539: £6 (Cross and Vickers, 1995, p. 115); *and see* **Berwik.**

Bisham: *see* Bysham.

Blackborne/Blackburn, Thomas: Whalley, *disp.* 1537 (*FOR*, 110).

Blackborne, William: Bruern; *ac.* 1497, *sd.*and *d.* 1498 (Lincoln; *Reg. W. Smith*, n. f.).

Blagdene, John: Stanley; *sd.* 1530, *d.* 1532, *p.* 1533 (Salisbury; *Reg. L. Campeggio*, n.f.).

Blake, William: St Mary Graces; *d.* 1520, *p.* 1521 (London; *Reg. R. Fitzjames*, ff. 181r [192r], 183v [194v]).

Blakeborne, James: Sawley; *sd.* and *d.* 1535, *p.* 1536 (Cross and Vickers. 1995, pp. 201, 203).

Blakede/Blecheden, Robert: Boxley, but apostate, 1512 (TNA, C81/1788/7).

Blankpayne/Blancpayne, Richard: former abbot of Kingswood with pension, 1487, when residing in the Dursley deanery (Worcester: *Reg. R. Morton*, f. 28; Smith, 2008, p. 303). Could he be Richard *Wotwan*, q.v.

Blethyn, Morgan: son of William Blethyn of Malpas, Monm., abbot, Llantarnam, 1500–1532/33 (Williams, 1976, pp. 85–86; 2001. p. 71).

Blith, William: Fountains, *sd.* 1499, *p.* 1501 (York; Cross and Vickers, 1995, p. 112).

Blythe: *see also* **Scarborough.**

Blomer, Edward: Furness, signed deed of surrender and *disp.* 1537 (*FOR*, p. 97; TNA, E322/91).

Blower, Robert: abbot, Sawtry, 1501–?1509 (Smith, 2008, p. 330).

Bloxham: *see* Inglis.

Blunham/Blinham, Lawrence: Woburn; *ac.* 1511 (Lincoln; *Reg. W. Smith*, n–f.), *p.* 1519 (*Reg. W. Atwater*, f. 131r); *disp.* 1538 (*FOR*, p. 145); opposed to the 'New Learning'; on the community being ministered the oath of supremacy salved his conscience by saying that because of the press of monks he could not touch the book; was hanged at Woburn in 1538 (Knowles, 1963, pp. 188–90; Gasquet, 1899, pp. 284–90).

Blymmyl: *see* Aklbrighton.

Blyton, Roland: Rufford; *sd.* 1496, *d.* 1497 (York; *Reg. T. Rotherham*, n.f.); *p.* 22 December 1498 [in Rotherham parish church]; abbot, Rufford, 1516–33 (Nottinghamshire Archives, DD/SR.208/64, 95); last abbot, Rievaulx, on deposition of Edward Kirkby in 1533; said in 1537 to be 'very aged' (Aveling, 1952, p. 104); signed deed of surrender and *disp.* 1538 (*DKR*, p. 38; *FOR*, p. 156; *RC*, **2**, pp. 388–89 [No. 732]; pension, 100 marks; perhaps settled on former abbey property at Welburn, Notts., in 1555 signed letters testimonial for a former novice (Cross and Vickers, 1995, pp. 170–71).

Bocking, John: Coggeshall, gave evidence at an inquiry in 1536 (*LP* **10**, pp. 59–60 [No. 164]); *disp.* 1538 (*FOR*, p. 124).

Boland/Bowland, Thomas: Woburn; *sd.* 1498, *d.* 1500, *p.* 1505 (Lincoln; *Reg. W. Smith*, f. 24r, n–f.).

Boland, Thomas: Sawley; *ac.* 1506, *sd.* 1507, *p.* 1510 (York; Cross and Vickers, 1995, p. 200).

Bolingbroke, Robert: Kirkstall; commissary of the vicar–general of the diocese of York, 1496 (*Reg. T. Rotherham*, p. 88 [No. 714]).

Bolland, Giles: Furness; signed deed of surrender and *disp.* 1537 (*DKR*, p. 21; TNA, E322/91).

Bolland/Robard, Thomas: Whalley; *p.* 1518 (York; *Reg. T. Wolsey*, f.181v); cellarer, Whalley, 1536 (TNA, SC6/HENVIII/1796; E315/427/3, f. 1r, – the same deed (f. 3) also names him as proctor of the abbey's possessions in Rochdale).

Bolton, Edmund: 'reward' £2–0–0 (Walcott, 1871, p. 216), *disp.* 1538; pension, £5 (Hibbert, 1910, pp. 239, 242; *FOR*, p. 160; Staffordshire Archives 2/32/00, p. 45).

Bolton/Bilton, Richard: Meaux; *sd.* 1491, *d.* 1492, *p.* 1495 (York; Cross and Vickers, 1995, p. 153).

Bolton, Richard: Hailes; *d.* and *p.* 1528 (Worcester; *Reg. R. Morton*, ff. 166, 168); sub–prior, 1537/38 (*CHA*, p. 85).

Bolton, Robert: Swineshead; *ac.* 1511, *d.* 1513 (Lincoln; *Reg. W. Smith*, n–f.); *p.* 1515 (*Reg. W. Atwater*, f. 112v).

Bolton, Thomas: Sawley; *d.* 1505 (York; Cross and Vickers, pp. 200, 202–03; abbot's chaplain, 1522; penultimate abbot, Sawley, by 1527 (Harland, 1853, p. 42); played a prominent role in the Northern Rising, and condemned to die, but appears to have been spared or have died of natural causes before execution (Baskerville, 1937, p. 165; disp. 1536 (*FOR*, p. 58); pension, £20 (*LP* **13**, Part 1, p. 574 [No. 1520/iii]; TNA, E244, no. 31 – where listed as last abbot, as also by: Smith, 2008, p. 329.

Bolton, Thomas: *see also* Poulton, Yarome.

Bolyake, John: Rewley, perhaps the John Bawe listed above; *d.* 1498 (Lincoln; *Reg. W. Smith*, n.f.).

Bonfay, George: Byland, *p.* 1480 (Cross and Vickers, 1995, p. 98).

Bongay: *see* Bungey.

Bordesley, John: Bordesley; *sd.* 1487 (Lichfield; *Reg. J. Hales*, f. 233v); *d.* 1488, *p.* 1490 (Worcester; *Reg. R. Morton*, ff. 142, 149).

Bordesley/Borsley, John: Bordesley; *ac.* 1507, *d.* 1510, *p.* 1515 (Worcester; *Reg. S. Gigli*, ff. 296, 302, 325).

Bordesley, John: Bordesley; *d.* 1532 (Worcester; *Reg. R. Morton addenda*, f. 172).

Bordesley, Thomas: Hailes; *sd.* 1504 (Worcester; *Reg. S. Gigli* , f. 289).

Brodesley. /Bordesley, William: Bordesley; *d.* and *p.* 1516 (Worcester; *Reg. S. Gigli*, ff. 330–31, where perhaps given wrongly as a monk of Hailes): *see*: **Brodesley.**.

Boreman: *see* Bourman.

Borought, Walter: St Mary Graces; *ex.* and *ac.* 1528 (London; *Reg. C. Tunstall*, f. 160v).

Borow, John: Byland; *sd.* 1499, *p.* 1504 (York; Cross and Vickers, 1995, p. 98).

Borreby/Borrowby, al. Moreland, William: Louth Park; *sd.* 1523, *d.* 1525, *p.* 1527 (Lincoln; *Reg. J. Longland*, ff. 6v, 11v, 19v); *disp.* 14–09–1536, thereafter lived at nearby Kedington (Gasquet, 1899, *204*); played a prominent role in the Lincolnshire Rising of 1536 (Shaw, 1999, pp. 94, 100, 102); hanged at Tyburn, 29–03–1537 (Dodds, 1915, **2**, pp. 153–54).

Borrowdale/Boradall, Gavin/Gawin: monk, Holm Cultram, 1531, when suspected of poisoning his abbot, and held for a time in custody at Furness abbey (Gilbanks, 1899, pp. 91–97); last abbot, Holm Cultram, 1537–1538 (TNA, LR1/173, f. 132r–v); signed deed of surrender and *disp.*1538 (TNA, E314/20/11, f. 3r; *FOR*, p. 123); after dissolution received the grant of part of the site from the Crown and the rectory of Holm Cultram (TNA, L1/173, ff. 12–143); died 1553 (Smith, 2008, p. 301).

Borsley: *see* Bordesley.

Bosforns: *see* Oxford.

Bossall, Marmaduke: monk, Rievaulx; *ac.* and *d.* 1490, *p.* 1493 (York; Cross and Vickers, 1995, p. 167).

Boston, John: Coggeshall; *sd.* and *d.* 1495, *p.* 1496 (London; *Reg. R. Hill*, ff. 30r, 30v, 31r).

Boston, **John:** Swineshead; *sd.* 1531, *d.* 1533 (Lincoln; *Reg. J. Longland*, ff. 30r, 33v).

Boteler: *see* Butler.

Bothe, Christopher: Fountains; *p.*1484 (Cross and Vickers, 1995, p. 111).

Bothe/Beche, William: Croxden, signed deed of surrender and *disp.* 1538 (TNA, E314/20/11, ff. 7d–8r; *FOR*, p. 151); pension, £4 (TNA, E315/233, f. 18v; BL. Add. MS 11041, f. 5).

Bourman, William: Dunkeswell, *disp.* 1539; pension, £6 (*DKR*, p. 19; TNA, E322/76; Sparks, 1978, pp. 109–10). Died at Hemyock, Devon, 1553 (Snell, 1967, p. 146).

Boxley, Mr: monk, present in Canterbury on Sunday 2 November 1533, supping with a monk, Mr Goodnestone (Canterbury Cathedral Archives, CC/JQ/333/vii).

Boys, William: Fountains; *sd.* 1494 (York; Cross and Vickers, 1995, p. 111). Was he the monk under–named?

Boys, William: Sibton, *disp.* 1536 (*FOR*, p. 70).

Brackley, al. Maiowe/Mayhoo, Richard: Biddlesden, *sd.* 1496, *d.* 1498, *p.* 1500 (Lincoln; *Reg. W. Smith*, f. 24v); *disp.* 1538; pension, £5–6–8, still received in 1555 (*FOR*, p. 179; Green, 1974, pp. 63–64; TNA, E164, f. 24r.

Bradacke, Richard: *see* Adams.

Bradford, Henry: Rievaulx; *sd.* 1487, *d.* 1488, *p.* 1490 (York; Cross and Vickers, 1995, p. 167).

Bradford/Brydeforth, Henry: Sawley; *sd.* and *d.* 1535, *p.* 1536 (York; Cross and Vickers, 1995, p. 201); *disp.* 1536 (*FOR*, p. 58); was slightly involved in the aftermath of the Pilgrimage of Grace (Dodds **2**, 1915, pp. 83–85).

Bradford, James: Byland; *ac.* 1490, *d.* 1491, *p.* 1493 (York; Cross and Vickers, 1995, p. 98).

Bradford/Bradforth, Thomas: Fountains, *d.* 1508, *p.* 1511 (York; Cross and Vickers, 1995, p. 113).

Bradham, John: Rewley, *disp.* 1536 (*FOR*, p. 78).

Bradley, Bernard: Sawley; *sd.* 1506, *d.* 1507 (York); transferred to Byland on Sawley's closure, 1536; *disp.* 1539, pension £5 – this later struck through (*FOR*, p. 181; Cross and Vickers, 1995, pp. 100, 103, 200).

Bradley, al. Kelyng, John: Biddlesden; *sd.* 1529, *d.* 1530, *p.* 1531 (Lincoln; *Reg. J. Longland*, ff. 24v, 26v, 28v); *disp.* 1538; pension, £5–6–8 (Green, 1974, pp. 63–6; TNA, E322/22).

Bradley, Marmaduke: Fountains, *sd.* 1503, *d.* 1504, *p.* 1508 (York); abbot's chaplain, 1509 (*FLB*, p. 118 [No. 130]), bursar, 1515–17 (*FLB*, pp. 16–17 [No. 17], 26 [No. 30]; later a .wayward monk rehabilitated by the abbot of Cîteaux, 1517/21 (*Letters*, pp. 267–68 [No. 139]); last abbot, 1536–39; pension, £100, 1539; later resided in Ripon where he held the prebend of Thorpe, and was master of the hospital of St Mary Magdalene (Cross, 1995, pp. 113, 115–16). In January 1536 Layton and Legh described him as 'a wealthy fellow;' had been able to promise Cromwell a gift of 600 marks for his appointment to the abbacy (Fletcher, 1919, pp. 254–55)

Bradley, William: *see also* Ffarlington.

Bradley/Kyllyng, Robert: Croxden; *sd.* 1501, *p.* 1504 (Lichfield; *Reg. J. Arundel*, f. 297; *Reg G.* Blyth, n–f.).

Bradmynch, John: Newenham; *ac. sd.* and *d.* 1490, *p.* 1491 (Exeter; *Reg. R. Fox*, ff. 155, 156v, 158r).

Bradmynch, Walter: Newenham; *p.* 1499 (Exeter; *Reg. O. King*, f. 40v)

Bragwen: *see* Brangwen.

Braintree: *see* Clerk.

Brampton, Mark: Sawtry; *p.* 1526 (Lincoln; *Reg. J. Longland*, f. 16r).

Brampton, Richard: Sawtry; *d.* 1527, *p.* 1530 (Lincoln; *Reg. J. Longland*, ff. 20v, 25v).

Brampton/*al.* Sawyer, Warin: prior, Sawtry, *c.* 1533 (TNA, STAC2/32/154); *disp.* 1536/37 (*FOR*, pp. 66, 110, 116).

Bramley/Bromeley: *see* Ryton.

Brancheley, John: Boxley; *d.* 1493 (*LPL*; *Reg. J. Morton* **2**, f. 141v.

Brangwayen/Brangwyn/Braneswice, Richard: Woburn; *sd.* 1496, *d.* 1497, *p.* 1500 (Lincoln; *Reg. W. Smith*, f. 24v); last abbot, Medmenham; *disp.* 1536 (*FOR*, p. 67); pension, £6–13–4 (TNA, E315/244, no. 7).

Brasiar, William: Tintern; *p.* 1511 (Worcester; *Reg. S. Gigli*, f. 401).

Brawnebone, John: Llantarnam; *sd.* 1473 (Hereford; *Reg. J. Stanbury*, p. 170).

Bray, Stephen: Buckland; *sd.* and *d.* 1507, *p.* 1508 (Exeter; *Reg. H. Oldham*, ff. 89v, 92r, 97v).

Brantre/Branctre/Braintree, John: monk, Tilty; *sd.* 1509, *d.* and *p.* 1510 (London; *Reg. R. Fitzjames*, ff. 157v [168v], 158r [169r], 159r [170v]).

Brayntrey/Braintree/Clerke, Richard: Coggeshall, *sd.* and *d.* 1522 (Canterbury; *Reg. W. Warham*, *London sede vacante*, f. 298v; London, *Reg. C. Tunstall*, f.152v); aged thirty-one in January 1536, when testified against his abbot (*LP* **10**, pp. 59–60 [No. 164]); *disp.* 1538 (*FOR*, p. 124).

Bredwater, Robert: Netley; *d.* 1500 (Winchester; *Reg. T. Langton*, f. 35v); in community, 1518, by which time priested (TNA, E314/101).

Breken/Breckynden, William: Robertsbridge, *c.*1497; abbot, by 1513 to 1523 (when dies), instituted in 23–10–1516 as vicar of, Salehurst, Sussex (Chichester; *Reg. R. Sherburne* **1**, f. 12r; Smith, 2008, p. 326); died by 5–09–1523 (SAL, MS 14, ff. 58v–59v).

Brekisley/Brikesley, Thomas: Coggeshall; *p.* 1515 (London; *Reg. R. Fitzjames*, f. 181v); *disp.* 1538 (*FOR*, p. 124); pension, £7 p.a. (TNA, SC12/7/34).

Brereton, John: Rievaulx; monk, Rievaulx; *sd.* and *d.* 1485, *p.* 1486 (York; Cross and Vickers, 1995, p. 167).

Brewarne: *see* Hanney, King.

Bridgewater, *al.* Stone, John: Ford; *sd.* 1504 (Canterbury; *Reg. W. Warham, Exeter sede v.*, f. 208r); *d.* 1507 (Wells; *Reg. H. de Castello*, f. 145); *p.* 1508 (Exeter; *Reg. H. Oldham*, f. 97v); *disp.* 1539; pension, £8 (*DKR*, p. 21, Youings, 1971, p. 186); still in receipt of pension in 1555 (TNA, E164/31, f. 34v).

Bridley, Richard: Rievaulx; *d.* 1452 (York; *Reg. W. Booth*, f. 413r).

Brighouse, William: Kirkstall, *sd.* 1505, *d.* 1506, *p.* 1507 (York). May have been the former monk *William Northes/Northives*, who testified around 1545 that he had been a monk of Kirkstall for about thirty years before the dissolution, and bursar for half that time (Cross and Vickers, 1995, pp. 140,

142, 149–50). If so, pension, 1539, £6; very probably curate of Adel, of which Kirkstall formerly had the advowson, in 1541/1551 (Lonsdale, 1972, p. 208).

Bright, John: abbot, Warden, 1491– (*Statuta* **6**, p. 22 [No. 1491/51]); in 1492/93 an attempt was allegedly made to poison him (Cross and Vickers, 1995, pp. 346–47).

Brikehed, Robert: Kirkstead, *disp.* 1537 (*FOR*, p. 96).

Brikelsey: *see* Brekisley.

Bristow/Bristol, *al.* Stephens, John: Cwmhir ['Cwmbie', St David's diocese], *disp.* 1511 (*CPL* **19**, p. 267 [No. 458]).

Bristowe, John: Hailes; prior, 1480, but had more or less abandoned monastic life and was vicar of Rodbourne Cheney, though returning to a corrody at the abbey in 1494 (*CHA*, pp. 37–8; Harper–Bill, 1980, p. 113).*).*

Bristowe, Matthew: Swineshead; *sd.* 1511, *d.* 1512, *p.* 1513 (Lincoln; *Reg. W. Smith*, n–f.).

Bristol/Brysto, Richard: Thame; signed deed of surrender, 1539 (*DKR*, p. 43); perhaps by 1550, rector, Crowmarsh Gillard, Oxon., died 1557 (Baskerville, 1930, p. 336). Not in an early pension list (TNA, E314/77).

Bristol/Bristowe, Thomas: Hailes; *p.* 1489 (Worcester; *Reg. R. Morton*, f. 144).

Bristow, Thomas: Rewley; *p.* 1521 (Lincoln; *Reg. J. Longland*, f. 1v).

Bristol/Bristowe, Thomas: Dore; *d.* 1533 (Hereford; *Reg. C. Bothe*, p. 330).

Brivel: *see* Bennett, Alan.

Brokenen/Brykenden, William: Robertsbridge, by 1461; abbot *c.*1511–1523 when dies (SAL, MS 14).

Brocweir, Matthew: ? monk, Tintern; *p.* 1518 (Hereford; *Reg. C. Bothe*, p. 306).

Brode, Philip: *see* Acton.

Brodebelte/? Lethley, Robert: Fountains; *sd.* 1503, *d.* 1504, *p.* 1506 (York); pension, 1539: £6. If Lethley, then early in 1536 he was reported as wishing to leave the religious life; still in receipt of his pension in 1554 (Cross and Vickers, 1995, pp. 113, 115, 118).

Broderton/?Herde, Thomas: Sawley; *sd.* and *d.* 1520, *p.* 1521 (York; Cross and Vickers, 1995, pp. 200, 205).

Brodesley/Borsley, William: Hailes: *ac.* 1516, *sd.* 1517, *d.* n.d., *p.* 1517 (Worcester; *Reg. S. Gigli*, ff. 331, 333, 335).

Brodle, Wiliam: Kirkstall, *ac.* 1484, *sd.* and *d.* 1485, *p.* 1489 (York; Cross and Vickers, 1995, p. 139).

Broke, Richard: Kirkstall; pension, 1539, £6–13–4; Perhaps the same monk as *Richard Spofforth*, q.v. (Lonsdale, 1972, p. 207), or *Richard Newall/Newton*, q.v. (Cross and Vickers, 1995, pp. 144).

Broke, Thomas: Vaudey; *p.* 1485 (Lincoln; *Reg. J. Russell*, f.18v).

Brombron, William: Vale Royal; *d.* 1506 (Lichfield; *Reg. G. Blyth*, n–f.).

Brom(e)feld, John: Stratford; *sd.* 1514, *d.* and *p.* 1516 (London; *Reg. R. Fitzjames*, ff. 178r [167r], 182v [171v], 184r [173r [184r]).

Bromley/*al.* Crocket/Brokehill, Edmund: Merevale; *ac.* and *sd.* 1519, *d.* 1520, *p.* 1521 (Lichfield; *Reg. G. Blyth*, n–f.); present in house at suppression (TNA, E322/151).), in receipt of pension of £5–6–8 in 1555 (TNA, E164/31, f. 48r). Not mentioned in the Faculty Office register.

Bromley, John: Boxley; *p.* 1494 (London; *Reg. R. Hill*, f. 29v).

Bromley, John: Stoneleigh; *sd.* 1499, *d.* 1500 (Lichfield; *Reg. J. Arundel*, ff. 282, 286).

Bromley/Bromfield, Richard: Valle Crucis; the bastard son of a monk; visited Rome in 1504, prior in 1528 (when passed over for the abbacy) to at least 1534 (when declined the abbacy); on account of infirmity permitted in 1528 to wear leggings and a 'head warmer'; said at the suppression to be 'a virtuous and well–disposed man', *disp.* 1538; he moved to Wrexham and was still alive in 1542 (Pratt, 1997, p. 29; Price, 1952, pp. 52–53, 186; *FOR*, p. 156).

Bromley, Thomas: Merevale; *ac.* and *sd.* 1519, *d.* 1520, *p.* 1521 (Lichfield; *Reg. G. Blyth*, n–f.).

Bromfelde, Robert: Valle Crucis; *ac.* 1499 (Lichfield; *Reg. J. Arundel*, f.281v; it is possible he is the above–mentioned monk, *Richard Bromley.*

Brompton, Ralph: Jervaulx; *sd.* 1513, *p.* 1515 (York; Cross and Vickers, 1995, p. 130).

Bromsgrove, Richard: Bordesley; *ac.* 1504, *sd.* 1506, *d.*1508, *p.* 1511 (Worcester; *Reg. S. Gigli*, ff. 289, 294, 298, 310).

Bromsgrove, Richard: *see* Deane.

Brondavert, Robert: Netley; in community, 1518, by which time priested (TNA, E314/101).

Broseyerde, John: kitchener, Sibton, 1520 (Ridgard and Norton, 2011, p. 39).

Brotherton, Thomas: Whalley; *d.* 1520 (York; *Reg. T. Wolsey*, f. 188v).

Brotun, John: Rewley; *p.* 1496 (Lincoln; *Reg. W. Smith*, n.f.).

Broughton, John: monk, Sawley, then at Furness; gave evidence in 1537 that 'he knew of the prophecies of the Holy Maid of Kent and others' (Gasquet, 1899, p. 274); he was opposed to the royal supremacy (Shaw, 1999, p. 97); probably imprisoned at the time of suppression (Haigh, 1969, p. 120).

Broughton/Broghton/*al.* Watson, Oliver: Rievaulx; *ac.* and *sd.* 1531, *d.* 1532, *p.* 1534 (York); listed in 1533 (TNA, STAC2/7/217); signed deed of surrender. Watson complained in 1552 that his pension was more than a year in arrears; .not listed in the 1564 pension list, but if he became in 1555 the vicar of Ormesby, he may have not died before 1582 (Cross and Vickers, 1995, pp. 169–70, 183–84).

Browne, Geoffrey: Buildwas; *sd.* 1496, *p.* 1497 (Lichfield; *Reg. J. Arundel*, ff. 258v, 264).

Browne/Cambridge, George: Tilty, *sd.* 1520, *d.* and *p.* 1521 (London; *Reg. R. Fitzjames*, ff. 181r [192r], 182v [193v], 183v [194v]); *disp.* 1536 (*FOR*, p. 60; *DKR*, p. 45).

Browne, Gilbert: Kirkstall; pension, 1539, £6 (Cross and Vickers, 1995, p. 142). See also: *Gilbert Wymmersley.*

Browne, Hugh: Furness; *sd.* 1521, *p.* 1522 (York; *Reg. T. Wolsey*, ff. 189v, 193v); signed deed of surrender and *disp.* 1537 (TNA, E322/91; *FOR*, p. 97); chaplain in Cambridgeshire, 1542 (Haigh, 1969, p. 120); but giving evidence in 1543 he was said to resident at 'Ayrton,' (possibly, Airton, Yorkshire, or near Grange–on–Sands), and aged about 47 years (*AF*, p. xc).

Browne, John: Kirkstall, *sd.* and *d.* 1491, *p.*1495 (York); last prior, 1539; pension, given as £66–13–4 must have been confusion with John Ripley, the last abbot (Lonsdale, 1972, p. 216).

Brown, John: procurator, St Mary Graces, 1522 (*LPL*; *Reg. W. Warham* **2**, f. 296v).

Brown/Bryan, John: Cistercian monk of unnamed house, ordained acolyte on letters dimissory from the Holy See, 1495 (Salisbury; *Reg. J. Blyth*, n.f.).

Browne, Richard: Rewley; *ac.* 1485, *sd.* 1488, *p.* 1489 (Lincoln; *Reg. J. Russell*, ff. 18v, 19r, 27r, 33v).

Browne, Roger: Swineshead, *disp.* 1536 (*FOR*, p. 67).

Brown, Thomas: Sawley; *sd.* 1504 (York; Cross and Vickers, 1995, p. 199).

Browne, Thomas: Fountains; *sd.* and *d.* 1521, *p.* 1524 (York); in February 1536 charged by the Visitors, Layton and Leigh perhaps spuriously, with self–abuse and sodomy with a boy; pension, 1539, £5–6–8; may have later been curate of Bilton or Walton, Yorkshire (Cross and Vickers, 1995, pp. 114–15, 118–19).

Browne, Thomas: rent–collector, Holm Cultram; gave evidence in an enquiry, 1533 (LP **6**, p. 426 [No. 988]), signed deed of surrender and *disp.* 1538 (*DKR*, p. 23; *FOR*, pp. 123–24). In receipt of his pension of £4–13–4 in 1555 (TNA, E164/31, f. 73v).

Browne, William: Roche; *d.* 1509 (York); in community, 1531 (*LP* **5**, p. 107 [No. 226]; TNA, E135/3/6); his name does not appear in the pension list, but three clerics of this name were known in post–Suppression Yorkshire (Cross and Vickers, 1995, pp. 187–90).

Browne, William, *al.* **Oxford/Oxenford:** Merevale; *ac.* 1506, *sd.* 1507, *d.* 1508, *p.* 1510 (Lichfield; *Reg. G. Blyth*, n–f.); as 'Bron' signed surrender deed, 1538 and *disp.* (TNA, E322/151); in receipt of pension of £5 as late as 1555 (TNA, E164/31, f. 48r), and also of a £5 pension from previous employment as a chantry priest until 1548 of the Church of St Augustine near St Paul's, London; was married but noted in 1555 as being divorced and as being 'an honest poor man' with no income save his pensions; he was then living at Claydon, Suffolk (Baskerville, 1933, pp. 62, 222).

Browne, William: *see* **Oxford.**

Brown: *see also* Whalley.

Brownyng, John: Waverley; *p.* 1508 (Lincoln; *Reg. W. Smith*, n–f.); abbot, 1526–1533; abbot, Beaulieu, 1533–36 (Smith, 2008, pp. 267, 348).

Browning, John: Robertsbridge, *c.*1491 (SAL, MS 14, f. 5v); *disp.* 1496 (*CPL* **16**, pp. 357 [No. 529], 426–27 [No. 649].

Brugge, Richard: Ford, 1538 (TNA, E322/151). This is probably an *alias* of another monk of Ford.

Bryan, John: abbot, Bindon; 1486 to 1504, when deposed (TNA, C/115/60, C1/198/48; C1282/25); rector of Keynstone, Dorset, 9 January 1504, granted a general pardon, 1493 (*Patent* 1493, p. 430). died 1511 (Smith, 2008, p. 269); proctor in convocation, n.d. (Salisbury; *Reg. T. Langton*, p. 98 [No. 565];

Brygge/Bridge, John: Bindon; *ac.* and *sd.* 1525, *d.* 1526, *p.* 1527 (Salisbury; *Reg. L. Campeggio*).

Brykhyll, Laurence: Woburn; *ac.* 1491, *sd.* 1492 (Lincoln; *Reg. J. Russell*, ff. 42r, 47/48r).

Byrkhill, Richard: Woburn; *p.* 1497 (Lincoln, *Reg. W. Smith*, n.f.).

Brynkelowe/*al.* **Percy/Perse, William:** Combe, *disp.* 1538 (*DKR*, pp. 16–17, *FOR*, p. 176); in receipt of pension of £5–6–8 as late as 1555 (TNA, E164/31, f. 48v).

Buckland, John: Bindon; *ac.* and *sd.* 1491, *d.* 1493 (Salisbury; *Reg. T. Langton*, pp. 109 [No. 565], 111 [No. 578], 117 [No. 585]); *p.* 1496 (Salisbury; *Reg. J. Blyth*, n.f.).

Buckland, Nicholas: Cleeve; *sd.* 1509 (Wells; *Reg. H. de Castello*, f. 150); *d.* and *p.* 1511 (Exeter; *Reg. H. Oldham*, ff. 105r, 106v).

Buckland/Bukland, William: Quarr; *sd.* 1487 (Chichester; *Reg. E. Story*, f. 180r); *d.* 1488 (Winchester; *Reg. P. Courtenay*, f. 14r).

Buildwas: *see* Rothwell.

Bucknall/Hucknall, John: Hulton; *p* 1504 (Lichfield; *Reg. G. Blyth* n–f.); signed deed of surrender and *disp.* 1538 (TNA, E322/106; *FOR*, p. 154); pension, £4–13–4 (TNA, E315/233, f. 22v).

Budelar: *see* Butler.

Bulde, Robert: Combe; *sd.* 1500 (Lichfield; *Reg. J. Arundel*, f. 288); *d.* 1503 (Lichfield; *sede v.*, CCA, DCc–Reg. f.287r); *p.* 1505 (Lichfield; *Reg G. Blyth*, n.f.).

Bulkington, William: Stoneleigh, *sd.* 1529, *d.* 1530, *p.* 1532 (Lichfield; *Reg. G. Blyth*, n–f.); *disp.* 1537 (*FOR*, p. 88).

Bulkyng: *see* Parkyng.

Bulvynoe/Bulymer, Henry: Thame; signed deed of surrender, 1539 (*DKR*, p. 43).

Bune: *see:* Woburn.

Bungey/Bongay, *al.* **Sabyn, Robert:** sub–prior and sacrist, Sibton, 1509 (*SAE*, p. 139); prior, when *disp.* 1536 (*SBC* **4**, p. 110–11 [No. 1187]; *LP* **10**, p. 520 [No. 1247]).

Bungey, William: Sibton, 1536 (*SBC* **4**, pp. 110–11 [No. 1187]).

Burcester/Bissetyr, ?Bicester, John: Biddlesden; *ac.* 1485, *sd.* 1487, *d.* 1489, *p.* 1490 (Lincoln; *Reg. J. Russell*, ff. 18v, 25v, 33r, 36v).

Burford, Richard: Dore, born *c.*1501; *ac.* and *sd.* 1522, *d.* 1525, *p.*1526 (Hereford; *Reg. C. Bothe*, pp. 311, 312, 319, 322); staying at Vale Royal, a daughter–house, 1531–1533; sub–prior, Dore, 1536, when about thirty–five years old (TNA, E315/109, ff. 127–34; Williams, 1976, pp. 28, 32).

Burford, Robert: Bruern; *sd.* 1510, *d.* and *p.* 1511 (Lincoln; *Reg. W. Smith*, n–f.).

Burford, William: Cleeve; *sd.* 1517, *d.* 1518 (Exeter; *Reg. H. Oldham*, ff. 127v, 130r); *p.* 1519 (Wells; *Reg. T. Wolsey*, f. 26); after being 'dismissed from his monastery', he signed the oath of supremacy in the Usk deanery, Monmouthshire, in 1535 (TNA, E36/63; *LP* 7, p. 396 [No. 1025/21]).

Burgess, John: Kirkstall, *sd.* 1505, *d.* 1506, *p.* 1509 (York; Cross and Vickers, 1995, p. 140).

Burges, William: prior, Stratford, 1516 (London; *Reg. R. Fitzjames*, f. 173r [184r]).

Burges, John: abbot, Netley, 1497–1525, previously cellarer (Smith, 2008, p. 316; *LP* 13, Part 1, p. 244 [No. 646].

Burghase/? Iden, Geoffrey: Robertsbridge; *sd.* 1519 (London; *Reg. R. Fitzjames*, f.188v).

Burghe, Stephen: Rievaulx; *sd.* 1501, *d.* 1502, *p.* 1504; 'monk of the bakehouse', Rievaulx, 1533, when spoke out against the deposition of Abbot Kirkby (TNA, STAC2/7/217; Cross and Vickers, 1995, pp. 168, 174); *disp.* 1538 and not traced thereafter (*FOR*, p. 156); may have died before the suppression (Aveling, 1952, p. 106).

Burley, George: Rievaulx; *sd.* and *d.* 1485, *p.* 1486 (York; Cross and Vickers, 1995, p. 167).

Burne, Robert/Richard: Louth Park; *sd.* 1510, *d.* 1511 (Lincoln; *Reg. W. Smith*, n–f.)

Burnell, Maurice: Tintern; *disp.* 1536 (*FOR*, p. 80); perpetual curate, Wootton–under–Edge, Gloucs., 1549–54, when perhaps deprived (*MA* 23, p. 68; Gloucestershire Archives, GDR 2a, ff. 44, 107).

Burnell, Thomas: Buckland; *sd.* 1491 (Canterbury for Bath and Wells; *Reg. J. Morton* 2, p. 13 [No. 53]).

Burslem, **Thomas:** Croxden; *sd.* and *d.* 1520 (Lichfield; *Reg. G. Blyth*, n–f.).

Burtall, Thomas: Aberconwy, *disp.* 1537 (*FOR*, p. 91).

Burton/Barton, John: Dore; *ac. sd.* 1522; *p.* 1523 (Hereford; *Reg. C. Bothe*, pp. 311–14).

Burton, John: abbot, Rievaulx, 1497– at least 1510; dispensed to hold a benefice in order to sustain his abbatial dignity, 1497 (*CPL* 16, pp. 530 [No. 776]); instituted as vicar of Normanton, West Yorkshire, 1499 (Smith, 2008, p. 324; York: *Reg. T. Rotherham*, p. 130 [No. 1077]).

Burton, Richard: Hailes; *ac.* 1528 (Canterbury;*Reg. J. Morton addenda*, p. 167; sacristan, 1537/38 (*CHA*, p. 85).

Burton, Robert: Merevale; *p.* 1532 (Lichfield; *Reg. G. Blyth*, n–f.). Could he be *Robert Sany*, q.v. Burton, Robert: *see also* Cornwall.

Burton, Thomas: abbot, Sawley, 1502–?1506 (Smith, 2008, p. 329).

Burton/Barton, Thomas: Newminster, thirty–five years old in 1536 (TNA, 12/13/65); *disp.* 1536 (*FOR*, p.77).

Burton, Thomas: Beaulieu, *disp.* 1538 (TNA, E314/20/11, f. 1d–2r; *DKR*, p. 9; *FOR*, p. 131); pension, £4 (TNA, E314/77).

Burton, William: abbot, Roche, 1488–1493 (*York; Reg. T. Rotherham*, pp. 227 [No. 1800]; 234 [No. 1850]).

Burton, William: Meaux; *sd.* 1525, *d.* 1526, *p.* 1528 (York); pension, 1539, £6 p..a. In 1546 owed the last abbot £6–6–8; may have served as curate of North Frodingham, Yorkshire; died 1558 (Cross and Vickers, 1995, pp. 155, 158).

Burton, ... : Combermere, 1530–33 (Aveling and Pantin, 1967, pp. 44, 215–16).

Burton: *see also* Barton.

Buseyn, Richard: Furness, *disp.* 1537 (*FOR*, p. 97); perhaps also known as *Richard Skales*, q.v.

Butler, John: Warden, 1492 (*Letters*, p. 156 [No. 79]).

Butler/Boteler,/Buckley, John: Stratford; *ac.* and *p.* 1503 (London; *Reg. W. Warham*, ff. 87r, 87d); sub–prior, 1510–16 (London; *Reg. R. Fitzjames*, ff. 158r [169v], 164r [175r], 172r [183r]). Could this be the *John Budelar* mentioned in 1510 (*Letters*, p. 232 [No. 117]); abbot, Vale Royal, 1517–1535, when dies; about 1530 some of his monks made accusations against him and Cardinal Wolsey ordered a visitation; he may have temporarily been suspended but by May 1530 was again abbot, though his rebellious monks were imprisoned in Chester Castle (Smith, 2008, p. 343).

Butler, John [perhaps wrongly entered as Thomas on one occasion]: Buildwas: *ac.* 1519, *sd.* and *d.* 1520 (Lichfield; *Reg. G. Blyth*, n–f.).

Butteler, Richard: Meaux; *ac.* 1517, *sd.* 1518, *d.* 1519, *p.* 1520; pension, £6 (York); seemingly owed as late as 1546 £6–6–8 to his former abbot, Richard Stopes; sixty years old in 1552; he may have acted as curate of North Frodingham, Yorkshire, and died there in 1558 (Cross and Vickers, 1995, pp. 154, 156, 158).

Butler/Boteler, Robert: Stratford; *ac.* 1495, *sd.* 1496 (when named 'Ralph'), *d.* 1500, *p.* 1502 (London; *Reg. R. Hill*, ff. 32v, 34r; *Reg. T. Savage*, f. 62v; *Reg. W. Warham*, f.83r).

Butler, Thomas: Aberconwy, 1515 – not perhaps abbot as once thought (*Augm.*, p. 97; *Flintshire Hist. Soc. Transactions* 7, pp. 78, 81).

Byculey, John: abbot, Waverley, 1476–85 (Smith, 2008, p. 348).

Bydall, John: Louth Park, *disp.* 4–05–1537 (*FOR*, p. 95).

Bydford/Bydforth, John: Bordesley; *ac.* and *sd.* 1532, *d.* 1533 (Worcester; *Reg. R. Morton addenda*, ff. 171, 174).

Byfleet/Bysyll, John: Beaulieu; *ac., sd.* and *d.* 1488, *p.* 1489 (Winchester; *Reg. P. Courtenay*, ff. 13r, 13v, 14r).

Bykerton, John: Dieulacres, *disp.* 1538; 'reward' £2–0–0 (Walcott, 1871, p. 216); pension, £2 (Hibbert, 1910, pp. 239, 242; TNA, E314/20/11, f. 9d; *FOR*, p. 160).

Byland, John: Rievaulx; *sd.* and *d.* 1495, *p.* 1497 (York; Cross and Vickers, 1995, p. 168).

Bylbroke, David: Cleeve; *d.* 1517 (Exeter; *Reg. H. Oldham*, f. 127v).

Byleigh: see Dey.

?Bylisle, James: Revesby; *d.* 1507 (Lincoln; *Reg. W. Smith*, n–f.).

Bylly: *see* Lylly.

Bynley/Byndeley, *al.* Wasdale/Wastell, Richard: Combe, *d.* and *p.* 1517 (Lichfield; *Reg. G. Blyth*, n–f.); *disp.* 1538 (*DKR*, pp. 16–17, *FOR*, p. 176); pension, £5–6–8 (TNA, E314/77).

Bynley/Byngley, Thomas: Combe, *sd.* 1531, *d.* 1532 (Lichfield; *Reg. G. Blyth*, n–f.). Does not appear in the pension list (TNA, E314/77).

Byrmycham/Byrmyngham/*al.* Starkey, Humphrey: Combe; *sd.* 1505, *p.* 1508 (Lichfield; *Reg. G. Blyth*, n.f); *disp.* 1538 (*DKR*, pp. 16–17; *FOR*, p. 176); in receipt of pension of £6 in 1555 (TNA, E164/31, f.48v).

Byrmencham, Richard: Pipewell; *sd.* 1508, *d.* 1509 (Lincoln; *Reg. W. Smith*, n–f.); *p.* 1515 (*Reg. W. Atwater*, f. 112v).

Byrmyncham, Thomas: Bordesley; *ac.* and *sd.* 1478, *d.* 1480 (*Reg. J. Alcock*, ff. 251, 261).

Brymyngham, William: order and house not stated; *d.* 1518 (Hereford; *Reg. C. Bothe*, p. 306).

Byrell, Robert: Rewley, *disp.* 1536 (*FOR*, p. 78).

Bysham, Thomas: Coggeshall; *ac.* and *sd.* 1522, *d.* 1523 (Canterbury; LPL: *Reg. W. Warham, London sede vacante* 2, ,f. 298r; London, *Reg. C. Tunstall*, ff.152r, 153r); *disp.* 1538 (*FOR*, p. 124); pension, £5 p.a. (TNA, SC12/7/34).

Byste, William: Cleeve; *sd.* 1493, *d.* 1494 (Wells; *Reg. R. Fox*, ff. 42, 44)

Cabull: *see* Ilminster.

Cadde/Cade, Robert: Croxden; *ac.* 1501 (Lichfield; *Reg. J. Arundel*, f.294v); signed deed of surrender and *disp.* 1538 (TNA, E314/20/11, ff. 7d–8r; *FOR*, p. 151); pension, £5–6–8 (TNA, E315/233, f.17v).

Cadde, Stephen: abbot (?23ʳᵈ) of Croxden, 1509–1516 (Smith, 2008, p. 286); general pardon, 1509 (*LP* **1**, Part 1, p. 208 [No. 438/1, n.10]. He may well be the monk *Stephen Croxden* noted later. Cadenham: *see* Todenham.

Caldbeck, Robert: Fountains; *d.* 1521 (York); pension, 1539, £5; chaplain of Little Burton in 1554 when aged fifty–three; drew his pension until 1582 when seemingly he died, requested burial in Kirk Hammerton church (Cross and Vickers, 1995, pp. 114–15, 119–20).

Caldecott(e)s, Richard: Newminster; *sd.* 1531 (Durham; *Reg. C. Tunstall,* p. 126 [No. 373]; thirty years old in 1536 (TNA, SC12/13/65); *disp.* 1536 (*FOR,* p. 77).

Caldre, Thomas: curate, Shildon, a church of Dunkeswell, perhaps a monk, *c.*1492 (LPL; *Reg. J. Morton,* f. 120).

Calers, John: Tintern; *p.* 1511 (Worcester; *Reg. S. Gigli,* f. 401).

Calne, *al.* Morley, Thomas: Stanley; *sd., d.* and *p.* 1506 (Salisbury; *Reg. E. Audley,* n–f); last abbot, by 1527–36 (Somerset Archives, DD/WHb/988); pension, £24 (TNA, E315/255, no. 144); bishop of Marlborough, suffragan of Salisbury, consecrated 28 August 1537 (VCH, *Wiltshire* **3**, 1956, p. 274; *LP* **12**, Part 2, p. 354 [No. 1008/34]; Smith, 2008, p. 333).

Calne, Thomas: Stanley; *sd.* 1530, *d.* 1531, *p.* 1532 (Salisbury; *Reg. L. Campeggio*).

Calne, William: Stanley; *p.* 1527 (Salisbury; *Reg. L. Campeggio*).

Cambridge, George: *see* Browne.

Cambrugge/Cambridge, John: Sawtry; *sd.* 1516, *d.* 1517 (Lincoln; *Reg. W. Atwater,* ff. 118v, 123v).

Cambridge, John: Sawtry; *sd.* 1530 (Lincoln; *Reg. J. Longland,* f. 25v).

Cambrygge/Cambridge, Robert: Croxden; *ac.* 1493, *sd.* and *d.* 1495, *p.* 1497 (Lichfield; *Reg. W. Smith, ff.* 171, 183v, 188v; *Reg. J. Arundel,* f. 261).

Cambridge, Thomas: Warden, 1492 (*Letters,* p. 157 [No. 79]).

Camillus ... : sub–prior, Stratford, 1503 (*Letters,* p. 230 [No. 114]).

Camp(e)den, William: Bruern; *sd., d.* and *p.* 1494 (Lincoln; *Reg. J. Russell,* ff. 51v, 52r, 54v).

Cannon, John: Whitland, in receipt of pension, £3, 1556 (TNA, E164/31, f. 75r).

Capron, *al.* Skegby, Thomas: Rufford; *sd.* 1534 (York; *Reg. E. Lee,* ff. 191r, 192r [repeated]). At Rufford on its suppression in 1536, moving then to Rievaulx where his former abbot, Roland Blyton, was now abbot; still a sub–deacon, he signed the deed of surrender and *disp.* 1538; pension, £4 (*DKR,* p. 38; *FOR,* pp. 74, 156). Involved in a family dispute regarding lands in Mansfield after the dissolution (TNA, C1/972/4–6); perhaps buried, 1556/57, Epperstone churchyard, Nottinghamshire, having returned to the county after Rievaulx's closure (Cross and Vickers, 1995, pp. 170, 174).

Carhill, John: Roche; *sd.* 1503, *d.* 1504, *p.* 1505 (York; Cross and Vickers, 1995, p. 186).

Carlelyle/Karliel/Carlile, Robert: Louth Park; *sd.* 1502, *d.* 1503, *p.* 1504 (Lincoln; *Reg. W. Smith,* ff. 35r, 40v, 46v).

Carpenter, Thomas: Waverley; *sd.* and *d.* 1522 (Winchester; *Reg. R. Fox* **4**, f. 72v; **5**, f. 30r); *disp.* 1536 (*FOR,* pp. 67–68). Baskerville, 1941, p. 18, names him as John.

Carr, Christopher: Furness; *p.* 1520 (York; *Reg. T. Wolsey,* f. 189r); signed deed of surrender and *disp.* 1537 (TNA, E322/91; *FOR,* p. 97).

Carr, Hugh: ? Furness; *p.* 1515 (York; *Reg. T. Wolsey,* f. 168r).

Carre, Richard: Furness; *p.* 1520 (York; *Reg. T. Wolsey,* f. 188v).

Carr, William: Calder, 1535–36; accused, perhaps spuriously, of sodomy in Crown visitation of 1535 (*LP* **10**, p. 138 [No. 364]); Loftie, 1888, p. 237; 1892, p. 80; VCH, *Cumberland* **2**, 1968, p. 177).

Carrington, John: Warden; *p.* 1510 (Lincoln; *Reg. W. Smith,* n–f.); either he, or the next mentioned monk, signed deed of surrender, when sub–prior, 1538 (TNA, E314/20/11, f. 1r–d; E314/77), and in receipt of his pension of £6–13–4 as late as 1555 (TNA, E164/31, f. 25v)..

Carynton, John: Warden: *d.* 1530 (Lincoln; *Reg. J. Longland,* f.26v).

Carrington, William: Warden; *d.* 1504 (Lincoln; *Reg. W. Smith*, f.44r); said around 1535 by Abbot Emery to be 'a common drunkard (*LC*, p. 59 [No. XXIX]); signed deed of suppression, when sexton, 1538 (*DKR*, p. 47; TNA, E314/20/11, f. 1r–d); pension, £6–13–4 (TNA, E314/77).

Carter, Laurence: Vaudey; *d.* 1506, *p.* 1507 (Lincoln; *Reg. W. Smith*, n–f.).

Carter, Thomas: short–lived abbot, Holm Cultram, 1536–37; allegedly had immoral relations with three women, 1535/36; alleged in 1537 to have aided the rebels in the northern rising, but died 10 August that year of natural causes (*LP* **10**, p. 138 [No. 364]; **11**, p. 115 [No. 276], Shaw, 1999, pp. 102–03; Smith, 2008, p. 301).

Carter, William: Roche, 1531 (TNA, E135/3/6); *sd.* 1531, *p.* 1533 (York); signed deed of surrender, 1538 (TNA, E322/204); *disp.* 1538 (*FOR*, p. 144); in receipt of £5 pension.as late as 1573 (Cross and Vickers, 1995, pp. 187, 190). Three local clerics held this name after the Suppression.

Cartwright, John: Robertsbridge, 1523 (SAL, *MS 14*, f. 59v); signed deed of surrender, 1536 (*DKR*, p. 45); *disp.* 1536; perhaps the cleric who witnessed wills in the parish of St Clement's, Hastings, between 1552 and 1558; deprived of the rectory of Ore in 1554, as he had married and bore a son, Adam (Salzman, 1954, pp. 35–36).

Caryngton: *see* **Baryngton**.

Carvegh, John: Rewley; *disp.* 1512, but retaining his 'monastic portion and place and voice in choir and chapter' (*CPL* **19**, p. 503 [No. 868]).

Cassom, John: described as a monk of Furness, Staffs! *disp.* 1538 (*FOR*, p. 154).

Castell/Castle, Henry: Newminster, *ac., sd.* and *d.* 1533 (Durham; *Reg. C. Tunstall*, ff. 13, 15–16; published version, pp. 47 [No. 77], 52 [No. 90], 54 [No. 95]); twenty–six years old in 1536 and then a deacon (TNA, SC12/13/65);.*disp.* 1536 (*FOR*, p. 77).

Castell/? Hebden/Shebden, Richard: Fountains, *sd.* and *d.* 1497, *p.* 1502 (York); pension, £6–13–4 (Cross and Vickers, 1995, pp. 112, 115).

Castell, William: Stoneleigh; *sd.* and *d.* 1507, *p.* 1510 (Lichfield; *Reg. G. Blyth*, n–f.).

Castelton, Ranulph/Ralph: *see* Goldsmith.

Castu, Roger: Hailes; *sd.* 1522 (Worcester; *Reg. G. Ghinucci*, f. 182).

Caterwalle/Catterall, Ralph: Whalley, *disp.* 1537 (*FOR*, p. 91); chaplain, Ince in Chester deanery, by 1541 (Haigh, 1969, p. 119).

Catworth, Robert: Sawtry; *sd.* 1512, *d.* 1513 (Lincoln; *Reg. W. Smith*, n–f.).

Caukfed, John: Coggeshall; *sd.* 1494 (London; CL, *Reg. R. Hill*, f. 11r).

?Cawce, George: Furness; *p.* 1486 (York; *Reg. T. Rotherham*, n–f).

Cawod, Thomas: Kirkstall, *sd.*and *d.* 1495, *p.* 1499 (York; Cross and Vickers, 1995, p. 139).

Cawton: *see* **Thirsk**.

Caxton, Roger: Newenham; *ac.* 1491 (Exeter; *Reg. O. King*, f. 159r).

Cercedon/Chercheden/Crecedon, John: Bruern; *ac.* 1497, *sd.* 1498, *d.* and *p.* 1502 (Lincoln; *Reg. W. Smith*, ff. 36r, 38r).

Chadulton/Chadleton, Thomas: Croxden; *sd.* and *d.* 1520, *p.* 1521 (Lichfield; *Reg. G. Blyth*, n–f.)

Chafern, John: monk, ?Bindon; *sd.* 1527 (Salisbury; *Reg. L. Campeggio*).

Chaffcom(be), al. Macy, John: Ford: *sd.* 1511, *d.* 1512, *p.* 1515 (Exeter; *Reg. H. Oldham*, ff. 106v, 109r, 120v); abbot, Bruern; 1527–1533, for gaining the abbacy he gave Cardinal Wolsey 250 marks and 280 of the monastery's finest oaks for building Cardinal's College in Oxford (Baskerville, 1937. Pp. 63, 106]; temporarily evicted by rioters, 1529 (*LP* **4**, Part 3, p. 2363 [No. 5373]; deposed, 1533, when given a pension of £13–6–8 (*VE*, **2**, p. 204); seems to have remained at the abbey until at its suppression, 1536 (Baskerville, 1930, p. 334); living at Hook Norton, Oxfordshire, in 1548, may have been vicar of Weston by Bath, Somerset, dying in 1555/56 (Smith, 2008, p. 272).

Chalner, Hugh: Vale Royal; *sd.* 1521, *d.* 1522, *p.* 1523 (Lichfield; *Reg. G. Blyth*, n–f.); committed suicide in 1536 by stabbing himself in the refectory, although blame was attached to the abbot (Gasquet, 1899, p. 343).

Chalner, Thomas: Croxden; professed *c.*1509 (Laurence, 1952, B.17); *sd.* ?1519 (Lichfield, R.O., *Reg. G. Blythe*, n.f.); last abbot, Croxden, blessed as abbot at Beaudesert by the bishop of Lichfield 21 May 1531 (*Reg. G. Blyth*, f.31r); was a student at St Bernard's College, Oxford, 1529, and owned a copy of R. Holcot, *super iv libros Sententiarum* (*BRUO* **2**, 1974, p. 109); re–appointed abbot on continuance of the monastery, 2 July 1537 (*LP* **12**, Part 2, p. 165 [No. 411/2]); signed deed of surrender and disp. 1538 (TNA, E314/20/11, ff. 7d–8r; *FOR*, p. 151; Smith, 2008, p. 286); pension, £26–13–4 (TNA, E315/233, f. 17r).

Chalner/Chawner, William: Hulton, brother of the later abbot of Croxden; *sd.* and *d.* 1510, *p.* 1511 (Lichfield; *Reg. G. Blyth*, n–f); a division of opinion as to his character prevented him gaining the abbacy of Hulton in 1534 (VCH. *Staffordshire* **2**, 1967, p. 236); alleged that he forged the foundation charter of Hulton to benefit a lay owner after the dissolution (Tomkinson, 1994, pp. 77–81); signed deed of surrender and *disp.* 1538 (*DKR*, p. 24; *FOR*, p. 151); pension, £4 (TNA, E315/233, f.22v).

Chamber(s), Robert: abbot, Holm Cultram, 1502–1527 (TNA, L1/173, f. 135); mitred, with right to confer the four minor orders, 1508 (*CPL* **19**, p. 57 [No. 98]); Cumbria R.O. PR/122/199 has him as dying *c.* 1519, this is incorrect and so may be the assertion that he was abbot for thirty years (Smith, 2008, 300).

Chambre/Chambers, Thomas: abbot, Furness, 1491–1497, when dies (York; *Reg. T. Rotherham*, p. 235 [No. 1853]; *Letters*, p. 200 [No. 99]; Smith, 2008, p. 295); on 3–09–1491, Archbishop of Rotherham of York issued a commission to the bishops of Carlisle, Sodor and St Asaph to receive Chambers' profession of obedience (*AF*, p. 299).

Chao/Choo, William, 'senior', Hailes, *disp.* 1540 (*FOR*, p. 208); pension, £6 (Baskerville, 1927, p. 89).

Chaptor: *see* Shaptor.

Chard, *al.* Tybbes, Thomas: probably born in Chard, Somerset; monk, Buckfast, student at St Bernard's College, Oxford, possibly provisor *c.*1503; B.D. *c*1504, B. Can. Law, 1506; D.Th. 1507 (*BRUO* **1**, p. 389), then described as 'a man of great learning and pure virtue.' In 1506 had sought leave of General Chapter to study for his doctorate at Oxford (*Statuta* **6**, p. 325 [No. 1506/16]); last abbot, Ford, 1505 to 1539 (Smith, 2008, pp. 291, 319); 1516, became a commissary for the Order in south and south–west England; built the abbey's new refectory and cloister; signed abbey's surrender on 8 March 1539, vicar of Thorncombe, Devon, until his death in 1544 (Pring, 1889, pp. 199–211; Lyte, 1928, p. 59; Stevenson, 1939, pp. 29, 43); pension: £80 and forty wainloads of firewood (Youings, 1971, p. 186). Could he be the Thomas Ford ordained in 1497, *q.v*?

Charles/Sharle/Scharyll, Francis: Dieulacres; *ac.* 1509; *d.* and *p.* 1510 (Lichfield; *Reg. G. Blyth*, n–f.).

Charlton/Chilton, Robert de: abbot, Newminster, by 1484–1499 (Smith, 2008, p. 318).

Chatborne, William: last bursar, Whalley, *disp.* 1537 (*FOR*, p. 91).

Chawerd/Chaverd, Richard: St Mary Graces; *ex.* and *ac.* 1528 (London; *Reg. C. Tunstall*, f. 160v).

Chedworth, Richard: Kingswood; *d.* 1503 (Wells; *Reg. O. King*, f. 122).

Checkley, John: see Walton.

Checkerley, *al.* Rolleston: Merevale, 1497 (TNA, E315/283, f.1).

Chekley, Richard: Croxden; *ac.* 1530, *sd.* 1531 (Lichfield; *Reg. G. Blyth*, n–f.).

Chelt(e)nham, Reginald: Hailes; *sd.* and *d.* 1527 (Worcester; *Reg. R. Morton addenda*, f. 165); succentor, 1537/38 (*CHA*, p. 85).

Chepenham: *see* Chippenham. William.

Cheryngton/Seerington/Sheryngton, Robert: Dieulacres, *ac.* 1528, *sd.* 1529, *d.* 1531 (Lichfield; *Reg. G. Blyth*, n–f.); *disp.* 1538; 'reward', £2–0–0 (Walcott, 1871, p. 216); pension, £5–6–8 (Hibbert, 1910, pp. 239, 242; *FOR*, p. 160.

Chester, ?Benedict: Vale Royal; *p.* 1493 (York; *Reg. T. Rotherham*, n–f.).

Chester, Edmund: Dieulacres; *sd.* and *d.* 1507, *p.* 1508 – when named Edward (Lichfield; *Reg. G. Blyth*, n–f.).

Chester, Humphrey: Combermere; *sd.* 1525, *d.* and *p.* 1526 (Lichfield; *Reg. G. Blyth*, n–f.); a bibliophile and to be equated with the monk, *Humphrey Lightfoot*, present at the suppression (VCH, *Cheshire* 3, 1980, p. 154), *q.v.* A keen reader of Scripture, he suffered from a fever in June 1531, and had an adversary in the community, 1532 (Aveling, 1967, pp. 146 [No. 96], 187–88 [No. 121], 240–41 [No. 163]).

Chester, John: Biddlesden: *p.* 1485 (Lincoln; *Reg. J. Russell*, f. 18v).

Chester, John: Dieulacres; *ac.* 1489 (perhaps 1487 more correctly), *p.* 1489 (Lichfield; *Reg. J. Hales*, ff. 243v, 245v).

Chester, John: Whalley; *p.* 1516 (*Reg. G. Blyth*, n–f.); *disp.* 1537 (*FOR*, p. 110); one source names him as the last bursar; stipendiary priest, Leyland, Lancs., 1541 (Haigh, 1966, pp. 119, 247).

Chester, John: Boxley; *sd.* and *d.* 1520 (Rochester; *Reg. J. Fisher*, f. 89v).

Chester, John: Vale Royal; *ac.* and *sd.* 1521, *d.* 1522, *p.* 1523 (Lichfield; *Reg. G. Blyth*, n–f.).

Chester, John: Sawley, *disp.* 1536 (*FOR*, p. 58); a cleric of this name was a chantry priest in Nottingham in 1548 (Cross, 1995, p. 203).

Chester, Richard: Cwmhir, *c.*1530 (*Early Chancery Proceedings Concerning Wales*, ed. E. A. Lewis; Cardiff: University of Wales Press, 1937, p. 273).

Chester, Thomas: Woburn; *ac.* 1485, *d.* 1487, *p.* 1489 (Lincoln; *Reg. J. Russell*, ff. 18v, 26v, 33r).

Chester, Thomas: Pipewell; signed deed of surrender and *disp.* 1538 (*DKR*, p. 37; *FOR*, p. 160); pension, £5–6–8 (TNA, SC6/HENVIII/7339); by 1554 had married a woman and was curate of Loddington [Leicestershire/Northamptonshire – two villages of this name]; living at East Norton, Leicestershire. in 1573 (Hodgett, 1959, pp. 85, 144); in receipt of pension as late as 1555 (TNA, E164/31, f.43r).

Chester, William: Combermere: *sd.* ?1487 and *p.* 1487 (Lichfield; *Reg. J. Hales*, ff. 225, 243v: there is a dating error on the last folio).

Chester, William: Dieulacres; *ac.* and *sd.* 1527, *d.* 1528, *p.* 1529 (Lichfield; *Reg. G. Blyth*, n–f.).

Chicheley, John: Tilty, signed deed of surrender and *disp.* 1536 (*DKR*, p. 45, *FOR*, p. 60).

Chichester, Thomas: Stratford; *ac.* and *sd.* 1492; monk, St Mary Graces; *d.* 1493, *p.* 1496 (London; *Reg. R. Hill*, ff. 25r, 26r, 27r, 31r).

Chilton, John: Bruern; *ac.* 1497, *sd.* 1498 (Lincoln; *Reg. W. Smith*, n. f).

Chilton: *see also* Charlton.

Chinnor, Richard: Thame; *d.* 1509, *p.* 1512 (Lincoln; *Reg. W. Smith*, n–f.); indicted at the Oxford Assizes *c.*1525, and rebuked at Thame's 1526 visitation (Baskerville, 1937, p. 91).

Chippenham, William: Stanley; *sd.* and *d.* 1521 (Salisbury; *Reg. E. Audley*, f.[45r]).

Chirk, John: Basingwerk; *p.* 1486 (Lichfield; *Reg. J. Hales*, f. 217v).

Chomundeley, Ranulph: Dieulacres; *ac.* and *sd.* 1527, *d.* 1528, *p.* 1529 (Lichfield; *Reg. G. Blyth*, n–f.).

Chorley, Robert: former abbot, Woburn; abbot of Loos, France, told how he was in a state of destitution and sought a pension for him; his pension and free movement confirmed by the abbot of Cîteaux and the General Chapter, 1491 (*Letters*, pp. 113–14 [No. 52], 145–46 [No. 72]; *Statuta* 5, pp. 22–23 [No. 1491/53]).

Christall, Robert: *see* **Shakilton.**

Christlo/Chrstelo, Marmaduke: *see* **Ampleforth.**

Christalowe: *see* Ampleforth.

Chrystylton: *see* Crystylton.

Chubbe, John: Stratford; *sd.* 1527 (London; *Reg. C. Tunstall,* f. 160v).

Church, Augustine: abbot, Thame, 1472 until at least 1495; titular bishop of Lydda, suffragan of Lincoln, 1488–1512; also acted in the dioceses of Exeter and Salisbury; instituted to the churches of Boscombe, diocese Bath and Wells, (1497) and Washingborough, Lincolnshire (1509) (Smith, 1982, p. 26; 2008, p. 339).

Churchman, John: Combe; *sd.* and *d.* 1494; *p.* 1495 (Lichfield; *Reg. W. Smith,* ff. 178v, 181, 187).

?Chyldersley, James: Revesby; signed deed of surrender, March 1538 (Essex R.O., D/DRg 1/104). Could he be *John Clerke* infra?

Chydyngfold, Robert: Waverley; *d.* and *p.* 1497 (Winchester; *Reg. T. Langton,* ff. 30v, 31v).

Clacton, William: abbot, Waverley, 1509–? at least 1523 (Smith, 2008, p. 348); pardoned for unspecified offences, 1532 (West Sussex R.O. SAS–BA/12); perhaps an error for 1522.

Claghton/Clayton, Henry: Sawley, *disp.* 1536 (*FOR,* p. 58); perhaps transferring to Kirkstall on Sawley's closure, where pension, 1539, £2, suggests he was not yet a priest (Cross and Vickers, 1995, pp. 139); in receipt of pension in 1555 (TNA, E164/31, f. 53v). Possibly vicar of Rokeby, Yorkshire, 1543–1554.

Clapham, John: abbot, Meaux, 1488–at least 1509; blessed by the bishop of Dromore, 4 September 1488 (York; *Reg. T. Rotherham,* p. 137 [Nos. 1137–38]; Smith, 2008, pp. 312–13.

Clapham, John: Furness, and kinsman of Abbot Alexander Banks; made procurator there, by 1517 (*Letters,* p. 249 [No. 129]); in community, 1521 (*DCL,* p. 96).

Clapeham, John: abbot, Calder, 1488–1525 (VCH, *Cumberland* 2, 1968, p. 178; Smith, 2008, p. 278); profession of obedience before the bishop of Dromore, 4–09–1488 (York; *Reg. T. Rotherham*).

?Clappe, Richard: Revesby; signed deed of surrender, March 1538 (Essex R.O., D/DRg 1/104).

Clarebrough, John: abbot, Garendon, 1487 (Smith, 2008, p. 296).

Clark: *see* Clerk.

Claypole: *see* Cleypole.

Cliderowe, Elias/Helias: Combermere; *sd.* ?1487 and *p.* 1487 (Lichfield; *Reg. J. Hales,* ff. 225, 243v: there is a dating error on the last folio).

Clederow/Clitherow, Richard: Sawley, *d.* 1486, *p.* 1490 (York; Cross and Vickers, 1995, p. 199).

Clyderow, Richard: Sawley; *sd.* 1504, *d.* 1505, *p.* 1506 (York; Cross and Vickers, 1995, p. 199); *disp.* 1536 (*FOR,* p. 58).

Cliderow, Robert: Hailes; *sd.* 1501, *d.* 1503 (Worcester; *Reg. S. Gigli,* ff. 402–03).

Clederow, William: Hailes; *ac.* 1516, *sd.* 1517 (Worcester; *Reg. S. Gigli,* ff. 331, 333).

Cleeve/Clyve/Cliffe, Hugh: Cleeve; *sd.* 1509 (Wells; *Reg. H. de Castello,* f. 150); *d.* 1510, *p.* 1511 (Exeter; *Reg. H. Oldham,* ff. 103r, 105r).

Cleeve, Richard: Cleeve; *ac.* and *sd.* 1475; *d.* 1480 (Wells; *Reg. R. Stillington,* ff.192, 206v).

Clement, Robert: Holm Cultram, in house,10–08–1536 (*LP* 11, p. 115 [No. 276]); signed deed of surrender and *disp.* 1538 (*DKR,* p. 23; *FOR,* pp. 123–24). In receipt of his pension of £2–10–0 in 1555 (TNA, E164/31, f. 73v; £5 in TNA, LR1/173, f. 147).

Clerk, Anthony: Stratford; *sd.* 1527, *d.* 1528 (London; *Reg. C. Tunstall,* ff. 160v, 161r); *p.* 1532 (London; *Reg. R. Stokesley,* f. 128v); at St Bernard's College, 1534–37; B.Th. Oxon. 1537, after seven years study at Oxford and elsewhere (*BRUO* 2, vol. 1, p. 118); signed deed of surrender and *disp.* 1538 (*DKR,* p. 42; *FOR,* p. 129); canon of Chichester, prebendary of Highleigh and headmaster of Chichester Grammar School, 1541 to not later than 1550; vicar of Oving, Sussex, 1547–55. In receipt of £8 pension in 1555 (TNA, E164/31, f. 9v); prebendary of Firles in Chichester diocese; vicar of

Cowfold, Suxssex, 1552, vicar of East Dean, Sussex, 1555, deprived in 1560 for refusing to take the oath of supremacy, but then became chaplain to Lord Montague at Cowdray who preferred the old ways of worship (Baskerville, 1937, pp. 268–69.).

Clerk/Clark, Edward: Vaudey; *sd.* 1524, *d.* and *p.* 1525 (Lincoln; *Reg. J. Longland*, ff. 10v, 11r, 12r); *disp.* 1536 (*FOR*, p. 67); said by Cromwell in 1533 to have 'greatly misordered himself' (*LP* **6**, p. 348 [No. 778].

Clerk, Henry: abbot, Cleeve, 1501 (TNA, C1/907/56–59; Smith, 2008, p. 279).

Clerk/Clark, John: Revesby, *sd.* 1528, *d.* 1529, *p.* 1531 (Lincoln; *Reg. J. Longland*, ff. 21r, 24r, 28r); disp. 1538 (*FOR*, p. 128).

Clerke/Braintree, Richard: Coggeshall; *sd.* 1522 (LPL,: *Reg. W. Warham* **2**, f. 298v); aged thirty–one in 1536 (*LP* **10**, pp. 59–60 [No. 164/ii].

Clerke, Robert: Calder; *d.* 1529 (York; *Reg. T. Wolsey*, f. 215v).

Clerk/Clarke, Robert: Croxden, signed deed of surrender and *disp.* 1538 (TNA, E314/20/11, ff. 7d–8r; *FOR*, p. 151); pension, £5–6–8 (TNA, E315/233, f.17r.)

Clerk, Thomas: Combe; disp. 1539 (*FOR*, p. 176); pension of £5–6–8 received as late as 1555 (TNA, E164/31, f. 48v).

Clarke, William: Vale Royal; signed deed of surrender, 1538 (*DKR*, p. 46); in receipt of his £5 pension in 1555 (TNA, E164/31, f. 69r).

Clarke: *see also* Skipsee.

Clerkenwell, John: abbot,, Stoneleigh, by 1490–1499 (Smith, 2008, p. 334; SSC, DR 10/996–97, DR18/3/52/37a, suggest a longer reign).

Clerkeson, Christopher: Dieulacres; *ac., sd. and d.* 1486, *p.* 1487 (Lichfield: *Reg. J. Hales*, ff. 216v, 217n, 219, 223v).

Clerkson, William: Fountains, *sd.* 1494 (York; Cross and Vickers, 1995, p. 112).

Cleubery, Thomas: Dore, son probably of Thomas Cleubery (*d.* 1479/80) of Cleubery Mortimer,Shropshire (*CPA*, p. 87); *p.* by 1511; abbot, 1516–23, when forced to resign; granted a residential corrody in 1526; assessed in 1540 for subsidy on his pension of £6–13–4 (Bodleian Library, Oxford, Tanner MS 343); a bibliophile, he resided in Hereford after the suppression and was still alive, aged seventy–one, in 1554; he was the collator of at least two composite works (See Chapter 2); There is no mention of him in the Dore entry of Cardinal Pole's pension list of 1555 (TNA, E164/31, f.45v).

Cleve(d)land, John: *see* **Jervaulx.**

Cley: *see* Henley:

Cleypoole/Claypole, Andrew: Thame; *sd.* and *d.* 1505, *p.* 1506 (Lincoln; *Reg. W. Smith*, n.f.).

Cleysland, Simon: Jervaulx, *disp.* 1537 (*FOR*, p. 119); may have been the chantry priest of St Lawrence's altar in Busby chapel in Stokesley parish, Yorkshire, who was aged seventy in 1548 (Cross and Vickers, 1995, p. 133).

Clifton/Clyston, John: Warden; *ac.* 1485, *d.* and *p.* 1487 (Lincoln; *Reg. J. Russell*, ff. 17v, 23r, 26v); at a visitation in 1492 he alleged that the rule of silence was not well kept (*Letters*, p. 158 [No. 79]; abbot [John V], Sibton, 1505–1520 (*SBC* **4**, pp. 68 [No. 1121], 93 [No. 1157]); 1509, general pardon (*LP* **1**, Part 1, p. 209 [No. 438/1, m.12].

Clifton, John: Warden; *sd.* and *d.* 1518, *p.* 1520 (Lincoln; *Reg. W. Atwater*, ,ff.125r, 127r, 134r). He was described about 1535 by Abbot Emery as being 'a common drunkard;' still a monk there at its suppression in 1538 (*DKR*, p. 47); pension, £5–6–8 (TNA, E314/77).

Clifton/?Norton, Robert: Fountains; pension, 1539: £6; if Norton, then *sd.* 1501, *d.* 1502 (Cross and Vickers, 1995, pp. 115, 120).

Clifton, Thomas: Pipewell; *p.* 1535 (Lincoln; *Reg. J. Longland,* f. 43r). Might he be the monk, *Thomas Chester* or *Thomas Hadley*? q.v.

Clifton, William: Fountains, *sd.* 1499, *p.* 1501 (York; Cross and Vickers, 1995, p. 112).

Clopton, Henry: Warden, *ac.* 1485, *sd.* 1487, *d.* 1490 (Lincoln; *Reg. J. Russell,* ff. 17v, 23r, 34r); asserted at a visitation in 1492 that its monks wore linen garments (*Letters,* pp. 157–58 [No. 79]); abbot, Sawtry, by 1524–*c.*1527; granted a pension of £6 p.a. on his cessation as abbot (*LP* **10**, p. 499 [No. 1191/4]); still alive in *c.*1536. A jubilarian..

Clughe/Clough, Henry: Kirkstall; *sd.* 1501, *d.* 1502, *p.* 1504 (York); pension, 1539, £6–13–4 (Cross and Vickers, 1995, pp. 142, 144).

Clugh, Thomas: Kirkstall, *sd.* 1501, *d.* 1502, *p.* 1504 (York; Cross and Vickers, 1995, p. 140).

Clyderowe, John: Croxden; *disp.*1500 (*CPL,* **17,** Part 1, p. 303 [No. 468]).

Clydero, Henry: Whalley, *disp.* 1537 (*FOR,* p. 91).

Clyft/Clys/Cliffe, Henry: Buckfast; *ac.* 1530, *sd.* 1533 (Exeter; *Reg. J. Vesey,* ff. 172v, 181v). Clyston, John: *see* Clifton. Clyve: *see* Cleeve.

Cobbys/Cobbe: *see* Coke.

Cock, Richard: Netley, *disp.* 1496 (*CPL* **16,** p. 334 [No. 488]).

Cockerell, George: Coggeshall, *disp.* 1538 (*FOR,* 124); pension, £5 p.a. (TNA, SC12/7/34). May he be the same monk as *George Cambridge.*

?Coditrave, William: Swineshead; *p.* 1523 (Lincoln; *Reg. J. Longland,* f.6v). Could he be William Cotgham, *q.v.?*

Coffe/Case/Cofe/Cogg, John: Buckfast; *ac.* and *sd.* 1517, *d.* 1518, *p.* 1521 (Exeter; *Reg. H. Oldham,* ff. 127v, 128r, 130r, *Reg. J. Vesey,* f.144v). Could he be the *John Doyge* noted later?

Cogan, Robert: last prior, Newenham; *sd.* 1492 (Wells – in the collegiate church of Ottery St Mary; *Reg. J. Morton* **2,** p. 86 [No. 323]); *d.* 1493 (Exeter; *Reg. O. King,* f.173r); *disp.* 1540 (*FOR,* p.216); pension, £6–13–4 (*LP* 14, Part 1, p. 184 [No. 469]).

Coggeshall/Coxall, John: Coggeshall; *sd.* 1510, *d.* 1515 (London; *Reg. R. Fitzjames,* ff.160r [171r], 169r [180r]).

Coggeshall, John: Coggeshall; *sd.* 1522, *d.* 1523 (Canterbury; *Reg. W. Warham, London sede–v.,* **2,** f. 298v, *Reg. C. Tunstall,* f. 153r). Either he, or the above named monk, was the *John Coxall, al. Roydon, disp.* 1538 (*FOR,* p. 124).

Coke, John: *ac.* 1470 (house not stated; Hereford; *Reg. J. Stanbury,* p. 165); monk, Margam; *p.* 1471 (Wells; *Reg. R. Stillington,* f.185v). If the same monk, then from 1479 to 1491 an influential but somewhat disliked confidant of the abbot of Woburn, a reformator of the Order in England; latterly he may have been a monk of Cîteaux and was described as 'a zealot of the Order'; his origin may have lain in Ireland (*Letters,* 63–64, 73, 79–80, 86, 89, 94, 112–13, 140–41).

Coke/Cobbys, Thomas: Stratford; *ac.* 1495, *sd.* 1498 (London; *Reg. T. Savage,* f. 57r; *Reg. R.Hill,* f. 32v).

Coke, John: Jervaulx; *d.* 1510 (York; Cross and Vickers, 1995, p. 130).

Coke/Cocks/Cobbe, Thomas: Rewley; *sd.* 1508 (Salisbury; *Reg. E. Audley,* f. 9v, *d.* 1509 (Lincoln; *Reg. W. Smith* ,n.f.); *p.* 1512 (Salisbury; *Reg. E. Audley,* f. 15v).

Cokerham, John: Cleeve; *sd.* and *d.* 1487, *p.* 1488 (Wells; *Reg. R. Stillington,* ff. 223–24, 226).

Cokermouth, Robert: Kirkstead; *d.* 1523, *p.* 1527 (Lincoln; *Reg. J. Longland,* ff. 7v, 19v).

Cokse(e)/ Cokesy, John: Combermere, *disp.* 1538 (TNA, E314/20/11, f. 10v; *FOR,* p. 154); in receipt of pension of £5 as late as 1555 (TNA, E164/31, f. 69r).

Coles, James: *see* **Schalster.**..

Cole/Cowle/Coole, John: Buckfast; *ac.* and *sd.* 1517, *d.* 1518, *p.* 1521 (Exeter; *Reg. H. Oldham*, ff. 127v, 128r, 130r; *Reg. J. Vesey*, f. 144v); a monk there still in 1539 (*DKR*, p. 11); pension, £6 ; seemingly chaplain or vicar of Tedburn, Devon, 1540/41 (Stéphan, 1970, p. 213).

Colles/Collys/Colas, *al.* Toller, Nicholas: Roche; *d.* 1509 (York; Cross and Vickers, 1995, p. 187, 190). signed deed of fraternity, 1531 (TNA, E135/3/6) and of surrender, 1538 (*DKR*, p. 39); *disp.* 1538 (*FOR*, p. 144) in receipt of £5 pension as late as 1555 (TNA, E164/31, f. 53r); until 1548 probably a chantry priest at Tickhill, Yorkshire.

Collet, Geoffrey [Geoffrey II]: abbot, Sibton; 1482–1505 (*SBC*, pp. 63 [No. 1116], 70 [No. 1124]; *Close*, 1506, p. 246 [No. 647/vii]; Norwich R.O., *Reg. James Goldwell*, f. 245r).

Collys, Meoland/Maelar: Roche, 1531 (TNA, E135/3/6); signed deed of surrender, 1538 (TNA, E322/204).

Collis, William: prior, Bordesley, 1486/87 (TNA, E328/146/2[18].

Colopp, John: Tilty; *sd.* 1520, *d.* and *p.* 1521 (London; *Reg. R. Fitzjames*, ff. 181r [192r], 182v [193v], 183v [194v]).

Colston, Thomas: cellarer, Tintern, 1459; abbot, 1460–86, indult of plenary indulgence, 1469; dead by 1487 (*Patent*, 1462, p. 229; *CPL* 12, p. 703; Williams, 1976, p. 109).

Colynton, Hugh: Tintern; *d.* 1524, *p.* 1525 (Hereford; *Reg. C. Bothe*, pp. 317, 319).

Combe, John: Kingswood; *ac., sd.* and *d.* 1492 (Worcester; *Reg. R. Morton*, pp. 152, 154).

Combe, John: Dunkeswell, *sd.* 1509, *d.* 1510, *p.* 1511 (Exeter; *Reg. H. Oldham*, ff. 99r, 103r, 105r).

Combe, Robert: Stanley; *sd.* and *d.* 1496, *p.* 1497 (Salisbury; *Reg. J. Blyth*, ff. 108v, 109v).

Combe, Robert: provisor, St Bernard's College, Oxford, 1533 (Smith, 2008, p. 319; *BRUO* **2**, p. 157).

Combe, William: Combe; *sd.* 1485 (Lichfield; *Reg. J. Hales*, f. 211).

Combermere, Robert: Combermere; *ac.* 1493 (Lichfield; *Reg. W. Smith*, f. 171). [This, and the next name, may mask a monk with an different family name].

Combermere, Thomas: Combermere; *d.* and *p.* 1512 (Lichfield; *Reg. G. Blyth*, n–f.).

Compyn/Company, William: Newenham; *ac.* 1516, *sd.* and *d.* 1517 (Exeter; *Reg. H. Oldham*, ff. 125r–v, 126v); *p.* 1519 (Canterbury; LPL, *Reg. W. Warham* **2**, f. 274v).

?Condler, Nicholas: Rewley; *p.* 1521 (Lincoln; *Reg. J. Longland*, f. 1v).

Consburgh, Nicholas: Roche; *p.* 1481 (York; Cross and Vickers, 1995, p. 186).

Constable, Thomas: Boxley; *sd.* 1517, *d.* 1518 (Rochester; *Reg. J. Fisher*, ff. 57v, 59v).

Conway/Cannon, John: Whitland; pension, £3 p.a., 1539; *disp.* 1540, alive in 1553 (*FOR*, p. 206, TNA, E315/233/258); in receipt of his pension in 1555 (TNA, E164/31, f. 75r).

Conysby, Robert: Stanley; *ac.* 1459 (Worcester; *Reg. J. Carpenter*, f. 548).

Conyngston, Simon: Meaux; *sd.* 1453 (York; *Reg. W. Booth*, f. 418r.)

Cooke, William: Dunkeswell; *sd.* 1522 (Exeter; *Reg. J. Vesey*, f.149r).

Cooper, Richard: *see* Cowper.

Cooper/Cowper/Copar, Robert: Robertsbridge, signed deed of surrender and *disp.* 1538 (*DKR*, p. 39; *FOR*, p. 135); still alive in 1555 with pension of £4 (Salzman, 1954, p. 34; TNA, E164/31, f.25v).

Copeland, William: Calder; *p.* 1507 (York; *Reg. T. Savage*, f. 140r).

Corbet, Antony: Buildwas; *ac.* 1520, *sd.* 1522, *d.* and *p.* 1523 (Lichfield; *Reg. G. Blyth*, n–f.).

Cordell: *see* London.

Cordon, Richard: Dieulacres, *disp.* 1538; 'reward' £2 (Walcott, 1871, p. 216); pension, £2 (Hibbert, 1910, pp. 239, 242; *FOR*, p. 160).

Corne/Cory, John: Netley; *sd.* and *d.* 1496, *p.* 1497 (Winchester; *Reg. T. Langton*, ff. 27v, 30r, 31v); prior when elected abbot; 11–11–1509 (Baigent, 1883, p. 196); blessed as abbot 22 December 1509 in Esher manor chapel by the bishop of Winchester (*Reg. R. Fox*, ff. 25v–26r); still abbot in 1523 (Smith, 2008, p. 316).

Corntown, William: abbot, Margam, 1468–87 (Birch, 1897, p. 376).

Cornwall *al.* Burton, Robert: Kirkstead; about 1460 left the Order and later became vicar of Broughton by Kettering, Northmaptonshire (*CPL* **15**, pp. 358–59; his holding of the church was challenged in 1492 (*CPL* **16**, pp. 5–6).

Cory/Coty, John: Ford; *sd.* 1504 (Canterbury; *Reg. W. Warham, Exeter sede v.*, f. 208r); *d.* 1505 (Exeter; *Reg H. Oldham*, f. 84r); *p.* 1507 (Wells; *Reg. H. de Castello*, f. 146).

Coscomb, Roger: Hailes, 1517, when a scholar at Oxford (Bell, 2010, pp. 346–47).

Cosgrave/Codgrave, Richard: Garendon; *sd.* 1512, *d.*1513 (Lincoln; *Reg. W. Smith*, n–f.).

Cosyn(s), John: Ford, 1539; pension, 1539, £6–13–4 (*DKR*, p. 21; Youings, 1971, p. 186).

Cotgham, William: Swineshead, *disp.* 1536 (*FOR*, p. 67).

Coth/Clolp, John: Revesby; *ac.* 1487, *sd.* and *d.* 1488, *p.* 1489 (Lincoln; *Reg. J. Russell*, ff. 24r, 28r, 28v, 31v).

Cottingham, William: Meaux; *sd.* 1493, *d.* 1495, *p.* 1496 (York; Cross and Vickers, 1995, p. 154). Did he transfer to Swineshead?, see *William* Cotgham.

Cottman, Richard: Quarr; *d.* 1495 (Winchester; *Reg. T. Langton*, f. 26r).

Cotton/Coton/Cooton John: Stoneleigh; *d.* 1514, *p.* 1517 (Lichfield; *Reg. G. Blyth*, n–f.); *disp.* 1537 (*FOR*, p. 88).

Coty: *see* Cory.

Cotyngham/Cottingham, Robert: Kirkstead; *sd.* 1524, *d.* 1526, *p.* 1528 (Lincoln; *Reg. J. Longland*, ff. 9r, 13v, 21v).

Cotyngham/Downey, Vincent: Meaux; *sd.* 1531, *d.* 1533, *p.* 1535 (York); pension, £5; fifty years old in 1552, still alive in 1564; it is possible that in 1559 he was curate of Sutton, Yorkshire (Cross and Vickers, 1995, pp. 155–56, 159).

Coventry, John: Pipewell; *sd.* and *d.* 1508, *p.* 1512 (Lincoln; *Reg. W. Smith*, n–f.).

Coventry, John: Garendon; *sd.* 1515, *d.* 1518, *p.* 1520 (Lincoln; *Reg. W. Atwater*, ff. 117r, 126v, 132r); in house 15–03–1536 (*LP* **10**, p. 194 [No. 475]); *disp.* 1536 (*FOR*, p. 76).

Coventry, John: Combe; *d.* June, 1536 (Lincoln; *Reg. J. Longland*, f. 52v). Not listed in the pension list (TNA, E314/77).

Coventry, Richard: Bruern; *sd.* 1494 (Lincoln; *Reg. J. Russell*, f. 51v).

Coventry, Richard: Hailes; *sd.* 1504 (Worcester; *Reg. S. Gigli*, f. 289).

Coventry/Symyng, Richard: Combe; *sd.* and *d.* 1500 (Lichfield; *Reg. J. Arundel*, ff. 288–89); *p.* 1503 (Canterbury, *Lichfield, sede v.*, CCA–~DCc–Reg. f.287); sub–prior, 1538, if not the undermentioned monk (*DKR*, pp. 16–17); pension, £6 (TNA, E314/77).

Coventry, Richard: Combe; *sd.*, *d.* and *p.* 1517 (Lichfield; *Reg. G.Blyth*, n–f.).

Coventry, Roger: Merevale; *ac.* 1506; *sd.* 1507, *d.* 1508, *p.* 1510 (Lichfield; *Reg. G. Blyth*, n–f.).

Coventry, Roger: St Mary Graces, 1533 (Grainger and Phillpotts, 2011, p. 93).

Coventry, Thomas: Stoneleigh; *sd.* and *d.* 1485, *p.* 1486 (Lichfield; *Reg. J. Hales*, ff. 212v, 214, 216v).

Coventry, William: Stoneleigh; *sd.* and *d.* 1485, *p.* 1488 (Lichfield; *Reg. J. Hales*, ff. 212v, 214, 240v).

Coventry, William: Combe; *p.* 1494 (Lichfield; *Reg. W. Smith*, f. 180v).

Coventry, William: Pipewell; *sd.* 1529, *d.* 1531, *p.* 1532 (Lincoln; *Reg. J. Longland*, ff. 23r, 28v, 31v).

Coventry, William: Beaulieu, *disp.* 1538, pension, £6 p.a. (TNA, E314/20/11, f. 1d–2r; *FOR*, p. 131).

Cowin, John: Warden; *sd.* 1510 (Lincoln; *Reg. W. Smith*, n–f.).

Cowle: see Cole.

Cowper, Richard: Netley; *sd.* 1489 (Winchester; *Reg. P. Courtenay,* f. 14v); in community, 1518, by which time priested (TNA, E314/101); sub–prior, 1536; *disp.* 1536 (*FOR,* p. 66).

Cowper, Robert: Robertsbridge; pension of £4 still received in 1555 (Ray, 1931, p. 144).

Cowper, Thomas: Buildwas; *sd.* 1511; *d.* and *p.* 1512 (Lichfield; *Reg. G. Blyth,* n–f.).

Cowper, William: abbot, Coggeshall, 1506 (Smith, 2008, p. 280).

Cowpar, William: prior, Stratford, 1513 (London; *Reg. R. Fitzjames,* f. 165v [175v]).

Cowper: *see also* Kirkby.

Coxall: *see* Coggeshall.

Craddok/Cradocke Richard: Hulton; *ac.* and *d.* 1517, *p.* 1521 (Lichfield; *Reg. G. Blyth,* n–f.); said to be one of the 'wisest priests' of the house', 1534 (VCH, Staffordshire **2**, 1967, p. 236); signed deed of surrender and *disp.* 1538 (TNA, E322/106; *FOR,* p. 154); pension, £4 (TNA, E315/233, f. 23r).

Crambroke, John: Boxley; *p.* 1506 (Canterbury; *Reg. W. Warham 2, f.* 262v); abbot, ?1509–1511 and later (Smith, 2008, p. 271).

Cramer/Cramar, Richard: Buildwas; *ac.* and *sd.* 1518, *d.* and *p.* 1519 (Lichfield; *Reg. G. Blyth,* n–f.); *disp.* 1537 (*FOR,* p. 92).

Crane, John: Coggeshall; *sd.* 1505, *d.* 1506, *p.* 1507 (London; *Reg. R. Fitzjames,* ff. 91r, 95r, 95v); sacristan, 1522 (London; *Reg. C. Tunstall,* f. 152r); *disp.* 1538 (*FOR,* p. 124).

Crawne/Craham, Robert: Meaux; *ac.* 1517, *sd.* 1518, *d.* 1519 (York; Cross and Vickers, 1995, p. 154).

Craythorne, Robert: Stratford; *sd.* 1492, *d.* 1493, *p.* 1496 (London; *Reg. R. Hill,* ff. 26r, 27v, 34r).

Creswell, Thomas: Rufford; *sd.* snd *d.* 1489, *p.* 1492 (York; *Reg. T. Rotherham,* n–f).

C(h)ristylton, Robert: abbot, Combermere, by 1472–1496 (Smith, 2008, p. 283).

Cristylton, Roger: Combermere; *sd.* 1500, *d.* 1501 (Lichfield; *Reg. J. Arundel,* ff. 288, 293).

Crocub', Robert: Cleeve; *ac.* and *sd.* 1475 (Wells; *Reg. R. Stillington, f.* 192).

Crocket, Thomas: Croxden, professed *c.*1509 (Laurence, 1952, p. B. 17).

Croft, Thomas: Kirkstall, *p.* 1501 (York; Cross and Vickers, 1995, p. 140).

Crokesden, Christopher: Combermere; *ac.* 1521, *sd.* and *d.* 1522, *p.* 1523 (Lichfield; *Reg. G. Blyth,* n–f.).

Crokysden, John: Croxden; *sd.* 1501 (Lichfield; *Reg. J. Arundel,* f. 297).

Crokesden, Richard: Croxden; *ac.* 1507, *sd.*and *d.* 1508 (Lichfield; *Reg. G. Blyth,* n–f.).

Crokesden [Croxden], Stephen: Croxden; *sd.* ?1487, *p.* 1487/88 (Lichfield; *Reg. J. Hales,* ff. 225, 235, 241v; some dating problems here). He may well be the later abbot, *Stephen Cadde,* q.v.

Crokesden, Thomas: Croxden; *d.* 1513, *p.* 1514 (Lichfield; *Reg. G. Blyth,* n–f.). For some reason his entry of ordination as a priest, and that of John Alton, *q.v.,* given in the episcopal register for 10 June 1514 is repeated in the list of 18 September the same year.

Crokesden, William: Croxden; *ac.* 1493, *sd.* and *d.* 1495, *p.* 1497 (Lichfield; *Reg. W. Smith,* ff. 171, 183v, 188v; *Reg. J. Arundel,* f. 261).

Crole, Richard: Fountains; *p.*1493 (Cross and Vickers, 1995, p. 111).

Cromboke/Cramocke, Christopher: Whalley; *d.* 1534, *p.* 1535 (York; *Reg. E. Lee,* ff. 190r, 192v); *disp.* 1537 (*FOR,* pp. 91, 181); monk, Byland, by 1535 when ordained priest, and to which he transferred by letters dimissory. Pension of £5–6–8 received as late as 1556; died 1561 at Monk Fryston where perhaps vicar by 1558 (Aveling, 1955, p. 11; Cross and Vickers, 1995, pp. 100, 104).

Cromboke, John: abbot of Hailes, by 1480, when appointed one of the Reformators of the Order for England and Wales (Harper–Bill, 1980, pp. 103–04) to 1483 (*CHA,* p. 92; Worcester, *Reg. J. Alcock,* ff. 72, 135).

Crombok, Thomas: Hailes; *ac.* 1532 (Worcester, *Reg. R. Morton addenda,* f. 171).

Cropthorne, William: Hailes, 1537/38 (*CHA,* p. 85).

Crosse, John: Revesby, *disp.* 1538 (*FOR*, p. 128; Essex R.O., D/DRg 1/104).

Crosse, William: Dieulacres, *disp.* 1538; 'reward' £2–0–0 (Walcott, 1871, p. 216); pension, £5–6–8 (Hibbert, 1910, pp. 239, 242).

Crosthwaite, Gavin: Fountains; *sd.* 1521, *p.* 1527 (York; Cross and Vickers, 1995, p. 114).

Croston, Thomas: Kirkstall, *sd.* and *d.* 1497 (York; Cross and Vickers, 1995, p. 139). Perhaps the same monk as *Thomas Croft*, q.v.

Croston, Thomas: Vale Royal, *c.*1500 (*LB*, p. 153).

Crokehill: *see* Bromley.

Crowe, ...: Woburn; *c.*1537 complained of the bread supplied the monks (Gasquet, 1899, p. 286).

Croxhall/Croxsale/Croxsall, William: Merevale; *sd., d.* and *p.* 1494 (Lichfield; *Reg. W. Smith*, ff. 176v, 179v, 181v). In community, 1497 (TNA, E315/283, f. 1).

Croxton/al. West, John: Woburn; *sd.* 1527, *d.* 1528, *p.* 1532 (Lincoln; *Reg. J. Longland*, ff. 18v, 22v, 31v); *disp.* 1538 (*FOR*, p. 145); alleged to have adopted 'the new world' (Gasquet, 1899, pp. 285–86).

C[r]undall, Henry: Roche, *sd.* and *d.* 1497, *p.* 1498 (York); last abbot, 1531–38 (TNA, E314/20/11, m. 4d; *FOR*, p. 144; DKR 39); in receipt of £33–6–8 pension until his death in 1555 (Cross and Vickers, 1995, pp. 168–89; TNA, E164/31, f. 53r). At the suppression he was also allowed to take with him his books, a fourth part of the abbey plate, a chalice and a vestment, and cattle and household effects (VCH, *County of York* 3, p. 154. Became vicar of Tickhill; Yorkshire., bequeathed forty shillings to the poor of Tickhill and twenty shillings to the poor of Crowle; died by 4 May 1555 (CIY project); probate granted, 4 May 1555 (Smith, 2008, p. 327).

Cundall, Thomas: Roche, *sd.* 1516, *d.* 1517, *p.* 1518 (Cross and Vickers, 1995, pp. 188, 191); signed deed of surrender, 1538; pension, £5 (TNA, E322/204; *disp.* 1538 (TNA, E314/20/11, 4d). Alive in 1555.

Curlew, Richard: Quarr; *p.* 1508 (Winchester, *Reg. R. Fox* **2**, f. 23v). At Quarr's closure in 1536 he moved to Beaulieu; *disp.* 1538 (*DKR*, p. 9, *FOR*, p. 131); pension, £5 (TNA, E314/77).

Curtes, Thomas: Fountains, *sd.* and *d.* 1497, *p.* 1502 (York); probably dead by July 1535 when his chamber allocated to a corrodian (Cross and Vickers, 1995, pp. 112, 120).

Curtes, William: Kirkstead; *sd.* 1510 (Lincoln; *Reg. W, Smith*, n–f.); *disp.* 1537 (*FOR*, p. 96).

Curteys, William (? Thomas): Basingwerk; *sd.* and *d..* 1478 (Lichfield; *Reg. J. Hales*, ff. 248r, 249r).

Cuthbert ... :: Strata Florida, 1534 (Williams, 1889, Appx. p. lxxix).

Cuthbert, Robert: Meaux; *ac.* and *sd.* 1488, *d.* 1489, *p.* 1490 (York; Cross and Vickers, 1995, p. 153).

Cutmore, Thomas: Vale Royal; *sd.* 1506 (Lichfield; *Reg. G. Blyth*, n–f.).

Dady, Thomas: Rewley; *d.* 1507, *p.* 1508 (Salisbury; *Reg. E. Audley*, ff. 7v, 9v).

Dady, William: Stratford; *ac.* 1511, *sd.* 1512, *d.* 1513 (London; *Reg. R. Fitzjames*, ff. 160v [171v], 164r [175r], 165v [175v]).

?Daffell, Richard: Medmenham; *d.* 1513, *p.* 1515 (Lincoln; *Reg. W. Smith*, n–f., *Reg. W. Atwater*, f. 115v.).

Dagel, Thomas: Rewley; *sd.* 1507, *d.* 1508 (Salisbury; *Reg. E. Audley*, ff. 7v, 9v).

Dalton, John: Furness; involved in a case concerning missing money (TNA, E111/79); abbot of Furness by 1514, troubled and imprisoned by his predecessor, Alexander Banks, held in the Fleet prison in 1516/17 (TNA, E135/2/30), and in 1532 was a simple monk of the house (*Letters*, pp. 248–49 [No. 128]; *LP* **2**, Part 2, p. 1529 [Appx. No. 200]; Smith, 2008, pp. 295–96).

Damport, Humphrey: Vale Royal; *sd.* 1526, *p.* 1527 (Lichfield; *Reg. G. Blyth*, n–f.).

Dane/?Davy, John: Kingswood; *d.* 1503 (Wells; *Reg. O. King*, f. 122).

Danfeld, Nicholas: Cleeve, 1518/29 (TNA, C1/521/20).

Danyell/*al.* Snead, Geoffrey: Combe, *d.* March, 1537 (Lincoln; *Reg. J. Longland,* f. 54r); *disp.* 1538 (*DKR,* pp. 16–17, *FOR,* p. 176); pension, £5–6–8 (TNA, E314/77).

Danyell, Richard: Bindon; *sd. d.* and *p.* 1498 (Salisbury; *Reg. J. Blyth,* ff. 113r, 114r, 115r).

Danyell, Robert: Stratford; *ac.* and *sd.* 1492, *d.* 1493, *p.* 1496 (London; *Reg. R. Hill,* ff. 24v, 25r, 27v, 34r).

Danyell, William: Stratford; *ac.* 1532, *sd.* and *d.* 1533, *p.* 1534 (London; *Reg. R. Stokesley,* ff. 128v, 129r, 129v, 130r); signed deed of surrender and *disp.* 1538 (*FOR,* p. 129; TNA, E314/20/11, f. 2r–v); pension, £5 (TNA, E315/232, f. 28v).

Darby, Henry: Buckland; *p.* 1501 (Wells; *Reg. O. King,* f. 116); pension, £5 (TNA, E314/77).

Darby/*al.* Hepworth/Hipworth, Robert: Combe, *disp.* 1538 (*DKR,* pp. *16–17, FOR,* p. 176); pension, £5–6–8 (TNA, E315/77).

Darby: *see also* Paynter.

Darcy, Robert: Rushen, 1540, when given a gift of 1–16–4 on the closure of the monastery, but his name does not appear in the next pension account (Davey and Roscow, 2010, pp. 159, 174; TNA, SC6/HENVIII/5682).

Darfford/Baforde/Bafford, John: Pipewell; a + appears by his name on the deed of surrender; it may be his infirmity precluded his signing; *disp.* 1538 (TNA, E314/20/11, f. 9r; *FOR,* p. 160); pension, £6 (TNA,E315/233, f. 87r).

Darley, John: Rufford; *sd.* 1505, *d.* 1506, *p.* 1508 (York; *Reg. T. Savage,* ff. 131v, 133r; *Reg. Sede vacante,* f. 604r).

Darneton, John: cellarer, then 30th abbot, Fountains, 1479–1495, when dies; 'a faithful man of integrity towards the abbot of Cîteaux' – this following tensions in the Order (*Statuta* **5**, p. 387; *Letters,* pp. 172 [No. 86], 183 [No. 89]); (*FLB,* p. 82 [No. 93]; Smith, 2008, p. 293.

Darneton, John: Jervaulx; *sd. d.* and *p.* 1511 (York; Cross and Vickers, 1995, p. 130).

Darneton, William: Louth Park; *ac.* 1522, *sd.* 1523, *d.* 1525, *p.* 1527 (Lincoln; *Reg. J. Longland,* ff. 3v, 6v, 11v, 19v).

Darnehall, ?Christopher: Vale Royal; *sd.* 1521 (Lichfield; *Reg. G. Blyth,* n–f.). Darnhall was a grange and the first site of the monastery.

Darnton/Daunton, William: Rievaulx; *sd.* 1531, *p.* 1535 (York); listed in 1533 when he objected strongly, young as he was, to the deposition of Abbot Kirkby (TNA, STAC2/7/217; Cross and Vickers, 1995, pp. 169, 175).

Darnston/Darton, William: Vaudey; *sd.* 1519 (Lincoln; *Reg. W. Atwater,* f. 128r); *disp.* 1536 (*FOR,* p. 67).

Darnton: *see also* Dawnton.

Daryngton, William: Fountains; *d.* 1517 (York; Cross and Vickers, 1995, p. 114; **and see: Hobson**.

Dauncey, Cuthbert: Stanley; *sd.* and *d.* 1521 (Salisbury; *Reg. E. Audley,* f. 45r).

Daventry, John: Pipewell; *ac.* 1496, *sd.* 1497, *d.* 1498, *p.* 1502 (Lincoln; *Reg. W. Smith,* f. 34v.).

Dafydd ap Ieuan: Cistercian monk and 'scholar', diocese of Bangor, house not named in 1457 when he requests a dispensation being the son of an unmarried woman. It is very likely that he is the next named monk, later abbot of Aberconwy, but seeking in 1457 his first dispensation allowing his profession as a monk (*SAP,* p. 196 [No. 925]); *p.* 1478 (Lichfield; *Reg. J. Hales,* f.263v.)

David ap Ieuan ap Iorwerth: perhaps the monk of Aberconwy, *David ap John (Ieuan),* dispensed in 1480 on account of illegitimacy, being the son of a Cistercian monk and an unmarried woman; thus allowing him to be abbot of Valle Crucis from 1480 to 1503 (*CPL* **17**, pp. 380–81 [Nos. 594–95]; Smith, 2008, p. 344). Dafydd was in 1485 appointed as a deputy to the abbots of Fountains and Woburn as 'reformators'. A supporter of Henry VII, shortly after the king's accession he headed a commission set up 'to make inquisition regarding the succession of the monarch through his grandfather, Owain Tudor's line;' much praised by the Celtic poets, he perhaps built the new abbatial quarters at Valle Crucis and restored its church. By 1496 he held in plurality the wardenship of the College of St Peter, Ruthin, with an income of £200 p.a., and when named bishop on 8 January 1500, kept *in commendam* both his abbacy and the wardenship (*CPL* **17**, Part 1, p. 381 [No. 596]); bishop, St Asaph, 1500–1503, dying in the latter part of that year. For a fuller bibliography, see: *ODNB online edition.*

David ap Owain: monk, Strata Marcella; *d.* and *p.* 1466 (Lichfield cathedral; *Reg. J. Hales*, ff. 184, 185v); abbot, Strata Marcella (1485–), Strata Florida (*c.*1496–1500), Aberconwy (1501–13); bishop of St Asaph concurrently, 1504–13; D.C.L. (Oxford; Williams, 2001, pp. 71–72; *LP* **1**, Part 1, 246 [438/3, m.18]); *ODNB online*); named as bishop, 18–12–1503, with leave to retain the abbey *in commendam,* licence to consecrate issued the next day (*CPL* **18**, p. 205 [Nos. 201, 202, 203]).

David ap Rhys:

David ap Thomas ap Hywel: abbot, Margam, 1500–1517, when deposed; may have married later, and had several illegitimate children (Birch, 1897, p. 376; *Letters*, p. 251 [No. 129]; general pardon, 1510 (*LP* **1**, Part 1, p. 230 [No. 438/2, m. 27].

David, Einion: Margam; *p.* 1487 (St David's; *EPD* **2**, p. 509).

David, Geoffrey: Margam; *p.* 1471 (Wells; *Reg. R. Stillington,* f. 184r.)

David, Lewis, *al.* Llanfadder/Llansadder: Strata Florida; *disp.* 26–01–1539, pension, £3 (*FOR,* p. 206). In receipt of that pension in 1555 (TNA, E164/31, f. 75v). Alive in 1558 (Williams, 1889, Appx. pp. xciii).

David, Owain: Margam, *d.* 1487 (St David's; *EPD* **2**, pp. 491, 509).

David … : *see* Owain ap.

Davis, Geoffrey: (and see Geoffrey ap David *infra*); abbot, Cwmhir, 1532–34 (TNA, E329/B.S.244; SC6/5412, m. 3d).

Davis, Richard: Rewley, *disp.* 1536 (*FOR,* p. 78).

Davy, John: Margam; *p.* 1471 (Wells; *Reg. R. Stillington,* f. 185v).

Davye, Matthew: St Mary Graces, *disp.* 1539 (*FOR,* p. 182); pension, £5–6–8 (*LP* **14**, Part 1, p. 340 [No. 688].

Davye, Richard: St Mary Graces, *disp.* 1539 (*FOR,* p. 182); pension, £5–6–8 (*LP* **14**, Part 1, p. 340 [No. 688]).

Davye/Pavy/Dive, Robert: Pipewell; signed deed of surrender and *disp.*1538 (TNA, E314/20/11, f. 9r; *FOR,* p. 160); pension, 1538, £6 (TNA,SC6/HENVIII/7339).

Davy, William: Stratford; *p.* 1514 (London; *Reg. R. Fitzjames,* f. 178v).

Dawkyns: *see* Northampton.

Dawnsar/Dawnser, Richard: last sub–prior,Hailes, *disp.* 1540 (*FOR,* p. 208); pension, £5–6–8; perhaps curate of Stanley Pontlarge (chapelry of Toddington, a Hailes living) in 1541; of Cirencester in 1545 (Baskerville, 1927, p. 90).

Dawson, John: B.D., last prior, Hailes; pension, £8; living at Staunton, Gloucestershire, in 1552 (Baskerville, 1927, p. 90).

Dawson, Nicholas: Jervaulx; *p.* 1486 (York; Cross and Vickers, 1995, p. 129).

Daye, John: monk, Fountains, *sd.* 1503, *d.* 1504 (York; Cross and Vickers, 1995, p.113).

Day/Dey, John, *al.* Beley: Bordesley; *sd.* 1488, *d.* 1489 (Worcester; *Reg. R. Morton,* ff. 141, 144); abbot, 1519–38; said in 1538 to be 'aged, impotent, sick, and also not of perfect remembrance'; surrendered house, 17 July, 1538; pension, £50 (*VCH, Worcestershire* **2**, 1971, pp. 153–54); *disp.* 1538 (*FOR,* p. 149; TNA, E322/26); still alive in 1540 (Bodleian LIbrary, Oxford; Tanner MS 343).

Dayes, John: Rufford, 1486/87 (Nottinghamshire. Archives, DD/SR/A11/27).

Daykhill, Robert: Woburn; *d.* 1490 (Lincoln; *Reg. J. Russell,* f.37v).

Dayley, Thomas: Rewley; *sd.* 1506 (Lincoln; *Reg. W. Smith*, n–f,); *d.* 1507 (Salisbury; *Reg. E. Audley*, n–f); *p.* 1509 (Lincoln; *Reg. W. Smith*, n–f.).

Daye/Dey,/Dee, John: Vale Royal, signed deed of surrender and *disp.* 1538 (*DKR*, p. 46; *FOR*, p. 162); in receipt of his £5 pension in 1555 (TNA, E164/31, f. 69r).

Deane, John: Jervaulx, *disp.* 1537 (*FOR*, p. 119; Cross, 1995, p. 133).

Dean, Philip: Kingswood; *ac.,sd. sd.* 1492 (Worcester; *Reg. R. Morton*, ff. pp. 152, 154).

Dean, Richard: Flaxley; *ac.* and *sd.* 1483 (Hereford; *Reg. T. Myllyng*, pp. 168–69).

Dean, Richard: Kingswood; *ac.* 1459 (Worcester; *Reg. J. Carpenter*, f. 548).

Deane, Richard: Dore; *ac.* 1525, *sd.* 1527, *d.* 1531 (Hereford; *Reg. C. Bothe*, pp. 318, 323, 329); *p.* 1532 (Worcester; *Reg. R. Morton addenda*, f. 172); on dissolution in 1536 seem to have moved to Hailes, where pension in 1539 of £1–6–8 (*FOR*, p. 208).

Deane, *al.* Bromsgrove, Richard: monk, Hailes; *p.* 1513 (Worcester; *Reg. S. Gigli*, f. 319); pension in 1539 of £1–6–8 (*FOR*, p. 208); vicar. Longborough (a Hailes living) 1527–28; died 1545 (Baskerville, 1927, p. 90).

Deane, Thomas: monk, Dore; *d.* 1513 (Hereford, *Reg. R. Mayew*, p. 262); *p.* 1518 (Hereford; *Reg. C. Bothe*, p. 306).

Dean, Thomas: cellarer, Tintern, 1524–1525 (NLW, Badminton Deeds, Group 2, Nos. 1661, 1663).

Dean, Walter: abbot, Vale Royal, early 16th C., (Cheshire Archives, DBC1621/26/4).

Dean, William: cellarer, Tintern, 1525 (NLW, Badminton Deeds, Group 2, No. 1661).

Dean: and see Donne.

Delfe, William: sub–prior, Robertsbridge, *c.*1491 (SAL, MS 14, f. 59v).

Denby, John: ? Whalley, 1536 (TNA, SC6/HENVIII/1796).

Denby, John: Kirkstall; pension, 1539, £2 (Cross and Vickers, 1995, p. 142).

Denlay, John: Jervaulx; *d.* 1481, *p.* 1483 (York; Cross and Vickers, 1995, p. 129).

Dent, Thomas: Jervaulx; *d.* 1534 (York; Cross and Vickers, 1995, pp. 132–33).

Denton, Richard: Kirkstall, *ac.* 1533, *d.* 1534, *p.* 1537 (York; Cross and Vickers, 1995, p. 142); *and see:* **Leaveaxe.**

Denton, Thomas: Fountains, *sd.* 1501, *d.* 1502, *p.* 1503 (York; Cross and Vickers, 1995, p. 112; *and see:* **Grenewood..**

Denton, William: Sawtry; *ac.* 1506, *sd.* and *d.* 1507 (Lincoln; *Reg. W. Smith*, n–f.).

Denyngton/Donyngton, *al.* Wylshire: William: Ford; *p.* 1538 (Exeter; *Reg. J. Vesey*, f. 189r); pension, 1539, £5 (Youings, 1971, p. 186; Weaver, 1891, p. 5); still in receipt of £5 pension in 1555 (TNA, E164/31, f. 34v).

Dere, Thomas: 'canon', Kingswood; *ac.* and *sd.* 1484 (Hereford; *Reg. T. Myllyng*, pp. 169–70).

Derham, Robert: Vaudey, *disp.* 1536 (*FOR*, p. 67).

Derham, William: Coggeshall; *sd.* and *d.* 1495 (London; *Reg. R. Hill*, ff. 30r, 30v).

Derley/Derleygh, John: Vale Royal; *sd.* 1487, *d.* and *p.* 1489 (Lichfield; *Reg. J. Hales*, ff. 233v, 238v, 243).

Derneton, William: Fountains; *sd.* 1514, *d.* 1516, *p.* 1517 (York; Cross and Vickers, 1995, p. 113).

Dervall, Richard: Vale Royal; *d.* 1522, *p.* 1523 (Lichfield; *Reg. G. Blyth*, n–f.);

Deveys/Devins, Matthew: at St Bernard's College, Oxford; B.Th. 1531 (*BRUO* **2**, p. 168); abbot, Holm Cultram, 1531–1532, when died of suspected poisoning (Gilbanks, 1899, pp. 91– 95; *LP* **6**, pp. 425–26 [No. 988]).

Devizes: *see* Vizes.

Dewyche, Peter: Sibton, 1536 (*SBC*, **4**, pp. 110–11 [No. 1187]).

Dey, John: last abbot, Bordesley, *see* **Day.**

Dixon, Diconson/Dykenson, Thomas: Fountains; *sd.* 1514, *d.* 1516; in February 1536 the Visitors said that he wished to leave the religious life, but pension, 1539, £5–6–8; if the later vicar of Hampsthwaite, Yorkshire, of this name then he died at the close of 1587 (Cross and Vickers, 1995, pp. 113, 115, 120).

Dixson, Christopher: Jervaulx, *disp.*1537 (*FOR*, p. 119); may have later been the chantry priest of this name at Dale Grange in Aysgarth parish; if so, he was forty–six and well–learned in 1548 (Cross and Vickers, 1995, p. 133).

Dobb(y)s, John: last abbot, Boxley; said in February 1538 to be 'sore sick'; pension, £50 (TNA, E314/77); *disp.* 1538 (*FOR*, p. 123; TNA, E314/20/11, f. 1r). He may well be *John Birde*, q.v. (Smith, 2008, p. 272).

Dobibee, William: Louth Park; *disp.* 6–08–1536 (*FOR*, p. 69). Might this be a transcription error for *William Rokeby*, q.v.?.

Doby, Richard: *see* Dovell.

Dodds, Christopher: Fountains; *sd.* 1533, *d.* and *p.* 1534 (York; Cross and Vickers, 1995, pp. 114, 120).

Dodgson, Robert: Fountains; pension, 1539: £5. If the monk named *Robert Wells*, then *sd.* 1521, and accused, perhaps spuriously, by the Visitors in February 1536 of immoral relations with a married woman (Cross and Vickers, 1995, pp. 115, 120).

Dod(s)worth, John: Roche, *sd. d.* and *p.* 1522; 1531 (*TNA, E135/3/6*); bursar there, and accused, perhaps spuriously, of self–abuse in 1535/36 by Henry VIII's commissioners; signed deed of surrender, 1538 (TNA, E322/204); *disp.* 1538 (*FOR*, P. 144); in receipt of £6 pension.as late as 1555 (TNA, E164/31, f. 53r). Moved to Kirkstall abbey after Roche's suppression, may have obtained a chantry in Kirk Bramworth parish church by 1540, and later became rector of Armthorpe, Yorkshire, formerly appropriated to Roche, dying in May 1574 and being buried in its churchyard (CIY project); said that he was seventy in 1569 (Cross and Vickers, 1995, pp. 187, 191)..

Domet, Thomas: Coggeshall; in 1450, when described as a priest of the London diocese, he asserted that when a boy his parents forced him to enter the monastery, and now seeks leave from the papal penitentiary to remain in the world (*SAP*, p. 147 [No. 664]).

Doncaster, John: Rufford; *sd.* 1505, *d.* 1506 (York; *Reg. T. Savage*, ff. 131v, 133r).

Doncaster, John: Swineshead; *sd.* 1531 (Lincoln; *Reg. J. Longland*, f. 27v).

Doncaster, Richard: Kirkstead; *ac.* 1506, *d.* and *p.* 1507 (Lincoln; *Reg. W. Smith*, n–f.).

Doncaster, Thomas: Kirkstead; *ac.* and *sd.* 1485, *d.* 1486, *p.* 1487 (Lincoln; *Reg. J. Russell*, ff. 17r, 18r, 21v, 25r).

Donc(h)aster, Thomas: Rufford; *sd.* and *d.* 1500 (York; *Reg. T. Rotherham*, n–f.); *p.* 1501 (York; *Reg. T. Savage*, f. 110r); last abbot, 1533–1536; disp. 1536 (*FOR*, p. 74); accused, perhaps spuriously, in 1535/36 of immoral relations with two married women and four others (*LP* **10**, p. 138 [No. 364]); rector, Rotherham, Yorkshire, 1538, in *lieu* of a £25 pension (Cross, 1993, p. 202; 1995, p. 171; Smith, 2008, p. 328); alive in 1555 (Aveling, 1967, pp. 269–70).

Doncaster, William: Roche; *p.* 1481 (York; Cross and Vickers, 1995, p. 186).

Donkaster, William: St Mary Graces, 1533 (Grainger and Phillpotts, 2011, p. 93).

Donham: see Dunham.

Donne/Doune/Dene, John: Merevale; *sd.* 1528, *d.* and *p.* 1529 (Lichfield; *Reg. G. Blyth*, n–f.); in monastery at suppression, 1538 (TNA, E322/151, where *Thomas Donne*); died *c.*1558 (Hodgett, 1959, p. 135); in receipt of pension of £5–6–8 as late as 1555 (TNA, E164/31, f.48r).

Donne, Gabriel: *see* Dunne.

Donwell/?White, William: Fountains; *d.* 1509, *p.* 1514; at 1536 visitation reported as wishing to leave the religious life; if Donwell, then received pension of £6 from 1539 until at least 1564 (Cross and Vickers, 1995, p. 121).

Donyngton: *see* Denyngton.

Dorchier, Roger: Beaulieu, 1538 (*DKR*, p. 9). Not mentioned in one pension list (*LP* 14, Part 1, p. 596 [No. 1355/iii]).

Dore, Lewis: Garendon, *disp.* 1536 (*FOR*, p. 78). Might he have been a visitor, for his signature does not appear on a deed of 15–03–1536 (*LP* **10**, p. 194 [No. 475]).

Dore, William: Dore; *ac.* 1485, *d.* 1486 (Hereford; *Reg. T. Myllyng*, pp. 173, 182). He is probably the same monk as *William Morse*, q.v.

Dorset, Richard: Bruern; *sd.* and *d.* 1512 (Lincoln; *Reg. W. Smith*, n–f.); a *Robert Dorset* was still a monk there in 1536 (Baskerville, 1930, p. 334).

Dorston, Richard: Dore, *d.* 1466, *p.* 1469 (Hereford; *Reg. J. Stanbury*, pp. 157, 163); abbot, Grace Dieu, 1486–95; abbot, Dore, 1495–1500, when effectively deposed 'for inordinate rule and governance'; abbot, Strata Florida, *c.*1505–13 (Williams, 1976, p. 23; 2001, pp. 69–70, 221); three impressions of his counter–seal are known (Carmarthen R.O., Lort Deed 11/554).

Dovell, David: Cleeve; *sd.* and *d.* 1525 (Wells; *Reg. J. Clarke*, ff.121, 126). His brother was prior of Augustinian Barlinch.

Dovyll/Dobyll, Richard: Cleeve; *sd.* and *d.* 1504 (LPL; *Reg. W. Warham, Wells sede v.*, ff. 198r, 208v: SRO, D/D/B Reg.29, f. 6v); *p.* 1505 (Wells; *Reg. H. de Castello*, f. 141).

Dovell, William: Cleeve; *d.* and *p.*1505 (Wells; *Reg. H. de Castello*, ff. 140–41); abbot, 1510–1536 (Smith, 2008, p. 280); said to be 'a man of great substance' (TNA, C (1/1001/24); in receipt of his £26–13–4 pension as late as 1555 (TNA, E164/31, f.31r; E315/244, No. 111).

Dovell: *see also* Doby.

Dovery, Maurice: Strata Florida; *ac.* 1515 (Hereford; *Reg. R. Mayew*, p. 271); *sd.* and *d.* 1516 (Worcester; *Reg. S. Gigli*, f. 334).

Downe, John: Flaxley, *disp.* 1536 (*FOR*, p. 73).

Downehan, Richard: Sawley; *sd.* 1517, *d.* 1518, *p.* 1519 (York; Cross and Vickers, 1995, p. 200).

Downey: *see* Cotyngham.

Doyge, John: Buckfast, –1539 (*DKR*, p. 12); pension, £6–13–4 (Stéphan, 1970, p. 213). Could he be the *John Coffe* al. *Cogg* noted above?

Draicot, John: St Mary Graces; *sd.* and *d.* 1504 (London; *Reg. W. Barons*, ff. 88v, 89r).

Draycote, Hugh: Pipewell; *ac.* 1496, *sd.* 1497, *d.* 1498, *p.* 1500 (Lincoln; *Reg. W. Smith*, f. 25v).

Drake, Thomas: Stratford; *ac.* 1533 (London; *Reg. R. Stokesley*, f. 129v); signed deed of surrender and *disp.* 1538, when still a deacon (*FOR*, p. 129; TNA, E314/77); in receipt of £3–6–8 pension in 1555 (TNA, E164/31, f. 9v); died before 1540 (Cross and Vickers, 1995, pp. 186, 192).

Drax, Richard: Roche; *ac.* and *d.* 1497, *p.* 1498 signed deed of surrender, 1538 (TNA, E322/204); *disp.* 1538 (*FOR*, p. 144); pension £5 (Cross and Vickers, 1995, p. 188).

Drew, William: Buckfast; *d.* 1504 (LPL,*Reg. W., Warham, Exeter sede v.*, f. 208v); *p.* 1506 (Exeter; *Reg. H. Oldham*, f. 86v).

Duffeld, John: Stratford; *ac.* 1495, *sd.* 1498, *d.* 1500 (London; *Reg. R. Hill*, f. 32v; *Reg. T. Savage*, ff. 57r, 62v); sub–prior, 1511 (London; *Reg. R. Fitzjames*, f. 160v [171v]).

Dugdale, Edmund: Combermere, *disp.* 1538 (*FOR*, p. 154); in receipt of pension of £4 as late as 1555 (TNA, E164/31, f. 69r).

Dugdale, Elyas/Elizeus: Hailes, *disp.* 1540 (*FOR*, p. 208); pension, £2–13–4; living in Fairford, Gloucestershire., 1552–53; rector of Stow–on–the–Wold, 1557–58, died 1574 (Baskerville, 1927, p. 90).

Dulton, Thomas: abbot, Dunkeswell, 1474–89 (Sparks, 1978, p. 119).

Dunham/Donham/Downeham, George: Boxley, *t.* and *ac.* 1520; 1520; *p.* 1526 (Rochester; *Reg. J. Fisher,* ff. 89v, 116v); *disp.* 1538 (*FOR,* p. 123); in receipt of pension of £4 in 1555 (TNA, E164/31, f.4; E315/77).

Dunne/Donne, Gabriel: Stratford; *sd.* 1510, *d.* 1511, *p.* 1516 (London; *Reg. R. Fitzjames,* ff. 158r [169v], 161v [172r], 182r); student at St Bernard's College, Oxford, where supplicated for the degree of B.D. in October 1521; then later at Louvain where wrongly associated with the capture of William Tyndale, 1535; a friend of Cromwell, last abbot, Buckfast, 1535–39, receiving a pension of £120 p.a.; 1541, in receipt that pension in 1555 (TNA, E164/31, f. 34r); prebendary of St Paul's Cathedral, London; 1544–1558, rector of Stepney without cure; 1549, buried 9 December 1558 at St Paul's; made a substantial scholarship bequest to Trinity Hall, Cambridge. His arms were: a wolf rampant, which described his standing in the eyes of Protestant reformers for his alleged part in the betrayal of Tyndale (Stéphan, 1970, pp. 203–12); Orme, 2001, pp. 97–108, gives the most accurate account of his life.

Dunster, John: Cleeve; *ac.* and *sd.* 1475 (Wells; *Reg. R. Stillington,* f. 192).

Dunwell, Christopher: Fountains; *sd.* and *d.* 1521, *p.* 1524 (York; Cross and Vickers, 1995, p. 114); *and see:* Jenkinson..

Dun(e)well, William: Fountains; pension, 1539: £6 (Cross and Vickers, 1995, p. 115).

Dunwich, William: Sibton, *disp.* 1536 (*FOR,* p. 70; *SBC* 4, pp. 110–11 [No. 1187]).

Durham/Deram/Heron, John: St Mary Graces; *sd.* 1520, *d.* 1521, *p.* 1521 (London; *Reg. R. Fitzjames,* ff. 180v [191v], 181v [192v], 183v [194v]); last abbot, Valle Crucis, 1535–36; paid composition fee of £40, 31–01–1536 (TNA, E334/1, f.35); pension, £23 p.a., (TNA, E315/2434, no. 145); alive in 1553 (Pratt, 1997, *passim;* Williams, 2001, pp. 76–77, 80–8, 87).

Dur(e)ham, Robert: Warden; *sd.* 1517, *d.* 1518 (Lincoln; *Reg. W. Atwater,* ff.120r 125v).

Durham, Thomas: Strata Florida, 1534–39; *disp.* 1540, pension, £4 p.a.; alive in 1558 (*FOR,* p. 206; Williams, 1889, p. 170, Appx. p. xciii).). In receipt of a pension of £4 in 1555 (TNA, E164/31, f. 75v).

Durham, Walter: Jervaulx; *sd.* and *d.* 1506, *p.* 1507 (York; Cross and Vickers, 1995, p. 130).

Durham, William: Quarr; *sd.* 1495, *d.* 1497, *p.* 1498 (Winchester; *Reg. T. Langton,* ff. 26r, 31v, 33r);

Duram, William: Fountains, *sd.* and *d.* 1497, *p.* 1502 (York; Cross and Vickers, 1995, p. 112).

Duxfeld, Gerard: abbot, Newminster, by ?1517–1527, when granted on retirement a residential corrody there (TNA, LR1/173, f. 62; Smith, 2008, p. 318); ninety–five years old in survey of 1536 (TNA, SC12/13/65); in receipt of a pension in 1538 (Gasquet, 1899, p. 269).

Dydebroke, John: born *c.*1497; monk, Dore, by 1528; *disp.* 1536; later resident chaplain at Llanfair Cilgoed grange chapel, Gwent, until death in 1570 (*FOR,* p. 98; *MW,* p. 89 [No. 28], Williams, 1976, pp. 27, 29). 89).

Dydbroke, Thomas: Hailes; *d.* 1483 (Worcester; *Reg. J. Alcock,* f. 273); a cleric of this name was a chaplain in the parish of Camden in 1487 (Worcester: *Reg. R. Morton,* f. 30). Ordained priest whilst under age (*SAP* 2, pp. 388–89 [No. 3142]).

Dydbroke, William: Hailes; *ac.* and *sd.* 1479, *d.* 1480, *p.* 1481 (Worcester; *Reg. J. Alcock,* ff. 257, 262, 265). Ordained priest whilst under age (*SAP* 2, pp. 388–89 [No. 3142]).

Dynkley, Edmund: sacristan, Whalley, 1527; of the abbey or the parish church? (*DCL,* p. 137).

Dynyngton, William:

Dyson/Tyson, Robert: Rushen; pension, 1540: £2–13–4).

Dyworth, Henry: Revesby; *d.* 1510 (Lincoln; *Reg. W. Smith,* n–f.).

Earl, John: Tintern, 1448–93; cellarer in 1448, 1476, 1488–89, 1493 (NLW, Badminton Deeds, Group 1, No. 1657; Group 2, Nos. 14473, 14481–82).

Easingwold, *al.* Smythson, William: Rievaulx; 1485, when sought a dispensation on account of apostasy and leave to transfer to another monastery (*SAP* **2**, pp. 328–29 [No. 2988]).

Eastgate: *see* Estgate.

Eaton: *see also* Eton.

Ebarson, Thomas: Rievaulx; ac. 1501, *sd.*and *d.* 1502, *p.* 1504 (York; Cross and Vickers, 1995, p. 168).

Ebsworth/Ellisworth, William: Buckland, *disp.* 1539 (*FOR*, p. 178); pension, £3–6–8, received as late as 1555 (TNA, E164/31, f. 34r); chaplain, Columpton, 1540/41 (*Devonshire Notes and Queries* **17**, 1932, p. 88).

Edham, John: Sawtry, 1470, when served as 'rector, called curate' of Sawtry church outside the monastery gates (*SAP* **2**, p. 286 [No. 2762]).

Everton/Enerton/Eberton, John: Stoneleigh; *sd.* 1485, *d.* 1486, *p.* 1489 (Lichfield; *Reg. J. Hales*, ff. 214, 216v, 245v).

Eccles, Alexander: Vale Royal; *d.* 1506 (Lichfield; *Reg. G. Blyth*, n–f.).

Ecclecell [? Ecclesall], Edward: Kirkstall, *sd.* 1527 (York; Cross and Vickers, 1995, pp. 141, 150–51).

Ecop, William: Kirkstall, *sd.* and *d.* 1513, *p.* 1515 (York; Cross and Vickers, 1995, p. 141).

Eddon: *see Hailes.*

Edlington, William: Kirkstead; *ac.* 1503, *sd.* 1504 (Lincoln; *Reg. W. Smith*, ff. 41v, 46r).

Edmonds/Eddon, Richard: *see* **Hailes.**

Edwards, William: Bordesley, signed suppression deed and *disp.* 1538 (*FOR*, p. 149; TNA, E322/26); in receipt of pension of £4 as late as 1555 (TNA, E164/31, f. 44r).

Effingham: Robert: Waverley; *sd.* and *d.* 1522 (Winchester; *Reg. R. Fox* **4**, f. 72v; **5.** f. 30r).

Egleston, Hugh: Furness; *p.* 1502 (York, Reg. T. Savage, f. 113r); mentioned, 1510 (*AF*, p. 303); detained in The Fleet, 1516/17 (TNA, 135/2/30).

Eherullegt, Cornelius de: St Mary Graces; *d.* 1502 (*CL*), possibly of foreign extraction.

Eignon, Thomas: Basingwerk; *d.* and *p.* 1472 (Lichfield; *Reg. J. Hales*, ff. 247v, 248v).

Einion, John: Whitland, 1539, still alive in 1555 (*MSS in BM* **4**, p. 932).

Ekynton, Gilbert: Swineshead; *sd.* 1508 (Lincoln; *Reg. W. Smith*, n–f.).

Elkham/Oltham/Olcam, Christopher: Netley, *p.* 1509 (Winchester; *Reg. R. Fox* **2**, f. 23r; *disp.* 1536 (*FOR*, p. 66).

Eliot, Thomas: Stratford; *sd.* 1501, *d.* 1503 (London; *Reg. W. Warham*, ff. 82v, 87r).

?Elleslake/Olteslake, John: Woburn: *d.* 1492 (Lincoln; *Reg. J. Russell*, f. 47/48r).

Elliott, Thomas: abbot, Bindon; by 1527–1534 (Smith, 2008, p. 269; Cornwall Record Office, PH/1 – reference of 1583 as once having been abbot).

Elliotts, Thomas: Tintern; *disp.* 1536 (*FOR*, p. 80).

Ellis, Richard: *see* **Birstall.**

Ellis, Thomas: Kirkstall; *sd.*1509, *p.*1513 (York); pension, 1539, £6 (Cross and Vickers, 1995, pp. 140, 142); he may have been the cleric, *Thomas Elyston*, who witnessed the wills of (1) Thomas Bartlett, priest, of Leeds (1542), who left him his best gown, and of (2) George Hall of Allerton Grange (1553). Ellis was still alive in 1558 (Lonsdale, 1972, p. 208); he may have become vicar of his abbey's church at Aldbrough, 1547–1557 (CIY).

Ellis, Owain: abbot, Cwmhir, 1490–?1491 (*Radnorshire Soc. Trans.* **34**, 1964, pp. 25, 29).

Ellisworth: *see* Ebsworth.

Elliton, John: Jervaulx; *ac.* 1505, *sd.* and *d.* 1506, *p.* 1507 (York; Cross and Vickers, 1995, p. 130).

Elley, John: Meaux; *p.* 1510 (York; Cross and Vickers, 1995, p. 154).

Elman, Robert: Sibton, 1536 (*SBC* **4**, pp. 110–11 [No. 1187]).

Elmyster: *see* Ilmister.

Elston/Elvestone, Thomas: Warden; *sd.* 1500, *d.* 1501 (Lincoln; *Reg. W. Smith*, ff. 21r, 26v).

Elston: *see also* Ayleston.

Eltryngham/Elthryngham/Eleryngyme, Roger: Stratford; *ac.* 1522 (LPL; *Reg. W. Warham* **2**, f. 297r); *sd.* 1523, *d.* 1525 (London; *Reg. C. Tunstall*, f. 154r); *p.* 1528 (*CL*); *disp.* to hold a benefice and wear the habit beneath that of a secular priest, a year before the suppression of his monastery; 20–04–1537 (*FOR*, p. 94).

Elyngham, John: Quarr; *d.* 1498, *p.* 1500 (Winchester; *Reg. T. Langton*, ff. 33r, 36r).

Elys, Henry: Buckfast; *sd.* 1533 (Exeter; *Reg. J. Vesey*, f. 181v).

Elys/Glys, John: abbot, Newenham; 1515 – 1523 at least (Smith, 2008, p. 317); papal *disp.* after appointment on account of defect of birth, 1514 (*LP* **1**, Part 2, p. 1531 [No. 3617]. Immediately after his decease two of his household allegedly immediately removed monastic deeds and cash from the monastery (TNA, C1/548/16).

Elys/Helys, Roger: Rewley; *d.* 1508, *p.* 1510 (Salisbury; *Reg. E. Audley*, ff. 9v, 15v).

Emden/Enders/Endon//Hendon: Thomas: Croxden, professed *c.*1509 (Laurence, 1952, B.17); signed deed of surrender and *disp.* 1538 (Hibbert, 1910, p. 222; *FOR*, p. 151); pension, £5; in receipt of pension of £4 as late as 1555 (TNA, E164/31, f. 46v); died at Ratby, Leics., 1567 (Hodgett, 1959, p. 144).

Emlyn: *see* Stratford.

Emery, Edmund: abbot, Tilty, 1530–32/33, when resigns or is deposed being called 'unthrifty' (Smith, 2008, p. 340), and awarded pension of £14 (*VCH, Essex* **2**, 1907, pp. 134–36); retired to a corrody at Warden abbey where his brother was abbot; in 1554 was married and living in Bedford (TNA, E101/76/26; E164/31, f. 10r; E315/92, f. 43v]. He had then no ecclesiastical preferments (Hodgett, 1959, p. 89).

Emmysworth: *see* Hemseworth.

Emery, Henry (III): abbot, Sibton, 1522–34 *SBC* **4**, p. 67 [No. 1120]); abbot, Warden, by 1535–1537; wished in 1535 to resign because of the hostility towards him of several of the community (*LC*, pp. 59–60 [No. XXIX]

Emory/Emery, Richard: Buildwas; *ac.* and *sd.* 1487 (Lichfield; *Reg. J. Hales*, f. 225, 243v); abbot, by 1519–1520 when deposed (Smith, 2008, p. 277); granted annuity of £12–6–8 which continued after the suppression in 1537 (*LP* **12** Part 2, p. 166 [411/13).

Emory, William: Buildwas; *d.* 1487 (Lichfield; *Reg. J. Hales*, f. 226v); could this be a copyist's error for Richard?

Engele, Thomas: Hailes; *d.* 1515 (Worcester; *Reg. S. Gigli*, f. 327).

Ensam, Edmund: Rewley; *p.* 1521 (Lincoln; *Reg. J. Longland*, f. 1v).

Erlyngham/Arlington, al. Fryer, Edward: Flaxley; *ac., sd., d.* 1524 (Hereford; *Reg. C. Bothe*, pp. 315, 316, 318); *disp.* 1536 (*FOR*, p. 73); then moved to Kingswood, where, as sexton, *disp.* 1538 (*DKR*, p. 25; *FOR*, p. 131); 'reward and finding', £2–13–4, pension, £4 (TNA, E36/152, f. 21); in receipt of his £4 pension as late as 1555 (TNA, E164/31, f. 29r); King Edward service priest, Newland, Gloucs., 1548; perpetual curate, Newnham, Gloucs., 1571; dies 1573 (Baskerville, 1927, p. 88). His will, made 16–12–1572, makes no allusion to his former monastic status (Gloucestershire R.O., Wills: Fryar 1573/31). Was he the monk, *Edward Freyer*, who as a monk of Bordesley was ordained priest in 1527?

Escoyd, Richard: Vale Royal; *ac.* 1521 (Lichfield; *Reg. G. Blyth*, n–f.).

Essex, Thomas: abbot, Boxley, 1481–1490 (Smith, 2008, p. 271).

Estgate, John: Whalley; *d.* 1536, *p.* February 1537 (York; *Reg. E. Lee*, ff.196v, 197v); after closure of Whalley appears to have moved to Furness but indicated a desire to transfer to Neath; the King wished to know why, but later (11 April 1537) permitted this (*LP* 12, Part 1, pp. 315 [No. 706], 399 [No. 896]; Haigh, 1969, p. 147). Not mentioned on the surrender deed of Furness.

Estgate, Richard: Sawley; *ac.* 1526, *sd.* and *d.* 1527 (York; Cross and Vickers, 1995, p. 200); *disp.* and permitted 'to hold a benefice with a stall in choir, a seat in the chapter, and a portion in any monastery to which the king may assign him', 20–05–1536 (*FOR*, p. 58). As abbot's chaplain he had some slight involvement in the aftermath of the Pilgrimage of Grace (Dodds **2**, 1915, pp. 83–85); on 24 March 1537, King commanded that he be 'sent up in safety' (*LP* **12**, Part 1, p. 315 [No. 706]; hung at Whalley, 12 March 1537 (Gasquet, 1899, p. 270; Baskerville, 1937, pp. 166–67).

Eston, William: Revesby, *disp.* 1538 (*FOR*, p. 128; (Essex R.O., D/DRg 1/104).

Estop(pe), Andrew: Buildwas; *ac.* and *sd.* 1487/89 there are dating problems), *p.* 1490 (Lichfield; *Reg. J. Hales*, ff. 226v, 229, 243v).

Etherway, al. Tetter, William: Stratford; *p.* 1492 (London; *Reg. R. Hill*, f. 26r); abbot, Stratford, 1516–1523, when died (Smith, 2008, p. 338); made his profession of obedience on 19 May 1516 before Thomas Hedde, vicar–general of London (London; *Reg. R. Fitzjames*, f. 64v [67r]).

Eton, Thomas: Woburn; *sd.* 1519, *d.* 1522, *p.* 1527 (Lincoln; *Reg. W. Atwater*, f. 130v; *Reg. J. Longland*, ff. 5r, 18v).

Eton/Eaton, Thomas: Combermere, 1538 (TNA, E314/20/11, f. 10d); in receipt of pension of £3–6–8 as late as 1555 (TNA, E164/31, f. 69r).

Euston/Enstone, Ralph: Bruern; *d.* 1531, *p.* 1532 (Lincoln; *Reg. J. Longland*, f.29r, 31v); still in community, 1535 (*VE* 2, p. 265).

Evans/Evance, Richard: Bordesley, *disp.* 1538 (*FOR*, p. 149; TNA, E322/26); in receipt of pension of £5 as late as 1555 (TNA, E164/31, f. 44r).

Evaw; *see* Ewalbre. Thomas:

Evaver: *see* Graver.

Everdon, Fulk: Biddlesden; *d.* 1485 (Lincoln; *Reg. J. Russell*, f. 18r).

Evershote/Eversholte, Robert: Woburn; *sd.* 1532, *d.* 1533, *p.* 1537 (Lincoln; *Reg. J. Longland*, ff. 31r, 36r, 55v); *disp.* 1538 (*FOR*, p. 145).

Evershotte, William: Thame; *sd.* 1538 (Lincoln; *Reg. J. Longland*, f. 58r); not mentioned at the suppression; could he be the *William Forrest* noted below?

Evesham, Thomas: Bordesley; *ac.* and *sd.* 1532, *d.* 1533 (Worcester; *Reg. R. Morton addenda*, ff. 171, 174). Could he be the next mentioned monk?

Evesham/Ebysham, Thomas: Bruern, 1535, when professed but not yet ordained priest (*VE* **2**, p. 265;
 Baskerville, 1930, p. 334).

Evesham, ... : Combermere (Aveling, 1967, p. 14).

Ewalbre/Evaw/ Galby/Gaulby, Thomas: monk perhaps of Netley transferring to Beaulieu, *disp.* 1538 (*FOR*, p. 131; TNA, E314/20/11, f. 1d–2r); pension of £4 received in 1555 (TNA, E164/31, f. 13r). Seemingly not priested in 1538 (TNA, E314/77).

Ewer, Robert: Vale Royal; *p.* 1487 (Lichfield; *Reg. J. Hales*, f.233v).

Excester, al. Where, William: Ford; *disp.* 1498 (*CPL* **17**, Part 1, p. 22 [No. 32]).

Exceter, John: Newenham; *sd.* 1508 (Exeter; *Reg. H. Oldham*, f. 97r).

Exeter, William: Tilty; *ac.* 1529 (London; *Reg. C. Tunstall*, f.162 v).

Exforth/Epphurth, Thomas: St Mary Graces; *p.* 1521 (London; *Reg. R. Fitzjames*, f. 183v [194v]); in community, 1533 (Grainger and Phillpotts, 2011, p. 93).

Exmester al. Were, Richard: Ford; pension, 1539, £8 (Youings, 1971, p. 186; *DKR*, p. 21).

Exestre, *al.* Where, William: Ford; : *disp.* 1498 (*CPL* **17**, Part 1, p. 22 [No. 32]).
Eykering: *see* Gykjering.
Eylston: *see* **Aylstone.**

Fabian, George: Coggeshall; *sd.* 1500, *d.* and *p.* 1501 (London; *Reg. T. Savage*, ff. 65v, 66v; *Reg. W. Warham*, f.78r); bequeathed 10s in 1524 by John Shote of Coggeshall 'to sing a trental of masses for my soul' (TNA, PROB11/21/451).
Fairclough, John: Waverley; *ac.* 1514, *sd.* and *p.* 1518 (Winchester; *Reg. R. Fox* **3**, f. 55v, **4**, ff. 69v, 70r).
Fairweather: see Gisburn.
Fanne/Vanne, Henry: Robertsbridge; *ac. and sd.* 1496, *d.* 1497, *p.* 1498 (Chichester; *Reg. E. Story*, ff. 190r, 190v, 192r, 193r); noted when not yet ordained priest, 1491 (SAL, *MS 14*, f. 59v).
Fante: *see* Westmester.
Faram/Ffarham, John: Boxley; *ac.* 1496 (Canterbury; *Reg. J. Morton*, p. 134 [No. 445a]); now a priest but apostate, 1512 (TNA, C81/1788/7).
Farlington/Farington, John: Byland; *ac. sd.* and *d.* 1482, *p.* 1485 (York; Cross and Vickers, 1995, p. 98); abbot, Byland, 1499–1509 (Smith, 2008, p. 278).
Farlington/? *al.* Lyn, John: Rievaulx; *sd.* and *d.* 1490, *p.* 1493; may have died by 1538 (York; Cross and Vickers, 1995, pp. 167, 178).
Farlington/?Leefe/Lease, Robert: Byland; *ac.* and *sd.* 1521, *d.* 1522, *p.* 1524 (York; Cross and Vickers, 1995, pp. 99, 106).
Farrington, Richard: Bruern; 1533 (*DCP*, p. 5), 1535, when professed but not yet ordained priest (*VE* **2**, p. 265); in house at its suppression, 1536 (Baskerville, 1930, p. 334).
Ffarlington/Farlington/*al.* Bradley, William: Rievaulx; *sd.* 1531, *p.* 1534 as 'Plington' (York); *disp.* 1538, pension, £5–6–8 (*FOR*, p. 156); perhaps curate of Grindale, Yorkshire, 1549, and vicar of Whenby, Yorkshire, 1554; seemingly died before 1564 (Cross and Vickers, 1995, pp. 169–70, 173–74).
?Farndale/Frandale, John: Kirkstead; *p.* 1532 (Lincoln; *Reg. J. Longland*, f. 30v).
Ffarnton, Thomas: Rufford *sd.* 1534, *p.* 1536 (York; *Reg. E. Lee*, ff. 192r, 195v).
Farny: *see* Fferny.
Farrand, William: Roche; *d.* 1509 (York; Cross and Vickers, 1995, p. 187).
Farre, *al.* Malvern, Thomas: last cellarer, Hailes, *disp.* 1540 (*FOR*, p. 208); rector of Pinnock, Gloucs., (by dispensation) 1530; dies 1552 (Baskerville, 1927, p. 89).
Farsy, Stephen: Bindon, 1539 (TNA, E322/21, when became the vicar of the parish (VCH, *Dorset* **2**, 1975, p. 86). Could he be *Stephen Sherborne*, q.v. At the suppression he was appointed with stipend of £5–6–8 to serve the cure of Bindon, but the king reserved 'all manner of tithes and oblations' (TNA, E314/77).
Fatherwed': *see* **Guisburn.**
Faucon/Fawkon, John: sub–sacrist and guest–master, Sibton, 1509 (*SAE*, pp. 140–41); sub–prior when *disp.* 1536 (*SBC* **4**, pp. 110–11 [No. 1187]; *LP* **10**, p. 520 [No. 1247]).
Fawcett, Gibert: Kirkstall, *sd.* and *d.* 1495, *p.* 1496 (York; Cross and Vickers, 1995, p. 139).
Ffawcett, Leonard: Furness: *sd.* 1516, *d.* and *p.* 1517 (York, *Reg. T. Wolsey*, ff. 174v, 175v, 177v).
Fawell/Fowell, John: John: Ford; *ac.* and *sd.* 1509; *d.* 1510, *p.* 1512 (Exeter; *Reg. H. Oldham*, ff. 99r, 101v, 102r, 108r); pension, 1539, £5–6–8, (Youings, 1971, p. 186; Weaver, 1891, p. 5; still in receipt of £5–6–8 pension in 1555 (TNA, E164/31, f. 34v).
Fawkon: *see* Facon.
?Fery, John: Furness, detained in The Fleet prison, 1516/17 (TNA, E135/2/30).

Ffacy: *see* Pfacye.

Ffeeste, Richard: prior, St Mary Graces, 1511 (London; *Reg. R. Fitzjames*, f. 160v [171v]).

Ffekenham, Thomas: Bordesley; *ac.* and *sd.* 1504, *d.* 1506 (Worcester; *Reg. S. Gigli*, ff. 289, 291, 294).

Fferney/Ferny(s)/Farny, George: monk, Dieulacres, *sd.* and *d.* 1514; *p.* 1515 (Lichfield; *Reg. G. Blyth*, n–f.); *disp.* 1538; 'reward' £2–10–0 (Walcott, 1871, p. 216); pension, £6 (Hibbert, 1910, pp. 239, 242; *FOR*, p. 160; Staffordshire Archives 2/32/00, p. 45).

Ffontes/Ffountance/Ffontanes, Richard: Buildwas; *ac.* 1523, *d.* 1524, *p.* 1525 (Lichfield; *Reg. G. Blyth*, n–f.).

Fforster, Richard: Rufford; *p.* 1533 (York; *Reg. E. Lee*, f.186r).

Ffox, Robert: Rufford; *sd.* and *d.* 1534 (York; *Reg. E. Lee*, ff. 188v, 192r).

Franck, John: professed at Fürstenfeld abbey, Bavaria; later transferring to Medmenham; *disp.* 1502 (*CPL* **17**, Part 1, p. 597 [No. 973].

Ffulburn, William: Sawtry; *sd.* 1517, *d.* 1519, *p.* 1520 (Lincoln; *Reg. W. Atwater*, ff. 123v, 128r, 133r).

Ffurber/Ferber, Robert: Combermere, *disp.* 1538 (*DKR*, p. 17, *FOR*, p. 154); pension, £4 (TNA, E315/233, f. 77v).

Ffynkell/Ffynkill, Robert: Stratford; *ac*, 1514, *sd.*, *d.* and *p.* 1516 (London; *Reg. R. Fitzjames*, ff.178r [167r], 182v [171v], 183r [172r], 184r [173r].

Finch: *see* Fynch.

Fishburne/Fishborne, Richard: Roche, *sd., d.* and *p.* 1522 (York); signed deed of surrender, 1538 (TNA, E322/204); *disp.* 1538 (*FOR*, p. 144); in receipt of £5 pension.as late as 1555 (TNA, E164/31, f.53r); signed letters testimonial, 1555; probably vicar, North Muskham, 1557–1563 when died (Cross, 1993, pp. 201, 203).

Fisher, Henry: Rewley; *sd.* 1485, *d.* 1487, *p.* 1488 (Lincoln; *Reg. J. Russell*, ff. 19v, 25r, 27r, 28v).

Fisher, John: Kirkstead; *sd.* 1486; *p.* 1490 (Lincoln; *Reg. J. Russell*, ff. 21v, 37r).

Fisher, William: *see* London.

?Fishwick, John: Woburn; *ac.* 1490 (Lincoln; *Reg. J. Russell*, f.37r).

Flatbury/Fladbury William: cellarer, Warden, 1534; (*LP* **7**, p. 568 [No. 1518]); last abbot, Sibton; 1534–36 (*SBC* **4**, pp. 6, 64 [No. 1117]); subject of complaint that he had tried to sell the abbey before the dissolution (TNA, C1/815/40; Smith, 2008, p. 332); *disp.* 1536 (*FOR*, 70; *LP* **10**, p. 520 [No. 1247]).

Flaxford, John: Waverley; *p.* 1491 (Winchester; *Reg. P. Courtenay*, f. 18v).

Flaxley, Richard: Flaxley; *d.* 1486 (Hereford; *Reg. T. Myllyng*, p. 183).

Flaxley, Richard: Kingswood; *p.* 1481 (Worcester; *Reg. J. Alcock*, f. 263).

Flaxley, *al.* Haneys, Richard: Bordesley; *d.* 1497 (Lichfield; *Reg. J. Arundell*, f. 261); *disp.* 1509 (*CPL* **19**, p. 154 [No. 263]).

Ffleming, John: Calder; *sd.* and *d.* 1516 (York; *Reg. T. Wolsey*, ff. 175r, 176r).

Fletcher, John: Stratford; *sd.* 1501, *d.* 1503 (London; *Reg. W. Warham*, ff. 82v, 87r).

Fle(t)cher, Thomas: cellarer, Vale Royal, when signed deed of surrender and *disp.* 1538 (*DKR*, p. 46; *FOR*, p. 162); in receipt of his £6 pension in 1555 (TNA, E164/31, f.69r).

Flitton, John: Woburn; *sd.* 1491 (Lincoln; *Reg. J. Russell*, f. 42r).

Flynt, Nicholas: Fountains; *ac., sd. d.,* and *p.* 1517 (York; Cross and Vickers, 1995, p. 114).

Fole, William: Buckfast, sometime after 1515 (Stéphan, 1970, p. 183).

Ford, John: Kirkstall, *sd.* 1482, *d.*1483, *p.* 1487 (York; Cross and Vickers, 1995, p. 139).

Forde, John: Woburn; *sd.* 1522, *d.* 1527, *p.* 1528 (Lincoln; *Reg. J. Longland*, ff. 5r, 18v, 22v); *disp.* 1538 (*FOR*, p. 145).

Ford, Thomas: Ford; *d.* 1495 (Salisbury; *Reg. J. Blyth*, f.104v); *p.* 1497 (Lincoln; *Reg. W. Smith*, n.f.).

Ford: *see also* Ilmystre.

Forest, John: Sawley; *sd.* 1517, *d.* 1518, *p.* 1519 (York; Cross and Vickers, 1995, p. 200); *disp.* 1536 (*FOR*, p. 58).

Forest, Laurence: Whalley; examined re plate of abbey, 1537 (*LP* **12**, Part 1, p. 280 [No. 621]); procurator, as distinct from cellarer, 1536 (TNA, E315/427/3, f. 2v).

Fforest, William: Quarr; *sd., d.* and *p.* 1509 (Winchester; *Reg. R. Fox* **2**, ff. 24r, 25r). May be the next but one named monk, having moved to Thame.

Forest, William: Furness; signed deed of surrender, 1537 (TNA, E322/91).

Forrest, William: Thame; signed deed of surrender, 1539 (*DKR*, p. 43); perhaps by 1542 Minor Canon, Cardinal's College: Christchurch, Oxford, with his monastic pension of £5; ministered at Thame, 1551–1552; vicar, Bledlow, Oxfordshire., 1553–1576; vicar, Adwell, Oxon., 1576; resigned, 1585 (Baskerville, 1930, p. 336).

Forester/Forster, James: Furness, signed deed of surrender and *disp.* 1537 (*FOR*, p. 97; TNA, E322/91); perhaps mis–transcribed as James Procter who *disp.* with licence of non–residence, 4–08–1535, fee of £4–10–0 (*FOR*, p. 21); acquired land in the Whalley area (Haigh, 1969, pp. 97, 114).

Forster, John: Furness; *p.* 1496 (York; *Reg. T. Rotherham*, n–f.).

Forster, Roger: Sawley; *ac.* 1488, *d.* and *p.* 1489 (York; Cross and Vickers, 1995, p. 199).

Forward, John: abbot, Quarr, 1479–1493 (Smith, 2008, p. 321).

Foster/Forster, John: Whalley; *p.* 1518 (York; *Reg. T. Wolsey*, f.181v); pitancier, Whalley, 1536 (TNA, SC6/HENVIII/1796; E315/427/3, .f. 1r–v); *disp.* 1537 (*FOR*, p. 91).

Foston, James: Byland; *sd.* 1493, *p.* 1496 (York; Cross, 1995, p. 98).

Foston, *al.* Leefe/Lease/Lerisse, Robert: Byland; *ac.* and *sd.* 1521, *d.*1522, *p.* 1524 (York); *disp.* 1539 (*DKR*, p. 13, *FOR*, p. 181); pension, £5–6–8; died 1552 (Cross, 1995, pp. 99–100, 106).

Fote/Faute, *see*: Westmester.

Fountains, James: Hailes; *p.* 1512 (Worcester; *Reg. S. Gigli*, f. 315).

Fountains, Thomas: Hailes; *sd.* 1492, *d.* 1493 (Worcester; *Reg. R. Morton*, ff. 156, 158).

Fountners/Fountance, Alexander: Sawley; *sd.* 1504, *d.* 1505, *p.* 1506 (York; Cross and Vickers, 1995, pp. 200, 204 [1995]); *disp.* 1536 (*FOR*, p. 58).

Fowler, John: Dunkeswell; *disp.* 1497 (*CPL* **17**, Part 1,p. 8 [No. 13]).

Fowler, John: Kirkstall, *ac.*1504, *sd.* and *d.* 1505 (York; Cross, 1995, p. 140).

Foxwist, Roger: Vale Royal; *d.* 1506, *p.* 1509 (Lichfield; *Reg. G. Blyth*, n–f.).

Frampton, William: *see* Hampton.

Freman/*al.* Aylson, William: Combe, *disp.* 1538 (*DKR*, pp. 16–17, *FOR*, p. 176); pension of £6 received as late as 1555 (TNA, E164/31, f. 48v).

Freman, Richard: Merevale; *sd., d.* and *p.* 1494 (Lichfield; *Reg. W. Smith*, ff.176v, 179v, 181v). In community, 1497 (TNA, E315/283, f. 1).

Freyer, Edward: Bordesley; *p.* 1527 (Worcester;*Reg. R. Morton addenda*, f. 164); could he be *Edward Erlingham* cited above?

Froddeshym [Frodsham], Richard: Buildwas; *ac.* 1511 (Lichfield; *Reg. G. Blyth*, n–f.)

Frye, Richard: last cellarer, Beaulieu, 1538; the last abbot appealed for an increase in his pension from £5 to £6–13–4, but he became rector of Farley, Wiltshire, on 17–09–1539 (*DKR*, p. 9; Hockey, 1976, pp. 182, 186–87).

Fuller, John: Tilty; *sd.* and *d.* 1493, *p.* 1494 (London; *Reg. R. Hill*, ff. 27r, 29r [bis]).

Fylay, John: last cellarer/bursar, Revesby, *disp.* 1538 (Essex Archives., D/DRg 1/103–104; *FOR*, p. 128).

Fynch, William: Stratford; *d.* 1489 (London; *Reg. T. Kemp*, f. 226).

Fyngale, Christopher: Jervaulx; *sd.* 1496, *d.* 1497, *p.* 1499 (York; Cross and Vickers, 1995, p. 129).
Fysher, 'Fraternus': Llantarnam; *d.* 1513 (Hereford; *Reg. R. Mayew*, p. 263).

Game, *al.* London, Augustine: Warden; *d.* 1485, *p.* 1487 (Lincoln; *Reg. J. Russell*, ff. 20r, 26v); abbot, 1500–1533 (Smith, 2008, p. 347; *LP* **1**, Part 1, p. 232 [No. 438/2, m. 31]).
Gamlynghey, John: Sawtry; *ac.* and *sd.* 1500, *d.* 1501, *p.* 1504 (Lincoln; *Reg. W. Smith*, ff. 21r, 26v, 44r).
Gardner/Garner, Brian: last prior, Furness; *p.* 1502 (York, *Reg. T. Savage*, f. 113r); accused of a rebellious assembly, but signed deed of surrender and *disp.* 1537 (TNA, E322/91; *FOR*, p. 97; Gasquet, 1899, p. 274).
Gardiner, Roger: Waverley; *ac., sd., d.* and *p.* 1509 (Winchester; *Reg. R. Fox* **2**, ff. 23v, 24r, 25r, 25v).
Gardener, Roger: Vale Royal, signed deed of surrender and *disp.* 1538 (*DKR*, p. 46; *FOR*, p. 162).
Garford/Carford, William: Fountains; pension, 1539, £6 (Cross and Vickers, 1995, pp. 115, 121).
Garforth, Thomas: Kirkstead, *disp.* 1498, and permitted to wear habit under a secular priest's attire (*CPL* **17**, Part 1, p. 294 [No. 447]).
Gargrave, George: Pipewell; *p.* 1515 (Lincoln; *Reg. W. Atwater*, f. 114r).
Gargrave, John: Roche; *sd.* and *d.* 1490, *p.* 1493 (Cross and Vickers, 1995, p. 186).
Gargrave, John: Swineshead; *sd.* 1513, *d.* 1514 (Lincoln; *Reg. W. Smith*, n–f.; *Reg. T. Wolsey*, f. 15r.)
Garlond, Richard: Newenham; *disp.* 1498 (*CPL* **17**, Part 1, p. 242 [No. 37]).
Garner: see Gardner.
Garnforth/Garnethorpe, Martin: Louth Park; *ac.* 1501, *sd.* 1502, *d.* 1503 (Lincoln; *Reg. W. Smith*, ff. 28r, 35r, 40v).
Gatyns/Gavitins/Gabitus/Gabatus, Thomas: Pipewell; signed deed of surrender and *disp.* 1538 (*DKR*, p. 37; *FOR*, p. 160); in receipt of pension of £5 as late as 1555 (TNA, E164/31, f. 43r).
Gaulby: *see* Ewalbre.
Gawdstrenght, William: Swineshead; *sd.* 1523 (Lincoln; *Reg. J. Longland*, f. 6v). *See also:* **Goldisborough.**
Gay, John: Cleeve; *sd.* and *d.* 1500, *p.* 1502 (Wells; *Reg. O. King*, ff. 113–14, 120). Very probably he is the under–mentioned monk, having moved from Cleeve at its earlier suppression in 1537.
Gaye/Saye, John: monk, Dunkeswell, at its suppression, 1539; pension, £6–13–4, and appointed to the 'cure' of Sheldon, but if he was impotent, pension reduced to £5–6–8; perhaps he was sick or old (*DKR*, p. 19; TNA, E322/76; Sparks, 1978, pp. 109–10).
Gayes, Thomas: Margam, *disp.* 1537 (*FOR*, p. 93).
Gaykney, Thomas: Revesby; *p.* 1487 (Lincoln; *Reg. J. Russell*, f.24v).
Geddyngton, Thomas: Pipewell; *sd.* and *d.* 1524; *p.* 1528 (Lincoln; *Reg. J. Longland*, ff.8r, 9r, 22v).
Genynge(s), John: Dunkeswell, *sd.* 1530, (Exeter; *Reg. J. Vesey*, ff. 170v); present at its suppression, 1539 (*DKR*, p. 19); pension, £4–13–4 (*LP* **14**, Part 1, p. 115 [No. 293]; in 1540/41 was a chaplain or vicar of Dunkeswell (*Devonshire Notes and Queries* **17**, 1932, p. 85; Sparks, 1978, pp. 109–10, 113). Died at Norlegh, Devon,1567 (Snell, 1967, p. 146).
Geoffrey ap David: perhaps the same monk as Geoffrey David, the later abbot of Cwmhir, *q.v.*; monk, Whitland, *p.* 1502 (*EPD* **2**, p. 733).
Geoffrey, Gruffydd: 'Gruffydd, by the name of Geoffrey'; abbot, Cymer, 1499–1506 (TNA, LR1/213, f. 271; University of Bangor, Nannau Deeds 20, 914).
Gerves: *see* Langton.
Gest, Henry: Rewley, *disp.* 1536 (*FOR*, p. 78).
Gethin, John: Dore; *d.* 1450 (Worcester; *Reg. J. Carpenter*, f. 528).

Gethin, John: Tintern; *ac.* 1511 (Worcester; *Reg. S. Gigli*); moved at Tintern's suppression in 1537 to Kingswood abbey where parish priest; *disp.* 1538; 'reward and finding', £2–13–4, pension, £4–13–4 (TNA, E36/152); ; involved in later litigation with his former abbot of Tintern, Richard Wyche; at some stage then became parish priest of Newnham, Gloucestershire, (*DKR*, p. 25, FOR, p. 131; *MA* **23**, p. 68).

?Gewby, John: Revesby; *d.* 1507 (Lincoln; *Reg. W. Smith, n–f.*). Perhaps the same cleric as *John Grebbe*, q.v.

Gibbes, John: Stratford; *sd.* 1528, *p.* 1532 (London; *Reg. C. Tunstall*, f. 162r; *Reg. R. Stokesley*, f. 128v); signed deed of surrender and *disp.* 1538 (*DKR*, p. 42, FOR, p. 129); in receipt of £5 pension in 1555 (TNA, E164/31, f. 9v).

Gibson, Richard: Tilty; *p.* 1525 (London; *Reg. C. Tunstall*, f. 152v); signed deed of surrender, 1536 (*DKR*, p. 45).

Gilbert, *al.* Atherston, Richard: Merevale, 1497 (TNA, E315/283, f. 1).

Gilboye, Wybert: formerly monk of Stratford and now of St Mary Graces – *disp.* to wear the habit of his Order beneath that of a secular priest,. £4 fee; 31–12–1537 (*FOR*, p. 118).

Gill/Gyll, Alfred/Avery; Buckfast; *d.* and *p.* 1489 (Exeter; *Reg. R. Fox*, ff. 153r, 154r); abbot, Buckfast; blessed, 12–04–1512, dies, 1525 (Stéphan, 1970, pp. 177, 181–86).

Gill, Richard: Newenham; *sd.* 1524, *d.* and *p.* 1525 (Exeter; *Reg. J. Vesey*, ff. 154r, 154v, 157r); last abbot, 1530–1539; *disp.* 1540 (*FOR*, p. 216); pension of £48 received as late as 1555 (TNA, E164/31, f.34v); allegedly misused the abbey seal; may have been chaplain after the Suppression at the altar of St Cross in Exeter Cathedral until 1548 with a stipend of £4 (*Devon and Cornwall Notes and Queries* **17**, 1932–33, p. 336; Orme, 1979, p. 94); then held the Devonshire living of Farway and Offwell until his death in 1573 (Baskerville, 1937, pp. 200–01).

Gyll, Thomas: Buckfast; *ac.* 1530, *sd.* 1533, *d.* 1535 (Exeter; *Reg. J. Vesey*, ff. 172v, 181v, 187r); *disp.* 1539 (*DKR*, p. 12); in receipt of pension of £5 in 1555 (TNA, E164/31, f. 34r); seemingly a chaplain, Woodland, Devon, 1540/41 (Stéphan, 1970, p. 214).

Gilling: *see* Gyllyng.

Gilman: *see* Gyllam.

Gisburght, *al.* Whalley, John: Rievaulx; *sd.* 1531 (York); *disp.* 1538. Not mentioned in the pension lists (Cross, 1995, pp. 170, 185; *FOR*, p. 156).

Gisburgh, Robert: Rievaulx; *sd.* 1497, *d.* 1498 (York; Cross and Vickers, 1995, p. 168).

Gisburne/Guisburgh, *al.* Fairweather, James: Rievaulx: *ac.* 1531, *d.* 1532, *p.* 1534 (York); objected to the deposition of Abbot Kirkby in 1533 (TNA, STAC2/7/217); signed deed of surrender and *disp.* 1538; pension, £5; perhaps the later vicar of Marton in Cleveland of that name in 1542, dying as its incumbent in 1565 (*DKR*, p. 38, FOR, p. 156, Cross and Vickers, 1995, pp. 170, 176).

Gisburne/Gisborne, John: Calder; *sd.* and *d.* 1525 (York; *Reg. T. Wolsey*, ff. 204v, 205v); accused, perhaps spuriously, of sodomy in Crown visitation of 1535, when alleged to desire release from his monastic vows (*LP* **10**, p. 138 [No. 364]); VCH, *Cumberland* **2**, 1968, p. 177).

Gisburn, John: Sawley; *ac., sd.,* and *d.* 1486; *p.* 1489 (York; Cross and Vickers, 1995, p. 199).

Gisburne, Robert: Sawley; *ac.* 1526, *sd., d.* and *p.* 1527 (York; Cross and Vickers, 1995, p. 200); *disp.* 1536 (*FOR*, p. 58).

Gisburn, Thomas: Sawley; *sd.* 1517 (York; Cross and Vickers, 1995, p. 200).

Gladwyn, Stephen: Revesby; *sd.* 1490, *d.* 1491, *p.* 1492 (Lincoln; *Reg. J. Russell*, ff. 35r, 40v, 44/45v).

Glassynbury, Robert: Boxley; *ac.* 1496 (Canterbury, *Reg. J. Morton*, p. 134 [No. 445a]).

Glaston: *see* Woolaston.

Glewe, Richard: Rewley; *ac.* 1498, *d.* and *p.* 1501 (Lincoln; *Reg. W. Smith*, ff. 30v, 31v).

Gloucester, Nicholas: Kingswood; *p.* 1457 (Worcester; *Reg. J. Carpenter*, f. 544).

Gloucester, Walter: Kingswood; *d.* 1503 (Wells; *Reg. O. King*, f. 122).

Gloucester, William: Hailes; *ac.* 1479, *d.* 1483 (Worcester; *Reg. J. Alcock*, ff. 257, 273). Ordained priest whilst under age (*SAP* **2**, pp. 388–89 [No. 3142]).

Gloucester, William/Walter: Tintern; *p.* 1525, *disp.* 1537 (*Reg. C. Bothe*, p. 319, *FOR*, p. 91).

Glyn(n), John: abbot, Dore, 1524–1528 – when dismissed for negligence; blessed, Whitbourne manor, 22 March 1526 (Hereford; *Reg. C. Bothe*, p. 177); last abbot, Cwmhir, 1535–36; had also been an unsuccessful superior of another house; mis-transcribed as 'Elin' in *LP* 13, Part 1, p. 577 [No. 1520]; Williams, 1976, pp. 26–27; 2001, p. 77).

Gobston/Gosberton, George: Swineshead; *sd.* 1525, *d.* 1526, *p.* 1527 (Lincoln; *Reg. J. Longland*, ff. 11v, 13v, 19r); *disp.* 1536 (*FOR*, p. 67).

Goch, Gruffydd: prior, Aberconwy, 1482–90, ? abbot, Cymer, 1495 (Williams, 1981, p. 44; 2001, pp. 65–66).

Godalmyng, *al.* Smyth, Thomas: Waverley; *ac.* 1487; *sd.* 1488; *d.* 1489, *p.* 1491 (Winchester; *Reg. P. Courtenay*, ff. 13r, 15r, 18v; Baigent, 1883, p. 209).

Goday, John: Coggeshall; 1496, when previously dispensed to hold a benefice (*CPL* **16**, p. 416 [No. 626]).

Godesave/Goodefore, John: St Mary Graces; *d.* and *p.* 1492 (London; *CL*). Might he be *John Goday*?

Godfrey, John: Pipewell; signed deed of surrender and *disp.* 1538 (*DKR*, p. 37; *FOR*, p. 160); in receipt of pension of £5–6–8 as late as 1555 (TNA, E164/31, f. 43r).

Godfrey, John: Boxley, *t.* and *a.* 1522, *sd.* 1523 (Rochester; *Reg. J. Fisher*, f. 92r); *disp.* 1538 (TNA, E314/20/11, f. 1r; *FOR*, p. 123); pension, £2–13–4 (TNA, E314/77).

Godfrey, Richard: Holm Cultram, by 1533 (Gilbanks, 1899, p. 94; *LP* **6**, pp. 425–26 [No.988]); signed deed of surrender and *disp.* 1538; pension, £4 (*DKR*, p. 23; TNA, LR1/173, f. 147; *FOR*, pp. 123–24).

Godson, Benjamin: Fountains, *d.* 1509, *p.* 1511 (York; Cross and Vickers, 1995, p. 113); monk, Strata Marcella, *disp.* 1515 (*CPL* **20**, p. 359 [No. 510]).

Godwyn: *see* Goodwyn.

Golde, Henry: Coggeshall, *disp.* 1487 (*CPL* **16**, p. cxix).

Goldington, John: Warden; *p.* 1510 (Lincoln; *Reg. W. Smith*, n–f.).

Goldisborough/Golesbury, William: Swineshead; *d.* 1525, *p.* 1527 (Lincoln; *Reg. J. Longland*, ff.11v, 19r). He may be the monk, *William Gawdstrenght*, q.v.

Goldsmith/*al.* Castleton, Ralph: Vale Royal, *ac.* and *sd.* 1521, *d.* 1522, *p.* 1523 (Lichfield; *Reg. G. Blyth*, n–f.); proposed for the abbacy in 1535, but this was not to be (VCH, *Cheshire* **3**, 1980, p. 162); *disp.* before closure of his monastery, and permitted to wear the Cistercian habit beneath that of a secular priest; £4 fee; 1–03–1538 (*FOR*, p. 125).

Goll, William: Roche; *sd.* 1503, *d.* 1504, *p.* 1505 (York; Cross and Vickers, 1995, p. 187).

Golson, Randulph: possibly the preceding monk but one; monk, Vale Royal, 1535; favoured by William Brereton, esq., for election as abbot, but the community chose another (TNA, C1/902/16–18).

Gonell/Garnell, Thomas: Coggeshall; *sd.* 1527 (London; *Reg. C. Tunstall*, f. 160r); *p.* 1530 (*Reg. W. Warham, London sede–v.*, 2, f. 314r).

Goodals/Goodale, Francis: Dieulacres; *ac.* 1509, *d.* 1510 (Lichfield; *Reg. G. Blyth*, n–f.).

Goodwin, John (VI): Robertsbridge, *c.*1490 (SAL, *MS* 14, f. 59v); abbot, Robertsbridge, 1491 – at least 1511 (East Sussex R.O., RYE/123/4; Smith, 2008, p. 326); blessed, 12 November 1491, by the bishop of Chichester in the chapel of his Aldingbourne manor (West Sussex R.O., EPI/1/3, f. 92); general pardon, 1509 (*LP* 1, Part 1, p. 258 [No. 4/m.4]; *disp.* to receive a secular benefice *in* *commendam*, 1501 (*CPL* **17**, Part 1, p. 338 [No. 527]); held the rectory of Haythorne, Kent, until 1507 (LPL, CM51/41).

Goodwyn, John (VI): abbot, Sibton, 1520–22 (SBC, **4**, pp. 6, 65 [No. 1118], 74 [No. 1129]). Was he earlier abbot of Robertsbridge?

Gores, Nicholas: cellarer for a time, Tintern, 1484–85 (NLW, *Badminton Deeds,* Group 2, Nos. 14,476–78)

Gorynge, Richard: Waverley; *sd.* and *d.* 1487, *p.* 1490 (Winchester: *Reg. P. Courtenay,* ff. 13r, 16r).

Gosfelde/Goswell, Robert: Coggeshall; *ac.* 1522 (*Reg. W. Warham, London sede–v.* **2**, f. 298r)., *sd.* 1523, *p.* 1527 (London; *Reg. C. Tunstall,* ff. 2r, 8r); allegedly 'unlawfully used' by his abbot before he became a monk, *c.*1526; (*LP* **10**, pp. 59–60 [No. 164/2/i]); *disp.* 1538 (*FOR,* p. 124).

Gosse, John: Stratford; *ac.* 1510, *sd.* 1511 (London, *Reg. R. Fitzjames,* ff. 158r [169v], 160v [170v]).

Goston, William: Newminster, thirty–six years old in 1536 (TNA, SC12/13/65); *disp.* 1536 (*FOR,* p. 77).

Grace, John: Stoneleigh; *sd.* 1529, *d.* 1531, *p.* 1532 (Lichfield; *Reg. G. Blyth,* n–f.); *disp.* 1537 (*FOR,* p. 88).

Grace, John: Woburn; *sd.* 1527, *d.* 1528, *p.* 1532 (Lincoln; *Reg. J. Longland,* ff. 18v, 22v, 31v); *disp.* 1538 (*FOR,* p. 145); at the visitation in 1538 he complained of the quality of bread served (VCH, *County of Bedford* **1**, 1972, p. 367n): lived for some time at Woburn after the suppression (Thomson, 1933, p. 141)

Graffham/Gressham, Robert: Warden; *sd.* 1508, *d.* 1509, *p.* 1510 (Lincoln; *Reg. W. Smith,* n–f.).

Graffon/Graffeham/Gresham, Richard: Sawtry; *sd.* 1512, *d.* 1513 (Lincoln: *Reg. W. Smith,* n–f.); *p.* 1516 (*Reg. W. Atwater,* f. 119r); *disp.* 1536/37 (*FOR,* pp. 66, 116).

Grafton, John: : Pipewell; *ac.* 1503, *sd.* and *d.* 1505, *p.* 1506 (Lincoln; *Reg. W. Smith,* f.42v, n–f.).

Grafton, Richard: Hailes; *sd.* 1501, *d.* 1503, *p.* 1504 (Worcester; *Reg. S. Gigli,* ff. 289, 402–03). Grafton: *see also* Graston.

Graison, Roger: Meaux; *sd.* 1510, *p.* 1513 (York; Cross and Vickers, 1995, p. 154).

Grame/Graham/Graym, Thomas: Holm Cultram; proctor of its Wigton church, 1533 (*LP* **6**, pp. 348–49 *No.* [781]); in 1537 he laid several accusations against his abbot, and wanted the abbacy for himself but was unsuccessful (Gasquet, 1899, pp. 279–81; Harrison, 1981, p. 129); last cellarer, 1538 (*DKR,* p. 23; *LP* **13**, Part 1, pp. 160–61 [No. 434]); signed deed of surrender and *disp.* 1538 (*FOR,* pp. 123–24); pension, £6–13–4 (TNA, LR1/173, f.147).

Grantham, William: Swineshead; *sd.* 1531, *d.* 1532, *p.* 1533 (Lincoln; *Reg. J. Longland,* ff. 27v, 30v, 34r).

Graston/Grafton, Peter: Meaux; *sd.* 1489, *d.* 1491, *p.* 1492 (York; Cross and Vickers, 1995, p. 153).

Graver, John: Boxley, *disp.* 1538 (*FOR,* p. 123); pension, £2–13–4 (TNA, E315/77).

Gray, John: abbot, Roche; resigned 5–06–1479 (Aveling, 1870, p. 62).

Grebbe, John: Revesby; *p.* 1508 (Lincoln; *Reg. W. Smith,* n–f.). Perhaps the same monk as *John Gewby,* q.v.

Green/Greyn Francis: Whalley; *sd.* 1523, *p.* 1525 (Lichfield; *Reg. G. Blyth,* n–f.); *disp.* 1537 (*FOR,* p. 110).

Green, Gilbert: Combermere, *sd.* 1532 (*Reg. G. Blyth,* n–f.); *disp.* 1538 (*DKR,* p. 17, *FOR,* p. 154); in receipt of pension of £5 as late as 1555 (TNA, E164/31, f. 69r).

Green/Greyn/Groyn John: Furness; detained in The Fleet prison, 1516/17 (TNA, C1/586/63; E135/2/30); accused, perhaps spuriously, of immoral relations with a woman, 1535 (*AF,* p. 324); alleged to have uttered treasonable words, but signed deed of surrender and *disp.* 1537 (TNA, E322/91; *FOR,* p. 97; Gasquet, 1899, p. 274.

Grene, John: St Mary Graces; *disp.* 1491 (*CPL* **15**, p. 385 [No. 727]).

Grene, John: Cleeve; *p.* 1498 (Wells; *Reg. O. King*, f. 109).

Green, John: perhaps cellarer, Sibton, 1520 (Ridgard and Norton, 2011, pp. 40–41).

Grene, John: Louth Park; *disp.* 6–08–1536; (*FOR*, p. 69).

Grene, Richard: Garendon; *sd.* 1516, *d.* 1518 (Lincoln; *Reg. W. Atwater*, ff. 118r, 125v); *p.* 1523 (*Reg. J. Longland*, f. 7v).

Green, Richard: Biddlesden; last abbot, 1535–1538, recommended to Cromwell by one Thomas Bedyll; commission to bless directed to Bishop Robert King, 4 May 1535 (Lincoln; *Reg. J. Longland*, f. 259v); *disp.* 1538, pension, £40 (*FOR*, p. 179; *LP* 8, p. 259 [No. 688]; Smith, 2008, p. 268). Either he, or the prior of Thame of the same name, supplicated for the B. Th, (Oxford) in 1529 and to oppose, 1533 (*BRUO* 2, p. 245). On the continuance of the monastery (8 August 1536) he was renamed as abbot (*LP* 11, p. 156 [No. 385/21]) pension, £40 (VCH, *County of Buckingham*, 1, 1905, p.367).

Greene/Grey, Richard: last prior, Thame; signed deed of surrender, 1539 (*DKR*, p. 43). Could he be the former abbot of Biddlesden? His position as prior gave him a pension of £7 (TNA, E314/77) which he still enjoyed in 1555 (TNA, E164/31, f. 42v).

Greyne, Robert: highly praised monk, Stratford, 1489–90; on business concerning St Bernard's College, Oxford, including restoration and new building there 1491–93 (*Letters*, pp. 121 [No. 59], 132 [No. 66], 196 [No. 97]).

Grene/Green, Stephen: Meaux; *ac.* 1490, *d.* 1491, *p.* 1495 (York; Cross and Vickers, 1995, p. 153).

Green, Stephen: abbot, Grace Dieu, 1515–17; last abbot, Buildwas, by 1521–1536 (Williams, 1976, p. 64; TNA, SC6/2496, f. 2v); pension, £16 (TNA, E315/244, No. 106; *LP* 12, Part 2, p. 166 [No. 411/13]); involved in a dispute re price of kine and cheese, *c.* 1530 (TNA, C1/645/31).

Grene, Thomas: Vaudey; *sd.* 1510, *d.* 1511 (Lincoln; *Reg. W. Smith*, n–f.).

Grene, William: Louth Park; *sd.* 1533 (Lincoln; *Reg. J. Longland*, f.33r).

Green, William: Ford; pension, 1539, £5–6–8 (Youings, 1971, p. 186; Weaver, 1891, p.5).

Greenslade/Greneslade, Thomas: Cleeve, ?1518/29 (TNA, C1/521/20).

Grenewood, Richard: Buildwas; *sd.* 1523 (Lichfield; *Reg. G. Blyth*, n–f.).

Grenewood/?Denton, Thomas: Fountains; *sd.* 1501; *d.* 1502, *p.* 1503; pension, 1539, £6, received until 1562; appears to have settled in Ripon (Cross and Vickers, 1995, pp. 115, 121).

Gregg/Gregges, William: Jervaulx, *disp.* 1537 (*FOR*, p. 119); may have become rector of Leven, Yorkshire, in 1557 and still so in 1575 (Cross and Vickers, 1995, pp. 133–34; *Patent*, 1575, p. 366).).

Grentham, William: Swineshead, *disp.* 1536 (*FOR*, p. 67).

Grenton, John: Jervaulx; *d.* 1509, *p.* 1510 (York; Cross and Vickers, 1995, p. 130).

Gresham: *see* Graffham.

Gresley/Grysley, John: Pipewell; *sd.* 1509, *d.* 1510, *p.* 1512 (Lincoln; *Reg. W. Smith*, n–f.).

Gresnen, Robert: Sawtry; *sd.* 1512 (Lincoln; *Reg. W. Smith*, n–f.).

Greston, Thomas: Furness, 1510 (*AF*, p. 303).

Grimsby: *see* Grymesby.

Gruffydd, John: abbot, Margam, 1517–1528, when forced to resign; plea by the king who desired that 'he may be sent home again' (*LP* 4, p. 2005 [Nos. 4604, 4606]); he may have been the last abbot of Grace Dieu, 1534–36, *disp.* 1537; pension, £4 p.a., (TNA. E315/244, no. 151); perhaps therefore not the John Griffith who was a monk of Hailes at its suppression (*FOR*, pp. 100, 208; Williams, 1976, p. 64; 2001, p. 71; TNA, E315/92/75).The John Gruffydd of Hailes was in receipt of pension of £6 as late as 1555 (TNA, E164/31, f.40r), and was perhaps successively chantry priest in Goshill, Isle of Wight, from 1540; rector, Holy Rood, Southampton, 1552–53; deprived for marriage, 1554, but rector, West Woodhay, Berks. 1554–64 (the accounts of John Gruffydd are confusing: Baskerville, 1927, p. 89).

Gruffydd, John ap Rhys ap: house not noted; disp. to hold a benefice, to wear habit of his Order under that of a secular priest, despite defect of birth, 23–02–1536 (*FOR*, p. 45).

Grymesby, Henry: Rewley; *p.* 1514 (Lincoln; *Reg. W. Atwater*, f. 111r).

Grymesby, William: Revesby; *sd.* 1490, *d.* 1491, *p.* 1492 (Lincoln; *Reg. J. Russell*, ff. 35r, 40v, 44v/45).

Grysome/ Upgrypyth, Richard: Bindon; pension, 1539, £4 (TNA, E314/77; E322/21).

Gudman/Guddam, Adam: Combermere; *ac.* and *sd.* 1512 (Lichfield; *Reg. G. Blyth*, n–f.).

Guerne,Henry: Whalley; *p.* 1516 (Lichfield; *Reg. G. Blyth*, n–f.).

Guisburn: *see* Gisburne.

Guiseley/Gyseley, Thomas: Roche; *sd.* and *d.* 1490, *p.* 1491 (Cross and Vcikers, 1995, p. 186).

Gwilym Moris ap Hywel Vachan: Neath, 1468, when seeks a dispensation on account of defect of birth (*SAP* 2, p. 63 [No. 1519).

Guy, *al.* Ewyl/Symbs', John: Beaulieu; *disp.* 1496 (*CPL* **16**, p. 357 [No. 530]).

Gye, Arnold/Arnald: Buckfast; *ac.* 1500, *sd.* 1502, *p.* 1503 (Exeter; *Reg. R. Redmayne*, ff.41r, 42v; *Reg. J. Arundell*, f.14r); B. D. (Oxon.) 1518 (Stevenson, 1939, p. 43); provisor, St Bernard's College, Oxford, 1528–1531; last prior, Buckfast –1539 (*DKR*, p. 12); pension, £8 plus a 'reward' of £2 (Stéphan, 1970, pp. 177, 212; Smith, 2008, p. 319; allegedly later left St Bernard's College, with unpaid bills (TNA, C1/1125/15).

Gye, William: Buckland; *sd.* and *d.* 1514, *p.* 1518 (Exeter; *Reg. H. Oldham*, ff. 115r, 117v, 129r); *disp.* 1539 (*FOR*, p. 178); pension, £5, received as late as 1555 (TNA, E164/31, f. 34r); chaplain, Columpton, Devon, 1540/41 (*Devonshire Notes and Queries* **17**, 1932, p. 88).

Gykering/Eykering, Robert: Rufford; *sd.* and *d.* 1500, *p.* 1501 (York; *Reg. T. Rotherham*, n–f.; *Reg. T. Savage*, f. 110r).

Gylford (Guildford), Richard: Beaulieu, cellarer in 1530 (Winchester R.O. 5M53/67); *disp.* 1538 (*FOR*, p. 131); pension, £5 (TNA, E314/77).

Gyll: *see* Gill.

Gyllam/Gilman, Thomas: *see* Lenton.

Gyllete, Edward: Kirkstead; *disp.* 1513 (*CPL* **20**, p. 148 [No. 225]).

Gylling/*al.* Hall, Robert: Rievaulx; *sd.* and *d.* 1495, *p.* 1499 (York); opposed the deposition of Abbot Kirkby in 1533 (TNA, STAC2/7/217), signed deed of surrender and *disp.* 1538; pension, £5–6–8 (*DKR*, p. 38, *FOR*, p. 156); was perhaps later a chantry priest in Holy Trinity, Hull, until 1548, and later incumbent of Laytham, Yorkshire. Dying in 1556, he left a number of books including a New Testament in English (Cross, 1995, pp. 168, 170, 176–77).

Gilling, Richard: Rievaulx; *p.* 1531 (York; Cross and Vickers, 1995, p. 169).

Gyllyng, Robert: Jervaulx; *sd.* 1496, *d.* 1497, *p.* 1499 (York; Cross and Vickers, 1995, p. 129).

Gyllyng, William: *see* Wetherall.

Gysse: *see* Gibbs.

Hacker/Halker, Simon: kitchener, Beaulieu, *disp.* 1538 (*DKR*, p. 9; *FOR*, p. 131); pension, £5 (TNA, E314/77). Perhaps the same monk as *Simon* Skerwhitt, q.v.

Haddington, Thomas: Rewley, *disp.* 1536 (*FOR*, p. 78).

Hadley/Hadleigh/Hadliam, Thomas: cellarer, Sibton, 1536 (*SBC* **4**, pp. 110–11 [No. 1187]): *disp.* 1536 (*FOR*, p. 70); then may have moved to Pipewell where a monk of the same name signed the deed of surrender and *disp.* 1538 (*DKR*, p. 37; *FOR*, p. 160); pension, £5–6–8 (TNA,E315/233, ff. 88v–89r).

Hadocke: *see* Haydoke.

Haeth/Heythe, Geoffrey: *see* Heath..

Hafferstone.Heverston, Robert: Vale Royal; *ac.* 1523, *sd.* 1525, *d.* and *p.* 1526 (Lichfield; *Reg. G. Blyth*, n–f.).

Hageley: *see* Baguley.

Hagforth, Thomas: Jervaulx; *d.* 1509, *p.* 1510 (York; Cross and Vickers, 1995, p. 130).

Hagger, Robert: Woburn; *sd.* and *d.* 1503 (Lincoln; *Reg. W. Smith*, ff. 38v, 41r).

Hagmond/Haymond, John: Whalley; *p.* 1518 (York; *Reg. R. Wolsey*, f. 181v).

Hagneby, Adam: Revesby; *d.* 1507 (Lincoln; *Reg. W. Smith*, n–f.).

Hailes/*al.* Eddon/Eden', Richard: Hailes: *sd.* 1527 (Worcester; *Reg. R. Morton addenda*, f. 165); scholar, St Bernard's College, Oxford, 1538–39; B.D. 1538 (Stevenson, 1939, pp. 44–45); precentor, Hailes, 1537/38 (*CHA*, p. 85); *disp.* 1540 (*FOR*, p. 208); in receipt of pension of £7 as late as 1555 (TNA, E164/31, f. 40r); living in Wells, Somerset, 1552–53; rector, North Petherton, Somerset, and a prebendary of Winchester Cathedral, 1554; from 1557 a member of the restored community of Westminster Abbey (Baskerville, 1927, p. 89; 1937, p. 191); principal, Gloucester Hall, Oxford, 1563; pensioner, St John's College, Oxford, 1564 (Bell, 2010, p. 349).

Halford, William: abbot, Bordesley, 1452–1497, possibly to 1504 (Worcester; *Reg. J. Alcock*, ff. 72, 135, 151; *Reg. R. Morton*, ff. 9, 118; *Reg. S. Gigli*, f. 33; Smith, 2008, p.270).

Haliday, Nicholas: Roche; *d.* 1509 (York; Cross and Vickers, 1995, p. 187).

Halifax, Thomas: Kirkstead; *sd.* 1526, *p.* 1528 (Lincoln; *Reg. J. Longland*, ff. 13v, 21v).

Halifax/Hallyfax, William: Vaudey; *ac.* and *sd.* 1496, *d.* 1498 (Lincoln; *Reg. W. Smith*, n.f.)

Halyfax, William: Sawley; *sd.* 1491, *d.* 1493, *p.* 1498 (York; Cross and Vickers, 1995, p. 199).

Hall, John: Hailes, *disp.* 1540 (*FOR*, p. 208); pension, £2–13–4, died at Christmas 1540 (Baskerville, 1927, p. 90; *LP* **14**, Part 1, p. 291 (No.771).

Hall, Robert [?John]: Roche; *sd.* 1516, *d.* 1517, *p.* 1518 (York; Cross, 1995, p. 187).

Hall, Robert: Bruern, 1535 (*VE* **2**, p. 265); still in house at its suppression, 1536 (Baskerville, 1930, p. 334).

Hall, William: Netley; *d.* 1509 (Winchester; *Reg. R. Fox* **2**, f. 25r); in community, 1518, by which time priested (TNA, E314/101).

Hall, William: Bruern; *sd.* 1517 (Lincoln; *Reg. W. Atwater*, f. 122r); in community, 1533 (, p. 5).

Hall, William: Jervaulx, *disp.* 1537 (*FOR*, p. 119).

Hall: *see also* **Gyllyng**.

Halliday, Anthony: Fountains; *sd.* and *d.* 1521 (York; Cross and Vickers, 1995, p. 114); *and see:* **Kendall.**

Halliday, *al.* Holydaye, William: Hailes; *disp.* 1540 (*FOR*, p. 208); vicar, Toddington, Gloucs., a Hailes living, 1541; died 1546 (Baskerville, 1927, p. 90).

Halton, John: prior, Furness, 1521 (*DCL*, p. 97).

Halton, Nicholas: Furness, 1510 (*AF*, p. 303).

Halton, William: Revesby; *d.* 1507 (Lincoln; *Reg. W. Smith*, n–f.).

Halton: *see also* Alton, Hilton.

Hamerton/Hamilton/Hampton, Michael: Furness, detained in The Fleet prison, 1516/17 (TNA, C1/586/63; E135/2/30); last prior; signed deed of surrender, 1537; could he be the same monk as *Michael Thornbrae?* q.v. (*DKR*, p. 21; TNA, E322/91). Did he transfer to another house? (Haigh, 1969, p. 120).

Hamerton, Thomas: Rievaulx, but apostate, 1489/90 or 1513/14 (TNA, C81/1788/42).

Hamirton, William: prior, Fountains, 1509 (*FLB*, p. 118 [No. 130])

Hamond/Hammond/Hawmond, Henry: Sawley; *sd.* 1497, *d.* 1498 (York; Cross and Vickers, 1995, p. 199; abbot, Sawley, 1506–?1527 (Harland, 1853, p. 42; *MCP*, p. 130 [No. 131]).

Hamond/Haymond/Hartmund, Thomas: Combermere; *sd.* 1487, *p.* 1488 (Lichfield; *Reg. J. Hales,* ff. 228v, 243v); prior, 1520 (*LCCS,* p. 129); *disp.* 1538 (*FOR,* p. 154); pension, £8 (TNA, E315/233, f. 76r). A jubilarian.

Hampole. John: Roche; *sd.* and *d.* 1490, *p.* 1493 (Cross and Vickers, 1995, p. 186).

Hampton, Griffin/Griffith [Graffinus]: Beaulieu; *ac., sd.,* and *d.* 1488, *p.* 1490 (Winchester; *Reg. P. Courtenay,* ff. 13r, 13v, 14r, 17r); *disp.* 1538; pension, £6 (TNA, E314/20/11, ff. 1v–2r, FOR, p. 131; Hockey, 1976, p. 187). A jubilarian.

Hampton, Harman: Beaulieu, *disp.* 1538 (*DKR,* p. 9; *FOR,* p. 131); curate of Eling and Ower, Hants., 1545 (Hockey, 1976, p. 187); pension of £5 received in 1555 (TNA, E164/31, f. 13r).

Hampton, John: Swineshead; *sd.* 1485, *d.* and *p.* 1486 (Lincoln; *Reg. J. Russell,* ff. 18r, 21r, 22v).

Hampton, John: Thame; *sd. and d.* 1505, *p.* 1506 (Lincoln; *Reg. W. Smith,* n.f.).

Hampton/Hartman/Hortun/Hunting, John: Bordesley; *ac.* 1533 (Worcester; *Reg. R. Morton addenda,* f. 173); *disp.* 1538 (*FOR,* p. 149; TNA, E322/26); pension, £4 – assessed for subsidy in 1540 (Bodleian Library, Oxford, Tanner MS 343).

Hampton, Nicholas: sub-prior, Kingswood, signed deed of surrender and *disp.* 1538 (*DKR,* p. 25, FOR, p. 131); 'reward and finding', 1538, £2–13–4 (TNA, E36/152, f. 21); in receipt of his £4 pension as late as 1555 (TNA, E164/31, f. 29r). Possibly, with the *alias* of Andrews, was curate of Kingswood in 1547 (Baskerville, 1927, p. 88).

HamptonHamerton, Thomas: Stratford; *sd.* 1501, *p.* 1505 (London; *Reg. W. Warham,* f. 82v; *Reg. W. Barons,* f. 90v).

Hampton/al. Sutton, Thomas: Combe; *sd.* 1511, *p.* 1512 (Lichfield; *Reg. G. Blyth,* n–f); cellarer, 1538, when *disp.* (*FOR,* p. 176; TNA, E315/245, f. 42); pension of £6 received as late as 1555 (TNA, E164/31, f. 48v). Perhaps the twin brother of:

Hampton/al. Sutton, William: Combe; *sd.* 1511, *p.* 1512 (Lichfield; *Reg. G. Blyth,* n–f); *disp.* 1538 (*FOR,* p. 176); pension of £6 received as late as 1555 (TNA, E164/31, f.48v); kitchener at time of suppression (*LP* 14, Part 1, pp. 44 [No. 111], 602 [No. 1355]; TNA, E315/245, f. 42).

Hampton, William: Stoneleigh; *ac.* 1505, *sd.* and *d.* 1507 (Lichfield; *Reg. G. Blyth,* n–f).

Hampton, William: Woburn; *sd.* 1522, *d.* 1527, *p.* 1528 (Lincoln; *Reg. J. Longland,* ff. 5r, 18v, 22v); abbot Hobbes's secretary, and at his request transcribed a book entitled 'Of the Power of Peter' (Gasquet, 1899, pp. 286, 288); *disp.* 1538 (*FOR,* p. 145).

Hancock, John: Cleeve; *sd.* and *d.* 1504 (Canterbury; *Reg. W. Warham, Wells sede v.,* ff. 198r, 208v; SRO, D/D/B Reg.29, f. 6v); *p.* 1505 (Wells; *Reg. H. de Castello,* f. 141).

Hanley, Roger: Bordesley; *ac.* and *sd.* 1532 (Worcester; *Reg. R. Morton addenda,* f. 171).

Hanley, Thomas: Hailes; *sd.* 1459 (Worcester; *Reg. J. Carpenter,* f. 549).

Hanley/Henley, William: Hailes; *ac.* and *sd.* 1479; *p.* 1489 (but the latter may be the ordination of a monk of similar name (Worcester; *Reg. J. Alcock,* f. 257; *Reg. R. Morton,* f. 144). Could he be *William Halliday,* q.v.

Hanney: *see* Brewarne, King.

Happa/Harper, John: Roche, 1531 (TNA, E135/3/6); signed deed of surrender and *disp.* 1538 (TNA, E322/204; FOR, p. 144). Pension, £5 (TNA, E314/20/11, f. 4v); died by Michaelmas 1543 (Cross and Vickers, 1995, pp. 188, 192).

Harbotell, William: Coggeshall; *disp.* 1516, but to retain his place in the monastery (*CPL* 20, p. 457 [No. 643], *Cf.* p. 456 [No. 639]).

Harcote/Harcourt/Haryett, John: Pipewell; signed deed of surrender and *disp.* 1538 (*DKR,* p. 37; FOR, p. 160); in receipt of pension of £6 as late as 1555 (TNA, E164/31, f. 43r).

Hardest, Thomas: Bruern; *sd.* 1512 (Lincoln; *Reg. W. Smith,* n-f.).

Hardford, William: Jervaulx; *sd.* 1526, *d.* 1527 (York; Cross and Vickers, 1995, pp. 131, 134).

Hardwyn, Oliver: Combe; *disp.* 1538 (*FOR*, p. 176); pension, £5–6–8 (TNA, E314/77).

Hardy/Hordy, Henry: Revesby; *ac.* 1502, *sd.* 1505, *p.* 1507 (Lincoln; *Reg. W. Smith*, f. 36v, n–f.); *disp.* 1538 (*FOR*, p. 128; Essex R.O., D/DRg 1/104).

Hardy, Roger: Fountains; *sd.* 1514, *d.* 1516, *p.* 1517 (York; Cross and Vickers, 1995, pp. 113–14, 122).

Hare/Harye, Thomas: Revesby; *p.* 1502 (Lincoln; *Reg. W. Smith*, f. 37r); *disp.* 1538 (*FOR*, p. 128; Essex R.O. D/DRg 1/104).

Hareware/Harwood, John: abbot, Hulton, by 1528 – 1535; became abbot of Vale Royal in 'free election', 1535; Sir John Brereton, a royal officer, was angered by the election saying that he 'would do unto Harwood such a displeasure that it should be very heavy and hard for him to abide in Cheshire' (TNA, C1/902/16–18); charged with divers offences at Vale Royal by Cromwell in person on 31 March 1539, but given a pension of £60 p.a. and the abbey's plate; the trial being a ruse to ensure the monastery surrendered quietly; signed deed of surrender and *disp.* 1538 (*DKR*, p. 46; *FOR*, p. 162); still alive in 1546 (Tomkinson, 1985, p. 66; *LB*, p. 23; Baskerville, 1937, p. 68–9; Smith, 2008, p. 301).

Harfeld/Herwet, William: Coggeshall; *sd., d.* and *p.* 1507 (London; *Reg. R. Fitzjames*, ff. 95r, 96r, 96v); *disp.* 1511 (*CPL* **19**, p. 249 [No. 426]); possibly the same monk as *William Harbotell*, q.v..

Harington, John: Furness; *p.* 1502 (York, *Reg. T. Savage*, f. 113r); detained in The Fleet prison, 1516/17 (TNA, C1/586/63; E135/2/30); signed deed of surrender and *disp.* 1537 (TNA, E322/91; *FOR*, p. 97).

Harpeham: *see* Austen.

Haryngton/Haryton/Honyngton, John: Bruern; *sd.* 1532, *d.* 1533, *p.* 1534 (Lincoln; *Reg. J. Longland*, ff. 32r, 34v, 38r); perhaps the monk also transcribed as *John Hymingyon*, and *John Emmington*; if so, still in house at its suppression, 1536 (Baskerville, 1930, p. 334).

Harper, John: *see* Happa.

Harper/Harry, William: St Mary Graces, *disp.* 1539 (*FOR*, p. 182); in receipt of pension of £5–6–8 in 1555 (TNA, E164/31, f. 4) when parson of North Pykenham, Norfolk and of Sampford Courtenay, Devon, bringing in a total income of £51–18–8; in addition his pension of £5–6–8 which was paid to him at Bury St Edmund's, and a further £1–6–8 pension from Stoke College, Suffolk, where perhaps he had been a chaplain or chantry priest – that pension was paid to him by the hands of one Mr Chester. William was 'reputed as a Catholic man and never married;' holding his parishes from 1542, he died in 1558 (Baskerville, 1933, p. 214).

Harries, John: Tintern; *d.* 1514 (Worcester; *Reg. S. Gigli*, f. 401).

Harries, Thomas: Margam; *d.* 1498 (Worcester; *Reg. G. Gigli*, f. 27).

Harrietsam, John: Boxley; *sd.* 1518 (Rochester; *Reg. J. Fisher*, f. 59v).

Harrison/Herison, John: Byland; *d.* 1512, *p.* 1518 (York); Crown grant, awarded before the dissolution, for life of the church of Old Byland; original pension of 40s cancelled because of his Crown presentation (Cross and Vickers, 1995, pp. 99, 100, 104; *FOR*, p. 92; *LP* **14**, Part 1, p. 67 [No 185]).

Harrison, Richard: abbot, Kirkstead, 1528–1537 (TNA, C1/656/35); hanged at Lincoln, 7 March 1537 (Dodds **2**, 1915, p. 152; Nash, 1965, p. 103; *LP* **13**, Part 1, p. 564 [No. 1519/21]).

Harrison/Herryson, Thomas: Roche, *sd., d.* and *p.* 1522 (York); *disp.* 1538 (*FOR*, p. 144; in receipt of £5 pension 5 (TNA, E164/31, f. 53r); perhaps rector of Hemsworth, Yorkshire, from 1564, still alive in 1571 (Cross and Vickers, 1995, p. 193).

Harrison: *and see* Herryson.

Hart, George; Buckfast; *t. ac.,* and *sd.* 1533 (Exeter; *Reg. J. Vesey*, f. 181v; Stéphan, 1970, p. 178).

Hart/Herte, Richard: Bindon, 1539 (TNA, E322/21); pension, £2 (TNA, E314/77).

Hart/Hert, Robert: Louth Park; *d.* 1510, *p.* 1511 (Lincoln; *Reg. W. Smith*, n–f.); *disp.* 6–08–1536 (*FOR*, p. 69); staying in Louth town shortly after the suppression of the monastery (Gasquet, 1899, pp. 205–06).

Haretopp/Harelope, John: Coggeshall; *ex.* and *ac.* 1509 (London; *Reg. R. Fitzjames*, f. 168r [157r]).

Hartilbury, John: Dore; *p.* 1511 (Hereford, *Reg. R. Mayew*, p. 256); still in the monastery in 1526 (Williams, 1976, p. 26).

Hartely, Thomas: Furness, instituted as vicar of Urswick, Cumbria, , 27 April 1536 (*FOR*, p. 53); seems to have left the monastery before its suppression in 1537.

Hartlepool/Hartipoole, Robert (Roger): Robert: Jervaulx; *ac.* 1526, *sd.* and *d.* 1527 (York); was involved in the aftermath of the Pilgrimage of Grace and fled to Scotland (Cross and Vickers, 1995, pp. 131, 134; Dodds **2**, 1915, p. 107).

Hartmund: *see* Hamond.

Harvy/Hervye, Robert: Buckland; *ac., d.* and *p.* 1526 (Exeter; *Reg. J. Vesey*, ff. 169v, 160v, 161r); *disp.* 1539 (*DKR*, p. 12; *FOR*, p. 178). Gill, 1968, p. 42, gives his Christian name as Hugh, with a pension of £4–13–4..

Harwood, Henry: Kirkstall, *p.* 1482 (York; Cross and Vickers, 1995, p. 139).

Harwood, William: Sawley; *ac.* 1526, *sd.* and *d.* 1527 (York; Cross and Vickers, 1995, p. 201); *disp.* 1536 (*FOR*, p. 58).

Harwood: *see also* Hareware, Horwodd.

Haryet/Haryat/Hotnett, Christopher: Pipewell; signed deed of surrender and *disp.* 1538 (*DKR*, p. 37; *FOR*, p. 160); pension, 1538, £6 (TNA, SC6/HENVIII/7339)..

Hasby, Richard: Merevale; *sd., d.* and *p.* 1494 (Lichfield; *Reg. W. Smith*, ff. 176v, 179v, 181v). In community, 1497 (TNA, E315/283, f. 1).

Hashenhurst, William: *see* **Asshenhurst.**

Hatham/Hathorn, William: Garendon; *sd.* 1503, *d.*1504, *p.* 1505 (Lincoln; *Reg. W. Smith*, ff. 42v, 46v, n–f.); *disp.* 1536 (*FOR*, p. 76).

Hatherley, Edward: Robertsbridge; *ac.* 1512, *sd.* 1514 (Canterbury; *Reg. W. Warham* **2**, f. 266r–v); *d.* 1514, *p.* 1515 (London; *Reg.R. Fitzjames*, ff. 178v, 190r).

Hatton/Halton, William: Dieulacres; *sd.* 1495 (Lichfield; *Reg. W. Smith*, ff. 188,199); *d.* 1496 (Canterbury, for Coventry and Lichfield; *Reg. J. Morton* **2**, p. 118 [No. 428]); *p.* 1496 (*Reg. J. Arundel*, f.259v).

Hawker: *see* Hacker, Simon.

Hawkland: *see* Awkeland.

Hawnes, John: Warden; *sd.* and *p.* 1492 (Lincoln; *Reg. J. Russell*, ff. 43r, 46v).

Hawnes, Richard: Woburn; *ac.* 1491 (Lincoln; *Reg. J. Russell*, f. 42r); disp. 1538 (*FOR*, p. 145).

Hawnes, Richard: Woburn; *sd.* 1532, *d.* 1533, *p.* 1537 (Lincoln; *Reg. J. Longland*, ff. 31r, 36r, 55v).

Hawnsley, John: Meaux; *ac.* 1536, *sd.* 1537; pension, £5; died 1551; probably to be identified with either *John Mapleton* or *John Wythornwike*, q.v. (Cross and Vickers, 1995, p. 159).

Hawthley/Hoothby, Edward: Robertsbridge; *sd.* 1514, *p.* 1515 (London; *Reg. R. Fitzjames*, ff. 167r [178r], 180r).

Hawthorne, William: *see* Hatham.

Hawthorne: *see also* Heythorne.

Haxby, Robert: Roche; *sd.* and *d.* 1525, *p.* 1526 (York; Cross, 1995, pp.187, 193).

Haydocke/Hadocke, William: Whalley; *sd.* 1523, *d.* 1524 (Lichfield; *Reg. G. Blyth*, n–f.); penultimate prior there, 'attainted of treason' (TNA, E315427/3, f. 3); executed by hanging at Whalley, 13 March 1537 (Gasquet, 1899, p. 270; Baskerville, 1937, pp. 166–67; Dodds **2**, 1915, p. 142).

Hayne, John: Combe; *disp.* 1486 (*CPL* **15**, p. 64 [No. 125]).

Hayster, John: Rewley; *p.* 1514 (Lincoln; *Reg. W. Atwater*, f.111r).

Hayter: *see* Studley.

Hayton, William: Fountains; *sd.* 1486, *d.* 1487 (Cross and Vickers, 1995, p. 111).

Hayward, John: Dunkeswell, 1539 (TNA, E322/76; Sparks, 1978, p. 109). Does not appear in the pension list (*LP* **14**, Part 1, p. 115 [No. 293]), unless an *alias* for *John Genyng* or *John Segar*.

Haywood, Thomas: Netley; *ac.* 1489, *sd.* 1491 (Winchester; *Reg. P. Courtenay*, ff. 15v, 18v).

Headingley, Christopher: Kirkstall, *d.* 1534 (York; Cross and Vickers, 1995, pp. 141, 151); *p.* 1536 (London; *Reg. R. Stokesley*, f. 136v). His family name may have been *Wilson*.

Healaugh, Richard of: prior, Sawtry, *c.*1530 (Smith, 2008, p. 330).

Heath/Heithe, Geoffrey: Hulton, signed deed of surrender and *disp.* 1538 (TNA, E322/106; *FOR*, p. 154); pension of only £1–13–0 (TNA, E315/233, f. 23r). so perhaps only a novice at the dissolution; by 1557 he was perhaps curate of Bentley, West Midlands (Tomkinson, 1985, p. 68).

Hebden, John: Meaux; *ac.* and *sd.* 1488, *d.* 1489, *p.* 1493 (York; Cross and Vickers, 1995, p. 153).

Hebden/Shebden, Richard: Fountains; pension, 1539, £6–13–4 (Cross and Vickers, 1995, 1995, p. 115); *and see:* **Castell**.

Hebstote/Hepiscote, Ralph/Ranulph: Newminster, thirty years old in 1536 (TNA, SC12/13/65); *disp.* 1536 (*FOR*, p. 77).

Hed, Peter: Rewley, *disp.* 1536 (*FOR*, p. 78).

Hede, John: Waverley; *ex.* and *sd.* 1510, *d.* 1511 (Winchester; *Reg. R. Fox* **3**, ff. 26v, 51r); *p.* 1512 (London; *Reg. R. Fitzjames*, f. 162v [172r]).

Heggys, Robert: Bruerne; *disp.* 1515, and permitted to wear his habit under the dress of a secular priest (*CPL* **20**, p. 577 [No. 55].

Helier: *see* Helyer.

Hellay/Helagh/Hylye/Hole, al. Wyke, Willian: Roche, by 1531 (*LP* **5**, p.107 [No. 226]; *sd.* 1535, *d.* 1536 (York); charged, perhaps spuriously, with self–abuse at the visitation of February 1536; *disp.* 1538, pension, £3–6–8, when still a deacon and a novice (TNA, E314/77); later sold his pension but was assessed on it in 1573 (Cross and Vickers, 1995, pp. 188, 193; TNA, E322/204; *FOR*, p. 144; TNA, E314/20/11, f. 4v).

Helmeden: *see* Holmeden.

Helmsley/al/ Symondson, Christopher: Rievaulx; *ac.* and *sd.* 1531, *d.* 1532, *p.* 1534 (York; Cross and Vickers, 1995, p. 170); signed deed of surrender and *disp.* 1538; pension, £5–6–8 (*DKR*, p. 38; *FOR*, p. 156). In receipt of his pension as late as 1556, he may have become vicar of Kirkby Fleetham, Yorkshire, and accused of recusancy in 1570 (Cross, 1995, p. 182).

Helmesley, Henry: Revesby; *disp.* 1499 (*CPL* 17, Part 1, p. 111 [No. 171]).

Helmsley, Richard: *see* Pereson.

Helmesley, William: Rievaulx; *sd.* and *d.* 1490, *p.* 1493 (York; Cross and Vickers, 1995, p. 167); at St Bernard's College, *c.* 1510; D. Th. 1511, after 18 years study (*BRUO* **2**, p. 905); abbot, Rievaulx, 1513–1528; commission to bless issued to the bishop of Negroponte by the archbishop of York, 18 November 1513 (*Reg. C. Bainbridge, f. 45r*); member of York Corpus Christi Guild, 1515 (Smith, 2008, p. 325).

Helmsley, William: Fountains, *sd.* 1503, *d.* 1504, *p.* 1506 (York; Cross and Vickers, 1995, p. 113).

Helperby, John: Rievaulx; *sd.* 1482, *d.* 1483 (York; *Cross* [1995] 167).

Helyer, Edward: Buckfast; *ac.* 1500 (Exeter; *Reg. R. Redmayne*, f. 41r); *d.* 1503 (London; *Reg. W. Warham*, f. 87r); later may have been chaplain and Master of St Lawrence's Grammar School, Ashburton, Devon; dies, 1509/10 (Stéphan, 1970, pp. 176–77).

Helys: *see* Elys.

Hemseworth/Emmysworth, *al.* Preston, Robert: Kirkstall; *sd.* 1527 (York); pension, 1539, £5–6–8 (Cross and Vickers, 1995, pp. 141–142, 146); recorded as in receipt of pension in 1555 (TNA, E164/31, f.53v) – but this cannot be as his will was proved 1553 when he was resident at Preston in the parish of Kippax, Yorkshire; earlier he may have been curate of Swillingford (Lonsdale, 1972, p. 209).

Hemyng, John: Vaudey, *disp.* 1536 (*FOR*, p. 67).

Henbury, William: Bordesley, *d.* 1516 (Worcester; *Reg. S. Gigli*, f. 334).

Heney, John: monk, Kingswood; *p.* 1511 (Worcester; *Reg. S. Gigli*, f. 308).

Hendon: *see* Emden.

Hengham/Heygham, John: Sibton; papal leave to acquire a benefice, 1494 (*CPL* **16**, p. 278 [No. 382]; he took to wearing secular dress while holding a parochial chaplaincy, but mended his ways, 1499 (Canterbury; *Reg. J. Morton* **3**, p. 172 [No. 351].

Henley, John: Whalley, examined regarding the abbey plate, 1537 (*LP* **12**, Part 1, p. 280 [No. 621]); *disp.* 1537 (*FOR*, p. 91).

Henley, *al.* Cley, William: abbot, Netley, by 1504–1509; dispensed to hold a benefice *in commendam*, 1506 (*CPL* **18**, p. 446 [No. 630]); general pardon, 1509 (*LP* **1**, Part 1, p. 239 [No. 438/3, m. 9]); resigned 11–11–1509 (Winchester; *Reg. R. Fox* **2**, ff. 25v–26r), and collated to the vicarage of Hound, 23–09–1510; still alive in 1521 (Smith, 2008, p. 316).

Henley: *see also* **Hanley**.

Henry ... : Neath; *ord.* 1486, but grade not stated (St David's; *EPD* **2**, pp. 464–65).

Henry ... : abbot, Hulton 1502 (Smith, 2008, p. 301).

Henryson, John: Kirkstall; pension, 1539, £6–13–4 (Cross and Vickers, 1995, pp. 142, 145); he may have been *John Potter* or *John Spoinge*, q.v. Perhaps the cleric of this name buried in Leeds parish church in 1545 (Lonsdale, 1972, p. 206).

Hepford, Thomas: St Mary Graces; *d.* 1520 (London; *CL*).

Hepham, Edmund: Vaudey; *disp.*1487, but to 'continue to enjoy all the privileges of his Order' (*CPL* **15**, p. 41 [No. 73].

Heptonstall/*al.* Pomfret, Edward: Kirkstall; *sd.* 1505, *d.* 1506, *p.* 1507 (York); pension, 1539, £6–13–4; still paid in 1555 (TNA, E164/31, f. 53v); priest in Leeds (CIY); made his will in 1558 in favour of his monastery should it be re-founded, leaving it the chest full of books he had brought from the abbey, and requesting burial in Leeds parish church (Cross, 1993, pp. 200–01; 1995, pp. 142, 146; Sitch, 2000, p. 25).

Hepworth/Hipworth: *see* Darby.

Herde/?Broderton, Thomas: Sawley, *disp.* 1536 (*FOR*, p. 58; Cross and Vickers, 1995, p. 205).

Hereford, Thomas: Dore; *ac.* 1486, *d.* 1488, *p.* 1489 (Hereford; *Reg. T. Myllyng*, pp. 173, 175, 177).

Herison: *and see* Harrison.

Herryson/Harrison, William: Vale Royal, signed deed of surrender and *disp.* 1538 (*DKR*, p. 46; *FOR*, p. 162); pension, £5 (TNA, E315/233,f. 67v).

Herman, Thomas: novice, Buildwas, *disp.* 1537 (*FOR*, p. 92).

Hermesley, John: Revesby; *d.* 1507 (Lincoln; *Reg. W. Smith*, n–f.).

Herncastre, Richard: Kirkstead; *sd.* 1499, *d.* 1500 (Lincoln; *Reg. W. Smith*, f. 22v.).

Heron: *see* Durham.

Hert, John: Rufford; *sd.* 1485, *d.* 1487, *p.* 1488 (York; *Reg. T. Rotherham*, f. 398r and n–f.).

Hertilpole: *see* Hartlepool.

Hertwith, John: Kirkstall, *ac.* 1533, *sd.* 1537 (York; Cross and Vickers, 1995, pp. 142, 151). He may be the monk, *John Snawe*, q.v. Alive in 1582.

Hertynton, William: Hulton; *ac.*, and *sd.* 1487, *d.* and *p.* 1488 (Lichfield; *Reg. J. Hales*, ff. 222, 223v, 236v, 240v).

Herwith, Thomas: prior, Fountains, 1501 (*FLB*, p. 69 [No. 77]).

Heryng, Dr: the abbot of St Mary Graces at Coggeshall on 2 September 1536 conversed with 'Dr Heryng, my predecessor, sometime abbot of Coggeshall' (*LP* **11**, p. 161 [No. 393]). He must be the same as *John Sampford*, q.v.

Heslerton/Eslerton/?Thompson, William: Meaux; *ac.* and *sd.* 1523, *d.* 1524, *p.* 1525 (York); pension, £6; may have been a chantry priest of Yokefleet, 'Howdenshire,' 1540; aged forty–six in 1548, he may then have become curate of Whitgift, Yorkshire; in 1552, aged fifty, he was living in Hull; alive in 1564 (York; Cross and Vickers, 1995, pp. 155, 164).

Heslington, John: Fountains; *sd.* 1491, *d.* 1492, *p.* 1495 (Cross and Vickers, 1995, p. 111); abbot, Roche, 1503 until at least 1531 (Smith, 2008, p. 327; *Cf.*. Stevenson, 1939, p. 45); in 1515 refused to deliver up title deeds entrusted to his deceased predecessor, John Morpeth (TNA, C1/323/18).

Heslington, William: abbot, Jervaulx, 1475, late abbot, 1487, when granted a general pardon, 1487 (Smith, 2008, p. 302; *Statuta* **5**, p. 336; *Patent* 1487, p. 191).

Heslington, William: Jervaulx; *p.* 1516 (York; Cross and Vickers, 1995, p. 131.

Hester/Hirst./Heth, 'Chrestannus' [?Christian]: Dieulacres; *p.* 1508 (Lichfield; *Reg. G. Blyth*, n–f.).

Hethe: *see* Rydforth.

Hethgerne/Hetharnoke, Henry: Woburn; *sd.* 1487, *d.* 1490 (Lincoln; *Reg. J. Russell*, ff. 26r, 37v). **Heverstone:** *see* Hafferstone.

Heythorne/Hethorne/Hawthorne, John: Waverley; *sd.* 1524, *d.* 1527, *p.* 1528 (Winchester; *Reg. R. Fox* 5, ff. 35v, 37v, 39r); *disp.* 1536 (*FOR*, pp. 67–68); curate of Waverley, 1541; rector of East Clandon, Surrey, 1545–71, when dies. Married in 1564, and bore a son, John (Baskerville, 1941, p. 18).

Heywood, Stephen: Bindon, 1539 (TNA, E322/21); pension, £5 (TNA, E314/77). Could he be *Stephen Sherborne*, q.v.

Hichson, Peter: Sibton, *disp.* 1536 (*FOR*, p. 70). Could this be an *alias* for *Peter Dewych*, q.v.? **Hickman:** *see* Hycheman.

Higgins: *see* Mynsternort.

Higham Ferrers/Hamferys, William: Biddlesden; *sd.* 1512, *d.* 1515 (Lincoln; *Reg. W. Smith*, n–f,, *Reg. W. Atwater*, f. 117v); *p.* (if same monk) 1523 (*Reg. J. Longland*, f. 6r).

Hill, William: Fountains; *p.* 1537 (York); nothing more is known of him (Cross and Vickers, 1995, pp. 114, 122).

Hilton, John: Hailes; *p.* 1515 (Worcester; *Reg. S. Gigli*, f. 327).

Hilton, Oliver: Jervaulx; *sd.* and *p.* 1513 (York; Cross and Vickers, 1995, p. 130).

Hilton/Halton, Robert: Sawley; *ac.*, *sd.* and *d.* 1486; *p.* 1488 (York; Cross and Vickers, 1995, p. 199); mentioned in chancery proceedings, 1493/1500 (TNA, C1/201/54).

Hilton: *see also* Hylton.

Hipworth: *see* Darby.

Hirst/Herste/Hyrste/Heth, Christopher: monk, Roche, *sd.* 1532 (York); in community, 1531 (TNA, E135/3/6); signed deed of surrender, 1538 (TNA, E322/204); *disp.* 1538 (*FOR*, p. 144; Cross and Vickers, 1995, pp. 188, 193–94); pension, £5 p.a. (TNA, E314/77).

Hirst, Nicholas: Roche; *p.* 1533 (Cross and Vickers, 1995, pp. 188, 194).

Hirst, William: Kirkstall, *sd.* and *d.* 1491; *p.* 1495 (York; Cross and Vickers, 1995, p. 139).

Hiw/How, David: Margam; *d.* and *p.* 1487 (St David's; *EPD* **2**, pp. 491, 509).

Hobbes, Robert: abbot, Woburn, by 1509–10–01–1538 (Bedfordshire Archives, Z813/3); general pardon, 1509 (*LP* **1**, Part 1, p. 214 [No. 438/1, m. 22]; executed at Woburn 14 June 1538 – although a very ill man (Knowles 1963, pp. 187–91).

Hobley, Thomas: Stratford; *d.* 1492, *p.* 1495 (London; *Reg. R. Hill*, ff. 25r, 32v).

Hobson/?Darington, William: Fountains; *d.* 1517 (York); pension, 1539: £5–6–8; may have become a chantry priest in Knaresborough, and in 1578 vicar of Aldbrough in Holderness (Cross and Vickers, 1995, pp. 114–15, 122).

Hoby, Thomas: Merevale; *ac.* and *sd.* 1525, *p.* 1526 (Lichfield; *Reg. G. Blyth*, n–f.).

Hodgeson/Hocheson, John: Kirkstead: *sd.* 1529, *p.* 1533 (Lincoln; *Reg. J. Longland*, ff. 24r, 34r); at one stage in the Lincolnshire rebellion of October 1536 he held two passports (*LP* **11**, p. 325 [No. 828/2viii–ix]).

Hogarth/Hogard, *al.* **York, Thomas:** Byland, *p.* 1515 (York); *disp.* 1539; pension, £8 (TNA, E314/77) altered from £6–13–4 (*LP* **14**, Part 1. 602 [No. 1355]); died 1545, whilst resident at Coxwold, Yorkshire (*DKR*, p. 13; *FOR*, p. 181; Cross and Vickers, 1995, pp. 99, 105).

Hoge/?York, Thomas: Holm Cultram; in house, 10–08–1536 (*LP* **11**, p. 115 [No. 276]); not ordained priest by 1538 when *disp.* (TNA, E314/20/11, f. 3r–v; *FOR*, pp. 123–24); does not appear in the pension list (TNA, LR1/173, f.147).

Ho(d)geson, Christopher: Hailes, *disp.* 1540 (*FOR*, p. 208); in receipt of pension of £2–13–4 as late as 1555 (TNA, E164/31, f. 40r); living at Lichfield, Staffs. 1552–53; perhaps rector, Newton Regis, Warwickshire, 1572–88 (Baskerville, 1927, p. 90).

Hogeson, Thomas: abbot, Woburn, 1500–1505 (Smith, 2008, p. 351); papal dispensation for 'incompatibility', 1501/02 (*CPL* **17**, Part 1, p. 650 [No. 1269]).

Hodgeson, William: Meaux; pension, £5; chantry priest in Knaresborough church, Yorkshire, in 1546; acted later as curate of Knaresborough, 1565; alive in 1571 (Cross and Vickers, 1995, pp. 156, 159).

Hogeson: *see also* **Thaxted.**

Hoghell, Christopher: Newminster, thirty–nine years old in 1536 (TNA, SC12/13/65).

Hoghton, Thomas: Roche; *d.* 1509 (York; Cross and Vickers, 1995, p. 187). Perhaps the monk known as *Thomas Smyth*, q.v.

Hokeson, Thomas: Whalley, *disp.* 1537 (*FOR*, p. 91).

Hola/Helsey/Hylye/Helay: *see* Hellay.

Holb: *see* Hobley;.

Holland, Edmund: Rushen; pension: £2–13–4 (TNA, SC6/HENVIII/5677 of 1540–41; Davey and Roscow, 2010, p. 175).

Holand/Hyland, John: Roche; in community by 1531 (*LP* **5**, p. 107 [No. 226]); *sd.* 1535, *d.* 1536 (York); probably the 'John Whelan' charged, perhaps spuriously, with self–abuse at the visitation of February 1536; seems to have left the house before the dissolution (Cross and Vickers, 1995, pp. 188, 194).

Holand, Thomas: Basingwerk; *d.* 1498, and *p.* 1500 (Lichfield; *Reg. J. Arundel*, ff. 272v, 287).

Holden, John: Whalley, *disp.* 1537 (*FOR*, p. 91).

Holgate, Thomas: Sawley; *d.* 1481, *p.* 1486 (York; Cross and Vickers, 1995, p. 199).

Holingbury/Holybery/Holinsbery, John: Boxley; *sd.* 1496, *d.* and *p.* 1497 (London; *Reg. T. Savage*, ff. 53r, 54r, 56v).

Holyngbourn', Stephen: Boxley; *ac.* 1514 (Canterbury; LPL, *Reg. W. Warham* **2**, f. 266v).

Holme, John: monk,, 'Ruffyn'; *p.* 1495 (York; *Reg. T. Rotherham*, n–f.).

Holme/Hombe, *al.* Milton, John: Hailes, *p.* 1489 (Worcester; *Reg. R. Morton,* f. 144); *disp.* 1540 (*FOR,* p. 208), pension, £2–13–4;; vicar, Didbrook, Gloucestershire., a Hailes living, from 1530 until death, either in 1547 or later (Baskerville, 1927, p. 90). A jubilarian.

Holme, Thomas: Rufford; *sd.* 1485, *d.* 1486, *p.* 1489 (York; *Reg. T. Rotherham,* n–f.).

Holme, Thomas: Combe; *disp.* 1539 (*FOR,* p. 176); in receipt of pension of £5–6–8 as late as 1555 (TNA, E164/31, f. 48v).

Holme: *see also* Beke.

Holmeden/Helmeden, Edward: Biddlesden; *ac.* 1523, *sd.* 1525, *p.* 1528 (Lincoln; *Reg. J. Longland,* ff. 5v, 10v, 22r).

Holt, William: Roche; *sd.* 1525 (York); did not sign suppression deed (Cross and Vickers, 1995, pp. 187, 194).

Holydaye: *see* **Halliday, William.** .

Holywell, William: Newminster; *p.* 1497 (Durham; *Reg. R. Fox* **2,** p. 49).

Hombe, John: *see* Holme.

?Hombre, John: Sawtry; *p.* 1527 (Lincoln; *Reg. J. Longland,* f. 20v).

Honyngton, John: prior, Bindon, 1535 (*VE* **1,** p. 24).

Honyngton: *see also* Haryngton.

Hooper, John: Cleeve; bishop of Gloucester and Worcester; executed 1555 (See Chapter 3).

Hooper/Hoper, Thomas: Buckland; *d.* 1514, *p.* 1518 (Exeter; *Reg. H. Oldham,* ff. 118v, 130v); *disp.* 1539 (*DKR,* p. 12; *FOR,* p. 178); pension, £5, received as late as 1555 (*TNA,* E164/31, f. 34r).

Hope, John: Robertsbridge, *disp.* 1536, before the monastery's closure (*FOR,* p. 44; Salzman, 1954, p. 34).

Hope, Richard: Valle Crucis; *ac.* 1499 (Lichfield; *Reg. J. Arundel,* f. 281v; the entry is confusing for it mistakenly reads: 'of the Carmelite Order, house of Valle Crucis.')

Hoper: *see* Pyttermister.

Hopkin, John: Margam, 1487–97 (Birch, 1897, pp. 351, 376; Smith, 2008, p. 310).

Hopkin, John: Margam, *disp.* 1536 (*FOR,* p. 68).

Hopkyns, John: Llantarnam; *sd.* 1528, *d.* 1529/30 (Worcester; *Reg. R. Morton addenda,* ff. 166, 170).

Hopkyns, Thomas: Hailes, *disp.* 1540 (*FOR,* p. 208); played an active role in the demolition of his monastery and the unauthorised sale of goods there; chaplain for a time to Robert Acton to whose custody the monastery was initially committed (Barnard, 1928, pp. 7, 9, 12); in receipt of pension of £5–6–8 as late as 1555 (TNA, E164/31, f. 40r); rector, Robbesford–cum.Bewdley, Worcestershire, 1544–45, died 1556 (Baskerville, 1927, p. 90).

Hopkins, William: Tintern; *disp.* 1537 (*FOR,* p. 92).

Hopworth, Richard: Woburn; *sd.* and *d.* 1509, *p.* 1513 (Lincoln; *Reg. W. Smith,* n–f.); *disp.* 1538 (*FOR,* p. 145).

Hornby, Richard: Jervaulx; *sd.* 1489, *d.* 1490, *p.* 1492 (York; Cross and Vickers, 1995, p. 129).

Hornby, Richard: Bruern; *sd.* and *d.* 1512 (Lincoln; *Reg. W. Smith,* n–f.).

Hornby, Thomas: Furness; accused, perhaps spuriously, of immoral relations with five women, 1535 (*AF,* p. 324); signed deed of surrender, 1537 (TNA, E322/91).

Horewood/Horwood, Thomas: monk, Hailes; *ac.* 1497, *d.* 1499 (Worcester; *Reg. S. Gigli,* ff. 25, 395). Could this be the undermentioned monk recorded much later at Whalley?

Horncastell, James: Revesby; *ac.* 1528, *sd., d.* and *p.* 1529 (Lincoln; *Reg. J. Longland,* ff. 21r, 23v, 24r, 25r).

Horncastell, Richard: Kirkstead; *ac.* 1506, *d.* and *p.* 1507 (Lincoln; *Reg. W. Smith,* n–f.).

Horncastell, Richard: Revesby; *d.* 1507, *p.* 1510 (Lincoln; *Reg. W. Smith,* n–f.).

Horncastre: *see* Herncastre.

Horowode, Thomas: Whalley, examined regarding the abbey's plate, 1537 (*LP* **12**, Part 1, p. 280 [No. 621]); *disp.* 1537 (*FOR*, p. 91).

Horsehed, Robert: Kirkstead, *disp.* 1537 (*FOR*, p. 96).

Horsforth/Horfford, George: Kirkstall, *d.* 1512, *p.* 1513 (York; Cross and Vickers, 1995, p. 141).

Horton, John: Stanley; *d.* 1458 (ordained in the conventual church of St James, Bristol, by the bishop of Worcester, 27 May; *Reg. J. Carpenter*, f. 546);.abbot, Stanley, by 1469 until at least 1490 (Smith, 2008, p. 333).

Horton, Richard: Newminster, twenty-five years old in 1536 and then a deacon (TNA, SC12/13/65); *disp.* 1536 (*FOR*, p. 77).

Horwodd/Harwood, John: Kirkstall; pension, 1539, £6–13–4 (Cross and Vickers, 1995,p. 142). He may have been either *John Potter* or *John Sponge.*

Hothe, Thomas: novice, Buildwas, *disp.* 1537 (*FOR*, p. 92).

Hothom, William: abbot, Revesby, 1484; possibly still abbot in 1497 (Smith, 2008, p. 322).

Hoton/Hooton/Hutton, John: Fountains; *sd.* 1514, *d.* 1516, *p.* 1517 (York); in February 1536 it was reported that he wished to leave the religious life, but pension of £5–6–8, received until 1559 (Cross and Vickers, pp. 114–15, 123).

Hoton, Thomas: Revesby; *ac.* 1487/92, *d.* 1493, *p.* 1494 (Lincoln; *Reg. J. Russell*, ff. 43/44v, 48/49v, 52r).

Houghton/Howhton, Thomas: Pipewell; *sd.* 1508, *d.* 1509 (Lincoln; *Reg. W. Smith*, n–f.); *p.* 1515 (*Reg. W. Atwater*, f. 112v).

House/Howys/Howes, Thomas: Warden; *sd.* and *d.* 1514 (Lincoln: *Reg. T. Wolsey*, ff. 13r, 14r); *p.* 1517 (*Reg. W. Atwater*, f. 123v); in house at suppression, 1538 (TNA, E314/20/11, f. 1r–v); in 1554 was resident at Stanground, Bedfordshire, was unmarried, and had his pension of £6–13–4 but no other ecclesiastical preferments (Hodgett, 1959, p. 92); was in receipt of his pension as late as 1555 (TNA, E164/31, f. 25v).

Howe, Edmund: Thame; signed deed of surrender, 1539 (*DKR*, p. 43); pension of £10, 1538 (TNA, E314/77); perhaps by 1544, rector of South Weston, Oxfordshire; living in Oxford, 1548; died 1549 (Baskerville, 1930, p. 33).

Howe, George: Cleeve; *sd.* 1525 (Wells; *Reg. J. Clerk*, f. 126).

Howells, Edward: possibly a monk of Stoneleigh; *p.* 1509 (Lichfield; *Reg. G. Blyth*, n–f.).

Howton(e), Henry: Strata Florida; *ac.* and *sd.* 1515 (Hereford; *Reg. R. Mayew*, pp. 270–71); *d.* and *p.* 1516 (Worcester; *Reg. S. Gigli*, f. 331).

Huby, Marmaduke: Fountains; *sd.* 19-09-1467 (in the Church of the Friars Minor, York); *d.* 17-03-1469 (in the Church of the Austin Friars, York); *p.* 19-09-1472 (in the Benedictine Conventual Church of the Holy Trinity, York; *Reg. G. Neville*, ff. 187v, 203r, 217r), 'a faithful and prudent man', 1488; bursar, 1489–90; (*Letters*, pp. 107 [No. 48], 113–14 [No. 53], 128–30 [No. 64], 239–40 [No. 125]; 31st abbot, 1495–1526; in 1519 was aged 80 and in ill–health: paralysis and the stone. A jubilarian. (See Chapter 3).

Huby, William: abbot, Warden, *c.*1477, when granted residential rights at Stoneleigh (Bearman, 2004, p. 212).

Huddleston, William: Stratford; *sd.* 1507, *d.* 1508, *p.* 1509 (London; *Reg. R. Fitzjames*, ff. 95r, 99v, 100r); kitchener, 1514 (*Reg. R. Fitzjames*, f. 167r [178r]); sub–prior, 1521 (London; *Reg. R. Fitzjames*, f. 183v [194v]); last abbot, Stratford, 1524–1538; signed deed of surrender and *disp.* 1538 (*DKR*, p. 42, *FOR*, p. 129); pension, £66–13–4 (TNA, E314/77). (See Chapters 3 and 4 in especial).

Hugh ap Robert ap Rhys/Price: abbot, Aberconwy, 1528; elected whilst a minor and died when studying at Cambridge, buried at Saffron Walden, 1528 (Hays, 1963, pp. 139, 141)

? Hugh/Hyn', John: Rievaulx, 1533 (TNA, STAC2/7/217).

Hughes, William: Kingswood, signed deed of surrender and *disp.* 1538 (*DKR*, p. 25, *FOR*, p. 131); 'reward and finding', 1538, £2–13–4 (TNA, E36/152, f..20); pension, £4; perhaps the cleric of this name who a stipendiary priest at Berkeley, Gloucestershire, in 1540 (Baskerville, 1927, p. 88). Huknall: *see* Bucknall.

Hull, Thomas: Revesby; *p.* 1487 (Lincoln; *Reg. J. Russell*, f. 24v).

Hull, William: Meaux; *sd.* 1492, *d.* 1493, *p.* 1495 (York; Cross and Vickers, 1995, p. 153); as a wayward monk of Meaux rehabilitated before 1521 (*Letters*, pp. 268–69 [No. 140]).

Hulton, John: Croxden; *ac.* 1530, *sd.* 1531 (Lichfield; *Reg. G. Blyth*, n–f.).

Humphrey ... : abbot, Cwmhir, 1491–94 (*Trans. Radnorshire Historical Soc.,* 34, 1964, pp. 25, 29).

Hunte, John: Rewley; *sd.* 1497, *d.* 1498 (Lincoln; *Reg. W. Smith*, n–f.).

Hunting: *see* Hampton.

Huntingdon, Edward: Sawtry; *p.* 1526 (Lincoln; *Reg. J. Longland*, f. 16r).

Huntingon, Robert: Vaudey; *sd.* and *d.* 1506, *p.* 1508 (Lincoln; *Reg. W. Smith*, n–f.)

?Huntley, William: Revesby; *d.* 1531 (Lincoln; *Reg. J. Longland*, f. 28r).

Huschwayte, Thomas: Jervaulx; *disp.* 1482, and held the church of St Medard, Oye, near Calais; allowed in 1491 to hold two more benefices (*CPL* 13, Part 1, p. 744; 15, p. 385 [No. 728])

Huskin, Henry: Neath; *? d.* 1524 (Lichfield; *Reg. G. Blyth*, n–f., where 'Henry Neth'; *disp.* to live as a secular 1535 (*FOR*, p. 38).

Hutton, James: Furness; *p.* 1502 (York, *Reg. T. Savage*, f. 113r).

Hycheman/Hickman, William: abbot, Stratford, 1490–1516; as Reformator of the Order in England was at variance with Abbot Huby of Fountains, confirmed the election of a new abbot of Rewley and received the resignation of an abbot of Waverley, 1490/91 (*Letters*, pp. 142, 144, 247); and certified the election of a new abbot of Netley, 1509 (Winchester: *Reg. R. Fox* 3, ff.25v–26); held a canonry of Wells, 1502–1506 (Smith, 2008, p. 337); presented to the parish church of Bircham, Norfolk, in 1506, in the king's gift on the 'free resignation' of the previous incumbent (*Patent*, 1506, p. 447); in receipt of an annuity of £5 paid by the King (*LP* 2, Part 1, p. 876 [No. 2736]).

Hyde, Simon: Beaulieu; *ac.* 1507 (London; *Reg. R. Fitzjames*, f. 95r).

Hyde: *see also* Wynsor.

Hyland, William: Hailes; *sd.* 1504 (*Reg. S. Gigli*, f. 289). Could he have then transferred to Dore, and be the next mentioned monk?; the alternative is that a scribe wrote down the name of the wrong abbey.

Hyland, William: Dore; *d.* 1505 (Hereford; *Reg. R. Mayew*, p. 237).

Hylton, Henry: Combermere; *sd.* 1500, *d.* 1501 (Lichfield; *Reg. J. Arundel*, ff. 288, 293v).

Hylton, John: Hulton; *p.* 1493 (Lichfield; *Reg. W. Smith*, f. 176).

Hylton/Hilton, John: abbot, Combermere, ?1498–1518 (Smith, 2008, p. 283).

Hylton: *see also* Hilton, Hulton.

Hyrd/Hirde, William: Byland, *disp.* 1539, pension: £5; dead by Michaelmas 1543 (*DKR*, p. 13; *FOR*, p. 181; Cross and Vickers, 1995, p.105).

Iden, Geoffrey: Robertsbridge, 1523 (SAL, *MS 14*, f. 59v); *disp.* before the closure of the monastery – to give up the habit and hold a benefice, 1536 (*FOR*, p. 57); vicar of Warbleton, Sussex, 1540; vicar of Dallington, 1541–51; until 1548 held Langton's chantry in Chichester cathedral – for which he received a pension of £3–10–0; vicar choral of Chichester cathedral and vicar of Jevington and Wilmington, Sussex, until his death in 1558 (Salzman, 1954, p. 34).

Idyell/Idle: *see* Ydel.

Ieuan ap Dafydd: Aberconwy; alleged in 1450 that he had been persuaded to enter the monastery at the age of twelve, and made profession, but then left after three months; sought a papal declaration that he is not bound to that monastery or to the Cistercian Order (*SAP*, pp. 155–56 [No. 704]).

Ieuan ap Reginald: Aberconwy; 'scholar', 1468; illegitimate son of Abbot Reginald. Monk by 1481 (*SAP* **2**, p. 63 [No. 1518]).

Ilmy(n)ster, *al.* Cabull, John: Newenham; *ac.* 1516, *sd.* and *d.* 1517, *p.* 1520 (Exeter; *Reg. H. Oldham*, ff. 125r–v, 126v; *Reg. J. Vesey*, f. 144r); provisor, St Bernard's College, Oxford, 1517–18 (*Statuta* **6**, p. 540 [No. 1518/69]); D.D. (Oxon.) 1528 (Stevenson, 1939, p. 43); abbot, Newenham, 1525 until at least 1527 (Smith, 2008, pp. 317, 319); may have had to resign, 1529 (*LP* **4**, Part 3, p. 2670 [No. 6001]; in 1531 he laid unspecified charges against Bishop Skevington and the abbots of Ford, St Mary Graces and Thame (*Statuta* **6**, pp. 700–01 [No. 1531/40]).

Ilymster/Ylmyster, John: curate, Dunkeswell parish, *c.*1492 (LPL, *Reg. J. Morton*, f. 120).

Ilmyster, *al.* Roose, Robert: Ford; *sd.* 1504 (Canterbury; *Reg. W. Warham, Exeter sede v.*, f. 208r); *d.* 1505 (Exeter; *Reg. H. Oldham*, f. 84r); *p.* 1507 (Wells; *Reg. H. de Castello*, f. 146); pension, 1539, £7 (Youings, 1971, p. 186).

Ince, William: Byland; *d.* 1480 (York; Cross and Vickers, 1995, p. 98).

Inglis, *al.* Bloxham, William: Bruern; 1535, when professed but not yet ordained priest (*VE* **2**, p. 265); still in house at its suppression, 1536; later of Aston Somerville, Gloucs., died 1563 (Baskerville, 1930, p. 334).

Ingram, John: Rewley; *d.* 1507, *p.* 1508 (Salisbury; *Reg. E. Audley*, ff. 7v, 9v).

Inkberrow, John: Bordesley; *d.* 1527 (Worcester; *Reg. R. Morton addenda*, f. 163).

Ipsley/Islip, William; Flaxley; *ac.* and *sd.* 1517, *d.* 1519, *p.* 1524 (Hereford; *Reg. C. Bothe*, pp. 305, 309, 318); abbot, Grace Dieu, resigning in 1533; monk again at Flaxley, 1536; *disp.* 1536, vicar of Littledean, Gloucs., 1544 (*FOR*, p. 73; Williams, 1976, p. 64).

Irby, Robert: monk, Revesby, and vicar of St Mary, Wymondham, 1479–1499 (personal comm. Richard Barton–Wood); being in 1490 permitted to wear a 'decent gown' over his Cistercian habit (*CPL* **15**, pp. 270–71 [No. 537]).

Ireby/Yreby, Thomas: abbot, Holm Cultram, 1532–1536; dies 10–08–1536 (*LP* **11**, p. 115 [No. 276]); paid £50 in 1533 for grant of temporalities (TNA, LR1/173, f.131r–v; Gilbanks, 1899, pp. 93–97; Smith, 2008, pp. 300–01).

Ireby, Thomas: novice, Holm Cultram, at time of surrender, 1538 (TNA, SC6/HENVIII/931, f. 2); signed deed of surrender (*DKR*, p. 23): In receipt of his pension of £2 in 1555 (TNA, E164/31, f. 3v).

Irton, Robert: Fountains; *sd.* 1492 (York; Cross and Vickers, 1995, p. 111).

Isake, William: Swineshead; died 1567 (Hodgett, 1959, p. 131).

Iveson, Richard: Sawley; *sd.* 1492, *d.* 1493, *p.* 1496 (York; Cross and Vickers, 1995, p. 199).

Ivynge, John : Warden, convicted of attempting to poison his abbot, 1492, and sent to confinement first to Sibton and then to Stratford (Letters, pp. 154–55 [No. 78], 163–64 [No. 81]).

Jackson/Jakeson, *al.* Adell, Anthony: Kirkstall; *sd.* 1509, *p.* 1514 (York); bursar, *c.*1528–1539; pension, 1539, £8 (Cross, 1995, pp. 140, 142; 146; CIY); in receipt of pension of £8 in 1555 (TNA, E164/31, f. 53v); in 1550 he was 'of Horsforth' when he witnessed the will of a former Kirkstall monk, Richard Elles, *q.v.*; who left him his best gown, a horse and a vestment. He was the godfather of Thomas Pepper, another Kirkstall monk, *q.v.*, In 1555 he was curate of Otley; in 1558 chaplain at Horsforth Hall, Guiseley (Lonsdale, 1972, p. 205). Mentioned in later litigation, 1544/51 (TNA, C1/1206/55–58). Alive in 1564.

Jackson, Henry: last abbot, Rushen; in receipt of his pension of £10 in 1555 (TNA, E164/31, f. 74v; Davey, 2010, p. 174).

Jackson/Jakeson, Henry: Fountains; *sd.* 1533, *d.* and *p.* 1534 (York); pension, 1539, £5, received until 1570 when seemingly he had died; three other local clerics bore this name (Cross and Vickers, 1995, pp. 114–15, 123).

Jackson (Jakson), John: Holm Cultram, in house, 1533 (*LP* **6**, pp. 425–26 [No. 988]); signed deed of surrender and *disp.* 1538 (*DKR*, p. 23; *FOR*, pp. 123–24); pension, £5–6–8 (TNA, LR1/173, ff. 147, 148).

Jacksun/Jackson, *al.* Norton, Peter: Byland, *sd.* 1532, *d.* and *p.* 1535; *disp.* 1539, pension £5–6–8 (*DKR*, p. 13; *FOR*, p. 181; Cross and Vickers, 1995, pp. 98, 105, 188). Described erroneously in 1532 as 'of Roche'.

Ja(c)kson, Roger: Furness: *p.* 1492 (York; *Reg. T. Rotherham*, n–f.).

Jackson/*al.* Richmond, Thomas: Rievaulx; *sd.* 1517, *d.* 1519, *p.* 1520 (York); B.D. (Oxon.) 1529 (Stevenson, 1939, p. 48); *disp.* 1538 when perhaps the prior; pension, £6–13–4 (*FOR*, p. 156; *DKR*, p. 38); in 1548 he was a chantry priest at Pockley in Helmsley parish, but maintained contacts with other former Rievaulx monks. In 1548 he was noted as being 'sixty years old, honest and learned'. He perhaps died *c.* 1560 (Cross, 1995, pp. 169, 177)..

James ap Jevan (Ieuan): Valle Crucis; in arrears to late Cardinal Wolsey for a faculty granted prior to 23–10–1530 (*LP* **4**, Part 3, p. 3048 [No. 6748/14].

James, William: perhaps a former monk of Sibton; vicar, Cransford, Suffolk, from 1564 (Baskerville, 1933, p. 61).

?Jamisley, Thomas: St Mary Graces; *sd.* 1498, *p.* 1501 (London; *Reg. T. Savage*, f. 56v; *Reg. W. Warham*, f. 78r).

Jasper ap Roger: *see* Thomas.

Jenkinson/?Dunwell, Christopher: Fountains; *sd.* and *d.* 1521; in February 1536 accused, perhaps spuriously, of self–abuse by Cromwell's commissioners; *p.* 1524 pension, 1539: £5–6–8; then became one of Magdalen's chantry priests in Ripon; died 1558 (Cross and Vickers, 1995, pp. 115, 123–24).

Jenkinson, Henry: Vaudey; *ac.* and *sd.* 1524, *d.* 1525, *p.* 1527 (Lincoln; *Reg. J. Longland*, ff. 8v, 10v, 11r, 19r); overseer of the granary and home granges, 1531/32 (TNA, SC6/HENVIII/2005B, f. 7); *disp.* 1536 (*FOR*, p. 67); moved to Kirkstead abbey where, with two of his confrères, took an active part in the Lincolnshire Rising, examined at Lincoln, 4–11–1536, and subsequently executed (Shaw, 1999, p. 94; *LP* **11**, pp. 320 [No. 827/ii], 325 [No. 828/2viii])

Jenkinson/?Awdefeld, Marmaduke: Fountains; *sd.* and *d.* 1521, *p.* 1524 (York); pension, 1539, £5–6–8; thereafter priest of Skelton, Yorkshire; making his will in 1558 he requested burial 'in the churchyard of St Peter and St Wilfrid near to the Palm Cross' (Cross and Vickers, 1995, pp. 114–15, 124).

Jenkynson, Richard: *see* **Ripon/Rypon**.

Jenkinson, Robert: *see* Middleham.

Jens, *al.* Yens, Thomas: abbot, Garendon, 1499–1504 on, when instituted to church of St George, Stamford, Lincs., (Smith, 2008, p. 296–97); pardon to Thomas Jens *al.* Yens, monk, *alias* prior of St James, London, 'in the wall', *alias* abbot of Garodon, co. Leicester. This is a reference to Garendon's cell at Cripplegate, London (*Patent*, 1504, p. 344).

Jervalles/Jervaux, *al.* Cleveland, John: Byland, *sd.* 1532, *d.* 1532 – when described as a monk of Roche; *p.* 1535 (York); *disp.* 1538 (*DKR*, p. 13; *FOR*, p. 181). Died 1556/64, meanwhile may have been: chantry priest in Batley parish church, Yorkshire, 1548; curate of Barnby, 1549; curate (perhaps vicar) of Tunstall, 1552; received pension of £5 as late as 1556, but died by 1564 (Cross and Vickers,

1995, pp. 99–100, 103–04, 188); involved in post–suppression litigation of 1547+ (TNA, C1/1263/56). See also *John Robinson*.

Jobe, John: Kirkstall, *sd.* 1515 (York; Cross and Vickers, 1995, p. 141).

John ... : abbot, Netley, 1466–1495 (Smith, 2008, p. 316).

John ... : 'lord of the old abbey'; abbot, Llantarnam, 1476–96 (Williams, 1976, p. 85).

John ... : abbot, Aberconwy, 1490 (*Letters*, p. 127 [No. 63]).

John ... : abbot, Vaudey, 1491–1508 (Smith, 2008, p. 346).

John ... : abbot, Coggeshall, 1492 (Smith, 2008, p. 280).

John ... : abbot, Strata Florida, 1495, when refusing to cooperate in collection of a subsidy for the Order, was declared excommunicate and deposed; previously he had been prior of another house (*Letters*, pp. 175 [No. 87], 180–81 [No. 88]).

John ... : abbot, Beaulieu, 1495 (Smith, 2008, p. 267).

John ... : abbot, Buckland, *c.*1496–1510 (Smith, 2008, p. 317).

John ... : abbot, Jervaulx, 1500 (Smith, 2008, p. 302).

John ... : abbot, Strata Florida, 1501 (*Patent*, 1501, p. 221).

John ... : abbot, Sawley, 1501 (Smith, 2008 p. 329).

John ... : abbot, Neath, 1502–07 (TNA, LR1/229, f.101d; SC6/5156).

John ... : abbot, Coggeshall, 1507 (Smith, 2008, p. 280).

John ... : abbot, Newminster, 1507 to at least 1514 (Smith, 2008, p. 318); *disp.* to receive a secular benefice *in commendam*, 1511 (*CPL* **19**, p. 462 [No. 791]).

John ....: abbot, Byland, 1515 (Smith, 2008, p. 278).

John ....: abbot, Flaxley, 1509–1523 (Smith, 2008, p. 290).

John ap David: no house stated; *ac.* 1496 (St David's; *EPD* **2**, p. 761).

John ap Hywel ap Morgan: Neath, 1496, when imprisoned for murder (Williams, 2001, p. 63).

John ap Rhydderch: Margam, *disp.* 1536 (*FOR*, p. 68).

John ap Rhys ap Gruffydd: O. Cist. , no monastery noted; *disp.* to hold a benefice if given consent of his superior, and to wear his habit beneath that of a secular priest, and despite defect of birth; no fee charged, 23–02–1536 (*FOR*, p. 45).

John ap Robert ap Rhys/Price: born about 1503; B.D. (Oxon.) 1529; last abbot, Strata Marcella, 1527–1536; in arrears to late Cardinal Wolsey for a faculty granted prior to 23–10–1530 (*LP* 4, Part 3, p. 3048 [No. 6748/14]); brother of Abbots Hugh and Richard ap Rhys of Aberconwy *(q.v.)*; pension, £6–13–4; portioner of Pontesbury from 1536 and rural dean; alive in 1553 (Owen, 1919, pp. 28–30; Williams, 2001, pp. 77, 79, 86]. In receipt of his £6–13–4 pension in 1555 (TNA, E164/31, f. 78v).

John ap Roger: Margam; *d.* 1498 (Worcester; *Reg. G. Gigli*, f. 27).

John ap Roger: Margam; *ac.* 1502 (St David's; *EPD* **2**, p. 735). This must be the same monk as the foregoing, and one of the copies of the ordination lists must be wrongly dated.

Johns, Geoffrey: abbot, Aberconwy, 1529–35, when resigns unwillingly; pension then of £9 p.a., (Hays, 1963, pp. 140, 160–61; *LP* **9**, p. 83; **10**, pp. 340, 434 [No. 1046]).

Johnson, John: Hulton; *ac.* and *d.* 1517, *p.* 1521 (Lichfield; *Reg. G. Blyth*, n–f.); said to be one of the 'wisest priests' of the house, 1534 (*VCH, Staffordshire* **2**, 1967, 236); signed deed of surrender and *disp.* 1538 (TNA, E322/106; *FOR*, p. 154); pension, £4 (TNA, E315/233, f. 23r).

Jonson/Johnson, John: Bordesley, *disp.* 1538 (*FOR*, p. 149; TNA, E322/26); in receipt of pension of £5 as late as 1555 (TNA, E164/31, f. 44r).

Johnson, Thomas: Meaux; *p.* 1510 (York); pension, £6; dead by October 1540 (Cross and Vickers, 1995, pp. 154, 159).

Johnson, Thomas: ? monk, Beaulieu, 1528 (Hockey, 1976, p. 226).

Jonys [Jones], John: no monastery stated, quite possibly a monk of Neath, Wales; *d.* 1524 (Lichfield; *Reg. G. Blyth*, n–f.).

Jones, Matthew: cellarer, Tintern, 1525–26 (NLW, Badminton Deeds, Group 2, Nos. 661, 1663).

Johns/Jones, Morgan: Margam, *disp.* 1537 (*FOR* p. 68.)

Johns, Morgan (ap): *see* **Morgan ap Johns**

Johns/Jones, William: resigns as abbot of Cwmhir in 1516, when granted an annuity of 40s (or perhaps £2–13–4); still resident at Cwmhir in 1529; but probably the monk of that name at Strata Florida, 1539; and granted a pension on 6 May 1537 by the Court of Augmentations of 40s. p.a. plus arrears of 60s; plus his abbatial pension of £2–13–4 (*LP* **14** Part 1, p. 362 [No. 748]); *disp.* 1540, died shortly thereafter (TNA, C24/29 (part 2); E315/91/56v; E315/92/91v; Williams, 2001, pp. 86, 88).

Jordan/Jurden, John: Buckland, *disp.* 1539 (*DKR*, p. 12, *FOR*, p. 178); pension, £3–6–8, received as late as 1555 (TNA, E164/31, f. 34r).

Judson, Richard: *see* Baxby.

Kaingham, John: Meaux; *p.* 1510 (York; Cross and Vickers, 1995, p. 154).

Kandall: *see Randall.*

Kechyn/Kytchyng, Robert: Furness, signed deed of surrender and *disp.* 1537 (TNA, E322/91; *FOR*, p. 97). He may be the *Robert Legate* mentioned below.

Kele/Keel, William: Revesby; *ac.* 1502, *sd.* 1503, *d.* 1505 (Lincoln; *Reg. W. Smith*, ff. 36v, 41v, n–f.).

Kelsall, John: Basingwerk; *ac.* 1488, *d.* and *p.* 1490 (Lichfield; *Reg. J. Hales*, ff. 228–29, 231). It seems very likely that he is the same monk as the next mentioned.

Kelsall, Richard: Basingwerk; *sd.* 1490 (Hereford; *Reg. T. Myllyng*, p. 177).

Kelsaye, William: Louth Park, *disp.* 1537 (*FOR*, p. 95).

Kelyng(e)/Kelling, Thomas: Croxden, signed deed of surrender and *disp.* 1538 (Hibbert, 1910, p. 222; *FOR*, p. 151); in receipt of pension of £4–6–8 as late as 1555 (TNA, E164/31, f. 46v).

Kelyng: *see also* Bradley, Kyllyng.

Kelyngbeck, Robert: Kirkstall; *ac.* 1453 (York; *Reg. W. Booth*, f. 418r.)

Kempton/?Bingham, William: Tilty; *p.* 1525 (London; *Reg. C. Tunstall*, n. f., *CL*).

Kendall, Anthoy: Fountains; *sd.* and *d.* 1521 (York); pension, 1539, £5; 1546–1553, when dies, curate of Kilnwick on the Wolds, Yorkshire (Cross and Vickers, 1995, pp. 114–15, 124–25).

Kendale, Christopher: Jervaulx; *p.* 1522 (York; Cross and Vickers, 1995, p. 131).

Kendall, James: Bruern; *sd.* 1531, *p.* 1532 (Lincoln; *Reg. J. Longland*, ff. 29r, 32r); in community, 1535 (*VE* **2**, p. 265).

Kendall/Skendall: Robert: Fountains; *sd.* 1533, *d.* and *p.* 1534 (York; Cross, 1995, pp. 115, 127).

Kendell, Thomas: Kirkstead, *disp.* 1537 (*FOR*, p. 96).

Kenilworth/Kyllyngworth, Richard: Stoneleigh; *sd.* 1506, *d.* 1507, *p.* 1508 (Lichfield; *Reg. G. Blyth*, n–f).

Kepas/Kippax, James: provisor, St Bernard's College, Oxford, 1495–1498 (*BRUO* **2**, p. 1054; Smith, 2008, p. 319; *Letters*, pp. 172–73 [No. 86]).

Kepas/?Tewisdaye, John: monk, Fountains, *sd.* and *d.* 1497, *p.* 1499 (York); pension, 1539: £6 (Cross and Vickers, 1995, pp. 112, 115, 128).

Kere, William: cellarer at times of Tintern, 1476–86; abbot, 1488–93 (NLW, Badminton Deeds, Group 2, Nos. 14473, 14475–78, 14481–82; *CPL* **16**, pp. 3–4 [No. 5]).

Ker(r)y, John: Waverley; *ac.* 1514, *sd.* and *p.* 1518 (Winchester; *Reg. R. Fox* **3**, f. 55v, **4**, ff. 69v, 70r). Moved to Beaulieu on the suppression of Waverley in 1536; pension of £5 p.a. received in 1555 (TNA, E314/20/11, f. 1v–2r; E164/31, f. 13r; Hockey, 1976, pp. 183, 187). Perhaps curate of Puttenham,

Surrey, in 1541, and of Lasham, Hants. 1551–55 (Baskerville, 1941, p. 18). He was perhaps the monk, *John Bere*, q.v.

Kettering, Henry: Biddlesden; *d.* 1496, *p.* 1498 (Lincoln; *Reg. W. Smith*, n.f.).

Keynes/Kemes, William: Neath; *disp.* 1539; pension, £4 p.a., alive in 1553 (Birch, 1902, pp. 150, 154; *FOR*, p. 170).

Keynston, William: Ford, in house at its suppression, 1539 (*DKR*, p. 21). This name does not appear in the pension list, so this monk may have had an *alias* (Weaver, 1891, p. 5).

Kidderminster: *see* Kitterminster.

Kighley, Richard: Fountains; *sd.* 1492, *d.* 1493, *p.* 1494 (Cross and Vickers, 1995, p. 111).

Kilburn, Thomas: Byland; *sd.* 1452 (York; *Reg. W. Booth*, f. 413r): abbot, Byland, 1479–1497, when resigned (Smith, 2008, p. 278).

Kilburn, William: Byland; *ac.* and *sd.* 1503; *d.* 1504, *p.* 1506 (York; Cross and Vickers, 1995, p. 99). Perhaps the same monk as *William Baxter*, q.v. (Aveling, 1955, p. 9).

Kilewile/Kilwylle/Kyldwick, Richard: Swineshead; *ac., sd.* and *d.* 1508, *p.* 1509 (Lincoln; *Reg. W. Smith*, n–f.).

Killingbeck, Robert: abbot, Kirkstall, 1499 (Smith, 2008, p. 305).

Killinsmarche/Killingworth, John:: Stoneleigh; *d.* 1514, *p.* 1518 (Lichfield; *Reg. G. Blyth*, n–f.).

Kilnesey, William: Fountains; *d.* and *p.* 1509 (York; Cross and Vickers, 1995, p. 113).

King, Edward: St Mary Graces; *ex.* and *ac.* 1526 (London; *Reg. C. Tunstall*, f. 158v); *sd., d.* and *p.* 1530 (Canterbury; *Reg. W. Warham, London sede–v.*, **2**, ff. 313r–v, 314r).

King, John: prior, Buckfast, by 1460, when appointed provisor, St Bernard's College, Oxford; but alleged in 1464 to spend much of his time at Buckfast where he was still prior; abbot, Buckfast, 1466–?1497/98 (Stéphan, 1970, pp. 163–172). The abbot in the later years of that period may have been *John Belworthy*, q.v. (Smith, 2008, p. 274).

King, *al.* Brewarne, Hanney, Richard: Bruern, by 1532 (Stevenson, 1939, p. 42); prior, 1533 (*DCP*, p. 5); last abbot, 1533–1536; pension of £22 received as late as 1555 (TNA, E164/31, f. 42r); rector, Wigginton, Oxfordshire, 1544 (Baskerville, 1930, p. 333); will dated 19–05–1557 (Smith, 2008, pp. 272–73).

King, Robert: St Bernard's Coll. Oxford, B.Th. 1507, D.Th. 1519; may have been a secular priest before entering the monastery; abbot, Bruern, 1515–1527 and later abbot of Thame from 1527–1539, where he built a fine new abbot's lodging (*BRUO* **2**, p. 172). Blessed as abbot of Thame and made profession of obedience before Bishop Longland in his private chapel at Lincoln, 12 May 1527 (*Reg. J. Longland*, f. 135v); consecrated 13 May 1527 at Lincoln as titular bishop of Rheon [Transcaucasus] and suffragan in the diocese of Lincoln, 1517–1542 (Smith, 1982, p. 27); 1537, abbot–commendatory also of Oseney, 1537; signed deed of suppression, 1539 (*DKR*, p. 43). In 1542 King became the first Bishop of Oxford. Under Mary, King returned to Catholicism, and was a judge at the trial of Cranmer. Died 4–12–1557, buried in Christ Church Cathedral, Oxford. (VCH, *County of Oxford* **2**, 1907, pp. 83–86).

Kyngsbery/Kingsbury, *al.* Sherman, Richard: Ford; *p.* 1538 (Exeter; *Reg. J. Vesey*, f. 189r); *disp.* 1539 (*DKR*, p. 21); pension, 1539, £5, substantial for a newly ordained monk (Youings, 1971, p. 186).

Kingsley, *al.* Berdmore, Hugh: abbot, Medmenham; general pardon, 1510 (*LP* **1**, Part 1, p. 232 [No. 438/2, m. 30].

Kingsley, John: Woburn; *ac.* 1490 (Lincoln; *Reg. J. Russell*, f. 37r).

Kippax: *see* **Kepas.**

Kirby, Francis: Kirkstead, *disp.* 1537 (*FOR*, p. 96).

Kirby, Matthew: Furness, signed deed of surrender and *disp.* 1537 (TNA, E322/91; *FOR*, p. 97).

Kirkby/*al.* Cowper, Edward: monk, Rievaulx; *sd.* 1504 (York); at St Bernard's College, Oxford, 1518, B.D.1525 (*BRUO* **2**, p. 335); abbot, Rievaulx, 1530–33 when deposed (Smith, 2008, p. 325), and given a pension of £44 p.a., *disp.* 1537. Vicar of Newport, Essex, 1539–46; 1543, incumbent of Kirby Misterton, Yorkshire, and in 1546 also rector of St Nicholas Olave, London. Made his will in 1551, alive in 1554 but died by 1557 (Cross and Vickers, 1995, pp. 168, 172–73); disp. 1537 (*FOR*, p. 96).

Kirkeby, John: Jervaulx; *sd.* 1501, *d.* 1502, *p.* 1503 (York; Cross and Vickers, 1995, p. 130).

Kyrkby, Reginald: Vaudey; *ac., sd., d.* and *p.* 1535 (Lincoln; *Reg. J. Longland*, ff 42r, 43v, 45v, 46r), by October 1536 a monk of Kirkstead and involved in the Lincolnshire rebellion; examined at Lincoln, 4–11–1536, and subsequently executed (*LP* **11**, pp. 320 [No. 827/ii], 325 [No. 828/2viii]).

Kirkby, William: Rievaulx; *sd.* 1452 (York; *Reg. W. Booth*, f. 413r).

Kirkby/? Lupton, William: Kirkstall, *sd.* 1531, *d.* and *p.* 1533 (York; Cross and Vickers, 1995, pp. 142, 147–48).

Kyrkby, William: Llantarnam; *d.* 1513 (Hereford; *Reg. R. Mayew*, p. 263).

Kirkby, William: Louth Park; *disp.* 6–08–1536 (*FOR*, p. 69).

Kirkby, William: *see also* Walton.

Kirkham/Aland, Edmund: Fountains; *sd.* and *d.* 1521, *p.* 1524 (York); pension, 1539, £6; may later have held Holme's chantry and Langtoft's chantry in Holy Trinity church, Goodramgate, York (Cross and Vickers, 1995, pp. 114;117).

Kirkham, Guy: Fountains; *d.* 1521 (York; Cross and Vickers, 1995, p. 114).

Kirkham, Robert: Vale Royal, *c.*1500 (*LB*, p. 153).

Kirkham, Thomas: abbot, Vale Royal; bishop of Sodor, 1458, holding the abbacy *in commendam* (*CPL* **11**, pp. 343–44, 359).

Kirkstall, Thomas: Kirkstall, *ac.* 1533, *sd. d.* and *p.* 1534 (York; Cross and Vickers, 1995, p. 142). Might he be *Thomas Pepper*, q.v.

Kirkstall: *see also* Shakilton/Christall.

Kitterminster, Richard: sub–prior, Dore, 1528 (TNA, E315/51/53; Williams, 1976, p. 27).

Knabrough/Knaresborough, Edward: Rufford; *p.* 1531 (York; *Reg. E. Lee*, f. 184v); *disp.* 1536 (*FOR*, p. 74). Signed letters testimonial in 1555 (Cross, 1993, p. 201; Cross and Vickers, 1995, p. 171).

Kniston, John: Rewley, *disp.* 1536 (*FOR*, p. 78).

Knoll(es), Thomas: Bordesley; *ac.* and *d.* 1516 (*Reg. S. Gigli*, pp. 329, 334).

Knottyfford, Ranulph: Vale Royal; *sd.* 1532 (Lichfield; *Reg. G. Blyth*, n–f.).

Knyver, John: *see* Kynvar.

Kubery/Kirbery, John: Rewley; *ac.* and *sd.* 1497, *d.* 1498 (Lincoln; *Reg. W. Smith*, n. f).

Kydd, John: Fountains, *d.* 1494 (York; Cross and Vickers, 1995, p. 112).

Kyd(de), Thomas: monk, Fountains; *sd.* 1492, *p.* 1495 (York); prior, 1539, pension: £8; alive in 1555 (Cross and Vickers, 1995, pp. 111, 115, 125).

Kydwely (*Cedweli*), Maurice: Margam, *disp.* 1536 (*FOR*, p. 68).

Kyffin, Geoffrey: 'Geoffrey the Red'; abbot, Aberconwy, ?1513–26 (Hays, 1963, pp. 138–39, 156–57; TNA, LR1/213, ff. 129–30, 210d). A cleric of this name, Geoffrey Kyffin, Ll. B. became vicar of Llanrwst in 1551 (*Jnl. of the Historical Society of the Church in Wales* **6**, 1956, p. 36).

KyfteKyte, William: Cleeve; *sd.* and *d.* 1493 Wells; *Reg. R. Fox*, pp. 148, 152).

Kylburn: *see* Kilburn.

Kyllyng, John: Croxden; in 1439 appeals to the papal penitentiary saying that he had been ejected from his monastery without cause, had accompanied an army overseas for five weeks and supported but did not commit looting, killing and arson; seeks absolution and dispensation for irregularity;

receiving that, then seeks a declaration that he might be promoted in his Order (*SAP*, pp. 41–42 [No. 118], 47 [No. 149]).

Kylner, John: abbot, Rewley, by 1513–1529 (Smith, 2008, p. 323; VCH, *County of Oxford* **2**, 1907, p. 83).

Kynggsbure/Kingsbury: *see above.*

Kyngston, John: Rewley; *p.* 1534 (Lincoln; *Reg. J. Longland*, f. 37r).

Kynnersley/Kyngsley, Richard: Dieulacres (possibly earlier at Merevale); *d.* and *p.* 1497 (Lichfield; *Reg. J. Arundel*, ff. 263v, 266v).

Kynvane, Robert: Bordesley; *p.* 1478 (Worcester; *Reg. J. Alcock*, f. 251).

Kynvar/Kynfar, John: Stoneleigh; *ac.* 1505, *sd.* 1506, *d.* 1507, *p.* 1508 (Lichfield; *Reg. G. Blyth*, n–f); *disp.* 1537 (*FOR*, p. 88).

Kynvar//Kym', *al.* Bate, Robert: Combe; *sd.* 1520, *d.* and *p.* 1522 (Lichfield; *Reg. G. Blyth*, n–f); B.D. (Oxon.) 1534 (Stevenson, 1939, p. 46); last abbot, Combe, 1538–1539 (TNA, C1/1188/31–33; SSC, DR10/1332); *disp.* 1539 (*DKR*, pp. 16–17; *FOR*, p. 176); pension of £80, received as late as 1555 (TNA, E164/31, f. 48v). The commissioner, Dr London, wrote that 'Combe has been surrendered. The abbot the same day twelve months after being made abbot left the house again' (Smith, 2008, p. 282). Was probably rector of Church Lawford, Worcestershire., 1547–1560.

Kynvar, William: Combe; *sd.* and *d.* 1494, *p.* 1495 (Lichfield; *Reg. W. Smith*, ff. 178v, 181, 187).

Kyrkby: *see* Kirkby.

Kyrkbystenyn, Richard: Cistercian monk, diocese Lincoln; *sd.* 1495 (Salisbury; *Reg. J. Blyth*,, f. 103v).

Kyrke, Thomas: Beaulieu; *p.* 1477 (Worcester; *Reg. J. Alcock*, f. 247).

Kyrketon, John: Swineshead; *sd.* 1485, *d.* 1486, *p.* 1487 (Lincoln; *Reg. J. Russell*, ff. 8r, 21r, 24v).

Kyrketon, Robert: Swineshead; *sd.* 1492, *d.* 1493 (Lincoln; *Reg. J. Russell*, ff. 45/46v, 48/49v).

Kyry: *see* Kerr.

Kytchyng, Robert: *see* Kechen.

Kytheby, Richard: abbot, Vaudey, 1509 (Smith, 2008, p. 346)

Laborne: *see* Laylord.

Lacoke/Lacock Thomas: Kingswood, 1538 (TNA, E314/20/11, f. 1v); pension, £2–13–4 'and a warrant for his capacity free'; was absent at the time of suppression as he was 'about the ministration of the Gospel' (*LP* **13**, Part 1, p. 387 [No. 1051]).

Lake, Robert: Swineshead, *disp.* 1536 (*FOR*, p. 67).

Laken, William: Cwmhir; *disp.* 1537 (*FOR*, p.101); could he be the *William Laykyn/Larkin*, formerly a monk of St Mary Graces?: *d.* and *p.* 1506 (London; *Reg. W. Barons*, f. 91v; *Reg. R. Fitzjames*, f. 92v).

Lambe/Lanne, Peter: St Mary Graces; *d.* 1506, *p.* 1511 (London; *Reg. R. Fitzjames*, ff. 92v, 160v [171v]).

Lambert, William: Stratford; *p.* 1492 (London; *Reg. R. Hill*, f. 26r).

La'mesley: *see* Jamisley.

Lamport, William: Bindon; *sd.* 1520, *p.* 1521 (Salisbury; *Reg. E. Audley*, ff. 43r, 44v).

Lancaster, John: Croxden; *ac.* 1507, *sd.* and *d.* 1508, *p.* 1510 (Lichfield; *Reg. G. Blyth*, n–f.).

Lancaster, John: Stanley; *d.* 1532 (Salisbury; *Reg. L. Campeggio*).

Lancaster, Nicholas: Vale Royal, signed deed of surrender and *disp.* 1538 (*DKR*, p. 46; *FOR*, p. 162); pension, £3–6–8 (TNA, E315/233, f. 69v).

Lancaster, William: Merevale; *p.* 1532 (Lichfield; *Reg. G. Blyth*, n–f).

Landon, William: Dore, *c.*1440, when priest of its Bacton church, Herefordshire (TNA, E315/405, f. 20).

Lane, John: Warden, 1492 (*Letters*, p. 158 [No. 79]).

Lane, Raynold/Reginald: Hailes, *disp.* 1540 (*FOR*, p. 208); pension of £5 received as late as 1555 (TNA, E164/31, f. 40r); perhaps a chantry priest of Stone in 1548, and curate of Dursley in 1551–53 (Baskerville, 1927, p. 89).

Lang, Richard: Furness; *p.* 1486 (York; *Reg. T. Rotherham*, n–f.).

Langley, Richard: Woburn; *sd.* 1496; *d.* 1497, *p.* 1500 (Lincoln; *Reg. W. Smith*, f. 24v.).

Lanston', William: Cleeve; *sd.* 1493 (Wells; *Reg. R. Fox*, f. 42).

Langton, *al.* Gerves, John: abbot, St Mary Graces, by 1483–1514, when dies; papal leave to acquire a secular benefice, 1493 (*CPL* **16**, pp. 166–67 [No. 233]); instituted to Stoke Daubeney church, Northamptonshire, 1498 (Smith, 2008, p. 308); general pardon, 1509 (*LP* **1**, Part 1, p. 245 [No. 438/3, m. 16]). His alternative surname might suggest that he was originally a monk of Jervaulx.

Langton, John: abbot, Newminster, by 1507 to at least 1514 (Oliver, 1915, p. 207; Smith, 2008, p. 318).

Langton, Robert: Holm Cultram; in house, 1533 (*LP* **6**, pp. 425–26 [No. 988]); bursar, Holm Cultram, 1538 (*DKR*, p. 23; *LP* **13**, Part 1, pp. 160–61 [No. 434]); *disp.* 1538 (*FOR*, pp. 123–24). In receipt of his pension of £6 in 1555 (TNA, E164/31, f. 73v; LR1/173, f. 147).

Langton, Thomas: Sibton; *disp.* 1492 (*CPL* **15**, p. 496 [No. 902]).

Lasynby/Lazenby, George: Jervaulx; *sd.* and *d.* 1524, *p.* 1526 (York); a visionary, who publicly espoused papal not royal supremacy and was executed at York in 1535; a fellow–monk preserved his head as a relic (Cross, 1995, pp. 131, 134–35; Shaw, 1999, p. 97).

Latom: *see* Layton.

Laucliff/Longcliff, James: Furness; *sd.* 1521, *p.* 1522 (York; *Reg. T. Wolsey*, ff. 189v, 193v.); signed deed of surrender and *disp.* 1537 (TNA, E322/91; *FOR*, p. 97).

Laverocke/Laverde, Richard: St Mary Graces, *d.* 1520, *p.* 1521 (London; *Reg. R. Fitzjames*, ff. 181r [192r], 183v [194v]); *disp.* 1539 (*FOR*, p. 182); in receipt of pension of £5–6–8 in 1555 (TNA, E164/31, f. 4).

Law(e), John: Whalley; *sd.* 1523, *d.* 1524, *p.* 1525 (Lichfield; *Reg. G. Blyth*, n–f.); sacrist, Whalley, 1536 (TNA, SC6/HENVIII/1796); *disp* 1537 (*FOR*, p. 110).

Lawrence ...: abbot, Furness, 1461–1491; papal indult to wear the mitre, 1481/82 (Smith, 2008, p. 295).

Laurence, John: Furness; *d.* 1487 (York; *Reg. T. Rotherham*, n.f.)

Lawrence, John: Bindon, sub–prior, 1539; pension, £7 (TNA, E314/77; E322/21).

Lawrence, Nicholas: monk, Jervaulx; *sd.* 1484, *d.* 1486 (York; Cross and Vickers, 1995, p. 129).

Lawrence/Laverence, Richard: St Mary Graces; *ex.* and *ac.* 1528 (London; *Reg. C.: Tunstall*, f. 160v); *disp.* 1539 (*FOR*, p. 182); in receipt of pension of £5–6–8 in 1555 (TNA, E164/31).

Lawrence, Thomas: *see* Seymour.

Lawrenson, Nicholas: Vale Royal, signed deed of surrender and *disp.* 1538 (*DKR*, p. 46; *FOR*, p. 162); in receipt of his £5 pension in 1555 (TNA, E164/31, f. 69r);

Layborn(e), Thomas: Netley; *sd.* 1497, *d.* 1499 (Winchester; *Reg. T. Langton*, ff. 31r, 35r).

Laye: *see* Ley.

Laylorn/Laborne, Lancelot: Newminster, *sd.* 1531 (Durham; *Reg. C. Tunstall*, p. 126 [No.373]; twenty–eight years old in 1536 (TNA, SC12/13/65); *disp.* 1536 (*FOR*, p. 77).

Layton/Leyton/Laton, Henry: Revesby; *ac.* 1528, *sd.* and *d.* 1529, *p.* 1531 (Lincoln; *Reg. J. Longland*, ff.21r, 23v, 24r, 28r); *disp.* 1538 (*FOR*, p. 128; Essex R.O., D/DRg 1/104).

Layton/Lanton/Latom, Richard: Revesby; *d.* 1507, *p.* 1510 (Lincoln; *Reg. W. Smith*, n–f.); *disp.* 1538 (*FOR*, p. 128; Essex R.O., D/DRg 1/104).

Layton, Robert: Fountains, *sd.* and *d.* 1494, *p.* 1495 (York; Cross and Vickers, 1995, p. 112).

Lazenby, George: *see* Lasynby.

Lazony/Laromby, Richard; Rewley; *d.* 1488 (Lincoln; *Reg. J. Russell*, f.28v).

Leavesaxe, Richard: Kirkstall, perhaps *Richard Denton*, q.v; if so, *d.* 1534, *p.* 1535; pension, 1539, £5 (Cross and Vickers, 1995, pp. 142, 147). After the Suppression had an assured place in the family home in Drighlington, Yorkshire (Lonsdale, 1972, p. 211).

Ledbury, Henry: Kingswood; *ac.* and *sd.* 1492 (Worcester; *Reg. R. Morton*, f. 152); *d.* 1502 (Wells; *Reg. O. King*, f. 119).

Ledes, John: *see* Alanbridge.

Ledeburn, *al.* Mardio, John: Dore, 1490, when given by the prior permission to live for seven years in whatsoever place he wished (TNA, E315/35/29; Williams, 1976, p. 22); *disp.* 1506 (*CPL* **18**, p. 493 [No. 714]).

Ledney, Hugh: Kirkstead; involved in the Lincolnshire rebellion, October 1536 (*LP* **11**, p. 320 [No.827/ii]).

Ledys/?Leeds, John: Kirkstall, *sd.*1488, *d.* 1489, *p.* 1490 (York; Cross and Vickers, 1995, p. 139).

Leeds, Robert: Boxley; *sd.* 1497, *d.* and *p.* 1498 (London; *Reg. T. Savage*, f. 53r, 54r, 56v).

Lee, Robert: Woburn; *sd.* 1498, *d.* 1500, *p.* 1505(Lincoln; *Reg. W. Smith*, f. 24r, n–f.).

Lee/Ley, Thomas: Combermere; *sd.* 1532 (*Reg. G. Blyth*, n–f.); *disp.* 1538 (*DKR*, p. 17; *FOR*, p. 154); pension of £5 received as late as 1555 (TNA, E164/31, f. 69r).

Lee, William: Croxden; *ac.* 1530, *sd.* 1531 (Lichfield; *Reg. G. Blyth*, n–f.).

Leek(e), John: Croxden; *sd.* and *d.* 1520, *p.* 1521 (Lichfield; *Reg. G. Blyth*, n–f.)

Leke (Leek)/Loke, Thomas: Dieulacres, *disp.* 1538; 'reward' £2–0–0 (Walcott, 1871, p. 216); pension, £2 (Hibbert, 1910, pp. 239, 242; *FOR*, 160).

Leefe/Lease: *see* Farlington.

Legate, Robert: Furness, *disp.* 1537 (*FOR*, p. 97). His signature does not appear on the deed of surrender (TNA, E322/91). Quite possibly he had an *alias* of *Kytchyng*, q.v.

Legate/Lygate, Thomas: Neath, 1539; *disp.* 1539, pension, £4 p.a., alive in 1553 (Birch, 1902, pp. 150, 154; *FOR*, p. 170; was he a late entry from Buildwas, see *Leydyate* below. In receipt of his £4 pension in 1555 (TNA, E164/31, f. 77v).

Leicester, Bartholomew: Combe; *sd.* 1505, *p.* 1508 (Lichfield; *Reg. G. Blyth*, n.f.).

Leicester, John: Combe; *sd., d.* and *p.* 1517 (Lichfield; *Reg. G.Blyth*, n–f.).

Leicester, John: Pipewell; *sd.* 1529, *d.* 1531, *p.* 1532 (Lincoln; *Reg. J. Longland*, ff. 23r, 28v, 31v).

Leicester, Richard: Garendon; in house, 15–03–1536 (*LP* **10**, p. 194 [No. 475]).

Leicester, Thomas: Biddlesden; *sd.* 1489, *d.* 1490, *p.* 1491 (Lincoln; *Reg. J. Russell*, ff. 33r, 36v, 40v).

Leicester, William: abbot, Garendon, 1490 (Farnham, 1927, p. 275; Smith, 2008, p. 296).

Leicester, William: Cwmhir, by 1494 to 1534 – when passed over for the abbacy; after the suppression lived in Llanfihangel–in–Ceri (TNA, C24/29 (part 2); Williams, 2001, pp. 77, 88).

Leicester, William: Pipewell; *sd.* 1497 (Lincoln; *Reg. W. Smith*, n.f., *Reg. W. Atwater*, f. 115v);

Leicester, William: Medmenham; *d.* 1513, *p.* 1515 (Lincoln; *Reg. W. Smith*, n–f.).

Leke, *al.* ffeampton, John: Swineshead, *disp.* 1507 (*CPL* **18**, p. 517 [No. 756]).

Lemyng, John: Vaudey; *ac., sd., d.* and *p.* 1535 (Lincoln; *Reg. J. Longland*, ff. 42r, 43v, 45v, 46r).

Leominster, Thomas: Beaulieu; *ac.* and *sd.* 1488 (Winchester; *Reg. P. Courtenay*, ff. 13r, 13v).

Lenton, John: Merevale; *d.* 1503 (Canterbury; *Lichfield, sede v.*, CCA–~DCc–Reg. f. 287r); *p.* 1504 (Lichfield; *Reg. G. Blyth*, n–f.). He was a junior monk there in 1497 (TNA, E315/283, f. 1).

Lenton *al.* Gilman, Gyllam, Thomas: Pipewell; *ac.* 1506, *sd.* 1507, *d.* 1508, *p.* 1510 (Lincoln; *Reg. W. Smith*, n–f.); abbot by 1522 – 1538; was willing on 6 July 1538 to offer Cromwell £200 for the continuance of the abbey, but it closed that year on 5 November (Smith, 2008, p. 320); signed deed of surrender and *disp.* 1538 (*DKR*, p. 37; *FOR*, p. 160); pension, £66–13–4 (TNA, SC6/HENVIII/7339).

Leswell, John: Coggeshall; *sd.* 1527 (*CL*). Perhaps the same monk as *John Barking*, q.v.

Lete/Lote, John: Meaux; *ac.* and *sd.* 1523, *d.* 1524, *p.* 1525 (York); pension, £6; chantry priest, Wansford church, Yorkshire, of Meaux's appropriation, March 1539 (Cross and Vickers, 1995, pp. 155, 156, 160).

Letheley/Leitheley, Richard: Byland; *sd.* and *d.* 1493, *p.* 1498 (York); *disp.* 1539, pension, £6; died in late 1539 (*FOR*, p. 181; Aveling, 1955, p. 8; Cross and Vickers, 1995, pp. 98, 100, 106).

Lethley, Robert: Fountains, *sd.* 1503, *d.* 1504, *p.* 1506 (York; Cross and Vickers, p. 113), and *see* **Broadebelt.**

Lewis ap Thomas: Valle Crucis; *d.* 1514 (Lichfield, in Repingdon conventual church, Derbyshire; *Reg. G. Blyth*, n–f.); he may have been briefly abbot of Strata Marcella before being translated to Cymer where he was abbot from around 1517 to 1537. He was one of the abbots appointed to make good grave faults at Valle Crucis in 1534. Pension, £6–13–4, 20–03–1537; suffragan bishop of Shrewsbury from 1537 until his death in 1561; appointed bishop, 13 June 1537, consecrated, :Lambeth, 24 June 1537 (Williams, 2001, pp. 66–67, 218; *Letters*, p. 25; Smith, 2008, p. 287; BRUO 3, p. 1708). He was also vicar of Bloxham, Oxon, from 1545. He was a co–consecrator on 3 May 1545 in Westminster Abbey of Bishop Anthony Kitchin of Llandaff (Birch, 1912, p. 360).

Lewis, Hugh: Stanley; *sd.* 1534 (Salisbury; *Reg. L. Campeggio*); perhaps *Hugh London*, q.v.

Lewis, William: sub–prior, Tilty, 1520 (London; *Reg. R. Fitzjames*, f. 181r [192r]).

Lewes/Lewys/Lawes, William: Warden; *sd.* and *d.* 1514 (Lincoln; *Reg. T. Wolsey*, ff. 13r, 14r); *p.* 1518 (Reg. W. Atwater, f. 125r); in house at suppression, 1538 (*DKR*, p. 47); in 1554 was resident at Pertenhall, Bedfordshire, and in receipt of his £5–6–8 pension, together with a pension of £5 from a chantry at Blunham, Bedfordshire; was unmarried and had no other ecclesiastical preferments (Hodgett, 1959, p. 92); in receipt of his pension as late as 1555 (TNA, E164/31, f. 25v).

Ley/Laye, John: Dunkeswell; *sd.* 1515, *d.* 1517 (Exeter; *Reg. H. Oldham*, ff. 122r, 127r; last abbot, 1529–1539 (TNA, E322/76); pension, £50 p.a.; rector of Sheldon and Sainthill, Devon, and from 1556 vicar of Payhembury, dying there a few years later (Sparks, 1978, pp. 107–110).

Leydyate, Thomas: Buildwas, *disp.* 1537 (*FOR*, p. 92).

Leyerd/Leidyard, Thomas: monk, Meaux; *sd.* 1485, *d.* and *p.* 1488 (York; Cross, 1995, p. 153).

Leyff/Lerisse, Robert: Byland: *see* **Foston.**

Leylond, Ralph: Vale Royal; *sd.* 1487, *d.* 1488; *p.* 1489 (Lichfield; *Reg. J. Hales*, ff. 233v, 238v, 243).

Leyng, William: St Mary Graces; *p.* 1520 (London; *Reg. R. Fitzjames*, f. 181r [192r]).

Leyshon, John: Margam, 1537 (Evans, 1996, p. 99)./

Lichfield, Humphrey: Bordesley; *ac.* 1497, *d.* 1499 (Worcester; *Reg. G. Gigli*, f. 25; *S. Gigli*, f. 395).

Lichfield, John: Bordesley; *ac.* 1497 (Lichfield; *Reg. J. Arundell*, f. 259v); *sd.* 1499, *p.* 1505 (Worcester; *Reg. S. Gigli*, ff. 293, 395).

Lichfield, Thomas: Hailes; *p.* 1478 (Worcester; *Reg. J. Alcock*, f. 250); ordained priest whilst under age (*SAP* 2, pp. 388–89 [No. 3142]).

Lichfield, Thomas: Merevale; *ac.* and *sd.* 1528, *d.* 1529, *p.* 1531 (Lichfield; *Reg. G. Blyth*, n–f.).

Lightfoot, Humphrey: Combermere, *disp.* 1538 (*DKR*, p. 17, *FOR*, p. 154); pension of £5 received as late as 1555 (TNA, E164/31, f. 69r); perhaps *Humphrey Chester*, q.v.

Lighton, Christopher: Fountains; *sd.* and *d.* 1521, *p.* 1524; 1536, accused, perhaps spuriously, of having illicit relations with a single woman; pension, 1539, £6 (York; Cross and Vickers, 1995, pp. 114–15, 125).

Lilborne, James: Llantarnam; *d.* 1491 (Wells; Somerset R.O., D/D/B Reg. 7, f.239r).

Lilborne, Thomas: Louth Park; *d.* 1509, *p.* 1510 (when named Philip; Lincoln; *Reg. W. Smith*, n–f.); last sub–prior (Gasquet, 1899, p. 205), *disp.* 1537 (*FOR*, p. 95).

Lincoln, John: Vaudey; *ac.* 1489, *sd.* 1492, *d.* 1493, *p.* 1494 (Lincoln; *Reg. J. Russell*, ff. 30v, 44/45r, 48/49v, 54v).

Lincoln, John: Vaudey; *d.* 1521, *p.* 1524 (Lincoln; *Reg. W. Atwater*, ff. 135v, 9r).

Lincoln, John: Sawtry, *sd.* 1491, *d.* 1492, *p.* 1494 (Lincoln; *Reg. J. Russell*, ff. 38r, 43/44r, 51v).

Lincoln, John: Louth Park; *ac.* 1500, *sd.* 1501, *d.* 1502, *p.* 1504 (Lincoln; *Reg. W. Smith*, ,ff. 22r, 28v, 35r, 45v).

Lingow, John: Llantarnam, *disp.* 1537 (*FOR*, p. 88 – where wrongly attributed to Llanthony Prima; info. Dr M. Gray).

Lister, Percival: Fountains, *sd.* 1501, *d.* 1502, *p.* 1503 (York; Cross and Vickers, 1995, pp. 110, 112).

Liswill/Liswell, William: Ford; *ac.* and *sd.* 1509; *d.* 1510, *p.* 1512 (Exeter; *Reg. H. Oldham*, ff. 99r, 101v, 102r, 108r).

Litster/Lytster/Lyster, John: Kirkstall, *ac.* 1533, *d.* 1534, *p.* 1535 (York); pension, 1539, £5 (Cross, 1995, pp. 141–42, 147); possibly married and was perhaps the John Lister of Burley mentioned in the will of a confrère, Edward Heptonstall, in 1558 (Lonsdale, 1972, p. 211). He may have been the vicar of his abbey's former church at Hollym, Holderness; if so, he made his will in 1562 (CIY).

Littleworth, Robert: Combe; *d.* 1485 (Lichfield; *Reg. J. Hales*, f. 211).

Llanfadder, Lewis: *see* **Lewis David.**

Lleision ap Thomas: *d.* 24–03–1509 ('Sitientes'/Lent Ember Saturday, in Ledbury church, dio. Hereford; *Reg. R. Mayew*, p. 251); last abbot, Neath, 1510–39; general pardon, 1510, when said to be 'late of Oxford' (*LP* 1, Part 1, p. 230 [438/2, m. 27]); B. Canon Law (Oxford) 1511; B. D. (Oxford) 1512; Reformator of the Order in Wales; definitor for the family of Clairvaux (1517) and of Cîteaux (1518); named in a commission of the peace, 1513 and 1536; *disp.* 1539; pension, £40, together with the rectory of Cadoxton, alive in 1547; still rector of Neath in 1542, when referred to as Lewis Thomas (TNA, E334/2, f. 7v), but a new rector seems to have taken over in 1544 (TNA, E334/4, f. 169v; *FOR*, p. 170).

Lloyd/Ffloyd, David: abbot, Aberconwy, ? 1489–1501; abbot, Cymer, 1514–16; abbot, Strata Marcella, 1517–25 (*Letters*, pp. 252 [No. 129]). It is possible that this name represents two different personages (Smith, 2008, pp. 284–85).

Lloyd, David: Valle Crucis; *p.* 1507 (Lichfield: *Reg. G. Blyth*, n–f.).

Lloyd, John/Sîon Llwyd: abbot, Valle Crucis, 1503–?1527; a genealogist and 'doctor of both laws'; (Williams, 2001, pp. 66–67; *LP* 1, p. 681); recommended to Cardinal Wolsey to be appointed bishop of St Asaph, though not so (*LP* 2, Part 2, p. 1262 [No. 4070]).

Llywelyn: *see* Philip Morgan.

Lodlam, Richard: Byland, –1538 (*DKR*, p. 13). Perhaps the same monk as *Richard Letheley*, q.v.

Lofthouse, Gabriel: Kirkstall, *sd.* 1515, *d.* 1516, *p.* 1522 (York); pension, £6; until 1548, priest, St Katherine's chantry, Richmond parish church; in 1550 he was a chaplain in Richmond where he was buried; his will of 1552 suggests that he was far from wealthy, even impoverished (Cross, 1995, pp. 141, 147–48; Lonsdale, 1972, pp. 207). *See also:* **Gabriel Lostens.**

Lofthouse *al.* Watson, Thursinus: monk, Kirkstall; *sd.* 1467, *d.* 1468/69 (York; *Reg. G. Neville*, ff. 185, 195); about 1482, and having been a white monk for eleven years, left the Cistercians to join the Carthusians (*CPL* 15, p. 158 [No. 320]); visited Rome seeking absolution; wished to return to Kirkstall; abbot of Fountains reported the case to the abbot of Cîteaux for his decision, 1485 (*Letters*, pp. 95–96 [No. 38]; 135 [No. 66]; same year, the General of the Carthusian Order wished permission for him to stay as a Carthusian (*CPL* 15, p. 296 [No. 577]; *Statuta* 5, p. 501 [No. 26]).

Lofthouse, William: Rievaulx; *ac.* 1501, *sd.* and *d.* 1502, *p.* 1504 (York; Cross and Vickers, 1995, p. 168).

Lokton, Richard: Waverley; *disp.* 1488 (*CPL* 15, p. 161 [No. 325]).

London, Augustine: *see* Game.

London, Hugh: Stanley; *d.* 1535 (Salisbury; *Reg. L. Campeggio*). He may be the same monk as *Hugh Lewis*, q.v.

London, John: Warden; *d.* 1490 (Lincoln; *Reg. J. Russell*, f. 34r). At a visitation of the abbey in 1492 he asserted that the tabula did not summon the monks to Mass, and also that the Saturday mandatum was not observed (*Letters*, p. 158 [No. 79]).

London, John: St Mary Graces; *ac.* 1494, *sd.* and *d.* 1498, *p.* 1500 (London; *Reg. R. Hill*, f. 29v; *Reg. T. Savage*, ff. 56v, 57r, 62v); abbot, Tilty, blessed 7 April 1515 by John de Riperia, O.Pr. titular bishop of Gallipoli, in the church of the Hospital of St Thomas Martyr of Acon, London (*Reg. R. Fitzjames*, f. 59 [61] r.); Leo X allowed his election to take effect from 16 November 1512 (*LP* 1, Part 2, p. 1527 [No. 3617]. Ceased to be abbot by 1517 (Smith, 2008, p. 340).

London, John: Warden; *ac.* and *sd.* 1500, *d.* 1501, *p.* 1504 (Lincoln; *Reg. W. Smith*, ff. 21r, 26v, 44r).

London, Philip: Warden; *d.* 1485, *p.* 1487 (Lincoln; *Reg. J. Russell*, ff. 20r, 26v).

London, Richard: Coggeshall; *sd.* and *d.* 1495, *p.* 1496 (London; *Reg. R. Hill*, ff. 30r, 30v, 31r).

London, Richard: Boxley; *ac.* 1497, *sd.* 1498, *p.* 1500 (London; *Reg. T. Savage*, ff. 53r, 54r, 61v).

London, Richard: Cleeve; *sd.* 1510 (Wells; *Reg. H. de Castello*, f. 151); *d.* 1511, *p.* 1512 (Exeter; *Reg. H. Oldham*, ff. 105r, 108r). Could he be the next mentioned monk?

London, Richard: Strata Marcella, 1525 (*MSS in BM* 3, p. 704 [No. 1293]).

London, Robert: Sawtry; *sd.* 1517, *d.* 1518, *p.* 1519 (Lincoln; *Reg. W. Atwater*, ff. 123v, 127r).

London(er), Thomas: abbot, Quarr, 1492–1508, when dies (Hockey, 1970, p. 260; Smith, 2008, p. 321).

London/*al.* Cordell, Thomas: Warden; *sd.* and *d.* 1518, *p.* 1520 (Lincoln; *Reg. W. Atwater*, ff. 125r, 127r, 134r); when in about 1535 he was commanded to read the divinity lecture in the monastery he read instead from a book 'carnal and of a brutal understanding' (*LC*, p. 59 [No. XXIX]). He may be the monk of this name who supplicated for B.D. (Oxon.) 1530, and who attempted to become abbot. He is probably the *Thomas Cordell* al. *Warden*, vicar of Welwyn, Hertfordshire, 1540–1563 and rector of Cranford, Middlesex, 1542–1563 (Stevenson, 1939, p. 47).

London, Thomas: Quarr; *ac.* 1518, *sd.* 1521, *d.* 1522, *p.* 1523 (Winchester; *Reg. R. Fox* 4, ff.69v, 72v; 5, ff. 30v, 32r); *disp.* 1537 (*FOR*, p. 87).

London, Thomas: Holm Cultram, signed deed of surrender, 1538 (*DKR*, p. 23). His name does not occur in one pension list (LR1/173, f. 147).

London, William: Dore; alleges in 1450 to the papal penitentiary that he was persuaded at the age of eleven to enter the monastery, was forced to make profession while under age, but later escaped; sought a declaration that he is not bound to the Cistercian Order (*SAP*, p. 155 [No. 703]).

London, *al.* Fysscher, William: Waverley; *sd.* and *d.* 1487, *p.* 1491 (Winchester; *Reg. P. Courtenay*, ff.13r, 18v; Baigent, 1883, p. 209).

London, William: Warden; *sd.* and *d.* 1514 (Lincoln: *Reg. T. Wolsey*, ff. 13r, 14r); *p.* 1517 (*Reg. W. Atwater*, f. 123v); *p.* 1518 (repetition, or another monk of same name? (*Reg. W. Atwater*, f. 126v).

London: *see* Senden.

Long, John: Dunkeswell; *sd., d.* and *p.* 1522 (Exeter; *Reg. J. Vesey*, ff. 149r–v, 150v).

Long, William: Coggeshall; *ex.* and *ac.* 1514, *sd.* 1515 (London; *Reg. R. Fitzjames*, ff. 178r [167r], 181v).

Longborowe, James: *see* **Loughborough.**

Longbottom/Longbotham, Thomas: Revesby; *sd.* 1528, *d.* and *p.* 1529 (Lincoln; Reg. J. Longland, ff. 21r, 24r, 25r); *disp.* 1538 (*FOR*, p. 128); 'president', when signed deed of surrender, March 1538 (Essex R.O., D/DRg 1/104); vicar, Dersingham, Norfolk, 1544–1554, when seemingly deprived on account of marriage, but rector, Ashwellthorpe, Norfolk, from 1555; died 1560 (Baskerville, 1933, p. 52).

Longclif, James: *see* Laucliff.

Longdon/Langdon, John: Hailes; *p.* 1478 (Worcester; Reg. J. Alcock 250; ordained priest whilst under age (*SAP* **2**, pp. 388–89 [No. 3142]); *disp.* 1491, but to 'continue to enjoy the privileges of the Cistercian Order', 1491 (*CPL* **15**, p. 430 [No. 823])); in 1496 travelled to Rome on the business of his abbey; abbot of Dore, 1501–1516; keen on saffron and hunting; resigned or died, 1516 (Williams, 1976, pp. 23–24; TNA, E315/405 [ii]/22; E315/238/72v).

Loodes: *see* Dodd.

Lorkyn/Loxyn, William: Boxley, *ac.* 1518, *d.* and *p.* 1520 (Rochester; Reg. J. Fisher, ff. 59v, 89v); *disp.* 1538 (*FOR*, p. 123); in receipt of pension of £4 in 1555 (TNA, E164/31, f. 4).

Lostens, Gabriel: Kirkstall; pension, 1539, £6 (Cross and Vickers, 1995, p. 142). Very probably he was *Gabriel Lofthouse*, q.v.

Lote: *see* Lete.

Lotewich, William: Margam, *disp.* 1536 (*FOR*, p. 68).

Loughborough/Longborowe, James: Garendon; *sd.* 1518, *d.* 1519, *p.* 1525 (Lincoln; Reg. W. Atwater, ff. 125v, 129r; Reg. J. Longland, f. 12r); *disp.* 1536 (*FOR*, p. 85).

Loughborough, Robert: Garendon; *sd.* 1497, *d.* 1498, *p.* 1500 (Lincoln; Reg. W. Smith, f. 24v).

Louth, Thomas: Revesby; *sd.* 1499, *d.* 1500 (Lincoln; Reg. W. Smith, f. 22v).

Love/Lowe, William: Coggeshall; *ex.* and *ac.* 1509, *d.* 1510; *p.* 1512 (London; Reg. R. Fitzjames, ff. 167r [156v], 163v [174v], CL); abbot, Coggeshall; election on 16–10–1527 certified by abbots of St Mary Graces and Sibton; blessed 24 October 1527 by Thomas, suffragan bishop of London, in chapel of the Hospital of Blessed Mary–iuxta–Bishopsgate (Reg. C. Tunstall, f. 147r); subject of an investigation by the Earls of Oxford and Essex in 1536 but cleared (Baskerville, 1937, p. 181); on 31 August 1536, having 'freely resigned', *disp.* with licence of non–residence, 1538 (*FOR*, pp. 75, 90, 124). In retirement granted "Sympson's Lodging" in which to dwell (TNA, SC12/7/34). Vicar of Witham, Essex, until his death in 1559 when buried in the chancel there (Smith, 2008, p. 281).

Lovage/Loveage, Benedict: Buckland; *ac.*, *d.* and *p.* 1526 (Exeter; Reg. J. Vesey, ff. 169v, 160v, 161r); *disp.* 1539 (*DKR*, p. 12; *FOR*, p. 178); pension, £4–13–4, received as late as 1555 (TNA, E164/31, f. 34v); chaplain, 1540/41 at Hytzweke, Devon (*Devonshire Notes and Queries* **17**, 1932, p. 91).

Lowde, Edmund: Fountains; *sd.* 1533, *d.* and *p.* 1534 (York); pension, 1539: £5; perhaps curate of Bubwith, Yorkshire, in 1552–57; died around 1569 (Cross and Vickers, 1995, pp. 114–15, 125).

Lowyk/Lowik, Robert: Pipewell; *sd.* 1515; *d.* and *p.* 1519 (Lincoln; Reg. W. Atwater, ff. 117r, 128r, 129r).

Lucas, Richard: Calder; *sd.* and *d.* 1497 (York; Reg. T. Rotherham, n–f.).

Lucy ... : Warden, accused at a visitation of serious shortcomings, 1492 (*Letters*, pp. 156–57 [No. 79]).

Ludlow, Richard: Bordesley; *sd.* 1487 (Lichfield; Reg. J. Hales, f. 233v); *d.* 1488, *p.* 1489 (Worcester; Reg. R. Morton, ff. 142, 144); *disp.* 1508 (*CPL* **18**, p. 595 [No. 902]).

Lunde, Leonard: Kirkstead; *sd.* 1510, *d.* 1511, *p.* 1512 (Lincoln; Reg. W. Smith, n–f.); *disp.* 1537 (*FOR*, p. 96).

Lune: *see* Woburn.

?Lunt, William: Revesby; *sd.* 1529 (Lincoln; Reg. J. Longland, f. 24r).

Lupton, William: Kirkstall; pension, 1539, £6 (Cross and Vickers, 1995, pp. 142, 148); in receipt of pension of £6 in 1555 (TNA, E164/31, f.53v); perhaps curate of Huddersfield in 1545 (Lonsdale, 1972, p. 208). Thomas Pepper (1553), formerly a Kirkstall monk, bequeathed him a feather bed and his best gown. Perhaps the monk, *William Kirkby*, q.v.

Luton/Lenton, Thomas: monk, Warden; *d.* and *p.* 1487 (Lincoln; *Reg. J. Russell*, ff. 23r, 26v); at the visitation of his monastery in 1492, he was accused of irregularities in his clothing, and that he had concubines (*Letters*, p. 158 [No. 79]). Might he be the monk *'Lucy'*, q.v.

Lutterworth, Robert: Combe; *p.* 1488 (Lichfield; *Reg. J. Hales*, f. 240v).

Lydney, James: Dore; 1511–12, *sd.* 1512 (Hereford, *Reg. R. Mayew*, p. 259).

Lydney, John: Flaxley; *ac.* 1476, *sd.* and *d.* 1478, *p.* 1481 (Hereford; *Reg. T. Myllyng*, pp. 156, 159–60, 164).

Lydney, John: Kingswood; *sd.* 1511 (Worcester; *Reg. S. Gigli*, f. 307).

Lylly, Robert: abbot, Sawtry, by 1530 (Smith, 2008, p. 330); *c.*1533, accused of enormities (TNA, STAC2/32/154).

Lylly//Lytly/Sythyll, Thomas: Bordesley, *ac.* and *d.* 1516 (Worcester; *Reg. S. Gigli*, ff. 329, 334); *disp.* 1538 (*FOR*, p. 149; TNA, E322/26); pension, £6 (TNA, E314/77); assessed for subsidy in 1540 (Bodleian Library, Oxford, Tanner MS 343).

Lyllyng, William: Rievaulx; *sd.* 1482, *d.* 1483 (York; Cross and Vickers, 1995, p. 167).

Lyn: *see* Farlington.

Lynacre, Thomas: Basingwerk; *sd.* and *d..* 1478 (Lichfield; *Reg. J. Hales*, ff. 248r, 249r).

Lynaker, Henry: Dieulacres; *sd.* 1494, *p.* 1495 (Lichfield; *Reg. W. Smith*, ff. 176v, 184v).

Lyndesey, William: Bruern; *p.* 1485 (Lincoln; *Reg. J. Russell*, f. 20r).

Lyng(e): *see* Allerton.

Lynham, Thomas: Bruern; *sd.* and *d.* 1494 (Lincoln; *Reg. J. Russell*, ff. 51v, 52r).

Lynne, William: Revesby; *d.* 1510 (Lincoln; *Reg. W. Smith*, n–f.).

Lynney, Ralph: Whalley; procurator, then vicar, 1536–1555, of its church of Blackburn, Lancashire; at some stage a scholar at Oxford; chaplain, 1555, to the Catholic Sir John Byron of Newstead Abbey, Nottinghamshire (Haigh, 1969, pp. 84–85, 118–119, 247).

Lyse, Roger: Rewley; *sd.* 1506 (Lincoln; *Reg. W. Smith*, n–f.).

Lyttyng, Robert: Coggeshall; *p.* 1496 (London; *CL*).

Mabson/Mapson, Charles: St Mary Graces; *ex.* and *ac.* 1528 (London; *Reg. C. Tunstall*, f. 160v); pension, £5–6–8, 1539 (*LP* **14**, Part 1, p. 340 [No. 688].

Machyn, William: Tintern, *disp.* 1537 (*FOR*, p. 92).

Macy: *see* Chaffcombe.

Madeley, William: Combermere; *p.* 1488 (Lichfield; *Reg. J. Hales*, f. 228v).

Maddershead: *see* Motsett.

Maidstone/Mayston, Thomas: Boxley; *ac.* 1493, *sd.* and *d.* 1494, *p.* 1495 (Canterbury; *Reg. J. Morton*, pp. 132–33 [Nos. 442a, 443c]; *Reg. R. Hill*, ff. 29r, 30r).

Maiowe: *see* Brackley.

Maisterman, John: Jervaulx, *disp.* 1537 (*FOR*, p. 119, Cross and Vickers, 1995, p. 135).

Maldon, John: Stanley: *sd., d.* and *p.* 1519 (Salisbury; *Reg. E. Audley*, ff. 37r, 39r, 40r).

Male, Thomas: Newenham; *sd.* 1530, *d.* 1532 (Exeter; *Reg. J. Vesey*, ff. 171v, 179r); *disp.* 1540 (*FOR*, p. 216); pension of £5 received as late as 1555 (TNA, E164/31, f.34v).

Mallyng, Thomas: Boxley; *ac.* and *sd.* 1508 (Rochester; *Reg. J. Fisher*, f. 33r).

Mallyng/Myllys, William: Boxley, 1494; held the church of Leybourne, Kent., and now permitted to hold a second benefice (*CPL* **16**, pp. 199–200 [No. 281].

Malmesbury, Robert: Stanley; *ac.* and *sd.* 1499 (Salisbury; *Reg. J. Blyth*, ff. 115v, 117r.).

Malmesbury, Thomas: Stanley; *sd., d.* and *p.* 1506 (Salisbury; *Reg. E. Audley*, ff. 6r, 7r).

Malpas, John: Vale Royal; *sd.* 1532 (Lichfield; *Reg. G. Blyth*, n–f.).

Malton/al/ Pynder, John: Rievaulx; *sd.* 1517, *d.* 1519, *p.* 1522 (York); signed deed of surrender and *disp.* 1538; pension granted of £5–6–8, but this cancelled on his death (*DKR*, p. 38; *FOR*, p. 156). He had become curate of Thornton–le–Dale, Yorkshire, before the formal dissolution. He was buried at Thornton on 3 February 1539, having left gifts to that church, which show him to be then a person of some substance (Aveling, 1952, pp. 107–08; Cross and Vickers, 1995, pp. 169–70, 179–80). .

?Malvern, John; Hailes; *sd.* 1459 (Worcester; *Reg. J. Carpenter*, f. 549).

Mancone/Mantorn, Amphiabulus/Amphibole: Boxley, *disp.* 1538 (*FOR*, p. 123); pension, £2–13–4 (TNA, E315/77).

Manchester, *al.* Pedley, Edward: Whalley; *p.* 1523 (Lichfield; *Reg. G. Blyth*, n–f.); supplicated for degree of B.D. (Oxon.) 1535/37. 'scholar', of Whalley, 1537/38; vicar, Whalley, 1538, until his death in 1558 (Haigh, 1969, pp. 84–85; Stevenson, 1939, p. 47).

Maneste/Manesty/Manasty, Robert: Calder; *sd., d.* and *p.* 1523 (York; *Reg. T. Wolsey*, ff. 197v, 198v, 201v); accused, perhaps spuriously, of sodomy in Crown visitation of 1535 (*LP* **10**, p. 138 [No. 364]); acted as vicar of nearby parish of St John Baptist (Loftie, 1892, p. 80; VCH, *Cumberland* **2**, 1968, p. 177).

Manfield: *see* Ovafield.

Manwood, ?Richard: Netley; in community, 1518, by which time priested (TNA, E314/101).

Maownsarell, Robert: *see* Mountsorell.

Mapleton, John: *see* Barrow.

Marbroke, Thomas: Rewley, *disp.* 1536 (*FOR*, p. 78).

Marbye: *see* Merbury.

Marcus, John: Hailes; *p.* 1516 (Worcester; *Reg. S. Gigli*, f. 331).

Marden: *see* Marley.

Mardvode: *see* Sylyfim.

Marflett, Thomas: Meaux; *d.* 1482, *p.* 1485 (York; Cross and Vickers, 1995, p. 153).

Markam/Marcam, John: Combe; *sd.* 1511, *p.* 1512 (Lichfield; *Reg. G. Blyth*, n–f);

Marke/Marcus, John: Ford; *sd.* 1510, *d.* 1511 (Exeter; *Reg. H. Oldham*, ff.103r, 106r).

Marlborough, John: Stanley; *sd.* 1530 (Salisbury; *Reg. L. Campeggio*).

Marlborough, Thomas: Stanley; *sd.* 1510. *d.* and *p.* 1511 (Salisbury; *Reg. E. Audley*, ff. 15v, 16v, 17r.).

Marley/Marden, Peter: Boxley; *t.* and *ac.* 1520, *sd.* 1523 (Rochester; *Reg. J. Fisher*, ff. 89v, 92r).

Marlow, William: abbot, Strata Florida, 1487; caught up in tension between Cîteaux and Clairvaux, and briefly imprisoned, but received royal backing (*Letters*, pp. 97–100 [No. 40–42]; Williams, 2010, p. 255).

Marom, James: Revesby; *ac.* 1505 (Lincoln; *Reg. W. Smith*, n–f.).

Marom/Marum/Marian, John: Kirkstead; *ac.* 1486, *sd.* 1487, *d.* 1489, *p.* 1491 (Lincoln; *Reg. J. Russell*, ff. 21r, 24v, 32r, 40r).

Marome, Thomas: Revesby; *sd.* 1529 (Lincoln; *Reg. J. Longland*, f. 24r).

Marr: *see* Warre.

Marre, Lawrence: Furness, 1510 (*AF*, p. 303); abbot, Calder, 1514–16 (Loftie, 1888, p. 236; 1892, p. 78); commission to bless issued to bishop of Negroponte by archbishop of York, 3 February 1514 (York; *Reg. C. Bainbridge*, f. 47).

Marsey, Reginald: Fountains; *d.* 1521 (York; Cross and Vickers, 1995, p, 114).

Marshall, Nicholas: Newminster; *p.* 1497 (Durham; *Reg. R. Fox* **2**, p. 49); sixty–eight years old in 1536 (TNA, SC12/13/65); *disp.* 1536 (*FOR*, p. 77).

Marshall, Rowland: Newminster; *p.* 1497 (Durham; *Reg. R. Fox* **2**, p. 49).

Marshall, William: Holm Cultram, 1533 (*LP* **6**, pp. 425–26 [No. 988]); signed deed of surrender and *disp.* 1538 (TNA, E314/20/11, f. 3r–d; *FOR*, pp. 123–24). At the dissolution was living in a chamber 'in the eastern part of the monastery' (TNA, LR1/173, f.141–142). In receipt of his pension of £4–13–4 in 1555 (TNA, E164/31, f.73v).

Marshall, William: Kirkstall, *sd.* 1482, *d.* 1483, *p.* 1487 (York; Cross and Vickers, 1995, p. 139); profession of obedience as abbot of Kirkstall before John, titular bishop of Chalkis, 5 December 1509 (York; *Reg. C. Bainbridge*, f. 9v); abbot, 1509–1525 (Smith, 2008, p. 305).

Marston, Thomas: Stratford; *p.* 1495 (London; *Reg. R. Hill*, f. 32v).

Marstyn/Merstin, Richard: porter, Whalley, 1536 (TNA, SC6/HENVIII/1796); *disp.* 1537 (*FOR*, p. 91).

Marten/Martyn/Moreton, William: Holm Cultram, 1536 (*LP* **11**, p. 115 [No. 276]); not yet ordained priest when signed deed of surrender and *disp.* 1538 (*DKR*, p. 23; *FOR*, pp. 123–24). In receipt of his pension of £2 in 1555 (LR1/173, f. 147, where 'Mason').

Martin ... : Stratford, attending General Chapter in 1489 (*Letters*, pp. 122–23 [No. 60]).

Martyn, Peter: Rewley; *p.* 1534 (Lincoln; *Reg. J. Longland*, f .37r).

Martin: *see also* Marin.

Martindale/Maÿdall', Richard: Furness, signed deed of surrender and *disp.* 1537 (TNA, E322/91; *FOR*, p. 97).

Marton, Robert: Rievaulx; *sd.* 1495, *d.* 1497, *p.* 1499 (York; Cross and Vickers, 1995, p. 168).

Marton/Morton, Thomas: Byland; *p.* 1532 (York); in 1536 was seeking to leave the religious life, and his name does not appear in the faculty lists (Cross and Vickers, 1995, pp. 99, 107).

Maryott/Meryott/Merryotun/Meryell/Meryk, John: Stratford; *ex.* and *ac.* 1521 (London; *Reg. R. Fitzjames*, f.183v [194v]); *sd.* 1522 (Canterbury; *Reg. W. Warham, London sede v.*, **2**, f. 297r); *p.* 1525 (London; *Reg. C. Tunstall*, f.157); precentor, when signed deed of surrender and *disp.* 1538 (*DKR*, p. 42; *FOR*, p. 129); pension, £5 (TNA, E315/232, f. 28v).

Masbery, Christopher: Merevale; *p.* 1514 (Lichfield; *Reg. G. Blyth*, n–f.).

Masham/Marsham, al. Tamworth, Lewis: Garendon; *ac.* 1530, *sd.* 1531, *d.* 1533, *p.* 1534 (Lincoln; *Reg. J. Longland*, ff. 26v, 28v, 35r, 38v).

Masham, Simon: Jervaulx; *ac.* 1505, *sd.* and *d.* 1506, *p.* 1507 (York; Cross and Vickers, 1995, p. 130).

Mashorder/Massrudder: *see* Mersherudder.

Mason, George: Jervaulx, *disp.* 1537 (*FOR*, p. 119); a priest of this name was the chantry priest of St Nicholas's chapel in York Minster in 1546 (Cross and Vickers, 1995, p. 135).

Mason, John: Revesby; *d.* 1507, *p.* 1510 (Lincoln; *Reg. W. Smith*, n–f.).

Mason, Paul: Kirkstall, son of Thomas Mason of St Martin's, York; *sd.* 1531, *d.* 1533, *p.* 1534 (York); accused, perhaps spuriously, of sodomy in 1535/36; pension, 1539, £5–6–8; in receipt of pension in 1555 (TNA, E164/31, f.53v); living in Leeds, 1556, when proved a will (Lonsdale, 1972, pp. 209–10. He may have been vicar of Bishopthorpe, York (1563), and of St Mary, Castlegate, in plurality. If so, he was charged at a visitation in 1571 of overlooking the faults of a woman whom he had churched, and of another to whom he had administered Holy Communion. His will, of December 1571, shows that he was married with a son, two daughters and a 'baseborn' daughter (Cross, 1995, pp. 142, 148–49).

Mason, William: Buckfast; *d.* 1526 (Exeter; *Reg. J. Vesey*, f. 160).

Massey/Massy, John: Combermere; *ac.* and *sd.* 1512 (Lichfield; *Reg. G. Blyth*, n–f.); sub–prior, 1524 (Smith, 2008, p. 283). Last abbot, Combermere, by 1536 (Cheshire Archives, DCH/Z/3);

disp. 1538 (*FOR*, p. 154); seemed to hope that the community could remain in the monastery even after its suppression (Youings, 1971, pp. 174–75). For his background: *Cheshire Sheaf* **10**, 1913, p. 15.

Massey, Richard: Warden; *sd.* 1510 (Lincoln; *Reg. W. Smith*, n–f.).

Massy, Richard: Kirkstead; *d.* 1511 (Lincoln; *Reg. W. Smith*, n–f.). It is possible that this monk and the foregoing are the same person, and that there has been an error in naming the monk's monastery.

Matthew, John: Kirkstall; pension, 1539, £6. Still alive in 1556 when he proved a will together with another former monk, Paul Mason. Chantry priest in Leeds until 1548 and living there in 1558. He may be either *John Richmond* or *John Thorner*, q.v. (Lonsdale, 1972, p. 207), or *John Shadwell*, q.v. (Cross and Vickers, 1995, pp. 142, 149) . Probably B. D. (Oxon.) 1539 (*Stevenson*, 1939, p. 46).

Mathew, Robert: Newminster, thirty–five years old in 1536 (TNA, SC12/13/65); *disp.* 1536 (*FOR*, p. 77).

Matson, Richard: Stratford; *ac.* 1495, *sd.* 1498, *d.* 1500 (London; *Reg. R. Hill*, f. 32v; *Reg. T. Savage*, ff. 55v, 62v).

Maurice John ap Rhys : abbot, Whitland, 1469–1490 – when deposed, accused of serious short-comings; seemingly briefly studied at Oxford, where on enquiry in 1469 no record could be found of his having been banished from the university (*BRUO* **2**, p. 1245); may have been Maurice ap Ieuan, the 'pretended abbot' of Strata Marcella, deposed in 1496 (*Statuta* **6**, p. 22 [No. 1491/48]; *Letters*, pp.131–36 [No. 66], 191 [No. 94]).

Mauv/Mayvu/Mayun, William: Bindon; general pardon, 1505 (*Patent*, 1505, p. 420); *disp.* 1505 (*CPL* **18**, p. 332 [425]); 1492, sought leave to study and lecture in a studium for seven years (*SAP* **2**, p. 373 [No. 3102]).

Maxfelde, Christopher: Vale Royal; *sd.* 1532 (Lichfield; *Reg. G. Blyth*, n–f).

Maynard, Thomas: Buckland; *sd.* and *d.* 1514, *p.* 1518 (Exeter; *Reg. H. Oldham*, ff.1 15r, 118v, 130v); *disp.* 1539; pension, £5–6–8 (*DKR*, p. 12; *FOR*, p. 178; Gill, 1951, p. 38.

Mayott, Richard: Dieulacres; *sd.* 1495 (Lichfield; *Reg. W. Smith*, f. 188); monk, Strata Florida, 1539; pension, £2–13–4; in receipt of pension of £2–13–4 in 1555 (TNA, E164/31, f. 75v).

Mayot: *see also* Meyot.

Mayuv/Mayun: *see* Mauv.

Maysam/Maesham/Marson, John: Garendon; *sd.* 1515, *d.* 1516, *p.* 1518 (Lincoln; *Reg. W. Atwater*, ff. 117r, 118r, 126v).

Medborn/Medburn, William: Pipewell; *sd.* and *d.* 1508 (Lincoln; *Reg. W. Smith*, n–f.).

Mede, Robert: Kirkstead; *sd.* 1528, *p.* 1530 (Lincoln; *Reg. J. Longland*, ff. 21r, 26r); *disp.* 1537 (*FOR*, p. 96).

Medeley, Thomas: proctor for abbot and convent, Flaxley, 1530 (Hereford; *Reg. C. Bothe*, p. 359). Was he a monk?

Medylton/Myddleton, Thomas: Roche, *d.* and. *p.* 1522 (York); signed deed of surrender, 1538 (TNA, E322/204); *disp.* 1538 (*FOR*, p. 144); in receipt of £5 pension.in 1555 (TNA, E164/31, f. 53r); until 1548 may have been a chantry priest at Bedale, Yorkshire; if so, then fifty years old in 1548; may have held several curacies, including Birdsall in 1571, alive but old in 1577 (Cross and Vickers, 1995, pp. 187, 194–95). Signed letters testimonial, 1555 (Cross, 1993, p. 201).

Mee/Mere, William: Combermere, 1538 (*DKR*, p. 17); pension, £3–6–8 (TNA, E315/233, f. 78r).

Meeks, William: Roche; pension, £5–6–8, 1538 (TNA, E314/77).

Mekenes, Thomas: Revesby, *sd.* 1498, *d.* 1499, *p.* 1500 (Lincoln; *Reg. W. Smith*, n.f.).

Melford: *see* Mylford.

Melsonby, John: Fountains; *d.* and *p.* 1509; abbot's chaplain, 1513; 1536, accused, perhaps spuriously, of having illicit relations with two single women; pension, 1539, £6 (York; Cross and Vickers, 1995, pp. 113, 115, 125–26).

Meltham/Meltoun/Moltam, John: Vale Royal, *ac.* 1530 (Lichfield; *Reg. G. Blyth*, n–f.); signed deed of surrender and *disp.* 1538 (*DKR*, p. 46; *FOR*, p. 162); pension, £5 (TNA, E315/233, f. 69v).

Melton, Antony: Hailes, ordained priest whilst under age (*SAP 2*, pp. 388–89 [No. 3142]). Abbot, Hailes, 1504–1527, when dies (*CHA*, p. 92; Smith, 2008, p. 299); general pardon, 1509 (*LP* **1**, Part 1, p. 247 [No. 438/3, m. 20]).

Melton, John: Hailes; *d.* 1512 (Worcester; *Reg. S. Gigli*, f. 315).

Melton, Richard: Rufford; *sd., d.* and *p.* 1522 (York; *Reg. T. Wolsey*, ff. 194r, 195v, 196v); *disp.* 1536 (*FOR*, p. 74).

Melton/al. Wurmell, William: Garendon; *sd.* 1512, *d.* 1513, *p.* 1514 (Lincoln; *Reg. W. Smith*, n–f; *Reg. T. Wolsey*, f. 15v.); *disp.* 1536, when last prior (*FOR*, p. 74; TNA, E315/278, f. 40).

Merbury, William: Dore; *d.* 1532 (Hereford; *Reg. C. Bothe*, p. 329); *p.* 1532 (Worcester; *Reg. R. Morton addenda*, f. 172); *disp.* 1537 (*FOR*, p. 98). After Dore's suppression served the local parishioners for a year or two (Williams, 1976, p. 32).

Merell/Merelde, John: Coggeshall; *sd.* 1500, *d.* and *p.* 1501 (London; *Reg. T. Savage*, ff. 65v, 66v; *Reg. W. Warham*, f. 78r); prior, 1509 (London; *Reg. R. Fitzjames*, f.157r [168r].

Merevale, John: Merevale; *d.* 1520 (Lichfield; *Reg. G. Blyth*, n–f.).

Meriot: *see* Maryott.

Mersherudder, Christopher: Furness, signed deed of surrender and *disp.* 1537 (TNA, E322/91; *FOR*, p. 97; *LP* **12**, Part 1, p. 372*n*).

Merston, Thomas: Fountains, *sd.* 1491 (York; Cross and Vickers, 1995, p. 111); abbot's chaplain, 1499–1501; bursar, 1507; cellarer, 1509–17 (*FLB*, pp. 16–17 [No. 17], 26 [No. 30], 67 [No. 74], 69 [No. 77], 78 [No. 89], 85 [No. 96], 118 [No. 130], 105 [No. 120]).

Metcalfe, Richard: Jervaulx; if his *alias* was York, then *p.* 1515 (York); *disp.* 1537 (*FOR*, p. 119); perhaps priest at Askrigg, Yorkshire, in 1548 (Cross and Vickers, 1995, p. 135).

Metcalf, Thomas: Byland, if his *alias* was York, then *p.* 1515 (York); *disp.* 1538 (*DKR*, p. 13; *FOR*, p. 181); pension, £5–6–8; died and buried at the local village of Kilburn, 1558, leaving his best silver spoon to his former abbot, John Alanbridge (Aveling, 1955, p. 9; Cross and Vickers, 1995, pp. 100, 107–08).

Meyer, Thomas: Robertsbridge, by *c.* 1491 (SAL, *MS 14*, f. 59v).

Meyot/Metall/Mayot, John: Hulton; *ac.* and *d.* 1517, *p.* 1521 (Lichfield; *Reg. G. Blyth*, n–f.)

Meyram, Geoffrey: Vale Royal; *p.* 1487 (Lichfield; *Reg. J. Hales*, f. 233v).

Meyre/Mayre/More, Richard: Croxden, signed deed of surrender and *disp.* 1538 (Hibbert,1910, p. 222; *FOR*, p. 151); in receipt of pension of £4 as late as 1555 (TNA, E164/31, f. 46v).

Michael, John: Beaulieu, abbot's trusted emissary, 1488 (*Letters*, p. 111 [No.51]).

Micklewright, John: Hulton; said in 1518 to have been apostate for twenty years (TNA, REQ 2/11/40).

Middleham, ?Jenkinson, Robert: Rievaulx; *sd.* 1522, *d.* 1524, *p.* 1526; does not feature in the pension lists (York; Cross and Vickers, 1995, pp. 169, 178–79; Aveling, 1952, p. 110.

Middleton/Mitulton, John: abbot, Grace Dieu, 1473–1484, when resigns, being harrassed by 'enemies' (Williams, 1976, pp. 62–63; TNA, E315/36/228).

Middelton, John: Warden; *d.* 1504 (Lincoln; *Reg. W. Smith*, f.44r); if same monk, *p.* 1515 (Lincoln; *Reg. W. Atwater*, f. 112r.)

Middleton, Thomas: Swineshead, 1532; *disp.* 1536 (TNA, REQ 2/13/99; *FOR*, p. 67).

Mydylton/Middleton, William: Croxden; *sd.* 1508 (Lichfield; *Reg. G. Blyth*, n–f.).

Midilton/Middleton, Robert: Whalley; *sd.* 1523, *d.* 1524 (Lichfield; *Reg. G. Blyth*, n–f.).

Midhurst, William: Waverley; *ac.* 1514 (Winchester; *Reg. R. Fox* **3**, f. 55v).

Midilham, Water: Jervaulx; *sd.* 1484, *d.* and *p.* 1486 (York; Cross and Vickers, 1995, p. 129).

Milford, Thomas: Roche; *sd.* and *d.* 1490, *p.* 1493 (York; Cross and Vickers, 1995, p. 186).

Milford: *see also* Mylford.

Milton, John: Hulton; *ac.* and *sd.* 1487, *d.* 1488 (Lichfield; *Reg. J. Hales*, ff. 222, 223v, 236v).

Milton, John: Rewley; *sd.* 1525, *d.* 1526 (Lincoln; *Reg. J. Longland*, ff. 14v, 17r); in house at its suppression, 1536 (Baskerville, 1930, p. 335).

Milton, Roger: Beaulieu, but apostate, 1489/90 or 1513/14 (TNA, C81/1788/2).

Milton, William: Pipewell; *sd.* and *d.* 1488, *p.* 1489 (Lincoln; *Reg. J. Russell*, ff. 27v, 29r, 33r).

Milton, William: Boxley, but apostate, 1512 (TNA, C81/1788/7).

Milward, Richard: Dunkeswell; *ac.* and *sd.* 1489; *d.* and *p.* 1490 (Exeter; *Reg. R. Fox*, ff. 153v–154r, 156r).

Minsterworth: *see* Mynsterworth.,

Mitchell, James: Whalley, *disp.* 1537 (*FOR*, p. 91).

Moke/Mooke/Monke, Thomas: Rufford; *d.* 1534 (York; *Reg. E. Lee*, f. 188v). On Rufford's suppression he moved to Kirkstall, and was in receipt of pension of £5 in 1555. Thomas was a chantry priest at Thorpe–by–Newark, Nottinghamshire. until 1548, when said to be fifty years old and 'unlearned.' His will of 1586, asked for burial in Farndon church or churchyard, Notts.; at that time his pensions from Thorpe and Kirkstall were in arrears (Cross and Vickers, 1995, p. 149; Lonsdale, 1972, p. 202).

?Mole, John: ? Garendon; *d.* 1488 (Lincoln; *Reg. J. Russell*, f. 21r; Cross and Vickers, 1995, p. 149).

Moll', Thomas: Combermere; *sd.* 1512 (Lichfield; *Reg. G. Blyth*, n–f.).

Moltam: *see* **Meltham.**

Molton, Anthony: Ford; *d.* 1526 (Exeter; *Reg. J. Vesey*, f. 161r).

Monmouth, John: Stanley; *sd.* 1459 (Worcester; *Reg. J. Carpenter*, f. 549).

Monmouth, Robert of: cellarer, Tintern, 1487–88 (NLW, Badminton Deeds, Group 2, Nos. 14478–79).

Mook, Thomas: *see* Moke.

Mordan, Hugh: Warden; *ac.* 1492 (Lincoln; *Reg. J. Russell*, f. 42v/43v).

More, Henry: last abbot, St Mary Graces, 1516–1539; blessed as abbot by John de Riperia, O. Pr. titular bishop of Gallipoli on 7 May 1516 at St Mary Graces (LMA, *Reg. R. FitzJames*, f. 147r; BL, Harley MS 6955, p. 74) ; chancery case between him and John Palmer, sub–prior, regarding theft of keys from previous abbot, John Prehest, on his death–bed (Smith, 2008, p. 309); permitted in 1536 (on resignation of William Love) to hold the monastery of Coggeshall *in commendam*, on payment of a fee of £125–11–0 (*FOR*, p. 75); post–1535, was granted by Sir Thomas Seymour, kt., an annual rent from and in the manor of Great and Little Coggeshall (TNA, E211/344); *disp.* 1539 (*FOR*, pp. 75, 182). Surrendered abbey of Coggeshall, 5 February 1538; as abbot of St Mary Graces, .pension £66–13–4, 1539 (*LP* **14**, Part 1, p. 340 [No. 688]).

More, James: sub–cellarer/kitchener, Whalley, 1536 (TNA, SC6/HENVIII/1796; E315/427, ff. 4, 39, 40); *disp.* 1537 (*FOR*, p. 91). Did he move to Rushen?, *vide infra*. Curate, Ribchester, by 1548–1554 (Haigh, 1969, p. 119).

More, James: Rushen; in receipt of his pension of £2–13–4 in 1555 (TNA, E164/31, f. 74v; Davey and Roscow, 2010, p. 174).

More, Richard: abbot, Woburn, *c.* 1490 or 1507 (Smith, 2008, p. 351).

More, Richard: *see* Meyre.

More, Thomas: St Mary Graces; 'president' there, 1521/22, when presenting a monk for ordination (London, *Reg. R. Fitzjames*, f.183v [194v]; Canterbury; *Reg. W. Warham*, f. 296v); kitchener, *c.*1530 (TNA, C1/990/41); rent–collector, 1533, 1538 (Grainger and Phillpotts, 2011, p. 92); *disp.* 1539 (*FOR*, p. 182); in receipt of pension of £5–6–8 in 1555 (TNA, E164/31, f. 4).

Moreby, Robert: Fountains; *d.* and *p.* 1509 (York); moved for a time to a Welsh abbey; executed in York in August 1538 for saying that the Welsh commons were ready to rise (Cross and Vickers, 1995, pp. 113, 126; *LP* **13**, Part 2, pp. 51 [No. 142], 60 [No. 156]).

Moreland, William: *see* Borrowby.

Moresley/Morisley, Richard: novice, Roche, 1538, when signed deed of surrender (TNA, E314/77, 322/204); a deacon living in Kellington, Yorkshire, in 1555, when a group of former Cistercian monks of Rufford and Roche signed letters testimonial enabling his ordination the the priesthood; still drawing his monastic pension of £3–6–8 in 1556 (Cross, 1993, pp.]201, 203; Cross and Vickers, 1995, pp. 171, 195; TNA, E164/31, f. 53r).

Moreton, Richard: Whalley, *disp.* 1537 (*FOR*, p. 91).

Moreton, Richard: St Mary Graces; ex. and ac. 1528 (London; *Reg. C. Tunstall*, f. 160v).

Moreton: and see *Morton*.

Morgan ap John: Neath; *sd.* 1503 (St David's; *EPD* **2**, p. 757).

Morgan ap Johns/Jones: Strata Florida; *d.* 1532 (Hereford; *Reg. C. Bothe*, p. 329); *disp.* 1540; pension, £3; possibly rector, Aberedw, Radnorshire, 1554 (TNA, E334/4, f.92 v); still alive in 1558 (*BW* **2**, p. 311; *FOR*, p. 206; Williams, 1889, Appx. p. xciii); in receipt of his pension in 1555 (TNA, E164/31, f. 75v).

Morgan ap Rhys: abbot, Strata Florida, 1444 (when dispensed on account of illegitimacy) to 1486; a genealogist and church restorer (*CPL* **9**, p. 413; Williams, 2001, p. 59; 2010, p. 254).

Morgan *al.* Talley, David: Strata Florida, 1539; *disp.* 1540, pension: £2 p.a., alive in 1553 (*FOR*, p. 206; TNA, E315/232/219). In receipt of pension of £3 in 1555 (TNA, E164/31, f. 75v).

Morgan, Philip/Philip de Llywelyn: Dore; *ac.* 1455, *sd.* and *d.* 1456; *p.* 1458 (Hereford; *Reg. J. Stanbury*, pp. 139, 140, 144); abbot, 1476–*c.*1495, when forced to step down being 'of great age'; professed then as a monk of Whitland, but lived in retirement in the house of the Dominicans in Hereford; died in early sixteenth century (TNA, C1/304/36; E303/5, f. 104; Williams, 1976, p. 22).

Morland, Matthew: Fountains; *sd.* 1533, *d.* and *p.* 1534 (York); pension, 1539, £5; dead by 1560 (Cross and Vickers, 1995, pp. 114–15, 126).

Morley: *see* Calne.

Morpeth, Cuthbert: Fountains, *sd.* 1499, *p.* 1501 (York; Cross, 1995, p. 112).

Morpeth, Edward: Newminster; *sd.* 1531 (Durham; *Reg. C. Tunstall*, p. 126 [No. 373]; twenty–seven years old in 1536 (TNA, SC12/13/65); *disp.* 1536 (*FOR*, p. 77).

Morpath, John: abbot, Roche, 1491–1503 (*Reg. T. Rotherham*, p. 234 [No. 1850]; Smith, 2008, p. 327); received title deeds from laity for safe keeping (TNA, C1/323/18), but also refused to deliver up title deeds when requested (TNA, C1/272/28).

Morpeth/Morpath, Roger: of Newminster; *disp.* 1491 (*CPL*, **15**, p. 401 [No. 759]); abbot by 1516 (Oliver, 1915, p. 207).

Morpeth, Thomas: Newminster, fifty–two years old in 1536 (TNA, SC12/13/65); *disp.* 1536 (*FOR*, p. 77).

Morreby: *see* Moreby.

Morris, John: Margam; *disp.* 1537 (*FOR*, p. 93).

Morys, Nicholas: Netley; *ac.* 1511, *p.* 1520 (Winchester; *Reg. R. Fox* **3**, f. 51r; **4**, f. 71r.).

Morris, Thomas: Grace Dieu, 1509–10; *p.* 1510 (Hereford; *Reg. R. Mayew*, p. 254).

Morse, William: Dore; *sd.* 1486 (Hereford; *Reg. T. Myllyng,* p. 172). He is probably the same monk as *William Dore,* q.v.

Mortok, John: prior, Robertsbridge, *c.*1491 (SAL, *MS 14,* f. 59v).

Mrtu'/?Mayhoo: *see* Brackley.

Morton, Hugh: Furness; *p.* 1502 (York; *Reg. T. Savage,* f.113r); detained in The Fleet prison, 1516/17 (TNA, E 135/2/30).

Morton, John: Stoneleigh; *sd.* and *d.* 1529, *p.* 1530 (Lichfield; *Reg. G. Blyth,* n–f.); *disp.* 1537 (*FOR,* p. 88).

Morton, Richard: *see* Norton.

Mor(e)ton, Robert: Bordesley; *sd.* 1506, *d.* 1510, *p.* 1516 (*Reg. S. Gigli,* ff. 294, 302, 330, where said to be of Hailes*); disp.* 1538 (*DKR,* p. 11; *FOR,* p. 149); signed deed of surrender, 1538 (TNA, E322/26); dispensation to practice medicine anywhere, 10–12–1536 (*FOR,* p. 81); pension, £8; may be the monk of this name, B.D. (Oxon.) 1519 (Stevenson, 1939, 47). Assessed for subsidy in 1540 (Bodleian Library, Oxford, Tanner MS 343).

Morton, Thomas: cellarer, Tintern, 1505–06, abbot, 1513–17 (Williams, 1976, pp. 109–10).

Morton: *see also* Marton.

Motsett/Motessett, Ralph: Dieulacres, *disp.* 1538; 'reward' £2–0–0 (Walcott, 1871, p. 216); pension, £5–6–8 (Hibbert, 1910, pp. 239, 242; *FOR,* p. 160). If *Ralph Maddershead,* then continued to live in the neighbourhood (Fisher, 1969, p. 58).

Motte, John: 'of the monastery of Robertsbridge'; made in 1502 an executor of Thomas Bishop of Whatlington, Sussex (*SW,* p. 90); he was possibly *John Mortok,* q.v.

Mounsorell, Robert: Garendon; *sd.* 1530, *d.* 1531, *p.* 1533 (Lincoln; *Reg. J. Longland,* ff. 26v, 28v, 35v); *disp.* 1536 (*FOR,* p. 76).

Mountsorell, Thomas: Garendon; *sd.* 1518, *d.* 1519 (Lincoln; *Reg. W. Atwater,* ff. 125v, 129r); *p.* 1521 (*Reg. J. Longland,* f.1v).

Mowdeley, William: Combermere; *sd.?*1487 (Lichfield; there is a dating error here; *Reg. J. Hales,* f. 243v).

Moyser, John: Byland; member of a local family; *disp.* 1539, was bequeathed £4 in 1541 to say Mass for a whole year for William Parker of Kilburn; in 1552 his pension was a year in arrears; still in receipt of his £6 pension in 1556, but dead by 1564 (Aveling, 1955, p. 8; *FOR,* p. 181; Cross and Vickers, 1995, pp. 100, 107).

Moysleye, Richard: *see* Moresley.

Mudde, Henry: Jervaulx; *disp.* 1478 (*CPL 13,* Part 2, p. 592).

Mudde/Madde, Thomas: Jervaulx, *disp.* 1537 (*FOR,* p. 119); after the Suppression he fled to Scotland taking the head of Blessed George Lazenby with him; returned to England in Mary's reign and taught children in Knaresborough; after Elizabeth's accession he became chaplain to the earl of Northumberland at Topcliffe, Yorkshire; after the Northern Rebellion he went into hiding; arrested at Boroughbridge in 1570, he was held in custody in York, and then in the North Block House at Hull where he died in 1583 (Gasquet, 1899, p. 458; Cross and Vickers, 1995, pp. 135–36).

Muldyclif, Ralph: Roche, *sd., d.* and *p.* 1522 (York; Cross and Vickers, 1995, p. 187).

Mykelton, John: Hailes; *sd.* 1459 (Worcester; *Reg. J. Carpenter,* f. 549); .sub–prior, 1478 (*Reg. J. Alcock,* f. 250).

Mylford/Milford/Melford, William: Quarr; *ac.* 1518, *d.* and *p.* 1527, (Winchester; *Reg. R. Fox 4,* f.69v; **5,** ff. 36r–v); moved to Buckland when Quarr was suppressed in 1536; *disp.* 1539, pension, £4, received as late as 1555 (TNA, E164/31, f. 34r; *DKR,* p. 12; *FOR,* p. 178).).

Mylward: *see* Milward.

Mynsterwoth, Raynald/Reginald: Llantarnam; *sd.* 1481 (Wells; *Reg. R. Stillington*, f. 210v); *disp.* 1506 (*CPL* **18**, pp. 408–09 [p.573]).

Mynty, Henry: Stanley; *ex.* and *ac.* 1518; *sd., d.* and *p.* 1519 (Salisbury; *Reg. E. Audley*, ff. 35r, 37r, 39r, 40r).

?Myntyard/Myntun, Richard: Revesby; *ac.* 1488, *d.* 1490 (Lincoln; *Reg. J. Russell*, ff. 28r, 35r).

Mysterton, Thomas: Combe; *ac.* 1500 (Lichfield; *Reg. J. Arundel*, f. 287v); *sd.* 1503 (Lichfield; *sede v.*, CCA, DCc–Reg. f. 287r).

Myvot, David: Aberconwy; *sd.* 1498 (Lichfield; *Reg. J. Arundel*, f. 271).

Nede/Neve, Robert: Woburn; *ac.* 1509, *sd.* 1511, *d.* 1513, (Lincoln; *Reg. W. Smith*, n–f); *p.* 1516 (*Reg. W. Atwater*, f. 120r); precentor, 1537 (Gasquet, 1899, pp. 286–87); *disp.* 1538 (*FOR*, p. 145).

Nele, Robert: St Mary Graces; *sd., d.* and *p.* 1530 (*Reg. W. Warham, London sede–v.*, **2**, ff.313r–314r).

Nelson, William: Jervaulx; sought out Abbot Sedbar on Witton Fell in 1536, and persuaded him to return to the abbey when the insurgents first arrived there. No ordination details available (Cross and Vickers, 1995, p. 136).

Nende, Thomas: abbot perhaps of Kingswood, 1468–1474; abbot, Beaulieu, 1475–1484 (Smith, 2008, pp. 267, 303).

Neth, Henry: *see* Huskin.

Nethertune, William: Hailes, *disp.* 1540 (*FOR*, p. 208); in receipt of pension of £5 as late as 1555 (TNA, E164/31, f. 40r); perhaps vicar, Great Coxwell, Berkshire, 1555–56, and of Ardington, Berks. 1556; died 1564 (Baskerville, 1927, p. 90).

Neve: *see* Nede.

Nuell'/?Nikoll, William: Cleeve; *sd.* 1504 (*Reg. W. Warham, Wells sede v.*, f. 198r; SRO, D/D/B Reg.29, f. 6v).

Nevinson, Christopher: Holm Cultram; in house, 1533 (*LP* **6**, pp. 425–26 [No. 988]); sub–prior by 10–08–1536 (*LP* **11**, p. 115 [No. 276]); last prior, *disp.* 1538 (*DKR*, p. 23; *FOR*, pp. 123–24); pension, £5–6–8, slightly above average for that monastery (TNA, LR1/173, f.147).

Newall, Gilbert: Kirkstall; *disp.* 1488 (*CPL* **15**, pp. 127–28 [No. 267]).

Newall, Richard: Kirkstall, *sd.* 1526, *d.* 1527, *p.* 1531 (York; Cross and Vickers, 1995, pp. 141, 144, 152). He may be the monk, *Richard Woodd*, q.v.

Newarke, Walter: Fountains; *d.* 1509, *p.* 1511 (York); 1536, accused, perhaps spuriously, of immoral relations with a single woman (Cross and Vickers, 1995, p. 113).

Newerke/Newark, William: Furness, signed deed of surrender and *disp.* 1537 (TNA, E322/91; *FOR*, p. 97).

Newchurche, Henry: Boxley; *ac.* 1487, *sd.* 1488 (Canterbury; *Reg. J. Morton*, pp. 124 [No. 431], 126 [No. 435]).

Newchurch, John: Quarr: *ac.* 1488, *sd.* 1489, *d.* 1490, *p.* 1491 (Winchester; *Reg. P. Courtenay*, ff. 13v, 15r, 17r, 18v); *disp.* 1507 (*CPL* **18**, p. 547 [No. 801])

Newenham, Philip: Kingswood; *ac.* and *sd.* 1484 (Hereford; *Reg. T. Myllyng*, pp. 169–70).

Newland, Henry: cellarer, Tintern, 1491–93; abbot, 1493–1506. His name suggests a local origin; in 1501 he gave the church house and green in Woolaston, Gloucestershire, to the villagers (Williams, 1976, pp. 109, 122).

Newland, Robert: Bordesley; *p.* 1478 (Worcester; *Reg. J. Alcock*, f. 251).

Newman, John: Waverley; *sd.* 1488, *d.* 1489, *p.* 1490; cellarer, 1510 (Winchester; *Reg. P. Courtenay*, ff. 13r, 15r, 16r, 26v).

Newman, John: Ford; pension, 1539, £6 (Youings, 1971, p. 186; *DKR*, p. 21).

Newport, John: Flaxley; *p.* 1452 (Worcester; *Reg. J. Carpenter*, f. 534).

Newport, John: Buildwas; *p.* 1521 (Lichfield; *Reg. G. Blyth*, n–f.).

Newport, Richard: Combe; *d.* 1485, *p.* 1488 (Lichfield; *Reg. J. Hales*, ff. 211, 240v). Might he have been the later *Abbot Richard*, q.v?

Newport, Richard: Woburn; *ac.* and *sd.* 1505, *d.* 1509, *p.* 1511 (Lincoln; *Reg. W. Smith*, n–f.); bursar, 1538 (Thomson, 1933, p. 132); *disp.* 1538 (*FOR*, p. 145).

Nestede, Thomas: Byland; *sd.* 1499, *p.* 1504 (York; Cross and Vickers, 1995, p. 99).

Newstede, Robert: Jervaulx; *d.* and *p.* 1486 (York; Cross and Vickers, 1995, p. 129).

Newstede, Thomas: Jervaulx; *ac.* 1527, *sd.* 1528, *p.* 1531 (York; Cross and Vickers, 1995, pp. 132, 136).

Newton, John: abbot, Dieulacres, 1490–1509 (*VCH, Staffordshire* **2**, 1967, p. 234).

Newton, John: Kirkstead; *d.* and *p.* 1523, (Lincoln; *Reg. J. Longland*, ff. 7v, 8r).

Newton, Richard: Kirkstall, *sd.* 1526, *d.* 1527, *p.* 1531 (York; Cross and Vickers, 1995, p. 141).

Newton, Richard: monk, Sawley; *sd.* 1517, *d.* 1518, *p.* 1519 (York; Cross and Vickers, 1995, p. 200); *disp.* 1536 (*FOR*, p. 58).

Newton, Robert: monk, Beaulieu, 1538 (*DKR*, p. 9); pension, £4 (TNA, E314/77). Could he be the monk, *Robert Pykton*, q.v.?

Nicholas ... : Warden, 1492; bore letters from the abbot of Warden to Cîteaux (*Letters*, p. 155 [No. 78]).

Nicholas, James: Whitland, 1539; alive in 1558 (*LP* **21**, Part 2, p. 442; in receipt of his pension of £3 in 1555 (TNA, E164/31, f. 75r).

Nic(h)ols, William: Thame; *sd.* 1514, *d.* and *p.* 1515 (Lincoln; *Reg. W. Atwater*, ff. 111r, 112r, 117v).

Nicholson, Anthony/Arthur: Holm Cultram, by 1533 (*LP* **6**, pp. 425–26 [No. 988]); signed deed of surrender and *disp.* 1538 (*DKR*, p. 23; *FOR*, pp. 123–24); pension, £4 (TNA, LR1/173, f. 147).

Nicholson/Nycholson, Francis: Vaudey; *sd.* 1524, *d.* and *p.* 1525 (Lincoln; *Reg. J. Longland*, ff. 10v, 11r, 12r); kitchener, 1531/32 (TNA, SC6/HENVIII/2005B, f. 7); *disp.* 1536 (*FOR*, p. 67).

Nicholson/Nycolson: John: abbot, Holm Cultram, 1530–1531 (TNA, L1/173, f. 173; Smith, 2008, p. 300).

Noble, William: Beaulieu; *sd.* and *d.* 1498 (Winchester; *Reg. T. Langton*, f. 32r).

Norman, John: last abbot, Bindon, 1534–1539 (Dorset History Centre, D/WLC/T3; VCH, *Dorset* **2**, 1908, p. 86; TNA, E322/21); pension, £50 (TNA, E314/77). Probably the monk, *John Salisbury*, q.v.

Norman, Peter: Kingswood; *ac.* and *sd.* 1484 (Hereford; *Reg. T. Myllyng*, pp. 169–70).

Norres(se), Richard: Fountains, *sd.* and *d.* 1497 (York); pension, 1539: £6–13–4; possibly vicar of Childwall, Merseyside, 1555; dead perhaps by 1560 (York; Cross and Vickers, 1995, pp. 112, 126–27).

Norris, Walter: Bindon; *disp.* 1491 (*CPL* **15**, p. 366 [No. 693]).

Northalderton, William: Thame; *p.* 1497 (Lincoln; *Reg. W. Smith*, n.f.).

Northampton, *al.* Dawkyns, John: Biddlesden; *ac.* 1496, *sd.* and *d.* 1498, *p.* 1500 (Lincoln; *Reg. W. Smith*, f. 24v); *disp.* 1538; pension, £5–6–8 (*FOR*, p. 179, Green, 1974, pp. 63–64).

Northampton/al. Taylor, Robert: Biddlesden, *disp.* 1538 (*FOR*, p. 179); pension, £5–6–8; in 1554 was vicar of Biddlesden, unmarried, with stipend of £8–17–1; died 1559 (Hodgett, 1959, p. 100, 139; Green, 1974, pp. 63–643. Was he originally, *Robert Taylor*, a monk of Stoneleigh? q.v.

Northampton, William: Thame; *sd.* 1514, *d.* and *p.* 1515 (Lincoln; *Reg. W. Atwater*, ff. 111r, 112r, 117v).

Northives, William: *see* Brighouse.

Northley/Nordley, William: Combe; *sd.* 1500, *d.* 1501 (Lichfield; *Reg. J. Arundel*, ff. 288, 293v); *p.* 1503 (Lichfield; *sede v.*, CCA; DCc–Reg. f. 287r).

Northyenell/Northill, William: Warden; *ac.* and *sd.* 1500, *d.* 1501, *p.* 1504 (Lincoln; *Reg. W. Smith*, ff. 21r, 26v, 44r).

Norton, Henry: Strata Marcella; *ac.* 1491 (Worcester; *Reg. R. Morton*, f. 147); *d.* 1491 (Hereford; *Reg. T. Myllyng*, p. 181); seems to have moved to the mother–house of Whitland, perhaps at Strata Marcella's suppression; at Whitland, *disp.* 1538, pension, £3 p.a., 1539 (*FOR*, p. 206).

Norton, John: Combe; *sd.* 1524, *d.* 1525, *p.* 1526 (Lichfield; *Reg. G. Blyth*, n–f.).

Norton, Peter: Byland; *see* Jackson.

Norton, Richard: Bruern; *sd.* and *d.* 1512 (Lincoln; *Reg. W. Smith*, n–f.); imprisoned in The Fleet prison 'for various crimes and offences' from 7 April 1526 to 22 June 1527 (TNA, C1/828/23–26); perhaps re–imprisoned, 1529 (*LP* 4, Part 3, p. 2741 [No. 6141]); prior, Bruern, by 1535 (*VE* 3, p. 265; Baskerville, 1930, p. 334).

Norton, Robert: Fountains, *sd.* 1501, *d.* 1502 (York; Cross and Vickers, 1995, p. 112); **and see: Clifton**.

Norton, Thomas: Jervaulx; *sd.* 1505, *d.* 1506, *p.* 1507 (York; Cross and Vickers, 1995, p. 130).

Norton, Thomas: Rewley; *sd.* 1525 (Lincoln; *Reg. J. Longland*, f.18r); accused in 1533 of treason by another monk; still in house at its suppression, 1536 (Baskerville, 1930, p. 335; VCH, *County of Oxford,* 2, 1907, p. 83)).

Norton, William: Hulton; *ac.* 1498, *sd.* 1499, *d.* 1500 (Lichfield; *Reg. J. Arundel*, ff. 271v, 277v, 289); signed deed of surrender and *disp.* 1538 (TNA, E322/106; *FOR*, p. 154); pension, £4–13–4 (TNA, E315/233, f. 22r).

Norwich, Thomas: Sibton; *disp.* 1486 (*CPL* **15**, p. 61 [No. 120]).

Nottingham, Thomas: Kirkstall, *sd.* 1501, *d.* 1502, *p* 1505 (York; Cross and Vickers, 1995, p. 140).

Nowell, Richard: Rushen; in receipt of his pension of £2–13–4 in 1555 (TNA, E164/31, f. 74v; Davey and Roscow, 2010, p. 174).

Nutt, Hugh: Stratford; *ac.* 1492, *sd.* 1493 (London; *Reg. R. Hill*, ff. 25v, 28v).

Nyrke, Robert: Louth Park; sought absolution from excommunication on account of apostasy, 1468 (*SAP* **2**, p. 33 [No. 1388]).

Offyngham: *see* Effingham.

Ogell/Ogle, Gilbert: Newminster, thirty–five years old in 1536 (TNA, SC12/13/65); *disp.* 1536 (*FOR*, p. 77).

Ogle, William: Rewley; *sd.* 1497, *d.* 1498 (Lincoln; Reg. W. Smith).

Okeborowe, John: Stanley; *ac.* 1518 (Salisbury; *Reg. E. Audley*, f. 35r).

Okeley, Thomas: Pipewell; *sd.* and *d.* 1488, *p.* 1491 (Lincoln; *Reg. J. Russell*, ff. 27v, 29r, 39v); abbot by 1493–1500, unless an earlier monk of that name (Smith, 2008, p. 320); plaintiff in a chancery case (TNA, C1/220/70).

Okeley, Thomas: Pipewell; *sd.* 1528, *d.* 1529, *p.* 1532 (Lincoln; *Reg. J. Longland*, ff. 22r, 23r, 31v).

Okley/Ocle, John: Warden; *sd.* 1508, *d.* 1509 (Lincoln; *Reg. W. Smith*, n–f.).

Oldfield, William: Byland; *sd.* 1521 (York; Cross and Vickers, 1995, pp. 99, 107).

Oliscombe/Olston/Alston, *al.* Potter, Elizeus [Ellis/Elys]: Ford; *sd.* 1511, *p.* 1515 (Exeter; *Reg. H. Oldham*, ff. 106v, 120v); pension, £7, 1539; received as late as 1555 (Youings, 1971, p. 186; TNA, E164/31, f. 34v).

Oliver, John: Buckfast; *d.* 1489 (Exeter; *Reg. R. Fox*, f. 154r); *p.* 1490 (*Reg. O. King*, f. 157r).

Olyver/Oliver, John: Combermere, *disp.* 1538 (*DKR*, p. 17; *FOR*, p. 154); received his pension of £5 as late as 1555 (TNA. E164/31, f. 69r).

Oliver, Thomas: Buckland, perhaps at St Bernard's College, Oxford, in 1462 when he obtained a sum of money owing to Buckland by an Oxford surgeon (*BRUO* **2**, pp. 1397–98); abbot, Buckland, blessed 20–03–1463 in Exeter Cathedral, but deprived a few years later by the abbot of Quarr, his father–abbot, and the prior, William Breton, installed as abbot by 1469; Oliver then held the monastery by force and remained *de facto* abbot, perhaps until 1508 (Gill, 1951, pp; 33–34; Smith, 2008, pp. 275–76; West Devon R.O. 70/126b, 126e, 139, 252); at some stage he visited Rome and had to borrow the equivalent of £4, presumably to see him safely home (TNA, C1/59/38).

Olston, William: Kingswood; *ac.* 1459 (Worcester; *Reg. J. Carpenter,* f. 548).

Oltham: *see* Elkham.

Omde, Henry: Warden; *p.* 1510 (Salisbury; *Reg. W. Smith,* n–f.).

Orchard, John: Ford; *disp.* 1490 (*CPL* **15**, p. 292 [No. 566]).

Orchard, Thomas: Cleeve; *ac.* 1518 (Exeter; *Reg. H. Oldham,* f. 130r); *d.* and *p.* 1519 (Wells; *Reg. T. Wolsey,* ff. 25– 26); might he have moved to Kingswood when Cleeve was suppressed?

Orchard, Thomas: Kingswood, signed deed of surrender and *disp.* 1538 (*DKR,* p. 25, *FOR,* p. 131); 'reward and finding', 1538, £2–13–4 (TNA, E36/152, f. 22); in receipt of his pension of £4 as late as 1555 (TNA, E164/31, f. 29r). He may have transferred from Stanley, and had the *alias* of Lacock, and may have been in 1566 the vicar of North Newton, Wiltshire, dying in 1573.

Ormeschede, Thomas: Fountains, *disp.* 1498 (*CPL* **16**, p. 575 [No. 852]).

Ormeshed, William: Meaux; *d.* 1513, *p.* 1517 (York); aged about thirty–four in 1527; may have died before the Suppression (Cross and Vickers, 1995, pp. 154, 160).

Orpe, John: Croxden; professed *c.*1509; *disp.* 1538 (*FOR,* p. 151; Laurence, 1952); pension, £5–6–8 (TNA, E315/233, f.18r; BL. Add MS 11041, f. 5).

Osburne/Osborn, William: Thame; *sd.* (in Thame church) and *d.* 1525 (Lincoln; *Reg. J. Longland,* ff. 11r, 17r); signed deed of surrender, 1539; pension, £6–13–4 (TNA, E314/77); after the suppression he may have held several livings before becoming vicar of St Giles', Oxford, in 1556 (Baskerville, 1930, p. 336).

Oswaldkirk, Guy: monk, Rievaulx, 1524, when the vicar of Oswaldkirk bequeathed him a number of books, and requested that he be an executor of his will 'if the abbot will suffer the same' (Cross and Vickers, 1995, p. 179).

Otewell, Thomas: Coggeshall; *sd.* 1505, *d.* 1506, *p.* 1507 (London; *Reg. R. Fitzjames,* ff. 91r, 95r, 95v).

Oteley, George: Vaudey; *sd.* 1524, *d.* and *p.* 1525 (Lincoln; *Reg. J. Longland,* ff. 10v, 11r, 12r).

Otteley, Richard: Buildwas; *ac.* 1523 (Lichfield; *Reg. G. Blyth,* n–f.).

Otteley, Roger: Swineshead; *sd.* 1522, *d.* 1523 (Lincoln; *Reg. J. Longland,* ff. 4r, 6v).

Otteleye, Thomas: Whalley, *sd.* 1511 (York; *Reg. C. Bainbridge,* f. 108r); monk, Sawley, *d.* 1512, *p.* 1512 (*Reg. C. Bainbridge,* f. 109v; Cross and Vickers, 1995, p. 200).

Ottewell, ... : Combermere; murdered 1520 by the monastery's tanner (Stewart–Brown, 1916, p. 129).

Otley, Thomas: Kirkstall, *sd.* 1531, *d.* 1533, *p.* 1534 (Cross and Vickers, 1995, p. 113).

Ottrey/Oty, William: Ford, *p.* 1518 (Exeter; *Reg. H. Oldham,* f. 130v); *disp.* 28–05–1536 (*FOR,* p. 56).

Ovafile/Ovafield/Manfield, William: Thame; signed deed of surrender, 1539 (*DKR,* p. 43); Cross and Vickers, 1995, pp. 153, 161); pension, £6 (TNA, E314/77).

Overton, Richard: Jervaulx; *d.* 1497, *p.* 1499 (York; Cross and Vickers, 1995, p. 130).

Oveton, Richard: Newminster; *ac., sd.* and *d.* 1533 (Durham; *Reg. C. Tunstall,* ff.13, 15–16; published version, pp. 47 [No. 77],52 [No. 90], 54 [No. 95].

Owain ap David: Cwmhir; *p.* 1458 (Hereford; *Reg. J. Stanbury,* pp. 142, 144); abbot, 1475–90 (*Radnorshire Society Transactions* **34**, 1964, pp. 25, 29). May have borne a son by an unmarried woman (*SAP* **2**, p. 402 [No. 3221]).

Owain, David: Margam; *d.* and *p.* 1487 (St David's; *EPD* **2**, pp. 491, 509).

Owain, David: monk of probably Aberconwy, 1536–37; passed over for the abbacy; may later have been vicar of Eglwys–bach, Gwynedd (Hays, 1963, p. 179).

Owain, David: *see also* **David ap Owain**.

Owndell/Orundell, Christopher: Pipewell; *ac.* 1506, *sd.* and *d.* 1508, *p.* 1512 (Lincoln; *Reg. W. Smith*, n–f.).

Oundall/Orundell/Candall, Thomas: Kirkstead: *sd.* 1523, *d.* 1524, *p.* 1526 (Lincoln; *Reg. J. Longland*, ff.8r, 9r, 14r).

Ownsbe, John: sub–prior, Merevale; signed deed of surrender, 1538 (TNA, E322/151); pension, £5–6–8 pension (TNA, E315/233, f. 62r).

Oxenford/Oxford, John: Tilty; *sd.* and *d.* 1495, *p.* 1496; later abbot, 1504–1513 (*VCH, Essex* **2**, pp. 134–36; Smith, 2008, p. 340), though TNA, C1/582/29; C1/607/19, suggest he held the abbacy later; B.D. (Oxon.) 1511 (Stevenson, 1939, p. 42; 42); *disp.* 1504 (*CPL* **18**, pp. 266–67 [No. 308]); by 1504 held for a time the living of Great Easton, Essex (TNA, C1/582/29;607/19); in 1520 resigned the rectory of Staines ad montem (BL, Harley MS 6955, f. 77 [No. 40r].

Oxforth, Richard: Rufford: *sd.* 1485, *d.* 1487, *p.* 1488 (York; *Reg. T. Rotherham*, f. 398r).

Oxford, Richard: Rewley; *p.* 1534 (Lincoln; *Reg. J. Longland*, f. 37r).

Oxford/Oxenford: *see* **Browne**.

'Ox. Ianikym', Lewis: Aberconwy, 1482; could he be the Abbot Lewis of Strata Marcella in 1492? (Hays, 1963, p. 136; *Statuta* **5**, pp. 438–39 [No. 1482/37], Williams, 2001, p. 65).

Packer (Pakker)/Parker, William: Kingswood, signed deed of surrender and *disp.* 1538 (*DKR*, p. 25; *FOR*, p. 131); 'reward and finding', 1538, £2–13–4 (TNA, E36/152, f. 21); in receipt of his £4 pension as late as 1555 (TNA, E164/31, f. 29r); may have witnessed a Frampton–on–Severn, Gloucestershire, will in 1544 (Baskerville, 1927, p. 88).

Paganis, Matthew de: Stratford; D.C.L; procurator for the Order in Rome, 1513–1518 (*Letters*, p. 256 [No. 130]).

Pakk/Packe, John: Boxley, *t,* and *a.* 1522, *sd.* 1523, *p.* 1526 (Rochester; *Reg. J. Fisher*, ff. 92v, 116r); *disp.* 1538 (*FOR*, p. 123); pension, £4 (TNA, E315/77).

Palfreyman: *see* **Shepyshed**.

Palmer, John: sub–prior, Tilty, 1521; prior, 1529 (London; *Reg. C. Tunstall*, f. 162v; *Reg. R. Fitzjames*, f. 182v [193v]); last abbot by 1533 (Smith, 2008, p. 340; signed deed of surrender and disp. 1536 (*DKR*, p. 45; *FOR*, p. 60); pension, £16 (TNA, E315/244, No. 42). Will made 9 January 1539, proved 22 February 1539, desiring to be buried in Great Easton Church, Essex, 'afore the rood' (Essex R.O., D/ABW 28/46). It is possible that he is the next mentioned monk.

Palmer, John: St Mary Graces; *sd.* 1498, *p.* 1502 (London; *Reg. T. Savage*, f. 56v; *Reg. W. Warham*, f. 84v); sub–prior, 1516, when stole the abbey keys on death of Abbot Prehest, then absconded and lived 'unreligiously' (Grainger, 2011, p. 92; TNA, C1/426/49. *LP* **2**, Part 1, p. 533 [No. 1861].

Palmer, William: St Mary Graces; *sd.* 1502 (London; *Reg. W. Warham*, f. 84r).

Pape, John: Fountains, *sd.* 1494 (York; Cross, 1995, p. 112).

Pardenham,: *see* **Todenham**.

Parish: *see* **Parysh**.

Parken: *see* **Parker**.

Parke(r), John: Calder; *d.* 1495 (York; *Reg. T. Rotherham*, n–f.); abbot, Calder, 1516– 1522 (Loftie, 1888, p. 236; 1892, p. 78; Smith [2008] 278).

Parker, John: Waverley; *d.* 1511 (Winchester; *Reg. R. Fox* **3**, f. 51r); *p.* 1512 (London; *Reg. R. Fitzjames*, f. 162v [172r]); *disp.* 1536 (*FOR*, pp. 67–68); curate of Wanborough, Surrey, 1541, presented by Sir William Fitzwillam who had been granted the monastery site (Baskerville, 1941, p. 18).

Parker, Lawrence: Beaulieu, *disp.* 1538 (*DKR*, p. 9; *FOR*, p. 131); pension, £4–13–4 (TNA, E315/77).

Parker, Robert: Revesby; *sd.* 1503 (Lincoln; *Reg. W. Smith*, f. 40r).

Parker, Robert: Stratford; *sd.* 1512, *d.* 1515, *p.* 1516 (London; *Reg. R. Fitzjames*, ff. 164r [175r]; 178v, 182r); intermediary in 1521 in borrowing £40 for the abbot from his step–father (Barber, 2004, pp. 57–58); died sometime after 1524 on a bed specially brought in by his mother (TNA, C1/874/21).

Parker/Parks, Thomas: Buildwas, *ac.* and *sd.* 1508; *d.* and *p.* 1509 (Lichfield; *Reg. G. Blyth*, n–f.); *disp.* 1537 (*FOR*, p. 92).

Parker/Parkyn, Perken, William: Meaux; pension of £5 paid as late as 1556; was probably the cleric of this name instituted as vicar of Great Edstone, Yorkshire, in 1546, dying there in 1560. His will of 1558 bequeathed his 'ballet' and plain books to one friend, Mr Brymelaye, and the whole Bible to another, Sir Thomas Akerygg (Cross and Vickers, 1995, p. 160).

Parker, William: *see also* Packer.

Parkyn, John: Kirkstead, *disp.* 1537 (*FOR*, p. 96).

Parkyng/?Bulkyng, John: Coggeshall; *d.* and *p.* 1500 (London; *Reg. T. Savage*, ff. 61r, 62v).

Parson(s), William: Newenham; an unsuccessful candidate favoured by the marquis of Dorset for the abbacy in 1523 (Smith, 2008, p. 317; *LP* **4**, Part 1, pp. 536–37 [No. 1228]); *disp.* to hold a benefice but be non–resident, if given his abbot's permission, 9 April 1535 (*FOR*, p. 26); received a family living from John Drake of Musbury, Devon, who was indebted to the monastery (Baskerville, 1937, p. 201).

Parish/Parysh, Richard: abbot, Sawley, by 1479–1493 (Smith, 2008, p. 329).

Parysh/Parish, Robert: Whalley; *p.* 1518 (York; *Reg. T. Wolsey*, f. 181v); *disp.* 1537 (*FOR*, p. 91); resigned the vicarage of Whalley in 1537, but remained in the parish and died there in 1572 (Haigh, 196, p. 114).

Parish, Christopher: Whalley; *p.* 1518 (York; *Reg. T. Wolsey*, f. 188v). Perhaps a brother of the foregoing monk?

Parysch/Parish, Christopher: Sawley; *sd.* and *d.* 1520, *p.* 1521 (York); was active in the Pilgrimage of Grace (Cross and Vickers, 1995, pp. 200, 205; Dodds **2**, 1915, pp. 83–85); *disp.* 1536 (FOR 58).

Paslew, John: 'scholar', Whalley (TNA, E163/22/2/5, f. 107); *sd.* 1489, *d.* 1490 (York; *Reg. T. Rotherham*, n–f.); last abbot, 1506–1537; permission to wear the mitre, 1516 (Smith, 2008, p. 350; tried at Lancaster, executed by hanging at Whalley, 10 March 1537 (Gasquet, 1899, p. 271; Dodds, **2**, 1915, p. 142). Believed to be in his sixties in 1530 (*DCL*, p. 204).

Paslew, John: Whalley; *p.* 1518 (York; *Reg. T. Wolsey*, f. 181v). Was he the abbot or a kinsman? (C. Haigh, 'Paslew, John', *ODNB* on line).

Pateman/Patenson/Pattinson, Richard: Holm Cultram, in house, 1533 (*LP* **6**, pp. 425–26 [No. 988]); signed deed of surrender and *disp.* 1538 (*DKR*, p. 23; *FOR*, pp. 123–24). In receipt of his pension of £3–6–8 in 1555 (TNA, E164/31, f.73v).

Patrick, Christopher: Louth Park; *ac.* 1498, *sd.* 1499, *d.* 1500, *p.* 1504 (Lincoln; *Reg. W. Smith*,f. 22v, 45v).

Patrington, John: Meaux; *ac.* and *sd.* 1504, *d.* 1505 (York; Cross and Vickers, 1995, p. 154).

Patryche, James: Cistercian monk, diocese Lincoln; *sd.* 1495 (Salisbury; *Reg. J. Blyth*, f. 103v).

Pavy, Robert: *see* Davy.

Pawton, John: Dunkeswell; *ac.* and *sd.* 1489; *d.* and *p.* 1490 (Exeter; *Reg. R. Fox*, ff. 153v–154r, 156r); mentioned in chancery proceedings, 1518/29 (TNA, C1/592/17).

Paycock, Robert: Coggeshall; *p.* 1490 (London; *Reg. R. Hill*, f. 20v).

Payne, Richard: Revesby; *ac.*and *sd.* 1493, *p.* 1498 (Lincoln; *Reg. J. Russell*, f. 48/49r; *Reg. W. Smith*, n.f.).

Paynter, Edward: apostate monk of Jervaulx, in prison in London in 1532 for possessing a copy of the New Testament in English; alleged that he was sold to the abbot of Jervaulx whilst an apprentice and only about thirteen years old, and forced to join the Order; he later married and lived with his wife in Colchester (Cross and Vickers, 1995, p. 136; Baskerville, 1937, p. 137).

Paynter/Peynter/ Poynter/*al.* Darby, John: Cleeve; *sd.* 1488, *d.* 1491 (Wells; *Reg. R. Stillington*, ff. 232v, 237r); *p.* 1492 (Canterbury; *Reg. J. Morton*, p. 19 [No. 65] – in the chapel of the Hospital of St John Baptist, Wells); abbot, by 1506–1510 (Smith, 2008, p. 279). TNA, C1/299/1, gives his Christian name as William..

Payte, Henry: Fountains; *d.* 1521 (York; Cross and Vickers, 1995, p. 114).

Pecke/Peke, John: Sawtry; *p.* 1527 (Lincoln; *Reg. J. Longland*, f. 20v); *disp.* 1537 (*FOR*, p. 116).

Peck, William: *see* Blonham.

Pedder, Robert: Revesby; *ac.* 1490, *sd.* 1492, *d.* 1493 (Lincoln; *Reg. J. Russell*, ff. 36v, f.44/45r, 48/49v); *disp.* 1538 (*FOR*, p. 128); signed deed of surrender, March 1538 (Essex R.O., D/DRg 1/104).

Pedder/Peddar, William: Waverley; *ac., sd., d.* and *p.* 1509 (Winchester; *Reg. R. Fox* **2**, ff. 23v, 24r, 25r, 25v).

Pedley: *see* Manchester.

Pedo, William: last sub–prior, Newenham, *disp.* 1540 (*FOR*, p. 216); pension, £5–6–8 (*LP* **14**, Part 1, p. 184 [No. 469]).

Peet, William: Warden, 1538 (*DKR*, p. 47).

Pele: . *see* Pyle.

Peln…, William: Buckland, –1539 (*DKR*, p. 12).

Penkerych, John: Waverley, *disp.* 1496 (*CPL* **16**, pp. 404–05 [No. 613]).

Pennant, Nicholas: last abbot, Basingwerk, ?1529–36; in demising lands and offices, he made the monastery something of a family concern; pension, £17 p.a., aged about fifty in 1545, dead by 1560, he requested burial in Holywell churchyard (Jones, 1933, p. 178; Williams, 2012, p. 49.)

Pennant, Thomas: Basingwerk, *disp.* on account of incompatibility, 1489/90 (*CPL* **15**, p. 552 [No. 1300]; abbot, ?1481–1522; praised by the bards, oversaw the building of the new Holywell chapel and of several mills, perhaps ran a monastic school, seemingly a forceful character, sired three sons, his youngest – Nicholas, succeeding him in the abbacy (Huws, 2000, pp. 23, 33, 62; Thomson, 1982, pp. 76–77; Williams, 2012, pp. 45–49). Might he be the Thomas Pennant, clerk, of the St Asaph diocese, seeking a dispensation in 1470 on account of defect of birth? (*SAP* **2**, p. 78 [No. 1624]).

Penney/Penne/Pen, John: Bordesley, *disp.* 1538 (*DKR*, p. 11; *FOR*, p. 149; TNA, E322/26); in receipt of pension of £4 as late as 1555 (TNA, E164/31, f. 44r).

Penreth, Richard: Jervaulx; *d.* 1481, *p.* 1483 (York; Cross and Vickers, 1995, p. 129).

Penreth, Richard: Jervaulx; *sd.* 1527 (York; Cross and Vickers, 1995, p. 136).

?Penton, John: Hailes; *p.* 1489 (Worcester; *Reg. R. Morton*, f. 144).

Pepper, *al.* Kirkstall, Thomas: Kirkstall; *ac.* 1533, *sd. d.* and *p.* 1534 ; pension, 1539, £5 (Cross and Vickers, 1995, pp. 142, 150); became rector of Adel, Yorkshire, in 1551 (Sitch, 2000, p. 25); in receipt of pension in 1555 (TNA, E164/31, f.53v). He may have been *Thomas Otley*, q.v (Lonsdale, 1972, p. 210); died in 1553 a fairly wealthy man, owning the Weetwood ironworks, Leeds, and leaving £86, he remembered three of his confrères in his will (CIY).

Pere, John: Buckfast; *p.* 1489 (Exeter; *Reg. R. Fox*, f. 153v)

Pere, *al.* Banbury, John: abbot, Bruern, by 1507 (Smith, 2008, p. 272); general pardon, 1509 (*LP* **1**, Part 1, p. 244 [No. 438/3, m. 15]).

Perse/Percy: *see* **Brynkelowe**.

Perte: *see* Thirsk.

Peyrson/Pereson/Pierson/al. Richmond, Henry: Byland; *sd.* 1537 (York); not yet a priest when *disp.* 1538 (*DKR*, p. 13; *FOR*, p. 181); pension, £4 (Cross, 1995, pp. 99–100, 107),

Pereson, John: manciple, St Bernard's College, Oxford, 1497 (*Letters*, p. 196 [No. 97]).

Pereson/Person, al. Helmsley, Richard: Byland, *sd.* 1499, *d.* 1500, *p.* 1502 (York); received 10s. in a will of 1506 (Aveling, 1955, p. 8); pension of £5–6–8; *disp.* 1539; alive in 1556, but dead by 1564 (Cross, 1995, pp. 98, 100, 108).

Pierson, Henry: Byland; *disp.* 1538 (*DKR*, p. 13; *FOR*, p. 181); in receipt of pension of £5–6–8 as late as 1555 (TNA, E1643/31, f. 55r).

Pest: *see* Prehest.

Perpin/Propin/Pierpoint Thomas: probably a monk of Flaxley; short–lived abbot of Grace Dieu, 1534; on resigning received an annuity of £3–6–8 but this was upgraded by the abbot of Dore to £4 p.a., *disp.* 1536, later chantry priest, Holy Trinity, Bristol, and then perpetual curate of Cirencester; alive in 1553 (*FOR*, p. 73, Baskerville, 1927, p. 108; Williams, 1976, p. 64). In receipt of pension in 1555 (TNA, E164/31, f. 77r).

Pershore, Richard: Dore; *ac.* 1485, *sd., d.* 1486 (Hereford; *Reg. T. Myllyng*, pp. 172–73, 182).

Person(s)/Parsons, William: Stratford; *ac.* 1510, *sd.* 1511, *d.* 1511, *p.* 1512 (London; *Reg. R. Fitzjames*, ff.158r [169v], 160v 71v], 161v [172r], 164r [175r]); last prior there, signed deed of surrender and *disp.* 1538 (*DKR*, p. 42; *FOR*, p. 129); in receipt of £8 pension in 1555 (TNA, E164/31, f. 9v).

Person/Pierson, William: Stratford; *ac.* 1532, *sd.* and *d.* 1533, *p.* 1534 (London; *Reg. R. Stokesley*, ff. 128v, 129r, 129v, 130r); signed deed of surrender and *disp.* 1538 (*DKR*, p. 42; *FOR*, p. 129); pension, 1538, £5 (TNA, E314/77).

Pest: *see* **Prehest.**.

Petersfield, William: Quarr; *d.* 1487 (Chichester; *Reg. E. Story*, f. 180r); *p.* 1488 (Winchester; *Reg. P. Courtenay*, f. 14r).

Pewson, Richard: Rufford, *disp.* 1536 (*FOR*, p. 74).

Pfacy/Pfarye, Ffacy, Christopher: Dunkeswell; *sd.* 1530, *d.* 1531 (Exeter; *Reg. J. Vesey*, ff. 170v, 175r).

Pharom, William: Jervaulx; *d.* 1452 (York; *Reg. W. Booth*, f. 413r).

Philip de Llywelyn: *see* **Morgan**.

Philip(p), John: Cleeve; *sd.* and d. 1487 (Wells; *Reg. R. Stillington*, ff. 22r, 224v; SRO, D/D/B Reg.2); *p.* 1488 (Exeter; *Reg. R. Fox*, f. 152r); *disp.* 1506 (*CPL* **19**, pp. 537 [No. 1232], 554 [No. 1446]; 565 [No. 1624]).

Philipps/Phillips, Thomas: Bordesley, *disp.* 1538 (*FOR*, p. 149; TNA, E322/26); in receipt of pension of £5 as late as 1555 (TNA, E164/31, f. 44r).

Philpott, Thomas: abbot, Grace Dieu, 1508 (TNA, LR1/228, f. 127v).

Pickburne, Christopher: Dore; *ac.* 1486 (Hereford; *Reg. T. Myllyng*, f. 171).

Pickering/al. Wardale, Robert: Rievaulx; *sd.* 1504 (York); cellarer, 1533 (TNA, STAC2/7/217); *disp.* 1538, pension, £5–6–8; died before Michaelmas 1540 (*FOR*, p. 156; Cross and Vickers, 1995, pp. 168, 170, 183).

Piell, Thomas: Tintern, 1536; *disp.* 1537 (*FOR*, p. 92).

Pierson: *see* Pereson.

Pingney: *see* Pyngney.

Pinnocke, Thomas: Hailes; *p.* 1513 (Worcester; *Reg. S. Gigli*, f. 319).

Pippesdon, William: Robertsbridge *c.*1491 (SAL, *MS 14*, f. 59v).; received a bequest of 6s 8d. in 1494 (*SW*, p. 90).

Pirley: *see* Pyrley.

Plington, William: Rievaulx; *p.* 1534 (York), but no further notice of him (Cross and Vickers, 1995, pp. 170, 179).

Plum(m)er, Anthony: Furness; signed deed of surrender, 1537 (*DKR*, p. 21; TNA, E322/91). His name does not appear in the dispensation lists, so possibly he sought refuge in another monastery.

Plumer, William: Kirkstall, *ac.* 1513, *sd. 1514, d.* and *p.* 1516 (York; Cross and Vickers, 1995, p. 141).

Pole, William: Stratford; *ac.* 1493, *sd.* 1494, *d.* and *p.* 1495 (London; *Reg. R. Hill*, ff. 28v, 29r, 30r, 30v).

Pole/Poole, Thomas: Hailes; *ac.* 1532 (Worcester; *Reg. R. Morton addenda*, f. 171); in house *c.*1537 (*CHA*, p. 85).

Pomfrett, Robert: Swineshead; *p.* 1522 (Lincoln; *Reg. J. Longland*, f. 4r).

Pomfret: *see also* Heptonstall.

Ponsonby, Matthew: Calder, 1535–36; accused, perhaps spuriously, of sodomy in Crown visitation of 1535 (*LP* **10**, p. 138 [No. 364]; Loftie, 1888, p. 237; 1892, p. 80).

Ponsonby, Richard: Calder; *p.* 1507 (York; *Reg. T. Savage*, f. 140r); probably of the Ponsonby family of Hale Hall in the parish adjoining Calder; last abbot, Calder, 1525–36 (Loftie, 1888, p. 236, 1892, p. 79); Smith, 2008, p. 279); pension, £12 p.a. (VCH, *Cumberland* **2**, 1968, p. 177)

Pontefrete, Edward: Kirkstall, *sd.*1505, *d.* 1506, *p.*1507 (York; Cross and Vickers, 1995, p. 140).

Pountefrete, Walter: Rievaulx; *sd.* and *d.* 1509, *p.* 1514 (York; Cross and Vickers, 1995, p. 168).

Pope, John: Buckfast, *sd.* 1501 (Exeter); alleged around 1520 to have taken part in the removal of monastic tenants from Staverton mill, Devon (TNA, STAC 2/29/169; Stéphan, 1970, pp. 183–84, 187–89).

Pope, Thomas: Buckfast; *ac.* 1500, *sd.* 1502 (Exeter; *Reg. R. Redmayne*, f.41r, 42v); *d.* 1504 (Canterbury; *Reg. W., Warham, Exeter sede v.*, f .208v).

Pores/Porysse/Powers, Hugh: Merevale; *ac.* and *sd.* 1525, *p.* 1526 (Lichfield; *Reg. G. Blyth*, n–f.).

Porestoke, John: abbot, Bindon; 1479–?1486 (Smith, 2008, p. 269); *disp.* to hold a benefice *in commendam*, 1482 (*CPL* **13**, Part 2, p. 784).

Porter, John: Aberconwy, *disp.* 10–04–1537 (*FOR*, p. 91).

Potter, John: Kirkstall, *ac.* 1504, *sd.* and *d.* 1505, *p.* 1509 (York; Cross and Vickers, 1995, p. 140); he may have been *John Horwood* or *John Henryson*, q.v. (Lonsdale, 1972, p. 206).

Potter: *see also* Oliscombe.

Poulson: *see* Yarom.

Poulton, Thomas: Byland, *disp.* 1538, pension: £5–6–8 (*DKR*, p. 13; *FOR*, p. 181; Cross, 1995, pp. 100, 103); died, 1558 (Aveling, 1955, p. 8).

Pountefrete: *see* Pontefrete.

Powell, Henry: Rewley; *sd.* 1506 (Lincoln; *Reg. W. Smith*, n–f.); *d.* 1507, *p.* 1508 (Salisbury; *Reg. E. Audley*, ff. 7v, 9v).

Powghwell, William: Cleeve; *sd.* 1493, *d.* 1494 (Wells; *Reg. R. Fox*, ff. 42, 44; printed version: pp. 148, 152).

Poynter: *see* Paynter.

Poynton, Laurence: Kirkstead; *ac.* 1503, *sd.* 1504, *d.* 1505 (Lincoln; *Reg. W. Smith*, ff. 41v, 46r, n–f.).

?Prald, Thomas: Meaux; *p.* 1496 (York; Cross and Vickers, 1995, p. 154).

Prall', Stephen: Robertsbridge, *c.*1491 (SAL, *MS 14*, f. 59v).

Pratt, John: Jervaulx, *disp.* 1537 (*FOR*, p. 119); perhaps later curate of Catterick (1548) and then vicar of Easingwould, Yorkshire (1549–57; Cross and Vickers, 1995, p. 136); involved in post–suppression litigation (TNA, C1/1263/56).

Prehest/Pest, Richard: abbot, St Mary Graces, 1514–1516; when dies (*LP* **2**, Part 1, p. 535 [No. 1861]; TNA, C1/426/49); seen as rebellious and a 'pretended' abbot (Smith, 2008, pp. 308–09; *Statuta* **6**, p. 475).

Prescote, John: Whitland, ? a monk, 1539 (*MSS in BM* **4**, pp. 931–32).

Preston, James: Kirkstead; *ac.* 1503, *sd.* 1504, *d.* 1505 (Lincoln; *Reg. W. Smith*, ff. 41v, 46r, n–f.).

Preston, John: Rievaulx: *sd.* 1531 (York; Cross and Vickers, 1995, p. 170).

Preston, John: Meaux; *d.* 1533 (York; Cross and Vickers, 1995, pp. 155, 160). Either he transferred from Rievaulx, or a mistake was made by the clerk entering the register).

Preston, Matthew: Buckfast; *sd.* 1522, *d.* and *p.* 1526, (Exeter; *Reg. J. Vesey*, ff. 149r, 160, 162v); in receipt of pension of £5–6–8 in 1555 (TNA, E164/31, f.34r); died, Rattery, Devon, 16–02–1567 (Stéphan, 1970, p. 214).

Preston, Nicholas: Bruern; *ac.* 1497, *sd.* and *d.* 1498 (Lincoln; *Reg. W. Smith*, n. f.).

Preston, Nicholas: Pipewell; *ac.* 1503, *sd.* and *d.* 1505, *p.* 1506 (Lincoln; *Reg. W. Smith*, f.42v, n–f.).

Preston, Richard: Calder, *sd.* and *d.* 1525 (York; *Reg. T. Wolsey*, ff.204v, 205v); accused, perhaps spuriously, of incontinence and sodomy in Crown visitation of 1535 (*LP* **10**, p. 138 [No. 364]); and allegedly desired release from his monastic vows (VCH, *Cumberland* **2**, 1968, p. 177), but still in the house at suppression (1536; Loftie, 1888, p. 23; 1892, p. 80)

Preston, Robert: *see* Hemsworth.

Preston/Pryston, Roger: Furness; *sd.* 1516, *d.* and *p.* 1517 (York; *Reg. T. Wolsey*, ff. 174v, 175v, 177v); signed deed of surrender and *disp.* 1537 (TNA, E322/91; *FOR*, p. 97).

Preston, Thomas: Pipewell; *ac.* 1506, *sd.* 1507, *d.* 1508 (Lincoln; *Reg. W. Smith*, n–f.).

Preston, William: Sawley; *ac.* 1526, *sd., d.* and *p.* 1527 (York; Cross and Vickers, 1995, p. 201).

Preston: *see also* Altam.

Price, Robert: Dore, *c.* 1495 (Williams, 1976, p. 23).

Price: *see also* Ap Rhys.

Procter, James: Furness, *disp.* to hold a benefice and licence of non–residence, 4–08–1535; fee, £4–10–0 (*FOR*, p. 21). This surname may be a mis–transcription for *Forster*, q.v.

Protache, James: Rewley; *ac.* 1488 (Lincoln; *Reg. J. Russell*, f. 26v).

Proudlove/rowloff, William: Dieulacres, *disp.* 1538 (*FOR*, p. 160); 'reward', £2–0–0 (Walcott, 1871, p. 216); pension, £5 (*LP* **13**, Part 2, p. 348 [No. 839/5]); in 1554 was unmarried, in receipt of his pension, and resident at Burton Lazars, Leicestershire., but had no ecclesiastical preferments (Hodgett, 1959, p. 86).

Pulford, Ralph: Buildwas; *ac.* and *sd.* 1518, *d.* 1519 (Lichfield; *Reg. G. Blyth*, n–f.).

Purforth, Robert: Waverley; *ac.* 1495, *d.* 1496 (Winchester; Reg. T. Langton, ff.26v, 29r).

Putterell/Pritwyll, Adam: last sub–prior, Revesby; *p.* 1510 (Lincoln; *Reg. W. Smith*, n–f.), *disp.* 1538 (*FOR*, p. 128; Essex R.O., D/DRg 1/103–104).

Pyerson, William: *see* Person.

Pykton/Piketon/Pyngleston/Pinckeston, Robert: monk, Beaulieu, *disp.* 1538 (*DKR*, p. 9, *FOR*, p. 131); pension of £4 received in 1555 (TNA, E164/31, f.13r). Could he be the monk, *Robert Newton*, q.v. Seemingly not priested in 1538 (TNA, E314/77).

Pyle/Pele, Roger: last abbot, Furness, 1531–1537; accused, perhaps spuriously, of immoral relations with women and others, 1535 (*LP* **10**, p. 138 [No. 364]; *AF*, p. 324); signed deed of suppression, 9 April 1537, in fear of the consequences of doing otherwise (TNA, E322/91; Gasquet, 1899, pp.

174–76); then became vicar of Dalton in Furness in lieu of a £66–13–4 pension (*LP* **13**, Part 1, pp. 22 [No. 67]; 583 [No. 1520]; dies 1541 (Smith, 2008, p. 296); for his will: *WIR*, pp. 21–23).

Pynder: *see* **Malton**.

Pyner, Thomas: cellarer, Tintern, 1521–22 (NLW, Badminton Deeds, Group 2, 1660).

Pyngney/Pyngham, Nicholas: Holm Cultram, in house, 1533 (*LP* **6**, pp. 425–26 [No. 988]); signed deed of surrender and *disp.* 1538 (*DKR*, p. 23; *FOR*, p. 123–24). In receipt of his pension of £4 in 1555 (TNA, E164/31, f. 73v).

Pyppysden, William: *see* Pippesden.

Pyrly/Purlee/Pirley, Richard: Quarr; *ac.* 1509, ; *sd.* 1511, *p.* 1513 (Winchester; *Reg. R. Fox* **3**, ff. 24r, 51r, 54r); granted release from all monastic obligations and *disp.* to hold a benefice by Cardinal Wolsey, 1526 (TNA, E326/8894); curate of St Helen's, Isle of Wight, 1527; priest–in–charge, chapel of the Holy Ghost, Limerston, Brighstone, Isle of Wight, 1528 – although suspended by the bishop of Winchester from officiating in the diocese (Hockey, 1970, pp. 201, 231); *disp.* 14–02–1538 (*FOR*, p. 87).

Pyrre, Edward: last abbot, Newminster; *see* **Tyrry**.

Pyrton, John: Stanley; *sd.* 1515, *d.* and *p.* 1516 (Salisbury; *Reg. E. Audley*, ff. 29v, 31v, 32v).

Pyrton, Thomas: abbot, Kingswood, 1481–1494; blessed, 21–03–1481 (Worcester; *Reg. J. Alcock*, ff. 72, 101, 135, 151; Smith, 2008, p. 303).

Pyrton, Thomas: Thame; *sd.* 1514, *d.* 1515 (Lincoln; *Reg. W. Atwater*, ff. 111r, 112r).

Pyttemister, *al.* Hoper, Richard: abbot, Dunkeswell, 1492–98 (Sparks, 1978, p. 120); borrowed money for church reparation (TNA, C1/216/36); as former abbot, and with a retirement pension, *disp.* 12–09–1499 (*CPL* **17**, Part 1, p. 91 [No. 148]).

Quicke, Humphrey: Cleeve; *ac.* 1456, *sd.* 1458, *d.* 1460, *p.* 1461 (Wells; *Reg. T. Bekynton* **2**, pp. 509, 515, 521, 532); abbot, Cleeve, 1479–88; abbot, Beaulieu, 1488–97; elected to Beaulieu on a unanimous vote, its community knowing Quicke to be a worthy and learned superior; confirmation by General Chapter, which gives Beaulieu as the immediate subject of Cîteaux (*Statuta* **5**, p. 631 [No. 1488/8–9]); appointed Reformator of the Order and commissary of the abbot of Cîteaux in England; this choice was not altogether welcome in the Order (Hockey, 1976, pp. 140–41; Smith, 2008, pp. 267, 279; *Letters*, pp. 102–05 [Nos. 44–47]; 108–10 [No. 50], 110–12 [No. 51]).

Quynell: *see* Overay.

Radelyf, Henry: Rushen, 1495; *disp.* to hold any two secular benefices (*CPL* **16**, p. 281 [No. 392]).

Radley, Thomas: Rewley; *sd.*, 1525, *d.* 1526 (Lincoln; *Reg. J. Longland*, ff.14v, 17r); in house at its suppression, 1536 (Baskerville, 1930, p. 335).

Raley/Ryley, Thomas: Meaux; *sd.* 1493, *d.* 1495 (York; Cross, 1995, p. 154).

Rampton/Ranton, John: Hailes; *sd.* 1504, *p.* 1511 (Worcester; *Reg. S. Gigli*, ff. 289, 308).

Randall, William: Waverley; *sd.* 1516 (London; *Reg. R. Fitzjames*, f. 182r).

Raner, Christopher: Byland, 1525, when witnessed a will (Cross and Vickers, 1995, p. 108). No ordination record.

Raspys/Raspes, John: Robertsbridge; *ac.* and *sd.* 1495, *d.* 1496, *p.* 1496 (Chichester; *Reg. E. Story*, ff. 189r, 190v, 192r); in community, 1523 (SAL, *MS 14*, f. 59v).

Ratton: *see* Ryston.

Rattrick, John: Fountains; *disp.* 1489 (*CPL* **15**, p. 221 [No. 442]).

Raworth, Robert: Roche; *sd.* 1503, *d.* 1504, *p.* 1505 (York; Cross and Vickers, 1995, p. 187).

Rawleston: *see* **Rolleston.**.

Rawlynson, John: Kirkstead; *d.* 1500, *p.* 1502 (Lincoln; *Reg. W. Smith*, ff. 22v, 35v); abbot, Kirkstead, 1509–1521; titular bishop of 'Ariensis,' suffragan of York (1512–1522) and of Lincoln (1519–1522; (Butler, 2000, p. 59), holding his abbacy *in commendam* (Smith, 2008, 306; *CPL* **19**, pp. 484–85 [Nos. 836–837]). There is no apparent note of his appointment in C. Eubel, *Hierarchia Catholica Medii Aevi.* Regensburg, 1910.

Rayfeld: *see* Reyfeld.

Raynes, John: Meaux; pension, £6; died 1551 (Cross and Vickers, 1995, pp. 156, 161).

Read: *see* Rede.

Reading/Radyng, Henry: Thame; *d.* 1509, *p.* 1512 (Lincoln; *Reg. W. Smith*, n–f.).

Reading: *see also* Redyng.

Redborne, John: St Mary Graces, *sd.* and *d.* 1498 (London; *Reg. T. Savage*, ff. 56v, 57r); *p.* 1500 *(CL)*; still in London, 1528; last abbot, Dore, 1529–36; blessed, St Mary's chapel, Hereford Cathedral, 24–03–1529 (Hereford; *Reg. C. Bothe*, p. 208); resident in Hereford, 1541, then about sixty–one years old, and the subject of an enquiry; in receipt of pension of £13 as late as 1555 (TNA, E164/31, f.45v); member of the restored community of Westminster Abbey, 1556–1557 – when died aged about seventy–seven years old (McCann, 1952, pp. 60, 62, 273; Williams, 1976, pp. 27–30).

Redborn/Redbury/Redlond, Thomas: St Mary Graces; *sd.* and *d.* 1510 (London; *Reg. R. Fitzjames*, ff. 158r [169r], 159r [170v]).

Reddysdale: *see* Ridsdale.

Rede, Edmund: Combermere; *p.* 1487 (Lichfield; *Reg. J. Hales*, f. 226v).

Rede, John I: abbot, Buckfast; blessed 4–11–1498; of a noted Dartmouth family (Stéphan, 1970, p. 173); general pardon, 1509 (*LP* **1**, Part 1, p. 240 [No. 438/3, m. 9]).

Rede/Read, John II: Buckfast, *ac.* 1500 (Exeter; *Reg. R. Redmayne*, f. 41r); *d.* 1504 (Canterbury; *Reg. W., Warham, Exeter sede v.,* f. 208v); *c.*1517, instigated the removal of monastic tenants from Staverton mill, Devon (TNA, STAC 2/29/169); abbot, 1525–35, blessed 23–04–1525; perhaps the nephew of Abbot John Rede I (Stéphan, 1970, pp. 173, 187–89). Mentioned under the name of *John Belworthy* in 1537).

Rede, John: Boxley, *disp.* 1538 (*FOR*, p. 123); in receipt of pension of £2–13–4 in 1555 (TNA, E164/31, f. 4).

Rede/Rode, Ranulph: Dieulacres; *d.* 1527, *p.* 1528 (Lichfield; *Reg. G. Blyth*, n–f.).

Rede/Reade/*al.* Whalley, Roger: Hailes; *d.* 1530 Worcester; *Reg. R. Morton, addenda,* f. 168); scholar, St Bernard's College, Oxford, 1538–39, B.D, 1538 (Stevenson, 1939, pp. 37–38); custodian of the Holy Blood, Hailes, 1537/38 (*CHA*, p. 85); *disp.* 1540 (*FOR*, p. 208); in receipt of pension of £5 as late as 1555 (TNA, E164/31, f. 40r); perhaps thereafter vicar of Rodbourne Cheney, Wiltshire, a Hailes living; died 1556 (Baskerville, 1927, p. 90).

Rede/Reade Thomas: Hailes, *disp.* 1540 (*FOR*, p. 208); in receipt of pension of £5 as late as 1555 (TNA, E164/31, f. 40r); perhaps the cleric who was in the Marshalsea prison, London, in 1579 (Gasquet, 1899, p. 458).

Rede/Read, William: Whalley; *sd.* 1460 (Lichfield; *Reg. J. Hales*, f. 180r); 24th abbot, Whalley, 1487–1507, when died (Smith, 2008, p. 350).

Rede, William: Stratford; *sd.* 1507, *d.* 1508, *p.* 1511 (London; *Reg. R. Fitzjames*, ff. 95r, .99v, 161v [172r]).

Rede, William: Sawley; *sd.* and *d.* 1520, *p.* 1521 (York; *Reg. T. Wolsey*, f. 188v; Cross and Vickers, 1995, p. 200).

Rede, William: *see* Sherborne, William.

Rediswell, John: Tilty; *sd.* 1507 (London; *Reg. R. Fitzjames*, f. 95v).

Redyng/Reading, Thomas: last prior, Kingswood, *disp.* 1538 (*FOR*, p. 131); signed deed of surrender, 1538 (*DKR*, p. 25); 'reward and finding', £3–6–8; pension, £6–13–4 (TNA, E36/152); in receipt of his pension as late as 1555 (TNA, E164/31, f. 29r). He may be the Thomas Kingswood, B.D. (Oxon.) 1533 (Stevenson, 1939, p. 46), who early in 1535 wrote to tell Cromwell that he had written a book upholding the king's supremacy (*LP* , p. 27 [No. 29]).

Redyng, William: Biddlesden; *d.* 1511 (Lincoln; *Reg. W. Smith*, n–f.).

Reginald 'ap Pigam': abbot, Aberconwy, died *c.*1481, had borne a son (Williams, 2001, pp. 65–66).

Reginald, John: Warden; *sd.* 1487 (Lincoln; *Reg. J. Russell*, f. 23r).

Regweke'Rugewike, Simon: Buckland, *disp.* 1539; pension, £4 (*DKR*, p. 12, *FOR*, p. 178).

Reme, Robert: Roche; in community by 1531 (*LP* **5**, p. 107 [No. 226]; *sd.* 1535 (York); accused, perhaps spuriously, of self–abuse in the visitation of February 1536; may have left before the Dissolution (Cross and Vickers, 1995, pp. 188, 194).

Remington, William: Furness; *sd.* 1516, *d.* and *p.* 1517 (York; *Reg. T. Wolsey*, ff. 174v, 175v, 177v).

Repeley, John: Pipewell; *d.* 1507 (Lincoln; *Reg. W. Smith*, n–f.).

Rewe, Nicholas: Cleeve; *sd.* 1506 (Wells; *Reg. H. de Castello*, f. 142).

Reyfeld, Robert: abbot, Boxley, 1498–?1509 (Smith, 2008, p. 271); in 1498 dispensed to hold a benefice in order to sustain his abbatial position (*CPL* **16**, pp. 612–13 [No. 917]); grant of the deanery of the college of St Mary in Shrewsbury, void by death, 1498 (*Patent*, 1498, p. 170); instituted to the vicarages of Headcorn and of Huntyngdon, Kent, 1499 (Canterbury; *Reg. J. Morton*, pp. 168–069 [Nos. 728, 742]).

Richard ap David: Whitland, 1489; *ac.* 1489, *sd.* 1490 *p.* 1491 (St David's; *EPD* **2**, pp. 579, 583, 591, 607); *disp.* to hold a secular benefice, 1500 (*CPL* **17**, Part 1, p. 202 [No. 319]).

Richard ap Jenkin: Neath; *sd.* 1503 (St David's; *EPD* **2**, p. 757).

Richard ap Morris/Mores: Whitland; *ac.* 1487 (St David's; *EPD* **2**, p. 509).

Richard ap Robert ap Rhys/Price: last abbot, Aberconwy; 1536–37; only twenty–four when appointed as a result of family influence and intrigue; one of the twelve sons of the influential Robert ap Rhys, vicar–general of St Asaph and a Crown Visitor of the monasteries; *disp.* 1537; from 1537–1589, rector of Eglwys–bach and Llanbadrig *in lieu* of a pension of £20, and for some years was parson of Cerrigydrudion – where he died in 1589. He married and his son, Thomas Wynn, was high sheriff of Denbighshire in 1595. Abbot Richard published a translation of a work on baptism and matrimony by Archbishop Herman of Cologne (1548), and in 1579 a work which contained instructions for those preparing to receive Holy Communion (M. D. Evans, 'Richard Rice [Price],' *ODNB* on–line; *FOR*, p. 91, Hays, 1963, pp. 140, 160–61, 178–79).

Richard ap … : Valle Crucis, 1486, when seeks a dispensation on account of illegitimate birth to permit him to have advancement in the Order (*SAP* **2**, p. 405 [No. 3239]).

Richard … : monk, Woburn, becoming abbot, Medmenham, 1482– (*Statuta* **5**, p. 432 [No. 1482/9]; Smith, 2008, p. 313).

Richard, … : abbot, Tilty: 1497–1501 (Smith, 2008, p. 340)..

Richard … : ?abbot, Medmenham, 1521 (Smith, 2008, p. 213).

Richard…… : abbot, Combe, 1486/93 or 1504/15 (Smith, 2008, p. 281).

Richard ….. : monk, Sawtry; *sd.* 1513 (Lincoln; *Reg. W. Smith*, n–f.).

Richard … : Valle Crucis – possibly Richard Bromley the prior; witnessed 12–06–1527 the will of the poet Lewis Môn (*AC*, 1880, p. 218).

Richard … : abbot, Sawtry, 1529 (Smith, 2008, p. 330).

Richards, John: Neath; *disp.* 1539; pension, £4., alive in 1553 (Birch, 1902, pp. 150, 154; *FOR*, p. 170; Cardinal Pole's pension list gives two monks of this name (TNA, E164/31, f. 77v).

Richardson, Anthony: Holm Cultram by 1533 (*LP* **6**, pp. 425–26 [No. 988]); kitchener, when signed deed of surrender and *disp.* 1538 (*DKR*, p. 23; *FOR*, pp. 123–24). In receipt of his pension of £5 in 1555 (TNA, E164/31, f.73v). His name was omitted from a community list of 1–08–1536 (*LP* **11**, p. 115 [No. 276]).

Richardson, Stephen: Meaux; *ac.* and *sd.* 1520, *d.* 1521, *p.* 1524 (York; Cross and Vickers, 1995, p. 155).

Riche, John: Newenham, *p.* 1536 (Exeter; *Reg. J. Vesey*, f. 187v); disp. 1540 (*FOR*, p. 216). Pension of £4–13–4 received as late as 1555 (TNA, E164/31, f. 34v). He allegedly benefited by the use of a counterfeit seal (Baskerville, 1937, p. 201).

Richmond, Henry: Byland; *sd.* 1537: *see* **Peyrson.**

Richmond, John: Kirkstall, *sd.* 1515, *d.* 1516, *p.* 1522 (York; Cross and Vickers, 1995, p. 141).

Richmond, John: Newminster; *ac., sd.* and *d.* 1533 (Durham; *Reg. C. Tunstall*, ff. 13, 15–16; published version, pp. 47 [No. 77], 52 [No. 90], 54 [No. 95]; twenty–six years old in 1536 when a deacon (TNA, SC12/13/65). No record of his dispensation.

Richmond, Ralph: Kirkstall, *sd.* 1509 (York; Cross and Vickers, 1995, p. 140).

Richmond, Richard: Jervaulx; *sd.* 1521 (York; Cross and Vickers, 1995, p. 131).

Richmond, Richard: *see also:* Helmsley.

Richemounte, Thomas: Robertsbridge; *d.* 1519 (London; *Reg. R. Fitzjames*, f. 188v [177v]).

Richmond, Thomas: *see* Jackson.

Richmund, William: Byland; *ac., sd.* and *d.* 1485, *p.* 1487 (York; Cross and Vickers, 1995, p. 98).

Ricson: *see* Ryston.

Riddsdale/Rysdale, John: Stratford, *ex.* and *ac.* 1521 (London; *Reg. R. Fitzjames*, f. 183v [194v]); *sd.* 1522 (Canterbury; *Reg. W. Warham, London sede v.*, **2**, f. 297r); *d.* 1523, *p.* 1525 (London; *Reg. C. Tunstall*, f. 157); sub–prior and sacristan when signed deed of surrender and *disp.* 1538 (*DKR*, p. 42, *FOR*, p. 129); in receipt of £6 pension in 1555 (TNA, E164/31, f. 9v).

Ridge/Ryge, William: Furness, signed deed of surrender and *disp.* 1537 (TNA, E322/91; *FOR*, p. 97).

Ripley, John: Louth Park; *d.* 1509 (Lincoln; *Reg. W. Smith*, n–f.)

Ripley/al. Brown, John: Kirkstall, *sd.* 1515, *d.* 1516, *p.* 1519 (York; Cross and Vickers, 1995, pp. 141, 143); elected abbot, 21–07–1528 to 22–11–1539; accused of detaining deeds pertaining to a layman (TNA, C1/56/2). Attended a meeting in Pontefract in December 1536 to discuss the Pilgrimage of Grace, but took no further part in that; said to be then 'a sober man and spoke little'. At the time of dissolution of his house was paying Cromwell an annual fee of £2–13–4. Pension of £66–13–8; in 1540 was left a gold noble; it is said that he lived on in the gatehouse of the abbey until his death (Lonsdale, 1972, p. 204).

Ripley, Thomas: Sawley; *sd.* 1510, *d.* 1511, *p.* 1512 (York; Cross and Vickers, 1995, p. 200).

Riplay, William: Jervaulx; *sd.* 1509, *d.* 1510, *p.* 1511 (York; Cross and Vickers, 1995, p. 130).

Ripon, James: Swineshead; *sd.* and *d.* 1508, *p.* 1509 (Lincoln; *Reg. W. Smith*, n–f.).

Ripon, John: Jervaulx; *ac.* 1466 (York; *Reg. G. Neville*, f. 193).

Ripon, John: cellarer, Fountains, 1499–1501 (*FLB*, pp. 69 [No. 77], 105 [No. 120]).

Ripon, Richard: monk, Fountains, *sd.* 1501, *d.* 1502, *p.* 1503; cellarer, 1521–35 (York; Cross and Vickers, 1995, pp. 112, 118); *disp.* 1539 (*FOR*, p. 25).

Ripon (Rypon)/al, Jenkynson, Richard: Rievaulx; *sd.* 1522, *d.* 1524, *p.* 1526 (York); signed deed of surrender and *disp.* 1538 (*DKR*, p. 38, *FOR*, p. 156); pension, £6–13–4; dying by 1553, perhaps in London (Aveling, 1952, p. 110, Cross and Vickers, 1995, pp. 169–70, 177–78).

Rippon, Thomas: Louth Park; *ac.* 1501, *sd.* 1502, *d.* 1503, *p.* 1504 (Lincoln; *Reg. W. Smith*, ff. 28r, 35r, 40v, 45v).

Ripon (Rypon), Thomas: cellarer, Fountains, before 1538 (TNA, LR1/174, f. 35.)

Ripon/Rypon, William: Beaulieu; *ac.* 1507 (London; *Reg. R. Fitzjames*, f. 9r); *p.* 1511 (Winchester; *Reg. R. Fox* **3**, f. 51r); last abbot, Quarr, 1525–36 (Hockey, 1970, p. 260); pension, £18 *(TNA, E315/244, No.129).*

Rip(p)on/Repin, William: Vaudey; *ac., sd.,*and *d.* 1535 (Lincoln; *Reg. J. Longland*, ff. 42r, 43v, 46r); later in the Kirkstead community and involved in the Lincolnshire rebellion, examined at Lincoln, 4 November 1536, and executed (*LP* **11**, pp. 320 [No. 827/ii], 325 [No. 828/2/viii].

Ritton, Thomas: Newminster; forty–seven years old in 1536 (TNA, SC12/13/65; *disp.* 1536, 1525–36 (*FOR*, p. 77).

Robbisley/Robesley, Andrew: Netley; *ac.* 1511, *p.* 1520 (Winchester; *Reg. R. Fox* **3**, f. 51r; **4**, f. 71r). Not in a community list of 1518 as not then priested (TNA, E314/101).

Robert … : prior, Basingwerk, 1532, when involved in an unseemly scuffle (Owen, 1919–20, p. 67; Williams, 2001, p. 69).

Robyns, Thomas: Tintern, 1536; *disp.* 1537 (*FOR*, p. 92).

Robyns, William: Buckfast; *ac.* and *d.* 1517, *d.* 1518, *p.* 1521 (Exeter; *Reg. H. Oldham*, ff. 127v, 128r, 130r, *Reg. J. Vesey*, f. 144v).

Robinson, John: Swineshead; seeks absolution from excommunication incurred by apostasy, 1465 (*SAP* **2**, p. 27 [No. 1364]).

Robynson (Robinson), John: Roche, as a novice was suspected of treason and imprisoned in York Castle, there in February 1536 and held in fetters he denied the charges and was released (CIY project); signed deed of surrender, 1538 (TNA, E322/204); still drawing his pension of £3–6–8 in 1555 (TNA, E164/31, f. 53r) and in 1564. Not noted in the Faculty Office register. Probably the same monk as *John Jervax*, q.v. (Cross and Vickers, 1995, pp. 193–94).

Robinson, John: *see* Auckland.

Robinson, Richard: Holm Cultram; in house,10–08–1536 (*LP* **11**, p. 115 [No. 276]); signed deed of surrender and *disp.* 1538 (*DKR*, p. 23; *FOR*, pp. 123–24); pension, £4–6–8 (LR1/173, f. 147).

Robinson, Richard: Meaux; pension, £5; forty–six years old in 1552; may have married (Cross and Vickers, 1995, pp. 156, 161).

Robinson, Robert: Meaux; studied at Cambridge, living in St Nicholas hostel; chantry priest at St William's altar in Beverley collegiate church,Yorkshire, 1540–1548; in 1548, said to be forty–two years old, 'honest and learned;' after suppression of the chantries he became a schoolmaster but retained his chantry annuity of £6–9–11. In addition he had his monastic pension of £5. No details of his ordination are known; he was still alive in Beverley in 1578 (Cross and Vickers, 1995, p. 162).

Robinson, William: St Mary Graces, *disp.* 1539 (*FOR*, p. 182); pension, £5–6–8 (*LP* **14**, Part 1, p. 340 [No. 688].

Robinson, William: Merevale; sacrist, 1538 (TNA, E322/151); pension, £5–6–8; in 1554 was unmarried, resident at Belton, Leics., and held no ecclesiastical preferments; died 1566/67 (Hodgett,1959, pp. 87, 136).

Robinson: *see also* Beverley.

Rocke, Thomas de: Tintern; *p.* 1528 (Worcester; *Reg. R. Morton*, f. 167). Could this be the same monk as *Thomas Rook*, infra?

Rode: *see* Rede.

Rodryke/Rotherithe, John: Neath; *disp.* 1539; pension £3–6–8; alive in 1553 (*FOR*, p. 170; Birch, 1902, pp. 150, 154). In receipt of his pension in 1555 (TNA, E164/31, f. 77v).

Rodyng, George Tilty; *sd.* 1504, *d.* 1507 (London; *CL*).

Roger, William: Boxley; *disp.* 1492 (*CPL* **15**, p. 511 [No. 934]); as priest of Our Lady's chantry in Ash church, Kent, 1512, might wear his habit beneath that of a secular priest (*CPL* **19**, p. 357 [No. 634]).

Rokeby, William: Louth Park; *sd.* 1533 (Lincoln; *Reg. J. Longland*, f. 33r).

Rolleston, Walter: Whalley; *p.* 1516 (Lichfield; *Reg. G. Blyth*, n–f.).

Rolleston/Rawleston, *al.* Checkerley, Thomas: Merevale; *sd.* 1487, *p.* 1488 (Lichfield; *Reg. J. Hales*, f.225, 235, 241v: some dating problems here). Signed deed of surrender, 1538 (Hibbert, 1910, p. 222; TNA, E314/20/11, ff. 7d–8r); pension, £5–6–8 (TNA, E315/233, f. 17r). A jubilarian.

Ronkorne, William: Jervaulx, *disp.* 1537 (*FOR*, p. 119, Cross and Vickers, 1995, p. 137).

Roobuk, William: Byland; *p.* 1483 (York; Cross and Vickers, 1995, p. 98).

Rook, Thomas: Tintern; *p.* 1525 (Hereford; *Reg. C. Bothe*, p. 319).

Ro(o)per, John: Newenham; *disp.* 1540 (*FOR*, p. 216); pension of £5 received as late as 1555 (TNA, E164/31, f. 34v); in 1582, now rector of West Stafford, Dorset, he gave evidence about wrongful use of his abbey's common seal (Baskerville, 1937, pp. 200–01).

Roose: *see* Ilmister.

Ros, Thomas: Swineshead; *disp.* 4–08–1536 (*FOR*, p. 67).

Ros, Thomas: Rewley; *disp.* 1536 (*FOR*, p. 78).

Rose/Roos/Roke, Robert: Revesby; *ac.* 1490; *sd.* 1492, *d.* 1493 (Lincoln; *Reg. J. Russell*, ff. 36v, 44/45r, 48/49v);

Roseter, William: Dunkeswell, 1539 (TNA, E322/76; Sparks, 1978, p. 109). Does not appear in the pension list (*LP* **14**, Part 1, p. 115 [No. 293]), unless an *alias* for *William Bourman*.

Ross, Thomas: Dore; *p.* 1479 (Worcester; *Reg. J. Alcock*, f. 260).

Ros(s)e/Roysse, Thomas: Vaudey; *sd.*and *d.* 1506, *p.* 1508 (Lincoln; *Reg. W. Smith*, n–f.).

Ross, Thomas: Dore; *ac.* and *sd.* 1478, *d.* 1479 (Hereford; *Reg. T. Myllyng*, pp. 159–61).

Ross, William: Dore; *ac.*, 1482, *p.* 1484 (Hereford; *Reg. T. Myllyng*, pp. 165, 170).

Rotherham, John: Rufford; *sd.* 1534 (York; *Reg. E. Lee*, ff. 191r, 192r repeated).

Rotherwas, John: Buildwas; *d.* 1492 (Worcester; *Reg. R. Morton*, f. 162).

Rothwell, Henry: Croxden, signed deed of surrender and *disp.* 1538 (Hibbert, 1910, p. 222; *FOR*, p. 151); in receipt of pension of £2 in 1555 (TNA, E164/31, f. 46v)

Rothwell/*al.* Buildwas, John: Buildwas; *ac.* 1493 (Lichfield; *Reg. W. Smith*, f. 172v); abbot, Grace Dieu, 1530–32/33, when granted pension, £8 (Smith, 2008, p. 297); alive in 1539 (Williams, 1976, p. 64).

Rothwell, Peter: Kirkstall, *sd.* and *d.* 1497, *p.* 1499 (York; Cross and Vickers, 1995, pp. 139–40).

Rothewell/Rowell, William: Thame; *sd.* and *d.* 1501, *p.* 1504 (Lincoln; *Reg. W. Smith*, ff. 30v, 31v, 44r).

Rotter, Richard: said in 1518 to be an 'apostate monk' of Grace Dieu, with a chantry in St Briavel's church, Gloucestershire. (Williams, 1976, p. 63; 2001, p. 73).

Rotyngton, Gervase de: Medmenham; *d.* 1474 (*CL*).

Rowell, Thomas: Pipewell; *sd.* and *d.* 1524 (Lincoln; *Reg. J. Longland*, ff. 8r, 9r).

Rowland. John: Tilty; *d.* 1504, *p.* 1505 (London; *Reg. W. Barons*, ff. 89v, 90r).

Roydon, John: Coggeshall; pension, £5–13–4 (TNA, SC12/7/34). He must be equated with one of the other Coggeshall monks of these years named John.

Rufford, Thomas: Rufford; *sd.*, *d.* and *p.* 1522 (York; *Reg. T. Wolsey*, ff. 194r, 195v, 196v).

Rugewike, Simon: Quarr; *ac.*, *sd.* and *d.* 1527 (Winchester; *Reg. R. Fox* **5**, ff. 36r–37v); transferred to Buckland on Quarr's closure (*LP* **15**, p. 544 [No. 1032]).

Rutir, Richard: Roche; *sd.* 1484, *d.* 1485, *p.* 1487 (York; Cross and Vickers, 1995, p. 186).

Rydforth, *al.* **Hethe, Thomas:** apostate monk of Bruern, 5–12–1500, when absolved by the pope for apostasy; ordered to receive a suitable penance, but allowed to hold a secular benefice and to wear his habit under that of a secular priest (*CPL* **17**, Part 1, p. 176 [No. 177]).

?Ryeys, Richard: Whalley; *p.* 1518 (York; *Reg. T. Wolsey,* f. 181v). Might this be a mis–transcription for *Richard Wyche,* q.v.?

Rysdal: *see* Riddsdale.

Ryshton/Rushton, William: Pipewell; *ac.* 1498, *sd.*and *d.* 1500, *p. 1502* (Lincoln; *Reg. W. Smith,* ff. 21r, 25r, 34v).

Ryton, *al.* **Bramley.**

Ryton, *al.* **Bramley/Bromley Henry:** abbot, Rewley, by 1500–1512 (Smith, 2008, 323).

Ryton, John: Rewley, *disp.* 1510 (*CPL* **19**, p. 364 [No. 655]); abbot, by 1532–1533, when dies; member of Coventry Trinity Guild (Smith, 2008, p. 323. Might he have been the same monk as *John Kylner,* q.v?

Ry(s)ton/Ratton/Ritson[, John: Holm Cultram, by 1533 (Gilbanks, 1899, p. 94); signed deed of surrender and *disp.* 1538 (*DKR,* p. 23; *FOR,* p. 123–24); pension, £4 (TNA, LR1/173, f. 147).

Sabyn: *see* Bungey.

Safe, John: ? Garendon; *d.* 1486 (Lincoln; *Reg. J. Russell,* f. 21r).

Sagar/Segar, *al.* **Whalley, Stephen:** educated at Whalley abbey (Gasquet, 1899, p. 259); monk, Hailes; *sd.* and *d.* 1512, *p.* 1513 (Worcester; *Reg. S. Gigli,* ff. 312, 315, 321); last abbot, 1527–1539; surrendered his house in London (Gasquet, 1899, p. 349); *disp.* 1540 (*FOR,* p. 208); pension, £100; 1539, rector, Avening, Gloucestershire, 1541–43; rector, Adel, Yorks., 1541–45; chaplain to the King, 1537; prebend of Givendale in York minster, 1544–47; dies 1547/51; buried in Warmfield church, Yorkshire, with his brother, Otto (Baskerville, 1927, p. 89; 1937, pp. 190–91; Bell, 2011, pp. 283–318 (gives a full biography).

Sale, Bonaventure: Stratford; *ac.* 1514, *sd.* and *d.* 1516, *p.* 1517 (London; *Reg. R. Fitzjames,* ff. 178r [167r], 182r, 183r [172r], 185v).

Salehurst, Robert: Robertsbridge; *ac.* 1512, *sd.* 1514 (LPL: Canterbury; *Reg. W. Warham* **2**, f. 266r–v); *d.* 1514, *p.* 1516 (London; *Reg. R. Fitzjames,* ff. 178v, 180r).

Saleford/Salford, Richard: Woburn; *sd.* 1532, *d.* 1533, *p.* 1537 (Lincoln; *Reg. J. Longland,* ff. 31r, 36r, 55v).

Salford/Saltforth/Saleford, Robert: Woburn; *sd.* 1509, *d.* 1511, *p.* 1513 (Lincoln; *Reg. W. Smith,* n.f.). Robert Salford played an active role in the betrayal of his abbot to the Lord Privy Seal in 1538 (Knowles, 1963, p. 189).

Salisbury/Sarz/Sausbury, John: Bindon; *d.* 1512, *p.* 1513 (Salisbury; *Reg. E. Audley,* ff. 19v, 22r); *disp.* 1536 (*FOR,* p. 66). Perhaps the abbot there, *John Norman,* suggested by P. Cunich, *ODNB* on–line.

Salisbury, John: Netley; *disp.* 1536 (*FOR,* p. 66).

Salley/Swalla, Christopher: Jervaulx; *sd.* 1521, *d.* and *p.* 1522 (York; Cross and Vickers, 1995, p. 131).

Salley, Edward: Jervaulx; *sd.* 1484 (York; Cross and Vickers, 1995, p. 129).

Salley, Henry: Kirkstall, *d.* 1512, *p.* 1515 (York; Cross and Vickers, 1995, p. 141).

Salley, John: Sawley; *p.* 1485 (York; Cross and Vickers, 1995, p. 199).

Salley, William: Hailes; *ac.* 1532, *sd.* 1533 (Worcester; *Reg. R. Morton addenda,* ff. 171, 174); in community, 1537/38 (*CHA,* p. 85).

Sally/Salter, Thomas: Sawley, *disp.* 1536 (*FOR,* p. 58; Cross, 1995, p. 201).

Salusbury, Robert: young abbot of Valle Crucis, 1528–1535, when deprived; the cause of severe division in his community; sent to Oxford to study, he led in 1534 a robber band, and was later committed to prison; still in the Tower of London in 1537, and alive in 1542 (Pratt, 1997, pp. 30–33; Williams, 2001, pp. 67–68); he was in arrears to late Cardinal Wolsey for a faculty granted prior to 23–10–1530 (*LP* **4**, Part 3, p. 3048 (No. 6748/14).

Same, Ralph: abbot, Meaux, 1479–1486 (Smith, 2008, p. 312).

Sampford/Sanford, John: Coggeshall; *sd.* and *d.* 1495, *p.* 1496 (London; *Reg. R. Hill*, ff. 30r–v, 34v); abbot by 1516–1527, when resigned or deposed (BL, Harley MS 6955, p. 86 [44v]); still alive in 1536 (Smith, 2008, p. 281; *LP* **10**, pp. 59–60 [No. 164]); pension, £11–6–8 p.a. (TNA, SC12/7/34).

Sandall, Edward: Kirkstall; pension, 1539, £6; in receipt of pension in 1555 (TNA, E164/31, f. 53v); still alive in 1573, he may have become a chantry priest of St Thomas, St Fennis–on–Ouse Bridge, York; and for a time curate of Tadcaster; later he taught boys but in 1568 on charges of recusancy was sent to York Castle as a prisoner *(CIY)*, he was released after taking the oath of supremacy (Lonsdale, 1972, pp. 208–09; Cross and Vickers, 1995, pp. 142, 156–57). May have been the monk, *Edward Ecclecell*, q.v.

Sandaille, Thomas: Jervaulx, *disp.* 1537 (*FOR*, p. 119; Cross and Vickers, 1995, p. 137).

Sandbach, Ranulph: Combermere; *ac.* 1521, *sd.* and *d.* 1522, *p.* 1523 (Lichfield; *Reg. G. Blyth*, n–f.).

Sanderson, George: Louth Park, 1520s (TNA, C1/475/15).

Sandford/Penford, Richard: Bordesley; *ac.* and *sd.* 1504, *d.* 1505 (Worcester; *Reg. S. Gigli*, ff. 289, 291–92) *disp.* 1538 (*FOR*, p. 149; *TNA, E322/26)*; pension, £5–6–8 (TNA, E314/77). Not noted in subsidy list of Michaelmas 1540, so had perhaps died (Bodleian Library, Oxford, Tanner MS 343).

Sandherst: *see* Bekeryng.

Sands, Milo: Revesby, *sd.* 1528, *d.* and *p.* 1529 (Lincoln; *Reg. J. Longland*, ff. 21r, 24r, 25r).

Sandwich, William: Boxley; *ac.* 1487, *sd.* 1488 (Canterbury; *Reg. J. Morton*, pp. 124 [No. 431], 126 [No. 435]); now a priest but apostate, 1512 (TNA, C81/1788/7).

Sany/Savey/Seny, Robert: Merevale; pension £5, 1538 (TNA, E315/233, f. 63r–v). Could he be *Robert Burton*, q.v.

Sardyns, Richard: Thame; signed deed of surrender, 1539 (*DKR*, p. 43). Possibly the same cleric as *Richard Sydnam?* q.v.

Satforthwire, William: Furness; *p.* 1502 (York: *Reg. T. Savage*, f. 113r).

Saundeford, John: Coggeshall, *disp.* 1538 (*FOR*, p. 124).

Saunders: *see* Scarburgh.

Sawer, John: Revesby; *sd.* ?1487/92, *p.* 1494 (Lincoln; *Reg. J. Russell*, ff. 44/45r, 52r); penultimate abbot, 1535–1537 (Smith, 2008, p. 322); *disp.* 1538 (*FOR*, p. 128); signed the deed of surrender, 1538 (Lincs. R.O., D/DRg 1/104.. Possibly a jubilarian.

Sawere, Richard: Jervaulx, *disp.* 1537 (*FOR*, p. 119; Cross and Vickers, 1995, p. 137).

Sawley, al. Banaster Henry: Sawley; was one of the four monks returned by Furness when Sawley was closed; accused in 1537 of treasonable statements, and was tried but evaded execution, whilst in 1555 a cleric of this name was instituted as vicar of Bratoft, Lincolnshire (Cross and Vickers, 1995, pp. 199, 202–03; Baskerville, 1937, p. 166). He may be equated with the monk, *Henry Ha(w)mond*, q.v.

Sawley, John: Jervaulx; *sd.* 1514, *d.* 1516, *p.* 1517 (York; Cross and Vickers, 1995, p. 130).

Sawley, Thomas: Hailes; *p.* 1489 (Worcester; *Reg. R. Morton*, f. 144); prior, 1509–18 (Gloucestershire Archives, D6799/3).

Sawley: *see also* Salley.

Sawtry, John: Sawtry; *ac.*, and *sd.* 1500, *d.* 1501, *p.* 1504 (Lincoln; *Reg. W. Smith*, ff. 21r, 26v, 44r).

Saxton, Henry: Fountains; *sd.* 1492, *d.* 1493, *p.*1494 (Cross and Vickers, 1995, p. 111). Was he the same monk as the under–named, being promoted to the abbacy of its daughter–house?

Saxton: Henry: abbot, Vaudey, 1510–33 and later (Lincolnshire Archives, 1ANC3/30/8, 2ANC2/19/28); in 1533 offered to resign for a pension of £20 p.a., not entirely willingly, as the abbot of Woburn wanted his cousin to succeed at Vaudey (Smith, 2008, p. 346); *disp.* 20–05–1536, about two months before the closure of his monastery, to hold a benefice if granted his superior's consent (*FOR*, p. 56); granted by the Crown on 8–11–1536 the parish of Creton, Lincolnshire, being in the king's hands on the closure of his abbey (*LP* **11**, 564 [No. 417/1]. Died *c.*1546, when said to have been the last abbot of Vaudey, which he was not (Hodgett, 1959, p. 132).

Saxton, William: Vaudey; pension, £10, in receipt of this in 1552; *pen.* £10, in receipt of this in 1552 (Hodgett, 1959, p. 36).

Saye: *see* Gaye.

Sayer, Thomas: Grace Dieu; *sd.* 1481 (Wells; *Reg. R. Stillington,* f. 210v).

Sayle, Thomas: Rewley; *ac.* 1506 (Lincoln; *Reg. W. Smith,* n–f.).

Saymaure: *see* Seymour.

Says, Thomas: Whitland, 1539; *disp.* 1540, pension, £4 p.a., alive in 1558 (*FOR*, p. 206); in receipt of his pension in 1555 (TNA, E164/31, f. 75r); perhaps his pension was increased as £3 was awarded in 1539 (*LP*, Part 1, p. 362 [No. 747]).

Scanlon'/Stalon'/Staley, Edward: Boxley; *p.* 1511 Canterbury; LPL; *Reg. W. Warham* **2**, f. 265v).

Scarburgh (Scarborough)/*al.* Blythe, Richard: Rievaulx; *sd.* and *d.* 1509, *p.* 1514 (York); bursar, 1520 (Aveling, 1952, p. 106); in visitation of February 1536 accused of immorality with several women; signed deed of surrender and *disp.* 1538, pension, £6 (*DKR*, p. 38; *FOR*, p. 156). A '+' follows his signature; was this his mark, or added later after his death, *c.*1560 (Cross and Vickers, 1995, pp. 168–70, 173). His father and brother were buried in Scarborough church (Aveling, 1955, p. 15).

Scarburgh/?Saunders, William: Meaux; *d.* 1531, *p.* 1533; pension, £5 (York); forty years old in 1552, perhaps died in 1564, and in the 1550s curate of Keyningham, Yorkshire (Cross and Vickers, 1995, pp. 155, 163).

Sclater, Richard: Sawley; *sd.* 1483 (York; Cross and Vickers, 1995, p. 199).

Scott, *al.* Stickney, Thomas: provisor, St Bernard's College, Oxford, 1502 (Smith, 2008, p. 319; *BRUO* **2**, p. 1771); abbot, Revesby, by 1504 to at least 1527; general pardon, 1509 (*LP* **1**, Part 1, p. 260 [No. 4/m.8]; instituted to Claxby Pluckacres Church, Lincolnshire, 1512 (Smith, 2008, p. 322).

Scott: *see also* Stott.

Scrope: *see* /Stopes.

Skar(de)burgh, Walter: Revesby; *sd.* 1498, *d.* 1499, *p.* 1500 (Lincoln; *Reg. W. Smith,* n.f.).

Schalstu'/Shalstone, John: *see* Shaldeste.

Seale, Thomas: Beaulieu, *disp.* 1538, pension, £6 p.a. (TNA, E314/20/11, f. 1d–2r; *FOR*, p. 131); rector, Farley Chamberlain, Hampshire, from 1541 (Hockey, 1976, pp. 182, 186–87).

Sedbar/Sedbergh, Adam: Jervaulx; *sd.* 1526, *d.* and *p.* 1527 (York); last abbot, 1533–37; alleged to have sent meat and drink to the insurgents during the Pilgrimage of Grace, executed at Tyburn, 2–06–1537 (Cross, 1995, pp. 132–33; Gasquet, 1899, pp. 255–57, 263; said to have been 'a tall lusty man' (*LP*, Part 1, p. 165 [No. 369/2]).

Sedgwick, Christopher: Thame, signed deed of surrender, 1539 (*DKR*, p. 43); priest, Kirtlington, Oxon., died 1549 (Baskerville, 1930, p. 336); pension, £5–6–8 (TNA, E314/77).

Sedon/Sedown, Alexander: last prior, Vale Royal, 1538 (*DKR*, p. 46; *LP* **13**, Part 2, p. 118 [No. 297]); pension, £12 (TNA, E315/233,f. 18v).

Seerington: *see* Cheryngton.

Segar, John: Dunkeswell, 1539; pension, £5–6–8 (TNA, E322/76; Sparks, 1978, p. 109); curate, Plymptre, Devon , 1540/41 (*Devonshire Notes and Queries* **17**, 1932, p. 87).

Segar: *see also* Sagar.

Segefeld, William: Meaux; *d.* 1482, *p.* 1485 (York; Cross and Vickers, 1995, p. 153).

Selby, **Henry:** monk, Fountains; *sd.* 1521, *p.* 1527 (York); 1536, said to wish to leave the religious life (Cross and Vickers, 1995, pp. 114, 127).

Selby, Thomas: Stratford; *sd.* and *d.* 1533, *p.* 1534 (London; *Reg. R. Stokesley*, ff. 129r–v, 130r); signed deed of surrender and *disp.* 1538 (*DKR*, p. 42, *FOR*, p. 129); pension, £5 (TNA, E314/77).

Selle[r], Robert: Whalley, *sd.* 1511 (York; *Reg. C. Bainbridge*, f. 108r); monk, Sawley, *d.* 1512, *p.* 1515 (*Reg. C. Bainbridge,* f. 109v; Cross and Vickers, 1995, p. 200).

Seller/Salley, Henry: Sawley; *p.* 1482 (York); transferred to Furness on Sawley's closure in May 1536, where he was alleged to have said that 'no secular knave should be head of the Church' (Cross and Vickers, 1995, p. 206); perhaps in prison at time of suppression (Haigh, 1969, p. 120). A jubilarian. Was he *Henry Claghton,* q.v.?

Semer, William: Rievaulx; *sd.* 1522, *d.* 1524, *p.* 1525, but no further note of him (York; Cross and Vickers, 1995, pp. 169, 180).

Senden/Seyndon, William: Robertsbridge, signed deed of surrender and *disp.* 1538 (*DKR*, p. 39; *FOR*, p. 135); vicar of Bodiam, Sussex, 1542–49, of Iden, 1549–60 (Salzman, 1954, p. 35); in receipt of his pension of £6–13–4 as late as 1555 (TNA, E164/31, f. 25v; Cooper [1856] 171, where name as William London).

?Serfe, William: Meaux; *sd.* 1453 (York; *Reg. W. Booth*, f. 418r.)

Sesay, John: Byland; *ac.* and *sd.* 1503, *d.* 1504, *p.* 1506 (York; Cross and Vickers, 1995, p. 99).

Setell/Settyll/Settle, Thomas: Furness; accused, perhaps spuriously, of immoral relations with a woman, 1535 (*AF*, p. 324); signed deed of surrender and *disp.* 1537 (TNA, E322/91; *FOR*, p. 97; AF, p. 324).

Sevenok, John: Boxley; *p.* 1506 (Canterbury; *Reg. W. Warham* **2**, f. 262v).

Seymour, al. Lawrence, Thomas: *conversus,* Kingswood, made his mark on the surrender deed in 1538 (*DKR*, p. 25); may have had the *alias* of Lawrence; on the suppression of Kingswood, 5–03–1538, he received £1 pocket–money and no pension, but was to be at his request sent to another house (TNA, E36/152, f. 22).

Shadwell, John: Kirkstall, *sd.* 1526, *d.* 1517, *p.* 1531 (York; Cross and Vickers, 1995, p. 141).

Shaftesbury, Stephen: Bindon; *p.* 1507 (Salisbury; *Reg. E. Audley*, f. 7v).

Shakelton, John/Robert, al. Christall: Hailes, *disp.* 1540 (*FOR*, p. 208).

Shakespere, Roger: Bordesley, *disp.* 1538 (*FOR*, p. 149; TNA, E322/26); in receipt of pension of £5 as late as 1555 (TNA, E164/31, f. 44r); assessed for subsidy in 1540 (Bodleian Library, Oxford, Tanner MS 343).

S(c(hlaster/Shaldeste/Shalstone, al. Colles, James: Biddlesden; *sd.* 1528, *d.* 1529, *p.* 1530 (Lincoln; *Reg. J. Longland*, ff. 21v, 24v, 26v); *disp.* 1538; pension, £5–6–8 (*FOR*, p. 179; TNA, E322/22); in receipt of his pension in 1555 (TNA, E164, f. 24r).

Shapter, Thomas: Buckfast; *sd.* 1530, *d.* 1533, *p.* 1535 (Exeter; *Reg. J. Vesey*, ff. 172v, 182r (Stéphan, 1970, p. 178).

Shaptor/Shapcot, William: Buckfast; *ac.* and *sd.* 1517, *sd.* 1518, *p.* 1521 (Exeter; *Reg. H. Oldham*, f. 127v, 130r; *Reg. J. Vesey*, f. 144v); pension, £5–6–8, 1539 (Stéphan, 1970, p. 213).

Sharparow, John: Meaux; *sd.* 1493, *d.* 1495, *p.* 1496 (York; Cross and Vickers, 1995, p. 154).

Sharp, James: St Mary Graces; *sd.* 1495 (London; *Reg. R. Hill*, f. 30r).

Sharpe, John: Kirkstead; *ac.* 1503, *sd.* 1504 (Lincoln; *Reg. W. Smith*, ff. 41v, 46r).

Sharp, Richard/Robert: Rufford; *sd.* 1513 (York; *Reg. C. Bainbridge*, f. 122v).

Sharpe, Thomas: Jervaulx, *disp.* 1537 *(FOR 119)*; may later (1548) have been a priest in Huggate, Yorkshire, aged sixty–seven (Cross and Vickers, 1995, p. 137).

Sharp: *see also* Thorp.

Shaw, Reginald: Dieulacres, *sd.* and *d.* 1514; *p.* 1516 (Lichfield; *Reg. G. Blyth*, n–f.)

?Shead, Robert: Rufford; *p.* 1514 (York; *Reg. T. Wolsey*, f. 168r).

Shebynton, Thomas: Merevale; *disp.* 1488 (*CPL* **15**, p. 116 [No. 243]).

Shepherd, *al.* Swineshead, Stephen: Swineshead; *sd.* 1492 (Lincoln; *Reg. J. Russell*, f. 45/46v); *disp.* 1505 (*CPL* **18**, p. 372 [No. 494]).

Shepherd, William: Bindon, 1539 (TNA, E322/21; pension, £2 (TNA, E314/77).

Shepley/Shiplay, Nicholas: Kirkstall, *sd.*1505, *d.* 1506, *p.*1509 (York; Cross and Vickers, 1995, p. 140).

Sheppy/Shepey, John: Merevale; *ac. and sd.* 1519, (Lichfield; *Reg. G. Blyth*, n–f.).

Shepyshed/Shiphede, *al.* Palfreyman, John: Biddlesden; *ac.* 1515, *sd.* 1518, *d.* 1520, *p.* 1525 (Lincoln; *Reg. W. Atwater*, ff. 117r, 127r, 132r; *Reg. J. Longland*, f. 11r); *disp.* 1538; pension, £5–6–8 (*DKR*, p. 10, *FOR*, p. 179; TNA, E314/77, which gives his name as *Richard*.

Shepeshed, Richard: Garendon; *sd.* 1530, *d.* 1531, *p.* 1533 (Lincoln; *Reg. J. Longland*, ff. 26v, 28v, 35v); in house on 15–03–1536 (*LP* **10**, p. 194 [No. 475]). A *Richard Shepshed* was at Biddlesden at its suppression in 1538, *disp.* 30–11–1539 (*FOR*, p. 179; TNA, E322/22).

Shepished, Thomas: Garendon; *sd.* 1497, *d.* 1498, *p.* 1502 (Lincoln; *Reg. W. Smith*, f. 37r.). Could he be the same monk as Abbot *Thomas Sheston*? q.v.

Shirborne/Sherborne, Richard: Kirkstead; *ac.* 1489, *d.* 1490/91, *P.* 1493 (Lincoln; *Reg. J. Russell*, ff. 31v, 37r, 40r, 49v).

Shyrborn/Sherborne, Stephen: Bindon; *d.* and *p.* 1525 (Salisbury; *Reg. L. Campeggio*). Could he be either *Stephen Farsy* or *Stephen Heywood*, q.v. ?

Sherborne, *al.* Rede, William: Ford; *p.* 1486 (Wells; *Reg. R. Stillington*, f. 218: SRO, D/D/B Reg.7, f. 218v); last prior, pension [1539] £8 (Youings, 1971, p. 186). A jubilarian.

Sherman: *see* Kingsbury.

Sherwyn, Christopher: last prior, Revesby, *disp.* 1538 (*FOR*, p. 128; Essex R.O., D/DRg 1/104).

Sheryngton: *see* Cherynton.

Sheston: *see* Syston.

Shiers/Skipton, Gilbert: Swineshead; *d.* 1508 (Lincoln; *Reg. W. Smith*, n–f.); *disp.* 1537 (*FOR*, p. 102).

Shilton, John: Bruern; *d.* and *p.* 1505 (Lincoln; *Reg. W. Smyth*, n.f.).

Shipton, John: Beaulieu, 1495, when permitted to hold a benefice, and also to be absent from it whilst attending a *studium generale* (*CPL* **16**, p. 331, [No. 483]). Might he be the later abbot of Croxden of this name?

Shipton, John: Bruern; *sd.* 1517 (Lincoln; *Reg. W. Atwater*, f. 122r).

Shipton, John: abbot, Hulton, 1517; abbot, Croxden, (said to be the 24th) 1517–1531 (Smith, 2008, pp. 286, 301).

Shirley/Shirlay, William: Garendon; *sd.* 1506, *d.* 1507, *p.* 1508 (Lincoln; *Reg. W. Smith*, n–f.).

Shrewsbury, Richard: Buildwas; *sd.* and *d.* 1525, *p.* 1527 (Lichfield; *Reg. G. Blyth*, n–f.).

Sidenham: *see also* Sydenham, Sydnam.

Silvester, John: kitchener, Hailes, *disp.* 1540 (*FOR*, p. 208); in receipt of pension of £6–6–8; in 1553 was living at Longborough, Gloucestershire.

Simpson, William: St Mary Graces, 1533 (Grainger and Phillpotts, 2011, p. 93).

Sitibes, John: Stratford; *d.* 1528 (*CL*); probably the same monk as *John Gibbes*, q.v.

Skale(s), Richard: sub–cellarer, Furness; signed deed of surrender, 1537 (TNA, E322/91); monk, Rushen, 1537–39, when pension, £2–13–4 (Davey and Roscow, 2010, p. 174). He may have been *Richard Buseyn*, q.v.

Skegbye: *see* Capron.

Skerne, Richard: Meaux; *sd.* 1525, *d.* 1526 (York). Perhaps *Richard Sympson,* still receiving a pension of £5 in 1564; said in 1552 to be fifty years old, and who became rector of Sproatley, Yorkshire, in 1548, and was said in 1567 to 'say communion for the dead'"; his will was dated 1570 (Cross, 1995, pp. 155, 163).

Skerne, 'parson': monk, Louth Park; later, in October 1536, was a ringleader in the Lincolnshire uprising (*LP* **11, p.** 225 [No. 568]).

Skevington (*al.* Pace), Thomas: Merevale, *sd.* 1 June 1482; *d.* 19 September 1482; *p.* 22 February 1483 (Lichfield; *Reg. J. Hales,* ff. 279r, 280r, 281v); Oxford graduate; abbot, Waverley, 1492–1508 (Smith, 2008, p. 348); *disp.* 1500 (*CPL* **17,** Part 1, pp. 184–85; **19,** p. 612); abbot, Beaulieu, 1508; concurrently abbot, Beaulieu and bishop of Bangor, 1509–33, consecrated, Lambeth, 17 June 1509; holding the abbacy *in commendam;* lived mostly at Beaulieu, and licensed by the bishop of Winchester to hold ordinations, 1510 and 1511 (Winchester; *Reg. R. Fox* **2,** f. 146; **3,** f. 51r–v); 1531, fined £333–6–8 for unspecified offences against the ordinances of provisions and preamunire; 1532, placed on the commission of the peace for Hampshire (*LP* **4,** p. 2697 [No. 6047]; **5,** Part 1, p. 295 [No. 657]); died, 17 August 1533, body buried at Beaulieu, but heart buried at Bangor cathedral (Hockey, 1976, pp. 144–54, 225–28 – details his will).

Skyggs/Skuggs/Skirwhitt, Simon: Waverley; *ac.* and *sd.* 1514 (Winchester; *Reg. R. Fox* **3,** ff. 55v, 56r); *d.* 1516 (London; *Reg. R. Fitzjames,* f. 182r); *disp.* 1536 (*FOR,* pp. 67–68); and see *Simon Hacker.*

Skipsee/Clarke, Stephen: Meaux; *sd.* 1517, *p.* 1518 (York); pension, 1539, £6 (Cross and Vickers, 1995, pp. 154, 158).

Skipsee, Thomas: Meaux; *d.* 1517 (York; Cross and Vickers, 1995, p. 154).

Skypton, John: Sawley, *disp.* 1536 (*FOR,* p. 58).

Skypton, Richard: Rufford; *sd.* 1500 (York; *Reg. T. Rotherham,* n–f.); *d.* 1501, *p.* 1503 (*Reg. T. Savage,* ff.110r, 119v).

Skipton, Stephen: Furness; signed deed of surrender, 1537 (TNA, E322/91). His name is not in the pension lists, so did he move to another house?

Skipton, William: Sawtry; *d.* 1482, *p.* 1483 (York; Cross and Vickers, 1995, p. 199).).

Skipton: *see also* Shiers.

Slingsby, Robert: Woburn; *sd.* 1532, *d.* 1533, *p.* 1537 (Lincoln; *Reg. J. Longland,* ff. 31r, 36r, 55v); *disp.* 1538 (*FOR,* p. 145); later vicar, Stagsden, Bedfordshire, dying in 1585 when rector, Aston on the Walls, Northamptonshire (Thomson, 1933, p. 140).

Small/Smales, John: Roche; *sd.* 1484, *d.* 1485, *p.* 1487 (York; Cross and Vickers, 1995, p. 186); *disp.* 1503 (*CPL* **17,** Part 1, p. 589 [No. 961].

Smart, Thomas: Buckland; *sd.* 1514 (Exeter; *Reg. H. Oldham,* f. 115r).

Smekergill, Thomas: Fountains; pension, 1539: £6 (Cross and Vickers, 1995, pp. 115, 127).

Smerden, Alexander: Boxley; *sd.* 1487, *d.* 1488 (Canterbury; *Reg. J. Morton,* pp. 124 [No. 431c], 126 [No. 435b]).

Smerdon/Smardon/Saverdon, Richard: Boxley; *sd.* 1494 (London; *Reg. R. Hill,* f. 29r); *d.* 1494 (Canterbury; *Reg. J. Morton),* *p.* 1495 (London; *Reg. R. Hill,* f, 30r).

Smeton, Edward/Edmund: Woburn; *sd.* 1487, *d.* 1489, *p.* 1490 Lincoln; *Reg. J. Russell,* ff. 26r, 33r, 37v); *disp.* 1538 (*FOR,* p. 145). A jubilarian.

Smyth, Christopher: Whalley; *sd.* 1489, *d.* 1490 (York; *Reg. T. Rotherham*, n–f.); last prior, Whalley, *disp.* 1537 (*FOR*, p. 91); remained at Whalley as a chantry priest, with a stipend of £6–14–4, but died in 1538; in 1537 was said to be eighty years old; a jubilarian (Haigh, 1969, p. 117).

Smyth, John: Cleeve; *p.* 1481 (Wells; *Reg. R. Stillington*, f. 210v).

Smyth, John: Sawley; *d.* 1481 (York; Cross and Vickers, 1995, p. 199).

Smyth, John: Waverley, *disp.* 1536 (*FOR*, pp. 67–68).

Smyth, John: Kirkstall, *d.* 1499 (York; Cross and Vickers, 1995, p. 140).

Smyth, John: Hulton, *sd.* and *d.* 1510, *p.* 1511 (Lichfield; *Reg. G. Blyth*, n–f.); signed deed of surrender and *disp.* 1538 (TNA, E322/106; *FOR*, p.154); pension, £4 (TNA, E315/233, f. 2v).

Smyth, John: Whitland; 1539; *disp.* 1540; pension £4 p.a. (*FOR*, p. 206; TNA, E315/233/258); perhaps his pension was increased as £3 was awarded in 1539 (*LP* **14**, Part 1, p. 362 [No. 747]).

Smyth, Lawrence: Fountains; *sd.* 1491, *d.* 1492, *p.* 1496; accused, perhaps spuriously, of having immoral relations with two married women, 1536 (Cross and Vickers, 1995, p. 118). Was he the same monk as *Lawrence Benne*, q.v.?

Smyth(e), Ranulph/Ralph: Combermere, *disp.* 1538 (*DKR*, p. 17, *FOR*, p. 154); received his £5 pension as late as 1555 (TNA, E164/31, f. 69r).

Smith, Richard: Strata Florida, 1534, when forty years old, and accused of coining in his cell; in receipt of a pension of but £3 in 1555 (TNA, E164/31, f. 75v; **14**, Part 1, p. 362 [No. 747]; Williams, 1889, p. 169; 2001, p. 70).

Smythe, Richard: novice, Buildwas, *disp.* 1537 (*FOR*, p. 92).

Smythe, Robert: *see* Staynethorp.

Smyth, Thomas: *see*: Godalmyng.

Smyth, Thomas: novice, Roche; signed deed of surrender, 1538; pension, £3–6–8 (TNA, E314/20/11, f. 4v; *DKR*, p. 39). Might he be *Thomas Hoghton*, q.v.?

Smyth, William: Dunkeswell; *p.* 1502 (Exeter; *Reg. R. Redmayne*, f. 43r).

Smythe, William: last sub-prior, St Mary Graces, *disp.* 1539 (*FOR*, p. 182); in receipt of pension of £6–13–4 in 1555 (TNA, E164/31, f. 4). Could it be his name which is inscribed on folio 24v of SAL, MS 14?

Smythson: *see* **Easingwold**.

Snape, Richard: abbot, Croxden, 1529–1531 (when very ill and died; Lichfield; *Reg. G. Blyth*, f. 31; Smith, 2008, p. 286; *LP* **5**, p. 163 [No. 347])

Snath, John: Kirkstall, *sd.* 1499, *p.* 1504 (York; Cross and Vickers, 1995, p. 140).

Snaw, John: Kirkstall; possibly the foregoing monk; pension, 1539, £5; in receipt of pension in 1555 (TNA, E164/31, f. 53v). might he be the monk, *John Hertwith*, q.v. (Cross and Vickers, 1995, pp. 142, 151).

Snead/Sneyde: *see* Danyell.

Snell, Thomas: Furness; *sd.* 1521, *p.* 1522 (York; *Reg. T. Wolsey*, ff. 189v, 193v); signed deed of surrender and *disp.* 1537 (TNA, E322/91; *FOR*, p. 97).

Snodland/Sundland, Roger: Boxley; *ac.* 1496 (Canterbury, *Reg. J. Morton*, p. 134 [No. 445a]); *sd.* 1496, *d.* and *p.* 1498 (London; *Reg. T. Savage*, ff. 53r, 54r, 56v).

Snow, Christopher: Stratford; *sd.* 1527, *d.* 1528 (London; *Reg. C. Tunstall*, ff. 160v,.161r); *p.* 1532 (London; *Reg. R. Stokesley*, f. 128v); signed deed of surrender and *disp.* 1538 (*DKR*, p. 42, *FOR*, p. 129); pension, £5 (TNA, E314/77)..

Sobary/Sothebry, Thomas: cellarer, Tintern, 1525 (NLW, Badminton Deeds, Group 2, Nos. 1661, 1663).

Sodbury, John: Kingswood; *ac.* and *sd.* 1481, *d.* 1482 (Worcester; *Reg. J. Alcock*, ff. 263–64, 268); abbot by 1504 (Worcester; *Reg. S. Gigli*, f. 33); if same monk in retirement, then signed deed of surrender and *disp.* 1538 (*DKR*, p. 25, *FOR*, p. 131); 'reward and finding', 1538, £2–13–4 . If not a different monk of the same name, then a jubilarian, and in receipt of his £4 pension as late as 1555 (TNA, E164/31, f. 29r).

Sole, William: Buckfast, *c.*1517/25, when alleged to have taken part in the removal of monastic tenants from Staverton mill, Devon (TNA, STAC 2/29/169; Stéphan, 1970, pp. 183–84).

Somerfield/Summerfield, John: Beaulieu, *disp.* 1538 (*DKR*, p. 9, *FOR*, p. 131); pension of £4 received in 1555 (TNA, E164/31, f. 13r). Seemingly not priested in 1538 (TNA, E314/77). Sondland: *see* Snodland.

Sothbye, James: Revesby, *disp.* 1538 (*FOR*, p. 128; Essex R.O., D/DRg 1/104).

Sotheron, George: Newminster, thirty–five years old in 1536 (TNA, SC12/13/65); *disp.* 1536 (*FOR*, p. 77).

Sotherton, Thomas: Fountains; abbot's officer, 1492 (*FLB*, p. 41 [No. 51]).

Spenser, William: abbot, Rievaulx, by 1477 to 1489, but may have been abbot from 1463; member, York Corpus Christi Guild, from 1469/70 (Smith, 2008, p. 324).

Spere, John: Merevale; deacon at time of suppression, pension £2–13–4 (TNA, E315/233, f. 63v).

Sper, Thomas: Merevale; signed suppression deed, 1538 (TNA, E322/151).

Spillesby, Richard: Vaudey; *sd.* and *d.* 1506, *p.* 1507 (Lincoln; *Reg. W. Smith*, n–f.).

Splatt/Splatby/Slott, Richard: Buckfast; *sd.* 1530, *d.* 1533 (Exeter; *Reg. J. Vesey*, f. 172v, 182r); still in its community in 1539 (*DKR*, p. 12); in receipt of pension of £5–6–8 in 1555 (TNA, E164/31, f. 34r); seemingly a chaplain at or vicar of Chagford, Devon, 1540/41 (Stéphan, 1970, p. 213). Splott: *see* Splatt.

Sponge, John: Kirkstall; *p.* 1509; he may have been *John Horwood* or *John Henryson*, q.v. (Lonsdale, 1972, p. 206).

Spratt, Thomas: Robertsbridge, by 1523 (SAL, *MS 14*, f. 59v); *disp.* to give up the habit and hold a benefice, 1536, but still on the books of the monastery in 1538, when signed deed of surrender (*FOR*, pp. 57; 135; *DKR*, p. 39); still alive in 1553 with pension of £8 (Cooper, 1856, p. 171); by December 1536 he was vicar of Bodiam, Sussex, but was then taken ill and seemingly returned to the abbey; curate of Seaford, Sussex, 1544–45; and vicar–choral of Chichester cathedral when he made his will on 12 July 1551 (*Salzman*, 1954, p. 34). Despite this he was mentioned in Cardinal Pole's pension list of 1555/56 (Ray, 1931, p. 144).

Spufford/Spofforth, Richard: Kirkstall, *p.* 1512 (York). Perhaps *Richard Broke*, q.v. (Lonsdale, 1972, p. 207), or *Richard Bateson*, q.v. (Cross and Vickers, 1995, pp. 141, 144).

Squire/Squere, Gregory: Robertsbridge, *sd.* 1501 (Chichester; *Reg. E. Story*, f. 196r); noted in SAL, *MS 14*, f. 59v).

Squire, Henry: Robertsbridge, by 1523 (SAL, *MS 14*, f. 59v).

Squire, Walter/William): Robertsbridge, by 1523 (SAL, *MS 14*, f. 59v); signed deed of surrender and *disp.* 1538 (*DKR*, p. 39; *FOR*, p. 135); pension, £6 (TNA, E314/77). .

Squires/Squyer, George: Boxley, *disp.* 1538 (FOR, p. 123); in receipt of pension of £4 in 1555 (TNA, E164/31, f. 4).

Stafford, *al.* Bate, Thomas: Ford, *sd.* 1510, *d.* 1511, *p.* 1518 (Exeter; *Reg. H. Oldham*, ff. 103r, 106r, 130v); still in the community at its suppression, pension, 1539, £5–6–8 (*LP* **14**, Part 1, p. 184 [No. 468]); pension still received in 1555 (TNA, E164/31, f. 34v).

Stafford, Robert: Rewley; *p.* 1514 (Lincoln; *Reg. W. Atwater*, f. 111r).

Stafford, Thomas: abbot, Hailes, 1483–1504 (*CHA*, p. 92; Smith, 2008, p. 299); blessed as abbot, 11 December 1483; finds mention in several episcopal registers (Worcester; *Reg. J. Alcock*, f. 148; *Reg. S. Gigli*, f. 33; *Reg. R. Morton*, f. 118). Named as William in 1500/01: SSC, BRT 1/3/109).

Stamford, John: Vaudey; *ac.* 1491, *sd.*1492, *d.* 1493, *p.* (Lincoln; Reg. J. Russell, ff. 30v, 44/45r, 46/47r, 48/49v, 54v).

Stam(p)ford/Staunford, Robert: Pipewell; *sd.* ?1492, *p.* 1496 (Lincoln; *Reg. J. Russell*, f.44/45r; *Reg. W. Smith*, n.f.); abbot by 1504 to at least 1510 or later, when general pardon (*LP* **1**, Part 1, p. 208 [No. 438/1, n.11]; Smith, 2008, p. 320).

Stampar, John: Meaux; *sd.* 1510, *p.* 1513 (York; Cross and Vickers, 1995, p. 154).

Stamper, Peter: Meaux; *p.* 1528 (York; Cross and Vickers, 1995, pp. 155, 165); perhaps the same monk as *Peter Waghen*, q.v..

Standcliff, Richard: Kirkstall; pension, 1539, £6 (Cross and Vickers, 1995, p. 142).

Stan(d)forth, Stephen: Furness, signed deed of surrender and *disp.* 1537 (TNA, E322/91; *FOR*, p. 97).

Staneburn/Stayneburgh, Henry: Kirkstall, *d.* 1512, *p.* 1516 (York; Cross and Vickers, 1995, p. 141).

Staneburn, John: Fountains; *sd.* 1514 (York; Cross and Vickers, 1995, p. 114).

Staynbury/Staynbourne, John: provisor, St Bernard's College, Oxford, 1478–1488 (Smith, 2008, p. 319).

Staynthorpe/Stanethorp, *al.* Smythe: Robert: Rievaulx; *ac.* 1501, *sd.* and *d.* 1502, *p.* 1504 (York); 'monk of the brewhouse', 1533 (TNA, STAC2/7/217); accused, perhaps spuriously, at the Crown visitation in 1536 of having had immoral relations with a woman; *disp.* 1538 (*DKR*, p. 38, *FOR*, p. 156); pension, £5–6–8; in his will (proved 26 February 1550) requested burial in Helmsley churchyard, Yorkshire, and appointed a former confrère as an executor (Cross and Vickers, 1995, pp. 168, 170, 180).

Stanford/Staynforth/?*al.* Car, Christopher: Sawley, *sd.* 1497, *d.* 1498, *p.* 1499 (York; Cross and Vickers, 1995, pp. 199, 206); disp. 1536 (*FOR*, p. 58).

Stanford/Stainforth, Edmund: Furness, *sd.* 1516, *d.* and *p.* 1517 (York; *Reg. T. Wolsey*, ff. 174v, 175v, 177v); vicar of Millom, Cumbria, by 1535, *disp.* to wear the habit of a regular beneath that of a secular priest (*FOR*, p. 94; Haigh, 1969, p. 120). Not in the abbey at the time in 1537 of its suppression. For him, see also: *DCL*, pp. 93–98.

Stanford, John: prior, Warden, 1492, 'old in years' (*Letters*, p. 156 [No. 79]).

Stanford, Robert: Furness; *d.* 1487 (York; *Reg. T. Rotherham*, n-f.).

Stanford, Robert: *see also* Stampford.

Stanley, John: Stanley; *sd.*, *d.* and *p.* 1506 (Salisbury; *Reg. E. Audley*, n.f.).

Stanley/Standeley/Standlow, John: Croxden, professed *c.*1509 (Laurence, 1952, p. B.17); signed deed of surrender and *disp.* 1538 (Hibbert, 1910, p. 222; *FOR*, p. 151); vicar, Alton, Hampshire, from 1546 to his death in 1569, when still receiving his pension of £5–13–4 as late as 1555 (TNA, E164/31, f. 46v).

Stanley: *see also* Wigstone.

Stanton/Staynton, John: Jervaulx; *sd.* and *d.* 1519, *p.* 1520 (York); involved in the Pilgrimage of Grace but appears to have escaped execution; perhaps was in 1546 the chantry priest of this name in Melton parish, Yorkshire (Cross and Vickers, 1995, pp. 131, 137).

Stanton, Richard: Stratford; *ac.* 1533, *sd.* 1534 (London; *Reg. R. Stokesley*, ff. 129v, 130r); signed deed of surrender and *disp.* 1538, when still a deacon (*DKR*, p. 42, *FOR*, p. 129; TNA, E314/77; in receipt of £3–6–8 pension in 1555 (TNA, E164/31, f. 9v).

Stanyern(t), Christopher: Pipewell; *sd.* and *p.* 1488 (Lincoln; *Reg. J. Russell*, ff. 27v, 30r); *disp.* 1503 (*CPL* **18**, p. 251 [No. 278]).

Stapford, T . . . . . ; monk, Rewley; *ac.* 1533 (Lincoln; *Reg. J. Longland*, f. 36v).

Stapleton, William: monk, Louth Park, *disp.* 1536 (*FOR*, p. 63).

Stapylton: *see* **Bedale**.

Starke/Starkey: *see* Byrmycham.

Staunford: *see* Stampford.

?Staunton, John: Rewley; *sd.* 1526 (Lincoln; *Reg. J. Longland*, f. 14v).

Staveley/Staley, *al.* Wilsdon, Thomas: Rufford; *sd.* and *d.* 1492, *p.* 1496 (York; *Reg. T. Rotherham*, n–f.); *disp.* 1505 (*CPL* **18**, p. 410 [No. 577]).

Stayerdn, William: Furness; *p.* 1502 (York: *Reg. T. Savage*, f. 113r).

Staynton/Staymerton, Lawrence: Calder; *sd.* and *d.* 1517 (York; *Reg. T. Wolsey*, ff. 175r, 176r).

Staynton,Richard: Rufford; *sd., d.* and *p.* 1522 (York; *Reg. T. Wolsey*, ff. 194r, 195v, 196v).

Staynton, Richard: Jervaulx, *disp.* 1537 (*FOR*, p. 119).

Stebbing, Richard: monk, Coggeshall; *sd.* 1505, *d.* 1506, *p.* 1507 (London; *Reg. R. Fitzjames*, ff. 95r, 95d; Reg. W. Barons, f. 91r).

Steynson, William: *see* **Yersley**.

Steynestone, John: Rufford; Signed letters testimonial in 1555 (Cross and Vickers, 1995, p. 171).

Stephyn, Richard: Thame; *ac.* 1494, *p.* 1497 (Lincoln; *Reg. J. Russell*, f. 54r; *Reg. W. Smith*, n.f.).

Stevens, Thomas: Netley; *ac.* 1509, *d.* 1510 (Winchester, *Reg. R. Fox* **2**, ff. 25r, 26v); priest by 1518 (*TNA, E314/101*); receiver of Netley, then abbot, Netley, 1529–1536; last abbot, Beaulieu, 1536–38 (Smith, 2008, pp. 267, 316), *disp.* 1538; pension, £33–6–8 (*DKR*, p. 9; *FOR*, p. 131); suffered in his abbacy at Beaulieu from uncooperative monks, after the surrender took up the plight of its sanctuary debtors, retired first to St Leonards before becoming rector of Bentworth, Hampshire, on 20 February 1539; he was appointed treasurer of Salisbury Cathedral in 1548, dying in 1550 (Hockey, 1976, pp. 183–85, 195).

Stephens: *see also* Bristow, Sydenham.

Stevenson, John: Meaux; *d.* 1513, *p.* 1517; pension, £6 (York; Cross and Vickers, 1995, pp. 154, 156, 163).

Steward/Stuarde, William: Bordesley, *disp.* 1538 (*FOR*, p. 149; TNA, E322/26); in receipt of pension of £5 as late as 1555 (TNA, E164/31, f. 44r)

Stickford, John: Revesby; in 1450, on account of old age seeks dispensation to read by candlelight and wear linen clothes (*SAP*, pp. 143 [No. 637], 156 [No. 709]).

Stickforde, Robert: Revesby; *d.* 1507 (Lincoln; *Reg. W. Smith*, n–f.); last abbot there, 1537–1538 (Smith, 2008, p. 322); *disp.* 1538 (*FOR*, p. 128); no pension details.

Stickney: *see* Scott.

Stile/Stele/Woburn/Webure, William: Woburn; *sd.* 1509, *p.* 1511 (Lincoln; *Reg. W. Smith*, n–f.); cellarer, 1533, and cousin to its abbot; abbot, Vaudey, 1533–1536 (Smith, 2008, p. 346); *disp.* 1536; in 1554 was living at Woburn, Bedfordshire, unmarried; had a pension of £20, but no other ecclesiastical preferments (Hodgett, 1959, pp. 36, 57, 90); still in receipt of pension in 1555 (TNA, E315/164, f. 18r).

Stilfelde, Richard: Netley; in community, 1518, by which time priested (TNA, E314/101); *disp.* 1536 (*FOR*, p. 66); incumbent, Eling, Hampshire, by December 1541 (Hockey, 1976, p. 187).

Stillington, Thomas: Rievaulx; *sd.* 1482, *d.* 1483, *p.* 1486 (York; Cross and Vickers, 1995, p. 167).

Stillyngton, William: monk, Byland; *ac., sd.* and *d.* 1482, *p.* 1485 (York; Cross and Vickers, 1995, p. 98).

Stock/Storke, Gavin/Gawin: monk, Fountains; *d.* 1521 (York); pension, 1539, £5; 1554 until death in 1556, incumbent in plurality of Wiggenhall St Mary, Norfolk, and Rickinghall Superior, Suffolk, a Marian appointment (Cross and Vickers, 1995, pp. 114–15, 127; Baskerville, 1933, p. 228).

Stockdale, William: Kirkstall, *p.*1482 (York; Cross and Vickers, 1995, p. 139; abbot, 1501–09; his brother was an alderman and merchant of York (Smith, 2008, p. 305).

Stockes, George: Merevale, 1497 (TNA, E315/283, f. 1).

Stode, Richard: Warden, 1538, but entry struck through (TNA, E314/20/11, f. 1r–d).

Stodeley, Thomas: Bordesley; *ac.* 1507 (Worcester; *Reg. S. Gigli,* f. 296).

Stodeley, John: Stanley; *ex.* and *ac.* 1518, *sd., d.* and *p.* 1519 (Salisbury; *Reg. E. Audley,* ff. 35r, 37r, 39r, 40r).

Stodeley, Walter: Stanley; *sd., d.* and *p.* 1506 (Salisbury; *Reg. E. Audley,* n–f.).

Stodeard/Stodeart: John: Strata Florida; *sd.* 1491; monk, Cymer; *d.* 1491 (St David's; *EPD* 2, pp. 609, 615; possibly the registrar recorded the wrong monastery).

Stoke, Henry: no house given, but Cistercian; *d.* 1472 (Worcester; *Reg. J. Carpenter* 2, f. 187).

Stoke, John: Pipewell; *sd.* 1508, *s.* 1509 (Lincoln; *Reg. W. Smith,* n–f.).

Stoke, Richard/Roger: Vale Royal; *p.* 1493 (York; *Reg. T. Rotherham,* n.f.).

Stoke(s), Richard: Thame; *sd.* and *d.* 1525 (Lincoln; *Reg. J. Longland,* ff. 11r, 17r).

Stoke, Thomas: Pipewell; *sd.* and *d.* 1488, *p.* 1491 (Lincoln; *Reg. J. Russell,* ff. 27v, 29r, 39v).

Stoke, Thomas: Pipewell; *sd.* 1528, *d.* 1529, *p.* 1532 (Lincoln; *Reg. J. Longland,* ff. 22r, 23r, 31v).

Stoke, William: Combe: *sd.* and *d.* 1494 (Lichfield; *Reg. W. Smith,* f. 178v, 181).

Stokeland, John: Hailes; *p.* 1516 (Worcester; *Reg. S. Gigli,* f. 331).

Stokland, John: Ford; *d.* and *p.* 1511 (Exeter; *Reg. H. Oldham,* ff. 105r, 106r).

Stockelonde, John: Newenham; *sd.* 1530, *d.* 1532 (Exeter; *Reg. J. Vesey,* ff. 171v, 179r).

Stockland, John: Cistercian monk; B.Th. 1525, probably one of the foregoing (*BRUO* 2, p. 541).

Stokes, George: Merevale, *sd.* 1–06–1482; *d.*19–09–1482; *p.* 22–02–1483 (Lichfield Cathedral (Lichfield; *Reg. J. Hales,* ff. 279r, 280r, 281v).

Stone: *see* Bridgewater.

Stonely, John: novice, Kingswood, signed deed of surrender and *disp.* 1538 (*DKR,* p. 25, *FOR,* p. 131); in receipt of his pension of only £2 as late as 1555 (TNA, E164/31, f. 29r); 'reward and finding', 1538, £2 (TNA, E36/152, f. 22).

Stonley, Richard: Bordesley; *d.* 1497 (Lichfield; *Reg. J. Arundell,* f. 261).

Stoneley, William: Stoneleigh; *sd.* 1485, *d.* 1486, *p.* 1487 (Lichfield; *Reg. J. Hales,* ff. 214, 216v, 225).

Stonnton, Richard: Rufford, *disp.* 1536 (*FOR,* p. 74).

Stope, William: Kirkstall, *d.* 1514 (York; Cross and Vickers, 1995, p. 141).

Stopes/Scrope: Richard: Meaux; *sd.* 1500, *p.* 1504 (York); last abbot, Meaux, 1523–1539; B.Th. (Oxon.) 1521, after ten years of study; pension, 1539, £40 (TNA, E315/246, f. 118); possibly vicar, Thrybergh, Yorkshire, 1542 until death in 1546, though he requested burial in the choir of Skerne church (Cross and Vickers, 1995, pp. 154, 156–57; Smith, 2008, p. 156).

Storror/Storer, William: Rievaulx; native of Hawnby, Yorkshire; *sd.* 1504 (York; Aveling, 1955, p. 14); sub–prior, Rievaulx, 1533 (TNA, STAC2/7/217); signed deed of surrender and *disp.* 1538, pension, £5–6–8 (*DKR,* p. 38, *FOR,* p. 156); not mentioned in the pension lists (Cross and Vickers, 1995, pp. 168, 170, 181–82).

Stotesbury, John: Biddlesden, 1497, by which year dispensed to hold a benefice, and now vicar of Little Horwood, Buckinghamshire (*CPL* 16, p. 504 [No. 762]).

Stott/Scott, John: Stratford; *ac.* and *sd.* 1533, *d.* 1534 (London; *Reg. J. Stokesley,* ff. 129r–v, 130r); signed deed of surrender and *disp.* 1538 (*DKR,* p. 42, *FOR,* p. 129); in receipt of £5 pension in 1555 (TNA, E164/31, f. 9v).

Stradlyng, Richard: Margam, 1484–86; cellarer in 1486 (Birch, 1897, p. 211).

Stratford/Stretforth, Edward: Kirkstead; *ac.* 1506, *d.* and *p.* 1507 (Lincoln; *Reg. W. Smith,* n–f.).

Stratford, Humphrey, *al.* Emlyn: St Mary Graces; *sd.* and *d.* 1510, *p.* 1511 (London; *Reg. R. Fitzjames,* ff. 158r [169r], 159r [170v], 160v [171r]).

Stratford, John: Hailes; presented monastic candidates from Hailes for ordination in Worcester diocese, 1479 (Worcester; *Reg. J. Alcock,* f. 257); abbot, Cymer, 1482–87; he may be the monk *John Stretford,* q.v., and was a trusted courier for the Crown and the Order (*Letters,* pp. 97 [No. 39], 99 [No. 41]; Williams, 2001, pp. 65–66; *Statuta* 5, p. 432 [No. 1482/13; Smith, 2008, p. 287).

Stratford, Richard: Hailes: *ac.* and *sd.* 1479, *d.* 1480 (Worcester; *Reg. J. Alcock,* ff. 257, 262); ordained priest whilst under age (*SAP,* 2, pp. 388–89 [No. 3142]).

Stratford, William: abbot, Vale Royal, *c.*1476 to 1516; though the names of Thomas as abbot occur 1495–1496 and of Richard in 1505 (Smith, 2008, p. 343; Warrington Archives, MS 596); general pardon, 1509 (*LP* 1, Part 1, p. 212 [No. 438/1, m. 18]. In 1517 he was described as 'William, late abbot of Vale Royal, otherwise William Stratford, S.T.P., brother–monk of John, abbot of Vale Royal (*LB,* p. 22); at St Bernard's College, Oxford, perhaps before 1481; B.Th. (Oxon)., and granted a grace to incept as D. D. (Cantab.; *BRUO* 2, Vol. 3, p.1801.

Stratford, William: Woburn; *ac.* and *sd.* 1509, *d.* 1511, *p.* 1513 (Lincoln; *Reg. W. Smith,* n–f.); *disp.* 1538 (*FOR,* p. 145).

Stratton/Stretton, John: Pipewell; *sd.* and *d.* 1519, *p.* 1521 (Lincoln; *Reg. W. Atwater,* ff.127v, 128v; *Reg. J. Longland,* f. 2r).

Stretford, John: Stoneleigh: *d.* 1486, *p.* 1488 (Lichfield; *Reg. J. Hales,* ff. 216v, 240v).

Stretford, John: Kingswood; *disp.* 1489 (*CPL* 15, p. 226 [No. 457]).

Stretforth/Stratford, William: abbot, Vale Royal, 1495–1509+ (Warrington Archives, MS 596); *Close,* 1506, p. 246 [No. 647/xix]. general pardon, 1509 (*LP* 1, Part 1, p. 212 [No. 438/1, m. 18].

Stringshall/Strenshall, Guy: Medmenham; *d.* 1513, *p.* 1515 (Lincoln; *Reg. W. Smith,* n–f., *Reg. W. Atwater,* f. 115v); in community, 1535 (Plaisted, 1925, p. 185).

Strother, William: Newminster; *p.* 1497 (Durham; *Reg. R. Fox,* p. 49).

Studley/*al.* Hayter, John: Stanley, *disp.* 1536 (*FOR* 62); probably same monk as *John Stodeley,* q.v.

Sudeley, Thomas: Hailes, 1530/32 (Aveling, 1967, pp. 115, 131–32, 215–16)

Surdenalle, Ralph: Meaux; *sd.* 1525, *d.* 1526, *p.* 1528; pension, 1539, £6 (York; Cross and Vickers, 1995, pp. 155, 163).

?Sursett, Conrad: Croxden; *p.* 1493 (Lichfield; *Reg. W. Smith,* f. 171).

Sutton, Christopher: Jervaulx; *sd.* 1514, *d.* 1516, *p.* 1517 (York; Cross and Vickers, 1995, pp. 131, 137).

Sutton, Richard: Kirkstead, *disp.* 1537 (*FOR,* p. 96).

Sutton, Robert: Thame; *sd.* and *d.* 1505 (Lincoln; *Reg. W. Smith,* n.f.).

Sutton, Robert/Robarde: abbot, Stoneleigh, by 1504 (*Close,* 1506, p. 245 [No. 647/xviii]; general pardon, 1509 (*LP* 1, Part 1, p. 266 [No. 4/m. 17]); resigned 29 July 1532 with pension of £9–6–8 but continued to reside in the monastery (SSC, DR 10/996–97, 1194; DR18/1/721; 8/1/733; 18/30/24/74, f. 5; TNA, E36/154, ff.146v–147r).

Sutton, Thomas: Fountains; *sd.* 1486, *d.* 1487, *p.* 1491 (Cross and Vickers, 1995, p. 111).

Sutton, Thomas: Pipewell; *d.* 1514 (Lincoln; *Reg. T. Wolsey,* f. 14r); *p.* 1515 (*Reg. W. Atwater,* f. 112v).

Sutton, Thomas: abbot, Byland, 1497–1499 (Smith, 2008, p. 278).

Sutton, William: Byland; *sd.* and *d.* 1493, *p.* 1497 (York; Cross and Vickers, 1995, p. 98).

Sutton, William: Meaux; *ac.* 1517, *sd.* and *d.* 1518, *p.* 1520 (York; Cross and Vickers, 1995, p. 154).

Sutton: *see also* **Hampton**.

Swadell, John: Kirkstead; *d.* 1531, *p.* 1532 (Lincoln; *Reg. J. Longland,* ff. 28r, 30v).

Swaledale/Swadell, Thomas: Jervaulx; *sd.* 1505, *d.* 1506, *p.* 1507 (York); allegedly detained land deeds belonging to a layman 1533/38 (TNA, C1/785/21–22); at the Crown visitation in 1536 was alleged, perhaps spuriously, to have had illicit relations with a single woman. He may have been a chantry priest in Bedale parish, Yorkshire, in 1546–48, and in the latter year was said to be seventy–four and indifferently learned (Cross and Vickers, 1995, pp. 130, 137–38).

Swan, Edward: Meaux; *sd.* 1500, *p.* 1505 (York; Cross and Vickers, 1995, p. 154).

Swansea/Swensey, John: monk, Margam; *d.* 1498 (Worcester; *Reg. S. Gigli*, f. 27); *p.* 1498/9 (St. David's; *EPD* **2**, p. 719).

Swansea, John: Margam; *ac.* 1502 (St David's; *EPD* **2**, p.735; either this or the preceding entry were wrongly dated).

Swyneshed/Swineshead, John: Swinehead; *ac.* 1500, *sd.* 1501, *d.* 1502, *p.* 1505 (Lincoln; *Reg. W. Smith*, ff. 21r, 27r, 36v).

Swyneshed/Swineshead, Lambert: Swinehead; *ac.* 1500, *sd.* 1501, *d.* 1502, *p.* 1505 (Lincoln; *Reg. W. Smith*, ff. 21r, 27r, 36v, n–f.).

Swyneshed/Swineshead, Richard: Swinehead; *ac.* and *sd.* 1500, *d.* 1501, *p.* 1502 (Lincoln; *Reg. W. Smith*, ff. 21r, 22r, 27v, 37r). These three monks may not have been brothers; rather the registrar may have just adopted their monastery name as their common surname.

Swineshead: see also Shepherd.

Swyngton/Swynton, John: Biddlesden; *sd.* 1531, *d.* 1532, *p.* 1534 (Lincoln; *Reg. J. Longland*, ff. 28v, 31r, 38v).

Swynton, John: Jervaulx; *sd.* and *d.* 1521, *p.* 1522 (York; Cross and Vickers, 1995, p. 131).

Sydenham, John: Thame; *sd.* and *d.* 1525 (Lincoln; *Reg. J. Longland*, ff. 11r, 17r).

Sydnam, *al.* Stevens, Richard: Thame; *d.* 1538 (Lincoln; ordained in Thame church: *Reg. J. Longland*, f. 58r). May have been by 1542 a Minor Canon of Cardinal's College, Oxford, with a pension of £5; curate, Sydenham, Oxon. 1552 (Baskerville, 1930, p. 336); see also: *Richard Sardyns.*

Sygyswyk, Christopher: *see* Sedgwick.

Sylyfim/? *al.* Mardvode, William: Netley; *ac.* 1509, *d.* 1510 (Winchester, *Reg. R. Fox* **2**, ff. 25r, 26v).

Symmynge: *see* Coventry.

Symmyngs, Richard: Coggeshall, *disp.* 1538 (*FOR*, p. 124), and see: *Oliver Adams.*

Symondson, Henry: Rievaulx; *sd.* and *d.* 1492, *p.* 1495 (York; Cross and Vickers, 1995, p. 167).

Symond(s)/Simon, William: Stratford; *sd.* and *d.* 1533, *p.* 1534 (London; *Reg. R. Stokesley*, ff. 129r–v, 130r); signed deed of surrender and *disp.* 1538 (*DKR*, p. 42; *FOR*, pp. 123–24, 129); pension, £5 (TNA, E314/77).

Symondson, William: Holm Cultram; in house, 1533 (*LP* 6, pp. 425–26 [No. 988]); provisioner, when signed deed of surrender and disp. 1538 (*DKR*, p. 23; TNA, E314/20/11, f. 3r–d). In receipt of his pension of £5 in 1555 (TNA, E164/31, f.73). Called William Simpson in Gilbanks, 1899, p. 110.

Symondson: see also Helmsley.

Sympson: *see* Skerne.

Symyng/Symmynge: *se* Adams, Coventry.

Symys, Thomas: Roche, in 1486/1515; allegedly one of three who refused to deliver up property deeds to a layman, Richard Blyth (TNA, C1/119/26).

Syston, Thomas: last abbot, Garendon, by 1519–1536; held silver plate in safe keeping, ? 1515/18 (TNA, C1/390/ 26); involved in land dispute, 1533 (TNA, C1/736/7); alleged to have used seditious words early in 1536 to the effect that 'the king should be expelled from the realm and slain on his return' (*LP* **10**, p. 194 [No. 475]; *LP* **12**, Part 2, p. 283 [No. 800]); disp. 20–09–1536 (*FOR*, p. 74); pension, £30 p.a. (TNA, E315/278, f.47; E315/244, no. 53); later involved in proceedings regarding the possession of an inn called *The Sign of the George* in Loughborough, Leicestershire (Smith, 2008, p. 297).

Sythyll/Sillyl: *see* Lylly.

Tadcaster, Christopher: Kirkstead; *ac.* 1489, *d.* 1490/91, *p.* 1493 (Lincoln; *Reg. J. Russell*, ff. 31v, 37v, 40r, 49v).

Tadcaster, John: Kirkstead; *sd.* 1503 (Lincoln; *Reg. W. Smith*, f. 41v); abbot, 1522 (Smith, 2008, p. 306).

Talbot, John: abbot, Medmenham, 1535 (Smith, 2008, p. 313; *VE* 4, p. 251).

Talley, Richard: monk, Strata Florida; *sd., d.* and *p.* 1513 (Hereford; *Reg. R. Mayew*, pp. 261–63); B.Th. (Oxon.) 1526 (*BRUO* 2, p. 555); last abbot, ?1516–39, surviving an attempt in 1534 to oust him; *disp.* 1540 (*FOR*, p. 206), pension, £40 (*LP* 14, Part 1, p. 362 [No. 748]); vicar, Llangathen, Carms., 1544–, rector, Eglwys Gymun, Carmarthenshire. 1548–, held the prebendal church of Llandyfrïog, Cardiganshire., 1555– (TNA, E334/2, ff. 68, 165v; E334/4, f.192); *may* have become archdeacon of Cardigan, but not cited as such in E. Yardley, *Menevia Sacra*, AC Supplement, 1927; alive in 1558 (Williams, 2001, pp. 70, 87). In receipt of his pension in 1555 (TNA, E164/31, f. 75v).

? Talley, *al.* Atherston, Thomas: monk and chaplain, Merevale, 1497 (TNA, E315/283, f. 1).

Tamworth, Andrew: Merevale, 1497 (TNA, E315/283, f. 1).

Tamworth, Henry: Stoneleigh; *sd.* and *d.* 1529, *p.* 1530 (Lichfield; *Reg. G. Blyth*, n–f.); *disp.* 1537 (*FOR*, p. 88).

Tamworthe, John: Merevale; *d.* 1503 (Lichfield; *sede v.*, CCA, DCc–Reg. f. 287r); *p.* 1504 (Lichfield; *Reg. G. Blyth*, n.f.). Listed as a monk there in 1497 (TNA, E315/283, f. 1).

Tamworth, Meredith: Merevale, *sd.* 1–06–1482; *d.* 19–09–1482; *p.* 22–02–1483 (Lichfield Cathedral; *Reg. J. Hales*, ff. 279r, 280r, 281v.

Tamworth: *see also* Masham/Marsham.

Tamworth, William: Bordesley; *d.* 1528 (Worcester; *Reg. R. Morton addenda*, f. 166); three monks of Bordesley bore this Christian name, and given that Tamworth perhaps indicates his place of origin, he may be one of those monks bearing the family surname of *Edwards* or *Steward*.

Tanfeld, William: Fountains; *sd.* 1486, *d.* 1487, *p.* 1491 (Cross and Vickers, 1995, p. 111).

Tanfield, William: Rievaulx; *p.* 1534 (York; Cross [1995] 170, 185); listed in 1533 (TNA, STAC2/7/217). Perhaps the same monk as *William Wordale*, q.v.

Tate, Thomas: Stratford; *ac.* 1522 (LPL; *Reg. W. Warham* 2, f. 297r).

Tate: *see also* Drake.

Tat(er)sall/Tatteshall, John: Kirkstead; *p.* 1502 (Lincoln; *Reg. W. Smith*, f. 35v); *disp.* 1537 (FOR, p. 96).

Tatersall, John: Kirkstead; *d.* 1530 (Lincoln; *Reg. J. Longland*, f. 26r).

Taunton, Robert: Cleeve; *sd.* 1487, *d.* and *p.* 1488 (Wells; *Reg. R. Stillington*, ff. 222r, 226v, 230v).

Taylor, Giles: former monk of Furness; giving evidence in 1543 he said that he was now 'thirty years and above' (*AF*, p. lxxxix). Perhaps he was *Giles Bolland*, q.v.

Taylor, John: Tilty; *sd.* 1493, *d.* and *p.* 1494 (London; *Reg. R. Hill*, ff. 28v, 29r, 29v).

Taylor, Richard: Jervaulx; *d.* 1499 (Winchester; *Reg. T. Langton*, f. 34r).

Taylor, Richard: Buckfast; *sd.* and *d.* 1512, *p.* 1515 (Exeter; *Reg. H. Oldham*, ff. 107v, 110r, 122v); present at its suppression, 1539 (*DKR*, p. 12); in receipt of pension of £5–6–8 in 1555 (TNA, E164/31, f. 34r); chaplain, Widecombe, Devon, 1540/41, chantry priest, Ermyngton, Devon (Stéphan, 1970, p. 214).

Taylor, Richard: native of Northampton; monk, Biddlesden; later vicar of Thornborough, Buckinghamshire, where, unmarried, was still alive in 1552 (Green, 1974, p. 25). Not listed in the pension list (TNA, E314/77) unless he had an *alias*.

Taylor, Robert: 'Stanlake', probably Stoneleigh; visited Rome, 1507 (Foley, 1880, p. 546).

Taylor, Robert: *see* Robert Northampton.

Taylor, Thomas: Boxley; last abbot, Robertsbridge, elected 5 September 1523 (SAL, *MS 14*, ff. 58v–59v); probably B.D. (Oxon). 1532 (Stevenson, 1939, p. 48); signed deed of surrender and *disp.* 1538 (*DKR*, p. 39; *FOR*, p. 135); pension, £50 (TNA, E314/77),; still alive in 1553 (Cooper, 1956, pp. 170–71); seemingly dead by 1555 (Salzman, 1954, p. 34).

Taylor, Thomas: two monks of this name at Bordesley, *disp.* 1538 (*FOR*, p. 149; TNA, E322/26); the more senior was in receipt of pension of £5–6–8 as late as 1555, the junior of £4 (TNA, E164/31, f. 44r).

Taylor, Thomas: *see also* Toller.

Tayntour, John: Revesby; *p.* 1488 (Lincoln; *Reg. J. Russell*, f. 28v).

Terell, John: Fountains, *sd.* 1503, *d.* 1504, *p.* 1506 (York; Cross, 1995, p. 112)

Terne, Thomas: Furness; *p.* 1502 (York; *Reg. T. Savage*, f. 113r).

Tery, Edward: Fountains, *sd.* 1499, *p.* 1501 (York; Cross, 1995, p. 112).

Tetbury, Walter: Kingswood; *ac.* and *sd.* 1492 (Worcester; *Reg. R. Morton*, f. 152); *d.* 1502 (Wells; *Reg. O. King*, f. 119).

Tetter/Tyder: *see* Etherway.

Tewisdaye, John: Fountains; pension, 1539: £6 (Cross and Vickers, 1995, p. 115); and see: *Kepas.*

?Thamworth, James: Rewley; *p.* 1514 (Lincoln; *Reg. W. Atwater*, f. 111r).

Thaxted, John: abbot, Tilty, in 1485–1487 (Smith, 2008, p. 340).

Thaxted/Hogeson, John: monk, Tilty; *sd.* 1523 (London; *Reg. C. Tunstall*, 1v; *CL*); signed deed of surrender and *disp.* 1536; could he have moved to Coggeshall and was his family name, *Hogeson*? (*DKR*, p. 45, *FOR*, p. 50).

Thaxted, John: Coggeshall, *disp.* 1538 (*FOR*, p. 124).

Therniworth/*al.* Clarke, Thomas: Combe, *disp.* 1538 (*DKR*, pp. 16–17, *FOR*, p. 176).

Thirsk, *al.* Cawton, Harry/Henry: Rievaulx; *p.* 1531 (York); listed in 1533 (TNA, STAC2/7/217); once relayed a prophecy that Rievaulx would be no more (Aveling, 1952, p. 111); signed deed of surrender and *disp.* 1538; pension, £6 (*DKR*, p. 38; *FOR*, p. 156); a native of Thirsk where his brother still resided, he was curate of Hovingham, Yorkshire, in 1546 and perhaps later vicar of Strensall; he still drew his pension in 1582 (Cross and Vickers, 1995, pp. 170, 174–75).

Thirsk, Robert: Byland; *ac* and *sd.* 1521, *d.* 1522, *p.* 1524 (York; Cross and Vickers, 1995, p. 99).

Thirsk, William: son of Alice Perte of Thirsk; monk, Fountains, *sd.* 1503, *d.* 1504, *p.* 1506 (York); scholar, St Bernard's College, Oxford, 1519; B.Th., 1521; D. Th. 1528; 32nd abbot, 1526–1536 (Smith, 2008, p. 293; *LP* **4**, p. 3103 [No. 85]); forced to resign in 1536, when granted a pension from the abbey of £66–13–4; moved to Jervaulx, implicated in the Pilgrimage of Grace, executed at Tyburn, 25 May 1537 (Cross and Vickers, 1995, pp. 113, 116–17; Dodds **2**, 1915, p. 213; Gasquet, 1899, pp. 257–58, 263)

Thomas ap Harry: monk, Margam; *p.* 1497 (St David's); the same name is repeated for the grade of acolyte in 1502. Could there be an error in compilation of the episcopal register? (St David's; *EPD* **2**, pp. 719, 735).

Thomas ap Rhys: abbot, Whitland, 1491–?1527; alive in 1531 (*Statuta* **6**, p. 22 [No. 1491/50]; TNA, E315/92/91d; SC6/4903, mm. 26d–27r; Williams, 2001, pp. 63, 65, 72); *c.*1491/92 an enquiry of unknown date, but perhaps of the 1490s, heard that he was alleged to have distrained a total of three horses, thirty oxen and twelve loads of hay from some seven tenants and of evicting one of them; perhaps he saw these as dues (four oxen in most cases) on his accession as abbot (Oxfordshire R.O., P6/32D/1).

Thomas ... : abbot, Stoneleigh, by 1480 until at least 1493 (Smith, 2008, p. 334).

Thomas ../. : abbot, Tilty, 1495 (Smith, 2008, p. 340).

Thomas ... : abbot, Stanley, 1495–1523 (Smith, 2008, p. 333).

Thomas ... : abbot, Margam, ?c. 1497 (but there may be an error in dating; E.A. Lewis (ed.), *Early Chancery Proceedings Concerning Wales*, Cardiff: University of Wales Press, 1937, p. 192).

Thomas ... : abbot, Netley, 1496 (Smith, 2008, p. 316).

Thomas ... : abbot, Cwmhir, 1499–1508 (*Radnorshire Historical Soc. Transactions* **34**, 1964, pp. 25–29).

Thomas ... : abbot, Kirkstead, 1503–1505 (Smith, 2008, p. 306).

Thomas ....: abbot, Byland, 1509–... (Smith, 2008, p. 278).

Thomas ...: abbot, Garendon, 1510–1514; either *Jens* or *Syston* (Smith, 2008, p. 297).

Thomas ... : abbot, Sawtry, *c.*1530 (Smith, 2008, p. 330).

Thomas, David: Neath; *disp.* 1539 (*FOR*, p. 170); in receipt of his pension of pension of £3–6–8 p.a. In 1555 (TNA, E164/31, f. 77v).

Thomas, Jasper *al.* **Jasper ap Roger:** Llantarnam; *p.* 1528 (Worcester; *Reg. R. Morton addenda*, f. 167); last abbot, by 1533–1536; pension, £15 p.a. (TNA, E315/244, No. 152; Williams, 1976, pp. 86–87).

Thomas, John: Margam; *d.* 1498 (Worcester; *Reg. G. Gigli*, f. 27); *p.* 1498/9 (St David's; *EPD* **2**, p. 719).

Thomas, John: Neath; *disp.* 1539 (*FOR*, p. 179); last prior (TNA, E314/77); pension, £4 (Birch, 1897, pp. 150, 154). In receipt of his pension in 1555 (TNA, E164/31, f. 77v).

Thomas, Lewis: monk, Neath; *d.* 1523 (London; LMA, *Reg. C. Tunstall*, f. 2v; ordained in St Bartholomew's Hospital by Thomas Bale, OSA, Bishop of Lydda; *p.* 1524 (Lincoln, ordained in Buckden parish church, *Reg. J. Longland*, f. 10r); in 1527 accompanied the abbot of Bective on a visitation of Mellifont abbey, Ireland (Fr Colmcille, *The Story of Mellifont*, Dublin: M.H. Gill & Son, 1958, pp. 162–63); last abbot, Margam, 1529–36; a definitor of the Order and confessor at General Chapter, 1530; *disp.* 1537, pension, £20 p.a. (Birch, 1897, pp. 358–59; *Letters*, p. 252, p. 71; *FOR*, p. 90). Either Lewis or Lewis ap Thomas, *q.v.* was admitted to the B.C.L. degree at Oxford in 1534 (*BRUO* **2**, pp. 562–63).

Thomas, Robert: Tintern, *disp.* 1536; there was a Robert Thomas at Thame at its later dissolution in 1539 (*FOR*, p. 80, *DKR*, p. 43); Robert Thomas [Thame], pension, £5–6–8 (TNA, E314/77).

Thomas, Robert: Margam, *disp.* 1536 (*FOR*, p. 68).

Thomas, William: Cleeve; *sd.* and *d.* 1500, *p.* 1502 (Wells; *Reg. O. King*, ff. 113–14, 120).

Thomas, William: Cwmhir; *sd.* 1527 (Hereford; *Reg. C. Bothe*, pp. 322–23); perhaps the later William ap Thomas, stipendiary priest serving Cwmhir's former Gwernygo grange chapel in 1547 (Williams, 2001, p. 87).

Thomson, Robert: Sawtry; *sd.* 1512 (Lincoln; *Reg. W. Smith*, n–f.).

T(h)ompson, Thomas: Netley; *d.* 1509 (Winchester; *Reg. R. Fox* **2**, f. 25r); in community, 1518, by which time priested (TNA, E314/101).

Thomson/Thompson, Thomas: Coggeshall; *ex.* and *ac.* 1514, *d.* 1515 (London; *Reg. R. Fitzjames*, ff. 178r [167r], 180r [169r]).

T(h)omson, Thomas: Meaux; *ac.* and *sd.* 1520, *d.* 1521, *p.* 1524 (York); pension, £6; may have been either vicar of Humbleton, Holderness, 1540–1559, or rector of Hemingford Abbots, Cambridge-shire, 1555 (Cross and Vickers, 1995, pp. 155–56, 164); died in Lincolnshire, 1563 (Hodgett, 1959, p. 134).

Thompson, William: *see* Heslerton.

Thorlis, Denis/Throppele. Dener: Newminster, thirty–five years old in 1536 (TNA, SC12/13/65); *disp.* 1536 (*FOR*, p. 77).

Thormonby, William: Byland; *d.* 1480, *p.* 1482 (York; Cross and Vickers, 1995, p. 98).

Thornbergh/Thornebarr, Christopher: Whalley; *p.* 1464 (Lichfield; *Reg. J. Hales*, f. 194v); abbot, Whalley, 1481–1487 (Smith, 2008, p. 350).

Thornbrae/Thornborough, Michael: Furness, *disp.* 1537 (*FOR*, p. 97); after suppression became vicar of St Michael's–on–Wyre, Lancashire (Haigh, 1969, p. 120). Could he be also known as *Michael Hamilton/Hampton*, q.v.

Thornor, John: Kirkstall, *sd.* 1509, *p.* 1515 (York; Cross and Vickers, 1995, p. 140).

Thornton, *al.* Topinger, Toppyng, Henry: Byland; *ac.* and *sd.* 1503, *p.* 1504 (York); denounced, perhaps spuriously, for self abuse at the Crown visitation in 1536; *disp.* 1538 (*DKR*, p. 13, *FOR*, p. 181); pension £5–6–8; possibly vicar of Hockerton, Nottinghamshire, in 1560, and later prebendary of Southwell and alive in 1571 (Cross and Vickers, 1995, pp. 99–100, 108).

Thorn(e)ton, John: Jervaulx; *ac.* and *sd.* 1522, *d.* and *p.* 1524 (York; Cross and Vickers, 1995, p. 131).

Thornton, John: Furness, Signed suppression deed (Haigh, 1969, pp. 97, 145).

Thornton, John: Croxden, signed deed of surrender and *disp.* 1538 (Hibbert, 1910, p. 222; *FOR*, p. 151); pension, £4 (TNA, E315/233, f.17v).

Thornton, Percival: Sawley; *sd.* and *d.* 1535, *p.* 1536 (York; Cross and Vickers, 1995, p. 201); *disp.* 1536 (*FOR*, p. 58).

Thornton, Robert: Jervaulx; *sd.* 1501, *d.* 1503 (York; Cross and Vickers, 1995, p. 130); *? p.* 1503 (Lincoln; *Reg. W. Smith*, f.41r); 22nd abbot of Jervaulx, 1511–1532; disp. to hold a benefice *in commendam*, 1516 (*CPL* **20**, pp. 387–88 [No. 555]; member of the Corpus Christi Guild of York; his personal black chasuble survives in the Victoria and Albert Museum (M. Carter, 'Thornton, Robert,' *ODNB* on–line); grave slab now in Middleham church, Yorkshire (Smith, 2008, p. 302).

Thornton, Thomas: Biddlesden; *ac.* 1487, *d.* 1491, *p.* 1493 (Lincoln; *Reg. J. Russell*, ff. 25v, 40v, 50r).

Thornton, William: Rievaulx; *sd.* and *d.* (York) 1492, *p.* 1495 (Cross and Vickers, 1995, p. 168).

Thornton, William: Calder; *p.* 1507 (York; *Reg. T. Savage*, f. 140r); acted as a chaplain in the local parish of St Bridget; accused, perhaps spuriously, of sodomy in Crown visitation of 1535 (*LP* **10**, p. 138 [No. 364]; Loftie, 1892, p. 80).

Thorp, Richard: Jervaulx; *sd.* 1484, *d.*1496 (York; Cross and Vickers, 1995, p. 129).

Thorpe, Thomas: Byland; *ac.* and *sd.* 1485, *d.* 1487, *p.* 1489 (York; Cross and Vickers, 1995, p. 98).

Thorp/Sharp, William: Rievaulx; *sd.* 1497, *d.* 1498 (York; Cross and Vickers, 1995, p. 168).

Thorp, William: Kirkstall, *ac.* 1513, *sd.* 1514, *d.* 1516, *p.* 1519 (York; Cross and Vickers, 1995, p. 141).

Thourne, William: Meaux; *p.* 1509 (York; Cross and Vickers, 1995, p. 154).

Thresher, William: Stratford; *sd.* 1507, *d.* 1508, *p.* 1511 (London; *Reg. R. Fitzjames*, ff. 95r, 99v, 161v [172r]).

Throstill, George: Meaux; *ac.* and *sd.* 1504, *d.* 1505 (York); bursar, 1538, then last prior; pension of only £6; died 1545 (Cross and Vickers, 1995, pp. 154, 156, 165). Sometimes mis–transcribed as *Chrastell*.

Thrower/Thower, Lawrence: Robertsbridge, 1523 (SAL, *MS 14*, f. 59v); signed deed of surrender and *disp.* 1538 (*DKR*, p. 39; *FOR*, p. 135); in receipt of his pension of £6 in 1555 (TNA, E164/31, f. 25v).

Thurgood/Thorowgood, Robert: sub–prior, Robertsbridge, 1523 *(SAL MS 14*, f. 59v); signed deed of surrender, 1538 (*DKR*, p. 39); pension, £8 (TNA, E314/77).

Thurne, Thomas: abbot, Roche, briefly from 19–12–1486 (Aveling, 1870, p. 64).

Tibbe/Tibbs, John: Dunkeswell; *sd.* 1509, *d.* 1510, *p.* 1515 (Exeter; *Reg. H. Oldham*, ff. 99r, 103r, 122v).

Ticehurst, Lawrence: Robertsbridge; *ac.* 1512, *sd.* 1514 (LPL; *Reg. W. Warham* **2**, f. 266r–v); *d.* 1514, *p.* 1515 (London; *Reg. R. Fitzjames*, ff. 178v, 180r). Might he be *Lawrence Thrower?* q.v.

Tichemarshe/Titchmarshh, John: Pipewell; *d.* 1514, *p.* 1519 (Lincoln; *Reg. T. Wolsey*, f. 14r; *Reg. W. Atwater*, f. 129r).

Tickhill, William: abbot, Roche, 1479 (Aveling, 1870, pp. 62–3).

Ti(c)khill, William: Rufford; *sd.* 1505, *d.* 1506, *p.* 1508 (York; *Reg. T. Savage*, ff. 131v, 133r; *sede vacante*, f. 604r).

Tintern, John: Tintern; 1513–28, cellarer at times (NLW, Badminton Manorial 1657, mm. 1d, 4d, 13d).

Tintern, Thomas: Tintern, *sd.* 1524, *p.* 1525, *disp.* 1537 (Hereford; *Reg. C. Bothe*, pp. 317, 319; FOR, p. 91). The next entry suggests that his entry as priest in 1525 was in error, and that in fact he was made deacon then.

Tintern, Thomas: Tintern; *p.* 1528 (Worcester; *Reg. R. Morton addenda*, f. 167)

***Tiverton*, Nicholas:** Cleeve; *d.* 1509 (Wells; *Reg. H. de Castello, f.* 150); *p.* 1510 (Exeter; *Reg. H. Oldham*, f. 103r).

Todd *al* Alkelond/Auckland, Thomas: sub–prior, Biddlesden, *disp.* 1538; pension, £6 (FOR, p. 179; Green, 1974, pp. 63–64; TNA, E322/22). He is listed as cellarer in *TNA, E314/77*; and as both sub–prior and cellarer in *LP* **13**, Part 2, p. 162 [Nos. 421–22].

Todenham/Todman//Cadenham, John: Bruern; *sd.* and *d.* 1512 (Lincoln; *Reg. W. Smith*, n–f.); *p.* 1517 (*Reg. W. Atwater*, f. 122v); still in house at its suppression, 1536 (Baskerville, 1930, p. 334).

Toker/Tucker, John: Buckland; *sd.* and *d.* 1503; *p.* 1505 (Exeter; *Reg. J. Arundell*, ff. 13v–14r; *Reg. H. Oldham*, f. 83v); blessed as abbot, Exeter Cathedral, 7 June 1528 (Gill, 1968, p. 40); in 1533 received a loan of £40, repayment of which was delayed (TNA, C1/1034/53–54); last abbot, *disp.* 1539 (*DKR*, p. 12; *FOR*, p. 178); pension, £60, received as late as 1555 (TNA, E164/31, f. 34r); after suppression, said to have been employed by John Peter senior, as a chaplain in 1540/41 at Torre Bryant, Devon (*Devonshire Notes and Queries* **17**, 1932, p. 92).

Toker, John: Newenham; *sd.* 1530, *d.* 1532 (Exeter; *Reg. J. Vesey*, ff. 171v, 179r).

Toller, Thomas: Woburn; *sd.* 1500, *d.* 1501, *p.* 1505 (Lincoln; *Reg. W. Smith*, ff. 24r, 26v, n–f.); curate, Woburn, 1538; by 1558, became rector, Stibbington, Huntingdonshire (Thomson, 1933, p. 140).

Toller: *see also* Colles.

Topclif, David/?Richard: Rievaulx; *sd.* 1522, *d.* 1524, *p.* 1526; not mentioned in the pension lists (York; Cross and Vickers, 1995, pp. 169, 182).

Topclif, Robert: Jervaulx; *p.* 1513 (York; Cross and Vickers, 1995, p. 130). Perhaps a mistaken entry.

Topclif, Robert: Jervaulx; *sd.* 1513, *d.* 1515, *p.* 1517 (York; Cross and Vickers, 1995, p. 131).

Topinger/ Tappyng, Henry: Byland: *see* **Thornton**. *disp.* 1538 (*DKR*, p. 13, FOR, p. 181).

Toppe/Tappe/Toope,/Topy, Robert: Buckland; *sd.* 1508, *d.* 1509, *p.* 1510 (Exeter; *Reg. H. Oldham*, ff. 98r–v, 103r); disp. 1538; pension, £5–6–8 (TNA, E314/20/11, f. 2r; FOR, p. 135; Gill, 1951, p. 38).

Tort: *see* Ampleforth.

Toton: *see* Towton.

Tottenham/Totnam, Richard: abbot, Quarr; blessed 3 March 1509 in Esher manor chapel by the bishop of Winchester (*Reg. R. Fox* **2**, f. 24r); general pardon, 1509 (*LP* **1**, Part 1, p. 270 [4/m.24]; dispensed to receive a secular benefice *in commendam* (*CPL* **19**, p. 374 [No. 679]); resigns, 1525; dies 1533 (Hockey, 1970, p. 260).

Touclif, Robert: Kirkstall, *sd.* 1505, *d.* 1506, *p.* 1507 (York; Cross and Vickers, 1995, p. 140).

Towell: *see* Twells.

Townesman, William: *see* Turner.

Towton/Toton, John: abbot, Combe, 1495–1512 (Smith, 2008, pp. 281–82); general pardon, 1509 (*LP* **1**, Part 1, p. 260 [No. 4/m.8]).

Toye, Hugh: Buildwas; *sd.* and *d.* 1514, *p.* 1515 (Lichfield; *Reg. G. Blyth*, n–f.).

Trafford, William: very doubtfully ascribed as last abbot, Sawley; second son of Sir John Trafford; hanged at Lancaster, 10 March 1537 (Gasquet, 1899, p. 270; Harland, 1853, p. 47). Not listed as abbot by Smith, 2008, p. 329.

Trebbe: *see* Tibbe.

Trennethde, Paul: Hailes, 1517 (*CHA*, p. 104 [No. 37]).

Trent, Roger: Buckfast; *d.* 1489 (Exeter; *Reg. R. Fox*, f. 153r); *p.* 1490 (*Reg. O. King*, f. 157r).

Trewinan, William: sub–prior, Bordesley, 1480, when he presented monks of the abbey for ordination (Worcester; *Reg. J. Alcock*, f. 261).

Troughton, John: Furness; *sd.* 1516, *d.* and *p.* 1517 (York; *Reg. T. Wolsey*, ff. 174v, 175v, 177v).signed deed of surrender and *disp.* 1537 (TNA, E322/91; *FOR*, p. 97). Might he be the *John Broughton* mentioned above?

Tunstall, William: Combe, *sd.* 1531, *d.* 1532 (Lichfield; *Reg. G. Blyth*, n–f.).

Turnar/Townesman, William: Merevale; signed suppression deed, 1538 (TNA, E322/151); pension, £5–6–8 TNA,E315/233, f. 62v).

Tutbury, Henry: Hailes; *ac.* 1497, *d.* 1499 (Worcester; *Reg. G. Gigli*, f. 25, *S. Gigli*, f. 395); moved to Dore 'for many reasons' including age and peace of mind, 1516 (SSC, DR 18/31/5, f. 17r).

Tutbury, Thomas: Bordesley; *sd.* 1486 (Lichfield; *Reg. J. Hales*, f. 216v); *p.* 1488 (Worcester; *Reg. R. Morton*, f. 142).

Tutbury, Thomas: Stoneleigh; *sd.* 1506, *d.* 1507, *p.* 1509 (Lichfield; *Reg. G. Blyth*, n–f.); last abbot, Stoneleigh, by 1533 (SSC, DR 10/1304; DR 18/30/24/74 [his account book for 1536/37]; *disp.* 1537 (*FOR*, p. 88); in receipt of pension of £23 as late as 1555 (TNA, E164/31, f. 48r); said in 1554 to be sixty–four but that cannot be correct, and in 1559 gave evidence in disputes regarding former lands of his monastery (SSC, DR18/1/1061; 18/3/47/43).

Tutbury, William: Bordesley; *d.* 1485, *p.* 1487 (Lichfield; *Reg. J. Hales*, ff. 216v, 233v).

Tutbury, William: abbot, Flaxley, 1487–1503 (Gloucestershire Archives, D1448/T31; Smith, 2008, p. 290). Could he be the preceding monk?

Tutylle, Thomas: Fountains; pension, 1539, £6; alive in 1555; *may* have been *Thomas Bradford* or *Thomas Wentbrig*, monks of Fountains (Cross and Vickers, 1995, pp. 115, 128).

Twells/Twellis/Towell, Thomas: Roche; *sd., d.* and *p.* 1522 (York); sub–prior, signed deed of surrender, 1538 (TNA, E322/204); *disp.* 1538 (*FOR*, p. 144). In receipt of £6–13–4 pension as late as 1555 (TNA, E164/31, f.53r); signed letters testimonial, 1555. In his will of 16–11–1558, he describes himself as 'Sir Thomas Twelves of Blyth, a Nottinghamshire priest'. Thomas left money to the poor of Blyth and surrounding villages, and a chalice to Sheffield parish church in return for a mass for his father and himself (*CIY* project; Cross and Vickers, 1995, pp. 187, 196–97, 201).

Tybbes: *see* Chard.

Tybsun, Thomas: Dunkeswell, at its suppression, 1539; pension, £4–13–4 (TNA, E322/76; Sparks, 1978, pp. 109–10); chaplain or vicar, Uffcolme, Devon, 1540/41 (*Devonshire Notes and Queries* **17**, 1932, p. 83); later ministered at Sampford Peverell, Devon, and died in 1566 (Snell, 1967, pp. 113, 146).

Tyler, Adam: Hailes, *disp.* 1540 (*FOR*, p. 208); in receipt of pension of £5 as late as 1555 (TNA, E164/31, f. 40r); living in Abingdon, Berks. 1552–53; may have been vicar of Bramford, Suffolk, 1541; rector, Barking, Suffolk, 1554–64; rector, Tattingstone, Suffolk, 1552–59 (Hailes had property in Suffolk: Baskerville, 1927, p. 90).

Tyllesley, James: Revesby; *p.* 1508 (Lincoln; *Reg. W. Smith,* n–f.); died 1556/57 (Hodgett, 1959, p. 149).

Tyrrell, John: a wayward monk of Fountains, but rehabilitated by Abbot Darnton of Fountains, who died in 1495 *(Letters,* pp. 266–67 [No. 138], 269 [No. 140]).

Tyrry, Edward: Fountains, 1520, when rehabilitated after plotting to oust his abbot, Marmaduke Huby *(Letters,* p. 259 [No. 131]; at Newminster by 1523 when described by Lord Dacre as 'my monk' *(LP* **3**, Part 2, p. 1324 [No. 3171]); last abbot, Newminster, 1527–1536 (TNA, LR1/173, ff. 62, 65, 74–75; Smith, 2008, p. 318); fifty-five years old in 1536 (TNA, SC12/13/645); pension, 1536, £30 p.a., (TNA,E315/244, no. 97); in receipt of pension, 1538 (Gasquet, 1899, p. 269).

Tyseherst: *see* Ticehurst.

Tyson: *see* Dyson.

Ulharston/Ulverston: Fountains; *sd.* 1486, *d.* 1487, *p.* 1491 (Cross and Vickers, 1995, p. 111).

Upgrypyth: *see* Grysome.

Upton, Robert: Sawtry, *sd.* 1491, *d.* 1492, *p.* 1494 (Lincoln; *Reg. J. Russell,* ff. 38r, 43/44r, 51v).

Valode, Richard: Fountains; *sd.* 1511 (York; Cross and Vickers, 1995, p. 113).

Van': *see* Fanne.

Vachan, Gwilym: Llantarnam, 1470, when seeks dispensation on account of defect of birth; could he be Gwilym Moris ap Hywel Vachan previously of Neath, *q.v.*? *(SAP* **2**, p. 71 [No. 1591]. Sought a further dispensation in 1482 permitting his advancement to an abbacy *(SAP* **2**, p. 246 [No. 2480]).

Vaughan, David: Aberconwy, *disp.* 10–04–1537 *(FOR,* p. 91; Hays, 1963, p. 179).

Vayn/Vaughan, Richard: abbot, Cwmhir, 1516–30 (Williams, 2001, p. 70); noted in a lease of 1520 (NLW, Powis Castle Deed 12645). A Richard Vaughan was rector of Bishopston, Glamorgan, in 1554 – but he is very unlikely to have been the former abbot (TNA, E334/2, f. 187v).

Vaghane, William: Rewley; *sd.* 1507, *d.* 1508 (Salisbury; *Reg. E. Audley,* ff. 7v, 9v).

Vayn/Vaughan, *al.* **ap Thomas, William:** last abbot, Whitland, 1527–39; in arrears to late Cardinal Wolsey for a faculty granted prior to 23–10–1530 *(LP* **4**, Part 3, p. 3048 (No. 6748/14); *disp.* 1540; pension, £40 p.a. *(FOR,* p. 206, Williams, 2001, p. 72).

Vaynsworth, Henry: Kirkstall, *sd.* 1488, *d.* 1489, *p.* 1491 (York; Cross and Vickers, 1995, p. 139).

Veyr, Thomas: Dunkeswell; *p.* 1509 (Exeter; *Reg. H. Oldham,* f. 100v).

Vhythy, John: Buckland; *disp.* 1488 *(CPL* **15**, p. 164 [No. 336]).

Vizes (De Vizes), John: Stanley; *sd., d.* and *p.* 1507 (Salisbury; *Reg. E. Audley,* ff.7v, 8r, 8v).

Vizes, Roger: Stanley; *sd.* 1510, *d.* and *p.* 1511 (Salisbury; *Reg. E. Audley,* ff. 15v, 16v, 17r).

Wacy/Wasy, John: Dunkeswell; *ac.* and *sd.* 1489; *d.* and *p.* 1490 (Exeter; *Reg. R. Fox,* ff. 153v–154r, 156r).

Wadell: *see* **Wordyll.**

Wadderell: *see* **Wetherall.** .

Wade, John: Netley; in community, 1518, by which time priested (TNA, E314/101); died 1530 (E. Kell, 'Netley Abbey.' In: *Collectanea Archaeologica* **2**, 1871, p. 68.

Wade, Richard: Tintern; *disp.* 1536 *(FOR,* p. 80).

Wadworth/Walworth, John: son of William Walworth of Ripon; monk, Fountains; *p.* April, 1538 (Lincoln; *Reg. J. Longland,* f. 57v); pension, 1539: £5 (Cross and Vickers, 1995, pp. 115, 128).

Waghen, Peter: Meaux; *sd.* 1525, *d.* 1526 (York; Cross, 1995, pp. 155; 165); perhaps the same monk as *Peter Stamper,* q.v.

Waghorn, William: Rewley; *ac.* 1506, *p.* 1509 (Lincoln; *Reg. W. Smith,* n–f.).

Wainflet, John: sub–prior, Merevale, 1497 (TNA, E315/283, f. 1).

Waite: *see* Whitby.

Wakefield, Richard: Sawley; ac. 1506, sd. 1507, p. 1510 (York; Cross and Vickers, 1995, p. 200); *disp.* 1536 (*FOR*, p. 58).

Wakefield, Thomas: Jervaulx; sd. and d. 1521, p. 1522 (York; Cross and Vickers, 1995, p. 131).

Waker, Robert: Furness, *disp.* 1537 (*FOR*, p. 97). His signature is not on the surrender deed (*DKR*, p. 21). Could he have been the monk, *Robert Kechen*?

Wakering, Stephen: Boxley, *disp.* 1505 (*CPL* **18**, p. 403 [No. 561]).

Wakerley, John: Stoneleigh; sd. 1499, d. 1500 (Lichfield; *Reg. J. Arundel*, ff. 282, 286); p. 1503 (Lincoln; *Reg. W. Smith*, f. 41v); sub–prior, 1510 (SSC, DR18/1/907).

Waldegrave, William: Pipewell; collector of contributions for the Cistercian Order, 1505–1506 (TNA, E328/26/vi, xvii).

Walenger, George: Boxley; *t.* and *ac.* 1520 (Rochester; *Reg. J. Fisher*, f. 89v).

Wal(l)ingford, William: Thame; sd. and d. 1525 (Lincoln; *Reg. J. Longland*, ff. 11r, 17r).

Walker, George: Louth Park; d. 1494, p. 1499 (Lincoln; *Reg. J. Russell*, f. 52r; *Reg. W. Smith*, n. f.); last abbot there, by 1509–1536; general pardon, 1509; *disp.* 4–05–1537 (FOR, p. 95); still in receipt of £26–13–4 pension in 1552, though for a time in arrears; in 1554 was resident at Saltfleetby, Lincolnshire, aged eighty–six years, and too ill to travel; was unmarried; died 1558 (Hodgett, 1959, pp. 37, 57, 103, 130).

Walker, Thomas: Flaxley; sd. 1475, d. and p. 1476 (Hereford; *Reg. T. Myllyng*, pp. 155, 157–58).

Wall, Thomas: Bordesley, *disp.* 1538 (*FOR*, p. 149; TNA, E322/26); pension, £6 (TNA, E314/77); assessed for subsidy in 1540 (Bodleian Library, Oxford, Tanner MS 343).

Wallas/Waller, John: Meaux; d. 1531, p. 1533 (York); pension, £5; probably curate of Winestead, 1547, and of Welwick, Yorkshire, 1551, perhaps in plurality; aged fifty in 1552; alive in 1556 (Cross and Vickers, pp. 155–56, 165).

Waller, Roger: Furness; vicar, Dalton, by 1535–1551 (Haigh, 1969, p. 120; *FOR*, p. 97).

Wallingford, William: Quarr; sd. 1497 Winchester; *Reg. T. Langton*, f. 31v).

Walmesley, Roger: Roche; sd. 1484, d. 1485, p. 1487 (Cross and Vickers, 1995, p. 186).

Walshe/Waleys, John: abbot, Bindon, by 1515–1523 (TNA, C1/282/25; Smith, 2008, p. 269).

Walter … : procurator, Newminster; a line missing in the script makes it impossible to determine his date (TNA, LR1/173, ff. 64d–65r).

Walter, Reinald: Hailes; d. 1527 (Worcester; *Reg. G. Ghinucci*, f. 186).

Walton, John, *al.* Checkley: ?1467–1507, abbot, said to be the 22nd' of Croxden, though a John Blundell is noted in 1476 (Smith, 2008, p. 286).

Walton, Lionel [*Leonellus*]: Stanley; *ex.* and *ac.* 1499 (Salisbury; *Reg. J. Blyth*, f. 115v).

Walton, Robert: Tilty; p. 1486 (Lincoln; *Reg. J. Russell*, f. 22v).

Walton, Robert: abbot, Sawtry; general pardon, 1510 (*LP* **1**, Part 1, p. 229 [No. 438/2, m. 25]. Mentioned as a pensioner in 1526 (Smith, 2008, p. 330).

Walton, William: Biddlesden; ac. and sd. 1509 (Lincoln; *Reg. W. Smith*, n–f.).

Walton, *al.* Waulton/ Kirkby, William: Byland; sd. 1537 (York); *disp.* 1539 (*DKR*, p. 13); d. and p. 1539 (after suppression of his monastery); pension, £4; probably vicar of West Markham (from May 1538) and later Barlborough, Yorkshire, in plurality until 1572, when exchanged latter for North Wheatley, but that year lost both livings for failing to subscribe to the articles or religion (Cross and Vickers, 1995, p. 109).

Wardale, Peter: Stratford: *ex.* and *ac.* 1521 (London; *Reg. R. Fitzjames*, f. 183v [194v]); sd. 1522, d. 1523 (Canterbury; *Reg. W. Warham, London sede v.*, **2**, f. 297r; London, *Reg. C. Tunstall*, f. 3v; *CL*).

Wardale, Robert: *see* Pickering.

Warde, John: Netley; *ac.* 1509, *d.* 1510 (Winchester, *Reg. R. Fox* **2**, ff. 25r, 26v); in community, 1518, by which time priested (TNA, E314/101); *disp.* 1536 (FOR, p. 66).

Warden, Christopher: Warden; *sd.* 1527, *d.* and *p.* 1530 (Lincoln; *Reg. J. Longland*, ff. 19v, 26v, 27v); in monastery at suppression, 1538 (*DKR*, p. 47); said in 1535 by Abbot Emery to be 'a common drunkard' (*LC*, p. 59); pension, £5–6–8 (TNA, E314/77).

Warden, John: Sawtry; *sd.* 1530 (Lincoln; *Reg. J. Longland*, f. 25v); abbot's chaplain *c.*1533 (TNA, STAC2/32/154).

Warden, John: Warden: *d.* and *p.* 1530 (Lincoln; *Reg. J. Longland*, ff. 26v, 27v); in the monastery at its suppression, 1538 (*DKR*, p. 47); in receipt of his pension of £5–6–8 as late as 1555 (TNA, E164/31, f. 25v).

Warden, Thomas: Warden; *sd.* and *d..* 1518, *p.* 1520 (Lincoln; *Reg. W. Atwater*, ff. 125r, 127r, 134r); when sent on business by Abbot Emery about 1535 spent all night in an ale–house in Shesford, refused correction and stirred up the monks against the abbot (*LC*, p. 59 [No. XXIX]); in house at its suppression, 1538 (*DKR*, p. 47), when still a deacon (TNA, E314/77); in 1554 was resident at Clothall, Hertfordshire, unmarried, with pension of £5–6–8 but no other ecclesiastical preferments (Hodgett, 1959, p. 92).

Wardlaw: *see* Wordyll.

Wardrop, Henry: Kirkstall, *sd.* and *d.* 1499, *p.* 1502 (York; Cross and Vickers, 1995, p. 140

Ware: *see* Were.

Warkeworth, William: Bruern; *ac.* 1497, *sd.* and *d.* 1498 (Lincoln; *Reg. W. Smith*, n. f.).

Warminster, Nicholas: Stanley; *sd.* and *d.* 1513, *p.* 1514 (Salisbury; *Reg. E. Audley*, ff. 21r, 23r, 26v).

Warner, William: Revesby, *disp.* 1538 (FOR, p. 128; Essex R.O., D/DRg 1/104).

Warre, Stephen: Robertsbridge; *ac.* 1496, *sd.* 1498, *d.* 1501 (Chichester; *Reg. E. Story*, ff. 190r, 193r, 196v); signed deed of surrender and *disp.* 1538 (*DKR*, p. 39, FOR, p. 135); pension, £6 (TNA, E314/77).

Warren, John: Waverley; *sd.* 1486 (Baigent, 1883, p. 209); *d.* 1487 (Winchester; *Reg. P. Courtenay*, f. 13r); perhaps the abbot of this name of Thame, 1495 – 1525 (Smith, 2008, p. 339) and after; criticised in 1526 for extravagant living (Baskerville, 1937, p. 91); inventory of the abbey's goods drawn up on 4 February 1525 (*Reg. J. Longland*, f. 109r–110r); died 18–01–1529 (VCH, *County of Oxford* **2**, 1907, pp. 83–86).

Warwick, Edward: *sd.* 1507 (Lichfield; *Reg. G. Blyth*, n–f.).

Warwick, William: Bordesley; *d.* 1528 (Worcester; *Reg. R. Morton addenda*, f. 166).

? Waryn, Stephen: Buckland; *p.* 1501 (Wells; *Reg. O. King*, f. 116).

Wartham, Thomas: Quarr, *disp.* 1537 (FOR, p. 87).

Warwick, Edward: Stoneleigh; *ac.* 1505, *d.* 1507 (Lichfield; *Reg. G. Blyth*, n–f);

Wasdale/Wastell: *see* Bynley.

Washford: *see* Wayshford.

Watchett, John: Cleeve; *ac.* and *sd.* 1475 (Wells; *Reg. R. Stillington*, f. 192).

Water, John: Bindon; *sd.* 1526, *d.* 1528 (Salisbury; *Reg. L. Campeggio*).

Water, John: Waverley, *disp.* 1536 (FOR, pp. 67–68).

Waterall/Watishall, Robert: Rufford; *sd.* 1500 (York; *Reg. T. Rotherham*, n–f.); *d.* 1501, *p.* 1503 (*Reg. T. Savage*, ff. 110r, 119v); *disp.* 1536 (FOR, p.74).

Watford, Hugh: abbot, Stratford Langthorne, by 1466–1490 (Smith, 2008, p. 337); permitted to hold a benefice *in commendam*, 1476 (*CPL* **13**, Part 1, 495).

Watkyns: *see* Wilkins.

Watson, John: Meaux; *ac.* and *sd.* 1520, *d.* 1521, *p.* 1525 (York; Cross and Vickers, 1995, p. 155).

Watson, Oliver: *see* **Broughton**.

Watson, Roger: *see* Whitby.

Watson: *see also* Lofthouse.

Watson, William: Fountains, *sd.* and *d.* 1497, *p.* 1499 (York; Cross and Vickers, 1995, p. 112).

Watson, William: Byland; *p.* 1532 (York; Cross and Vickers, 1995, p. 99); *disp.* to hold any benefice with cure, if licensed by his abbot; 26 March 1535 (*FOR*, p. 21); *disp.* 1538 (*FOR*, p. 181; fee of £4); may later have been rector of Levisham and then of Heslerton, Yorkshire (1554; Aveling, 1955, p. 12).

Watson, William: Revesby, *disp.* 1538 (*FOR*, p. 128); Could he have transferred from Byland?

Watson, William: Holm Cultram, 1533 (Gilbanks, 1899, p. 94; *LP* **6**, pp. 425–26 [No. 988]); alleged, perhaps spuriously, that he had immoral relations with three women, 1535/36 (*LP* **10**, p. 138 [No. 364]).

Watson: *see also* Wigston.

Watton, John: Pipewell; *ac.* 1500, *sd.* 1502, *d.* 1503 (Lincoln; *Reg. W. Smith*, ff. 21r, 33v, 42v).

Watts, Christopher: Buckfast; *p.* 1489 (Exeter; *Reg. R. Fox*, f. 154r).

Watt(ys), John: Buckfast; *sd.* and *d.* 1512, *p.* 1515 (Exeter; *Reg. H. Oldham*, ff. 107v, 110r, 122v); present at Suppression in 1539 (*DKR*, p. 12); in receipt of pension of £5–6–8 in 1555 (TNA, E164/31, f. 34r); vicar or curate of Buckfastleigh, 1540/41 (Stéphan, 1970, p. 213).

Wayford, John: Cleeve; *d.* 1489 (Exeter; *Reg. R. Fox*, f. 153v)

Wayshford, John: Cleeve: *sd.* 1514, *d.* and *p.* 1515 (Exeter; *Reg. H. Oldham*, ff. 118r, 119v, 120v).

Wayshford, William: Cleeve; *d.* 1517 (Exeter; *Reg. H. Oldham*, f. 127v).

Webbe, John: Cleeve; *p.* 1489 (Wells; *Reg. R. Stillington*, f. 233v; SRO, D/D/B Reg.7). Might he have transferred from Cleeve to Dunkeswell in 1537?

Webbe, John: Bruern, 1535 (*VE* **2**, p. 265).

Webbe, John: Dunkeswell; 'cellarer/steward' there at its suppression, 1539; pension, £6 p.a. (TNA, E322/76; Sparks, 1978, pp. 109–110).

Webster, John: Meaux; *sd.* 1493, *d.* 1495, *p.* 1496 (York; Cross and Vickers, 1995, p. 154).

Webster/Weston, John: Pipewell; signed deed of surrender and *disp.* 1538 (*DKR*, p. 37; *FOR*, p. 160); in receipt of pension of £1–6–8 as late as 1555 (TNA, E164/31, f.43 r) – perhaps not long professed..

Webster *al.* Foston, Robert: Byland, *ac.* 1521 (York), possibly confused with Robert Foston; *disp.* 1539; pension, £5; three clerics of this name held local positions in 1548 (*DKR*, p. 13, *FOR*, p. 181, Cross, 1995, pp. 100, 109); on 17 November 1536 Byland presented Robert Webster, 'sometime our fellow brother and monk', to the rents and profits of its rectory of Bubwith (TNA, LR1/175, f. 314r).

Weche, William: Valle Crucis; *ac.* 1499 (Lichfield; *Reg. J. Arundel*, f. 281v).

Wedderall: *see* Wetheral.

Weitwang, John: Fountains; *sd.* 1492, *d.* 1493, *p.* 1495 (Cross and Vickers ,1995, p. 111).

Welbery, Alexander: St Mary Graces; *sd.* 1510, *d.* 1511 (London; *Reg. R. Fitzjames*, ff. 158r [169r], 160v [171v]).

Welling, William: Pipewell; *sd.* 1488 (Lincoln; *Reg. J. Russell*, f. 29v).

Welington/Willimgton, Thomas: Warden; *ac.* 1500, *p.* 1504 (Lincoln; *Reg. W. Smith*, f. 44r).

Wellington/Wellyngton/Willington, William: Merevale; *ac.* and *sd.* 1528, *d.* and *p.* 1529 (Lichfield; *Reg. G. Blyth*, n–f.).

Wellington/Welyngton, William: Buildwas; *ac.* 1528, *sd.* 1529, *d.* 1530 (Lichfield; *Reg. G. Blyth*, n–f.).

Wells, Robert: Fountains; *sd.* 1521 (York; Cross and Vickers, 1995, p. 114); ***and see* Dodgeson**..

Wellis, John: Tilty; *d.* 1508, *p.* 1509 (London; *Reg. R. Fitzjames*, ff. 98r, 100r).

Wellis/Wells, Richard: Netley; *ac.* 1489, *sd.* 1491, *p.* 1495 (Winchester; *Reg. P. Courtenay*, ff. 15v, 18v; *Reg. T. Langton*, f. 26v); in community, 1518 (TNA, E314/101).

Wellis, Thomas: Rufford; *sd.* 1498, *d.* 1499, *p.* 1503 (York; *Reg. T. Rotherham*, n–f., *T. Savage*, f. 119v); last sub–prior, Rufford, *disp.* 1536 (*FOR*, p. 74); moving then to Roche; monk, Roche, signed deed of surrender, 1538 (TNA, E322/204); *disp.* 1538 (*FOR*, p. 144); signed letters testimonial in 1555, when said to be at St Clement's, Lincoln. Previously, chaplain, the Stretton Wolfe chantry in Lincoln until 1548; never married, said in 1554 to be 'decrepit,' and died *c.*1564. Was in receipt of two pensions, £5 on the dissolution of Roche, and £3–11–8 from his chantry chaplaincy (Hodgett, 1959, p. 125; Cross and Vickers, 1995, pp. 171, 197, 201; (TNA, E164/31, f. 53r; CIY).

Welys: *see also:* Wyke.

?Wenlok, Roger: Rewley; *p.* 1521 (Lincoln; *Reg. J. Longland*, f. 1v).

Wensley, Thomas: Byland; *d.* 1512 (York; Cross and Vickers, 1995, p. 99); abbot's chaplain, 1533 (Brown, 1911, p. 47).

Wentbrig, Thomas: Fountains; *d.* 1509, *p.* 1511 (York; Cross and Vickers, 1995, p. 113).

Were: *see* Exmester.

Were, Thomas: Dunkeswell; *sd.* and *d.* 1504 (Canterbury; *Reg. W. Warham, Exeter sede v.*, ff. 205v, 208v).

Were/Ware, Thomas: perhaps the foregoing monk; abbot, Kingswood, 1525–1529; last abbot, Flaxley, 1533–1536; pension, £15 (TNA, E315/222, no. 43); said to have moved after his abbey's surrender to Thame, and later lived with the vicar of Aston Rowant, Oxfordshire, where he was buried in 1546 (Baskerville, 1927, p. 91; 'Dispossessed Religious of Oxfordshire,' 1930, pp. 282, 288–89; Smith, 2008, pp. 290, 304).

West, John: Buckland; *sd.* 1508, *d.* 1509, *p.* 1510 (Exeter; *Reg. H. Oldham*, ff. 98r–v, 103r); *disp.* 1539 (*DKR*, p. 12, *FOR*, p. 178); pension, £5, received as late as 1555 (TNA, E164/31, f. 34r).

West, William: Fountains, *sd.* and *d.* 1497 (York; Cross and Vickers, 1995, p. 112).

West: *see also* Croxton.

Westbrook, Richard: Beaulieu; *p.* 1507 (London; *Reg. R. Fitzjames*, f. 95v).

Westbury, John: Kingswood; signed deed of surrender and *disp.* 1538 (*DKR*, p. 25, *FOR*, p. 131); 'reward and finding', 1538, £2–13–4 (TNA, E36/152, f. 20); pension, £4–6–8 (Baskerville, 1927, p. 88).

Westbury/Westbye, Ralph: Dore; *ac.* 1525, *sd.* 1526, *d.* 1527 (Hereford; *Reg. C. Bothe*, pp. 318, 321, 32); monk, Flaxley; *p.* 1529/30 (Worcester; *Reg. R. Morton addenda*, f. 170); *disp.* 1537 (*FOR*, p. 98). May have transferred to Flaxley for a short period, unless there is a copying error in one of the registers.

Westby, William: Vale Royal, 1500 (*LB*, p. 153).

Westhede, Robert: Jervaulx; *sd.* 1484 (York; Cross and Vickers, 1995, p. 129).

Westmester/Westmon/Faute/Fote, William: Newenham; *p.* 1499 (Exeter; *Reg. R. Redmayne*, f. 40v); *disp.* 1540 (*FOR*, p. 216); pension of £6 received as late as 1555 (TNA, E164/31, f. 34v). Became incumbent of South Molton, Devon., died at Membury, 1552 (Snell, 1967, pp. 114, 146).

Weston, John: *see* Webster.

Weston, Richard: Bordesley, *disp.* 1538 (*FOR*, p. 149; TNA, E322/26); pension, £6 (TNA, E314/77); assessed for subsidy in 1540 (Bodleian Library, Oxford, Tanner MS 343).

Weston, *al.* Bertelet, Robert: Biddlesden, *d.* and *p.* 1496 (Lincoln; *Reg. W. Smith*, n.f.); *disp.* 1538; pension, £5–6–8 (*FOR*, p. 179; Green, 1974, pp. 63–64; TNA, E322/22).

Weston, Thomas: abbot, Pipewell, 1483–at least 1493 (Smith, 2008, p. 320).

Weston, William: Combe; *sd.* 1511, *p.* 1512 (Lichfield; *Reg. G. Blyth*, n–f).

Weston, William: Stoneleigh; *d.* 1514 (Lichfield; *Reg. G. Blyth*, n–f.).

Wetherall, Anthony: Holm Cultram, 1533 (*LP* **6**, pp. 425–26 [No. 988]); perhaps the same monk as *Anthony Ryston*, q.v.

Wetherall, Edward: Newminster, thirty–seven years old in 1536 (TNA, SC12/13/65); *disp.* 1536 (*FOR*, p. 77).

Wetherall/Wederall, *al*. Gilling, William: Byland, *ac.* 1533, *sd.* 1537 (York); *disp.* 1538 (*DKR*, p. 13, *FOR*, p. 181); *d.* and *p.* 1539 (after suppression, on title of Sir Nicholas Fairfax), perhaps vicar of Laneham, Nottinghamshire, from 1548; and of Epperstone, from 1554; in receipt of pension of £5 in 1555 (TNA, E164/31, f. 55r); made his will in 1566 (Aveling, 1955, p. 13; Cross and Vickers, 1995, pp. 99, 109–110).

Whalley, Christopher: Combermere; *ac.* 1521, *sd.* and *d.* 1522, *p.* 1523 (Lichfield; *Reg. G. Blyth*, n–f.); abbot, Combermere, by 1518 to 1533 (Smith, 2008, p. 283); not highly thought of in a letter to Cromwell of 1528/29 (*LP* **4**, pp. 3176–77 [Appendix 227]).

Whalley, *al*. Brown, Christopher: Furness; signed deed of surrender, 1537 (TNA, E322/91).

Whalley, Edmund: Fountains; *sd.* 1533, *d.* and *p.* 1534 (York; Cross and Vickers, 1995, p. 114); and see: *Lowde*.

Whalley, John: Croxden; *ac.* 1501 (Lichfield; *Reg. J. Arundel*, f. 294v).

Whalley, John: *see also* Gisburght.

Whalley, John: Louth Park; *d.* 1502 (Lincoln; *Reg. W. Smith*, f. 35r).

Whalley, Ornelius/Otiwelinus: Combermere: *ac.* 1487, *sd.* 1489 (Lichfield; *Reg. J. Hales*, ff. 226v, 243).

Whalley/Walley, Richard: Hailes; *sd.* 1483 (Worcester; *Reg. J. Alcock*, f. 273); *disp.* 1491 (*CPL* **15**, p. 388 [No. 735]).

Whalley, Robert: Louth Park; *ac.* 1500, *sd.* 1501, *p.* 1504 (Lincoln; *Reg. W. Smith*, ff. 22r, 28v, 45v).

Whalley *al*. Rede, Roger: Hailes; *d.* 1530 (Worcester; *Reg. R. Morton addenda*, f. 168); scholar, St Bernard's College, Oxford, and custodian of the Holy Blood, Hailes, ?1537/38 (*CHA*, p. 85).

Whalley, Stephen: *see* Sagar.

Whalley, Thomas: Kirkstall, *sd.* and *d.* 1522, *p.* 1525 (York; Cross and Vickers, 1995, p. 141).

Whalley, William: abbot, Buildwas, by 1485 to 1512 (TNA, C1/59/110; Smith, 2008, p. 277).

Whalley, William: Vaudey; *ac.*and *sd.* 1496, *d.* 1498 (Lincoln; *Reg. W. Smith*, n.f.)

Whalley, William: examined re plate of abbey, 1537 (*LP* **12**, Part 1, p. 280 [No. 621]); *disp.* 1537 (*FOR*, p. 91).

Where: *see* **Excester.**

Whatles/Watloos, Christopher: Thame; *sd.* and *d.* 1505, *p.* 1506 (Lincoln; *Reg. W. Smith*, n.f.).

Whiston, William: Woburn; *sd.* 1485, *p.* 1487 (Lincoln; *Reg. J. Russell*, ff. 18v, 26v).

Whitacre/Whitaker, Miles: Whalley, *disp.* 1537 (*FOR*, p. 91).

Whitby/Witters,/Wytty/Waite, Richard: Holm Cultram; in house, 1533 (*LP* **6**, pp. 425–26 [No. 988]); signed deed of surrender and *disp.* 1538 (*DKA*, p. 23; *FOR*, pp. 123–24). In receipt of his pension of £5 in 1555 (TNA, E164/31, f. 73v).

Whitby/Watson, Roger: monk, Rievaulx, *sd.* 1517, *d.* 1519, *p.* 1522 (York); *disp.* 1538 (*FOR*, p. 156); pension, £5–6–8; seemingly employed by 1555 as a curate of Whenby, Yorkshire, the incumbent being William Bradley, formerly a fellow monk at Rievaulx. In his will of 1555 Watson left 12d. each to any of the brethren of Rievaulx still alive. He was living then at Farlington in the parish of Sheriff Hutton, and desired to be buried there (Aveling, 1952, p. 109, Cross and Vickers, 1995, pp. 169, 171, 173–74, 184).

Whitchurch, William: abbot, Hailes; dies 1479 (Worcester; *Reg. J. Alcock*, f. 7r).

Whitcliff/Wyclyff, John: Fountains; *sd.* 1533, *d.* 1534 (York; Cross and Vickers, 1995, pp. 114, 128).

Whyt/White, John: last sub–prior, Thame, 1539; but only allocated a £6 pension (TNA, E314/77; DKR, p. 43); seemingly continued to live in Thame, dying there in 1552 (Baskerville, *Religious of Oxfordshire*, 1930, p. 335).

White, Stephen: Quarr; *ex.* and *ac.* 1510, *sd.* 1511, *p.* 1513 (Winchester; *Reg. R. Fox* **2**, f. 26r; **3**, ff. 51r, 54r).

White, Thomas: abbot, Buckland, in 1500–1528; the marquis of Exeter wished him to resign but he begged to be allowed to continue in office (Chapter 3; Smith, 2008, p. 276; West Devon R.O., 70/141, 143, 144, 145, 146, 215, 216, 334/2); Gill, 1951, p. 34, gives a *John Brundon* as abbot in 1508.

Whytt, Thomas: Newenham; *sd.* 1524, *d.* and *p.* 1525 (Exeter; *Reg. J. Vesey*, ff. 154r, 154v, 157r); *disp.* 1540 (*FOR*, p. 216); pension of £4–13–4 received as late as 1555 (TNA, E164/31, f. 34v), but awarded £5–6–8 at dissolution (*LP* **14**, Part 1, p. 184 [No. 469]).

White/Whyett, Thomas: Beaulieu, *disp.* 1538 (*DKR*, p. 9; *FOR*, p. 131); perhaps vicar of New-church, Isle of Wight, from 20 December 1541 (Hockey, 1976, p. 187); pension of £5 received in 1555 (TNA, E164/31, f. 13r).

White, William: abbot, Ford, by ?1484–1501, when dies (Smith, 2008, p. 291).

White, William: Fountains; *d.* 1509, *p.* 1514 (York; Cross and Vickers, 1995, p. 113); *and see* **Donwell**.

Whitechurch, Thomas: Combermere: *d.* 1506, *p.* 1507 (Lichfield; *Reg. G. Blyth*, n–f.).

Whit(e)more, John: Dunkeswell; *ac.* and *sd.* 1490 (Exeter; *Reg. R. Fox*, f. 155v); *d.* 1490 ((Salisbury; *Reg. T. Langton*, n–f.); *p.* 1490 (Salisbury; *Reg. T. Langton*, p. 106 [No. 572]); abbot, 1501–29; post–1500, refused to pay back a loan (TNA, C1/216/36); involved in land dispute, 1508 (TNA, C1/386/36; C1/382/1; Sparks, 1978, pp. 103–04).

Whitford/Whyteforde, William: Newenham; *ac.* 1513, *d.* 1520, *p.* 1521 (Exeter; *Reg. H. Oldham*, f. 113v; *Reg. J. Veysey*, f. 144v, 145v).

Whitkyrk, Richard: Swineshead; *sd.* 1531, *d.* 1533 (Lincoln; *Reg. J. Longland*, ff. 27v, 33v).

Whitland, John: Margam, *disp.* 1536 (*FOR*, p. 68).

Whitney, James: Strata Florida; *sd.* 1515 (Hereford; *Reg. R. Mayew*, p. 270).

Whitney: *see also* **Witney.**

Whitwell/Whittle, Hugh: Basingwerk; *sd.* and *d.* 1498, *p.* 1500 (Lichfield; *Reg. J. Arundel*, ff. 272, 274v, 287).

Whityngdon, John: Bordesley; *ac.* 1499 (Worcester; *Reg. S. Gigli*, f. 395).

Whittington, Richard: Combe, 1497 (TNA, E315/283, f.1).

Whityngdon, Richard: Bordesley; *ac.* and *sd.* 1504, *d.* 1505 (Worcester; *Reg. S. Gigli*, ff. 289, 291–92); cellarer, 1538, when he tried to engineer the abbacy for himself, and its surrender to Cromwell (VCH, *Worcestershire* **2**, 1971, pp. 153, 154n; Youings, 1971, pp. 69, 173). His signature does not occur in the deed of surrender, 12–07–1538 (TNA, E322/26); but he may be identified with *Richard Weston*, q.v.

Whityngton, William: abbot, Combe, 1476–1491 when resigned (, 2008, p. 281), dead by 1498 (*Patent*, 1498, p. 141).

Whome, Thomas: Combe; pension, £6; living at Ibstock, Leicestershire, in 1573 (Hodgett, 1959, p. 144).

Whytt: *see* White.

Whytty, John: Margam, *disp.* 1536 (*FOR*, p. 68).

Wich, John: Bordesley; *d.* 1497 (Lichfield; *Reg. J. Arundell*, f. 261);

Wiche, John: Combermere; *sd.* 1500, *d.* 1501 (Lichfield; *Reg. J. Arundel*, ff. 288, 293v).

Wiche, Nicholas: Vale Royal; *p.* 1509 (Lichfield; *Reg. G. Blyth*, n–f.).

Wiche, Robert: Dieulacres; *ac.* 1528, *sd.* 1529, *d.* 1531 (Lichfield; *Reg. G. Blyth*, n–f.).

Wich: *see also:* **Weche, Wyche.**

Wigston/Watston/*al*. Stanley: Thomas: Garendon; *sd.* 1497, *d.* 1498, *p.* 1500 (Lincoln; *Reg. W. Smith,* f. 24v.); *disp.* 1536 (*FOR,* p. 76).

Wigtoft, William: Swineshead; *sd.* 1492, *d.* 1493 (Lincoln; *Reg. J. Russell,* ff. 45/46v, 48/49v).

Wilkins/Watkyns, Edward: last abbot, Hulton, 1536; confirmed as abbot on renewal of monastery (Staffordshire Archives, D1798/H.M.ASTON/6/2, of 1 October 1537; *Cf. LP* **12**, Part 2p. 349 [No. 1008/1]., signed deed of surrender and *disp.* 1538 (TNA, E322/106; *FOR,* p. 154; pension, £20 (Tomkinson, 1985, p. 68).

Wilkinson, Robert: Revesby; *disp.* 1507 (*CPL* **18**, p. 548 [No. 803]).

Wilkinson, Robert: Byland, *ac.* and *sd.* 1521; *d.* 1522, *p.* 1524 (York); *disp.* 1539 (*DKR,* p. 13, *FOR,* p. 181); perhaps chantry priest of St Nicholas in Gilling church, Yorkshire, in 1548, when said to be 'of no learning'; pension of £5 received as late as 1573 (Cross and Vickers, 1995, p. 110).

William … : abbot, Robertsbridge, by 1481 to 1492 (Smith, 2008, p. 326).

William … : abbot, Cymer, 1487–91 (Williams, 2001, p. 66; *Statuta* **5**, p. 536 [No. 1486/18]).

William … : Stratford, attending General Chapter in 1489, probably its later sub–prior – 'a good zealot of the Order', 1500 (*Letters,* pp. 122–23 [No. 60]; 221 [No. 109]; 225–228 [No. 110]).

William … : abbot, Coggeshall, 1508–10 (*Smith [2008] 280). Could this possible be William Cowper,* q.v. although an Abbot John occurs in 1507.

William, William: Pipewell; *d.* and *p.* 1489 (Lincoln; *Reg. J. Russell,* ff. 31v, 33r).

Williams, Rhys: Dore, in 1536, when about twenty–seven years old (TNA, E315/109, ff. 127–34).

William, Stephen: prior, Bindon, 1509 (TNA, STAC2/1, ff. 28–30).

Williamson, George: Revesby, *disp.* 1538 (*FOR,* p. 128; Essex R.O. D/DRg, 1/104).

Williamson/*al*. Harwode, John: Kirkstead, *disp.* to hold a benefice if given his abbot's consent, 12 February 1537 (*FOR,* p. 86); pension, 1539, £6–13–4 (Cross and Vickers, 1995, p. 142); died 1554 (Hodgett, 1959, p. 130).

Williamson, Robert: Revesby; *ac.*and *sd.* 1502, *d.* and *p.* 1503 (Lincoln; *Reg. W. Smith,* ff. 36v, 37v, 40v, 42r).

Wilmalow: see *Wynneslow.*

Wyllys/Wylls, John: Buckland; *sd.* and *d.* 1503; *p.* 1505 (Exeter; *Reg. J. Arundell, ff.* 13v–14r; *Reg. H. Oldham,* f. 83v).

Wilsdon: see *Stavley.*

Wilsemsted/Wilshamstede, William: Warden; *ac.* and *sd.* 1500, *p.* 1504 (Lincoln; *Reg. W. Smith,* .ff. 21r, 44r).

Wilson, Christopher: Kirkstall; pension, £6–13–4 (*Lonsdale, 1972, p. 207); and see* **Headingley**.

Wilson, Henry: Roche; *sd.* and *d.* 1525, *p.* 1526 (York; Cross and Vickers, 1995, pp. 187, 198); charged with self–abuse, perhaps spuriously, at the Crown visitation of February 1536; signed deed of surrender, 1538 (TNA, E322/204); *disp.* 1538 (*FOR,* p. 144); in receipt of £5 pension.as late as 1564 and a pension of £3–12–0 from Heckington (TNA, E164/31, f. 53r), After the dissolution of Roche he may have moved to Kirkstall abbey and later became a chantry priest at Heckington, Lincolnshire. He seemingly never married, and died at Brauncewell on 10 April 1573 (CIY project; Hodgett, 1959, p. 149)

Wilson/*al*. Mardersey, John: Kirkstead; *disp.* if given his abbot's consent, 12 February 1537 (*FOR,* p. 86).

Wilson, Robert: : Stoneleigh; *d.* 1514 (Lichfield; *Reg. G. Blyth,* n–f.).

Wilson, Thomas: bursar, Kirkstead; 1533 (TNA, DL41/326); died 1543 (Hodgett, 1959, p. 130).

Wilson: *see also* Wylson.

Winchcombe, John: Hailes; *p.* 1527 (Worcester; *Reg. R. Morton addenda,* f. 165); a monk–bibliophile, 1529/30 (Aveling, 1967, p. 106 [74]).

Winchcombe: *see also* Wynchcombe.

Winchester, Henry: Cistercian monk in diocese of London; *d.* 1511 (Salisbury; *Reg. E. Audley,* n–f.).

Winchester, John: Netley, *disp.* 1536 (*FOR,* p. 66).

Winchester, Thomas: Bordesley; *sd.* 1486 (Lichfield; *Reg. J. Hales,* f . 216v).: *p.* 1488 (Worcester; *Reg. R. Morton,* f. 142).

Winchester, Thomas: Beaulieu; *sd.* and *d.* 1498 (Winchester; *Reg. T. Langton,* f. 32v); *p.* 1507 (London; *Reg. R. Fitzjames,* f. 95v).

Winchester, William: Beaulieu; *ac.* 1488 (Winchester; *Reg. P. Courtenay,* f. 13r).

Winchester, William: Cleeve; *d.* 1523 (Wells; *Reg. T. Wolsey,* f. 30).

Windsor: *see also* Wynsor.

Winslow: *see* Wynneslow.

Wisbeche: *see* Wysbech.

Wise/Wyse, John: Holm Cultram; in house,10–08–1536 (*LP* **11**, p. 115 [No. 276]); signed deed of surrender and *disp.* 1538 (*DKR,* p. 23; *FOR,* pp. 123–24). In receipt of his pension of £3–6–8 in 1555 (TNA, E164/31, f.73v).

Wises: see Vizes.

Wistow, John: abbot, Louth Park, 1498–?1501 (Smith, 2008, p. 310); A *John Wistow* still in the community, perhaps a name sake, when *disp.* 6–08–1536 (*FOR,* p. 69).

Witham, Robert: Woburn; *ac.* 1487 (Lincoln; *Reg. J. Russell,* f. 20r).

Witham, William: Coggeshall; *sd.* and *d.* 1496, *p.* 1497 (London; *Reg. R. Hill,* ff. 31r; 32r; *Reg. T. Savage,* f. 53r).

Withibroke/Wethebroke, Thomas: Stoneleigh; *sd.* 1499, *d.* 1500 (Lichfield; *Reg. J. Arundel,* ff. 282, 286).

Withyngton, William: St Mary Graces, 1533 (Grainger and Phillpotts, 2011, p. 93).

W(h)itney, Thomas: Dieulacres, *sd.* and *d.* 1514, *p.* 1515 (Lichfield; *Reg. G. Blyth,* n–f.); last abbot, by.1524 to 1538 (Smith, 2008, p. 288); alleged to have forcibly evicted a tenant, 1529 (TNA, STAC 2/21/245); *disp.* 1538; pension, £60 (Hibbert, 1910, pp. 239, 242; *FOR,* p. 160; Staffordshire R.O., 2/32/00, p. 45). After the Suppression he lived in Mill Street, Leek, where in 1540 in financial difficulties as his pension was in arrears; died in 1558 requesting burial in Westminster Abbey (TNA, PROB11/40/398).

Whitney/Wytney, Thomas: Cleeve; *d.* 1523 (Wells; *Reg. T. Wolsey,* f. 30). Did he move to Ford?

Witney, Thomas: Ford; *p.* 1525 (Exeter; *Reg. J. Vesey,* f. 155v).

Witton, John: Jervaulx; *sd.* 1496, *d.* 1497, *p.* 1499 (York; Cross and Vickers, 1995, pp. 129–30).

Wixe: *see* Wilkys.

Woborne, *al.* Lune/Bune, Edward: Woburn; *sd.* 1532, *d.* 1533, *p.* 1537 (Lincoln; *Reg. J. Longland,* ff. 31r, 36r, 55v); *disp.* 1538 (*FOR,* p. 145); rector, Fortho, Northamptonshire, 1533; rector, Grafton,Regis, 1560 and rector, Eversholt, Bedfordshire., 1561, in plurality; unmarried (Thomson, 1933, p. 140).

Woburn, *al.* Barnes, Ralph: Woburn; *d.* 1519, *p.* 1522 (Lincoln; *Reg. W. Atwater,* f. 131r; *Reg. J. Longland,* f. 5r); perhaps B.D., Oxon., 1533 (Stevenson, 1939, p. 49); sub–prior, 1537, upheld papal authority and hanged, 1538 (Gasquet, 1899, pp. 288–90).

Woborne, Robert: Woburn; *sd.* 1532, *d.* 1533, *p.* 1537 (Lincoln; *Reg. J. Longland,* ff. 31r, 36r, 55v); *disp.* 1538 (*FOR,* p. 145).

Woburn, William: *see* Stele/Stile.

Wodd/Wood, Richard: Kirkstall; pension; *sd.* 1526 (York); 1539, £5–6–8 (Cross and Vickers, 1995, pp. 142, 152); in receipt of pension in 1555 (TNA, E164/31, f. 53v); Wodd perhaps an *alias* for *Richard Newall* or *Newton*, q.v. (Lonsdale, 1972, p. 209).

Wode, Alexander: Thame; *p.* 1491 (Lincoln; *Reg. J. Russell*, f. 40r).

Wode, Richard: Fountains; *disp.* 1486 (*CPL* **15**, p. 61 [No.119]).

Wode, William: Thame; visited Rome in 1507 (Foley, 1880, p. 546).

Wodelond, Thomas: Dore; 1473 (Worcester; *Reg. J. Carpenter* **2**, f. 190).

Wodestrete, John: Bindon; *sd.* 1520, *p.* 1521 (Salisbury; *Reg. E. Audley*, ff. 43r, 44v); sub–prior, 1535 (*VE* **1**, p. 24).

Wodeward: *see* **Woodward.**

Wodill, Richard: Quarr; *sd.* 1495 (when named *Roger*), *d.* 1498, *p.* 1500 (Winchester; *Reg. T. Langton*, ff. 26r, 33r, 36r); *disp.* 1537 (*FOR*, p. 87).

Wodmard, Richard: Flaxley, rehabilitated by the General Chapter after various crimes, including forging money (*Statuta* **5**, pp. 562–63 [No. 1486/120].

Woldham/Woldgrove, al. Acon, Nicholas: Boxley; *ac.* 1497, *sd.* and *d.* 1498, *p.* 1500 (London; *Reg. T. Savage*, ff. 53r, 54r, 61v).

Wolston/Wolsunton/Stanton, Oliver: Combe, *sd.* and *d.* 1494, *p.* 1495 (Lichfield; *Reg. W. Smith*, ff. 178v, 181, 187); signed deed of surrender, 1538 (*DKR*, pp. 16–17).

Wolston, Robert: Stoneleigh; *p.* 1517 (Lichfield; *Reg. G. Blyth*, n–f.).

Wood/Wodnett, George: Pipewell; signed deed of surrender and *disp.* 1538 (*DKR*, p. 37; *FOR*, p. 160); in receipt of pension of £1–6–8 as late as 1555 (TNA, E164/31, f.43r); he was perhaps not long professed before the abbey closed.

Woode, Richard: grain receiver, Whalley, 1536 (TNA, SC6/HENVIII/1796); the only monk of his house accused, perhaps spuriously, of immoral behaviour in 1535/36 (*LP* **10**, p. 138 [No. 364]); *disp.* 1537 (*FOR*, p. 91); from 1535 probably until his death in 1560, chaplain at Great Harwood in Whalley's Blackburn parish, and buried in his chapel (Haigh, 1969, p. 119).

Woodlands, John: abbot, Dieulacres, 1520; deposed by 1523 for wasting the abbey's wealth (*VCH, Staffordshire* **2**, 1967, p. 235; Fisher, 1969, pp. 47–48).

Woodward, Gabriel: Flaxley, *d.* 1492 (Worcester; *Reg. R. Morton*, f. 162); *disp.* 1536 (*FOR*, p. 73).

Woodward, John: Garendon; *sd.* 1515, *d.* 1516, *p.* 1522 (Lincoln; *Reg. W. Atwater*, ff. 117r, 118r; *Reg. J. Longland*, f. 4r); *disp.* 1536 (*FOR*, p. 76).

Woodward, Richard: Hailes, *disp.* 1540 (*FOR* 208); at the suppression of Hailes he took away, perhaps as souvenirs, four little pieces of glass and twenty bars of iron (Barnard, 1928, p. 10); in receipt of pension of £5 as late as 1555 (TNA, E164/31, f. 40r); vicar, Chedworth, Gloucestershire, 1555; died 1580, wishing to be buried in the church porch; his will mentions his 'long, black gown' (Winkless, 1990, p. 61); in 1571 subscribed to the Thirty–Nine Articles (Baskerville, 1927, p. 90).

Woolaston, al. Glaston, Robert: Kingswood; *ac., sd.* and *d.* 1492 (Worcester; *Reg. R. Morton*, ff. 152, 154); abbot by 1512 (Worcester; *Reg. S. Gigli*, f. 149); summoned to Convocation, 1515 (*Reg. S. Gigli*, f. 274); noted in 1516 as 'Glaston' (Somerset Archives, DD/SE/15/1);.his deposition in 1517 was not well received locally (TNA, STAC2/15, ff. 159–62; 2/17/259); his surname suggests that he was originally a monk from Tintern's Woolaston manor (*Letters*, pp. 249, 252, 282; Williams, 1976, pp. 109–110; 2001, pp. 63–64).

Wooton/Wotton, William: Kingswood; *p.* 1457 (Worcester; *Reg. J. Carpenter*, f. 544).

Wooton/Wotton, William: Kingswood; *sd.* 1511 (Worcester; *Reg. S. Gigli*, f. 307); food provider/granary keeper, Kingswood, signed deed of surrender and *disp.* 1538 (*DKR*, p. 25, *FOR*, p. 131); 'reward and finding', 1538, £2–13–4 (TNA, E36/152, f. 20); pension, £4–6–8 (Baskerville, 1927, p. 88).

Worcester, John: Bruern; *sd.* 1485 (Lincoln; *Reg. J. Russell,* f. 20r).

Worcester, John: Croxden; *ac.* 1493 (Lichfield; *Reg. W. Smith,* f. 171).

Worcester, John: Hailes; *ac.* 1497, *d.* 1499 (Worcester; *Reg. G. Gigli,* f. 25, *S. Gigli,* f. 395).

Worcester, Richard: Hailes; *ac.* 1532 (Worcester; *Reg. R. Morton addenda,* f. 171).

Worcester, Thomas: Bordesley; *ac.* and *sd.* 1478 (Worcester; *Reg. J. Alcock, f. 261*).

Wordyll/Worlde, William: Rievaulx; in community, 1533, when he spoke in favour of Abbot Kirkby (Aveling, 1952, p. 111; accused, perhaps spuriously, by the Crown Visitors early in 1536 of self–abuse and wishing to leave the Order; still in the house at its suppression, 1538; *disp.* 1538 (*FOR,* p. 156);. pension, £5; may have become vicar of Hunsingore, Yorkshire, from 1546 to 1554; in 1553 complained that his pension was half–a–year in arrears (DKR, p. 38; Cross and Vickers, 1995, pp. 170, 185). Might he be the next mentioned monk switching houses?

Worlde, William: Whalley, *d.* 1524, *p.* 1525 (Lichfield; *Reg. G. Blyth,* n–f.); *disp.* 1537 (*FOR,* p. 91).

Wortley, Henry: Rievaulx; *sd.* 1497 (York; Cross and Vickers, 1995, p. 168).

Wottan/'Wotwan', Richard: Hailes; on 13 April 1479 the bishop of Worcester commissions the bishop of Connor to bless Richard Wotton as abbot of Hailes, though by 1480 John Crombock is abbot there; as late abbot of Kingswood Richard was declared contumacious and excommunicated by General Chapter, 1486 (*Statuta* **5**, p. 536 [1486/18]).

Wren, Martin: Meaux; *ac.* 1517, *sd.* 1518, *d.* 1519, *p.* 152; pension, £6 (York; Cross and Vickers, 1995, pp. 155–56, 165–66); B.D. (Oxon.) 1526. Vicar of Darton, Yorkshire, from 1542 until his death in 1558 (Stevenson, 1939, p. 49).

Wrenbury, John: Combermere; *ac.* 1521, *sd.* and *d.* 1522, *p.* 1523 (Lichfield; *Reg. G. Blyth,* n–f.).

Wright/Wyght, John: Stratford, when made his mark on the deed of surrender, 1538, it being noted 'which can not wrytte'; he may have been a monk debilitated by a stroke, and his name does not appear in the dispensation list possibly because he had died (DKR, p. 52).

Wright, Robert: Fountains; *sd.* 1491, *d.* 1492, *p.* 1493 (Cross and Vickers, 1995, p. 111).

Wright, Thomas ['White' in one entry]**:** Vale Royal; *ac.* and *sd.* 1521, *d.* 1522, *p.* 1523 (Lichfield; *Reg. G. Blyth,* n–f.).

Wright, William: scholar, Byland; visited Rome in 1506 (Aveling, 1955, p. 4; Foley, 1880, p. 547).

Wright, William: Vale Royal, signed deed of surrender and *disp.* 1538 (DKR, p. 46; *FOR,* p. 162); in receipt of his £5 pension in 1555 (TNA, E164/31, f. 69r).

Wyche, Nicholas: Vale Royal; *sd.* 1506 (Lichfield; *Reg. G. Blyth,* n–f.).

Wyche, Richard: Whalley, B.Th. (Oxon.) 1521; last abbot, Tintern, 1521/22–36; in 1534 delayed answering a summons from Cromwell so as to be in his monastery for the feast of the Nativity of BVM; *disp.* 30 Nov. 1536 (*FOR,* p. 80); pension, £23 p.a., later assistant curate of Woolaston, Gloucestershire, with stipend of £4–13–4; dies in the opening days of January 1553 after making his will (*MA* **23**, 2007, pp. 67–74).

Wyche: *see also* Wiche.

Wydon, Henry: Cleeve; *sd.* and *d.* 1505 (Wells; *Reg. H. de Castello,* ff. 140–41). Seemingly he moved to Llantarnam abbey perhaps to fill depleted ranks; prior, Llantarnam, *disp.* 1537 (*FOR,* p. 88 – where wrongly attributed to Llanthony Prima (information from Dr M. Gray).

Wyght: *see* Wright.

Wyke/?Welys, John: Robertsbridge, *c.*1523 (SAL, MS 14, f.59v); signed deed of surrender and *disp.* 1538 (DKR, p. 39, FOR, p. 135); pension, £6 (TNA, E314/77).

Wyke: *see also* Hellay.

Wykyn, John: Pipewell; *sd.* and *d.* 1519, *p.* 1521 (Lincoln; *Reg. W. Atwater,* ff. 127v, 128v, *Reg. J. Longland,* f. 2r).

Wylkys/Wixe/Wykes, William: Thame; *sd.* in Thame church, 14 June 1538; perhaps originally a monk of Woburn (Baskerville, 1930, p. 336); signed deed of surrender, 1539 (*DKR*, p. 43); in receipt of £5–6–8 pension as late as 1555 (TNA, E164/31, f. 42r).

Wyllyngham, William: Kingswood, disp. 1538 (*FOR*, p. 131).

Wylshire: *see* Denyngton.

Wylson, Christopher: Kirkstall; pension, 1539, £6–13–4 (Cross and Vickers, 1995, p. 142).

Wylson, Henry: *see* Wilson.

Wylson, Thomas: Kirkstall; pension, 1539, £5 (Cross and Vickers, 1995, pp. 142, 151); in receipt of pension in 1555 (TNA, E164/31, f. 53v); he may have been resided in Leeds and have been *Thomas Kirkstall* or *Thomas Otley*, q.v.

Wymbirslay, Thomas: abbot, Kirkstall, 1468–1493 (Smith, 2008, p. 304).

Wymmersley, Gilbert: Kirkstall, *sd.* and *d.* 1522, *p.* 1525 (York; Cross and Vickers, 1995, pp. 141, 144). His family name may have been *Browne*.

Wymmyngdon/Wemelton/Wymbleton, John: Waverley; *ac.* 1487; *sd.* 1488; *d.* 1489 (Winchester; *Reg. P. Courtnay*, ff. 13r, 15r).

Wymiswold/Wynmesswold, Thomas: Garendon; *sd.* 1512, *d.* and *p.* 1513 (Lincoln; *Reg. W. Smith*, n–f.).

Wynborne, Peter: abbot, Bruern, from 1468 to at least 1486; blessed, 8 September 09–1468 (Lincoln; Smith, 2008, p. 272).

Wynchcombe, David: Hailes, 1461, when permitted 'out of consideration for his ailments' by the abbot of Cîteaux to wear linen (Harper–Bill, 1980, p. 112); abbot, Aberconwy, 1482 (*Statuta* 5, p. 432 [No. 1482/14]; blessed as abbot on commission from the bishop of Bangor at Hartlebury Castle by the bishop of Worcester, 13–01–1482 (*Reg. J. Alcock 93*); his rule and abbacy challenged by David Lloyd (*q.v.*) may have ended after a few years; resident at Hailes in 1495, he became abbot briefly of Cymer (1495–96), and then of Strata Marcella (1496–1513; in 1496, appointed a definitor of the Order for the line of Pontigny, and in 1510 for the line of La Ferté; Marmaduke Huby of Fountains thought highly of him (*Statuta* 5, pp. 123, 151–52, 377; Hays, 1963, pp. 135–37; *Letters*, p. 191).

Wynchcombe, Thomas: Hailes; *sd.* 1459 (Worcester; *Reg. J. Carpenter*, f. 549).

Wynchcombe, Walter: Bruern; *sd.* 1485 (Lincoln; *Reg. J. Russell*, f. 20r).

Wynchester: *see* Winchester.

Wyndresse, *al.* York, Leonard; Kirkstall, *sd.* and *d.* 1499, *p.* 1504 (York); sub–prior at suppression (Lonsdale, 1972, p. 205); pension, 1539, £8 (Cross and Vickers, 1995, pp. 140, 142, 152); in receipt of pension in 1555 (TNA, E164/31, f. 53v).

Wynmerhurst/Wymstherst, *al. ?* Drinkhurst, Alexander: Boxley, *disp.* 1538 (*FOR*, p. 123); in receipt of pension of £4 in 1555 (TNA, E164/31, f. 4).

Wynneslow/Wilmslow, *al.* Golson, Ranulph/Randal: Vale Royal; *ac.* and *sd.* 1521, *d.* 1522, *p.* 1523 (Lichfield; *Reg. G. Blyth*, n–f.); Recommended unsuccesfully in 1535 by Sir Piers Dutton to Cromwell for appointment as abbot there calling him 'a good religious man, discreet and well grounded in learning' (*LC*, pp. 122–23. No. LXXIII]).

Wynsor/Wynson, *al.* Hyde, William: Ford; signed surrender deed, 1539 (*DKR*, p. 21); pension, £5 (Youings, 1971, p. 186).

Wysbeche, William: Sawtry; *ac.* 1506, *sd.* and *d.* 1507 (Lincoln; *Reg. W. Smith*, n–f.).

Wythornwike: *see* Barrowe.

Yakesley, Richard: *see* Yaxley.

Yambson, Gabriel: Louth Park; *disp.* 1536 (*FOR*, p. 69).

Yansted, Geoffrey: Louth Park; *sd.* and *d.* 1533 (Lincoln; *Reg. J. Longland*, ff. 33r).

Yarom, John: Stratford; *ac.* 1495, *sd.* and *d.* 1498 (London; *Reg. R. Hill*, f. 30r; *Reg. T. Savage*, ff. 55v, 59r).

Yarom/Yarm, Thomas: *see* **Barker.**

Yarom/*al.* Poulson, Thomas: Rievaulx: *sd.* and *d.* 1509, *p.* 1514 (York); sacristan, 1525; present at the suppression, pension £5–6–8; not noted in the 1552 pension list (*DKR*, p. 38, Cross and Vickers, 1995, pp. 169–70, 179).

Yaxley/Yakesley, Richard: Thame; *ac.* 1497, *sd.* and *d..* 1501, *p.* 1504 (Lincoln; *Reg. W. Smith*, ff. 30v, 31v, 44r; in 1538 preached a sermon in St Mary Magdalene's Church, Oxford, upholding purgatory and the veneration of saints (Stevenson, 1939, p. 49); possessed of a pension of £5 until at least 1556.

Yaxley, Thomas: abbot, Sawtry, by 1479–1487; instituted to the church of Holcot, Lincolnshire, 1480 (Smith, 2008, p. 330).

Ydele/Ydell, John: Holm Cultram, by 1533 (Gilbanks, 1899, p. 94).signed deed of surrender and *disp.* 1538 (*DKR*, p. 23; *FOR*, pp. 123–24). In receipt of his pension of £4 in 1555 (TNA, E164/31, f. 73v).

Ydle, Thomas: Beaulieu, 1538 (*DKR*, p. 9).

Yens: *see* Jens.

Yerdley, John: Pipewell; *p.* 1493 (Lincoln; *Reg. J. Russell*, f. 50r).

Yerd(e)ley/Yardley, Thomas: Bordesley, *disp.* 1538 (*FOR*, p. 149; TNA, E322/26); in receipt of pension of £5–6–8 as late as 1555 (TNA, E164/31, f. 44r).

Yer(e)sley/*al.* Steynson, William: Rievaulx; *ac.* and *d.* 1490, *p.* 1493 (York); *disp.* 1538, pension: £5–6–8 (*FOR*, p. 156, *DKR*, p. 38); perhaps the cleric of that name who held the chantry of St Saviour in York Minster in 1546; dead by 1553 (Cross and Vickers, 1995, pp. 167, 181).

Ylmister: *see* Ilmister.

Yong, Alan: Stratford: *sd.* 1492 (London; *Reg. R. Hill*, f. 26v).

Yong/Yonges, John: Fountains; *sd.* 1514, *d.* 1516, *p.* 1517 (York; Cross and Vickers, 1995, pp. 114–15, 128).

Yong, John: Margam, *disp.* 1536 (*FOR*, p. 68).

Yong/Yonge, Thomas: Boxley; *d..* 1511, *p.* 1514 (Canterbury; LPL, *Reg. W. Warham* **2**, ff. 265v, 266v).

Yong, William: Basingwerk; *d.* and *p.* 1472 (Lichfield; *Reg. J. Hales*, ff. 247v, 248v).

York, James: Roche; *sd.* and *d.* 1490, *p.* 1493 (York; Cross and Vickers, 1995, p. 186).

York, John: Furness; *p.* 1486 (York; *Reg. T. Rotherham*, n–f.).

York, John: monk–bailiff at Strata Florida's granges at Abermîwl and Cwmdeuddwr granges, 1532–39; pension, £2–13–4 plus £1–6–8 granted him under convent seal on account of his duties; in receipt of both pensions in 1555; was still bailiff in 1543 and alive in 1558; in the years immediately following the Suppression he acted as chaplain at Strata Florida for the local populace (Williams, 1889, Appx. pp. xcii; TNA, E164/31, f. 75v; E315/233/219; *LP* **14**, Part 1, p. 362 [No. 748]).

York, Thomas: see Hoge.

York, Laurence: Rufford; *sd.* 1505, *d.* 1506, *p.* 1508 (York; *Reg. T. Savage*, ff. 131v, 133r; *sede vacante*, f. 604r).

York, Leonard: see Wyndresse.

York, Roger: Jervaulx; *sd.*and *d.* 1486, *p.* 1489 (York; Cross and Vickers, 1995, p. 129).

York, Thomas: Byland; *see* **Hogarth, Metcalfe.**

York, Thomas: St Mary Graces; *ac.* 1494, *d.* and *p.* 1495 (London; *Reg. R. Hill*, ff. 29v, 30v, 31r).

York, Thomas: Meaux; *ac.* and *sd.* 1485, *d.* and *p.* 1488 (York; Cross and Vickers, 1995, p. 153).

York, William: Jervaulx; *sd.* 1484, *d.* and *p.* 1486 (York; Cross and Vickers, 1995, p. 129).

Yorke, William: Jervaulx; *sd.* 1509, *d.* 1510, *p.* 1511 (York; Cross and Vickers, 1995, p. 130).
York, William: Vaudey; *ac., sd.,*and *d.* 1535 (Lincoln; *Reg. J. Longland,* ff. 42r, 43v, 46r).

CISTERCIAN NUNS, 1485–1540

(The nuns of Arthington and Wallingwells, claiming to be Cistercian at the time, are bracketed).

Abson, Joan: Basedale/Baysdale, 1528 (TNA, LR1/169, f. 445r).

Adlard, Margaret: Stixwould, 1525 (*VDL* **3**, p. 103).

Adleson/Addeson/Adderton, Agnes: Basedale, 1528 (TNA, LR1/169, f. 445r); aged forty in 1539; pension: £1 (Purvis, 1931, pp. 79–80) and 10s. 'reward' (TNA, SP5/2, f. 20 r). Dead by late 1543 (Cross and Vickers, 1995, p. 557).

Alcoke, Katherine: prioress, Wykeham, from 1521, dead by September 1528 (Smith, 2008, p. 677).

Alleyn/Alan, Alice: Hampole; fifty–nine years old in 1536 (Purvis, 1931, p. 114); pension £2–13–4 (Cross and Vickers, 1995, pp. 567–68).

Alston, Alice: prioress, Stixwould, 1505 (Smith, 2008, p. 694).

Amian/Amyas, Katherine: Fosse; in receipt of pension of 16s 8d in 1555 (TNA, E164/31, f. 19r).

Amcotts/Amcettes, Jane: Stixwould, moving then to Heynings (*LP* **14**, Part 1, p. 563 [No. 1280]); pension, £1–10–0; in 1554 was single and living in Asthorpe, Lincs. (Hodgett, 1959, p. 81).

Amcettes, Joan: Heynings; pension, 1539, £1–10–0 (*LP* **14**, Part 1, p. 563 [No. 1280]).

Anlaby, Katharine: prioress, Keldholme, by 1467 (VCH, *County of York* **3**, 1974, pp. 169–70); resigns, 1497, and appears to remain in the community (Smith, 2008, p. 659).

Anne … : prioress, Cook Hill, 1502 (Smith, 2008, p. 639).

Annes … : abbess, Llanllŷr, perhaps late 15th C. (Williams, 1975, p. 165).

Arley, Elizabeth: prioress, Hampole: 1504–1512 (Smith, 2008, p. 652); profession of obedience, 10–01–1504 (York; *Reg. T. Savage*, f. 36v).

Arte, Elizabeth: Swine; pension, 1539, £2–6–8; living in Riccall, North Yorkshire, aged forty in 1552; alive in 1556 (Cross and Vickers, 1995, pp. 589–90).

Arthynton, Agnes: Nun Appleton; sixty years old in 1553; pension, £2–6–8, received as late as 1555 (Cross and Vickers, 1995, p. 581; TNA, E164/31, f. 53r).

Arthyngton, Elizabeth: Hampole; pension of £2 received as late as 1555 (TNA, E164/31, f. 55r). Perhaps a blood relative of the foregoing nun; might it be that she transferred to Hampole on the closure of her house? (Cross and Vickers, 1995, p. 568).

Arthyngton, Isabella: last prioress, Hampole, 1518–1539 (Smith, 2008, p. 652); fifty years old in 1536 (Purvis, 1931, p. 114); pension of £10 received as late as 1573, but dead by 1582 (TNA, E164/31, f. 55r). Cross and Vickers, 1995, p. 567, has her becoming prioress only after 1532.

Aslaby, Agnes: Ellerton, transferring on its closure in 1537 to Nun Appleton; pension, £1–13–4, received as late as 1555; when forty–two years old; benefited by £6–13–4 and various goods under her father's will in 1542; married Brian Spofforth, rector of Burton in Ryedale, Yorkshire, in the early 1550s; in April 1554 he was deprived of his rectory and made to divorce from Agnes (Cross and Vickers, 1995, pp. 561, 581; TNA, E164/31, f. 53r); pension of £2–13–4 recorded by TNA, LR1/169, f. 473. Might she be *Agnes Simpson*, q.v?; seemingly alive in 1582

Augur/Aunger, Agnes: Nun Appleton; pension, £2 (*LP* **14**, Part 2, p. 232 [No. 636]). After the Suppression lived with her brother–in–law, Henry Burton of Bardsey, , Lincs., until his death in 1558; his executors then made provision for her (Woodward, 1966, p. 155).

Badersley/Badersby, Joan: prioress, Rosedale, from 1505 to ?1521 (Smith, 2008, p. 685; Seekings, 2005, p. 9); profession of obedience, 1–06–1505 (York; *Reg. T. Savage*, f. 65).

Bakbyse, Joan: prioress, Catesby, 1486–1502 (Smith, 2008, p. 636).

Bakeby, Joan: prioress, Sewardesley, by 1483 to at least 1488 (Smith, 2008, p. 688).

Bakpuys, Avise: infirmarian, Catesby, 1520 (*VDL* **3**, p. 102).

Banham: *see* **Baynham.**

Bank, Mary: Swine; pension, 1539, £2; in receipt of pension in 1556 (Cross and Vickers, 1995, pp. 589–90).

Barowe, Agnes: Stixwould, 1525 ((*VDL* **3**, p. 103).

Barton, Joan: *see* Gascon.

Battell/Bartell, Martha: Swine; pension, 1539, £2–6–8; was seventy–four years old in 1552, alive in 1556 (Cross and Vickers, 1995, pp. 589–90).

Bayn(e), Agnes: Esholt; said in 1536 to be 'continuing in religion'; although she had given birth to a child; aged fifty–five in 1539, pension: 26s 8d (Cross and Vickers, 1995, p. 563, Purvis, 1931, p. 81).

Bayne, Ellen: Nun Appleton; pension of £1–13–4 received as late as 1555 (TNA, E164/31, f. 53r) and 1582 (Cross and Vickers, 1995, pp. 580, 582).

Baynham, Elizabeth: prioress, Llanllŷr, 1532–1537 (Williams, 1975, pp. 165, 172); pension, £4 (*LP* **13**, Part 1, p. 577)>

Beydynghe, Ellen de., *al.* Weswyck: Sinningthwaite, 1482, when seeks dispensation allowing her to be promoted within the Order, although the daughter of a priest and an unmarried woman (*SAP* **2**, p. 237 [No. 2440]).

Belamy, Joan: Cook Hill; assessed in 1540 for subsidy on her pension of £2–13–4 (Bodleian Library, Oxford, Tanner MS 343; TNA, E315/245, f. 114). Could she be *Jane Bilbye*, q.v.

Bennyson/Beryson, Anna: Handale; daughter of Thomas Bennison of Liverton, Yorkshire; aged twenty–seven in 1536; pension, 1539, £1–6–8 (Cross and Vickers, 1995, p. 574; Purvis, 1931, pp. 75, 77).

Beswyk, Katherine: sub–sacrist, Gokewell, 1519 (*VDL* **2**, p. 154).

Bykley, Agnes: Catesby, 1530 (*VDL* **3**, p. 103).

Bikerley/Bykley, Joyce: prioress, Catesby, by 1508–1536; *disp.* to leave the religious life, 26–06–1537 (*FOR*, p. 101); the king's commissioners in 1536 praised her as 'a pure, wise, discreet and very religious woman,' who wished her house to stand; pension, £20 p.a. (warrant, 3–07–1536 (*TNA, E315/244, E315/278*, f. 107); Gasquet, 1899, pp. 296–97; Smith, 2008, p. 636).

Bikerley/Bykley, Joyce: a second nun of this name, perhaps a niece, occurs in the 1530 visitation of Catesby (*VDL* **3**, p. 103).

Bilbye, June/Jane: Fosse; pension, 1539, 16s 8d (*LP* **14**, Part 1, p. 556 [No. 1256]).

Billesby Elizabeth: sub–prioress, Greenfield, 1519–1521, when dead (Smith, 2008, p. 651); at a visitation in 1519 it was said that she regularly entertained two layfolk, Margaret Billesby and Agnes Stanley, at her table (*VDL* **2**, pp. 160–62).

Bird, Joan: Gokewell; pension of £2 received in 1555 (TNA, E164/31, f. 18v).

Bolner/Balner, Joan: Tarrant; pension, 1539, £3–6–8 (TNA, E315/245, f. 200; *DKR*, p. 43).

Borseley: *see* Worsley.

Bosome, Elizabeth: Stixwould, 1525 (*VDL* **3**, p. 103).

Bothe, Elizaberh: Gokewell, 1519 (*VDL* **2**, p. 154).

Bowarde, Alice: Gokewell; pension of £2 received in 1555 (TNA, E164/31, f. 18v).

Bragge, Mary: Tarrant, when suppressed, 1539 (TNA, E322/233). Her name does not appear in a pension list (TNA, E315/245, f. 200), unless 'Bragge' is an *alias* for *Mary Newborowe*, q.v.

Bramley, Joan: Rosedale, 1437, when given a dispensation on account of illegitimacy; sub–prioress when elected prioress, in 1468 (Smith, 2008, p. 685).

Brampton, Alice: Handale; allegedly bore a child, 1536/36 (*LP* **10**, p. 139 [No. 364]); pension, 1539, £1–13–4 (TNA, LR1/169, f. 414v), when seventy–three years old (TNA, SP5/2, f.1), so if this allegation was true she must have given birth many years earlier; dead by 1553 (Cross, 1995, p. 574).

Brathwayt, Joan: Wykeham; thirty years old in 1536, pension: £1–6–8 (Purvis, 1931, p. 94); pension in arrears in 1552, but still received in 1564 (Cross and Vickers, 1995, p. 596).

Brewer/Brewarne/Bruane/Browyng, Jane/Joan: precentrix, Nun Cotham; 1525 (*VDL* **3**, p. 37); in receipt of pension, £1–10–0, in 1555 (TNA, E164/31, f. 18v).

Bride, Isabel: precentrix, Stixwould, 1525 (*VDL* **3**, p. 103).

Broke, Agnes: Kirklees, forty years old in 1539 (Chadwick, 1902, p. 335); pension, £1–13–4; perhaps the Dame Agnes Broke of the Woodhouse, who made her will in 1558, asking to be buried in the parish church of Huddersfield (Cross and Vickers, 1995, pp. 577–78).

Bromley/Brownley/Brynlaw, Barbara: Basedale; sub–chantress, 1524, aged 30 in 1536, pension: £1, received as late as 1582 – she being the last survivor of Basedale (Burton, 1975/78, p. 146; Purvis, 1931, pp. 79–80; Cross and Vickers, 1995, p. 557).

Broune, Elizabeth: Legbourne, by 1525 (*VDL* **2**, p. 183), *disp.* 1536 (*FOR*, p. 73). Could she be the under–mentioned nun?

Browne, Elizabeth: Keldholme, 1497 (York; *Reg. T. Rotherham*, p. 152 [No. 1268]).

Bryneholme, Matilda: Nun Appleton; forty–four years old in 1536 (Harrison, 2001, p. 21).

Bucke, Dorothy: Nun Cotham; in house, 1525 (*VDL* **3**, p. 36); pension, 1539, £1–10–0 (*LP* **14**, Part 1, p. 563 [No. 1280]).

Bukton, Margaret: prioress, Basedale, 1523 –1524, when dies (Cross and Vickers, 1995, p. 557).

Bulmer/Dulmer, Anna: nun at its suppression, Basedale (TNA, SP5/2); aged thirty–two in 1536; pension: £1, gratuity, 10s. (Cross and Vickers, 1995, p. 558; Purvis, 1931, pp. 79–80).

Burghe, Elizabeth: Heynings; pension, 1539, £1–10–0 (*LP* **14**, Part 1, p. 563 [No. 1280]).

Burghill/Burrell, Joan: last prioress, Whistones; in receipt of pension of £5–10–0,, 1537 (TNA, E315/244/138) as late as 1555 (TNA, E164/31, f. 44v; Smith, 2008, p. 705).

Burton, Joan: Esholt; 29 in 1539 when awarded pension of 26s 8d, of which she was still in receipt in 1582 (Cross and Vickers, 1995, pp. 563–64; Purvis, 1931, p. 82).

Bussell: *see* Russell.

Buttre, Emma/Emeta: Wykeham; fifty–one years old in 51 in 1539, pension: £2–13–4 (Purvis, 1931, pp. 93–94).

Bykley: *see* Bikerley.

Calcote/Calcott, Ellen: last prioress, Douglas, Isle of Man; in receipt of her pension of £3–6–8 in 1555 (TNA, E164/31, f.74v; SC6/HENVIII/5677; Davey and Roscow, 2010, p. 175); it has been thought that as Margaret Goodman she married Robert Calcott, who was comptroller of the Isle of Man in 1538, but it is more likely she was his sister (*Manx Note Book* **3**, 1887).

Campbell, Elizabeth: last prioress, Sewardsley, by 1534–1536 (Smith, 2008, p. 688); pension, £5 (TNA, E315/244, No. 90).

Cartwright, Christine: Gokewell; pension of £10 received in 1555 (TNA, E164/31, f. 18v).

Cartar, Agnes: prioress, Sewardsley: her election quashed by the bishop on 21 March 1530, as she was allegedly 'a corrupt, apostate woman' who had borne a child, yet on 4 April that year the bishop appointed her: there may well be an error in dating in the register? (Smith, 2008, p. 688).

Carter, Elizabeth: Hampole; pension, 1539, £2 (TNA, LR1/169, f. 473).

Carter, Elizabeth: Nun Appleton; pension, £2 (Cross and Vickers, 1995, p. 580); forty–five years old in 1536 (Harrison, 2001, p. 21).

Carter, Margaret: Nun Appleton; pension, £2; by 1536 had borne a child (Cross and Vickers, 1995, pp. 580, 582); forty-seven years old in 1536 (Harrison, 2001, p. 21).

Carver: *see* Gawen.

Castelforth, Ann: Gokewell, granted dispensation on payment of £5, to be head of a religious house, despite being only twenty-six, 14 May 1534 (*FOR*, p. 1); last prioress, Gokewell, *disp.* 1536 (*FOR*, p. 80); alive and in receipt of £4 pension in 1554, when living in Amcotts, Lincolnshire, having married Robert Staynton (Hodgett, 1959, pp. 37, 78; Smith, 2008, p. 649); still in receipt of £4 pension in 1555 (TNA, E164/31, f. 18r).

Chapman, al. Derton, Felicity: Wykeham; aged twenty–nine in 1539, pension: £1-6-8 (TNA, LR1/169, f. 449; Purvis, 1931, p. 94); in 1552, came before the Yorkshire commissioners, and complained that her pension had not been paid for a whole year; alive in 1564 (Cross and Vickers, 1995, p. 596).

Cheverall, Anne: last sub–prioress, Tarrant, by 1535 (*VE* **1**, p. 267); pension, 1539, £5 (TNA, E315/245, f. 200; *DKR*, p. 43).

Christina ... : prioress, Sewardsley, 1502 (Smith, 2008, p. 688).

Christina ... : prioress, Nun Cotham, 1505 (Smith, 2008, p. 677).

Clayton, Elizabeth: Legbourne, *disp.* 1536 (*FOR*, p. 73).

Clayton, Joan: Heynings; pension, 1539, £1–10–0 (*LP* **14**, Part 1, p. 563 [No. 1280]).

Clifton, Alice: prioress, Stixwould, 1509 (Smith, 2008, p. 694).

Clifton, Elizabeth: Swine; aged twenty–four in 1536, still alive in 1573 (Purvis, 1931, p. 97); pension, £3–6–8 (TNA, LR1/169, f. 406r), which reportedly she had sold by 1553, though assessed on it as late as 1582 ; she may have been the daughter of Hezekiah Clifton, esq., of Burton Agnes, Yorkshire (Cross and Vickers, 1995, pp. 590–91)..

Clithero, Elizabeth: Swine; pension, 1539, £2–13–4 (Cross and Vickers, 1995, p. 589).

?Clithero, Isabel: Handale; pension, £2–13–4 (TNA, LR1/169, f. 414v). Was she *Isabel Norman*, q.v.?

Cockeson/Coxson, Isabel: Hampole; only nineteen in 1536 (Purvis, 1931, p. 114); pension of £2 received as late as 1555 (TNA, E164/31, f. 55r). Alive in 1602, when she must have been about eighty–five years old (Cross and Vickers, 1995, p. 568).

Coker, Edith: abbess, Tarrant, by 1525–1535, dead by 9 August 1535 (*LP* **9**, p. 79 [No. 236/6]; Smith, 2008, p. 699).

[**Cokyll, Katherine:** Arthington, 1539; pension, £1–6–8 (*LP* **14**, Part 2, p. 209 [No. 588])]

Cokyn/Collyn, Agnes: Esholt; forty–nine years old in 1539; said in 1536 to wish to continue in religious life, pension: 26s 8d; may have died by 1552. (Purvis, 1931, pp. 81–82, Cross and Vickers, 1995, pp. 563–64).

Colman, Alice: Nun Cotham; sacristan, 1525 (*VDL* **3**, p. 36); in receipt of pension, £2, in 1555 (TNA, E164/31, f. 18v).

Conyers, Cecily: Ellerton, disp. for illegitimacy, 1474 (Power, 1922, p. 31).

Copley, Elizabeth: Swine; aged 29 in 1536 (Purvis, 2001, 97); by 1536 allegedly had a child fathered by a priest (*LP* **10**, p. 138 [No. 364]), not in the pension list unless this surname was an *alias* (Thompson, 1824, pp. 68, 70–71); probably dead by 1543 (Cross and Vickers, 1995, 591).

[**Coventry, Alice:** Wallingwells; pension, £2 (*LP* **14**, Part 2, p. 249 [No. 681]).]

Cowper/Cockspear, Elizabeth: nun, Basedale; aged fifty–seven in 1536; pension, £1; in arrears in 1552, gratuity, 10s (Cross and Vickers, 1995, p. 558; Purvis, 1931, pp. 79–80). TNA, LR1/169, f. 442v, gives an *Isabel Cowper* with a pension of £1–6–8.

Cowper, Margaret: nun at its suppression, Basedale; aged 31 in 1536; pension: £1, but died shortly after the suppression (TNA, SP5/2; Purvis, 1931, pp. 79–80).

Cranmer, Alice: sister of Archbishop Thomas Cranmer and of Edmund Cranmer, archdeacon of Canterbury; nun, Stixwould; sacrist in 1525 (*VDL* **3**, p. 103); 'receiver' and in fact business manager, 1529 (BL. Add. Ch. 67119); leave in 3 June 1534 [fee of £10] to join any other order or community of nuns, and act as abbess or prioress, if so elected (*FOR*, p. 2). On 11 November 1534 she was elected, on the nomination of her brother, as abbess of Benedictine Minster, Kent. She had, in 1525, been a severe critic of the then prioress of Stixwould. Pension, 1536, £14, and given the lease from 1544 of Ashoverland rectory, Kent; dead by 1556 (Baskerville, 1936, pp, 287–89; 1937, p. 213).

Crober, Agnes: Greenfield; *disp.* 1538 (*FOR*, p. 71; *VDL* **3**, p. 102).

[**Croft, Isabel:** prioress, Wallingwells, 1508–?1517 (Smith, 2008, p. 701).

Crofts, Alice: Catesby, 1530 (*VDL* **3**, p. 103).

Curston, Alice: Fosse; pension, 1539, 16s 8d.(*LP* **14**, p. 256 [No. 1256]).

Cutler/Cuther/Cutlane, Agnes: Hampole; aged thirty–two in 1536 (Purvis, 1931, p. 114); pension of £2 received as late as 1555 (TNA, E164/31, f. 55r). She may have been the Anne Dodgeson *alias* Cutler of York, who made her will in 1557 wishing to be buried in St Cuthbert's church there. If so, she was not poor when she died, and had been in a position to lend money to her father and her nieces (Cross and Vickers, 1995, p. 569).

Cyes, Katherine: *see* **Tyas**.

Dalalyne/Delalyne/Lyne/Lynde, Margaret: last prioress, Tarrant by 1535 (*VE* 1, p. 267); pension, 1539, £6–13–4 (*DKR*, p. 43 – where noted as sub–prioress; TNA, E315/245, f. 200).

Davell, Elizabeth: prioress, Basedale, 1482–1497, after dispensation to be elected notwithstanding defect of age, 1481 (Smith, 2008, p. 626); resigns on being elected prioress of Keldholme, 20–08–1497; made profession of obedience before the official of the archdeacon of Cleveland. (York; *Reg. T. Rotherham*, p. 15 [Nos. 113–14]; dies, 1534, when still prioress (Power, 1922, p. 360n; (VCH, *County of York* **3**, 1974, p. 159).

Davell, Joan: prioress, Keldholme, *c.*1525 until her death in 1534 (Cross, 1995, p. 576).

Dene/Deyn, Eleanor: penultimate prioress, Swine, 1521–1537, when probably died (Cross, 1995, p. 590); profession of obedience, 18–03–1521 (York, *Reg. T. Wolsey*, f. 53r; Purvis, 1934, pp. 136–37 [No. 140]); on continuance of her house re–instated as prioress, 1 October 1537 (*LP* **12**, Part 2, p. 349 [No. 1008/2]..

Dodsworth, Margaret: Sinningthwaite, by 1520, when left by her mother a feather bed, a cover and a casket, two kerchiefs and ten yards of harden cloth (Cross and Vickers, 1995, p. 587).

Dogeson, Agnes: Esholt; forty years old in 1536; pension: 26s 8d; alive in 1556, seems to have died by 1564 (Cross and Vickers, 1995, pp. 563–64, Purvis, 1931, p. 82).

Dogeson, Barbara: Esholt; thirty–seven years old in 1536; pension: 26s 8d; perhaps dead by 1552 (Cross and Vickers, 1995, pp. 563, 565; Purvis, 1931, p. 82).

Dowe, Joan: Gokewell; pension of £2 received in 1555 (TNA, E164/31, f. 18v).

Duffelde, Joan: Heynings; pension, 1539, £1–13–4 (*LP* **14**, Part 1, p. 563 [No. 1280]).

Dunward, Grace: sacrist, Catesby, 1520 (*VDL* **3**, p. 102).

Dydmyll, Elizabeth: Tarrant, when suppressed, 1539 (*DKR*, p. 43; TNA, E322/233).

Dymock, Elizabeth: prioress, Stixwould, 1487 (Smith, 2008, p. 694).

Dynnell/Dennell/Dynwell, Margaret: Nun Cotham; in receipt of pension, £1–10–0, which was still paid in 1555 (TNA, E164/31, f. 18v).

Dyson/Dowsone, Margaret/Margery: Cook Hill; in receipt of pension of £2–13–4 as late as 1555 (TNA, E164/31, f. 44v); may previously have been a nun of Ellerton transferring on her house's closure in 1536; appointed in 1550 executrix of her will by Joan Harkey, former prioress of Ellerton (Cross and Vickers, 195, p. 561); assessed in 1540 for subsidy on her pension of £2–13–4 (Bodleian Library, Oxford, Tanner MS 343).

Edmundson, Elizabeth: prioress, Wykeham, dies by February 1488 (York; *Reg. T. Rotherham*, p. 58 [No. 471]).

Eglestone/Eccleston, Margaret: Douglas, Isle of Man, in receipt of her pension of £1–6–8 in 1555 (TNA, E164/31, f. 74v; Davey and Roscow, 2010, p. 175).

Eland, Cecily: Swine, prioress from 1506 (Smith, 2008, p. 697); profession of obedience, 23–09–1506 (Thompson, 1824, p. 54).

Elizabeth ... : prioress, Greenfield, 1483–1485 (Smith, 2008, p. 651).

Ellys, Helen: sub–prioress, Stixwould, 1525 (*VDL* 3, p. 103).

Elton, Margery: Nun Appleton; pension, 1539, of £2 (Cross and Vickers, 1995, pp. 580, 582).

Elsley, Elizabeth: Swine; pension, 40s, 1539; later lived in Northallerton and alive in 1564 (Thompson, 1824, p. 54).

Esquier, Elizabeth: prioress, Sinningthwaite, 1489–1509 (Smith, 2008, p. 691), general pardon, 1509 (*LP* 1, Part 1, p. 271 [No. 4/m. 25].

Etton, Alice: Sinningthwaite; sought dispensation to be advanced to any dignity of her Order, except the principal one, on account of defect of birth, 1467 (*SAP* 2, p. 60 [No. 1496]); further dispensation on account of illegitimate birth, 29–05–1482; four days later elected prioress; dead by early 1489 (Smith, 2008, p. 691).

Eursbye, Isabel: Nun Cotham; pension, `1539, £1–10–0 (*LP* 14, Part 1, p. 563 [No. 1280]).

Fairfax, Joan/Jane/Janet: Sinningthwaite, by 1526, when bequeathed by her father a maser with a band of silver and gilt, and 'a quy to make a cow upon' to the use of the house in return for the convent's prayers for his soul; on the suppression of Sinningthwaite, transferred to Nun Appleton; pension, £1–13–4, received as late as 1555 (TNA, E164/31, f. 53r). TNA, LR1/169, f. 473, gives pension as £2–13–4; out in the world she was close to one Guy Fairfax of Laysthorpe, having a child by him around 1552; the Court of Chancery in 1555 ordered her to perform public penance in Stonegrave church and to separate entirely from Fairfax's company (Cross and Vickers, 1995, pp. 582, 587).

Felton, Matilda/Maud: Rosedale; prioress, 1521 to at least 1524 (Smith, 2008, p. 685); profession of obedience, 5–12–1522 (York; *Reg. T. Wolsey*, f. 42r).

Feny, Alice: Stixwould, 1525 (*VDL* 3, p. 103).

? Ffownter, Katherine: Wintney, 1501 (CCA, DCc/Register R, f. 139r).

Fillbaron, Alice: Legbourne, 1525; alleged by one witness at the visitation that year of being of levity in her speech (*VDL* 2, p. 182).

FitzRichard, Joan: Nun Appleton; no date given (Power, 1922, p. 326).

FitzWilliam, Margaret: Legbourne, *disp.* 1536 (*FOR*, p. 73).

Fleshewer, Joan: Keldholme, 1497 (York; *Reg. T. Rotherham*, p. 152 [No. 1268]).

Fletcher, Joan: Rosedale, professed, 1503; aged thirty–five in when became prioress of Basedale; profession of obedience, 13 August 1524 (York; *Reg. T. Wolsey*, f.72v); in 1527 when forced to resign on account of immorality for sometime she lived outside the cloister, and then at Rosedale, *c.*1530–34, but was readmitted to Basedale in 1534; by 1536 she had borne a child (TNA, *LP* 10, p. 139 [No. 364]); pension of £1 (granted on closure of Basedale) and £3–6–8 (awarded on her resignation as prioress). Dead before 1564 (Burton, 1978, pp. 146–151; Cross and Vickers, 1995, p. 557; Smith, 2008, p. 626).

Fletcher, Margaret: prioress, Kirklees, 1506 (Chadwick, 1902, p. 321; Smith, 2008, 660); profession of obedience, 10 March 1506 (York; *Reg. T. Savage*).

Foderby, Dorothy: Stixwould, 1525 *(VDL 3, p. 103)*.

Foster, Helen: sub–prioress, Nun Appleton, 1509 (Harrison, 2001, p. 14).

Foster/Fforster, Katherine: Sinningthwaite; last prioress, election confirmed, 14 January 1535 (York; *Reg. E. Lee*, f. 11r–v; *VDY*, p. 439n; pension, £6–13–4 (TNA, E315/244, No. 29). In her will, made 11 September 1543, she desired burial 'within her parish church of Tadcaster,' Yorkshire; amongst her bequests was a white satin cope for Stainburn chapel (Cross and Vickers, 1995, p. 586). Frampton: *see* Brampton.

Frances, Joan: Legbourne, 1453, when sought dispensation on account of old age to remain in her room, and eat, drink and pray there, and to be excused from choir (*SAP*, p. 164 [No. 729]).

Franklyn, Johanna: prioress, Cookhill, 1490, when deposed, accused of serious shortcomings (*Letters*, pp. 131–32 [No. 66], 138–39 [No. 67]; 146–47 [73]).

Frith/Firth, Agnes; prioress, Esholt, 1505–07;profession of obedience, 16–11–1505 (York; *Reg. T. Savage*; no author named, *The Cistercian Priory of S. Leonard at Esholt in Airedale*, London: J.C. Hotten, 1866, pp. 33–34; Smith, 2008, p. 644). Named as 'Agnes' in the archbishop's commissary's deed, in her vow she calls herself 'Margaret.' Presumably a copying error.

Frobisher/Furbisher, Agnes: Hampole; aged thirty–six in 1536 (Purvis, 1931, p. 114); pension, £2–6–8 (TNA, LR1/169, f. 454). May have been the daughter of John Frobysher of Altofts, who provided for his daughter, Agnes, in his will of 1542 (Cross and Vickers, 1995, p. 569).

Fyddell/Fiddle/Feddle, Alice: Nun Cotham; cellarer, 1525 *(VDL 3*, p. 36); in receipt of pension, £1–10–0, in 1554, when unmarried and living at Barton–on–Humber, Lincs (Hodgett, 1959, pp. 42, 109), and 1555 (TNA, E164/31, f. 18v).

Fishwick/Fysswyke, Amea/Ann: Legbourne, by 1525 *(VDL 2*, p. 183); *disp.* 1536 *(FOR, 73)*.

Garrett, Agnes: Legbourne, 1525 *(VDL 2*, p. 182).

Gascoyn/Gaston, Isabel: Nun Appleton; pension, £2 (TNA, LR1/169, f. 473; Cross and Vickers, 1995, p. 580); aged fifty–four in 1536 (Harrison, 2001, p. 21).

Gascoyne, Joan: last sub–prioress, Hampole; 63 in 1536 (Purvis, 1931, p. 114); pension of £3–6–8 received as late as 1555 (TNA, LR1/169, f. 454). She appears at the end of the Nun Appleton list of nuns but with a cancellation line (TNA, LR1/169, f. 473).

Gawen/Carver, Anne: Tarrant, when suppressed, 1539 (TNA, E322/233); pension, £3–6–8 (TNA, E315/245, f. 200).

Gayle, Catherine: Wykeham; aged twenty–eight in 1539, pension: £1–6–8 (Purvis, 1931, p. 94); god–daughter of the last prioress, Catherine Nendyk; alive in 1564 (Cross and Vickers, 1995, pp. 596–97).

Gill, Elizabeth: Wykeham; aged forty in 1536, pension: £1–6–8 (Purvis, 1931, p. 94); paid as late as 1582 (Cross and Vickers, 1995, p. 597).

Gimmeld, Agnes: Legbourne, 1525 *(VDL 2*, p. 182).

Godehand, Joan: Legbourne, by 1525; prioress 1529–1535 (Smith, 2008, p. 663; *VDL 2*, p. 183).

Goderne/Goderick/Goodrich, Anne/Agnes: Stixwould, 1525 *VDL 3*, p. 103); prioress, Greenfield; 1530–1538 (Lincoln R.O. 2ANC1/18/11); disp. 1536 *(FOR*, p. 73); alive in 1550 (Smith, 2008, p. 651).

Goldesburgh, Anne: prioress, Sinningthwaite, by 1529 (Smith, 2008, p. 691); resigned in 1535 after an unsatisfactory visitation report, awarded a pension of £10 (*VDY*, p. 439n) and allowed a parlour with a chamber in the convent (York; *Reg. E. Lee*, f. 11v); accused of detention of deeds (TNA, C1/833/46). Dead by Michaelmas 1543 (Cross and Vickers, pp. 586–87).

Goldesburgh, Joan: Sinningthwaite, 1520 (Cross and Vickers, 1995, p. 588).

Goldsmith, Katherine: Whistones, 1485 (Worcester; *Reg. J. Alcock*, f. 214).

[**Goldsmyth, Margaret:** last prioress, Wallingwells, 1522–1535; pension, £6 (*LP* **14**, Part 2, p. 249 [No. 681]); profession of obedience, 22–01–1522 (York; *Reg. T. Wolsey*, ff. 43v–44r)].

Golybright vergh Llywelyn ap Johns: prioress, Llanllugan, 1524–1536 (*LP* **13**, Part 1, p. 576; TNA, SC6/5257). She may perhaps be equated with *Rose Lewis*, q.v. (Williams, 1975, p. 159).

Goold, Edith: abbess, Tarrant, 1486/93 or 1504/15 (TNA, C1/137/40; Smith, 2008, p. 699).

Gore/Gower, Joan: Nun Appleton, by 1520, when left 6s 8d in a will; in 1527 the vicar of Masham bequeathed her 'his bed covering of new work' whilst Thomas Ryther left her £1–6–8; pension, £2, received in 1555, when fifty–two years old (TNA, E164/31, f. 53r; Cross and Vickers, 1995, p. 583) but, if the same nun, was sixty years old in 1536 (Harrison, 2001, pp. 14, 21). Perhaps there were two nuns of like name.

Graunde/Growance, Agnes: Greenfield, 1525, accused at the visitation that year of being a scold; of a weak disposition and friendly with one James Smyth (*VDL* **2**, p. 163; see Chapter 8).

Grice, Katherine: Kirklees, aged twenty-five in 1539 (Chadwick, 1902, p. 335); pension, £1–13–4 (Cross and Vickers, 1995, pp. 577–78).

Grimston, Elizabeth: Swine; aged twenty-four in 1536 (Purvis, 1931, p. 97); pension, £2–6–8 (TNA, LR1/169, f. 408); *disp.* 1538 (*FOR*, p. 73). She married one Pykkerd of Welwick, Yorkshire, and was still in receipt of her pension in 1582: Cross and Vickers, 1995, p. 591 give her as aged only nineteen in 1536.

Growannce: *see* Graunde.

Grymston, Joan: Stixwould, 1525 (*VDL* **3**, p. 103).

Gudband: *see* Godehand.

[**Hall, Elizabeth:** said to be the prioress of Cistercian Arthington when that house was exempted from suppression, 11–03–1538 (*LP* **13**, Part 1, p. 242 [Grant 17]; pension, £5 (*LP* **14**, Part 2, p. 209 [No. 588])].

Harkey, Joan: last prioress, Ellerton, by 1534 (Warwickshire R.O., CR26/1/12/L/69); made her will in 1550 (Cross and Vickers, 1995, p. 561; Smith, 2008, p. 642).

Harte/Herte, Ales/Alice: sacrist, Tarrant, 1535 (*VE* **1**, 267); in house when suppressed 1539 (TNA, E322/233); pension, 1539, £4 (TNA, E315/245, f. 200).

[**Hayles, Joan:** Arthington; pension, 1539, £1–6–8 (*LP* **14**, Part 2, p. 209 [No. 588]).]

Heigham, Joan: abbess, Marham, 1480–1502 (Smith, 2008, p. 669 ; the convent accounts exist for 1492–93 (Norwich R.O., Hare 2211).

Herryson/Haryson, Joan: Hampole; aged fifty in 1536 (Purvis, 1931, p. 114); pension, £2–13–4 (TNA, LR1/169, f. 454).

Higden, Isabel: Nun Cotham; in house, 1525 (*VDL* **3**, p. 36).

Hillerde/Hylyarde/Heliarde, Eleanor: Nun Cotham; in house, 1525 (*VDL* **3**, p. 36); was left 6s. 8d. in will of James Myssenden of Great Limber, Lincolnshire, 1529 (Power, 1922, p. 326); in receipt of pension, £1–13–4, in 1555 (TNA, E164/31, f. 18v).

Hobe, Joan: sacristan, Basedale, 1525 (Cross and Vickers, 1995, p. 558).

Holwall/Hoswall, Elizabeth: at Tarrant, when suppressed, 1539 (TNA, E322/233); pension, £4 (TNA, E315/245, f. 200).

Hollynraws/Hollynraker, Joan: Esholt; aged seventy–four in 1536, when said that she was 'lame and not able to ride'; she appeared to be living with friends but wearing her habit; her name is not in the 1539 pension list, so perhaps had died (Purvis, 1931, pp. 81–82, Bell, 1938, p. 31; Cross and Vickers, 1995, p. 565).

Hopton, Isabella: Kirklees; aged fifty in 1536/39 (Chadwick, 1902, p. 335); pension, £2–13–4 (TNA, LR1/169, f. 416); £1–13–4: *LP* **14**, Part 2, p. 577 [No. 1520].

Horneby, Alice: prioress, Wykeham, 1502 to 1508, when dies (Smith, 2008, p. 710); profession of obedience, 18 September 1502 (York; *Reg. T. Savage*).

Horseman, Agnes: Hampole; pension of £2 received as late as 1555 (TNA, E164/31, f. 55r). She is not mentioned in the 1536 list of the community (Purvis, 1931, p. 114), but alive in 1564. She may have transferred to Hampole from another house between 1536 and 1539 (Cross and Vickers, 1995, p. 570).

Horsolde/Horsforth, Joan: Legbourne, 1525 (*VDL* **2**, p. 183); disp. 1536 (*FOR*, p. 73).

Hostbye/Osteby, Margaret: Nun Cotham; in house, 1525 (*VDL* **3**, p. 36); pension, 1539, £1–10–0 (*LP* **14**, Part 1, p. 563 [No. 1280]).

Hughes, Elizabeth: Gokewell; last prioress Cook Hill, 1537–1539 (*VCH, County of Worcester* **2**, 1906, p. 158; Smith, 2008, p. 639; in receipt of pension of £8 as late as 1555 (TNA, E164/31, f. 44r).

Hunt, Sybil: Catesby, 1530 (*VDL* **3**, p. 103).

Hutton/Huson, Joan/Jonetta: Esholt; aged thirty in 1536, when intending not to continue in the religious life. By September 1535, she had given birth to a child, and was penanced by the archbishop of York; pension: 26s 8d (TNA, LR1/169, f. 349r; Cross and Vickers, 1995, pp. 563, 565; Purvis, 1931, p. 82).

Hyk, Cecilia: prioress, Kirklees, 1472–1491 (Smith, 2008, p. 660); she was bequeathed 10s. in 1487; died *c.*1491 (Chadwick, 1902, pp. 321, 364, 366).

Hyll, Cecilia: Catesby, 1530 (*VDL* **3**, p. 103).

Hyltoft, Joan: Nun Cotham, before 1482 (Bell, 1938, pp. 170–71).

Ithell, Elen: Douglas; pension, £1–6–8, 1540 (TNA, SC6/HENVIII/5677; Davey and Roscow, 2010, p. 175).

Jacklyng, Margaret: Nun Cotham; pension, 1539, £1–10–0 (*LP* **14**, Part 1, p. 563 [No. 1280]).

[**Jacson, Joan:** Wallingwells; pension, £2 (*LP* **14**, Part 2, p. 249 [No. 681]).]

Joan ... : prioress, Nun Cotham, 1500 (Smith, 2008, p. 677).

Joan ... : prioress, Stixwould, 1503–04 (Smith, 2008, p. 694).

Jenkinson, Isabel: Swine; still alive in 1582 (Cross and Vickers, 1995, p. 591); pension, £2–13–4 (TNA, LR1/169, f. 406r).

Jenkins(on), Joan: last prioress, Esholt, by 1536 (when aged forty) to 1539 (Smith, 2008, p. 644; pension, £6–13–4 (TNA, LR169, f. 349r);. dead by 1556 (Bell, 1938, p. 32).

Johnson, Agnes: Greenfield, by 1525 (*VDL* **2**, p. 161); disp. 1538 (*FOR*, p. 73).

Johnson, Anna: Nun Appleton; pension, £2, received as late as 1555 (TNA, E164/31, f. 53r); aged forty in 1553, and still alive in 1564 (Cross and Vickers, 1995, p. 583). An 'Agnes' Johnson, but not Anne, is noted in 1536 by Harrison, 2001, p. 21.

Johnson, Margaret; sub–prioress, Nun Cotham, 1525 (*VDL* **3**, p. 36); left 6s. 8d. in will of James Myssenden of Great Limber, Lincolnshire, 1529 (Power, 1922, p. 326).

?Julowe/Ineleron/ine Lewin, Agnes: Douglas, I.O.M., in receipt of her pension of £1–6–8 in 1555 (TNA, E164/31, f. 74v; Davey and Roscow, 2010, p. 175).

Kelk, Joan: prioress, Swine, 1483–1498 (Smith, 2008, p. 697); profession of obedience, 4–03–1483 (Thompson, 1824, p. 54).

Kelk, Margaret: Nun Cotham; in house, 1525 (*VDL* **3**, p. 36); but resident in 1530 at Catesby where deponents in the visitation there that year said that she absented herself from choir, that she was disobedient, and was a source of discord (*VDL* **3**, p. 103).

Kereston/Cheriston, Elena: Wykeham; aged forty–four in 1539, pension: £1–13–4 (Purvis, 1931, p. 94); still in receipt of pension in 1556 (Cross and Vickers, 1995, p. 596).

Key, Ellen/Helen: prioress, Stixwould, 1514–36 (Smith, 2008, pp. 694–95; TNA, E118/1/31, ff. 52–60).

Kirby, Joan: Wykeham; aged forty in 1536, pension: £1–6–8 (Purvis, 1931, p. 94; in receipt of pension in 1556 (Cross and Vickers, 1995, p. 597).

Kirkeby, Elizabeth: prioress, Fosse, by 1498, when dies (Smith, 2008, p. 647).

Knight, Dorothy: last prioress, Swine, 1538/39; pension, £13–6–8. after only a short period as prioress; in receipt of pension as late as 1582 (Cross and Vickers, 1995, p. 589; Purvis, 1931, p. 97; TNA, LR1/169, ff. 368–400; (Smith, 2008, p. 697).

Kylburne, Matilda/Magdalene: Nun Appleton; forty–two years old in 1536 (Harrison, 2001, p. 21); pension, £2, received as late as 1555 (TNA, E164/31, f. 53r); aged sixty in 1553, she seems to have died by 1564 (Cross and Vickers, 1995, p. 583).

Kyppes/Kyppax/Janet, Joan: last prioress, Kirklees, 1539, aged 50; pension, only £2 (*LP* **14**, Part 2, p. 577 [No. 1520]); then lived with four sisters at Mirfield and buried in Mirfield church, 5–02–1562 (Chadwick, 1902, pp. 322, 335; Cross and Vickers, 1995, p. 577).

[**Kyrkeby, Elizabeth:** Wallingwells; prioress there, profession of obedience, ?20–07–1505 (York; *Reg. T. Savage*); pension, £2–13–4 (*LP* , Part 2, p. 249 [No. 681]).]

Lacy, Dorothy: Stixwould; ?of the Cistercian foundation; pension: £2; living in 1554 at Brigsley, Lincolnshire (Hodgett, 1959, p. 112).

Langton, Anne: penultimate prioress, Nun Appleton, 1507–1539 (Sheffield Archives EM/844–45; Smith, 2008, p. 676); profession of obedience, 28 February 1507 (York; *Reg. T. Savage*); was eighty years old in 1536 but died in the interval between the survey of the monastery and its closure in December 1539 (Cross and Vickers, 1995, p. 580; Harrison, 2001, p. 21).

Lasingby, Elizabeth: prioress, Esholt, 1475–1480, then prioress again (unless another nun of like name), 1497–1505; profession of obedience, 3–08–1497 (York; *Reg. T. Rotherham*, p. 126 [Nos. 1045–46]; Smith, 2008, p. 644).

Lasinge/Lasyn, Isabel: Hampole; aged thirty–eight in 1536 (Purvis, 1931, p. 114); pension of £2–6–8 received as late as 1555 (TNA, E164/31, f. 55r).

[**Lendford, Elizabeth:** Wallingwells; pension, £2 (*LP* **14**, Part 2, p. 249 [No. 681]).

Lenney/Lumney, Meriall: Handale; aged thirty–four in 1536; pension of 26/8d (Purvis, 1931, pp. 75, 77); dead by 1540 (Cross and Vickers, 1995, p. 575).

Lenthe, Dorothy: licence to be professed as a nun of Whistones, 4–08–1531 (Worcester R.O., ; *Reg. Various*: BA 2648/8 (ii)].

Lenthorpe/Leventhorpe, Joan: Kirklees; aged sixty in 1539; pension, £2 (Fletcher, 1919, p. 317; Chadwick, 1902, p. 335; TNA, LR1/169, f. 349v).

Lewys, Rose: prioress, Llanllugan, 1536; pension, £3–6–8 (*LP* **13**, Part 1, p. 577). See *Elizabeth Baynham* above. Rose might be an *alias*, or she might have been sub–prioress but unlikely.

Lightfoot, Elizabeth: Marham, 1536; seems to have continued in religion on its closure (TNA, E117/14/22).

Li.ster, Alice: Stixwould; solemnly professed in 1529/29 (BL. Add Ch. 67119).

Logham/Loghan, Margaret: Handale; aged forty–two in 1536; pension, 1539, of £1–6–8 was upgraded to £1–13–4; it was noted that 'she is lame' (Purvis, 1931, pp. 75, 77).

Lovell, Dorothy: Marham; 1536 (TNA, E117/14/22).

Lowe, Beatrix: prioress, Swine, 1498–1506 (*MCP*, pp. 136–37 [No. 140]; TNA, C1/227/68; Smith, 2008, p. 697). Profession of obedience, 22 December 1489 (Thompson, 1824, p. 54).

Lutton, Anna: last prioress, Handale, 1532–1539 aged fifty–one in 1536; pension, £6–13–4 (Purvis, 1931, pp. 74, 77); may later have lived at New Malton, Yorkshire, dying in 1551(Smith, 2008, p. 653; Cross and Vickers, 1995, p. 573).

Lyndley, Isabel: Heynings; pension, 1539, ££1–10–0 (*LP* **14**, Part 1, p. 563 [No. 1280]).

Lyne: *see* Delalyne.

Lyon, Elizabeth: last prioress, Keldholme, 1534–1536 (Smith, 2008, p. 659); pension, £2; alive in 1582 (Cross and Vickers, 1995, p. 576).

Maltby, Joan: Stixwould, 1525 (*VDL* **3**, p. 103).

Margaret ... : prioress, Llanllŷr, 1488 (Williams, 1975, p. 165).

Margery ... : prioress, Ellerton, 1521 (Smith, 2008, p. 642).

Marre, Agnes: last prioress, Fosse, 1539 (Smith, 2008, p. 647); pension, £2–13–4 (TNA, E315/245, f. 23).

Marshall, Mary: Nun Appleton; prioress, Rosedale, 1527–1536; profession of obedience, 6 May 1526 (York; *Reg. T. Wolsey*, f. 84v); pension, £6; probably dead by 1552 (Cross and Vickers, 1995, p. 585).

Marshall/Martiall, Matilda: reputedly a nun of Esholt who retired nearby, dying only about 1607, but her name does not occur in the pension lists (Bell, 1938, pp. 32–33, Cross and Vickers, 1995, p. 565).

Martyn, Elizabeth: Legbourne, *disp.* 1536 (*FOR*, p. 73).

Martyn, Elizabeth: prioress, Wintney, 1534–1536 (Smith, 2008, p. 708; *LP* **11**, p. 155 [No. 385/3]); still receiving a pension of £10 in 1555 (TNA, E164/31, f. 13r).

Mason, Barbara: last abbess, Marham, 1507–37, when dispensed (TNA, E117/14/22); accused in 1535/36 of illicit relations with the prior of nearby Pentney (*LP* 10, pp. 138–39 [No. 364]); after suppression lived with family at 'Hayle', Suffolk; died between 4 and 14 September 1538, and willed to have a marble tombstone (Smith, 2008, p. 669; *WIB*, pp. 133–35).

Matilda ....: prioress, Heynings, to 1524 (Smith, 2008, p. 654).

Mawde (Maud)/Malor/Man', Dorothy: Nun Appleton; pension, £2, received as late as 1555 (TNA, E164/31, f. 53r); forty–six years old in 1553, but still alive in 1564 (Cross and Vickers, 1995, pp. 580, 5833). See *Dorothy Robinson* below.

Mawde/Mandy. Elizabeth: Esholt; aged forty–nine in 1539 when awarded pension of 26s 8d (Purvis, 1931, pp. 81–82, Cross and Vickers, 1995, pp. 563, 566).

Mershall, Margaret: Heynings; pension, 1539, £`1–10–0 (*LP* **14**, Part 1, p. 563 [No. 1280]).

Messodyn/Missenden, Joan: Legbourne, by 1525 (*VDL* **2**, p. 183); last prioress, *disp.* 1536 (*FOR*, p. 73); in receipt of £7 pension, in arrears in 1552 (Hodgett, 1959, pp. 37, 57); pension still paid in 1555 (TNA, E164/31, f. 18r). In 1554 she was living at Corby, Lincolnshire and was married to William Ottbie, gent. (Hodgett, 1959, p. 112; Smith, 2008, p. 663).

Michell, Eleanor: Tarrant, when suppressed, 1539 (TNA, E322/233); pension, 1539, £4 (TNA, E315/245, f. 200).

Milkyn: *see* Wilkin.

Mol(l)ens, Joan: Tarrant, when suppressed, 1539 (TNA, E322/233); pension, £4 (TNA, E315/245, f. 200).

Moigne, al. Maye, Elizabeth: infirmarian, Stixwould, 1519 to at least 1525 (*VDL* **3**, pp. 102–03).

[**Moore, Elizabeth:** Arthington; pension, 1539, possibly sub–prioress; £1–13–4 (*LP* **14**, Part 2, p. 209 [No. 588]).

Mor', Juliana: Wintney, 1501 (CCA, DCc/Register R, f. 139r).

More, Joan: Tarrant; cellarer, 1535 (*VE* **1**, p. 267); in house when suppressed, 1539 (TNA, E322/233); pension, 1539, £4 (TNA, E315/245, f. 200).

Morgan, Anne: Cook Hill; assessed in 1540 for subsidy on her pension of £3–6–8 (Bodleian Library, Oxford, Tanner MS 343).

Morton, Joan: Whistones; prioress from 1485 to at least 1492; blessed, 15–12–1485 (Worcester; *Reg. J. Alcock*, f. 214; Smith, 2008, p. 704).

Morton/Norton, Elizabeth: Tarrant, when suppressed, 1539 (TNA, E322/233); pension, 1539, £4 (TNA, E315/245, f. 200).

Nellys, Agnes: Basedale, by 1524 (TNA, LR1/169, f. 445r; Cross and Vickers, 1995, p. 558); aged twenty–nine in 1536; pension: £1 (Purvis, 1931, pp. 79–80). She must have been a teenager when she was professed.

Nelson, Margaret: Heynings; pension, 1539, £`1–10–0 (*LP* **14**, Part 1, p. 563 [No. 1280]).

Nendyk/Nandyke, Catherine: last prioress, Wykeham, from about 1508 to 1536, when aged seventy, being granted a pension of £6–13–4. By her will, proved in 1541, she left 6s 8d., to each of her former nuns, and made several other bequests showing that she was comfortably off (Chapter 8); she desired burial in the chancel of Kirkby Moorside church where her father and mother were buried, leaving money for a £4 stipend for priest for a year to offer Mass for her and good friends' souls there (CIY project; Cross and Vickers, 1995, pp. 595–96; Purvis, 1931, pp. 93–94, 145–46, 149; Smith, 2008, p. 711).

Nendyk, Isabella: Wykeham; aged forty–four in 1539, probably a relative of the above–mentioned nun; pension: 26s 8d (Purvis, 1931, p. 94) or £2–13–4 (TNA, LR1/169, f. 449); in 1552, her pension had not been paid for a whole year; alive in 1564 (Cross and Vickers, 1995, p. 597).

Newborrowe, Mary: Tarrant, when suppressed, 1539 (TNA, E322/233); pension, 1539, £4 (TNA, E315/245, f. 200).

Newcombe, Margaret: Greenfield; at the visitation of 1525, it was alleged that she had borne a child, had been disobedient and absented herself from divine office (Chapter 8); *disp.* 1538 (*VDL* **2**, pp. 160–63); *disp.* 1538 (*FOR*, p. 73).

Nicolson, Alice: Swine; pension, £2 (TNA, LR1/169, f. 406r), which she still drew in 1582 (Cross and Vickers, 1995, p. 592).

Norman, Isabella: Handale; aged twenty–nine in 1539; pension of 26/8d (Purvis, 1931, pp. 75, 77); daughter of George Norman of Thirkleby, Lincolnshire, who provided for her in his will of 29–01–1539 (Cross and Vickers, 1995, p. 575).

Nornabell/Normavelle, Eleanor: Nun Appleton, by 1520; by 1536 had given birth to a child; last prioress, but only for three months, 1539/40 (Cross and Vickers, 1995, pp. 580–81; Smith, 2008, p. 676); pension £2–6–8 (TNA, E315/246, f. 21 – where noted as sub–prioress; fifty–six years old in 1536. The Normaville family had connections with the convent going back to 1303 (Harrison, 2001, p. 21).

Norton, Alice: Keldholme, 1497 (York; *Reg. T. Rotherham*, p. 152 [No.1268]).

Nutting, Agnes: Heynings; pension, 1539, £1–10–0 (*LP* **14**, Part 1, p. 563 [No. 1280]).

?Olwarde, Anne: Gokewell; pension of £2 received in 1555 (TNA, E164/31, f. 18v).

Osborne, Agnes: 'president', Whistones, 1485 (Worcester; *Reg. J. Alcock*, f. 214).

Osgarby, Joan/Jane: Gokewell; *disp.* 1536 (*FOR*, p. 80); then moved to Fosse until its closure in 1539 (*LP* **14**, p. 256 [No. 1256]); receiving pension of 16s 8d as late as 1555 (TNA, E164/31, f. 19r).
Otteley, Agnes: prioress, Legbourne, by 1519–1529 when dies; criticised at a visitation in 1525 for the lack of instruction given to the junior nuns (*VDL* 2, pp. 182–83).
Owley, Elen: Cook Hill; assessed in 1540 for subsidy on her pension of £2–13–4 (Bodleian Library, Oxford, Tanner MS 343).

Palmer, Joan: Catesby, 1520 (when sub–precentrix) to 1530 or later (*VDL* **3**, pp. 102–03).
Parker, Ales/Alice: Tarrant, when suppressed, 1539 (TNA, E322/233); pension, 1539, £4 (TNA, E315/245, f. 200).
Parker, Elizabeth: Ellerton; transferring on its closure in 1537 to Nun Appleton; in 1550, was left 12d. in will of Joan Harkey, the last prioress of Ellerton, but died about that time (Cross and Vickers, 1995, pp. 561, 583); pension, £2–13–4 (TNA, LR1/169, f. 473); £1–13–4 (*LP* **14**, Part 2, p. 232 [No. 636]).
Patericke/Patricke, Elizabeth: Swine; pension, £2 (TNA, LR1/169, f. 406r), which she received as late as 1557; seemingly lived in Hull with a another nun of Swine, Elizabeth Thorne, who in 1557 left Elizabeth her house and made her executrix of her will (Cross and Vickers, 1995, p. 592).
Percy/Pieroy, Elizabeth: Wykeham; aged twenty–four in 1536, pension: £1–6–8 (Purvis, 1931, p. 94; Cross and Vickers, 1995, pp. 597–598); she was probably related to Katherine, Countess of Northumberland. .
[**Pettye, Agnes:** Arthington; pension, 1539, £1–6–8 (*LP* **14**, Part 2, p. 209 [No. 588])
[**Petyngher, Agnes:** Wallingwells; pension, £2 (*LP* **14**, Part 2, p. 249 [No. 681]).]
Pigeon, Petronilla: Wintney; prioress, 1460–1498 (Smith, 2008, p. 708).
Pighan, Agnes: Handale; aged seventy–five in 1539; pension of £1–13–4 (Purvis, 1931, pp. 75, 77).
Passemer/Plasmer/Placemer/Passmire, Alice: sacrist, Gokewell, 1519 (*VDL* 2, p. 154); nun, Nun Cotham; in receipt of pension, £2, in 1555 (TNA, E164/31, f. 18v).
Pinchebeck, Elizabeth: Legbourne, 1525 (*VDL* **2**, p. 182).
Plumer, Elizabeth: Marham, 1536; seems to have continued in religion on its closure (TNA, E117/14/22).
[**Porter, Dorothy:** Arthington; pension, 1539, £1–6–8 (*LP* **14**, p. 209 [No. 588]).
Prytfeld, Isabella: Greenfield, 1525 (*VDL* **2**, p. 161).
Pudsey, Eliabeth: prioress, Esholt, 1512–1535 ; blessed 9–03–1512; no longer prioress when said in 1536 to be 70, 'decrepid and not able to ride' and desiring of living with friends; pension unknown – she may have died by 1539 (Cross and Vickers, 1995, p. 564; Bell, 1938, p. 31; Purvis, 1931, pp. 81–82). Her fragmented tombstone is built into a wall at Esholt Hall. She was perhaps a younger daughter of Henry Pudsey of Bolton near Gisburn, Yorkshire (*S Leonard at Esholt*, 1866, p.34).
Pulley, Barbara: Swine; pension, £2–13–4 (TNA, LR1/169, f. 405v).
Pulleyne, Joan: Hampole; aged only nineteen in 1536 (Purvis, 1931, p. 114); pension of £2 received in 1555 (TNA, E164/31, f. 55r).
Pykhaver, Alice: Hampole; aged thirty in 1536 (Purvis, 1931, p. 114); pension, £2 (TNA, LR1/169, f. 454). Probably dead by 1552 (Cross and Vickers, 1995, p. 571).
Pynder, Margaret: Greenfield, by 1525 (*VDL* **2**, p. 161); *disp.* 1538 (*FOR*, p. 73).
[**Pye, E…eyn:** Wallingwells; pension, £2 (*LP* **14**, Part 2, p. 249 [No. 681]).]

Raighton/Raughton: *see* Roughton.
Ratclyff, Effama: Arthington; pension, 1539, £1–6–8 (*LP* **14**, Part 2, p. 209 [No. 588]).

Ratlyfte/Rokclyff, Joan: Hampole; aged fifty in 1536 (Purvis, 1931, p. 114); pension of £2–13–4 received as late as 1555 (TNA, E164/31, f. 55r); TNA, LR1/169, f. 454 gives a £2 pension..

Rawlins, Edith: Tarrant, when suppressed, 1539 (TNA, E322/233); pension, 1539, £4 (TNA, E315/245, f. 200).

Reder, Elizabeth: Heynings; pension, 1539, £1–10–0 (*LP* **14**, Part 1, p. 563 [No. 1280]).

Redesdale, Christine: Keldholme, 1497 (York; *Reg. T. Rotherham*, p. 152 [No. 1268]).

Renborowe: *see* Newborowe.

Res, Mary: Marham; *disp.* 1536 (TNA, E117/14/22).

Reve, Anne: Cook Hill; assessed in 1540 for subsidy on her pension of £2–13–4 (Bodleian Library, Oxford, Tanner MS 343).

Ripon, Margaret: prioress, Rosedale, by 1503–1505, when dies (Smith, 2008, p. 685).

Robynson, Alice: Nun Cotham; in house, 1525 (*VDL* **3**, p. 36); in receipt of pension, £1–10–0, in 1555 (TNA, E164/31, f. 18v).

Robinson, Dorothy: Nun Appleton, 1536 (Harrison, 2001, p. 21). Might her name be an *alias* for *Dorothy* Mawde, q.v.?

Roche, Margaret: prioress, Esholt, 1507–1513, when resigns (Smith, 2008, p. 644).

[**Roden, Anne:** Wallingwells; pension, £2–13–4 (*LP* **14**, Part 2, p. 249 [No. 681]).

Rodes/Rhodes/Rodys, Isabella: Kirklees, aged forty in 1539; said then to be 'criminous', having borne a child (Chadwick, 1902, p. 335); pension, £2–13–4 (TNA, LR1/169, f. 416); £1–13–4 (Cross and Vickers, 1995, p. 579); perhaps dead by 1564..

Roese, Margaret: prioress, Cook Hill, 1524 (Smith, 2008, p. 639).

Roughton/Raighton, Elizabeth: Keldholme, then last prioress, Basedale, 1527–39 (Cross and Vickers, 1995, p. 557; Smith, 2008, p. 626; York: *Reg. T. Wolsey*, f.85r–v); aged forty–one in 1539, pension: £6–13–4 (Purvis, 1931, pp. 79–80); £5–6–8 + 'reward and wages' of 13s 4d (TNA, SP5/2, f. 20r).

Russell, Margaret: last abbess, Tarrant; signed surrender deed, 3 March 1539 (TNA, E322/233; Smith, 2008, p. 699); pension, £40 (TNA, E315/245, f. 200).

Saltynstall, Isabella; Kirklees, aged twenty–four in 1539 (Chadwick, 1902, p. 335); pension, £2–13–4 (TNA, LR1/169, f. 416); £1–13–4 (*LP* **14**, Part 2, p. 577 [No. 1520]); lived in Halifax after the Suppression; in 1577 was cleared of calling one Marjory Hall a whore; still alive in 1582 (Cross and Vickers, 1995, p. 577).

Samford, Joan: last prioress, Heynings, 1533–1539 (Smith, 2008, p. 654); surrenders nunnery, 11 July 1539 (TNA, E322/98); pension, £6–13–4 (LP **14**, Part 1, p. 563 [No. 1280]).

Scanebury: *see* Staneburn.

Scaresbrig, Eleanor: prioress, Sewardsley, 1526–1530, when dies (Smith, 2008, pp. 688–89).

Scott, Joan: prioress, Handale, 1504–1532 (Smith, 2008, p. 652); profession of obedience, 2 July 1504 (York; *Reg. T. Savage*); blind and aged ninety in 1536, dead by 1539 (Purvis, 1931, p. 74); Cross and Vickers, 1995, pp. 571–72).

Seloo, Anna: Wykeham; 33 in 1536, pension: £1 4s 4d (Purvis, 1931, p. 94).

Semfold/Somfeld, Elizabeth: nun, Keldholme, 1497 (York; *Reg. T. Rotherham*, p. 152 [No. 1268]).

Sheffelde, Alice: Sinningthwaite, 1536, when it was reported she had borne a child; on its closure transferred to Nun Appleton; pension, 1539, £2 (Cross and Vickers, 1995, pp. 580, 588).

Sherewood, Margaret: Greenfield by 1525 (*VDL* **2**, p. 161); *disp.* 1538 (*FOR*, p. 73).

Skipwith, Elizabeth: Nun Cotham; in house, 1525 (*VDL* **3**, p. 36); assessed on her pension of £1–13–4 in 1552, but she had sold her pension for £7 to Henry Alamby in 1550; in 1554 was said to be married to Thomas Billesby, gent. (Hodgett, 1959, pp. 42, 69, 104). Still alive in 1555 (TNA, E164/31, f. 18v).

Skipwith, Jane/Joan: prioress, Greenfield, 1490–1518 (Lincolnshire R.O. 2ANC1/18/10; Smith, 2008, p. 651).

Simpson, Agnes: Nun Appleton; pension, £2–6–8, received as late as 1555 (TNA, E164/31, f. 53r). Said to be forty years old in 1536, sixty years old in 1553 (Cross and Vickers, 1995, p. 584; Harrison, 2001, p. 21).

Smyth, Alice: Swine; pension, £3–6–8 (TNA, LR1/169, f.406r).

Smyth, Elizabeth: Tarrant, 1539 (TNA, E322/233).

Smyth, Emma: Handale; 35 years old in 1539; pension of 26/8d (Purvis, 1931, pp. 75, 77); may have died by 1552 (Cross and Vickers, 1995, p. 575).

Smyth, Isabella: Stixwould, when collated by the bishop as prioress, Greenfield, 1521 until her death in 1530 (Smith, 2008, p. 651). At the visitation of 1525 she rejected the rumour of her enemies that a year before she had born a child, but it was also laid against her that she burdened the house by admitting relatives and neighbours (Chapter 8; *VDL* **2**, pp. 161–62). In 1528/39 another seemingly erroneous source gives her as sub–prioress of Stixwould (BL, Add Ch. 67119).

Snawdon, Agnes: Hampole; aged thirty in 1536 (Purvis, 1931, p. 114). No pension assigned, so she may have died before the dissolution of Hampole in 1539 (Cross and Vickers, 1995, p. 571), but could she be the next mentioned nun?

Snoutone/Snaynton, Agnes: Nun Appleton; said to have been aged thirty–eight in 1536, fifty–six in 1553. Pension of £3 received as late as 1555, but perhaps deceased by 1584 (TNA, E164/31, f. 53r; Cross and Vickers, 1995, p. 584; Harrison, 2001, p. 21). Is it possible that she had transferred from Hampole?

Snow/Snawe, Alive: Catesby, 1520 (when precentrix) – 1530 (*VDL* **3**, p. 103).

Sorell/Surell, Alice: Wykeham; 46 in 1539, pension: £1–13–4 (Purvis, 1931, p. 94).

Stable, Alice: nun at its suppression, Basedale, 1539; eighty years old in 1536, and granted a pension of 26s 8d (slightly more than the £1 accorded the rest of the community); (TNA, LR1/196, ff. 441–442; died by 1552 (Cross and Vickers, 1995, p. 559; Purvis, 1931, pp. 79–80).

Staneburn, Beatrix: sub–prioress, Nun Appleton, 1520, when bequeathed 6s 8d with a request for prayers for soul of William Normanville (Cross and Vickers, 1995, p. 584; Harrison, 2001, p. 14).

Stainburn, Margaret: nun and 'receiver'/business manager, Stixwould, until 1528/29 (BL, Add Ch. 67119).

Standyke/Standish, Elen/Eleanor: Hampole; pension, £2–6–8, 1539 (TNA, LR1/169, f. 454); not in a 1536 list of its nuns, so may have transferred from another house; pension received as late as 1583 (Cross and Vickers, 1995, p. 571).

Stansfield, Joan: prioress, Kirklees, elected 1491, when promises obedience to archbishop of York; dies 1499 (Chadwick, 1902, pp. 321, 364, 367 ; York: *Reg. T. Rotherham*, p. 124 [No.1021]).

Stapleton, Dorothy: Swine; pension, 1539, £2, in receipt of which in 1564; aged sixty in 1552 (Cross and Vickers, 1995, pp. 589, 592).

Stapleton, Isabel: Sinningthwaite, 1520 (Cross and Vickers, 1995, p. 588).

Stephenson, Cecily: Greenfield; *disp.* 1538 (*FOR*, p. 73).

Steward, Cecilia: Fosse; pension, 16s 8d, 1539 (*LP* **14**, Part 1, p. 556 [No. 1256]); resident at nearby Torksey in 1554, single, but 'too decrepit to work' (Hodgett, 1959, p. 81); in receipt of her pension in 1555 (TNA, E164/31, f. 19r).

Steynton, Adeline: prioress, Catesby, 1472–1484 (Smith, 2008, p. 636).

Stichenall/Stycherer, Joan: sub–prioress, Catesby, 1520; in house, 1530 (TNA, C1/187/15; *VDL* **3**, p. 103).

Stokes/Stocks, Katherine: Sinningthwaite, 1536, when reported she had borne a child; after its closure, transferred to Hampole; pension of £2–13–4 received as late as 1555; alive in 1564 (TNA, E164/31, f. 55r; Cross and Vickers, 1995, pp. 571 588). She may be the nun, *Katherine Tyas*, q.v.

Stockewith, Joan: Gokewell; pension of £2 received in 1555 (TNA, E164/31, f. 18v).

Strowed, Elizabeth: Tarrant, when suppressed, 1539 (TNA, E322/233); pension, 1539, £4 (TNA, E315/245, f. 200).

Sturney, Margaret: probably sub–prioress, Whistones, 1485 (Worcester; *Reg. J. Alcock*, f. 214; Smith, 2008, p. 704). Might she have been the nun of that name who was one of the electors in the choosing of a new prioress in 1427, and perhaps born about 1410 .

Swale/Sewall, Cecilia: Ellerton; the visitation of February 1536 found that she had given birth to a child (*LP* 10, pp. 138–39 [No. 364]); on closure of Ellerton in 1536 she transferred to Swine; received 1s. in 1550 in will of Joan Harkey, *q.v.*, in receipt of £2 pension in 1582 (Cross and Vickers, 1995, p. 561).

Swayne, Joan: sacrist, Wintney, 1501 (CCA, DCc/Register R, f.139r).

Swer, Elizabeth: prioress, Sinningthwaite, 1489–1529 (*MCP*, p. 135 [No. 138]; TNA, C1/356/27). Swinfey: *see* Sturney.

Swinson, Margery: prioress, Whistones, in 1476–1485 when dies (Worcester; *Reg. J. Alcock*, ff. 214, 241; Smith, 2008, p.704).

Syddenham, Dorothy: Tarrant, 1539 (TNA, E322/233); pension, £4 (TNA, E315/245, f. 200).

Synelde, Agnes: Legbourne, *disp.* 1536 (*FOR 73*).

Tailbus, Matilda: prioress, Nun Appleton, 1489–1507, when dies (York; *Reg. T. Savage*; Smith, 2008, p. 676).

Talbot, Margaret: Keldholme, 1497 (York; *Reg. T. Rotherham*, p. 152 [No. 1268]).

Tallboys, Isabel: prioress, Nun Cotham; by 1519–1521 when dead (TNA, E118/1/55; Smith, 2008, p. 677).

Tarleton, Margaret: prioress, Kirklees, elected 1499; 24–April 1499, promises obedience to archbishop of York (York; *Reg. T. Rotherham*, p. 130 [No. 1074]; Chadwick, 1902, pp. 321, 364).

Tathewell/Taylwode, Ursula: Legbourne, criticised at a visitation of 1 July 1525 for disobedience to the prioress, for over–familiarity with local priests and outsiders (Chapter 8; *VDL* 2, pp. 182–83); *disp.* 1536 (*FOR*, p. 73).

Thomas, Anne: prioress, Wintney, 1498–1534 (Smith, 2008, p. 708); alleged to have been involved in 1527 in the abduction of animal stock from a lay farmer (TNA, STAC2/3, f.314; STAC10/1/7).

Thomlynson, Agnes: prioress, Basedale, 1497– (York; *Reg. T. Rotherham*, p. 152 [Nos.1270–71]); named as former prioress in 1529/32 (Smith, 2008, p. 626); nun, Wykeham; aged sixty–nine in 1536, pension:£2–6–8 (Purvis, 1931, pp. 93–94).

Thompson/Tomson, Alice: Ellerton; remembered in the will of her former prioress, Joan Harkey, *q.v.* (Cross and Vickers, 1995, p. 562).

Thompson, Isabel: 'late prioress,' Basedale; pension, £6–13–4 (TNA, LR1/169, f. 442v). It is difficult to find the dates of her holding that office.

Thompson, Jane/Joan: last prioress, Nun Cotham, by 1525 (*VDL* 3, p. 36); was left £2 in will of James Myssenden of Great Limber, Lincolnshire, 1529 (Power, 1922, p. 326); surrendered nunnery, 9 July 1539 (TNA, E322/181); in receipt of pension, £6, in 1555 (TNA, E164/31, f. 18v); in 1554 was living at Kelsey, Lincolnshire, and was said to be too old and infirm to travel; died 1565 (Hodgett, 1959, pp. 109, 131).

[**T(h)ompson, Janet:** Arthington; pension, 1539, £1–6–8 (*LP* 14, Part 2, p. 209 [No. 588]).]

Thompson/Tanson, Margaret: Nun Cotham; in receipt of pension, £1–10–0, in 1555 (TNA, E164/31, f. 18v).

Thorne, Elizabeth: Swine; aged thirty in 1536 (Purvis, 1931, p. 97); pension, £3 (TNA, LR1/169, f. 406r); aged sixty in 1552 when living in Hull; her will, made at Hull on 17 September 1557, showed a concern for the welfare of that city and especially for its poor, as well as the mending of the highways; she left her house to another Swine nun, Elizabeth Patricke, for her life. The will shows her to have been a lady of not inconsiderable means with much household furniture and utensils and over £10 in cash. She made Patricke her sole executrix, calling her her 'well beloved in Christ' (Cross and Vickers, 1995, p. 593).

Thorney, Sybil: prioress, Gokewell, 1519 (*VDL* **2**, p. 154).

Thurland, Margaret: Hampole; pension, £2 (TNA, LR1/169, f. 454). Not in the 1536 list of its nuns, so may have transferred there from a house closed earlier (Cross, 1995, pp. 571–72).

Thymbelbye, Isabel: Gokewell; pension of £2 received in 1555 (TNA, E164/31, f. 18v).

Thymbelbye, Margaret: Gokewell; pension of £2 received in 1555 (TNA, E164/31, f. 18v).

Tomlynson, Dorothy: Swine; pension, 1539, £2; alive in 1556 (Cross and Vickers, 1995, pp. 589, 593).

Topcliffe/Toplys, Cecilia: prioress, Kirklees, 1516; prioress, profession of obedience, 19–07–1527 (York; *Reg. T. Wolsey*, f. 85v; resigns, 1538; still in community at the suppression, 1539, when said to be aged sixty–two 62 (Chadwick, 1902, pp. 321, 335; TNA, LR1/169, ff. 431, 434; Smith, 2008, p. 661).

Turtilby, Agnes: Basedale; age not stated, but pension of £1 accorded in 1539; dead by 1564 (Cross and Vickers, 1995, p. 559; Purvis, 1931, pp. 79–80).

Tyas, Elizabeth: Swine; pension, 1539, £2; in 1552 she was living in Tickhill, South Yorkshire, married to John Swyne, gent; still alive in 1564 (Cross and Vickers, 1995, pp. 589, 593).

Tyas, Katherine: Hampole; aged thirty in 1536; pension, 1539, £2 (Cross, 1995, pp. 567, 572).

Tyndall, Margaret: Heynings; pension, 1539, £1–13–4 (TNA, E315/245, f. 44v).

Vaughan, Elizabeth: Catesby, 1520–1530 (*VDL* **3**, pp. 102–03).

Vavasour, Agnes: Swine, 1486 (Bell, 1995, p. 171]).

[**Vavasour, Elizabeth:** Arthington; pension, 1539, £1–6–8 (*LP* **14**, Part 2, p. 209 [No. 588]).

Vavasour, Isabella: Gokewell; precentrix, 1519 (*VDL* **2**, p. 154); *disp.* 1536 (*FOR*, p. 80).

[**Vynes, Agnes:** Wallingwells; pension, £2 (*LP* **14**, Part 2, p. 249 [No. 681]).

Wade, Mald/Matilda: prioress, Swine; resigned 1482 (Bell, 1995, pp. 170–71).

Wakefield, Agnes: Stixwould, 1525 (*VDL* **3**, p. 103).

Walbanke, Joan: Greenfield, by 1525; at the visitation that year, she accused several sisters of shortcomings, but was herself found at fault (*VDL* **2**, pp. 161–63); *disp.* 1538 (*FOR*, p. 73).

Walsh: *see* Welys.

Waltham, Dorothy: Stixwould, 1525 (*VDL* **3**, p. 103).

Walton/Walter, Matilda/Magdalen/Maud: Hampole; aged thirty–six in 1536 (Purvis, 1931, p. 14); pension of £2–6–8 received as late as 1555 (TNA, E164/31, f. 55r).

Warde, Joan: Esholt, *disp.* on account of illegitimacy, 1471/72 (Power, 1922, p. 31; *SAP* **2**, p. 211 [No. 2235])); prioress, Esholt, by 1480, resigns, 1497 (York; *Reg. T. Rotherham*, p. 126 [Nos. 1045–46]; Smith, 2008, p. 644. She may have been a member of the founding Ward family (*S. Leonard in Esholt*, Hotten, 1866, p. 34).

Warde, Katherine: prioress, Wykeham, profession of obedience, 14–02–1488 (York; *Reg. T. Rotherham*, p. 58 [Nos. 471–472]).

Wastle, Alys: Cook Hill; assessed in 1540 for subsidy on her pension of £2–13–4 (Bodleian Library, Oxford, Tanner MS 343).

Watson, Cecilia: Handale; aged thirty–one in 1539; pension of 26s 8d (Purvis, 1931, pp. 75, 77); still alive in 1564 (Cross and Vickers, 1995, p. 575).

Watson, Joan; prioress, Fosse, profession of obedience, 24–12–1498 (Lincoln; *Reg. W. Smith*, f. 163r) until at least 1518 (Smith, 2008, p. 647). Did she retire to Nun Appleton?

Watson, Joan/Jane: Nun Appleton; pension, £2, received as late as 1555 (TNA, E164/31, f. 53r). Aged sixty in 1553 (Cross and Vickers, 1995, p. 584); but given as fifty–six years old in 1536 (Harrison, 2001, p. 21).Were there two sisters of this name?

Webbe, Elizabeth: prioress, Cookhill, in 1485, and the again from 1490 until at least 1493 (Smith, 2008, p. 639); cited with the abbot of Hailes in 1491 by the dean of the Arches to explain why Joan Frankelyn was removed from office. Confirmed in office by the General Chapter, 1491 (Chapter 8; *Letters*, pp. 134 [No. 66], 138 [No. 67]; 146–47 [No. 73]).

Welys/Welshe, Margaret: prioress, Whistones, by 1502 to at least 1515 (Smith, 2008, p. 704); assessed in 1540 for subsidy on her pension of £2 (Bodleian Library, Oxford, Tanner MS 343).

Wetherall, Elizabeth: Hampole; pension, £2–13–4 (TNA, LR1/169, f. 454). May have transferred to Hampole between 1536 and 1539? (Cross and Vickers, 1995, p. 572).

Whately/Wheateley, Isabel: prioress, Hampole, 1483–1503, when dies; *disp.* for defect of birth, prior to election (Smith, 2008, p. 652; VCH, *County of York* **3**, p. 165); c.1493/1500; accused of detention of valuables (TNA, C1/202/6; *MCP*, p. 54 [No. 47]). Cross and Vickers, 1995, p. 567, have her as prioress as late as 1532; *LP* **5**, No. 780/5, has her as prioress on 30 November 1512.

[**Whitehead, Isabel:** Arthington; pension, 1539, £1–6–8 (*LP* **14**, Part 2, p. 209 [No. 588]).]

Whitfield, Margaret: Swine; aged thirty–six in 1536, still alive in 1573 (Purvis, 1931, p. 97); pension, £3 (TNA, LR1/169, f. 406r); in 1534, her mother, Isabel Whitfeld, widow of a York alderman, left her £3–6–8 to be kept by her brother and given to her in instalments as she needed it; fifty years old in 1553 (Cross and Vickers, 1995, p. 594).

Wigston, Margery: Catesby, 1520 (*VDL* **3**, p. 102); last prioress, Pinley, 1534–1536, when house dissolved (TNA, E315/290/1, f. 25v; Smith, 2008, p. 680); pension, £4 (warrant, 20–`11–1536: TNA, E315/244, No. 132). She was the brother of Roger Wigston, M.P., and influential in monastic affairs; his son, John, received the monastery site.

[**Wilcocks, Elizabeth:** prioress, Wallingwells, but dying or resigning about 1505 (York; *Reg. T. Savage*).]

Wilkin, Agnes: Fosse; in receipt of pension of 16s 8d in 1555 (TNA, E164/31, f. 19r).

Williamson, Joan: Gokewell; conversus, 1519 (*VDL* **2**, p. 154); disp. 1536 (*FOR*, p. 80).

Wilson, Walliam: Gokewell; pension of £2 received in 1555 (TNA, E164/31, f. 18v); could she be the nun, *Elizabeth Wales*, listed in 1519, when sub–prioress? (*VDL* **2**, p. 154).

Wilton, Alice: prioress, Heynings, 1530 (Smith, 2008, p. 654).

Wise, Grace: Fosse; in receipt of pension of 16s 8d in 1555 (TNA, E164/31, f. 19r).

Wood, Agnes: Esholt; said in 1536, perhaps spuriously, to be unchaste; aged twenty–nine in 1539 when awarded pension of 26s 8d; still alive in 1564 (Cross and Vickers, 1995, pp. 563, 566, Purvis, 1931, p. 82).

Wooton, Elizabeth: prioress, Whistones, *ante*–1476 (Worcester; *Reg. J. Alcock*, f. 241).

[**Wormewell, Elizabeth:** Arthington; pension, 1539, £1–6–8 (*LP* **14**, Part 2, p. 209 [No. 588]).]

Worsley, Elizabeth: Tarrant, when suppressed, 1539 (TNA, E322/233); pension, 1539, £4 (TNA, E315/245, f. 200).

Wright, Agnes: Keldholme, 1497 (York; *Reg. T. Rotherham*, p. 152 [No. 1268]).

Wright, Ann: Legbourne, disp. 1536 (*FOR*, p. 73).

Wright, Katherine: Greenfield; disp. 1538 (*FOR*, p. 73).

Ync(h)e, Agnes: prioress, Hampole; 1512–1516 (VCH, *County of York* **3**, 1974, p. 163–65; TNA, LR1/169, f. 463).

Yooderson, Elizabeth: Swine; aged twenty–nine in 1536 (Purvis, 1931, p. 97).

BIBLIOGRAPHY

Alphonse, T., *Llantarnam Abbey*, Llantarnam: cyclostyled, 1979.

Ashmore, O., *Whalley Abbey*, Blackburn: Diocesan Board of Finance; 6th edn., 2003.

Austin, J. D., *Merevale Church and Abbey*, Studley: Brewin, 1998.

Aveling, J. H., *The History of Roche Abbey*, London: John Russell Smith and Worksop: Robert White, 1870.

Aveling, M., 'The Rievaulx Community after the Dissolution.' In: *Ampleforth Jnl.* **57**, 1952, pp. 101–12.

—————, 'The Monks of Byland after the Dissolution'. In: *Ampleforth Jnl.,* **60**, 1955, pp. 3–15.

Aveling, H. and Pantin, W. A. (ed.), *The Letter Book of Robert Joseph*, OHS, N.S. **19**, 1967.

Baddeley, St Clair., 'The Holy Blood of Hailes.' In: *TBGA* **23**, 1900, pp. 276–84.

Baigent, F. G, 'On the Abbey of the Blessed Mary of Waverley' In: *SAC* **8**, 1883, pp. 157–210.

Barber, B., et al., *The Cistercian Abbey of St Mary, Stratford Langthorne, Essex,* Museum of London, 2004.

Barnard, E. A. B., *The Last Days of Hailes Abbey and of Gretton Chapel*, Evesham: Evesham Journal, 1928.

Barnes, G. D., *Kirkstall Abbey, 1147–1539.* In: PTS, **58**: No. 128 (for 1982).

Baskerville, G., 'The Dispossessed Religious of Gloucestershire'. In: *TBGAS* **49**, 1927, pp. 63–122.

—————, 'The Dispossessed Religious of Oxfordshire', Oxfordshire Archaeological Society Report **75**, 1930, pp. 327–45.

—————, 'Some Ecclesiastical Wills'. In: *TBGAS* **52**, 1930, pp. 281–94.

—————, 'Married Clergy and Pensioned Religious in Norwich Diocese, 1555'. In: *EHR* **48**, 1933, pp. 43–64, 222–28.

—————, 'A Sister of Archbishop Cranmer'. In: EHR **51**, 1936.

—————, *English Monks and the Suppression of the Monasteries,* London: Jonathan Cape, 1937.

—————, 'The Dispossessed Religious in Surrey'. In: *SAC* **47**, 1941, pp. 12–28.

Bearman, R., *Stoneleigh Abbey*, Stoneleigh: Stoneleigh Abbey Ltd., 2004.

Bell, D. N., 'The English Cistercians and the Practice of Medicine'. In: *Cîteaux* **40**, 1989, pp. 139–74.

—————, *An Index of Authors and Works in Cistercian Libraries in Great Britain*, Kalamazoo: Cistercian Publications, 1992.

—————, *What Nuns Read*, Kalamazoo: Cistercian Publications, 1995.

—————, 'Hailes Abbey and its Books'. In: *Cîteaux* **61**, 2010, pp. 301–64.

—————, 'A Tudor Chameleon: The Life and Times of Stephen Sagar, Last Abbot of Hailes.' In: *Cîteaux* **62**, 2011.

Bell, H. E., 'Esholt Priory'. In: *YAJ* **33**, 1938, pp. 5–34.

Bell, H. I., 'Translations from the Cywyddwyr'. In: *THSC*, 1940–1942, pp. 221–253.

Bettey, J. H., *Suppression of the Monasteries in the West Country*, Gloucester: Alan Sutton, 1989.

Beverley Smith, L., 'Disputes and Settlements in Medieval Wales'. In: *EHR* **106**, 1991, pp. 835–60.

Birch, W. de Gray, *A History of Margam Abbey*, London: privately printed, 1897.

—————, *A History of Neath Abbey*, Neath: Richards, 1902.

—————, *Memorials of the See and Cathedral of Llandaff*, Neath: J.E. Richards, 1912.

Blackwell, A. E., 'Lundy's Ecclesiastical History.' In: *RTDA* **92**, 1960, pp. 88–100.

Bloxam, M. H., 'Merevale Abbey.' In: *TLAS* **2**, 1870, pp. 324–34.

Bostock, T. and Hogg, S., *Vale Royal Abbey, 1277–1538*, Vale Royal Borough Council, 1999.

Bridge, M., *Tree–Ring Analysis of Timbers, The Conference Centre, Whalley Abbey*, London: English Heritage, Research Dept. Report Series, No. **66**/2007, 2007.

Brooking Rowe, J., 'Buckland Abbey.' In: *RTDA* **7**, 1875, pp. 329–66.

—————, 'Ford Abbey.' In: *RTDA* **10**, 1878, pp. 349–76.

Brown, G., *Stanley Abbey and its Estates, 1151–c.1640*, BAR British Series **566**, 2012.

Brown, W., 'Edward Kirkby, Abbot of Rievaulx.' In: *YAJ* **21**, 1911, pp. 44–51.

Bryant–Quinn, M. P. (ed.), *Gwaith Ieuan ap Llywelyn Fychan, Ieuan Llwyd Brydydd a Lewys Aled*, Aberystwyth University: Centre for Advanced Welsh and Celtic Studies, 2003.

Burton, J. E., 'The election of Joan Fletcher as prioress of Basedale.' In: *Borthwick Institute Bulletin* **1**, 1975–8, pp. 145–53.

Bush, M. L., 'The Richmondshire Uprising of October 1536 and the Pilgrimage of of Grace.' In: *NH* **29**, 1993, pp. 64–98.

Butler, L. A. S., 'Suffragan Bishops in the Medieval Diocese of York.' In: *NH* **37**, 2000, pp. 49–60.

Cameron, A., 'Some Social Consequences of the Dissolution of the Monasteries in Nottinghamshire.' In: *Trans. Thoroton Soc.* **79**, 1975, pp. 50–59.

Carter, M., 'Late Medieval Relief Sculptures from Rievaulx and Fountains.' In: *Cîteaux* **60**, 2009.

—————, 'The Tower of Marmaduke Huby of Fountains Abbey: Hubris or Piety?' In: *YAJ* **82**, 2010, pp. 269–85.

—————, 'The mourning vestment of Robert Thornton, abbot of Jervaulx.' In: *Textile History* **41**, 2010, pp. 145–60.

Cartwright, J., 'Abbes Annes and the Ape.' In: J. Burton and K. Stöber, ed. *Monastic Wales*, Cardiff: University of Wales Press, 2013, pp. 191–207.

Chadwick, S. J., 'Kirklees Priory.' In: *YAJ* **16**, 1902, pp. 319–368.

Cherry, B. and Pevsner, N. (eds), *Devon*, London: Penguin, 2nd edn., 1989.

Cirket, A. F., *English Wills, 1498–1526, BHRS* **37**, 1957.

Clancy, J. P., (ed.), *Medieval Welsh Lyrics*, London: Macmillan, 1965.

Clarence, L. B., 'Church Bells of Dorset.' In: *Proc. Dorset Natural History and Antiquarian Field Club* **19**, 1898, pp. 25–42.

Clark–Maxwell, W. G., 'Buildwas Abbey, – The Survey of 1536.' In: *Trans. Shropshire Archaeol. Soc.,* **16**, 1931, pp. 65–69.

Clay, J. W., *Yorkshire Monasteries Suppression Papers, YASRS* **48**, 1912.

Collinson, M., 'Monastic Cash at the Dissolution.' In: *YAJ* **80**, 2008, pp. 239–44.

Connor, W., 'The Esholt Priory Charter of 1485 and its Decoration.' In: *YAJ* **80**, 2008, pp. 121–52.

Cooper, G. M: 'Notices of the Abbey of Robertsbridge.' In: *SxAC* **8**, 1856, pp. 141–76.

Coppack, G., *Fountains Abbey*, Stroud: Tempus, 2003.

—————, *Abbeys and Priories*, Stroud: Amberley, 2009.

—————, 'How the Other Half Lived: Cistercian Nunneries in Early Sixteenth–Century Yorkshire.' In: *Cîteaux* **59**, 3–4, 2008, pp. 253–98.

Coppack, G. and Gilyard–Beer, R., *Fountains Abbey*, London: English Heritage, 1993.

Cross, C., 'Community Solidarity among Yorkshire Religious after the Dissolution.' In: *MS* **1**, 1990, pp. 245–54.

—————, 'The Reconstitution of Northern Monastic Communities in the Reign of Mary Tudor.' In: *NH* **29**, 1993, pp. 200–04.

—————, 'The End of Medieval Monasticism in the North Riding of Yorkshire.' In: *YAJ* **78**, 2006, pp. 145–58.

Cross, C. and Vickers, N., *Monks, friars and nuns in sixteenth century Yorkshire*, Leeds: Yorkshire Archaeological Society, 1995.

Davey, P. J. and Roscow, J. R., *Rushen Abbey and the Dissolution of the Monasteries in the Isle of Man*, Isle of Man Natural History and Antiquarian Society, Monograph **1**, 2010.

Davidson, J., *The History of Newenham Abbey, Devon*, London: Longman @ Co., 1843.

D'Elboux, R. H., *Surveys of the Manors of Robertsbridge*, Sussex Record Society **47**, 1944.

Dickens, A. G., *Reformation Studies*, London: Blades, East and Blades, 1982.

Dineley, T., *The Official Progress of the First Duke of Beaufort through Wales*, ed. R. W. Banks, London: Hambledon,1888.

Dodds, M. H., *The Pilgrimage of Grace and the Exeter Conspiracy*, Cambridge U.P., 1915.

Ellis, T. P., *The Welsh Benedictines of the Terror*, Newtown: Welsh Outlook Press, 1936.

Evans, A. L., *Margam Abbey*, Port Talbot Historical Society, 2nd. edn., 1996.

Evans, D. H., *Valle Crucis Abbey*, Cardiff: CADW, revised edn.1995.

Farnham, G. F., 'The Charnwood Manors' In: *TLAS* **15**, 1927, pp. 139–281.

Fergusson, P. and Harrison, S., *Rievaulx Abbey*, Yale U.P., 1999.

Figueiredo, P. de., and Treuherz, J., *Cheshire Country Houses*, Chichester: Phillimore, 1981.

Fisher, Fisher, M. J. C., *Dieulacres Abbey, Staffordshire*, Leek: Hill Bros., 1969.

Fletcher, J. S., *The Cistercians in Yorkshire*, London: S.P.C.K., 1919.

Foley, H., 'The Pilgrim Book of the Ancient English Hospice, Rome.In: *Records of the English Province of the Society of Jesus*, London: Burns and Oates, **6**, 1880.

Foss, D. B., 'Marmaduke Bradley, Last Abbot of Fountains.' In: *YAJ* **61**, 1989, pp. 103–10..

Fowler, R. C., 'Essex Monastic Inventories.' In: *TEAS*, N.S. **10**, 1909, pp. 14–18.

Freeman, E., 'Houses of a Peculiar Order: Cistercian Nunneries in Medieval England.' In: *Cîteaux* **55**, Parts 3–4, 2004, pp. 245–87.

Gasquet, F. A., *Henry VIII and the English Monasteries*, London: J.C. Nimmo, 2nd. edn., 1899.

————, *The Greater Abbeys of England*, London: Chatto and Windus, 1908

Gibson, E. W., Tilty Abbey.' In: *Essex Review* **5**, 1896, pp. 94–102.

Gilbanks, G. E., *Some Records of a Cistercian Abbey; Holm Cultram, Cumberland*, Cumberland, s.n. 1899.

Gill, C., *Buckland Abbey*, Plymouth, s.n., 1st edn. 1951, 3rd edn., 1968.

Gilyard–Beer, R., *Cleeve Abbey, Somerset*, London: Historic Buildings and Monuments Commission, 1960.

Goodrich, M., *Worcester Nunneries*, Chichester: Phillimore, 2008.

Grainger, F., 'The Chambers Family of Raby Cote.' In: *TCWAA* N.S. **1**, 1901, pp. 194–234.

Grainger, I. and Phillpotts, C., *The Cistercian Abbey of St Mary Graces, East Smithfield*, London: Museum of London, 2011.

Greatorex, J., *Coggeshall Abbey and Abbey Mill*, Colchester: J. Greatorex, 1999.

Green, C. W., *Biddlesden and its Abbey*, Buckingham: E.N. Hiller and Sons., 1974.

Green, F., 'Early Wills in West Wales.' In: *West Wales Historical Records* **7**, 1917–18, pp. 143–64.

Haigh, C., *The Last Days of the Lancashire Monasteries and the Pilgrimage of Grace*, Manchester U.P., for the Chetham Society, 1969.

Hall, J., *Croxden Abbey: buildings and community*, York University: Ph. D. thesis, 2003.

————, 'Croxden Abbey Church,' In: *JBAA* **160**, 2007.

Harland, J., *A History of Sawley in Craven*, London, 1853; Felinfach, Ceredigion: Llanerch press reprint, 1993.

Harper–Bill, C., 'Cistercian Visitation.' In: *Bulletin of the Institute of Historical Research,***53**, 1980, pp. 103–113.

Harries, L., *Gwaith Huw Cae Llwyd ac eraill*, Cardiff: Gwasg Prifysgol Cymru, 1953.

Harrison, M. J., *The Nunnery of Nun Appleton*, University of York: Borthwick Paper **98**, 2001.

Harrison, S., *Cleeve Abbey*, London: English Heritage, 2000.

Harrison, S. M., *The Pilgrimage of Grace in the Lake Counties, 1536–7*, Royal Historical Soc., 1981.

Hartwell, C. and Pevsner, N., *Lancashire North*, Yale U.P., and London: Penguin, 2009.

Hartwell, C. *et al,. Cheshire*, Yale U.P. and London: Penguin, 2011.

Hays, R. W., *History of the Abbey of Aberconway*, Cardiff, University of Wales Press, 1963.

Heath, S., *The Story of Ford Abbey*, London: Francis Griffiths, 1911.

Hibbert, F. A., *The Dissolution of the Monasteries*, London: Pitman, 1910.

Hills, G. M., 'Fountains Abbey.' In: *Collectanea Archaeologica* **2**, London, 1871, pp. 251–302.

Hockey, S. F., *Quarr Abbey and its Lands*, Leicester U.P., 1970.

————, *Beaulieu, King John's Abbey*, Beaulieu: Pioneer Publns., 1976.

Hodgett, C. A. J., *The state of the ex–Religious and former Chantry priests in the Diocese of Lincoln*, Lincoln Record Society, **53**, 1959

Holden, J., 'The Fate of Monastic Churches in Cumbria.' In: *MS* **1**, 1990.

Hook, D. and Ambrose, A, *Boxley: The story of an English parish*, Maidstone: The Authors, 1999.

(St John) Hope, W. H. and Bilson, J., *Architectural Description of Kirkstall Abbey*, Leeds: *PTS* **16**, 1907.

Howard, R. E., Laxton, R. R., and Litton, C. D., *Tree–Ring Analysis of Oak Timbers from Combermere Abbey*, London: English Heritage, Centre for Archaeology Report, **83**, 2003.

Hoyle, R., 'Monastic Leasing Before the Dissolution.' In: *YAJ* **61**, 1989, pp. 111–38.

Humphrey, W., *Garendon Abbey*, Loughborough University: East Midlands Study Unit, 1982.

Huws, D., *Medieval Welsh Manuscripts*, Cardiff: University of Wales Press, 2000.

Jennings, B., *Yorkshire monasteries*, Otley: Smith Settle, 1999.

Jones, A., 'Basingwerk Abbey.' In: J. G. Edwards *et al.* (ed.), *Historical Essays in honour of James Tait*, Manchester, printed for the subscribers, 1933, pp. 169–78.

————, 'The Estates of the Welsh Abbeys at the Dissolution.'In: *AC* **92**, 1937, pp. 269–86.

Kell, E., 'Netley Abbey.' In: *Collectanea Archaeologica* **2**, London, 1871, pp. 65–92.

Knowles, D., *Saints and Scholars*, Cambridge U.P., 1963.

————, *The Religious Orders in England* **3**: *The Tudor Age*, Cambridge U.P., 1971.

————, *Bare Runied Choirs*, Cambridge U.P., 1976 edn.

Laurence, M. 'Notes on Croxden Abbey.' In: *Trans. N. Staffordshire Field Club*, **87**, 1952, Appx. pp. B.51–B.74.

Lekai, L. J., *The Cistercians, Ideals and Reality*, Kent State U.P., U.S.A., 1977.

Lloyd, J. Y. W., *The history of the princes, the lords marcher, and the ancient nobility of Powys Fadog*, III, London: T. Richards Whiting, 1883.

Loftie, A. G., 'Calder Abbey, Part II.' In: *TCWAAS* **9**, 1888, pp. 206–39.

————, *Calder Abbey*, London: Bemrose and Sons, 1892.

Lonsdale, A. ,'The Last Monks of Kirkstall Abbey.' In: *PTS* **53**, No. 118; Part 3, 1972, pp. 201–16.

Mathew, D. and A., 'The Survival of the Dissolved Monasteries in Wales.' In: *Dublin Review* **184**, 1929, pp. 70–81.

Maxwell–Lyte, H. C., 'Thomas Chard, Abbot of Ford.' In: *Proc. Somerset Archaeological and Natural History Soc.* **74**, 1928, pp. 57–60.

McCann, J. and Cary–Elwes, C (eds.), *Ampleforth and its Origins*, London: Burns and Oates and Washbourne, 1952.

Moore, J. L. M., 'Sibton Church.' In: *Proceedings of the Suffolk Insitute of Archaeology and History*, **8**, Part 1, pp. 65–75.

Moorhouse, G., *The Pilgrimage of Grace*, London: Weidenfeld and Nicolson, 2002.

Mowforth, E. H., *Rosedale Priory and the Church of St Laurence*, s.n., 1962.

Nash, C., 'The Fate of the English Cistercian Abbots in the Reign of Henry VIII.' In: *Cîteaux* **2**, 1965, pp. 97–113..

Nichols, J. A., 'Medieval English Cistercian Nunneries', Chauvin, B (ed.), In: *Mélanges à la Mémoire du Père Anselme Dimier*, Arbois, France: Benoît Chauvin Pupillin, **5**/III, 1982, pp. 151–75.

Oliva, M., *The Convent and Community in Late Medieval England*, Woodbridge: Boydell Press, 1998.

Oliver, A. M., 'A List of the Abbots of Newminster.' In: *Archaeologia Aeliana* 3rd Ser. **12**, 1915, pp. 206–25.

Orme, N., 'The Dissolution of the Chantries in Devon, 1546–48.' In: *RTDA* **111**, 1979, pp. 75–124.

————, 'The Last Medieval Abbot of Buckfast,' In: *RTDA*, **133**, 2001, pp. 97–108.

Owen, E., 'Strata Marcella immediately before and after its Dissolution.' *Y Cymmrodor*, **29**, 1919, pp. 1–32.

————, 'The Monastery of Basingwerk.' In: *Jnl. Flintshire Historical Soc.*, **7**, 1919/20, pp. 47–89.

————, 'Vale Crucis Abbey.' In: *Wrexham Guardian*, 4 November 1931, p. 1.

Owen, G. D., *Agricultural Conditions in West Wales*, University of Wales: Ph. D. thesis, 1935.

Oxley, J. E., *The Reformation in Essex*, Manchester U.P., 1965.

Pearce, E. H., *The Monks of Westminster*, Cambridge U.P., 1916.

Peacock, E., 'Injunctions of John Longland, Bishop of Lincoln.' In: *Archaeologia* **47**, Part 1, 1882, pp. 55–64.

Perry, G. G., ''The Visitation of the Monastery of Thame, 1526.' In: *EHR* **3**, 1888, pp. 704–22.

Pevsner, N., *South and West Somerset*, Harmondsworth: Penguin, 1958.

————, *Yorkshire: The North Riding*, Harmondsworth: Penguin, 1966.

————, *Yorkshire: The West Riding*, revised by Enid Radcliffe, Harmondsworth: Penguin, 1974.

Pevsner, N. and Harris, J: *Lincolnshire*, London: Penguin, 1989.

Pevsner, N. and D. Neave, *Yorkshire: York and the East Riding*, London: Penguin, 2nd. edn., 1995.

Plaisted, A. H., *The Manor and Parish Records of Medmenham*, London: Longmans, Green and Co., 1925.

Power, E., *Medieval English Nunneries*, Cambridge U.P., 1922.

Pratt, D., *The Dissolution of Valle Crucis Abbey*, Wrexham: Bridge Books, 1997.

————, 'The Impact of the Cistercians on Welsh Life and Culture in North and Mid–Wales'. In: *Denbighshire Historical Society Transactions* **50**, 2001, pp. 13–23.

————, 'Valle Crucis Abbey: lands and.,' In: *Denbighshire Historical Society Transactions*, **59**, 2011, pp. 9–55.

Price, G. V., *Valle Crucis Abbey*, Liverpool: Hugh Evans and Son, 1952.

Pring, J. H., 'Memoir of Thomas Chard, D.D.' In: *JBAA* **18**, 1862, pp. 187–219.

Pryce, A. I., *The Diocese of Bangor in the Sixteenth Century*, Bangor: Jarvis and Foster, 1923.

Purvis, J. S., *A Selection of Monastic Rentals and Dissolution Papers*, YASRS **80**, 1931.

Ray, J. E., 'Sussex Chantry Records.' In: *Sussex Record Society* **36**, 1931, p. 144.

Ridgard, J. and Norton, R., *Food and Ale, Farming and Worship: Daily Life at Sibton Abbey*, Leiston: Suffolk; Leiston Press, 2011.

Roberts, T., *The Poetical Works of Dafydd Nanmor*, Cardiff: University of Wales Press, 1923.

Robinson, D. M., *Tintern Abbey*, Cardiff: CADW, 1990.

————, *Buildwas Abbey*, London: English Heritage, 2002.

Robson, P., *Fountains Abbey*, York: Cundall Manor, Helperby, 1983.

Salter, H. E. (ed.), *Snappe's Formulary*, Oxford U.P., 1924.

Salzman, L. F., 'Sussex Religious at the Dissolution.' In: *SxAC* **92**, 1954, pp. 24–36..

Saunders, E. J., 'Lleision ap Thomas.' In: *The Dictionary of Welsh Biography down to 1940*, London: Honourable Society of Cymmrodorion, 1959, pp. 567–68.

Seekings, K and Herd, D., *Rosedale Abbey*, Lastingham, Yorkshire: United Benefice of Lastingham, 2005).

Shaw, A. N., 'The Northern Visitation of 1535/6: Some New Observations.' In: *Downside Review* **116**, No. 405; October 1998, pp. 279–99.

————, 'The Involvement of the Religious Orders in the Northern Risings of 1536/7: Compulsion or Desire.' In: *Downside Review* **117**, No. 407; April, 1999, pp. 89–114.

Shaw, H., 'Cistercian Abbots in the Service of British Monarchs.' In: *Cîteaux* **58**, 2007, pp. 225–45.

Sheppard, J. M., *The Buildwas Books*, Oxford: Oxford: Bibliographical Soc., 1997.

Sherwin, C., 'The History of Ford Abbey.' In: *RTDA* **59**, 1927, pp. 249–64.

Sherwood, J. and Pevsner, N., *Oxfordshire*, Harmondsworth, Penguin, 1974.

Siddons, M. P (ed.), *Visitations by the Heralds in Wales*, London: Harleian Soc., 1966.

Sitch, B., *Kirkstall Abbey*, Leeds: Leeds City Council, 2000.

Smith, D. M., 'Suffragan Bishops in the Medieval Diocese of Lincoln.' In: Lincolnshire History and Archaeology **17**, 1982, pp. 17–27.

Smith, D. M. and London, V.C.H. (ed.), *The Heads of Religious Houses, England and Wales*, II, *1216–1377*, Cambridge U.P., 2002.

Smith, D. M. (ed.), *The Heads of Religious Houses, England and Wales* III: *1377–1540*, Cambridge U.P., 2008.

Smith, W. C., *The History of Farnham and the Ancient Cistercian Abbey of Waverley*, Farnham: no publisher cited, 1829.

Snell, L. S., *The Suppression of the Religious Foundations of Devon and Cornwall*, Marazion: Wordens of Cornwall Ltd., 1967.

Sparks, J. A., *In the Shadow of the Blackdowns*, Bradford–on–Avon: Moonraker Press, 1978.

Sparvel–Bayly, J. A., 'The Cistercian Abbey of Stratford Langthorne.' In: *Essex Review* **4**, 1895, pp. 249–58.

Spear, V. G., *Leadership in Medieval English Nunneries*, Woodbridge: Boydell Press, 2005.

Squire, A., *Aelred of Rievaulx*, London: S.P.C.K., 1969.

Stéphan, J., *A History of Buckfast Abbey*, Bristol: Burleigh Press, 1970.

Stevenson, W. H. and Salter, H. E., *The Early History of St John's College, Oxford*, Oxford; Oxford Historical Soc., 1939.

Straker, E., 'Westall's Book of Panningridge.' In: *SxAC* **72**, 1931, pp. 253–60.

Talbot, C. H., 'The English Cistercian Martyrs, I: George Lazenby, Monk of Jervaulx.' In: *Collectanea Cisterciensia* **2**, 1935, pp. 70–75.

————, 'Marmaduke Huby, Abbot of Fountains, 1495–1526.' In: *Analecta Sacri Ordinis Cisterciensis* **20**, 1964, pp. 165–84.

Thomas, L., *The Reformation in the Old Diocese of Llandaff*, Cardiff: William Lewis, 1930.

Thompson, D., 'Cistercians and Schools in Late Medieval Wales.' In: *Cambridge Medieval Celtic Studies* **3**, 1982. pp. 76–80.

Thompson, T., *The History of the Church and Priory of Swine in Holderness*, Hull: T. Topping, 1824.

Thomson, G. S., 'Woburn Abbey and the Dissolutiom of the Monasteries.' In: *Trans. Royal Historical Society*, 4th Series **16**, 1933, pp. 129–60.

Thorley, J., 'The Estates of Calder Abbey.' In: *TCWAA* 3rd Ser., **4**, 2004, pp. 133–62.

Tomkinson, J. L, 'The History of Hulton Abbey,' In: *Staffordshire Archaeological Studies* N.S. **2**, 1985.

————, 'The Documentation of Hulton Abbey: ?Two Cases of Forgery.' In: *Staffordshire Studies* **6**,

1994, pp. 73–102.

————, *A History of Hulton Abbey*, Staffordshire Archaeological Studies N.S. **10**, 1997.

Tyers, I., *Tree–Ring Analysis of Oak Timbers from the Frater Roof of Cleeve Abbey*, London: English Heritage, Centre for Archaeology, 2003.

Tyler, R., *Forde Abbey*, St Ives: Beric Tempest Co., 1995.

Walcott, M. E. C. (ed.), 'Inventory of Whalley Abbey.' In: *THSLC* N.S. **7**, 1867, pp. 103–110. [The original is: TNA, E36/154, ff. 183r–189r].

————, 'Inventory of Stanlow.' In: *THSLC* N.S. **12**, 1871, pp. 53–56.

————, 'Inventories and Valuations of Religious Houses.' In: *Archaeologia* **43**, 1871, pp. 201–49.

————, 'Chantries of Leicestershire.' In: *TLAS* **4**, 1874, where a loose sheet inserted.

Waller, W. C., 'An Account of Some Records of Tilty Abbey preserved at Easton Lodge.' In: *TEAS*, N.S. **8**, 1902; **9**, 1903.

Ward, J., 'Our Lady of Penrhys.' In: *AC*, 1914, pp. 395–405.

Ware, *The White Monks of Waverley*, Farnham: Farnham District Museum Soc., 1976.

Watkins, A., 'Merevale Abbey in the Late 1490s.' In: *Warwickshire History* **9**:No. 3, Summer, 1994, pp. 87–104..

Watson, A. G., 'A book belonging to Thomas Cleubery.' In: *Transactions of the Woolhope Naturalists Field Club*, **40**, Part 1, 1970, pp. 133–36.

Weaver, F. W., 'Thomas Chard, D.D., the last abbot of Ford.' In: *Proc. Somerset Archaeological and Natural History Soc.*, **37**, 1891, pp. 1–14.

West, T., *The Antiquities of Furness*, London: T. Spilsbury, 1774; Ulverston: G. Ashburner, 1805.

Whitworth , M., 'Original Document.' In: *The Lincolnshire Historian* **2**, No. 5, 1958, pp. 32–37.

Wild, J., *The history of Castle Bytham*, Stamford: Johnson, Houlson, 1871.

Williams, D(avid) H., 'Cistercian Nunneries in Medieval Wales.' In: *Cîteaux* **26**, 1975, pp. 151–174.

————, *White Monks in Gwent and the Border*, Pontypool: Griffin Press, 1976.

————, 'White Monks in Powys.' In: *Cistercian Studies* **11**, 1976, pp. 73–101, 155–91.

————, 'Sale of Goods at Abbey Dorc.' In: *MA* **3**, Parts 3–4, 1975, pp. 192–97.

————, 'Corrodians and Residential Servants in Tudor Cistercian Monasteries.' In: *Cîteaux* **34**, 1–2, 1983, pp. 77–91, 284–310.

————, *The Cistercians in the Early Middle Ages*, Leominster: Gracewing, 1998.

——————, 'Cistercian Bridges.' In: *Tarmac Papers* **3**, 1999, pp. 149–64.

——————, *The Welsh Cistercians*, Leominster: Gracewing, 2001.

——————, 'The Last Abbot of Tintern.' In: *MA* **23**, 2007, 67–74.

——————, 'The Cistercians in West Wales, I. Cymmer Abbey.' In: *AC* **130**, 1981, pp. 36–58.

——————, 'The Cistercians in West Wales, II: Ceredigion.' In: *AC* **159**, 2010, pp. 241–86.

——————, 'Exeter College, Oxford, MS 1.' In: *Cîteaux* **62**, 2011, pp. 119–139.

——————, 'The Monks of Basingwerk: Foreigners in Wales?' In: *Flintshire Historical Soc. Jnl.* **39**, 2012, pp. 33–52.

Williams, G(lanmor), *Welsh Church from Conquest to Reformation*, Cardiff: University of Wales Press, 1962.

——————, *Welsh Reformation Essays*, Cardiff: University of Wales Press, 1967.

——————, 'Neath Abbey.' In: E. Jenkins, ed., *Neath and District: A Symposium*, Neath: Elis Jenkins, 1974, pp. 73–91.

Williams, S(tephen) W., *The Cistercian Abbey of Strata Florida*, London: Whiting & Co., 1889.

Winkless, D., *Hailes Abbey, Gloucestershire*, Stocksfield: Spredden, 1990.

Wood, B. J., 'Llanderfil,. In: *Pontypool and District Review* **5**, 1970.

Woodward, G. W. O., *The Dissolution of the Monasteries*, London: Blandford Press, 1966.

Wright, T., *Three Chapters of Letters relating to the Suppresson of the Monasteries*, London: Camden Soc., 1843.

Youings, J., *The Dissolution of the Monasteries*, London: Allen and Unwin, 1971.

No Author cited

A Short History of Dunkeswell Abbey, Honiton: Abbey Preservation Fund, 2nd. ed. 1974.

The Cistercian Priory of S. Leonard at Esholt in Airedale, London: J.C. Hotten, 1866.

INDEX OF PERSONS

ab. abbot/abbess; bp. bishop, m. monk; n. nun; pr. prior/prioress.

INDEX OF PLACES

INDEX OF SUBJECTS

Lightning Source UK Ltd.
Milton Keynes UK
UKOW06f0543220814

237339UK00001B/1/P